abnormalpsychology

Ninth Edition

IN A CHANGING WORLD

JEFFREY S.
NEVID
St. John's University

SPENCER A.
RATHUS
The College of New Jersey

BEVERLY
GREENE
St. John's University

PEARSON

Boston   Columbus   Indianapolis   New York   San Francisco   Upper Saddle River
Amsterdam   Cape Town   Dubai   London   Madrid   Milan   Munich   Paris   Montreal   Toronto
Delhi   Mexico City   Sao Paulo   Sydney   Hong Kong   Seoul   Singapore   Taipei   Tokyo

Senior Acquisitions Editor: Erin Mitchell
Editorial Assistant: Sarah Henrich
VP, Director of Marketing: Brandy Dawson
Senior Marketing Manager: Jeremy Intal
Marketing Assistant: Frank Alarcon
Director of Development: Sharon Geary
Development Editor: Amber Mackey
Director of Production: Lisa Iarkowski
Senior Managing Editor: Linda Behrens
Project Manager: Shelly Kupperman
Program Manager: Annemarie Franklin

Operations Supervisor: Mary Fischer
Operations Specialist: Diane Peirano
Creative Design Director: Leslie Osher
Interior/Cover Design: DeMarinis Design LLC
Digital Media Editor: Tom Scalzo
Digital Media Project Manager: Pam Weldin
Full-Service Project Management: PreMediaGlobal
Printer/Binder: R. R. Donnelley and Sons
Cover Printer: Lehigh-Phoenix Color/Hagerstown
Cover Image: Ostill/Shutterstock
Text Font: Adobe Garamond Pro, 10.5/12.5

Library of Congress Cataloging-in-Publication Data

Nevid, Jeffrey S., author.
    Abnormal psychology in a changing world / Jeffrey S. Nevid, Spencer A. Rathus,
    Beverly Greene. — Ninth Edition.
        pages cm
    ISBN 978-0-205-96171-9
    1. Psychology, Pathological—Textbooks.   I. Nevid, Jeffrey S., author.
    II. Rathus, Spencer A., author.   III. Greene, Beverly, author.   IV. Title.
    RC454.N468 2014
    616.89—dc23
                                            2013019033

10 9 8 7 6 5 4 3 2 1

Student Edition
ISBN-10:   0-205-96171-1
ISBN-13: 978-0-205-96171-9

Books à la Carte
ISBN-10:   0-205-96230-0
ISBN-13: 978-0-205-96230-3

brief contents

contents

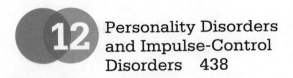

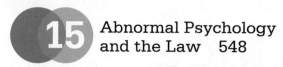

15 Abnormal Psychology and the Law 548

preface

What's New in the Ninth Edition?

Welcome to the ninth edition of *Abnormal Psychology in a Changing World*. We continue to bring readers the latest research developments that inform contemporary understandings of abnormal behavior in a way that both stimulates student interest and makes complex material understandable. Highlights of this new edition include the following:

- **Full integration of *DSM-5***—The *DSM-5* is integrated throughout the text, including reorganization of some chapters to parallel *DSM-5* classification

- **Inclusion of *DSM-5* Criteria Tables**—Updated diagnostic tables highlight *DSM-5* changes for selected disorders

- **Integration of Latest Scientific Developments**—Full updating of latest scientific research, including more than 1,000 new references since the last edition

- **Expanded Coverage of Disorders**—Expansion of coverage of disorders to include Hoarding Disorder, Premenstrual Dysphoric Disorder, Disruptive Mood Dysregulation Disorder, Major and Mild Neurocognitive Disorders, Somatic Symptom Disorder, Illness Anxiety Disorder, Intermittent Explosive Disorder, Pyromania, REM Sleep Behavior Disorder, and Social (Pragmatic) Communication Disorder, among others

- **@*Issue* Critical Thinking features**—This critical thinking boxed feature highlights current controversies in the field and poses critical thinking questions students can answer

- **Learning Objectives**—Learning objectives are now integrated throughout the chapters and tied to levels in Bloom's taxonomy using the unique IDEA model of course assessment

- **Introduction of QR Codes**—Use of QR codes students enables students to directly access sample video case vignettes on their smartphones or computers

- **Chapter Consolidation**—Now organized in 15 chapters to match up with a typical semester, the new edition combines previous chapters on theories and methods of treatment into one chapter (Chapter 2)

Putting a Human Face on the Study of Abnormal Psychology

We approach the teaching of abnormal psychology with five fundamental goals in mind:

- To help students distinguish abnormal from normal behavior and acquire a better understanding of abnormal behavior patterns

- To put a human face on the study of abnormal psychology and increase student sensitivity to the struggles of people suffering from these types of problems

- To help students understand the conceptual bases of abnormal behavior patterns

- To help students understand how our knowledge of abnormal behavior is informed by research developments in the field

- To help students understand how psychological disorders are classified and treated

We recognize there is a basic human dimension to the study of abnormal psychology. We invite students to enter the world of people struggling with psychological disorders by including many illustrative case examples and video case interviews of real people diagnosed with different disorders, and by including a unique pedagogical feature that takes this approach an important step further—the **"I"** feature.

The **"I"** feature brings students directly into the world of people affected by psychological disorders. The **"I"** feature consists of first-person narratives of people with psychological disorders as they tell their own stories in their own words. Incorporating first-person narratives helps break down barriers between "us" and "them," encouraging students to recognize that mental health problems are a concern to us all. At the beginning of every chapter and then integrated in the text, students will discover these poignant personal stories. Examples include the following:

- "Jerry Has a Panic Attack on the Interstate" (Panic Disorder)

- "Jessica's Little Secret" (Bulimia Nervosa)

- "I Hear Something You Can't Hear" (Schizophrenia)

- "Now Is the Last Best Time" (Alzheimer's Disease)

NEW! "@Issue" Critical Thinking Feature Puts a Spotlight on Controversies in the Field

Students may begin the course with an expectation that our knowledge of abnormal psychology is complete and incontrovertible. They soon learn that while we have learned much about the underpinnings of psychological disorders, much more remains to be learned. They also learn that there are many current controversies in the field. By spotlighting these controversies, we encourage students to think critically about these important issues and examine different points of view.

In this edition, we consolidate critical thinking about controversial issues in a boxed feature entitled **@*Issue***. Here students learn about major controversies and are challenged with critical thinking questions. Instructors may encourage their students to answer the critical thinking questions as required or elective writing assignments. Examples include the following:

- Should Therapists Treat Clients Online?
- What Accounts for the Gender Gap in Depression?
- Should We Use Drugs to Treat Drug Abuse?
- Is Mental Illness a Myth?

Two of the **@Issue** features in this edition are written by outside contributors who are leading authorities in the field: Dr. Thomas Widiger of the University of Kentucky ("The *DSM*: The Bible of Psychiatry"); and Dr. Jerry Deffenbacher of Colorado State University ("Anger Disorders and the *DSM:* Where Has All the Anger Gone?").

NEW! Interactive Concept Maps in Abnormal Psychology: A Unique Visual Learning Tool

Concept Maps in Abnormal Psychology are unique visual learning diagrams crafted to help students visualize linkages between specific disorders, underlying causal factors, and treatment approaches. Students learn best when they are actively engaged in the learning process. To engage students in active learning, we converted the Concept Maps in this edition to an interactive, online format hosted on *MyPsychLab*. The maps are presented in a fill-in-the-blanks format in which key words and terms are omitted so that students can fill in the missing pieces to complete these knowledge structures. The completed maps may be used as an active study tool or submitted to instructors as required course assignments or extra credit assignments.

Keeping Pace with an Ever-Changing Field

The text integrates the latest research findings and scientific developments in the field that inform our understanding of abnormal psychology. We present these research findings in a way that makes complex material engaging and accessible to the student.

Focus on Neuroscience

As part of our continuing efforts to integrate important advances in neuroscience that inform our understanding of abnormal behavior patterns, we have built upon the very solid foundations in previous editions to include new material from neuroscience research throughout the text. Students will read about the search for endophenotypes in schizophrenia, the emerging field of epigenetics, use of brain scans to diagnose psychological disorders, efforts to probe the workings of the meditative brain, potential use of drugs to enhance effectiveness of exposure therapy, and emerging research exploring whether disturbing memories linked to PTSD might be erased.

The Fully Integrated Textbook

Integrating the *DSM-5*

After years of development and debate, the *DSM-5* is finally here. **The ninth edition of the text is fully integrated with the** ***DSM-5***. Instructors are challenged to revise their instructional materials in light of the many changes introduced in the *DSM-5*. We integrated the *DSM-5* throughout the text to allow a seamless transition in teaching abnormal psychology. We apply *DSM-5* criteria in the body of the text and in the many accompanying overview charts throughout the text. Although we recognize the importance of the *DSM* system in the classification of psychological or mental disorders, we believe a course in abnormal psychology should not be taught as a training course in the *DSM* or as a psychodiagnostic seminar. We also recognize the many limitations of the *DSM* system, even in its latest version.

Integrating Diversity

We examine abnormal behavior patterns in relation to factors of diversity such as ethnicity, culture, gender, sexual orientation, and socioeconomic status. We believe students need to understand how issues of diversity affect the conceptualization of abnormal behavior as well as the diagnosis and treatment of psychological disorders. We also believe that coverage of diversity should be integrated directly in the text, not separated off in boxed features.

Integrating Theoretical Perspectives

Students often feel as though one theoretical perspective must ultimately be right and all the others wrong. We examine the many different theoretical perspectives that inform contemporary understanding of abnormal psychology and help students integrate these diverse viewpoints in the ***Tying It Together*** feature. We also explore potential causal pathways involving interactions of psychological, sociocultural, and biological factors. We hope to impress upon students the importance of taking a broader view of the complex problems we address by considering the influences of multiple factors and their interactions.

NEW! Integrating Video Case Examples with Student-Enabled QR Codes

Video case examples provide students with opportunities to see and hear individuals who are diagnosed with different types of psychological disorders. Students can read about the clinical features of specific disorders and, with a few clicks of a computer mouse, see a video case example that illustrates concepts discussed in the text. The video case examples are highlighted in the margins of the text with an icon and can be accessed through *MyPsychLab* at www.mypsychlab.com. We also introduce student-enabled fast response or QR codes that allow students to directly access the first video case in a chapter for display on their smartphones or personal computers.

The video case examples supplement the many illustrative case examples included in the text itself. Putting a human face on the subject matter helps make complex material more accessible. Many of these case examples are drawn from our own clinical files and those of leading mental health professionals.

Integrating Critical Thinking

We encourage students to think more deeply about key concepts in abnormal psychology by including two sets of critical thinking items in each chapter. First, the *@Issue* feature highlights current controversies in the field and includes critical thinking questions that challenge students to think further about the issues discussed in the text. Second, the critical thinking questions at the end of each chapter challenge students to think carefully and critically about concepts discussed in the chapter and to reflect on how these concepts relate to their own experiences or experiences of people they know. To integrate writing-across-the-curriculum (WAC) objectives, instructors may wish to assign the critical thinking questions in the *@Issue* features and the critical thinking questions at the end of each chapter as required or extra-credit writing assignments.

NEW! Integrating Learning Objectives with Bloom's Taxonomy

This edition introduces learning objectives at the start of each chapter. The learning objectives in this text are integrated with the IDEA model of course assessment, which comprise four key acquired skills in the study of abnormal psychology that spell out the convenient acronym, IDEA:

1. **Identify** ... criteria used to determine whether behavior is abnormal, categories of psychotropic or psychiatric drugs, specific types of disorders within diagnostic categories, risk factors for suicide among adolescents, etc.
2. **Define** or **Describe** ... key features of different psychological disorders and theoretical understandings, etc.
3. **Explain** or **Evaluate** ... major perspectives on abnormal psychology, effectiveness of psychotherapy, how cocaine affects the brain, etc.
4. **Apply** ... key features of critical thinking, knowledge of healthy sleeping habits, the diathesis-stress model to the development of schizophrenia, etc.

The IDEA model is integrated with the widely used taxonomy of educational objectives developed by the renowned educational researcher Benjamin Bloom. Bloom's taxonomy is arranged in increasing levels of cognitive complexity. The lowest levels comprise basic knowledge and understanding. The middle level involves application of knowledge and the upper levels involve higher level skills of analysis, synthesis, and evaluation.

The learning objectives identified in the IDEA model represent three basic levels of cognitive skills in Bloom's taxonomy. *Identify*, *Describe*, and *Define* learning objectives represent basic levels of cognitive skills (i.e., knowledge and comprehension in the original Bloom taxonomy, or remembering and understanding in the revised Bloom taxonomy). The *Apply* learning objective reflects an intermediate level of cognitive skills involved in application of psychological concepts. *Evaluate* and *Explain* learning objectives assess more complex, higher-order skills in the hierarchy involving analysis, synthesis, and evaluation of

psychological knowledge (or analyzing and evaluating domains as represented in the revised taxonomy). By building exams around these learning objectives, instructors can assess not only overall student knowledge, but also acquisition of skills at different levels of cognitive complexity in Bloom's taxonomy.

Maintaining Our Focus

Abnormal Psychology in a Changing World is a complete learning and teaching package that brings into focus four major objectives: (1) integrating an interactionist or biopsychosocial model of abnormal behavior, (2) underscoring the importance of issues of diversity to the understanding and treatment of psychological disorders, (3) maintaining currency, and (4) adopting a student-centric pedagogy.

Focus on the Interactionist Approach

We approached our writing with the belief that a better understanding of abnormal psychology is gained by adopting a biopsychosocial orientation that takes into account the roles of psychological, biological, and sociocultural factors and their interactions in the development of abnormal behavior patterns. We emphasize the value of taking an interactionist approach as a running theme throughout the text. We highlight a prominent interactionist model, the diathesis–stress model, to help students better understand the factors contributing to different forms of abnormal behavior.

Focus on Exploring Key Issues in Our Changing World

The *A Closer Look* feature provides opportunities for further exploration of selected topics that reflect cutting-edge issues in the field. A number of the *A Closer Look* features focus on advances in neuroscience research.

Focus on Student-Centric Pedagogy

We continually examine our pedagogical approach to find even better ways of helping students succeed in this course. To foster deeper understanding, we include many pedagogical aids, such as *Truth or Fiction* chapter openers to capture student attention and interest, *self-scoring questionnaires* to encourage active learning through self-examination, and *overview charts,* which are capsulized summaries of disorders that students can use as study charts.

"TRUTH OR FICTION" CHAPTER OPENERS

Each chapter begins with a set of *Truth or Fiction* questions to whet the student's appetite for the subject matter within the chapter. Some items challenge preconceived ideas and common folklore and debunk myths and misconceptions, whereas others highlight new research developments in the field. Instructors and students have repeatedly reported to us that they find this feature stimulating and challenging.

The *Truth or Fiction* questions are revisited and answered in the sections of the chapter where the topics are discussed. Students are thus given feedback concerning the accuracy of their preconceptions in light of the material being addressed.

SELF-SCORING QUESTIONNAIRES

These questionnaires on various topics involve students in the discussion at hand and encourage them to evaluate their own attitudes and behavior patterns. In some cases, students may become more aware of troubling concerns, such as states of depression or problems with drug or alcohol use, which they may want to bring to the attention of a helping professional. We have carefully developed and screened the questionnaires to ensure they will provide students with useful information to reflect on as well as serve as a springboard for class discussion.

OVERVIEW CHARTS

These visually appealing overview charts provide summaries of various disorders. We are gratified by the many comments from students and professors regarding the value of these "at-a-glance" study charts.

"SUMMING UP" CHAPTER SUMMARIES

Summing Up chapter summaries provide brief answers to the learning objectives posed at the beginning of the chapter. These summaries provide students with feedback they can use to compare their own answers to those provided in the text.

Ancillaries

No matter how comprehensive a textbook is, today's instructors and students require a complete teaching package to advance teaching and comprehension. *Abnormal Psychology in a Changing World* is accompanied by the following ancillaries:

MyPsychLab for Abnormal Psychology

MyPsychLab is an online homework, tutorial, and assessment program that truly engages students in learning. It helps students better prepare for class, quizzes, and exams—resulting in better performance in the course. It provides educators a dynamic set of tools for gauging individual and class performance. To order the ninth edition with MyPsychLab, use ISBN 0205965016.

Speaking Out: Interviews with People Who Struggle with Psychological Disorders

This set of video segments allows students to see firsthand accounts of patients with various disorders. The interviews were conducted by licensed clinicians and range in length from 8 to 25 minutes. Disorders include major depressive disorder, obsessive-compulsive disorder, anorexia nervosa, PTSD, alcoholism, schizophrenia, autism, ADHD, bipolar disorder, social phobia, hypochondriasis, borderline personality disorder, and

adjustment to physical illness. These video segments are available on DVD or through MyPsychLab.

> Volume 1: ISBN 0-13-193332-9
> Volume 2: ISBN 0-13-600303-6
> Volume 3: ISBN 0-13-230891-6

Instructor's Manual (020597189X)

A comprehensive tool for class preparation and management, each chapter includes learning objectives, a chapter outline, lecture and discussion suggestions, "think about it" discussion questions, activities and demonstrations, suggested video resources, and a sample syllabus. Available for download on the Instructor's Resource Center at www.pearsonhighered.com.

Test Bank (0205971881)

The Test Bank has been rigorously developed, reviewed, and checked for accuracy, to ensure the quality of both the questions and the answers. It includes fully referenced multiple-choice, true/false, and concise essay questions. Each question is accompanied by a page reference, difficulty level, skill type (factual, conceptual, or applied), topic, and a correct answer. Available for download on the Instructor's Resource Center at www.pearsonhighered.com.

MyTest (020597838X)

A powerful assessment-generation program that helps instructors easily create and print quizzes and exams. Questions and tests can be authored online, allowing instructors ultimate flexibility and the ability to efficiently manage assessments anytime, anywhere. Instructors can easily access existing questions and edit, create, and store questions using a simple drag-and-drop technique and word-like controls. Data on each question provide information on difficulty level and the page number of corresponding text discussion. For more information, go to www.PearsonMyTest.com.

Lecture PowerPoint Slides (ISBN 0205979610)

The PowerPoint slides provide an active format for presenting concepts from each chapter and feature relevant figures and tables from the text. Available for download on the Instructor's Resource Center at www.pearsonhighered.com.

Enhanced Lecture PowerPoint Slides with Embedded Videos (ISBN 0205997430)

The lecture PowerPoint slides have been embedded with select Speaking Out video pertaining to each disorder chapter, enabling instructors to show videos within the context of their lecture. No internet connection is required to play videos.

PowerPoint Slides for Photos, Figures, and Tables (ISBN 0205979629)

Contain only the photos, figures, and line art from the textbook. Available for download on the Instructor's Resource Center at www.pearsonhighered.com.

CourseSmart (ISBN 0205968368)

CourseSmart Textbooks Online is an exciting choice for students looking to save money. As an alternative to purchasing the print textbook, students can subscribe to the same content online and save up to 60 percent off the suggested list price of the print text. With a CourseSmart eTextbook, students can search the text, make notes online, print out reading assignments that incorporate lecture notes, and bookmark important passages for later review. For more information or to subscribe to the CourseSmart eTextbook, visit www.coursesmart.com.

Acknowledgments

With each new edition, we try to capture a moving target, as the literature base that informs our understanding continues to expand. We are deeply indebted to the thousands of talented scholars and investigators whose work has enriched our understanding of abnormal psychology. Thanks to our colleagues who reviewed our manuscript through earlier editions and continue to help us refine and strengthen our presentation of this material:

REVIEWERS OF THE PREVIOUS EDITIONS

Laurie Berkshire, *Erie Community College*

Sally Bing, *University of Maryland Eastern Shore*

Christiane Brems, *University of Alaska Anchorage*

Wanda Briggs, *Winthrop University*

Joshua Broman-Fulks, *Appalachian State University*

Barbara L. Brown, *Georgia Perimeter College*

Ann Butzin, *Owens State Community College*

Gerardo Canul, *UC Irvine*

Dennis Cash, *Trident Technical College*

Lorry Cology, *Owens Community College*

Michael Connor, *California State University*

Charles Cummings, *Asheville-Buncombe Technical Community College*

Nancy T. Dassoff, *University of Illinois—Chicago*

David Dooley, *University of California at Irvine*

Kristina Faimon, *Southeast Community College—Lincoln Campus*

Jeannine Feldman, *San Diego State University*

Heinz Fischer, *Long Beach City College*

John H. Forthman, *Vermillin Community College*

Pam Gibson, *James Madison University*

Colleen Gift, *Blackhawk Technical College*

Karla J. Gingerich, *Colorado State University*

Bernard Gorman, *Nassau Community College*

Gary Greenberg, *Connecticut College*

Nora Lynn Gussman, *Forsyth Technical Community College*

John K. Hall, *University of Pittsburgh*

Marc Henley, *Delaware County Community College*

Jennifer Hicks, *Southeastern Oklahoma State University*

Bob Hill, *Appalachian State University*

Kristine Jacquin, *Mississippi State University*

Ruth Ann Johnson, *Augustana College*

Robert Kapche, *California State University at Los Angeles*

Stuart Keeley, *Bowling Green State University*

Cynthia Diane Kreutzer, *Georgia Perimeter College*

Jennifer Langhinrichsen-Rohling, *University of South Alabama*

Marvin Lee, *Tennessee State University*

John Lloyd, *California State University, Fresno*

Don Lucas, *Northwest Vista College*

Tom Marsh, *Pitt Community College*

Sara Martino, *Richard Stockton College of New Jersey*

Shay McCordick, *San Diego State University*

Donna Marie McElroy, *Atlantic Cape Community College*

Lillian McMaster, *Hudson County Community College*

Mindy Mechanic, *California State University, Fullerton*

Linda L. Morrison, *University of New England*

C. Michael Nina, *William Paterson University*

Gary Noll, *University of Illinois at Chicago*

Martin M. Oper, *Erie Community College*

Joseph J. Palladino, *University of Southern Indiana*

Carol Pandey, *L. A. Pierce College*

Ramona Parish, *Guilford Technical Community College*

Jackie Robinson, *Florida A&M University*

Esther D. Rosenblum, *University of Vermont*

Sandra Sego, *American International College*

Harold Siegel, *Nassau Community College*

Nancy Simpson, *Trident Technical College*

Ari Solomon, *Williams College*

Robert Sommer, *University of California—Davis*

Linda Sonna, *University of New Mexico, Taos*

Charles Spirrison, *Mississippi State University*

Stephanie Stein, *Central Washington University*

Joanne Hoven Stohs, *California State University—Fullerton*

Larry Stout, *Nicholls State University*

Tamara Sullivan, *SUNY Brockport*

Deborah Thomas, *Washington State Community College*

Amber Vesotski, *Alpena Community College*

Theresa Wadkins, *University of Nebraska—Kearny*

Naomi Wagner, *San Jose State University*

Sterling Watson, *Chicago State University*

Thomas Weatherly, *Georgia Perimeter College*

Max Zwanziger, *Central Washington University*

We also wish to recognize the exemplary contributions of the publishing professionals at Pearson who helped guide the development of this edition, especially Erin Mitchell, executive editor, who has brought a distinctive vision to enrich the text and make it an even more effective learning platform; Amber Mackay, associate editor, for beautifully coordinating the many editorial features that comprise this work; production editor Lindsay Bethoney for so skillfully bringing together the various components of the text; and photo editor Kate Cebik, who worked tirelessly to find just the right images to illustrate key concepts.

We especially wish to thank the two people without whose inspiration and support this effort never would have materialized or been completed: Judith Wolf-Nevid and Lois Fichner-Rathus. We invite students and instructors to contact us at the following email address with any comments, suggestions, and feedback. We'd love to hear from you.

—J.S.N
New York, New York
jeffnevid@gmail.com

—S.A.R.
New York, New York
srathus@aol.com

—B.A.G
Brooklyn, New York

about the authors

Jeffrey S. NEVID

is Professor of Psychology at St. John's University in New York, where he directs the Doctoral Program in Clinical Psychology, teaches at the undergraduate and graduate levels, and supervises doctoral students in clinical practicum work. He received his Ph.D. in Clinical Psychology from the University at Albany and was a staff psychologist at Samaritan Hospital in Troy, New York. He later completed a National Institute of Mental Health Post-Doctoral Fellowship in Mental Health Evaluation Research at Northwestern University. He holds a Diplomate in Clinical Psychology from the American Board of Professional Psychology, is a Fellow of the American Psychological Association and the Academy of Clinical Psychology, and has served on the editorial boards of several psychology journals and as Associate Editor of the *Journal of Consulting and Clinical Psychology*. He has published more than 70 articles in professional journals and has authored or coauthored more than 50 editions of textbooks and other books in psychology and related fields. His research publications have appeared in such journals as *Journal of Consulting and Clinical Psychology*, *Health Psychology*, *Journal of Occupational Medicine*, *Behavior Therapy*, *American Journal of Community Psychology*, *Professional Psychology: Research and Practice*, *Journal of Clinical Psychology*, *Journal of Nervous and Mental Disease*, *Teaching of Psychology*, *American Journal of Health Promotion*, and *Psychology and Psychotherapy*. Dr. Nevid is also author of the book *Choices: Sex in the Age of STDs* and the introductory psychology text, *Psychology: Concepts and Applications*, as well as several other college texts in the fields of psychology and health that he coauthored with Dr. Spencer Rathus. Dr. Nevid is also actively involved in a program of pedagogical research focusing on helping students become more effective learners.

Spencer A. RATHUS

received his Ph.D. from the University at Albany. He is on the faculty of the College of New Jersey. His areas of interest include psychological assessment, cognitive behavior therapy, and deviant behavior. He is the originator of the Rathus Assertiveness Schedule, which has become a Citation Classic. He has authored several books, including *Psychology in the New Millennium*, *Essentials of Psychology*, and *The World of Children*. He coauthored *Making the Most of College* with Lois Fichner-Rathus; *AIDS: What Every Student Needs to Know* with Susan Boughn; *Behavior Therapy*, *Psychology and the Challenges of Life*, *Your Health*, *Health in the New Millennium*, and *HLTH* with Jeffrey S. Nevid; and *Human Sexuality in a World of Diversity* with Jeffrey S. Nevid and Lois Fichner-Rathus. His professional activities include service on the American Psychological Association Task Force on Diversity Issues at the Precollege and Undergraduate Levels of Education in Psychology, and on the Advisory Panel, American Psychological Association, Board of Educational Affairs (BEA) Task Force on Undergraduate Psychology Major Competencies.

Beverly A. GREENE

is Professor of Psychology at St. John's University and is a Fellow of eight divisions of the American Psychological Association and the Academy of Clinical Psychology. She is Board Certified in Clinical Psychology and serves on the editorial boards of numerous scholarly journals. She received her Ph.D. in Clinical Psychology from Adelphi University's Derner Institute. She was founding coeditor of the APA Society for the Study of Lesbian, Gay, and Bisexual Issues series, *Psychological Perspectives on Lesbian, Gay, and Bisexual Issues*. She is also coauthor of *What Therapists Don't Talk About and Why: Understanding Taboos That Hurt Ourselves and Our Clients*, and has more than 100 professional publications that are the subject of eleven national awards. Dr. Greene was recipient of the APA 2003 Committee on Women in Psychology Distinguished Leadership Award, the 1996 Outstanding Achievement Award from the APA Committee on Lesbian, Gay, and Bisexual Concerns, the 2004 Distinguished Career Contributions to Ethnic Minority Research Award from the APA Society for the Study of Ethnic Minority Issues, the 2000 Heritage Award from the APA Society for the Psychology of Women, the 2004 Award for Distinguished Senior Career Contributions to Ethnic Minority Research (APA Division 45), and the 2005 Stanley Sue Award for Distinguished Professional Contributions to Diversity in Clinical Psychology (APA Division 12). Her coedited book, *Psychotherapy with African American Women: Innovations in Psychodynamic Perspectives and Practice*, was also honored with the Association for Women in Psychology's 2001 Distinguished Publication Award. In 2006, she was the recipient of the Janet Helms Award for Scholarship and Mentoring from the Teacher's College, Columbia University Cross Cultural Roundtable. She also received the 2006 Florence Halpern Award for Distinguished Professional Contributions to Clinical Psychology (APA Division 12). In 2009, she was honored as recipient of the APA Award for Distinguished Senior Career Contribution to Psychology in the Public Interest. She is also the 2012 recipient of the Association for Women in Psychology's Jewish Women's Caucus award for scholarship for *A Minyan of Women: Family Dynamics, Jewish Identity, and Psychotherapy Practice* (with Dorith Brodbar) and that Association's 2012 Espin Award for scholarship. She is also active in APA governance and is coeditor of the forthcoming publications, *The Psychologist's Desk Reference* (Oxford, with Gerald Koocher and John Norcross) and *The Psychological Health of Women of Color* (Praeger, with Lillian Comas Diaz).

Introduction and Methods of Research

1

learning objectives

1.1
Define the term psychological disorder.

1.2
Identify criteria professionals use to determine whether behavior is abnormal.

1.3
Apply these criteria to case examples discussed in the text.

1.4
Describe the cultural bases of abnormal behavior.

1.5
Describe the historical changes that have occurred in conceptualizations and treatment of abnormal behavior through the course of Western culture.

1.6
Describe the major contemporary perspectives on abnormal behavior.

1.7
Identify the objectives of science and the steps in the scientific method.

1.8
Identify the ethical principles that guide research in psychology.

1.9
Describe the major types of research methods scientists use to study abnormal behavior and evaluate the strengths and weaknesses of these methods.

1.10
Apply key features of critical thinking to the study of abnormal behavior.

truth OR fiction

T☐ F☐ About one in ten American adults suffer from a diagnosable mental or psychological disorder in any given year. (p. 4)

T☐ F☐ Although effective treatments exist for some psychological disorders, we still lack the means of effectively treating most types of psychological disorders. (p. 5)

T☐ F☐ Unusual behavior is abnormal. (p. 5)

T☐ F☐ Psychological problems like depression may be experienced differently by people in different cultures. (p. 9)

T☐ F☐ A night's entertainment in London a few hundred years ago might have included gaping at the inmates at the local asylum. (p. 12)

T☐ F☐ Despite changing attitudes in society toward homosexuality, the psychiatric profession continues to classify homosexuality as a mental disorder. (p. 18)

T☐ F☐ Recent evidence shows there are literally millions of genes in the nucleus of every cell in the body. (p. 28)

T☐ F☐ Case studies have been conducted on dead people. (p. 29)

"I" "Pretty Grisly Stuff"

I never thought I'd ever see a psychologist or someone like that, you know. I'm a police photographer and I've shot some pretty grisly stuff, corpses and all. Crime scenes are not like what you see on TV. They're more grisly. I guess you kind of get used to it. It never bothered me, just maybe at first. Before I did this job, I worked on a TV news chopper. We would take shots of fires and rescues, you know. Now I get uptight sitting in the back seat of a car or riding an elevator. I'll avoid taking an elevator unless I really have no other choice. Forget flying anymore. It's not just helicopters. I just won't go in a plane, any kind of plane.

I guess I was younger then and more daring when I was younger. Sometimes I would hang out of the helicopter to shoot pictures with no fear at all. Now, just thinking about flying makes my heart race. It's not that I'm afraid the plane will crash. That's the funny thing. Not ha-ha funny, but peculiar, you know. I just start trembling when I think of them closing that door, trapping us inside. I can't tell you why.
Source: From the Author's Files

Phil, 42, a police photographer

"I" Cowering Under the Covers

When I start going into a high, I no longer feel like an ordinary housewife. Instead I feel organized and accomplished and I begin to feel I am my most creative self. I can write poetry easily. I can compose melodies without effort. I can paint. My mind feels facile and absorbs everything. I have countless ideas about improving the conditions of mentally retarded children, of how a hospital for these children should be run, what they should have around them to keep them happy and calm and unafraid. I see myself as being able to accomplish a great deal for the good of people. I have countless ideas about how the environment problem could inspire a crusade for the health and betterment of everyone. I feel able to accomplish a great deal for the good of my family and others. I feel pleasure, a sense of euphoria or elation. I want it to last forever. I don't seem to need much sleep. I've lost weight and feel healthy and I like myself. I've just bought six new dresses, in fact, and they look quite good on me.

I feel sexy and men stare at me. Maybe I'll have an affair, or perhaps several. I feel capable of speaking and doing good in politics. I would like to help people with problems similar to mine so they won't feel hopeless.

It's wonderful when you feel like this. . . . The feeling of exhilaration—the high mood—makes me feel light and full of the joy of living. However, when I go beyond this stage, I become manic, and the creativeness becomes so magnified I begin to see things in my mind that aren't real. For instance, one night I created an entire movie, complete with cast, that I still think would be terrific. I saw the people as clearly as if watching them in real life. I also experienced complete terror, as if it were actually happening, when I knew that an assassination scene was about to take place. I cowered under the covers and became a complete shaking wreck. . . . My screams awakened my husband, who tried to reassure me that we were in our bedroom and everything was the same. There was nothing to be afraid of. Nevertheless, I was admitted to the hospital the next day.
Source: Fieve, 1975, pp. 27–28

> *A firsthand account of a 45-year-old woman with bipolar disorder*

"I" **Thomas Hears Voices**

I've been diagnosed as having paranoid schizophrenia. I also suffer from clinical depression. Before I found the correct medications, I was sleeping on the floor, afraid to sleep in my own bed. I was hearing voices that, lately, had turned from being sometimes helpful to being terrorizing. The depression had been responsible for my being irritable and full of dread, especially in the mornings, becoming angry over frustrations at work, and seemingly internalizing other people's problems. . . .

The voices, human sounding, and sounding from a short distance outside my apartment, were slowly turning nearly all bad. I could hear them jeering me, plotting against me, singing songs sometimes that would only make sense later in the day when I would do something wrong at work or at home. I began sleeping on the floor of my living room because I was afraid a presence in the bedroom was torturing good forces around me. If I slept in the bedroom, the nightly torture would cause me to make mistakes during the day. A voice, calling himself Fatty Acid, stopped me from drinking soda. Another voice allowed me only one piece of bread with my meals.
Source: Campbell, 2000, reprinted with permission of the National Institute of Mental Health

> *Thomas, a young man diagnosed with schizophrenia and major depression*

These three people—like many you will meet in this text—struggle with problems that mental health professionals classify as psychological or mental disorders. A **psychological disorder** is a pattern of abnormal behavior that is associated with states of significant emotional distress, such as anxiety or depression, or with impaired behavior or ability to function, such as difficulty holding a job or even distinguishing reality from fantasy. **Abnormal psychology** is the branch of psychology that studies abnormal behavior and ways of helping people who are affected by psychological disorders.

The problem of abnormal behavior might seem the concern of only a few. After all, relatively few people are ever admitted to a psychiatric hospital. Most people never seek the help of a mental health professional, such as a psychologist or psychiatrist. Fewer still ever plead not guilty to crimes on grounds of insanity. Most of us probably have at least one relative we consider "eccentric," but how many of us have relatives we consider "crazy"? And yet, the truth is that abnormal behavior affects all of us in one way or another. Let's break down the numbers.

If we limit the discussion to diagnosable mental disorders, nearly one in two of all Americans (46%) are directly affected at some point in their lives (Kessler, Berglund, Demler, Jin, & Walters, 2005; see Figure 1.1). About one in four adult Americans (26%)

1.1 Define the term psychological disorder.

FIGURE 1.1

Lifetime and past-year prevalences of psychological disorders. This graph is based on a nationally representative sample of 9,282 English-speaking U.S. residents aged 18 and older. We see percentages of individuals with diagnosable psychological disorders either during the past year or at some point in their lives for several major diagnostic categories. The mood disorders category includes major depressive episode, manic episode, and dysthymia (discussed in Chapter 7). Anxiety disorders include panic disorder, agoraphobia without panic disorder, social phobia, specific phobia, and generalized anxiety disorder (discussed in Chapter 5). Substance use disorders involving alcohol or other drugs are discussed in Chapter 8.

Source: Kessler, Chiu, Demler, & Walters, 2005; Kessler, Bergland, Demler, et al., 2005.

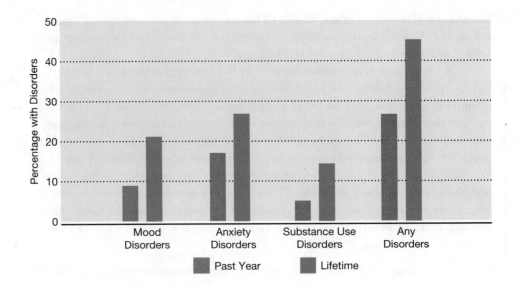

truth OR fiction

About one in ten American adults suffer from a diagnosable mental or psychological disorder in any given year.

☑ **FALSE** It's actually about one in four American adults.

experience a diagnosable psychological disorder in any given year (Kessler, Chiu, Demler, & Walters, 2005). **T / F**

According to the World Health Organization, the United States has the highest rates of diagnosable psychological disorders among 17 countries they surveyed (Kessler et al., 2009). American women are more likely than men to suffer from psychological disorders, especially mood disorders (discussed in Chapter 7) ("Women More at Risk," 2012). In addition, twice as many young adults (ages 18–25) are affected by psychological disorders than are people over 50.

If we also include the mental health problems of our family members, friends, and coworkers and take into account those who foot the bill for treatment in the form of taxes and health insurance premiums as well as lost productivity due to sick days, disability leaves, and impaired job performance inflating product costs, then clearly all of us are affected to one degree or another.

The study of abnormal psychology is illuminated not only by the extensive research on the causes and treatments of psychological disorders reported in scientific journals but also by the personal stories of people affected by these problems. In this text, we will learn from these people as they tell their stories in their own words. Through first-person narratives, case examples, and video interviews, researchers enter the world of people struggling with various types of psychological disorders that affect their moods, thinking, and behavior. Some of these stories may remind you of the experiences of people close to you, or perhaps even yourself. We invite you to explore with us the nature and origins of these disorders and ways of helping people who face the many challenges they pose.

Let's pause for a moment to raise an important distinction. Although the terms *psychological disorder* and *mental disorder* are often used interchangeably, we prefer using the term *psychological disorder*. The major reason is that the term *psychological disorder* puts the study of abnormal behavior squarely within the purview of the field of psychology. Moreover, the term *mental disorder* (also called *mental illness*) is derived from the **medical model** perspective that views abnormal behavior patterns as symptoms of underlying illness. Although the medical model is a major contemporary model for understanding abnormal behavior, we believe we need to take a broader view of abnormal behavior by incorporating psychological and sociocultural perspectives as well.

SURGEON GENERAL'S REPORT ON MENTAL HEALTH The U.S. Surgeon General issued a report at the turn of the new millennium that is still pertinent today in terms of focusing the nation's attention on problems of mental health. Here are some key conclusions from the report (Satcher, 2000; U.S. Department of Health and Human Services, 1999):

- Mental health reflects the complex interaction of brain functioning and environmental influences.

- Effective treatments exist for most mental disorders, including psychological interventions such as psychotherapy and counseling and psychopharmacological or drug therapies. Treatment is often more effective when psychological and psychopharmacological treatments are combined. **T / F**

- Progress in developing effective prevention programs in the mental health field has been slow because we do not know the causes of mental disorders or ways of altering known influences, such as genetic predispositions. Nonetheless, some effective prevention programs have been developed.

- Although 15% of American adults receive some form of help for mental health problems each year, many who need help do not receive it.

- Mental health problems are best understood when we take a broader view and consider the social and cultural contexts in which they occur.

- Mental health services need to be designed and delivered in a manner that takes into account the viewpoints and needs of racial and ethnic minorities.

The Surgeon General's report provides a backdrop for our study of abnormal psychology. As we shall see throughout the text, we believe that understandings of abnormal behavior are best revealed through a lens that takes into account interactions of biological and environmental factors. We also believe that social and cultural (or *sociocultural*) factors need to be considered in the attempt to both understand abnormal behavior and develop effective treatment services.

In this chapter, we first address the difficulties of defining *abnormal behavior*. We see that throughout history, abnormal behavior has been viewed from different perspectives. We chronicle the development of concepts of abnormal behavior and its treatment. We see that in the past, treatment usually referred to what was done *to*, rather than *for*, people with abnormal behavior. We then describe the ways in which psychologists and other scholars study abnormal behavior today.

How Do We Define *Abnormal Behavior?*

We all become anxious or depressed from time to time, but is this abnormal? Anxiety in anticipation of an important job interview or a final examination is perfectly normal. It is appropriate to feel depressed when you have lost someone close to you or when you have failed at a test or on the job. So, where is the line between normal and abnormal behavior?

One answer is that emotional states such as anxiety and depression may be considered abnormal when they are not appropriate to the situation. It is normal to feel down when you fail a test, but not when your grades are good or excellent. It is normal to feel anxious before a college admissions interview, but not to panic before entering a department store or boarding a crowded elevator.

Abnormality may also be suggested by the magnitude of the problem. Although some anxiety is normal enough before a job interview, feeling that your heart might leap from your chest—and consequently your canceling the interview—is not. Nor is it normal to feel so anxious in this situation that your clothing becomes soaked with perspiration **T / F**.

Criteria for Determining Abnormality

Mental health professionals apply various criteria in making judgments about whether behavior is abnormal. The most commonly used criteria include the following:

1. *Unusualness.* Behavior that is unusual is often considered abnormal. Only a few of us report seeing or hearing things that are not really there; "seeing things" and "hearing things" are almost always considered abnormal in our culture, but such experiences are sometimes considered normal in certain types of spiritual

truth OR fiction

Although effective treatments exist for some psychological disorders, we still lack the means of effectively treating most types of psychological disorders.

☑ **FALSE** The good news is that effective treatments exist for most psychological disorders.

truth OR fiction

Unusual behavior is abnormal.

☑ **FALSE** Unusual or statistically deviant behavior is not necessarily abnormal. Exceptional behavior also deviates from the norm.

1.2 Identify criteria professionals use to determine whether behavior is abnormal.

experiences. Moreover, hearing voices and other forms of hallucinations under some circumstances are not considered unusual in some preliterate societies.

However, becoming overcome with feelings of panic when entering a department store or when standing in a crowded elevator is uncommon and considered abnormal. Uncommon behavior is not in itself abnormal. Only one person can hold the record for swimming the fastest 100 meters. The record-holding athlete differs from the rest of us but, again, is not considered abnormal. Thus, rarity or statistical deviance is not a sufficient basis for labeling behavior abnormal; nevertheless, it is often one of the yardsticks used to judge abnormality.

2. *Social deviance.* All societies have norms (standards) that define the kinds of behavior that is acceptable in given contexts. Behavior deemed normal in one culture may be viewed as abnormal in another. For example, people in our culture who assume that all male strangers are devious are usually regarded as unduly suspicious or distrustful. But such suspicions were justified among the Mundugumor, a tribe of cannibals studied by anthropologist Margaret Mead (1935). Within that culture, male strangers *were* typically malevolent toward others, and it was normal to feel distrustful of them. Norms, which arise from the practices and beliefs of specific cultures, are relative standards, not universal truths.

Thus, clinicians need to weigh cultural differences when determining what is normal and abnormal. Moreover, what strikes one generation as abnormal may be considered normal by the next. For example, until the mid-1970s, homosexuality was classified as a mental disorder by the psychiatric profession (see the *Thinking Critically About Abnormal Psychology* feature on page 18). Today, however, the psychiatric profession no longer considers homosexuality a mental disorder, and many people argue that contemporary societal norms should include homosexuality as a normal variation in behavior.

When normality is judged on the basis of compliance with social norms, nonconformists may incorrectly be labeled as mentally disturbed. We may come to brand behavior that we do not approve of as "sick" rather than accept that the behavior may be normal, even though it offends or puzzles us.

3. *Faulty perceptions or interpretations of reality.* Normally, our sensory systems and cognitive processes permit us to form accurate mental representations of the environment. Seeing things and hearing voices that are not present are considered hallucinations, which in our culture are generally taken as signs of an underlying mental disorder. Similarly, holding unfounded ideas or *delusions,* such as ideas of persecution that the CIA or the Mafia are out to get you, may be regarded as signs of mental disturbance—unless, of course, they *are real.* (As former U.S. Secretary of State Henry Kissinger is said to have remarked, "Even paranoid people have enemies.")

It is normal in the United States to say that one talks to God through prayer. If, however, a person insists on having literally seen God or heard the voice of God—as opposed to, say, being divinely inspired—we may come to regard her or him as mentally disturbed.

4. *Significant personal distress.* States of personal distress caused by troublesome emotions, such as anxiety, fear, or depression, may be abnormal. As we noted earlier, however, anxiety and depression are sometimes appropriate responses to the situation. Real threats and losses do occur in life, and *lack* of an emotional response to them would be regarded as abnormal. Appropriate feelings of distress are not considered abnormal unless the feelings persist long after the source of anguish has been removed (after most people would have adjusted) or if they are so intense that they impair the individual's ability to function.

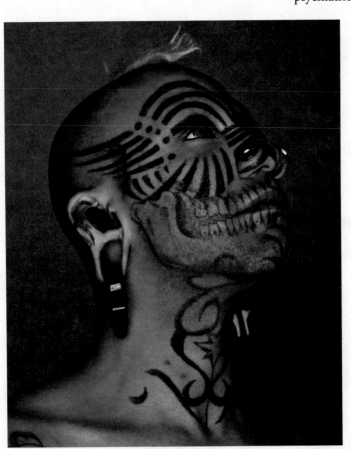

Is this man abnormal? Judgments of abnormality take into account the social and cultural standards of society. Do you believe this man's body adornment is a sign of abnormality or merely a fashion statement?

5. *Maladaptive or self-defeating behavior.* Behavior that leads to unhappiness rather than self-fulfillment can be regarded as abnormal. Behavior that limits one's ability to function in expected roles, or to adapt to one's environments, may also be considered abnormal. According to these criteria, heavy alcohol consumption that impairs health or social and occupational functioning may be viewed as abnormal. Agoraphobic behavior, characterized by intense fear of venturing into public places, may be considered abnormal in that it is both uncommon and maladaptive because it impairs the individual's ability to fulfill work and family responsibilities.

6. *Dangerousness.* Behavior that is dangerous to oneself or other people may be considered abnormal. Here, too, the social context is crucial. In wartime, people who sacrifice their lives or charge the enemy with little apparent concern for their own safety may be characterized as courageous, heroic, and patriotic. But people who threaten or attempt suicide because of the pressures of civilian life are usually considered abnormal.

When is anxiety abnormal? Negative emotions such as anxiety are considered abnormal when they are judged to be excessive or inappropriate to the situation. Anxiety is generally regarded as normal when it is experienced during a job interview, so long as it is not so severe that it prevents the interviewee from performing adequately. Anxiety is deemed to be abnormal if it is experienced whenever one boards an elevator.

Football and hockey players who occasionally get into fistfights or altercations with opposing players may be normal enough. Given the nature of these sports, unaggressive football and hockey players would not last long in college or professional ranks. But players involved in frequent altercations may be regarded as abnormal. Physically aggressive behavior is most often maladaptive in modern life. Moreover, physical aggression is ineffective as a way of resolving conflicts—although it is by no means uncommon.

Abnormal behavior thus has multiple definitions. Depending on the case, some criteria may be weighted more heavily than others. But in most cases, a combination of these criteria is used to define abnormality.

APPLYING THE CRITERIA Let's return to the three cases we introduced at the beginning of the chapter. Consider the criteria we can apply in determining whether the behaviors reported in these vignettes are abnormal. For one thing, the abnormal behavior patterns in these three cases are unusual in the statistical sense. Most people do not encounter these kinds of problems, although we should add that these problems are far from rare. The problem behaviors also meet other criteria of abnormality, as we shall see.

1.3 Apply these criteria to case examples discussed in the text.

Phil suffered from *claustrophobia,* an excessive fear of enclosed spaces. (This is an example of an anxiety disorder and is discussed more fully in Chapter 5.) His behavior was unusual (relatively few people are so fearful of confinement that they avoid flying in airplanes or riding on elevators) and was associated with significant personal distress. His fear also impaired his ability to carry out his occupational and family responsibilities. But he was not hampered by faulty perceptions of reality. He recognized that his fears exceeded a realistic appraisal of danger in these situations.

What criterion of abnormality applies in the case of the woman who cowered under the blankets? She was diagnosed with *bipolar disorder* (formerly called manic-depression), a type of mood disorder in which a person experiences extreme mood swings, from the heights of elation and seemingly boundless energy to the depths of depression and despair. (The vignette described the manic phase of the disorder.) Bipolar disorder, which is discussed in Chapter 7, is associated with extreme personal distress and difficulty functioning effectively in normal life. It is also linked to self-defeating and dangerous behavior, such as reckless driving or exorbitant spending during manic phases and attempted suicide during depressive phases. In some cases, like the one presented here, people in manic phases sometimes have faulty perceptions or interpretations of reality, such as hallucinations and delusions.

Thomas suffered from both schizophrenia and depression. It is not unusual for people to have more than one disorder at a time. In the parlance of the psychiatric profession, these clients present with *comorbid* (co-occurring) diagnoses. Comorbidity complicates treatment because clinicians need to design a treatment approach that focuses on treating two or more disorders. Schizophrenia meets a number of criteria of abnormality, including statistical infrequency (it affects about 1% of the general population). The clinical features of schizophrenia include socially deviant or bizarre behavior, disturbed perceptions or interpretations of reality (delusions and hallucinations), maladaptive behavior (difficulty meeting responsibilities of daily life), and personal distress. (See Chapter 11 for more detail on schizophrenia.) Thomas, for example, was plagued by auditory hallucinations (terrorizing voices), which were certainly a source of significant distress. His thinking was also delusional, because he believed that "a presence" in his bedroom was "torturing good forces," surrounding him and causing him to make mistakes during the day. In Thomas's case, schizophrenia was complicated by depression that involved feelings of personal distress (irritability and feelings of dread). Depression is also associated with dampened or downcast mood, maladaptive behavior (difficulty getting to work or school or even getting out of bed in the morning), and potential dangerousness (possible suicidal behavior).

It is one thing to recognize and label behavior as abnormal; it is another to understand and explain it. Philosophers, physicians, natural scientists, and psychologists have used various approaches, or *models,* in the effort to explain abnormal behavior. Some approaches have been based on superstition; others have invoked religious explanations. Some current views are predominantly biological; others are psychological. In considering various historical and contemporary approaches to understanding abnormal behavior, let's first look further at the importance of cultural beliefs in determining which behavior patterns are deemed abnormal.

1.4 Describe the cultural bases of abnormal behavior.

Cultural Bases of Abnormal Behavior

As noted, behavior that is normal in one culture may be deemed abnormal in another. Australian aborigines believe they can communicate with the spirits of their ancestors and that other people, especially close relatives, share their dreams. These beliefs are considered normal within Aboriginal culture. But were such beliefs to be expressed in our culture, they would likely be deemed delusions, which professionals regard as a common feature of schizophrenia. Thus, the standards we use in making judgments of abnormal behavior must take into account cultural norms.

Kleinman (1987) offers an example of "hearing voices" among Native Americans to underscore the ways in which judgments about abnormality are embedded within a cultural context:

> Ten psychiatrists trained in the same assessment technique and diagnostic criteria who are asked to examine 100 American Indians shortly after the latter have experienced the death of a spouse, a parent or a child may determine with close to 100% consistency that those individuals report hearing, in the first month of grieving, the voice of the dead person calling to them as the spirit ascends to the afterworld. [Although such judgments may be consistent across observers] the determination of whether such reports are a sign of an abnormal mental state is an interpretation based on knowledge of this group's behavioural norms and range of normal experiences of bereavement. (p. 453)

A traditional Native American healer. Many traditional Native Americans distinguish between illnesses believed to arise from influences external to their own culture ("White man's sicknesses") and those that emanate from a lack of harmony with traditional tribal life and thought ("Indian sicknesses"). Traditional healers such as the one shown here may be called on to treat Indian sickness, whereas "White man's medicine" may be sought to help people deal with problems whose causes are seen as lying outside the community, such as alcoholism and drug addiction.

To these Native Americans, bereaved people who report hearing the spirits of the deceased calling to them as they ascend to the afterlife are normal. Behavior that is normative within the cultural setting in which it occurs should not be considered abnormal.

Concepts of health and illness vary across cultures. Traditional Native American cultures distinguish between illnesses that are believed to arise from influences outside the culture, called "White man's sicknesses," such as alcoholism and drug addiction, and those that emanate from a lack of harmony with traditional tribal life and thought, which are called "Indian sicknesses" (Trimble, 1991). Traditional healers, shamans, and medicine men and women are called on to treat Indian sickness. When the problem is thought to have its cause outside the community, help is sought from "White man's medicine."

Abnormal behavior patterns take different forms in different cultures. Westerners experience anxiety, for example, in the form of worrying about paying the mortgage and losing a job. Yet "in a number of African cultures, anxiety is expressed as fears of failure in procreation, in dreams and complaints about witchcraft" (Kleinman, 1987). Australian aborigines can develop intense fears of sorcery, accompanied by the belief that one is in mortal danger from evil spirits (Spencer, 1983). Trancelike states in which young aboriginal women are mute, immobile, and unresponsive are also quite common. If these women do not recover from the trance within hours or, at most, a few days, they may be brought to a sacred site for healing.

The very words that we use to describe psychological disorders—words such as *depression* or *mental health*—have different meanings in other cultures, or no equivalent meaning at all. This doesn't mean that depression doesn't exist in other cultures. Rather, it suggests we need to learn how people in different cultures experience emotional distress, including states of depression and anxiety, rather than imposing our perspectives on their experiences. People in China and other countries in the Far East generally place greater emphasis on the physical or somatic symptoms of depression, such as headaches, fatigue, or weakness, than on feelings of guilt or sadness, as compared to people from Western cultures such as our own (Kalibatseva & Leong, 2011; Ryder et al., 2008; Zhou et al., 2011). **T / F**

These differences demonstrate how important it is that we determine whether our concepts of abnormal behavior are valid before we apply them to other cultures. Research efforts along these lines have shown that the abnormal behavior pattern associated with our concept of schizophrenia exists in countries as far flung as Colombia, India, China, Denmark, Nigeria, and the former Soviet Union, as well as many others (Jablensky, Sartorius, Ernberg, & Anker, 1992). Furthermore, rates of schizophrenia appear similar among the countries studied. However, differences have been observed in some of the features of schizophrenia across cultures (Myers, 2011).

Views about abnormal behavior vary from society to society. In Western culture, models based on medical disease and psychological factors are prominent in explaining abnormal behavior. But in traditional native cultures, models of abnormal behavior often invoke supernatural causes, such as possession by demons or the Devil. For example, in Filipino folk society, psychological problems are often attributed to the influence of "spirits" or the possession of a "weak soul" (Edman & Johnson, 1999).

Historical Perspectives on Abnormal Behavior

Throughout the history of Western culture, concepts of abnormal behavior have been shaped, to some degree, by the prevailing worldview of the particular era. For hundreds of years, beliefs in supernatural forces, demons, and evil spirits held sway. (And, as we've just seen, these beliefs still hold true in some societies.) Abnormal behavior was often taken as a sign of possession. In modern times, the predominant—but by no means universal—worldview has shifted toward beliefs in science and reason. In Western culture, abnormal behavior has come to be viewed as the product of physical and psychosocial factors, not demonic possession.

The Demonological Model

Why would anyone need a hole in the head? Archaeologists have unearthed human skeletons from the Stone Age with egg-sized cavities in the skull. One interpretation of these holes is that our prehistoric ancestors believed abnormal behavior was caused by the inhabitation of evil spirits. These holes might be the result of **trephination**—the drilling of the skull to provide an outlet for those irascible spirits. Fresh bone growth indicates that some people did survive this "medical procedure."

Just the threat of trephining may have persuaded some people to comply with tribal norms. Because no written accounts of the purpose of trephination exist, other explanations are possible. For instance, perhaps trephination was simply a form of surgery

truth OR fiction

Psychological problems like depression may be experienced differently by people in different cultures.

☑ **TRUE** For example, depression is more likely to be associated with the development of physical symptoms among people in East Asian cultures than in Western cultures.

1.5 Describe the historical changes that have occurred in conceptualizations and treatment of abnormal behavior through the course of Western culture.

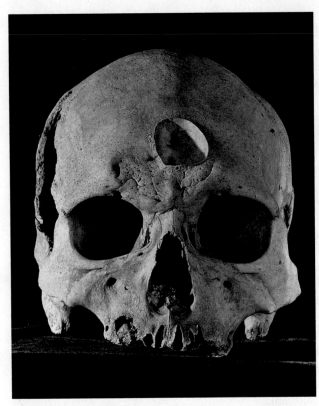

Trephination. Trephination refers to a procedure by which a hole is chipped into a person's skull. Some investigators speculate that the practice represented an ancient form of surgery. Perhaps trephination was intended to release the "demons" responsible for abnormal behavior.

Source: Photo by Bierwert. American Museum of Natural History Library.

to remove shattered pieces of bone or blood clots that resulted from head injuries (Maher & Maher, 1985).

The notion of supernatural causes of abnormal behavior, or demonology, was prominent in Western society until the Age of Enlightenment. The ancients explained nature in terms of the actions of the gods: The Babylonians believed the movements of the stars and the planets expressed the adventures and conflicts of the gods. The Greeks believed that the gods toyed with humans, that they unleashed havoc on disrespectful or arrogant humans and clouded their minds with madness.

In ancient Greece, people who behaved abnormally were sent to temples dedicated to Aesculapius, the god of healing. The Greeks believed that Aesculapius would visit the afflicted while they slept in the temple and offer them restorative advice through dreams. Rest, a nutritious diet, and exercise were also part of the treatment. Incurables were driven from the temple by stoning.

Origins of the Medical Model: In "Ill Humor"

Not all ancient Greeks believed in the demonological model. The seeds of naturalistic explanations of abnormal behavior were sown by Hippocrates and developed by other physicians in the ancient world, especially Galen.

Hippocrates (ca. 460–377 B.C.E.), the celebrated physician of the Golden Age of Greece, challenged the prevailing beliefs of his time by arguing that illnesses of the body and mind were the result of natural causes, not possession by supernatural spirits. He believed the health of the body and mind depended on the balance of **humors,** or vital fluids, in the body: phlegm, black bile, blood, and yellow bile. An imbalance of humors, he thought, accounted for abnormal behavior. A lethargic or sluggish person was believed to have an excess of phlegm, from which we derive the word *phlegmatic.* An overabundance of black bile was believed to cause depression, or *melancholia.* An excess of blood created a *sanguine* disposition: cheerful, confident, and optimistic. An excess of yellow bile made people "bilious" and *choleric*—quick-tempered.

Though scientists no longer subscribe to Hippocrates's theory of bodily humors, his theory is important because of its break from demonology. It foreshadowed the modern medical model, the view that abnormal behavior results from underlying biological processes. Hippocrates made other contributions to modern thought and, indeed, to modern medical practice. He classified abnormal behavior patterns, using three main categories, which still have equivalents today: *melancholia* to characterize excessive depression, *mania* to refer to exceptional excitement, and *phrenitis* (from the Greek "inflammation of the brain") to characterize the bizarre behavior that might today typify schizophrenia. To this day, medical schools honor Hippocrates by having students swear an oath of medical ethics that he originated, the Hippocratic oath.

Galen (ca. 130–200 C.E.), a Greek physician who attended Roman emperor–philosopher Marcus Aurelius, adopted and expanded on the teachings of Hippocrates. Among Galen's contributions was the discovery that arteries carry blood, not air, as had been formerly believed.

Medieval Times

The Middle Ages, or medieval times, cover the millennium of European history from about 476 C.E. through 1450 C.E. After the passing of Galen, belief in supernatural causes, especially the doctrine of possession, increased in influence and eventually dominated medieval thought. This doctrine held that abnormal behaviors were a sign of possession by evil spirits or the Devil. This belief was part of the teachings of the Roman Catholic Church, the central institution in Western Europe after the decline of the Roman Empire. Although belief in possession preceded the Church and is found in ancient Egyptian and Greek writings, the Church revitalized it. The Church's treatment of choice for possession was exorcism. Exorcists were employed to persuade evil spirits that the bodies of the "possessed" were no longer habitable. Methods of persuasion included prayer, incantations, waving a cross at the victim, and beating and flogging, even starving, the victim. If the victim continued to display unseemly behavior, there were yet more persuasive remedies, such as the rack, a device of torture. No doubt, recipients of these "remedies" desperately wished the Devil would vacate them immediately.

The Renaissance—the great revival of classical learning, art, and literature—began in Italy in the 1400s and spread throughout Europe. Ironically, although the Renaissance is considered the transition from the medieval to the modern world, the fear of witches also reached its height during this period.

Witchcraft

The late 15th through the late 17th centuries were especially bad times to annoy your neighbors. These were times of massive persecutions, particularly of women, who were accused of witchcraft. Church officials believed that witches made pacts with the Devil, practiced satanic rituals, ate babies, and poisoned crops. In 1484, Pope Innocent VIII decreed that witches be executed. Two Dominican priests compiled a notorious manual for witch-hunting, called the *Malleus Maleficarum* (The Witches' Hammer), to help inquisitors identify suspected witches. Many thousands would be accused of witchcraft and put to death in the next two centuries.

Exorcism. This medieval woodcut illustrates the practice of exorcism, which was used to expel the evil spirits that were believed to have possessed people.

Witch-hunting required innovative "diagnostic" tests. In the case of the water-float test, suspects were dunked in a pool to certify they were not possessed by the Devil. The test was based on the principle in smelting, during which pure metals settle to the bottom, whereas impurities bob up to the surface. Suspects who sank and drowned were ruled pure. Suspects who kept their heads above water were judged to be in league with the Devil. As the saying went, you were "damned if you do and damned if you don't."

Modern scholars once believed these so-called witches were actually people with psychological disorders who were persecuted because of their abnormal behavior. Many suspected witches did confess to bizarre behaviors, such as flying or engaging in sexual intercourse with the Devil, which suggests the types of disturbed behavior associated with modern conceptions of schizophrenia. Yet these confessions must be discounted because they were extracted under torture by inquisitors who were bent on finding evidence to support accusations of witchcraft (Spanos, 1978). We know today that the threat of torture and other forms of intimidation are sufficient to extract false confessions. Although some who were persecuted as witches probably did show abnormal behavior patterns, most did not (Schoenman, 1984). Rather, it appears that accusations of witchcraft were a convenient means of disposing of social nuisances and political rivals, of seizing property, and of suppressing heresy (Spanos, 1978). In English villages, many of the accused were poor, unmarried elderly women who were forced to beg for food from their neighbors. If misfortune befell the people who declined to give help, the beggar might be accused of having cast a curse on the household. If the woman was generally unpopular, an accusation of witchcraft was likely to follow.

Demons were believed to play roles in both abnormal behavior and witchcraft. However, although some victims of demonic possession were perceived to be afflicted as retribution for their own wrongdoing, others were considered to be innocent victims—possessed by demons through no fault of their own. Witches were believed to have renounced God and voluntarily entered into a pact with the Devil. Witches were generally seen as more deserving of torture and execution (Spanos, 1978).

The water-float test. This so-called test was one way in which medieval authorities sought to detect possession and witchcraft. Managing to float above the waterline was deemed a sign of impurity. In the lower right hand corner, you can see the bound hands and feet of one poor unfortunate who failed to remain afloat, but whose drowning would have cleared away any suspicions of possession.

Historical trends do not follow straight lines. Although the demonological model held sway during the Middle Ages and much of the Renaissance, it did not completely supplant belief in naturalistic causes. In medieval England, for example, demonic possession was only rarely invoked in cases in which a person was held to be insane by legal authorities (Neugebauer, 1979). Most explanations for unusual behavior involved natural causes, such as physical illness or trauma to the brain. In England, in fact, some disturbed people were kept in hospitals until they were restored to sanity (Allderidge, 1979). The Renaissance Belgian physician Johann Weyer (1515–1588) also took up the cause of Hippocrates and Galen by arguing that abnormal behavior and thought patterns were caused by physical problems.

Asylums

By the late 15th and early 16th centuries, asylums, or madhouses, began to crop up throughout Europe. Many were former leprosariums, which were no longer needed because of the decline in leprosy after the late Middle Ages. Asylums often gave refuge to beggars as well as the mentally disturbed, but conditions were appalling. Residents were chained to their beds and left to lie in their own waste or to wander about unassisted. Some asylums became public spectacles. In one asylum in London, St. Mary's of Bethlehem Hospital—from which the word *bedlam* is derived—the public could buy tickets to observe the antics of the inmates, much as we would pay to see a circus sideshow or animals at the zoo **T / F**.

The Reform Movement and Moral Therapy

The modern era of treatment begins with the efforts of the Frenchmen Jean-Baptiste Pussin and Philippe Pinel in the late 18th and early 19th centuries. They argued that people who behave abnormally suffer from diseases and should be treated humanely. This view was not popular at the time; mentally disturbed people were regarded as threats to society, not as sick people in need of treatment.

From 1784 to 1802, Pussin, a layman, was placed in charge of a ward for people considered "incurably insane" at La Bicêtre, a large mental hospital in Paris. Although Pinel is often credited with freeing the inmates of La Bicêtre from their chains, Pussin was actually the first official to unchain a group of the "incurably insane." These unfortunates had been considered too dangerous and unpredictable to be left unchained. But Pussin believed that if they were treated with kindness, there would be no need for chains. As he predicted, most of the shut-ins were manageable and calm after their chains were removed. They could walk the hospital grounds and take in fresh air. Pussin also forbade the staff from treating the residents harshly, and he fired employees who ignored his directives.

Pinel (1745–1826) became the medical director for the incurables' ward at La Bicêtre in 1793 and continued the humane treatment Pussin had begun. He stopped harsh practices, such as bleeding and purging, and moved patients from darkened dungeons to well-ventilated, sunny rooms. Pinel also spent hours talking to inmates, in the belief that showing understanding and concern would help restore them to normal functioning.

The philosophy of treatment that emerged from these efforts was labeled *moral therapy*. It was based on the belief that providing humane treatment in a relaxed and decent environment could restore functioning. Similar reforms were instituted at about this time in England by William Tuke and later in the United States by Dorothea Dix. Another influential figure was the American physician Benjamin Rush (1745–1813)—also a signatory to the Declaration of Independence and an early leader of the antislavery movement. Rush, considered the father of American psychiatry, penned the first American textbook

"Bedlam." The bizarre antics of the patients at St. Mary's of Bethlehem Hospital in London in the 18th century were a source of entertainment for the well-heeled gentry of the town, such as the two well-dressed women in the middle of the painting.

on psychiatry, in 1812: *Medical Inquiries and Observations Upon the Diseases of the Mind.* He believed that madness is caused by engorgement of the blood vessels of the brain. To relieve pressure, he recommended bloodletting, purging, and ice-cold baths. He did advance humane treatment by encouraging the staff of his Philadelphia Hospital to treat patients with kindness, respect, and understanding. He also favored the therapeutic use of occupational therapy, music, and travel (Farr, 1994). His hospital became the first in the United States to admit patients for psychological disorders.

Dorothea Dix (1802–1887), a Boston schoolteacher, traveled about the country decrying the deplorable conditions in the jails and almshouses where mentally disturbed people were placed. As a result of her efforts, 32 mental hospitals devoted to treating people with psychological disorders were established throughout the United States.

A Step Backward

In the latter half of the 19th century, the belief that abnormal behaviors could be successfully treated or cured by moral therapy fell into disfavor. A period of apathy ensued in which patterns of abnormal behavior were deemed incurable (Grob, 1994, 2009). Mental institutions in the United States grew in size but provided little more than custodial care. Conditions deteriorated. Mental hospitals became frightening places. It was not uncommon to find residents "wallowing in their own excrements," in the words of a New York State official of the time (Grob, 1983). Straitjackets, handcuffs, cribs, straps, and other devices were used to restrain excitable or violent patients.

Deplorable hospital conditions remained commonplace through the middle of the 20th century. By the mid-1950s, the population in mental hospitals had risen to half a million. Although some state hospitals provided decent and humane care, many were described as little more than human snake pits. Residents were crowded into wards that lacked even rudimentary sanitation. Mental patients in back wards were essentially *warehoused;* that is, they were left to live out their lives with little hope or expectation of recovery or a return to the community. Many received little professional care and were abused by poorly trained and supervised staffs. Finally, these appalling conditions led to calls for reforms of the mental health system. These reforms ushered in a movement toward **deinstitutionalization,** a policy of shifting the burden of care from state hospitals to community-based treatment setting, which led to a wholesale exodus from state mental hospitals. The mental hospital population across the United States has plummeted from nearly 600,000 in the 1950s to about 40,000 today ("Rate of Patients," 2012). Some mental hospitals were closed entirely.

Another factor that laid the groundwork for the mass exodus from mental hospitals was the development of a new class of drugs—the *phenothiazines.* This group of antipsychotic drugs, which helped quell the most flagrant behavior patterns associated with schizophrenia, was introduced in the 1950s. Phenothiazines reduced the need for indefinite hospital stays and permitted many people with schizophrenia to be discharged to halfway houses, group homes, and independent living.

The Role of the Mental Hospital Today

Most state hospitals today are better managed and provide more humane care than those of the 19th and early 20th centuries, but here and there, deplorable conditions persist. Today's state hospital is generally more treatment-oriented and focuses on preparing residents to return to community living. State hospitals function as part of an integrated, comprehensive approach to treatment. They provide a structured environment for people who are unable to function in a less-restrictive community setting. When hospitalization has restored patients to a higher level of functioning, the patients are reintegrated in the community and given follow-up care and transitional residences, if needed. If a community-based hospital is not available or if they require more extensive care, patients may be rehospitalized as needed in a state hospital. For younger and less intensely disturbed people,

The unchaining of inmates at La Bicêtre by 18th-century French reformer Philippe Pinel. Continuing the work of Jean-Baptiste Pussin, Pinel stopped harsh practices, such as bleeding and purging, and moved inmates from darkened dungeons to sunny, airy rooms. Pinel also took the time to converse with inmates, in the belief that understanding and concern would help restore them to normal functioning.

the state hospital stay is typically briefer than it was in the past, lasting only until their condition allows them to reenter society. Older, chronic patients, however, may be unprepared to handle the most rudimentary tasks of independent life (shopping, cooking, cleaning, and so on)—in part because the state hospital may be the only home such patients have known as adults.

The Community Mental Health Movement

The U.S. Congress in 1963 established a nationwide system of *community mental health centers* (CMHCs), which was intended to offer an alternative to long-term custodial care in bleak institutions. CMHCs were charged with providing continuing support and mental health care to former hospital residents, released from state mental hospitals. Unfortunately, not enough CMHCs have been established to serve the needs of hundreds of thousands of formerly hospitalized patients and to prevent the need to hospitalize new patients by providing comprehensive, community-based care and structured residential treatment settings, such as halfway houses.

The community mental health movement and the policy of deinstitutionalization were developed in the hope that mental patients could return to their communities and assume more independent and fulfilling lives. But deinstitutionalization has often been criticized for failing to live up to its lofty expectations. The discharge of mental patients from state hospitals left many thousands of marginally functioning people in communities that lacked adequate housing and other forms of support they needed to function. Although the community mental health movement has had some successes, a great many patients with severe and persistent mental health problems fail to receive the range of mental health and social services they need to adjust to life in the community (Frank & Glied, 2006; Lieberman, 2010). As we shall see, one of the major challenges facing the community mental health system is the problem of psychiatric homelessness.

The mental hospital. Under the policy of deinstitutionalization, mental hospitals today provide a range of services, including short-term treatment of people in crisis or in need of a secure treatment setting. They also provide long-term treatment in a structured environment for people who are unable to function in less-restrictive community settings.

Deinstitutionalization and the Psychiatric Homeless Population

Many of the homeless wandering city streets and sleeping in bus terminals and train stations are discharged mental patients or persons with disturbed behavior who might well have been hospitalized in earlier times, before deinstitutionalization was in place. Lacking adequate support, they often face more dehumanizing conditions on the street than they did in the hospital. Many compound their problems by turning to illegal street drugs such as crack. Also, some of the younger psychiatric homeless population might have remained hospitalized in earlier times but are now, in the wake of deinstitutionalization, directed toward community support programs when they are available. The problem of psychiatric homelessness is not limited to the United States. A recent study in Denmark showed that about 60% of the homeless population had diagnosable psychiatric disorders (Nielsen, Hjorthøj, Erlangsen, & Nordentoft, 2011).

The federal government estimates that about one-third of homeless adults in the United States suffer from severe psychological disorders (National Institutes of Health, 2003). A large percentage of the homeless also have significant neuropsychological impairments, such as problems with memory and concentration, which leaves them disadvantaged in terms of finding and holding jobs (Bousman et al., 2011; Rosenheck, 2012). The lack of available housing, transitional care facilities, and effective case management plays an important role in homelessness among people with psychiatric problems (Folsom et al., 2005; Rosenheck, 2012). Some homeless people with severe psychiatric problems are repeatedly hospitalized for brief stays in community-based hospitals during acute episodes. They move back and forth between the hospital and the community as though caught in a revolving door. Frequently, they are released from the hospital with inadequate arrangements for housing and community care. Some are essentially left to fend for themselves. Although many state hospitals closed their doors and others slashed the number of beds, the states failed to provide sufficient funds to support services needed in the community to replace the need for long-term hospitalization.

The mental health system alone does not have the resources to resolve the multifaceted problems faced by the psychiatric homeless population. Helping the psychiatric homeless escape from homelessness requires matching services to their needs in an integrated effort involving mental health and alcohol and drug abuse programs; access to decent, affordable housing; and provision of other social services (Price, 2009; Rosenheck, Kasprow, Frisman, & Liu-Mares, 2003).

Another difficulty is that homeless people with severe psychological problems typically do not seek out mental health services. Many have become disenfranchised from mental health services because of previous bad hospital stays, during which they had been treated poorly or felt disrespected, dehumanized, or simply ignored (Price, 2009). Society needs not only more intensive outreach and intervention efforts to help homeless people connect with the services they need but also programs that provide a better quality of care to homeless individuals (Coldwell & Bender, 2007; Price, 2009). All in all, the problems of the psychiatric homeless population remain complex, vexing problems for the mental health system and society at large.

Psychiatric homelessness. Many homeless people have severe psychological problems but fall through the cracks of the mental health and social service systems.

Deinstitutionalization: A Promise as Yet Unfulfilled

Although the net results of deinstitutionalization may not yet have lived up to expectations, a number of successful community-oriented programs are available. However, they remain underfunded and unable to reach many people needing ongoing community support. If deinstitutionalization is to succeed, patients need continuing care and opportunities for decent housing, gainful employment, and training in social and vocational skills. Most people with severe psychiatric disorders, such as schizophrenia, live in their communities, but only about half of them are currently in treatment (Torrey, 2011).

New, promising services exist to improve community-based care for people with chronic psychological disorders—for example, psychosocial rehabilitation centers, family psychoeducational groups, supportive housing and work programs, and social skills training. Unfortunately, too few of these services exist to meet the needs of many patients who might benefit from them. The community mental health movement must have expanded community support and adequate financial resources if it is to succeed in fulfilling its original promise.

Contemporary Perspectives on Abnormal Behavior

1.6 Describe the major contemporary perspectives on abnormal behavior.

As noted, beliefs in possession or demonology persisted until the 18th century, when society began to turn toward reason and science to explain natural phenomena and human behavior. The nascent sciences of biology, chemistry, physics, and astronomy promised knowledge derived from scientific methods of observation and experimentation. Scientific observation in turn uncovered the microbial causes of some kinds of diseases and gave rise to preventive measures. Scientific models of abnormal behavior also began to emerge, including models representing biological, psychological, sociocultural, and biopsychosocial perspectives. We briefly discuss each of these models here, particularly in terms of their historical background, which will lead to a fuller discussion in Chapter 2.

The Biological Perspective

Against the backdrop of advances in medical science, the German physician Wilhelm Griesinger (1817–1868) argued that abnormal behavior was rooted in diseases of the brain. Griesinger's views influenced another German physician, Emil Kraepelin (1856–1926), who wrote an influential textbook on psychiatry in 1883 in which he likened mental disorders to physical diseases. Griesinger and Kraepelin paved the way for the modern medical model, which attempts to explain abnormal behavior on the basis of underlying biological defects or abnormalities, not evil spirits. According to the medical model, people behaving abnormally suffer from mental illnesses or disorders that can be classified, like physical illnesses, according to their distinctive causes and symptoms. Adopters of the medical model don't necessarily believe that every mental disorder is a product of defective biology, but they maintain that it is useful to classify patterns of abnormal behavior as disorders that can be identified on the basis of their distinctive features or symptoms.

Kraepelin specified two main groups of mental disorders or diseases: **dementia praecox** [from roots meaning "precocious (premature) insanity"], which we now call *schizophrenia,* and manic–depressive insanity, which we now label *bipolar disorder* (Zivanovic & Nedic, 2012). Kraepelin believed that dementia praecox is caused by a biochemical imbalance and manic–depressive psychosis by an abnormality in body metabolism. His major contribution was the development of a classification system that forms the cornerstone of current diagnostic systems.

The medical model gained support in the late 19th century with the discovery that an advanced stage of *syphilis*—in which the bacterium that causes the disease directly invades the brain—led to a form of disturbed behavior called **general paresis** (from the Greek *parienai,* meaning "to relax"). General paresis is associated with physical symptoms and psychological impairment, including personality and mood changes, and with progressive deterioration of memory functioning and judgment. With the advent of antibiotics for treating syphilis, the disorder has become extremely uncommon.

General paresis is of interest to scientists mostly for historical reasons. With the discovery of the connection between general paresis and syphilis, scientists became optimistic that other biological causes would soon be discovered for many other types of disturbed behavior. The later discovery of Alzheimer's disease (discussed in Chapter 14), a brain disease that is the major cause of dementia, lent further support to the medical model. Yet, it is now known that the great majority of psychological disorders involve a complex web of factors scientists are still struggling to understand.

Much of the terminology used in abnormal psychology has been "medicalized." Because of the medical model, we commonly speak of people whose behavior is abnormal as being mentally ill, and we commonly refer to the symptoms of abnormal behavior, rather than the features or characteristics of abnormal behavior. Other terminological offspring of the medical model include *mental health, syndrome, diagnosis, patient, mental patient, mental hospital, prognosis, treatment, therapy, cure, relapse,* and *remission.*

The medical model is a major advance over demonology. It inspired the idea that abnormal behavior should be treated by learned professionals, not punished. Compassion supplanted hatred, fear, and persecution. But the medical model has also led to controversy over the extent to which certain behavior patterns should be considered forms of mental illness. We address this topic in the *@Issue* feature on page 18.

Charcot's teaching clinic. Parisian neurologist Jean-Martin Charcot presents a female patient who exhibits the highly dramatic behavior associated with hysteria, such as falling faint at a moment's notice. Charcot was an important influence on the young Sigmund Freud.

The Psychological Perspective

Even as the medical model was gaining influence in the 19th century, some scientists argued that organic factors alone could not explain the many forms of abnormal behavior. In Paris, a respected neurologist, Jean-Martin Charcot (1825–1893), experimented with hypnosis in treating *hysteria,* a condition characterized by paralysis or numbness that cannot be explained by any underlying physical cause. [Interestingly, cases of hysteria were common in the Victorian period, but are rare today (Spitzer, Gibbon, Skodol, Williams, & First, 1989).] The thinking at the time was that people with hysteria must have an affliction of the nervous system, which caused their symptoms. Yet, Charcot and his associates demonstrated that these symptoms could be removed in hysterical patients or, conversely, induced in normal patients, by means of hypnotic suggestion.

Among those who attended Charcot's demonstrations was a young Austrian physician named Sigmund Freud (1856–1939) (Esman, 2011). Freud reasoned that if hysterical symptoms could be made to disappear or appear through hypnosis—the mere "suggestion of ideas"—they must be psychological, not biological, in origin (E. Jones, 1953). Freud concluded that whatever psychological factors give rise to hysteria, they must lie outside the range of conscious awareness. This insight underlies the first psychological perspective on abnormal behavior—the **psychodynamic model.** "I received the proudest impression," Freud wrote of his experience with Charcot, "of the possibility that there could be powerful mental processes which nevertheless remained hidden from the consciousness of men" (as cited in Sulloway, 1983, p. 32).

Freud was also influenced by the Viennese physician Joseph Breuer (1842–1925), 14 years his senior. Breuer too had used hypnosis, to treat a 21-year-old woman, Anna O., with hysterical complaints for which there were no apparent medical basis, such as paralysis in her limbs, numbness, and disturbances of vision and hearing (E. Jones, 1953). A "paralyzed" muscle in her neck prevented her from turning her head. Immobilization of the fingers of her left hand made it all but impossible for her to feed herself. Breuer believed there was a strong psychological component to her symptoms. He encouraged her to talk about her symptoms, sometimes under hypnosis. Recalling and talking about events connected with the appearance of the symptoms—especially events that evoked feelings of fear, anxiety, or guilt—provided symptom relief, at least for a time. Anna referred to the treatment as the "talking cure" or, when joking, as "chimney sweeping."

The hysterical symptoms were taken to represent the transformation of these blocked-up emotions, forgotten but not lost, into physical complaints. In Anna's case, the symptoms disappeared once the emotions were brought to the surface and "discharged." Breuer labeled the therapeutic effect *catharsis,* or emotional discharge of feelings (from the Greek word *kathairein,* meaning to clean or to purify).

Sigmund Freud and Bertha Pappenheim (Anna O.). Freud is shown here at around age 30. Pappenheim (1859–1936) is known more widely in the psychological literature as "Anna O." Freud believed that her hysterical symptoms represented the transformation of blocked-up emotions into physical complaints.

THINKING CRITICALLY about abnormal psychology

@Issue: What Is Abnormal Behavior?

The question of where to draw the line between normal and abnormal behavior continues to be a subject of debate within the mental health field and the broader society. Unlike medical illness, a psychological or mental disorder cannot be identified by a spot on an X-ray or from a blood sample. Classifying these disorders involves clinical judgments, not findings of fact; and as we have noted, these judgments can change over time and can vary from culture to culture. For example, medical professionals once considered masturbation a form of mental illness. Although some people today may object to masturbation on moral grounds, professionals no longer regard it as a mental disturbance.

Consider other behaviors that may blur the boundaries between normal and abnormal: Is body-piercing abnormal, or is it simply a fashion statement? (How much piercing do you consider "normal"?) Might excessive shopping behavior or overuse of the Internet be forms of mental illness? Is bullying a symptom of an underlying disorder, or is it just bad behavior? Mental health professionals base their judgments on the kinds of criteria we outline in this text. But even in professional circles, debate continues about whether some behaviors should be classified as forms of abnormal behavior or mental disorders.

One of the longest of these debates concerns homosexuality. Until 1973, the American Psychiatric Association classified homosexuality as a mental disorder. In that year, the organization voted to drop homosexuality from its listing of classified mental disorders in its diagnostic manual, the *Diagnostic and Statistical Manual of Mental Disorders,* or *DSM* (discussed in Chapter 3). This decision to declassify homosexuality, however, was not unanimous among the nation's psychiatrists. Many argued that the decision was motivated more by political reasons than by good science. Some objected to basing such a decision on a vote. After all, would it be reasonable to drop cancer as a recognized medical illness on the basis of a vote? Shouldn't scientific criteria determine these kinds of judgments, rather than a popular vote?

What do you think? Is homosexuality a variation in the normal spectrum of sexual orientation, or is it a form of abnormal behavior? What is the basis of your judgment? What criteria did you apply in forming a judgment? What evidence do you have to support your beliefs?

truth OR fiction

Despite changing attitudes in society toward homosexuality, the psychiatric profession continues to classify homosexuality as a mental disorder.

☑ **FALSE** The psychiatric profession dropped homosexuality from its listing of mental disorders in 1973.

Is homosexuality a mental disorder? Until 1973, homosexuality was classified as a mental disorder by the American Psychiatric Association. What criteria should be used to form judgments about determining whether particular patterns of behavior comprise a mental or psychological disorder?

Within the *DSM* system, mental disorders are recognized on the basis of behavior patterns associated with either emotional distress and/or significant impairment in psychological functioning. Researchers find that people with a gay male or lesbian sexual orientation tend to have a greater frequency of suicide and of states of emotional distress, especially anxiety and depression, than people with a heterosexual orientation (Cochran, Sullivan, & Mays, 2003; King, 2008). But even if gay males and lesbians are more prone to develop psychological problems, it doesn't necessarily follow that these problems are the result of their sexual orientation.

Gay adolescents in our society come to terms with their sexuality against a backdrop of deep-seated prejudices and resentment toward gays. The process of achieving a sense of self-acceptance against this backdrop of societal intolerance can be so difficult that many gay adolescents seriously consider or attempt suicide. As adults, gay men and lesbians often continue to bear the brunt of prejudice and negative attitudes toward them, including negative reactions from family members that often follow the disclosure of their sexual orientation. The social stress associated with stigma, prejudice, and discrimination that gay people encounter may directly cause mental health problems (Meyer, 2003).

Understood in this context, it is little wonder that many gay males and lesbians develop psychological problems. As a leading authority in the field, psychologist J. Michael Bailey (1999, p. 883) wrote, "Surely, it must be difficult for young people to come to grips with their homosexuality in a world where homosexual people are often scorned, mocked, mourned, and feared."

Should we then accept the claim that societal intolerance is the root cause of psychological problems in people with a homosexual orientation? As critical thinkers, we should recognize that other factors may be involved. Scientists need more evidence before they can arrive at any judgments concerning why gay males and lesbians are more prone to psychological problems, especially suicide.

Imagine a society in which homosexuality was the norm and heterosexual people were shunned, scorned, or ridiculed. Would we find that heterosexual people are more likely to have psychological problems? Would this evidence lead us to assume that heterosexuality is a mental disorder? What do you think?

In thinking critically about the issue, answer the following questions:

• How do you decide when any behavior, such as social drinking or even shopping or Internet use, crosses the line from normal to abnormal?

• Is there a set of criteria you use in all cases? How do your criteria differ from the criteria specified in the text?

• Do you believe that homosexuality is abnormal? Why or why not?

Freud's theoretical model was the first major psychological model of abnormal behavior. As we'll see in Chapter 2, other psychological perspectives on abnormal behavior based on behavioral, humanistic, and cognitive models soon followed. Each of these perspectives, as well as the contemporary medical model, spawned particular forms of therapy to treat psychological disorders.

The Sociocultural Perspective

Mustn't we also consider the broader social context in which behavior occurs to understand the roots of abnormal behavior? Sociocultural theorists believe the causes of abnormal behavior may be found in the failures of society rather than in the person. Accordingly, psychological problems may be rooted in the ills of society, such as unemployment, poverty, family breakdown, injustice, ignorance, and lack of opportunity. Sociocultural factors also focus on relationships between mental health and social factors such as gender, social class, ethnicity, and lifestyle.

Sociocultural theorists also observe that once a person is called "mentally ill," the label is hard to remove. It also distorts other people's responses to the "patient." People classified as mentally ill are stigmatized and marginalized. Job opportunities may disappear, friendships may dissolve, and the "patient" may feel increasingly alienated from society. Sociocultural theorists focus peoples' attention on the social consequences of becoming labeled as a "mental patient." They argue that society needs to provide access to meaningful societal roles, as workers, students, and colleagues, to those with long-term mental health problems, rather than shunt them aside.

The Biopsychosocial Perspective

Aren't patterns of abnormal behavior too complex to be understood from any one model or perspective? Many mental health professionals endorse the view that abnormal behavior is best understood by taking into account multiple causes representing the biological, psychological, and sociocultural domains (Levine & Schmelkin, 2006). The **biopsychosocial model,** or interactionist model, informs this text's approach toward understanding the origins of abnormal behavior. We believe it's essential to consider the interplay of biological, psychological, and sociocultural factors in the development of psychological disorders. Although our understanding of these factors may be incomplete, we must consider all possible pathways and account for multiple factors, influences, and interactions.

Perspectives on psychological disorders provide a framework not only for explanation but also for treatment (see Chapter 2). The perspectives scientists use also lead to the predictions, or *hypotheses,* that guide their research or inquiries into the causes and treatments of abnormal behavior. The medical model, for example, fosters inquiry into genetic and biochemical treatment methods. In the next section, we consider the ways in which psychologists and other mental health professionals study abnormal behavior.

Research Methods in Abnormal Psychology

Abnormal psychology is a branch of the scientific discipline of psychology. Research in the field is based on the application of the **scientific method**. Before we explore the basic steps in the scientific method, let us consider the four overarching objectives of science: description, explanation, prediction, and control.

Description, Explanation, Prediction, and Control: The Objectives of Science

To understand abnormal behavior, we must first learn to describe it. Description allows us to recognize abnormal behavior and provides the basis for explaining it. Descriptions should be clear, unbiased, and based on careful observation. Let us pose a vignette that challenges you to put yourself in the position of a graduate student in psychology who is asked to describe the behavior of a laboratory rat the professor places on the desk:

Imagine you are a brand-new graduate student in psychology and are sitting in your research methods class on the first day of the term. The professor, a distinguished woman of about 50, enters the class. She is carrying a small wire-mesh cage containing a white rat. The professor removes the rat from the cage and places it on the desk. She asks the class to observe its behavior. As a serious student, you attend closely. The animal moves to the edge of the desk, pauses, peers over the edge, and seems to jiggle its whiskers at the floor below. It maneuvers along the edge of the desk, tracking the perimeter. Now and then the rat pauses and vibrates its whiskers downward in the direction of the floor.

The professor picks up the rat and returns it to the cage. She asks the class to describe the animal's behavior.

A student responds, "The rat seems to be looking for a way to escape."

Another student says, "It is reconnoitering its environment, examining it." "Reconnoitering"? You think. That student has seen too many war movies.

The professor writes each response on the blackboard. Another student raises her hand. "The rat is making a visual search of the environment," she says. "Maybe it's looking for food."

The professor prompts other students for their descriptions.

"It's looking around," says one.

"Trying to escape," says another.

Your turn arrives. Trying to be scientific, you say, "We can't say what its motivation might be. All we know is that it's scanning its environment."

"How so?" the professor asks.

"Visually," you reply, confidently.

The professor writes the response and then turns to the class, shaking her head. "Each of you observed the rat," she said, "but none of you described its behavior. Instead, you made inferences that the rat was 'looking for a way down' or 'scanning its environment' or 'looking for food,' and the like. These are not unreasonable inferences, but they are inferences, not descriptions. They also happen to be wrong. You see, the rat is blind. It's been blind since birth. It couldn't possibly be looking around, at least not in a visual sense."

The vignette about the blind rat illustrates that our descriptions of behavior may be influenced by our expectations. Our expectations reflect our preconceptions or models of behavior, and they may incline us to perceive events—such as the rat's movements and other people's behavior—in certain ways. Describing the rat in the classroom as "scanning" and "looking" for something is an inference, or conclusion, we draw from our observations based on our model of how animals explore their environments. In contrast, description would involve a precise accounting of the animal's movements around the desk, measuring how far in each direction it moves, how long it pauses, how it bobs its head from side to side, and so on.

Nevertheless, inference is important in science. Inference allows us to jump from the particular to the general—to suggest laws and principles of behavior that can be woven into a model or **theory** of behavior. Without a way of organizing our descriptions of phenomena in terms of models and theories, we would be left with a buzzing confusion of unconnected observations.

Theories help scientists explain puzzling data and predict future data. Prediction entails the discovery of factors that anticipate the occurrence of events. Geology, for example, seeks clues in the forces affecting the earth, interpretation of which can forecast natural events such as earthquakes and volcanic eruptions. Scientists who study abnormal behavior seek clues in overt behavior, biological processes, family interactions, and so forth, to predict the development of abnormal behaviors as well as factors that might predict response to various treatments. It is not sufficient that theoretical models help scientists explain or make sense of events or behaviors that have already occurred. Useful models and theories allow them to predict the occurrence of particular behaviors.

The idea of controlling human behavior—especially the behavior of people with serious problems—is controversial. The history of societal response to abnormal behaviors, including abuses such as exorcism and cruel forms of physical restraint, renders the idea particularly distressing. Within science, however, the word *control* does not imply that people are coerced into doing the bidding of others, like puppets dangling on strings. Psychologists, for example, are committed to the dignity of the individual, and the concept of human dignity requires that people be free to make decisions and exercise choices. Within this context, *controlling behavior* means using scientific knowledge to help people shape their own goals and more efficiently use their resources to accomplish them. Today, in the United States, even when helping professionals restrain people who are violently disturbed, the goal is to assist them in overcoming their agitation and regaining the ability to exercise meaningful choices in their lives. Ethical standards prohibit the use of injurious techniques in research or practice.

Psychologists and other scientists use the *scientific method* to advance the description, explanation, prediction, and control of abnormal behavior.

The Scientific Method

The scientific method tests assumptions and theories about the world through gathering objective evidence. Gathering evidence that is objective requires thoughtful observational and experimental methods. Here let us focus on the basic steps involved in using the scientific method in experimentation.

1. *Formulating a research question.* Scientists derive research questions from previous observations and current theories. For instance, on the basis of their clinical observations and theoretical understanding of the underlying mechanisms in depression, psychologists may formulate questions about whether certain experimental drugs or particular types of psychotherapy help people overcome depression.

2. *Framing the research question in the form of a hypothesis.* A **hypothesis** is a prediction tested in an experiment. For example, scientists might hypothesize that people who are clinically depressed will show greater improvement on measures of depression if they are given an experimental drug than if they receive an inert placebo (a sugar pill).

3. *Testing the hypothesis.* Scientists test hypotheses through experiments in which variables are controlled and the differences are observed. For instance, they can test the hypothesis about the experimental drug by giving the drug to one group of people with depression and giving another group the placebo. They can then test to see if the people who received the active drug showed greater improvement over a period of time than those who received the placebo.

4. *Drawing conclusions about the hypothesis.* In the final step, scientists draw conclusions from their findings about the accuracy of their hypotheses. Psychologists use statistical methods to determine the likelihood that differences between groups are significant, as opposed to chance fluctuations. Psychologists can be reasonably confident that group differences are significant—that is, not because of chance—when

there is a probability of less than 5% that chance alone can explain the differences. When well-designed research findings fail to bear out hypotheses, scientists rethink the theories from which the hypotheses are derived. Research findings often lead to modifications in theory, new hypotheses, and in turn, subsequent research.

Before we consider the major research methods used by psychologists and others in studying abnormal behavior, let us consider some of the principles that guide ethical conduct in research.

1.8 **Identify** the ethical principles that guide research in psychology.

1.9 **Describe** the major types of research methods scientists use to study abnormal behavior and **evaluate** the strengths and weaknesses of these methods.

Ethics in Research

Ethical principles are designed to promote the dignity of the individual, protect human welfare, and preserve scientific integrity (American Psychological Association, 2002). Psychologists are prohibited by the ethical standards of their profession from using methods that cause psychological or physical harm to their subjects or clients. Psychologists also must follow ethical guidelines that protect animal subjects in research.

Institutions such as universities and hospitals have review committees, called *institutional review boards* (IRBs), that review proposed research studies in light of ethical guidelines. Investigators must receive IRB approval before they are permitted to begin their studies. Two of the major principles on which ethical guidelines are based are (a) *informed consent* and (b) *confidentiality.*

The principle of **informed consent** requires that people be free to choose whether they want to participate in research studies. They must be given sufficient information in advance about the study's purposes and methods, and its risks and benefits, to make an informed decision about their participation. Research participants must be free to withdraw from a study at any time without penalty. In some cases, researchers may withhold certain information until all the data are collected. For instance, participants in placebo-control studies of experimental drugs are told that they may receive an inert placebo rather than the active drug. In studies in which information was withheld or deception was used, participants must be debriefed afterward. That is, they must receive an explanation of the true methods and purposes of the study and why it was necessary to keep them in the dark. After the study is concluded, participants who received the placebo would be given the option of receiving the active treatment, if warranted.

Research participants also have a right to expect that their identities will not be revealed. Investigators are required to protect their **confidentiality** by keeping the records of their participation secure and by not disclosing their identities to others.

We now turn to discussion of the research methods used to investigate abnormal behavior.

The Naturalistic Observation Method

In **naturalistic observation,** the investigator observes behavior in the field, where it happens. Anthropologists have observed behavior patterns in preliterate societies to study human diversity. Sociologists have followed the activities of adolescent gangs in inner cities. Psychologists have spent weeks observing the behavior of homeless people in train stations and bus terminals. They have even observed the eating habits of slender and overweight people in fast-food restaurants, searching for clues to obesity.

Scientists try to ensure that their naturalistic observations are unobtrusive, so as to minimize interference with the behavior they observe. Nevertheless, the presence of the observer may distort the behavior that is observed, and this must be taken into consideration.

Naturalistic observation provides information on how people behave, but it does not reveal why they do so. It may reveal, for example, that men who frequent bars

Naturalistic observation. In naturalistic observation, psychologists take their research into the streets, homes, restaurants, schools, and other settings where behavior can be directly observed. For example, psychologists have unobtrusively positioned themselves in school playgrounds to observe how aggressive or socially anxious children interact with peers.

and drink often get into fights. But such observations do not show that alcohol *causes* aggression. As we shall see, questions of cause and effect are best approached by means of controlled experiments.

The Correlational Method

One of the primary methods used to study abnormal behavior is the **correlational method,** which involves the use of statistical methods to examine relationships between two or more factors that can vary, called *variables.* For example, in Chapter 7 we will see that there is a statistical relationship, or *correlation,* between the variables of negative thinking and depressive symptoms. The statistical measure used to express the association or correlation between two variables is called the **correlation coefficient,** which can vary along a continuum ranging from –1.00 to +1.00. When higher values in one variable (negative thinking) are associated with higher values in the other variable (depressive symptoms), there is a *positive correlation* between the variables. If higher levels of one variable are associated with lower values of another variable, there is a *negative correlation* between the variables. Positive correlations carry positive signs; negative correlations carry negative signs. The higher the correlation coefficient—meaning the closer it is to either −1.00 or +1.00—the stronger the relationship between the variables.

The correlational method does not involve manipulation of the variables of interest. In the previous example, the experimenter does not manipulate people's depressive symptoms or negative thoughts. Rather, the investigator uses statistical techniques to determine whether these variables tend to be associated with each other. Because the experimenter does not directly manipulate the variables, a correlation between two variables does not prove that they are causally related to each other. It may be the case that two variables are correlated but have no causal connection. For example, children's foot size is correlated with their vocabulary, but growth in foot size does not cause the growth of vocabulary. Depressive symptoms and negative thoughts are correlated, as we shall see in Chapter 7. Though negative thinking may be a causative factor in depression, it is also possible that the direction of causality works the other way—that depression gives rise to negative thinking. Or perhaps the direction of causality works both ways, with negative thinking contributing to depression and depression in turn influencing negative thinking. Then again, depression and negative thinking may both reflect a common causative factor, such as stress, and not be causally related to each other at all. In sum, we cannot tell from a correlation alone whether or not variables are causally linked. To address questions of cause and effect, investigators use experimental methods in which the experimenter manipulates one or more variables of interest and observes their effects on other variables or outcomes under controlled conditions.

Although the correlational method cannot determine cause-and-effect relationships, it does serve the scientific objective of prediction. When two variables are correlated, scientists can use one to predict the other. Although causal connections are complex and somewhat nebulous, knowledge, for example, of correlations among alcoholism, family history, and attitudes toward drinking helps scientists predict which adolescents are at greater risk of developing problems with alcohol. Knowing which factors predict future problems helps direct preventive efforts toward high-risk groups.

THE LONGITUDINAL STUDY The **longitudinal study** is a type of correlational study in which individuals are periodically tested or evaluated over lengthy periods of time, perhaps for decades. By studying people over time, researchers seek to identify factors or events in people's lives that predict the later development of abnormal behavior patterns, such as depression or schizophrenia. Prediction is based on the *correlation* between events or factors that are separated in time. However, this type of research is time-consuming and costly. It requires a commitment that may literally outlive the original investigators. Therefore, long-term longitudinal studies are relatively uncommon. In Chapter 11, we examine one of the best-known longitudinal studies, the Danish high-risk study that tracked a group of children whose mothers had schizophrenia and who were themselves at increased risk of developing the disorder.

The Experimental Method

The **experimental method** allows scientists to demonstrate causal relationships by manipulating the causal factor and measuring its effects under controlled conditions that minimize the risk of other factors explaining the results.

The term *experiment* can cause some confusion. Broadly speaking, an experiment is a trial or test of a hypothesis. From this vantage point, any method that seeks to test a hypothesis could be considered experimental—including naturalistic observation and correlational studies. But investigators usually limit the use of the term *experimental method* to refer to studies in which researchers seek to uncover cause-and-effect relationships by directly manipulating possible causal factors.

In experimental research, the factors or variables hypothesized to play a causal role are manipulated or controlled by the investigator. These are called **independent variables.** Factors that are observed in order to determine the effects of manipulating the independent variable are labeled **dependent variables.** Dependent variables are measured, but not manipulated, by the experimenter. Examples of independent and dependent variables of interest to investigators of abnormal behavior are shown in Table 1.1.

In an experiment, subjects are exposed to an *independent variable,* for example, the type of beverage (alcoholic vs. nonalcoholic) they consume in a laboratory setting. They are then observed or examined to determine whether the independent variable makes a difference in their behavior, or more precisely, whether the independent variable affects the dependent variable—for example, whether they behave more aggressively if they consume alcohol. Studies need to have a sufficient number of participants (subjects) to be able to detect statistically meaningful differences between experimental groups.

EXPERIMENTAL AND CONTROL GROUPS Well-controlled experiments randomly assign subjects to experimental and control groups (Mauri, 2012). The **experimental group** is given the experimental treatment, whereas the **control group** is not. Care is taken to hold other conditions constant for each group. By using **random assignment** and holding other conditions constant, experimenters can be reasonably confident that it was the experimental treatment, and not uncontrolled factors, such as room temperature or differences between the types of people in the experimental and control groups, that explained the experimental findings.

Why should experimenters assign subjects to experimental and control groups at random? Consider a study intended to investigate the effects of alcohol on behavior. Let's suppose we allowed subjects themselves to decide whether they wanted to be in an experimental group, which drank alcohol, or a control group, which drank a nonalcoholic beverage. If this were the case, differences between the groups might be due to an underlying **selection factor** rather than the experimental manipulation.

TABLE **1.1**

Examples of Independent and Dependent Variables in Experimental Research

Independent Variables	Dependent Variables
Type of treatment: different types of drug treatments or psychological treatments	Behavioral variables: measures of adjustment, activity levels, eating behavior, smoking behavior
Treatment factors: brief vs. long-term treatment, inpatient vs. outpatient treatment	Physiological variables: measures of physiological responses such as heart rate, blood pressure, and brain wave activity
Experimental manipulations: types of beverage consumed (alcoholic vs. nonalcoholic)	Self-report variables: measures of anxiety, mood, or marital or life satisfaction

For example, subjects who *chose* the alcoholic beverage might differ in their personalities from those who chose the control beverage. They might be more willing to explore or to take risks, for example. Therefore, the experimenter would not know whether the independent variable (type of beverage) or a selection factor (difference in the kinds of subjects making up the groups) was ultimately responsible for observed differences in behavior. Random assignment controls for selection factors by ensuring that subject characteristics are randomly distributed across both groups. Thus, it is reasonable to assume that differences between groups result from the treatments they receive rather than from differences between the subjects making up the groups. Still, it is possible that apparent treatment effects stem from subjects' expectancies about the treatments they receive rather than from the active components in the treatments themselves. In other words, knowing that you are being given an alcoholic beverage to drink might affect your behavior, quite apart from the alcoholic content of the beverage itself.

CONTROLLING FOR SUBJECT EXPECTANCIES To control for subject expectancies, experimenters rely on procedures that render subjects **blind,** or uninformed about the treatments they are receiving. For example, participants in a study designed to test an investigational medication for depression would be kept uninformed about whether they are receiving the actual drug or a **placebo,** an inert drug that physically resembles the active drug. Experimenters use placebos to control for the possibility that treatment effects result from a person's hopeful expectancies rather than from the chemical properties of the drug itself or from the specific techniques used in psychotherapy (Bradford & Meston, 2010; Moerman, 2011).

In a *single-blind placebo-control study,* subjects are randomly assigned to treatment conditions in which they receive either an active drug (experimental condition) or an inert placebo (placebo-control condition), but are kept blind, or uninformed, about which drug they receive. It is helpful to keep the researchers as well blind as to which substances the subjects receive, so as to prevent the researchers' own expectations from affecting the results. So in the case of a *double-blind placebo-control design,* neither the researcher nor the subject knows who is receiving the active drug or the placebo.

Double-blind studies control for both subject and experimenter expectancies. But a major limitation of single-blind and double-blind studies is that participants and experimenters can sometimes "see through" the blind (Mooney, White, & Hatsukami, 2004). Telltale side effects or obvious drug effects, or differences in the taste or smell between the placebo and the active drug, may provide clues for identifying the active drug, making the double-blind seem like a Venetian blind with the slats slightly open (Perlis et al., 2010). Still, the double-blind placebo control is among the strongest and most popular experimental designs, especially in drug treatment research. Although placebos are routinely used in clinical research, evidence indicates that the effects of placebos are generally weak (Bailar, 2001; Hrobjartsson & Gotzsche, 2001). Placebo effects are generally strongest in pain studies, presumably because pain is a subjective experience that may be influenced more by the power of suggestion than other physiological factors that rely on objective measures, such as blood pressure.

Placebo-control groups are also used in psychotherapy research to control for subject expectancies. Assume you were to study the effects of therapy method A on mood. You could randomly assign research participants to either an experimental group in which they receive the new therapy or to a (no-treatment) "waiting-list" control group. But in that case, the experimental group might show greater improvement because participation in treatment engendered hopeful expectations, not because of the particular therapy method used. Although a waiting-list control group might control for positive effects due simply to the passage of time, it would not account for placebo effects, such as the benefits of therapy resulting from instilling a sense of hope and expectations of success.

To control for placebo effects, experimenters sometimes use an *attention-placebo* control group in which participants are exposed to a believable or credible treatment that contains the nonspecific factors that all therapies share—such as the attention and

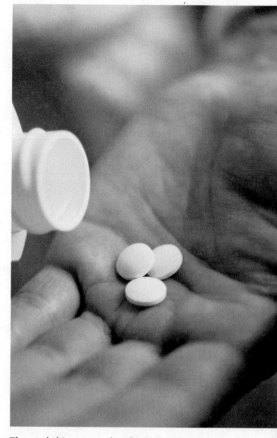

The real thing or a placebo? Placebos are inert pills that physically resemble active drugs.

emotional support of a therapist—but not the specific therapeutic ingredients represented in the active treatment. Attention-placebo treatments commonly substitute general discussions of participants' problems for the specific ingredients of therapy contained in the experimental treatment. Unfortunately, although experimenters may keep attention-placebo subjects blind as to whether they are receiving the experimental treatment, their therapists are generally aware of which treatment is being administered. Therefore, the attention-placebo method may not control for therapists' expectations.

EXPERIMENTAL VALIDITY Experimental studies are judged on whether they are valid, or sound. There are many aspects of validity, including *internal validity, external validity,* and *construct validity.* We will see in Chapter 3 that the term *validity* is also applied in the context of tests and measures to refer to the degree to which these instruments measure what they purport to measure.

Experiments have **internal validity** when the observed changes in the dependent variable(s) can be causally related to changes in the independent or treatment variable. Assume that a group of depressed subjects is treated with a new antidepressant medication (the independent variable), and changes in their mood and behavior (the dependent variables) are tracked over time. After several weeks of treatment, the researcher finds most subjects have improved and claims the new drug is an effective treatment for depression. Not so fast! How does the experimenter know that the independent variable and not some other factor was causally responsible for the improvement? Perhaps the subjects improved naturally as time passed, or perhaps they were exposed to other events responsible for their improvement. Experiments lack internal validity to the extent that they fail to control for other factors (called *confounds,* or threats to validity) that might pose rival hypotheses for the results.

Experimenters *randomly assign* subjects to treatment and control groups to control for rival hypotheses (Mitka, 2011). Random assignment helps ensure that subjects' attributes—intelligence, motivation, age, race, and so on—are randomly distributed across the groups and are not likely to favor one group over the other. Through the random assignment to groups, researchers can be reasonably confident that significant differences between the treatment and control groups reflect the effects of independent (treatment) variables and not confounding selection factors. Well-designed studies include the large-enough samples of research participants needed to be able to discern statistically significant differences between experimental and control groups.

External validity refers to the generalizability of results of an experimental study to other subjects, settings, and times. In most cases, researchers are interested in generalizing the results of a specific study (e.g., effects of a new antidepressant medication on a sample of people who are depressed) to a larger population (people in general who are depressed). The external validity of a study is strengthened to the degree that the *sample* is representative of the target population. In studying the problems of the urban homeless, it is essential to recruit a representative sample of the homeless population, for example, rather than focusing on a few homeless people who happen to be available. One way of obtaining a representative sample is by means of random sampling. In a *random sample,* every member of the target population has an equal chance of being selected.

Researchers may seek to extend the results of a particular study by means of *replication,* which refers to the process of repeating the experiment in other settings, with samples drawn from other populations, or at other times. A treatment for hyperactivity may be helpful with economically deprived children in an inner-city classroom but not with children in affluent suburbs or rural areas. The external validity of the treatment may be limited if its effects do not generalize to other samples or settings. That does not mean the treatment is less effective, but rather that its range of effectiveness may be limited to certain populations or situations.

Construct validity is a conceptually higher level of validity. It is the degree to which treatment effects can be accounted for by the theoretical mechanisms or constructs represented in the independent variables. A drug, for example, may have predictable effects but not for the theoretical reasons claimed by the researchers.

Consider a hypothetical experimental study of a new antidepressant medication. The research may have internal validity in the form of solid controls and external validity in the form of generalizability across samples of seriously depressed people. However, it may lack construct validity if the drug does not work for the reasons proposed by the researchers. Perhaps the researchers assumed that the drug would work by raising the levels of certain chemicals in the nervous system, whereas the drug actually works by increasing the sensitivity of receptors for those chemicals. "So what?" we may ask. After all, the drug still works. True enough—in terms of immediate clinical applications. However, a better understanding of why the drug works can advance theoretical knowledge of depression and give rise to the development of yet more effective treatments.

Scientists can never be certain about the construct validity of research. They recognize that their current theories about why their results occurred may eventually be toppled by other theories that better account for the findings.

Epidemiological Studies

Epidemiological studies examine the rates of occurrence of abnormal behavior in various settings or population groups. One type of epidemiological study is the **survey method,** which relies on interviews or questionnaires. Surveys are used to ascertain the rates of occurrence of various disorders in the population as a whole and in various subgroups classified according to factors such as race, ethnicity, gender, or social class. Rates of occurrence of a given disorder are expressed in terms of **incidence,** the number of new cases occurring during a specific period of time, and **prevalence,** the overall number of cases of a disorder existing in the population during a given period of time. Prevalence rates, then, include both new and continuing cases.

Epidemiological studies may point to potential causal factors in medical illnesses and psychological disorders, even though they lack the power of experiments. By finding that illnesses or disorders "cluster" in certain groups or locations, researchers can identify distinguishing characteristics that place these groups or regions at higher risk. Yet, such epidemiological studies cannot control for selection factors—that is, they cannot rule out the possibility that other unrecognized factors will play a causal role in putting a certain group at greater risk. Therefore, they must be considered suggestive of possible causal influences that must be tested further in experimental studies.

SAMPLES AND POPULATIONS In the best of possible worlds, researchers would conduct surveys in which every member of the population of interest would participate. In that way, they could be sure the survey results accurately represent the population they want to study. In reality, unless the population of interest is rather narrowly defined (say, for example, designating the population of interest as the students living on your dormitory floor), surveying every member of a given population is extremely difficult, if not impossible. Even census takers can't count every head in the general population. Consequently, most surveys are based on a sample, or subset, of the population. Researchers must take steps when constructing a sample to ensure that it *represents* the target population. For example, a researcher who sets out to study smoking rates in a local community by interviewing people drinking coffee in late-night cafés will probably overestimate its true prevalence.

One method of obtaining a representative sample is random sampling. A **random sample** is drawn in such a way that each member of the population of interest has an equal probability of selection. Epidemiologists sometimes construct random samples by surveying at random a given number of households within a target community. By repeating this process in a random sample of U.S. communities, the overall sample can approximate the general U.S. population, based on even a tiny percentage of the overall population.

Random sampling is often confused with random assignment. *Random sampling* refers to the process of randomly choosing individuals within a target population to participate in a survey or research study. By contrast, *random assignment* refers to the process by which members of a research sample are assigned at random to different experimental conditions or treatments.

Kinship Studies

Kinship studies attempt to disentangle the roles of heredity and environment in determining behavior of the subjects. Heredity plays a critical role in determining a wide range of traits. The structures we inherit make our behavior possible (humans can walk and run) and at the same time place limits on us (humans cannot fly without artificial equipment). Heredity plays a role in determining not only our physical characteristics (hair color, eye color, height, and the like) but also many of our psychological characteristics. The science of heredity is called *genetics.*

Genes are the basic building blocks of heredity. They regulate the development of traits. *Chromosomes,* rod-shaped structures that house our genes, are found in the nuclei of the body's cells. A normal human cell contains 46 chromosomes, organized into 23 pairs. Chromosomes consist of large, complex molecules of *deoxyribonucleic acid* (DNA). Genes occupy various segments along the length of chromosomes. Scientists believe there are about 20,000 to 25,000 genes in the nucleus of a human body cell (Lupski, 2007; Volkow, 2006). **T / F**

The set of traits specified by our genetic code is referred to as our **genotype.** Our appearance and behavior are not determined by our genotype alone. We are also influenced by environmental factors such as nutrition, learning, exercise, accidents and illnesses, and culture. The constellation of observable or expressed traits is called a **phenotype.** Our phenotype represents the interaction of genetic and environmental influences. People who possess genotypes for particular psychological disorders have a *genetic predisposition* that makes them more likely to develop the disorder in response to stressful life events, physical or psychological trauma, or other environmental factors (Kendler, Myers, & Reichborn-Kjennerud, 2011).

The more closely people are related, the more genes they have in common. Children receive half of their genes from each parent. Thus, there is a 50% overlap in genetic heritage between each parent and his or her offspring. Siblings (brothers and sisters) similarly share half their genes in common.

To determine whether abnormal behavior runs in a family, as one would expect if genetics plays a role, researchers locate a person with the disorder and then study how the disorder is distributed among the person's family members. The case first diagnosed is referred to as the index case, or **proband.** If the distribution of the disorder among family members of the proband approximates their degree of kinship, there may be a genetic component to the disorder. However, the closer their kinship, the more likely people are to share environmental backgrounds as well. For this reason, twin and adoptee studies are of particular value.

TWIN STUDIES Sometimes a fertilized egg cell (or *zygote*) divides into two cells that separate, so each develops into a separate person. In such cases, there is a 100% overlap in genetic makeup, and the offspring are known as identical twins, or monozygotic (MZ) twins. Sometimes a woman releases two egg cells, or ova, in the same month, and they are both fertilized. In such cases, the *zygotes* develop into fraternal twins, or dizygotic (DZ) twins. DZ twins overlap 50% in their genetic heritage, just as other siblings do.

Identical, or MZ, twins are important in the study of the relative influences of heredity and environment because differences between MZ twins are the result of environmental rather than genetic influences. In twin studies, researchers identify individuals with a specific disorder who are members of an MZ or DZ twin pair and then study the other twin in the pairs. A role for genetic factors is suggested when MZ twins (who have 100% genetic overlap) are more likely than DZ twins (who have 50% genetic overlap) to share a disorder in common. The term *concordance rate* refers to the percentage of cases in which both twins have the same trait or disorder. As we shall see, investigators find higher concordance rates for MZ twins than DZ twins for some forms of abnormal behavior, such as schizophrenia and major depression.

Even among MZ twins, though, environmental influences cannot be ruled out. Parents and teachers, for example, often encourage MZ twins to behave in similar ways. Put in another way: If one twin does X, everyone expects the other to do X also. Expectations have a way of influencing behavior and making for self-fulfilling prophecies. Because twins might not be typical of the general population, researchers are cautious when generalizing the results of twin studies to the larger population.

ADOPTEE STUDIES Adoptee studies provide powerful arguments for or against a role for genetic factors in the appearance of psychological traits and disorders. Assume that children are reared by adoptive parents from a very early age—perhaps from birth. The children share environmental backgrounds with their adoptive parents but not their genetic heritages. Then assume that we compare the traits and behavior patterns of these children with those of their biological parents and their adoptive parents. If the children show a greater similarity to their biological parents than to their adoptive parents on certain traits or disorders, we have strong evidence for genetic factors in these traits and disorders.

The study of monozygotic twins reared apart can provide even more dramatic testimony to the relative roles of genetics and environment in shaping abnormal behavior. However, this situation is so uncommon that few examples exist in the literature. Although adoptee studies may represent the strongest source of evidence for genetic factors in explaining abnormal behavior patterns, we should recognize that adoptees, like twins, may not be typical of the general population. In later chapters, we explore the role that adoptee and other kinship studies play in ferreting out genetic and environmental influences in many psychological disorders.

Twin studies. Identical twins have 100% of their genes in common, as compared with the 50% overlap among fraternal twins or any two other siblings. Establishing that identical twins are more likely to share a given disorder than are fraternal twins provides strong evidence for a genetic contribution to the disorder.

Case Studies

Case studies have been important influences in the development of theories and treatment of abnormal behavior. Freud developed his theoretical model primarily on the basis of case studies, such as the case of Anna O. Therapists representing other theoretical viewpoints have also reported cases studies.

TYPES OF CASE STUDIES Case studies are intensive studies of individuals. Some case studies are based on historical material, involving subjects who have been dead for hundreds of years. Freud, for example, conducted a case study of the Renaissance artist and inventor Leonardo da Vinci. More commonly, case studies reflect an in-depth analysis of an individual's course of treatment. They typically include detailed histories of the subject's background and response to treatment. The therapist attempts to glean information from a particular client's experience in therapy that may be of help to other therapists treating similar clients. **T / F**

Despite the richness of material that case studies can provide, they are much less rigorous as research designs than experiments. Distortions or gaps in memory are bound to occur when people discuss historical events, especially those of their childhoods. Some people may intentionally color events to make a favorable impression on the interviewer; others aim to shock the interviewer with exaggerated or fabricated recollections. Interviewers themselves may unintentionally guide subjects into reporting histories that mirror their theoretical preconceptions.

SINGLE-CASE EXPERIMENTAL DESIGNS The lack of control available in the traditional case-study method led researchers to develop more sophisticated methods, called **single-case experimental designs** (sometimes called *single-participant research designs*),

FIGURE **1.2**

An A-B-A-B reversal design.

1.10 Apply key features of critical thinking to the study of abnormal behavior.

in which subjects serve as their own controls. One of the most common forms of the single-case experimental design is the A-B-A-B, or **reversal design** (see Figure 1.2). This method involves repeated measurement of behavior across four successive phases:

1. *A baseline phase (A).* This phase occurs prior to treatment and allows the experimenter to establish a baseline rate for the behavior before treatment begins.
2. *A treatment phase (B).* Now the target behaviors are measured as the client undergoes treatment.
3. *A second baseline phase (A, again).* Treatment is now temporarily withdrawn or suspended. This is the reversal in the reversal design, and it is expected that the positive effects of treatment should now be reversed because the treatment has been withdrawn.
4. *A second treatment phase (B, again).* Treatment is reinstated, and the target behaviors are assessed again.

The investigator looks for evidence that change in the observed behavior occurred coincident with treatment. If the problem behavior declines whenever treatment is introduced (during the first and second treatment phases) but returns (is "reversed") to baseline levels during the reversal phase, the experimenter can be reasonably confident the treatment had the intended effect.

A reversal design is illustrated by a case study in which Azrin and Peterson (1989) used a controlled blinking treatment to eliminate a severe eye tic—a form of squinting the eyes shut tightly for a fraction of a second—in a 9-year-old girl. The tic occurred about 20 times a minute when the girl was at home. In the clinic, the rate of eye tics or squinting was measured for 5 minutes during a baseline period (A). Then the girl was prompted to blink her eyes softly every 5 seconds (B). The experimenters reasoned that voluntary "soft" blinking would activate motor (muscle) responses incompatible with those producing the tic, thereby suppressing the tic. As you can see in Figure 1.3, the tic was virtually

FIGURE **1.3**

Use of an A-B-A-B reversal design in the Azrin and Peterson study. Notice how the target response, eye tics per minute, decreased when the competing response was introduced in the first B phase. The rate then increased to near baseline levels when the competing response was withdrawn during the second A phase. It decreased again when the competing response was reinstated in the second B phase.

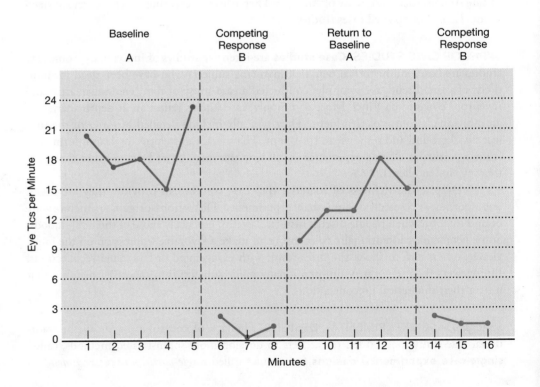

Thinking Critically About Abnormal Psychology

We are exposed to a flood of information about mental health streaming through the popular media—television, radio, and print media, including books, magazines, and newspapers, and increasingly, the Internet. We may hear a news report touting a new drug as a "breakthrough" in the treatment of anxiety, depression, or obesity, only to later learn that the so-called breakthrough doesn't live up to expectations or carries serious side effects. Some reports in the media are accurate and reliable, whereas others are misleading or biased or contain half-truths, exaggerated claims, or unsupported conclusions.

To sort through the welter of confusion, we need to use critical-thinking skills, to adopt a questioning attitude toward the information we hear and read. Critical thinkers weigh evidence to see if claims stand up to scrutiny. Becoming a critical thinker means never taking claims at face value. It means looking at both sides of the argument. Most of us take certain "truths" for granted. Critical thinkers, however, evaluate assertions and claims for themselves.

We encourage you to apply critical-thinking skills as you study this book. Adopt a skeptical attitude toward information you receive. Carefully examine the definitions of terms. Evaluate the logical bases of arguments. Evaluate claims in the light of available evidence. Here are some key features of critical thinking:

1. *Maintain a skeptical attitude.* Don't take anything at face value, not even claims made by respected scientists or textbook authors. Consider the evidence yourself. Seek additional information. Investigate the credibility of your sources.

2. *Consider the definitions of terms.* Statements may be true or false depending on how the terms they use are defined. Consider the statement, "Stress is bad for you." If we define *stress* in terms of hassles and work or family pressures that stretch our ability to cope to the max, then there is substance to the statement. However, if we define *stress* (see Chapter 4) as conditions that require us to adjust, which may include life events such as a new marriage or the birth of a child, then certain types of stress can be positive, even if they are difficult. Perhaps, as we'll see, we all need some amount of stress to be energized and alert.

3. *Weigh the assumptions or premises on which arguments are based.* Consider a case in which we are comparing differences in the rates of psychological disorders across racial or ethnic groups in our society. Assuming we find differences, should we conclude that ethnicity or racial identity accounts for these differences? This conclusion might be valid if we can assume that all other factors that distinguish one racial or ethnic group from another are held constant. However, ethnic or racial minorities in the United States and Canada are disproportionately represented among the poor, and the poor are more apt to develop more severe psychological disorders. Thus, differences we find among racial or ethnic groups may be a function of poverty, not race or ethnicity. These differences may also be due to stereotyping of minorities by clinicians in making diagnostic judgments, rather than to true differences in underlying rates of the disorder.

4. *Bear in mind that correlation is not causation.* Consider the relationship between depression and stress. Evidence shows a positive correlation between these variables, which means depressed people tend to encounter high levels of stress (e.g., Drieling, Calker, & Hecht, 2006; Kendler, Kuhn, & Prescott, 2004). But does stress cause depression? Perhaps it does. Or perhaps depression leads to greater stress. After all, depressive symptoms are stressful in themselves and may lead to additional stress as the person finds it increasingly difficult to meet life responsibilities, such as keeping up with work at school or on the job. Perhaps the two variables are not causally linked at all but are linked through a third variable, such as an underlying genetic factor. Is it possible that people inherit clusters of genes that make them more prone to both depression and stress?

5. *Consider the kinds of evidence on which conclusions are based.* Some conclusions, even seemingly "scientific" conclusions, are based on anecdotes and personal endorsements, not sound research. There is much controversy today about so-called recovered memories that are said to suddenly resurface in adulthood, usually during psychotherapy or hypnosis, and usually involving incidents of sexual abuse committed during childhood by the person's parents or family members. Are such recovered memories accurate? (See Chapter 6.)

6. *Do not oversimplify.* Consider the statement "Alcoholism is inherited." In Chapter 8, we review evidence suggesting that genetic factors may create a predisposition to alcoholism, at least in males. But the origins of alcoholism, as well as of schizophrenia, depression, and physical health problems such as cancer and heart disease, are complex and reflect the interplay of biological and environmental factors. For instance, people may inherit a predisposition to develop a particular disorder but may be able to avoid developing it if they live in a healthy environment or learn to manage stress effectively.

7. *Do not overgeneralize.* In Chapter 6, we consider evidence showing that a history of severe abuse in childhood figures prominently in the great majority of people who later develop multiple personalities. Does this mean that most abused children go on to develop multiple personalities? Not at all. Actually, very few do.

eliminated in but a few minutes of practicing the incompatible, or competing, response (soft blinking) but returned to near baseline levels during the reversal phase (A), when the competing response was withdrawn. The positive effects were quickly reinstated during the second treatment period (B). The child was also taught to practice the blinking response at home during scheduled 3-minute practice periods and whenever the tic occurred or she felt an urge to squint. The tic was eliminated during the first six weeks of the treatment program and remained absent at a follow-up evaluation two years later.

No matter how well controlled the design, or how impressive the results, single-case designs suffer from weak external validity because they cannot show whether a treatment that is effective for one person is effective for others. Replication can help strengthen external validity. But results from controlled experiments on groups of individuals are needed to provide more convincing evidence of treatment effectiveness and generalizability.

Scientists use different methods to study phenomena of interest to them. But all scientists share a skeptical, hard-nosed way of thinking called **critical thinking.** When thinking critically, they adopt a willingness to challenge the conventional wisdom that many take for granted. Scientists maintain an open mind and seek *evidence* to support or refute beliefs or claims rather than rely on feelings or gut impressions.

summing up

How Do We Define Abnormal Behavior?

1.1 Define the term psychological disorder.

Psychological disorders are patterns of abnormal behavior that involve marked personal distress or impaired functioning or behavior.

1.2 Identify the criteria that professionals use to determine whether behavior is abnormal.

Psychologists consider behavior abnormal when it meets some combination of the following criteria: when behavior is (a) unusual or statistically infrequent, (b) socially unacceptable or in violation of social norms, (c) fraught with misperceptions or misinterpretations of reality, (d) associated with states of severe personal distress, (e) maladaptive or self-defeating, or (f) dangerous. Psychological disorders are patterns of abnormal behavior associated with states of emotional distress or impaired behavior or ability to function.

1.3 Apply these criteria to case examples discussed in the text.

The case of Phil illustrated the psychological disorder of claustrophobia, which involves an excessive fear of enclosed spaces. His behavior was abnormal on the basis of the criteria of unusualness, personal distress, and impaired ability to meet occupational and family responsibilities. The case of the woman who cowered under the blankets was diagnosed with bipolar disorder, a psychological disorder characterized by personal distress and difficulty functioning effectively, as well as by possible self-defeating behavior, dangerous behavior (self-harm), and, as in this case, faulty perception or interpretations of reality. Thomas suffered from both schizophrenia and depression. His behavior demonstrated unusualness (deviant or bizarre behavior), disturbed perceptions or interpretations of reality (delusions and hallucinations), maladaptive behavior (difficulty meeting responsibilities of daily life), and personal distress. These disorders may also involve dangerous behavior, as in suicidal behavior.

1.4 Describe the cultural bases of abnormal behavior.

Behaviors deemed normal in one culture may be considered abnormal in another. Concepts of health and illness are also different in different cultures. Abnormal behavior patterns also take different forms in different cultures, and societal views or models explaining abnormal behavior vary across cultures.

Historical Perspectives on Abnormal Behavior

1.5 Describe the historical changes that have occurred in conceptualizations and treatment of abnormal behavior through the course of Western culture.

Ancient societies attributed abnormal behavior to divine or supernatural forces. In medieval times, abnormal behavior was considered a sign of possession by the Devil, and exorcism was intended to rid

the possessed of the evil spirits that afflicted them. The 19th-century German physician Wilhelm Griesinger argued that abnormal behavior was caused by diseases of the brain. He and another German physician who followed him, Emil Kraepelin, were influential in the development of the modern medical model, which likens abnormal behavior patterns to physical illnesses.

Asylums, or madhouses, arose throughout Europe in the late 15th and early 16th centuries. Conditions in these asylums, however, were dreadful. With the rise of moral therapy in the 19th century, conditions in mental hospitals improved. Proponents of moral therapy believed that mental patients could be restored to functioning if they were treated with dignity and understanding. The decline of moral therapy in the latter part of the 19th century led to the belief that the "insane" could not be treated successfully. During this period of apathy, mental hospitals deteriorated, offering little more than custodial care. Not until the middle of the 20th century did public concern about the plight of mental patients lead to the development of community mental health centers as alternatives to long-term hospitalization.

Mental hospitals today provide structured treatment environments for people in acute crisis and for those who are unable to adapt to community living. Deinstitutionalization has greatly reduced the population of state mental hospitals, but it has not yet fulfilled its promise of providing the quality of care needed to restore discharged patients to a reasonable quality of life in the community. One example of the challenges yet to be met is the large number of homeless people with severe psychological problems who are not receiving adequate care in the community.

Contemporary Perspectives on Abnormal Behavior

1.6 Describe the major contemporary perspectives on abnormal behavior.

The medical model conceptualizes abnormal behavior patterns, like physical diseases, in terms of clusters of symptoms, called syndromes, which have distinctive causes presumed to be biological in nature. Psychological models focus on the psychological roots of abnormal behavior and derive from psychoanalytic, behavioral, humanistic, and cognitive perspectives. The sociocultural model emphasizes a broader perspective that takes into account the social contexts in which abnormal behavior occurs. Today, many theorists subscribe to a biopsychosocial model that posits that multiple causes—representing biological, psychological, and sociocultural domains—interact in the development of abnormal behavior patterns.

Research Methods in Abnormal Psychology

1.7 Identify the objectives of science and the steps in the scientific method.

The scientific approach focuses on four general objectives: description, explanation, prediction, and control. There are four steps to the scientific method: formulating a research question, framing the research question in the form of a hypothesis, testing the hypothesis, and drawing conclusions about the correctness of the hypothesis. Psychologists follow the ethical principles of the profession that govern research.

1.8 Identify the ethical principles that guide research in psychology.

The guiding ethical principles governing research in psychology include (a) informed consent and (b) protecting the confidentiality of records of research participants and not disclosing their identities to others.

1.9 Describe the major types of research methods scientists use to study abnormal behavior and evaluate the strengths and weaknesses of these methods.

In naturalistic observation, the investigator carefully observes behavior under naturally occurring conditions. The correlational method of research explores relationships between variables, which may help predict future behavior and suggest possible underlying causes of behavior. However, correlational research cannot directly demonstrate cause-and-effect relationships. Longitudinal research is a correlational method in which a sample of subjects is repeatedly studied at periodic intervals over long periods of time, sometimes spanning decades.

In the experimental method, the investigator manipulates or controls the independent variable under controlled conditions to identify cause-and-effect relationships. Experiments use random assignment as the basis for determining which subjects (called experimental subjects) receive an experimental treatment and which others (called control subjects) do not. Investigators may use single-blind and double-blind research designs to control for possible subject and experimenter expectances. Experiments are evaluated in terms of internal, external, and construct validity.

Epidemiological studies examine the rates of occurrence of abnormal behavior in various population groups or settings. They may indicate possible causal relationships, but lack the power of experimental studies to isolate causal factors. Kinship studies, such as twin studies and adoptee studies, attempt to differentiate the contributions of environment and heredity to behavior. Environmental factors may affect twin studies, whereas adoptees may not be typical of the general population.

Case studies provide rich material, but are limited by difficulties in obtaining accurate and unbiased client histories, by possible therapist biases, and by the lack of control groups. Single-case experimental designs help researchers overcome some of these limitations.

1.10 Apply key features of critical thinking to the study of abnormal behavior.

The features of critical thinking include maintaining a skeptical attitude, considering the definitions of terms, weighing assumptions or premises on which arguments are based, distinguishing correlation from causation, examining evidence on which conclusions are based, avoiding oversimplification, and avoiding overgeneralization.

critical thinking questions

On the basis of your reading of this chapter, answer the following questions:

- Give an example of a behavior (other than behaviors in the text) that might be deemed normal in one culture but abnormal in another.

- How have beliefs about abnormal behavior changed over time? What changes have occurred in how society treats people whose behavior is deemed abnormal?

- Why should we not assume that because two variables are correlated they are causally linked?

- What are the two major types of placebo-control studies? What are they intended to control? What is the major limitation of these designs?

- How do investigators separate the effects of heredity and environment in the study of abnormal behavior?

key terms

psychological disorder 3
abnormal psychology 3
medical model 4
trephination 9
humors 10
deinstitutionalization 13
dementia praecox 16
general paresis 16
psychodynamic model 17
biopsychosocial model 19
scientific method 20
theory 20

hypothesis 21
informed consent 22
confidentiality 22
naturalistic observation 22
correlational method 23
correlation coefficient 23
longitudinal study 23
experimental method 24
independent variables 24
dependent variables 24
experimental group 24
control group 24

random assignment 24
selection factor 24
blind 25
placebo 25
internal validity 26
external validity 26
construct validity 26
epidemiological studies 27
survey method 27
incidence 27
prevalence 27
random sample 27

genotype 28
phenotype 28
proband 28
adoptee studies 29
case studies 29
single-case experimental
  designs 29
reversal design 30
critical thinking 32

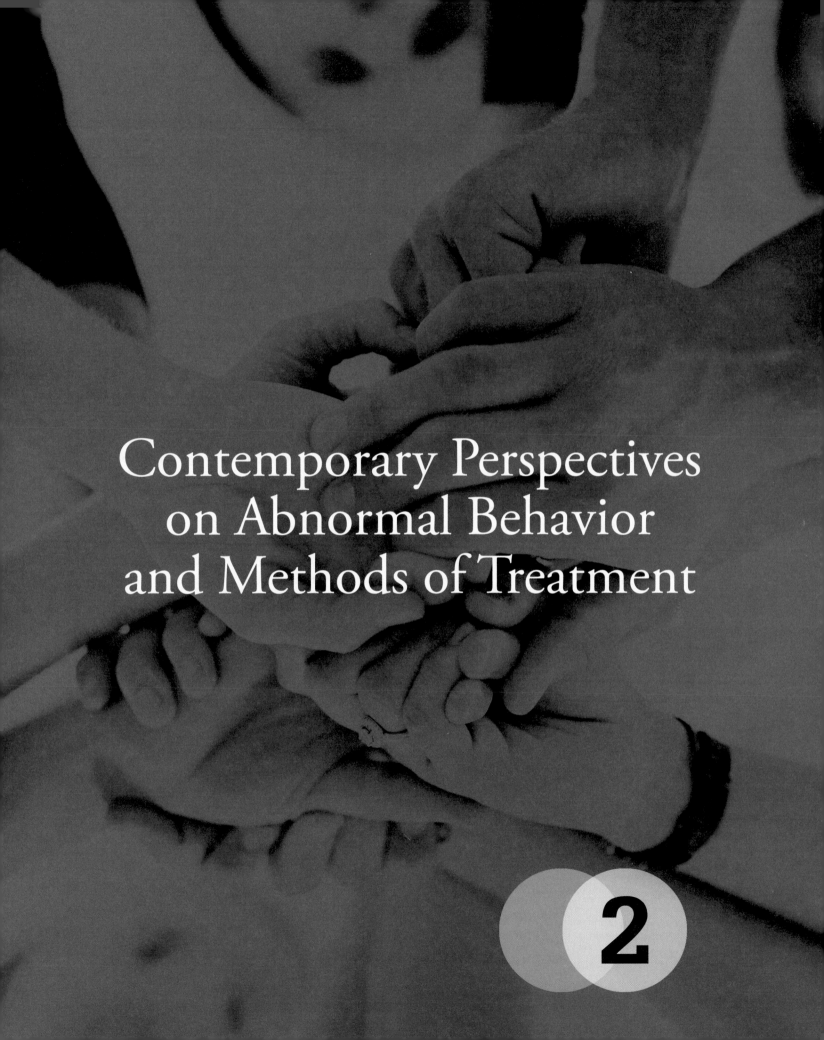

Contemporary Perspectives on Abnormal Behavior and Methods of Treatment

2

learning objectives

2.1
Identify the parts of the neuron and describe their functions.

2.2
Identify the major parts of the nervous system and the cerebral cortex and describe their functions.

2.3
Evaluate biological perspectives on abnormal behavior.

2.4
Describe the major psychological models of abnormal behavior, identify the major theorists, and evaluate these models.

2.5
Describe the sociocultural perspective and evaluate its importance in understanding abnormal behavior.

2.6
Describe and evaluate the biopsychosocial perspective on abnormal behavior and identify a major biopsychosocial model.

2.7
Identify the major types of helping professionals and describe their training backgrounds and professional roles.

2.8
Describe the goals and techniques of various forms of psychotherapy: psychodynamic therapy, behavior therapy, person-centered therapy, cognitive therapy, cognitive behavior therapy, eclectic therapy, group therapy, family therapy, and couple therapy.

2.9
Evaluate the effectiveness of psychotherapy and the role of nonspecific factors in therapy.

2.10
Describe the importance of multicultural factors in psychotherapy and barriers to use of mental health services by ethnic minorities.

2.11
Identify the major categories of psychotropic or psychiatric drugs and examples of drugs in each type, and evaluate their strengths and weaknesses.

2.12
Describe the use of electroconvulsive therapy and psychosurgery and evaluate their effectiveness.

2.13
Evaluate biomedical treatment approaches.

truth OR fiction

T ☐ F ☐   Anxiety can give you indigestion. (p. 42)

T ☐ F ☐   Scientists are unlikely to discover any particular gene that causes any psychiatric disorder. (p. 44)

T ☐ F ☐   Children may acquire a distorted self-concept that mirrors what others expect them to be, but that does not reflect who they truly are. (p. 57)

T ☐ F ☐   According to a leading cognitive theorist, people's beliefs about their life experiences cause their emotional problems, not the experiences themselves. (p. 59)

T ☐ F ☐   Some psychologists have been trained to prescribe drugs. (p. 67)

T ☐ F ☐   In classical psychoanalysis, clients are asked to express whatever thought happens to come to mind, no matter how seemingly trivial or silly. (p. 67)

T ☐ F ☐   Psychotherapy is no more effective than simply letting time take its course. (p. 76)

T ☐ F ☐   Antidepressants are used only to treat depression. (p. 85)

T ☐ F ☐   Sending jolts of electricity into a person's brain can often help relieve severe depression. (p. 85)

"I" Jessica's "Little Secret"

I don't want Ken (her fiancé) to find out. I don't want to bring this into the marriage. I probably should have told him, but I just couldn't do it. Every time I wanted to I just froze up. I guess I figured I'd get over this before the wedding. I have to stop bingeing and throwing up. I just can't stop myself. You know, I want to stop, but I get to thinking about the food I've eaten and it sickens me. I picture myself getting all fat and bloated and I just have to rush to the bathroom and throw it up. I would go on binges, and then throw it all up. It made me feel like I was in control, but really I wasn't.

I have this little ritual when I throw up. I go to the bathroom and run the water in the sink. Nobody ever hears me puking. It's my little secret. I make sure to clean up really well and spray some Lysol before leaving the bathroom. No one suspects I have a problem. Well, that's not quite true. The only one who suspects is my dentist. He said my teeth were beginning to decay from stomach acid. I'm only 20 and I've got rotting teeth. Isn't that awful?

. . . Now I've started throwing up even when I don't binge. Sometimes just eating dinner makes me want to puke. I've just got to get the food out of my body—fast, you know. Right after dinner, I make some excuse about needing to go to the bathroom. It's not every time but at least several times a week. After lunch sometimes, too. I know I need help. It's taken me a long time to come here, but you know I'm getting married in three months and I've got to stop.
Source: From the Author's Files

Jessica, a 20-year-old communications major

Jessica excuses herself from the dinner table, goes to the bathroom, sticks a finger down her throat to gag, and throws up her dinner. Sometimes she binges first and then forces herself to throw up. You'll recall that in Chapter 1 we described the criteria that mental health professionals generally use to classify behavior patterns as abnormal. Jessica's behavior clearly meets several of these criteria. Bingeing and throwing up is a source of personal distress and is maladaptive in the sense that it can lead to serious health consequences, such as decaying teeth (see Chapter 9), and social consequences (which is why Jessica kept it a secret and feared it would damage her upcoming marriage). It is also statistically infrequent, although perhaps not as infrequent as you might think. Jessica was diagnosed with *bulimia nervosa,* a type of eating disorder we discuss in Chapter 9.

How can we understand such unusual and maladaptive behavior? Since earliest times, humans have sought explanations for strange or deviant behavior, often relying on superstitious or supernatural explanations. In the Middle Ages, the predominant view was that abnormal behavior was caused by demons and other supernatural forces. But even in ancient times, there were some thinkers, such as Hippocrates and Galen, who looked for natural explanations of abnormal behavior. Today, of course, superstition and demonology have given way to theoretical models from the natural and social sciences. These approaches have paved the way not only for a scientifically based understanding of abnormal behavior but also for ways of treating people with psychological disorders.

In this chapter, we examine contemporary approaches to understanding abnormal behavior from the vantage points represented by biological, psychological, and sociocultural perspectives. Many scholars today believe that abnormal behavior patterns are complex phenomena that are best understood by taking into account these multiple perspectives. Each perspective provides a window for examining abnormal behavior, but none captures a complete view of the subject. As we shall see later in this chapter, the biological and psychological perspectives on abnormal behavior give rise to specific treatments for these problems.

The Biological Perspective

The *biological perspective,* inspired by scientists and physicians since the time of Hippocrates, focuses on the biological underpinnings of abnormal behavior and the use of biologically based approaches, such as drug therapy, to treat psychological disorders. The biological perspective gave rise to the development of the *medical model,* which remains a powerful force in contemporary understanding of abnormal behavior. People who adopt the medical model believe that abnormal behaviors represent symptoms of underlying disorders or diseases, called *mental illnesses,* that have biological root causes. The medical model is not synonymous with the biological perspective, however. We can speak of biological perspectives without adopting the tenets of the medical model. For example, a behavior pattern such as shyness may have a strong genetic (biological) component but not be considered a "symptom" of any underlying "disorder" or illness.

Our understanding of the biological underpinnings of abnormal behavior has grown in recent years. In Chapter 1, we focused on the methods for studying the role of heredity or genetics. Genetics plays a role in many forms of abnormal behavior, as we shall see throughout the text.

We also know that other biological factors, especially the functioning of the nervous system, are involved in the development of abnormal behavior. To better understand the role of the nervous system in abnormal behavior patterns, we first need to learn how the nervous system is organized and how nerve cells communicate with each other. In Chapter 4, we examine another body system, the *endocrine system,* and the important roles that it plays in the body's response to stress.

The Nervous System

Perhaps if you did not have a nervous system, you would never feel nervous—but neither would you see, hear, or move. However, even calm people have nervous systems. The nervous system is made up of **neurons**, nerve cells that transmit signals or "messages" throughout the body. These messages allow us to sense an itch from a bug bite, coordinate

2.1 Identify the parts of the neuron and **describe** their functions.

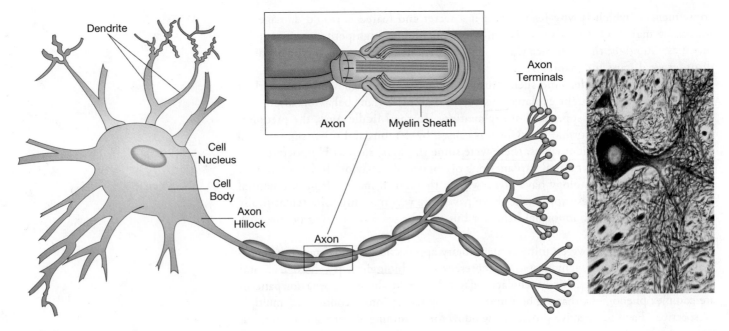

FIGURE 2.1

Anatomy of a neuron. The three basic parts of the neuron are the cell body, the dendrites, and the axon. The axon of this neuron is wrapped in a myelin sheath, which insulates it from the bodily fluids surrounding the neuron and facilitates transmission of neural impulses (messages that travel within the neuron).

👁 **Watch** the **Video** *BioFlix: Neurons Work* on **MyPsychLab**

our vision and muscles to ice skate, write a research paper, solve a math problem, and in the case of hallucinations, hear or see things that are not really there.

Every neuron has a cell body that contains the nucleus of the cell and metabolizes oxygen to carry out the work of the cell (see Figure 2.1). Short fibers called **dendrites** project from the cell body to receive messages from adjoining neurons. Each neuron has an **axon** that projects trunklike from the cell body. Axons can extend as long as several feet, if they are conveying messages between the toes and the spinal cord. Axons terminate in small branching structures that are aptly called **terminals.** Some neurons are covered with a **myelin sheath,** an insulating layer that helps speed transmission of neural impulses. 👁

Neurons convey messages in one direction, from the dendrites or cell body along the axon to the axon terminals. The messages are then conveyed from the terminals to other neurons, muscles, or glands.

Neurons transmit messages to other neurons by means of chemical substances called **neurotransmitters.** Neurotransmitters induce chemical changes in receiving neurons. These changes cause axons to conduct the messages in electrical form.

The connecting points between neurons is the **synapse,** which is a junction or small gap between a transmitting neuron and a receiving neuron. The message does not jump across the synapse like a spark. Instead, axon terminals release neurotransmitters into the cleft like myriad ships casting off into the sea (Figure 2.2).

Each kind of neurotransmitter has a distinctive chemical structure. Each will fit into only one kind of harbor, or **receptor site,** on the receiving neuron. Consider the analogy of a lock and key. Only the right key (neurotransmitter) operates the lock, causing the *postsynaptic* (receiving) neuron to forward the message.

When released, some molecules of a neurotransmitter reach port at receptor sites of other neurons. "Loose" neurotransmitters may be broken down in the synapse by enzymes, or be reabsorbed by the axon terminal (a process termed *reuptake*), to prevent the receiving cell from continuing to fire.

Psychiatric drugs, including drugs used to treat anxiety, depression, and schizophrenia, work by affecting the availability of neurotransmitters in the brain. Consequently, it appears that irregularities in the workings of neurotransmitter systems in the brain play important roles in the development of these abnormal behavior patterns (see Table 2.1).

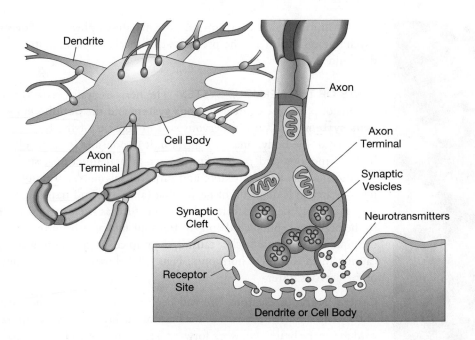

Dendrite

Axon

Cell Body

Axon Terminal

Axon Terminal

Axon Terminal

Synaptic Vesicles

Synaptic Cleft

Neurotransmitters

Receptor Site

Dendrite or Cell Body

FIGURE 2.2

Transmission of neural impulses across the synapse. Shown are the structure of the neuron and the mode of transmission of neural impulses between neurons. Neurons transmit messages, or neural impulses, across synapses, which consist of the axon terminal of the transmitting neuron, the gap or synapse between the neurons, and the dendrite of the receiving neuron. The "message" is carried by neurotransmitters that are released into the synapse and taken up by receptor sites on the receiving neuron. Patterns of firing of many thousands of neurons give rise to psychological events such as thoughts and mental images. Different forms of abnormal behavior are associated with irregularities in the transmission or reception of neural messages.

Depression, for example, is linked to chemical imbalances in the brain involving irregularities in the functioning of several neurotransmitters, especially serotonin (see Chapter 7). Serotonin is a key brain chemical involved in regulating moods, so it is not surprising that it plays a role in depression. Two of the most widely used antidepressant drugs—Prozac and Zoloft—belong to a class of drugs that increase the availability of serotonin in the brain. Serotonin is also linked to anxiety disorders, sleep disorders, and eating disorders. 👁

Alzheimer's disease, a brain disease in which there is a progressive loss of memory and cognitive functioning, is associated with reductions in the levels of the neurotransmitter *acetylcholine* in the brain (see Chapter 14). Irregularities involving the neurotransmitter *dopamine* are implicated in the development of schizophrenia (see Chapter 11). Antipsychotic drugs used to treat schizophrenia apparently work by blocking dopamine receptors in the brain.

2.2 **Identify** the major parts of the nervous system and the cerebral cortex and **describe** their functions.

👁 **Watch the Video**
How the Brain Works Part 1: The Basics
on **MyPsychLab**

TABLE 2.1

Neurotransmitter Functions and Relationships with Abnormal Behavior Patterns

Neurotransmitter	Functions	Associations with Abnormal Behavior
Acetylcholine	Control of muscle contractions and formation of memories	Reduced levels found in patients with Alzheimer's disease (see Chapter 14)
Dopamine	Regulation of muscle contractions and mental processes involving learning, memory, and emotions	Overutilization in the brain may be involved in the development of schizophrenia (see Chapter 11)
Norepinephrine	Mental processes involved in learning and memory	Irregularities linked with mood disorders such as depression (see Chapter 7)
Serotonin	Regulation of mood states, satiety, and sleep	Irregularities are implicated in depression and eating disorders (see Chapters 7 and 9)

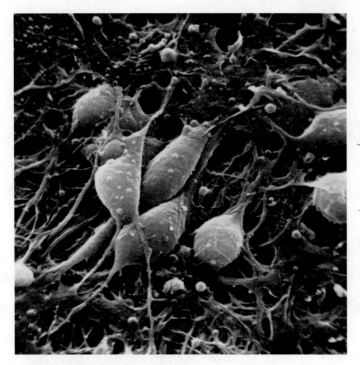

This remarkable electron microscope photograph shows connections between neurons.

Although neurotransmitter systems are implicated in many psychological disorders, the precise causal mechanisms remain to be determined.

PARTS OF THE NERVOUS SYSTEM The nervous system consists of two major parts, the **central nervous system** and the **peripheral nervous system.** The central nervous system consists of the brain and spinal cord, the body's master control unit responsible for controlling bodily functions and performing higher mental functions, such as sensation, perception, thinking, and problem solving. The peripheral nervous system is made up of nerves that (a) receive and transmit sensory messages (messages from sense organs such as the eyes and ears) to the brain and spinal cord and (b) transmit messages from the brain or spinal cord to the muscles, causing them to contract, and to glands, causing them to secrete hormones. Figure 2.3 shows the organization of the nervous system.

Central Nervous System We will begin our overview of the parts of the central nervous system at the back of the head, where the spinal cord meets the brain, and work forward (see Figure 2.4). The lower part of the brain, or hindbrain, consists of the *medulla, pons,* and *cerebellum.* The **medulla** plays roles in vital life-support functions such as heart rate, respiration, and blood pressure. The **pons** transmits information

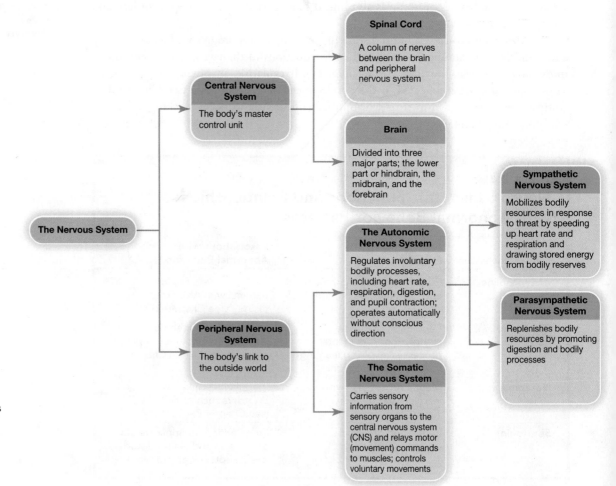

FIGURE 2.3

The organization of the nervous system. *Source:* Adapted from J. S. Nevid (2007). *Psychology: Concepts and applications,* 2nd ed. (p. 56). Boston: Houghton Mifflin Company. Reprinted by permission.

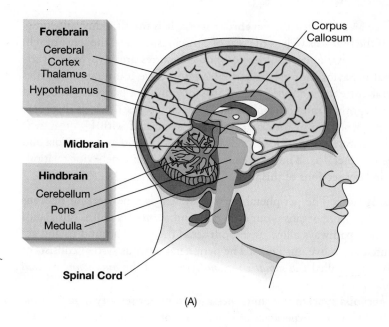

(A)

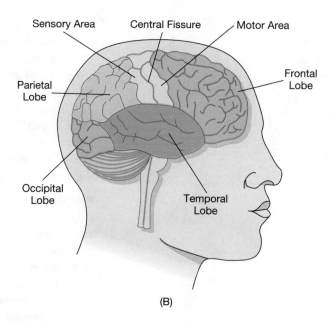

(B)

FIGURE **2.4**

The geography of the brain. Part A shows parts of the hindbrain, midbrain, and forebrain. Part B shows the four lobes of the cerebral cortex: frontal, parietal, temporal, and occipital. In Part B, the sensory (tactile) and motor areas lie across the central fissure from one another. Researchers are investigating the potential relationships between various patterns of abnormal behavior and abnormalities in the formation or functioning of the structures of the brain.

👁 **Watch** the **Video**
How the Brain Works Part 2: The Basics
on **MyPsychLab**

about body movement and is involved in functions related to attention, sleep, and respiration.

Behind the pons is the **cerebellum** (Latin for "little brain"). The cerebellum regulates balance and motor (muscle) behavior. Injury to the cerebellum can impair one's ability to coordinate one's movements, causing stumbling and loss of muscle tone.

The *midbrain* lies above the hindbrain and contains nerve pathways linking the hindbrain to the upper region of the brain, called the *forebrain*. The **reticular activating system** (RAS) starts in the hindbrain and rises through the midbrain into the lower part of the forebrain. The RAS is a weblike network of neurons that play important roles in regulating sleep, attention, and states of arousal. Stimulation of the RAS heightens alertness. On the other hand, use of *depressant drugs,* such as alcohol, dampens central nervous system activity, which reduces RAS activity and can induce states of grogginess or even stupor. (Effects of depressants and other drugs are discussed further in Chapter 8.) 👁

The large frontal area of the brain, called the *forebrain,* includes structures such as the thalamus, hypothalamus, basal ganglia, and cerebrum. The **thalamus** relays sensory information (such as tactile and visual stimulation) to the higher regions of the brain. The thalamus, in coordination with the RAS, is also involved in regulating sleep and attention.

The **hypothalamus** (*hypo* means "under") is a tiny, pea-sized structure located under the thalamus. Despite its small size, the hypothalamus plays a key role in many vital bodily functions, including regulation of body temperature, concentration of fluids in the blood, and reproductive processes, as well as emotional and motivational states. By implanting electrodes in parts of the hypothalamus of animals and observing the effects when a current is switched on, researchers have found that the hypothalamus is involved in a range of motivational drives and behaviors, including hunger, thirst, sex, parenting behaviors, and aggression.

The hypothalamus, together with parts of the thalamus and other nearby interconnected structures, makes up the brain's **limbic system.** The limbic system plays important roles in emotional processing and memory. It also serves important functions regulating more basic drives involving hunger, thirst, and aggression. The **basal ganglia** lie at the base of the forebrain and are involved in regulating postural movements and coordination.

The **cerebrum** is the brain's crowning glory. It is responsible for higher mental functions, such as thinking and problem solving, and also accounts for the delightfully rounded shape of the human head. The surface of the cerebrum is convoluted with ridges and valleys. This surface area is called the **cerebral cortex.** It is the thinking, planning, and executive center of the brain, as well as the seat of consciousness and the sense of self.

Structural or functional abnormalities of brain structures are involved in various forms of abnormal behavior. For example, investigators have found abnormalities in parts of the cerebral cortex and limbic system in schizophrenia patients (discussed in Chapter 11). The hypothalamus is implicated in certain types of sleep disorders (see Chapter 9), and deterioration of the basal ganglia is associated with Huntington's disease—a degenerative disease that can lead to disturbances of mood and paranoia and even to dementia (see Chapter 14). These are but a few of the brain–behavior relationships we shall discuss in later sections of this text.

Peripheral Nervous System The peripheral nervous system is a network of neurons connecting the brain to our sense organs—our eyes, ears, and so on—as well as our glands and muscles. These neural pathways allow us to both sense the world around us and act on it by using our muscles to move our limbs. The peripheral nervous system consists of two main parts or divisions, called the *somatic nervous system* and the *autonomic nervous system* (see Figure 2.3).

The **somatic nervous system** transmits messages from our sensory organs to the brain for processing, leading to the experience of visual, auditory, tactile, and other sensations. Commands emanating from the brain pass downward through the spinal cord to nerves of the somatic nervous system that connect to our muscles, allowing us to voluntarily control our movements, such as when raising an arm or walking.

Psychologists are especially interested in the workings of the **autonomic nervous system** (ANS) because of its role in emotional processing. *Autonomic* means "automatic." The ANS regulates the glands and involuntary processes such as heart rate, breathing, digestion, and dilation of the pupils of the eyes, even when we are sleeping.

The ANS has two branches, the **sympathetic nervous system** and the **parasympathetic nervous system.** These have mostly opposing effects. Many organs and glands are served by both branches of the ANS. The sympathetic division is most involved in processes that mobilize the body's resources during physical exertion or responses to stress, such as when drawing energy from stored reserves to prepare the person to deal with imposing threats or dangers (see Chapter 4). When we face a threatening or dangerous situation, the sympathetic branch of the ANS kicks in by accelerating our heart rate and breathing rate, thereby preparing our body to either fight or flee from a threatening stressor. Sympathetic activation in the face of a threatening stimulus is associated with emotional responses such as fear or anxiety. When we relax, the parasympathetic branch decelerates the heart rate. The parasympathetic division is most active during processes that replenish energy reserves, such as digestion. Because the sympathetic branch dominates when we are fearful or anxious, fear or anxiety can lead to indigestion: Activation of the sympathetic nervous system interferes with parasympathetic control of digestive activity. **T / F**

The Cerebral Cortex The parts of the brain responsible for higher mental functions, such as thought and use of language, are the two large masses of the cerebrum called the right and left *cerebral hemispheres.* The outer layer or covering of each hemisphere is called the cerebral cortex. (The word *cortex* literally means "bark" and is so used because the cerebral cortex can be likened to the bark of a tree.) Each hemisphere is divided into four parts, called *lobes,* as shown in Figure 2.4. The *occipital lobe* is primarily involved in processing visual stimuli; the *temporal lobe* is involved in processing sounds or auditory stimuli. The *parietal lobe* is involved in processing sensations of touch, temperature, and pain. The *sensory area* of the parietal lobe receives messages from receptors in the skin all over the body. Neurons in the motor area (also called the *motor cortex*) in the *frontal lobes* control muscle movements, allowing us to walk and move our limbs. The *prefrontal cortex* (the part of the frontal lobe that lies in front of the motor cortex) regulates higher mental functions such as thinking, problem solving, and use of language.

Evaluating Biological Perspectives on Abnormal Behavior

Biological structures and processes are involved in many patterns of abnormal behavior, as we will see in later chapters. Genetic factors, as well as disturbances in neurotransmitter functioning and underlying brain abnormalities or defects, are implicated in many psychological disorders. For some disorders, such as Alzheimer's disease, biological processes play the direct causative role. (Even then, however, the precise causes remain unknown.) But for most disorders, we need to examine the interaction of biological and environmental factors.

We each possess a unique genetic code that plays an important role in determining our risks of developing various physical and mental disorders (Hyman, 2011; Kendler et al., 2011b). A large body of evidence connects genetic factors to a wide range of psychological disorders, including schizophrenia, bipolar (manic–depressive) disorder, major depression, alcoholism, autism, dementia due to Alzheimer's disease, anxiety disorders, dyslexia, and antisocial personality disorder (e.g., Bassett, Scherer, & Brzustowicz, 2010; Kendler et al., 2011a; NIMH, 2003; Psychiatric GWAS Consortium Bipolar Disorder Working Group, 2011; Vacic et al., 2011). The heritable characteristics that increase our risk of psychological disorders include genetic variations (variations in particular genes among people) and genetic mutations (changes in genes from generation to generation).

Scientists are now searching for specific genes involved in psychological disorders such as schizophrenia, mood disorders, and autism (e.g., Boot et al., 2012; Dennis et al., 2012; Sakai et al., 2011; Serretti & Mandelli, 2008). The hope is that in the not-too-distant future, it will be possible to block the actions of defective or harmful genes or enhance the actions of beneficial genes.

Questions about the genetic bases of abnormal behavior touch upon a long-standing debate in psychology, arguably the longest debate—the so-called *nature versus nurture* debate. The debate has shifted from one pitting nature against nurture to one framed in terms of how much of our behavior is a product of nature (genes) and how much is a product of nurture (environment). Scientists today are studying complex interactions between genes and environmental factors to better understand the determinants of abnormal behavior patterns (Hardy & Low, 2011; Karg, Burmeister, Shedden, & Sen, 2011; Kendler, 2011b; Lee, Glass, James, Bandeen-Roche, & Schwartz, 2011). As the debate continues, let us offer a few key points to consider:

1. *Genes do not dictate behavioral outcomes.* Evidence of a genetic contribution in psychological disorders is arguably strongest in the case of schizophrenia. But as discussed in Chapter 11, even in the case of monozygotic twins who share 100% genetic overlap, when one of the monozygotic twins has schizophrenia, the chance of the other twin having the disorder is slightly less than 50%. In other words, genetics alone does not account for schizophrenia, or any other psychological disorder. As Kenneth Kendler, a leading genetics researcher, explained it, "We do not have and are not likely to ever discover 'genes' for psychiatric illness" (Kendler, 2005, p. 1250).

2. *Genetic factors create a predisposition or likelihood—not a certainty—that certain behaviors or disorders will develop.* Genes do not directly cause psychological disorders. Rather, they create predispositions that increase the risk or likelihood of developing particular disorders. Our genes are carried in our chromosomes from the moment of conception and are not affected

A human being, decoded. Here we see a portion of the human genome, the genetic code of a human being. Scientists recognize that genes play an important role in determining predispositions for many psychological traits and disorders. But whether these predispositions are expressed depends on the interactions of genetic and environmental influences.

Scientists are unlikely to discover any particular gene that causes any psychiatric disorder.

☑ **TRUE** Scientists believe that many genes contribute to the complex behavior patterns associated with psychiatric disorders, not any one gene.

2.4 Describe the major psychological models of abnormal behavior, **identify** the major theorists, and **evaluate** these models.

directly by the environment. However, the effects that genes have on the body and mind may be influenced by environmental factors such as life experiences, family relationships, and life stress (Kendler, 2005; Moffitt, Caspi, & Rutter, 2006). Even ethnicity and gender may influence how genes operate in the body (Williams et al., 2003).

3. *Multigenic determinism affects psychological disorders.* In disorders in which genetic factors play a role, multiple genes are involved, not individual genes acting alone (Hamilton, 2008; Uhl & Grow, 2004). Scientists have yet to find any psychological disorder that can be explained by defects or variations on a single gene. **T / F**

4. *Genetic factors and environmental influence interact with each other in shaping our personalities and determining our vulnerability to a range of psychological disorders.* The contemporary view of the nature–nurture debate is best expressed in terms of nature and nurture *acting together,* not nature *versus* nurture.

One example of the gene–environment interaction occurs when genes increase sensitivity to environmental influences (Dick, 2011). For example, harsh or neglectful parenting may lead to psychological problems. But not all children exposed to a harsh upbringing go on to develop psychological disorders. Some people have genetic tendencies that make them more sensitive to negative effects of these environmental influences (Polanczyk et al., 2009). Complicating the picture further is that environmental influences can also affect the expression of genetic traits, a topic we examine in the *A Closer Look* section on *epigenetics.*

As we continue to learn more about the biological foundations of abnormal behavior patterns, we should recognize that the interface between biology and behavior is a two-way street. Researchers have uncovered links between psychological factors and many physical disorders and conditions (see Chapter 4). Researchers are also investigating whether the combination of psychological and drug treatments for problems such as depression, anxiety disorders, and substance abuse disorders may improve upon the therapeutic benefits of either of the two approaches alone.

The Psychological Perspective

At about the time that biological models of abnormal behavior were becoming prominent in the late 19th century with the contributions of Kraepelin, Griesinger, and others, another approach to understanding abnormal behavior began to emerge. This approach emphasized the psychological roots of abnormal behavior and was most closely identified with the work of the Austrian physician Sigmund Freud. Over time, other psychological models would emerge from the behaviorist, humanistic, and cognitivist traditions. Let us begin our study of psychological perspectives with Freud's contribution and the development of psychodynamic models.

Psychodynamic Models

Psychodynamic theory is based on the contributions of Sigmund Freud and his followers. Freud's **psychoanalytic theory** is based on the belief that the roots of psychological problems involve unconscious motives and conflicts that can be traced back to childhood. Freud put the study of the unconscious mind on the map (Lothane, 2006). To Freud, unconscious motives and conflicts revolve around primitive sexual and aggressive instincts and the need to keep these primitive impulses out of consciousness. But why must the mind keep impulses hidden from conscious awareness? Because, on the Freudian account, were we to become fully aware of our most basic sexual and aggressive urges—which, according to Freud, include incestuous and violent impulses—our conscious self would be flooded with crippling anxiety. By the Freudian account, abnormal behavior patterns represent "symptoms" of these dynamic struggles taking place within the unconscious mind. The patient is aware of the symptom, but not the unconscious conflict that lies at its root. Let's take a closer look at the key elements in psychoanalytic theory.

Epigenetics—The Study of How the Environment Affects Genetic Expression

The genetic code imprinted in an organism's DNA provides a set of instructions for building an organism. It determines, for example, that certain cells will differentiate into lungs (for humans) rather than gills (for fish), as well as physical traits such as eye color, height, and hair color and texture. The genetic code also influences the development of behavioral characteristics, including intelligence, personality traits, and tendencies to develop various psychological disorders. Throughout this text, we examine the role of genetics in many of these disorders, from anxiety disorders to mood disorders to schizophrenia, among others. The great majority of psychological disorders, perhaps even all to a certain extent, are influenced by genetic factors. But what about the reverse? Can environment influence the workings of our genes? Indeed it can.

The field of **epigenetics** focuses on how environmental factors influence genetic expression (Dick, 2011; Labonté et al., 2012; Mischel & Brooks, 2011). The ability of genes to influence physical or behavioral characteristics depends on whether they are actively expressed. Each human cell contains the full complement or set of genes, excepting sperm and ova, which contain half the genetic complement. But perhaps only about 10% to 20% of genes in a given cell are active (Coila, 2009). Thus, genes that code for eye color are active in the eyes, but not in other parts of the body, such as the liver. Environmental influences can affect gene expression by influencing the release of certain bodily chemicals that either turn genes on or turn them off, even though the genetic content (or code) itself remains unchanged.

Think of it this way. Embedded in your computer are codes (software) directing it to perform all of its programs, including web-browsing programs that allow you to surf the net. But you first need to turn on the power to activate the instructions encoded in the software. Otherwise, the computer is merely a black box that sits there until you flick the power switch. In a similar way, the codes embedded in our genes are a kind of biological software, but whether or not they become expressed or active can be affected by environmental influences that either turn on or turn off these genetic switches (T. B. Franklin et al., 2011; Murphy et al., 2013). For example, early life experiences, such as stress, diet, sexual or physical abuse, and exposure to toxic chemicals, may determine whether certain genes become switched on or remain dormant later in life. Investigators find that severe abuse in early childhood can alter gene expression, perhaps setting the stage later in life for the development of depression or other emotional disorders (Labonté et al., 2012).

Environmental factors may lead to chemical processes in the body that "tag" or mark certain genes for either activation or suppression but do not change the genetic code or DNA sequence itself. These "tags" may become part of the organism's genetic inheritance that is passed along to offspring, affecting the workings of genes in future generations (Cloud, 2010). Recently, scientists discovered chemical changes that affect the functioning of DNA in patients with schizophrenia (Melas et al., 2012).

The field of epigenetics is still in its infancy, but scientists hope that by learning more about how environmental factors influence gene expression, they may someday be able to silence certain genes or activate others to treat or prevent mental and physical disorders (Dempster et al., 2011; Dubovsky, 2010; Nestler, 2011).

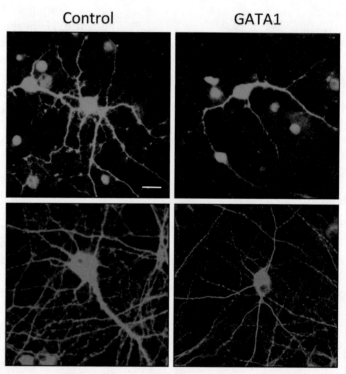

Control   GATA1

Gene expression in psychological disorders. Scientists are studying gene expression in psychological disorders like depression. Some genes are expressed (turned on and off) differently in the brains of depressed people as compared to those of other people. Investigators found that turning-on a particular gene that is linked to depression in humans decreased the density of synaptic connections (right) in the rat brain as compared to controls (left). The growth of synaptic connections may play a role in depression in humans. Research along these lines may eventually lead to new targets for treating depression or other psychological disorders.

THE STRUCTURE OF THE MIND We can liken Freud's model of the mind to an iceberg with only the tip visible above the surface of awareness (Figure 2.5). Freud called this region "above the surface," the **conscious** part of the mind. It is the part of the mind that corresponds to our present awareness. The larger part of the mind remains below the surface of consciousness. The regions that lie beneath the surface of awareness were labeled the *preconscious* and the *unconscious.*

In the **preconscious** are memories that are not in awareness but that can be brought into awareness by focusing on them. Your telephone number, for example, remains in the preconscious until you focus on it. The **unconscious,** the largest part of the mind, remains shrouded in mystery. Its contents can be brought to awareness only with great difficulty, if at all. Freud believed the unconscious is the repository of our basic biological impulses or drives, which he called instincts—primarily sexual and aggressive instincts.

THE STRUCTURE OF PERSONALITY According to Freud's structural hypothesis, the human personality is divided into three mental entities, or psychic structures: the *id, ego,* and *superego.*

The **id** is the original psychic structure, present at birth. It is the repository of our baser drives and instinctual impulses, including hunger, thirst, sex, and aggression. The id, which operates completely in the unconscious, follows the **pleasure principle:** It demands instant gratification of instincts without consideration of social rules or customs or the needs of others.

During the first year of life, the child discovers that every demand is not instantly gratified. He or she must learn to cope with the delay of gratification. The **ego** develops during this first year to organize reasonable ways of coping with frustration. Standing for "reason and good sense" (Freud, 1933/1964, p. 76), the ego seeks to curb the demands of the id and to direct behavior in keeping with social customs and expectations. Gratification can thus be achieved, but not at the expense of social disapproval. Let's say the id floods your consciousness with hunger pangs. Were it to have its way, the id might prompt you to wolf down whatever food is at hand or even to swipe someone else's plate. But the ego creates the idea of walking to the refrigerator, making a sandwich, and pouring a glass of milk.

The ego is governed by the **reality principle.** It considers what is practical and possible, as well as the urgings of the id. The ego lays the groundwork for developing a conscious sense of ourselves as distinct individuals.

During middle childhood, the **superego** develops from the internalization of the moral standards and values of our parents and other key people in our lives. The superego serves as a conscience, or internal moral guardian, which monitors the ego and passes judgment on right and wrong. When it finds that the ego has failed to adhere to the superego's moral standards, it metes out punishment in the form of guilt and shame. Ego stands between the id and the superego. It endeavors to satisfy the cravings of the id without offending the moral standards of the superego.

FIGURE 2.5

The parts of the mind, according to Freud. The human mind in classic Freudian theory can be likened to an iceberg; only a small part of it rises to conscious awareness at any moment in time. Although material in the preconscious mind may be brought into consciousness by focusing one's attention on it, the impulses and wishes in the id remain veiled in mystery in the unconscious recesses of the mind. The ego and superego operate at all three levels of consciousness; the workings of the id are mired in the unconscious.

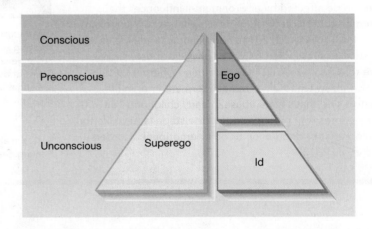

DEFENSE MECHANISMS Although part of the ego rises to consciousness, some of its activity is carried out unconsciously. In the unconscious, the ego serves as a kind of watchdog, or censor, which screens impulses from the id. It uses **defense mechanisms** (psychological defenses) to prevent socially unacceptable impulses from rising into consciousness. If not for these defense mechanisms, the darkest sins of our childhoods, the primitive demands of our ids, and the censures of our superegos might disable us psychologically. *Repression,* or motivated forgetting, by which unacceptable wishes, urges, and impulses are banished to the unconscious, is the most basic of the defense mechanisms (Boag, 2006). Others are described in Table 2.2.

A dynamic unconscious struggle thus takes place between the id and the ego. Biological drives that are striving for expression (the id) are pitted against the ego, which seeks to restrain them or channel them into socially acceptable outlets. When these conflicts are not resolved smoothly, they can lead to the development of behavior problems or psychological disorders. Because one cannot view the unconscious mind directly, Freud developed a method of mental detective work called *psychoanalysis,* which is described later in the chapter.

The use of defense mechanisms to cope with feelings such as anxiety, guilt, and shame is considered normal. These mechanisms enable us to constrain impulses from the id as we go about our daily business. Freud believed that slips of the tongue and ordinary forgetfulness could represent hidden motives that are kept out of consciousness by repression. If a friend means to say, "I hear what you're saying," but it comes out, "I hate what you're saying," perhaps the friend is expressing a repressed hateful impulse. If a lover storms out in anger but forgets his umbrella, perhaps he is unconsciously creating an excuse for returning. Defense mechanisms may also give rise to abnormal behavior, however. The person who regresses to an infantile state under pressures of enormous stress is clearly not acting adaptively to the situation.

TABLE 2.2

Types of Defense Mechanisms in Psychodynamic Theory

Defense Mechanism	Description	Example
Repression	Banishment of unacceptable urges, wishes, or impulses to the unconscious mind	A man is unaware of having hateful or destructive impulses toward his own father.
Denial	Refusal to accept the reality of a threatening impulse or unsafe behavior	A person with a heart condition refuses to acknowledge the seriousness of the condition and avoids seeking medical attention or making healthy changes in his lifestyle.
Rationalization	Self-justifications for unacceptable behavior used as a form of self-deception	A man accused of rape justifies his behavior to himself by thinking that the woman had dressed and acted so provocatively that she was "just asking for it."
Displacement	Directing one's unacceptable impulses toward threatening objects onto safer or less-threatening objects	After a woman is chewed out by her boss at work, she picks a fight with her daughter upon returning home.
Projection	Attributing one's own impulses or wishes to another person	A hostile and argumentative person perceives others as having difficulty controlling their tempers.
Reaction formation	Taking the opposite stance to what one truly wishes or believes so as to keep one's genuine impulses repressed	A woman who has difficulty accepting her own sexual impulses mounts a crusade against pornography.
Regression	Return of behaviors associated with earlier stages of development, generally during times of stress	After his marriage ends, a man becomes completely dependent on his parents.
Sublimation	Channeling one's own unacceptable impulses into more socially appropriate pursuits or activities	A woman channels her aggressive impulses into her artistic pursuits.

Denial? Denial is a defense mechanism in which the ego fends off anxiety by preventing awareness of an underlying threat. Failing to take seriously the warnings of health risks from smoking may be considered a form of denial.

STAGES OF PSYCHOSEXUAL DEVELOPMENT Freud argued that sexual drives are the dominant factors in the development of personality, even in childhood. Freud believed that the child's basic relationship to the world in the child's first several years of life is organized around the pursuit of sensual or sexual pleasure. In Freud's view, all activities that are physically pleasurable, such as eating or moving one's bowels, are in essence "sexual." (What Freud meant by *sexual* is probably closer in present-day meaning to the word *sensual*.)

The drive for sexual pleasure represents, in Freud's view, the expression of a major life instinct, which he called Eros—the basic drive to preserve and perpetuate life. He called the energy contained in Eros that allows it to fulfill its function *libido*, or sexual energy. Freud believed libidinal energy is expressed through sexual pleasure in different body parts, called *erogenous zones*, as the child matures. In Freud's view, the stages of human development are psychosexual in nature because they correspond to the transfer of libidinal energy from one erogenous zone to another. Freud proposed the existence of five psychosexual stages of development: oral (first year of life), anal (second year of life), phallic (beginning during the third year of life), latency (from around age 6 to age 12), and genital (beginning in puberty).

In the first year of life, the *oral stage*, infants achieve sexual pleasure by sucking their mothers' breasts and by mouthing anything that happens to be nearby. Oral stimulation, in the form of sucking and biting, is a source of both sexual gratification and nourishment. During the *anal stage* of psychosexual development, the child experiences sexual gratification through contraction and relaxation of the sphincter muscles that control elimination of bodily waste.

The next stage of psychosexual development, the *phallic stage*, generally begins during the third year of life. The major erogenous zone during this stage is the phallic region (the penis in boys, the clitoris in girls). Perhaps the most controversial of Freud's beliefs was his suggestion that phallic-stage children develop unconscious incestuous desires for the parent of the opposite sex and begin to view the parent of the same sex as a rival. Freud dubbed this conflict the *Oedipus complex*, after the legendary Greek king Oedipus, who unwittingly slew his father and married his mother. The female version of the Oedipus complex has been named by some followers (although not by Freud himself) the *Electra complex*, after Electra, who, according to Greek legend, avenged the death of her father, King Agamemnon, by slaying her father's murderers—her own mother and her mother's lover. Freud believed the Oedipus conflict represents a central psychological conflict of early childhood and that failure to successfully resolve the conflict can set the stage for the development of psychological problems in later life.

Successful resolution of the Oedipus complex involves the boy repressing his incestuous desires for his mother and identifying with his father. This identification leads to development of the aggressive, independent characteristics associated with the traditional masculine gender role. For the girl, successful resolution involves repression of incestuous desires for her father and identification with her mother, leading to the acquisition of the more passive, dependent characteristics traditionally associated with the feminine gender role.

The Oedipus complex comes to a point of resolution, whether fully resolved or not, by about the age of 5 or 6. From the identification with the parent of the same gender comes the internalization of parental values in the form of the superego. Children then enter the *latency stage* of psychosexual development, a period of late childhood during which sexual impulses remain in a latent state. Interests become directed toward school and play activities.

Sexual drives are once again aroused with the *genital stage*, beginning with puberty, which reaches fruition in mature sexuality, marriage, and the bearing of children. The sexual feelings toward the parent of the opposite sex that had remained repressed during the latency period emerge during adolescence but are displaced, or transferred, onto socially appropriate members of the opposite sex. In Freud's view, successful adjustment during the genital stage involves attaining sexual gratification through sexual intercourse with someone of the opposite sex, presumably within the context of marriage.

One of Freud's central beliefs is that the child may encounter conflict during each of the psychosexual stages of development. Conflict in the oral stage, for example, centers on whether or not the infant receives adequate oral gratification. Too much gratification could lead the infant to expect that everything in life is given with little or no effort on his or her part. In contrast, early weaning might lead to frustration. Too little or too much gratification at any stage could lead to **fixation** in that stage, which leads to the development of personality traits characteristic of that stage. Oral fixations could include an exaggerated desire for "oral activities," which could become expressed in later life in smoking, alcohol abuse, overeating, and nail biting. Like the infant who depends on the mother's breast for survival and for gratification of oral pleasure, orally fixated adults may also become clinging and dependent in their interpersonal relationships. In Freud's view, failure to successfully resolve the conflicts of the phallic stage (i.e., the Oedipus complex) can lead to the rejection of the traditional masculine or feminine roles and to homosexuality.

OTHER PSYCHODYNAMIC THEORISTS Psychodynamic theory has been shaped over the years by the contributions of psychodynamic theorists who shared certain central tenets in common with Freud, for example, that behavior reflects unconscious motivation, inner conflict, and the operation of defensive responses to anxiety. However, many psychodynamic theorists deviated sharply from Freud's positions on many issues. For example, they tended to place less emphasis than Freud on basic instincts such as sex and aggression, and greater emphasis on conscious choice, self-direction, and creativity.

Carl Jung Swiss psychiatrist Carl Jung (1875–1961) was a member of Freud's inner circle. His break with Freud came when he developed his own psychodynamic theory, which he called *analytical psychology*. Jung believed that an understanding of human behavior must incorporate self-awareness and self-direction as well as impulses of the id and mechanisms of defense. He believed that not only do we have a *personal* unconscious, a repository of repressed memories and impulses, but we also inherit a collective unconscious. The collective unconscious contains primitive images, or **archetypes**, which reflect the history of our species, including vague, mysterious, mythical images like the all-powerful God; the fertile and nurturing mother; the young hero; the wise old man; the dark, shadowy evil figure; and themes of rebirth or resurrection. Although archetypes remain in the unconscious, in Jung's view, they influence our thoughts, dreams, and emotions and render us responsive to cultural themes in stories and films.

Alfred Adler Like Jung, Alfred Adler (1870–1937) held a place in Freud's inner circle, but broke away as he developed his own beliefs, that people are basically driven by an inferiority complex, not by the sexual instinct, as Freud maintained. For some people, feelings of inferiority are based on physical deficits and the resulting need to compensate for them. But all of us, because of our small size during childhood, encounter feelings of inferiority to some degree. These feelings lead to a powerful drive for superiority, which motivates us to achieve prominence and social dominance. In the healthy personality, however, strivings for dominance are tempered by devotion to helping other people.

Adler, like Jung, believed self-awareness plays a major role in the formation of personality. Adler spoke of a *creative self,* a self-aware aspect of personality that strives to overcome obstacles and develop the individual's potential. With the hypothesis of the creative self, Adler shifted the emphasis of psychodynamic theory from the id to the ego. Because our potentials are uniquely individual, Adler's views have been termed *individual psychology.*

Karen Horney Some psychodynamic theorists, such as Karen Horney (1885–1952) (pronounced HORN-eye), stressed the importance of child–parent relationships in the development of emotional problems. She maintained that when parents are harsh or

The oral stage of psychosexual development? According to Freud, the child's early encounters with the world are largely experienced through the mouth.

An oral fixation? Freud believed that too little or too much gratification at a particular stage of psychosexual development can lead to fixation, resulting in personality traits associated with that stage, such as exaggerated oral traits.

uncaring, children come to develop a deep-seated form of anxiety called *basic anxiety,* which she described as a feeling of "being isolated and helpless in a potentially hostile world" (cited in Quinn, 1987, p. 41). Children who harbor deep-seated resentment toward their parents may develop a form of hostility she labeled *basic hostility.* She shared with Freud the view that children repress their hostility toward their parents because of an underlying fear of losing them or of suffering reprisals or punishment. However, repressed hostility generates more anxiety and insecurity. With Horney and other psychodynamic theorists who followed Freud, the emphasis shifted from a focus on sexual and aggressive drives toward a closer examination of social influences on development.

More recent psychodynamic models also place a greater emphasis on the self or the ego and less emphasis on the sexual instinct than Freud's model. Today, most psychoanalysts see people as motivated on two tiers: by the growth-oriented, conscious pursuits of the ego as well as by the more primitive, conflict-ridden drives of the id. Heinz Hartmann (1894–1970) was one of the originators of **ego psychology,** which posits that the ego has energy and motives of its own. The choices to seek an education, dedicate oneself to art and poetry, and further humanity are not merely defensive forms of sublimation, as Freud had seen them.

Erik Erikson Erik Erikson (1902–1994) was influenced by Freud but became an important theorist in his own right. He focused on psychosocial development in contrast to Freud's emphasis on psychosexual development. Erikson attributed more importance to social relationships and formation of personal identity than to unconscious processes. Whereas Freud's developmental theory ends with the genital stage, Erikson's developmental theory, beginning in early adolescence, posits that our personalities continue to be shaped throughout adulthood as we deal with the psychosocial challenges or crises we face during each period of life. In Erikson's view, for example, the major psychosocial challenge faced by adolescents is development of *ego identity,* a clearly defined sense of who they are and what they believe in.

Margaret Mahler One popular contemporary psychodynamic approach, **object-relations theory,** focuses on how children come to develop symbolic representations of important others in their lives, especially their parents (Blum, 2010). The object-relations theorist Margaret Mahler (1897–1985) saw the process of the child separating from the mother during the first three years of life as crucial to the child's personality development (discussed further in Chapter 12).

According to psychodynamic theory, we introject, or incorporate, into our own personalities parts of parental figures in our lives. For example, you might introject

Karen Horney

Erik Erikson

Margaret Mahler

your father's strong sense of responsibility or your mother's eagerness to please others. Introjection is more powerful when we fear losing others because of death or rejection. Thus, we might be particularly apt to incorporate elements of people who *disapprove* of us or who see things differently.

In Mahler's view, these symbolic representations, which are formed from images and memories of others, come to influence our perceptions and behavior. We experience internal conflict as the attitudes of introjected people battle with our own. Some of our perceptions may be distorted or seem unreal to us. Some of our impulses and behavior may seem unlike us, as if they come out of the blue. With such conflict, we may not be able to tell where the influences of other people end and our "real selves" begin. The aim of Mahler's therapeutic approach was to help clients separate their own ideas and feelings from those of the introjected objects so they could develop as individuals—as their own persons.

PSYCHODYNAMIC VIEWS ON NORMALITY AND ABNORMALITY In the Freudian model, mental health is a function of the dynamic balance among the mental structures id, ego, and superego. In mentally healthy people, the ego is strong enough to control the instincts of the id and to withstand the condemnation of the superego. The presence of acceptable outlets for the expression of some primitive impulses, such as the expression of mature sexuality in marriage, decreases the pressures within the id and, at the same time, lessens the burdens of the ego in repressing the remaining impulses. Being reared by reasonably tolerant parents might prevent the superego from becoming overly harsh and condemnatory.

In people with psychological disorders, the balance among the psychic structures is lopsided. Some unconscious impulses may "leak," producing anxiety or leading to psychological disorders, such as hysteria and phobias. The symptom expresses the conflict among the parts of the personality while it protects the self from recognizing the inner turmoil. A person with a fear of knives, for example, is shielded from becoming aware of her own unconscious aggressive impulses to use a knife to murder someone or attack herself. So long as the symptom is maintained (and the person avoids knives), the murderous or suicidal impulses are kept at bay. If the superego becomes overly powerful, it may create excessive feelings of guilt and lead to depression. People who intentionally hurt others without feeling guilty about it are believed to have an underdeveloped superego.

Freud believed that the underlying conflicts that give rise to psychological disorders originate in childhood and are buried in the depths of the unconscious. Through psychoanalysis, he sought to help people uncover the underlying conflicts and learn to deal with them. This way, they can free themselves of the need to maintain the overt symptoms.

Perpetual vigilance and defense take their toll, however. The ego can weaken and, in extreme cases, lose the ability to keep a lid on the id. When the urges of the id spill forth, untempered by an ego that is either weakened or underdeveloped, **psychosis (a loss of touch with reality)** results. Psychosis is characterized, in general, by bizarre behavior and thoughts and by faulty perceptions of reality, such as hallucinations (hearing voices or seeing things that are not present). Speech may become incoherent; there may be bizarre posturing and gestures. Schizophrenia is the major form of psychosis (see Chapter 11).

Freud equated psychological health with the *abilities to love and to work.* The normal person can care deeply for other people, find sexual gratification in an intimate relationship, and engage in productive work. To accomplish these ends, sexual impulses must be expressed in a relationship with a partner of the opposite gender. Other impulses must be channeled (sublimated) into socially productive pursuits, such as work, enjoyment of art or music, or creative expression. Other psychodynamic theorists, such as Jung and Adler, emphasized the need to develop a differentiated self—the unifying force that provides direction to behavior and helps develop a person's potential. Adler also believed that psychological health involves efforts to compensate for feelings of inferiority by striving to excel in one or more of the arenas of human endeavor. For Mahler, similarly, abnormal behavior derives from failure to develop a distinctive and individual identity.

The power of archetypes. One reason adventure stories such as Harry Potter and the *Star Wars* saga are so compelling may be that they feature archetypes represented in the struggle between good and evil characters.

Evaluating Psychodynamic Models

Psychodynamic theory has pervaded the general culture (Lothane, 2006). Even people who have never read Freud look for symbolic meanings in slips of the tongue and assume that abnormalities can be traced to early childhood. Terms such as *ego* and *repression* have become commonplace, although their everyday meanings do not fully overlap with those intended by Freud.

The psychodynamic model led us to recognize that we are not transparent to ourselves (Panek, 2002)—that our behavior may be motivated by hidden drives and impulses of which we are unaware or only dimly aware. Moreover, Freud's beliefs about childhood sexuality were both illuminating and controversial. Before Freud, children were perceived as pure innocents, free of sexual desire. Freud recognized, however, that young children, even infants, seek pleasure through stimulation of the oral and anal cavities and the phallic region. Yet, his beliefs that primitive drives give rise to incestuous desires, intrafamily rivalries, and conflicts remain controversial, even within psychodynamic circles.

Many critics, including even some of Freud's followers, believe he placed too much emphasis on sexual and aggressive impulses and underemphasized social relationships. Critics have also argued that the psychic structures—the id, ego, and superego—may be little more than useful fictions, poetic ways to represent inner conflict. Many critics argue that Freud's hypothetical mental processes are not scientific concepts because they cannot be directly observed or tested. Therapists can speculate, for example, that a client "forgot" about an appointment because "unconsciously" she or he did not want to attend the session. Such unconscious motivation may not be subject to scientific verification, however. On the other hand, psychodynamically oriented researchers have developed scientific approaches to test many of Freud's concepts. They believe that a growing body of evidence supports the existence of unconscious processes that lie outside ordinary awareness, including defense mechanisms such as repression (Cramer, 2000; Westen & Gabbard, 2002).

Learning-Based Models

The psychodynamic models of Freud and his followers were the first major psychological theories of abnormal behavior. Other relevant psychologies also took shape early in the 20th century. The behavioral perspective is identified with the Russian physiologist Ivan Pavlov (1849–1936), the discoverer of the conditioned reflex, and the American

Ivan Pavlov. Russian physiologist Ivan Pavlov (center, with white beard) demonstrates his apparatus for classical conditioning to students. How might the principles of classical conditioning explain the acquisition of excessive irrational fears that psychologists refer to as phobias?

psychologist John B. Watson (1878–1958), the father of **behaviorism.** The behavioral perspective focuses on the role of learning in explaining both normal and abnormal behavior. From a learning perspective, abnormal behavior represents the acquisition, or learning, of inappropriate, maladaptive behaviors.

From the medical and psychodynamic perspectives, respectively, abnormal behavior is *symptomatic* of underlying biological or psychological problems. From the learning perspective, however, the abnormal behavior itself is the problem. In this perspective, abnormal behavior is learned in much the same way as normal behavior. Why do some people behave abnormally? It may be that their learning histories differ from most people's. For example, a person who was harshly punished as a child for masturbating might become anxious, as an adult, about sexuality. Poor child-rearing practices, such as capricious punishment for misconduct and failure to praise or reward good behavior, might lead to antisocial behavior. Children with abusive or neglectful parents might learn to pay more attention to inner fantasies than to the world outside and have difficulty distinguishing reality from fantasy.

Watson and other behaviorists, such as Harvard University psychologist B. F. Skinner (1904–1990), believed that human behavior is the product of our genetic inheritance and environmental or situational influences. Like Freud, Watson and Skinner discarded concepts of personal freedom, choice, and self-direction. But whereas Freud saw us as driven by forces in the unconscious mind, behaviorists see us as products of environmental influences that shape and manipulate our behavior. Behaviorists also believe that we should limit the study of psychology to behavior itself rather than focus on underlying motivations. Therapy, in this view, consists of shaping behavior rather than seeking insight into the workings of the mind. Behaviorists focus on the roles of two forms of learning in shaping both normal and abnormal behavior: classical conditioning and operant conditioning.

ROLE OF CLASSICAL CONDITIONING Ivan Pavlov discovered the conditioned reflex (now called a *conditioned response*) quite by accident. In his laboratory, he harnessed dogs to an apparatus like that in Figure 2.6 to study their salivary response to food. Along the way he observed that the animals would salivate and secrete gastric juices even before they started to eat. These responses appeared to be elicited by the sound of the food cart as it was wheeled into the room. So Pavlov undertook an experiment that showed that animals could learn to salivate in response to other stimuli, such as the sound of a bell, if these stimuli were *associated* with feeding. 👁

Because dogs don't normally salivate to the sound of bells, Pavlov reasoned that they had acquired this response. He called it a **conditioned response** (CR), or conditioned reflex, because it had been paired with what he called an **unconditioned stimulus**

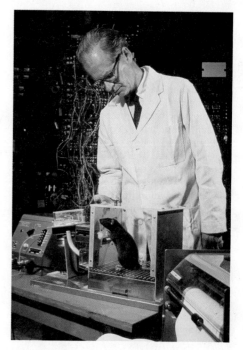

B. F. Skinner

👁 **Watch** the **Video**
Pavlov's Salivary Conditioning Experiment
on **MyPsychLab**

FIGURE 2.6

The apparatus used in Ivan Pavlov's experiments on conditioning. Pavlov used an apparatus such as this to demonstrate the process of conditioning. To the left is a two-way mirror, behind which a researcher rings a bell. After the bell is rung, meat is placed on the dog's tongue. Following several pairings of the bell and the meat, the dog learns to salivate in response to the bell. The animal's saliva passes through the tube to a vial, where its quantity may be taken as a measure of the strength of the conditioned response.

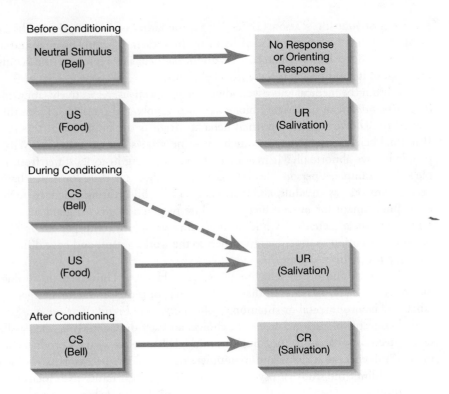

FIGURE 2.7

Schematic representation of classical conditioning. Before conditioning, food (an unconditioned stimulus, or US) placed on a dog's tongue will naturally elicit salivation (an unconditioned response, or UR). The bell, however, is a neutral stimulus that may elicit an orienting response but not salivation. During conditioning, the bell (the conditioned stimulus, or CS) is rung while food (the US) is placed on the dog's tongue. After several conditioning trials have occurred, the bell (the CS) will elicit salivation (the conditioned response, or CR) when it is rung, even though it is not accompanied by food (the US). The dog is said to have been conditioned, or to have learned to display the conditioned response (CR) in response to the conditioned stimulus (CS). Learning theorists have suggested that irrational, excessive fears of harmless stimuli may be acquired through principles of classical conditioning.

(US)—in this case, food—which naturally elicited salivation (see Figure 2.7). The salivation in response to food, an unlearned response, Pavlov called the **unconditioned response** (UR), and the bell, a previously neutral stimulus, he called the **conditioned stimulus** (CS).

Can you recognize examples of **classical conditioning** in your everyday life? Do you flinch in the waiting room at the sound of the dentist's drill? The sound of the drill may be a conditioned stimulus that elicits conditioned responses of fear and muscle tension.

Phobias or excessive fears may be acquired by classical conditioning. For instance, a person may develop a phobia for riding on elevators following a traumatic experience on an elevator. In this example, a previously neutral stimulus (elevator) becomes paired or associated with an aversive stimulus (trauma), which leads to the conditioned response (phobia).

Watson himself had demonstrated how a fear response could be acquired through classical conditioning. Together with his research assistant Rosalie Rayner, who was later to become his wife, Watson classically conditioned an 11-month-old boy, who is well-known in the annals of psychology as "Little Albert," to develop a fear response to a white rat (Watson & Rayner, 1920). Prior to conditioning, the boy showed no fear of the rat and had actually reached out to stroke it. Then, as the boy reached for the animal, Watson banged a steel bar with a hammer just behind the boy's head, creating a loud, aversive sound. After repeated pairings of the jarring sound and the presence of the animal, Albert sure enough showed a conditioned response, displaying fear of the rat alone.

From the learning perspective, normal behavior involves responding adaptively to stimuli, including conditioned stimuli. After all, if we do not learn to be afraid of putting our hand too close to a hot stove after one or two experiences of being burned or nearly burned, we might repeatedly suffer unnecessary burns. On the other hand, acquiring inappropriate and maladaptive fears on the basis of conditioning may cripple our efforts to function in the world. Chapter 5 explains how conditioning may help explain anxiety disorders such as phobias.

ROLE OF OPERANT CONDITIONING Classical conditioning can explain the development of simple, reflexive responses, such as salivating to cues associated with food, as well as the emotional response of fear to stimuli that have been paired with painful or aversive stimuli. But classical conditioning does not account for more complex behaviors, such as studying, working, socializing, or preparing meals. The behavioral psychologist B. F. Skinner (1938) called these types of complex behaviors *operant responses* because they operate on the environment to produce effects or consequences. In **operant conditioning,** responses are acquired and strengthened by their consequences.

We acquire responses or skills, such as raising our hand in class, that lead to **reinforcement.** Reinforcers are changes in the environment (stimuli) that increase the frequency of the preceding behavior.

Behaviors that lead to rewarding consequences are strengthened—that is, they are more likely to occur again. Over time, such behaviors become habits (Staddon & Cerutti, 2003). For example, you likely acquired the habit of raising your hand in class on the basis of experiences early in grade school when your teachers responded to you only if you first raised your hand.

TYPES OF REINFORCERS Skinner identified two types of reinforcers. **Positive reinforcers,** which are commonly called *rewards,* boost the frequency of a behavior when they are introduced or presented. Most of Skinner's work focused on studying operant conditioning in animals, such as pigeons. If a pigeon gets food when it pecks a button, it will continue to peck a button until it has eaten its fill. If we get a friendly response from people when we hold the door open for them, we're more likely to develop the habit of opening the door for others. **Negative reinforcers** increase the frequency of behavior when they are *removed.* If picking up a crying child stops the crying, the behavior (picking up the child) is negatively reinforced (made stronger) because it removes the negative reinforcer (the crying, an aversive stimulus).

Adaptive, normal behavior involves learning responses or skills that lead to reinforcement. We learn behaviors that allow us to obtain positive reinforcers or rewards, such as food, money, and approval, and that help us remove or avoid negative reinforcers, such as pain and disapproval. But if our early learning environments do not provide opportunities for learning new skills, we might be hampered in our efforts to develop the skills needed to obtain reinforcement. A lack of social skills, for example, may reduce our opportunities for social reinforcement (approval or praise from others), which in turn may lead to depression and social isolation. In Chapter 7, we examine links between changes in reinforcement levels and the development of depression. In Chapter 11, we examine how principles of reinforcement are incorporated in learning-based treatment programs to help people with schizophrenia develop more adaptive social behaviors.

Punishment Versus Reinforcement Punishment can be considered the flip side of reinforcement. Punishments are aversive stimuli that *decrease* the frequency of the behavior they follow. Punishment may take many forms, including physical punishment (spanking or use of other painful stimuli), removal of a reinforcing stimulus (turning off the TV), assessment of monetary penalties (parking tickets, etc.), taking away privileges ("You're grounded!"), or removal from a reinforcing environment ("time-out").

Before going further, let us distinguish between two terms that are often confused: *negative reinforcement* and *punishment.* The confusion arises because an aversive or painful stimulus can serve as either a negative reinforcer or a punishment, depending on the situation. With punishment, the *introduction* or application of the aversive or painful stimulus weakens the behavior it follows. With negative reinforcement, the removal of the aversive or painful stimulus strengthens the behavior it follows. A baby's crying can be a punishment (if it weakens the preceding behavior, such as turning your attention away from the baby) or a negative reinforcer (if it strengthens the behavior that leads to its removal, such as picking the baby up).

Punishment, especially physical punishment, may not eliminate undesirable behavior, although it may suppress it for the moment. The behavior may return when the punishment is withdrawn. Another limitation of punishment is that it does not lead to the development of more desirable alternative behaviors. It may also encourage people to withdraw from such learning situations. Punished children may cut classes, drop out of school, or run away. Moreover, punishment may generate anger and hostility rather than constructive learning and may cross the boundary into abuse, especially when it is repetitive and severe. Child abuse figures prominently in many abnormal behavior patterns, including some types of personality disorders (Chapter 12) and dissociative disorders (Chapter 6).

Psychologists recognize that reinforcement is more desirable than punishment. But rewarding good behavior requires paying attention to it, not just to misbehavior. Some children who develop conduct problems gain attention from others only when they misbehave. Consequently, other people may be inadvertently reinforcing these children for undesirable behavior. Learning theorists point out that adults need to teach children desirable behavior and regularly reinforce them for displaying it.

Let us now consider a contemporary model of learning, called *social-cognitive theory* (formerly called *social-learning theory*), which considers the role of cognitive factors in learning and behavior.

SOCIAL-COGNITIVE THEORY Social-cognitive theory represents the contributions of theorists such as Albert Bandura (1925–), Julian B. Rotter (1916–), and Walter Mischel (1930–). Social-cognitive theorists expanded traditional learning theory by including roles for thinking, or cognition, and learning by observation, which is also called **modeling** (Bandura, 2004). A phobia for spiders, for example, may be learned by observing the fearful reactions of others in real life, on television, or in the movies.

Social-cognitive theorists believe that people have an impact on their environment, just as their environment has an impact on them (Bandura, 2004). Social-cognitive theorists agree with traditional behaviorists such as Watson and Skinner that theories of human nature should be tied to observable behavior. However, they argue that factors *within* the person, such as **expectancies** and the values placed on particular goals as well as observational learning, also need to be considered in explaining human behavior. For example, we will see in Chapter 8 that people who hold more positive expectancies about the effects of a drug are more likely to use the drug and to use larger quantities of the drug than are people with less positive expectancies.

Evaluating Learning Models

Learning perspectives have spawned a model of therapy, called *behavior therapy* (also called *behavior modification*), that involves systematically applying learning principles to help people change their undesirable behavior. Behavior therapy techniques have helped people overcome a wide range of psychological problems, including phobias and other anxiety disorders, sexual dysfunctions, and depression. Moreover, reinforcement-based programs are now widely used in helping parents learn better parenting skills and helping children learn in the classroom.

Critics contend that behaviorism alone cannot explain the richness of human behavior and that human experience cannot be reduced to observable responses. Many learning theorists, too—especially social-cognitive theorists—have been dissatisfied with the strict behavioristic view that environmental influences—rewards and punishments—mechanically control our behavior. Humans experience thoughts and dreams and formulate goals and aspirations; behaviorism does not seem to address much of what it means to be human. Social-cognitive theorists have broadened the scope of traditional behaviorism, but critics claim that social-cognitive theory places too little emphasis on genetic contributions to behavior and doesn't provide a full enough account of subjective experience, such as self-awareness and the flow of consciousness. As we'll see next, subjective experience takes center stage in humanistic models.

Observational learning. According to social-cognitive theory, much human behavior is acquired through modeling, or observational learning.

Humanistic Models

Humanistic psychology emerged during the mid-20th century and departed from both the psychodynamic and behavioral or learning-based models by emphasizing the personal freedom human beings have in making conscious choices that imbue their lives with a sense of meaning and purpose. American psychologists Carl Rogers (1902–1987) and Abraham Maslow (1908–1970), two principal figures in humanistic psychology, believed that people have an inborn tendency toward **self-actualization**—to strive to become all they are capable of being. Each of us possesses a singular cluster of traits and talents that gives us our own set of feelings and needs and our own perspective on life. By recognizing and accepting our genuine needs and feelings, by being true to ourselves, we live *authentically,* with meaning and purpose. We may not decide to act out every wish and fancy, but awareness of our authentic feelings and subjective experiences can help us make more meaningful choices.

To understand abnormal behavior in the humanist's view, we need to understand the roadblocks that people encounter in striving for self-actualization and authenticity. To accomplish this, psychologists must learn to view the world from clients' own perspectives because clients' subjective views of their world lead them to interpret and evaluate their experiences in either self-enhancing or self-defeating ways. The humanistic viewpoint involves the attempt to understand the subjective experience of others, the stream of conscious experiences people have of "being in the world."

HUMANISTIC CONCEPTS OF ABNORMAL BEHAVIOR Rogers held that abnormal behavior results from a distorted concept of the self. Parents can help children develop a positive self-concept by showing them **unconditional positive regard,** that is, by prizing them and showing them that they are worthy of love irrespective of their behavior at any given time. Parents may disapprove of a certain behavior but need to convey to their children that the behavior is undesirable, not the child. However, when parents show children **conditional positive regard**—accepting them only when they behave in the way the parents want them to behave—the children may learn to disown all the thoughts, feelings, and behaviors their parents have rejected. Children will learn to develop *conditions of worth;* that is, they will think of themselves as worthwhile only if they behave in certain approved ways. For example, children whose parents seem to value them only when they are compliant may deny to themselves that they ever feel angry. Children in some families learn that it is unacceptable to hold their own ideas, lest they depart from their parents' views. Parental disapproval causes them to see themselves as "bad" and their feelings as wrong, selfish, or even evil. To retain their self-esteem, they may have to deny their genuine feelings or disown parts of themselves. The result can be a distorted *self-concept:* the children become strangers to their true selves.

Rogers believed we become anxious when we sense that our feelings and ideas are inconsistent with the distorted concept we have of ourselves that mirrors what others expect us to be—for example, if our parents expect us to be docile and obedient but we sense ourselves becoming angry or defiant. Because anxiety is unpleasant, we may deny to ourselves that these feelings and ideas even exist. And so the actualization of our authentic self is bridled. We channel our psychological energy not toward growth but toward continued denial and self-defense. Under such conditions, we cannot hope to perceive our genuine values or personal talents. The result is frustration and dissatisfaction, which set the stage for abnormal behavior.

According to the humanists, we cannot fulfill all the wishes of others and remain true to ourselves. This does not mean that self-actualization invariably leads to conflict. Rogers believed that people hurt one another or become antisocial in their behavior only when they are frustrated in their endeavors to reach their unique potentials. When parents and others treat children with love and tolerance for their differences, children, too, grow up to be loving and tolerant—even if some of their values and preferences differ from their parents' choices. T / F

Self-actualization. Humanistic theorists believe that there exists in each of us a drive toward self-actualization—to become all that we are capable of being. No two people follow quite the same pathway toward self-actualization.

truth OR fiction

Children may acquire a distorted self-concept that mirrors what others expect them to be, but that does not reflect who they truly are.

☑ **TRUE** According to Rogers, children can develop a distorted self-concept that mirrors what others expect them to be but is not true to themselves.

In Rogers's view, the pathway to self-actualization involves a process of self-discovery and self-acceptance, of getting in touch with our true feelings, accepting them as our own, and acting in ways that genuinely reflect them. These are the goals of Rogers's method of psychotherapy, called *client-centered therapy* or *person-centered therapy*.

Evaluating Humanistic Models

The strength of humanistic models in understanding abnormal behavior lies largely in their focus on conscious experience and their therapy methods that guide people toward self-discovery and self-acceptance. The humanistic movement brought concepts of free choice, inherent goodness, personal responsibility, and authenticity into modern psychology. Ironically, the primary strength of the humanistic approach—its focus on conscious experience—may also be its primary weakness. Conscious experience is private and subjective, which makes it difficult to quantify and study objectively. How can psychologists be certain they accurately perceive the world through the eyes of their clients? Humanists may counter that we should not shrink from the challenge of studying consciousness because to do so would deny an essential aspect of what it means to be human.

Critics also claim that the concept of self-actualization—which is so basic to Maslow and Rogers—cannot be proved or disproved. Like a psychic structure, a self-actualizing force is not directly measurable or observable. It is inferred from its supposed effects. Self-actualization also yields circular explanations for behavior. When someone is observed engaging in striving, what do we learn by attributing striving to a self-actualizing tendency? The source of the tendency remains a mystery. Similarly, when someone is observed *not* to be striving, what do we gain by attributing the lack of endeavor to a blocked or frustrated self-actualizing tendency? We must still determine the source of frustration.

Cognitive Models

The word *cognitive* derives from the Latin *cognitio*, meaning "knowledge." Cognitive theorists study the cognitions—the thoughts, beliefs, expectations, and attitudes—that accompany and may underlie abnormal behavior. They focus on how reality is colored by our expectations, attitudes, and so forth, and how inaccurate or biased processing of information about the world—and our place within it—can give rise to abnormal behavior. Cognitive theorists believe that our interpretations of the events in our lives, and not the events themselves, determine our emotional states.

INFORMATION-PROCESSING MODELS Cognitive psychologists often draw upon concepts in computer science in explaining how humans process information and how these processes may break down, leading to problems involving abnormal behavior. In computer terms, information is input into a computer by striking keys on a keyboard (encoded so that it can be accepted by the computer as input) and placed in working memory, where it can be manipulated to solve problems, such as performing statistical or arithmetic operations. Information can also be placed permanently in a storage medium, such as a hard drive or a flash drive, from which it can later be retrieved and output in the form of a print-out or a display on a computer screen.

In humans, information about the outside world is *input* through the person's sensory and perceptual processes, *manipulated* (interpreted or processed), *stored* (placed in memory), *retrieved* (accessed from memory), and then *output* in the form of acting upon the information. Psychological disorders may represent disruptions or disturbances in how information is processed. Blocking or distortion of input or faulty storage, retrieval, or manipulation of information can lead to distorted output (e.g., bizarre behavior). People with schizophrenia, for example, may have difficulty accessing and organizing their thoughts, leading to jumbled output in the form of incoherent speech or delusional thinking. They may also have difficulty focusing their attention and filtering out

Carl Rogers and Abraham Maslow. Two of the principal forces in humanistic psychology.

extraneous stimuli, such as distracting noises, which may represent problems in the initial processing of input from their senses.

Manipulation of information may also be distorted by what cognitive therapists call *cognitive distortions,* or errors in thinking. For example, people who are depressed tend to develop an unduly negative view of their personal situation by exaggerating the importance of unfortunate events they experience, such as receiving a poor evaluation at work or being rejected by a dating partner. Cognitive theorists such as Albert Ellis (1913–2007) and Aaron Beck (1921–) have postulated that distorted or irrational thinking patterns can lead to emotional problems and maladaptive behavior.

Social-cognitive theorists, who share many basic ideas with the cognitive theorists, focus on the ways in which social information is encoded. For example, aggressive boys and adolescents are likely to incorrectly encode other people's behavior as threatening (see Chapter 13). They assume that other people intend them ill when they do not. Aggressive children and adults may behave in ways that elicit coercive or hostile behavior from others, which serves to confirm their aggressive expectations. Rapists, especially date rapists, may misread a woman's expressed wishes. They may wrongly assume, for example, that the woman who says "no" really means "yes" and is merely playing "hard to get."

ALBERT ELLIS Psychologist Albert Ellis (e.g., Ellis, 1977, 1993; Ellis & Ellis, 2011), a prominent cognitive theorist, believed that troubling events in themselves do not lead to anxiety, depression, or disturbed behavior. Rather, it is the irrational beliefs people hold about unfortunate experiences that foster negative emotions and maladaptive behavior. Consider someone who loses a job and becomes anxious and despondent about it. It may seem that being fired is the direct cause of the person's misery, but the misery actually stems from the person's beliefs about the loss, not directly from the loss itself.

Ellis used an *ABC approach* to explain the causes of misery. Being fired is an *activating event (A).* The ultimate outcome, or *consequence* (C), is emotional distress. But the activating event (A) and the consequence (C) are mediated by various *beliefs* (B). Some of these beliefs might include "that job was the major thing in my life," "what a useless washout I am," "my family will go hungry," "I'll never be able to find another job as good," "I can't do a thing about it." These exaggerated and irrational beliefs compound depression, nurture helplessness, and distract people from evaluating what to do.

The situation can be diagrammed like this:

ACTIVATING EVENT $\longrightarrow$ BELIEF $\longrightarrow$ CONSEQUENCES

Ellis pointed out that apprehension about the future and feelings of disappointment are perfectly normal when people face losses. However, the adoption of irrational beliefs leads people to catastrophize their disappointments, leading to profound distress and states of depression. Irrational beliefs—"I must have the love and approval of nearly everyone who is important to me or else I'm a worthless and unlovable person"—impair coping ability. In his later writings, Ellis emphasized the demanding nature of irrational or self-defeating beliefs—tendencies to impose "musts" and "shoulds" on ourselves (Ellis, 1993). Ellis noted that the desire for others' approval is understandable, but it is irrational to assume that one must have it to survive or to feel worthwhile. It would be marvelous to excel in everything we do, but it's absurd to demand it of ourselves or believe that we couldn't stand it if we failed to measure up. Ellis developed a model of therapy, called *rational-emotive behavior therapy,* to help people dispute these irrational beliefs and substitute more rational ones (discussed later in the chapter). **T / F**

Ellis recognized that childhood experiences are involved in the origins of irrational beliefs, but he maintained that it is repetition of these beliefs in the "here and now" that continues to make people miserable. For most people who are anxious and depressed, the key to greater happiness does not lie in discovering and liberating deep-seated conflicts, but in recognizing and modifying irrational self-demands.

The makings of unconditional positive regard? Rogers believed that parents can help their children develop self-esteem and set them on the road toward self-actualization by showing them unconditional positive regard—prizing them on the basis of their inner worth, regardless of their behavior of the moment.

truth OR fiction

According to a leading cognitive theorist, people's beliefs about their life experiences cause their emotional problems, not the experiences themselves.

☑ **TRUE** Ellis believed that emotional distress is determined by the beliefs people hold about events they experience, not by the events themselves.

Albert Ellis. Cognitive theorist Albert Ellis believed that negative emotions arise from judgments we make about events we experience, not from the events themselves.

Aaron Beck. Aaron Beck, a leading cognitive theorist, focuses on how errors in thinking, or cognitive distortions, set the stage for negative emotional reactions in the face of unfortunate events.

AARON BECK Another prominent cognitive theorist, psychiatrist Aaron Beck, proposed that depression may result from errors in thinking or "cognitive distortions," such as judging oneself entirely on the basis of one's flaws or failures and interpreting events in a negative light (through blue-colored glasses, as it were) (A. T. Beck et al., 1979). Beck stressed four basic types of cognitive distortions that contribute to emotional distress:

1. *Selective abstraction.* People may *selectively abstract* (focus exclusively on) the parts of their experiences that reveal their flaws and ignore evidence of their competencies. For example, a student may focus entirely on the one mediocre grade received on a math test and ignore all the higher grades.

2. *Overgeneralization.* People may *overgeneralize* from a few isolated experiences. For example, a person may believe he will never marry because he was rejected by a date.

3. *Magnification.* People may blow out of proportion, or *magnify,* the importance of unfortunate events. For example, a student may catastrophize a bad test grade by jumping to the conclusion that she will flunk out of college and her life will be ruined.

4. *Absolutist thinking.* Absolutist thinking is seeing the world in black-and-white terms, rather than in shades of gray. For example, an absolutist thinker may assume that a work evaluation that is less than a total rave is a complete failure.

Like Ellis, Beck developed a major model of therapy, called *cognitive therapy,* which focuses on helping individuals with psychological disorders identify and correct faulty ways of thinking (see discussion later in the chapter).

Evaluating Cognitive Models

As we'll see in later chapters, cognitive theorists have had an enormous impact on our understanding of abnormal behavior patterns and development of therapeutic approaches. The overlap between the learning-based and cognitive approaches is best represented by the emergence of *cognitive-behavioral therapy,* a form of therapy that focuses on modifying self-defeating beliefs as well as overt behaviors.

A major issue concerning cognitive perspectives is their range of applicability. Cognitive therapists have largely focused on emotional disorders relating to anxiety and depression. They have had less impact on the development of treatment approaches, or conceptual models, of more severe forms of disturbed behavior, such as schizophrenia. Moreover, in the case of depression, it remains unclear, as we will see in Chapter 7, whether distorted thinking patterns are causes of depression or are themselves effects of depression.

2.5 Describe the sociocultural perspective and **evaluate** its importance in understanding abnormal behavior.

The Sociocultural Perspective

Does abnormal behavior arise from forces within the person, as the psychodynamic theorists propose, or from learned maladaptive behaviors, as the learning theorists suggest? Or, as the *sociocultural perspective* proposes, does a fuller accounting of abnormal behavior require that we consider the roles of social and cultural factors, including factors relating to ethnicity, gender, and social class? As we noted in Chapter 1, sociocultural theorists seek causes of abnormal behavior in the failures of society rather than in the person. Some of the more radical psychosocial theorists, such as Thomas Szasz, even deny the existence of psychological disorders or mental illness. Szasz (1961, 2000) argues that "abnormal" is merely a label society attaches to people whose behavior deviates from accepted social norms. According to Szasz, this label is used to stigmatize social deviants.

Throughout the text, we examine relationships between abnormal behavior patterns and sociocultural factors such as gender, ethnicity, and socioeconomic status. Here, we examine recent research on relationships between ethnicity and mental health.

Ethnicity and Mental Health

Given the increasing ethnic diversity of the population, researchers have begun to study ethnic group differences in the prevalence of psychological disorders. Knowing that a disorder disproportionately affects one group or another can help planners direct prevention and treatment programs to the groups that are most in need (Pole et al., 2005).

We need to take income level or socioeconomic status into account when comparing differences in rates of particular disorders across ethnic groups. Ethnic minority groups tend to be disproportionally represented among lower socioeconomic status levels. People with household incomes near or below the poverty line stand an increased risk of developing various psychological disorders, including mood disorders and drug-related disorders, than do those with higher incomes (Sareen, Afifi, McMillan, & Asmundson, 2011).

Researchers also need to account for differences among ethnic subgroups, such as differences among the various subgroups that comprise the Hispanic American and Asian American populations. For example, depression is more prominent a problem among Hispanic immigrants to the United States from Central America than from Mexico, even when considering differences in educational backgrounds (Salgado de Snyder, Cervantes, & Padilla, 1990).

Researchers need to be cautious—and to think critically—when interpreting ethnic group differences in rates of diagnoses of psychological disorders. Might these differences reflect ethnic or racial differences, or differences in other factors on which groups may vary, such as socioeconomic level, living conditions, or cultural backgrounds?

An analysis of ethnic group differences in rates of mental disorders revealed an interesting pattern (Breslau et al., 2005). Using data from a nationally representative sample of adult Americans, investigators found that traditionally disadvantaged groups (non-Hispanic Black Americans and Hispanic Americans) had either significantly lower rates of psychological disorders or comparable rates as compared to European Americans (non-Hispanic Whites) (see Figure 2.8). However, when the investigators looked at the persistence, or *chronicity*, of psychological disorders, they found that Hispanic Americans and Black Americans tended to experience more persistent mental disorders than European Americans.

What might we make of these findings on persistence of mental disorders? Additional analysis showed that differences in persistence were not a function of socioeconomic level. But might they reflect differences in access to quality care? The question needs to be addressed in further research, but it is conceivable that White European Americans benefit from better access to quality mental health care, which shortens the length of psychological disorders they experience.

Native Americans are a traditionally disadvantaged minority group with high rates of mental disorders (Gone & Trimble, 2012). They also happen to be among the most impoverished ethnic groups in both the United States and Canada. Native Americans

FIGURE 2.8

Ethnicity and psychological disorders in the United States. We can see that European Americans (non-Hispanic Whites) tend to have higher prevalence rates of psychological disorders than either Hispanic Americans (Latinos) or (non-Hispanic) Black Americans. Though not all of these differences were statistically significant, in none of these comparisons were there significantly higher prevalence rates among Hispanic Americans and Black Americans than among European Americans. *Source:* Breslau et al., 2005, based on data from the National Comordibity Survey (NCS).

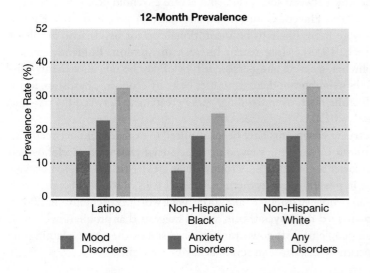

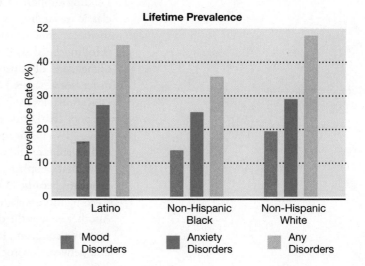

Roots of abnormal behavior? Sociocultural theorists believe that the roots of abnormal behavior are found not in the individual but in the social ills of society, such as poverty, social decay, discrimination based on race and gender, and lack of economic opportunity.

suffer from a much greater prevalence of mental health problems than other ethnic groups, most commonly alcohol dependence, posttraumatic stress disorder, and depression (Beals et al., 2005). The rate of alcohol-related disorders among Native Americans is six times that of other Americans (Rabasca, 2000). The death rate due to suicide among adolescents in the 10- to 14-year-old age range is about four times higher among Native Americans than among other ethnic groups. Male Native American adolescents and young adults have the highest suicide rates in the nation (USDHHS, 1999).

Asian Americans typically show lower rates of psychological disorders than the general U.S. population (Sue, Yan Cheng, Saad, & Chu, 2012). But there are exceptions. When you envision stereotypes such as hula dancing, luaus, and wide tropical beaches, you may assume that Native Hawaiians are a carefree people. Reality paints a different picture, however. One reason for studying the relationship between ethnicity and abnormal behavior is to debunk erroneous stereotypes. Native Hawaiians, like other Native American groups, are economically disadvantaged and suffer a disproportionate share of physical diseases and mental health problems. Native Hawaiians tend to die at a younger age than other residents of Hawaii, largely because they face an increased risk of serious diseases, including hypertension, cancer, and heart disease (Johnson et al., 2004). They also show higher rates of risk factors associated with these life-threatening diseases, such as smoking, alcohol abuse, and obesity. Compared to other Hawaiians, Native Hawaiians also experience higher rates of mental health problems, including higher suicide rates among men, higher rates of alcoholism and drug abuse, and higher rates of antisocial behavior.

The mental health problems, as well as the economic disadvantage, of Native Americans, including Native Hawaiians, may at least partly reflect alienation and disenfranchisement from the land and a way of life that resulted from colonization by European cultures (Rabasca, 2000). Native peoples often attribute mental health problems, especially depression and alcoholism, to the collapse of their traditional culture brought about by colonization. The depression so common among indigenous or native peoples may reflect the loss of a relationship with the world that was based on maintaining harmony with nature. Whatever the underlying differences in psychopathology among ethnic groups, members of ethnic minority groups tend to underutilize mental health services compared to White European Americans (USDHHS, 1999, 2001). Native Americans, for example, commonly seek help from traditional healers rather than from mental health professionals (Beals et al., 2005). Members of other ethnic minority groups often turn to members of the clergy or to spiritualists. Those who do seek services are more likely to drop out of treatment prematurely. Later in the chapter, we consider barriers that limit the use of mental health services by various ethnic minority groups in American society.

Evaluating the Sociocultural Perspective

Lending support to the link between social class and severe psychological disturbance, a classic research study in New Haven, Connecticut, showed that people from the lower socioeconomic groups were more likely to be institutionalized for psychiatric problems (Hollingshead & Redlich, 1958). More recent research in London, England, showed higher rates of schizophrenia, a severe and persistent type of psychological or mental disorder (see Chapter 11), in neighborhood communities beset by economic hardship, lower educational levels, high crime rates, overcrowding, and a greater gap between the rich and the poor (Kirkbride et al., 2012).

Two major theoretical viewpoints have been advanced to explain links between SES and severe mental health problems. One viewpoint is the **social causation model,** which holds that people from lower socioeconomic groups are at greater risk of severe behavior problems because living in poverty subjects them to a greater level of social stress than that faced by more well-to-do people (Costello et al., 2003; Wadsworth & Achenbach, 2005). Another view is the **downward drift hypothesis,** which suggests that problem behaviors, such as alcoholism, lead people to drift downward in social status, thereby explaining the link between low socioeconomic status and severe behavior problems.

Sociocultural theorists have focused much-needed attention on the social stressors that can lead to abnormal behavior. Throughout the text, we consider how sociocultural factors relating to gender, race, ethnicity, and lifestyle inform our understanding of abnormal behavior and our response to people deemed mentally ill. Later in this chapter, we consider how issues relating to race, culture, and ethnicity affect the therapeutic process.

The Biopsychosocial Perspective

2.6 Describe and evaluate the biopsychosocial perspective on abnormal behavior and identify a major biopsychosocial model.

Contemporary views of abnormal behavior are informed by several models or perspectives representing biological, psychological, and sociocultural perspectives. The fact that there are different ways of looking at the same phenomenon doesn't mean that one model must be right and the others wrong. No one theoretical perspective accounts for the many complex forms of abnormal behavior we will discuss in this text. Each perspective contributes something to our understanding, but none offers a complete view. Table 2.3 presents an overview of these perspectives.

The final perspective we discuss, the *biopsychosocial perspective*, takes a broader view of abnormal behavior than other models. It examines contributions of multiple factors spanning biological, psychological, and sociocultural domains, as well as their interactions, in the development of psychological disorders. As we'll see in later chapters, most

TABLE 2.3
Perspectives on Abnormal Behavior

	Model	Focus	Key Questions
Biological perspective	**Medical model**	Biological underpinnings of abnormal behavior	What role is played by neurotransmitters in abnormal behavior? By genetics? By brain abnormalities?
Psychological perspective	**Psychodynamic models**	Unconscious conflicts and motives underlying abnormal behavior	How do particular symptoms represent or symbolize unconscious conflicts? What are the childhood roots of a person's problem?
	Learning models	Learning experiences that shape the development of abnormal behavior	How are abnormal patterns of behavior learned? What role does the environment play in explaining abnormal behavior?
	Humanistic models	Roadblocks that hinder self-awareness and self-acceptance	How do a person's emotional problems reflect a distorted self-image? What roadblocks did the person encounter in the path toward self-acceptance and self-realization?
	Cognitive models	Faulty thinking underlying abnormal behavior	What styles of thinking characterize people with particular types of psychological disorders? What role do personal beliefs, thoughts, and ways of interpreting events play in the development of abnormal behavior patterns?
Sociocultural perspective		Social ills, such as poverty, racism, and prolonged unemployment, contributing to the development of abnormal behavior; relationships among abnormal behavior and ethnicity, gender, culture, and socioeconomic level	What relationships exist between social-class status and risks of psychological disorders? Are there gender or ethnic group differences in various disorders? How are these explained? What are the effects of stigmatization of people who are labeled mentally ill?
Biopsychosocial perspective		Interactions of biological, psychological, and sociocultural factors in the development of abnormal behavior	How might genetic or other factors predispose individuals to psychological disorders in the face of life stress? How do biological, psychological, and sociocultural factors interact in the development of complex patterns of abnormal behavior?

Source: Adapted from Nevid, J. S. (2013). *Psychology: Concepts and applications* (4th ed.). Belmont, CA: Cengage Learning.

psychological disorders involve multiple causal factors, as well as the interactions among these factors. For some disorders, especially schizophrenia, bipolar disorder, and autism, biological influences appear to be more prominent causal factors. For other disorders, such as anxiety disorders and depression, there appears to be a more intricate interplay of biological, psychological, and environmental causal factors (Weir, 2012).

Researchers are only beginning to unravel the complex web of factors that underlie many of the disorders we discuss in this text. Even disorders that are primarily biological may be influenced by psychological or environmental factors, or vice versa. For example, some phobias may be learned behaviors that are acquired through experiences in which particular objects became associated with traumatic or painful experiences (see Chapter 5). Yet, some people may inherit certain traits that make them susceptible to the development of acquired or conditioned phobias.

Here, we take a closer look at one of the leading examples of a biopsychosocial model, the *diathesis–stress model,* which posits that psychological disorders arise from an interaction of vulnerability factors (primarily biological in nature) and stressful life experiences.

The Diathesis–Stress Model

The **diathesis–stress model** was originally developed as a framework for understanding schizophrenia (see Chapter 11). The model holds that certain psychological disorders, such as schizophrenia, arise from a combination or interaction of a **diathesis** (a vulnerability or predisposition to develop the disorder, usually genetic in nature) with stressful life experiences (see Figure 2.9). The diathesis–stress model has recently been applied to other psychological disorders, including depression and attention-deficit hyperactivity disorder (e.g., see Pennington et al., 2009).

Whether a disorder actually develops depends on the nature of the diathesis and the type and severity of stressors the person experiences in life. The life stressors that may contribute to the development of disorders include birth complications, trauma or serious illness in childhood, childhood sexual or physical abuse, prolonged unemployment, loss of loved ones, or significant medical problems (Jablensky et al., 2005).

In some cases, people with a diathesis for a particular disorder, say schizophrenia, will remain free of the disorder or will develop a milder form of the disorder if the level of stress in their lives remains low or if they develop effective coping responses for handling the stress they encounter. However, the stronger the diathesis, the less stress is generally needed to trigger the disorder. In some cases, the diathesis may be so strong that the disorder develops even under the most benign life circumstances.

A diathesis or predisposition is usually genetic in nature, such as having a particular genetic variant that increases the risk of developing a particular disorder. However, a diathesis may take other forms. A psychological diathesis, such as maladaptive personality traits and negative ways of thinking, may increase vulnerability to psychological disorders in the face of life stress (Morris, Ciesla, & Garber, 2008; Zvolensky et al., 2005). For example, the tendency to blame oneself for negative life events such as a divorce or the loss of a job may put a person at greater risk of developing depression in the face of these stressful events (see Chapter 7) (Just, Abramson, & Alloy, 2001).

FIGURE 2.9

The diathesis–stress model.

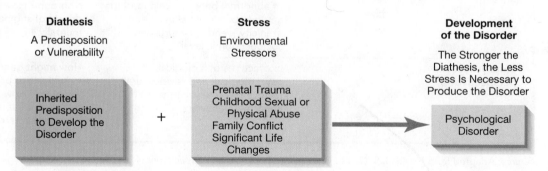

Diathesis
A Predisposition or Vulnerability

Stress
Environmental Stressors

Development of the Disorder
The Stronger the Diathesis, the Less Stress Is Necessary to Produce the Disorder

Inherited Predisposition to Develop the Disorder

+

Prenatal Trauma
Childhood Sexual or Physical Abuse
Family Conflict
Significant Life Changes

Psychological Disorder

Evaluating the Biopsychosocial Perspective

The strength of the biopsychosocial model—its very complexity—may also be its greatest weakness. The model holds the view that with few exceptions, psychological disorders or other patterns of abnormal behavior are complex phenomena that arise from multiple causes. We cannot pinpoint any one cause that leads to the development of schizophrenia or panic disorder, for example. In addition, different people may develop the same disorder because of different sets of causal influences. Yet, the complexity of understanding the interplay of underlying causes of abnormal behavior patterns should not deter researchers from the effort. The accumulation of a body of knowledge is a continuing process. We know a great deal more today than we did a few short years ago. We will surely know more in the years ahead.

The Case of Jessica—A Final Word

Let us briefly return to the case of Jessica, the young woman with bulimia whom we introduced at the beginning of the chapter. The biopsychosocial model leads us to consider the biological, psychological, and sociocultural factors that might account for bulimic behavior. As we shall consider further in Chapter 9, evidence points to biological influences, such as genetic factors and irregularities in neurotransmitter activity. Evidence also points to contributions of sociocultural factors, such as the social pressures imposed on young women in our society to adhere to unrealistic standards of thinness, as well as psychological influences such as body dissatisfaction, cognitive factors such as thinking in perfectionistic and dichotomous ("black or white") terms, and underlying emotional and interpersonal problems. In all likelihood, multiple factors interact in leading to bulimia and other eating disorders. For example, we might apply the diathesis–stress model to frame a potential causal model of bulimia. From this perspective, we can propose that a genetic predisposition (diathesis) affecting the regulation of neurotransmitters in the brain interacts in some cases with stress in the form of social and family pressures, leading to the development of eating disorders.

We will return to consider these causal influences in Chapter 9. For now, let us simply note that psychological disorders such as bulimia are complex phenomena that are best approached by considering the contributions and interactions of multiple factors.

Methods of Treatment

Carla, a 19-year-old college sophomore, had been crying more or less continuously for several days. She felt her life was falling apart, that her college aspirations were in shambles, and that she was a disappointment to her parents. The thought of suicide had crossed her mind. She could not seem to drag herself out of bed in the morning. She had withdrawn from her friends. Her misery had seemed to descend on her from nowhere, although she could pinpoint some pressures in her life: a couple of poor grades, a recent breakup with a boyfriend, some adjustment problems with roommates.

The psychologist who examined her arrived at a diagnosis of major depressive disorder. Had she broken a leg, she would have received a fairly standard course of treatment from a qualified professional. Yet, the treatment that Carla or someone else with a psychological disorder receives is likely to vary not only with the type of disorder involved but also with the therapeutic orientation and professional background of the helping professional. A psychiatrist might recommend a course of antidepressant medication, perhaps in combination with some form of psychotherapy. A cognitively oriented psychologist might suggest a program of cognitive therapy to help Carla identify dysfunctional thoughts that may underlie her depression, whereas a psychodynamic therapist might recommend she begin therapy to uncover inner conflicts originating in childhood that may lie at the root of her depression.

In these next sections, we focus on ways of treating psychological disorders. Yet, despite the widespread availability of mental health services, there remains a large unmet need, as most people with diagnosed mental disorders remain either untreated or undertreated (Kessler et al., 2005c; González et al., 2010).

In later chapters, we examine treatments of particular disorders, but here we focus on the treatments themselves. We will see that the biological and psychological perspectives on abnormal behavior have spawned corresponding approaches to treatment. First, however, we consider the major types of mental health professionals who treat psychological or mental disorders and the different roles they play.

Types of Helping Professionals

2.7 Identify the major types of helping professionals and describe their training backgrounds and professional roles.

Many people are confused about the differences in qualifications and training of the various types of professionals who provide mental health care. It is little wonder people are confused, because there are different types of mental health professionals who represent a wide range of training backgrounds and areas of practice. For example, clinical psychologists and counseling psychologists have completed advanced graduate training in psychology and obtained a license to practice psychology. Psychiatrists are medical doctors who specialize in the diagnosis and treatment of emotional disorders. The major professional groupings of helping professionals, including clinical and counseling psychologists, psychiatrists, social workers, nurses, and counselors, are described in Table 2.4.

TABLE 2.4
Major Types of Helping Professionals

Type	Description
Clinical psychologists	Have earned a doctoral degree in psychology (a Ph.D. [Doctor of Philosophy]; a Psy.D. [Doctor of Psychology]; or an Ed.D. [Doctor of Education]) from an accredited college or university. Training in clinical psychology typically involves four years of graduate coursework, followed by a year-long internship and completion of a doctoral dissertation. Clinical psychologists specialize in administering psychological tests, diagnosing psychological disorders, and practicing psychotherapy. Until recently, they were not permitted to prescribe psychiatric drugs. However, as of this writing, two states (New Mexico and Louisiana) have enacted laws granting prescription privileges to psychologists who complete specialized training programs (Bradshaw, 2010; De Leon, 2012). The granting of prescription privileges to psychologists remains a hotly contested issue between psychologists and psychiatrists and within the field of psychology itself.
Counseling psychologists	Also hold doctoral degrees in psychology and have completed graduate training preparing them for careers in college counseling centers and mental health facilities. They typically provide counseling to people with psychological problems falling in a milder range of severity than those treated by clinical psychologists, such as difficulties adjusting to college or uncertainties regarding career choices.
Psychiatrists	Have earned a medical degree (M.D.) and completed a residency program in psychiatry. Psychiatrists are physicians who specialize in the diagnosis and treatment of psychological disorders. As licensed physicians, they can prescribe psychiatric drugs and may employ other medical interventions, such as electroconvulsive therapy (ECT). Many also practice psychotherapy based on training they receive during their residency programs or in specialized training institutes.
Clinical or psychiatric social workers	Have earned a master's degree in social work (M.S.W.) and use their knowledge of community agencies and organizations to help people with severe mental disorders receive the services they need. For example, they may help people with schizophrenia make a more successful adjustment to the community once they leave the hospital. Many clinical social workers practice psychotherapy or specific forms of therapy, such as marital or family therapy.
Psychoanalysts	Typically are either psychiatrists or psychologists who have completed extensive additional training in psychoanalysis. They are required to undergo psychoanalysis themselves as part of their training.
Counselors	Have typically earned a master's degree by completing a graduate program in a counseling field. Counselors work in many settings, including private practices, schools, college testing and counseling centers, and hospitals and health clinics. Many specialize in vocational evaluation, marital or family therapy, rehabilitation counseling, or substance abuse counseling. Counselors may focus on providing psychological assistance to people with milder forms of disturbed behavior or those struggling with a chronic or debilitating illness or recovering from a traumatic experience. Some are clergy members who are trained in pastoral counseling programs to help parishioners cope with personal problems.
Psychiatric nurses	Typically are registered nurses (R.N.s) who have completed a master's program in psychiatric nursing. They may work in a psychiatric facility or in a group medical practice where they treat people suffering from severe psychological disorders.

Source: Adapted from Nevid, J. S. (2013). *Psychology: Concepts and applications* (4th ed.). Belmont, CA: Cengage Learning. T / F

Unfortunately, many states do not limit the use of the titles *therapist* or *psychotherapist* to trained professionals. In such states, anyone can set up shop as a psychotherapist and practice "therapy" without a license. Thus, people seeking help should inquire about the training and licensure of helping professionals. We now consider the major types of psychotherapies and their relationships to the theoretical models from which they are derived. **T / F**

Psychotherapy

Psychotherapy, commonly referred to as "talk therapy," is a structured form of treatment based on a psychological framework and comprising one or more verbal interchanges between a client and a therapist. Psychotherapy is used to treat psychological disorders, to help clients change maladaptive behaviors or solve problems in living, or to help them develop their unique potentials.

Psychodynamic Therapy

Sigmund Freud developed the first model of psychotherapy, which he called **psychoanalysis,** which he used to treat people with psychological disorders. Psychoanalysis was also the first form of **psychodynamic therapy,** a general term referring to forms of psychotherapy based on the Freudian tradition that seeks to help people gain insight into, and resolve, the dynamic struggles or conflicts between forces within the unconscious mind believed to lie at the root of abnormal behavior. Working through these conflicts, the ego would be freed of the need to maintain defensive behaviors—such as phobias, obsessive–compulsive behaviors, and symptoms of hysteria—that shield it from awareness of the inner turmoil.

Freud summed up the goal of psychoanalysis by saying, "Where id was, there shall ego be." This meant, in part, that psychoanalysis could help shed the light of awareness, represented by the conscious ego, on the inner workings of the id. Through this process, a man might come to realize that unresolved anger toward his dominating or rejecting mother has sabotaged his intimate relationships with women during his adulthood. A woman with a loss of sensation in her hand that cannot be explained medically might come to see that she harbors guilt over urges to masturbate. The loss of sensation might have prevented her from acting on these urges. Through confronting hidden impulses and the conflicts they produce, clients learn to sort out their feelings and find more constructive and socially acceptable ways of handling their impulses and wishes. The ego is then freed to focus on more constructive interests.

The major methods that Freud used to accomplish these goals were free association, dream analysis, and analysis of the transference relationship.

FREE ASSOCIATION Free association is the process of expressing whatever thoughts come to mind. Free association is believed to gradually break down the defenses that block awareness of unconscious processes. Clients are told not to censor or screen out thoughts, but to let their minds wander "freely" from thought to thought. Although free association may begin with small talk, it may eventually lead to more personally meaningful material.

The ego continues to try to shield the self from awareness of threatening impulses and conflicts. As deeper and more conflicted material is touched upon, the ego may throw up a "mental stop sign" in the form of *resistance,* or unwillingness or inability to recall or discuss disturbing or threatening material. Clients may report that their minds suddenly go blank when they venture into sensitive areas, such as hateful feelings toward family members or sexual yearnings. They may switch topics abruptly or accuse the analyst of trying to pry into material that is too personal or embarrassing to talk about. Or they may conveniently "forget" the next appointment after a session in which sensitive material was touched on. Signs of resistance are often suggestive of meaningful material. Now and then, the analyst brings interpretations of this material to the client's attention to help the client gain better insight into deep-seated feelings and conflicts. **T / F**

DREAM ANALYSIS To Freud, dreams represented the "royal road to the unconscious." During sleep, the ego's defenses are lowered and unacceptable impulses find expression in

truth OR fiction

Some psychologists have been trained to prescribe drugs.

☑ **TRUE** Some psychologists have received specialized training that prepares them to prescribe psychiatric medications.

2.8 Describe the goals and techniques of various forms of psychotherapy: psychodynamic therapy, behavior therapy, person-centered therapy, cognitive therapy, cognitive behavior therapy, eclectic therapy, group therapy, family therapy, and couple therapy.

truth OR fiction

In classical psychoanalysis, clients are asked to express whatever thought happens to come to mind, no matter how seemingly trivial or silly.

☑ **TRUE** In classical psychoanalysis, clients are asked to report any thoughts that come to mind. The technique is called free association.

The therapeutic relationship. In the course of successful psychotherapy, a therapeutic relationship is forged between the therapist and client. Therapists use attentive listening to understand as clearly as possible what the client is experiencing and attempting to convey. Skillful therapists are also sensitive to clients' nonverbal cues, such as gestures and posture, that may indicate underlying feelings or conflicts.

dreams. Because the defenses are not completely eliminated, the impulses take a disguised or symbolized form. In psychoanalytic theory, dreams have two levels of content:

1. *Manifest content:* the material of the dream the dreamer experiences and reports.
2. *Latent content:* the unconscious material the dream symbolizes or represents.

A man might dream of flying in an airplane. Flying is the apparent or manifest content of the dream. Freud believed that flying may symbolize erection, so perhaps the latent content of the dream reflects unconscious issues related to fears of impotence. Because such symbols may vary from person to person, analysts ask clients to free-associate to the manifest content of the dream to provide clues to the latent content. Although dreams may have a psychological meaning, as Freud believed, researchers lack any independent means of determining what they may truly mean.

TRANSFERENCE Freud found that clients responded to him not only as an individual but also in ways that reflected their feelings and attitudes toward other important people in their lives. A young female client might respond to him as a father figure, displacing, or transferring, onto Freud her feelings toward her own father. A man might also view him as a father figure, responding to him as a rival in a manner that Freud believed might reflect the man's unresolved Oedipus complex.

The process of analyzing and working through the **transference relationship** is considered an essential component of psychoanalysis. Freud believed that the transference relationship provides a vehicle for the reenactment of childhood conflicts with parents. Clients may react to the analyst with the same feelings of anger, love, or jealousy they felt toward their own parents. Freud termed the enactment of these childhood conflicts the *transference neurosis.* This "neurosis" had to be successfully analyzed and worked through for clients to succeed in psychoanalysis.

Childhood conflicts usually involve unresolved feelings of anger, rejection, or need for love. For example, a client may interpret any slight criticism by the therapist as a devastating blow, transferring feelings of self-loathing that the client had repressed from childhood experiences of parental rejection. Transference may also distort or color the client's relationships with others, such as a spouse or an employer. A client might relate to a spouse as to a parent, perhaps demanding too much or unjustly accusing the spouse of being insensitive or uncaring. Or a client who had been mistreated by a past lover might not give new friends or lovers the benefit of a fair chance. The analyst helps the client recognize transference relationships, especially the therapy transference, and work through the residues of childhood feelings and conflicts that lead to self-defeating behavior in the present.

According to Freud, transference is a two-way street. Freud felt he transferred his underlying feelings onto his clients, perhaps viewing a young man as a competitor or a woman as a rejecting love interest. Freud referred to the feelings that he projected onto clients as **countertransference.** Psychoanalysts in training are expected to undergo psychoanalysis themselves to help them uncover motives that might lead to countertransferences in their therapeutic relationships. In their training, psychoanalysts learn to monitor their own reactions in therapy, so as to become better aware of when and how countertransferences intrude on the therapy process.

Although the analysis of transference is a crucial element of psychoanalytic therapy, it generally takes months or years for a transference relationship to develop and be resolved. This is one reason why psychoanalysis is typically a lengthy process.

MODERN PSYCHODYNAMIC APPROACHES Although some psychoanalysts continue to practice traditional psychoanalysis in much the same manner as Freud did, briefer and less intensive forms of psychodynamic treatment have emerged. They are able to reach clients who are seeking briefer and less costly forms of treatment, perhaps once or twice a week (Grossman, 2003).

Like traditional psychoanalysts, modern psychodynamic therapists explore their clients' psychological defenses and transference relationships—a process described as "peeling an onion" (Gothold, 2009). But unlike traditional psychoanalysis, they focus more on clients' present relationships and less on sexual issues (Knoblauch, 2009). They also place greater emphasis on making adaptive changes in how their clients relate to others. Many contemporary psychodynamic therapists draw more heavily on the ideas of Erik Erikson, Karen Horney, and other theorists than on Freud's ideas. Treatment entails a more open dialogue and direct exploration of the client's defenses and transference relationships than was traditionally the case. The client and therapist generally sit facing each other, and the therapist engages in more frequent verbal give-and-take with the client, as in the following vignette. Note how the therapist uses interpretation to help the client, Mr. Arianes, achieve insight into how his relationship with his wife involves a transference of his childhood relationship with his mother:

OFFERING AN INTERPRETATION

MR. ARIANES: I think you've got it there, Doc. We weren't communicating. I wouldn't tell her [his wife] what was wrong or what I wanted from her. Maybe I expected her to understand me without saying anything.

THERAPIST: Like the expectations a child has of its mother.

MR. ARIANES: Not my mother!

THERAPIST: Oh?

MR. ARIANES: No, I always thought she had too many troubles of her [his mother] own to pay attention to mine. I remember once I got hurt on my bike and came to her all bloodied up. When she saw me she got mad and yelled at me for making more trouble for her when she already had her hands full with my father.

THERAPIST: Do you remember how you felt then?

MR. ARIANES: I can't remember, but I know that after that I never brought my troubles to her again.

THERAPIST: How old were you?

MR. ARIANES: Nine. I know that because I got that bike for my ninth birthday. It was a little too big for me still, that's why I got hurt on it.

THERAPIST: Perhaps you carried this attitude into your marriage.

MR. ARIANES: What attitude?

THERAPIST: The feeling that your wife, like your mother, would be unsympathetic to your difficulties. That there was no point in telling her about your experiences because she was too preoccupied or too busy to care.

MR. ARIANES: But she's so different from my mother. I come first with her.

THERAPIST: On one level you know that. On another, deeper level there may well be the fear that people—or maybe only women, or maybe only women you're close to—are all the same, and you can't take a chance at being rejected again in your need.

MR. ARIANES: Maybe you're right, Doc, but all that was so long ago, and I should be over that by now.

THERAPIST: That's not the way the mind works. If a shock or a disappointment is strong enough, it can permanently freeze our picture of ourselves and our expectations of the world. The rest of us grows up—that is, we let ourselves learn about life from experience and from what we see, hear, or read of the experiences of others, but that one area where we really got hurt stays unchanged. So what I mean when I say you might be carrying that attitude into your relationship with your wife is that when it comes to your hopes of being understood and catered to when you feel hurt or abused by life, you still feel very much like that 9-year-old boy who was rebuffed in his need and gave up hope that anyone would or could respond to him.

—*Offering an Interpretation, from M. F. Basch,* Doing Psychotherapy *(Basic Books, 1980), pp. 29–30. Reprinted by permission of Basic Books, a member of Perseus Books Group.*

What does it mean? Freud believed that dreams represent the "royal road to the unconscious." Dream interpretation was one of the principal techniques Freud used to uncover unconscious material.

Contemporary psychodynamic therapy. Modern psychodynamic therapy is generally briefer than traditional Freudian psychoanalysis and involves more direct, face-to-face interactions with clients.

Some modern psychodynamic therapists focus more on the role of the ego and less on the role of the id. These therapists, such as Heinz Hartmann, are generally described as *ego analysts*. Other modern psychoanalysts, such as Margaret Mahler, are identified with *object-relations* approaches to psychodynamic therapy. They focus on helping people separate their own ideas and feelings from the elements of significant others they have incorporated or *introjected* onto themselves. Clients can then develop more as individuals—as their own persons, rather than trying to meet the expectations they believe others have of them.

Though psychodynamic therapy is no longer the dominant force it once was, it remains widely practiced and is supported by accumulating evidence of its effectiveness (e.g., Knekt et al., 2011; Leichsenring & Rabung, 2008; Levy & Scala, 2012; Town et al., 2012; Wolitzky, 2011). Let us now turn to other forms of therapy, beginning with behavior therapy.

Behavior Therapy

Behavior therapy is the systematic application of the principles of learning to the treatment of psychological disorders. Because the focus is on changing behavior—not on personality change or deep probing into the past—behavior therapy is relatively brief, typically lasting from a few weeks to a few months. Behavior therapists, like other therapists, seek to develop warm therapeutic relationships with clients, but they believe the special efficacy of behavior therapy derives from the learning-based techniques rather than from the nature of the therapeutic relationship.

Behavior therapy originally gained widespread attention as a means of helping people overcome fears and phobias, problems that had proved resistant to insight-oriented therapies. Among the methods used are systematic desensitization, gradual exposure, and modeling. **Systematic desensitization** involves a therapeutic program of exposure of the client (in imagination or by means of pictures or slides) to progressively more fearful stimuli while he or she remains deeply relaxed. First the client uses a relaxation technique, such as progressive relaxation (discussed in Chapter 6), to become deeply relaxed. The client is then instructed to imagine (or perhaps view, as through a series of slides) progressively more anxiety-arousing scenes. If fear is evoked, the client again practices a relaxation exercise to restore a relaxed state. The process is repeated until the client can tolerate the scene without anxiety. The client then progresses to the next scene in the *fear-stimulus hierarchy*. The procedure is continued until the person can remain relaxed while imagining the most distressing scene in the hierarchy.

In **gradual exposure** (also called in vivo, meaning "in life," exposure), people seeking to overcome phobias put themselves in situations in which they engage fearful stimuli in real-life encounters. As with systematic desensitization, the person moves at his or her own pace through a hierarchy of progressively more anxiety-evoking stimuli. The person with a fear of snakes, for example, might first look at a harmless, caged snake from across the room and then gradually approach and interact with the snake in a step-by-step process, progressing to each new step only when feeling completely calm at the prior step. Gradual exposure is often combined with cognitive techniques that focus on replacing anxiety-arousing irrational thoughts with calming rational thoughts.

In **modeling,** individuals learn desired behaviors by observing others performing them. For example, the client may observe and then imitate others who successfully interact with fear-evoking situations or objects. After observing the model, the client may be assisted or guided by the therapist or the model in performing the target behavior. The client receives ample reinforcement from the therapist for each attempt. Modeling approaches were pioneered by Albert Bandura and his colleagues, who had remarkable success using modeling techniques with children to treat various phobias, especially fear of animals, such as snakes and dogs.

Behavior therapists also use reinforcement techniques based on operant conditioning to shape desired behavior. For example, parents and teachers may be trained to systematically reinforce children for appropriate behavior by showing appreciation for it and to extinguish inappropriate behavior by ignoring it. In institutional settings, **token economy** systems seek to increase adaptive behavior by rewarding residents with tokens for performing appropriate behaviors, such as self-grooming and making their beds. The tokens can eventually be exchanged for desired rewards. Token systems have also been used to treat children with conduct disorders.

Other techniques of behavior therapy discussed in later chapters include *aversive conditioning* (used in the treatment of substance abuse problems such as smoking and alcoholism) and *social skills training* (used in the treatment of social anxiety and skills deficits associated with schizophrenia).

"You say 'off with her head,' but what I'm hearing is, 'I feel neglected.'"

DRAWING BY MIKE EWERS. REPRINTED BY PERMISSION.

Humanistic Therapy

Psychodynamic therapists tend to focus on clients' unconscious processes, such as internal conflicts. By contrast, humanistic therapists focus on clients' subjective, conscious experiences. The major form of humanistic therapy is **person-centered therapy** (also called *client-centered therapy*), which was developed by the psychologist Carl Rogers (Rogers, 1951; Raskin, Rogers, & Witty, 2011).

PERSON-CENTERED THERAPY To Rogers, psychological disorders result largely from roadblocks that other people place in our path toward self-actualization. When others are selective in their approval of our childhood feelings and behavior, we may disown the criticized parts of ourselves. To earn social approval, we may don social masks or facades. We learn "to be seen and not heard" and may even become deaf to our own inner voices. Over time, we may develop distorted self-concepts that are consistent with others' views of us but are not of our own making and design. As a result, we may become poorly adjusted, unhappy, and confused as to who and what we are.

Person-centered therapy creates conditions of warmth and acceptance in the therapeutic relationship that help clients become more aware and accepting of their true selves. Rogers did not believe therapists should impose their own goals or values on their clients. His focus of therapy, as the name implies, is the person.

Person-centered therapy is *nondirective.* The client, not the therapist, takes the lead and directs the course of therapy. The therapist uses *reflection*—the restating or paraphrasing of the client's expressed feelings without interpreting them or passing judgment on them. This encourages the client to further explore his or her feelings and to get in touch with deeper feelings and parts of his or her self that had been disowned because of social condemnation.

Rogers stressed the importance of creating a warm, therapeutic relationship that would encourage the client to engage in self-exploration and self-expression. The effective person-centered therapist possesses four basic qualities or attributes: *unconditional positive regard, empathy, genuineness,* and *congruence.* First, the therapist must be able to express unconditional positive regard for clients. In contrast to the conditional approval the client may have received from parents and others in the past, the therapist must be unconditionally accepting of the client as a person, even if the therapist sometimes finds the client's choices or behaviors to be objectionable. Unconditional positive regard provides clients with a sense of security that encourages them to explore their feelings without fear of disapproval. As clients feel accepted or prized for themselves, they are encouraged to accept themselves in turn.

Therapists who display **empathy** are able to accurately reflect or mirror their clients' experiences and feelings. Therapists try to see the world through their clients' eyes or frames of reference. They listen carefully to clients, setting aside their own judgments and interpretations of events. Showing empathy encourages clients to get in touch with feelings of which they may be only dimly aware. **Genuineness** is the ability to be open about one's feelings. Rogers admitted he had negative feelings at times during therapy sessions, typically boredom, but he attempted to express these feelings openly rather than hide them (Bennett, 1985). **Congruence** refers to the coherence or fit among one's thoughts, feelings, and behaviors. The congruent person is one whose behavior, thoughts, and feelings are integrated and consistent. Congruent therapists serve as models of psychological integrity for their clients.

Cognitive Therapy

There is nothing either good or bad, but thinking makes it so.

—Shakespeare, *Hamlet*

Shakespeare did not mean to imply that misfortunes or ailments are painless or easy to manage. His point, it seems, was that the ways in which we evaluate upsetting events can heighten or diminish our discomfort and affect our ability to cope. Several hundred years later, cognitive therapists such as Aaron Beck and Albert Ellis adopted this simple but elegant expression as a kind of motto for their approach to therapy.

Cognitive therapists focus on helping clients identify and correct faulty thinking, distorted beliefs, and self-defeating attitudes that create or contribute to emotional problems. They argue that negative emotions such as anxiety and depression are caused by interpretations people place on troubling events, not on events themselves. Here, we focus on two prominent types of **cognitive therapy:** Albert Ellis's rational emotive behavior therapy and Aaron Beck's cognitive therapy.

RATIONAL EMOTIVE BEHAVIOR THERAPY Albert Ellis (1993, 2001, 2011) believed that negative emotions such as anxiety and depression are caused by the irrational ways in which we interpret or judge negative events, not by the negative events themselves. Consider the irrational belief that we must almost always have the approval of the people who are important to us. Ellis finds it understandable to want other people's approval and love, but he argues that it is irrational to believe we cannot survive without it. Another irrational belief is that we must be thoroughly competent and achieving in virtually everything we seek to accomplish. We are doomed to eventually fall short of these irrational expectations, and when we do, we may experience negative emotional consequences, such as depression and lowered self-esteem. Emotional difficulties such as anxiety and depression are not directly caused by negative events, but rather by how we distort the meaning of these events by viewing them through the dark-colored glasses of self-defeating beliefs. In Ellis's **rational emotive behavior therapy** (REBT), therapists actively *dispute* clients' irrational beliefs and the premises on which they are based and help clients develop alternative, adaptive beliefs in their place.

Rational emotive behavior therapists help clients substitute more effective interpersonal behavior for self-defeating or maladaptive behavior. Ellis often gave clients specific tasks or homework assignments, such as disagreeing with an overbearing relative or asking someone for a date. He also assisted them in practicing or rehearsing adaptive behaviors.

BECK'S COGNITIVE THERAPY Psychiatrist Aaron Beck (e.g., Beck, 2005; Beck & Weishaar, 2011) developed cognitive therapy, which, like rational emotive behavior therapy, focuses on helping people change faulty or distorted thinking. Cognitive therapy is the fastest growing and most widely researched model of psychotherapy today (Beck & Dozois, 2011).

Cognitive therapists encourage their clients to recognize and change errors in thinking, called *cognitive distortions,* such as tendencies to magnify the importance of negative events and minimize one's personal accomplishments. These self-defeating ways of thinking, Beck argues, underlie negative emotional states such as depression. Like tinted glasses, these distorted or faulty thoughts color a person's perception of life experiences and his or her reactions to the outside world (Smith, 2009). Cognitive therapists ask clients to record their thoughts in response to upsetting events and note connections between their thoughts and their emotional responses. They then help clients dispute distorted thoughts and replace them with rational alternatives.

Cognitive therapists also use behavioral homework assignments, such as encouraging depressed people to fill their free time with structured activities like gardening or completing work around the house. Another type of homework assignment involves *reality testing,* whereby clients are asked to test their negative beliefs in light of reality. For example, a depressed client who feels unwanted by everyone might be asked to call two or three friends on the phone to gather data about the friends' reactions to the calls. The therapist might then ask the client to report on the assignment: "Did they immediately hang up the phone, or did they seem pleased you called? Did they express any interest at all in talking to you again or getting together sometime? Does the evidence support the conclusion that *no one* has any interest in you?" Such exercises help clients replace distorted beliefs with rational alternatives.

The therapies developed by Beck and Ellis can be classified as forms of cognitive-behavioral therapy, which is the treatment approach we turn to next. We will then consider a growing movement among therapists toward incorporating principles and techniques derived from different schools of therapy. Before reading further, you may wish to review Table 2.5, which summarizes the major approaches to psychotherapy.

Cognitive-Behavioral Therapy

Today, most behavior therapists identify with a broader model of behavior therapy called **cognitive-behavioral therapy** (CBT) (also called *cognitive behavior therapy*). Cognitive-behavioral therapy attempts to integrate therapeutic techniques that help individuals make changes not only in their overt behavior but also in their underlying thoughts, beliefs, and attitudes. Cognitive-behavioral therapy draws on the assumption that thinking patterns and beliefs affect behavior and that changes in these cognitions can produce desirable behavioral and emotional changes. Cognitive-behavioral therapists focus on helping clients identify and correct the maladaptive beliefs and negative, automatic thoughts that may underlie their emotional problems.

Cognitive-behavioral therapists use an assortment of cognitive techniques, such as changing maladaptive thoughts, and behavioral techniques, such as exposure to fear-invoking situations. Cognitive-behavioral therapy has produced impressive results in controlled trials in treating a wide range of emotional disorders, including depression, panic disorder, generalized anxiety disorder, social phobia, posttraumatic stress disorder, agoraphobia, and obsessive–compulsive disorder, as well as other disorders such as bulimia and personality disorders (e.g., DiMauro et al., 2012; Hofmann, Asnaani, Vonk, Sawyer, & Fang, 2012; McEvoy, Nathan, Rapee, & Campbell, 2012; Resick, Williams, Suvak, Monson, & Gradus, 2012; Roy-Byrne et al., 2010; Stewart & Chambless, 2009). Yet, like other forms of treatment, including drug therapy, cognitive-behavioral therapy is not effective in all cases, with many patients either failing to respond to treatment or showing symptoms when evaluated years afterward (David & Szentagotaia, 2006; Durham, Higgins, Chambers, Swan, & Dow, 2012). This only underscores the need for efforts to further improve current treatment approaches.

Eclectic Therapy

Each of the major psychological models of abnormal behavior—the psychodynamic, behaviorist, humanistic, and cognitive approaches—has spawned its own approaches to psychotherapy. Although many therapists identify with one or another of these schools of therapy, some others practice **eclectic therapy,** which incorporates principles and techniques from different therapeutic orientations that they believe will produce the greatest benefit in treating a particular client (Norcross & Beutler, 2011; Prochaska & Norcross, 2010). An eclectic or integrative therapist might use behavior therapy techniques to help

TABLE 2.5

Overview of Major Types of Psychotherapies

Type of Therapy	Major Figure(s)	Goal	Length of Treatment	Therapist's Approach	Major Techniques
Classical psychoanalysis	Sigmund Freud	Gaining insight and resolving unconscious psychological conflicts	Lengthy, typically lasting several years	Passive, interpretive	Free association, dream analysis, interpretation
Modern psychodynamic approaches	Various	Focus on developing insight, but with greater emphasis on ego functioning, current interpersonal relationships, and adaptive behavior than traditional psychoanalysis	Briefer than traditional psychoanalysis	More direct probing of client defenses; more back-and-forth discussion	Direct analysis of client's defenses and transference relationships
Behavior therapy	Various	Directly changing problem behavior through use of learning-based techniques	Relatively brief, typically lasting 10 to 20 sessions	Directive, active problem solving	Systematic desensitization, gradual exposure, modeling, reinforcement techniques
Humanistic, client-centered therapy	Carl Rogers	Self-acceptance and personal growth	Varies, but briefer than traditional psychoanalysis	Nondirective; allowing client to take the lead, with therapist serving as an empathic listener	Use of reflection; creation of a warm, accepting therapeutic relationship
Ellis's rational emotive behavior therapy	Albert Ellis	Replacing irrational beliefs with rational alternative beliefs; making adaptive behavioral changes	Relatively brief, typically lasting 10 to 20 sessions	Direct, sometimes confrontational challenging of client's irrational beliefs	Identifying and challenging irrational beliefs, behavioral homework assignments
Beck's cognitive therapy	Aaron Beck	Identify and correcting distorted or self-defeating thoughts and beliefs, making adaptive behavioral changes	Relatively brief, typically lasting 10 to 20 sessions	Collaboratively engaging client in process of logically examining thoughts and beliefs and testing them out	Identifying and correcting distorted thoughts; behavioral homework, including reality testing
Cognitive-behavioral therapy	Various	Use of cognitive and behavioral techniques to change maladaptive behaviors and cognitions	Relatively brief, typically lasting 10 to 20 sessions	Direct, active problem solving	Combination of cognitive and behavioral techniques

a client change specific maladaptive behaviors, for example, along with psychodynamic techniques to help the client gain insight into the childhood roots of the problem.

The largest percentage of clinical psychologists today (22%) identify with an eclectic/integrative theoretical orientation, not counting, however, the cognitive approach (31%) (Norcross & Karpiak, 2012) (see Figure 2.10). Therapists who adopt an eclectic approach tend to be older and more experienced (Beitman, Goldfried, & Norcross, 1989). Perhaps they have learned through experience the value of drawing on diverse contributions to the practice of therapy.

There are two general types of eclecticism, *technical eclecticism* and *integrative eclecticism*. Therapists who practice technical eclecticism draw on techniques from different schools of therapy without necessarily adopting the theoretical positions that spawned those techniques. They assume a pragmatic approach in using techniques from different therapeutic approaches that they believe are most likely to work with a given client.

Therapists who practice integrative eclecticism attempt to synthesize and integrate diverse theoretical approaches—to bring together different theoretical concepts and approaches under the roof of one integrated model of therapy. Although various

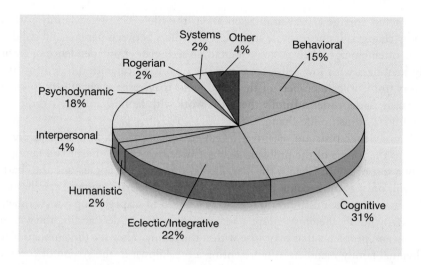

FIGURE 2.10

Therapeutic orientations of clinical psychologists. A recent national survey showed that the cognitive and the eclectic/integrative therapeutic orientations were the most popular among clinical psychologists today. *Source:* Adapted from Norcross & Karpiak (2012).

approaches to integrative psychotherapy have been proposed, the field has yet to arrive at a consensus regarding a therapeutic integration of principles and practices. Not all therapists subscribe to the view that therapeutic integration is a desirable or achievable goal. They believe that combining elements of different therapeutic approaches will lead to a hodgepodge of techniques that lack a cohesive conceptual framework. Still, interest in the professional community in therapeutic integration is growing, and we expect to see new models emerging that aim to tie together the contributions of different approaches.

Group, Family, and Couple Therapy

Some approaches to therapy expand the focus of treatment to include groups of people, families, and couples.

GROUP THERAPY In **group therapy,** a group of clients meets together with a therapist or a pair of therapists. Group therapy has several advantages over individual treatment. For one, group therapy is less costly to individual clients, because several clients are treated at the same time. Many clinicians also believe that group therapy is more effective in treating groups of clients who have similar problems, such as complaints relating to anxiety, depression, lack of social skills, or adjustment to divorce or other life stresses. Clients learn how people with similar problems cope and receive social support from the group as well as the therapist. Group therapy also provides members with opportunities to work through their problems in relating to others. For example, the therapist or other group members may point out how a particular member's behavior in a group session mirrors the person's behavior outside the group. Group members may also rehearse social skills with one another in a supportive atmosphere.

Despite these advantages, clients may prefer individual therapy for various reasons. For one, clients might not wish to disclose their problems in a group. Some clients prefer the individual attention of the therapist. Others are too socially inhibited to feel comfortable in a group setting. Because of such concerns, group therapists require that group disclosures be kept confidential, that group members relate to each other supportively and nondestructively, and that group members receive the attention they need.

FAMILY THERAPY In **family therapy,** the family, not the individual, is the unit of treatment. Family therapy aims to help troubled families resolve their conflicts and problems so the family functions better as a unit and individual family members are subjected to less stress from family conflicts. In family therapy, family members learn to communicate more effectively and to air their disagreements constructively (Gehar, 2009). Family

Group therapy. What are some of the advantages of group therapy over individual therapy? What are some of its disadvantages?

Family therapy. In family therapy, the family, not the individual, is the unit of treatment. Therapists help family members communicate more effectively with one another, for example, by airing disagreements in ways that are not hurtful to individual members. Therapists also try to prevent one member of the family from becoming the scapegoat for the family's problems.

2.9 Evaluate the effectiveness of psychotherapy and the role of nonspecific factors in therapy.

truth OR fiction

Psychotherapy is no more effective than simply letting time take its course.

☑ **FALSE** There is ample evidence that psychotherapy produces better results than control treatments in which people are placed on waiting lists that allow time to take its course.

conflicts often emerge at transitional points in the life cycle, when family patterns are altered by changes in one or more members. Conflicts between parents and children, for example, often emerge when adolescent children seek greater independence or autonomy. Family members with low self-esteem may be unable to tolerate different attitudes or behaviors from other members of the family and may resist their efforts to change or become more independent. Family therapists work with families to resolve these conflicts and help them adjust to life changes.

Family therapists are sensitive to tendencies of families to scapegoat one family member as the source of the problem, or the "identified client." Disturbed families seem to adopt a sort of myth: Change the identified client, the "bad apple," and the "barrel," or family, will once again become functional. Family therapists encourage families to work together to resolve their disputes and conflicts, instead of scapegoating one member.

Many family therapists adopt a *systems approach* to understanding the workings of the family and problems that may arise within the family. They see the problem behaviors of individual family members as representing a breakdown in the system of communications and role relationships within the family. For example, a child may feel in competition with other siblings for a parent's attention and develop enuresis, or bed-wetting, as a means of securing attention. Operating from a systems perspective, the family therapist may focus on helping family members understand the hidden messages in the child's behavior and make changes in their relationships to meet the child's needs more adequately.

COUPLE THERAPY Couple therapy focuses on resolving conflicts in distressed couples, including married and unmarried couples (Baucoma, Sevier, Eldridge, Doss, & Christensen, 2011; Christensen et al., 2010). Like family therapy, couple therapy focuses on improving communication and analyzing role relationships. For example, one partner may play a dominant role and resist any request to share power. The couple therapist helps bring these role relationships into the open, so that partners can explore alternative ways of relating to one another that would lead to a more satisfying relationship.

Evaluating the Methods of Psychotherapy

What, then, of the effectiveness of psychotherapy? Does psychotherapy work? Are some forms of therapy more effective than others? Are some forms of therapy more effective for some types of clients or for some types of problems than for others?

USE OF META-ANALYSIS That psychotherapy is effective receives strong support from the research literature. Reviews of the scientific literature often use a statistical technique called *meta-analysis*, which averages the results of a large number of studies to determine an overall level of effectiveness.

A classic example of a meta-analysis of psychotherapy outcomes involved some 375 controlled studies, each of which compared psychotherapy (of different types, including psychodynamic, behavioral, and humanistic) against control groups (M. L. Smith & Glass, 1977). Across these studies, the average client receiving psychotherapy was better off than 75% of clients who remained untreated. A larger analysis of 475 controlled outcome studies showed the average person who received therapy to be better off at the end of treatment than 80% of those who did not (M. L. Smith, Glass, & Miller, 1980). **T / F**

Later meta-analyses also showed positive outcomes for particular types of therapy, including cognitive-behavioral therapy and psychodynamic therapy (e.g., Butler et al., 2006; Cuijpers, Hofmann et al., 2010; Shedler, 2010; Tolin, 2010; Town et al., 2012). Psychotherapy has proven to be effective not only in the confines of clinical research centers but also in settings more typical of ordinary clinical practice (Shadish et al., 2000).

The greatest gains in psychotherapy typically occur in the first several months of treatment. At least 50% of patients in controlled research studies show clinically significant improvement in about 13 treatment sessions; by 26 sessions, this figure rises to more than 80% (E. M. Anderson & Lambert, 2001; Hansen, Lambert, & Forman, 2002;

THINKING CRITICALLY about abnormal psychology

@Issue: Should Therapists Treat Clients Online?

Might better mental health be only a few keystrokes away? You can do almost anything on the Internet these days, from ordering concert tickets to downloading music (legally, of course) or even whole books. You can also receive counseling or therapy services from an online therapist. Online counselors and therapists are using video chat services, such as Skype, as well as e-mail, and other electronic and telephonic services to provide help to people with emotional problems and relationship issues. As the number of online counseling services continues to increase, so does the controversy concerning their use.

Many professionals voice concerns about clinical, ethical, and legal issues of online counseling services (Gabbard, 2012; Harris & Younggren, 2011; Van Allen & Roberts, 2011; Yuen, Goetter, Herbert, & Forman, 2012). One problem is that psychologists are licensed in particular states, but Internet communications easily cross state borders (DeAngelis, 2012). It remains unclear, therefore, whether psychologists or other mental health professionals can legally provide online services to residents of states in which they are not licensed.

Ethical problems and liability issues also arise when psychologists and other helping professionals offer services to clients they actually never meet in person. Many therapists also express concern that interacting with a client only by computer or by other means, such as by telephone, would prevent them from evaluating nonverbal cues and gestures that might signal deeper levels of distress than could be communicated by typing words on a keyboard or talking on the telephone (Rehm, 2008).

Therapists are rightfully concerned, however, about the ethical problems in using technology in therapy—problems such as unauthorized access to client records and dissemination (posting) of client information on social websites (van Allen & Roberts, 2011). Yet another problem is that online therapists may live at great distances from their clients, so they may not be able to provide the more intensive services clients need during times of emotional crisis. Professionals also express concerns about the potential for unsuspecting clients to be victimized by unqualified practitioners or quacks. There is not yet a system to ensure that only licensed and qualified practitioners offer online therapeutic services.

On the other hand, therapists are demonstrating therapeutic benefits in using the Internet to deliver guided self-help treatment programs for a wide range of problems, including posttraumatic stress disorder, panic disorder, insomnia, social phobia, obsessive–compulsive disorder, pathological gambling, alcohol abuse, and smoking addiction (e.g., Andersson et al., 2012; Beard, Weisberg, & Amir, 2011; Blankers, Koeter, & Schippers, 2011; Carlbring et al., 2011; Choi et al., 2012; Dear et al., 2011; Herbst et al., 2012; Lancee, van den Bout,

van Straten, & Spoormaker, 2012; Newman et al., 2011a, b; Sunderland, Wong, Hilvert-Bruce, & Andrews, 2012). In these cases, therapists oversee the quality of the online treatment services they provide. In some cases, therapists provide additional support to supplement online treatment protocols via the use of e-mail or periodic telephone contact, in a similar way that a person might access a help line for using computer software programs. Mental health professionals are also incorporating computerized therapy tools as part of a traditional treatment program.

One advantage of online treatment is that it can reach people who may have avoided seeking help because of shyness or embarrassment. Online consultation may make some people feel more comfortable about receiving help, making it a first step toward meeting a therapist in person. Online therapy and teleconferencing services may also provide needed services to people who might not otherwise receive help because they lack mobility or live in remote areas (McCord et al., 2011). A recent study showed that online therapy used in the treatment of adolescents with anxiety disorders combined with minimal therapist contact was just as effective as regular, face-to-face sessions with a therapist and had the advantage of reaching families who might have difficulty arranging clinic visits (Spence, 2011).

All in all, psychologists are not writing off electronic forms of therapy, but they do remain cautious about its use (Mora, Nevid, & Chaplin, 2008). Psychologists are seeking to put client protections into place for using the Internet and other forms of computerized or electronically delivered psychological services

Internet Therapy. Online therapeutic services are popping up on the Internet. Although Internet-based counseling or therapy services may have therapeutic benefits, many mental health professionals express concerns about potential clinical, ethical, and legal issues associated with these services.

before they are disseminated for widespread use (DeAngelis, 2012; Hadjistavropoulos et al., 2011; Perle, Langsam, & Nierenberg, 2011).

What do you think about the value of online psychological services? In thinking critically about this issue, answer the following questions:

- What ethical and practical problems do therapists who offer online therapy face?

- What are the potential benefits of online therapy? What are the potential risks?

- If you were in need of psychological services, would you seek an Internet-based treatment? Why or why not?

Messer, 2001a). Yet, we should recognize that many clients drop out prematurely, before therapeutic benefits are achieved.

Although evidence supports the effectiveness of psychotherapy, researchers lack clarity about why it works—that is, what factors or processes account for therapeutic change (Carey, 2011). Different forms of therapy produce about the same level or size of benefits when each is compared to control (untreated) groups (Cuijpers, van Straten et al., 2008; Wampold et al., 2011). This suggests that the effectiveness of different forms of psychotherapy may have more to do with the common features that cut across different types of psychotherapy, called **nonspecific treatment factors,** than with the specific techniques that set them apart.

Nonspecific or common factors include expectations of improvement and features of the therapist–client relationship: (1) empathy, support, and attention shown by the therapist; (2) *therapeutic alliance,* or the attachment the client develops toward the therapist and the therapy process; and (3) the *working alliance,* or the development of an effective working relationship in which the therapist and client work together to identify and confront the important problems and concerns the client faces (Crits-Christoph, Gibbons, Hamilton, Ring-Kurtz, & Gallop, 2011; Prochaska & Norcross, 2010; Smith, Msetfi, & Golding, 2010). These factors may have therapeutic benefits in themselves, quite apart from the specific benefits associated with particular forms of therapy (Bjornsson, 2011; Goldfried, 2012).

Should we conclude that different therapies are about equally effective? Not necessarily. Different therapies may be more or less equivalent in their effects overall, but some may be more effective for some patients or some types of problems. We should also allow that the effectiveness of therapy may have more to do with the effectiveness of the therapist than with the particular form of therapy (Wampold, 2001).

All in all, the question of whether some forms of therapy are more effective than others remains unresolved. Perhaps the time has come for investigators to turn more of their attention to examining the active ingredients that make some therapists more effective than others, such as their interpersonal skills, ability to show empathy, and ability to develop a good therapeutic relationship or alliance with their clients (Karver et al., 2006; Prochaska & Norcross, 2010). A stronger therapeutic alliance, especially when formed early in therapy, is associated with better treatment outcomes (Crits-Christoph et al., 2011; Strunk et al., 2012; Zuroff & Blatt, 2006).

Another question researchers pose is whether specific therapies work as well in the clinic as they do in the research lab. Two types of research studies, *efficacy studies* and *effectiveness studies,* examine these types of effects. Efficacy studies speak to the issue of whether particular treatments work better than control procedures under tightly controlled conditions in a research lab setting. But the fact that a given treatment works well in the research lab does not necessarily mean it also works well in a typical clinic setting. This question is addressed by effectiveness studies, which examine the effects of treatment when it is delivered by therapists in real-world practice settings with the kinds of clients they normally see in their practices.

EMPIRICALLY SUPPORTED TREATMENTS Empirically supported treatments are specific psychological treatments that have been demonstrated to be effective in treating

TABLE 2.6
Examples of Empirically Supported Treatments

Treatment	Conditions for Which Treatment Is Effective
Cognitive therapy	Headache (Chapter 6)
	Depression (Chapter 7)
Behavior therapy or behavior modification	Depression (Chapter 7)
	Persons with developmental disabilities (Chapter 13)
	Enuresis (Chapter 13)
Cognitive-behavioral therapy	Panic disorder (Chapter 5)
	Generalized anxiety disorder (Chapter 5)
	Bulimia nervosa (Chapter 9)
Exposure treatment	Agoraphobia and specific phobia (Chapter 5)
Exposure and response prevention	Obsessive–compulsive disorder (Chapter 5)
Interpersonal psychotherapy	Depression (Chapter 7)
Parent training programs	Children with oppositional behavior (Chapter 13)

Note. Chapter in text in which treatment is discussed is in parentheses.

particular types of problem behaviors or disorders in carefully designed research studies (see Table 2.6) (APA Presidential Task Force on Evidence-Based Practice, 2006; Lohr, 2011; Wells & Miranda, 2006). The designation of empirically supported treatments (also called *evidence-based practice*) may change, as other treatments may be added to the list as scientific evidence of their efficacy in treating specific types of problems becomes available. We should note, however, that inclusion of a particular treatment in the listing of empirically supported treatments does not mean the treatment is effective in every case.

Let us conclude by noting that it is insufficient to ask which therapy works best. Instead, we must ask: Which therapy works best for which type of problem? Which clients are best suited for which type of therapy? What are the advantages and limitations of particular therapies? Although the effort to identify empirically supported treatments moves us in the direction of matching treatments to particular disorders, determining which treatment, practiced by whom, under what conditions is most effective for a given client remains a challenge.

All in all, psychotherapy is a complex process that incorporates common features along with specific techniques that foster adaptive change. Practitioners need to take into account the contributions to therapeutic change of both specific and nonspecific factors, as well as their interactions (Gibbons et al., 2009).

Multicultural Issues in Psychotherapy

We live in an increasingly diverse, multicultural society in which people bring to therapy not only their personal backgrounds and individual experiences but also their cultural learning, norms, and values. Normal and abnormal behaviors occur in a context of culture and community. Clearly, therapists need to be culturally competent to provide appropriate services to people of varied backgrounds (Stuart, 2004).

Therapists need to be sensitive to cultural differences and how they affect the therapeutic process. Cultural sensitivity involves more than good intentions. Therapists must also have accurate knowledge of cultural factors, as well as the ability to use that knowledge effectively in developing culturally sensitive approaches to treatment (Comas-Diaz, 2011a,b; Hwang, 2011; Leong & Kalibatseva, 2011; Sue, Zane, Hall, & Berger, 2009). Moreover, they need to avoid ethnic stereotyping and demonstrate

2.10 Describe the importance of multicultural factors in psychotherapy and barriers to use of mental health services by ethnic minorities.

Cultural sensitivity. Therapists need to be sensitive to cultural differences and how they may affect the therapeutic process. They also need to avoid ethnic stereotyping and to demonstrate sensitivity to the values, languages, and cultural beliefs of members of racial or ethnic groups that are different from their own. Clients who are not fluent in English profit from having therapists who can conduct therapy in the languages their clients speak.

sensitivity to the values, languages, and cultural beliefs of members of racial or ethnic groups that are different from their own. Perhaps it shouldn't surprise practicing therapists that clients who rate their therapists high on multicultural competence also tend to perceive them as having skills of empathy and general competence (Fuertes & Brobst, 2002). However, a survey of professional psychologists showed that they applied relatively few of the recommended multicultural psychotherapy competencies in their practices (Hansen et al., 2006).

Just because a given therapy works with one population does not necessarily mean it will work with another population. Researchers and practitioners need evidence that speaks directly to whether particular therapies are effective with different populations and whether specific cultural adaptations of particular therapies offer greater benefits than their standard versions (see, for example, Hayes, Muto, & Masuda, 2011; Franko et al., 2012; López, Barrio, Kopelowicz, & Vega, 2012). A recent study showed that a culturally specific form of behavior therapy for phobias was more effective in treating Asian Americans than a standard behavioral treatment, especially for less well acculturated clients (Pan, Huey, & Hernandez, 2011). This finding suggests that therapists using established treatments should consider how they can incorporate culturally specific elements to boost treatment benefits in working with people from different ethnic or racial groups (Burrow-Sanchez & Wrona, 2012; Comas-Diaz, 2011b).

We next touch on factors involved in treating members of the major ethnic minority groups in American society: African Americans, Asian Americans, Hispanic Americans, and Native Americans.

AFRICAN AMERICANS The cultural history of African Americans must be understood in the context of persistent racial discrimination and its toxic effects on the psychological adjustment of people of color (Greene, 2009). African Americans have needed to develop coping mechanisms for managing the pervasive racism they encounter in areas such as employment, housing, education, and access to health care (Greene, 1993a, 1993b; Jackson & Greene, 2000). For example, the sensitivity of many African Americans to the potential for maltreatment and exploitation is a survival tool and may take the form of a heightened level of suspiciousness or reserve. Therefore, therapists need to be aware of the tendency of African American clients to minimize their vulnerability by being less self-disclosing, especially in early stages of therapy (Sanchez-Hucles, 2000). Therapists should not confuse such suspiciousness with paranoia.

In addition to the psychological problems African American clients may present, therapists often need to help their clients develop coping mechanisms to deal with racial barriers they encounter in daily life. Contrary to what some believe, the election of an African American president does not alter the day-to-day experiences of prejudice and discrimination that many African Americans across social classes continue to encounter. Therapists also need to be attuned to the tendencies of some African Americans to internalize the negative stereotypes about Blacks that are perpetuated in the dominant culture.

African Americans encounter racism in various forms. There are blatant forms of discrimination in housing and job opportunities, for example, that leave no doubt about what in fact they are; however, some forms are more subtle and harder to identify, such as a suspicious glance by a store security guard. Sue (2010) argues that subtle forms of discrimination can be even more damaging because they leave the victim with a sense of uncertainty about how to respond, if at all.

To be culturally competent, therapists not only must understand the cultural traditions and languages of the groups with which they work, but also recognize their own racial and ethnic attitudes and how these underlying attitudes affect how they practice. Therapists are exposed to the same negative stereotypes about African Americans as other people in society and must recognize how these stereotypes, if left unexamined, can become destructive to the therapeutic relationships they form with African American clients. A core principle in working within a diverse society is the willingness to openly examine one's own racial attitudes and the influences these attitudes may have on the therapeutic process. In addition, Snowden (2012) points out that therapists must be aware of environmental risk factors that affect the mental and physical health of African Americans, such as a lack of access to quality health care.

Therapists must also be aware of the cultural characteristics of African American families, such as strong kinship bonds, often including people who are not biologically related (e.g., a close friend of a parent may have some parenting role and may be addressed as "aunt"); strong religious and spiritual orientation; multigenerational households; adaptability and flexibility of gender roles (African American women have a long history of working outside the home); and distribution of child care responsibilities among different family members (Greene, 1990, 1993a; Jackson & Greene, 2000; USDHHS, 1999).

ASIAN AMERICANS Culturally sensitive therapists not only understand the beliefs and values of other cultures but also integrate this knowledge within the therapy process. Generally speaking, Asian cultures, including Japanese culture, value restraint in talking about oneself and one's feelings. Public expression of emotions is also discouraged in Asian cultures, which may inhibit Asian clients from revealing their feelings in therapy. In traditional Asian cultures, the failure to keep one's feelings to oneself, especially negative feelings, may be perceived as reflecting poorly on one's upbringing. Asian clients who appear passive or emotionally restrained when judged by Western standards may be responding in ways that are culturally appropriate and should not be judged as shy, uncooperative, or avoidant by therapists (Hwang, 2006).

Clinicians also note that Asian clients often express psychological complaints such as anxiety through development of physical symptoms such as tightness in the chest or a racing heart (Hinton et al., 2009). However, the tendency to *somaticize* emotional problems may be explained in part by differences in communication styles (Zane & Sue, 1991). That is, Asians may use more somatic terms to convey emotional distress.

In some cases, the goals of therapy may conflict with the values of a particular culture. The individualism of American society, which is expressed in many forms of psychotherapy that focus on the development of the self, may conflict with the group- and family-centered values of Asian cultures. Therapists working with Asian clients might also emphasize more of a we/us orientation than a me/I orientation to underscore the importance of socially connectedness with their Asian clients (Hayes et al., 2011).

Framing the therapy process in culturally appropriate terms may help build bridges, for example, by emphasizing the strong links in Asian cultures among mind, body, and spirit (Hwang, 2006). Therapists may incorporate techniques that reflect East Asian philosophical or cultural traditions, such as *mindfulness meditation,* a widely practiced Buddhist form of meditation (Hall, Hong, Zane, & Meyer, 2011) (discussed in Chapter 4). They also need to draw upon culturally relevant resources in treatment, such as a strong religious faith tradition, strong extended families, and culturally specific programs in the community (Hays, 2011).

HISPANIC AMERICANS Although Hispanic American subcultures differ in various respects, many share certain cultural values and beliefs, such as the importance placed on the family and kinship ties, as well as on respect and dignity (Calzada, Fernandez, & Cortes, 2010). Therapists need to recognize that the traditional Hispanic American value of interdependency within the family may conflict with the values of independence and self-reliance that are stressed in the mainstream U.S. culture (De la Cancela & Guzman, 1991).

Therapists need to respect differences in values rather than attempt to impose the values of majority cultures. Therapists should also recognize that psychological disorders may manifest differently across ethnic groups. For example, the culture-bound syndrome of *ataques de nervios* (see Chapter 3) affects about 5% of Hispanic children, according to a recent study of children in the Bronx, New York, and San Juan, Puerto Rico (López et al., 2009).

Therapists should also be trained to reach beyond the confines of their offices to work within the Hispanic American community itself, in settings that have an impact on the daily lives of Hispanic Americans, such as social clubs, *bodegas* (neighborhood groceries), and neighborhood beauty and barber shops.

NATIVE AMERICANS Traditionally underserved groups, including people of color, have the greatest unmet needs for mental health treatment services (Wang et al., 2005). A case in point are Native Americans, who remain underserved, partly as the result of the underfunding of the Indian Health Service that was designated to serve this population (Gone & Trimble, 2012). Also contributing to the disparity in mental health services is the cultural gap between providers and Native American recipients (Duran et al., 2005). Mental health professionals can be successful in helping Native Americans if they work within a context that is relevant and sensitive to Native Americans' customs, culture, and values (Gone & Trimble, 2012). For example, many Native Americans expect that the therapist will do most of the talking and they will play a passive role in treatment. These expectations are in keeping with the traditional healer role in Native American culture, but in conflict with the client-focused approach of many forms of conventional therapy. There may also be differences in gestures, eye contact, facial expression, and other modes of nonverbal expression that can impede effective communication between therapist and client (Renfrey, 1992).

Psychologists recognize the importance of bringing elements of tribal culture into mental health programs for Native Americans (Csordas, Storck, & Strauss, 2008). For example, therapists can use indigenous ceremonies that are part of the client's cultural or religious traditions. Purification and cleansing rites have therapeutic value for many Native American peoples in the United States and elsewhere, as *Santeria* is among the African Cuban community, *umbanda* in the Brazilian community, and *vodou* in the Haitian community (Lefley, 1990). People who believe their problems are caused by failure to placate malevolent spirits or to perform mandatory rituals often seek out cleansing rites.

Respect for cultural differences is a key feature of culturally sensitive therapies. Training in multicultural therapy is becoming more widely integrated into training programs for therapists. Culturally sensitive therapies adopt a respectful attitude that encourages people to tell their own personal stories as well as the story of their culture (Coronado & Peake, 1992).

Barriers to Use of Mental Health Services by Ethnic Minorities

A report by the U.S. Surgeon General concluded that members of racial and ethnic minority groups typically have less access to mental health care and receive lower-quality care than do other Americans (USDHHS, 2001). A major reason for this disparity is that a disproportionate number of minority group members remain uninsured or underinsured, leaving them unable to afford mental health care (Snowden, 2012). Consequently, members of ethnic minorities shoulder a greater burden of mental health problems that go undiagnosed and untreated (Neighbors et al., 2007).

Ethnic minorities are also more likely to seek help for psychological problems from other sources than psychologists or psychiatrists, in part to avoid the perceived stigma of mental illness from consulting a mental health provider (Kouyoumdjian, Zamboanga, & Hansen, 2003; Vega, Rodriguez, & Ang, 2010). They may turn first to the church or local emergency room or general hospital than mental health providers.

We can better understand low rates of use of outpatient mental health services by ethnic minorities by examining the barriers to receiving treatment, including the following (based on Cheung, 1991, López et al., 2012, Sanders Thompson, Bazile, & Akbar, 2004, Sue et al., 2012; Venner et al., 2012; and other sources):

1. *Cultural mistrust.* People from minority groups often fail to use mental health services because of a lack of trust. Mistrust may stem from a cultural or personal history of oppression and discrimination, or experiences in which service providers were unresponsive to their needs. When ethnic minority clients perceive majority therapists and the institutions in which they work to be cold or impersonal, they are less likely to place their trust in them.

2. *Mental health literacy.* Latinos may not make use of mental health services because they lack knowledge of mental disorders and how to treat them. Increasing public knowledge among Latinos about the features of schizophrenia and depression, for example, may lead to more referrals to mental health professionals for these kinds of problems.

3. *Institutional barriers.* Facilities may be inaccessible to minority group members because they are located at a considerable distance from their homes or because of lack of public transportation. Moreover, minority group members often feel that staff members make them feel stupid for not being familiar with clinic procedures, and their requests for assistance often become tangled in red tape.

4. *Cultural barriers.* Many recent immigrants, especially those from Southeast Asian countries, have had little, if any, previous contact with mental health professionals. They may hold different conceptions of mental health problems or view mental health problems as less severe than physical problems. In some ethnic minority subcultures, the family is expected to take care of members who have psychological problems and may resist use of outside assistance. Other cultural barriers include cultural differences between typically lower socioeconomic strata minority group members and mostly White middle class staff members and the stigma and shame that is often associated with seeking mental health treatment in ethnic minority communities.

5. *Language barriers.* Differences in language make it difficult for minority group members to describe their problems or obtain needed services. Mental health facilities may lack the resources to hire mental health professionals who are fluent in the languages of minority residents in the communities they serve.

6. *Economic and accessibility barriers.* As mentioned earlier, financial burdens are often a major barrier to use of mental health services by ethnic minorities, many of whom live in economically distressed areas. Moreover, many minority group members live in rural or isolated areas where mental health services may be lacking or inaccessible.

Greater use of mental health services will depend to a large extent on the ability of the mental health system to develop programs that take cultural factors into account and to build staffs comprising culturally sensitive providers, including minority staff members and professionals with competencies in the languages used by community residents (Le Meyer et al., 2009; Sue et al., 2012). Cultural mistrust of the mental health system among minority group members may be grounded in the perception that many mental health professionals are racially biased in how they evaluate and treat members of minority groups.

Biomedical Therapies

There is a growing emphasis in American psychiatry on the use of biomedical therapies, especially *psychotropic drugs* (also called psychiatric drugs). Today, roughly one in five adult Americans takes psychotropic drugs, an increase of about 20% from 2001 to 2010 (Smith, 2012). Biomedical therapies are generally administered by medical doctors, many of whom have specialized training in psychiatry or **psychopharmacology.** Many family physicians or general practitioners also prescribe psychotherapeutic drugs for their patients.

Biomedical approaches have had dramatic success in treating some forms of abnormal behavior, although they also have their limitations. For one, drugs may have unwelcome or dangerous side effects. Psychosurgery has been all but eliminated as a form of treatment because of serious harmful effects of earlier procedures.

Drug Therapy

Different classes of psychotropic or psychiatric drugs are used in treating many types of psychological disorders. But all the drugs in these classes act on neurotransmitter systems in the brain, affecting the delicate balance of chemicals that ferry nerve impulses from neuron to neuron. Psychiatric drugs do not cure mental or psychological disorders, but they can often help control the troubling symptoms or features of these disorders. The

2.11 **Identify** the major categories of psychotropic or psychiatric drugs and examples of drugs in each type, and **evaluate** their strengths and weaknesses.

major classes of psychiatric drugs are antianxiety drugs, antipsychotic drugs, and antidepressants, as well as lithium and other drugs used to treat mania and mood swings in people with bipolar disorder. The use of other psychotropic drugs, such as stimulants, will be discussed in later chapters.

ANTIANXIETY DRUGS Antianxiety drugs (also called *anxiolytics,* from the Greek *anxietas,* meaning "anxiety," and *lysis,* meaning "bringing to an end") combat anxiety and reduce states of muscle tension. They include mild tranquilizers, such as those of the *benzodiazepine* class of drugs, for example, *diazepam* (Valium) and *alprazolam* (Xanax), as well as hypnotic sedatives, such as *triazolam* (Halcion). Xanax is currently the largest selling psychiatric drug in the United States (Henig, 2012).

Antianxiety drugs depress the level of activity in certain parts of the central nervous system. In turn, the central nervous system decreases the level of sympathetic nervous system activity, reducing the respiration rate and heart rate and lessening states of anxiety and tension.

Side effects of using antianxiety drugs include fatigue, drowsiness, and impaired motor coordination that can impair the ability to function or to operate an automobile. There is also the potential for abuse. One of the most commonly prescribed minor tranquilizers, Valium, has become a major drug of abuse among people who become psychologically and physiologically dependent on it. When used on a short-term basis, antianxiety drugs can be safe and effective in treating anxiety and insomnia. Yet, drugs by themselves do not teach people new skills or more adaptive ways of handling their problems. Instead, people may simply learn to rely on chemical agents to cope with their problems. **Rebound anxiety** is another problem associated with regular use of tranquilizers. Many people who regularly use antianxiety drugs report that anxiety or insomnia returns in a more severe form once they discontinue the drugs.

ANTIPSYCHOTIC DRUGS Antipsychotic drugs, also called *neuroleptics,* are commonly used to treat the more flagrant features of schizophrenia and other psychotic disorders, such as hallucinations, delusions, and states of confusion. Introduced during the 1950s, many of these drugs, including *chlorpromazine* (Thorazine), *thioridazine* (Mellaril), and *fluphenazine* (Prolixin), belong to the *phenothiazine* class of chemicals. Phenothiazines appear to control psychotic features by blocking the action of the neurotransmitter dopamine at receptor sites in the brain. Although the underlying causes of schizophrenia remain unknown, researchers suspect an irregularity in the dopamine system in the brain may be involved (see Chapter 11). *Clozapine* (Clozaril), a neuroleptic of a different chemical class than the phenothiazines, is effective in treating many people with schizophrenia whose symptoms were unresponsive to other neuroleptics. The use of clozapine must be carefully monitored, however, because of potentially dangerous side effects.

The use of neuroleptics has greatly reduced the need for more restrictive forms of treatment for severely disturbed patients, such as physical restraints and confinement in padded cells, and has lessened the need for long-term hospitalization.

Neuroleptics are not without their problems, including potential side effects such as muscular rigidity and tremors. Although these side effects are generally controllable by use of other drugs, long-term use of antipsychotic drugs (possibly excepting clozapine) can produce a potentially irreversible and disabling motor disorder called *tardive dyskinesia* (see Chapter 11), which is characterized by uncontrollable eye blinking, facial grimaces, lip smacking, and other involuntary movements of the mouth, eyes, and limbs.

ANTIDEPRESSANTS Four major classes of **antidepressants** are in use today: *tricyclics* (TCAs), *monoamine oxidase (MAO) inhibitors, selective serotonin-reuptake inhibitors* (SSRIs), and *serotonin-norepinephrine reuptake inhibitors* (SNRIs). Tricyclics and MAO inhibitors increase the availability of the neurotransmitters norepinephrine and serotonin in the brain. Some commonly used tricyclics are *imipramine* (Tofranil), *amitriptyline* (Elavil), and *doxepin* (Sinequan). The MAO inhibitors include drugs such as *phenelzine* (Nardil). Tricyclics antidepressants are favored over MAO inhibitors because they cause fewer potentially serious side effects.

Selective serotonin-reuptake inhibitors have more specific effects on serotonin levels in the brain. Drugs in this class include *fluoxetine* (Prozac) and *sertraline* (Zoloft). SSRIs increase the availability of serotonin in the brain by interfering with its reuptake (reabsorption) by transmitting neurons. *Serotonin-norepinephrine reuptake inhibitors,* such as *venlafaxine* (Effexor), work specifically on increasing levels of two neurotransmitters linked to mood states, serotonin and norepinephrine, by means of interfering with the reuptake of these chemicals by transmitting neurons.

Antidepressants have beneficial effects in treating a wide range of psychological disorders as well, including panic disorder, social phobia, obsessive–compulsive disorder (see Chapter 5), and bulimia, the type of eating disorder (see Chapter 9) described earlier in the case of Jessica. As research into the underlying causes of these disorders continues, we may find that irregularities of neurotransmitter functioning in the brain play a key role in their development. T / F

LITHIUM AND ANTICONVULSIVE DRUGS Lithium carbonate, a salt of the metal lithium in tablet form, helps treat manic symptoms and stabilize mood swings in people with bipolar disorder (formerly *manic depression*) (discussed further in Chapter 7). However, people with bipolar disorder may have to continue using lithium indefinitely to control the disorder. Further, because of the potential toxicity associated with lithium, the blood levels of people maintained on the drug must be carefully monitored. Anticonvulsive drugs (e.g., Depakote) used in the treatment of epilepsy also have anti-manic and mood stabilizing effects and are sometimes used in people with bipolar disorder who cannot tolerate lithium (see Chapter 7).

Table 2.7 lists psychotropic drugs according to their drug class and category.

Electroconvulsive Therapy

The use of **electroconvulsive therapy (ECT)** seems barbaric and remains controversial. An electric shock is sent through the patient's brain, sufficient to induce convulsions of the type found in epilepsy patients. Although many people with major depression who have failed to respond to antidepressants show significant improvement following ECT (Ebmeier, Donaghey, & Steele, 2006; Faedda et al., 2009; UK ECT Review Group, 2003), electroconvulsive therapy is associated with memory loss for events occurring around the time of treatment and high relapse rates (see Chapter 7). ECT is generally considered a treatment of last resort after less intrusive methods have been tried and failed. T / F

Psychosurgery

Psychosurgery is even more controversial than ECT and is rarely practiced today. The most common form of psychosurgery, no longer performed today, was the *prefrontal lobotomy.* This procedure involved surgically severing nerve pathways linking the thalamus to the prefrontal lobes of the brain. The operation was based on the theory that extremely disturbed patients suffer from overexcitation of emotional impulses emanating from lower-brain centers, such as the thalamus and hypothalamus. It was believed that by severing the connections between the thalamus and the higher-brain centers in the frontal lobe of the cerebral cortex, the patient's violent or aggressive tendencies could be controlled. The procedure was abandoned, because of lack of evidence of its effectiveness and because it often produced serious complications and even death. The advent in the 1950s of psychiatric drugs that could be used to control violent or disruptive behavior all but eliminated the use of psychosurgery (Hirschfeld, 2011).

TABLE 2.7
Major Psychotropic Drugs

	Generic Name	Brand Name	Clinical Uses	Possible Side Effects or Complications
Antianxiety Drugs	Diazepam	Valium	Anxiety, insomnia	Drowsiness, fatigue, impaired coordination, nausea
	Chlordiazepoxide	Librium		
	Lorazepam	Ativan		
	Alprazolam	Xanax		
Antidepressant Drugs	**Tricyclics (TCAs)**			
	Imipramine	Tofranil	Depression, bulimia, panic disorder	Changes in blood pressure, heart irregularities, dry mouth, confusion, skin rash
	Amitriptyline	Elavil		
	Doxepin	Sinequan		
	Monoamine Oxidase Inhibitors (MAOIs)			
	Phenelzine	Nardil	Depression	Dizziness, headache, sleep disturbance, agitation, anxiety, fatigue
	Selective Serotonin-Reuptake Inhibitors (SSRIs)			
	Fluoxetine	Prozac	Depression, bulimia, panic disorder, obsessive–compulsive disorder, posttraumatic stress disorder (Zoloft), social anxiety disorder (Paxil)	Nausea, diarrhea, anxiety, insomnia, sweating, dry mouth, dizziness, drowsiness
	Sertraline	Zoloft		
	Paroxetine	Paxil		
	Citalopram	Celexa		
	Escitalopram	Lexapro		
	Serotonin-Norepinephrine Reuptake Inhibitors (SNRIs)			
	Duloxetine	Cymbalta	Depression, generalized anxiety disorder	Nausea, stomachache, loss of appetite, dry mouth, blurred vision, drowsiness, joint or muscle pain, weight gain
	Venlafaxine	Effexor	Depression	Nausea, constipation, dry mouth
	Desvenlafaxine	Pristiq	Depression	Drowsiness, insomnia, dizziness, anxiety
	Other Antidepressant Drugs			
	Bupropion	Wellbutrin Zyban	Depression, nicotine dependence	Dry mouth, insomnia, headaches, nausea, constipation, tremors
Antipsychotic Drugs	**Phenothiazines**			
	Chlorpromazine	Thorazine	Schizophrenia and other psychotic disorders	Movement disorders (e.g., tardive dyskinesia), drowsiness, restlessness, dry mouth, blurred vision, muscle rigidity
	Thioridazine	Mellaril		
	Trifluoperazine	Stelazine		
	Fluphenazine	Prolixin		
	Atypical Antipsychotics			
	Clozapine	Clozaril	Schizophrenia and other psychotic disorders	Potentially lethal blood disorder, seizures, fast heart rate, drowsiness, dizziness, nausea
	Risperidone	Risperdal	Schizophrenia and other psychotic disorders	Feeling unable to sit still, constipation, dizziness, drowsiness, weight gain
	Olanzapine	Zyprexa	Schizophrenia and other psychotic disorders	Low blood pressure, dizziness, drowsiness, heart palpitations, fatigue, constipation, weight gain
	Aripiprazole	Abilify	Schizophrenia, mania, depression when used along with an antidepressant	Headache, nervousness, drowsiness, dizziness, heartburn, constipation, diarrhea, stomach pain, weight gain

(Continued)

TABLE 2.7 (*continued*)

	Other Antipsychotic Drugs			
	Haloperidol	Haldol	Schizophrenia and other psychotic disorders	Similar to phenothiazines
Antimanic Drugs	Lithium carbonate	Eskalith	Manic episodes and mood stabilization in bipolar disorder	Tremors, thirst, diarrhea, drowsiness, weakness, lack of coordination
	Divalproex sodium	Depakote	Manic episodes and mood stabilization in bipolar disorder	Nausea, vomiting, dizziness, abdominal cramps, sleeplessness
Stimulant Drugs	Methylphenidate	Ritalin, Concerta	Attention–deficit/ hyperactivity disorder (ADHD)	Nervousness, insomnia, nausea, dizziness, heart palpitations, headache; may temporarily retard growth
	Amphetamine with dextroamphetamine	Adderall		

Source: Adapted from J. S. Nevid (2013). *Psychology: Concepts and applications,* 4th ed., p. 629. Belmont, CA: Cengage Learning. Reprinted by permission.

Today, more sophisticated psychosurgery techniques have been introduced. Guided by a better understanding of the brain circuitry involved in certain disorders, such as obsessive–compulsive disorder, modern surgical techniques target smaller parts of the brain and produce less damage than the prefrontal lobotomy. These techniques have been used in treating patients with severe forms of obsessive–compulsive disorder, bipolar disorder, and major depression who have failed to respond to other treatments (Carey, 2009b; Shields et al., 2008; Steele et al., 2008). Yet the safety and effectiveness of these procedures remains to be demonstrated, so it is best to classify them as experimental treatments (Anderson & Booker, 2006; Lipsman, Neimat, & Lozano, 2007).

Evaluation of Biomedical Approaches

2.13 **Evaluate** biomedical treatment approaches.

There is little doubt that biomedical treatments have helped many people with severe psychological problems. Many thousands of people with schizophrenia who were formerly hospitalized are able to function in the community because of antipsychotic drugs. Antidepressant drugs can help relieve depression in many cases and show therapeutic benefits in treating other disorders, such as panic disorder, obsessive–compulsive disorder, and eating disorders. ECT is helpful in relieving depression in many people who have been unresponsive to other treatments. However, psychiatric drugs and other biomedical treatments such as ECT are not a cure, nor a panacea. There are often troubling side effects of drug treatment and ECT and potential risks for physiological dependence, such as in the case of Valium. Moreover, psychotherapy may be as effective as drug therapy in treating anxiety disorders and depression (see Chapters 5 and 7).

Medical practitioners are sometimes too willing to look for a quick fix by using their prescription pads rather than conducting careful evaluations and helping patients examine their lives or referring them for psychological treatment (Boodman, 2012). We should not expect to solve all of the problems we face in life with a pill (Sroufe, 2012). Physicians often feel pressured, of course, by patients who seek a chemical solution to their life problems.

Researchers are also gathering evidence showing that a combination of psychological and drug treatments for problems such as depression, anxiety disorders, and substance abuse disorders may be more helpful in some cases than either treatment alone (e.g., Cuijpers et al., 2011; Lynch et al., 2011; Oestergaard & Møldrup, 2011; Schneier et al., 2012 Sudak, 2011).

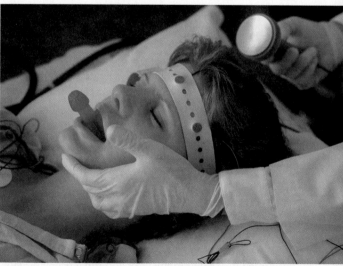

Electroconvulsive therapy (ECT). ECT is helpful in many cases of severe or prolonged depression that do not respond to other forms of treatment. Still, it remains a controversial form of treatment.

2 summing up

The Biological Perspective

2.1 Identify the parts of the neuron and describe their functions.

The nervous system is composed of neurons, nerve cells that communicate with one another through chemical messengers, called neurotransmitters, which transmit nerve impulses across the tiny gaps, or synapses, between neurons.

The parts of the neuron include the cell body (or soma), which performs the cell's metabolic functions; dendrites, or filaments that receive messages (nerve impulses) from neighboring neurons; axons, which are long cable-like structures that carry nerve impulses across the neuron; terminal buttons, or small branching structures at the tips of axons; and the myelin sheath, the insulating layer in some neurons that speeds transmission of nerve impulses.

2.2 Identify the major parts of the nervous system and cerebral cortex and describe their functions.

The nervous system consists of two major parts, the central nervous system and the peripheral nervous system. The central nervous system consists of the brain and spinal cord and is responsible for controlling bodily functions and performing higher mental functions. The peripheral nervous system consists of two major divisions, the somatic nervous system, which transmits messages between the central nervous system and the sense organs and muscles, and the autonomic nervous system, which controls involuntary bodily processes. The autonomic nervous system has two branches or subdivisions, the sympathetic and the parasympathetic. These two branches have largely opposing effects, with the sympathetic nervous system mobilizing the body's resources needed for physical exertion or responding to stress, and the parasympathetic system, which replenishes bodily resources and takes control during times of relaxation.

The cerebral cortex consists of four parts or lobes: (1) the occipital lobe, which is involved in processing visual stimuli; (2) the temporal lobe, which is involved in processing sounds or auditory stimuli; (3), the parietal lobe, which is responsible for sensations of touch, temperature, and pain, and the (4) frontal lobes, which are responsible for controlling muscle movement (motor cortex) and higher mental functions (prefrontal cortex).

2.3 Evaluate biological perspectives on abnormal behavior.

Biological factors such as disturbances in neurotransmitter functioning in the brain, heredity, and underlying brain abnormalities are implicated in the development of abnormal behavior. However, biology is not destiny and genes do not dictate behavior outcomes. There is a complex interaction of nature and nurture, of environment and heredity, in the development of abnormal behavior. Genetics creates a predisposition or likelihood—not a certainty—that certain behavior patterns or disorders will develop. Where genetic factors play a role, multiple genes, not any individual gene, are involved.

The Psychological Perspective

2.4 Describe the major psychological models of abnormal behavior, identify the major theorists, and evaluate these models.

Psychodynamic perspectives reflect the views of Freud and those who follow in this tradition, including Carl Jung, Alfred Adler, Karen Horney, Erik Erikson, and Margaret Mahler, who believed that abnormal behavior stemmed from psychological causes based on underlying psychic forces within the personality. Learning theorists such as John B. Watson and B. F. Skinner posited that the principles of learning can be used to explain both abnormal and normal behavior. Humanistic theorists such as Carl Rogers and Abraham Maslow believed it is important to understand the obstacles that people encounter as they strive toward self-actualization and authenticity. Cognitive theorists such as Aaron Beck and Albert Ellis focus on the role of distorted and self-defeating thinking in explaining abnormal behavior.

The psychodynamic model led to the development of psychodynamic models of treatment and focused attention on the importance of unconscious processes, but it has been criticized largely on the basis of the degree of importance placed on sexual and aggressive impulses and the difficulty subjecting some of the more abstract concepts to scientific tests. Learning-based theories spawned the development of behavior therapy and a broader conceptual model called social-cognitive theory, but have been criticized for not providing a fuller account of self-awareness and subjective experience and the importance of genetic factors. Humanistic models increased attention on the importance of conscious, subjective experience, but it has been criticized for the difficulty posed by studying private mental experiences and self-actualization objectively. Cognitive models spawned cognitive approaches to therapy and the emergence of cognitive-behavioral therapy, but has been criticized that it is too narrowly focused on emotional disorders and nagging questions about whether distorted thinking is a cause or an effect of depression.

The Sociocultural Perspective

2.5 Describe the sociocultural perspective and evaluate its importance in understanding abnormal behavior.

Sociocultural theorists broaden our outlook on abnormal behavior by taking into account sociocultural factors relating to the development of psychological disorders, including roles of social class, ethnicity, and exposure to poverty and racism. Sociocultural theorists focus much-needed attention on the role of social stressors in abnormal behavior. Research supports the link between social class and severe psychological disorders.

The Biopsychosocial Perspective

2.6 Describe and evaluate the biopsychosocial perspective on abnormal behavior and identify a major biopsychosocial model.

The biopsychosocial perspective seeks an understanding of abnormal behavior based on the interplay of biological, psychological, and sociocultural factors. A leading example is the diathesis–stress model, which holds that a person may have a predisposition, or diathesis, for a particular disorder, but whether the disorder actually develops depends on the interaction of the diathesis with stress-inducing life experiences. Although the biopsychosocial model has emerged as a leading conceptual model, its complexity may also be its greatest weakness.

Methods of Treatment

2.7 Identify the major types of helping professionals and describe their training backgrounds and professional roles.

Clinical psychologists complete graduate training in clinical psychology, typically at the doctoral level. Psychiatrists are medical doctors who specialize in psychiatry. Clinical or psychiatric social workers are trained in graduate schools of social work or social welfare, generally at the master's level.

2.8 Describe the goals and techniques of various forms of psychotherapy: psychodynamic therapy, behavior therapy, person-centered therapy, cognitive therapy, cognitive behavior therapy, eclectic therapy, group therapy, family therapy, and couple therapy.

Psychodynamic therapy originated with psychoanalysis, the approach to treatment developed by Freud. Psychoanalysts use techniques such as free association and dream analysis to help people gain insight into their unconscious conflicts and work through them in light of their adult personalities. Contemporary psychodynamic therapy is typically briefer and more direct in its approach to exploring the patient's defenses and transference relationships.

Behavior therapy applies the principles of learning to help people make adaptive behavioral changes. Behavior therapy techniques include systematic desensitization, gradual exposure, modeling, operant conditioning approaches, and social skills training. Cognitive-behavioral therapy integrates behavioral and cognitive approaches in treatment.

Humanistic therapy focuses on the client's subjective, conscious experience in the here and now. Rogers's person-centered therapy helps clients increase their awareness and acceptance of inner feelings that had met with social condemnation and been disowned. The effective person-centered therapist possesses the qualities of unconditional positive regard, empathy, genuineness, and congruence.

Cognitive therapy focuses on modifying the maladaptive cognitions believed to underlie emotional problems and self-defeating behavior. Ellis's rational emotive behavior therapy focuses on disputing irrational beliefs that cause emotional distress and substituting adaptive beliefs and behavior. Beck's cognitive therapy focuses on helping clients identify, challenge, and replace distorted cognitions, such as tendencies to magnify negative events and minimize personal accomplishments. Cognitive-behavioral therapy is a broader form of behavior therapy that integrates cognitive and behavioral techniques in treatment.

There are two general forms of eclectic therapy, *technical eclecticism*, a pragmatic approach that draws on techniques from different schools of therapy without necessarily subscribing to the theoretical positions represented by these schools, and *integrative eclecticism*, a model of therapy that attempts to synthesize and integrate diverse theoretical approaches.

Group therapy provides opportunities for mutual support and shared learning experiences within a group setting to help individuals overcome psychological difficulties and develop more adaptive behaviors. Family therapists work with conflicted families to help them resolve their differences. Family therapists focus on clarifying family communications, resolving role conflicts, guarding against scapegoating of individual members, and helping members develop greater autonomy. Couple therapists focus on helping couples improve their communications and resolve their differences.

2.9 Evaluate the effectiveness of psychotherapy and the role of nonspecific factors in therapy.

Evidence from meta-analyses of psychotherapy outcome studies that compare psychotherapy with control groups strongly supports the effectiveness of psychotherapy. The question remains, however, whether there are differences in the relative effectiveness of different types of psychotherapy. Empirically supported therapies are those that have demonstrated significant benefits in comparison to control procedures in scientific studies.

Nonspecific factors, including empathy, support, attention from a therapist, and the development of a therapeutic alliance and a working alliance, are common factors shared among different types of therapy. Questions remain about the degree to which therapeutic gains are due to the specific treatments clients receive or to the nonspecific factors that different therapies share in common.

2.10 Describe the importance of multicultural factors in psychotherapy and barriers to use of mental health services by ethnic minorities.

Therapists need to be sensitive to cultural differences and how they affect the therapeutic process. Some forms of therapy may vary in effectiveness when used with members of different cultural groups. Culturally competent therapists both understand and respect cultural differences that may impact the practice of psychotherapy. Factors that limit use of mental health services by ethnic minorities include cultural factors regarding preferences for other forms of help, cultural mistrust of the mental health system, cultural barriers, linguistic barriers, and financial and accessibility barriers.

2.11 Identify the major categories of psychotropic or psychiatric drugs and examples of drugs in each type, and evaluate their strengths and weaknesses.

The three major classes of psychiatric drugs are antianxiety drugs, antidepressants, and antipsychotics. Antianxiety drugs, such as Valium, may relieve short-term anxiety but do not directly help people solve their problems or cope with stress. Antidepressants, such as Prozac and Zoloft, can help relieve depression, but are not a cure and also carry risks of side effects. Antianxiety and antidepressant drugs may be no more effective than psychological approaches to treatment. Lithium and anticonvulsive drugs are helpful in many cases in stabilizing mood swings in people with bipolar disorder. Antipsychotic drugs help control flagrant psychotic symptoms, but regular use of these drugs is associated with the risk of serious side effects.

2.12 Describe the use of electroconvulsive therapy and psychosurgery and evaluate their effectiveness.

ECT involves administration of a series of electric shocks to the brain that can lead to dramatic relief from severe depression, even in people who have failed to respond to other treatments. However, ECT is an invasive form of treatment, is associated with high relapse rates, and carries risk of memory loss, especially for events occurring around the time of treatment. Psychosurgery has all but disappeared as a form of treatment because of adverse consequences.

2.13 Evaluate biomedical treatment approaches.

Biomedical therapies in the form of drug therapy and ECT can help relieve troubling symptoms such as anxiety, depression, and mania, help stabilize mood swings in bipolar patients, and control hallucinations and delusions in schizophrenia patients, but they are not a cure. Moreover, psychotherapy may be as effective as drug therapy in treating many problems relating to anxiety and depression without the risk of drug side effects and possible physiological dependence. In some cases, a combination of psychological and drug therapy may be more effective than either treatment approach alone.

critical thinking questions

Based on your reading of this chapter, answer the following questions:

- Give an example or two of your own behavior, or the behavior of others, in which defense mechanisms may have played a role. Which particular defense mechanisms were at play?

- Give an example from your personal experiences in which your thinking reflected one or more of the cognitive distortions identified by Beck—selective abstraction, overgeneralization, magnification, or absolutist thinking. What effects did these thought patterns have on your moods? On your level of motivation? How might you change your thinking about these experiences?

- Why is it necessary to consider multiple perspectives in explaining abnormal behavior?

- How do the different types of mental health professionals differ in their training backgrounds and the roles they perform?

- What type of therapy would you prefer if you were seeking treatment for a psychological disorder? Why?

- Why is it important for therapists to take cultural factors into account when treating members of diverse groups? What cultural factors are important to consider?

key terms

neurons 37
dendrites 38
axon 38
terminals 38
myelin sheath 38
neurotransmitters 38
synapse 38
receptor site 38
central nervous system 40
peripheral nervous system 40
medulla 40
pons 40
cerebellum 41
reticular activating system 41
thalamus 41
hypothalamus 41
limbic system 41
basal ganglia 41
cerebrum 41
cerebral cortex 42
somatic nervous system 42
autonomic nervous system 42
sympathetic nervous system 42
parasympathetic nervous
   system 42

psychoanalytic theory 44
epigenetics 45
conscious 46
preconscious 46
unconscious 46
id 46
pleasure principle 46
ego 46
reality principle 46
superego 46
defense mechanisms 47
fixation 49
archetypes 49
ego psychology 50
object-relations theory 50
psychosis 51
behaviorism 53
conditioned response 53
unconditioned stimulus 53
unconditioned response 54
conditioned stimulus 54
classical conditioning 54
operant conditioning 55
reinforcement 55
positive reinforcers 55

negative reinforcers 55
punishment 55
social-cognitive theory 56
modeling 56
expectancies 56
self-actualization 57
unconditional positive
   regard 57
conditional positive
   regard 57
social causation model 62
downward drift
   hypothesis 62
diathesis–stress model 64
diathesis 64
psychotherapy 67
psychoanalysis 67
Psychotherapy 67
psychodynamic therapy 67
free association 67
transference relationship 68
countertransference 68
behavior therapy 70
systematic desensitization 70
gradual exposure 70

modeling 70
token economy 71
person-centered
   therapy 71
empathy 71
genuineness 72
congruence 72
cognitive therapy 72
rational emotive behavior
   therapy 72
cognitive-behavioral
   therapy 73
eclectic therapy 73
group therapy 75
family therapy 75
couple therapy 76
nonspecific treatment
   factors 78
psychopharmacology 83
antianxiety drugs 84
rebound anxiety 84
antipsychotic drugs 84
antidepressants 84
electroconvulsive therapy
   (ECT) 85

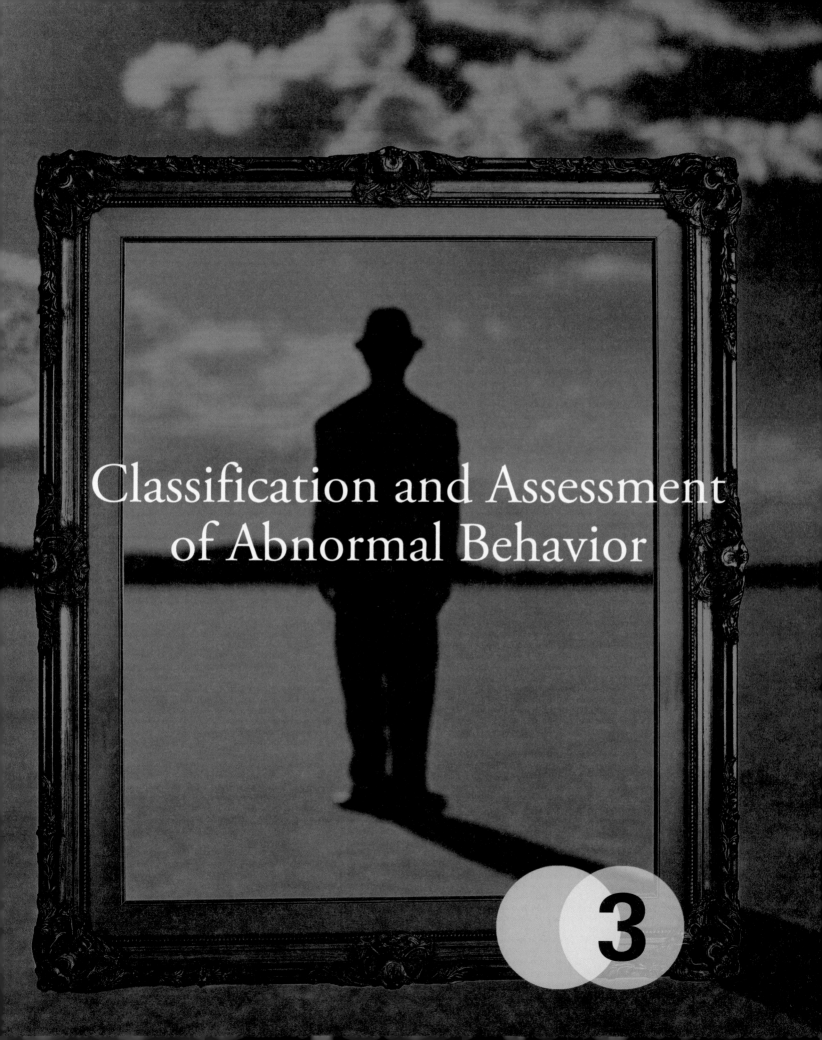

Classification and Assessment of Abnormal Behavior

3

3

learning objectives

3.1
Describe the key features of the *DSM* system of diagnostic classification.

3.2
Describe the concept of culture-bound syndromes and identify some examples.

3.3
Explain why the new edition of the *DSM*, the *DSM-5*, is controversial.

3.4
Evaluate the *DSM* system, listing its strengths and weaknesses.

3.5
Describe the standards of clinical assessment.

3.6
Describe the major methods used in clinical assessment: the clinical interview, psychological tests, neuropsychological assessment, behavioral assessment, cognitive assessment, and physiological measurement.

3.7
Describe objective and projective personality tests and evaluate their usefulness.

3.8
Describe the role of sociocultural aspects of psychological assessment.

truth or fiction?

T☐ F☐ Some men in India have a psychological disorder in which they are troubled by anxiety over losing semen. (p. 98)

T☐ F☐ A psychological test can be highly reliable but also invalid. (p. 104)

T☐ F☐ Although it is not an exact science, the measurement of the bumps on an individual's head can be used to determine his or her personality traits. (p. 105)

T☐ F☐ One of the most widely used personality tests asks people to interpret what they see in a series of inkblots. (p. 113)

T☐ F☐ Despite advances in technology, physicians today must still perform surgery to study the workings of the brain. (p. 122)

T☐ F☐ Undergoing an MRI scan is like being stuffed into a large magnet. (p. 123)

T☐ F☐ Cocaine cravings in people addicted to cocaine have been linked to parts of the brain that are normally activated during pleasant emotions. (p. 124)

T☐ F☐ Advances in brain scanning allow physicians to diagnose schizophrenia with a MRI scan (p. 126)

"I" *"Jerry Has a Panic Attack on the Interstate"*

Interviewer: Can you tell me a bit about what it was that brought you to the clinic?

Jerry: Well, ... after the first of the year, I started getting these panic attacks. I didn't know what the panic attack was.

Interviewer: Well, what was it that you experienced?

Jerry: Uhm, the heart beating, racing ...

Interviewer: Your heart started to race on you.

Jerry: And then uh, I couldn't be in one place, maybe a movie, or a church ... things would be closing in on me and I'd have to get up and leave.

Interviewer: The first time that it happened to you, can you remember that?

Jerry: Uhm, yeah I was ...

Interviewer: Take me through that, what you experienced.

Jerry: I was driving on an interstate and, oh I might've been on maybe 10 or 15 minutes.

Interviewer: Uh huh.

Jerry: All of a sudden I got this fear. I started to ... uh race.

Interviewer: So you noticed you were frightened?

Jerry: Yes.

Interviewer: Your heart was racing and you were perspiring. What else?

Jerry: Perspiring and uh, I was afraid of driving anymore on that interstate for the fear that I would either pull into a car head on, so uhm, I just, I just couldn't function. I just couldn't drive.

Interviewer: What did you do?

Jerry: I pulled, uh well at the nearest exit. I just got off ... uh stopped and, I had never experienced anything like that before.

Interviewer: That was just a ...

Jerry: Out of the clear blue ...

Interviewer: Out of the clear blue? And what'd you think was going on?

Jerry: I had no idea.

Jerry: I thought maybe I was having a heart attack.

Interviewer: You just knew you were ...

Interviewer: Okay.

Source: Excerpted from "Panic Disorder: The Case of Jerry," found on the *Videos in Abnormal Psychology* CD-ROM that accompanies this textbook.

Jerry begins to tell his story, guided by the interviewer. Psychologists and other mental health professionals use clinical interviews and a variety of other means to assess abnormal behavior, including psychological testing, behavioral assessment, and physiological monitoring. The clinical interview is an important way of assessing abnormal behavior and arriving at a diagnostic impression—in this case, panic disorder. The clinician matches the presenting problems and associated features with a set of diagnostic criteria in forming a diagnostic impression.

The diagnosis of psychological or mental disorders represents a way of classifying patterns of abnormal behavior on the basis of their common features or symptoms. Abnormal behavior has been classified since ancient times. Hippocrates classified abnormal behaviors according to his theory of *humors* (vital bodily fluids). Although his theory proved to be flawed, Hippocrates's classification of some types of mental health problems generally corresponds to diagnostic categories clinicians use today (see Chapter 1). His description of melancholia, for example, is similar to current conceptions of depression. During the Middle Ages, some "authorities" classified abnormal behaviors into two groups, those that resulted from demonic possession and those due to natural causes.

The 19th-century German physician Emil Kraepelin was the first modern theorist to develop a comprehensive model of classification on the basis of distinctive features, or symptoms, associated with abnormal behavior patterns (see Chapter 1). The most commonly used classification system today is largely an outgrowth and extension of Kraepelin's work: the *Diagnostic and Statistical Manual of Mental Disorders (DSM)*, published by the American Psychiatric Association.

Why is it important to classify abnormal behavior? For one thing, classification is the core of science. Without labeling and organizing patterns of abnormal behavior, researchers could not communicate their findings to one another, and progress toward understanding these disorders would come to a halt. Moreover, important decisions are made on the basis of classification. Certain psychological disorders respond better to one therapy than to another or to one drug than to another. Classification also helps clinicians predict behavior: schizophrenia, for example, follows a more or less predictable course. Finally, classification helps researchers identify populations with similar patterns of abnormal behavior. By classifying groups of people as depressed, for example, researchers might be able to identify common factors that help explain the origins of depression.

This chapter reviews the classification and assessment of abnormal behavior, beginning with the *DSM*.

How Are Abnormal Behavior Patterns Classified?

The *DSM* was introduced in 1952. The latest version, published in 2013, is the *DSM-5*. The *DSM* is used widely in the United States; however, the most widely used diagnostic manual worldwide is the *International Statistical Classification of Diseases and Related Health Problems (ICD)*, now in a tenth revision (the *ICD-10*) (Clay, 2012). Published by the World Health Organization, it is a compendium of both mental and physical disorders. The *ICD* is presently undergoing a revision scheduled for 2015. The *DSM* is compatible with the *ICD*, so that *DSM* diagnoses can be coded in the *ICD* system as well.

The *DSM* has been widely adopted by mental health professionals, which is why we focus on it here. Yet, we recognize that many psychologists and other mental health professionals criticize the *DSM* on several grounds, such as relying too strongly on the medical model.

In the *DSM*, abnormal behavior patterns are classified as mental disorders. *Mental disorders* involve emotional distress (typically depression or anxiety), significantly impaired functioning (difficulty meeting responsibilities at work, in the family, or in society at large), or behavior that places people at risk for personal suffering, pain, disability, or death (e.g., suicide attempts, repeated use of harmful drugs).

Let us also note that a behavior pattern that represents an expected or culturally appropriate response to a stressful event, such as signs of bereavement or grief following the death of a loved one, is not considered disordered within the *DSM,* even if behavior is significantly impaired. If a person's behavior remains significantly impaired over an extended period of time, however, a diagnosis of a mental disorder might become appropriate.

3.1 Describe the key features of the *DSM* system of diagnostic classification.

The *DSM* and Models of Abnormal Behavior

The *DSM* system, like the medical model, treats abnormal behaviors as signs or symptoms of underlying disorders or pathologies. However, the *DSM* does not assume that abnormal behaviors necessarily stem from biological causes or defects. It recognizes that the causes of most mental disorders remain unclear: Some disorders may have purely biological causes, whereas others may have psychological causes. Still others, probably most, are best explained within a multifactorial model that takes into account the interaction of biological, psychological, social (socioeconomic, sociocultural, and ethnic), and physical environmental factors.

The developers of the *DSM* recognize that their use of the term *mental disorder* is problematic because it perpetuates a long-standing but dubious distinction between mental and physical disorders (American Psychiatric Association, 2000). They point out that there is much that is physical in mental disorders and much that is mental in physical disorders. The manual continues, however, to use the term *mental disorder* because its developers have not been able to agree on an appropriate substitute. In this text, we use the term *psychological disorder* in place of *mental disorder* because we believe it is more appropriate to place the study of abnormal behavior squarely within a psychological context. Moreover, the term *psychological* has the advantage of encompassing behavioral patterns as well as strictly "mental" experiences, such as emotions, thoughts, beliefs, and attitudes.

The *DSM* classifies disorders people have, not the people themselves. Consequently clinicians don't classify a person as a *schizophrenic* or a *depressive.* Rather, they refer to *an individual with schizophrenia* or *a person with major depression.* This difference in terminology is not simply a matter of semantics. To label someone a schizophrenic carries an unfortunate and stigmatizing implication that a person's identity is defined by the disorder the person has.

FEATURES OF THE DSM The *DSM* is *descriptive,* not *explanatory.* It describes the diagnostic features—or, in medical terms, symptoms—of abnormal behaviors; it does not attempt to explain their origins or adopt any particular theoretical framework, such as psychodynamic or learning theory. Using the *DSM* classification system, the clinician arrives at a diagnosis by matching a client's behaviors with the specific criteria that define particular mental disorders. The *DSM-5* is organized in 20 general categories of mental disorders, including anxiety disorders, schizophrenia spectrum and other psychotic disorders, and personality disorders. Table 3.1 lists the 20 diagnostic categories or groupings of disorders in the *DSM-5,* along with examples of disorders in each category and where in the text they are discussed. The *DSM-5* diagnostic table on the next page shows the diagnostic criteria for a particular type of anxiety disorder called generalized anxiety disorder.

The examining clinician determines whether a person's symptoms or problem behaviors match the *DSM*'s criteria for a particular mental disorder, such as major depressive disorder or schizophrenia. A diagnosis is given only when the minimum number of symptoms or features is present to meet the diagnostic criteria for the particular diagnosis. The *DSM* is based on a *categorical model of classification,* which means that clinicians needs to make a categorical or *yes–no* type of judgment about whether the disorder is present in a given case. Categorical judgments are commonplace in modern medicine, such as in determining whether or not a a person has cancer. One limitation of the categorical model is that it does not directly provide a means

TABLE 3.1
DSM-5 Categories of Mental Disorders

Diagnostic Categories (Where Discussed in Text)	Examples of Specific Disorders
Neurodevelopmental Disorders (Chapter 13)	Autism spectrum disorder Specific learning disorder Communication disorders
Schizophrenia Spectrum and Other Psychotic Disorders (Chapter 11)	Schizophrenia Schizophreniform disorder Schizoaffective disorder Delusional disorder Schizotypal personality disorder (see Chapter 12)
Bipolar and Related Disorders (Chapter 7)	Bipolar disorder Cyclothymic disorder
Depressive Disorders (Chapter 7)	Major depressive disorder Persistent depressive disorder (Dysthymia) Premenstrual dysphoric disorder
Anxiety Disorders (Chapter 5)	Panic disorder Phobic disorders Generalized anxiety disorder
Obsessive-Compulsive and Related Disorders (Chapter 5)	Obsessive–compulsive disorder Body dysmorphic disorder Hoarding disorder Trichotillomania (Hair-pulling disorder)
Trauma- and Stressor-Related Disorders (Chapter 4)	Adjustment disorder Acute stress disorder Posttraumatic stress disorder
Dissociative Disorders (Chapter 6)	Dissociative amnesia Depersonalization/derealization disorder Dissociative identity disorder
Somatic Symptom and Related Disorders (Chapter 6)	Somatic symptom disorder Illness anxiety disorder Factitious disorder
Feeding and Eating Disorders (Chapter 9)	Anorexia nervosa Bulimia nervosa Binge-eating disorder
Elimination Disorders (Chapter 13)	Enuresis (bed wetting) Encopresis (soiling)
Sleep-Wake Disorders (Chapter 9)	Insomnia disorder Hypersomnolence disorder Narcolepsy Breathing-related sleep disorders Circadian rhythm sleep-wake disorders Nightmare disorder
Sexual Dysfunctions (Chapter 10)	Male hypoactive sexual desire disorder Erectile disorder Female sexual interest/arousal disorder Female orgasmic disorder Delayed ejaculation Premature (early) ejaculation
Gender Dysphoria (Chapter 10)	Gender dysphoria
Disruptive, Impulse-Control, and Conduct Disorders (Chapters 12 and 13)	Conduct disorder Oppositional defiant disorder Intermittent explosive disorder

Substance Related and Addictive Disorders (Chapter 8)	Alcohol use disorder Stimulant use disorder Gambling disorder
Neurocognitive Disorders (Chapter 14)	Delirium Mild neurocognitive disorder Major neurocognitive disorder
Personality Disorders (Chapter 12)	Paranoid personality disorder Schizoid personality disorder Histrionic personality disorder Antisocial personality disorder Borderline personality disorder Dependent personality disorder Avoidant personality disorder Obsessive–compulsive personality disorder
Paraphilic Disorders (Chapter 10)	Exhibitionistic disorder Fetishistic disorder Transvestic disorder Voyeuristic disorder Pedophilic disorder Sexual masochism disorder Sexual sadism disorder
Other Mental Disorders	Other specified mental disorder

Source: Based on American Psychiatric Association (2013).

criteria for
Generalized Anxiety Disorder

DSM-5

A. Excessive anxiety and worry (apprehensive expectation), occurring more days than not for at least 6 months, about a number of events or activities (such as work or school performance).

B. The individual finds it difficult to control the worry.

C. The anxiety and worry are associated with three (or more) of the following six symptoms (with at least some symptoms having been present for more days than not for the past 6 months):

Note: Only one item is required in children.

1. Restlessness or feeling keyed up or on edge.
2. Being easily fatigued.
3. Difficulty concentrating or mind going blank.
4. Irritability.
5. Muscle tension.
6. Sleep disturbance (difficulty falling or staying asleep, or restless, unsatisfying sleep).

D. The anxiety, worry, or physical symptoms cause clinically significant distress or impairment in social, occupational, or other important areas of functioning.

E. The disturbance is not attributable to the physiological effects of a substance (e.g., a drug of abuse, a medication) or another medical condition (e.g., hyperthyroidism).

F. The disturbance is not better explained by another mental disorder (e.g., anxiety or worry about having panic attacks in panic disorder, negative evaluation in social anxiety disorder [social phobia], contamination or other obsessions in obsessive-compulsive disorder, separation from attachment figures in separation anxiety disorder, reminders of traumatic events in posttraumatic stress disorder, gaining weight in anorexia nervosa, physical complaints in somatic symptom disorder, perceived appearance flaws in body dysmorphic disorder, having a serious illness in illness anxiety disorder, or the content of delusional beliefs in schizophrenia or delusional disorder).

Source: Reprinted with permission from the Diagnostic and Statistical Manual of Mental Disorders, Fifth Edition, (Copyright 2013). American Psychiatric Association.

of evaluating the severity of a disorder. Two people might have the same number of symptoms of a given disorder to warrant a diagnosis but differ markedly in the severity of the disorder.

A major difference between the *DSM-5* and the previous version, the *DSM-IV,* is that the new version dispenses with the *multiaxial* framework of the previous version. The *DSM-IV* included five axes or dimensions, enabling a clinician to arrive at a more comprehensive evaluation of the person's psychological functioning than merely a diagnosis. These five axes, which constituted a multiaxial system of assessment, comprised an inventory of mental disorders (coded on Axis I and Axis II), as well as symptoms indicating presence of medical conditions and diseases (Axis III) and of psychosocial and environmental problems or sources of stress affecting the patient's psychological functioning (Axis IV), and a rating scale used to judge the person's overall level of functioning (Axis V). However, because the multiaxial system proved too cumbersome to use, the developers of the *DSM-5* replaced it with a simpler system that clinicians can use to render diagnostic judgments as well as identify stressful factors affecting the person's psychological functioning and disability factors that should be taken into account to provide the most appropriate level of care.

Another major change in the *DSM-5* was the adoption of a dimensional component in assessment and diagnosis. To put this change in context, recall that the *DSM* is built on a categorical model of assessment, which means that a diagnosis is given only when a person shows a minimum number of symptoms or features needed to meet the diagnostic criteria for the particular disorder. As noted, making a diagnosis of a mental disorder involves a *yes–no* type of categorical judgment—that is, determining whether a particular person meets or does not meet criteria for a specific disorder. A categorical model is often used in classification, such as in the case of making a categorical judgment that a woman is either pregnant or not pregnant.

The *DSM-5* did not abandon the categorical model, but expanded it to include a dimensional component for many disorders (Frances & Widiger, 2012; Shedler et al., 2010). This dimensional component gives the evaluator the opportunity to identify "shades of gray." For many disorders, the evaluator is charged not only with determining whether a disorder is present but also with rating the severity of the symptoms of a disorder along a scale ranging from "mild" to "very severe."

CULTURE-BOUND SYNDROMES Some patterns of abnormal behavior, called **culture-bound syndromes,** occur in some cultures but are rare or unknown in others.

Culture-bound syndromes may reflect exaggerated forms of common folk superstitions and belief patterns within a particular culture. For example, the psychiatric disorder *taijin-kyofu-sho* (TKS) is common among young men in Japan but rare elsewhere. The disorder is characterized by excessive fear of embarrassing or offending other people (Kinoshita et al., 2008). The syndrome is associated with the value placed in traditional Japanese culture on not causing others to feel embarrassed or ashamed. People with TKS may dread blushing in front of others, not because they are afraid of embarrassing themselves, but for fear of embarrassing others. People with TKS may also fear mumbling their thoughts aloud, lest they inadvertently offend others.

Culture-bound syndromes in the United States include anorexia nervosa (discussed in Chapter 9) and dissociative identity disorder (formerly called *multiple personality disorder;* discussed in Chapter 6). These abnormal behavior patterns are essentially unknown in less-developed cultures. Table 3.2 lists some other culture-bound syndromes identified in the *DSM.*

Determining level of care The assessment of a person's functioning takes into account the individual's ability to manage the responsibilities of daily living. Here, we see a group home for people with mental retardation; the residents assume responsibility for household functions.

3.2 **Describe** the concept of culture-bound syndromes and **identify** some examples.

TABLE 3.2

Examples of Culture-Bound Syndromes from Other Cultures

Culture-Bound Syndrome	Description
Amok	A disorder principally occurring in men in southeastern Asian and Pacific Island cultures, as well as in traditional Puerto Rican and Navajo cultures in the West, it describes a type of dissociative episode (a sudden change in consciousness or self-identity) in which an otherwise normal person suddenly goes berserk and strikes out at others, sometimes killing them. During these episodes, the person may have a sense of acting automatically or robotically. Violence may be directed at people or objects and is often accompanied by perceptions of persecution. A return to the person's usual state of functioning follows the episode. In the West, people use the expression "running amuck" to refer to an episode of losing oneself and running around in a violent frenzy. The word *amuck* is derived from the Malaysian word *amoq*, meaning "engaging furiously in battle." The word passed into the English language during colonial times when British rulers in Malaysia observed this behavior among the native people.
Ataque de nervios ("attack of nerves")	A way of describing states of emotional distress among Latin American and Latin Mediterranean groups, it most commonly involves features such as shouting uncontrollably, fits of crying, trembling, feelings of warmth or heat rising from the chest to the head, and aggressive verbal or physical behavior. These episodes are usually precipitated by a stressful event affecting the family (e.g., receiving news of the death of a family member) and are accompanied by feelings of being out of control. After the attack, the person returns quickly to his or her usual level of functioning, although there may be amnesia for events that occurred during the episode.
Dhat syndrome	A disorder (described further in Chapter 6) affecting males, found principally in India, that involves intense fear or anxiety over the loss of semen through nocturnal emissions, ejaculations, or excretion with urine (in fact, semen doesn't mix with urine). In Indian culture, there is a popular belief that loss of semen depletes a man of his vital natural energy. **T / F**
Falling out or blacking out	Occurring principally among southern U.S. and Caribbean groups, the disorder involves an episode of sudden collapsing or fainting. The attack may occur without warning or be preceded by dizziness or feelings of "swimming" in the head. Although the eyes remain open, the individual reports an inability to see. The person can hear what others are saying and understand what is occurring but feels powerless to move.
Ghost sickness	A disorder occurring among American Indian groups, it involves a preoccupation with death and with the "spirits" of the deceased. Symptoms include bad dreams, feelings of weakness, loss of appetite, fear, anxiety, and a sense of foreboding. Hallucinations, loss of consciousness, and states of confusion may also be present, among other symptoms.
Koro	Found primarily in China and some other south and east Asian countries, the syndrome (discussed further in Chapter 6) refers to an episode of acute anxiety involving the fear that one's genitals (the penis in men and the vulva and nipples in women) are shrinking and retracting into the body and that death may result.
Zar	A term used in a number of countries in North Africa and the Middle East to describe the experience of spirit possession. Possession by spirits is often used in these cultures to explain dissociative episodes (sudden changes in consciousness or identity) that may be characterized by periods of shouting, banging the head against a wall, laughing, singing, or crying. Affected people may seem apathetic or withdrawn or refuse to eat or carry out their usual responsibilities.

Source: Adapted from the *DSM-5* (American Psychiatric Association, 2013); Dzokoto & Adams (2005); and other sources.

truth OR fiction

Some men in India have a psychological disorder in which they are troubled by anxiety over losing semen.

☑ **TRUE** Dhat syndrome is a culture-bound syndrome found in India in which men develop intense fears over loss of semen.

EVALUATING THE *DSM* SYSTEM To be useful, a diagnostic system must demonstrate **reliability** and **validity.** The *DSM* may be considered reliable, or consistent, if different evaluators using the system are likely to arrive at the same diagnoses when they evaluate the same people. The system may be considered valid if diagnostic judgments correspond with observed behavior. For example, people diagnosed with social phobia should show abnormal levels of anxiety in social situations. Another form of validity is *predictive validity*, or ability to predict the course the disorder is likely to follow or its response to treatment. For example, people diagnosed with bipolar disorder typically respond to the drug lithium (see Chapter 7). Likewise, persons diagnosed with specific phobias (such as fear of heights) tend to be highly responsive to behavioral techniques for reducing fears (see Chapter 5). **T / F**

Overall, evidence supports the reliability and validity of many *DSM* categories, including many anxiety disorders and mood disorders, as well as alcohol and drug use disorders (e.g., B. F. Grant et al., 2006; Hasin, Hatzenbuehler, Keyes, & Ogburn., 2006). Yet, questions about validity persist for some diagnostic categories (e.g., Smith et al., 2011; Widiger & Simonsen, 2005). Many observers also believe the *DSM* needs to become more sensitive to the importance of cultural and ethnic factors in diagnostic assessment (e.g., Alarcón et al., 2009). We should understand that the symptoms or problem behaviors included as diagnostic criteria in the *DSM* were determined by a consensus of mostly U.S.-trained psychiatrists, psychologists, and social workers. Had the American Psychiatric Association asked Asian-trained or Latin American–trained professionals to develop their diagnostic manual, for example, there might have been some different diagnostic criteria or even different diagnostic categories.

In fairness to the *DSM*, however, the more recent editions place greater emphasis than earlier editions on weighing cultural factors when assessing abnormal behavior. The *DSM* system recognizes that clinicians who are unfamiliar with an individual's cultural background may incorrectly classify that individual's behavior as abnormal when in fact it falls within the normal spectrum in that individual's culture. The *DSM* also recognizes that abnormal behaviors may take different forms in different cultures and that some abnormal behavior patterns are culture-specific (see Table 3.2). Although every edition of the *DSM* has had its critics, the *DSM-5*, as we see next, has sparked a firestorm of criticism.

CHANGES IN THE *DSM-5* The *DSM* system has been periodically revised ever since it was introduced in 1952. The latest revision, the *DSM-5*, was years in the making and was published in 2013. It represents a major overhaul of the manual. The committees charged with revising the manual comprised experts in their fields. They closely examined the previous edition, the *DSM-IV*, taking a careful look at what parts of the diagnostic system were working well and what parts needed to be revised to improve the manual's clinical utility (how it is used in practice) and to address concerns raised by clinicians and researchers.

Some new disorders have sprung into being with the introduction of the *DSM-5* (see Table 3.3). Some existing disorders were reclassified or consolidated with other disorders under new diagnostic labels. For example, Asperger's disorder and autistic disorder were reclassified under a general category of *autism spectrum disorder* (discussed in Chapter 13). Trichotillomania (hair-pulling disorder) was moved from a category of impulse control disorders to a new category of *Obsessive Compulsive and Related Disorders* (discussed in

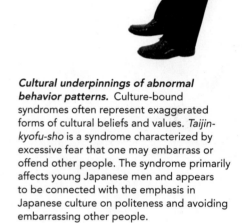

Cultural underpinnings of abnormal behavior patterns. Culture-bound syndromes often represent exaggerated forms of cultural beliefs and values. *Taijin-kyofu-sho* is a syndrome characterized by excessive fear that one may embarrass or offend other people. The syndrome primarily affects young Japanese men and appears to be connected with the emphasis in Japanese culture on politeness and avoiding embarrassing other people.

3.3 Explain why the new edition of the DSM, the DSM-5, is controversial.

TABLE 3.3
Examples of New Disorders in the *DSM-5*

Disorder	Major Feature	Diagnostic Classification	Where Discussed in Text
Hoarding Disorder	Compulsive need to accumulate things, such as books, clothing, household items, and even junk mail	Obsessive-Compulsive and Related Disorders	Chapter 5
Disruptive Mood Dysregulation Disorder	Frequent, excessive temper tantrums in children	Depressive Disorders	Chapter 13
Mild and Major Neurocognitive Disorders	Significant declines in mental functioning involving thinking, memory, and attention	Neurocognitive Disorders	Chapter 14

Chapter 5). Pathological (compulsive) gambling was moved from the impulse control disorder category to a new category called *Substance Use and Addictive Behaviors* (discussed in Chapter 8). Posttraumatic stress disorder (PTSD) was moved from the category of anxiety disorders to a new category, *Trauma- and Stressor-Related Disorders* (discussed in Chapter 4).

Despite many years of debate, editing, and review, the final version of the *DSM-5* remains steeped in controversy. Controversy has been a constant companion of the *DSM* system, in part because of difficulties involved in forging a consensus. Trying to weave together a consensus by committee reminds many of the old adage that a camel is a horse designed by committee.

Here are some of points of controversy about the *DSM-5*:

- **Expansion of diagnosable disorders.** One of the most common criticisms concerns the proliferation of new mental disorders—a problem dubbed *diagnostic inflation* (Frances & Widiger, 2012). Two disorders, *premenstrual dysphoric mood disorder* and *binge-eating disorder* (discussed in Chapters 7 and 9, respectively), that had previously been placed in an appendix of the *DSM* containing proposed diagnoses in need of further study, were moved up in the ranks to become officially recognized mental disorders in the *DSM-5*. Other disorders are new to the diagnostic manual, including *mild neurocognitive disorder* (see Chapter 14). The result of diagnostic inflation may be to greatly expand the numbers of people labeled as suffering from a mental disorder or mental illness.

- **Changes in classification of mental disorders.** Another frequent criticism is that the *DSM-5* changes the ways in which many disorders are classified. As noted, a number of diagnoses were reclassified or folded into broader categories, including Asperger's disorder. Many families of children who had an Asperger's diagnosis are concerned that their children's needs may not be met as effectively if Asperger's is no longer held to be a distinct diagnosis. Mental health professionals accustomed to using the earlier diagnostic categories have questioned whether changes in classification are justified and whether they will lead to more diagnostic confusion (e.g., Tanguay, 2011). The debate over classification will likely continue until the next edition of the *DSM* manual is developed.

- **Changes in diagnostic criteria for particular disorders.** Another criticism is that changes in the clinical definitions or diagnostic criteria for various disorders in the *DSM-5* may change the numbers of cases in which these diagnoses are applied. Critics contend that many of the changes in the diagnostic criteria have not been sufficiently validated. Particular concerns have been raised about the substantial changes made in the set of symptoms or features used to diagnose autism spectrum disorder, which may have profound effects on the numbers of children identified as suffering from autism and related disorders (Carey, 2012).

- **Process of development.** Other criticisms of the *DSM-5* include the contention that the process of development was shrouded in secrecy, that it failed to incorporate input from many leading researchers and scholars in the field, and that changes to the diagnostic manual were not clearly documented on the basis of an adequate body of empirical research.

One significant change in the *DSM-5* that has been generally well received is a greater emphasis on *dimensional assessment* across most categories of disorders. By conceptualizing disorders more broadly as representing dimensions of dysfunctional behavior rather than simply as "present or absent" diagnostic categories allows clinicians to make judgments about the relative severity of disorders, such as by indicating the frequency of symptoms or the level of suicide risk or anxiety. Still, many psychologists believe that the developers of the *DSM-5* did not go far enough in shifting from a categorical model of assessment to a dimensional model (as discussed further in Chapter 12 with respect to the dimensional model of personality disorders).

In summing up, let's reference the comments of a leading psychologist, Marsha Linehan, who remarked that the approval of the *DSM-5* ended years of editing but began years of debate ("Critic Calls," 2012). Ironically, the chairperson of the *DSM-IV* task force, psychiatrist Allen Frances, is now one of the leading critics of the *DSM-5*. Frances called the approval of the *DSM-5* a "sad day for psychiatry" (cited in "Critic Calls," 2012). In a scathing criticism, Frances argued that the introduction of new disorders and changes in the definition of existing disorders may medicalize behavioral problems like repeated temper tantrums in children (now classified as a new type of mental disorder called *disruptive mood dysregulation disorder*) and expectable life challenges, such as mild cognitive changes or everyday forgetting in older adults (now classified as a new disorder called *mild neurocognitive disorder*).

Why are these changes and controversies important to anyone other than psychologists and psychiatrists? The answer is that the diagnostic manual affects how clinicians identify, conceptualize, classify, and ultimately treat mental or psychological disorders. Changes in diagnostic practices can have far-reaching consequences. For example, Allen Frances argues that bringing behavior problems like recurrent temper tantrums under the umbrella of mental disorders will further increase the "excessive and inappropriate use of [psychiatric] medication in young children" (cited in "Critic Calls," 2012). Under the best of circumstances, however, changes in diagnostic practices lead to improved patient care. Time will tell how successful the *DSM-5* will be and whether it will continue to be the most widely used diagnostic system in the United States or be replaced by yet another revision or perhaps with an alternative system, such as the *ICD*.

All in all, the *DSM-5* remains a work in progress, a document that will continue to be argued about and subjected to continuing scrutiny for the foreseeable future.

ADVANTAGES AND DISADVANTAGES OF THE *DSM* SYSTEM The major advantage of the *DSM* may be its designation of specific diagnostic criteria. The *DSM* permits the clinician to readily match a client's complaints and associated features with specific standards to see which diagnosis best fits the symptoms. For example, auditory hallucinations ("hearing voices") and delusions (fixed, but false, beliefs, such as thinking that other people are devils) are characteristic symptoms of schizophrenia.

Criticisms are also leveled against the *DSM* system. Critics challenge the utility of particular symptoms or features associated with a particular syndrome or of specified diagnostic criteria, such as the requirement that major depression be present for two weeks before a diagnosis is reached. Others challenge the reliance on the medical model. In the *DSM* system, problem behaviors are viewed as symptoms of underlying mental disorders in much the same way that physical symptoms are seen as signs of underlying physical disorders. The very use of the term *diagnosis* presumes the medical model is an appropriate basis for classifying abnormal behaviors. But some clinicians feel that behavior, abnormal or otherwise, is too complex and meaningful to be treated as merely symptomatic. They assert that the medical model focuses too much on what may happen within the individual and not enough on external influences on behavior, such as social factors (socioeconomic, sociocultural, and ethnic) and physical environmental factors.

Another concern is that the medical model focuses on categorizing psychological (or mental) disorders rather than on describing a person's behavioral strengths and weaknesses. Similarly, many investigators question whether the diagnostic model should retain its categorical structure (a disorder is either present or not). Perhaps, they argue, it should be replaced with a full dimensional approach in which abnormal behavior patterns such as anxiety, depression, and personality disorders represent extreme variations along a spectrum of emotional states and psychological traits found in the general population (e.g., Akiskal & Benazzi, 2006; First, 2006). Some experts favor a *mixed model* similar to the *DSM-5* approach that includes elements of both categorical and dimensional classification (e.g., Drabick, 2009; Kamphuis & Noordhof, 2009; Maser et al., 2009).

3.4 Evaluate the *DSM* system in terms of its strengths and weaknesses.

To behaviorally oriented psychologists, the understanding of behavior, abnormal or otherwise, is best approached by examining the interaction between the person and the environment. The *DSM* aims to determine what "disorders" people "have"—not how well they can function in particular situations. The behavioral model, alternatively, focuses more on behaviors than on underlying processes—more on what people *do* than on what they "are" or "have." Behaviorists and behavior therapists also use the *DSM,* of course, in part because mental health centers and health insurance carriers require the use of a diagnostic code and in part because they want to communicate in a common language with other practitioners. Many behavior therapists view the *DSM* diagnostic code as a convenient means of labeling patterns of abnormal behavior, a shorthand for a more extensive behavioral analysis of the problem.

Critics also complain that the *DSM* system might stigmatize people by labeling them with psychiatric diagnoses. Our society is strongly biased against people who are labeled as mentally ill. They are often shunned by others, even family members, and subjected to discrimination—or **sanism** (Perlin, 2002-2003), the counterpart to other forms of prejudice, such as racism, sexism, and ageism—in housing and employment.

The *DSM* system, despite its critics, has become part and parcel of the everyday practice of most U.S. mental health professionals. It may be the one reference manual found on the bookshelves of nearly all professionals and dog-eared from repeated use. In the *@Issue* feature in this chapter, a prominent investigator in the field, Thomas Widiger, shares his views on the *DSM,* or what he refers to as the "bible of psychiatry". Dr. Widiger also discusses the dimensional approach to assessing personality disorders such as antisocial personality disorder. (See Chapter 12 for a description of the features of antisocial personality disorder and other personality disorders.)

Now let's consider various ways of assessing abnormal behavior. We begin by considering the basic requirements for methods of assessment—that they be reliable and valid.

3.5 Describe the standards of clinical assessment.

Standards of Assessment

Clinicians make important decisions on the basis of classification and assessment. For example, their recommendations for specific treatment techniques vary according to their assessment of the behaviors clients exhibit. Therefore, methods of assessment, like diagnostic categories, must be *reliable* and *valid.*

Reliability

The reliability of a method of assessment, like that of a diagnostic system, refers to its consistency. A gauge of height, for example, would be unreliable if it showed a person to be taller or shorter at every measurement. Also, different people should be able to check the yardstick and agree on the measured height of the subject. A yardstick that shrinks and expands with the slightest change in temperature will be unreliable. So will be one that is difficult to read. A reliable measure of abnormal behavior must yield the same results on different occasions.

An assessment technique has *internal consistency* if the different parts of the test yield consistent results. For example, if responses to the different items on a depression scale are not highly correlated, the items may not be measuring the same characteristic or trait—in this case, depression. On the other hand, some tests are designed to measure a set of different traits or characteristics. For example, the widely used personality test, the Minnesota Multiphasic Personality Inventory (MMPI) (now in a revised edition, called the MMPI-2), contains subscales measuring various traits related to abnormal behavior.

An assessment method has *test–retest reliability* if it yields similar results on separate occasions. We would not trust a bathroom scale that yielded different results each time we weighed ourselves—unless we had stuffed or starved ourselves between weighings. The same principle applies to methods of psychological assessment.

THINKING CRITICALLY about abnormal psychology

@Issue: The *DSM*—The Bible of Psychiatry—Thomas Widiger

If you are a clinical psychologist, there are probably many reasons to dislike the American Psychiatric Association's *Diagnostic and Statistical Manual of Mental Disorders*. First, it is under the control of a profession with which clinical psychologists are in professional and economic competition. Second, it can be perceived as being used by, or perhaps is in fact used by, insurance companies as a means of limiting coverage of clinical practice. For example, a managed care company might limit the number of sessions they will cover depending on the patient's diagnosis. (They might not even cover the treatment of some disorders.) I am not too sure that these are necessarily valid reasons for disliking the *DSM,* but I do believe they contribute to some of the criticism that it receives. But, third, and most fundamentally important, it doesn't really work that well. A diagnosis of a disorder should lead to the identification of that specific disorder that has a specific pathology that accounts for it and a specific therapy that can be used to cure the patient of that pathology. That hasn't been the case for mental disorders diagnosed by the *DSM* system, not yet at least.

Despite its shortcomings, the *DSM* is a necessary document. Clinicians and researchers need a common language with which to communicate with each other about patterns of psychopathology, and that is the primary function of the *DSM*. Before the *DSM*'s first edition, the clinical practice was awash with a confusing plethora of different names for the same thing and the same name for quite different things. It was, simply put, chaotic.

Many helping professionals are critical of the *DSM* for placing labels on persons. We work with our clients. We don't want to categorize or label them; however, labeling is a necessity. Persons who object to labeling must also use terms (e.g., categories) that describe the problems that clients present. It is not that labeling per se is the problem. It is perhaps in part the negative connotations of receiving a psychiatric diagnosis and the stereotyping of patients diagnosed with various disorders. Each of these concerns will be briefly discussed in turn.

Regrettably, many persons feel shame or embarrassment upon receiving a psychiatric diagnosis or undergoing psychological or psychiatric treatment. In part, the embarrassment or shame reflects the myth that only a small minority of the population experiences psychological problems that warrant a diagnosis of a mental disorder. It's never been clear to me why we believe that we have not suffered, do not suffer, or will not suffer from a mental disorder. All of us have suffered, do suffer, and will suffer from quite a few physical disorders. Why should it be so different for mental disorders? It's not as if any of us are born with perfect genes, or are raised by perfect parents, or go through life untouched by stress, trauma, or psychological problems.

The difficulty with stereotyping is also problematic. People receiving psychiatric diagnoses are lumped into diagnostic categories that seem to treat all members of a particular diagnostic grouping as having the same characteristics. The diagnostic system fails to take individual profiles of psychopathology into account with respect to identifying the distinctive patterns of symptoms and presenting problems that particular individuals present.

Most (if not all) mental disorders appear to result from a complex array of interacting biological vulnerabilities and dispositions with a number of significant environmental and psychosocial factors that often exert their effects over a period of time. The symptoms and pathologies of mental disorders appear to be influenced by a wide range of neurobiological, interpersonal, cognitive, and other factors, leading to the development of particular constellations of symptoms and complaints that characterize an individual's psychopathology profile. This complex web of causal factors and the distinctiveness of individual psychopathology profiles are unlikely to be captured by any single diagnostic category. I prefer the more individualized description of persons provided by dimensional models of classification, for example, the *five-factor model* for the classification of personality disorders.

These five broad domains have been identified as extraversion, agreeableness versus antagonism, conscientiousness, neuroticism or emotional instability, and openness or unconventionality. Each of the five domains can also be differentiated into more specific facets. For example, the domain of agreeableness can be broken down into its underlying components of trust versus mistrust, straightforwardness versus deception, self-sacrifice versus exploitation, compliance versus aggression, modesty versus arrogance, and softheartedness versus callousness.

Most important for clinical psychology, all of the personality disorders are described well in terms of the domains and facets of the five-factor model. For example, antisocial personality disorder includes many of the facets of low conscientiousness (low deliberation, self-discipline, and dutifulness) and high antagonism (callousness, exploitation, and aggression). The glib charm and fearlessness seen in the psychopath are represented by abnormally low levels of the neuroticism facets of self-consciousness, anxiousness, and vulnerability. This approach to describing patients provides a more individualized description of each patient, and it might even help somewhat with the stigmatization of a mental disorder diagnosis. All persons vary in the extent of their neuroticism, in the extent to which they are agreeable versus antagonistic, and in the extent to which they're conscientious. Persons with personality disorders would no longer be said to have disorders that are qualitatively distinct from normal

(continued)

psychological functioning but would instead be seen simply as persons who have relatively extreme and maladaptive variants of the personality traits that are evident within all of us.

In thinking critically about the issue, answer the following questions:

• Do we really need an authoritative diagnostic manual? Why or why not?

• How can we fix the problems of negative, pejorative connotations of diagnoses of mental disorders in our society?

Thomas A. Widiger is Professor of Psychology at the University of Kentucky. He received his Ph.D. in clinical psychology from Miami University (Ohio) and completed his internship at Cornell University Medical College. He currently serves as Associate Editor of *Journal of Abnormal Psychology* and *Journal of Personality Disorders,* as well as the *Annual Review of Clinical Psychology.* He was a member of the *DSM-IV* Task Force and served as the Research Coordinator for *DSM-IV.*

Finally, an assessment method that relies on judgments from observers or raters must show *interrater reliability.* That is, raters must show a high level of agreement in their ratings. For example, two teachers may be asked to use a behavioral rating scale to evaluate a child's aggressiveness, hyperactivity, and sociability. The scale would have good interrater reliability if both teachers rated the same child in similar ways.

Validity

Assessment techniques must also be valid; that is, instruments used in assessment must measure what they intend to measure. Suppose a measure of depression actually turned out to be measuring anxiety. Using such a measure might lead an examiner to an incorrect diagnosis. There are different ways of measuring validity, including *content, criterion,* and *construct validity.* T / F

The **content validity** of an assessment technique is the degree to which its content represents the behaviors associated with the trait in question. For example, depression includes features such as sadness and refusal to participate in activities the person once enjoyed. To have content validity, then, techniques that assess depression should include items that address these areas.

Criterion validity represents the degree to which the assessment technique correlates with an independent, external criterion (standard) of what the technique is intended to assess. *Predictive validity* is a form of criterion validity. A test or assessment technique shows good predictive validity if it can be used to predict future performance or behavior. For example, a test measuring antisocial behavior would show predictive validity if people scoring high on the measure later showed more evidence of delinquent or criminal behavior than did low scorers.

Another way of measuring criterion validity of a diagnostic test for a particular disorder is to see if it is able to identify people who meet diagnostic criteria for the disorder. Two related concepts are important here: sensitivity and specificity. *Sensitivity* refers to the degree to which a test correctly identifies people who have the disorder the test is intended to detect. Tests that lack sensitivity produce a high number of *false negatives*—individuals identified as not having the disorder who truly do have the disorder. *Specificity* refers to the degree to which the test avoids classifying people as having a particular disorder who truly do not have the disorder. Tests that lack specificity produce a high number of *false positives*—people identified as having the disorder who truly do not have the disorder. By taking into account the sensitivity and specificity of a given test, clinicians can determine the ability of a test to classify individuals correctly.

Construct validity is the degree to which a test corresponds to the theoretical model of the underlying construct or trait it purports to measure. Let's say we have a test that purports to measure anxiety. Anxiety is not a concrete object or phenomenon. It can't be measured directly, counted, weighed, or touched. Anxiety is a theoretical construct that helps explain phenomena such as a pounding heart or the sudden inability to

truth OR fiction

A psychological test can be highly reliable but also invalid.

☑ **TRUE** A psychological test can indeed be highly reliable yet also invalid. A test of musical aptitude may have superb reliability but be invalid as a measure of personality or intelligence.

speak when you are asking someone out on a date. Anxiety may be indirectly measured by such means as self-report (the client rates his or her personal level of anxiety) and physiological techniques (measuring the level of sweat on the palms of the client's hands).

The construct validity of a test of anxiety requires the results of the test to predict other behaviors that would be expected, given your theoretical model of anxiety. Let's say your theoretical model predicts that socially anxious college students will have greater difficulties than calmer students in speaking coherently when asking someone for a date, but not when they are merely rehearsing the invitation in private. If the results of an experimental test of these predictions fit these predicted patterns, we could say the evidence supports the test's construct validity (Smith, 2005).

A test may be reliable (give you consistent responses) but still not measure what it purports to measure (be invalid). For example, 19th-century phrenologists believed they could gauge people's personalities by measuring the bumps on their heads. Their calipers provided reliable measures of their subjects' bumps and protrusions; the measurements, however, did not provide valid estimates of subjects' psychological traits. The phrenologists were bumping in the dark, so to speak. **T / F**

Methods of Assessment

Clinicians use different methods of assessment to arrive at diagnoses, including interviews, psychological testing, self-report questionnaires, behavioral measures, and physiological measures. The role of assessment, however, goes further than classification. A careful assessment provides a wealth of information about clients' personalities and cognitive functioning. This information helps clinicians acquire a broader understanding of their clients' problems and recommend appropriate forms of treatment. In most cases, the formal assessment involves one or more clinical interviews with the client, leading to a diagnostic impression and a treatment plan. In some cases, more formal psychological testing probes the client's psychological problems and intellectual, personality, and neuropsychological functioning.

3.6 Describe the major methods used in clinical assessment: the clinical interview, psychological tests, neuropsychological assessment, behavioral assessment, cognitive assessment, and physiological measurement.

The Clinical Interview

The *clinical interview* is the most widely used means of assessment. The interview is usually the clinician's first face-to-face contact with a client. Clinicians often begin by asking clients to describe the presenting complaint in their own words, saying something like, "Can you describe to me the problems you've been having lately?" (Therapists learn not to ask, "What brings you here?" to avoid the possibility of receiving such answers as "a car," "a bus," or "my social worker.") The clinician will then usually probe aspects of the presenting complaint, such as behavioral abnormalities and feelings of discomfort, the circumstances surrounding the onset of the problem, history of past episodes, and how the problem affects the client's daily functioning. The clinician may explore possible precipitating events, such as changes in life circumstances, social relationships, employment, or schooling. The interviewer encourages the client to describe the problem in her or his own words to understand it from the client's viewpoint. For example, the interviewer in the case vignette that opened the chapter asked Jerry to discuss the concerns that prompted him to seek help.

Although the format may vary, most interviews cover these topics:

1. *Identifying data.* This refers to information regarding the client's sociodemographic characteristics: address and telephone number, marital status, age, gender, racial/ethnic characteristics, religion, employment, family composition, and so on.

Building rapport. By developing rapport and feelings of trust with a client, the skillful interviewer helps put the client at ease and encourages candid communication.

2. *Description of the presenting problem(s).* How does the client perceive the problem? What troubling behaviors, thoughts, or feelings are reported? How do they affect the client's functioning? When did they begin?
3. *Psychosocial history.* Information describing the client's developmental history: educational, social, and occupational history; early family relationships.
4. *Medical/psychiatric history.* Here, the clinician elicits the client's history of medical and psychiatric treatment and hospitalizations: Is the present problem a recurrent episode of a previous problem? If yes, how was the problem handled in the past? Was treatment successful? Why or why not?
5. *Medical problems/medication.* This refers to a description of present medical problems and present treatment, including medication. The clinician is alert to ways in which medical problems may affect the presenting psychological problem. For example, drugs for certain medical conditions can affect people's moods and general levels of arousal.

The interviewer is attentive to the client's nonverbal as well as verbal behavior, forming judgments about the appropriateness of the client's attire and grooming, apparent mood, and ability to focus attention. Clinicians also judge the clarity or soundness of clients' thought and perceptual processes and level of orientation, or awareness of themselves and their surroundings (who they are, where they are, and what the present date is). These clinical judgments form an important part of the initial assessment of the client's mental state.

INTERVIEW FORMATS There are three general types of clinical interviews. In an **unstructured interview,** the clinician adopts his or her own style of questioning rather than following a standard format. In a **semistructured interview,** the clinician follows a general outline of questions designed to gather essential information but is free to ask the questions in any particular order and to branch off into other directions to follow up on important information. In a **structured interview,** the interview follows a preset series of questions in a particular order.

The major advantage of the unstructured interview is its spontaneity and conversational style. Because the interviewer is not bound to use any specific set of questions, there is an active give-and-take with the client. The major disadvantage is the lack of standardization. Different interviewers may ask questions in different ways. For example, one interviewer might ask, "How have your moods been lately?" whereas another might pose the question, "Have you had any periods of crying or tearfulness during the past week or two?" The clients' responses may depend to a certain extent on how the questions are worded. Also, the conversational flow of the interview may fail to touch on important clinical information needed to form diagnostic information, such as suicidal tendencies.

A semistructured interview provides more structure and uniformity, but at the expense of some spontaneity. Some clinicians prefer to conduct a semistructured interview in which they follow a general outline of questions but allow themselves the flexibility to depart from the interview protocol when they want to pursue issues that seem important.

Structured interviews (also called *standardized interviews*) provide the highest level of reliability in reaching diagnostic judgments, which is why they are used frequently in research settings. The *Structured Clinical Interview for the DSM* (SCID) includes closed-ended questions to determine the presence of behavior patterns that suggest specific diagnostic categories and open-ended questions that allow clients to elaborate on their problems and feelings. The SCID guides the clinician in testing diagnostic hypotheses as the interview progresses. Evidence supports the reliability of the SCID across various clinical settings (Zanarini et al., 2000).

No matter what type of interview is conducted, the interviewer arrives at a diagnostic impression by compiling all the information available: from the interview, from review of the client's background, and from the presenting problems.

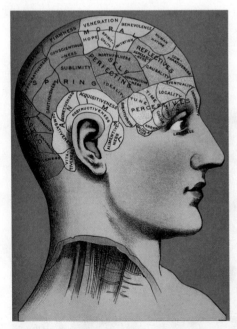

Phrenology. The 19th-century belief in phrenology held that personality and mental faculties were based on the size of certain parts of the brain and could be assessed by measuring the pattern of bumps on a person's head.

Computerized Interviews

Do clinical interviews need to be conducted by a trained, live interviewer? Today, many of us do our banking by computer, order airline tickets over the Internet, and organize our schedules electronically. Might the clinical interviewer be replaced by a computer?

Computerized assessment protocols are becoming more widely used, although it is unlikely they will replace human interviewers anytime soon. In a computerized clinical interview, clients respond to questions about their psychological symptoms and related concerns that are posed to them on a computer screen. The computer interview may help identify problems that clients may be embarrassed or unwilling to report to a live interviewer (Taylor & Luce, 2003). People may actually reveal more information about themselves to a computer than to a human interviewer. Perhaps people feel less self-conscious if someone isn't looking at them when they are interviewed. Or perhaps the computer seems more willing to take the time to note all complaints.

Computerized interview. Would you be more likely to tell your problems to a computer than to a person? Computerized clinical interviews have been used for more than 25 years, and some research suggests that the computer may be more effective than its human counterpart in teasing out problems.

On the other hand, computers may lack the human touch needed to delve into sensitive concerns such as a person's deepest fears, relationship problems, and sexual matters. A computer also lacks the means of judging the nuances in people's facial expressions that may reveal more about their innermost concerns than their typed or verbal responses. All in all, however, evidence shows that computer programs are as capable as skilled clinicians at obtaining information from clients and reaching an accurate diagnosis (Taylor & Luce, 2003). Computer programs are also less expensive and more time efficient than personal interviews.

Most of the resistance to using computer interviews seems to come from clinicians rather than clients. Some clinicians believe that personal, eye-to-eye contact is necessary to tease out a client's underlying concerns. Clinicians should also recognize that because computer-administered diagnostic interviews sometimes yield misleading findings, computer assessments should be combined with clinical judgment by a trained clinician (Garb, 2007). Although the computer may never completely replace the human interviewer, a combination of computerized and interviewer-based assessment may strike the best balance of efficiency and sensitivity.

Another change in the offing is the development of online assessments. Some psychologists are now conducting psychological assessments via email, videoconferencing, and the Internet (Naglieri et al., 2004; Shore, Savin, Orton, Beals, & Manson, 2007).

Psychological Tests

A psychological test is a structured method of assessment used to evaluate reasonably stable traits, such as intelligence and personality. Tests are usually standardized on large numbers of subjects and provide norms that compare a client's scores with the average. By comparing test results from samples of people who are free of psychological disorders with those of people who have diagnosable psychological disorders, researchers gain some insights into the types of response patterns that are indicative of abnormal behavior. Although researchers tend to think of medical tests as a gold standard of testing, evidence shows that psychological tests are actually on par with many medical tests in their ability to predict criterion variables, such as underlying conditions or future outcomes (Meyer et al., 2001).

Here, we examine two major types of psychological tests: intelligence tests and personality tests.

INTELLIGENCE TESTS The assessment of abnormal behavior often includes an evaluation of the client's intelligence. Formal intelligence tests are used to help diagnose intellectual disability (formerly labeled mental retardation). They evaluate the intellectual impairment that may be caused by other disorders, such as organic mental disorders caused by damage to the brain. They also provide a profile of the client's intellectual strengths and weaknesses to help develop a treatment plan suited to the client's competencies.

Attempts to define intelligence continue to stir debate in the field. David Wechsler (1975), the originator of the most widely used intelligence tests, the Wechsler scales, defined intelligence as "capacity ... to understand the world ... and ... resourcefulness to cope with its challenges." From his perspective, intelligence has to do with the ways in which people (a) mentally represent the world and (b) adapt to its demands.

The first formal intelligence test was developed by a Frenchman, Alfred Binet (1857–1911). In 1904, Binet was commissioned by school officials in Paris to develop a mental test to identify children who were unable to cope with the demands of regular classroom instruction and who required special classes to meet their needs. Binet and a colleague, Theodore Simon, developed an intelligence test consisting of memory tasks and other short tests of mental abilities that children were likely to encounter in daily life, such as counting. A later version of their test, called the Stanford-Binet Intelligence Scale, is still widely used to measure intelligence in children and young adults.

Intelligence, as given by a person's scores on intelligence tests, is usually expressed in the form of an intelligence quotient, or IQ. An IQ score is typically based on the relative difference (deviation) of a person's score on an intelligence test from the norms for the person's age group. A score of 100 is defined as the mean. People who answer more items correctly than the average obtain IQ scores above 100; those who answer fewer items correctly obtain scores of less than 100.

Wechsler's intelligence scales are today the most widely used intelligence tests. Different versions are used for different age groups. The Wechsler scales group questions into subtests or subscales, with each subscale measuring a different intellectual ability. (Table 3.4 shows examples from the adult version of the test.) The Wechsler scales are thus designed to offer insight into a person's relative strengths and weaknesses, not to simply yield an overall score.

The Wechsler scales include subtests of verbal skills, perceptual reasoning, working memory, and processing speed. Scores on these subtests are combined to yield an overall intelligence quotient. [Figure 3.1 shows items similar to those on two of the perceptual reasoning tests on the Wechsler Adult Intelligence Scale (WAIS).]

The Wechsler IQ scores are based on how respondents' answers deviate from those attained by their age-mates. The mean whole test score at any age is defined as 100. Wechsler distributed IQ scores so that 50% of the scores of the population would lie within a "broad average" range of 90 to 110.

TABLE 3.4
Examples of Items Similar to Those on the Wechsler Adult Intelligence Scale

Comprehension: Why do people need to obey traffic laws? What does the saying "the early bird catches the worm" mean?

Arithmetic: John wanted to buy a shirt that cost $31.50, but only had $17. How much more money would he need to buy the shirt?

Similarities: How are a stapler and a paper clip alike?

Digit span: Forward order: Listen to this series of numbers and repeat them back to me in the same order: 6 4 5 2 7 3; backward order: Listen to this series of numbers and then repeat them in reverse order: 9 4 2 5 8 7.

Vocabulary: What does *capricious* mean?

Picture completion: Identify the missing part from a picture, such as the picture of the watch in Figure 3.1.

Block design: Using blocks such as those in Figure 3.1, match the design shown.

Letter-number sequencing: Listen to this series of numbers and letters and repeat them back, first saying the numbers from least to most, and then saying the letters in alphabetical order: S-2-C-1.

Source: Adapted from J. S. Nevid (2013). *Psychology: Concepts and applications,* 4th ed. (p. 270). Belmont, CA: Wadsworth/ Cengage Learning. Reprinted by permission.

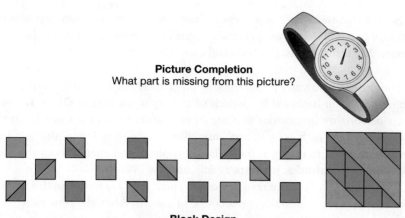

Picture Completion
What part is missing from this picture?

Block Design
Put the blocks together to make this picture.

FIGURE 3.1

Items similar to those found on two of the perceptual reasoning subtests of the Wechsler Adult Intelligence Scale (WAIS).   The perceptual reasoning subtests measure such skills as nonverbal reasoning ability, spatial perception and problem solving, and ability to perceive visual details.   *Source*: From the Wechsler Intelligence Scales for Adults and Children. Copyright © 1949, 1955, 1974, 1981, 1991, 1997, 2003, by The Psychological Corporation, a Harcourt Assessment Company. Reproduced by permission. All rights reserved. Wechsler® is a trademark of The Psychological Corporation registered in the United States of America and/or other jurisdictions.

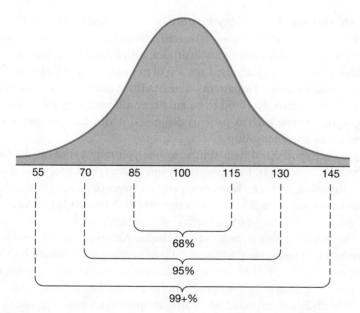

FIGURE 3.2

Normal distribution of IQ scores. The distribution of IQ scores resembles a bell-shaped curve, which is referred to by psychologists as a normal curve. Wechsler defined the deviation IQ so that the average (mean) score was 100 and the standard deviation of scores was 15. A standard deviation is a statistical measure of the variability or dispersion of scores around the mean. Here, we see the distribution of scores at one, two, and three standard deviations from the mean. Note that about two-thirds of people score within one standard deviation of the mean (85 to 115).

Most IQ scores cluster around the mean (see Figure 3.2). Just 5% of them are above 130 or below 70. Wechsler labeled people who attained scores of 130 or above as "very superior" and those with scores below 70 as "intellectually deficient."

Clinicians use IQ scales to evaluate a client's intellectual resources and to help diagnose mental retardation. IQ scores below 70 are one of the criteria used in diagnosing intellectual disability.

Next, we consider two major types of tests used to assess personality: *objective tests* and *projective tests*. Clinicians use personality tests to learn more about the client's underlying personality traits, needs, interests, and concerns.

3.7 Describe objective and projective personality tests and **evaluate** their usefulness.

OBJECTIVE TESTS Do you like automobile magazines? Are you easily startled by noises in the night? Are you bothered by periods of anxiety or shakiness? **Objective tests** are self-report personality inventories that use items similar to the ones just listed to measure personality traits such as emotional instability, masculinity/femininity, and introversion. People are asked to respond to specific questions or statements about their feelings, thoughts, concerns, attitudes, interests, beliefs, and the like.

What makes personality tests *objective*? These tests are not objective in the sense that a bathroom scale is an objective measure of weight. After all, personality tests rely on subjects' giving subjective reports of their interests, feeling states, and so on. Rather, researchers consider these tests objective in the sense that they limit the range of possible responses and so can be scored objectively. They are considered objective also because they were developed on the basis of empirical evidence supporting their validity. Subjects might be instructed to check adjectives that apply to them, to mark statements as true or false, to select preferred activities from lists, or to indicate whether items apply to them "always," "sometimes," or "never." For example, a test item may ask you to check either "true" or "false" to a statement like, "I feel uncomfortable in crowds." Here, we focus on two of the more widely used objective personality tests in clinical settings, the Minnesota Multiphasic Personality Inventory and the Millon Clinical Multiaxial Inventory (MCMI).

Minnesota Multiphasic Personality Inventory The revised version of the MMPI, the MMPI-2, contains more than 567 true–false statements that assess interests, habits, family relationships, physical health complaints, attitudes, beliefs, and behaviors characteristic of psychological disorders. It is widely used as a test of personality as well as to assist clinicians in diagnosing abnormal behavior patterns. The MMPI-2 comprises a number of individual scales made up of items that tend to be answered differently by members of carefully selected diagnostic groups, such as patients diagnosed with schizophrenia or depression, than by members of reference groups.

Consider a hypothetical item similar to one you might find on the MMPI-2: "I often read detective novels." If, for example, groups of depressed people tended to answer the item in a direction different from non-patient reference groups, the item would be placed on the depression scale. The items on the MMPI-2 are divided into various clinical scales (see Table 3.5). A score of 65 or higher on a particular scale is considered clinically significant. The MMPI-2 also includes validity scales that assess clients' tendencies to distort test responses in a favorable ("faking good") or unfavorable ("faking bad") direction. Other scales on the tests, called *content scales,* measure an individual's specific complaints and concerns, such as anxiety, anger, family problems, and low self-esteem.

The MMPI-2 is interpreted according to individual scale elevations and interrelationships among scales. For example, a 2–7 profile, commonly found among people seeking therapy, refers to a test pattern in which scores for Scales 2 ("Depression") and 7 ("Psychasthenia") are clinically significant. Clinicians may refer to *atlases*, or descriptions, of people who usually attain various profiles.

MMPI-2 scales are regarded as reflecting continua of personality traits associated with the diagnostic categories represented by the test. For example, a high score on Scale 4, psychopathic deviation, suggests that the respondent holds a higher-than-average number of nonconformist beliefs and may be rebellious, which are characteristics often found in people with antisocial personality disorder. However, because it is not tied specifically to *DSM* criteria, this score cannot be used to establish a diagnosis. The MMPI, which was originally developed in the 1930s and 1940s, cannot be expected to provide diagnostic judgments consistent with the current version of the *DSM* system, the *DSM-5*. Even so, MMPI profiles may suggest possible diagnoses that can be considered in light of other evidence. Moreover, many clinicians use the MMPI to gain general information about

TABLE 3.5
Clinical Scales of the MMPI-2

Scale Number	Scale Label	Items Similar to Those Found on MMPI Scale	Sample Traits of High Scorers
1	Hypochondriasis	My stomach frequently bothers me. At times, my body seems to ache all over.	Many physical complaints, cynical defeatist attitudes, often perceived as whiny, demanding
2	Depression	Nothing seems to interest me anymore. My sleep is often disturbed by worrisome thoughts.	Depressed mood, pessimistic, worrisome, despondent, lethargic
3	Hysteria	I sometimes become flushed for no apparent reason. I tend to take people at their word when they're trying to be nice to me.	Naive, egocentric, little insight into problems, immature, develops physical complaints in response to stress
4	Psychopathic deviate	My parents often disliked my friends. My behavior sometimes got me into trouble at school.	Difficulties incorporating values of society, rebellious, impulsive, antisocial tendencies, strained family relationships, poor work and school history
5	Masculinity-femininity	I like reading about electronics. (M) I would like to work in the theater. (F)	Males endorsing feminine attributes: have cultural and artistic interests, effeminate, sensitive, passive; females endorsing male attributes: aggressive, masculine, self-confident, active, assertive, vigorous
6	Paranoia	I would have been more successful in life but people didn't give me a fair break. It's not safe to trust anyone these days.	Suspicious, guarded, blames others, resentful, aloof, may have paranoid delusions
7	Psychasthenia	I'm one of those people who have to have something to worry about. I seem to have more fears than most people I know.	Anxious, fearful, tense, worried, insecure, difficulties concentrating, obsessional, self-doubting
8	Schizophrenia	Things seem unreal to me at times. I sometimes hear things that other people can't hear.	Confused and illogical thinking; feels alienated and misunderstood; socially isolated or withdrawn; may have blatant psychotic symptoms such as hallucinations or delusional beliefs; may lead detached, schizoid lifestyle
9	Hypomania	I sometimes take on more tasks than I can possibly do. People have noticed that my speech is sometimes pressured or rushed.	Energetic, possibly manic, impulsive, optimistic, sociable, active, flighty, irritable, may have overly inflated or grandiose self-image or unrealistic plans
10	Social introversion	I don't like loud parties. I was not very active in school activities.	Shy, inhibited, withdrawn, introverted, lacks self-confidence, reserved, anxious in social situations

respondents' personality traits and attributes that may underlie their psychological problems, rather than to make a diagnosis per se.

The validity of the MMPI-2 is supported by a large body of research findings (Butcher, 2011; Graham, 2011). The test successfully discriminates between psychiatric patients and controls and between groups of people with different psychological disorders, such as anxiety versus depressive disorders. Moreover, the content scales of the MMPI-2 provide additional information to that provided by the clinical scales, which can help clinicians learn more about the client's specific problems (Graham, 2011).

The Millon Clinical Multiaxial Inventory (MCMI) The MCMI was developed to help clinicians formulate diagnoses, especially for personality disorders (Millon, 1982). The MCMI (now in a third edition, called the MCMI-III) is the only objective personality test that focuses specifically on personality disorders. The MMPI-2, by contrast, focuses on personality traits associated with other clinical disorders, such as mood disorders, anxiety disorders, and schizophrenia. Some clinicians may use both instruments to capture a wider range of personality traits. The MCMI-III also has scales to assess depression and anxiety, but the validity of these scales has been called into question (Saulsmana, 2011).

Evaluation of Objective Tests Objective or self-report tests are relatively easy to administer. Once examiners read the instructions to clients and make sure they can read and understand the items, clients themselves can complete the tests unattended. Because tests permit limited response options, such as requiring the person to mark each item either true or false, they can be scored with high interrater reliability. These tests often reveal information that might not be gleaned from a clinical interview or by observing the person's behavior. For example, we might learn that a person holds negative views of himself or herself—self-perceptions that might not be directly expressed outwardly in behavior or revealed openly during an interview. All things considered, clinicians might gain more valuable information from self-report tests in some cases and from clinician interviews in others (Cuijpers, Hofmann, & Andersson, 2010). Consequently, a combination of assessment methods may be used.

A disadvantage of self-rating tests is that they rely on individuals themselves as the sole source of information. Test responses may therefore reflect underlying response biases, such as tendencies to give socially desirable responses that may not reflect the individual's true feelings. For this reason, self-report inventories, such as the MMPI, contain validity scales to help ferret out response biases. However, built-in validity scales may not be able to detect all sources of bias. Examiners may also look for corroborating information, such as interviewing others who are familiar with the client's behavior.

Further, if a test does nothing more than identify people who are likely to have a particular disorder, its utility is usurped by more economical means of arriving at a diagnosis, such as a structured clinical interview. Clinicians expect more from personality tests than diagnostic classification, and the MMPI has shown its value in providing a wealth of information about underlying personality traits, problem behaviors, interpersonal relationships, and interest patterns. However, psychodynamically-oriented critics suggest that self-report instruments tell us little about unconscious processes. The use of self-report tests may also be limited to relatively high-functioning individuals who can read well, respond to verbal material, and focus on a potentially tedious task. Clients who are disorganized, unstable, or confused may not be able to complete the tests.

PROJECTIVE TESTS A **projective test,** unlike an objective test, offers no clear, specified response options. Clients are presented with ambiguous stimuli, such as inkblots, and asked to respond to them. The word *projective* is used because these personality tests derive from the psychodynamic belief that people impose, or "project," their own psychological needs, drives, and motives, much of which lie in the unconscious, onto their interpretations of ambiguous stimuli.

The psychodynamic model holds that potentially disturbing impulses and wishes, often of a sexual or aggressive nature, may be hidden from consciousness by our defense mechanisms. Indirect methods of assessment, such as projective tests, may offer clues to unconscious processes. More behaviorally oriented critics contend, however, that the results of projective tests are based more on clinicians' subjective interpretations of test responses than on empirical evidence.

Many projective tests have been developed, including tests based on how people fill in missing words to complete sentence fragments or how they draw human figures and other objects. The two most prominent projective techniques are the Rorschach Inkblot Test and the Thematic Apperception Test (TAT).

The Rorschach Inkblot Test The Rorschach test was developed by a Swiss psychiatrist, Hermann Rorschach (1884–1922). As a child, Rorschach was intrigued by the game of dripping ink on paper and folding the paper to make symmetrical figures. He noted that people saw different things in the same blot, and he believed their "percepts" reflected their personalities as well as the stimulus cues provided by the blot. Rorschach's fraternity

FIGURE 3.3

"What does this look like?"
In the Rorschach test, a person is presented with
ambiguous stimuli in the form of inkblots and
asked to describe what each of the blots looks like.
Rorschach assumed that people project aspects
of their own personalities into their responses, but
controversy whirls around the question of whether
the test yields scientifically valid conclusions.

nickname was *Klex,* which means "inkblot" in German. As a psychiatrist, Rorschach experimented with hundreds of blots to identify those that could help in the diagnosis of
psychological problems. He finally found a group of 15 blots that seemed to do the job and
could be administered in a single session. Ten blots are used today because Rorschach's pub-
lisher did not have the funds to reproduce all 15 blots in the first edition of the text on the
subject. Rorschach never had the opportunity to learn how popular and influential his inkblot test would become. Sadly, seven months after the publication of the test that bears his
name, Rorschach died at age 37 of complications from a ruptured appendix (Exner, 2002).

Five of the inkblots are black and white, and the other five have color (see Figure 3.3).
Each inkblot is printed on a separate card, which is handed to subjects in sequence. Subjects
are asked to tell the examiner what the blot might be or what it reminds them of. Then, they
are asked to explain what features of the blot (its color, form, or texture) they used to form
their perceptions. **T / F**

Clinicians who use the Rorschach make interpretations on the basis of the content
and the form of the responses. For example, they may infer that people who use the entire
blot in their responses show an ability to integrate events in meaningful ways. Those who
focus on minor details of the blots may have obsessive–compulsive tendencies, whereas
people who respond to the negative (white) spaces may see things in their own idiosyncratic ways, suggesting underlying negativism or stubbornness.

A response consistent with the form or contours of the blot is suggestive of adequate
reality testing. People who see movement in the blots may be revealing intelligence and
creativity. Content analysis may shed light on underlying conflicts. For example, adult
clients who see animals but no people may have problems relating to people. Clients who
appear confused about whether or not percepts of people are male or female may, according to psychodynamic theory, be in conflict over their own gender identity.

The Thematic Apperception Test The Thematic Apperception Test was developed by
psychologist Henry Murray at Harvard University in the 1930s. *Apperception* is a French
word that can be translated as "interpreting (new ideas or impressions) on the basis of
existing ideas (cognitive structures) and past experience." The TAT consists of a series of
cards, each depicting an ambiguous scene (see Figure 3.4). It is assumed that clients' responses to the cards will reflect their experiences and outlooks on life—and, perhaps, shed
light on their deep-seated needs and conflicts.

Respondents are asked to describe what is happening in each scene, what led up to
it, what the characters are thinking and feeling, and what will happen next. Psychodynamic
theorists believe that people will identify with the protagonists in their stories and project

truth OR fiction

One of the most widely used tests of
personality asks people to interpret what
they see in a series of inkblots.

☑ **TRUE** The Rorschach is a widely
used personality test in which a person's
responses to inkblots are interpreted to
reveal aspects of his or her personality.

FIGURE 3.4

"Tell me a story." In the Thematic Apperception Test (TAT), a person is presented with a series of pictures, similar to the one depicted here, and asked to tell a story about what is happening in the scene. The person is also asked to describe what events led up to the scene and how the story will turn out. How might the stories you tell reveal underlying aspects of your personality? *Source:* Reprinted by permission of the publishers from Henry A. Murray, Thematic Apperception Test, Cambridge, Mass.: Harvard University Press, © 1943 by the President and Fellows of Harvard College, © 1971 by Henry A. Murray.

underlying psychological needs and conflicts into their responses. More superficially, the stories suggest how respondents might interpret or behave in similar situations in their own lives. TAT results may also be suggestive of clients' attitudes toward others, particularly family members and partners.

Evaluation of Projective Techniques The reliability and validity of projective techniques continue to be a subject of extensive research and debate. For one thing, interpretation of a person's responses depends to some degree on the subjective judgment of the examiner. For example, two examiners may interpret the same Rorschach or TAT response differently.

Although more comprehensive scoring systems have improved standardization of scoring the Rorschach, the reliability of the test continues to be debated. Even if a Rorschach response can be scored reliably, the interpretation of the response—what it means—remains an open question (Garb, Wood, Lilienfeld, & Nezworski, 2005).

Evidence supports some limited use of Rorschach responses (e.g., Baer & Blais, 2010; Meyer, 2001). For example, the Rorschach may help distinguish among different types of psychological disorders (Dao & Prevatt, 2006), as well as detect underlying needs for dependency (Garb et al., 2005) and forms of disturbed thinking (Lilienfeld, Fowler, & Lohr, 2003). Although some proponents of the Rorschach believe its overall validity is generally on par with that of other psychological tests such as the MMPI (e.g., Meyer et al., 2001; Weiner, Spielberger, & Abeles, 2003), critics claim the test fails to meet standards of scientific utility or validity (e.g., Garb, Wood, Lilienfeld, & Nezworski, 2002; Hamel, Shafer, & Erdberg, 2003; Hunsley & Bailey, 2001). The debate over the validity and clinical utility of the Rorschach continues to rage between supporters and detractors with no clear resolution in sight.

The validity of the TAT in eliciting deep-seated material or tapping underlying psychopathology also remains to be demonstrated. A person's responses to the test may say more about the features of the drawings than the person's underlying personality.

Proponents of projective methods point out that allowing subjects freedom of expression through projective testing reduces their tendency to offer socially desirable responses. Psychologist George Stricker (2003, p. 728) appraised the standoff in the field: "The field remains divided between believers and nonbelievers, and each is able to marshal considerable evidence and discount the evidence of their opponents to support their point of view."

Neuropsychological Assessment

Neuropsychological assessment involves the use of tests to help determine whether psychological problems reflect underlying neurological impairment or brain damage. When neurological impairment is suspected, a neurological evaluation may be requested from a *neurologist*—a medical doctor who specializes in disorders of the nervous system. A clinical *neuropsychologist* may also be consulted to administer neuropsychological assessment techniques, such as behavioral observation and psychological testing, to reveal signs of possible brain damage. Neuropsychological testing may be used together with brain-imaging techniques such as the MRI and CT to shed light on relationships between brain function and underlying abnormalities. The results of neuropsychological testing may not only suggest whether patients suffer from brain damage but also point to the parts of the brain that may be affected.

THE BENDER VISUAL MOTOR GESTALT TEST One of the first neuropsychological tests to be developed and still one of the most widely used neuropsychological tests is the Bender Visual Motor Gestalt Test, now in its second edition, the Bender-Gestalt II (Brannigan & Decker, 2006). The Bender consists of geometric figures that illustrate various Gestalt principles of perception. The client is asked to copy geometric designs. Signs of possible brain damage include rotation of the figures, distortions in shape, and incorrect sizing of the figures in relation to one another (see Figure 3.5). The examiner then asks the client to reproduce the designs from memory, because neurological damage can impair memory functioning. Although the Bender remains a convenient and economical means of uncovering possible organic impairment, more sophisticated test batteries have been developed for this purpose, including the widely used Halstead-Reitan Neuropsychological Battery.

THE HALSTEAD-REITAN NEUROPSYCHOLOGICAL BATTERY Psychologist Ralph Reitan developed the battery by adapting tests used by his mentor, Ward Halstead, an experimental psychologist, to study brain–behavior relationships among organically

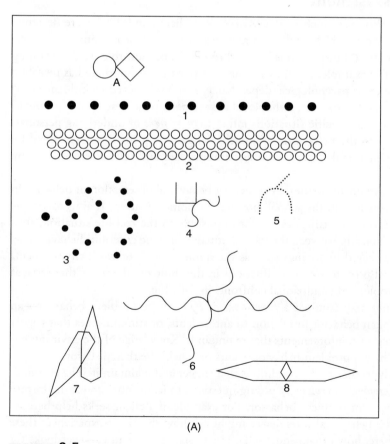

(A)

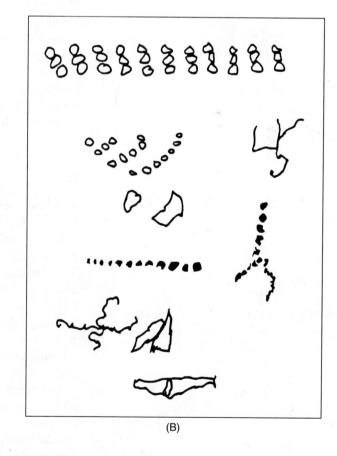

(B)

FIGURE 3.5

The Bender Visual Motor Gestalt Test. The Bender is intended to assess organic impairment. Part A shows the series of figures respondents are asked to copy. Part B shows the drawings of a person who is known to have brain damage.

impaired individuals. The battery contains tests that measure perceptual, intellectual, and motor skills and performance. A battery of tests permits the psychologist to observe patterns of results, and various patterns of performance deficits are suggestive of certain kinds of brain defects, such as those occurring following head trauma (Allen, Thaler, Ringdahl, Barney, & Mayfield, 2011; Holtz, 2011; Reitan & Wolfson, 2012). The Halstead-Reitan test battery comprises a number of subtests, including the following:

1. *The Category Test.* This test measures abstract thinking ability, as indicated by the individual's proficiency at forming principles or categories that relate different stimuli to one another. A series of groups of stimuli that vary in shape, size, location, color, and other characteristics are flashed on a screen. The subject's task is to discern the principle that links them, such as shape or size, and to indicate which stimuli in each grouping represent the correct category by pressing a key. By analyzing the patterns of correct and incorrect choices, the subject normally learns to identify the principles that determine the correct choice. Performance on the test is believed to reflect functioning in the frontal lobes of the cerebral cortex.

2. *The Rhythm Test.* This is a test of concentration and attention. The subject listens to 30 pairs of recorded rhythmic beats and indicates whether the beats in each pair are the same or different. Performance deficits are associated with damage to the right temporal lobe of the cerebral cortex.

3. *The Tactual Performance Test.* This test requires the blindfolded subject to fit wooden blocks of different shapes into corresponding depressions on a form board. Afterward, the subject draws the board from memory as a measure of visual memory.

Behavioral Assessment

Traditional personality tests such as the MMPI, Rorschach, and TAT were designed to measure underlying psychological traits and dispositions. Test responses are interpreted as *signs* of traits and dispositions believed to play important roles in determining people's behavior. For example, certain Rorschach responses are interpreted as revealing underlying traits, such as psychological dependency, that are believed to influence how people relate to others. In contrast, **behavioral assessment** treats test results as *samples* of behavior that occur in specific situations rather than as *signs* of underlying personality traits. According to the behavioral approach, behavior is primarily determined by environmental or situational factors, such as stimulus cues and reinforcement, not by underlying traits.

Behavioral assessment focuses on clinical or behavioral observation of behavior in a particular setting, such as in the school, hospital, or home situation. It aims to sample an individual's behavior in settings as similar as possible to the real-life situation, thus maximizing the relationship between the testing situation and the criterion. Behavior may be observed and measured in settings such as the home, school, or work environment. The examiner may also try to simulate situations in the clinic or laboratory that serve as analogues of the problems the individual confronts in daily life.

The examiner may conduct a *functional analysis* of the problem behavior—an analysis of the problem behavior in relation to antecedents, or stimulus cues that trigger it, and consequences, or reinforcements that maintain it. Knowledge of the environmental conditions in which a problem behavior occurs may help the therapist work with the client and the family to change the conditions that trigger and maintain it. The examiner may conduct a *behavioral interview* by posing questions to learn more about the history and situational aspects of problem behavior. For example, if a client seeks help because of panic attacks, the behavioral interviewer might ask how the client experiences these attacks—when, where, how often, under what circumstances. The interviewer looks for precipitating cues, such as thought patterns (e.g., thoughts of dying or losing control) or situational factors (e.g., entering a department store) that may provoke an attack. The interviewer also seeks information about reinforcers that may maintain the panic. Does the client flee the situation when an attack occurs? Is escape reinforced by relief from anxiety? Has the client learned to lessen anticipatory anxiety by avoiding exposure to situations in which attacks have occurred?

The examiner may also use observational methods to connect the problem behavior to the stimuli and reinforcements that help maintain it. Consider the case of Kerry.

> ## Kerry, the "Royal Terror"
>
> *A 7-year-old boy, Kerry, is brought by his parents for evaluation. His mother describes him as a "royal terror." His father complains he won't listen to anyone. Kerry throws temper tantrums in the supermarket, screaming and stomping his feet if his parents refuse to buy him what he wants. At home, he breaks his toys by throwing them against the wall and demands new ones. Sometimes, though, he appears sullen and won't talk to anyone for hours. At school he appears inhibited and has difficulty concentrating. His progress at school is slow, and he has difficulty reading. His teachers complain he has a limited attention span and doesn't seem motivated.*
>
> *From the Author's Files*

The psychologist may use direct home observation to assess the interactions between Kerry and his parents. Alternatively, the psychologist may observe Kerry and his parents through a one-way mirror in the clinic. Such observations may suggest interactions that explain the child's noncompliance. For example, Kerry's noncompliance may follow parental requests that are vague (e.g., a parent says, "Play nicely now," and Kerry responds by throwing toys) or inconsistent (e.g., a parent says, "Go play with your toys but don't make a mess," to which Kerry responds by scattering the toys). Observation may suggest ways in which Kerry's parents can improve communication and cue and reinforce desirable behaviors.

Direct observation, or behavioral observation, is the hallmark of behavioral assessment. Through direct observation, clinicians can observe and quantify problem behavior. Observations may be videotaped to permit subsequent analysis to identify behavioral patterns. Observers are trained to identify and record targeted patterns of behavior. Behavior coding systems have been developed that enhance the reliability of recording.

There are both advantages and disadvantages to direct observation. One advantage is that direct observation does not rely on the client's self-reports, which may be distorted by efforts to make a favorable or unfavorable impression. In addition to providing accurate measurements of problem behavior, behavioral observation can suggest strategies for intervention. A mother might report that her son is so hyperactive he cannot sit still long enough to complete homework assignments. By using a one-way mirror, the clinician may discover that the boy becomes restless only when he encounters a problem he cannot solve right away. The child may then be helped by being taught ways of coping with frustration and of solving certain kinds of academic problems.

Direct observation also has its drawbacks. One issue is the possible lack of consensus in defining problems in behavioral terms. In coding the child's behavior for hyperactivity, clinicians must agree on which aspects of the child's behavior represent hyperactivity. Another potential problem is a lack of reliability of measurement, that is, inconsistency, across time or between observers. Reliability is reduced when an observer is inconsistent in the coding of specific behaviors or when two or more observers code the same behavior inconsistently.

Observers may also show response biases. An observer who has been sensitized to expect that a child is hyperactive may perceive normal variations in behavior as subtle cues of hyperactivity and erroneously record them as instances of hyperactive behavior. Clinicians can help minimize these biases by keeping observers uninformed or "blind" about the target subject they are observing.

Reactivity is another potential problem. Reactivity refers to the tendency for the behavior being observed to be influenced by the way in which it is measured. For example, people may put their best feet forward when they know they are being observed. Using covert observation techniques, such as hidden cameras or one-way mirrors, may reduce reactivity. Covert observation may not be feasible, however, because of ethical concerns or practical constraints. Another approach is to accustom subjects to observation by watching them a number of times before collecting data. Another potential problem is *observer drift*—the tendency of observers, or groups of raters, to deviate from the coding system in which they were trained as time elapses. One suggestion to help control this problem is to regularly retrain observers to ensure continued compliance with the coding system (Kazdin, 2003). As time elapses, observers may also become fatigued or distracted. It may be helpful to limit the duration of observations and to provide frequent breaks.

Behavioral observation is limited to measuring overt behaviors. Many clinicians also wish to assess subjective or private experiences—for example, feelings of depression and anxiety or distorted thought patterns. Such clinicians may combine direct observation with forms of assessment that permit clients to reveal internal experiences. Staunch behavioral clinicians tend to consider self-reports unreliable and to limit their data collection to direct observation.

In addition to behavioral interviews and direct observation, behavioral assessment may involve the use of other techniques, such as self-monitoring, contrived or analogue measures, and behavioral rating scales.

SELF-MONITORING Training clients to record or monitor the problem behavior in their daily lives is another method of relating the problem behavior to the settings in which it occurs. In **self-monitoring,** clients assume the responsibility for assessing the problem behavior in the settings in which it naturally occurs.

Behaviors that can easily be counted, such as food intake, cigarette smoking, nail biting, hair pulling, study periods, or social activities, are well suited for self-monitoring. Self-monitoring can produce highly accurate measurement, because the behavior is recorded as it occurs, not reconstructed from memory.

There are various devices for keeping track of the targeted behavior. A behavioral diary or log is a handy way to record calories ingested or cigarettes smoked. Such logs can be organized in columns and rows to track the frequency of occurrence of the problem behavior and the situations in which it occurs (time, setting, feeling state, etc.). A record of eating may include entries for the type of food eaten, the number of calories, the location in which the eating occurred, the feeling states associated with eating, and the consequences of eating (e.g., how the client felt afterward). In reviewing an eating diary with the clinician, a client can identify problematic eating patterns, such as eating when feeling bored or in response to TV food commercials, and devise better ways of handling these cues.

Behavioral diaries can also help clients increase desirable but low-frequency behaviors, such as assertive behavior and dating behavior. Unassertive clients might track occasions that seem to warrant an assertive response and jot down their actual responses to each occasion. Clients and clinicians then review the log to highlight problematic situations and rehearse assertive responses. A client who is anxious about dating might record social contacts with potential dating partners. To measure the effects of treatment, clinicians may encourage clients to engage in a baseline period of self-monitoring before treatment is begun. Today, clinicians are turning to the use of handheld electronic devices, such as smart phones, to help clients track specific behaviors (see the Closer Look section on smart phones later).

Self-monitoring, though, is not without its disadvantages. Some clients are unreliable and do not keep accurate records. They become forgetful or sloppy, or they underreport undesirable behaviors, such as overeating or smoking, because of embarrassment or fear of criticism. To offset these biases, clinicians may, with clients' consent, corroborate

Symptom Monitoring Enters the Smartphone Era

Therapists are now using smartphones to monitor their clients' problem behaviors and symptoms on a real-time basis. Therapists are tweeting and texting or otherwise prompting their patients to report on their moods, symptoms, and drug and tobacco use in their day-to-day life (Aguilera & Muñoz, 2011; Ehrenreich, Righter, Rocke, Dixon, & Himelhoch, 2011; Swendsen Ben-Zeev, & Granholm, 2010; Yager, 2011). In a recent example, patients with eating disorders reported about their symptoms by texting their therapists, who then provided them with tailored feedback and suggestions (Bauer, Okon, Meermann, & Kordy, 2012). In another example, a compulsive hoarder whose house was cluttered with mountains of books, magazines, cardboard boxes, and other assorted items, sent digital pictures of her living space so that her therapist could monitor her progress (Eonta et al., 2011).

Therapy apps are making treatment resources available on smart phones for a wide range of problems, including anxiety and depression (Carey, 2012; Clough & Casey, 2011; Kazdin & Blasé, 2011; Shapiro et al., 2010). In one example, therapists used an app called Mobile Therapy to prompt clients to report on their mood levels at specific times during the day by touching icons on a *mood map* on their cell phones (Morris et al., 2010).

Another example is the PTSD Coach, an app developed by the U.S. government to help people with PTSD manage their symptoms and to link them to services they may need (Kuehn, 2011b). The app is intended to be used as a supplement to regular treatment by a qualified professional.

In a treatment program for smoking cessation, participants texted the word *crave* to their therapists whenever they felt a strong craving for cigarettes, prompting the therapists to reply with suggestions they could use to resist smoking temptations (Free et al., 2011). Field Coach is an app designed to help clients with borderline personality disorder, a type of personality

The PTSD Coach. The U.S. government has developed an app called the PTSD Coach to help PTSD patients manage their symptoms and access services they need. *Source: U.S. Department of Veterans Affairs.*

disorder discussed in Chapter 12. This app provides resources such as supportive video and audio messages to help patients cope with difficult situations they face in their daily lives (Dimeff, Paves, Skutch, & Woodcock, 2011). The future promise of therapy apps as therapeutic tools is limited only by the developer's and therapist's imagination.

the accuracy of self-monitoring by gathering information from other parties, such as clients' spouses. Private behaviors such as eating or smoking alone cannot be corroborated in this way, however. Sometimes other means of corroboration, such as physiological measures, are available. For example, blood alcohol levels can be used to verify self-reports of alcohol use, or analysis of carbon monoxide levels in clients' breath samples can be used to corroborate reports of abstinence from smoking.

Recording undesirable behaviors may make people more aware of the need to change them. Thus, self-monitoring can be put to therapeutic use if it leads to adaptive behavioral changes, such as focusing attention of people in weight management programs on the calorie contents of foods they consume. However, self-monitoring alone may not be sufficient to produce desired behavioral changes. Motivation to change and skills needed to make behavior changes are also important.

ANALOGUE MEASURES *Analogue measures* are intended to simulate the setting in which the behavior naturally takes place but are carried out in laboratory or controlled settings. Role-playing exercises are common analogue measures. Suppose a client has difficulty challenging authority figures, such as professors. The clinician might describe a scene to the client as follows: "You've worked very hard on a term paper and received a very poor grade, say a D or an F. You approach the professor, who asks, 'Is there some problem?' What do you do now?" The client's enactment of the scene may reveal deficits in self-expression that can be addressed in therapy or assertiveness training.

The Behavioral Approach Task, or BAT, is a widely used analogue measure of a phobic person's approach to a feared object, such as a snake (e.g., Ollendick, Allen, Benoit, & Cowart, 2011; Vorstenbosch, Antony, Koerner, & Boivin, 2011). Approach behavior is broken down into levels of response, such as looking in the direction of the snake from about 20 feet, touching the box holding the snake, and touching the snake. The BAT provides direct measurement of a response to a stimulus in a controlled situation. The subject's approach behavior can be quantified by assigning a score to each level of approach. The BAT is widely used as a measure of treatment effectiveness based on measuring how much more closely the phobic person can approach the feared object during the course of treatment.

BEHAVIORAL RATING SCALES A *behavioral rating scale* is a checklist that provides information about the frequency, intensity, and range of problem behaviors. Behavioral rating scales differ from self-report personality inventories, in that items assess specific behaviors rather than personality characteristics, interests, or attitudes.

Behavioral rating scales are often used by parents to assess children's problem behaviors. The Child Behavior Checklist (CBCL) (Achenbach & Dumenci, 2001; Ang et al., 2011), for example, asks parents to rate their children on more than 100 specific problem behaviors, including the following:

- ❐ refuses to eat
- ❐ is disobedient
- ❐ hits
- ❐ is uncooperative
- ❐ destroys own things

The scale yields an overall problem-behavior score and subscale scores on dimensions such as delinquency, aggressiveness, and physical problems. The clinician can compare the child's score on these dimensions with norms based on samples of age-mates.

Cognitive Assessment

Cognitive assessment involves measurement of *cognitions*—thoughts, beliefs, and attitudes. Cognitive therapists believe that people who hold self-defeating or dysfunctional cognitions are at greater risk of developing emotional problems, such as depression, in the face of stressful or disappointing life experiences. They help clients replace dysfunctional thinking patterns with self-enhancing, rational thought patterns.

Several methods of cognitive assessment have been developed. One of the most straightforward is the thought record or diary. Depressed clients may carry such diaries to record dysfunctional thoughts as they arise. In early work, Aaron Beck (Beck, Rush, Shaw, & Emery, 1979) designed a thought diary, a daily record of dysfunctional thoughts, to help clients identify thought patterns connected with troubling emotional states. Each time the client experiences a negative emotion, such as anger or sadness, the client makes entries to identify

1. the situation in which the emotional state occurred;
2. the automatic or disruptive thoughts that passed through the client's mind;

Behavioral approach task. One form of behavioral assessment of phobia involves measurement of the degree to which the person can approach or interact with the phobic stimulus. Here, we see a woman with a snake phobia reach out to touch a (harmless) snake. Other people with snake phobia would not be able to touch the snake or even remain in its presence unless it was securely caged.

3. the type or category of disordered thinking that the automatic thought(s) represented (e.g., selective abstraction, overgeneralization, magnification, or absolutist thinking—see Chapter 2);
4. a rational response to the troublesome thought;
5. the emotional outcome or final emotional response.

A thought diary can become part of a treatment program in which the client learns to replace dysfunctional thoughts with rational alternative thoughts.

The Automatic Thoughts Questionnaire (ATQ-30-Revised) (Hollon & Kendall, 1980) asks people to rate both the frequency of occurrence and the strength of belief associated with 30 automatic negative thoughts. (Automatic thoughts seem to just pop into our minds.) Sample items on the ATQ include the following:

- I don't think I can go on.
- I hate myself.
- I've let people down.

A total score is obtained by summing the frequencies of occurrence of each item. Higher scores are suggestive of depressive thought patterns. Items similar to those found on the ATQ are shown in Table 3.6. The ATQ is widely used to measure changes in cognitions of depressed people undergoing treatment, especially cognitive-behavioral therapy (e.g., Hamilton et al., 2012).

Another cognitive measure, the Dysfunctional Attitudes Scale (DAS) (A. N. Weissman & Beck, 1978), consists of an inventory of a relatively stable set of underlying attitudes or assumptions associated with depression. Examples include, "I feel like I'm nothing if someone I love doesn't love me back." Subjects use a 7-point scale to rate the degree to which they endorse each belief. The DAS taps underlying assumptions believed to predispose individuals to depression, so it may be useful in detecting vulnerability to depression (Chioqueta & Stiles, 2007).

Cognitive assessment opens a new domain to the psychologist in understanding how disruptive thoughts are related to abnormal behavior. Only in the past two decades or so have cognitive and cognitive-behavioral therapists begun to explore what

---

TABLE 3.6

Items Similar to Those on the Automatic Thoughts Questionnaire

Negative automatic thoughts such as those shown below may pop into a person's head and have a depressing effect on the person's mood and level, such as those shown below, of motivation. Therapists use questionnaires such as the ATQ to help clients identify their automatic thoughts and replace them with rational alterative thoughts.

- I'm a loser.
- I wonder what's the matter with me.
- I think the worst is about to happen.
- What's wrong with me?.
- Things always go wrong.
- I'm just worthless.
- I'm incompetent.
- I wish I were someone else.
- I think I'm going to fail.
- I'm just not as good as other people.
- I'm never going to succeed.
- I'm really disappointed in myself.

Source: Adapted from Hollon & Kendall (1980).

B. F. Skinner labeled the *black box*—people's internal states—to learn how thoughts and attitudes influence emotional states and behavior.

The behavioral objection to cognitive techniques is that clinicians have no direct means of verifying clients' subjective experiences, their thoughts and beliefs. These are private experiences that can be reported but not observed and measured directly. However, even though thoughts remain private experiences, reports of cognitions in the form of rating scales or checklists can be quantified and validated by reference to external criteria.

Physiological Measurement

Physiological assessment is the study of people's physiological responses. Anxiety, for example, is associated with arousal of the sympathetic division of the autonomic nervous system (see Chapter 2). Anxious people therefore show elevated heart rates and blood pressure, which can be measured directly by means of the pulse and a blood pressure cuff. People also sweat more heavily when they are anxious. When we sweat, our skin becomes wet, increasing its ability to conduct electricity. Sweating can be measured by means of the *electrodermal response* or *galvanic skin response* (GSR). (*Galvanic* is named after the Italian physicist and physician Luigi Galvani, who was a pioneer in research in the study of electricity.) Measures of the GSR assess the amount of electricity that passes through two points on the skin, usually of the hand. Researchers assume the person's anxiety level correlates with the amount of electricity conducted across the skin.

The GSR is just one example of a physiological response measured through probes or sensors connected to the body. Another example is the *electroencephalograph* (EEG), which measures brain waves by attaching electrodes to the scalp (Figure 3.6).

Changes in muscle tension are also often associated with states of anxiety or tension. They can be detected through the *electromyograph* (EMG), which monitors muscle tension through sensors attached to targeted muscle groups. Placement of EMG probes on the forehead can indicate muscle tension associated with tension headaches.

BRAIN-IMAGING AND RECORDING TECHNIQUES Advances in medical technology have made it possible to study the workings of the brain without the need for surgery. One of the most common is the EEG, which is a record of the electrical activity of the brain. The EEG detects minute amounts of electrical activity in the brain, or *brain waves,* which are conducted between electrodes placed on the scalp. Certain brain wave patterns are associated with mental states such as relaxation and with the different stages of sleep. The EEG is used to examine brain wave patterns associated with psychological disorders, such as schizophrenia, and with brain damage. The EEG is also used by medical personnel to reveal brain abnormalities such as tumors.

Brain-imaging techniques generate images that reflect the structure and functioning of the brain. In a *computed tomography* (CT) scan, a narrow X-ray beam is aimed at the head (Figure 3.7). The radiation that passes through is measured from multiple angles. The CT scan (also called a CAT scan, for *computerized axial tomography*) reveals abnormalities in brain shape and structure that may be suggestive of lesions, blood clots, or tumors. The computer enables scientists to integrate the measurements into a three-dimensional picture of the brain. Evidence of brain damage that was once detectable only by surgery may now be displayed on a monitor. **T / F**

Another imaging method, *positron emission tomography* (PET) scan, is used to study the functioning of various parts of the brain (Figure 3.8). In this method, a small amount of a radioactive compound or tracer is mixed with glucose and injected into the bloodstream. When it reaches the brain, patterns of neural activity are revealed by

FIGURE 3.6

The electroencephalograph (EEG). The EEG can be used to study differences in brain waves between groups of normal people and people with problems such as schizophrenia or organic brain damage.

truth OR fiction

Despite advances in technology, physicians today must still perform surgery to study the workings of the brain.

☑ **FALSE** Advances in brain-imaging techniques make it possible to observe the workings of the brain without invasive surgery.

measurement of the *positrons*—positively charged particles—emitted by the tracer. The glucose metabolized by parts of the brain generates a computer image of neural activity. Areas of greater activity metabolize more glucose. The PET scan has been used to learn which parts of the brain are most active (metabolize more glucose) when we are listening to music, solving a math problem, or using language. It can also be used to reveal abnormalities in brain activity in people with schizophrenia (see Chapter 11).

A third imaging technique is *magnetic resonance imaging* (MRI). In MRI, the person is placed in a donut-shaped tunnel that generates a strong magnetic field. The basic idea of the MRI, in the words of its inventor, is to stuff a human being into a large magnet (Weed, 2003). Radio waves of certain frequencies are then directed at the head. As a result, the brain emits signals that can be measured from several angles. As with the CT scan, the signals are integrated into a computer-generated image of the brain, which can reveal brain abnormalities associated with psychological disorders, such as schizophrenia and obsessive–compulsive disorder. T / F

A type of MRI, called *functional magnetic resonance imaging* (fMRI), is used to identify parts of the brain that become active when people engage in particular tasks, such as seeing, recalling from memory, or speaking (see Figure 3.9). The fMRI tracks demands for oxygen in different parts of the brain, which reveals their relative level of activity or engagement during particular tasks. In an illustration of an fMRI study, investigators found that when cocaine-addicted subjects experienced cocaine cravings, their brains showed greater activity in areas that become engaged when healthy subjects watch depressing videotapes (Wexler et al., 2001). This suggests that feelings of depression may be involved in triggering drug cravings. T / F

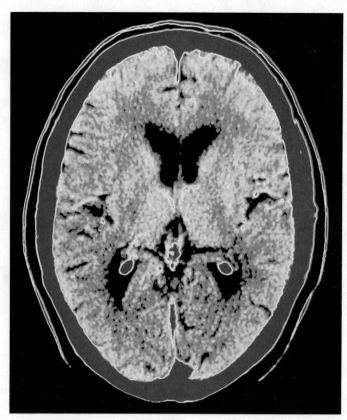

FIGURE 3.7

The computed tomography (CT) scan. The CT scan aims a narrow X-ray beam at the head, and the resultant radiation is measured from multiple angles as it passes through. The computer enables researchers to consolidate the measurements into a three-dimensional image of the brain. The CT scan reveals structural abnormalities in the brain that may be implicated in various patterns of abnormal behavior.

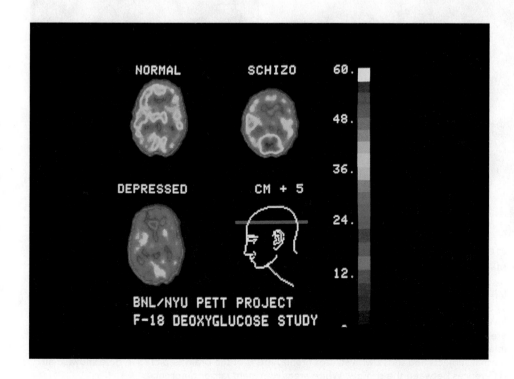

truth OR fiction

Undergoing an MRI scan is like being stuffed into a large magnet.

☑ **TRUE** The MRI is like a large magnet that generates a strong magnetic field that can be used to create images of the brain when radio waves are directed toward the head.

FIGURE 3.8

The positron emission tomography (PET) scan. These PET scan images suggest differences in the metabolic processes of the brains of people with depression and schizophrenia and controls who are free of psychological disorders.

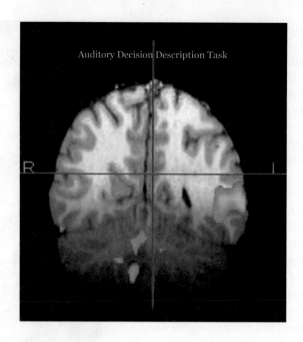

Auditory Decision Description Task

FIGURE 3.9

Functional Magnetic Resonance Imaging (fMRI). An fMRI is a specialized type of MRI that allows investigators to determine the parts of the brain that are activated during particular tasks. The areas depicted in orange/red are activated during a task in which the person is instructed to indicate whether two words in a word pair match. The large area of orange/red in the left hemisphere (depicted here on the right) corresponds to a part of the cerebral cortex involved in processing language.

truth OR fiction

Cocaine cravings in people addicted to cocaine have been linked to parts of the brain that are normally activated during pleasant emotions.

☑ **FALSE** Just the opposite was the case. Cravings were associated with activation of parts of the brain that normally become active when watching depressing videotapes.

Finally, investigators also use sophisticated EEG recording techniques to provide a picture of the electrical activity of various parts of the brain in people with schizophrenia and other psychological disorders. As you can see in Figure 3.10, multiple electrodes are attached to various areas on the scalp to feed information about a person's brain activity

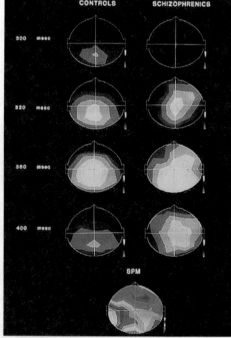

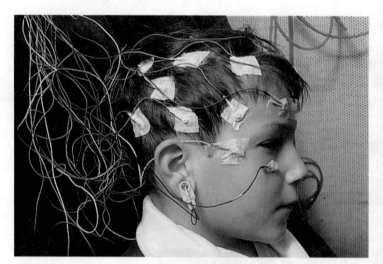

FIGURE 3.10

Mapping the electrical activity of the brain. By placing electrodes on the scalp (left), researchers can use the EEG to record electrical activity in various regions of the brain. The left column of the brain scans (right) shows the average level of electrical activity in the brains of 10 normal people (controls) at four time intervals. The right column shows the average level of activity of subjects with schizophrenia during the same intervals. Higher activity levels are represented in increasing order by yellows, reds, and whites. The computer-generated image in the bottom center summarizes differences in activity levels between the brains of normal subjects and those with schizophrenia. Areas of the brain depicted in blue show small differences between the groups. White areas represent larger differences.

Can Brain Scans See Schizophrenia?

The answer is ... not yet, but efforts in this direction are well under way (e.g., Bullmore, 2012; Ehlkes, Michie, & Schall, 2012). Scientists hope that brain scans will help clinicians better diagnose and treat psychological disorders such as mood disorders, schizophrenia, and attention-deficit/hyperactivity disorder. Investigators are looking for telltale signs in brain scans of psychiatric patients, in much the same way that physicians today use imaging techniques to reveal the presence of tumors, tissue injuries, and brain damage. **T / F**

Early enthusiasm in the mental health community that brain scans would herald a new era in the diagnosis of psychological problems proved to be premature. Dr. Steven Hyman, Harvard University professor and former director of the National Institute of Mental Health, explained it this way: "I think that, with some notable exceptions, the community of scientists was excessively optimistic about how quickly imaging would have an impact on psychiatry ... In their enthusiasm, people forgot that the human brain is the most complex object in the history of human inquiry, and it's not at all easy to see what's going wrong" (Carey, 2005).

One of the problems facing investigators is that signs of brain abnormalities in such disorders as schizophrenia are subtle or fall within a normal range of variation in the general population. Some abnormalities also occur in other disorders. However, there is emerging evidence of identifiable brain abnormalities that might be detected by brain scans in the early phases of schizophrenia (Ehlkes, Michie, & Schall, 2012). Investigators are now trying to lock down specific indicators of these brain abnormalities using sophisticated brain imaging techniques. Looking ahead, it is conceivable that brain scans will someday be used as widely in diagnosing schizophrenia as they are today in diagnosing brain tumors.

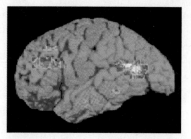
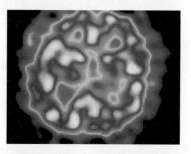
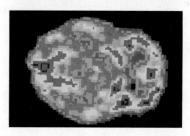

Which of these brain scans shows schizophrenia? We can't yet say, but investigators hope they will someday be able to diagnose mental disorders such as schizophrenia and depression by using brain scans to detect telltale signs of the disorders.

to a computer. The computer analyzes the signals and displays a vivid image of the electrical activity of the working brain. In later chapters, we will see how modern imaging techniques further scientists' understanding of different types of psychological disorders.

Might brain scans be used to diagnose mental disorders? We consider this intriguing question in the *A Closer Look* section. **T / F**

Sociocultural Factors in Psychological Assessment

Researchers and clinicians must keep sociocultural and ethnic factors of clients in mind when assessing personality traits and psychological disorders. For example, in testing people from other cultures, careful translations are essential to capture the meanings of the original items. Clinicians also need to recognize that assessment techniques that may be reliable and valid in one culture may not be in another, even when they are translated accurately (Cheung, Kwong, & Zhang, 2003).

3.8 Describe the role of sociocultural factors in psychological assessment.

truth OR fiction

Advances in brain scanning allow physicians to diagnose schizophrenia with an MRI scan.

☑ **FALSE** Not yet, but perhaps one day we will be able to diagnose psychological disorders by using brain-imaging techniques.

Researchers need to disentangle psychopathology from sociocultural factors so as not to introduce cultural biases in assessment. Translations of assessment instruments should not only translate words, but also provide instructions that encourage examiners to address the importance of cultural beliefs, norms, and values, so that examiners will consider the client's background when making assessments of abnormal behavior patterns. Examiners need to ensure they are not labeling cultural differences in beliefs or practices as evidence of abnormal behaviors.

Investigators also need to put psychological instruments under a cultural microscope. For example, the Beck Depression Inventory (BDI), an inventory of depressive symptoms used widely in the United States, has good validity when used with ethnic minority groups in the United States and in other cultures in the world in distinguishing between depressed and nondepressed people (Grothe et al., 2005; Yeung et al., 2002). A recent study in China that showed that the MMPI-2 was able to predict the level of adjustment of recruits to army life in the Chinese military (Xiao, Han, & Han, 2011).

Other investigators have found no evidence of clinically significant cultural bias on the MMPI-2 in comparing African American and European American (non-Hispanic White) patients in outpatient and inpatient settings (Arbisi, Ben-Porath, & McNulty, 2002). In other research, investigators found that the MMPI-2 was sensitive to detecting problem behaviors and symptoms in American Indian tribal members (Greene, Robin, Albaugh, Caldwell, & Goldman., 2003; Robin, Greene, Albaugh, Caldwell, & Goldman, 2003).

Therapists must recognize the importance of considering clients' language preferences when conducting multicultural assessments. Meanings can get lost in translation, or worse, distorted. For example, Spanish-speakers are often judged to be more disturbed when interviewed in English than in Spanish (Fabrega, 1990). Therapists, too, may fail to appreciate the idioms and subtleties of different languages. We recall, for instance, one clinician, a foreign-born and -trained psychiatrist whose native language was not English, reporting that a patient had exhibited the delusional belief that he was outside his body. The clinician based this assessment on the patient's response when asked if he was feeling anxious. "Yes, doc," the patient had replied, "I feel like I'm jumping out of my skin at times."

summing up

How Are Abnormal Behavior Patterns Classified?

3.1 Describe the key features of the DSM system of diagnostic classification.

The *DSM*, now in its fifth edition (the *DSM-5*), classifies a wide range of abnormal behavior patterns in terms of categories of mental disorders and identifies specific types of disorders within each category that are diagnosed on the basis of applying specified criteria.

3.2 Describe the concept of culture-bound syndromes and identify some examples.

Culture-bound syndromes are abnormal behavior patterns found exclusively or predominantly in particular cultures. Examples include the Koro syndrome in China and the dhat syndrome in India.

3.3 Explain why the new edition of the DSM, the DSM-5, is controversial.

Many concerns have been raised about the *DSM-5*, including concerns over the expansion of diagnosable disorders, changes in classification of mental disorders, changes in diagnostic criteria for particular disorders, and lack of research evidence during the process of development.

3.4 Evaluate the DSM system in terms of its strengths and weaknesses.

The major strength of the *DSM* system is the use of specified diagnostic criteria for each disorder. Weaknesses include questions about reliability and validity of certain diagnostic categories and, to some, the adoption of a medical model framework for classifying abnormal behavior patterns.

Standards of Assessment

3.5 Describe the standards of clinical assessment.

Methods of assessment must be reliable and valid. Reliability of assessment techniques is shown in various ways, including internal consistency, test–retest reliability, and interrater reliability. Validity is measured by means of content validity, criterion validity, and construct validity.

Methods of Assessment

3.6 Describe the major methods used in clinical assessment: the clinical interview, psychological tests, neuropsychological assessment, behavioral assessment, cognitive assessment, and physiological measurement.

The clinical interview involves the use of a set of questions designed to elicit relevant information from people seeking treatment. The three major types of clinical interviews are unstructured interviews (clinicians use their own style of questioning rather than follow a particular script), semistructured interviews (clinicians follow a preset outline in directing their questioning but are free to branch off in other directions), and structured interviews (clinicians strictly follow a preset order of questions).

Psychological tests are structured methods of assessment used to evaluate reasonably stable traits such as intelligence and personality. Tests of intelligence, such as the Wechsler scales, are used for various purposes in clinical assessment, including determining evidence of intellectual disability or cognitive impairment, and assessing strengths and weaknesses.

Neuropsychological assessment involves the use of psychological tests to indicate possible neurological impairment or brain defects. The Halstead-Reitan Neuropsychological Battery uncovers skill deficits that are suggestive of underlying brain damage.

Methods of behavioral assessment include behavioral interviewing, self-monitoring, use of analogue or contrived measures, direct observation, and behavioral rating scales. The behavioral examiner may conduct a functional analysis, which relates the problem behavior to its antecedents and consequences.

Cognitive assessment focuses on the measurement of thoughts, beliefs, and attitudes to help identify distorted thinking patterns. Specific methods of assessment include the use of a thought record or diary and the use of rating scales such as the Automatic Thoughts Questionnaire and the Dysfunctional Attitudes Scale.

Measures of physiological functioning include heart rate, blood pressure, galvanic skin response, muscle tension, and brain wave activity. Brain-imaging and recording techniques such as EEG, CT scans, PET scans, and MRI and fMRI, probe the inner workings and structures of the brain.

3.7 Describe objective and projective personality tests and evaluate their usefulness.

Objective personality tests, such as the MMPI, use structured items to measure psychological characteristics or traits, such as anxiety, depression, and masculinity-femininity. These tests are considered objective in the sense that they make use of a limited range of possible responses to items and are based on an empirical, or objective, method of test construction. Objective tests are easy to administer and have high reliability because the limited response options permit objective scoring. However, they may be limited by underlying response biases. Projective personality tests, such as the Rorschach and TAT, require subjects to interpret ambiguous stimuli in the belief their answers may shed light on their unconscious processes. However, the reliability and validity of projective techniques continue to be debated.

Sociocultural Factors of Psychological Assessment

3.8 Describe sociocultural factors in psychological assessment.

Tests that are reliable and valid in one culture may not be so when used with members of another culture, even when they are translated accurately. Examiners also need to protect against cultural biases when evaluating people from other ethnic or cultural backgrounds. For example, they need to ensure they do not label behaviors as abnormal that are normative within the person's own cultural or ethnic group.

critical thinking questions

On the basis of your reading of this chapter, answer the following questions:

- Why is it important for clinicians to take cultural factors into account when diagnosing psychological disorders?

- Consider the debate over the use of projective tests. Do you believe that a person's response to inkblots or other unstructured stimuli might reveal aspects of that person's underlying personality? Why or why not?

- Have you ever taken a psychological test, such as an intelligence test or a personality test? What was the experience like? What, if anything, did you learn about yourself from the testing experience?

- Jamie complains of feeling depressed since the death of her brother in a car accident last year. What methods of assessment might a psychologist use to evaluate her mental condition?

key terms

culture-bound syndromes 97
reliability 98
validity 98
sanism 102
content validity 104

criterion validity 104
construct validity 104
unstructured interview 106
semistructured interview 106
structured interview 106

objective tests 110
projective test 112
reality testing 113
neuropsychological assessment 114

behavioral assessment 116
self-monitoring 118
cognitive assessment 120
physiological assessment 122

Stress-Related Disorders

4

learning objectives

4.1
Evaluate the effects of stress on health.

4.2
Identify and describe the stages of the general adaptation syndrome.

4.3
Evaluate evidence on the relationship between life changes and psychological and physical health.

4.4
Evaluate the role of acculturative stress in psychological adjustment.

4.5
Identify psychological factors that moderate the effects of stress.

4.6
Define the concept of an adjustment disorder and describe the key features of this disorder.

4.7
Describe the key features of acute stress disorder and posttraumatic stress disorder.

4.8
Describe ways of understanding and treating PTSD.

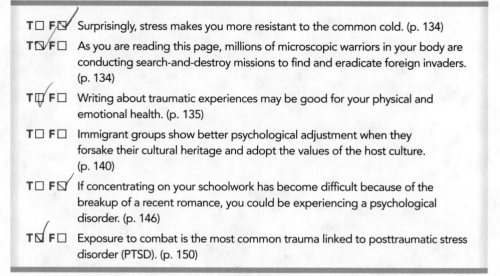
"Is there a problem?" I (J. Nevid) asked as I entered my classroom at St. John's University in Queens, New York, on the morning of September 11, 2001. Many years have passed since that terrible day, but my memory remains vivid. The students were gathered around the window. None replied, but one pointed out the window with a pained expression on her face that I'll never forget. Moments later, I saw for myself the smoke billowing out of one of the towers of the World Trade Center, clearly visible some 15 miles to the west. Then the second tower suddenly burst into flames. We watched in stunned silence. Then the unthinkable occurred. Suddenly one tower was gone and then the other. A student who had come into the room asked, "Where are they?" Another answered that they were gone. The first replied, "What do you mean, gone?"

We watched from a distance the horror that we knew was unfolding. But many other New Yorkers experienced the World Trade Center disaster firsthand, including thousands like New York City police officer Terri Tobin, who risked their lives to save others. Here, Officer Tobin tells of her experience:

"I" "Go! It's Coming Down"

Then I saw people running toward me, and they were screaming. "Go! Go! It's coming down!" Just for a second, I looked up and saw it. I thought, *I'm not going to outrun this*. But then I thought, *Maybe I can make it back to my car and jump in the back seat*. Before I could make a move, the force of the explosion literally blew me out of my shoes. It lifted me up and propelled me out, over a concrete barrier, all the way to the other side of the street. I landed face-first on a grassy area outside the Financial Center, and after I landed there, I just got pelted with debris coming out of this big black cloud.

And then I felt it, but what sticks with me is hearing it: The whomp of my helmet when I got hit in the head. The helmet literally went crack, split in half, and fell off my head. I realized then that I'd just taken a real big whack in the head. I felt blood going down the back of my neck, and when I was able to reach around, I felt this chunk of cement sticking out three or four inches from the back of my head. It was completely embedded in my skull.

Then it got pitch black, and I thought, *I must have been knocked unconscious, because it's totally black.* But then I thought, *I wouldn't be thinking about how black it is if I'm unconscious.* And it was really hard to breathe. All I heard were people screaming. Screaming bloody murder. All sorts of cries. At that moment, I thought, *This is it. We're all going to die on the street.*

→ *From Hagen & Carouba, 2002*

Exposure to stress, especially traumatic stress like that experienced by many thousands of people on 9/11, can have profound and enduring effects on our mental and physical health. This chapter focuses on the effects of stress on the mind and body, including stress associated with everyday life experiences as well as traumatic forms of stress.

Many sources of stress are psychological or situational in nature, such as stress associated with holding down a job (or two), preparing for exams, balancing the family budget, or caring for a sick child or loved one. These and other sources of stress can have profound effects on our physical and emotional health. Psychologists who study interrelationships between psychological factors, including stress, and physical health are called **health psychologists.**

Before we begin to examine the effects of stress, let us define our terms. The term *stress* refers to pressure or force placed on a body. In the physical world, tons of rock that crash to the ground in a landslide, for example, cause stress on impact, forming indentations or craters when they land. In psychology, we use the term **stress** to refer to pressures or demands placed on organisms to adapt or adjust. A **stressor** is a source of stress. Stressors (or stresses) include psychological factors, such as examinations in school and problems in social relationships, and life changes, such as the death of a loved one, divorce, or a job termination. They also include daily hassles, such as traffic jams, and physical environmental factors, such as exposure to extreme temperatures or noise levels. The term *stress* should be distinguished from *distress,* which refers to a state of physical or mental pain or suffering. Some amount of stress is probably healthy for us; it helps keep us active and alert. But stress that is prolonged or intense can overtax our coping ability and lead to states of emotional distress, such as anxiety or depression, and to physical complaints, such as fatigue and headaches.

Stress is implicated in a wide range of physical and psychological problems. We begin our study of the effects of stress by discussing relationships between stress and health. We then examine stress-related psychological disorders that involve maladaptive reactions to stress.

Stress and Health

4.1 Evaluate the effects of stress on health.

Psychological sources of stress not only diminish our capacity for adjustment but also may adversely affect our health. Many visits to physicians, perhaps even most, can be traced to stress-related illness. Stress is associated with an increased risk of various types of physical illnesses, ranging from digestive disorders to heart disease.

Many Americans feel that the level of stress in their lives is on the rise. According to a recent nationwide study by the American Psychological Association, nearly half of Americans polled reported that their level of stress had increased during the preceding five years; about one in three said they face extreme levels of stress (American Psychological Association, 2007a, 2007b, 2010). Americans recognize that stress is taking its toll. Many say they are experiencing psychological symptoms, such as irritability or anger, and physical symptoms such as fatigue as a result or stress (see Figure 4.1).

The field of *psychoneuroimmunology* studies relationships between psychological factors, especially stress, and the workings of the immune system (Kiecolt-Glaser, 2009). Here, we examine what scientists have learned about these relationships.

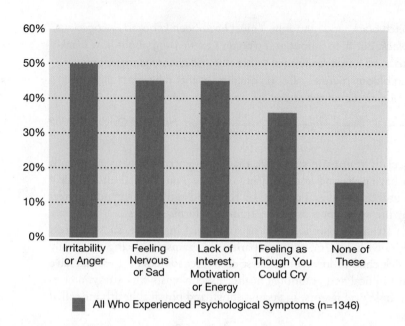

All Who Experienced Psychological Symptoms (n=1346)

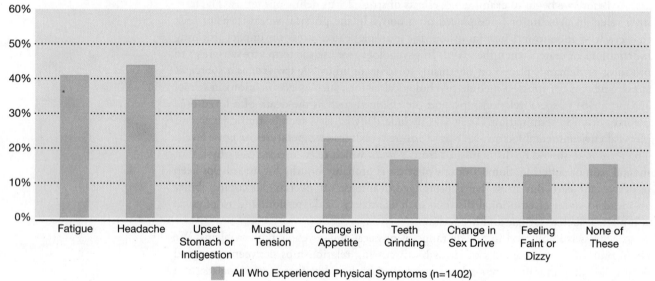

All Who Experienced Physical Symptoms (n=1402)

FIGURE 4.1

Psychological and physical symptoms resulting from stress. Americans report a range of symptoms resulting from stress, including both psychological symptoms such as irritability, anger, and nervousness, and physical symptoms, such as fatigue, headaches, and upset stomach. How does stress affect you?

Source of data: Adapted from American Psychological Association (2010). *Stress in America 2011: Executive summary.* Retrieved from http://www.apa.org/news/press/releases/stress-exec-summary.pdf.

Stress and the Endocrine System

Stress has a domino effect on the **endocrine system,** the body's system of glands that release their secretions, called **hormones,** directly into the bloodstream. (Other glands, such as the salivary glands that produce saliva, release their secretions into a system of ducts.) Figure 4.2 shows the major endocrine glands, which are distributed throughout the body.

Several endocrine glands are involved in the body's response to stress. First, the hypothalamus, a small structure in the brain, releases a hormone that stimulates the nearby pituitary gland to secrete the *adrenocorticotrophic hormone* (ACTH). ACTH, in turn, stimulates the adrenal glands, which are located above the kidneys. Under the influence of ACTH, the outer layer of the adrenal glands, called the *adrenal cortex,* releases a group of hormones called *cortical steroids* (cortisol and cortisone are examples). Cortical steroids (also called *corticosteroids*) have a number of functions in the body. They boost resistance to stress, foster muscle development, and induce the liver to release sugar, which provides needed bursts of energy for responding to a threatening stressor (e.g., a lurking predator or assailant) or an emergency situation. They also help the body defend against allergic reactions and inflammation.

The sympathetic branch of the autonomic nervous system, or ANS, stimulates the inner layer of the adrenal glands, called the *adrenal medulla,* to release a mixture of epinephrine (adrenaline) and norepinephrine (noradrenaline). These chemicals function as hormones when released into the bloodstream. Norepinephrine is also produced in the nervous system, where it functions as a neurotransmitter. Together, epinephrine and norepinephrine mobilize the body to deal with a threatening stressor by accelerating the heart rate and stimulating the liver to release stored glucose (a form of sugar used as fuel by cells in the body). The stress hormones produced by the adrenal glands help the body prepare to cope with an impending threat or stressor. Once the stressor has passed, the body returns to a normal state. This is perfectly normal and adaptive. However, when stress is enduring or recurring, the body regularly pumps out stress hormones and mobilizes other systems, which over time can tax the body's resources and impair health (Gabb, Sonderegger, Scherrer, Ehlert, 2006; Kemeny, 2003). Chronic or repetitive stress can damage many bodily systems, including the cardiovascular system (heart and arteries) and the immune system.

Stress and the Immune System

Given the intricacies of the human body and the rapid advance of scientific knowledge, we might consider ourselves dependent on highly trained medical specialists to contend with illness. However, our bodies cope with most diseases on their own, through the functioning of the immune system.

The **immune system** is the body's system of defense against disease. Your body is constantly engaged in search-and-destroy missions against invading microbes, even as you're reading this page. Millions of white blood cells, or *leukocytes,* are the immune system's foot soldiers in this microscopic warfare. Leukocytes systematically envelop and kill pathogens such as bacteria, viruses, and fungi, worn-out body cells, and cells that have become cancerous.

Leukocytes recognize invading pathogens by their surface fragments, called *antigens,* literally *anti*body *gen*erators. Some leukocytes produce *antibodies,* specialized proteins that lock into position on an antigen, marking it for destruction by specialized "killer" lymphocytes that act like commandos on search-and-destroy missions (Greenwood, 2006; Kay, 2006). **T / F**

Special "memory lymphocytes" (lymphocytes are a type of leukocyte) are held in reserve rather than marking foreign bodies for destruction or going to war against them. They can remain in the bloodstream for years and form the basis for a quick immune response to an invader the second time around (Jiang & Chess, 2006).

Occasional stress may not impair our health, but persistent or prolonged stress can eventually weaken the body's immune system (Fan et al., 2009; Kemeny, 2003). A weakened immune system increases our susceptibility to many illnesses, including the common cold and the flu, and may increase the risk of developing chronic diseases, including cancer.

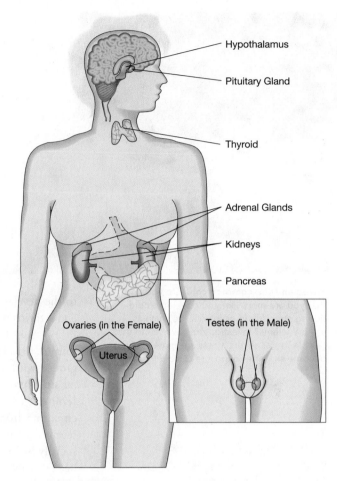

FIGURE 4.2

Major glands of the endocrine system. The glands of the endocrine pour their secretions—called hormones—directly into the bloodstream. Although hormones may travel throughout the body, they act only on specific receptor sites. Many hormones are implicated in stress reactions and various patterns of abnormal behavior. ⊙➤ **Simulate the Experiment** *The Endocrine System* in **MyPsychLab**

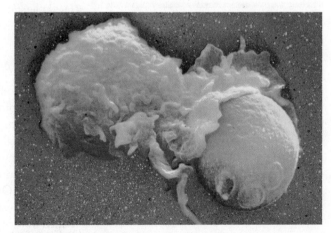

The war within. White blood cells, shown here (colored blue) attacking and engulfing a pathogen, form the major part of the body's system of defense against bacteria, viruses, and other invading organisms.

Stress and the common cold. Do you find that you are more likely to develop a cold during stressful times in your life, such as around exams? Investigators have found that people under severe stress are more likely to become sick after exposure to cold viruses.

truth OR fiction

Surprisingly, stress makes you more resistant to the common cold.

☑ **FALSE** Stress increases the risk of developing a cold.

truth OR fiction

As you are reading this page, millions of microscopic warriors in your body are conducting search-and-destroy missions to find and eradicate foreign invaders.

☑ **TRUE** Your immune system is always on guard against invading microbes and continuously dispatches specialized white blood cells to identify and eliminate infectious organisms.

Psychological stressors can dampen the response of the immune system, especially when the stress is intense or prolonged (Segerstrom & Miller, 2004). Even relatively brief periods of stress, such as final exam time, can weaken the immune system, although these effects are more limited than those associated with chronic or prolonged stress. The kinds of life stressors that can take a toll on the immune system, leaving us more vulnerable to disease, include marital conflict, divorce, and chronic unemployment and traumatic stress, such as natural disasters and terrorist attacks (e.g., Kiecolt-Glaser, McGuire, Robles, Glaser, 2002).

But just how does a psychological factor—stress—translate into physical health problems? Scientists believe they have an answer—inflammation (Cohen et al., 2012: Gouin, Glaser, Malarkey, Beversdorf, Kiecolt-Glaser, 2012). Normally, the immune system regulates the body's inflammatory response to infection or injury. Under stress, the immune system becomes less capable of toning down the inflammatory response, leading to persistent inflammation that may contribute to the development of many physical disorders, including cardiovascular disease, asthma, and arthritis (Cohen et al., 2012).

Social support may help moderate or buffer the harmful effects of stress on the immune system. Several early studies showed poorer immune system functioning in groups with less available social support, such as lonely students and medical and dental students with fewer friends (Glaser, Kiecolt-Glaser, Speicher, Holliday, et al., 1985; Jemmott et al., 1983; Kiecolt-Glaser, Speicher, Holliday, Glaser, 1984). The picture emerging from this research is that loneliness may be damaging to your health. More recent evidence from epidemiological studies supports this view, showing that lonely and socially isolated people tend to have shorter life spans and more often suffer from physical health problems such as infections and heart disease (Miller, 2011).

Exposure to stress is linked to greater risk of developing the common cold. However, investigators found that more sociable people tended to have greater resistance to developing the common cold than their less sociable peers after both groups voluntarily received injections of a cold virus (Cohen, Doyle, Turner, Alper, Skoner, 2003). This result points to a possible role of socialization or social support in buffering the effects of stress. T / F

We should caution that much of the research in psychoneuroimmunology is correlational. Researchers examine immunological functioning in relation to different indices of stress, but do not (nor would they!) directly manipulate stress to observe its effect on subjects' immune systems or general health. Correlational research helps scientists better understand relationships among variables and may point to possible underlying causal factors, but it does not in itself demonstrate causal connections.

Writing About Stress and Trauma as a Coping Response

Expressing our emotions in the form of writing about stressful or traumatic events in our lives is a coping response that can have positive effects on both psychological and physical health (Frattaroli, 2006). Many research studies show that expressive writing can reduce psychological and physical symptoms (e.g., Low, Stanton, & Danoff-Burg, 2006; Sloan, Marx, & Epstein, 2005; Sloan, Marx, Epstein, Lexington, 2007). T / F

Scientists don't yet know how expressive writing produces beneficial effects on our health. One possibility is that keeping thoughts and feelings about highly stressful or traumatic events tightly under wraps places a burden on the autonomic nervous system, which in turn may weaken the immune system and increase susceptibility to stress-related disorders. Writing about stress-related thoughts and feelings may lessen their effects on the immune system.

Terrorism-Related Trauma

The 9/11 terrorist attacks on America changed everything. Before 9/11, we may have felt secure in our homes, offices, and other public places from the threat of terrorism. But now, terrorism looms as a constant threat to our safety and sense of security. Still, we endeavor to maintain a sense of normalcy in our lives. We travel and attend public gatherings, although the ever-present security regulations are a constant reminder of the heightened concern about terrorism. Many of us who were directly affected by 9/11 or lost friends or loved ones may still be trying to cope with the emotional consequences of that day. Many survivors, like those of other forms of trauma, such as floods and tornadoes, may experience prolonged, maladaptive stressful reactions, such as posttraumatic stress disorder (PTSD). Evidence from a community-based study in Michigan showed that the number of suicide attempts jumped in the months following the 9/11 attacks (Starkman, 2006).

Although most people exposed to traumatic events do not develop PTSD, many do experience symptoms associated with the disorder, such as difficulties concentrating and high levels of arousal. In more than 60% of households in New York City, parents reported that their children were upset by the attacks of 9/11. Since the attacks, many Americans have become sensitized to the emotional consequences of traumatic stress. A Closer Look on page 136 focuses on coping with trauma-related stress.

People vary in their reactions to traumatic stress. Investigators trying to pinpoint factors that account for resiliency in the face of stress suggest that positive emotions can play an important role. Evidence gathered since 9/11 shows that experiencing positive emotions, such as feelings of gratitude and love, helped buffer the effects of stress (Fredrickson, Tugade, Waugh, Larkin, 2003).

The General Adaptation Syndrome

Stress researcher Hans Selye (1976) coined the term **general adaptation syndrome (GAS)** to describe a common biological response pattern to prolonged or excessive stress. Selye pointed out that our bodies respond similarly to many kinds of unpleasant stressors, whether the source of stress is an invasion of microscopic disease organisms, a divorce, or the aftermath of a flood. The GAS model suggests that our bodies, under stress, are like clocks with alarm systems that do not shut off until their energy is perilously depleted.

The GAS consists of three stages: the alarm reaction, the resistance stage, and the exhaustion stage. Perception of an immediate stressor (e.g., a car that swerves in front of you on the highway) triggers the **alarm reaction.** The alarm reaction mobilizes the body to prepare for challenge or stress. We can think of it as the body's first line of defense against a threatening stressor. The body reacts with a complex, integrated response involving activation of the sympathetic nervous system, which increases bodily arousal and triggers release of stress hormones by the endocrine system.

In 1929, Harvard University physiologist Walter Cannon termed this response pattern the **fight-or-flight reaction.** We noted earlier how the endocrine system responds to stress. During the alarm reaction, the adrenal glands, controlled by the pituitary gland in the brain, pump out cortical steroids and stress hormones that help mobilize the body's defenses (see Table 4.1).

The fight-or-flight reaction most probably helped our early ancestors cope with the many perils they faced. The reaction may have been provoked by the sight of a predator or by a rustling sound in the undergrowth. But our ancestors usually did not experience prolonged activation of the alarm reaction. Sensitive alarm reactions increased their chances of survival: Once a threat was eliminated—they either fought off predators or fled quickly—the body reinstated a lower level of arousal; it did not remain for long in a state of heightened arousal after the immediate danger was past. In contrast, people today are continually bombarded with stressors—everything from battling traffic every workday to

4.2 Identify and **describe** the stages of the general adaptation syndrome.

IN THE BLEACHERS © 2006 Steve Moore. Reprinted with permission of Universal Press Syndicate. All rights reserved.

Coping with Trauma-Related Stress

People normally experience psychological distress in the face of trauma. If anything, it would be abnormal to remain blasé at a time of crisis or disaster. The American Psychological Association offers the following suggestions for coping with traumatic experiences.

How Should I Help Myself and My Family?

There are many steps you can take to help restore emotional well-being and a sense of control following a disaster or other traumatic experience, including the following:

- *Give yourself time to adjust.* Anticipate that this will be a difficult time in your life. Allow yourself to mourn the losses you have experienced. Try to be patient with changes in your emotional state.
- *Ask for support from people who care about you and who will listen and empathize with your situation.* But keep in mind that your typical support system may be weakened if those who are close to you also have experienced or witnessed the trauma.
- *Communicate your experience.* Communicate in whatever ways you feel comfortable with—such as by talking with family or close friends, or keeping a diary.
- *Find out about local support groups that often are available.* Support groups, such as for those who have suffered from natural disasters or other traumatic events, can be especially helpful for people with limited personal support systems.

- *Try to find groups led by appropriately trained and experienced professionals.* Group discussion can help people realize that other individuals in the same circumstances often have similar reactions and emotions.
- *Engage in healthy behaviors to enhance your ability to cope with excessive stress.* Eat well-balanced meals and get plenty of rest. If you experience ongoing difficulties with sleep, you may be able to find some relief through relaxation techniques. Avoid alcohol and drugs.
- *Establish or reestablish routines such as eating meals at regular times and following an exercise program.* Take some time off from the demands of daily life by pursuing hobbies or other enjoyable activities.
- *Avoid major life decisions such as switching careers or jobs if possible.* These activities tend to be highly stressful.

Stress reactions that linger for two or more months and affect an individual's ability to function in everyday life can be a cause for concern. If you or a loved one is experiencing persistent emotional effects of traumatic stress, it may be worthwhile to seek professional mental health assistance. Assistance is available through your college health services (for registered students) or through networks of trained professionals. For more information or a referral, you may contact your local American Red Cross chapter or the American Psychological Association at 202-336-5800.

Source: Reprinted from "Managing traumatic stress: Tips for recovering from disasters and other traumatic events," with permission of the American Psychological Association, http://www.apa.org/helpcenter/recovering-disasters.aspx

balancing school and work or rushing from job to job. Consequently, our alarm system is turned on much of the time, which may eventually increase the likelihood of developing stress-related disorders.

When a stressor is persistent, we progress to the **resistance stage,** or adaptation stage, of the GAS. Endocrine and sympathetic nervous system responses

---

TABLE 4.1

Stress-Related Changes in the Body Associated with the Alarm Reaction

Corticosteroids are released.
Epinephrine and norepinephrine are released.
Heart rate, respiration rate, and blood pressure increase.
Muscles tense.
Blood shifts from the internal organs to the skeletal muscles.
Digestion is inhibited.
Sugar is released by the liver.
Blood-clotting ability is increased.

(e.g., release of stress hormones) remain at high levels, but not quite as high as during the alarm reaction. During the resistance stage, the body tries to renew spent energy and repair damage. But when stressors continue or new ones appear, we may progress to the final stage of the GAS: the **exhaustion stage.** Although there are individual differences in capacity to resist stress, all of us will eventually exhaust our bodily resources. The exhaustion stage is characterized by dominance of the parasympathetic branch of the ANS. Consequently, our heart and respiration rates decelerate. Do we benefit from the respite? Not necessarily. If the source of stress persists, we may develop what Selye termed *diseases of adaptation.* These range from allergic reactions to heart disease—and, at times, even death. The lesson is clear: Chronic stress can damage our health, leaving us more vulnerable to a range of diseases and other physical health problems.

For better or for worse. Life changes such as marriage and the death of loved ones are sources of stress that require adjustment. The death of a spouse may be one of the most stressful life changes a person ever faces.

Cortical steroids are perhaps one reason that persistent stress may eventually lead to health problems. Although cortical steroids help the body cope with stress, they also suppress the activity of the immune system. They have negligible effects when they are released only periodically. Continuous secretion, however, weakens the immune system by disrupting the production of antibodies, which can increase vulnerability to colds and other infections over time.

Although Selye's model speaks to the general response pattern of the body under stress, different bodily responses may occur in response to particular kinds of stressors (Denson, Spanovic, & Miller, 2009). For example, exposure to excessive noise may invoke different bodily processes than other sources of stress, as might overcrowding or psychological stressors such as divorce or separation.

Stress and Life Changes

Researchers have investigated the stress–illness connection by quantifying life stress in terms of life changes (also called *life events*). Life changes are sources of stress because they force us to adjust. They include both positive events, such as getting married, and negative events, such as the death of a loved one. You can gain insight into the level of stressful life changes you may have experienced during the past year by completing the College Life Stress Inventory on page 138.

4.3 Evaluate evidence on the relationship between life changes and psychological and physical health.

People who experience a greater number of life changes are more likely to suffer from psychological and physical health problems than those with fewer life events (Dohrenwend, 2006). Again, however, researchers need to be cautious when interpreting these findings. These reported links are correlational and not experimental. In other words, researchers did not (and would not!) assign subjects to conditions in which they were exposed to either a high or a low level of life changes to see what effects these conditions might have on their health over time. Rather, existing data are based on observations of relationships, say, between life changes on the one hand and physical health problems on the other. Such relationships are open to other interpretations. It could be that physical symptoms are sources of stress in themselves and lead to more life changes. Physical illness may cause disruptions of sleep or financial burdens, and so forth. Hence, in some cases at least, the causal direction may be reversed: Health problems may lead to life changes. Scientists can't yet tease out the possible cause-and-effect relationships.

Although both positive and negative life changes can be stressful, it is reasonable to assume that positive life changes are generally less disruptive than negative life changes. In other words, marriage tends to be less stressful than divorce or separation. Or, to put it another way, a change for the better may be a change, but it is less of a hassle.

Acculturative Stress: Making It in America

Should Hindu women who immigrate to the United States give up the sari in favor of California casuals? Should Russian immigrants continue to teach their children Russian in the home? Should African American children be acquainted with the music and art of African peoples? Should women from traditional Islamic societies remove the veil and enter the competitive workplace? How do the stresses of acculturation affect the psychological well-being of immigrants and their families?

questionnaire

Going Through Changes

How stressful has your life been lately? Life changes or events, such as those listed below, can impose a stressful burden on a person's adjustment. These life events are similar to those reported by samples of college students and are scaled according to the level of stress they impose (Renner & Mackin, 1998). Place a checkmark next to each event you have experienced during the past year. Then look at the guide at the end of the chapter to interpret your score. (check all that apply)

Low Level of Stress
_____ Registering for classes
_____ Rushing a fraternity or sorority
_____ Making new friends
_____ Commuting to work or school
_____ Going out on a first date
_____ Beginning a new semester
_____ Dating someone steadily
_____ Getting sick
_____ Maintaining a stable romantic relationship
_____ Living away from home for the first time

Medium Level of Stress
_____ Being in a class you hate
_____ Getting involved with drugs
_____ Having difficulties with a roommate
_____ Cheating on a boyfriend or girlfriend
_____ Changing jobs or having hassles at work
_____ Missing sleep
_____ Having conflicts with parents
_____ Moving or adjusting to a new residence
_____ Experiencing negative consequences from using alcohol or drugs
_____ Having to talk in front of class

High Level of Stress
_____ Death of a close friend or family member
_____ Missing an exam because you overslept
_____ Failing a class
_____ Terminating a long-standing dating relationship
_____ Learning that a boyfriend or girlfriend is cheating on you
_____ Having financial problems
_____ Dealing with a serious illness of a friend or family member
_____ Getting caught cheating
_____ Being raped
_____ Having someone accuse you of rape

Sociocultural theorists have alerted us to the importance of accounting for social stressors in explaining abnormal behavior. One of the primary sources of stress imposed on immigrant groups, or on native groups living in the larger mainstream culture, is the need to adapt to a new culture. We can define *acculturation* as the process of adaptation by which immigrants, native groups, and ethnic minority groups adjust to the new culture or majority culture through making behavioral and attitudinal changes. **Acculturative stress** is pressure that results from the demands placed on immigrant, native, and ethnic minority groups to adjust to life in the mainstream culture. Acculturative stress can be a factor among first and second generation immigrant groups in emotional problems such as anxiety and depression (Katsiaficas et al., 2013).

There are two general theories of the relationships between acculturation and psychological adjustment. One theory, dubbed the *melting pot theory,* holds that acculturation helps people adjust to living in the host culture. From this perspective, Hispanic Americans, for example, might adjust better by replacing Spanish with English and adopting the values and customs associated with mainstream American culture. A competing theory, the *bicultural theory,* holds that psychosocial adjustment is marked by identification with both traditional and host cultures. That is, a person's ability to adapt to the ways of the new society combined with a supportive cultural tradition and a sense of ethnic identity may predict good adjustment. From a bicultural perspective, immigrants maintain their ethnic identity and traditional values while learning to adapt to the language and customs of the host culture.

Maintaining ethnic identity. Recent immigrants may be better able to cope with the stress of adjusting to a new culture when they make an effort to adapt while maintaining their ties to their traditional cultures.

RELATIONSHIPS BETWEEN ACCULTURATION AND PSYCHOLOGICAL ADJUSTMENT Relationships between acculturation and psychological adjustment are complex. Some research links higher acculturation status to a greater likelihood of developing psychological problems, whereas other research shows the opposite to be the case. First, let's note some findings from research with Hispanic (Latino) Americans that highlight psychological effects associated with acculturation:

- *Increased risk of heavy drinking among women.* Evidence shows that highly acculturated Hispanic American women are more likely than relatively unacculturated Hispanic American women to become heavy drinkers (Caetano, 1987). In Latin American cultures, men tend to drink much more alcohol than women, largely because gender-based cultural prohibitions on drinking constrain alcohol use among women. These constraints appear to have loosened among Hispanic American women who adopt "mainstream" U.S. attitudes and values.

- *Increased risk of smoking and sexual intercourse among adolescents.* In Latino adolescents, higher levels of acculturation are also linked to increased risks of smoking (Ribisl et al., 2000) and engaging in sexual intercourse (Adam, McGuire, Walsh, Basta, LeCroy, 2005; Lee & Hahm, 2010).

- *Increased risk of disturbed eating behaviors.* Highly acculturated Hispanic American high school girls were found more likely than their less acculturated counterparts to show test scores associated with anorexia (an eating disorder characterized by excessive weight loss and fears of becoming fat—see Chapter 8) on an eating attitudes questionnaire (Pumariega, 1986). Acculturation apparently made these girls more vulnerable to the demands of striving toward the contemporary American ideal of the (very!) slender woman. More recently, investigators found that acculturative stress was linked to poorer body image and internalization of the thin ideal among male and female Hispanic undergraduates in West Texas (Menon & Harter, 2012).

From this evidence, we might gather that acculturation has a negative influence on psychological adjustment, perhaps by contributing to an erosion of traditional family networks and values, which in turn may increase susceptibility to psychological disorders in the face of stress (Ortega, Rosenheck, Alegría, Desai, 2000). Yet we need to balance this view by taking into account other evidence of psychological benefits of bicultural identification. People with a bicultural identity seek to adjust to the host (American) culture while also maintaining their identity with their traditional culture. In an early study of elderly Mexican Americans, researchers found that subjects who were minimally acculturated showed higher levels of depression than either their highly acculturated or their bicultural counterparts (Zamanian et al., 1992). More recently, a large-scale study of Native American youth in 67 American Indian tribes showed that those who were biculturally competent (i.e., had the ability to adapt to both Indian and White cultures) reported lower levels of hopelessness than did those with competencies in only one culture or neither culture (LaFromboise, Albright, & Harris, 2010).

Why would low acculturation status be linked to increased risk of depression? The answer may be that low acculturation status is often a marker for low socioeconomic status (SES). People who are minimally acculturated often face economic hardship and tend to occupy the lower strata of socioeconomic status. Social stress resulting from financial difficulties, lack of proficiency in the host language, and limited economic opportunities add to the stress of adapting to the host culture, all of which may contribute to increased risk of depression and other psychological problems (Ayers et al., 2009; Yeh, 2003). Not surprisingly, one study found that Mexican Americans who were more proficient in English generally had fewer signs of depression and anxiety than did their less-English-proficient counterparts (Salgado de Snyder, 1987). Yet socioeconomic status and language proficiency are not the only, or necessarily the most important, determinants of mental health among immigrant groups. Consider the findings from a northern California sample that showed better mental health profiles among Mexican immigrants than among people of Mexican descent born in the United States, despite the greater socioeconomic disadvantages faced by the immigrant group (Vega et al., 1998). "Americanization" may have damaging effects on the mental health of acculturated minority groups, but such effects may be buffered to a certain extent by retaining cultural traditions. **T / F**

In sum, the erosion of traditional family networks and traditional values that may accompany acculturation among immigrant groups might increase the risk of psychological problems (Ortega et al., 2000). Evidence points to the benefits of adapting to the larger culture while maintaining ties to the traditional culture. For example, development of a strong sense of ethnic identity and pride is associated with higher self-esteem and better adjustment in ethnic minority children (Oyserman, 2008; Rodriguez, Umaña-Taylor, Smith, Johnson, 2009; Smith, Levine, Smith, Dumas, Prinz, 2009). Let's also note the results of a study of Asian immigrant adolescents in the United States that showed that feelings of being alienated or caught between two cultures—the United States and the traditional culture—can lead to mental health problems (Yeh, 2003).

Moreover, some outcomes need careful interpretation. For example, does the finding that highly acculturated Hispanic American women are more likely to drink heavily argue in favor of placing greater social constraints on women? Perhaps a loosening of restraints is a double-edged sword, and all people—male and female, Hispanic and non-Hispanic—encounter adjustment problems when they gain new freedoms.

Finally, we need to consider gender differences in acculturation. In an early study, female immigrants showed higher levels of depression than male immigrants (Salgado de Snyder, Cervantes, & Padilla, 1990). Their higher levels of depression may be linked to the greater level of stress women typically encounter in adjusting to changes in family patterns and personal issues, such as the greater freedom of gender roles for men and women in U.S. society. Because they were reared in cultures in which men are expected to be breadwinners and women homemakers, immigrant women may encounter more family and internal conflict when they enter the workforce, regardless of whether they work because of economic necessity or personal choice. Given these factors, we shouldn't be surprised that wives in more acculturated Mexican American couples tend to report greater marital distress than those in less acculturated couples (Negy & Snyder, 1997). The lead author of this study, psychologist Charles Negy of the University of Central Florida, explores the role of acculturation among Latinos in the following Closer Look section.

a CLOSER look

Coming to America: The Case of Latinos—Charles Negy

As a young man of part Mexican American heritage, I worked in a grocery store in East Los Angeles and was intrigued by the wide range of people of Mexican ancestry I encountered. Many recent immigrants from Mexico seemed eager to practice the little English they knew and were interested in learning more about mainstream American culture. I also knew many immigrants, including many who had lived in California for more than 20 years, who spoke barely any English and hardly ever ventured beyond the local community.

When I entered graduate school, it seemed natural for me to study acculturation among Latino or Hispanic Americans. Acculturation refers to adopting the values, attitudes, and behaviors of a host culture. In my early studies, I quickly observed what other researchers had already discovered, namely, that Latinos in the United States varied greatly in their degree of acculturation toward the U.S. culture. In general, the longer they had lived in the United States, the more acculturated they tended to be, and the more acculturated they were, the more they resembled non-Hispanic Whites in their values, attitudes, and customs.

In my early studies (e.g., Negy & Woods, 1992a; 1993), I found that the more acculturated Mexican American college students were, the more similar their scores were to those of non-Hispanic Whites on standardized personality tests. I wasn't surprised to find that those who were more acculturated tended to come from higher socioeconomic backgrounds (Negy & Woods, 1992b). I also found that among lower-income Mexican American adolescents who showed signs of depression, the more acculturated they were, the more likely they were to have experienced thoughts of committing suicide (Rasmussen, Negy, Carlson, & Burns, 1997).

I later began a line of research examining ethnic differences in marital relationships by comparing Mexican American couples with (non-Hispanic) White couples and Mexican couples (Negy & Snyder, 1997; Negy, Snyder, & Diaz-Loving, 2004). As a group, Mexican couples reported more verbal and/or physical aggression in their relationships than did Mexican American couples, who in turn reported more aggression in their relationships than did (non-Hispanic) White couples. I also observed that Mexican American couples had more egalitarian (equal) relationships and higher levels of marital satisfaction

than Mexican couples (Negy & Snyder, 2004). I learned from these findings that living in the United States was associated with relationship patterns among Mexican Americans that were closer to the Americanized ideal of mutual respect and shared decision making.

These findings suggested that more highly acculturated Hispanic couples have less conflicted, more egalitarian, and more satisfying marriages. On the other hand, acculturation is linked to some mental health problems, such as increased likelihood of suicidal thinking as a way of dealing with depression. This mixed picture of acculturation among Latinos is consistent with the complex and sometimes conflicting results from studies examining relationships between acculturation and mental health reported in this chapter.

I also observed in my study of Mexican American couples that more highly acculturated women reported less satisfaction with the sexual component of their relationships than did less well-acculturated women. These findings lead me to wonder whether American culture imparts greater expectations of female sexual satisfaction in marriages that translate into lower satisfaction when these expectations are not fulfilled.

There are important issues to keep in mind when interpreting these research findings. For starters, the research is correlational in nature. As you may recall about correlational data, we cannot say whether one variable causes another variable. For example, on the basis of the findings from my study of marital couples, I cannot conclude that acculturation is causally related to the development of more egalitarian marriages. It is possible that causation works in the opposite direction—that having an egalitarian marriage influences acculturation. How? We can speculate that Mexican Americans with more egalitarian relationships may be more accepted by mainstream society, and the more interactions they have within the general society, the more opportunities they have to acculturate. Therefore, having egalitarian marriages tends to be associated (correlated) with acculturation, but there is no causal link between the two.

In more recent research, my colleagues and I focused on the role of acculturative stress among Latino immigrants. We found that Latino immigrants reporting the highest levels of acculturative stress tended to be those for whom the experience of living in the United States deviated the most from what they had expected would be the case before they immigrated (Negy, Schwartz, & Reig-Ferrer, 2009). In another sample of Hispanic immigrant women, we found that acculturative stress appeared to both exacerbate previous relationship difficulties among couples and to contribute to stress among married Latinas (Negy, Hammons, Reig-Ferrer, Carper, 2010). Most recently, I conducted a study on deported Salvadorans who are struggling to transition back to life in El Salvador. I found that despite being back in their home country, they experience a modest amount of stress related to having to adapt to a life they left behind when they had emigrated from El Salvador to the United States.

Learning more about the adjustment and acculturation challenges many Latinos face as they endeavor to maintain family relations while striving for a better life may help inform the treatment programs and interventions clinicians can offer to Latino individuals and families.

Charles Negy, Ph.D., is Associate Professor of Psychology at the University of Central Florida and is a licensed psychologist in the state of Florida. His research primarily focuses on the acculturation of Hispanic Americans.

4.5 **Identify** psychological factors that moderate the effects of stress.

Psychological Factors That Moderate Stress

Stress may be a fact of life, but the ways in which we handle stress help determine our ability to cope with it. Individuals react differently to stress depending on psychological factors such as the meaning they ascribe to stressful events. Let's consider, for example, a major life event, such as pregnancy. Whether it is a positive or negative stressor depends on the couple's desire for a child and their readiness to care for one. We can say the stress of pregnancy is moderated by the perceived value of children in the couple's eyes and their self-efficacy—their confidence in their ability to raise a child. As we see next, psychological factors such as coping styles, self-efficacy expectancies, psychological hardiness, optimism, social support, and ethnic identity may moderate or buffer the effects of stress.

STYLES OF COPING What do you do when faced with a serious problem? Do you pretend it does not exist? Like Scarlett O'Hara in the classic film *Gone with the Wind,* do you say to yourself, "I'll think about it tomorrow," and then banish it from your mind? Or do you take charge and confront it squarely?

Pretending that problems do not exist is a form of denial. Denial is an example of **emotion-focused coping** (Lazarus & Folkman, 1984). In emotion-focused coping, people take measures that immediately reduce the impact of the stressor, such as denying its existence or withdrawing from the situation. Emotion-focused coping, however, does not eliminate the stressor (a serious illness, for example) or help the individual develop better ways of managing it. In **problem-focused coping,** by contrast, people examine the stressors they face and do what they can to change them or modify their own reactions to render stressors less harmful. These basic styles of coping—emotion-focused and problem-focused—have been applied to ways in which people respond to illness.

Denial of illness can take various forms, including the following.

1. Failing to recognize the seriousness of the illness
2. Minimizing the emotional distress the illness causes
3. Misattributing symptoms to other causes (e.g., assuming the appearance of blood in the stool represents nothing more than a local abrasion)
4. Ignoring threatening information about the illness

Denial can be dangerous to your health, especially if it leads to avoidance of, or noncompliance with, needed medical treatment. Avoidance is another form of emotion-based coping. Like denial, avoidance may deter people from complying with medical treatments, which can lead to a worsening of their medical conditions. Evidence supports the negative consequences of avoidant coping. In one study, people who had an avoidant style of coping with cancer (e.g., by trying not to think or talk about it) showed greater disease progression when evaluated a year later than did people who more directly confronted the illness (Epping-Jordan, Compas, & Howell, 1994). Other investigators link avoidance to the later development of depression and PTSD among combat veterans (Holahan, Moos, Holahan, Brennan, Schutte, 2005; Stein et al., 2005).

Another form of emotion-focused coping, the use of wish-fulfillment fantasies, is also linked to poor adjustment in coping with serious illness. Examples of wish-fulfillment fantasies include ruminating about what might have been had the illness not occurred and longing for better times. Wish-fulfillment fantasy offers the patient no means of coping with life's difficulties other than an imaginary escape.

Does this mean that people are invariably better off when they know all the facts concerning their illnesses? Not necessarily. Whether you will be better off knowing all the facts may depend on your preferred style of coping. A mismatch between the individual's style of coping and the amount of information provided may hamper recovery. In an important early study, cardiac patients with a repressive style of coping (relying on denial) who received information about their conditions showed a higher incidence of medical complications than repressors who were largely kept in the dark (Shaw, Cohen, Doyle, Pelesky, 1985). Sometimes ignorance helps people manage stress—at least temporarily.

Problem-focused coping involves strategies that address the sources of stress, such as seeking information about the illness through self-study and medical consultation. A person receiving a cancer diagnosis may feel more optimistic or hopeful by receiving information from medical providers about the successful outcomes of treatment.

SELF-EFFICACY EXPECTANCIES Self-efficacy expectancies refer to our expectations regarding our abilities to cope with the challenges we face, to perform certain behaviors skillfully, and to produce positive changes in our lives (Bandura, 1986, 2006). We may be better able to manage stress, including the stress of coping with illness, if we feel confident (have higher self-efficacy expectancies) in our ability to cope effectively. A forthcoming exam may be more or less stressful depending on your confidence in your ability to achieve a good grade.

In a classic study, psychologist Albert Bandura and colleagues found that spider-phobic women showed high levels of the stress hormones epinephrine and norepinephrine when they interacted with the phobic object, for example, by allowing a spider to crawl on their laps (Bandura, Taylor, Williams, Medford, Barchas, 1985). However, as their confidence or self-efficacy expectancies for coping with these tasks increased, the levels of these stress hormones declined. These hormones make us feel shaky, have "butterflies in the stomach," and feel generally nervous. Because high self-efficacy expectancies appear to be associated with lower secretion of these stress hormones, people who believe they can cope with their problems are less likely to feel nervous.

PSYCHOLOGICAL HARDINESS Psychological hardiness refers to a cluster of traits that may help people manage stress. Suzanne Kobasa (1979) and her colleagues investigated business executives who resisted illness despite heavy burdens of stress. Three key traits distinguished the psychologically hardy executives (Kobasa, Maddi, & Kahn, 1982, pp. 169–170):

1. *Commitment.* Rather than feeling alienated from their tasks and situations, hardy executives involved themselves fully. That is, they believed in what they were doing.
2. *Challenge.* Hardy executives believed change was the normal state of things, not sterile sameness or stability for the sake of stability.
3. *Control over their lives.* Hardy executives believed and acted as though they were effectual rather than powerless in controlling the rewards and punishments of life. In terms suggested by social-cognitive theorist Julian Rotter (1966), psychologically hardy individuals have an *internal locus of control.*

Coping with stress. Psychologically hardy people appear to cope more effectively with stress by adopting active, problem-solving approaches and by perceiving themselves as choosing high-stress situations.

Psychologically hardy people appear to cope more effectively with stress by using more active, problem-solving approaches. They are also likely to report fewer physical symptoms and less depression in the face of stress than nonhardy people (Pengilly & Dowd, 2000). Kobasa suggests that hardy people are better able to handle stress because they perceive themselves as *choosing* their stress-creating situations. They perceive the stressors they face as making life more interesting and challenging, not as simply burdening them with additional pressures. A sense of control is a key factor in psychological hardiness.

OPTIMISM Seeing the proverbial glass as half full rather than half empty is linked to better physical health and emotional well-being (Carver, Scheier, & Segerstrom, 2010; Forgeard & Seligman, 2012). For example, one recent research study links greater optimism in women to lower rates of heart disease and greater longevity (Tindle et al., 2009).

Pain patients who express more pessimistic thoughts during flare-ups tend to report more severe pain and distress than counterparts who have sunnier thoughts (Gil, Williams, Keefe, Beckham, 1990). Examples of these pessimistic thoughts include, "I can no longer do anything," "No one cares about my pain," and "It isn't fair I have to live this way." To date, research shows only correlational links between optimism and health. Perhaps we shall soon discover whether learning to alter attitudes—learning to see the glass as half filled—plays a causal role in maintaining or restoring health. You can evaluate your own level of optimism by completing the optimism scale on page 145.

The study of optimism falls within a broader contemporary movement in psychology called **positive psychology.** The developers of this movement believe that psychology should focus more of its efforts on the positive aspects of the human experience, rather than just the deficit side of the human equation, such as problems of emotional disorders, drug abuse, and violence (Donaldson, Csikszentmihalyi, & Nakamura, 2011; McNulty & Fincham, 2012; Seligman, Steen, Park, Peterson, 2005). Although researchers shouldn't turn away from the study of emotional problems, they need to explore how positive attributes, such as optimism, love, and hope, affect peoples' ability to lead satisfying and fulfilling lives. Another positive aspect of the human experience is the ability to help others in need and to be helped by others in turn, as in the case of social support.

SOCIAL SUPPORT People with a broad network of social relationships, such as having a spouse, having close family members and friends, and belonging to social organizations, not only show greater resistance to fending off the common cold but also tend to live longer lives than people with narrower social networks (Cohen & Janicki-Deverts, 2009; Cohen, Doyle, Turner, Alper, Skoner, 2003). Having a diverse social network may provide a wider range of social support that helps protect the body's immune system by serving as a buffer against stress.

ETHNIC IDENTITY African Americans, on the average, stand a greater risk than Euro-Americans of suffering chronic health problems, such as obesity, hypertension, heart disease, diabetes, and certain types of cancers (Brown, 2006; Ferdinand & Ferdinand, 2009; Shields, Lerman, & Sullivan, 2005). The particular stressors that African Americans often face, such as racism, poverty, violence, and overcrowded living conditions, may contribute to their heightened risks of serious health-related problems.

Evidence links perceived discrimination among ethnic minorities to poorer mental and physical health and to higher rates of substance abuse (Chou, Asnaani, & Hofmann, 2012; Delgado, Updegraff, Roosa, Umaña-Taylor, 2010; Huynh, Devos, & Dunbar, 2012; Torres, Driscoll, & Voell, 2012). Studies of Latino and Navajo youth show that negative effects of discrimination may be offset to a certain extent by having strong connections to one's traditional culture and by having parents with strong culturally based orientations and values (Delgado et al., 2010; Galliher, Jones, & Dahl, 2011).

African Americans often demonstrate a high level of resiliency in coping with stress. Among the factors that help buffer stress among African Americans are strong social networks of family and friends, beliefs in one's ability to handle stress (self-efficacy), coping skills, and ethnic identity. Interestingly, African Americans who reported more active attempts to seek social support were less affected by the effects of perceived racism, a significant life stressor, than were those who were less active in support seeking (Clark, 2006).

Ethnic identity is associated with perceptions of a better quality of life among African Americans (Utsey, Payne, Jackson, Jones, 2002) and appears to be more strongly related to psychological well-being among African Americans than among White Americans (Gray-Little & Hafdahl, 2000). Acquiring and maintaining pride in their racial identity and cultural heritage may help African Americans and other ethnic minorities withstand stresses imposed by racism. Evidence links stronger racial identity in African Americans to lower levels of depression (Settles, Navarrete, Pagano, Abdou, Sidanius, 2010). Conversely, African Americans and other ethnic minorities who become alienated from their culture or ethnic identity may be more vulnerable to the effects of stress, which in turn may increase risks of physical and mental health problems.

Ethnic pride as a moderator of the effects of stress. Pride in one's racial or ethnic identity may help the individual withstand the stress imposed by racism and intolerance.

Questionnaire

Are You an Optimist?

Are you someone who looks on the bright side of things? Or do you expect bad things to happen? The following questionnaire may give you insight into whether you are an optimist or a pessimist.

Directions: Indicate whether or not each of the items represents your feelings by writing a number in the blank space according to the following code. Then turn to the scoring key at the end of the chapter.

5 = strongly agree
4 = agree
3 = neutral
2 = disagree
1 = strongly disagree

1. _____ I believe you're either born lucky or like me, born unlucky.

2. _____ My attitude is that if something can wrong, it probably will.

3. _____ I think of myself more as an optimist than a pessimist.

4. _____ I generally expect things will work out in the end.

5. _____ I have these doubts about whether I will eventually succeed.

6. _____ I am hopeful about what the future holds for me.

7. _____ I tend to believe that "every cloud has a silver lining."

8. _____ I think of myself as a realist who thinks the proverbial class is half-empty rather than half-filled.

9. _____ I think the future will be rosy.

10. _____ Things don't generally work out the way I planned.

Adjustment Disorders

Adjustment disorders are the first psychological disorders we discuss in this book, and they are among the mildest. Adjustment disorders are classified in the *DSM-5* within a category of Trauma- and Stressor-Related Disorders, which also includes traumatic stress disorders such as acute stress disorder and posttraumatic stress disorder. We begin with adjustment disorders.

An **adjustment disorder** is a maladaptive reaction to a distressing life event or stressor that develops within 3 months of the onset of the stressor. The stressful event may be either a traumatic experience, such as a natural disaster or a motor vehicle accident with serious injury, or a nontraumatic life event, such as the breakup of a romantic relationship or starting college. According to the *DSM*, the maladaptive reaction is characterized by significant impairment in social, occupational, or other important area of functioning, such as academic work, or by marked emotional distress exceeding what would normally be expected in coping with the stressor. Prevalence estimates of the rates of the disorder in the population vary widely. However, the disorder is common among people seeking outpatient mental health care, with estimates indicating that between 5% and 20% of people receiving outpatient mental health services present with a diagnosis of adjustment disorder (APA, 2013).**T / F**

If your relationship with someone comes to an end (an identified stressor) and your grades are falling off because you are unable to keep your mind on schoolwork, you may fit the bill for an adjustment disorder. If Uncle Harry has been feeling down and pessimistic since his divorce from Aunt Jane, he too may be diagnosed with an adjustment disorder. So too might Cousin Billy if he has been cutting classes and spraying obscene words on the school walls or showing other signs of disturbed conduct.

The concept of "adjustment disorder" as a *mental disorder* highlights some of the difficulties in attempting to define what is normal and what is not. When something important goes wrong in life, we should feel bad about it. If there is a crisis in business, if we are victimized by a crime, or if there is a flood or a devastating hurricane, it is understandable that we might become anxious or depressed. There might, in fact, be something more seriously wrong with us if we did not react in a "maladaptive" way, at least temporarily. However, if our emotional reaction exceeds an expected response, or our ability to function is impaired (e.g., avoidance of social interactions, difficulty getting out of bed, or falling behind in schoolwork), then a diagnosis of adjustment disorder may be indicated. Thus, if you are having trouble concentrating on your schoolwork following the breakup of a romantic relationship and your grades are slipping, you may have an adjustment disorder. There are several specific types of adjustment disorders that vary in terms of the type of maladaptive reaction (see Table 4.2).

For the diagnosis of an adjustment disorder to apply, the stress-related reaction must not be sufficient to meet the diagnostic criteria for other clinical syndromes, such as traumatic stress disorders (acute stress disorder

Difficulty concentrating or adjustment disorder? An adjustment disorder is a maladaptive reaction to a stressor that may take the form of impaired functioning at school or at work, such as having difficulties keeping one's mind on one's studies.

TABLE 4.2

Specific Types of Adjustment Disorders

Disorder	Chief Features
Adjustment disorder with depressed mood	Sadness, crying, and feelings of hopelessness.
Adjustment disorder with anxiety	Worrying, nervousness, and jitters (or in children, fear of separation from primary attachment figures).
Adjustment disorder with mixed anxiety and depressed mood	A combination of anxiety and depression.
Adjustment disorder with disturbance of conduct	Violation of the rights of others or violation of social norms appropriate for one's age; sample behaviors include vandalism, truancy, fighting, reckless driving, and defaulting on legal obligations (e.g., stopping alimony payments).
Adjustment disorder with mixed disturbance of emotion and conduct	Both emotional disturbance, such as depression or anxiety, and conduct disturbance (as described above).
Adjustment disorder unspecified	A residual category that applies to people not classifiable in one of the other subtypes.

Source: Based on the *DSM-5* (American Psychological Association, 2013).

or posttraumatic stress disorder), or anxiety or mood disorders or mood disorders (see Chapters 5 and 7). The maladaptive reaction may be resolved if the stressor is removed or the individual learns to cope with it. If the adjustment disorder lasts for more than six months after the stressor (or its consequences) has been removed, the diagnosis may be changed. Although the *DSM* system distinguishes adjustment disorder from other clinical syndromes, it may be difficult to identify distinguishing features of adjustment disorders that are distinct from other disorders, such as depression (Casey et al., 2006).

Traumatic Stress Disorders

In adjustment disorders, people may have difficulty adjusting to stressful life events such as business or marital problems, termination of a romantic relationship, or death of a loved one. But with traumatic stress disorders, the focus shifts to how people cope with disasters and other traumatic experiences. Exposure to trauma can tax anyone's ability to adjust. For some people, traumatic experiences lead to the development of traumatic stress disorders, which are characterized by maladaptive patterns of behavior in response to trauma that involve marked personal distress or significant impairment of functioning. Here we focus on the two major types of traumatic stress disorders, *acute stress disorder* and *posttraumatic stress disorder*. Table 4.3 provides an overview of these disorders and Table 4.4 identifies some of their common features.

4.7 Describe the key features of acute stress disorder and posttraumatic stress order.

Acute Stress Disorder

In **acute stress disorder,** the person shows a maladaptive pattern of behavior for a period of three days to one month following exposure to a traumatic event. The traumatic event may involve exposure to either actual or threatened death, a serious accident, or a sexual violation. The person with acute stress disorder may have been directly exposed to the trauma, witnessed other people experiencing the trauma, or learned about a violent or accidental traumatic event experienced by a close friend or family member. First responders who are responsible for collecting human remains or police officers who regularly interview children about the details of child abuse may also develop acute stress disorder.

People with acute stress disorder may feel they are "in a daze" or that the world seems like a dreamlike or unreal place. Acute stress disorder may occur in response to

TABLE 4.3

Overview of Traumatic Stress Disorders

Type of Disorder	Lifetime Prevalence in Population (approx.)	Description	Associated Features
Acute stress disorder	Varies widely with the type of trauma	Acute maladaptive reaction in the days or weeks following a traumatic event	Features similar to those of PTSD, but limited to a period of one month following direct exposure to the trauma, witnessing other people exposed to the trauma, or learning about a trauma experienced by a close family member or friend
Posttraumatic stress disorder (PTSD)	About 9%	Prolonged maladaptive reaction to a traumatic event	Reexperiencing the traumatic event, avoidance of cues or stimuli associated with the trauma; general or emotional numbing, hyperarousal, emotional distress, and impaired functioning

Sources: American Psychological Association, 2013; Conway, Compton, Stinson, & Grant, 2006; Kessler, Sonnega, Bromet, et al., 1995, Ozer & Weiss, 2004.

battlefield trauma or exposure to natural or technological disasters. A soldier may have come through a horrific battle, not remembering important features of the battle and feeling numb and detached from the environment. People who are injured or who nearly lose their lives in a hurricane may walk around "in a fog" for days or weeks afterward; be bothered by intrusive images, flashbacks, and dreams of the disaster; or relive the experience as though it were happening again.

The symptoms or features of acute stress disorder vary and may include disturbing, intrusive memories or dreams about the trauma; reexperiencing the trauma in the form of flashbacks; feelings of unreality or detachment ("dissociation") from one's surroundings or from oneself; avoidance of external reminders of the trauma (such as places or people associated with the trauma); problems sleeping; and development of irritable or aggressive behavior or an exaggerated startle response to sudden noises.

Stronger or more persistent symptoms of dissociation around the time of the trauma is associated with a greater likelihood of later development of PTSD (Cardeña & Carlson, 2011). (Dissociation experiences are discussed further in Chapter 6 in the discussion of dissociative disorders.) Symptoms of acute stress disorder parallel the lingering effects of trauma associated with PTSD, as we'll see next.

TABLE 4.4

Common Features of Traumatic Stress Disorders

Avoidance behavior	The person may avoid cues or situations associated with the trauma. A rape survivor may avoid traveling to the part of town where she was attacked. A combat veteran may avoid reunions with soldiers or watching movies or feature stories about war or combat.
Reexperiencing the trauma	The person may reexperience the trauma in the form of intrusive memories, recurrent disturbing dreams, or momentary flashbacks of the battlefield or being pursued by an attacker.
Emotional distress, negative thoughts, and impaired functioning	The person may experience persistent negative thoughts and emotions, feel detached or estranged from others, or have difficulty functioning effectively.
Heightened arousal	The person may show signs of increased arousal, such as becoming hypervigilant (always on guard); have difficulty sleeping and concentrating; become irritable or have outbursts of anger; or show an exaggerated startle response, such as jumping at any sudden noise.
Emotional numbing	In PTSD, the person may feel "numb" inside and lose the ability to have loving feelings.

Posttraumatic Stress Disorder

Whereas is limited to the several weeks following a traumatic event, **posttraumatic stress disorder** is a prolonged maladaptive reaction that lasts longer than one month after the traumatic experience. PTSD presents with a similar symptom profile as acute stress disorder, but may persist for months, years, or even decades, and may not develop until many months or even years after the traumatic event.

Many people with acute stress disorder, but certainly not all, go on to develop PTSD (Kangas, Henry, & Bryant, 2005). Researchers find both types of traumatic stress disorders in soldiers exposed to combat and among rape survivors, victims of serious motor vehicle and other accidents, and people who have witnessed the destruction of their homes and communities by natural disasters, such as floods, earthquakes, or tornadoes, or technological disasters, such as railroad or airplane crashes. For Margaret, the trauma involved a horrific truck accident.

Trauma. Trauma associated with the development of PTSD may involve combat, acts of terrorism, or violent crimes, including crimes such as the mass murders in Newtown, Connecticut, and Virginia Tech. However, the most frequent source of traumas linked to PTSD are serious motor vehicle accidents.

→ "I Thought the World Was Coming to an End:" A Case of PTSD

Margaret was a 54-year-old woman who lived with her husband, Travis, in a small village in upstate New York. Two winters earlier, in the middle of the night, a fuel truck had skidded down one of the icy inclines that led into the village center. Two blocks away, Margaret was shaken from her bed by the explosion ("I thought the world was coming to an end") when the truck slammed into the general store. The store and the apartments above were immediately engulfed in flames. The fire spread to the church next door. Margaret's first and most enduring visual impression was of shards of red and black that rose into the air in an eerie ballet. On their way down, they bathed the centuries-old tombstones in the church graveyard in hellish light. A dozen people died, mostly those who had lived above and behind the general store. The old caretaker of the church and the truck driver were lost as well.

Margaret shared the village's loss, took in the temporarily homeless, and did her share of what had to be done. Months later, after the general store had been leveled to a memorial park and the church was on the way toward being restored, Margaret started to feel that life was becoming strange, that the world outside was becoming a little unreal. She began to withdraw from her friends, and scenes of the night of the fire would fill her mind. At night she now and then dreamed the scene. Her physician prescribed a sleeping pill, which she discontinued because "I couldn't wake up out of the dream." Her physician turned to Valium, to help her get through the day. The pills helped for a while, but "I quit them because I needed more and more of the things and you can't take drugs forever, can you?"

Over the next year and a half, Margaret tried her best not to think about the disaster, but the intrusive recollections and the dreams came and went, apparently on their own. By the time Margaret sought help, her sleep had been seriously distressed for nearly two months and the recollections were as vivid as ever.

→ *From the Author's Files*

Like acute stress disorder the traumatic event associated with PTSD involves direct exposure to a trauma involving actual or threatened death, serious physical injury, or a sexual violation; witnessing other people experiencing trauma; or learning that a close friend or family member has experienced an accidental or violent traumatic event (death due to natural causes does not apply). In some cases, however, the affected person is exposed to the horrific consequences of traumatic events, such as first responders who collect human remains in the aftermath of an explosion or bombing.

Counseling veterans with posttraumatic stress disorder. Storefront counseling centers have been established across the country to provide supportive services to combat veterans suffering from PTSD.

truth OR fiction

Exposure to combat is the most common trauma linked to posttraumatic stress disorder (PTSD).

☑ **FALSE** Motor vehicle accidents are the most common trauma linked to PTSD.

👁 **Watch** the **Video** Bonnie: Posttraumatic Stress Disorder on **MyPsychLab**

PTSD is found in many cultures. High rates of PTSD are found among earthquake and hurricane survivors in many countries, for example, survivors of the devastating earthquake in Pakistan in 2010, as well as among civilians who have suffered the ravages of war, for example, the "killing fields" of the 1970s Pol Pot war in Cambodia, the Balkan conflicts of the 1990s, and the wars in Iraq (e.g., Ali, Farooq, Bhatti, Kuroiwa, 2012; Wagner, Schulz, & Knaevelsrud, 2011). Cultural factors may play a role in determining how people manage and cope with trauma as well as their vulnerability to traumatic stress reactions and the specific form the disorder might take.

PTSD is closely linked to combat experience (Polusny et al., 2011). Among U.S. soldiers who served in the Vietnam War, the prevalence of PTSD was pegged at about one in five (19%) (Dohrenwend et al., 2006). Similarly, about 13% of combat veterans returning from the wars in Iraq and Afghanistan have developed PTSD (Kok, Herrell, Thomas, Hoge, 2012). In total, as many as 300,000 American soldiers returning from the war zones in Iraq and Afghanistan show symptoms of posttraumatic stress disorder or depression (Miller, 2011). Veterans with PTSD often have other problem behaviors, including substance abuse, marital problems, poor work histories, and in some cases, physical aggression against partners in intimate relationships (Taft, Watkins, Stafford, Street, Monson, 2011).

Although exposure to combat or terrorist attacks may be the types of trauma the public most strongly links to PTSD (Pitman, 2006), the traumatic experiences most commonly associated with PTSD are serious motor vehicle accidents (Blanchard & Hickling, 2004). However, traumas involving terrorist attacks and other violent acts, particularly rape and assault, are more likely to lead to PTSD than other forms of trauma (Norris et al., 2003; North et al., 2012). For example, investigators found that survivors of terrorist acts had double the rate of PTSD as compared with survivors of motor vehicle accidents (Shalev & Freedman, 2005). **T / F**

Traumatic events are actually quite common, as more than two-thirds of people suffer a traumatic experience at some point in their lives (Galea, Nandi, & Vlahov, 2005). But most people are resilient in the face of traumatic stress and recover without any professional help (Amstadter, Broman-Fulks, Zinzowa, Ruggiero, Cercone, 2009; Elwood et al., 2009). Fewer than one in ten go on to develop PTSD (Delahanty, 2011a). 👁

Investigators have identified certain factors that increase a person's risk of developing PTSD in the face of traumatic stressors (see Table 4.5). Some vulnerability

---

TABLE 4.5

Factors Predictive of PTSD in Trauma Survivors

Factors Relating to the Event	Factors Relating to the Person or Social Environment
Degree of exposure to trauma	History of childhood sexual abuse
Severity of the trauma	Genetic predisposition or vulnerability
	Lack of social support
	Lack of active coping responses in dealing with the traumatic stressor
	Feeling shame
	Detachment or "dissociation" shortly following the trauma, or feeling numb
	Prior psychiatric history

Sources: Afifi et al., 2010; Elwood et al., 2009; Goenjian et al., 2008; Koenen, Stellman, & Stellman, 2003; North et al., 2012; Ozer, Best, Lipsey, Weiss, 2003; Xie et al., 2009.

factors relate to the traumatic event itself, such as the degree of exposure to the trauma, whereas others relate to the person or the social environment (Delahanty, 2011b; Furr, Comer, Edmunds, Kendall, 2010; Gabert-Quillen, Fallon, & Delahanty, 2011; North et al., 2012). The more direct the exposure to the trauma, the greater the person's likelihood of developing PTSD. Children in the Gulf Coast region of the United States who were more directly exposed to Hurricane Katrina suffered more PTSD symptoms, on average, than did those with less direct exposure (Weems et al., 2007). People who were in the buildings that were struck in the 9/11 terrorist attack were nearly twice as likely to develop PTSD as those who witnessed the attacks but were outside the buildings at the time (Bonanno, Galea, Bucciarelli, Vlahov, 2006). Of the more than 3,000 people who evacuated the Twin Towers when it was attacked, nearly all (96%) developed some PTSD symptoms and about 15% developed diagnosable PTSD two to three years after the disaster ("More Than 3,000," 2011).

Another factor relating to the likelihood of developing PTSD is gender. Although men more often have traumatic experiences, women are more likely to develop PTSD, about twice as likely (Parto, Evans, & Zonderman, 2011; Tolin & Foa, 2006). However, women's greater vulnerability to PTSD may have more to do with their greater incidence of sexual victimization and with their younger ages at the time of trauma than with gender itself (Cortina & Kubiak, 2006; Olff, Langeland, Draijer, Gersons, 2007).

Other vulnerability factors relate to personal and biological factors. Genetic factors involved in regulating the body's response to stress appear to play a part in determining a person's susceptibility to PTSD in the wake of trauma (Afifi, Asmundson, Taylor, Jang, 2010; Xie et al., 2009). Recently, investigators reported that the *amygdala*, a small structure in the brain's limbic system that triggers the body's fear response, was smaller in a group of combat veterans with PTSD than in combat veterans without PTSD (Morey et al., 2012). Although more research is needed, these intriguing findings point to a possible biological factor that may account for why some people develop PTSD in the face of trauma whereas others don't.

Other factors linked to increased vulnerability to PTSD include a history of childhood sexual abuse, lack of social support, and limited coping skills (Lowe, Chan, & Rhodes, 2010; Mehta et al., 2011; Mercer et al., 2011). Personality factors such as lower levels of self-efficacy and higher levels of hostility are also linked to increased risk of PTSD (Heinrichs et al., 2005). People who experience unusual symptoms during or immediately after the trauma, such as feeling that things are not real or feeling as though one were watching oneself in a movie as the events unfold, stand a greater risk of developing PTSD than do other trauma survivors (Ozer & Weiss, 2004). (As we noted, these unusual reactions are called *dissociative* experiences; see Chapter 6.) On the other hand, finding a sense of purpose or meaning in the traumatic experience, for example, believing that the war one is fighting is just, may bolster one's ability to cope with the stressful circumstances and reduce the risk of PTSD (Sutker, Davis, Uddo, Ditta, 1995).

Theoretical Perspectives

4.8 Describe ways of understanding and treating PTSD.

The major conceptual understanding of PTSD derives from the behavioral or learning perspective. Within a classical conditioning framework, traumatic experiences are unconditioned stimuli that become paired with neutral (conditioned) stimuli such as the sights, sounds, and even smells associated with the trauma—for example, the battlefield or the neighborhood in which a person has been raped or assaulted. Consequently, anxiety becomes a conditioned response that is elicited by exposure to trauma-related stimuli.

Cues that reactivate negative arousal or anxiety are associated with thoughts, memories, or even dream images of the trauma; with hearing someone talking about the trauma; or with visiting the scene of the trauma. Through operant conditioning, the person may learn to avoid any contact with trauma-related stimuli. Avoidance behaviors are operant responses that are negatively reinforced by relief from anxiety. Unfortunately, by avoiding trauma-related cues, the person also avoids opportunities to overcome the

Can Disturbing Memories Be Erased?

Might it be possible to erase troubling memories in people with PTSD or at least to blunt their emotional effects? Although such suggestions may have seemed far-fetched only a few years ago, recent scientific discoveries offer such possibilities.

Researchers are exploring drugs that can block disturbing memories or reduce the anxiety or fear associated with traumatic experiences (Andero et al., 2011). In one study, people with chronic PTSD were asked to recall and describe details of the PTSD-related traumatic event and were then given either a common blood pressure drug, *propranolol*, or a placebo (inactive drug) (Brunet et al., 2007). A week later, they were asked to reactivate mental images associated with the traumatic event while the investigators monitored their physiological reactions, including their heart rate and level of muscle tension. Those who had received propranolol showed lower physiological activity as compared with those who had received the placebo. It appears the drug may blunt the body's physiological response to traumatic memories.

Propranolol may also reduce acquired fear reactions. Investigators in the Netherlands conditioned a fear response in 60 healthy college students by showing them a picture of a spider while they received a mild electric shock (Kindt, Soeter, & Vervliet, 2009). The students quickly acquired a conditioned fear response; they showed a stronger startle response to a loud noise when they were again exposed to the fearful stimulus (the spider picture) but this time without the accompanying shock than when they were exposed to the control stimulus with no shock. The next day, participants received either propranolol or a placebo just before their fear response was reactivated by their viewing the fearful stimulus again. The following day, students who had received the drug the day before showed a weaker startle response while viewing the spider picture than did those who had received the placebo. The experimenters believe the drug interfered with the processing of the fearful memory when it was reactivated, which in turn dulled or erased the behavioral response to the feared stimulus. What's more, when students were then exposed to a second round of conditioning in which the spider picture was again paired with shock, the fear response returned in those who had received the placebo, but not in those given propranolol.

Now to understand these effects, we need to consider how the body responds to stress. When exposed to trauma or to a painful stimulus like electric shock, the body releases the stress hormone adrenaline (also called epinephrine). Adrenaline has many effects on the body, including activating the amygdala, the fear-processing center in the brain. Propranolol blocks adrenaline receptors in the amygdala, which may weaken memories of fearful stimuli.

In people with problems with anxiety or fear, the amygdala appears to be overreactive to cues relating to threat, fear, and

rejection. Drugs like propranolol may modulate the brain's response to fearful stimuli, providing a way of lessening or even erasing fear responses and blocking their return. It's conceivable that one day soon, drugs like propranolol may become part of the therapeutic arsenal clinicians use to quell anxiety responses in people with PTSD or other problems with anxiety, such as anxiety disorders. Researchers don't yet know whether such drugs can permanently erase painful memories, or whether they should even try to erase these personal memories. But if these drugs work on networks in the brain that house emotional memories, they may be useful in rendering troubling memories less painful.

Might drugs be used to prevent PTSD symptoms in soldiers who have suffered traumatic injuries in battle? Investigators are exploring whether use of morphine, a powerful opiate drug used to treat pain in wounded soldiers, might also disrupt the process of forming painful memories that can lead to PTSD (Holbrook, Galarneau, Dye, Quinn, Dougherty, 2010). Depending on the outcomes of more research, morphine may come to be used by battlefield medics not simply to treat pain in wounded soldiers but also to prevent the later emergence of PTSD symptoms. Other investigators find that in laboratory rats, sleep deprivation disrupts PTSD-like memories associated with trauma (Cohen et al., 2012). It is conceivable that sleep deprivation may have a similar effect in people exposed to trauma.

On a related research front, scientists probing the molecular underpinnings of memory are attempting to isolate and tamp down specific brain circuits associated with particular memories. Recently, investigators reported progress in blocking recall of aversive stimuli in laboratory rats, revealing a potential

Might Sleep Deprivation Prevent Traumatic Memories? Laboratory research with rats suggests that sleep deprivation may prevent the consolidation of newly formed memories of trauma. If these findings hold up with humans, people who experience trauma may decide to forgo sleep for a day in order to block the formation of disturbing memories.

pathway in the brain that may lead to ways of blocking disturbing memories in people with PTSD (Lauzon et al., 2013). Other investigators were able to erase a particular learned response in a sea snail using a chemical that interfered with biological processes needed to form long-term memories (Cai, Pearce, Chen, Glanzman, 2011). The sea snail is used to explore how memory works at the biochemical level. Although it has a much simpler nervous system than more advanced animals, the underlying processes involved in how new memories are laid down in neural circuits in the snail are also involved in memory formation in the brains of mammals, including memories of learned responses.

What scientists learn in the laboratory may lead to breakthrough treatments for PTSD. There may come a day when it becomes possible to identify and effectively control specific brain circuits that house traumatic memories while leaving intact other memories of life experiences.

Scientific advances may someday enable medical care providers to block or dull certain traumatic memories of traumatic survivors. But having the ability to control memories at the biochemical level raises important moral, legal, and ethical questions for both society and individuals themselves. We raise the following questions for reflection and debate:

- Who should decide whether memory blocking drugs are used in the immediate aftermath of trauma? The battlefield commander or medic? The health care provider? Or the trauma survivor?
- What if the trauma survivor is rendered unconscious or unable to make this decision? Should the law require a prior medical proxy, or legal agreement stipulating who should make these decisions and under what conditions?
- Is it right to obliterate a person's memories of a significant life event in the hopes that it may prevent later emotional suffering?
- Would you want to blot out traumatic memories? Or would rather keep your memories and deal with the emotional consequences that may unfold?

underlying fear. Extinction (gradual weakening or elimination) of conditioned anxiety can occur only when the person encounters the conditioned stimuli (the cues associated with the trauma) in the absence of any troubling unconditioned stimuli.

Treatment Approaches

Cognitive-behavioral therapy has produced impressive results in the treatment of PTSD (e.g., Ehlers et al., 2010; Henslee & Coffey, 2010; Resick, Williams, Suvak, Monson, Gradus, 2012). The basic treatment component is repeated exposure to cues and emotions associated with the trauma. In cognitive-behavioral therapy, the person gradually reexperiences the anxiety associated with the traumatic event in a safe setting, thereby allowing extinction to take its course. The PTSD patient may be encouraged to repeatedly talk about the traumatic experience, reexperience the emotional aspects of the trauma in imagination, view related slides or films, or visit the scene of the traumatic event. Survivors of serious motor vehicle crashes who have avoided driving since the accident might be instructed to make short driving trips around the neighborhood (Gray & Acierno, 2002). They might also be asked to repeatedly describe the incident and the emotional reactions they experienced. For combat-related PTSD, exposure-based homework assignments might include visiting war memorials or viewing war movies. Evidence shows that supplementing exposure with cognitive restructuring (challenging and replacing distorted thoughts or beliefs with rational alternatives) can enhance treatment gains (Bryant, Moulds, Guthrie, Dang, Nixon, 2003). Exposure therapy is also of benefit in treating people with ASD (Bryant et al., 2008).

Therapists may use a more intense form of exposure called *prolonged exposure,* in which the person repeatedly reexperiences the traumatic event in imagination during treatment sessions or directly confronts situations linked to the trauma in real life without seeking to escape from the anxiety (Leiner, Kearns, Jackson, Astin, Rothbaum, 2012; Resick et al., 2012; Schneier et al., 2012; Sharpless & Barber, 2011). For rape survivors, prolonged exposure may mean repeatedly recounting the horrifying ordeal within the supportive therapeutic setting.

@Issue: Is EMDR a Fad or a Find?

A controversial technique has emerged in the treatment of PTSD—**eye movement desensitization and reprocessing (EMDR)** treatment (Shapiro, 2001). In EMDR, the client is asked to form a mental picture of an image associated with the trauma while the therapist rapidly moves a finger back and forth in front of the client's eyes for about 20 to 30 seconds. While holding the image in mind, the client is asked to move his or her eyes to follow the therapist's finger. The client then relates to the therapist the images, feelings, bodily sensations, and thoughts that were experienced during the procedure. The procedure is then repeated until the client becomes desensitized to the emotional impact of this disturbing material.

Evidence from carefully controlled studies demonstrates the therapeutic benefits of EMDR in treating PTSD (e.g., Leiner et al., 2012; Oren & Solomon, 2012; Sharpless & Barber, 2011; Tarquinio, Rydberg, & Oren, 2012). The controversy is not about whether EMDR works, but *why* it works and whether the key feature of the technique—the eye movements themselves—is a necessary factor in explaining its effects (Karatzias et al., 2011; Lohr, Lilienfeld, & Rosen, 2012; van den Hout et al., 2011).

Researchers lack a compelling theoretical model explaining why rapid eye movements would relieve symptoms of PTSD, and this is an important factor in why some clinicians resist using it in practice (Cook, Biyanova, & Coyne, 2009). A related concern is whether the therapeutic effects of EMDR have anything to do with eye movements. Perhaps EMDR is effective because of the role of nonspecific factors it shares with other therapies, such as mobilizing a sense of hope and positive expectancies in clients. Another possibility is that EMDR works because it represents a form of exposure therapy, which is a well-established treatment for PTSD and other anxiety disorders (Taylor et al., 2003). The effective ingredient in EMDR may be repeated exposure to traumatic mental imagery, rather than the rapid eye movements. Although the controversy over EMDR is not yet settled, the technique may turn out to be nothing more than a novel way of conducting exposure-based therapy. Meanwhile, evidence from another study shows that more traditional exposure therapy

EMDR. A relatively new and controversial treatment for PTSD, EMDR involves the client holding an image of the traumatic experience in mind while moving his or her eyes to follow a sweeping motion of the therapist's finger.

worked better and faster in reducing avoidance behaviors than did EMDR, at least among people who completed treatment (Taylor et al., 2003).

As the debate over EMDR continues, it is worthwhile to consider the famous dictum known as *Occam's razor,* or the principle of parsimony. In its most widely used form today, the principle holds that the simpler the explanation, the better. In other words, if researchers can explain the effects of EMDR on the basis of exposure, there is no need to posit more complex explanations involving effects of eye movements per se in desensitizing clients to traumatic images.

In thinking critically about the issue, answer the following questions:

- Why is it important to determine why a treatment works and not simply whether it works?
- What types of research studies would be needed to determine whether rapid eye movements are a critical component of the benefits of EMDR?

Training in stress management skills, such as self-relaxation, can also improve the client's ability to cope with troubling symptoms of PTSD, such as heightened arousal and the desire to run away from trauma-related stimuli. Training in anger management skills may also be helpful, especially for combat veterans with PTSD. Treatment with antidepressant drugs, such as *sertraline* (Zoloft) or *paroxetine* (Paxil), may help reduce the anxiety components of PTSD (Schneier et al., 2012).

Thinking Critically About Abnormal Psychology discusses a controversial form of treatment for PTSD, eye movement desensitization and reprocessing. What is EMDR? Does it work? And if it does work, why does it work?

summing up

Stress and Health

4.1 Evaluate the effects of stress on health.
Evidence links exposure to stress to weakened immune system functioning, which in turn can increase vulnerability to physical illness. However, because this evidence is correlational, questions of cause and effect remain.

4.2 Identify and describe the stages of the general adaptation syndrome.
The general adaptation syndrome, a term coined by Hans Selye, refers to the body's generalized pattern of response to persistent or enduring stress, which is characterized by three stages: (1) the alarm reaction, in which the body mobilizes its resources to confront a stressor; (2) the resistance stage, in which bodily arousal remains high but the body attempts to adapt to continued stressful demands; and (3) the exhaustion stage, in which bodily resources become dangerously depleted in the face of persistent and intense stress, and stress-related disorders, or diseases of adaptation, may develop.

4.3 Evaluate evidence on the relationship between life changes and psychological and physical health.
Again, links are correlational, but evidence shows that people who experience more life stress in the form of life changes and daily hassles are at an increased risk of developing physical health problems.

4.4 Evaluate the role of acculturative stress in psychological adjustment.
The pressures of acculturation, or acculturate stress, can affect mental and physical functioning. The relationships between level of acculturation and psychological adjustment are complex, but evidence supports the value of developing a bicultural pattern of acculturation, which involves efforts to adapt to the host culture while maintaining one's traditional ethnic or cultural identity.

4.5 Identify psychological factors that moderate the effects of stress.
These factors include effective coping styles, self-efficacy expectancies, psychological hardiness, optimism, and social support.

Adjustment Disorders

4.6 Define the concept of an adjustment disorder and describe the key features of this disorder.
Adjustment disorders are maladaptive reactions to identified stressors. Adjustment disorders are characterized by emotional reactions that are greater than normally expected given the circumstances or by evidence of significant impairment in functioning. Impairment usually takes the form of problems at work or school or in social relationships or activities.

4.7 Describe the key features of acute stress disorder and post-traumatic stress disorder.
The two types of traumatic stress disorders are acute stress disorder and posttraumatic stress disorder. Both involve maladaptive reactions to traumatic stressors. Acute stress disorder occurs in the days and weeks following exposure to the traumatic event. Posttraumatic stress disorder persists for months, years, or even decades after the traumatic experience and may not begin until months or years after the event.

4.8 Describe ways of understanding and treating PTSD.
Learning theory provides a framework for understanding the conditioning of fear to trauma-related stimuli and the role of negative reinforcement in maintaining avoidance behavior. However, other factors come into play in determining vulnerability to PTSD, including degree of exposure to the trauma and personal characteristics, such as a history of childhood sexual abuse and lack of social support.

The major treatment approach is cognitive-behavioral therapy, which focuses on repeated exposure to cues associated with the trauma and may be combined with cognitive restructuring and training in stress management and anger management techniques. Eye movement desensitization and reprocessing is a relatively new but controversial form of treatment for PTSD.

critical thinking questions

On the basis of your reading of this chapter, answer the following questions:

- Does evidence presented in the text seem to argue for or against a melting pot model of American culture? What evidence suggests that maintaining a strong ethnic identity may be beneficial?

- Examine your own behavior patterns. Do you believe your behaviors in everyday life enhance or impair your ability to handle stress? What changes can you make in your lifestyle to adopt healthier behaviors?

- Consider the level of stress in your own life. How might stress be affecting your psychological or physical health? In what ways can you reduce the level of stress in your life? What coping strategies can you learn to manage stress more effectively?

key terms

health psychologist 131
stress 131
stressor 131
endocrine system 132
hormones 132
immune system 133
general adaptation syndrome (GAS) 135

alarm reaction 135
fight-or-flight reaction 135
resistance stage 136
exhaustion stage 137
acculturative stress 139
emotion-focused coping 142

problem-focused coping 142
self-efficacy expectancies 143
psychological hardiness 143
positive psychology 144
adjustment disorder 146
acute stress disorder 147

posttraumatic stress disorder (PTSD) 149
eye movement desensitization and reprocessing (EMDR) 154

Scoring Key for the "Going Through Changes" Questionnaire

Examining your responses can help you gauge how much life stress you have experienced during the past year. Though everyone experiences some degree of stress, if you checked many of these items, especially those at the higher stress levels, it is likely you have been experience a relatively high level of stress during the past year. Bear in mind, however, that the same level of stress may affect different people differently. Your ability to cope with stress depends on many factors, including your coping skills and the level of social support you have available. If you are experiencing a high level of stress, you may wish to examine the sources of stress in your life. Perhaps you can reduce the level of stress you experience or learn more effective ways of handling the sources of stress you can't avoid.

Scoring Key for Optimism Scale

To compute your overall score, you first need to reverse your scores on items 1, 2, 5, 8, and 10. This means that a 1 becomes 5, a 2 becomes a 4, a 3 remains the same, a 4 becomes a 2, and a 5 becomes a 1. Then sum your scores. Total scores can range from 10 (lowest optimism) to 50 (highest optimism). Scores around 30 indicate that you are neither strongly optimistic nor pessimistic. Although we do not have norms for this scale, you may consider scores in the 31 to 39 range as indicating a moderate level of optimism, whereas those in the 21 to 29 range indicate a moderate level of pessimism. Scores of 40 or above suggest higher levels of optimism, whereas those of 20 or below suggest higher levels of pessimism.

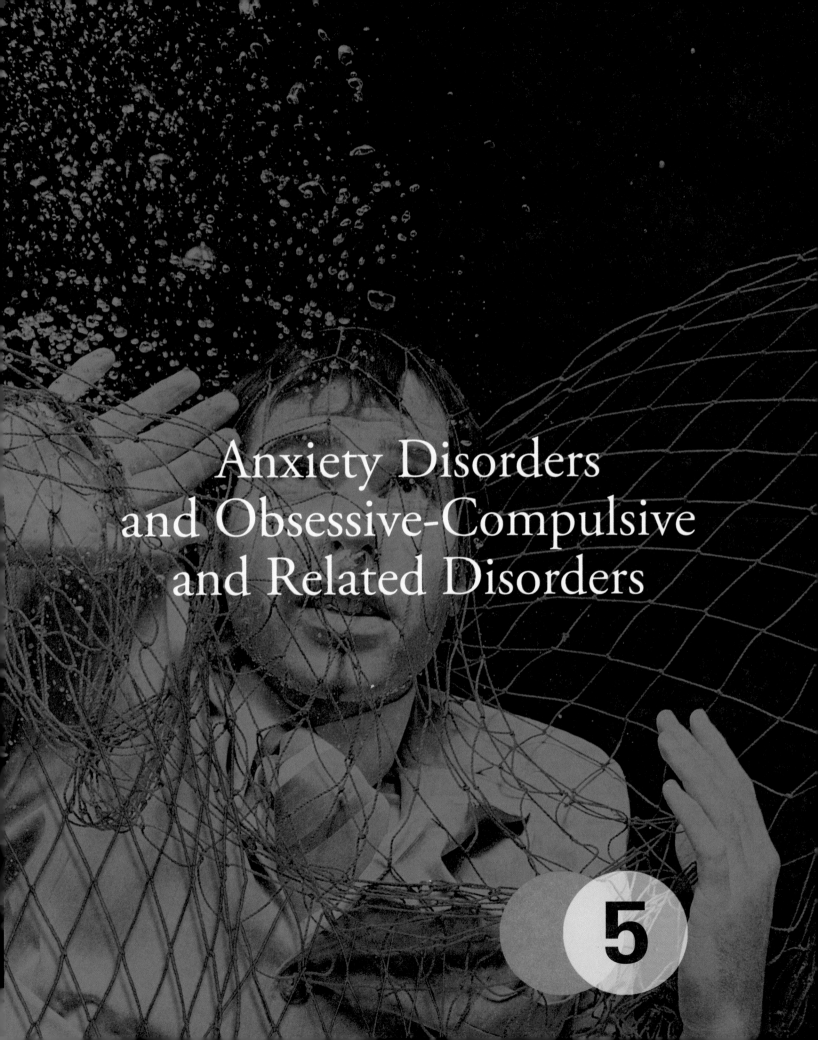

Anxiety Disorders
and Obsessive-Compulsive
and Related Disorders

5

5

learning objectives

5.1
Describe the physical, behavioral, and cognitive features of anxiety disorders.

5.2
Describe the key features of panic disorder.

5.3
Describe the leading conceptual model of panic disorder.

5.4
Evaluate methods used to treat panic disorder.

5.5
Describe the key features and specific types of phobic disorders and explain how phobias develop.

5.6
Evaluate methods used to treat phobic disorders.

5.7
Describe the key features of generalized anxiety disorder and ways of understanding and treating it.

5.8
Evaluate ethnic differences in rates of anxiety disorders.

5.9
Describe the key features of obsessive–compulsive disorder and ways of understanding and treating it.

5.10
Describe the key features of body dysmorphic disorder and hoarding disorder and explain why these disorders are classified within the obsessive–compulsive spectrum.

truth OR fiction

T☐ F☐   People who experience a panic attack often think they are having a heart attack. (p. 161)

T☐ F☐   Antidepressant drugs are used to treat people who are not depressed but are suffering from various anxiety disorders. (p. 166)

T☐ F☐   People with phobias believe their fears to be well founded. (p. 169)

T☐ F☐   Some people are so fearful of leaving their homes that they are unable to venture outside even to mail a letter. (p. 172)

T☐ F☐   We may be genetically predisposed to acquire fears of objects that posed a danger to ancestral humans. (p. 176)

T☐ F☐   If there is a spider in the room, the spider phobic in the group will likely be the first to notice it and point it out. (p. 177)

T☐ F☐   Therapists have used virtual reality to help people overcome phobias. (p. 181)

T☐ F☐   Obsessional thinking helps relieve anxiety. (p. 190)

T☐ F☐   Having skin blemishes leads some people to consider suicide. (p. 193)

"I" "I Felt Like I Was Going to Die Right Then and There"

I never experienced anything like this before. It happened while I was sitting in the car at a traffic light. I felt my heart beating furiously fast, like it was just going to explode. It just happened, for no reason. I started breathing really fast but couldn't get enough air. It was like I was suffocating and the car was closing in around me. I felt like I was going to die right then and there. I was trembling and sweating heavily. I thought I was having a heart attack. I felt this incredible urge to escape, to just get out of the car and get away.

I somehow managed to pull the car over to the side of the road but just sat there waiting for the feelings to pass. I told myself if I was going to die, then I was going to die. I didn't know whether I'd survive long enough to get help. Somehow—I can't say how—it just passed and I sat there a long time, wondering what had just happened to me. Just as suddenly as the panic overcame me, it was gone. My breathing slowed down and my heart stopped thumping in my chest. I was alive. I was not going to die. Not until the next time, anyway.

"The Case of Michael," from the Author's Files

What is it like to have a panic attack? People tend to use the word *panic* loosely, as when they say, "I panicked when I couldn't find my keys." Clients in therapy often speak of having panic attacks, although what they describe often falls in a milder spectrum of anxiety reactions. During a true panic attack, like the one Michael describes, the level of anxiety rises to the point of sheer terror. Unless you have suffered one, it is difficult to appreciate just how intense panic attacks can be. People who have panic attacks describe them as the most frightening experiences of their lives. The occurrence of panic attacks is the cardinal feature of a severe type of anxiety disorder called *panic disorder*.

There is much to be anxious about—our health, social relationships, examinations, careers, international relations, and the condition of the environment are but a few sources of possible concern. It is normal, even adaptive, to be somewhat anxious about these aspects of life.

Anxiety is a generalized state of apprehension or foreboding. Anxiety is useful because it prompts us to seek regular medical checkups or motivates us to study for tests. Anxiety is therefore a normal response to threats, but anxiety becomes abnormal when it is out of proportion to the reality of a threat, or when it seems to simply come out of the blue—that is, when it is not in response to life events.

In Michael's case, panic attacks began spontaneously, without any warning or trigger. This kind of maladaptive anxiety reaction, which can cause significant emotional distress or impair the person's ability to function, is labeled an **anxiety disorder**. Anxiety, the common thread that connects the various types of anxiety disorders, can be experienced in different ways, from the intense fear associated with a panic attack to the generalized sense of foreboding or worry in generalized anxiety disorder. Anxiety disorders are very common, affecting nearly one in five adults in the United States, which works out to more than 40 million people (Torpy, Burke, & Golub, 2011).

Overview of Anxiety Disorders

Anxiety is characterized by a wide range of symptoms that cut across physical, behavioral, and cognitive domains:

5.1 Describe the physical, behavioral, and cognitive features of anxiety disorders.

a) *Physical features* may include jumpiness, jitteriness, trembling or shaking, tightness in the pit of the stomach or chest, heavy perspiration, sweaty palms, lightheadedness or faintness, dryness in the mouth or throat, shortness of breath, heart pounding or racing, cold fingers or limbs, and upset stomach or nausea, among other physical symptoms.

b) *Behavioral features* may include avoidance behavior, clinging or dependent behavior, and agitated behavior.

c) *Cognitive features* may include worry, a nagging sense of dread or apprehension about the future, preoccupation with or keen awareness of bodily sensations, fear of losing control, thinking the same disturbing thoughts over and over, jumbled or confused thoughts, difficulty concentrating or focusing one's thoughts, and thinking that things are getting out of hand.

Although people with anxiety disorders don't necessarily experience all these features, it is easy to see why anxiety is distressing. The *DSM* recognizes the following major types of anxiety disorders: panic disorder, phobic disorders, and generalized anxiety disorder. Several other disorders that were previously classified in the category of anxiety disorders are placed in the *DSM-5* in new diagnostic categories with other disorders with which they share common features. Obsessive-compulsive disorder is now classified in a new diagnostic category of Obsessive-Compulsive and Related Disorders, which we discuss later in the chapter. Acute stress disorder and posttraumatic stress disorder, which we discussed in Chapter 4, are now classified in a new category of Trauma- and Stressor-Related Disorders.

Table 5.1 provides an overview of the major types of anxiety disorders. The anxiety disorders are not mutually exclusive. People frequently meet diagnostic criteria for more than one of them. Moreover, many people with anxiety disorders also have other types of disorders, especially mood disorders.

The anxiety disorders, along with dissociative disorders and somatic symptom and related disorders (see Chapter 6), were classified as neuroses throughout most of the 19th century. The term *neurosis* derives from roots meaning "an abnormal or diseased condition of the nervous system." The Scottish physician William Cullen coined the term *neurosis* in the 18th century. As the derivation implies, it was assumed that neurosis had biological origins. It was seen as an affliction of the nervous system.

At the beginning of the 20th century, Cullen's organic assumptions were largely replaced by Sigmund Freud's psychodynamic views. Freud maintained that neurotic behavior stems from the threatened emergence of unacceptable anxiety-evoking ideas into conscious awareness. According to Freud, disorders involving anxiety (as well as the dissociative and somatic symptom disorders discussed in Chapter 6) represent ways in which the ego attempts to defend itself against anxiety. Freud's views on the origins of these problems united them under the general category of neuroses. Freud's concepts

TABLE 5.1

Overview of Major Types of Anxiety Disorders

Type of Disorder	Approximate Lifetime Prevalence in Population (%)	Description	Associated Features
Panic Disorder	5.1%	Repeated panic attacks (episodes of sheer terror accompanied by strong physiological symptoms, thoughts of imminent danger or impending doom, and an urge to escape)	Fears of recurring attacks may prompt avoidance of situations associated with the attacks or in which help might not be available; attacks begin unexpectedly but may become associated with certain cues or specific situations; may be accompanied by agoraphobia, or general avoidance of public situations
Generalized Anxiety Disorder	9%	Persistent anxiety that is not limited to particular situations	Excessive worrying; heightened states of bodily arousal, tenseness, being on edge
Specific Phobia	12.5%	Excessive fears of particular objects or situations	Avoidance of phobic stimulus or situation; examples include acrophobia, claustrophobia, and fears of blood, small animals, or insects
Social Anxiety Disorder (Social Phobia)	12.1%	Excessive fear of social interactions	Characterized by an underlying fear of rejection, humiliation, or embarrassment in social situations
Agoraphobia	About 1.4% to 2%	Fear and avoidance of open, public places	May occur secondarily to losses of supportive others to death, separation, or divorce

Sources: Prevalence rates derived from APA, 2013; Conway et al., 2006; Grant et al., 2005a; Grant et al., 2006b, 2006c; Kessler et al., 2005a.

were so widely accepted in the early 1900s that they formed the basis for the classification systems found in the first two editions of the *Diagnostic and Statistical Manual of Mental Disorders* (*DSM*).

Since 1980, the *DSM* has not contained a category termed *neuroses*. The *DSM* today is based on similarities in observable behavior and distinctive features rather than on causal assumptions. Many clinicians continue to use the terms *neurosis* and *neurotic* in the manner in which Freud described them, however. Some clinicians use the term *neuroses* to group milder behavioral problems in which people maintain relatively good contact with reality. *Psychoses*, such as schizophrenia, are typified by loss of touch with reality and bizarre behavior, beliefs, and hallucinations.

Anxiety is not limited to the diagnostic categories traditionally termed *neuroses*, moreover. People with adjustment problems, depression, and psychotic disorders may also encounter problems with anxiety. Let's now consider the major types of anxiety disorders in terms of their features or symptoms, their causes, and the ways of treating them.

5.2 Describe the key features of panic disorder.

Panic Disorder

Panic disorder is characterized by repeated, unexpected *panic attacks*. Panic attacks are intense anxiety reactions that are accompanied by physical symptoms such as a pounding heart; rapid respiration, shortness of breath, or difficulty breathing; heavy perspiration; and weakness or dizziness (see Table 5.2). There is a stronger bodily component to panic attacks than to other forms of anxiety. The attacks are accompanied by feelings of sheer terror and a sense of imminent danger or impending doom and by an urge to escape the situation. They are usually accompanied by thoughts of losing control, "going crazy," or dying.

TABLE 5.2
Key Features of Panic Attacks

Panic attacks are episodes of intense fear or discomfort that develop suddenly and reach a peak within a few minutes. They are characterized by such features as the following:

- Pounding heart, tachycardia (rapid heart rate), or palpitations
- Sweating, trembling, or shaking
- Experience of choking or smothering sensations or shortness of breath
- Fears of either losing control and dying or going crazy
- Pain or discomfort in the chest
- Tingling or numbing sensations
- Nausea or stomach distress
- Dizziness, light-headedness, faintness, or unsteadiness
- Feelings of being detached from oneself, as if observing oneself from a distance, or sense of unreality or strangeness about one's surroundings
- Fear of losing control or going crazy
- Hot flashes or chills

During panic attacks, people tend to be keenly aware of changes in their heart rates and may think they are having a heart attack, even though there is really nothing wrong with their hearts. But since symptoms of panic attacks can mimic those of heart attacks or even severe allergic reactions, a thorough medical evaluation should be performed. **T / F**

As in the case of Michael, panic attacks generally begin suddenly and spontaneously, without any warning or clear triggering event. The attack builds to a peak of intensity within 10 to 15 minutes. Attacks usually last for minutes, but can last for hours. They tend to produce a strong urge to escape the situation in which they occur. For a diagnosis of panic disorder to be made, there must be the presence of recurrent panic attacks that begin unexpectedly—attacks that are not triggered by specific objects or situations. They seem to come out of the blue. However, subtle physical symptoms may precede an unexpected panic attack in the hour preceding an attack, even though the person may not be aware of it (Meuret et al., 2011).

The first panic attacks occur spontaneously or unexpectedly, but over time they may become associated with certain situations or cues, such as entering a crowded department store or boarding a train or airplane. The person may associate these situations with panic attacks in the past or may perceive them as difficult to escape from in the event of another attack.

People often describe panic attacks as the worst experiences of their lives. Their coping abilities are overwhelmed. They may feel they must flee. If flight seems useless, they may "freeze." There is a tendency to cling to others for help or support. Some people with panic attacks fear going out alone. Recurring panic attacks may become so difficult to cope with that panic sufferers become suicidal. People with panic disorder may avoid activities related to their attacks, such as exercise or venturing into places where attacks may occur or they fear may occur, or where they may be cut off from their usual supports. Consequently, panic disorder can lead to **agoraphobia**—an excessive fear of being in public places in which escape may be difficult or help unavailable (Berle et al., 2008). That said, panic disorder *without* accompanying agoraphobia is much more common than panic disorder *with* agoraphobia (Grant et al., 2006b).

Not all of the features in Table 5.2 need to be present during a panic attack. Nor are all panic attacks signs of panic disorder; about 10% of otherwise healthy people

People who experience a panic attack often think they are having a heart attack.

☑ **TRUE** People experiencing a panic attack may believe they are having a heart attack, even though their hearts are perfectly healthy.

Agoraphobia. People with agoraphobia fear venturing into open or crowded places. In extreme cases, they may become literally housebound out of fear of venturing away from the security of their home.

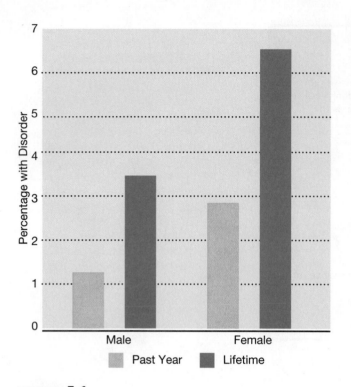

may experience an isolated attack in a given year (USDHHS, 1999). For a diagnosis of panic disorder to be made, the person must have experienced repeated, unexpected panic attacks, and at least one of the attacks must have been followed by a period of at least one month by either or both of the following features (Based on American Psychiatric Association, 2013):

a) Persistent fear of subsequent attacks or of the feared consequences of an attack, such as losing control, having a heart attack, or going crazy

b) Significant maladaptive change in behavior, such as limiting activities or refusing to leave the house or venture into public for fear of having another attack

According to recent national, representative survey, 5.1% of the general U.S. population develops panic disorder at some point in their lives (Grant et al., 2006b). Panic disorder usually begins in late adolescence through the mid-30s and occurs about twice as often among women than men (Grant et al., 2006b; Katon, 2006) (see Figure 5.1). This gender difference fits the general pattern that anxiety disorders are more common among women than men (McLean & Anderson, 2009; Seedat et al., 2009).

FIGURE 5.1

Prevalence of panic disorder by gender.
Panic disorder affects about two times as many women as men.

Source: Grant et al., 2006b.

> **Panic on the Golf Course**
>
> *Athletes are accustomed to playing through aches and pains and even injuries. But this was different. At a professional golf tournament in 2012, rookie golfer Charlie Beljan played through a panic attack that was so severe he feared he was having a heart attack (Crouse & Pennington, 2012). He spent that night in the hospital for medical tests, hooked up to medical equipment while still wearing his golf shoes. Fortunately, the tests revealed no signs of heart problems. All the more surprising, he went on to play another 36 rounds, winning the tournament—his first professional victory. The panic attack on the golf course was not his first. That happened a few months earlier, while he was on an airplane, requiring the pilot to make an emergency landing so he could receive medical treatment. Panic attacks typically occur spontaneously, so it may have just been an unfortunate coincidence he panicked during the tournament. Or the stress of playing in a major professional tournament may have increased his vulnerability to the cascading set of neurochemical changes in the body—the rapid heartbeat and difficulty breathing, for example—that accompany panic attacks. Along with further medical tests, Beljan also consulted a psychologist. As we'll see, psychological techniques can help cope with panic attacks.*
>
> *From the Author's Files*

Theoretical Perspectives

The prevailing view of panic disorder is that panic attacks involve a combination of cognitive and biological factors, of misattributions (misperceptions of underlying causes of changes in physical sensations) on the one hand and physiological reactions on the other. Figure 5.2 presents a schematic representation of the cognitive-biological model of panic disorder . Like Michael, who feared his physical symptoms were the first signs of a heart attack, panic-prone individuals tend to misattribute minor changes in internal bodily sensations to "underlying dire causes." For example, they may believe that sensations of momentary dizziness, light-headedness, or heart palpitations are signs of an impending heart attack, loss of control, or going crazy.

5.3 Describe the leading conceptual model of panic disorder.

FIGURE 5.2 Cognitive–biological model of panic disorder. In panic-prone people, perceptions of threat from internal or external cues lead to feelings of worry or fear, which are accompanied by changes in bodily sensations (e.g., heart racing or palpitations). Exaggerated, catastrophic interpretations of these sensations intensify perceptions of threat, resulting in yet more anxiety, more changes in bodily sensations, and so on in a vicious cycle that can culminate in a full-blown panic attack. Anxiety sensitivity increases the likelihood that people will overreact to bodily cues or symptoms of anxiety. Panic attacks may prompt avoidance of situations in which attacks have occurred or in which help might not be available.

Source: Adapted from Clark, 1986, and other sources.

As represented in Figure 5.2, the perception of bodily sensations as dire threats triggers anxiety, which is accompanied by activation of the sympathetic nervous system. Under control of the sympathetic nervous system, the adrenal glands release the stress hormones epinephrine (adrenaline) and norepinephrine (noradrenaline). These hormones intensify physical sensations by inducing accelerated heart rate, rapid breathing, and sweating. These changes in bodily sensations, in turn, become misinterpreted as evidence of an impending panic attack or, worse, as a catastrophe in the making ("My God, I'm having a heart attack!"). Catastrophic misattributions of bodily sensations reinforce perceptions of threat, which intensifies anxiety, leading to more anxiety-related bodily symptoms and yet more catastrophic misinterpretations in a vicious cycle that can quickly spiral into a full-fledged panic attack. In summary, the prevailing view of panic disorder reflects a combination of cognitive and biological factors, of misattributions (catastrophic misinterpretations of bodily sensations) on the one hand and physiological reactions and physical sensations on the other (Teachman, Marker, & Clerkin, 2010).

The changes in bodily sensations that trigger a panic attack may result from many factors, such as unrecognized *hyperventilation* (rapid breathing), exertion, changes in temperature, or reactions to certain drugs or medications. Or they may be fleeting, normally occurring changes in bodily states that typically go unnoticed. But panic-prone individuals may misattribute these bodily cues to dire causes, setting in motion a vicious cycle that can bring on a full-fledged attack.

Why are some people more prone to developing panic disorder? Here again, a combination of biological and cognitive factors come into play.

BIOLOGICAL FACTORS Evidence indicates that genetic factors contribute to proneness or vulnerability to panic disorder (e.g., Spatola et al., 2011). Genes may create a predisposition or likelihood, but not a certainty, that panic disorder or other psychological disorders will develop. Other factors play important roles, such as thinking patterns (Casey, Oei, & Newcombe, 2004). For example, people with panic disorder may misinterpret bodily sensations as signs of impending catastrophe. Panic-prone people also tend to be especially sensitive to their own physical sensations, such as heart palpitations.

The biological underpinnings of panic attacks may involve an unusually sensitive internal alarm system involving parts of the brain, especially the limbic system and frontal lobes, that normally become involved in responding to cues of threat or danger (Katon, 2006). Psychiatrist Donald Klein (1994) proposed a variation of the alarm model called the *suffocation false alarm theory*. He postulated that a defect in the brain's respiratory alarm system triggers a false alarm in response to minor cues of suffocation. In Klein's model, small changes in the level of carbon dioxide in the blood, perhaps resulting from hyperventilation, produce sensations of suffocation. These respiratory sensations trigger the respiratory alarm, leading to a cascade of physical symptoms associated with the classic panic attack: shortness of breath, smothering sensations, dizziness, faintness, increased heart rate or palpitations, trembling, sensations of hot or cold flashes, and feelings of nausea. Klein's intriguing proposal remains to be more fully tested and has received at best mixed support in the research literature to date (e.g., Vickers & McNally, 2005).

Let's also consider the role of neurotransmitters, especially *gamma-aminobutyric acid* (GABA). GABA is an *inhibitory* neurotransmitter, which means that it tones down excess activity in the central nervous system and helps quell the body's response to stress. When the action of GABA is inadequate, neurons may fire excessively, possibly bringing about seizures. In less dramatic cases, inadequate action of GABA may heighten states of anxiety or nervous tension. People with panic disorder tend to have low levels of GABA in some parts of the brain (Goddard et al., 2001). Also, we know that antianxiety drugs called benzodiazepines, which include the well-known Valium and Xanax, work specifically on GABA receptors, making these receiving stations more sensitive to the chemical, which enhances the calming effects of the neurotransmitter.

Other neurotransmitters, especially serotonin, help regulate emotional states (Weisstaub et al., 2006). Serotonin's role is supported by evidence, as discussed later in the chapter, that antidepressant drugs that specifically target serotonin activity in the brain have beneficial effects on some forms of anxiety as well as depression.

Further evidence of biological factors in panic disorder comes from studies comparing responses of people with panic disorder and control subjects to certain biological challenges that produce changes in bodily sensations (e.g., dizziness), such as infusion of the chemical *sodium lactate* or manipulation of carbon dioxide (CO_2) levels in the blood. CO_2 levels may be changed either by intentional hyperventilation (which reduces levels of CO_2 in the blood) or by inhalation of carbon dioxide (which increases CO_2 levels). Studies show that panic disorder patients are more likely than nonpatient controls to experience anxiety or symptoms of panic in response to these types of biological challenges (e.g., Coryell et al., 2006).

COGNITIVE FACTORS In referring to the anxiety facing the nation in the wake of the economic depression of the 1930s, President Franklin Roosevelt said in his 1932 inaugural address, "We have nothing to fear but fear itself." These words echo today in research on the role of *anxiety sensitivity* (AS) in the development of anxiety disorders, including panic disorder, phobic disorders, agoraphobia, and generalized anxiety disorder (Busscher et al., 2013; Ho et al., 2011; Naragon-Gainey, 2010; Wheaton et al., 2012).

Anxiety sensitivity, or *fear of fear itself*, involves fear of one's emotions and bodily sensations getting out of control. When people with high levels of AS experience bodily signs of anxiety, such as a racing heart or shortness of breath, they perceive these symptoms as signs of dire consequences or even an impending catastrophe, such as a heart attack. These catastrophic thoughts intensify their anxiety reactions, making them vulnerable to a vicious cycle of anxiety building on itself, which can lead to a full-blown panic attack. People with high levels of anxiety sensitivity also tend to avoid situations in which they have experienced anxiety in the past, a pattern we often see in people who have panic disorder accompanied by agoraphobia (Wilson & Hayward, 2006).

Anxiety sensitivity is influenced by genetic factors (Zavos et al., 2012). But environmental factors also play a role, including factors relating to ethnicity. A study of high school students showed that Asian and Hispanic students reported higher levels of anxiety sensitivity on the average than did Caucasian adolescents (Weems et al., 2002). However, anxiety sensitivity was less strongly connected to panic attacks in the Asian and Hispanic groups than in the Caucasian group. Other investigators find higher levels of anxiety sensitivity among American Indian and Alaska Native college students than among Caucasian college students (Zvolensky et al., 2001). These findings remind us of the need to consider ethnic differences when exploring the roots of abnormal behavior.

We shouldn't overlook the role that cognitive factors may play in determining oversensitivity of panic-prone people to biological challenges, such as manipulation of carbon dioxide levels in the blood. These challenges produce intense physical sensations that panic-prone people may misinterpret as signs of an impending heart attack or loss of control. Perhaps these misinterpretations—not any underlying biological sensitivities per se—are responsible for inducing the spiraling of anxiety that can quickly lead to a panic attack.

The fact that panic attacks often seem to come out of the blue seems to support the belief that the attacks are biologically triggered. However, the cues that set off many panic attacks may be internal, involving changes in bodily sensations, rather than external stimuli. Changes in internal (physical) cues, combined with catastrophic thinking, may lead to a spiraling of anxiety that culminates in a full-blown panic attack.

Treatment Approaches

5.4 Evaluate methods used to treat panic disorder.

The most widely used forms of treatment for panic disorder are drug therapy and cognitive-behavioral therapy. Drugs commonly used to treat depression, called *antidepressant drugs,* also have antianxiety and antipanic effects. The term *antidepressants* may be something of a misnomer since these drugs have broader effects than just treating depression.

Antidepressant drugs are used to treat people who are not depressed but are suffering from various anxiety disorders.

☑ **TRUE.** Antidepressant drugs also have antianxiety effects and are used to treat anxiety disorders such as panic disorder and social anxiety disorder, as well as obsessive-compulsive disorder.

Antidepressants help counter anxiety by normalizing activity of neurotransmitters in the brain. Antidepressants used for treating panic disorder include the tricyclics *imipramine* (Tofranil) and *clomipramine* (Anafranil) and the SSRIs *paroxetine* (Paxil) and *sertraline* (Zoloft) (Katon, 2006). However, some troublesome side effects may occur with these drugs, such as heavy sweating and heart palpitations, leading many patients to prematurely stop using the drugs. The high-potency antianxiety drug *alprazolam* (Xanax), a type of benzodiazepine, is also helpful in treating panic disorder, social anxiety, and generalized anxiety disorder. **T / F**

A potential problem with drug therapy is that patients may attribute clinical improvement to the drugs and not to their own resources. Let's also note that psychiatric drugs help control symptoms, but do not produce cures, and that relapses are common after patients discontinue medication. Reemergence of panic is likely unless cognitive-behavioral treatment is provided to help patients modify their cognitive overreactions to their bodily sensations (Clark, 1986).

Cognitive-behavioral therapists use a variety of techniques in treating panic disorder, including coping skills development for handling panic attacks, breathing retraining and relaxation training to reduce states of heightened bodily arousal, and exposure to situations linked to panic attacks and bodily cues associated with panicky symptoms. The therapist may help clients think differently about changes in bodily cues, such as sensations of dizziness or heart palpitations. By recognizing that these cues are fleeting sensations rather than signs of an impending heart attack or other catastrophe, clients learn to cope with them without panicking. Clients learn to replace catastrophizing thoughts and self-statements ("I'm having a heart attack") with calming, rational alternatives ("Calm down. These are panicky feelings that will soon pass."). Panic attack sufferers may also be reassured by having a medical examination to ensure that they are physically healthy and their physical symptoms are not signs of heart disease.

Breathing retraining is a technique that aims at restoring a normal level of carbon dioxide in the blood by having clients breathe slowly and deeply from the abdomen, avoiding the shallow, rapid breathing that leads to breathing off too much carbon dioxide. In some treatment programs, people with panic disorder are encouraged to intentionally induce panicky symptoms in order to learn how to cope with them, for example, by hyperventilating in the controlled setting of the treatment clinic or spinning around in a chair (Antony et al., 2006; Katon, 2006). Through firsthand experiences with panicky symptoms, patients learn to calm themselves down and cope with these sensations rather than overreact. Some commonly used elements in cognitive-behavioral therapy (CBT) for panic disorder are shown in Table 5.3.

TABLE 5.3
Elements of Cognitive-Behavioral Programs for Treatment of Panic Disorder

Self-monitoring	Keeping a log of panic attacks to help determine situational stimuli that might trigger them.
Exposure	A program of gradual exposure to situations in which panic attacks have occurred. During exposure trials, the person engages in self-relaxation and rational self-talk to prevent anxiety from spiraling out of control. In some programs, participants learn to tolerate changes in bodily sensations associated with panic attacks by experiencing these sensations within a controlled setting of the treatment clinic. The person may be spun around in a chair to induce feelings of dizziness, learning in the process that such sensations are not dangerous or signs of imminent harm.
Development of coping responses	Developing coping skills to interrupt the vicious cycle in which overreactions to anxiety cues or cardiovascular sensations culminate in panic attacks. Behavioral methods focus on deep, regular breathing and relaxation training. Cognitive methods focus on modifying catastrophic misinterpretations of bodily sensations. Breathing retraining may be used to help the individual avoid hyperventilation during panic attacks.

Coping with a Panic Attack

People who have panic attacks usually feel their hearts pounding such that they are overwhelmed and unable to cope. They typically feel an urge to flee the situation as quickly as possible. If escape is impossible, however, they may become immobilized and freeze until the attack dissipates. What can you do if you suffer a panic attack or an intense anxiety reaction? Here are a few coping responses.

- Don't let your breathing get out of hand. Breathe slowly and deeply.

- Try breathing into a paper bag. The carbon dioxide in the bag may help you calm down by restoring a more optimal balance between oxygen and carbon dioxide.

- Talk yourself down: Tell yourself to relax. Tell yourself you're not going to die. Tell yourself no matter how painful the attack is, it is likely to pass soon.

- Find someone to help you through the attack. Telephone someone you know and trust. Talk about anything at all until you regain control.

- Don't fall into the trap of making yourself housebound to avert future attacks.

- If you are uncertain about whether sensations such as pain or tightness in the chest have physical causes, seek immediate medical assistance. Even if you suspect your attack may "only" be one of anxiety, it is safer to have a medical evaluation than to diagnose yourself.

You need not suffer recurrent panic attacks and fears about loss of control. If your attacks are persistent or frightening, consult a professional. When in doubt, see a professional.

Michael, whom we introduced at the beginning of the chapter, was 30 when he suffered his first panic attack. Michael first sought a medical consultation with a cardiologist to rule out any underlying heart condition. He was relieved when he received a clean bill of health. Although the attacks continued for a time, Michael learned to gain a better sense of control over them. Here he describes what the process was like:

"I" "Glad They're Gone:" The Case of Michael

For me, it came down to not fearing them. Knowing that I was not going to die gave me confidence that I could handle them. When I began to feel an attack coming on, I would practice relaxation and talk myself through the attack. It really seemed to take the steam out of them. At first I was having an attack every week or so, but after a few months, they whittled down to about one a month, and then they were gone completely. Maybe it was how I was coping with them, or maybe they just disappeared as mysteriously as they began. I'm just glad they're gone.

From the Author's Files

A number of well-controlled studies attest to the effectiveness of CBT in treating panic disorder (e.g., Craske et al., 2009; Gloster et al., 2011; Gunter & Whittal, 2010). Investigators report average response rates to CBT treatment of more than 60% of cases (Schmidt & Keough, 2010). Despite the common belief that panic disorder is best treated with of cases psychiatric drugs, CBT compares favorably to drug therapy in the short-term and generally leads to better long-term results (Otto & Deveney, 2005; Schmidt & Keough, 2010).

Why does CBT produce longer-lasting results? In all likelihood, the answer is that CBT helps people acquire skills they can use even after treatment ends. Although psychiatric drugs can help quell panicky symptoms, they do not assist patients in developing new skills that can be used after drugs are discontinued. However, there are some cases in which a combination of psychological treatment and drug treatment is most effective. We should also note that other forms of psychological treatments may have therapeutic benefits. A recent study supported the treatment benefits of a form of psychodynamic therapy specifically designed to treat panic symptoms (Milrod et al., 2007).

5.5 Describe the key features and specific types of phobic disorders and **explain** how phobias develop.

TABLE 5.4

Typical Age of Onset for Various Phobias

	Mean Age of Onset
Animal phobia	7
Blood phobia	9
Injection phobia	8
Dental phobia	12
Social phobia	15
Claustrophobia	20
Agoraphobia	28

Source: Adapted from Grant et al., 2006c; Öst, 1987, 1992.

Phobic Disorders

The word **phobia** derives from the Greek *phobos,* meaning "fear." The concepts of fear and anxiety are closely related. *Fear* is anxiety experienced in response to a particular threat. A phobia is a fear of an object or situation that is disproportionate to the threat it poses. To experience a sense of gripping fear when your car is about to go out of control is not a phobia, because you truly are in danger. In phobic disorders, however, the fear exceeds any reasonable appraisal of danger. People with a driving phobia, for example, might become fearful even when they are driving well below the speed limit on a sunny day on an uncrowded highway. Or they might be so afraid that they will not drive or even ride in a car. Most, but not all, people with phobic disorders recognize their fears are excessive or unreasonable.

A curious thing about phobias is that they usually involve fears of the ordinary events in life, such as taking an elevator or driving on a highway, not the extraordinary. Phobias can become disabling when they interfere with daily tasks such as taking buses, planes, or trains; driving; shopping; or even leaving the house.

Different types of phobias usually appear at different ages, as noted in Table 5.4. The ages of onset appear to reflect levels of cognitive development and life experiences. Fears of animals are frequent subjects of children's fantasies, for example. Agoraphobia, in contrast, often follows the development of panic attacks beginning in adulthood.

Types of Phobic Disorders

The *DSM* recognizes three distinct phobic disorders: *specific phobia, social anxiety disorder (social phobia),* and *agoraphobia.*

SPECIFIC PHOBIAS A **specific phobia** is a persistent, excessive fear of a specific object or situation that is out of proportion to the actual danger these objects or situations pose. There are many types of specific phobias, including the following (APA, 2013):

- Fear of animals, such as fear of spiders, insects, and dogs
- Fear of natural environments, such as fear of heights (*acrophobia*), storms, or water
- Fear of blood-injection injury, such as fear of needles or invasive medical procedures
- Fear of specific situations, such as fear of enclosed spaces (*claustrophobia*), elevators, or airplanes

> **Carla Passes the Bar But Not the Courthouse Staircase: A Case of Specific Phobia**
>
> *Passing the bar exam was a significant milestone in Carla's life, but it left her terrified at the thought of entering the county courthouse. She wasn't afraid of encountering a hostile judge or losing a case, but of climbing the stairs leading to a second floor promenade where the courtrooms were located. Carla, 27, suffered from acrophobia, or fear of heights. "It's funny, you know," Carla told her therapist. "I have no problem flying or looking out the window of a plane at 30,000 feet. But the escalator at the mall throws me into a tailspin. It's just any situation where I could possibly fall, like over the side of a balcony or banister."*
>
> *People with anxiety disorders try to avoid situations or objects they fear. Carla scouted out the courthouse before she was scheduled to appear. She was relieved to find a service elevator in the rear of the building she could use instead of the stairs. She told her fellow attorneys with whom she was presenting the case that she suffered from a heart condition and couldn't climb stairs. Not suspecting the real problem, one of the attorneys said, "This is great. I never knew this elevator existed. Thanks for finding it."*
>
> *From the Author's Files*

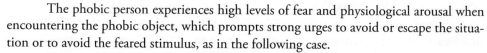

Three types of phobic disorder. The man in the photo directly above has a specific phobia for dogs, a common phobia that may have an evolutionary origin. The young woman in the top-right photo would like to join others but keeps to herself because of social anxiety, an intense fear of social criticism and rejection. The woman in the bottom-right photo has acrophobia, or a fear of heights, which makes her feel uncomfortable even on a second floor balcony.

The phobic person experiences high levels of fear and physiological arousal when encountering the phobic object, which prompts strong urges to avoid or escape the situation or to avoid the feared stimulus, as in the following case.

To rise to the level of a diagnosable disorder, the phobia must significantly affect the person's lifestyle or functioning or cause significant distress. You may have a fear of snakes, but unless your fear interferes with your daily life or causes you significant emotional distress, it would not warrant a diagnosis of phobic disorder.

Specific phobias often begin in childhood. Many children develop passing fears of specific objects or situations. Some, however, go on to develop chronic clinically significant phobias. Claustrophobia seems to develop later than most other specific phobias, with a mean age of onset of 20 years (see Table 5.4).

Specific phobias are among the most common psychological disorders, affecting about 9% of the general population at some point in their lives (Conway et al., 2006). The fear, anxiety, and avoidance associated with specific phobias typically persist for six months or longer, and often for years or even decades unless the phobia is successfully treated.

Anxiety disorders in general and phobic disorders in particular are more common in women than in men (McLean & Anderson, 2009). Gender differences in development of phobias may reflect cultural influences that socialize women into more dependent roles in society, for example, to be timid rather than brave or adventurous. Examiners also need to be aware of cultural factors when making diagnostic judgments. Fears of magic or spirits are common in some cultures and should not be considered a sign of a phobic disorder unless the fear is excessive for the culture in which it occurs and leads to significant emotional distress or impaired functioning.

People with specific phobias will often recognize that their fears are exaggerated or unfounded. But they still are afraid, as in the case of this young woman whose fear of medical injections almost prevented her from getting married. **T / F**

truth OR fiction

People with phobias believe their fears are well founded.

☑ **FALSE.** Actually, many people with phobias recognize that their fears are exaggerated or unfounded but remain fearful.

"I" "This Will Sound Crazy, But ...": A Case of Specific Phobia

This will sound crazy, but I wouldn't get married because I couldn't stand the idea of getting the blood test. [Blood tests for syphilis were required at the time.] I finally worked up the courage to ask my doctor if he would put me out with ether or barbiturates—taken by pills—so that I could have the blood test. At first he was incredulous. Then he became sort of sympathetic but said that he couldn't risk putting me under any kind of general anesthesia just to draw some blood. I asked him if he would consider faking the report, but he said that administrative procedures made that impossible.

Then he got me really going. He said that getting tested for marriage was likely to be one of my small life problems. He told me about minor medical problems that could arise and make it necessary for blood to be drawn, or to have an IV in my arm, so his message was I should try to come to grips with my fear. I nearly fainted while he was talking about these things, so he gave it up.

The story has half a happy ending. We finally got married in [a state] where we found out they no longer insisted on blood tests. But if I develop one of those problems the doctor was talking about, or if I need a blood test for some other reason, even if it's life-threatening, I really don't know what I'll do. But maybe if I faint when they're going to [draw blood], I won't know about it anyway, right?

People have me wrong, you know. They think I'm scared of the pain. I don't like pain—I'm not a masochist—but pain has nothing to do with it. You could pinch my arm till I turned black and blue and I'd tolerate it. I wouldn't like it, but I wouldn't start shaking and sweating and faint on you. But even if I didn't feel the needle at all—just the knowledge that it was in me is what I couldn't take.

→ *From the Author's Files*

SOCIAL ANXIETY DISORDER (SOCIAL PHOBIA) It is not abnormal to experience some degree of fear or anxiety in social situations such as dating, attending parties or social gatherings, or giving a talk or presentation to a class or group. Yet people with **social anxiety disorder** (also called *social phobia*) have such an intense fear of social situations that they may avoid them altogether or endure them only with great distress. The underlying problem is an excessive fear of negative evaluations from others—fear of being rejected, humiliated, or embarrassed.

Imagine what it's like to have social anxiety disorder. You are always fearful of doing or saying something humiliating or embarrassing. You may feel as if a thousand eyes are scrutinizing your every move. You are probably your own harshest critic and are likely to become fixated on whether your performance measures up when interacting with others. Negative thoughts run through your mind: "Did I say the right thing? Do they think I'm stupid?" You may even experience a full-fledged panic attack in social situations.

Stage fright, speech anxiety, and dating fears are common forms of social anxiety. People with social anxiety may find excuses for declining social invitations. They may eat lunch at their desks to avoid socializing with coworkers and avoid situations in which they might meet new people. Or they may find themselves in social situations and attempt a quick escape at the first sign of anxiety. Relief from anxiety negatively reinforces escape behavior, but escape prevents learning how to cope with fear-evoking situations. Leaving the scene while still feeling anxious only serves to strengthen the link between the social situation and anxiety. Some people with social anxiety are unable to order food in a restaurant for fear the server or their companions might make fun of the foods they order or how they pronounce them.

Social anxiety or fear can severely impair a person's daily functioning and quality of life. Fear may prevent people from completing educational goals, advancing in their

 **Watch** the **Video** *Steve: Social Phobia* on **MyPsychLab**

careers, or even holding a job in which they need to interact with others. In some cases, social fears are limited to speaking or performing in front of others, such as in the case of "stage fright" or in public speaking situations. People with this form of social anxiety disorder do not fear nonperformance social situations, such as when meeting new people or interacting with others in social gatherings.

People with social anxiety often turn to tranquilizers or try to "medicate" themselves with alcohol when preparing for social interactions (see Figure 5.3). In extreme cases, they may become so fearful of interacting with others that they become essentially housebound.

Nationally representative surveys show that about 5% of U.S. adults are affected by social anxiety disorder at some point in their lives (Conway et al., 2006; Grant et al., 2006c). The disorder is more common among women than men, perhaps because of the greater social or cultural pressures placed on young women to please others and earn their approval.

The average age of onset of social anxiety disorder is about 15 years (Grant et al., 2006c). About 80% of affected people develop the disorder by age 20 (Stein & Stein, 2008). Social anxiety is strongly associated with a history of childhood shyness (Cox, MacPherson, & Enns, 2004). Consistent with the *diathesis–stress model* (see Chapter 2), shyness may represent a diathesis or predisposition that makes a person more vulnerable to developing social anxiety in the face of stressful experiences, such as traumatic social encounters (e.g., being embarrassed in front of others). Social anxiety tends to be a chronic, persistent disorder, lasting about 16 years on average (Grant et al., 2006c). Yet despite its early development and the many negative effects it has on social functioning, people with social anxiety first receive help at an average age of 27 (Grant et al., 2006c).

AGORAPHOBIA The word *agoraphobia* is derived from Greek words meaning "fear of the marketplace," which suggests a fear of being out in open, busy areas. People with agoraphobia may fear shopping in crowded stores; walking through crowded streets; crossing a bridge; traveling by bus, train, or car; eating in restaurants; being in a movie theater; or even leaving the house. They may structure their lives around avoiding exposure to fearful situations and in some cases become housebound for months or even years, even to the

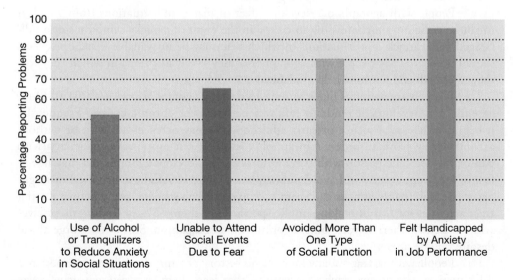

FIGURE 5.3

Percentage of people with social anxiety reporting specific difficulties associated with their fears of social situations. More than 90% of people with social anxiety feel handicapped by anxiety in their jobs.

Source: Adapted from Turner & Beidel, 1989.

@Issue: Where Does Shyness End and Social Anxiety Disorder Begin?

We began this chapter by noting that anxiety is a common emotional experience that may be adaptive in situations involving a threat to our safety or well-being. It is common and may even be expected to feel anxious on a job interview or when taking an important test. Anxiety becomes maladaptive, however, when it is either inappropriate to the situation (no real threat or danger exists) or excessive (beyond expectable reactions) and when it interferes significantly with a person's social, occupational, or other areas of functioning (e.g., turning down a job on a high floors in an office building because of a fear of heights).

But what about shyness, a common personality trait? Many of us are shy, but where should we draw a line between ordinary shyness and social anxiety disorder? As Bernardo Carducci, a prominent shyness researcher at Indiana University, points out, "shyness is not a disease, a psychiatric disorder, a character flaw, or a personality defect that needs to be 'cured'" (cited in Nevid & Rathus, 2013). Many famous people in history were reported to be shy, among them Charles Darwin, Albert Einstein, and Harry Potter creator, J. K. Rowling (Cain, 2011). Carducci speaks of shy people becoming successfully shy, not by changing who they are, but by accepting themselves and learning how to interact with others, such as by working in a volunteer organization, learning conversation starters,

and expanding social networks. As Carducci notes, "Successfully shy individuals do not need to change who they are—remember, there is nothing wrong with being a shy person. Successfully shy individuals change the way they think and act. They think less about themselves and more about others and take actions that are more other-focused and less self-focused" (cited in Nevid & Rathus, 2013).

We should be careful not to pathologize normal variations in personality traits such as shyness or make people who are naturally shy think of themselves as suffering from a psychological disorder in need of treatment. In the *DSM* system, a diagnosis of an anxiety disorder must be based on evidence of significant impairment of functioning or marked personal distress. Sometimes what the shy person needs is public speaking training, not psychotherapy or medication (Cain, 2011).

In thinking critically about the issue, answer the following questions:

- Think of someone you know who is painfully shy, perhaps even yourself? Does this person suffer from a diagnosable psychological disorder? Why or why not?
- What do you think it means to be successfully shy?

truth OR fiction

Some people are so fearful of leaving their homes that they are unable to venture outside even to mail a letter.

☑ **TRUE.** Some people with agoraphobia become literally housebound and unable to venture outside even to mail a letter.

extent of being unable to venture outside to mail a letter. Agoraphobia has the potential to become the most incapacitating type of phobia.

People with agoraphobia develop a fear of places and situations from which it might be difficult or embarrassing to escape in the event of panicky symptoms or a full-fledged panic attack or of situations in which help may be unavailable if such problems should occur. Elderly people with agoraphobia may avoid situations in which they fear they might fall and not have help available. T / F

Women are about as likely as men to develop agoraphobia (APA, 2013). Once agoraphobia develops, it tends to follow a persistent or chronic course. Frequently, it begins in late adolescence or early adulthood. It may occur either with or without accompanying panic disorder. Agoraphobia is often, but not always, associated with panic disorder. The person with panic disorder who develops agoraphobia may live in fear of recurrent attacks and avoid public places where attacks have occurred or might occur. Because panic attacks can seem to come out of nowhere, some people restrict their activities for fear of making public spectacles of themselves or finding themselves without help. Others venture outside only with a companion. Still others forge ahead despite intense anxiety.

People with agoraphobia who have no history of panic disorder may experience mild panicky symptoms, such as dizziness, that lead them to avoid venturing away from places where they feel safe or secure. They, too, tend to become dependent on others for support. The following case of agoraphobia without a history of panic disorder illustrates the dependencies often associated with agoraphobia.

Helen: A Case of Agoraphobia

Helen, a 59-year-old widow, became increasingly agoraphobic 3 years after the death of her husband. By the time she came for treatment, she was essentially housebound, refusing to leave her home except under the strongest urging of her daughter, Mary, age 32, and only if Mary accompanied her. Her daughter and 36-year-old son, Pete, did her shopping and took care of her other needs as best they could. However, the burden of caring for their mother, on top of their other responsibilities, was becoming too great for them to bear. They insisted that Helen begin treatment, and Helen begrudgingly acceded to their demands.

Helen was accompanied to her evaluation session by Mary. She was a frail-looking woman who entered the office clutching Mary's arm and insisted that Mary stay throughout the interview. Helen recounted that she had lost her husband and mother within 3 months of one another; her father had died 20 years earlier. Although she had never experienced a panic attack, she always considered herself an insecure, fearful person. Even so, she had been able to function in meeting the needs of her family until the deaths of her husband and mother left her feeling abandoned and alone. She had now become afraid of "just about everything" and was terrified of being out on her own, lest something bad would happen and she wouldn't be able to cope with it. Even at home, she was fearful that she might lose Mary and Pete. She needed continual reassurance from them that they too wouldn't abandon her.

→ *From the Author's Files*

Theoretical Perspectives

Theoretical approaches to understanding the development of phobias have a long history in psychology, beginning with the psychodynamic perspective.

PSYCHODYNAMIC PERSPECTIVES From the psychodynamic perspective, anxiety is a danger signal that threatening impulses of a sexual or aggressive (murderous or suicidal) nature are nearing the level of awareness. To fend off these threatening impulses, the ego mobilizes its defense mechanisms. In phobias, the Freudian defense mechanism of *projection* comes into play. A phobic reaction is a projection of the person's own threatening impulses onto the phobic object. For instance, a fear of knives or other sharp instruments may represent the projection of one's own destructive impulses onto the phobic object. The phobia serves a useful function. Avoiding contact with sharp instruments prevents these destructive wishes toward the self or others from becoming consciously realized or acted on. The threatening impulses remain safely repressed. Similarly, people with acrophobia may harbor unconscious wishes to jump that are controlled by avoiding heights. The phobic object or situation symbolizes or represents these unconscious wishes or desires. The person is aware of the phobia, but not of the unconscious impulses it symbolizes.

LEARNING PERSPECTIVES The classic learning perspective on phobias was offered by psychologist O. Hobart Mowrer (1960). Mowrer's **two-factor model** incorporated roles for both classical and operant conditioning in the development of phobias. The fear component of phobia is believed to be acquired through classical conditioning, as previously neutral objects and situations gain the capacity to evoke fear by being paired with noxious or aversive stimuli. A child who is frightened by a barking dog may acquire a phobia for dogs. A child who receives a painful injection may develop a phobia for hypodermic syringes. Many people with phobias had experiences in which the phobic object or situation was associated with aversive experiences (e.g., getting trapped on an elevator).

Consider the case of Phyllis, a 32-year-old writer and mother of two sons. Phyllis had not used an elevator in 16 years. Her life revolved around finding ways to avoid appointments and social events on high floors. She had suffered from a fear of elevators since the age of 8, when she had been stuck between floors with her grandmother. In conditioning terms, the unconditioned stimulus was the unpleasant experience of being stuck on the elevator and the conditioned stimulus was the elevator itself.

As Mowrer pointed out, the avoidance component of phobias is acquired and maintained by operant conditioning, specifically by *negative reinforcement*. That is, relief from anxiety *negatively reinforces* the avoidance of fearful stimuli, which thus serves to strengthen the avoidance response. Phyllis learned to relieve her anxiety over riding the elevator by opting for the stairs instead. Avoidance works to relieve anxiety, but at a significant cost. By avoiding the phobic stimulus (e.g., elevators), the fear may persist for years, even a lifetime. On the other hand, fear can be weakened and even eliminated by repeated, uneventful encounters with the phobic stimulus. In classical conditioning terms, *extinction* is the weakening of the conditioned response (e.g., the fear component of a phobia) when the conditioned stimulus (the phobic object or stimulus) is repeatedly presented in the absence of the unconditioned stimulus (an aversive or painful stimulus).

Conditioning accounts for some, but certainly not all, phobias. In many cases, perhaps even most, people with specific phobias can't recall any aversive experiences with the objects they fear. Learning theorists might counter that memories of conditioning experiences may be blurred by the passage of time or that the experience occurred too early in life to be recalled verbally. But contemporary learning theorists highlight the role of another form of learning—*observational learning*—that does not require direct conditioning of fears. In this form of learning, observing parents or significant others model a fearful reaction to a stimulus can lead to the acquisition of a fearful response. In an illustrative study of 42 people with severe phobias for spiders, observational learning apparently played a more prominent role in fear acquisition than did conditioning (Merckelbach, Arnitz, & de Jong, 1991). Moreover, simply receiving information from others, such as hearing others speak about the dangers posed by a particular stimulus, spiders, for example, can also lead to the development of phobias (Merckelbach et al., 1996).

Learning models help account for the development of phobias (Field, 2006). But why do some people seem to acquire fear responses more readily than others? The biological and cognitive perspectives may offer some insights.

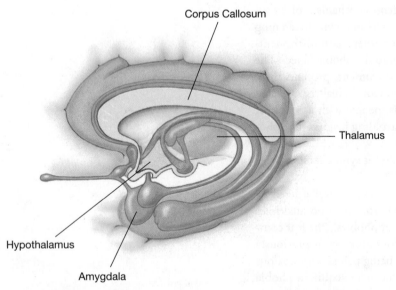

Corpus Callosum

Thalamus

Hypothalamus

Amygdala

FIGURE 5.4

The amygdala and limbic system. The amygdala, the brain's fear-triggering center, is part of the brain's limbic system, which comprises a group of interconnected structures located below the cerebral cortex, which also includes parts of the thalamus and hypothalamus and other nearby structures. The limbic system is involved in memory formation and emotional processing. Recent evidence links anxiety disorders to an overly excitable amygdala.

BIOLOGICAL PERSPECTIVES Genetic factors can predispose individuals to develop anxiety disorders such as panic disorder and phobic disorder (Coryell et al., 2006; Kendler, 2005; Smoller et al., 2008). But how do genes affect a person's likelihood of developing anxiety disorders?

For one thing, we've learned that people with variations of particular genes are more prone to develop fear responses and to have greater difficulty overcoming them (Lonsdorf et al., 2009). For example, people with a variation of a particular gene who are exposed to fearful stimuli show greater activation of a brain structure called the *amygdala,* an almond-shaped structure in the brain's limbic system (Hariri et al., 2002). Located below the cerebral cortex, the limbic system comprises a group of interconnected structures involved in memory formation and processing emotional responses.

The amygdala produces fear responses to triggering stimuli without conscious thought (Agren et al., 2012; Forgas, 2008). It works as a kind of "emotional computer" whenever we encounter a threat or danger (Coelho & Purkis, 2009) (see Figure 5.4). Higher brain centers, especially the *prefrontal cortex* in the frontal lobes of the cerebral cortex, have the job of evaluating threatening stimuli more carefully. As noted in Chapter 2, the prefrontal cortex, which lies directly under your forehead, is responsible for many higher mental functions, such as thinking, problem solving, reasoning, and decision making. So when you see an object in the road that resembles a snake, the amygdala bolts into action, inducing a fear response that makes you stop or jump backwards and sends quivers of fear racing through your body. But a few moments later, the prefrontal cortex sizes up the threat more carefully, allowing you to breathe a sigh of relief ("It's only a stick. Relax.").

In people with anxiety disorders, however, the amygdala may become overly excitable, inducing fear in response to mildly threatening situations or environmental cues (Nitschke et al., 2009). Supporting this view, researchers find increased levels of activation of the amygdala in people with social anxiety and in combat veterans with PTSD (Stein & Stein, 2008). In another recent study, anxious adolescents showed a greater amygdala response to faces with fearful expressions than did nonpatient controls (Beesdo et al., 2009). For people with anxiety disorders, the amygdala may become overreactive to cues of threat, fear, and rejection.

In related research, investigators used functional magnetic resonance imaging (fMRI) to examine how the brain responds to negative social cues (Blair et al., 2008). Investigators compared brain responses of people with the generalized form of social anxiety and nonphobic controls to negative social comments about them (e.g., "You are ugly."). The socially phobic individuals showed greater levels of activation in the amygdala and in the some parts of the prefrontal cortex (see Figure 5.5). The amygdala may trigger the initial fear response to negative social cues like criticism, while the prefrontal cortex may be engaged processes relating to self-reflection about these cues ("Why did he say that about me? Am I really so ugly?").

Investigators have also used experimental animals, such as laboratory rats, to explore how the brain responds to fearful stimuli. An influential study showed that a part of the prefrontal cortex in the rat's brain sends a kind of "all-clear" signal to the amygdala, quelling fearful reactions (see Figure 5.6) (Milad & Quirk, 2002). The investigators first conditioned rats to respond with fear to a tone by repeatedly pairing the tone with shock. The rats froze whenever they heard the tone. The investigators then extinguished the fear response by presenting the tone repeatedly without the shock. Following extinction, neurons in the middle of the prefrontal cortex fired up whenever the tone was sounded, sending signals through neural pathways to the amygdala. The more of these neurons that fired, the less the rats froze (NIH, 2002). The discovery that the prefrontal cortex sends a safety signal to the amygdala may eventually lead to new treatments for people with phobias that work by turning on the brain's all-clear signal.

Research on the biological underpinnings of fear is continuing. For example, investigators are targeting particular types of neurons involved in fear memories. Destroying these types of neurons in laboratory mice literally erased memories of earlier learned fear responses (Han et al., 2009). Although extending laboratory research with mice to helping people overcome phobic responses is a stretch, experimental work with animals may lead to the development of drugs that might selectively block or interfere with fear responses in humans.

Are humans genetically predisposed to acquire phobic responses to certain classes of stimuli ? People appear to be more likely to have fears of snakes and spiders than of rabbits, for example. This belief in a biological predisposition to acquire fears of certain types of objects or situations, called *prepared conditioning,* suggests that evolution favored the survival of human ancestors who were genetically predisposed to develop fears of potentially threatening objects, such as large animals, snakes, spiders, and other "creepy-crawlies"; of heights; of enclosed spaces; and even of strangers. This model may explain why we are more likely to develop fears of spiders or heights than of objects that appeared

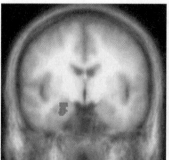
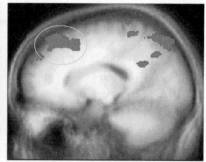

FIGURE 5.5

Brain responses to criticism in people with generalized social anxiety. fMRI scans of the brain in response to criticism showed greater activity in the amygdala (left) and parts of the prefrontal cortex (circled in yellow, right) in people with generalized social anxiety.
Source: NIMH, 2008.

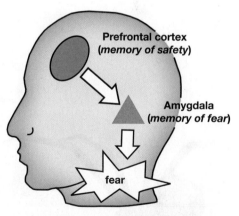

FIGURE 5.6

The "all-clear" signal quells fear. Evidence from animal studies shows that all-clear signals from the prefrontal cortex to the amygdala inhibit fear responses. This discovery may lead to treatments that can help quell fear reactions in humans.

Source: Milad & Quirk, 2002. Figure reprinted from "Mimicking brain's 'all clear' quells fear in rats," *NIH News Release,* Posted November 6, 2002.

We may be genetically predisposed to acquire fears of objects that posed a danger to ancestral humans.

☑ **TRUE.** Some theorists believe that we are genetically predisposed to acquire certain fears, such as fears of large animals and snakes. The ability to readily acquire these fears may have had survival value to ancestral humans.

much later on the evolutionary scene, such as guns or knives, although these later-appearing objects pose more direct threats to our survival today. **T / F**

COGNITIVE PERSPECTIVES Recent research highlights the importance of cognitive factors in determining proneness to phobias, including factors such as oversensitivity to threatening cues, overpredictions of dangerousness, and self-defeating thoughts and irrational beliefs (e.g., Armfield, 2006; Schultz & Heimberg, 2008; Wenzel et al., 2005):

1. *Oversensitivity to threatening cues.* People with phobias tend to perceive danger in situations most people consider safe, such as riding on elevators or driving over bridges. Similarly, people with social anxiety tend to be overly sensitive to social cues of rejection or negative evaluation from others (Schmidt et al., 2009).

   We all possess an internal alarm system that is sensitive to cues of threat. The amygdala in the brain's limbic system plays a key role in this early warning system. This system may have had evolutionary advantages for ancestral humans by increasing the chances of survival in a hostile environment. Early humans who responded quickly to signs of threat, such as a rustling sound in the bush that may have indicated a lurking predator about to pounce, may have been better prepared to take defensive action (to fight or flee) than those with less sensitive alarm systems.

   The emotion of fear is a key element in this alarm system and may have motivated our early ancestors to take defensive action, which in turn may have helped them survive. People today who have specific phobias and other anxiety disorders may have inherited an acutely sensitive internal alarm that leads them to become overly sensitive to threatening cues. They are always on high alert for threatening objects or stimuli. If there is a spider in the room, the spider phobic in the group will likely be the first to notice it and point it out (Purkis, Lester, & Field, 2011). Other research suggests that the more a person is afraid of spiders, the bigger he or she perceives them to be (Vasey et al., 2012). **T / F**

2. *Overprediction of danger.* Phobic individuals tend to overpredict how much fear or anxiety they will experience in the fearful situation. The person with a snake phobia, for example, may expect to tremble when he or she encounters a snake in a cage. People with dental phobia may have exaggerated expectations of the pain they will experience during dental visits. Typically speaking, the actual fear or pain experienced during exposure to the phobic stimulus is a good deal less than what people expect. Yet the tendency to expect the worst encourages avoidance of feared situations, which in turn prevents the individual from learning to manage and overcome anxiety.

   Overprediction of dental pain and fear may also lead people to postpone or cancel regular dental visits, which can contribute to more serious dental problems down the road. But actual exposure to fearful situations may lead to more accurate predictions of the person's level of fear. A clinical implication is that with repeated exposure, people with anxiety disorders may come to anticipate their responses to fear-inducing stimuli more accurately, leading to reductions of fear expectancies. This in turn may reduce avoidance tendencies.

3. *Self-defeating thoughts and irrational beliefs.* Self-defeating thoughts can heighten and perpetuate anxiety and phobic disorders. When faced with fear-evoking stimuli, the person may think, "I've got to get out of here," or "My heart is going to leap out of my chest." Thoughts like these intensify autonomic arousal, disrupt planning, magnify the aversiveness of stimuli, prompt avoidance behavior, and decrease self-efficacy expectancies concerning a person's ability to control the situation. Similarly, people with social anxiety may think, "I'll sound stupid," whenever they have an opportunity to speak in front of a group of people (Hoffmann et al., 2004). Such self-defeating thoughts may stifle social participation.

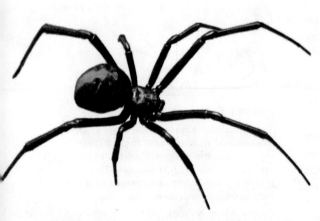

"It was as big as my head, I swear!" Investigators find that the more afraid people are of spiders, the larger they perceive them to be.

People with phobias also display more irrational beliefs of the type cataloged by Albert Ellis (see Chapter 2) than do nonfearful people. These irrational beliefs may involve exaggerated needs to be approved of by everyone they meet and to avoid any situation in which negative appraisal from others might arise. Consider these beliefs: "What if I have an anxiety attack in front of other people? They might think I'm crazy. I couldn't stand it if they looked at me that way." The results of an early study may hit close to home: College men who believed it was awful (not just unfortunate) to be turned down when requesting a date showed more social anxiety than those who were less likely to catastrophize rejection (Gormally et al., 1981).

Before going on, you may wish to review Figure 5.7, which illustrates a conceptual model for understanding phobias in terms of roles of learning influences and vulnerability factors such as a genetic predisposition and cognitive factors.

truth OR fiction

If there is a spider in the room, the spider phobic in the group will likely be the first to notice it and point it out.

☑ **TRUE.** People with specific phobias tend to be on high alert for detecting fearful stimuli or objects.

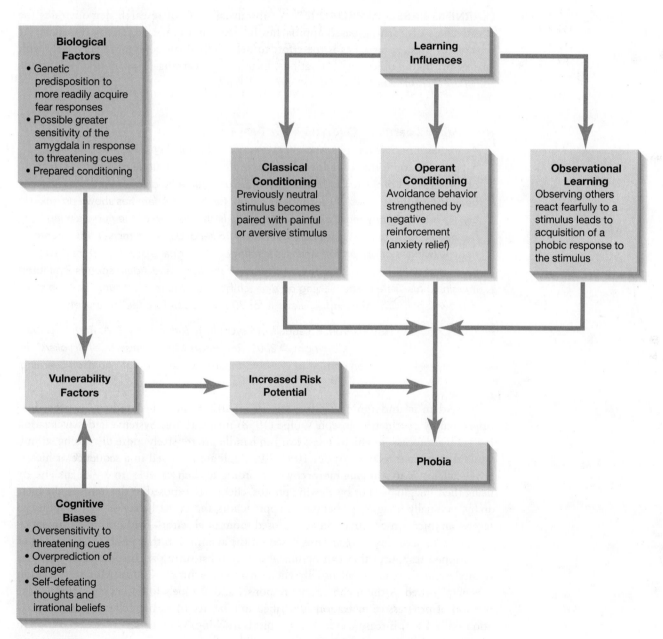

FIGURE 5.7

A multifactorial model of phobia. Learning influences play a key role in the acquisition of many phobias. But whether these learning experiences lead to the development of phobias may also depend on vulnerability factors, such as a genetic predisposition and cognitive factors.

Treatment Approaches

Traditional psychoanalysis fosters awareness of how clients' fears symbolize their inner conflicts, so the ego can be freed from expending its energy on repression. Modern psychodynamic therapies also foster clients' awareness of inner sources of conflict. They focus to a greater extent than do traditional approaches on exploring sources of anxiety that arise from current rather than past relationships, however, and they encourage clients to develop more adaptive behaviors. Such therapies are briefer and more directed toward specific problems than traditional psychoanalysis. Although psychodynamic therapies may prove to be helpful in treating some cases of anxiety disorders, there is little compelling empirical support documenting their overall effectiveness (USDHHS, 1999).

The major contemporary treatment approaches to specific phobias, as for other anxiety disorders, derive from the learning, cognitive, and biological perspectives.

LEARNING-BASED APPROACHES A substantial body of research demonstrates the effectiveness of learning-based approaches in treating a range of anxiety disorders. At the core of these approaches is the effort to help individuals cope more effectively with anxiety-provoking objects and situations. Examples of learning-based approaches include *systematic desensitization, gradual exposure,* and *flooding.*

> **Adam Learns to Overcome His Fear of Injections**
>
> *Adam has a phobia for receiving injections. His behavior therapist treats him as he reclines in a comfortable padded chair. In a state of deep muscle relaxation, Adam observes slides projected on a screen. A slide of a nurse holding a needle has just been shown three times, 30 seconds at a time. Each time Adam has shown no anxiety. So now a slightly more discomforting slide is shown: one of the nurse aiming the needle toward someone's bare arm. After 15 seconds, our armchair adventurer notices twinges of discomfort and raises a finger as a signal (speaking might disturb his relaxation). The projector operator turns off the light, and Adam spends 2 minutes imagining his "safe scene"—lying on a beach beneath the tropical sun. Then the slide is shown again. This time Adam views it for 30 seconds before feeling anxiety.*
>
> *From Essentials of Psychology (6th ed.) by S. A. Rathus, p. 537. Copyright © 2001. Reprinted with permission of Brooks/Cole, an imprint of Wadsworth Group, a division of Thomson Learning.*

Adam is undergoing **systematic desensitization,** a fear-reduction procedure originated by psychiatrist Joseph Wolpe (1958) in the 1950s. Systematic desensitization is a gradual process in which clients learn to handle progressively more disturbing stimuli while they remain relaxed. About 10 to 20 stimuli are arranged in a sequence or hierarchy—called a **fear-stimulus hierarchy**—according to their capacity to evoke anxiety. By using their imagination or by viewing photos, clients are exposed to the items in the hierarchy, gradually imagining themselves approaching the target behavior—be it ability to receive an injection or remain in an enclosed room or elevator—without undue anxiety.

Systematic desensitization is based on the assumption that phobias are learned or conditioned responses that can be unlearned by substituting an incompatible response to anxiety in situations that usually elicit anxiety (Rachman, 2000). Muscle relaxation is generally used as the incompatible response, and Wolpe's followers generally use the method of progressive relaxation (described in Chapter 6) to help clients acquire relaxation skills. For this reason, Adam's therapist is teaching Adam to experience relaxation in the presence of (otherwise) anxiety-evoking slides of needles.

Systematic desensitization creates a set of conditions that can lead to extinction of fear responses. The technique fosters extinction by providing opportunities for repeated exposure to phobic stimuli in imagination without aversive consequences.

Gradual exposure uses a stepwise approach in which phobic individuals gradually confront the objects or situations they fear. Repeated exposure to a phobic stimulus in the absence of any aversive event ("nothing bad happening") can lead to extinction, or gradual weakening, of the phobic response, even to the point that it is eliminated. Gradual exposure also leads to cognitive changes. The person comes to perceive the previously feared object or situation as harmless and perceives him- or herself as capable of handling the situation more effectively.

Exposure therapy can take several forms, including *imaginal exposure* (imagining oneself in the fearful situation) and *in vivo exposure* (actual encounters with phobic stimuli in real life). In vivo exposure may be more effective than imaginal exposure, but both techniques are often used in therapy. The effectiveness of exposure therapy for phobias is well established, making it the treatment of choice for many phobias (e.g., Gloster et al., 2011; Hofman, 2008; McEvoy, 2008).

Consider social anxiety, for example. In exposure therapy, socially phobic clients may be instructed to enter increasingly stressful social situations (e.g., eating and conversing with coworkers in the cafeteria) and to remain in those situations until the anxiety and urge to escape lessen. The therapist may help guide them during exposure trials, gradually withdrawing direct support so that clients become capable of handling the situations on their own. Exposure therapy for agoraphobia generally follows a stepwise course in which the client is exposed to increasingly fearful stimulus situations, such as walking through congested streets or shopping in department stores. A trusted companion or perhaps the therapist may accompany the person during the exposure trials. The eventual goal is for the person to be able to handle each situation alone and without discomfort or an urge to escape. Gradual exposure was used in treating the following case of claustrophobia.

Gradual exposure. The client confronts fearful stimuli in real-life situations in a step-by-step fashion and may be accompanied by a therapist or trusted companion serving in a supportive role. To encourage the person to accomplish the exposure tasks increasingly on his or her own, the therapist or companion gradually withdraws direct support. Gradual exposure is often combined with cognitive techniques that focus on helping the client replace anxiety-producing thoughts and beliefs with calming, rational alternatives.

→ Kevin Combats His Fear of Elevators: A Case of Claustrophobia

Claustrophobia (fear of enclosed spaces) is not very unusual, although Kevin's case was. Kevin's claustrophobia took the form of a fear of riding on elevators. What made the case so unusual was Kevin's occupation: He worked as an elevator mechanic. Kevin spent his work days repairing elevators. Unless it was absolutely necessary, however, Kevin managed to complete the repairs without riding in the elevator. He would climb the stairs to the floor where an elevator was stuck, make repairs, and hit the down button. He would then race downstairs to see that the elevator had operated correctly. When his work required an elevator ride, panic would seize him as the doors closed. Kevin tried to cope by praying for divine intervention to prevent him from passing out before the doors opened.

Kevin related the origin of his phobia to an accident three years earlier in which he had been pinned in his overturned car for nearly an hour. He remembered feelings of helplessness and suffocation. Kevin developed claustrophobia—a fear of situations from which he could not escape, such as flying on an airplane, driving in a tunnel, taking public transportation, and of course, riding in an elevator. Kevin's fear had become so incapacitating that he was seriously considering switching careers, although the change would require considerable financial sacrifice. Each night he lay awake wondering whether he would be able to cope the next day if he were required to test-ride an elevator.

Kevin's therapy involved gradual exposure in which he followed a stepwise program of exposure to increasingly fearful stimuli. A typical anxiety hierarchy for helping people overcome a fear of riding on elevators might include the following steps:

1. *Standing outside the elevator*
2. *Standing in the elevator with the door open*
3. *Standing in the elevator with the door closed*

4. *Taking the elevator down one floor*
5. *Taking the elevator up one floor*
6. *Taking the elevator down two floors*
7. *Taking the elevator up two floors*
8. *Taking the elevator down two floors and then up two floors*
9. *Taking the elevator down to the basement*
10. *Taking the elevator up to the highest floor*
11. *Taking the elevator all the way down and then all the way up*

Clients begin at step 1 and do not progress to step 2 until they are able to remain calm on the first. If they become anxious, they remove themselves from the situation and regain calmness by practicing muscle relaxation or focusing on soothing mental imagery. The encounter is then repeated as often as necessary to reach and sustain feelings of calmness. They then proceed to the next step, repeating the process.

Kevin was also trained to practice self-relaxation and to talk calmly and rationally to himself to help him remain calm during his exposure trials. Whenever he began to feel even slightly anxious, he would tell himself to calm down and relax. He was able to counter the disruptive belief that he was going to fall apart if he was trapped in an elevator with rational self-statements such as, "Just relax. I may experience some anxiety, but it's nothing that I haven't been through before. In a few moments I'll feel relieved."

Kevin slowly overcame his phobia but still occasionally experienced some anxiety, which he interpreted as a reminder of his former phobia. He did not exaggerate the importance of these feelings. Now and then it dawned on him that an elevator he was servicing had once occasioned fear. One day following his treatment, Kevin was repairing an elevator, which serviced a bank vault 100 feet underground. The experience of moving deeper and deeper underground aroused fear, but Kevin did not panic. He repeated to himself, "It's only a couple of seconds and I'll be out." By the time he took his second trip down, he was much calmer.

From the Author's Files

Flooding is a form of exposure therapy in which subjects are exposed to high levels of fear-inducing stimuli either in imagination or in real-life situations. *Why?* The belief is that anxiety represents a conditioned response to a phobic stimulus and should dissipate if the individual remains in the phobic situation for a long enough period of time without harmful consequences. Most individuals with phobias avoid confronting phobic stimuli or beat a hasty retreat at the first opportunity if they cannot avoid them. Consequently, they lack the opportunity to unlearn the fear response. In flooding, the person purposely engages in a highly feared situation, such as in the case of a person with social anxiety sitting down at a lunch table where people have already gathered and remain for a long enough period of time for anxiety to dissipate. Flooding has been used effectively in treating various anxiety disorders, including social anxiety and PTSD (Moulds & Nixon, 2006).

VIRTUAL THERAPY: THE NEXT BEST THING TO BEING THERE In the movie *The Matrix,* the lead character played by Keanu Reeves comes to realize that the world he believes is real is merely an illusion, a complex virtual environment so lifelike that people cannot tell it isn't real. *The Matrix* is science fiction, but the use of virtual reality as a therapeutic tool is science fact.

Virtual reality therapy (VRT) is a behavior therapy technique that uses computer-generated simulated environments as therapeutic tools. By donning a specialized helmet and gloves that are connected to a computer, a person with a fear of heights, for example, can encounter frightening stimuli in this virtual world, such as riding a glass-enclosed elevator to the top floor of an imaginary hotel, peering over a railing on a balcony on the 20th floor, or crossing a virtual Golden Gate Bridge. By a process of exposure to a series of increasingly frightening virtual stimuli, while progressing only when fear at each step diminishes, people can learn to overcome fears in virtual reality in much the same way they would had they followed a program of gradual exposure in real-life situations. **T / F**

Virtual therapy has been used successfully in helping people overcome phobias, such as fear of heights and fear of flying (Coelho et al., 2009; Parsons & Rizzo, 2008). In one research study, virtual reality was just as effective as real-life exposure in treating fear of flying, with both treatments showing better results than an untreated (waiting list) control condition (Rothbaum et al., 2002). Ninety-two percent of VRT participants succeeded in flying on a commercial airliner in the year following treatment. A recent review showed substantial treatment benefits for VRT in treating anxiety disorders; in fact, treatment effects for VRT were slightly larger than those for in vivo (actual) exposure treatment (Powers & Emmelkamp, 2008).

Overcoming fears with virtual reality. Virtual reality technology can be used to help people overcome phobias.

Virtual reality therapy offers some advantages over traditional exposure-based treatments. For one thing, it is often difficult or impossible to arrange in real life the types of exposure experiences that can be simulated in virtual reality, such as repeated airplane takeoffs and landings. Virtual therapy also allows for greater control over the stimulus environment, as when the participant controls the intensity and range of stimuli used during virtual exposure sessions (Zimand et al., 2002). Individuals may also be more willing to perform certain fearful tasks in virtual reality than in real life.

In order for virtual therapy to be effective, says psychologist Barbara Rothbaum, an early pioneer in the use of the technique, the person must become immersed in the experience and believe at some level that it is real and not like watching a videotape. "If the first person had put the helmet on and said, 'This isn't scary,' it wouldn't have worked," Dr. Rothbaum said. "But you get the same physiological changes—the racing heart, the sweat—that you would in the actual place" (cited in Goleman, 1995b, p. C11). Today, with advances in virtual reality technology, the simulated virtual environment is convincing enough to evoke intense anxiety in fearful people (Lubell, 2004).

We have only begun to explore the potential therapeutic uses of virtual technology. Therapists are using virtual therapy to treat many kinds of fears as well as other disorders, including posttraumatic stress disorder, social anxiety disorder, and even autism spectrum disorders (DeAngelis, 2012b). Therapists are helping substance abusers work toward recovery by placing them in virtual bars and other simulated situations, like family conflicts, that are linked to their addictive behaviors. Virtual therapy using simulated wartime scenes can help reduce combat-related PTSD symptoms in active duty soldiers and returning veterans (e.g., Reger et al., 2011). In other applications, virtual therapy may help clients work through unresolved conflicts with significant figures in their lives by allowing them to confront these "people" in a virtual environment.

COGNITIVE THERAPY Through rational emotive behavior therapy, Albert Ellis might have shown people with social anxiety how irrational needs for social approval and perfectionism produce unnecessary anxiety in social interactions. Eliminating exaggerated needs for social approval is apparently a key therapeutic factor.

Cognitive therapists seek to identify and correct dysfunctional or distorted beliefs. For example, people with social anxiety might think no one at a party will want to talk with them and that they will wind up lonely and isolated for the rest of their lives. Cognitive therapists help clients recognize the logical flaws in their thinking and to view situations rationally. Clients may be asked to gather evidence to test their beliefs, which may lead them to alter beliefs they find are not grounded in reality. Therapists may encourage

truth OR fiction

Therapists have used virtual reality to help people overcome phobias.

☑ **TRUE.** Virtual reality therapy has been used successfully in helping people overcome phobias, including fear of heights.

clients with social anxiety to test their beliefs that they are bound to be ignored, rejected, or ridiculed by others in social gatherings by attending a party, initiating conversations, and monitoring other people's reactions. Therapists may also help clients develop social skills to improve their interpersonal effectiveness and teach them how to handle social rejection, if it should occur, without catastrophizing.

One example of a cognitive technique is **cognitive restructuring,** a method in which therapists help clients pinpoint self-defeating thoughts and generate rational alternatives they can use to cope with anxiety-provoking situations. For example, Kevin (see earlier case study) learned to replace self-defeating thoughts with rational alternatives and to practice speaking rationally and calmly to himself during his exposure trials.

Cognitive-behavioral therapy is the general term used to apply to therapeutic approaches that combine behavioral and cognitive therapy techniques. CBT practitioners incorporate behavioral techniques, such as exposure, along with techniques drawn from the cognitive therapies of Ellis, Beck, and others. For example, in treating social anxiety, therapists often combine exposure treatment with cognitive restructuring techniques that help clients replace anxiety-inducing thoughts with calming alternatives (Rapee, Gaston, & Abbott, 2009). Evidence supports the effectiveness of CBT in treating many types of phobia, including social anxiety and claustrophobia (e.g., Choy, Fyer, & Lipsitz, 2007; McEvoy et al., 2012; Rachman, 2009).

DRUG THERAPY Evidence also supports the use of antidepressant drugs, including sertraline (Zoloft) and paroxetine (Paxil), in treating social anxiety (Liebowitz, Gelenberg, & Munjack, 2005; Schneier, 2006). A combination of psychotherapy and drug therapy in the form of antidepressant medication may be more effective in some cases than either treatment approach alone (Blanco et al., 2010).

Generalized Anxiety Disorder

5.7 Describe the key features of generalized anxiety disorder and ways of understanding and treating it.

Watch the Video *Philip: Generalized Anxiety Disorder* on **MyPsychLab**

Generalized anxiety disorder (GAD) is characterized by excessive anxiety and worry that is not limited to any one object, situation, or activity. Normally, anxiety can be an adaptive response, a kind of built-in bodily warning system to signal when something is threatening and requires immediate attention. But for people with generalized anxiety disorder, anxiety becomes excessive, becomes difficult to control, and is accompanied by physical symptoms such as restlessness, jumpiness, and muscle tension (Donegan & Dugas, 2012; Torpy, Burke, & Golub, 2011).

The central feature of GAD is excessive worry (Newman & Llera, 2011;Starcevic et al., 2012). People with GAD tend to be chronic worriers—even lifelong worriers. They may worry about many things, including their health, their finances, the well-being of their children, and their social relationships. They tend to worry about everyday, minor things, such as getting stuck in traffic, and about unlikely future events, such as going bankrupt. They may avoid situations or events in which they expect that something "bad" might happen. Or they might repeatedly seek reassurance from others that everything is okay. To reach a diagnostic level, GAD needs to be associated with either marked emotional distress or significant impairment in daily functioning. Children with generalized anxiety disorder tend to worry about academics, athletics, and social aspects of school life.

The emotional distress associated with GAD interferes significantly with the person's daily life. GAD frequently occurs together with other disorders, including depression or other anxiety disorders such as agoraphobia and obsessive–compulsive disorder. Other related features include restlessness; feeling tense, keyed up, or on edge; becoming easily fatigued; having difficulty concentrating or finding one's mind going blank; irritability; muscle tension; and disturbances of sleep, such as difficulty falling asleep, staying asleep, or having restless and unsatisfying sleep.

GAD tends to be a stable disorder that initially arises in the mid-teens to mid-20s and then typically follows a lifelong course. The lifetime prevalence of GAD in the

Take This Pill Before Seeing Your Therapist

The drug *D-cycloserine* (DSQ), an antibiotic used to treat tuberculosis, might one day be used for an entirely different purpose—to boost the effects of psychotherapy. The drug acts on synaptic connections in the brain involved in processes of learning and memory, so investigators suspect that it might enhance the effects of learning-based treatments such as cognitive-behavioral therapy. More about this in a moment, but first some background.

Experimental research with laboratory mice showed that DSQ boosted ability on tests of memory of particular objects seen earlier and places where these objects had been placed (Zlomuzica et al., 2007). Other research showed that DSQ sped up extinction of fear responses in rats (Davis et al., 2005). As you'll recall, extinction is the process by which a conditioned fear response is weakened as a result of repeated exposure to the conditioned stimulus (i.e., the fearful object or situation) in the absence of the aversive unconditioned stimulus (i.e., a painful or unpleasant stimulus).

The drug acts on a particular receptor for the neurotransmitter *glutamate,* a chemical in the brain that keeps the central nervous system aroused and kicking. The drug caffeine also increases glutamate activity, which explains why many people start their morning with a cup of caffeine-rich coffee or tea to increase their level of arousal and alertness.

The underlying brain mechanism explaining the effectiveness of DSQ in boosting extinction of fear responses remains unknown, but investigators suspect that the amygdala, the fear-triggering part of the brain, is involved (Davis et al., 2006). One possibility is that DSQ acts on glutamate receptors in the amygdala to speed up the process of extinction (Britton et al., 2007).

Might DSQ have similar effects on anxiety disorders in people? Evidence is building that DSQ can boost the effectiveness of exposure therapy in treating PTSD, especially in more severe cases that require longer treatment (Cukor et al., 2009; de Kleine et al, 2012). It appears that DCS may jump-start exposure treatment, speeding up its effects (Chasson et al., 2010).

Other studies find booster effects of DSQ when it is combined with behavioral exposure therapy in treating social anxiety (Guastella et al., 2008; Hofmann et al., 2006). In another study, people with a fear of heights received either DSQ or a placebo drug before participating in exposure sessions using a virtual reality simulation of height situations (Davis et al., 2006). Participants who received the active drug showed greater improvement than those who received the placebo.

The use of drugs to boost psychological interventions is still in its infancy, but a day may come when popping a pill before seeing your behavior therapist becomes routine.

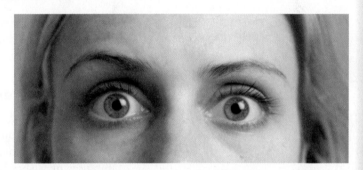

Can drugs boost the effects of behavior therapy? Investigators are exploring whether the drug D-cycloserine can boost the effects of behavior (learning-based) therapy of phobias and other anxiety disorders.

---

general U.S. population is estimated to be around 4% overall, but is about twice as common in women as in men (Conway et al., 2006). About 2% of adults are affected by GAD in any given year (Grant et al., 2005). In the following case, we find a number of features of generalized anxiety disorder.

→ **"Worrying About Worrying": A Case of Generalized Anxiety Disorder**
Earl was a 52-year-old supervisor at the automobile plant. His hands trembled as he spoke. His cheeks were pale. His face was somewhat boyish, making his hair seem grayed with worry.
    He was reasonably successful in his work, although he noted that he was not a "star." His marriage of nearly three decades was in "reasonably good shape," although sexual relations were "less than exciting—I shake so much that it isn't easy to get involved." The mortgage on the house was not a burden and would be paid off within five years, but "I don't know what it is; I think about money all the time."

The three children were doing well. One was employed, one was in college, and one was in high school. But "with everything going on these days, how can you not worry about them? I'm up for hours worrying about them."

"But it's the strangest thing," Earl shook his head. "I swear I'll find myself worrying when there's nothing in my head. I don't know how to describe it. It's like I'm worrying first and then there's something in my head to worry about. It's not like I start thinking about this or that and I see it's bad and then I worry. And then the shakes come, and then, of course, I'm worrying about worrying, if you know what I mean. I want to run away; I don't want anyone to see me. You can't direct workers when you're shaking."

Going to work had become a major chore. "I can't stand the noises of the assembly lines. I just feel jumpy all the time. It's like I expect something awful to happen. When it gets bad like that I'll be out of work for a day or two with shakes."

Earl had been worked up "for everything; my doctor took blood, saliva, urine, you name it. He listened to everything, he put things inside me. He had other people look at me. He told me to stay away from coffee and alcohol. Then from tea. Then from chocolate and Coca-Cola, because there's a little bit of caffeine [in them]. He gave me Valium [an antianxiety drug or minor tranquilizer] and I thought I was in heaven for a while. Then it stopped working, and he switched me to something else. Then that stopped working, and he switched me back. Then he said he was 'out of chemical miracles' and I better see a shrink or something. Maybe it was something from my childhood."

→ *From the Author's Files*

Theoretical Perspectives

Freud characterized the type of anxiety we see in GAD as "free floating" because people seem to carry it from situation or situation. From a psychodynamic perspective, generalized anxiety represents the threatened leakage of unacceptable sexual or aggressive impulses or wishes into conscious awareness. The person is aware of the anxiety but not its underlying source. The problem with speculating about the unconscious origins of anxiety is that they lie beyond the reach of direct scientific tests. We cannot directly observe or measure unconscious impulses.

From a learning perspective, generalized anxiety is precisely that: generalization of anxiety across many situations. People concerned about broad life themes, such as finances, health, and family matters, are likely to experience apprehension or worry in a variety of settings. Anxiety would thus become connected with almost any environment or situation.

The cognitive perspective on GAD emphasizes the role of exaggerated or distorted thoughts and beliefs, especially beliefs that underlie worry. People with GAD tend to worry just about everything. They also tend to be overly attentive to threatening cues in the environment (Amir et al., 2009), perceiving danger and calamitous consequences at every turn. Consequently, they feel continually on edge, as their nervous systems respond to the perception of threat or danger with activation of the sympathetic nervous system, leading to increased states of bodily arousal and the accompanying feelings of anxiety.

The cognitive and biological perspectives converge in evidence showing irregularities in the functioning of the amygdala in GAD patients and in its connections to the brain's thinking center, the prefrontal cortex (PFC) (Etkin et al., 2009) (see Figure 5.8). It appears that

FIGURE 5.8 The areas in red in the front part of this brain image show parts of the prefrontal cortex that have stronger connections to the amygdala in the brains of GAD patients than in the brains of nonpatient controls. These areas are involved in processes relating to distraction and worry.

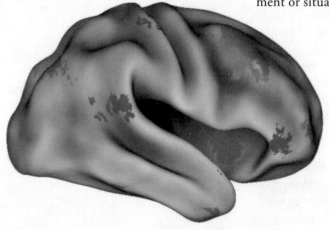

in people with GAD, the PFC may rely on worrying as a cognitive strategy for dealing with the fear generated by an overactive amygdala.

We also suspect irregularities in neurotransmitter activity in GAD. We mentioned earlier that antianxiety drugs such as the benzodiazepines *diazepam* (Valium) and *alprazolam* (Xanax) increase the effects of GABA, an inhibitory neurotransmitter that tones down central nervous system arousal. Similarly, irregularities of the neurotransmitter serotonin are implicated in GAD on the basis of evidence that GAD responds favorably to the antidepressant drug *paroxetine* (Paxil), which specifically targets serotonin (Sheehan & Mao, 2003). Neurotransmitters work on brain structures that regulate emotional states such as anxiety, so it is possible that an overreactivity of these brain structures (the amygdala, for example) is involved. 👁

👁 **Watch** the **Video** *Christy: Generalized Anxiety Disorder with Insomnia* in **MyPsychLab**

Treatment Approaches

The major forms of treatment of generalized anxiety disorder are psychiatric drugs and cognitive-behavioral therapy. Antidepressant drugs, such as *sertraline* (Zoloft) and *paroxetine* (Paxil), can help relieve anxiety symptoms (Allgulander et al., 2004; Liebowitz et al., 2002). Bear in mind, however, that although psychiatric drugs may help relieve anxiety, they do not cure the underlying problem. Once the drugs are discontinued, the symptoms often return.

Cognitive-behavioral therapists use a combination of techniques in treating GAD, including training in relaxation skills; learning to substitute calming, adaptive thoughts for intrusive, worrisome thoughts; and learning skills of decatastrophizing (e.g., avoiding tendencies to think the worst). Evidence from controlled studies shows substantial therapeutic benefits of cognitive-behavioral therapy in treating GAD (DiMauro et al., 2013; Donegan & Dugas, 2012; Newman et al., 2011). The effectiveness of CBT is comparable to that of drug therapy, but with lower dropout rates, which indicates that the psychological treatment is better tolerated by patients (Mitte, 2005). In one illustrative study, the great majority of GAD patients treated with either behavioral or cognitive methods, or the combination of these methods, no longer met diagnostic criteria for the disorder following treatment (Borkovec et al., 2002).

Ethnic Differences in Anxiety Disorders

5.8 **Evaluate** ethnic differences in rates of anxiety disorders.

Although anxiety disorders have been the subject of extensive study, little attention has been directed toward examining ethnic differences in the prevalence of these disorders. Are anxiety disorders more common in certain racial or ethnic groups? We might think that stressors that African Americans in our society are more likely to encounter, such as racism and economic hardship, might contribute to a higher rate of anxiety disorders in this population group. On the other hand, an alternative argument is that African Americans, by dint of having to cope with these hardships in early life, develop resiliency in the face of stress that shields them from anxiety disorders. Evidence from large epidemiological surveys lends support to this alternative argument.

According to the best available evidence drawn from a large national survey, the National Comorbidity Survey Replication (NCS-R), showed that African Americans (or non-Hispanic Blacks) and Latinos have lower rates of social anxiety disorder and generalized anxiety disorder than do European Americans (non-Hispanic Whites) (Breslau et al., 2006). We have evidence from yet another large national survey showing higher lifetime rates of panic disorder in European Americans than in Latinos, African Americans, or Asian Americans (Grant et al., 2006b).

Let's also note that anxiety disorders are not unique to our culture. Panic disorder, for example, is known to occur in many countries, perhaps even universally. However, the specific features of panic attacks, such as shortness of breath or fear of dying, may vary from culture to culture. Some culture-bound syndromes have features similar to panic attacks, such as *ataque de nervios* (see Table 3.2 in Chapter 3).

TYING it together

Many psychologists believe that the origins of anxiety disorders involve a complex interplay of environmental, physiological, and psychological factors. Complicating matters further is that different causal pathways may be at work in different cases. Given that multiple causes are at work, it is not surprising that different approaches to treating anxiety disorders have emerged.

To illustrate, let's offer a possible causal pathway for panic disorder. Some people may inherit a genetic predisposition, or diathesis, that makes them overly sensitive to minor changes in bodily sensations. Cognitive factors may also be involved. Physical sensations associated with changing carbon dioxide levels, such as dizziness, tingling, or numbness, may be misconstrued as signs of an impending disaster—suffocation, heart attack, or loss of control. This in turn may lead, like dominoes falling in line, to an anxiety reaction that quickly spirals into a full-fledged panic attack.

Whether this happens may depend on another vulnerability factor, the individual's level of anxiety sensitivity. People with high levels of anxiety sensitivity may be more likely to panic in response to changes in their physical sensations. In some cases, a person's anxiety sensitivity may be so high that panic ensues, even without a genetic predisposition. Over time, panic attacks may come to be triggered by exposure to internal or external cues (conditioned stimuli) that have been associated with panic attacks in the past, such as heart palpitations or boarding a train or elevator. As we saw in the case of Michael at the beginning of the chapter, changes in physical sensations may be misconstrued as signs of an impending heart attack, setting the stage for a cycle of physiological responses and catastrophic thinking that can result in a full-blown panic attack. Helping panic sufferers develop more effective coping skills for handling anxiety symptoms without catastrophizing can help break this vicious cycle.

5.9 Describe the key features of obsessive–compulsive disorder and ways of understanding and treating it.

👁 Watch the Video *Dave: Obsessive Compulsive Disorder (OCD)* on **MyPsychLab**

Obsessive–Compulsive and Related Disorders

The *DSM-5* category of Obsessive–Compulsive and Related Disorders contains a hodge-podge of disorders that have in common a pattern of compulsive or driven repetitive behaviors that are associated with significant personal distress or impaired functioning in meeting demands of daily life (see Table 5.5). In the following sections we focus on three major disorders in this category: *obsessive–compulsive disorder, body dysmorphic disorder,* and *hoarding disorder.* Two other related disorders, *trichotillomania (hair pulling disorder)* and *excoriation (skin picking) disorder,* are described in Table 5.5.

Obsessive–Compulsive Disorder

People with **obsessive–compulsive disorder (OCD)** are troubled by recurrent obsessions or compulsions, or both obsessions and compulsions, that are time-consuming, such as lasting more than an hour a day, or causing significant distress or interference with a person's normal routines or occupational or social functioning (APA, 2013; Parmet, Lynm, & Golub, 2011). An **obsession** is a recurrent, persistent, and unwanted thought, urge, or mental image that seems beyond the person's ability to control. Obsessions can be potent and persistent enough to interfere with daily life and can engender significant distress and anxiety. One may wonder endlessly whether one has locked the doors and shut the windows, for example. One may be obsessed with the urge to do harm to one's spouse. One can have intrusive mental images or fantasies, such as the recurrent fantasy of a young mother that her children had been run over by traffic on the way home from school. Obsessions generally cause anxiety or distress, but not in all cases (APA, 2013). 👁

A **compulsion** is a repetitive behavior (e.g., hand washing or checking door locks) or mental act (e.g., praying, repeating certain words, or counting) that the person feels compelled or driven to perform (APA, 2013). Compulsions typically occur in response to obsessional thoughts and are frequent and forceful enough to interfere with daily life or cause significant distress. Table 5.6 shows some relatively common obsessions and

TABLE 5.5
Overview of Obsessive-Compulsive and Related Disorders

Type of Disorder	Approximate Lifetime Prevalence in Population	Description	Associated Features
Obsessive–Compulsive Disorder	About 2% to 3%	Recurrent obsessions (recurrent, intrusive thoughts) and/or compulsions (repetitive behaviors the person feels compelled to perform)	• Obsessions generate anxiety that may be at least partially relieved by performance of the compulsive rituals
Body Dysmorphic Disorder	Unknown	Preoccupation with an imagined or exaggerated physical defect	• Person may believe that others think less of him or her as a person because of the perceived defect • Person may engage in compulsive behaviors, such as excessive grooming, that aim to correct the perceived defect
Hoarding Disorder (compulsive hoarding)	2% to 5%	Strong need to accumulate possessions, regardless of their value, and persistent difficulty or distress associated with discarding them	• Leads to cluttering the home with piles of collected materials, such as books, clothing, household items, and even junk mail • Can have a range of harmful effects including difficulty using the living space and conflicts with needs of family members and others • The person may feel a sense of security from accumulating and retaining otherwise useless or unnecessary stuff • The person may fail to recognize that the hoarding behavior is a problem, despite the obvious evidence
Trichotillomania (Hair-Pulling Disorder)	Unknown	Compulsive or repetitive hair pulling resulting in hair loss	• Hair pulling may involve the scalp or other parts of the body and may result in noticeable bald spots • Hair pulling may have self-soothing effects and be used as a coping response in dealing with stress or anxiety
Excoriation (Skin-Picking) Disorder	1.4% or higher (in adults)	Compulsive or repetitive picking of the skin, resulting in skin lesions or sores that may never completely heal because of repeated picking at scabs	• Skin picking may involve scratching, picking, rubbing, or digging into the skin • Skin picking may be an attempt to remove slight imperfections or irregularities in the skin or used as a coping response to stress or anxiety

Sources: Prevalence rates derived from APA, 2013, Mataix-Cols et al., 2010, and other sources.

compulsions. In the following first-person account, a man describes his obsessive concerns about having caused harm to other people (and even insects) as the result of his actions.

> ## "I" "Tormenting Thoughts and Secret Rituals"
>
> My compulsions are caused by fears of hurting someone through my negligence. It's always the same mental rigmarole. Making sure the doors are latched and the gas jets are off. Making sure I switch off the light with just the right amount of pressure, so I don't cause an electrical problem. Making sure I shift the car's gears cleanly, so I don't damage the machinery... .
>
> I fantasize about finding an island in the South Pacific and living alone. That would take the pressure off; if I would harm anyone it would just be me. Yet even if I were alone, I'd still have my worries, because even insects can be a problem. Sometimes when I take the garbage out, I'm afraid that I've stepped on an ant. I stare down to see if there is an ant kicking and writhing in agony. I took a walk last week by a pond, but I couldn't enjoy it because I remembered it was spawning season, and I worried that I might be stepping on the eggs of bass or bluegill.

I realize that other people don't do these things. Mainly, it's that I don't want to go through the guilt of having hurt anything. It's selfish in that sense. I don't care about them as much as I do about not feeling the guilt.

From Osborn, 1998

Most compulsions fall into two categories: cleaning rituals and checking rituals. Rituals can become the focal point of life. A compulsive hand washer, Corinne, engaged in elaborate hand-washing rituals. She spent 3 to 4 hours daily at the sink and complained, "My hands look like lobster claws." Some people literally take hours checking and rechecking that all the appliances are off before they leave home, and still remain in doubt.

Another woman with a checking compulsion described an elaborate ritual she insisted her husband perform to complete the simple act of taking out the garbage (Colas, 1998). The couple lived in an apartment and deposited their garbage in a common dumpster. The ritual was intended to keep the neighbors' germs out of her apartment. She insisted that after her husband tossed the garbage without ever touching the dumpster, he then needed to take his shoes off when returning to the apartment and wash his hands, using his clean hand to pump the soap dispenser so that it would not become contaminated. Her husband then needed to repeat the process 20 times, one time for each of 20 sealed bags of garbage. If she noticed a stain on his shirt, say a brown liquid stain, she insisted he go into the dumpster and find the bag matching the stain in order to identify the liquid. If he refused, she would hound him for hours until he relented.

Compulsions often accompany obsessions and may at least partially relieve the anxiety created by obsessional thinking. By washing their hands 40 or 50 times in a row each time they touch a public doorknob, compulsive hand washers may experience some relief from the anxiety engendered by the obsessive thought that germs or dirt still linger in the folds of skin. They may believe that the compulsive ritual will help prevent a dreaded event, such as germ contamination. However, the repetitive nature of the compulsive behavior far exceeds any reasonable steps one can take as a precaution. In effect, the solution (i.e., performing the compulsive ritual) becomes the problem (Salkovskis et al., 2003). The person becomes trapped in a vicious pattern of worrisome intrusive thoughts leading to compulsive rituals. People with OCD generally recognize that their obsessive concerns are excessive or irrational, but feel incapable of stopping them (Belkin, 2005).

Obsessive–compulsive disorder affects between 2% and 3% of the general population at some point in their lives (Keeley et al., 2008). It usually begins in adolescence or early adulthood, but may emerge in childhood, even in early childhood (Parmet, Lynm, &

Table 5.6

Examples of Obsessive Thoughts and Compulsive Behaviors

Obsessive Thought Patterns	Compulsive Behavior Patterns
Thinking that one's hands remain dirty despite repeated washing	Rechecking one's work time and time again
Difficulty shaking the thought that a loved one has been hurt or killed	Rechecking the doors or gas jets before leaving home
Repeatedly thinking that one has left the door to the house unlocked	Constantly washing one's hands to keep them clean and germ free
Worrying constantly that the gas jets in the house were not turned off	
Repeatedly thinking that one has done terrible things to loved ones	

Golub, 2011). A Swedish study found that although most OCD patients eventually showed some improvement, most also continued to have some symptoms of the disorder through the course of their lives (Skoog & Skoog, 1999). The disorder occurs about equally often in men and women. The nearby case example of Jack illustrates a checking compulsion.

THEORETICAL PERSPECTIVES Within the psychodynamic tradition, obsessions represent leakage of unconscious urges or impulses into consciousness, and compulsions are acts that help keep these impulses repressed. Obsessive thoughts about contamination by dirt or germs may represent the threatened emergence of unconscious infantile wishes to soil oneself and play with feces. The compulsion (in this case, cleanliness rituals) helps keep such wishes at bay. The psychodynamic model remains largely speculative, in large part because of the difficulty (some would say impossibility) of arranging scientific tests to determine the existence of unconscious impulses and conflicts.

Vulnerability to OCD is in part determined by genetic factors (Taylor, 2011; Taylor & Jang, 2011). Just what genes are involved in OCD remains under study, but research evidence points to a possible role for a gene that works to tone down the actions of a particular neurotransmitter, *glutamate,* at least in some cases of the disorder (Arnold et al., 2006; Dickel et al., 2006). On a related note, many people with OCD, especially those who developed the disorder during childhood, have a history of tic disorders, leading investigators to believe there is a genetic link between tic disorders and OCD (Eichstedt & Arnold, 2001; Stewart et al., 2007).

Another possibility is that the actions of particular genes affect chemical balances in the brain that lead to overarousal of a network of neurons called a *worry circuit,* a neural network that signals danger in response to perceived threats. In OCD, the brain may be continually sending messages through this "worry circuit" or neural circuit that something is wrong and requires immediate attention, leading to obsessional, worrisome thoughts and repetitive, compulsive behaviors. These signals may emanate from the brain's fear-triggering center, the amygdala, which is part of the limbic system. Normally, the prefrontal cortex modulates input from the amygdala and other lower brain structures. However, in people with OCD and other anxiety disorders, this process may break down as the prefrontal cortex fails to control excess neural activity emanating from the amygdala, leading to anxiety and worry (Harrison et al., 2009; Monk et al., 2008).

Let's consider other intriguing possibilities regarding the biological underpinnings of OCD. One possibility requiring further study is that compulsive aspects of OCD result from abnormalities in brain circuits that normally serve to constrain repetitive behaviors. As a result, people with OCD may feel compelled to perform repetitive behaviors as though they were "stuck in gear" (Leocani et al., 2001).

The frontal lobes in the cerebral cortex regulate brain centers in the lower brain that control bodily movements. Brain imaging studies implicate abnormal patterns of activation of brain circuits involving the frontal lobes in OCD patients (Harrison et al., 2009; Szeszko et al., 2008). Perhaps a disruption in these neural pathways explains the failure of people with compulsive behavior to inhibit repetitive, ritualistic behaviors. Changes in patterns of frontal lobe activation are also found among patients who respond favorably to cognitive-behavioral treatment, which suggests that CBT may directly affect parts of the brain implicated in OCD (Ingram & Siegle, 2001).

Other parts of the brain, including the basal ganglia, may also be involved in OCD (Baxter, 2003). The basal ganglia are involved in controlling body movements, so it is conceivable that a dysfunction in this region might help explain the ritualistic behaviors seen in OCD patients.

Psychological models of OCD emphasize cognitive and learning-based factors. People with OCD tend to be overly focused on their thoughts (Taylor & Jang, 2011). They can't seem to break the mental loop in which the same intrusive, negative thoughts keep reverberating in their minds. They also tend to exaggerate the risk that unfortunate events will occur. Because they expect terrible things to happen, people with OCD engage

An obsessive thought? One type of obsession involves recurrent, intrusive images of a calamity occurring as the result of one's own carelessness. For example, a person may not be able to shake the image of his or her house catching fire because of an electrical short in an appliance inadvertently left on.

truth OR fiction

Obsessive thinking helps relieve anxiety.

☑ **FALSE.** Obsessive thinking actually engenders anxiety. However, performing compulsive rituals may partially reduce the anxiety associated with obsessive thinking, thereby creating a cycle in which obsessive thinking prompts ritualistic behavior, which is reinforced by anxiety relief.

Exposure with response prevention. In exposure with response prevention, the therapist assists the client in breaking the obsessive–compulsive disorder cycle by confronting stimuli, such as dirt, that evoke obsessive thoughts but without performing the compulsive ritual.

in rituals to prevent them. An accountant who imagines awful consequences for slight mistakes on a client's tax forms may feel compelled to repeatedly check her or his work. Rituals may provide an illusion of control over stressful events (Reuven-Magril, Dar, & Liberman, 2008).

Another cognitive factor linked to the development of OCD is perfectionism, or belief that one must perform flawlessly (Moretz & McKay, 2009; Taylor & Jang, 2011). People who hold perfectionist beliefs exaggerate the consequences of turning in less-than-perfect work and may feel compelled to redo their efforts until every detail is flawless.

From a learning perspective, we can view compulsive behaviors as operant responses that are negatively reinforced by relief from anxiety triggered by obsessional thoughts. Put simply, "obsessions give rise to anxiety/distress and compulsions reduce it" (Franklin et al., 2002, p. 283). If a person obsesses that dirt or foreign bodies contaminate other people's hands, shaking hands or turning a doorknob may evoke powerful anxiety. Compulsive hand washing following exposure to a perceived contaminant provides some degree of relief from anxiety. Reinforcement, whether positive or negative, strengthens the behavior that precedes it. Thus, the person becomes more likely to repeat the compulsive ritual the next time he or she is exposed to anxiety-evoking cues, such as shaking hands or touching doorknobs. **T / F**

The question remains why some people develop obsessive thoughts whereas others do not. Perhaps those who develop obsessive–compulsive disorder are physiologically sensitized to overreact to minor cues of danger. Along these lines, we can speculate that the brain's worry circuit may be unusually sensitive to cues of danger. Deficits in memory may also play a role. For example, compulsive checkers may have difficulty remembering whether they have completed the task correctly, such as turning off the toaster oven before leaving for the day. The hypothesis that impaired memory contributes to compulsive checking remains to be more fully tested, however (Cuttler & Grafa, 2009; Harkin & Kessler, 2011).

TREATMENT APPROACHES Behavior therapists have achieved impressive results in treating obsessive–compulsive disorder with the technique of *exposure with response prevention* (ERP) (e.g., Franklin & Foa, 2011). The *exposure* component involves exposure to situations that evoke obsessive thoughts. For many people, such situations are hard to avoid. Leaving the house, for example, may trigger obsessive thoughts about whether the gas jets are turned off or the windows and doors are locked. Or clients may be instructed to purposely induce obsessive thoughts by leaving the house messy or rubbing their hands in dirt. The *response prevention* component involves preventing the compulsive behavior from occurring. Clients who rub their hands in dirt must avoid washing them for a designated period of time. The compulsive lock checker must avoid checking to see that the door was locked.

Through exposure with response prevention, people with OCD learn to tolerate the anxiety triggered by their obsessive thoughts while they are prevented from performing their compulsive rituals. With repeated exposure trials, the anxiety eventually subsides, and the person feels less compelled to perform the accompanying rituals. The underlying principle, yet again, is extinction. When cues that trigger obsessive thoughts and accompanying anxiety are repeatedly presented but the person sees that nothing bad happens, the bonds between these cues and the anxiety response should weaken.

Cognitive techniques are often combined with ERP within a cognitive-behavioral treatment program (Abramowitz, 2008; Hassija & Gray, 2010). The cognitive component involves correcting distorted ways of thinking (cognitive distortions), such as tendencies to overestimate the likelihood and severity of feared consequences (Whittal et al., 2008).

SSRI antidepresssants (selective serotonin reuptake inhibitors; discussed in Chapter 2) also have therapeutic benefits in treating OCD (Pampaloni et al., 2009; Simpson et al., 2008). This class of drugs includes *fluoxetine* (Prozac), *paroxetine* (Paxil), and *clomipramine* (Anafranil). These drugs increase the availability of the neurotransmitter serotonin in the brain. The effectiveness of these drugs suggests that problems with serotonin transmission play an important role in the development of OCD, at least in some cases. Bear in mind, however, that most people treated with SSRIs continue to experience significant OCD symptoms and some fail to respond at all (Simpson et al., 2008). We should also note that many patients fail to respond fully to cognitive-behavioral therapy (Fisher & Wells, 2005).

CBT produces at least as much benefit as drug treatment with SSRIs and may lead to more lasting results in treating OCD (Franklin & Foa, 2011). As with other forms of anxiety disorder, some people with OCD may benefit from a combination of psychological and drug treatment (Simpson et al., 2008). The Closer Look section in the following page explores an experimental treatment for OCD and other psychological disorders involving electrical stimulation of structures deep within the brain.

5.10 Describe the key features of body dysmorphic disorder and hoarding disorder and explain why these disorders are classified within the obsessive–compulsive spectrum.

Body Dysmorphic Disorder

People with **body dysmorphic disorder (BDD)** are preoccupied with an imagined or exaggerated physical defect in their appearance, such as skin blemishes, wrinkling or swelling of the face, body moles or spots, or facial swelling, causing them to feel they are ugly or even disfigured (Buhlmann, Marques, & Wilhelm, 2012; Marques et al., 2011). They fear others will judge them negatively on the basis of their perceived defect or flaw (Anson, Veale, & de Silva, 2012). They may spend hours examining themselves in the mirror and go to extreme measures to correct the perceived defect, even undergoing invasive or unpleasant medical procedures, including unnecessary plastic surgery. Some people with BDD remove all the mirrors from their homes so as not to be reminded of the "glaring flaw" in their appearance. People with BDD may believe that others view them as ugly or deformed and treat them negatively because of their physical flaws.

BDD is classified within the obsessive–compulsive spectrum because people with the disorder often become obsessed with their perceived defect and often feel compelled to check themselves in the mirror or engage in compulsive behaviors aimed at fixing, covering, or modifying the perceived defect. In the following case example of BDD, compulsive behavior takes the form of repetitive grooming, washing, and styling hair.

Can't you see it? A person with body dysmorphic disorder may spend hours in front of a mirror obsessing about an imagined or exaggerated physical defect in appearance.

A Pacemaker for the Brain?

Although psychosurgery remains an experimental and controversial treatment, emerging evidence points to a possible role for a surgical technique involving deep brain stimulation (DBS) in treating people with severe obsessive–compulsive disorder (Denys et al., 2010). DBS targets particular brain circuits linked to specific disorders, such as OCD (Beck, 2012) (see Figure 5.9). In deep brain stimulation, electrodes are surgically implanted in specific areas of the brain and attached to a small battery placed in the chest wall. When stimulated by a pacemaker-like device, the electrodes transmit electrical signals directly into surrounding brain tissue. Neuroscientists can't say exactly how DBS works, but it may involve interrupting aberrant brain signals (Beck, 2012).

One unanswered question in using deep brain stimulation is where to place the electrodes. As psychiatrist Wayne Goodman of the National Institute of Mental Health points out, "We're still not exactly sure where the sweet spot is in the brain to reduce the symptoms of OCD. Even if you think you're in the right neighborhood, you may be one block off. And one block off in the brain may be just 1 millimeter" (quoted in "Pacemaker for Brain," 2008).

Though deep brain stimulation remains an experimental treatment, recent research points to its potential use in treating other disorders in addition to OCD. Investigators find encouraging results in using DBS to treat severely depressed people who fail to respond to other treatments (e.g., Blomsted et al., 2011; Hirschfeld, 2011b; Holtzheimer et al., 2012; Kennedy et al., 2011; Keshtkar et al., 2012).

It is not too fanciful to conjecture that someday, perhaps someday soon, people with severe OCD, depression, or other psychological disorders may be able to self-administer bursts of electricity to precise areas of the brain to control their troublesome symptoms. On a related note, investigators are also evaluating whether brain stimulation from an MRI device might yield a therapeutic benefit similar to DBS. Preliminary results from this form of brain stimulation are promising, showing a reduction in depression in people with major depression (Vaziri-Bozorg et al., 2012).

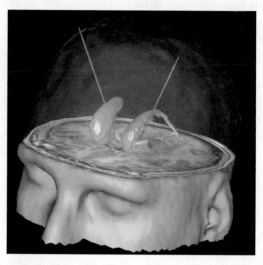

FIGURE 5.9

Deep brain stimulation for obsessive–compulsive disorder. This illustration shows the placement of the two electrodes inserted into nuclei of cell bodies that lie under the thalamus and used to stimulate the brain in patients with obsessive–compulsive disorder.

Source: "Pacemaker for Brain," 2008.

"I" "When My Hair Isn't Right ... I'm Not Right"

For Claudia, a 24-year-old legal secretary, virtually every day was a "bad hair day." She explained to her therapist, "When my hair isn't right, which is like every day, I'm not right." "Can't you see it?" she went on to explain. "It's so uneven. This piece should be shorter and this one just lies there. People think I'm crazy but I can't stand looking like this. It makes me look like I'm deformed. It doesn't matter if people can't see what I'm talking about. I see it. That's what counts." Several months earlier Claudia had a haircut she described as a disaster. Shortly thereafter, she had thoughts of killing herself: "I wanted to stab myself in the heart. I just couldn't stand looking at myself."

Claudia checked her hair in the mirror innumerable times during the day. She would spend two hours every morning doing her hair and still wouldn't be satisfied. Her constant pruning and checking had become a compulsive ritual. As she told her therapist, "I want to stop pulling and checking it, but I just can't help myself."

Having a bad hair day for Claudia meant that she would not go out with her friends and would spend every second examining herself in the mirror and fixing her hair. Occasionally she would cut pieces of her hair herself in an attempt to correct the mistakes of her last haircut. But cutting it herself inevitably made it even worse, in her view. Claudia was forever searching for the perfect haircut that would correct defects only she could perceive. Several years earlier she had what she described as a perfect haircut. "It was just right. I was on top of the world. But it began to look crooked when it grew in." Forever in search of the perfect haircut, Claudia had obtained a hard-to-get appointment with a world-renowned hair stylist in Manhattan, whose clientele included many celebrities. "People wouldn't understand paying this guy $375 for a haircut, especially on my salary, but they don't realize how important it is to me. I'd pay any amount I could." Unfortunately, even this celebrated hair stylist disappointed her: "My $25 haircut from my old stylist on Long Island was better than this."

Claudia reported other fixations about her appearance earlier in life: "In high school, I felt my face was like a plate. It was just too flat. I didn't want any pictures taken of me. I couldn't help thinking what people thought of me. They won't tell you, you know. Even if they say there's nothing wrong, it doesn't mean anything. They were just lying to be polite." Claudia related that she was taught to equate physical beauty with happiness: "I was told that to be successful you had to be beautiful. How can I be happy if I look this way?"

From the Author's Files

Although BDD is believed to be relatively common, we don't have specific data on the rates of the disorder because many people with the disorder fail to seek help or try to keep their symptoms a secret (Cororve & Gleaves, 2001; Phillips et al., 2006). We should not underplay the emotional distress associated with BDD, as evidence shows high rates of suicidal thinking and suicide attempts among people with the disorder (Buhlmann, Marques, & Wilhelm, 2012; Phillips & Menard, 2006). More encouraging is recent evidence based on a small group of people with BDD that showed most patients eventually recovered, although it often took five years or longer (Bjornsson et al., 2011). **T / F**

Exposure therapy with response prevention is often used in treating body dysmorphic disorder. Exposure can take the form of intentionally revealing the perceived defect in public, rather than concealing it with makeup or clothing. Response prevention may involve efforts to avoid mirror checking (e.g., by covering mirrors at home) and excessive grooming. ERP is generally combined with cognitive restructuring, in which therapists help clients challenge their distorted beliefs about their physical appearance and evaluate them in light of evidence (Phillips & Rogers, 2011).

Hoarding Disorder

Compulsive hoarding, which is classified by *DSM-5* as a newly recognized disorder called **hoarding disorder,** is characterized by the accumulation of and need to retain stacks of unnecessary and seemingly useless possessions, causing personal distress or making it difficult to maintain a safe, habitable living space. The piles of objects can become a fire hazard or render most of the living space effectively unusable. Visitors must carefully navigate around mounds of clutter. People who hoard cling to their possessions, leading to conflicts with family members and others who press them to discard the useless junk. According to recent estimates, hoarding disorder affects an estimated 2% to 5% of the general population (Mataix-Cols et al., 2010).

Hoarding disorder has an important emotional component characterized by the need to accumulate and retain possessions in order to feel a sense of security. People who hoard become unusually attached to their possessions and fearful of losing them, often because of the misfounded belief that they are somehow valuable or important. Typically, the person who hoards fails to recognize hoarding as a problem, as in the following case example.

truth OR fiction

Having skin blemishes leads some people to consider suicide.

☑ **TRUE.** People with BDD may become so consumed by their self-perceived flaws—even minor skin blemishes—that they think seriously of ending it all.

a CLOSER look

"Don't They See What I See?" Visual Processing of Faces in People with Body Dysmorphic Disorder

Findings from a brain imaging study resonate with impressions many clinicians have about people with body dysmorphic disorder. In the study, fMRI scans of people with BDD and non-BDD (control) participants were taken during a facial matching task (Feusner et al., 2007) (see Figure 5.10). Participants were shown a series of male and female faces and asked to match each face with one of three comparison faces shown directly below the target face. Brain scans during the matching task showed different patterns of brain activation between BDD and control participants.

The major difference was that participants with body dysmorphic disorder showed more activation in the left cerebral hemisphere than did control group members. For most people, the left hemisphere is dominant for tasks requiring analytic, evaluative processing, whereas the right hemisphere is dominant for holistic processing—the type of processing involved in recognizing faces. We typically perceive faces by holistic processing (i.e., recognizing faces as whole patterns) rather than by piecing together the component parts of the face in a piecemeal fashion.

Among people with BDD, visual processing in the brain involves greater left hemisphere activation consistent with detailed or piecemeal analysis, in contrast to the more global or contextual processing of the control group. In other words, the BDD group was more prone to overattend to visual details in piecing together parts of the face rather than recognizing faces as whole patterns. This tendency to hone in on details of physical appearance is a key clinical feature of BDD. People with BDD may wrongly assume that other people are as detail-oriented in their perception of physical appearance as they are. This may help explain why they often assume that other people will notice the minor blemishes or physical defects that stand out so clearly in their perceptions of their own faces.

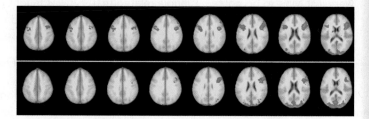

FIGURE 5.10 Brain activation patterns of people with dysmorphic disorder. These are brain scans showing activation of parts of the brain (shown by areas of red) in body dysmorphic disorder patients (top row) and controls (bottom row) in response to facial stimuli. BDD patients show activation in both the left and right prefrontal regions (top part of images) whereas controls show activation only in the right prefrontal regions.

Source: Image provided courtesy of Dr. Jamie Feusner.

The Neighbors Complain: A Case of Compulsive Hoarding

The 55-year-old divorced man did not regard his hoarding as a problem, but felt pressured to come for treatment because of complaints filed by neighbors who were concerned about a fire hazard (his house was one of a series of attached row houses). A home visit revealed the extent of the problem. The rooms were filled with all kinds of useless objects, including out-of-date food cans, piles of newspapers and magazines, and stacks of papers and even pieces of cloth. Most of the furniture was completely hidden by the clutter. A narrow path around the clutter led to the bathroom and to the man's bed. The kitchen was so cluttered that none of the appliances was accessible. The man reported that he hadn't used the kitchen in quite a while and routinely went out for his meals. There was a pervasive stale and dusty smell throughout the house. When asked why he had kept all this stuff, he replied he felt fearful of discarding "important papers" and "things he might need." But the observers were at a loss to explain how any of these objects could be important or needed.

Source: Adapted from Rachman & DeSilva, 2009

Hoarding disorder bears a close relationship to obsessive–compulsive disorder (Frost, Steketee, & Tolin, 2012). The obsessional features of hoarding disorder may involve recurring thoughts about acquiring objects and fears over losing them. The compulsive features may involve repeatedly rearranging stacks of possessions and stubbornly refusing to avoid discarding them, even in the face of strong protests from other people. Despite the similarities to OCD, hoarding disorder in the *DSM-5* is a distinct disorder, not a subtype of OCD. There are important shades of difference between hoarding disorder and OCD (Frost, Steketee, & Tolin, 2012). For one, obsessional thinking in hoarding disorder does not have the character of intrusive, unwanted thoughts that it does in OCD. These thoughts in people who hoard are typically experienced as a part of the normal stream of thoughts (Mataix-Cols et al., 2010). Moreover, people who hoard do not experience an urge to perform rituals to control disturbing thoughts. Distress associated with hoarding is not a result of intrusive, obsessive thinking, but is the result of difficulty adjusting to living amidst all the clutter and conflicts with other people about the clutter. Another difference with OCD is that people who hoard typically experience pleasure or enjoyment from collecting possessions and thinking about them, which is unlike the anxiety associated with obsessional thinking in OCD.

Hoarding. People who hoard compulsively acquire and retain piles of useless or unneeded possessions. They become emotionally attached to their possessions and fearful of parting with them.

Underlying causal factors in hoarding behavior continue to be studied, but recent research has probed its neurological basis. When thinking about acquiring and discarding possessions, people who hoard show abnormal patterns of activation in parts of the brain involved in such processes as decision making and self-regulation (Tolin et al., 2012). Further research along these lines may help us better understand the difficulties people with this disorder face in making decisions to accumulate objects and avoiding getting rid of them. Although hoarding has been difficult to treat, recent evidence shows promising results from cognitive-behavior therapy focused on helping the person change maladaptive beliefs about the need to accumulate and retain possessions and working on strategies to discard them (Steketee et al., 2010).

summing up

Overview of Anxiety Disorders

5.1 Describe the physical, behavioral, and cognitive features of anxiety disorders.

Anxiety disorders are characterized by disturbed patterns of behavior in which anxiety is the most prominent feature. They are characterized by physical symptoms such as jumpiness, sweaty palms, and a pounding or racing heart; by behavioral features such as avoidance behavior, clinging or dependent behavior, and agitated behavior; and by cognitive features, such as worry or a sense of dread or apprehension about the future and fear of losing control.

Panic Disorder

5.2 Describe the key features of panic disorder.

Panic disorder is characterized by often immobilizing, repeated panic attacks, which involve intense physical features, notably cardiovascular symptoms, that may be accompanied by sheer terror and fears of losing control, losing one's mind, or dying. Panic attack sufferers often limit their outside activities for fear of recurrent attacks. This can lead to agoraphobia, the fear of venturing into public places.

5.3 Describe the leading conceptual model of panic disorder.

The predominant model conceptualizes panic disorder in terms of a combination of cognitive factors (e.g., catastrophic misinterpretation of bodily sensations, anxiety sensitivity) and biological factors (e.g., genetic proneness, increased sensitivity to bodily cues). In this view, panic disorder involves physiological and psychological factors interacting in a vicious cycle that can spiral into full-blown panic attacks.

5.4 Evaluate methods used to treat panic disorder.

The most effective methods of treating are cognitive-behavioral therapy and drug therapy. CBT for panic disorder incorporates techniques such as self-monitoring, controlled exposure to panic-related cues, including bodily sensations, and development of coping responses for handling panic attacks without catastrophic misinterpretations of bodily cues. Biomedical approaches incorporate use of antidepressant drugs, which have antianxiety and antipanic effects as well as antidepressant effects.

Phobic Disorders

5.5 Describe the key features and specific types of phobic disorders and explain how phobias develop.

Phobias are excessive irrational fears of specific objects or situations. Phobias involve a behavioral component—the avoidance of the phobic stimulus—as well as physical and cognitive features of anxiety associated with exposure to the phobic stimulus. Specific phobias are excessive fears of particular objects or situations, such as mice,

spiders, tight places, or heights. Social anxiety involves an intense fear of being judged negatively by others. Agoraphobia involves fears of venturing into public places. Agoraphobia may occur with, or in the absence of, panic disorder.

Learning theorists explain phobias as learned behaviors that are acquired on the basis of the principle of conditioning and observational learning. Mowrer's two-factor model incorporates classical and operant conditioning in the explanation of phobias. Phobias appear to be moderated by cognitive factors, such as oversensitivity to threatening cues, overprediction of dangerousness, and self-defeating thoughts and irrational beliefs. Genetic factors also appear to increase proneness to development of phobias. Some investigators believe we are genetically predisposed to acquire certain types of phobias that may have had survival value for our prehistoric ancestors.

5.6 Evaluate methods used to treat phobic disorders.

The most effective methods of treatment are learning-based approaches, such as systematic desensitization and gradual exposure, as well as cognitive therapy and drug therapy, such as the use of antidepressants (e.g., Zoloft, Paxil) for treating social anxiety.

Generalized Anxiety Disorder

5.7 Describe the key features of generalized anxiety disorder and ways of understanding and treating it.

Generalized anxiety disorder is a type of anxiety disorder involving persistent anxiety that seems to be free floating or not tied to specific situations. Psychodynamic theorists view anxiety disorders as attempts by the ego to control the conscious emergence of threatening impulses. Feelings of anxiety are seen as warning signals that threatening impulses are nearing awareness. Learning-based models focus on the generalization of anxiety across stimulus situations. Cognitive theorists seek to account for generalized anxiety in terms of faulty thoughts or beliefs that underlie worry. Biological models focus on irregularities in neurotransmitter functioning in the brain. The two major treatment approaches are cognitive-behavioral therapy and drug therapy (typically *paroxetine*).

Ethnic Differences in Anxiety Disorders

5.8 Evaluate ethnic differences in rates of anxiety disorders.

Evidence from nationally representative samples of U.S. adults showed generally lower rates of some anxiety disorders among ethnic minorities as compared to (non-Hispanic) White Americans.

Obsessive–Compulsive and Related Disorders

5.9 Describe the key features of obsessive–compulsive disorder and ways of understanding and treating it.

Obsessive–compulsive disorder involves recurrent patterns of obsessions or compulsions, or a combination of the two. Obsessions are nagging, persistent thoughts that create anxiety and seem beyond the person's ability to control. Compulsions are apparently irresistible repetitious urges to perform certain behaviors, such as repeated elaborate washing after using the bathroom.

Within the psychodynamic tradition, obsessions represent leakage of unconscious urges or impulses into consciousness, and compulsions are acts that help keep these impulses repressed. Research on biological factors highlights roles for genetics and for brain mechanisms involved in signaling danger and controlling repetitive behaviors. Research shows roles for cognitive factors, such as overfocusing on one's thoughts, exaggerated perceptions of risk of unfortunate events, and perfectionism. Learning theorists view compulsive behaviors as operant responses that are negatively reinforced by relief from anxiety produced by obsessional thinking.

The major contemporary treatment approaches include learning-based models (exposure with response prevention), cognitive therapy (correction of cognitive distortions), and use of SSRI-type antidepressants.

5.10 Describe the key features of body dysmorphic disorder and hoarding disorder and explain why these disorders are classified within the obsessive–compulsive spectrum.

In body dysmorphic disorder, people are preoccupied with an imagined or exaggerated defect in their physical appearance. It is clas-

sified within the OCD spectrum because people with BDD typically experience obsessive thoughts related to their physical appearance and show compulsive checking behaviors and attempts to correct or cover up the problem. Hoarding disorder is characterized by excessive accumulation and retention of possessions to a point of causing personal distress or significantly interfering with the person's ability to maintain a safe and habitable living space. People who hoard have a strong attachment to objects they accumulate and have difficulty discarding them. Hoarding disorder shares characteristics with obsessive–compulsive disorder, such as obsessive thinking about acquiring objects and fears over losing them as well as compulsive behaviors involving rearranging possessions and rigidly resisting efforts to discard them.

critical thinking questions

On the basis of your reading of this chapter, answer the following questions:

- Anxiety may be a normal emotional reaction in some situations but not in others. Think of a situation in which anxiety would be a normal reaction and one in which it would be a maladaptive reaction. What are the differences? What criteria would you use to distinguish between normal and abnormal anxiety reactions?

- Do you have any specific phobias, such as fears of small animals, insects, heights, or enclosed spaces? What factors may have contributed to the development of the phobia (or phobias)? How has the phobia affected your life? How have you coped with it?

- John has been experiencing sudden panic attacks on and off for the past few months. During the attacks, he has difficulty breathing and fears that his heart is racing out of control. His physician checked him out and told him the problem is with his nerves, not his heart. What treatment alternatives are available to John that might help him deal with this problem?

- Do you know anyone who has received treatment for an anxiety disorder or OCD? What was the outcome? What other treatment alternatives might be available? Which approach to treatment would you seek if you suffered from a similar problem?

key terms

anxiety 158
anxiety disorder 159
panic disorder 160
agoraphobia 161
phobia 168
specific phobia 168
social anxiety disorder 170

two-factor model 173
systematic
  desensitization 178
fear-stimulus
  hierarchy 178
gradual exposure 179
flooding 180

virtual reality therapy 180
cognitive restructuring 182
generalized anxiety disorder
  (GAD) 182
obsessive–compulsive
  disorder (OCD) 186
obsession 186

compulsion 186
body dysmorphic disorder
  (BDD) 191
hoarding disorder 193

Dissociative Disorders, Somatic Symptom and Related Disorders, and Psychological Factors Affecting Physical Health

6

truth OR fiction

T☐ F☐ The term *split personality* refers to schizophrenia. (p. 201)

T☐ F☐ People with multiple personalities typically have two different personalities. (p. 204)

T☐ F☐ Very few of us have episodes in which we feel strangely detached from our own bodies or thought processes. (p. 210)

T☐ F☐ Most people with multiple personalities had normal and uneventful childhoods. (p. 214)

T☐ F☐ Some people lose all feeling in their hands or legs, although nothing is medically wrong with them. (p. 222)

T☐ F☐ Some men have a psychological disorder characterized by fear of the penis shrinking and retracting into the body. (p. 225)

T☐ F☐ The term *hysteria* derives from the Greek word for testicle. (p. 225)

T☐ F☐ People can relieve the pain of migraine headaches by raising the temperature in a finger. (p. 230)

T☐ F☐ Deaths from coronary heart disease are rising in the United States, largely the result of increased rates of smoking. (p. 236)

learning objectives

6.1
Describe the key features of these major types of dissociative disorders: dissociative identity disorder, dissociative amnesia, and depersonalization/derealization disorder.

6.2
Explain why the concept of dissociative identity disorder is controversial.

6.3
Describe different theoretical perspectives on dissociative disorders.

6.4
Describe the treatment of dissociative identity disorder.

6.5
Describe the key features of these types of somatic symptom and related disorders: somatic symptom disorder, illness anxiety disorder, conversion disorder, and factitious disorder.

6.6
Explain the difference between malingering and factitious disorder.

6.7
Describe the key features of koro and dhat syndromes.

6.8
Describe the theoretical understandings of somatic symptom and related disorders.

6.9
Describe methods used to treat somatic symptom and related disorders.

6.10
Describe the role of psychological factors in physical health problems such as headaches, cardiovascular disease, asthma, cancer, and AIDS.

"I" "We Share a Single Body"

Elaina is a licensed clinical therapist. Connie is a nurse. Sydney is a delightful little girl who likes to collect bugs in an old mayonnaise jar. Lynn is shy and has trouble saying her ls, and Heather—Heather is a teenager trying hard to be grown-up. We are many different people, but we have one very important thing in common: We share a single body. . . .

We have dozens of different people living inside us, each with our own memories, talents, dreams, and fears. Some of us "come out" to work or play or cook or sleep. Some of us only watch from inside. Some of us are still lost in the past, a tortured past full of incest and abuse. And there are many who were so damaged by this past and who have fled so deep inside, we fear we may never reach them. . . .

Many of our Alter personalities were born of abuse. Some came because they were needed, others came to protect.

Leah came whenever she heard our father say, "Come lay awhile with me." If she came, none of our other Alters would have to do those things he wanted. She could do them for us, and protect us from that part of our childhood.

Source: From "Quiet Storm," a pseudonym used by a woman who claims to have several personalities residing within her.

This is a first-hand description of a personality so fractured because of severe childhood abuse that it splinters into many pieces. Some of the pieces bear memories of the abuse, whereas others go about their business unaware of the pain and trauma. Now imagine that these separate parts develop their own unique characteristics. Imagine, too, that these alter personalities become so compartmentalized that they don't know of each other's existence. Even the core personality may not know of the existence of the others.

This is a description of *dissociative identity disorder,* known popularly as "multiple personality," perhaps the most perplexing and intriguing of all psychological disorders. The diagnosis is officially recognized in the *DSM* system, although it remains controversial, with many professionals doubting its existence or ascribing it to a form of role-playing. Dissociative identity disorder is classified as a type of *dissociative disorder,* a grouping of psychological disorders characterized by changes or disturbances in the functions of self—identity, memory, or consciousness—that make the personality whole.

Normally speaking, we know who we are. We may not be certain of ourselves in an existential, philosophical sense, but we know our names, where we live, and what we do for a living. We also tend to remember the salient events of our lives. We may not recall every detail, and we may confuse what we had for dinner on Tuesday with what we had on Monday, but we generally know what we have been doing for the past days, weeks, and years. Normally speaking, there is a unity to consciousness that gives rise to a sense of self. We perceive ourselves as progressing through space and time. In people with dissociative disorders, one or more of these aspects of daily living is disturbed— sometimes bizarrely so.

In this chapter, we explore the dissociative disorders as well as another class of puzzling disorders, *somatic symptom and related disorders.* People with these may have physical complaints that defy medical explanation and so are believed to involve underlying psychological conflicts or issues. People with these disorders may report blindness or numbness, although no organic basis can be detected. In other cases, people with somatic symptom and related disorders hold exaggerated beliefs about the seriousness of their physical symptoms, such as taking them as signs of life-threatening illnesses despite medical reassurances to the contrary.

In earlier versions of the *DSM,* dissociative and somatic symptom and related disorders were classified with the anxiety disorders under the general category of "neurosis." This grouping was based on the psychodynamic model, which holds that dissociative and somatic symptom and related disorders, as well as the anxiety disorders discussed in Chapter 5, involve maladaptive ways of managing anxiety. With anxiety disorders, disturbing levels of anxiety are expressed directly in behavior, such as the avoidance shown by a person with a phobic disorder toward the feared object or situation. By contrast, the role of anxiety in dissociative and somatic symptom and related disorders is *inferred* rather than directly *observed* in behavior. People with dissociative disorders have psychological problems, such as loss of memory or changes in identity, but don't typically show obvious signs of anxiety. From the psychodynamic model, we infer that dissociative symptoms serve a psychological purpose of shielding the self from the anxiety that would arise from conscious awareness of disturbing internal conflicts over sexual or aggressive wishes or impulses. Likewise, some people with conversion disorder, which is classified in the category of somatic symptom and related disorders, may show a strange indifference to their physical problems, such as loss of vision, that would greatly concern most of us. Here, too, we can theorize that the "symptoms" mask unconscious sources of anxiety. Some theorists interpret indifference to symptoms to mean that those symptoms have an underlying benefit; that is, they help prevent anxiety from intruding into consciousness.

The *DSM-5* separates the anxiety disorders from the other classical categories of neuroses—the dissociative and somatic symptom and related disorders—with which they were historically linked. Yet many practitioners continue to use the broad conceptualization of *neuroses* as a useful framework for grouping together anxiety disorders, dissociative disorders, and somatic symptom and related disorders.

6.1 **Describe** the key features of these major types of dissociative disorders: dissociative identity disorder, dissociative amnesia, and depersonalization/ derealization disorder.

Dissociative Disorders

The major **dissociative disorders** include *dissociative identity disorder, dissociative amnesia,* and *depersonalization/derealization disorder.* In each case, there is a disruption or dissociation ("splitting off") of the functions of identity, memory, or consciousness that normally make us whole. Table 6.1 presents an overview of the dissociative disorders discussed in the text.

Dissociative Identity Disorder

The Ohio State campus dwelled in terror as four college women were seized, coerced to cash checks or get money from automatic teller machines, and then raped. A cryptic phone call led to the capture of Billy Milligan, a 23-year-old drifter who had been dishonorably discharged from the Navy.

Billy was diagnosed with multiple personality disorder, which is now called **dissociative identity disorder** (DID). In dissociative identity disorder, two or more personalities—each with its own distinctive traits, memories, mannerisms, and even style of speech—"occupy" one person. Dissociative identity disorder, which is often called *multiple personality* or *split personality* by laypeople, should not be confused with schizophrenia. Schizophrenia (which comes from Greek roots meaning "split mind") occurs much more commonly than multiple personality and involves the "splitting" of cognition, affect, and behavior. In a person with schizophrenia, there may be little agreement between thoughts and emotions, or between perceptions of reality and what is truly happening. The person with schizophrenia may become giddy when told of disturbing events or may experience hallucinations or delusions (see Chapter 11). In people with multiple personality, the personality apparently divides into two or more personalities, but each of them usually shows more integrated functioning on cognitive, affective, and behavioral levels than is true of people with schizophrenia. **T / F**

Celebrated cases of multiple personality have been depicted in the popular media. One became the subject of the 1950s film *The Three Faces of Eve*. In the film, Eve White is a timid housewife who harbors two other personalities: Eve Black, a sexually provocative, antisocial personality, and Jane, a balanced, developing personality who could balance her sexual needs with the demands of social acceptability. The three faces eventually merged into one—Jane—providing a "happy ending." The real-life Eve, whose name was Chris Sizemore, failed to maintain this integrated personality. Her personality reportedly split into 22 subsequent personalities.

truth OR fiction

The term *split personality* refers to schizophrenia.

☑ **FALSE** The term *split personality* refers to multiple personality, not schizophrenia.

TABLE 6.1
Overview of Dissociative Disorders

Type of Disorder	Approximate Lifetime Prevalence in Population	Description	Associated Features
Dissociative Identity Disorder	Unknown	Emergence of two or more distinct personalities	• Alternates may vie for control • May represent a psychological defense against severe childhood abuse or trauma
Dissociative Amnesia	Unknown	Inability to recall important personal material that cannot be accounted for by medical causes	• Information lost to memory is usually of traumatic or stressful experiences • Subtypes include localized amnesia, selective amnesia, and generalized amnesia • May be associated with dissociative fugue, a rare condition in which the person may travel to a new location and start a new life under a different identity
Depersonalization/ Derealization Disorder	2%	Episodes of feeling detached from one's self or one's body or having a sense of unreality about one's surroundings (derealization)	• Person may feel as if he or she were living in a dream or acting like a robot • Episodes of depersonalization are persistent or recurrent and cause significant distress

Source: Prevalence rates derived from APA, 2013.

Not the Boy Next Door: A Case of Dissociative Identity Disorder

Billy wasn't quite the boy next door. He tried twice to commit suicide while he was awaiting trial, so his lawyers requested a psychiatric evaluation. The psychologists and psychiatrists who examined Billy deduced that ten personalities dwelled inside of him. Eight were male and two were female. Billy's personality had been fractured by a brutal childhood. The personalities displayed diverse facial expressions, memories, and vocal patterns. They performed in dissimilar ways on personality and intelligence tests.

Arthur, a sensible but phlegmatic personality, conversed with a British accent. Danny, 14, was a painter of still lifes. Christopher, 13, was normal enough, but somewhat anxious. A 3-year-old English girl went by the name of Christine. Tommy, a 16-year-old, was an antisocial personality and escape artist. It was Tommy who had enlisted in the Navy. Allen was an 18-year-old con artist. Allen also smoked. Adelena was a 19-year-old introverted lesbian. It was she who had committed the rapes. It was probably David who had made the mysterious phone call. David was an anxious 9-year-old who wore the anguish of early childhood trauma on his sleeve. After his second suicide attempt, Billy had been placed in a straitjacket. When the guards checked his cell, however, he was sleeping with the straitjacket as a pillow. Tommy later explained that he was responsible for Billy's escape.

*The defense argued that Billy was afflicted with multiple personality disorder. Several alternate personalities resided within him. The alternate personalities knew about Billy, but Billy was unaware of them. Billy, the core or dominant personality, had learned as a child that he could sleep as a way of avoiding the sexual and physical abuse of his father. A psychiatrist claimed that Billy had likewise been "asleep"—in a sort of "psychological coma"—when the crimes were **committed**. Therefore, Billy should be judged innocent by reason of insanity.*

Billy was decreed not guilty by reason of insanity. He was committed to a mental institution. In the institution, 14 additional personalities emerged. Thirteen were rebellious and labeled "undesirables" by Arthur. The fourteenth was the "Teacher," who was competent and supposedly represented the integration of all the other personalities. Billy was released 6 years later.

Adapted from Keyes, 1982

CLINICAL FEATURES DID is characterized by the emergence of two or more distinct personalities that may vie for control of the person. There may be one dominant or core personality and several subordinate personalities. The sudden transformation of one personality into another may be experienced as a form of possession. The more common alter personalities include children of various ages, adolescents of the opposite gender, prostitutes, and gay males and lesbians. Some of the personalities may show psychotic symptoms—a break with reality expressed in the form of hallucinations and delusional thinking.

In some cases, the host (main) personality is unaware of the existence of the other identities, whereas the other identities are aware of the existence of the host. In other cases, the different personalities are completely unaware of one another. In some isolated cases, alternate personalities (also called *alter personalities*) may even have different eyeglass prescriptions, different allergic reactions, and different responses to medication (e.g., Birnbaum, Martin, & Thomann, 1996; Spiegel, 2009). The person with DID may also have memory gaps, including events experienced by other alters and ordinary life events as well as important personal information (e.g., where the person attended high school or college) or prior traumatic experiences (APA, 2013).

Dissociative identity disorder. In dissociative identity disorder, multiple personalities emerge from within the same person, with each having its own well-defined traits and memories.

All in all, the clusters of alter personalities serve as a microcosm of conflicting urges and cultural themes. Themes of sexual ambivalence (sexual openness vs. restrictiveness) and shifting sexual orientations are particularly common. It is as if conflicting internal impulses cannot coexist or achieve dominance. As a result, each is expressed as the cardinal or steering trait of an alternate personality. The clinician can sometimes elicit alternate personalities by inviting them to make themselves known, as in asking, "Is there another part of you that wants to say something to me?"

In many cases, the dominant personality remains unaware of the existence of the alter personalities. It thus seems that unconscious processes control the underlying mechanism that results in dissociation, or splitting off of awareness. There may even be "interpersonality rivalry," in which one personality aspires to do away with another, usually in ignorance of the fact that murdering an alternate would result in the death of all.

Although dissociative identity disorder is diagnosed more frequently in women, it is not clear whether there are gender differences in the prevalence of the disorder in the general population. Cases of dissociative identity disorder typically present with several alter personalities, and sometimes with 20 or more alters. The key features of dissociative identity disorder are listed in Table 6.2. **T / F**

truth OR fiction

People with multiple personalities typically have two different personalities.

☑ **FALSE** Most report having several alters, sometimes even 20 or more alters.

Key Features of Dissociative Identity Disorder (Formerly Multiple Personality Disorder)

- Two or more distinct personalities exist within the person.
- Alter personalities may represent different ages, genders, interests, and ways of relating to others.
- Two or more alter personalities repeatedly take full control of the individual's behavior.
- Forgetfulness about ordinary life events and important personal information that cannot be explained by ordinary forgetfulness.
- The main or dominant personality may or may not know of the existence of the alter personalities.

6.2 **Explain** why the concept of dissociative identity disorder is controversial.

CONTROVERSIES Although multiple personality is generally considered rare, the very existence of the disorder continues to arouse debate. Many professionals continue to have doubts about the legitimacy of the diagnosis.

Only a handful of cases worldwide were reported from 1920 to 1970, but since then, the number of reported cases has skyrocketed into the thousands (Spanos, 1994). This may indicate that multiple personality is more common than was earlier believed. However, it is also possible that the disorder has been overdiagnosed in highly suggestible people who might simply be following suggestions that they might have the disorder. Increased public attention paid to the disorder in recent years may also account for the perception that its prevalence is greater than was commonly believed.

The disorder does appear to be culture-bound and largely restricted to North America (Spanos, 1994). Relatively few cases have been reported elsewhere, even in Western countries such as Great Britain and France. A recent survey in Japan failed to find even one case, and in Switzerland, 90% of the psychiatrists polled had never seen a case of the disorder (Modestin, 1992; Spanos, 1994). Even in North America, few psychologists and psychiatrists have ever encountered a case of multiple personality. Most cases are reported by a relatively small number of investigators and clinicians who strongly believe in the existence of the disorder. Critics wonder if they may be helping to manufacture that which they are seeking.

Some leading authorities, such as the late psychologist Nicholas Spanos, believe so. Spanos and others have challenged the existence of dissociative identity disorder (Reisner, 1994; Spanos, 1994). To Spanos, dissociative identity is not a distinct disorder, but a form of role-playing in which individuals first come to construe themselves as having multiple selves and then begin to act in ways that are consistent with their conception of the disorder. Eventually their role-playing becomes so ingrained that it becomes a reality to them. Perhaps their therapists or counselors unintentionally planted the idea in their minds that their confusing welter of emotions and behaviors may represent different personalities at work. Impressionable people may have learned how to enact the role of persons with the disorder by watching others on television and in the movies. Films such as *The Three Faces of Eve* and *Sybil* have given detailed examples of the behaviors that characterize multiple personalities. Or perhaps therapists provided cues about the features of multiple personality.

Once the role is established, it may be maintained through social reinforcement, such as attention from others and avoidance of accountability for unacceptable behavior. This is not to suggest that people with multiple personalities are "faking," any more than you are faking when you perform different daily roles as student, spouse, or worker. You may enact the role of a student (e.g., sitting attentively in class, raising your hand when you wish to talk) because you have learned to organize your behavior according to the nature of the role and because you have been rewarded for doing so. People with multiple personalities may have come to identify so closely with the role that it becomes real for them.

Relatively few cases of multiple personality involve criminal behavior, so the incentives for enacting a multiple personality role do not often relieve individuals of criminal responsibility for their behavior. But there still may be perceived benefits to enacting the role of a multiple personality, such as a therapist's expression of interest and excitement at discovering a multiple personality. People with multiple personalities were often highly imaginative during childhood. Accustomed to playing games of "make believe," they may readily adopt alternate identities, especially if they learn how to enact the multiple personality role and there are external sources of validation, such as a clinician's interest and concern.

The social reinforcement model may help to explain why some clinicians seem to "discover" many more cases of multiple personality than others. These clinicians may unknowingly cue clients to enact the role of a multiple personality and then reinforce the performance with extra attention and concern. With the right set of cues, certain clients may adopt the role of a multiple personality to please their clinicians. Some authorities have challenged the role-playing model (e.g., Gleaves, 1996), and it remains to be seen how many cases of the disorder in clinical practice the model can explain. Whether dissociative identity disorder is a real phenomenon or a form of role-playing, there is no question that people who display this behavior have serious emotional and behavioral difficulties.

We have personally noted a tendency for claims of multiple personality to spread on inpatient units. In one case, Susan, a prostitute admitted for depression and suicidal thoughts, claimed that she could exchange sex for money only when "another person" inside her emerged and took control. Upon hearing this, another woman, Ginny—a child abuser who had been admitted for depression after her daughter had been removed from her home by social services—claimed that she abused her daughter only when another person inside of her assumed control of her personality. Susan's chart recommended that she be evaluated further for multiple personality disorder (the term used at the time to refer to the disorder), but Ginny was diagnosed with a depressive disorder and a personality disorder, not with multiple personality disorder.

Dissociative disorders are associated with an increased risk of suicide attempts, including multiple suicide attempts (Foote et al., 2008). Suicide attempts are especially common among people with multiple personalities. In one Canadian study, 72% of multiple personality patients had attempted suicide, and about 2% had succeeded (Ross et al., 1989).

Dissociative Amnesia

Dissociative amnesia is believed to be the most common type of dissociative disorder (Maldonado, Butler, & Spiegel, 1998). *Amnesia* derives from the Greek roots *a-*, meaning "not," and *mnasthai*, meaning "to remember." In **dissociative amnesia** (formerly called *psychogenic amnesia*), the person becomes unable to recall important personal information, usually involving traumatic or stressful experiences, in a way that cannot be accounted for by simple forgetfulness. Nor can the memory loss be attributed to a particular organic cause, such as a blow to the head or a particular medical condition, or to the direct effects of drugs or alcohol. Unlike some progressive forms of memory impairment (such as dementia associated with Alzheimer's disease; see Chapter 14), the memory loss in dissociative amnesia is reversible, although it may last for days, weeks, or even years. Recall of dissociated memories may happen gradually but often occurs suddenly and spontaneously, as when the soldier who has no recall of a battle for several days afterward suddenly remembers being transported to a hospital away from the battlefield. 👁

Memories of childhood sexual abuse are sometimes recovered during the course of psychotherapy or hypnosis. The sudden emergence of such memories has become a source of major controversy within the field and the general community, as we explore in the *Thinking Critically About Abnormal Psychology* section on page 210.

👁 **Watch the Video**
Sharon: Dissociative Amnesia
on MyPsychLab

"Does Anybody Know Me"? Diagnosed with dissociative amnesia, 40-year old Jeffrey Ingram searched for more than a month for anyone who could tell him who he was. He was finally recognized by a family member who saw him on a TV news program. Even after returning home, he lacked any memory of his identity, but said that it felt like home to him. According to his mother, he had suffered earlier incidents of memory loss and had never fully recovered his memory.

Amnesia is not ordinary forgetfulness, such as forgetting someone's name or where you left your car keys. Memory loss in amnesia is more profound or wide ranging. Dissociative amnesia is divided into five distinct types of memory problems.

1. *Localized amnesia.* Most cases take the form of *localized amnesia* in which events occurring during a specific time period are lost to memory. For example, the person cannot recall events for a number of hours or days after a stressful or traumatic incident, such as a battle or a car accident.
2. *Selective amnesia.* In *selective amnesia,* people forget only the disturbing particulars that take place during a certain period of time. A person may recall the period of life during which he conducted an extramarital affair, but not the guilt-arousing affair itself. A soldier may recall most of a battle, but not the death of his buddy.
3. *Generalized amnesia.* In *generalized amnesia,* people forget their entire lives—who they are, what they do, where they live, whom they live with. This form of amnesia is very rare, although you wouldn't think so if you watch daytime soap operas. People with generalized amnesia cannot recall personal information, but they tend to retain their habits, tastes, and skills. If you had generalized amnesia, you would still know how to read, although you would not recall your elementary school teachers. You would still prefer French fries to baked potatoes—or vice versa.
4. *Continuous amnesia.* In this form of amnesia, the person forgets everything that occurred from a particular point in time up to and including the present.
5. *Systematized amnesia.* In *systematized amnesia,* the memory loss is specific to a particular category of information, such as memory about one's family or particular people in one's life.

People with dissociative amnesia usually forget events or periods of life that were traumatic—that generated strong negative emotions, such as horror or guilt. Consider the case of Rutger.

Rutger: A Case of Dissociative Amnesia

He was brought to the emergency room of a hospital by a stranger. He was dazed and claimed not to know who he was or where he lived, and the stranger had found him wandering in the streets. Despite his confusion, it did not appear that he had been drinking or abusing drugs or that his amnesia could be attributed to physical trauma. After staying in the hospital for a few days, he awoke in distress. His memory had returned. His name was Rutger and he had urgent business to attend to. He wanted to know why he had been hospitalized and demanded to leave. At the time of admission, Rutger appeared to be suffering from generalized amnesia: He could not recall his identity or the personal events of his life. But now that he was requesting discharge, Rutger showed localized amnesia for the period between entering the emergency room and the morning he regained his memory for prior events.

Rutger provided information about the events prior to his hospitalization that was confirmed by the police. On the day when his amnesia began, Rutger had killed a pedestrian with his automobile. There had been witnesses, and the police had voiced the opinion that Rutger—although emotionally devastated—was blameless in the incident. Rutger was instructed, however, to fill out an accident report and to appear at the inquest. Still nonplussed, Rutger filled out the form at a friend's home. He accidentally left his wallet and his identification there. After placing the form in a mailbox, Rutger became dazed and lost his memory.

Although Rutger was not responsible for the accident, he felt awful about the pedestrian's death. His amnesia was probably connected with feelings of guilt, the stress of the accident, and concerns about the inquest.

Adapted from Cameron, 1963, pp. 355–356. Personality development and psychopathology: A dynamic approach.

People sometimes claim they cannot recall certain events of their lives, such as criminal acts, promises made to others, and so forth. Falsely claiming amnesia as a way of escaping responsibility is called *malingering*, which refers to faking symptoms or making false claims for personal gain (such as avoiding work). Clinicians don't have any guaranteed methods for distinguishing people with dissociative amnesia from malingerers. But experienced clinicians can make reasonably well-educated guesses.

→ The Lady in the Water: A Case of Dissociative Amnesia

The captain of the Staten Island Ferry caught sight of the bobbing head in the treacherous waters about a mile off the southern tip of Manhattan. It was a woman floating face down in the water, and incredibly, she was alive. The crew rescued her from the river and she was taken to the hospital where she was treated for hypothermia and dehydration. Stories likes these seldom end well: A young woman mysteriously disappears. A body is found floating in the water. The body matches the description of the missing woman. Police suspect foul play or suicide. But this case was different, very different.

This was the case of a 23-year-old schoolteacher in New York City, Hannah Emily Upp, who one day went out jogging and three weeks later ended up being rescued from the river. What happened during the three weeks in which she was missing remains a mystery. Her doctors supplied an explanation: dissociative fugue, a subtype of dissociative amnesia in in which individuals suddenly lose their memory of their identity and may travel to other places, sometimes establishing whole new identities. The loss of personal memory may last for hours, days, or even years.

Hannah Emly Upp, months after her rescue, in the park near where which she went jogging the night she disappeared.

How did Hannah end up in the river? As best as we can tell, she hadn't jumped off a pier in an attempt to end her life; nor was she pushed. In a confused state, and suffering from a large blister on her foot from having walked around Manhattan for several weeks, she apparently sought relief by wading into the river on that warm August night. Hannah later reflected, "They think that just as I was wandering on land, I wandered in the water. . . . I don't think I had a purpose. But I had that really big blister, so maybe I just didn't want my shoes on anymore" (cited in Marx & Didziulis, 2009, p. CY7).

So many questions, so few answers. How had she survived for several weeks without any money or identification? (Her wallet, cell phone, and ID were found at her apartment.) Hannah herself could supply few answers. In her first interview some months after her rescue, she talked about her sense of responsibility for her disappearance: "How do you feel guilty for something you didn't even know you did? It's not your fault, but it's still somehow you. So it's definitely made me reconsider everything. Who was I before? Who was I then—is that part of me? Who am I now?" (cited in Marx & Didziulis, 2009, p. CY7). Months later, Hannah was reconnecting with friends and family, filling in the pieces of her past life and trying to come to terms with who she was.

A rare subtype of dissociative amnesia is characterized by *fugue,* or "amnesia on the run." The word *fugue* derives from the Latin *fugere,* meaning "flight." (The word *fugitive* has the same origin.) In dissociative fugue, the person may travel suddenly and unexpectedly from his or her home or place of work. The travels may either be purposeful, leading to a particular location, or involve bewildered wandering. During a fugue state, the person may be unable to recall past personal information and becomes confused about his or her identity or assumes a new identity (either partially or completely). Despite these odd behaviors, the person may appear "normal" and show no other signs of mental disturbance (Maldonado, Butler, & Spiegel, 1998). The person may not think about the past, or may report a past filled with false memories without recognizing them as false.

Whereas people with amnesia appear to wander aimlessly, people in a fugue state act more purposefully. Some stick close to home. They spend the afternoon in the park or in a theater, or they spend the night at a hotel under another name, usually avoiding contact with others. But the new identity is incomplete and fleeting, and the individual's former sense of self returns in a matter of hours or a few days. Less common is a pattern in which dissociative fugue lasts for months or years and involves travel to distant places and assumption of a new identity. These individuals may assume an identity that is more spontaneous and sociable than their former selves, which were typically "quiet" and "ordinary." They may establish new families and successful businesses. Although these events sound rather bizarre, the fugue state is not considered psychotic because people with the disorder can think and behave quite normally—in their new lives, that is. Then one day, quite suddenly, awareness of their past identity returns to them, and they are flooded with

Depersonalization. Episodes of depersonalization are characterized by feelings of detachment from oneself. It may feel as if one were walking through a dream or observing the environment or oneself from outside one's body.

old memories. Now they typically do not recall the events that occurred during the fugue state. The new identity, the new life—including all its involvements and responsibilities—vanish from memory.

Dissociative amnesia is relatively uncommon, but is most likely to occur in wartime or in the wake of another kind of disaster or extremely stressful event. The underlying notion is that dissociation protects the person from traumatic memories or other sources of emotionally painful experiences or conflict (Maldonado, Butler, & Spiegel, 1998).

Dissociative amnesia can also be difficult to distinguish from malingering. That is, people who were dissatisfied with their former lives could claim to have amnesia when they are discovered in their new locations and new identities. Let's consider a case that could lead to varying interpretations (Spitzer et al., 1989).

Burt or Gene? A Case of Dissociative Fugue?

A 42-year-old man had gotten into a fight at the diner where he worked. The police were called and the man, who carried no ID, identified himself as Burt Tate. He said he had arrived in town a few weeks earlier, but could not remember where he had lived or worked before arriving in town. Although no charges were pressed against him, the police prevailed upon him to come to the emergency room for evaluation. "Burt" knew the town he was in and the current date and recognized that it was somewhat unusual that he couldn't remember his past, but he didn't seem concerned about it. There was no evidence of any physical injuries, head trauma, or drug or alcohol abuse. The police made some inquiries and discovered that Burt fit the profile of a missing person, Gene Saunders, who had disappeared a month earlier from a city some 2,000 miles away. Mrs. Saunders was called in and confirmed that Burt was indeed her husband. She reported that her husband, who had worked in middle-level management in a manufacturing company, had been having difficulty at work before his disappearance. He was passed over for promotion and his supervisor was highly critical of his work. The job stress apparently affected his behavior at home. Once easygoing and sociable, he withdrew into himself and began to criticize his wife and children. Then, just before his disappearance, he had a violent argument with his 18-year-old son. His son called him a "failure" and bolted out the door. Two days later, the man disappeared. When he came face to face with his wife again, he claimed he didn't recognize her, but appeared visibly nervous.

Adapted from Spitzer et al., 1994, pp. 254–255

Although the presenting evidence supported a diagnosis of dissociative fugue, clinicians can find it difficult to distinguish true amnesia from amnesia that is faked to allow a person to start a new life.

Depersonalization/Derealization Disorder

Depersonalization is a temporary loss or change in the usual sense of our own reality. In a state of depersonalization, people feel detached from themselves and their surroundings. They may feel as if they are dreaming or acting like a robot (Sierra et al., 2006).

Derealization—a sense of unreality about the external world involving odd changes in the perception of one's surroundings or in the passage of time—may also be present. People and objects may seem to change in size or shape and sounds may seem different. All these feelings can be associated with feelings of anxiety, including dizziness and fears of going insane, or with depression.

Although these sensations are strange, people with depersonalization/derealization disorder maintain contact with reality. They can distinguish reality from unreality, even

THINKING CRITICALLY about abnormal psychology

@Issue: Are Recovered Memories Credible?

A high-level business executive's comfortable life fell apart one day when his 19-year-old daughter accused him of having repeatedly molested her throughout her childhood. The executive lost his marriage as well as his $400,000-a-year job. But he fought back against the allegations, which he insisted were untrue. He sued his daughter's therapists, who had helped her recover these memories. A jury sided with the businessman, awarding him $500,000 in damages from the two therapists.

This case is but one of many involving adults who claim to have only recently become aware of memories of childhood sexual abuse. Hundreds of people across the country have been brought to trial on the basis of recovered memories of childhood abuse, with many of these cases resulting in convictions and long jail sentences, even in the absence of corroborating evidence. Recovered memories often occur following suggestive probing by a therapist or hypnotist. The issue of recovered memories continues to be hotly debated in psychology and the broader community. At the heart of the debate is the question, "Are recovered memories believable?" No one doubts that childhood sexual abuse is a major problem confronting our society. But should recovered memories be taken at face value?

Several lines of evidence lead us to question the validity of recovered memories. Experimental evidence shows that false memories can be created, especially under the influence of leading or suggestive questioning during hypnosis or psychotherapy (Gleaves et al., 2004; McNally & Garaerts, 2009). Memory for events that never happened may actually be created and seem just as genuine as memories of real events (Bernstein & Loftus, 2009). If anything, genuine traumatic events are highly memorable, even if people may be a little sketchy about the details (McNally & Garaerts, 2009). A leading memory expert, psychologist Elizabeth Loftus (1996, p. 356), writes of the dangers of taking recovered memories at face value:

> After developing false memories, innumerable "patients" have torn their families apart, and more than a few innocent people have been sent to prison. This is not to say that people cannot forget horrible things that have happened to them; most certainly they can. But there is virtually no support for the idea that clients presenting for therapy routinely have extensive histories of abuse of which they are completely unaware, and that they can be helped only if the alleged abuse is resurrected from their unconscious.

Should we conclude, then, that recovered memories are bogus? Not necessarily. Both false memories and recovered true memories may exist (Gleaves et al., 2004). In all likelihood, some recovered memories are genuine, whereas others are undoubtedly false (Erdleyi, 2010).

In sum, we shouldn't think of the brain as a kind of mental camera that stores snapshots of events as they actually happened in the form of memories. Memory is more of a reconstructive process in which bits of information are pieced together in ways that can sometimes lead to a distorted recollection of events, although the person may be convinced the memory is accurate. Unfortunately, scientists don't have the tools needed to reliably distinguish true memories from false ones.

In thinking critically about the issue, answer the following questions:

1. Why should we not accept claims of recovered memories at face value?

2. How does human memory work differently than a camera in recording events and experiences?

---

truth OR fiction

Very few of us have episodes in which we feel strangely detached from our own bodies or thought processes.

☑ **FALSE** About half of all adults at some time experience an episode of depersonalization in which they feel detached from their own bodies or mental processes.

during the depersonalization episode. In contrast to generalized amnesia and fugue, they know who they are. Their memories are intact and they know where they are—even if they do not like their present state. Feelings of depersonalization usually come on suddenly and fade gradually.

Note that we have thus far described only normal feelings of depersonalization. Healthy people frequently experience transient episodes of depersonalization and derealization (Hunter et al., 2003). According to *DSM-5,* about half of all adults have experienced at least one episode of depersonalization/derealization at some point in their lives (APA, 2013). **T / F**

Given the commonness of occasional dissociative symptoms, Richie's experience, described in the following case study, is not atypical.

> **Richie's Experience of Depersonalization/Derealization at Disney World**
> *We went to Orlando with the children after school let out. I had also been driving myself hard, and it was time to let go. We spent three days "doing" Disney World, and it got to the point where we were all wearing shirts with mice and ducks on them*

Elizabeth Loftus. Research by Loftus and others has demonstrated that false memories of events that never actually occurred can be induced experimentally. This research calls into question the credibility of reports of recovered memories.

and singing Disney songs. On the third day I began to feel unreal and ill at ease while we were watching these middle-American Ivory-soap teenagers singing and dancing in front of Cinderella's Castle. The day was finally cooling down, but I broke into a sweat. I became shaky and dizzy and sat down on the cement next to the 4-year-old's stroller without giving [my wife] an explanation. There were strollers and kids and [adults'] legs all around me, and for some strange reason I became fixated on the pieces of popcorn strewn on the ground. All of a sudden it was like the people around me were all silly mechanical creatures, like the dolls in the "It's a Small World" [exhibit] or the animals on the "Jungle Cruise." Things sort of seemed to slow down, the way they do when you've smoked marijuana, and there was this invisible wall of cotton between me and everyone else.

Then the concert was over and my wife was like "What's the matter?" and did I want to stay for the Electrical Parade and the fireworks or was I sick? Now I was beginning to wonder if I was going crazy and I said I was sick, that my wife would have to take me by the hand and drive us back to the Sonesta Village [motel]. Somehow we got back to the monorail and turned in the strollers. I waited in the herd [of people] at the station like a dead person, my eyes glazed over, looking out over kids with Mickey Mouse ears and Mickey Mouse balloons. The mechanical voice on the monorail almost did me in and I got really shaky.

I refused to go back to the Magic Kingdom. I went with the family to Sea World, and on another day I dropped [my wife] and the kids off at the Magic Kingdom and picked them up that night. My wife thought I was goldbricking or something, and we had a helluva fight about it, but we had a life to get back to and my sanity had to come first.

→ *From the Author's Files*

Richie's depersonalization experience was limited to the one episode and would not qualify for a diagnosis of **depersonalization/derealization disorder.** The disorder is diagnosed only when these experiences become persistent or recurrent and cause significant distress or impairment in daily functioning. Depersonalization/derealization disorder

Key Features of Depersonalization/Derealization Disorder

- Repeated episodes of either or both depersonalization and derealization.
- Episodes are characterized by feelings of detachment from one's thoughts, feelings, or sensations (depersonalization) or from one's surroundings (derealization).
- Episodes may have the quality of seeming to be an outside observer of oneself.
- Episodes may have a dreamlike quality.
- During these episodes, the person can still distinguish reality from unreality.

can become a chronic or long-lasting problem. The *DSM* diagnoses depersonalization-derealization disorder according to the criteria shown in Table 6.3. Note the following case example.

➜ A Case of Depersonalization/Derealization Disorder

A 20-year-old college student feared he was going insane. For two years, he had increasingly frequent experiences of feeling "outside" himself. During these episodes, he experienced a sense of "deadness" in his body, and felt wobbly, frequently bumping into furniture. He was more apt to lose his balance when he was out in public, especially when he felt anxious. During these episodes, his thoughts seemed "foggy," which reminded him of his state of mind when he was given shots of a pain-killing drug for an appendectomy five years earlier. He tried to fight off these episodes when they occurred, by saying "stop" to himself and by shaking his head. This would temporarily clear his head, but the feeling of being outside himself and the sense of deadness would shortly return. The disturbing feelings would gradually fade away over a period of hours. By the time he sought treatment, he was experiencing these episodes about twice a week, each one lasting from three to four hours. His grades remained unimpaired, and had even improved in the past several months, because he was spending more time studying. However, his girlfriend, in whom he had confided his problem, felt that he had become totally absorbed in himself and threatened to break off their relationship if he didn't change. She had also begun dating other men.

Adapted from Spitzer et al., 1994, pp. 270–271

In terms of observable behavior and associated features, depersonalization and derealization may be more closely related to anxiety disorders such as phobias and panic disorder than to dissociative disorders. Unlike other forms of dissociative disorders that seem to protect the self from anxiety, depersonalization and derealization can lead to anxiety and in turn to avoidance behavior, as we saw in the case of Richie.

Cultural influences have an important bearing on the development and expression of abnormal behavior patterns, including dissociative syndromes such as depersonalization/derealization disorder. For example, evidence suggests that depersonalization and derealization experiences may be more common in individualistic cultures that emphasize individualism or self-identity, such as in the United States, than in collectivistic cultures, which emphasize group identity and responsibility to one's social roles and obligations (Sierra et al., 2006). As we explore next, dissociative disorders may also take very different forms in different cultures.

Culture-Bound Dissociative Syndromes

Similarities exist between the Western concept of dissociative disorder and certain culture-bound syndromes found in other parts of the world. For example, *amok* is a

An Inventory of Dissociative Experiences

Brief dissociative experiences, such as momentary feelings of depersonalization, are quite common in the general population (Bernstein & Putnam, 1986; Michal et al., 2009). Many of us experience them from time to time. Fleeting dissociative experiences may be quite common, but those reported by people with dissociative disorders are more frequent and problematic than those experienced by the general population (Waller & Ross, 1997). Dissociative disorders involve persistent and severe dissociative experiences.

The following is a sampling of dissociative experiences similar to those experienced by many people in the general population. Bear in mind that transient experiences like these are reported in varying frequencies by both normal and abnormal groups. Let's us suggest, however, that if these experiences become persistent or commonplace or cause you concern or distress, then it might be worthwhile to discuss them with a professional.

Have You Ever Experienced the Following?

1. Had a sense that objects or people around you seemed unreal.

2. Felt as if you were walking through a fog or a dream.

3. Weren't sure whether you were asleep or awake.

4. Not recognized yourself in a mirror.

5. Found yourself walking somewhere and not remembering where you were going or what you were doing.

6. Felt like you were watching yourself from a distance.

7. Felt detached or disconnected from yourself.

8. Didn't know who you were, or where you were, at a particular moment.

9. Felt distant or detached from what was happening around you.

10. Were in a familiar place that seemed unfamiliar or strange.

11. Finding yourself in a place but having no memory of how you got there.

12. Having such a vivid fantasy or daydream that it seemed like it was really happening at the moment.

13. Having a memory of an event that seemed like you were reliving it in the moment.

14. Felt like you were watching yourself doing something as if you were watching another person.

15. Spacing out when talking to someone and not knowing all or part of what the person was saying.

16. Becoming confused as to whether you had just done something or had just thought about doing it, such as wondering whether you had actually mailed or letter or just thought about mailing a letter.

---

culture-bound syndrome occurring primarily in southeast Asian and Pacific Island cultures that involves a trancelike state in which a person suddenly becomes highly excited and violently attacks other people or destroys objects (see Table 3.2 in Chapter 3). People who "run amuck" may later claim to have no memory of the episode or recall feeling as if they were acting like a robot. Another example is *zar,* a term used in countries in North Africa and the Middle East to describe spirit possession in people who experience dissociative states. During these states, individuals engage in unusual behavior, ranging from shouting to banging their heads against the wall.

Theoretical Perspectives

Dissociative disorders are fascinating and perplexing phenomena. How can one's sense of personal identity become so distorted that one develops multiple personalities, blots out large chunks of personal memory, or develops a new identity? Although these disorders remain in many ways mysterious, some clues provide insights into their origins.

6.3 Describe different theoretical perspectives on dissociative disorders.

PSYCHODYNAMIC VIEWS To psychodynamic theorists, dissociative disorders involve the massive use of repression, resulting in the splitting off from consciousness of unacceptable impulses and painful memories, typically involving parental abuse (Ross & Ness, 2010). Dissociative amnesia may serve an adaptive function of disconnecting or

Imaginary friends. It is normal for children to play games of make-believe and even to have imaginary playmates. In the case of multiple personalities, however, games of make-believe and the invention of imaginary playmates may be used as psychological defenses against abuse. Research indicates that most people with multiple personalities were abused as children.

truth OR fiction

Most people with multiple personalities had normal and uneventful childhoods.

☑ **FALSE** The great majority of people with multiple personalities report experiencing severe physical or sexual abuse during childhood.

dissociating one's conscious self from awareness of traumatic experiences or other sources of psychological pain or conflict. In dissociative amnesia and fugue, the ego protects itself from anxiety by blotting out disturbing memories or by dissociating threatening impulses of a sexual or aggressive nature. In dissociative identity disorder, people may express these unacceptable impulses through the development of alternate personalities. In depersonalization, people stand outside themselves—safely distanced from the emotional turmoil within.

SOCIAL-COGNITIVE THEORY From the standpoint of social-cognitive theory, we can conceptualize dissociation in the form of dissociative amnesia and fugue as a learned response involving the behavior of psychologically distancing oneself from disturbing memories or emotions. The habit of psychologically distancing oneself from these matters, such as by splitting them off from consciousness, is negatively reinforced by relief from anxiety or removal of feelings of guilt or shame. For example, shielding oneself from memories or emotions associated with past physical or sexual abuse by disconnecting (dissociating) them from ordinary consciousness is a way to avoid the anxiety or misplaced guilt these experiences may engender.

Some social-cognitive theorists, such as the late Nicholas Spanos, believe that dissociative identity disorder is a form of role-playing acquired through observational learning and reinforcement. This is not quite the same as pretending or malingering; people can honestly come to organize their behavior patterns according to particular roles they have observed. They might also become so absorbed in role-playing that they "forget" they are enacting a role.

BRAIN DYSFUNCTION Might dissociative behaviors be connected with underlying brain dysfunction? Research along these lines is still in its infancy, but preliminary evidence shows structural differences in brain areas involved in memory and emotion between patients with dissociative identity disorder and healthy controls (Vermetten et al., 2006). Although intriguing, the significance of these differences in explaining DID remains to be determined. Another study showed differences in brain metabolic activity between people with depersonalization/derealization disorder and healthy subjects (Simeon et al., 2000). These findings, which point to a possible dysfunction in parts of the brain involved in body perception, may help account for the feeling of being disconnected from one's body that is characteristic of depersonalization.

Recent evidence also points to another irregularity in brain functioning during sleep. Investigators suggest that disruption in the normal sleep-wake cycle may result in intrusions of dream-like experiences in the waking state that result in dissociative experiences, such as feeling detached from one's body (van der Kloet et al., 2012). Regulating the sleep-wake cycle may thus help prevent or treat dissociative experiences.

DIATHESIS–STRESS MODEL Despite widespread evidence of severe physical or sexual abuse in childhood in the great majority of people with dissociative identity disorder (Dale et al., 2009; Foote et al., 2005; Spiegel, 2006), very few children who experience extreme trauma eventually develop multiple personalities. Consistent with the diathesis–stress model, people who are prone to fantasize, are highly hypnotizable, and are open to altered states of consciousness, may be more likely than others to develop dissociative experiences in the face of traumatic abuse. (See Tying It Together on page 218.) These personality traits in themselves do not lead to dissociative disorders. They are actually quite common in the population. However, they may increase the risk that people who experience severe trauma will develop dissociative phenomena as a survival mechanism (Butler et al., 1996). Investigators continue to debate the role of fantasy proneness as a risk factor for dissociation in response to trauma (Dalenberg et al., 2012). Yet one possibility is that people who are not prone to fantasize will experience anxious, intrusive thoughts associated with posttraumatic stress disorder (PTSD) following traumatic stress, rather than dissociative disorders (Dale et al., 2009).

Perhaps most of us can divide our consciousness so that we become unaware of—at least temporarily—those events we normally focus on. Perhaps most of us can thrust the unpleasant from our minds and enact various roles—parent, child, lover, businessperson, and soldier—that help us meet the requirements of our situations. Perhaps the marvel is *not* that attention can be splintered, but that human consciousness is normally integrated into a meaningful whole.

Treatment of Dissociative Disorders

Dissociative amnesia and fugue are usually fleeting experiences that end abruptly. Episodes of depersonalization can be recurrent and persistent, and they are most likely to occur when people are undergoing periods of mild anxiety or depression. In such cases, clinicians usually focus on managing the anxiety or depression. Though research is limited, the available evidence shows that treating dissociative disorders does help reduce symptoms of dissociation, depression, and feelings of distress (Brand et al., 2009, 2012a).

Much of the research interest on treating dissociative identity disorder focuses on integrating the alter personalities into a cohesive personality structure. To accomplish this end, therapists seek to help patients uncover and work through memories of early childhood trauma. In doing so, they often recommend establishing connections with the dominant and alter personalities (Chu, 2011b; Howell, 2011). The therapist may ask the client to close his or her eyes and wait for the alter personalities to emerge (Krakauer, 2001). Wilbur (1986) points out that the analyst can work with whatever personality dominates the therapy session. The therapist asks any and all personalities that come out to talk about their troubling memories and dreams and assures them that the therapist will help them make sense of their anxieties, safely "relive" traumatic experiences, and make them conscious. The disclosure of abuse is considered essential to the therapeutic process (Krakauer, 2001). Wilbur notes that anxiety experienced during a therapy session may lead to a switch in personalities, because alter personalities were presumably developed as a means of coping with intense anxiety. But if therapy is successful, the person will be able to work through the traumatic memories and will no longer need to escape into alternate "selves" to avoid the anxiety associated with the trauma. Thus, reintegration of the personality becomes possible.

Through the process of integration, the disparate elements, or alters, are woven into a cohesive self. Here, a patient speaks about this process of "making mine" those parts of the self that had been splintered off.

"I" "Everybody's Still Here"

Integration made me feel alive for the first time. When I feel things now, I know I feel them. I'm slowly learning it's okay to feel all feelings, even unpleasant ones. The bonus is, I get to feel pleasurable feelings as well. I also don't worry about my sanity anymore.

It's difficult to explain even to people who try to understand what integration means to someone who has been "in parts" for a lifetime. I still talk in a "we" way sometimes. Some of my "before integration" friends assume I can now just get back to being "me"—whatever that is. They don't realize integration is like being three all over again. I don't know how to act in certain situations because "I" never did it before. Or I only know how to respond in fragmented ways. What does "sadness" mean to someone who doesn't feel it continually? I don't know sometimes when I feel sad if I really should. It's confusing and scary being responsible for me all by myself now.

The most comforting aspect of integration for me, and what I especially want other multiples to know is [this:] Nobody died. Everybody's still here inside me, in their correct place without controlling my body independently. There was not a scene where everybody left except one. I am a remarkably different "brand new" person. I've spent months learning how to access my alters' skills and emotions—and they are mine now. I have balance and perspective that never existed before. I'm happy and content. This isn't about dying. It's about celebrating living to the fullest extent possible.

From Olson, 1997

Wilbur describes the formation of another treatment goal in the case of a woman with dissociative identity disorder.

The "Children" Should Not Feel Ashamed

A 45-year-old woman had suffered from dissociative identity disorder throughout her life. Her dominant personality was timid and self-conscious, rather reticent about herself. But soon after she entered treatment, a group of "little ones" emerged, who cried profusely. The therapist asked to speak with someone in the personality system who could clarify the personalities that were present. It turned out that they included several children, all of whom were under 9 years of age and had suffered severe, painful sexual abuse at the hands of an uncle, a great-aunt, and a grandmother. The great-aunt was a lesbian with several voyeuristic lesbian friends. They would watch the sexual abuse, generating fear, pain, rage, humiliation, and shame.

It was essential in therapy for the "children" to come to understand that they should not feel ashamed because they had been helpless to resist the abuse.

Adapted from Wilbur, 1986, pp. 138–139

Does therapy for dissociative identity disorder work? We don't yet have sufficient empirical evidence to support any general conclusions (Brand, 2012b). In an early work, Coons (1986) followed 20 "multiples" aged between 14 and 47 at time of intake for an average of 3¼ years. Only five of the subjects showed a complete reintegration of their personalities. Yet other therapists report significant improvement in measures of dissociative symptoms and depressive symptoms in treated patients, even in those who failed to achieve integration. However, greater symptom improvement is also reported for those who achieved integration (Ellason & Ross, 1997).

Reports of the effectiveness of psychodynamic and other forms of therapy, such as behavior therapy, rely on uncontrolled case studies. Controlled studies of treatments of dissociative identity disorder or other forms of dissociative disorder are yet to be reported. The relative infrequency of the disorder has hampered efforts to conduct controlled experiments that compare different forms of treatments with each other and with control groups. Nor do scientists have evidence showing psychiatric drugs or other biological approaches are effective in bringing about integration of various alternate personalities. Though psychiatric drugs such as the antidepressant Prozac have been used to treat depersonalization/derealization disorder, there is a lack of evidence that they are any more effective than placebos (Simeon et al., 2004; Sierra et al., 2012). This lack of responsiveness suggests that depersonalization/derealization disorder may not be a secondary feature of depression.

The Three Faces of Eve. In the classic film *The Three Faces of Eve,* the actress Joanne Woodward (pictured here) won an Academy Award for playing Eve's three personalities: Eve White (left), a timid housewife, who harbors two alter personalities—Eve Black (middle), a libidinous and antisocial personality, and Jane (right), an integrated personality who can accept her sexual and aggressive urges but still engage in socially appropriate behavior. In the film, the therapist succeeded in helping Eve integrate her three personalities. In real life, however, Joanne Woodward reportedly split into 22 personalities later on.

Somatic Symptom and Related Disorders

The word *somatic* derives from the Greek *soma,* meaning "body." People with **somatic symptom and related disorders** (formerly called *somatoform disorders*) may have physical ("somatic") symptoms without an identifiable physical cause or have excessive concerns about the nature or meaning of their symptoms. The symptoms significantly interfere with the people's lives and often lead them to go "doctor shopping" in the hope of finding a medical practitioner who can explain and treat their ailments (Rief & Sharpe, 2004). Or they may hold the belief that they are gravely ill, despite reassurances from their doctors to the contrary. Some individuals fake or manufacture physical symptoms for no apparent reason other than to receive medical treatment.

The concept of somatic symptom and related disorders presumes that psychological processes affect physical functioning. For example, some people complain of problems in breathing or swallowing, or a "lump in the throat." Such problems can reflect overactivity of the sympathetic branch of the autonomic nervous system, which might result from anxiety. All in all, at least 20% of doctor visits involve complaints that cannot be explained medically (Rief & Sharpe, 2004).

There are several types of somatic symptom and related disorders. Here we consider the following major types: *somatic symptom disorder, illness anxiety disorder, conversion disorder*, and *factitious disorder*. Table 6.4 provides an overview of these disorders.

Somatic Symptom Disorder

Most people have physical symptoms somewhere along life's course. It is normal to feel concerned about one's physical symptoms and to seek medical attention. However, people with **somatic symptom disorder** (SSD) not only have troubling physical symptoms, but they are excessively concerned about their symptoms to the extent that it affects their thoughts, feelings, and behaviors in daily life. Thus, the diagnosis emphasizes the psychological features of physical symptoms, not whether the underlying cause or causes of

6.5 Describe the key features of these types of somatic symptom and related disorders: somatic symptom disorder, illness anxiety disorder, conversion disorder, and factitious disorder.

TYING it together

Although scientists have different conceptualizations of dissociative phenomena, evidence points to a history of childhood abuse in a great many cases. The most widely held view of dissociative identity disorder is that it represents a means of coping with and surviving severe, repetitive childhood abuse, generally beginning before the age of 5 (Burton & Lane, 2001; Foote, 2005). The severely abused child may retreat into alter personalities as a psychological defense against unbearable abuse. The construction of these alter personalities allows these children to psychologically escape or distance themselves from their suffering. In the case example in the opening of the chapter, one alter personality, Leah, bore the worst of the abuse for all the others. Dissociation may offer a means of escape when no other means is available. In the face of continued abuse, these alter personalities may become stabilized, making it difficult for the person to maintain a unified personality. In adulthood, people with multiple personalities may use their alter personalities to block out traumatic childhood memories and their emotional reactions to them, thus wiping the slate clean and beginning life anew in the guise of alter personalities. The alter identities or personalities may also help the person cope with stressful situations or express deep-seated resentments that the individual is unable to integrate within his or her primary personality. The diathesis–stress model, as represented in Figure 6.1, offers a conceptual framework for understanding the development of dissociative identity disorder on the basis of the combination of predisposing factors (a diathesis) and traumatic stress.

Compelling evidence indicates that exposure to childhood trauma, usually by a relative or caretaker, is involved in the development of dissociative disorders, especially dissociative identity disorder. Dissociative identity disorder is strongly linked to a history of sexual or physical abuse in childhood. In some samples, rates of reported childhood physical or sexual abuse have ranged from 76% to 95% (Ross et al., 1990; Scroppo et al., 1998). Evidence of cross-cultural similarity comes from a study in Turkey, which showed that the great majority of dissociative identity disorder patients in one research sample reported sexual or physical abuse in childhood (Sar, Yargic, & Tutkun, 1996). Childhood abuse is also linked to dissociative amnesia (Chu, 2011a).

Childhood abuse is not the only source of trauma linked to dissociative disorders. Trauma of warfare in both civilians and soldiers plays a part in some cases of dissociative amnesia. Significant life stress, such as severe financial problems and the wish to avoid punishment for socially unacceptable behavior, may precipitate episodes of dissociative amnesia or depersonalization.

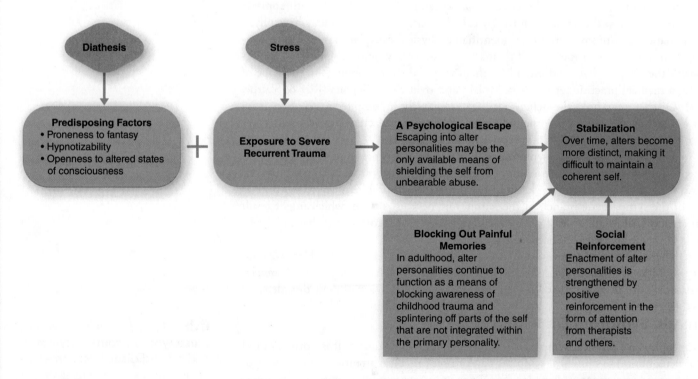

FIGURE 6.1

Diathesis–stress model of dissociative identity disorder. In this model, exposure to severe, recurrent trauma (stress), together with certain predisposing factors (diathesis), leads in some cases to the development of alter personalities, which over time become stabilized and strengthened by social reinforcement and blocking out of disturbing memories.

TABLE 6.4
Overview of Major Somatic Symptom and Related Disorders

Type of Disorder	Approximate Lifetime Prevalence in Population	Description	Associated Features
Somatic Symptom Disorder	Unknown, but may affect 5% to 7% of the general adult population	A pattern of abnormal behaviors, thoughts, or feelings relating to physical symptoms	• Symptoms prompt frequent medical visits or cause significant impairment of functioning
Illness Anxiety Disorder	Unknown	Preoccupation with the belief that one is seriously ill	• Fear of illness persists despite medical reassurance to the contrary • Tendency to interpret physical sensations or minor aches and pains as signs of serious illness
Conversion Disorder (Functional Neurological Symptom Disorder)	Unknown, but reported in 5% of patients referred to neurology clinics	Change in or loss of a physical function without medical cause	• Emerges in context of conflicts or stressful experiences, which lends credence to its psychological origins • May be associated with *la belle indifférence* (indifference to symptoms)
Factitious Disorder	Unknown, but an estimated 1% of medical patients in hospital settings may qualify for the diagnosis	Faking or manufacturing physical or psychological symptoms without any apparent motive	• Unlike malingering, the symptoms do not result in any obvious gain • There are two major types, factitious disorder imposed on self (fabricating or inducing symptoms in oneself, generally called Münchausen syndrome) and factitious disorder imposed on another (fabricating or inducing symptoms in others)

Source: Prevalence rates derived from APA, 2013.

the symptoms can be medically explained. The diagnosis of SSD requires that physical symptoms be persistent, lasting typically for a period of six months or longer (though any one symptom may not be continuously present) and that they are associated with either significant personal distress or interference with daily functioning. The symptoms may include such complaints as gastric (stomach) distress and various aches and pains.

People with SSD may have excessive concerns about the seriousness of their symptoms. Or they may be bothered by nagging anxiety about what their symptoms might mean and spend a great deal of time running from doctor to doctor seeking a cure or confirmation that their worries are valid. Their concerns may last for years and become a source of continuing frustration for themselves, as well as for their families and physicians (Holder-Perkins & Wise, 2002). A study that tracked use of medical care by patients with excessive somatic concerns found them to be heavy users of medical services (Barsky, Orav, & Bates, 2005).

Previous versions of the *DSM* included a disorder called **hypochondriasis**, which applied to people with physical complaints who believed their symptoms were due to a serious, undetected illness, such as cancer or heart disease, despite medical reassurance to the contrary. For example, a person suffering from headaches may fear that they are a sign of a brain tumor and believe doctors are wrong when they say these fears are groundless. At the core of hypochondriasis is health anxiety, a preoccupation that one's physical symptoms are signs of something terribly wrong with one's health (Abramowitz & Braddock, 2011; Skritskaya et al., 2012). Hypochondriasis is believed to affect about 1% to 5% of the general population and about 5% of patients seeking medical care (Abramowitz & Braddock, 2011; Barsky & Ahern, 2004). 👁

The term *hypochondriasis* is still in widespread use, but is no longer a distinct diagnosis in *DSM-5*. The great majority of cases previously diagnosed as hypochondriasis,

👁 **Watch** the **Video** *Henry: Hypochondriasis* in **MyPsychLab**

What to take? Hypochondriasis is a persistent concern or fear that one is seriously ill, although no organic basis can be found to account for one's physical complaints. People with this disorder frequently medicate themselves with over-the-counter medications and find little if any reassurance in doctors' assertions that their health is not in jeopardy.

perhaps as many as three fourths, would now be diagnosed as somatic symptom disorder (APA, 2013).

People with hypochondriasis do not consciously fake their symptoms. They feel real physical discomfort, often involving their digestive system or an assortment of aches and pains throughout the body. They may be overly sensitive to benign changes in physical sensations, such as slight changes in heartbeat and minor aches and pains (Barsky et al., 2001).

Anxiety about physical symptoms can produce its own physical sensations, however—for example, heavy sweating and dizziness, even fainting. Thus, a vicious cycle may ensue. Patients may become resentful when their doctors tell them that their own fears may be causing their physical symptoms. They frequently go doctor shopping in the hope that a competent and sympathetic physician will heed them before it is too late. Physicians, too, can develop hypochondriasis, as we see in the following case example.

→ The Doctor Feels Sick: A Case of Hypochondriasis

Robert, a 38-year-old radiologist, had just returned from a 10-day stay at a famous diagnostic center where he has undergone extensive testing of his entire gastrointestinal tract. The evaluation proved negative for any significant physical illness, but rather than feel relieved, he appeared resentful and disappointed with the findings. He had been bothered for several months with a variety of physical symptoms, including mild abdominal pain, feelings of "fullness," "bowel rumblings," and a feeling of a "firm abdominal mass." He had become convinced that his symptoms were due to colon cancer and began testing his stool for blood on a weekly basis and carefully palpating his abdomen for "masses" every few days while lying in bed. He also secretly performed X-ray studies on himself. There was a history of a heart murmur that was discovered when he was 13, and his younger brother had died of congenital heart disease in early childhood. Although the evaluation of his murmur showed it to be benign, he began worrying that something might have been overlooked. He developed a fear that something was terribly wrong with his heart, and while the fear eventually subsided, it never entirely left him. In medical school he worried about diseases he learned about in pathology. Since graduating, he repeatedly experienced concerns about his health that followed a typical pattern: noticing certain symptoms, becoming preoccupied with what the symptoms might mean, and undergoing physical evaluations that proved negative. His decision to seek a psychiatric consultation was prompted by an incident with his 9-year-old son. His son accidentally walked in on him while he was palpating his abdomen and asked, "What do you think it is this time, Dad?" He became tearful as he described this incident and reported feeling shame and anger—mostly at himself.

→ *Adapted from Spitzer et al., 1994, pp. 88–90*

People with hypochondriasis often report having been sick as children, having missed school because of health reasons, and having experienced childhood trauma, such as sexual abuse or physical violence (Barsky et al., 1994). Hypochondriasis and other forms of somatic symptom disorder can last for years and often occurs together with other psychological disorders, especially major depression and anxiety disorders.

About one in four people with hypochrondriasis complain of relatively minor or mild symptoms that they take to be signs of a serious undiagnosed illness. Because of the mildness of their symptoms, the diagnosis of somatic symptom disorder would not apply (APA, 2013). However, these individuals express such a high level of health anxiety or concern about their medical condition that they would likely receive a diagnosis of a newly recognized disorder in *DSM-5* called *illness anxiety disorder.*

Illness Anxiety Disorder

A common misconception is that physical symptoms in people with hypochondriasis are "made-up" or "all in their heads." However, in the great majority of cases, people with hypochondriasis have real symptoms that cause real distress and so would warrant a diagnosis of somatic symptom disorder (SSD). But there is a subgroup of people with hypochondriasis who complain of relatively minor or mild symptoms they take to be signs of a serious undiagnosed illness. The *DSM-5* introduced a new diagnostic category of **illness anxiety disorder** (IAD) to apply to this subgroup, with the emphasis placed on the anxiety associated with illness rather than the distress the symptoms cause. For these patients, it's not the symptoms they find so troubling—symptoms such as vague aches and pains or a passing feeling of tightness in the abdomen or chest. Rather, it's the fear of what these symptoms might mean. In some cases, there are no reported symptoms at all, but the person still expresses serious concerns about having a serious undiagnosed illness.

In some cases of illness anxiety disorder, the person has a family history of a serious disease (e.g., Alzheimer's disease) but becomes preoccupied with an exaggerated concern that he or she is suffering from the disease or is slowly developing it. The person may become preoccupied with checking his or her body for signs of the feared disease.

There are two general subtypes of the disorder. One subtype, the *care-avoidant subtype*, applies to people who postpone or avoid medical visits or lab tests because of high levels of anxiety about what might be discovered. The second subtype, called the *care-seeking subtype*, describes people who go doctor shopping, basically jumping from doctor to doctor in the hope of finding the one medical professional who might confirm their worst fears. These individuals may get angry at doctors who try to convince them that their fears are unwarranted.

Conversion Disorder

Conversion disorder (called *functional neurological symptom disorder* in *DSM-5*) is characterized by symptoms or deficits that affect the ability to control voluntary movements (inability to walk or move an arm, for example) or that impair sensory functions, such as an inability to see, hear, or feel tactile stimulation (touch, pressure, warmth, or pain). What qualifies these problems as a psychological disorder is that the loss or impairment of physical functions is either inconsistent or incompatible with known medical conditions or diseases. Consequently, conversion disorder is believed to involve the conversion or transformation of emotional distress into significant symptoms in the motor or sensory domain (Becker et al., 2013; Reynolds, 2012). In some cases, however, what appears to be conversion disorder actually turns out to be intentional fabrication or faking of symptoms for some external gain (malingering). Unfortunately, clinicians lack the ability to reliably determine that someone is faking.

The physical symptoms in conversion disorder usually come on suddenly in stressful situations. A soldier's hand may become "paralyzed" during intense combat, for example. The fact that conversion symptoms first appear in the context of, or are aggravated by, conflicts or stressors suggests a psychological connection. The prevalence of the disorder in the general population remains unknown, but the diagnosis is reported in about of 5% of patients referred to neurology clinics (APA, 2013). Like dissociative identity disorder, conversion disorder is linked in many cases to a history of childhood trauma or abuse (Sobot et al., 2012).

Conversion disorder is so named because of the psychodynamic belief that it represents the channeling, or *conversion*, of repressed sexual or aggressive energies into physical symptoms. Conversion disorder was formerly called *hysteria* or *hysterical neurosis*, and it played an important role in Freud's development of psychoanalysis (see Chapter 2). Hysterical or conversion disorders seem to have been much more common in Freud's day than they are today.

According to the *DSM,* conversion symptoms mimic neurological or general medical conditions involving problems with voluntary motor (movement) or sensory

Some people lose all feeling in their hands or legs, although nothing is medically wrong with them.

☑ **TRUE** Some people with conversion disorder have lost sensory or motor functions even though there is nothing medically wrong with them. (However, some people who are assumed to have conversion disorders may actually have medical problems that go unrecognized.)

6.6 **Explain** the difference between malingering and factitious disorder.

functions. Some classic symptom patterns take the form of paralysis, epilepsy, problems in coordination, blindness and tunnel vision, loss of the sense of hearing or of smell, or loss of feeling in a limb (anesthesia). The bodily symptoms found in conversion disorders often do not match the medical conditions they suggest. For example, *conversion epileptics*, unlike true epileptic patients, may maintain control over their bladders during an attack. People whose vision is supposedly impaired may walk through the physician's office without bumping into the furniture. People who become "incapable" of standing or walking may nevertheless perform other leg movements normally. Nonetheless, hysteria and conversion symptoms are sometimes incorrectly diagnosed in people who turn out to have underlying medical conditions (Stone et al., 2005).

If you suddenly lost your vision, or if you could no longer move your legs, you would probably show understandable concern. But some people with conversion disorders, like those with dissociative amnesia, show a remarkable indifference to their symptoms, a phenomenon termed *la belle indifférence* ("the beautiful indifference") (Stone et al., 2006). The *DSM* advises against relying on indifference to symptoms as a factor in making the diagnosis, however, because many people cope with real physical disorders by denying or minimizing their pain or concerns, which relieves anxieties—at least temporarily.

Factitious Disorder

Factitious disorder is a puzzlement. People with this disorder fake or manufacture physical or psychological symptoms, but without any apparent motive. Sometimes they are outright faking, claiming they cannot move an arm or a leg or claiming a pain that doesn't exist. Sometimes they injure themselves or take medication that causes troubling, even life-threatening symptoms. The puzzlement involves the lack of a motive for these deceitful behaviors. Factitious disorder is not the same as **malingering.** Because malingering is motivated by external rewards or incentives, it is not considered a mental disorder within the *DSM* framework. People may feign physical illness to avoid work or to qualify for disability benefits. They may be deceitful and even dishonest, but they are not deemed to be suffering from a psychological disorder.

But in factitious disorder, the symptoms do not bring about obvious gains or external rewards. Thus, factitious disorder serves an underlying psychological need involved in assuming a sick role; hence, it is classified as a type of mental or psychological disorder.

The two major subtypes of factitious disorder are (1) *factitious disorder on self* (characterized by faking or inducing symptoms in oneself) and (2) *factitious disorder imposed on another* (characterized by inducing symptoms in others).

Factitious disorder imposed on oneself is the most common form of the disorder and is popularly referred to as **Münchausen syndrome.** The syndrome is a form of feigned illness in which the person either fakes being ill or makes him- or herself ill (by ingesting toxic substances, for example). Although people with somatic symptom disorder may reap some benefits from having physical symptoms (e.g., drawing sympathy from others), they do not purposefully produce them. They do not set out to deceive others. But Münchausen syndrome is a type of factitious disorder in which there is deliberate fabrication or inducement of seemingly plausible physical complaints for no obvious gain, apart from assuming the role of a medical patient and receiving sympathy and support from others.

Münchausen syndrome was named after Baron Karl von Münchausen, one of history's great fibbers. The good baron, an 18th-century German army officer, entertained friends with tales of outrageous adventures. In the vernacular, *Münchausenism* refers to tellers of tall tales. In clinical terms, Münchausen syndrome refers to patients who tell tall tales or outrageous lies to their doctors. People who have Münchausen syndrome usually suffer deep anguish as they bounce from hospital to hospital and subject themselves to unnecessary, painful, and sometimes risky medical treatments, even surgery. "A Closer Look" explores this curious disorder in more depth.

Münchausen Syndrome

A woman staggered into the emergency room of a New York City hospital bleeding from the mouth, clutching her stomach, and wailing with pain (Lear, 1988). Even in that setting, forever serving bleeders and clutchers and wailers, there was something about her, some terrible star quality that held center stage. The story she told was one of horrible abuse and trauma. There was a man who had seduced her and then tied her, beaten her, and forced her to turn over her money and jewelry. She had other physical symptoms, including pain in her lower body and an intense headache. After she was admitted to the hospital, tests were run but to no avail. No physical cause of her bleeding and pain could be found. But a hospital aide noticed some objects on her bedside table, including a syringe and a blood thinner. Yes, she had injected herself before entering the hospital with the blood thinner, causing the bleeding. She denied it all, claiming the items on the bedside table were not hers. Someone had planted them on the table, she claimed. But finding no one who believed her, she soon checked herself out the hospital, claiming she would find other doctors who really cared. Later it was discovered that she had recently been admitted to two other hospitals, reporting the same symptoms.

Münchausen patients may go to great lengths to seek a confirmatory diagnosis, such as agreeing to exploratory surgery, even though they know there is nothing wrong with them. Some inject themselves with drugs to produce symptoms such as skin rashes. When confronted with evidence of their deception, they may turn nasty and stick to their guns. They are also skillful-enough actors to convince others that their complaints are genuine.

Why do patients with Münchausen syndrome fake illness or put themselves at risk by making themselves out to be sick or injured?

Perhaps enacting the sick role in the protected hospital environment provides a sense of security that was lacking in childhood. Perhaps the hospital becomes a stage on which they can act out resentments against doctors and parents that have been brewing since childhood. Perhaps they are trying to identify with a parent who was often sick. Or perhaps they learned to enact a sick role in childhood to escape from repeated sexual abuse or other traumatic experiences and continue to enact the role to escape stressors in their adult lives. No one is really sure, and the disorder remains one of the more puzzling forms of abnormal behavior.

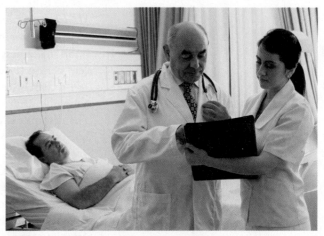

Is this patient really sick? Münchausen syndrome is characterized by the fabrication of medical complaints for no other apparent purpose than to gain admission to hospitals. Some Münchausen patients may produce life-threatening symptoms in their attempts to deceive doctors.

"I" Sickened: Factitious Disorder Imposed on Another

In her memoir entitled Sickened, Julie Gregory recounts how she was subjected to numerous X-rays and operations as a child, not because there was anything wrong with her, but to find the cause of an illness that existed only in her mother's mind (Gregory, 2003). At age 13, Julie underwent an invasive medical procedure, a heart catheterization, because of her mother's insistence to "... get to the bottom of this thing." When the cardiologist informed Julie's mother that the test results were within normal limits, her mother argued for an even more invasive test involving open-heart surgery. When the doctor refused, Julie's mother confronted him in Julie's presence:

"I can't believe it! I cannot believe this! You're not going to dig into this and do the open-heart? I thought we had agreed to follow this through to the end, Michael. I thought you said you were committed to me on this."

"I'm committed to finding Julie's illness, Ms. Gregory, but Julie doesn't need heart surgery. Usually parents are thrilled to—"

"Oh, that's just it? That's all you're going to do? Just drop me like a hot potato? I mean, for crying out loud, why can't I just have a normal kid like other mothers? I mean I'm a good mom . . . ."

I'm standing behind my mother's left leg, my eyes glued to the doctor, boring an SOS into his eyes: "Don't make me go, don't let her take me."

"Ms. Gregory, I didn't say you weren't a good mother. But I can't do anything else here. You need to drop the heart procedures. Period." And with that he turned on his heels.

"Well, you're the one who's going to be sorry," Mom screeches, "when this kid dies on you. That's what. Cause you're going to get sued out the yin-yang for being such an incompetent idiot. Can't even find out what's wrong with a thirteen-year-old girl! You are insane! This kid is sick, you hear me? She's sick!"

Source: Gregory, 2003.

Julie's case highlights a most pernicious form of child maltreatment called *Münchausen syndrome by proxy*, which in the *DSM-5* is now called *factitious disorder imposed on another*. People with this disorder intentionally falsify or induce physical or emotional illness or injury in another person, typically (and shockingly) a child or dependent person (Feldman, 2003).

Parents or caregivers who induce illness in their children may be trying to gain sympathy or experience the sense of control made possible by attending to a sick child. The disorder is controversial and remains under study by the psychiatric community. The controversy arises in large part because it appears to put a diagnostic label on abusive behavior. What is clear is that the disorder is linked to heinous crimes against children (Mart, 2003). In one sample case, a mother was suspected of purposely causing her 3-year-old's repeated bouts of diarrhea (Schreier & Ricci, 2002). Sadly, the child died before authorities could intervene. In another case, a foster mother is alleged to have brought about the deaths of three children by giving them overdoses of medicines containing potassium and sodium. The chemicals induced suffocation or heart attacks.

A review of 451 cases of Münchausen syndrome by proxy reported in the scientific literature showed that 6% of the victims died (Sheridan, 2003). Typical victims were 4 years of age or below. Mothers were perpetrators in three out of four cases. Cases of Münchausen syndrome by proxy often involve mysterious high fevers in children, seizures of unknown cause, and similar symptoms. Doctors typically find the illnesses to be unusual, prolonged, and unexplained. They require some medical sophistication on the part of the perpetrator.

6.7 Describe the key features of koro and dhat syndromes.

Koro and Dhat Syndromes: Far Eastern Somatic Symptom Disorders?

In the United States, it is common for people who develop hypochondriasis to be troubled by the idea that they have serious illnesses, such as cancer. The koro and dhat syndromes of the Far East share some clinical features with hypochondriasis. Although these syndromes may seem foreign to North American readers, each is connected with the folklore of its own culture.

KORO SYNDROME A culture-bound syndrome found primarily in China and some other Far Eastern countries, people with **koro syndrome** fear that their genitals are shrinking and retracting into their bodies, which they believe will result in death (Bhatia, Jhanjee, & Kumar, 2011). Koro is classified as a culture-bound syndrome, although some cases have been reported outside China and the Far East (e.g., Alvarez et al., 2012; Ntouros et al., 2010). The syndrome has been identified mainly in young men, although some cases have also been reported in women. Koro syndrome tends to be short-lived and to involve episodes of acute anxiety that one's genitals are retracting. Physiological signs of anxiety that approach panic are common, including profuse sweating, breathlessness, and heart palpitations. Men who suffer from koro have been known to use mechanical devices, such as chopsticks, to try to prevent the penis from retracting into the body (Devan, 1987).

Koro syndrome has been traced within Chinese culture as far back as 3000 B.C.E. Epidemics involving hundreds or thousands of people have been reported in China, Singapore, Thailand, and India (Tseng et al., 1992). In Guangdong Province in China, an epidemic of koro involving more than 2,000 people occurred during the 1980s (Tseng et al., 1992). Guangdong residents who developed koro tended to be more superstitious, lower in intelligence, and more accepting of koro-related folk beliefs (such as the belief that shrinkage of the penis will be lethal) than those who did not fall victim to the epidemic (Tseng et al., 1992). Medical reassurance that such fears are unfounded often quells koro episodes (Devan, 1987). Koro episodes among those who do not receive corrective information tend to pass with time but may recur. **T / F**

DHAT SYNDROME Found among young Asian Indian males, **dhat syndrome** involves excessive fears over the loss of seminal fluid in nocturnal emissions, in urine, or through masturbation (Bhatia, Jhanjee, & Kumar, 2011; Mehta, De, & Balachandran, 2009). Some men with this syndrome also believe (incorrectly) that semen mixes with urine and is excreted through urination. Men with dhat syndrome may roam from physician to physician seeking help to prevent nocturnal emissions or the (imagined) loss of semen mixed with excreted urine. There is a widespread belief within Indian culture (and other Near and Far Eastern cultures) that the loss of semen is harmful because it depletes the body of physical and mental energy. Like other culture-bound syndromes, dhat must be understood within its cultural context (Akhtar, 1988, p. 71):

> In India, attitudes toward semen and its loss constitute an organized, deep-seated belief system that can be traced back to the scriptures of the land ... [even as far back as the classic Indian sex manual, the *Kama Sutra*, which was believed to be written by the sage Vatsayana between the third and fifth centuries A.D.]. . . . Semen is considered to be the elixir of life, in both a physical and mystical sense. Its preservation is supposed to guarantee health and longevity.

It is a commonly held Hindu belief that it takes "forty meals to form one drop of blood; forty drops of blood to fuse and form one drop of bone marrow, and forty drops of this to produce one drop of semen" (Akhtar, 1988, p. 71). On the basis of the cultural belief in the life-preserving nature of semen, it is not surprising that some Indian males experience extreme anxiety over the involuntary loss of the fluid through nocturnal emissions (Akhtar, 1988). Dhat syndrome has also been associated with difficulty in achieving or maintaining erection, apparently due to excessive concern about loss of seminal fluid through ejaculation (Singh, 1985).

Theoretical Perspectives

Conversion disorder, or "hysteria," was known to the great physician of ancient Greece, Hippocrates, who attributed the strange bodily symptoms to a wandering uterus (*hystera* in Greek), creating internal chaos. Hippocrates noticed that these complaints were less common among married than unmarried women. He prescribed marriage as a "cure" on the basis of these observations and also on the theoretical assumption that pregnancy would satisfy uterine needs and fix the organ in place. Pregnancy fosters hormonal and structural changes that are of benefit to some women with menstrual complaints, but Hippocrates's mistaken belief in the "wandering uterus" has contributed throughout the centuries to degrading interpretations of women's complaints of physical problems. Despite Hippocrates's belief that hysteria is exclusively a female concern, it also occurs in men. **T / F**

truth OR fiction

Some men have a psychological disorder characterized by fear of the penis shrinking and retracting into the body.

☑ **TRUE** This culture-bound syndrome found in the Far East may have existed in China for at least 5,000 years.

truth OR fiction

The term *hysteria* derives from the Greek word for testicle.

☑ **FALSE** The term is derived from *hystera*, the Greek word for uterus.

6.8 Describe the theoretical understandings of somatic symptom and related disorders.

The wandering uterus. The ancient Greek physician Hippocrates believed that hysterical symptoms were exclusively a female problem caused by a wandering uterus. However, Hippocrates did not have opportunity to treat male aviators during World War II who developed "hysterical night blindness" that prevented them from carrying out dangerous nighttime missions.

Not much is known about the biological underpinnings of somatic symptom and related disorders. Brain imaging studies of patients with hysterical paralysis (a limb the person claims to be unable to move, despite healthy muscles and nerves) points to possible disruptions occurring in brain circuitry responsible for controlling movement and emotional responses (Kinetz, 2006). These imaging studies suggest that normal control of movement may be inhibited by activation of brain circuits involved in processing emotions. We should caution that scientists are only at the beginning stages of understanding the biological bases of conversion disorder and much remains unknown. Like the dissociative disorders, the scientific study of conversion disorder and other forms of somatic symptom disorder has been largely approached from the psychological perspective, which is our focus here.

PSYCHODYNAMIC THEORY Hysterical disorders provided an arena for some of the debate between the psychological and biological theories of the 19th century. The alleviation—albeit often temporary—of hysterical symptoms through hypnosis by Charcot, Breuer, and Freud contributed to the belief that hysteria was rooted in psychological rather than physical causes and led Freud to the development of a theory of the unconscious mind (see Chapter 2). Freud held that the ego manages to control unacceptable or threatening sexual and aggressive impulses arising from the id through defense mechanisms such as repression. Such control prevents the anxiety that would occur if the person were to become aware of these impulses. In some cases, the leftover emotion that is "strangulated," or cut off, from the threatening impulses becomes *converted* into a physical symptom, such as hysterical paralysis or blindness. Although the early psychodynamic formulation of hysteria is still widely held, empirical evidence has been lacking. One problem with the Freudian view is that it does not explain *how* energies left over from unconscious conflicts become transformed into physical symptoms (E. Miller, 1987).

According to psychodynamic theory, hysterical symptoms are functional: They allow the person to achieve *primary gains* and *secondary gains.* The primary gain of the symptoms is to allow the individual to keep internal conflicts repressed. The person is aware of the physical symptom but not of the conflict it represents. In such cases, the "symptom" is symbolic of, and provides the person with a "partial solution" for, the underlying conflict. For example, the hysterical paralysis of an arm might symbolize and also prevent the individual from acting on repressed unacceptable sexual (e.g., masturbatory) or aggressive (e.g., murderous) impulses. Repression occurs unconsciously, so the individual remains unaware of the underlying conflicts. *La belle indifférence,* first noted by Charcot, is believed to occur because the physical symptoms help relieve rather than cause anxiety. From the psychodynamic perspective, conversion disorders, like dissociative disorders, serve a purpose.

Secondary gains from the symptoms are those that allow the individual to avoid burdensome responsibilities and to gain the support—rather than condemnation—of those around them. For example, soldiers sometimes experience sudden "paralysis" of their hands, which prevents them from firing their guns in battle. They may then be sent to recuperate at a hospital rather than face enemy fire. The symptoms in such cases are not considered contrived, as would be the case in malingering. A number of bomber pilots during World War II suffered hysterical "night blindness" that prevented them from carrying out dangerous nighttime missions. In the psychodynamic view, their blindness may have achieved a primary gain of shielding them from guilt associated with dropping bombs on civilian areas. It may also have achieved a secondary purpose of helping them avoid dangerous missions.

LEARNING THEORY Theoretical formulations, including both psychodynamic theory and learning theory, focus on the role of anxiety in explaining conversion disorders. Psychodynamic theorists, however, seek the causes of anxiety in unconscious conflicts.

Learning theorists focus on the more direct reinforcing properties of the symptom and its secondary role in helping the individual avoid or escape anxiety-evoking situations.

From the learning perspective, people with somatic symptom and related disorders may also carry the benefits, or reinforcing properties, of the "sick role." People with conversion disorders, for instance, may be relieved of chores and responsibilities such as going to work or performing household tasks. Being sick also usually earns sympathy and support. See Figure 6.2 for a schematic representation of the psychodynamic and learning theory conceptualizations of conversion disorder.

Differences in learning experiences may explain why conversion disorders were historically more often reported among women than men. It may be that women in Western culture are more likely than men to be socialized to cope with stress by enacting a sick role (Miller, 1987). We are not suggesting that people with conversion disorders are fakers. We are merely pointing out that people may learn to adopt roles that lead to reinforcing consequences, regardless of whether they deliberately seek to enact these roles.

Some learning theorists link hypochondriasis to obsessive–compulsive disorder (e.g., Weck et al., 2011). People with hypochondriasis, which is now labeled somatic symptom disorder or illness anxiety disorder, are often bothered by obsessive, anxiety-inducing thoughts about the state of their health. Running from doctor to doctor may be a form of compulsive behavior that is reinforced by the temporary relief from anxiety that comes from doctors reassuring them that their fears are unwarranted. Yet the troublesome thoughts eventually return, prompting repeated consultations. The cycle then repeats.

COGNITIVE THEORY From a cognitive perspective, we can think about hypochondriasis in some cases as a type of self-handicapping strategy, a way of blaming poor performance on failing health. In other cases, diverting attention to physical complaints may serve as a means of avoiding thinking about other life problems.

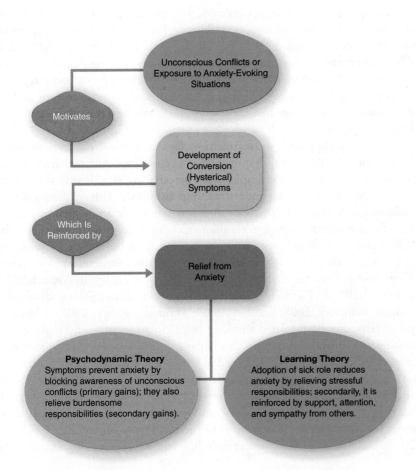

FIGURE 6.2

Conceptual models of conversion disorder. Psychodynamic and learning theories offer conceptual models of conversion disorder that emphasize the role of conversion symptoms that lead to escape or relief from anxiety.

Another cognitive explanation focuses on the role of distorted thinking. People with hypochondriasis have a tendency to exaggerate the significance of minor physical complaints (Fulton, Marcus, & Merkey, 2011; Hofmann, Asmundson, & Beck, 2011). They misinterpret benign symptoms as signs of a serious illness, which creates anxiety, which leads them to chase down one doctor after another in an attempt to uncover the dreaded disease they fear they have. The anxiety itself may lead to unpleasant physical symptoms, which are likewise exaggerated in importance, leading to more worrisome cognitions.

Anxiety about health concerns is a common feature of hypochondriasis and panic disorder (Abramowitz, Olatunji, & Deacon, 2008). Theorists speculate that both disorders may share a common cause involving a distorted way of thinking that leads to misinterpreting minor changes in bodily sensations as signs of pending catastrophe (Salkovskis & Clark, 1993). The differences between the two disorders may hinge on whether the misinterpretation of bodily cues carries a perception of an imminent threat that leads to a rapid spiraling of anxiety (panic disorder) or of a longer-range threat that leads to fear of an underlying disease process (hypochondriasis). Given the prominent role of anxiety in hypochondriasis, investigators question whether it should be classified, as it is now, as a form of somatic symptom disorder or illness anxiety disorder, or be moved to the category of anxiety disorders (Creed & Barsky, 2004; Gropalis et al., 2012).

BRAIN DYSFUNCTION Recently, investigators proposed that conversion symptoms may involve a disconnect or impairment in the neural connections between parts of the brain that control certain functions (speech, for example) and other parts involved in regulating anxiety (Bryant & Das, 2012). Research on the biological underpinnings of somatic symptom and related disorders is in its infancy, but it promises to help elucidate connections between anxiety and brain functions.

Treatment of Somatic Symptom and Related Disorders

6.9 Describe methods used to treat somatic symptom and related disorders.

The treatment approach that Freud pioneered, psychoanalysis, began with the treatment of hysteria, which is now termed *conversion disorder*. Psychoanalysis seeks to uncover and bring into conscious awareness unconscious conflicts that originated in childhood. Once the conflict is aired and worked through, the symptom is no longer needed and should disappear. The psychoanalytic method is supported by case studies, some reported by Freud and others by his followers. However, the infrequent occurrence of conversion disorders in contemporary times has made controlled studies of the psychoanalytic technique difficult to conduct.

The behavioral approach to treatment focuses on removing sources of secondary reinforcement (or secondary gain) that may become connected with physical complaints. Family members and others, for example, often perceive individuals with these disorders as sickly and incapable of carrying out normal responsibilities. This reinforces dependent and complaining behaviors. The behavior therapist may teach family members to reward attempts to assume responsibility and to ignore nagging and complaining. The behavior therapist may also work directly with patients, helping them learn more adaptive ways of handling stress or anxiety (through relaxation and cognitive restructuring, for example).

Cognitive-behavioral therapy has achieved good results in hypochondriasis, which is now classified as somatic symptom disorder or illness anxiety disorder (e.g., Abramowitz & Braddock, 2008; Kroenke, 2009; Thomson & Page, 2007). The cognitive technique of restructuring distorted thinking helps clients identify and replace exaggerated illness-related beliefs with rational alternatives. The behavioral technique of *exposure with response prevention,* which we discussed in Chapter 5, can help patients with somatic symptom disorder and illness anxiety disorder break the pattern of running to doctors for reassurance whenever they experience some worrisome, health-related concerns. These individuals can also benefit from breaking problem habits, such as repeatedly checking the Internet for illness-related information and reading newspaper obituaries (Barsky & Ahern, 2004). Unfortunately, many people with these types of disorders drop out of treatment when they are told that their problems are psychological in nature, not physical. As one leading expert, Dr. Arthur Barksy, put it, "They'll say, 'I don't need to talk about this, I need somebody to stick a biopsy needle in my liver, I need that CAT scan repeated'" ("Therapy and Hypochondriacs", 2004, p. A19). Although cognitive-behavioral therapy is the best established treatment for somatic symptom and related disorders, several studies also support the therapeutic value of antidepressants in treating hypochondriasis and factitious disorder (Münchausen syndrome) (Kroenke, 2009; Phillips, Albertini, & Rasmussen, 2002; Rief & Sharpe, 2004).

All in all, the dissociative disorders and somatic symptom and related disorders remain among the most intriguing and least understood patterns of abnormal behavior.

Psychological Factors Affecting Physical Health

The somatic symptom and related disorders open a window to the role of disturbed thoughts, behaviors, and emotions in our physical health. In this section, we take a broader view of the role of psychological factors in physical health. Whereas somatic symptom and related disorders are behavioral or psychological in nature, physical disorders are affected by psychological factors, as we will consider next. Physical disorders in which psychological factors are believed to play a causal or contributing role have traditionally been termed **psychosomatic** disorders. The term *psychosomatic* is derived from the Greek roots *psyche,* meaning "soul" or "intellect," and *soma,* which means "body." Disorders such as asthma and headaches have traditionally been labeled as psychosomatic because of the belief that psychological factors play an important role in their development.

Ulcers are another ailment traditionally identified as a psychosomatic disorder. Ulcers affect about 1 in 10 people in the United States. However, their status as a psychosomatic disorder has been reevaluated in light of recent landmark research showing that a bacterium, *H. pylori,* not stress or diet, is the major cause of the types of ulcers called *peptic ulcers,* which are sores in the lining of the stomach or upper part of the small intestine (Jones, 2006). Ulcers may arise when the bacterium damages the protective lining of the stomach or intestines. Treatment with a regimen of antibiotics may cure ulcers by attacking the bacterium directly. Scientists don't yet know why some people who harbor the bacterium develop ulcers and others do not. The virulence of the particular strain of *H. pylori* may determine whether infected people develop peptic ulcers. Stress may also play a role, although scientists lack definitive evidence that stress contributes to vulnerability (Jones, 2006).

The field of psychosomatic medicine explores health-related connections between the mind and the body. Today, evidence points to the importance of psychological factors in a much wider range of physical disorders than those traditionally identified as psychosomatic. In this section, we discuss several traditionally identified psychosomatic disorders as well as other diseases in which psychological factors may play a role in the course or treatment of the disease—cardiovascular disease, cancer, and HIV/AIDS.

Headaches

Headaches are symptoms of many medical disorders. When they occur in the absence of other symptoms, however, they may be classified as stress-related. By far the most frequent kind of headache is the *tension headache*. Stress can lead to persistent contractions of the muscles of the scalp, face, neck, and shoulders, giving rise to periodic or chronic tension headaches. Such headaches develop gradually and are generally characterized by dull, steady pain on both sides of the head and feelings of pressure or tightness.

6.10 Describe the role of psychological factors in physical health problems such as headaches, cardiovascular disease, asthma, cancer, and AIDS.

Migraine! Migraine headaches involve intense throbbing pain on one side of the head. They may be triggered by many factors, such as hormonal changes, exposure to strong light, changes in barometric pressure, hunger, exposure to pollen, red wine, and use of certain drugs and even monosodium glutamate.

Migraines, which affect about 30 million Americans, are more than simple headaches. They are complex neurological disorders that last for hours or days (Bigal et al., 2008; Dodick & Gargus, 2008). Although they can affect people of both genders and of all ages, about two out of three cases occur in women between 15 and 55 years of age.

Migraines may occur as often as daily or as seldom as every other month. They are characterized by piercing or throbbing sensations on one side of the head only or centered behind an eye. They can be so intense that they seem intolerable. Sufferers may experience an *aura,* or cluster of warning sensations that precedes the attack. Auras are typified by perceptual distortions, such as flashing lights, bizarre images, or blind spots. Coping with the misery of brutal migraine attacks can take its toll, impairing quality of life and leading to disturbances of sleep, mood, and thinking processes.

THEORETICAL PERSPECTIVES The underlying causes of headaches remain unclear and subject to continued study. One factor contributing to tension headaches may be increased sensitivity of the neural pathways that send pain signals to the brain from the face and head (Holroyd, 2002). Migraine headaches may involve an underlying central nervous system disorder involving nerves and blood vessels in the brain. The neurotransmitter serotonin is also implicated. Falling levels of serotonin may cause blood vessels in the brain to contract (narrow) and then dilate (expand). This stretching stimulates sensitized nerve endings, giving rise to the throbbing, piercing sensations associated with migraines. Evidence also points to a strong genetic contribution to migraine ("Scientists Discover," 2003).

Many factors can trigger a migraine attack, including emotional stress; stimuli such as bright lights and fluorescent lights; menstruation; sleep deprivation; altitude; weather and seasonal changes; pollen; certain drugs; the chemical monosodium glutamate (MSG), which is often used to enhance the flavor of food; alcohol; hunger; and weather and seasonal changes (Sprenger, 2011; Zebenholzer et al., 2011). In women, hormonal changes associated with the menstrual cycle can also trigger attacks, so it is not surprising that the incidence of migraines among women is about twice that among men.

TREATMENT Commonly available pain relievers, such as aspirin, ibuprofen, and acetaminophen, may reduce or eliminate pain associated with tension headaches. Drugs that constrict dilated blood vessels in the brain or help regulate serotonin activity are used to treat the pain from migraine headache.

Psychological treatment can also help relieve tension or migraine headache in many cases. These treatments include training in biofeedback, relaxation, coping skills training, and some forms of cognitive therapy (Holroyd, 2002; Nestoriuc & Martin, 2007). **Biofeedback training (BFT)** helps people gain control over various bodily functions, such as muscle tension and brain waves, by giving them information (feedback) about these functions in the form of auditory signals (e.g., "bleeps") or visual displays. People learn to make the signal change in the desired direction. Training people to use relaxation skills combined with biofeedback has also been shown to be effective. *Electromyographic* (EMG) biofeedback is a form of BFT that involves relaying information about muscle tension in the forehead. EMG biofeedback thus heightens awareness of muscle tension in this region and provides cues that people can use to learn to reduce it.

Some people have relieved the pain of migraine headaches by raising the temperature in a finger. This biofeedback technique, called *thermal BFT,* modifies patterns of blood flow throughout the body, including blood flow to the brain, helping to control migraine headaches (Smith, 2005). One way of providing thermal feedback is by attaching a temperature-sensing device to a finger. A console bleeps more slowly or rapidly as the temperature in the finger rises. The temperature rises when more blood flows to the fingers and away from the head. The client can imagine the finger growing warmer to bring about these desirable changes in the flow of blood in the body. T / F

truth OR fiction

People can relieve the pain of migraine headaches by raising the temperature in a finger.

☑ **TRUE** Some people have relieved migraine headaches by raising the temperature in a finger. This biofeedback technique modifies patterns of blood flow in the body.

Psychological Methods for Lowering Arousal

Stress induces bodily responses such as excessive levels of sympathetic nervous system arousal, which, if persistent, may impair our ability to function optimally and increase the risk of stress-related illnesses. Psychological treatments have been shown to lower states of bodily arousal that may be prompted by stress. Here, we consider two widely used psychological methods of lowering arousal: meditation and progressive relaxation.

Meditation

Meditation comprises several ways of narrowing consciousness to moderate the stressors of the outer world. Yogis (adherents to Yoga philosophy) study the design on a vase or a mandala. The ancient Egyptians riveted their attention on an oil-burning lamp, which is the inspiration for the tale of Aladdin's lamp. We've learned that meditation has measurable benefits in treating many psychological and physical disorders, especially those in which stress plays a contributing role, such as hypertension, chronic pain, and insomnia, as well as problems involving anxiety and depression (e.g., Arch et al., 2013; Chiesa & Serretti, 2011; Kenga, Smoski, & Robins, 2011; Manicavasgar, Parker, & Perich, 2011; Rapgay et al., 2011; Rosenberg, 2012; Sedlmeier et al., 2012; Treanor, 2011; Walsh, 2011). A recent study with African American heart patients showed that daily meditation reduced heart attack risk and deaths as compared to a health education (control) condition (Schneider et al., 2012).

There are many methods of meditation, but they all share the common thread of narrowing attention by focusing on repetitive stimuli. Problem solving, worrying, planning, and routine concerns may be temporarily suspended, and consequently, levels of sympathetic nervous system arousal are reduced.

Many thousands of Americans regularly practice *transcendental meditation (TM)*, a simplified kind of Indian meditation brought to the United States in 1959 by Maharishi Mahesh Yogi. Practitioners of TM repeat *mantras*—relaxing sounds such as *ieng* and *om.*

In *mindfulness meditation,* a form of meditation practiced by Tibetan Buddhists, the person focuses on increasing awareness of one's thoughts, feelings, and sensations on a moment-to-moment basis, without judging or evaluating them. We can liken it to observing the flow of a river. Meditation shows promise as a helpful treatment on its own or when combined with other psychological or medical treatments for problems such as hypertension, chronic pain, insomnia, anxiety, PTSD, and depression.

Functional magnetic resonance imaging (fMRI) shows that the brains of long-term practitioners of meditation, as compared to those of newly trained meditators, have higher levels of activity in the areas involved in attention and decision making (Brefczynski-Lewis et al., 2007) (see Figure 6.3). These findings lead scientists to speculate that regular practice of meditation may alter brain functioning in ways that may be therapeutic to children with *attention deficit/hyperactivity disorder* (ADHD), who have trouble maintaining attention. (ADHD is discussed further in Chapter 13.)

One of the lead investigators in the fMRI study, University of Wisconsin psychologist Richard Davidson, points out that it may be possible to train the brain through regular practice to become more efficient in performing certain cognitive processes, including attention. We can train the body through regular exercise, so perhaps we can also train the brain through systematic practice of attentional skills. As promising as these research findings may be, we await systematic research to determine whether psychological techniques can change the brain's attentional processes.

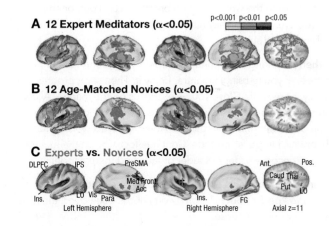

FIGURE 6.3

A well-trained brain. Here, we see brain scans of groups of expert meditators and novice meditators during an attentional task. Areas of greater activation are shown in hues of orange and red. Row C shows areas of the brains that were significantly different between the groups, with more activation in several parts of the brain involved in attentional processes, including the prefrontal cortex (toward the right side of the brain image).

Source: Brefczynski-Lewis et al., 2007 (Proceedings of the National Academy of Sciences).

Although there are differences among meditative techniques, the following suggestions illustrate some general guidelines.

1. Try meditation once or twice a day for 10 to 20 minutes at a time.

2. When you meditate, what you don't do is more important than what you do. So embrace a passive attitude: Tell yourself, "What happens, happens." In meditation, you take what you get. You don't strive for more. Striving of any kind hinders meditation.

3. Place yourself in a hushed, calming environment. For example, don't face a light directly.

4. Avoid eating for an hour before you meditate. Avoid caffeine (found in coffee, tea, many soft drinks, and chocolate) for at least two hours before meditation.

5. Get into a relaxed position. Modify it as needed. You can scratch or yawn if you feel the urge.

6. For a focusing device, you can concentrate on your breathing or sit in front of a serene object, such as a plant or burning incense. Benson suggests "perceiving" (not "mentally saying") the word once each time you breathe out. That is, think the word, but "less actively" than you normally would. Other researchers suggest thinking the word in as you breathe in and out, or ah-h-h, as you breathe out. They also suggest mantras, such as ah-nam, rah-mah, and shi-rim.

7. When preparing for meditation, repeat your mantra aloud many times—if you're using a mantra. Enjoy it. Then say it progressively more softly. Close your eyes. Focus on the mantra. Allow thinking the mantra to become more and more "passive" so you perceive rather than think it. Again, embrace your "what happens, happens" attitude. Continue focusing on the mantra. It may become softer or louder or fade and then reappear.

8. If unsettling thoughts drift in while you're meditating, allow them to "pass through." Don't worry about squelching them, or you may become tense.

9. Remember to take what comes. Meditation and relaxation cannot be forced. You cannot force the relaxing effects of meditation. Like sleep, you can only set the stage for it and then permit it to happen.

10. Let yourself drift. (You won't get lost.) What happens, happens.

Progressive Relaxation

Progressive relaxation was originated by University of Chicago physician Edmund Jacobson in 1938. Jacobson noticed that people tense their muscles under stress, intensifying their uneasiness. They tend to be unaware of these contractions, however. Jacobson reasoned that if muscle contractions contributed to tension, muscle relaxation might reduce tension. But clients who were asked to focus on relaxing muscles often had no idea what to do.

Jacobson's method of progressive relaxation teaches people how to monitor muscle tension and relaxation. With this method, people first tense, then relax, selected muscle groups in the arms; facial area; the chest, stomach, and lower back muscles; the hips, thighs, and calves; and so on. The sequence heightens awareness of muscle tension and helps people differentiate feelings of tension from relaxation. The method is progressive in that people progress from one group of muscles to another in practicing the technique. Since the 1930s, progressive relaxation has been used by a number of behavior therapists, including Joseph Wolpe and Arnold Lazarus (1966).

The following instructions from Wolpe and Lazarus (1966, pp. 177–178) illustrate how the technique is applied to relaxing the arms. Relaxation should be practiced in a favorable setting. Settle back on a recliner, a couch, or a bed with a pillow. Select a place and time when you're unlikely to be disturbed. Make the room warm and comfortable. Dim sources of light. Loosen tight clothing. Tighten muscles about two thirds as hard as you could if you were trying your hardest. If you sense that a muscle could have a spasm, you are tightening too much. After tensing, let go of tensions completely.

Relaxation of Arms (time: 4–5 minutes)

Settle back as comfortably as you can. Let yourself relax to the best of your ability. . . . Now, as you relax like that, clench your right fist, just clench your fist tighter and tighter, and study the tension as you do so. Keep it clenched and feel the tension in your right fist, hand, forearm … and now relax. Let the fingers of your right hand become loose, and observe the contrast in your feelings. . . . Now let yourself go and try to become more relaxed all over. . . . Once more, clench your right fist really tight … hold it, and notice the tension again. . . . Now let go, relax; your fingers straighten out, and you notice the difference once more. . . . Now repeat that with your left fist. Clench your left fist while the rest of your body relaxes; clench that fist tighter and feel the tension … and now relax. Again enjoy the contrast. . . . Repeat that once more, clench the left fist, tight and tense. . . . Now do the opposite of tension—relax and feel the difference. Continue relaxing like that for a while. . . . Clench both fists tighter and together, both fists tense, forearms tense, study the sensations … and relax; straighten out your fingers and feel that relaxation. Continue relaxing your hands and forearms more and more. . . . Now bend your elbows and tense your biceps, tense them harder and study the tension feelings … all right, straighten out your arms, let them relax and feel that difference again. Let the relaxation develop. . . . Once more, tense your biceps; hold the tension and observe it carefully. . . . Straighten the arms and relax; relax to the best of your ability. . . . Each time, pay close attention to your feelings when you tense up and when you relax. Now straighten your arms, straighten them so that you feel most tension in the triceps muscles along the back of your arms; stretch your arms and feel that tension. . . . And now relax. Get your arms back into a comfortable position. Let the relaxation proceed on its own. The arms should feel comfortably heavy as you allow them to relax. . . . Straighten the arms once more so that you feel the tension in the triceps muscles; straighten them. Feel that tension ... and relax. Now let's concentrate on pure relaxation in the arms without any tension. Get your arms comfortable and let them relax further and further. Continue relaxing your arms even further. Even when your arms seem fully relaxed, try to go that extra bit further; try to achieve deeper and deeper levels of relaxation.

Going with the flow. Meditation is a popular method of managing the stresses of the outside world by reducing states of bodily arousal. This young woman practices yoga, a form of meditation. She "goes with the flow," allowing the distractions of her environment to, in a sense, "pass through." Contrast her meditative state with the apparently stressful features of the young man sitting behind her.

Cardiovascular Disease

Your cardiovascular system, the network that connects your heart and blood vessels, is your highway of life. Unfortunately, there are accidents along this highway in the form of **cardiovascular disease** (CVD) or heart and artery disease. CVD is the leading cause of death in the United States, claiming about 830,000 lives annually and accounting for about one in every three deaths, most often as the result of heart attacks or strokes (American Heart Association, 2009). *Coronary heart disease* (CHD), the major form of cardiovascular disease, accounts for nearly 500,000 of these deaths. CHD is the leading cause of death for both men and women, claiming even more women's lives than breast cancer.

In coronary heart disease, the flow of blood to the heart is insufficient to meet the heart's needs. The underlying disease process in CHD is called *arteriosclerosis,* or "hardening of the arteries," a condition in which artery walls become thicker, harder, and less elastic, which makes it more difficult for blood to flow freely. The major underlying cause of arteriosclerosis is *atherosclerosis,* a process involving the buildup of fatty deposits along artery walls, which leads to the formation of artery-clogging plaque. If a blood clot should form in an artery narrowed by plaque, it may nearly or completely block the flow of blood to the heart. The result is a heart attack (also called a *myocardial infarction*), a life-threatening event in which heart tissue dies because of a lack of oxygen-rich blood. When a blood clot blocks the supply of blood in an artery serving the brain, a *stroke* can occur, leading to death of brain tissue, which can result in loss of function controlled by that part of the brain, coma, or even death.

We can lower our risks of developing cardiovascular disease by reducing risk factors we can directly control. Some risk factors are indeed beyond our control, such as age and family history. But other major risk factors are controllable through obtaining medical treatment and making healthy lifestyle changes—factors such as high blood levels of low-density lipoprotein (LDL) cholesterol, hypertension (high blood pressure), smoking, overeating, heavy drinking, consuming a high-fat diet, and leading a sedentary lifestyle (e.g., Cannon, 2011; Djoussé, Driver, & Gaziano, 2009; Mitka, 2012).

Fortunately, adoption of healthier behaviors can have beneficial effects on the heart and circulatory system (Roger, 2009). Even seasoned couch potatoes can reduce their risk of cardiovascular disease by becoming more physically active (Borjesson & Dahlof, 2005). Additional good news is that deaths from CHD have been declining since the 1980s, thanks largely to improved medical care and reductions in risk factors such as smoking (Levy, 2012; CDC, 2011a; National Center for Health Statistics, 2012a).

NEGATIVE EMOTIONS Frequent emotional distress in the form of anger, anxiety, and depression may have damaging effects on the cardiovascular system (e.g., Glassman, Bigger, & Gaffney, 2009; Lichtman et al., 2008; Whooley et al., 2008). Here, we focus on the effects of chronic anger.

Occasional anger may not damage the heart in healthy people, but chronic anger—the type you see in people who appear to be angry much of the time—is linked to increased risk of CHD (Chida & Steptoe, 2009; Denollet & Pedersen, 2009; Pressman & Cohen, 2005). Anger is closely associated with hostility—a personality trait characterized by quickness to anger and by tendencies to blame others and to perceive the world in negative terms. Hostile people tend to have short fuses and are prone to getting angry easily. Hostility is a component of the **Type A behavior pattern (TABP)**, a style of behavior that characterizes people who are hard driving, ambitious, impatient, and highly competitive. Although earlier research had linked the TABP to a higher risk of CHD, later research casts doubt on the relationship between this general behavior pattern and coronary risk (Geipert, 2007). On the other hand, evidence consistently links hostility, a component of the TABP, to increased risks of heart disease and other negative health outcomes (Chida & Steptoe, 2009; Denollet & Pedersen, 2009; Olson et al., 2006).

People high in hostility tend to be angry much of the time. But how might anger or other negative emotions translate into increased risk of coronary heart disease? Although we can't say with certainty, the stress hormones epinephrine and norepinephrine appear to play significant roles. Anxiety and anger trigger the release of these stress hormones by the adrenal glands. These hormones increase heart rate, breathing rate, and blood pressure, which results in pumping more oxygen-rich blood to the muscles to enable them to prepare for defensive action—to either fight or flee—in the face of a threatening stressor. In people who frequently experience strong negative emotions such as anger or anxiety, the body may repeatedly pump out these stress hormones, eventually damaging the heart and blood vessels.

Episodes of acute anger can actually trigger heart attacks and sudden cardiac death in people with established heart disease (Clay, 2001a). Moreover, people who are higher

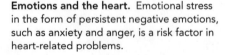

Emotions and the heart. Emotional stress in the form of persistent negative emotions, such as anxiety and anger, is a risk factor in heart-related problems.

in the psychological trait of hostility tend to have more cardiovascular risk factors, such as obesity and smoking, than do less hostile people (Bunde & Suls, 2006). Anxiety and anger may also compromise the cardiovascular system by increasing blood levels of cholesterol, the fatty substance that clogs arteries and increases the risk of heart attacks (Suinn, 2001).

Helping angry people learn to remain calm in provocative situations may have beneficial effects on the heart as well as the mind. Depression may also play a role in coronary heart disease, perhaps because it places additional stress on the body (Gordon et al., 2011; Huffman et al., 2008). As Jeff Huffman of Harvard Medical School, a leading researcher in this area, puts it, "There is good evidence that if a person has depression after a heart attack, they are more likely to die from cardiac causes in the following months and years" (cited in "Depression Ups Risk," 2008). But even people without already established heart disease who suffered major depression appear to be at greater risk than nondepressed people of dying from heart-related causes (Penninx et al., 2000). All in all, taking care of our emotional health may yield additional benefits for our physical health.

SOCIAL ENVIRONMENTAL STRESS *Social environmental stress* also appears to heighten the risk of CHD (Krantz et al., 1988). Factors such as overtime work, assembly-line labor, and exposure to conflicting demands are linked to increased risk of CHD (C. D. Jenkins, 1988). The stress–CHD connection is not straightforward, however. For example, the effects of demanding occupations may be moderated by factors such as psychological hardiness and whether or not people find their work meaningful (Krantz et al., 1988).

Other forms of stress are also linked to increased cardiovascular risk (Walsh, 2011). Researchers in Sweden, for example, find that among women, marital stress triples the risk of recurrent cardiac events, including heart attacks and cardiac death (Foxhall, 2001; Orth-Gomér et al., 2000).

a CLOSER look

Can You Die of a Broken Heart?

You've probably heard the expression "a broken heart" used in relation to a failed romantic relationship. But broken-heart syndrome is an actual medical condition that potentially can be deadly. Under high emotional stress, the body releases large amounts of stress hormones epinephrine and norepinephrine into the bloodstream. Physicians suspect that in broken-heart syndrome, these hormones effectively "stun" the heart, preventing it from pumping normally (Wittstein et al., 2006). The symptoms can be very similar to those of a true heart attack, including chest pain and problems breathing ("As Valentine's Day Approaches," 2012). Consider this case report:

The patient's heart was failing. She was only 45, but showed all the signs of having a heart attack. But it wasn't a heart attack. Were it a heart attack, there would have been blockage of blood flow through the arteries that service the heart. However, blood flowed freely to her heart. No, in this case, the woman's heart was failing because of the emotional shock of losing her husband in a car crash two days earlier. She had rushed to the crash site and collapsed next to his body, crying inconsolably and trying desperately but unsuccessfully to wake him. Two days later, she was rushed to the hospital complaining of chest pain and difficulty breathing. This woman's heart was pumping only a fraction of the expected amount of blood. Fortunately, the woman survived, as the levels of stress hormones receded and the heart returned to pumping at a nearly normal level. Later, she told a reporter, "If anyone had told me that you could die of a broken heart … I'd never have believed it. But I almost did." (Sanders, 2006, p. 28)

Although broken-heart syndrome was so named because of its association with intense grief, it may also be triggered by stressful events associated with strong emotional reactions of anxiety, fear, or even sudden surprise (Naggiar, 2012). Fortunately, broken-heart syndrome is a rare occurrence, but it may explain isolated cases of sudden death following an emotional shock, such as the unexpected death of a spouse. For people without a prior history of heart disease, the symptoms are usually short-lived and, unlike true heart attacks, they do not permanently damage the heart ("As Valentine's Day Approaches," 2012). But patients with established coronary heart disease may be especially susceptible to serious, even life-threatening coronary events in response to strong emotional stress (Strike et al., 2006).

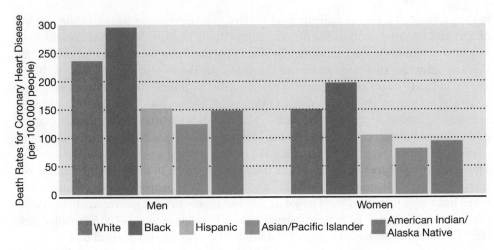

FIGURE 6.4

Coronary heart disease death rates in relation to race and ethnicity. Deaths due to CHD in our society fall disproportionately on White men and on Black (non-Hispanic) men and women.

Source: National Center for Health Statistics. (2012b). *Health, United States, 2011: With Special Feature on Socioeconomic Status and Health*. Hyattsville, MD.

ETHNICITY AND CHD Coronary heart disease is not an equal opportunity destroyer. European Americans (non-Hispanic Whites) and African Americans (non-Hispanic Blacks) have the highest rates of death due to coronary heart disease (see Figure 6.4) (Ferdinand & Ferdinand, 2009). Factors such as obesity, smoking, diabetes, and hypertension play important roles in determining relative risks of CHD and the rate of CHD-related deaths (CDC, 2011; Taubes, 2012). For example, African Americans have higher rates of hypertension relative to other U.S. population groups, as well as higher rates of obesity and diabetes. Moreover, a dual standard of care limits access to quality health care for minority group members. Black Americans with heart disease who suffer heart attacks, strokes, or heart failure generally do not receive the same level of care as Whites or have as much access to the latest cardiac care technologies, which likely contributes to their higher overall death rates due to cardiovascular disease (Chen et al., 2001; Peterson & Yancy, 2009). This dual standard of care may reflect discrimination as well as cultural factors limiting utilization of services, such as mistrust among many African Americans toward the medical establishment.

We finish this section with encouraging news. Americans have begun to take better care of their cardiovascular health. The incidence of CHD and deaths from heart disease have been declining steadily during the past 50 years, thanks largely to reductions in smoking, to improved treatment for coronary heart disease, and perhaps to other lifestyle changes, such as reduced intake of dietary fat. Better-educated people are also more likely to modify unhealthy behavior patterns and reap the benefits of change. Is there a message here for you? T / F

Asthma

Asthma is a respiratory disorder in which the main tubes of the windpipe—the bronchi—constrict and become inflamed, and large amounts of mucus are secreted. During asthma attacks, people wheeze, cough, and struggle to breathe in enough air. They may feel as though they are suffocating.

Asthma affects approximately 16 million adults and 7 million children in the United States (CDC, 2009b). Rates of asthma are on the rise, having more than doubled over the past 30 years. Attacks can last from just a few minutes to several hours and vary notably in intensity. A series of attacks can harm the bronchial system, causing mucus to collect and muscles to lose their elasticity. Sometimes the bronchial system is weakened to the point where a subsequent attack is lethal.

truth OR fiction

Deaths from coronary heart disease are rising in the United States, largely as a result of increased rates of smoking.

☑ **FALSE**   Just the opposite is the case.

THEORETICAL PERSPECTIVES Many causal factors are implicated in asthma, including allergic reactions; exposure to environmental pollutants, including cigarette smoke and smog; and genetic and immunological factors. Asthmatic reactions in susceptible people can be triggered by exposure to allergens such as pollen, mold spores, and animal dander; by cold, dry air and by hot, humid air; and by emotional responses such as anger or even laughing too hard. Psychological factors such as stress, anxiety, and depression can increase susceptibility to asthmatic attacks (see Schreier & Chen, 2008; Voelker, 2012). Asthma, moreover, has psychological consequences. Some sufferers avoid strenuous activity, including exercise, for fear of increasing their demand for oxygen and tripping attacks.

TREATMENT Although asthma cannot be cured, it can be controlled by reducing exposure to allergens, by desensitization therapy ("allergy shots") to help the body acquire more resistance to allergens, by use of inhalers, and by drugs that open bronchial passages during asthma attacks (called *bronchodilators*) and others (called *anti-inflammatories*) that reduce future attacks by helping to keep bronchial tubes open. Behavioral techniques may be used to help asthma sufferers develop breathing and relaxation skills to improve their breathing and cope more effectively with stress (e.g., Brody, 2009).

Cancer

The word *cancer* is arguably the most feared word in the English language, and rightly so: One out of every four deaths in the United States is caused by cancer. Cancer claims about half a million lives in the United States annually, one every 90 seconds or so. Men have a one in two chance of developing cancer at some point in their lives; for women the odds are one in three. Yet there is good news to report: The cancer death rate has been inching downward in recent years, in large part due to better screening and treatment (Jemal et al., 2007).

Cancer involves the development of aberrant, or mutant, cells that form growths (tumors) that spread to healthy tissue. Cancerous cells can take root anywhere—in the blood, bones, lungs, digestive tract, and reproductive organs. When it is not contained early, cancer may *metastasize,* or establish colonies throughout the body, leading to death.

There are many causes of cancer, including genetic factors, exposure to cancer-causing chemicals, and even exposure to some viruses. Yet more than half of all cancers could be prevented if people adopted healthier behaviors, especially avoiding smoking, limiting fat intake, controlling excess body weight, curtailing alcohol consumption, exercising regularly, and limiting exposure to the sun (i.e., ultraviolet light causes skin cancer) (e.g., Colditz, Wolin, & Gehlert, 2012; Li et al., 2009). Consider, for example, that death rates from cancer are much lower in Japan than in the United States, where people ingest more fat, especially animal fat. The difference is not genetic or racial, but one of lifestyle and diet; Japanese Americans whose dietary intake of saturated fat approximates that of the typical American diet show similar death rates from cancer as other Americans.

STRESS AND CANCER A weakened or compromised immune system may increase susceptibility to cancer. We've seen that psychological factors, such as exposure to stress, may affect the immune system. So it stands to reason that exposure to stress might increase a person's risk of developing cancer. However, links between stress and cancer remain inconclusive and in need of further study (Cohen, Janicki-Deverts, & Miller, 2007; Dougall & Baum, 2001).

On the other hand, we have ample evidence that psychological counseling and group support programs can help cancer patients cope with the emotional consequences of cancer, which often include depression, anxiety, and feelings of hopelessness (e.g., Antoni, 2012; Brothers et al., 2011; Hopko et al., 2011; Piet, Würtzen, & Zachariae, 2012). Investigators also recently reported that cognitive therapy that included a mindfulness meditation training component improved depression and anxiety in cancer patients (Foley et al., 2010). Promising findings from an 11-year study at Ohio State University showed that participation in coping skills training and stress learning management techniques increased survival rates in women with breast cancer (Anderson et al., 2008).

Cancer patients may also benefit from coping skills training programs aimed at relieving the stress and pain of coping with cancer, such as dealing with the unpleasant side effects of chemotherapy. Cues associated with chemotherapy, such as the hospital environment itself, may become conditioned stimuli that elicit nausea and vomiting even before the drugs are administered. Pairing relaxation, pleasant imagery, and attention distraction with these cues can help reduce nausea and vomiting associated with chemotherapy (Redd & Jacobsen, 2001).

Acquired Immunodeficiency Syndrome

Acquired immunodeficiency syndrome (AIDS) is a disease caused by the *human immunodeficiency virus* (HIV). HIV attacks the immune system, leaving it helpless to fend off diseases it normally would hold in check. HIV/AIDS is one of history's worst epidemics. HIV/AIDS has claimed more than 430,000 lives in the United States and some 24 million worldwide (Bongaarts, Pelletier, & Gerland, 2010a). More than 30 million people worldwide are believed to be infected with HIV (Kaiser Family Foundation, 2012). Approximately 55,000 new cases of HIV infection are reported annually in the United States (CDC, 2011a).

There are two primary reasons for including HIV/AIDS in our discussion of psychological factors in physical illness. First, people living with HIV/AIDS often develop significant psychological problems in adjusting to living with the disease. Second, behavioral patterns such as unsafe sexual and injection practices play the dominant role in determining the risk of contracting and transmitting the virus.

HIV can be transmitted by sexual contact, that is, vaginal and anal intercourse or oral–genital contact; direct infusion of contaminated blood, as from transfusions of contaminated blood, accidental pricks from needles used previously on an infected person, or needle sharing among injecting drug users; or from an infected mother to a child during pregnancy or childbirth or through breast-feeding. AIDS is not contracted by donating blood; by airborne germs; by insects; or by casual contact, such as using public toilets, holding or hugging infected people, sharing eating utensils with them, or living or going to school with them. Routine screening of the blood supply for HIV has reduced the risk of infection from blood transfusions to virtually nil. There is no cure or vaccine for HIV infection, but the introduction of highly effective antiretroviral drugs has revolutionized treatment of the disease (Thompson et al., 2012). Although not a cure, these drugs can keep the disease at bay for decades (Cohen, 2012). Fortunately, the number of AIDS-related deaths worldwide has declined in recent years as antiviral therapies become more widely available., However, the lack of a cure or effective vaccine means that prevention programs focusing on reducing or eliminating risky sexual and injection practices represent our best hope for controlling the epidemic.

ADJUSTMENT OF PEOPLE WITH HIV AND AIDS Given the nature of the disease and the stigma suffered by people with HIV and AIDS, it is not surprising that many people with HIV, although certainly not all, develop psychological problems, most commonly anxiety and depression.

Psychologists and other mental health professionals are involved in providing treatment services to people affected by HIV/AIDS. Coping skills training and cognitive-behavioral therapy can improve immune response, reduce feelings of depression and anxiety, enhance ability to handle stress, and improve quality of life in patients with HIV/AIDS (McCain et al., 2008; Scott-Sheldon et al., 2008; Stout-Shaffer & Page, 2008). Treatment may incorporate stress-management techniques, such as relaxation training and use of positive mental imagery, as well as cognitive strategies to control intrusive negative thoughts and preoccupations.

Antidepressant medication may also help patients with HIV/AIDS cope with a frequent emotional consequence of living with the disease—depression. Whether treatment of depression or stress management training can improve immunological functioning or prolong life in people with HIV and AIDS remains an open question.

PSYCHOLOGICAL INTERVENTIONS TO REDUCE RISKY BEHAVIORS Providing information about risk reduction alone is not sufficient to induce widespread changes in sexual behavior. Despite awareness of the dangers, many people continue to practice unsafe sexual and injection behaviors. Fortunately, psychological interventions are effective in helping people alter risky behaviors (e.g., Albarracín, Durantini, & Ear, 2006; Carey et al., 2004). These programs raise awareness about risky behaviors and help people practice more adaptive behaviors, such as assertively refusing invitations to engage in unsafe sex and communicate more effectively with partner about safer sexual practices. The likelihood of engaging in safer sexual practices is also linked to the avoidance of alcohol and drugs before sex and to the perception that practicing safer sex represents a social norm (expected behavior) within one's peer group.

We have focused on relationships between stress and health and on the psychological factors involved in health. Psychology has much to offer in the understanding and treatment of physical disorders. Psychological approaches may help in the treatment of physical disorders such as headaches and coronary heart disease. Psychologists can also help people develop healthier behaviors that reduce their risks of developing serious health problems such as cardiovascular disorders, cancer, and AIDS. Emerging fields such as psychoneuroimmunology promise to further enhance our knowledge of the intricate relationships between mind and body.

6 summing up

Dissociative Disorders

6.1 Describe the key features of these major types of dissociative disorders: dissociative identity disorder, dissociative amnesia, and depersonalization/derealization disorder.

In dissociative identity disorder, two or more distinct personalities, each possessing well-defined traits and memories, exist within the person and repeatedly take control of the person's behavior. In dissociative amnesia, the person experiences a loss of memory for personal information that cannot be accounted for by organic causes. In dissociative amnesia with fugue, the person suddenly travels away from home or the workplace, shows a loss of memory for his or her personal past, and experiences identity confusion or takes on a new identity. In depersonalization/derealization disorder, the person experiences persistent or recurrent episodes of depersonalization or derealization of sufficient severity to cause significant distress or impairment in functioning.

6.2 Explain why the concept of dissociative identity disorder is controversial.

Some theorists question whether dissociate identity disorder is a true disorder or rather an elaborate form of role-playing of a "multiple personality" that is reinforced by attention and interest from others, including therapists.

6.3 Describe different theoretical perspectives on dissociative disorders.

Psychodynamic theorists view dissociative disorders as a form of psychological defense by which the ego defends itself against troubling memories and unacceptable impulses by blotting them out of consciousness. There is increasing documentation of a link between dissociative disorders and early childhood trauma, which lends support to the view that dissociation may serve to protect the self from troubling memories. To learning and cognitive theorists, dissociative experiences involve ways of learning not to think about certain troubling behaviors or thoughts that might lead to feelings of guilt or shame. Relief from anxiety negatively reinforces this pattern of dissociation. Some social-cognitive theorists suggest that multiple personality may represent a form of role-playing behavior.

6.4 Describe the treatment of dissociative identity disorder.

The major form of treatment is psychotherapy aimed at achieving a reintegration of the personality by focusing on helping people with dissociative identity disorder uncover and integrate dissociated painful experiences from childhood.

Somatic Symptom and Related Disorders

6.5 Describe the key features of these types of somatic symptom and related disorders: somatic symptom disorder, illness anxiety disorder, conversion disorder, and factitious disorder.

Somatic symptom disorder applies to cases of excessive concern about physical symptoms to the extent that it affects one's thoughts, feelings, and behaviors in daily life. Illness anxiety disorder applies to cases of minor physical symptoms in which the person becomes preoccupied with the belief that they reflect serious underlying illness despite medical evidence to the contrary. Conversion disorder applies in cases in which people have symptoms or deficits in motor or sensory functioning that cannot be accounted for by known medical conditions or diseases.

6.6 Explain the difference between malingering and factitious disorder.

Malingering involves deliberate efforts to fake or exaggerate symptoms to reap personal gain or avoid unwanted responsibilities and so is not considered a mental or psychological disorder. The symptoms in factitious disorder are also fabricated. However, because of the absence of any obvious gain, the symptoms in factitious disorder are believed to reflect underlying psychological needs and hence they represent the features of a mental or psychological disorder. Münchausen syndrome is the major form of factitious disorder and is characterized by deliberate fabrication of physical symptoms for no apparent reason other than to assume a patient role.

6.7 Describe the key features of koro and dhat syndromes.

These are two examples of culture-bound syndromes. Koro disorder, which is found primarily in China, is characterized by excessive fear that one's genitals are shrinking and retracting into the body. Dhat syndrome, found primarily in India, involves excessive fears in men concerning the loss of seminal fluid.

6.8 Describe the theoretical understandings of somatic symptom and related disorders.

Much of the theoretical focus on somatic symptom and related disorders has centered on hypochondriasis, which is now classified as either somatic symptom disorder or illness anxiety disorder. One learning theory model likens hypochondriasis to obsessive–compulsive behavior. Cognitive factors in hypochondriasis include possible self-handicapping strategies and cognitive distortions involving exaggerated perceptions of the status of one's health. The psychodynamic model of conversion disorder holds that it represents the conversion into physical symptoms of leftover emotion or energy cut off from unacceptable or threatening impulses that the ego has prevented from reaching awareness. The symptom is functional in the sense that it allows the person to achieve both primary gains and secondary gains. Learning theorists focus on reinforcements associated with conversion disorders, such as the reinforcing effects of adopting a "sick role."

6.9 Describe methods used to treat somatic symptom and related disorders.

Psychodynamic therapists attempt to uncover and bring to the level of awareness underlying unconscious conflicts, originating in childhood, believed to be at the root of somatic symptom and related disorders. Once conflicts are uncovered and worked through, symptoms should disappear because they are no longer needed as a partial solution to the underlying conflict. Behavioral approaches focus on removing underlying sources of reinforcement that may be maintaining the abnormal behavior pattern. More generally, behavior therapists help people with somatic symptom and related disorders learn to handle stressful or anxiety-arousing situations more effectively. In addition, a combination of cognitive-behavioral techniques, such as exposure with response prevention and cognitive restructuring, may be used in treating hypochondriasis. Antidepressant medication may prove to be helpful in treating some cases of somatic symptom and related disorders.

Psychological Factors Affecting Physical Health

6.10 Describe the role of psychological factors in physical health problems such as headaches, cardiovascular disease, asthma, cancer, and AIDS.

The most common headache is the tension headache, which is often stress-related. Behavioral methods of relaxation training and biofeedback help in treating various types of headaches. Psychological factors that increase the risk of coronary heart disease include unhealthy patterns of consumption, leading a sedentary lifestyle, and persistent negative emotions. Psychological factors such as stress, anxiety, and depression may trigger asthma attacks in susceptible individuals. Although relationships between stress and risk of cancer remain under study, behavioral risk factors for cancer include unhealthy dietary practices (especially high fat intake), heavy alcohol use, smoking, and excessive sun exposure. Psychological interventions help cancer patients cope better with the symptoms of the disease and its treatment. Psychologists are also involved in prevention programs to reduce risky behaviors that can lead to HIV infection, and developing treatment programs, such as coping-skills training and cognitive-behavioral therapy, designed to help people affected by HIV/AIDS.

critical thinking questions

On the basis of your reading of this chapter, answer the following questions:

- Why is the diagnosis of dissociative identity disorder controversial? Do you believe that people with dissociative identity disorder are merely playing a role they have learned? Why or why not?

- How are dissociative and somatic symptom and related disorders distinguished from malingering? What difficulties arise in trying to make these determinations?

- Why is conversion disorder considered a treasure trove in the annals of abnormal psychology? What role did the disorder play in the development of psychological models of abnormal behavior?

- Does koro or dhat syndrome seem strange to you? How might your reaction depend on the culture in which you were raised? Can you give an example of a behavioral pattern in your culture that might be viewed as strange by members of other cultures?

key terms

dissociative disorder 200
dissociative identity
   disorder 201
dissociative
   amnesia 205
depersonalization 209
derealization 209

depersonalization/
   derealization disorder 211
somatic symptom
   disorder 217
Somatic symptom and related
   disorders 217
hypochondriasis 219

illness anxiety
   disorder 221
conversion disorder 221
factitious disorder 222
malingering 222
Münchausen syndrome 222
koro syndrome 224

dhat syndrome 225
psychosomatic 229
biofeedback training
   (BFT) 230
cardiovascular disease 233
Type A behavior pattern
   (TABP) 234

Mood Disorders and Suicide

7

truth OR fiction

T☐ F☐   Feeling sad or depressed is abnormal. (p. 245)

T☐ F☐   Major depression affects millions of Americans, but fortunately most get the help they need. (p. 248)

T☐ F☐   Most people who experience a major depressive episode never have another one. (p. 248)

T☐ F☐   The bleak light of winter casts some people into a diagnosable state of depression. (p. 251)

T☐ F☐   Men are about twice as likely as women to develop major depression. (p. 251)

T☐ F☐   Physical exercise not only helps tone the body but can help combat depression. (p. 262)

T☐ F☐   High levels of fish oil in the diet are linked to increased risk of bipolar disorder. (p. 270)

T☐ F☐   The ancient Greeks and Romans used a chemical to curb turbulent mood swings that is still used today. (p. 277)

T☐ F☐   Placing a powerful electromagnet on the scalp can help relieve depression. (p. 280)

T☐ F☐   People who threaten suicide are basically attention seekers. (p. 285)

learning objectives

7.1
Define the term mood disorder and describe the key features of major depressive disorder.

7.2
Evaluate factors that may account for the increased rates of depression among women.

7.3
Describe the key features of persistent depressive disorder and premenstrual dysphoric disorder.

7.4
Describe the key features of bipolar disorder and cyclothymic disorder.

7.5
Evaluate the role of stress in depression.

7.6
Describe the major psychological models of depression.

7.7
Describe biological factors in depression.

7.8
Describe causal factors in bipolar disorders.

7.9
Identify and describe methods used to treat mood disorders.

7.10
Identify risk factors in suicide.

7.11
Identify the major theoretical perspectives on suicide.

7.12
Apply your knowledge of factors in suicide to steps you can take if someone you knew was experiencing suicidal thoughts.

"I" Darkness Visible

At age 60, William Styron (1925–2006), the celebrated author of *The Confessions of Nat Turner* and *Sophie's Choice,* suffered from depression so severe that he planned to commit suicide. In a 1990 memoir, he speaks about this personal darkness and about reclaiming his commitment to life:

"I watched myself in mingled terror and fascination as I began to make the necessary preparation: going to see my lawyer in the nearby town—there rewriting my will—and spending part of a couple of afternoons in a muddled attempt to bestow upon posterity a letter of farewell. It turned out that putting together a suicide note, which I felt obsessed with a necessity to compose, was the most difficult task of writing that I had ever tackled. . . .

But even a few words came to seem to me too longwinded, and I tore up all my efforts, resolving to go out in silence. Late one bitterly cold night, when I knew that I could not possibly get myself through the following day, I sat in the living room of the house bundled up against the chill; something had happened to the furnace. My wife had gone to bed, and I had forced myself to watch the tape of a movie in which a young actress, who had been in a play of mine, was cast in a small part. At one point in the film, which was set in late-nineteenth-century Boston, the characters moved down the hallway of a music conservatory, beyond the walls of which, from unseen musicians, came a contralto voice, a sudden soaring passage from the *Brahms Alto* Rhapsody.

This sound, which like all music—indeed, like all pleasure—I had been numbly unresponsive to for months, pierced my heart like a dagger, and in a flood of swift recollection I thought of all the joys the house had known: the children who had rushed through its rooms, the festivals, the love and work, the honestly earned slumber, the voices and the nimble commotion, the perennial tribe of cats and dogs and birds. . . . All this I realized was more than I could ever abandon, even as what I had set out so deliberately to do was more than I could inflict on those memories, and

William Styron. The celebrated author William Styron suffered from severe depression—a "darkness visible" that led him to the precipice of suicide.

7.1 Define the term mood disorder and describe the key features of major depressive disorder.

upon those, so close to me, with whom the memories were bound. And just as powerfully I realized I could not commit this desecration on myself. I drew upon some last gleam of sanity to perceive the terrifying dimensions of the mortal predicament I had fallen into. I woke up my wife and soon telephone calls were made. The next day I was admitted to the hospital."

From Darkness Visible *by William Styron*

A distinguished author stands at the precipice of taking his own life. The depression that enshrouded him and that nearly cost him his life—this *darkness visible*—is an unwelcome companion for millions of people. Depression is a disturbance of mood that casts a long, deep shadow over many facets of life.

Moods are feeling states that color our psychological lives. Most of us experience changes in mood. We feel elated when we have earned high grades, a promotion, or the affections of Ms. or Mr. Right. We feel down or depressed when we are rejected by a date, flunk a test, or suffer financial reverses. It is normal and appropriate to be happy about uplifting events. It is just as normal, just as appropriate, to feel depressed by dismal events. It might very well be abnormal if we did not feel down or depressed in the face of tragic or deeply disappointing events or circumstances. But people with **mood disorders** experience disturbances in mood that are unusually severe or prolonged and impair their ability to function in meeting their normal responsibilities. Some people become severely depressed even when things appear to be going well or when they encounter mildly upsetting events that others take in stride. Still others experience extreme mood swings. They ride an emotional roller coaster with dizzying heights and abysmal depths when the world around them remains largely on an even keel. Let's begin our study of these types of emotional problems by examining the different types of mood disorders.

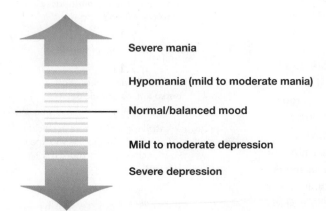

Severe mania

Hypomania (mild to moderate mania)

Normal/balanced mood

Mild to moderate depression

Severe depression

FIGURE 7.1

A mood thermometer. Mood states can be conceptualized as varying along a spectrum or continuum. One end represents severe depression and the other end severe mania, which is a cardinal feature of bipolar disorder. Mild or moderate depression is often called the blues but is classified as "dysthymia" when it becomes chronic. In the middle of the spectrum is normal or balanced mood. Mild or moderate mania is called hypomania and is characteristic of cyclothymic disorder. *Source:* NIMH, 2001.

Types of Mood Disorders

This chapter explores the two major forms of mood disorders: depressive disorders and bipolar disorders (mood swing disorders). Unlike previous editions of the *DSM, DSM-5* does not include a general category of mood disorders. Rather, mood disorders are now classified in separate categories called "Depressive Disorders" and "Bipolar and Related Disorders." Our study of mood disorders breaks down into a study of two's. There are two major types of depressive disorders, *major depressive disorder* and *persistent depressive disorder,* and two major types of bipolar disorders, *bipolar disorder* and *cyclothymic disorder* (also called *cyclothymia*). We'll also see that bipolar disorder is comprised of two distinct disorders, bipolar I disorder and bipolar II disorder.

Depressive disorders are also called *unipolar* disorders because the mood disturbance goes in only one emotional direction or pole: down. By contrast, mood swing disorders are called *bipolar* disorders because they involve states of both depression and elation, which often appear in an alternating pattern. Table 7.1 provides an overview of these disorders. A convenient way of conceptualizing differences in mood states corresponding to these disorders is shown in the form of a mood thermometer in Figure 7.1.

Many of us—probably most of us—have periods of sadness from time to time. We may feel down in the dumps, cry, lose interest in things,

TABLE 7.1

Overview of Mood Disorders

	Type of Disorder	Approximate Lifetime Prevalence Rates[*]	Major Features or Symptoms	Additional Comments
Depressive Disorders	Major Depressive Disorder (MDD)	12% in men; 21% in women; 16.5% overall	Episodes of severe depression characterized by downcast mood, feelings of hopelessness and worthlessness, changes in sleep patterns or appetite, loss of motivation, loss of pleasure in usual activities	Following a depressive episode, the person may return to his or her usual state of functioning, but recurrences are common. Seasonal affective disorder is a type of major depression.
	Persistent Depressive Disorder (Dysthymia)	4.3%	A chronic pattern of depression	Person experiences chronic mild or major depression or feels "down in the dumps" most of the time
	Premenstrual Dysphoric Disorder (PMDD)	Unknown	Marked changes in mood during the woman's premenstrual period	A new diagnostic category in *DSM-5*, it remains controversial as critics claim it unfairly stigmatizes women who have significant premenstrual symptoms by labeling them with a mental or psychological disorder.
Bipolar Disorders	Bipolar Disorder	About 1% for bipolar I disorder and bipolar II disorder	Periods of shifting moods, energy level, and level of activity between mania and depression, perhaps with intervening periods of normal mood; two general subtypes are bipolar I disorder (occurrence of one or more manic episodes) and bipolar II disorder (major depressive episode and hypomanic episode, but no full manic episode)	Manic episodes are characterized by pressured speech, greatly increased energy or activity, flight of ideas, poor judgment, high levels of restlessness and excitability, and inflated mood and sense of self
	Cyclothymic Disorder	About 0.4% to 1.0%	Mood swings that are milder in severity than those in bipolar disorder	Cyclothymia usually begins in late adolescence or early adulthood and tends to persist for years

[*]Lifetime prevalence refers to the percentage of people in the population affected by the disorder at some point in their lives.

Sources: Prevalence rates derived from APA, 2013; Conway et al., 2006; Merikangas et al., 2007; Merikangas & Pato, 2009; Van Meter, Youngstrom, & Findling, 2012. Table updated and adapted from Nevid, J. S. (2009). *Psychology: Concepts and applications* (3rd ed., p. 257). Boston: Houghton Mifflin Co. Reprinted with permission.

have trouble concentrating, expect the worst to happen, and even consider suicide. For most of us, mood changes pass quickly or are not severe enough to interfere with our lifestyle or ability to function. Among people with mood disorders, including depressive disorders and bipolar disorders, mood changes are more severe or prolonged and affect daily functioning. **T / F**

Major Depressive Disorder

The diagnosis of **major depressive disorder** (also called *major depression*) is based on the occurrence of at least one *major depressive episode* (MDE) in the absence of a history of **mania** or **hypomania.** A major depressive episode involves a clinically significant change in functioning involving a range of depressive symptoms, including depressed mood (feeling sad, hopeless, or "down in the dumps") and/or loss of interest or pleasure in all or virtually all activities for a period of at least two weeks (APA, 2013). Table 7.2 lists some of

truth OR fiction

Feeling sad or depressed is abnormal.

☑ **FALSE** Feeling depressed is not abnormal in the context of depressing events or circumstances.

When are changes in mood considered abnormal? Although changes in mood in response to the ups and downs of everyday life may be quite normal, persistent or severe changes in mood, or cycles of extreme elation and depression, may suggest the presence of a mood disorder.

 Watch the Video *Martha: Major Depressive Disorder* on **MyPsychLab**

TABLE 7.2
Common Features of Depression

Changes in emotional states	• Changes in mood (persistent periods of feeling down, depressed, sad, or blue) • Evidence of tearfulness or crying • Increased irritability, jumpiness, or loss of temper
Changes in motivation	• Feeling unmotivated, or having difficulty getting going in the morning or even getting out of bed • Reduced level of social participation or interest in social activities • Loss of enjoyment or interest in pleasurable activities • Reduced interest in sex • Failure to respond to praise or rewards
Changes in functioning and motor behavior	• Moving about or talking more slowly than usual • Changes in sleep habits (sleeping too much or too little, awakening earlier than usual and having trouble getting back to sleep in early morning hours—so-called early morning awakening) • Changes in appetite (eating too much or too little) • Changes in weight (gaining or losing weight) • Functioning less effectively at work or school; failing to meet responsibilities and neglecting one's physical appearance
Cognitive changes	• Difficulty concentrating or thinking clearly • Thinking negatively about oneself and one's future • Feeling guilty or remorseful about past misdeeds • Lack of self-esteem or feelings of inadequacy • Thinking of death or suicide

---

the common features of depression. The diagnostic criteria for a major depressive episode are listed in DSM box.

Major depression is not simply a state of sadness or the blues. People with *major depressive disorder* (MDD) may have poor appetite, lose or gain substantial amounts of weight, have trouble sleeping or sleep too much, and become physically agitated or—at the other extreme—show a marked slowing down in their motor (movement) activity. Here, a woman recounts how depression—the "beast" as she calls it—affects every fiber of her being.

"I" "The Beast is Back"

My body aches intermittently, in waves, as if I had malaria. I eat with no appetite, simply because the taste of food is one of my dwindling number of pleasures. I am tired, so tired. Last night I lay like a pile of old clothes, and when David came to bed I did not stir. Sex is a foreign notion. At work today I am forgetful; I have trouble forming sentences, I lose track of them halfway through, and my words keep getting tangled. I look at my list of things to do today, and keep on looking at it; nothing seems to be happening. Things are sad to me. This morning I thought of the woman who used to live in my old house, who told me she went to Sears to buy fake lace curtains. It seemed a forlorn act—having to save your pennies, not being able to afford genuine lace. (Why? A voice in my head asks. The curtains she bought looked perfectly nice.) I feel as if my brain were a lump of protoplasm with tiny circuits embedded in it, and some of the wires keep shorting out. There are tiny little electrical fires up there, leaving crispy sections of neurons smoking and ruined. . . .

I don't even know when this current siege began—a week ago? A month ago? The onset is so gradual, and these things are hard to tell. All I know is, the Beast is back.

It is called depression, and my experiences with it have shaped my life—altered my personality, affected my most intimate relationships, changed the course of my career—in ways I will probably never be fully aware of.

From Thompson, 1995

A. Five (or more) of the following symptoms have been present during the same 2-week period and represent a change from previous functioning; at least one of the symptoms is either (1) depressed mood or (2) loss of interest or pleasure.
   Note: Do not include symptoms that are clearly attributable to another medical condition.

   1. Depressed mood most of the day, nearly every day, as indicated by either subjective report (e.g., feels sad, empty, hopeless) or observation made by others (e.g., appears tearful). (**Note:** In children and adolescents, can be irritable mood.)

   2. Markedly diminished interest or pleasure in all, or almost all, activities most of the day, nearly every day (as indicated by either subjective account or observation).

   3. significant weight loss when not dieting or weight gain (e.g., a change of more than 5% of body weight in a month), or decrease or increase in appetite nearly every day. (**Note:** In children, consider failure to make expected weight gain.)

   4. Insomnia or hypersomnia nearly every day.

   5. Psychomotor agitation or retardation nearly every day (observable by others, not merely subjective feelings of restlessness or being slowed down).

   6. Fatigue or loss of energy nearly every day.

   7. Feelings of worthlessness or excessive or inappropriate guilt (which may be delusional) nearly every day (not merely self-reproach or guilt about being sick).

   8. Diminished ability to think or concentrate, or indecisiveness, nearly every day (either by subjective account or as observed by others).

   9. Recurrent thoughts of death (not just fear of dying), recurrent suicidal ideation without a specific plan, or a suicide attempt or a specific committing suicide.

B. The symptoms cause clinically significant distress or impairment in social, occupational, or other important areas of functioning.

C. The episode is not attributable to the physiological effects of a substance or to another medical condition.

Note: Criteria A–C represent a major depressive episode.
Note: Responses to a significant loss (e.g., bereavement, financial ruin, losses from a natural disaster, a serious medical illness or disability) may include the feelings of intense sadness, rumination about the loss, insomnia, poor appetite, and weight loss noted in Criterion A, which may resemble a depressive episode. Although such symptoms may be understandable or considered appropriate to the loss, the presence of a major depressive episode in addition to the normal response to a significant loss should also be carefully considered. This decision inevitably requires the exercise of clinical judgment based on the individual's history and the cultural norms for the expression of distress in the context of loss.

D. The occurrence of the major depressive episode is not better explained by schizoaffective disorder, schizophrenia, schizophreniform disorder, delusional disorder, or other specified and unspecified schizophrenia spectrum and other psychotic disorders.

E. There has never been a manic episode or a hypomanic episode.
Note: This exclusion does not apply if all of the manic-like or hypomanic-like episodes are substance-induced or are attributable to the physiological effects of another medical condition.

Major depression impairs people's ability to meet the ordinary responsibility of everyday life. People with major depression may lose interest in most of their usual activities and pursuits, have difficulty concentrating and making decisions, have pressing thoughts of death, and attempt suicide. They even show impaired driving skills in driving simulation tests (Bulmash et al., 2006).

Mired in the depths of depression in 1841, Abraham Lincoln said of himself, "I am now the most miserable man living. If what I feel were equally distributed to the whole human family, there would not be one cheerful face on the earth" (Lincoln 1841/1953, p. 230). These words of despair poignantly express just how disabling depression can be (Forgeard et al., 2011).

Many people don't seem to understand that people who are clinically depressed can't simply "shake it off" or "snap out of it." Many people still view depression as a sign of weakness, not a diagnosable disorder. Many people with major depression believe they can handle the problem themselves. These attitudes may help explain why, despite the availability of safe and effective treatments, about half of Americans with major depression fail to receive help from a mental health professional (González et al., 2010). Latinos and African Americans are less likely than other groups to receive care. Another factor

The melancholic president. Abraham Lincoln struggled with depression through much of his life.

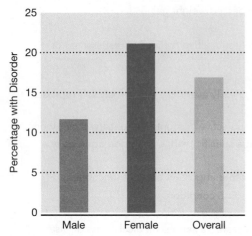

FIGURE 7.2

Lifetime prevalence rates for major depressive disorder. Major depressive episodes affect about twice as many women as men. *Source:* Conway et al., 2006.

FIGURE 7.3

Percentage of persons 12 years of age and older reporting difficulty with their work, home, and social activities by sex and depression severity. Depression affects people in many ways. Most people (55.1% with mild depression; 79.7% with moderate or severe depression) report difficulties with work, home, or social activities. *Source:* Pratt & Brody, 2008.

explaining the lack of care is that many depressed patients seek help from their family physicians, who often fail to either detect depression or make referrals to mental health professionals (Simon et al., 2004). **T / F**

Major depressive disorder is the most common type of diagnosable mood disorder. A recent nationally representative survey showed a lifetime prevalence for the disorder of about 12% for men, 21% for women, and 16.5% overall (Conway et al., 2006; Forgeard et al., 2011) (see Figure 7.2). Nearly 8% of U.S. adults currently suffer from the disorder (National Center for Health Statistics, 2012). More often than not, major depression frequently occurs together with other psychological disorders, such as anxiety disorders (Nolen-Hoeksema, 2008). Because of the high frequency of co-occurrence of depression and anxiety, the *DSM-5* requires clinicians to rate the level of anxious distress in individuals receiving a depressive or bipolar disorder diagnosis.

Major depression is a major public health problem, not only affecting psychological functioning but also impairing a person's ability to meet school, work, family, and social responsibilities (Pratt & Brody, 2008). As you can see in Figure 7.3, nearly 80% of people with moderate to severe depression report impaired work, family, or social functioning.

The economic costs of depression are staggering, costing many billions in lost productive work time. The average worker suffering from depression earns about 10% less than unaffected workers in similar jobs (McIntyre et al., 2011). Major depression costs the average worker about 27.2 lost workdays per year—for bipolar disorder, about 65 days are lost on the average (Kessler et al., 2006).

The economic toll of depression is as great if not greater than the costs of major medical illnesses, such as heart disease and diabetes (Stewart et al., 2003). On the other hand, effective treatment for depression leads not only to psychological improvement but also to more stable employment and increased income, as people are able to return to a more productive level.

Major depression, particularly in more severe episodes, may be accompanied by psychotic features, such as delusions that one's body is rotting from illness. People with major depression may also exhibit psychotic behaviors, such as hallucinations, as in "hearing" voices condemning the person for perceived misdeeds.

The following case illustrates the range of features connected with major depressive disorder. **T / F**

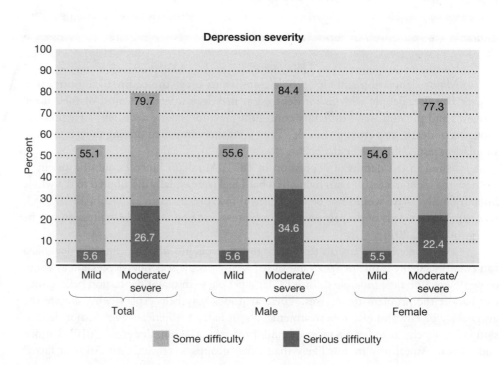

A 38-year-old female clerical worker has suffered from recurrent bouts of depression since she was about 13 years of age. Most recently, she has been troubled by crying spells at work, sometimes occurring so suddenly she wouldn't have enough time to run to the ladies room to hide her tears from others. She has difficulty concentrating at work and feels a lack of enjoyment from work she used to enjoy. She harbors severe pessimistic and angry feelings, which have been more severe lately because she has been putting on weight and has been neglectful in taking care of her diabetes. She feels guilty that she may be slowly killing herself by not taking better care of her health. She sometimes feels that she deserves to be dead. She has been bothered by excessive sleepiness for the past year and a half, and her driving license has been suspended because of an incident the previous month in which she fell asleep while driving, causing her car to hit a telephone pole. She wakes up most days feeling groggy and just "out of it," and remains sleepy throughout the day. She has never had a steady boyfriend, and lives quietly at home with her mother, with no close friends outside of her family. During the interview, she cried frequently and answered questions in a low monotone, staring downward continuously.

→ *Adapted from Spitzer et al., 1989, pp. 59–62*

Major depressive episodes may resolve in a matter of months or last for a year or more. Some people experience a single episode of major depression and then return to their earlier state of normal psychological functioning (Eaton et al., 2008). Yet, most people with MDD have episodes of major depression occurring from time to time through the course of their lives (Hölzel et al., 2011; Reifler, 2006). Evidence shows that risk of repeat episodes is related to genetic influences and the presence of other significant medical or psychiatric illnesses (Burcusa & Iacono, 2007; Richards, 2011). However, the good news is that the longer the period of recovery from an episode of major depression, the lower the risk of eventual relapse (Solomon et al., 2000).

RISK FACTORS IN MAJOR DEPRESSION Many factors are associated with an increased risk of depression, including age (initial onset is most common among young adults); socioeconomic status (people lower down the socioeconomic ladder are at greater risk than those who are better off); and marital status (people who are separated or divorced have higher rates than married or never-married people).

Women are about twice as likely as men to be diagnosed with major depressive disorder (major depression) (Addis, 2008; Hasin et al., 2005). The greater risk of depression in women begins in early adolescence (ages 13 to 15) and persists at least through middle age (Costello et al., 2008; Hyde, Mezulis, & Abramson, 2008). Noting the existence of a gender gap in the diagnosis of depression is one thing; explaining it is quite another (see Thinking Critically About Abnormal Psychology).

SEASONAL AFFECTIVE DISORDER Are you glum on gloomy days? Is your temper short during the brief days of winter? Are you dismal during the long, dark winter nights and sunny when spring and summer return?

Although our moods may vary with the weather, the changing of the seasons from summer to fall and winter can lead to a type of depression called *seasonal affective (mood) disorder* (SAD) (Madsen, Dam, & Hageman, 2011). In most cases, the depression lifts in the spring. SAD is not a diagnostic category in its own right but is a specifier or subcategory of major depression. For example, major depressive disorder that occurs seasonally would be diagnosed as major depressive disorder with seasonal pattern. Although the causes of SAD remain unknown, one possibility is that seasonal changes in light may alter the body's underlying biological rhythms that regulate processes such as body temperature and sleep–wake cycles (Gordijn, Mannetje, & Meesters, 2012). Another possibility is that seasonal changes might affect the availability or use of the mood-regulating neurotransmitter

7.2 Evaluate factors that may account for the increased rates of depression among women.

THINKING CRITICALLY about abnormal psychology

@Issue: What Accounts for the Gender Gap in Depression?

Women are about twice as likely as men to suffer from clinical depression, about 12% for men versus about 21% for women (Conway et al., 2006; Hyde, Mezulis, & Abramson, 2008). A greater prevalence of depression among women was found in each of 15 countries from various parts of the world in a recent cross-national study by the World Health Organization (Seedat et al., 2009). The question is, *why?*

Investigators believe that a number of factors are involved (Eagly et al., 2012). Hormonal fluctuations may contribute to depression in some cases, but investigators also need to consider the disproportionate burden of stress women in our society tend to shoulder, as well as the individual's way of coping with emotional distress. Women are more likely than men to experience stressful life factors such as physical and sexual abuse, poverty, single parenthood, and sexism, all of which may increase vulnerability to depression. Depressed women, especially those in young adulthood, tend to report more negative life events than depressed men—events such as loss of loved one's or changes in life circumstances (Harkness et al., 2010). On the other hand, a recent World Health Organization cross-national study showed that a narrowing of gender differences in major depression may be occurring, perhaps because of a loosening of traditional female gender roles in many cultures (Seedat et al., 2009).

The late psychologist Susan Nolen-Hoeksema focused on gender differences in coping styles. She proposed that women tend to ruminate or brood more about their problems, whereas men are more likely to distract themselves by doing something they enjoy, such as going to a favorite hangout to get their minds off their problems (Nolen-Hoeksema, 2006, 2012). Rumination tends to increase emotional distress, setting the stage for depression and other negative emotions, such as anxiety. But distracting oneself from one's problems by turning to alcohol or other drugs can lead to substance-related psychological and social problems.

Another view of the gender gap in depression is that women's self-esteem—how they view themselves—may hinge more than men's on their interpersonal relationships with their peers, friends, and romantic partners (Cambron, Acitelli, & Pettit, 2009). Positive events in relationships may bolster their self-esteem, but when problems arise (e.g., arguments, rejection), their self-esteem may plummet. This in turn may give rise to rumination about what's wrong with them and negative interpersonal behaviors such as excessive demands for reassurance of their self-worth, which in turn may lead to depression.

Rumination is not limited to women. Ruminating or brooding about one's problems are associated with both greater proneness to depression and longer durations of depression in both men and women (Joormann, Levens, & Gotlib, 2011; Koster et al., 2011;

Lo et al., 2008). People who continually mull over their problems tend to get stuck on bad thoughts. As University of Miami psychologist Jutta Joormann puts it, "They basically get stuck in a mindset where they relive what happened to them over and over again. . . . Even though they think, oh, it's not helpful, I should stop thinking about this, I should get on with my life—they can't stop doing it" (cited in "People with Depression," 2011).

Rumination tends to aggravate whatever moods people are experiencing at the time, making them feel sadder or more depressed if they are feeling down or more angry if they are feeling angry or irritated (Nolen-Hoeksema, 2008). Rumination may also play a role in other forms of abnormal behavior, including anxiety disorders and binge eating (Nolen-Hoeksema, Wisco, & Lyubomirksy, 2008).

Might the gender difference in depression be at least partially explained by a reporting bias that leads men to underreport depression? In our culture, men are expected to be tough and resilient. Consequently, they are less likely to report depression or seek treatment for it. Even physicians are not immune from these social expectations. As one male physician put it, "I'm the John Wayne generation. . . . I thought depression was a weakness—there was something disgraceful about it. A real man would just get over it" (cited in Wartik, 2000). The stigma associated with depression shows signs of lessening, but not disappearing. Although depression was long viewed by men as a sign of personal weakness, more men are coming forward to get help. The male ego has likely been battered by assaults from corporate downsizing and growing financial insecurity. **T / F**

Gender differences in depression. Women are about twice as likely to suffer from major depression as men. The question is, *why?*

serotonin in the brain during winter months. Cognitive factors may play a part, as people with SAD tend to report more automatic negative thoughts throughout the year than do nondepressed controls (Rohan, Sigmon, & Dorhofer, 2003). **T / F**

Whatever the underlying cause, the therapeutic use of bright artificial light, called *phototherapy*, often helps relieve depression in SAD (Gordijn, Mannetje, & Meesters, 2012; Reeves et al., 2012). The artificial light apparently supplements the meager sunlight the person otherwise receives. Patients can generally carry out some daily activities (e.g., eating, reading, or writing) during phototherapy sessions. Improvement typically occurs within several days of beginning treatment, but treatment often needs to be continued throughout the winter season. Antidepressant drugs, such as Prozac, may also help relieve depression in patients with seasonal affective disorder (Lam et al., 2006).

POSTPARTUM DEPRESSION   Many new mothers, perhaps as many as 80%, experience mood changes following childbirth (Friedman, 2009; Payne, 2007). These mood changes are commonly called the "maternity blues," "postpartum blues," or "baby blues." They usually last for a few days and may be a normal response to hormonal changes associated with childbirth. Given these turbulent hormonal shifts, it might be considered "abnormal" for most women *not* to experience some changes in feeling states shortly following childbirth. However, some new mothers, about one in seven according to recent estimates (Friedman, 2009), experience more severe mood changes that can be classified as a mood disorder called **postpartum depression (PPD)** (Navarro et al., 2008).

The word *postpartum* derives from the Latin roots *post,* meaning "after," and *papere,* meaning "to bring forth." PPD affects 10% to 15% of U.S. women in the first year following childbirth (CDC, 2008). It may persist for months or even a year or more. PPD is often accompanied by disturbances in appetite and sleep, low self-esteem, and difficulties in maintaining concentration or attention.

Women with postpartum depression experience a major depressive episode within four weeks of delivery. In 50% of cases, however, the depressive episode actually begins before delivery and continues into the postpartum period (APA, 2013). Fortunately, most episodes of postpartum depression don't typically last as long as other episodes of major depression and tend to be less severe. However, some suicides are linked to postpartum depression.

Women with a history of mood disorders or who experience the blues during pregnancy face an increased risk of PPD. Other risk factors include the following (Kornfeld et al., 2012; Leibenluft & Yonkers, 2010; Phillips et al., 2010; Reck et al., 2009; Viguera et al., 2011):

- Being a single or first-time mother
- Having financial problems or a troubled marriage
- Suffering domestic violence
- Lacking social support from partners and family members
- Having unwanted, sick, or temperamentally difficult infants

Light therapy. Exposure to bright artificial light for a few hours a day during the fall and winter months can often bring relief from seasonal affective disorder.

Genetic factors may also contribute to vulnerability to PPD (Friedman, 2009; Mahon et al., 2009). Having PPD increases the risk that a woman will suffer future depressive episodes. Fortunately, there are effective treatments available, including different forms of psychotherapy and antidepressant drugs (Sockol, Epperson, & Barber, 2011).

Postpartum depression needs to be distinguished from a much less common but more severe reaction, called *postpartum psychosis,* in which the new mother loses touch with reality and experiences symptoms such as hallucinations, delusions, and irrational thinking.

Postpartum depression is not limited to American culture. Researchers find high rates of PPD among South African women (Cooper et al., 1999) and Chinese women from Hong Kong (D. T. S. Lee et al., 2001). In the South African sample, a lack of psychological and financial support from the baby's father was associated with an increased risk of the disorder, mirroring findings with U.S. samples.

7.3 Describe the key features of persistent depressive disorder and premenstrual dysphoric disorder.

Persistent Depressive Disorder (Dysthymia)

Major depressive disorder is severe and marked by a relatively abrupt change from one's preexisting state and followed by remission after a period of a few weeks or months. But some forms of depression become chronic conditions that can last for years. The diagnosis of **persistent depressive disorder** is used to classify cases of chronic lasting for at least two years. Persons with persistent depressive disorder may have either chronic major depressive disorder or a chronic but milder form of depression called *dysthymia.* Dysthymia typically begins in childhood or adolescence and tends to follow a chronic course through adulthood. The word *dysthymia* derives from Greek roots *dys-,* meaning "bad" or "hard," and *thymos,* meaning "spirit."

People with dysthymia feel "bad spirited" or "down in the dumps" most of the time, but they are not as severely depressed as those with major depressive disorder. Whereas major depressive disorder tends to be severe and time limited, dysthymia is relatively mild and nagging, typically lasting for years. The risk of relapse is quite high (Keller et al., 2000), as is the risk of major depressive disorder: 90% of people with dysthymia eventually develop major depression (Friedman, 2002).

Dysthymia affects about 4% of the general population at some point in their lifetimes (Conway et al., 2006). Like major depressive disorder, dysthymia is more common in women than in men (see Figure 7.4). It is diagnosed only in people who have never had episodes of either mania or hypomania, which are characteristics of bipolar disorder (APA, 2013).

QUESTIONNAIRE

Are You Depressed?

This self-screening test can be used as an aid to understanding whether you may be suffering from depression. However, it is not intended for you to diagnose yourself, but should be used to raise awareness of concerns you may want to discuss further with a professional.

	Yes	No
1. I feel extremely sad all or most of the time.	_____	_____
2. I have no energy.	_____	_____
3. I cry a lot when I'm alone.	_____	_____
4. I've lost interest in most of the activities I used to enjoy.	_____	_____
5. I sleep much more (or much less) than usual.	_____	_____
6. I have suddenly gained (or lost) a lot of weight.	_____	_____
7. I have trouble concentrating, remembering, and making decisions.	_____	_____
8. I feel hopeless about the future.	_____	_____
9. I feel worthless.	_____	_____
10. I feel anxious.	_____	_____
11. I'm often irritable, and I never used to be that way.	_____	_____
12. I think about death and suicide.	_____	_____

Evaluating your responses: If you agree with two or more of these symptoms and they last for at least two weeks, then you should seek a consultation with a mental health professional for a more complete evaluation. If you said "yes" that you are thinking about death and suicide, you should seek an immediate consultation. If you don't know to whom to turn, contact your college counseling center, neighborhood mental health center, or health care provider.

Source: D. Blum & M. Kirchner (1997). Depression at work. *Customs Today,* Winter issue. Quotes used with permission of the National Mental Health Association. The Blum & Kirchner article is used with the authors' permission.

In dysthymia, complaints of depression may become such a fixture of people's lives that they seem to be intertwined with the personality structure. The persistence of complaints may lead others to perceive the person as whining and complaining. Although dysthymia is less severe than major depressive disorder, persistent depressed mood and low self-esteem can affect the person's occupational and social functioning, as in the following case.

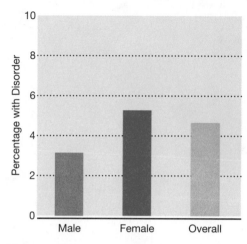

FIGURE 7.4

Lifetime prevalence rates for dysthymia. Like major depression, dysthymia occurs in about twice as many women as men. *Source of data:* Conway et al., 2006.

→ A Case of Dysthymia

The woman, a 28-year-old junior executive, complained of chronic feelings of depression since the age of 16 or 17. Despite doing well in college, she brooded about how other people were "genuinely intelligent." She felt she could never pursue a man she might be interested in dating because she felt inferior and intimidated. Although she had extensive therapy through college and graduate school, she could never recall a time during those years when she did not feel somewhat depressed. She got married shortly after college graduation to the man she was dating at the time, although she didn't think that he was anything "special." She just felt she needed the companionship of a husband and he was available. But they soon began to quarrel, and she's lately begun to feel that marrying him was a mistake. She has had difficulties at work, turning in "slipshod" work and never seeking anything more than what was basically required of her and showing little initiative. Although she dreams of acquiring status and money, she doesn't expect that she or her husband will rise in their professions because they lack "connections." Her social life is dominated by her husband's friends and their spouses, and she doesn't think that other women would find her interesting. She lacks interest in life in general and expresses dissatisfaction with all facets of her life—her marriage, her job, her social life.

→ *Adapted from Spitzer et al., 1994, pp. 110–112*

Some people are affected by both dysthymia and major depression at the same time. The term **double depression** applies to those who have a major depressive episode superimposed on a longer-standing dysthymia. People suffering from double depression generally have more severe depressive episodes than do people with major depression alone (Klein, Schwartz, et al., 2000).

Premenstrual Dysphoric Disorder

Premenstrual dysphoric disorder (PMDD) was introduced as a diagnostic category in *DSM-5* (Epperson, 2013). It had been classified in the previous edition of the *DSM* as a proposed diagnosis requiring further study. The inclusion of this new diagnostic category is intended to draw greater attention to the problem of mood swings associated with the premenstrual period and increase delivery of services to women suffering from these types of problems.

PMDD is a more severe form of *premenstrual syndrome* (PMS), which is a cluster of physical and mood-related symptoms occurring during the woman's premenstrual period. The diagnosis of PMDD is intended to apply to women who experience a range of significant psychological symptoms in the week before menses (and improvement beginning within a few days following the onset of menses). A range of symptoms need to be present to diagnose PMDD, including symptoms such as mood swings, sudden tearfulness or feelings of sadness, depressed mood or feelings of hopelessness, irritability or anger, feelings of anxiety, tension, being on edge, greater sensitivity to cues of rejection, and negative thoughts about oneself. These symptoms also need to be associated with significant emotional distress or interference with the woman's ability to function on the job, in school, or in usual social activities.

The diagnosis of PMDD brings into focus the difficulty establishing clear lines between normal and abnormal behavior. Most women have some mood-related premenstrual symptoms, with many women (upwards of 50%) experiencing moderate to severe symptoms (Freeman, 2011). Investigators report that nearly one in five women have premenstrual physical or mood-related symptoms that are severe enough to interfere with their daily functioning, such as causing absenteeism from work, or producing significant emotional distress (Halbreich et al., 2006; Heinemann et al., 2010).

The cause or causes of both PMS and premenstrual dysphoric disorder remain unclear. Investigators suspect that PMS involves a complex interaction between female sexual hormones and neurotransmitters (Bäckström et al., 2008; Kiesner, 2009). Psychological factors, such as the woman's attitudes about menstruation, may also play a role. Recent research suggests that normal levels of female sexual hormones may trigger negative emotional reactions in women with PMDD, but not in healthy women (Baller et al., 2013; Epperson, 2013).

The diagnosis of PMDD remains controversial. Critics fear it will pathologize the woman's natural menstrual cycle and may stigmatize women who have serious premenstrual complaints by labeling them with a psychiatric diagnosis. Although the new diagnosis of PMDD has been estimated to apply to perhaps only 2% to 5% of women overall ("PMDD Proposes," 2012), the question remains whether the diagnosis will become overextended to a much larger percentage of women who suffer from a wider range of premenstrual symptoms. Moreover, even if relatively few women are diagnosed with PMDD, is it fair to characterize them as suffering from a mental disorder when they may be suffering from a physical condition? Mental health professionals will need to contend with these questions as they begin to apply the PMDD diagnosis in clinical practice.

We have noted that major depressive disorder and dysthymia are depressive disorders in the sense that the disturbance of mood is only in one direction—down. Yet, people with mood disorders may have fluctuations in mood in both directions that exceed the usual ups and downs of everyday life. These types of disorders are called bipolar disorders. Here, we focus on the major types of mood swing disorders: (1) bipolar disorder and (2) cyclothymic disorder.

Bipolar Disorder

Bipolar disorder is characterized by extreme swings of mood and changes in energy and activity levels. Mood swings typically shift between the heights of elation to the depths of depression. The first episode may be either manic or depressive. Manic episodes typically last a few weeks or perhaps a month or two and are generally much shorter and end more abruptly than major depressive episodes. Some people with bipolar disorder attempt suicide "on the way down" from the manic phase. They report that they would do nearly anything to escape the depths of depression they know lies ahead. People with bipolar disorder ride an emotional roller coaster.

Some people with bipolar disorder experience mixed states characterized by episodes of both mania and depression (APA, 2013). During these mixed states, the person's mood may rapidly shift between mania and depression (Swann et al., 2013). Moreover, some people with major depressive disorder also experience mixed states in which they show some symptoms of mania but not of a sufficient number or magnitude to merit a diagnosis of a bipolar disorder.

Kay Redfield Jamison, a psychologist and leading authority on the treatment of bipolar disorder, suffers from the disorder herself. Within three months of beginning her first professional appointment as an assistant professor in the Department of Psychiatry at UCLA, she became, in her own words, "ravingly psychotic." Jamison has suffered from bipolar disorder since her teens but wasn't diagnosed until she was 28 (Ballie, 2002).

7.4 Describe the key features of bipolar disorder and cyclothymic disorder.

Watch the Video *Ann: Bipolar Disorder* on MyPsychLab

The *DSM -5* distinguishes between two types of bipolar disorder, *bipolar I disorder* and *bipolar II disorder.* The distinction can be confusing, so let's try to clarify.

The distinction is based on whether the person has ever experienced a full-blown manic episode (Youngstrom, 2009). The diagnosis of bipolar I disorder applies to people who have had at least one *full manic episode* at some point in their lives. Typically, bipolar I disorder involves extreme mood swings between manic episodes and major depression with intervening periods of normal mood. But it is possible for bipolar I disorder to apply to a person who does not have a history of a major depressive episode. It is assumed in these cases that major depression may have been overlooked in the past or will develop in the future.

Bipolar II disorder applies to people who have had *hypomanic episodes* (from the Greek prefix *hypo-,* meaning "under" or "less than") as well as a history of at least one major depressive episode, but have never had a full-blown manic episode. Hypomanic episodes are less severe than manic episodes and are not accompanied by the extreme social or occupational problems associated with full-blown mania (Tomb et al., 2012). During a hypomanic episode, a person might may feel unusually charged with energy and show a heightened level of activity and an inflated sense of self-esteem, and may be more alert, restless, and irritable than usual. The person may be able to work long hours with little fatigue or need for sleep.

Some, but not all, bipolar II patients go on to develop bipolar I disorder (Nusslock et al., 2012). The question remains, however, whether bipolar I and bipolar II disorders should be considered two distinct disorders or simply different points along a continuum of severity of a single bipolar disorder. About 1% of the adult population in the U.S. are affected by bipolar I disorder or bipolar II disorder at some point in their lives (Kupfer, 2005b; Merikangas et al., 2007). Bipolar disorder typically develops around age 20 in both men and women and tends to become a chronic, recurring condition requiring long-term treatment (Frank & Kupfer, 2003; Tohen, Zarate, et al., 2003). 👁

Unlike major depression, rates of bipolar I disorder appear about equal in men and women (Merikangas & Pato, 2009). In men, however, the onset of bipolar I disorder typically begins with a manic episode, whereas with women, it usually begins with a major depressive episode. The underlying reason for this gender difference remains unknown. It remains unclear whether there is a gender difference in rates of bipolar II disorder (APA, 2013).

In some cases of bipolar disorder, a pattern of "rapid cycling" occurs, in which the individual experiences two or more full cycles of mania and depression within a year

Catherine Zeta-Jones. The actress revealed that she suffers from a form of bipolar disorder. She said she hoped that making her condition known will draw public attention to the problem.

👁 **Watch** the **Video** *Feliziano: Living with Bipolar Disorder* on **MyPsychLab**

Is there a thin line between genius and madness? Many creative individuals, including the famed novelist Ernest Hemingway who is pictured here and the artist Vincent van Gogh, suffered from mood disorders. Whatever the links between creativity and mood disorders may be, we should bear in mind that the great majority of creative writers and artists did not suffer from serious mood disturbances.

without any intervening normal periods. Rapid cycling is relatively uncommon, but occurs more often in women than men (Schneck et al., 2004, 2008). It is usually limited to a year or less, but is associated with a more severe form of the disorder and with more serious suicide attempts.

Many observers draw attention to possible links between mood disorders, especially bipolar disorder, and creativity (e.g., McDermott, 2001; Nettle, 2001; Johnson et al., 2011). Many distinguished writers, artists, and composers seem to have suffered from major depression or bipolar disorder. The list of luminaries who suffered from mood disorders stretches from artists Michelangelo and Vincent van Gogh, to composers William Schumann and Peter Tchaikovsky, to novelists Virginia Woolf and Ernest Hemingway, and to poets Alfred Lord Tennyson, Emily Dickinson, Walt Whitman, and Sylvia Plath. Perhaps in some cases, creative people can channel the seemingly boundless energy and rapid stream of thoughts associated with mania into creative expressions. However, we should recognize that the vast majority of writers and artists did not suffer from serious mood disorders and that creativity does not typically spring from psychological disturbance. Moreover, not all studies find links between psychological disorders and creativity, so it's best to reserve judgment on the nature of any such relationship (Bailey, 2003).

MANIC EPISODE A **manic episode** typically begins abruptly, gathering force within days. A hallmark feature of a manic episode, as well as a hypomanic episode, is increased activity or energy (APA, 2013). The person may seem to be on overdrive and to have boundless energy. The basic difference between a full manic episode and a hypomanic episode is one of degree or severity. During a manic episode, the person experiences a sudden elevation or expansion of mood and feels unusually cheerful, euphoric, or optimistic. The person may become extremely sociable, although perhaps to the point of becoming overly demanding and overbearing toward others. Other people recognize the sudden shift in mood to be excessive in the light of the person's life situation. It is one thing to feel elated if one has just won the state lottery. It is another to feel euphoric because it's Wednesday. Here, a young man with bipolar disorder who dubbed himself "Electroboy" describes what a manic episode is like for him (Behrman, 2002):

> **"I" Electroboy**
>
> Manic depression is about buying a dozen bottles of Heinz ketchup and all eight bottles of Windex in stock at the Food Emporium on Broadway at 4 A.M., flying from Zurich to the Bahamas and back to Zurich in three days to balance the hot and cold weather (my "sweet and sour" theory of bipolar disorder), carrying $20,000 in $100 bills in your shoes into the country on your way back to Tokyo, and picking out the person sitting six seats away at the bar to have sex with only because he or she happens to be sitting there. It's about blips and burps of madness, moments of absolute delusion, bliss, and irrational and dangerous choices made in order to heighten pleasure and excitement and to ensure a sense of control. The symptoms of manic depression come in different strengths and sizes. Most days I need to be as manic as possible to come as close as I can to destruction, to get a real good high—a $25,000 shopping spree, a four-day drug binge, or a trip around the world. Other days a simple high from a shoplifting excursion at Duane Reade for a toothbrush or a bottle of Tylenol is enough. I'll admit it: There's a great deal of pleasure to mental illness, especially to the mania associated with manic depression. It's an emotional state similar to Oz, full of excitement, color, noise, and speed—an overload of sensory

stimulation—whereas the sane state of Kansas is plain and simple, black and white, boring and flat. Mania has such a dreamlike quality that often I confuse my manic episodes with dreams I've had. . . .

Mania is about desperately seeking to live life at a more passionate level, taking second and sometimes third helpings on food, alcohol, drugs, sex, and money, trying to live a whole life in one day. Pure mania is as close to death as I think I have ever come. The euphoria is both pleasurable and frightening. My manic mind teems with rapidly changing ideas and needs; my head is cluttered with vibrant colors, wild images, bizarre thoughts, sharp details, secret codes, symbols, and foreign languages. I want to devour everything—parties, people, magazines, books, music, art, movies, and television.

> *From* Electroboy *by Andy Behrman*

People in a manic episode tend to show poor judgment and to be argumentative, sometimes going so far as to destroy property. Roommates may find them abrasive and keep a distance from them. They may become extremely generous and make large charitable contributions they can ill afford or give away costly possessions.

People in a manic episode tend to speak very rapidly (with *pressured speech*). Their thoughts and speech may jump from topic to topic in a rapid *flight of ideas.* Others find it difficult to get a word in edgewise. They typically experience an inflated sense of self-esteem that may range from extreme self-confidence to wholesale delusions of grandeur (Schulze et al., 2005). They may feel capable of solving the world's problems or of composing symphonies, despite a lack of any special knowledge or talent. They may spout off about matters on which they know little, such as how to eliminate world hunger or create a new world order. It soon becomes clear that they are disorganized and incapable of completing their projects. They also become highly distractible. Their attention is easily diverted by irrelevant stimuli like the sounds of a ticking clock or people talking in the next room. They tend to take on multiple tasks, more than they can handle. They may suddenly quit their jobs to enroll in law school, wait tables at night, organize charity drives on weekends, and work on the great American novel in their "spare time." They may not be able to sit still and almost always show decreased need for sleep. They tend to awaken early yet feel well rested and full of energy. They sometimes go for days without sleep but without feeling tired. Although they may have abundant stores of energy, they seem unable to organize their efforts constructively. Their elation impairs their ability to work and to maintain normal relationships.

People in manic episodes fail to weigh the consequences of their actions. They may get into trouble as a result of lavish spending, reckless driving, or sexual escapades. In severe cases, they may experience hallucinations or become grossly delusional, believing, for example, that they have a special relationship with God.

Cyclothymic Disorder

Cyclothymia is derived from the Greek *kyklos,* which means "circle," and *thymos,* meaning "spirit." The notion of a circular-moving spirit is an apt description, because this disorder represents a chronic cyclical pattern of mood disturbance characterized by mild mood swings lasting at least two years (one year for children and adolescents).

Cyclothymic disorder (also called *cyclothymia*) usually begins in late adolescence or early adulthood and persists for years. Few, if any, periods of normal mood last for more than a month or two. However, the periods of elevated or depressed mood are not severe enough to warrant a diagnosis of bipolar disorder. Although cyclothymic disorder may be the most common of the bipolar disorders, with reported prevalence rates ranging from about 0.4% to 1.0%, it tends to be underdiagnosed in clinical practice (APA, 2013; van Meter, Youngstrom, & Findling, 2012).

During a period of at least two years, the adult with cyclothymia has numerous periods of hypomanic symptoms that are not severe enough to meet the criteria for a hypomanic episode and numerous periods of mild depressive symptoms that do not measure up to a major depressive episode (APA, 2013). In effect, the person fluctuates between periods of mildly high "highs" and mildly low "lows." When they are "up," people with cyclothymic disorder show elevated activity levels, which they direct toward accomplishing various professional or personal projects. But, when their moods reverse, they may leave their projects unfinished. Then they enter a mildly depressed mood state and feel lethargic and depressed, but not to the extent typical of a major depressive episode. Social relationships may become strained by shifting moods, and work may suffer. Sexual interest waxes and wanes with the person's moods.

The boundaries between bipolar disorder and cyclothymic disorder are not clearly established. Some forms of cyclothymic disorder may represent a mild, early type of bipolar disorder. Although cyclothymia is milder than bipolar disorder, it can significantly impair a person's daily functioning (Van Meter, Youngstrom, & Findling, 2012). Estimates are that about one in three people with cyclothymic disorder eventually go on to develop bipolar disorder (USDHHS, 1999). Clinicians presently lack the ability to distinguish those with cyclothymia who are likely to develop bipolar disorder. The following case presents an example of the mild mood swings that typify cyclothymic disorder.

→ **"Good Times and Bad Times": A Case of Cyclothymic Disorder**
The man, a 29-year-old car salesman, reports that since the age of 14 he has experienced alternating periods of "good times and bad times." During his "bad" periods, which generally last between four and seven days, he sleeps excessively and feels a lack of confidence, energy, and motivation, as if he were "just vegetating." Then his moods abruptly shift for a period of three or four days, usually upon awakening in the morning, and he feels aflush with confidence and sharpened mental ability. During these "good periods" he engages in promiscuous sex and uses alcohol, in part to enhance his good feelings and in part to help him sleep at night. The good periods may last upwards of 7 to 10 days at times, before shifting back into the bad periods, generally following a hostile or irritable outburst.

→ *Adapted from Spitzer et al., 1994, pp. 155–157*

Causal Factors in Depressive Disorders

Depressive disorders are best understood in terms of complex interactions of biological and psychosocial influences (NIMH, 2003). Although a full understanding of the causes of depressive and bipolar disorders presently lies beyond our grasp, researchers have begun to identify many of the important contributors to these disorders. In the next sections, we examine contemporary understandings of the causal factors in both depressive disorders and bipolar disorders. Many factors are implicated in the development of these disorders, including stressful life events and biological factors.

7.5 Evaluate the role of stress in depression.

Stress and Depression

Stressful life events increase the risk of mood disorders such as bipolar disorder and major depression (Kendler & Gardner, 2010; Monroe & Reid, 2008; Risch et al., 2009). Most people with major depression—perhaps as many as 80%—report experiencing a major source of life stress before the onset of the disorder (Monroe & Reid, 2009). Sources of life stress linked to depression include loss of a loved one, breakup of a romantic relationship, prolonged unemployment and economic hardship, serious physical illness, marital or relationship problems, separation or divorce, exposure to racism and discrimination, and living in unsafe, distressed neighborhoods (e.g., Drieling, van Calker, & Hecht, 2006; Kõlves, Ide, & De Leo, 2010; National Center for Health Statistics, 2012b). Any significant loss, whether it be death of a loved one, a failed relationship, or a job termination, can lead to depression (APA, 2013).

DSM-5 considers grief to be an expectable response to a significant loss, but not a mental disorder (APA, 2013). However, it recognizes that grief and depression may occur together after a loss and that some extreme or severe grief reactions (such as in the case of suicidal thinking or difficulty functioning) may indicate the presence of a major depressive disorder. However, it remains unclear whether practitioners will be able to distinguish between a normal or expectable grief reaction and a depressive disorder layered over the pain of grief in a bereaved individual.

A recent study suggests that stress associated with interpersonal problems with friends, family members, and romantic partners contributes to depression in young people, but only among those who tend to think negatively (Carter & Garber, 2011). This reminds us of the need to take multiple factors and their interactions into account—in this case, negative thinking and stress—in understanding causal pathways leading to mental disorders such as depression. For reasons that remain unclear, stressful life events are more closely connected to a first episode of major depression than to later episodes (Monroe et al., 2007; Stroud, Davila, & Moyer, 2008).

The relationship between stress and depression cuts both ways: Stressful life events may contribute to depression, whereas depressive symptoms may be stressful in themselves or lead to other sources of stress, such as divorce or loss of employment (Liu & Alloy, 2010; Uliaszek et al., 2012). For example, if you become depressed, you may find it more difficult to keep up with your work, which can lead to more stress as work backs up. Consider, too, that stress associated with unemployment and financial hardship may lead to depression, but depression may also lead to unemployment and lower income (Whooley et al., 2002).

Although stress is often implicated in depression, not everyone who encounters stress becomes clinically depressed. Factors such as coping skills, genetic endowment, and availability of social support may lessen the likelihood of depression in the face of stressful events. We also need to take into account gene–environment interactions in depression and suicidal behavior (Monroe & Reid, 2008; Shinozaki et al., 2013). Consistent with the *diathesis–stress model* outlined in Chapter 2, people who possess variants of certain genes may be more susceptible to developing depression if they have a history of severely stressful life experiences, such as maltreatment during childhood (Fisher et al., 2013).

We need to consider further the role of early life experiences. A lack of secure attachments to parents during infancy or childhood may also contribute to greater vulnerability to depression in later life following disappointment, failure, or other stressful life events (Morley & Moran, 2011). Adverse experiences early in life, such as parental divorce or physical abuse, are also linked to greater vulnerability to depression in adulthood (Wainwright & Surtees, 2002).

Some psychosocial factors may act as buffers against stress, providing a cushion against depression. A strong marital relationship, for instance, may be a source of support during times of stress. Not surprisingly, divorced or separated people, who lack a supportive marital relationship, show higher rates of depression and suicide attempts than do married people (Weissman et al., 1991). People who live alone, and may thus have more limited social support available, also face a greater risk of depression (Pulkki-Raback et al., 2012).

"Gotta have friends." Social support from friends and family members appears to buffer the effects of stress and may reduce the risk of depression. People who lack important relationships and who rarely join in social activities are more likely to suffer from depression.

7.6 Describe the major psychological models of depression.

Psychodynamic Theories

The classic psychodynamic theory of depression proposed by Freud (1917/1957) and his adherents (e.g., Abraham, 1916/1948) holds that depression represents anger directed inward rather than against significant others. Anger may become directed against the self following either the actual or the threatened loss of these important others.

Freud believed that mourning, or normal bereavement, is a healthy process by which one eventually comes to separate oneself psychologically from a person who has been lost through death, separation, divorce, or another reason. Pathological mourning, however, does not promote healthy separation. Rather, it fosters lingering depression. Pathological mourning is likely to occur in people who hold powerful ambivalent feelings—a combination of positive (love) and negative (anger, hostility) feelings—toward the person who has departed or whose departure is feared. Freud theorized that when people lose, or even fear losing, an important figure about whom they feel ambivalent, their feelings of anger turn to rage. Yet, rage triggers guilt, which in turn prevents the person from venting anger directly at the lost person (called an "object").

To preserve a psychological connection to the lost object, people *introject,* or bring inward, a mental representation of the object. They thus incorporate the other person into the self. Now anger is turned inward, against the part of the self that represents the inward representation of the lost person. This produces self-hatred, which in turn leads to depression.

From the psychodynamic viewpoint, bipolar disorder represents shifting dominance of the individual's personality between the ego and superego. In the depressive phase, the superego is dominant, producing exaggerated notions of wrongdoing and flooding the individual with feelings of guilt and worthlessness. After a time, the ego rebounds and asserts supremacy, producing feelings of elation and self-confidence that characterize the manic phase. The excessive display of ego eventually triggers a return of guilt, once again plunging the individual into depression.

Although they emphasize the importance of loss, more recent psychodynamic models shift the focus toward the individual's sense of self-worth or self-esteem. One model, called the *self-focusing model,* considers how people allocate their attentional processes after a loss, such as the death of a loved one or a personal failure or significant disappointment (Pyszczynski & Greenberg, 1987). In this view, depressed people have difficulty thinking about anything other than themselves and the loss they experienced.

Consider a person who must cope with the termination of a failed romantic relationship. The depression-prone individual gets wrapped up in thinking about the relationship and hopes of restoring it, rather than recognizing the futility of the effort and getting on with life. Moreover, the lost partner was a source of emotional support on whom the depression-prone individual had relied to maintain self-esteem. Following the loss, the depression-prone individual feels stripped of hope and optimism because these positive feelings had depended on the lost object. The loss of self-esteem and of feelings of security, not the loss of the relationship per se, precipitates depression. Similarly, loss of a specific occupational goal may trigger self-focusing and consequent depression. Only by surrendering the object or lost goal and fostering alternate sources of identity and self-worth can the cycle be broken.

RESEARCH EVIDENCE Psychodynamic theorists focus on the role of loss in depression. Evidence shows loss of significant others (through death or divorce, for example) to be associated with increased risk of depression (Kendler, Hettema, et al., 2003). Personal losses may also lead to other psychological disorders, however. There is yet a lack of research to support Freud's view that repressed anger toward the departed loved one is turned inward in depression.

Evidence supports the view that a self-focusing style—an inward or self-absorbed focus of attention—is associated with depression, especially in women (Mor & Winquist,

2002; Muraven, 2005). Yet, self-focused attention is not limited to depression and is often found in people with anxiety disorders and other psychological disorders. Thus, the general linkage between self-focused attention and psychopathology may limit the model's value as an explanation of depression.

Humanistic Theories

From the humanistic framework, people become depressed when they cannot imbue their existence with meaning and make authentic choices that lead to self-fulfillment. The world for them becomes a drab place. People's search for meaning gives color and substance to their lives. Guilt may arise when people believe they have not lived up to their potential. Humanistic psychologists challenge us to take a long hard look at our lives. Are they worthwhile and enriching? Or are they drab and routine? If the latter, perhaps we have frustrated our needs for self-actualization. We may be settling, coasting through life. Settling can give rise to a sense of dreariness that becomes expressed in depressive behavior—lethargy, sullen mood, and withdrawal.

Loss and depression. Psychodynamic theorists focus on the important role of loss in the development of depression.

Like psychodynamic theorists, humanistic theorists focus on the loss of self-esteem that can occur when people lose friends or family members or suffer occupational setbacks. We tend to connect our personal identity and sense of self-worth with our social roles as parents, spouses, students, or workers. When these role identities are lost, through the death of a spouse, the departure of children to college, or loss of a job, our sense of purpose and self-worth can be shattered. Depression is a frequent consequence of such losses. It is especially likely when we base our self-esteem on our occupational role or success. Job loss, demotion, or failure to achieve a promotion are common precipitants of depression, especially for individuals who value themselves on the basis of occupational success.

Learning Theories

Whereas the psychodynamic perspectives focus on inner, often unconscious, causes, learning theorists emphasize situational factors, such as the loss of positive reinforcement. We perform best when levels of reinforcement are commensurate with our efforts. Changes in the frequency or effectiveness of reinforcement can shift the balance so that life becomes unrewarding.

THE ROLE OF REINFORCEMENT Learning theorist Peter Lewinsohn (1974) proposed that depression results from an imbalance between behavior and reinforcement. A lack of reinforcement for one's efforts can sap motivation and induce feelings of depression. Inactivity and social withdrawal reduce opportunities for reinforcement; lack of reinforcement exacerbates withdrawal.

The low rate of activity typical of depressed individuals may also be a source of secondary reinforcement. Family members and other people may rally around people suffering from depression and release them from their responsibilities. Sympathy may thus become a source of reinforcement that helps maintain depressed behavior.

Reduction in reinforcement levels can occur for many reasons. A person who is recuperating at home from a serious illness or injury may find little that is reinforcing to do. Social reinforcement may plummet when people close to us, who were suppliers of reinforcement, die or leave us. People who suffer social losses are more likely to become depressed when they lack the social skills to form new relationships. Some first-year college students are homesick and depressed because they lack the skills to form rewarding new relationships. Widows and widowers may be at a loss as to how to start a new relationship.

Physical exercise not only helps tone the body but can help combat depression.

☑ **TRUE** Evidence supports the benefits of regular physical activity or exercise in the treatment of depression.

Changes in life circumstances may also alter the balance of effort and reinforcement. A prolonged layoff may reduce financial reinforcement, which may in turn force painful cutbacks in lifestyle. A disability or an extended illness may also impair one's ability to ensure a steady flow of reinforcements. Lewinsohn's model is supported by research findings that connect depression to a low level of positive reinforcement, and, importantly, by evidence that encouraging depressed patients to participate in rewarding activities and goal-oriented behaviors can help alleviate depression (Otto, 2006). Encouraging depressed patients to engage in regular physical activity or exercise also helps combat depression, especially in the face of major life stressors (Mata et al., 2012; Walsh, 2011; Wipfli et al., 2010). **T / F**

INTERACTIONAL THEORY Problems in interpersonal relationships may help explain the lack of positive reinforcement. Interactional theory, developed by psychologist James Coyne (1976), proposes that the adjustment to living with a depressed person can become so stressful that the partner or family member becomes progressively less reinforcing.

Interactional theory is based on the concept of *reciprocal interaction.* Our behavior influences how other people respond to us, and how they respond to us influences how we in turn respond to them. The theory holds that depression-prone people react to stress by seeking or demanding reassurance and support from their partners and significant others (Evraire & Dozois, 2011; Rehman, Gollan, & Mortimer, 2008). At first, this effort to garner support may succeed. But over time, persistent demands for emotional support begin to elicit more anger and annoyance than expressions of support. Although loved ones may keep these negative feelings to themselves, these feelings may surface in subtle ways that spell rejection. Depressed people may react to cues of rejection with deeper feelings of depression and by making greater demands for reassurance, triggering a vicious cycle of further rejection and more profound depression. They may also feel guilty about causing distress in the family, which can exacerbate their negative feelings about themselves.

Family members may find it stressful to adjust to the depressed person's behavior, especially latter's withdrawal, lethargy, despair, and constant demands for reassurance. Not surprisingly, evidence shows that people with spouses being treated for depression tend to report higher-than-average levels of emotional distress (Benazon, 2000; Kronmüller et al., 2011).

Evidence generally supports Coyne's model that depressed individuals' excessive needs for reassurance lead to rejection by the very people from whom they seek reassurance and support (Rehman, Gollan, & Mortimer, 2008; Starr & Davila, 2008). A lack of social skills may best explain this rejection. Depressed people tend to be unresponsive, uninvolved, and even impolite when they interact with others. For example, they tend to gaze very little at the other person, to take an excessive amount of time to respond, to show very little approval or validation of the other person, and to dwell on their problems and negative feelings. They even dwell on negative feelings when interacting with strangers. In effect, they turn other people off, setting the stage for rejection. Yet, relationships can work both ways, as partners who fail to meet each other's psychological needs or are critical or hurtful toward each other can affect each other's emotional well-being (Ibarra-Rovillard & Kuiper, 2010).

Cognitive Theories

Cognitive theorists relate the origin and maintenance of depression to the ways in which people see themselves and the world around them. One of the most influential cognitive theorists, psychiatrist Aaron Beck (Beck & Alford, 2009; Beck et al., 1979) links the development of depression to the adoption early in life of a negatively biased or distorted way of thinking—the **cognitive triad of depression** (see Table 7.3). The cognitive triad includes negative beliefs about oneself ("I'm no good"),

Working out to work it out. Recent evidence suggests that regular physical activity or exercise may be helpful in combating depression, especially in people facing significant life stressors.

TABLE 7.3 **The Cognitive Triad of Depression**	
Negative view of oneself	Perceiving oneself as worthless, deficient, inadequate, unlovable, and lacking the skills necessary to achieve happiness.
Negative view of the environment	Perceiving the environment as imposing excessive demands and/or presenting obstacles that are impossible to overcome, leading to continual failure and loss.
Negative view of the future	Perceiving the future as hopeless and believing that one is powerless to change things for the better. One expects of the future only continuing failure and unrelenting misery and hardship.

Note: According to Aaron Beck, depression-prone people adopt a habitual style of negative thinking—the so-called cognitive triad of depression.
Source: Adapted from Beck & Young, 1985; Beck et al., 1979.

the environment or the world at large ("This school is awful"), and the future ("Nothing will ever turn out right for me"). Cognitive theory holds that people who adopt this negative way of thinking are at greater risk of becoming depressed in the face of stressful or disappointing life experiences, such as getting a poor grade or losing a job.

Beck views these negative concepts of the self and the world as mental templates that are adopted in childhood on the basis of early learning experiences. Children may find that nothing they do is good enough to please their parents or teachers. As a result, they come to regard themselves as basically incompetent and to perceive their future prospects as dim. These beliefs may sensitize them later in life to interpret any failure or disappointment as a reflection of something basically wrong or inadequate about themselves. Even a minor disappointment becomes a crushing blow or a total defeat that can quickly lead to states of depression.

The tendency to magnify the importance of minor failures is an example of an error in thinking that Beck labels a *cognitive distortion*. He believes cognitive distortions set the stage for depression in the face of personal losses or negative life events. A colleague of Beck, psychiatrist David Burns (1980), identified a number of cognitive distortions associated with depression:

1. *All-or-nothing thinking: Seeing events as either all good or all bad, or as either black or white with no shades of gray.* For example, one may perceive a relationship that ended in disappointment as a totally negative experience, despite any positive feelings or experiences that may have occurred along the way. Perfectionism is an example of all-or-nothing thinking. Perfectionists judge any outcome other than perfect success to be complete failure. They may consider a grade of B or even an A– to be tantamount to an F. Perfectionism is connected with an increased vulnerability to depression as well as to poor treatment outcomes (Blatt et al., 1998; Minarik & Ahrens, 1996).

2. *Overgeneralization: Believing that if a negative event occurs, it is likely to occur again in similar situations in the future.* One may interpret a single negative event as foreshadowing an endless series of negative events. For example, receiving a letter of rejection from a potential employer leads one to assume that all other job applications will be similarly rejected.

3. *Mental filter: Focusing only on negative details of events, thereby rejecting the positive features of one's experiences.* Like a droplet of ink that spreads to discolor an entire beaker of water, focusing only on a single negative detail can darken one's vision of reality. Beck called this cognitive distortion *selective abstraction*, meaning the individual selectively abstracts the negative details from events and ignores the

"Why do I always screw up?" Cognitive theorists believe a person's self-defeating or distorted interpretations of life events, such as tendencies to blame oneself without considering other factors, can set the stage for depression in the face of disappointing life experiences.

events' positive features. One thus bases one's self-esteem on perceived weaknesses and failures, rather than on positive features or on a balance of accomplishments and shortcomings. For example, a person receives a job evaluation that contains both positive and negative comments but focuses only on the negative ones.

4. *Disqualifying the positive: The tendency to snatch defeat from the jaws of victory by neutralizing or denying one's accomplishments.* An example is dismissal of congratulations for a job well done by thinking and saying, "Oh, it's no big deal. Anyone could have done it." As a matter of fact, taking credit where credit is due may help people overcome depression by increasing their belief that they can make changes that will lead to a positive future.

5. *Jumping to conclusions: Forming a negative interpretation of events, despite a lack of evidence.* Two examples of this style of thinking are "mind reading" and "the fortune teller error." In *mind reading*, a person arbitrarily jumps to the conclusion that others don't like or respect him or her, as in interpreting a friend's not calling for a while as a rejection. The *fortune teller error* is the prediction that something bad is always about to happen. The person believes the prediction of calamity is factually based, even though there is no evidence to support it. For example, the person concludes that a passing tightness in the chest *must* be a sign of heart disease, discounting the possibility of more benign causes.

6. *Magnification and minimization: The tendency to make mountains out of molehills.* Also called *catastrophizing,* this type of distortion refers exaggeration of the importance of negative events, personal flaws, fears, or mistakes. Minimization is the mirror image, a type of cognitive distortion in which one minimizes or underestimates one's good points.

7. *Emotional reasoning: Basing reasoning on emotions.* A person with this distortion thinks, for example, "If I feel guilty, it must be because I've done something really wrong." One interprets feelings and events on the basis of emotions rather than on fair consideration of evidence.

8. *"Should" statements: Creating personal imperatives or self-commandments—"shoulds" or "musts."* For example, "I *should* always get my first serve in!" or "I *must* make Chris like me!" By creating unrealistic expectations, *musterbation*—the label given to this form of thinking by Albert Ellis—can lead one to become depressed when one falls short.

9. *Labeling and mislabeling: Explaining behavior by attaching negative labels to oneself and others.* Students may explain a poor grade on a test by thinking they were "lazy" or "stupid" rather than simply unprepared for the specific exam or, perhaps, ill. Labeling other people as "stupid" or "insensitive" can engender hostility toward them. Mislabeling involves the use of labels that are emotionally charged and inaccurate, such as calling oneself a "pig" because of a minor deviation from one's usual diet.

10. *Personalization: Assuming that one is responsible for other people's problems and behavior.* For example, an individual may feel blame if his or her partner or spouse is crying, rather than recognizing that other causes may be involved.

Consider the errors in thinking illustrated in the following case example.

Christie's Errors in Thinking

Christie was a 33-year-old real estate sales agent who suffered from frequent episodes of depression. Whenever a deal fell through, she would blame herself: "If only I had worked harder ... negotiated better ... talked more persuasively ... the deal would have been done." After several successive disappointments, each one followed by self-recriminations, she felt like quitting altogether. Her thinking became increasingly dominated by negative thoughts, which further depressed her mood and lowered her self-esteem: "I'm a loser ... I'll never succeed ... It's all my fault ... I'm no good and I'm never going to succeed at anything."

Christie's thinking included cognitive errors such as the following: (1) personalization (believing herself to be the sole cause of negative events); (2) labeling and mislabeling (labeling herself to be a loser); (3) overgeneralization (predicting a dismal future on the basis of a present disappointment); and (4) mental filter (judging her personality entirely on the basis of her disappointments). In therapy, Christie learned to think more realistically about events and not to jump to conclusions that she was automatically at fault whenever a deal fell through, or to judge her whole personality on the basis of disappointments or perceived flaws in herself. In place of this self-defeating style of thinking, she began to think more realistically when disappointments occurred, like telling herself, "Okay, I'm disappointed. I'm frustrated. I feel lousy. So what? It doesn't mean I'll never succeed. Let me discover what went wrong and try to correct it the next time. I have to look ahead, not dwell on disappointments in the past."

From the Author's Files

Distorted thinking tends to occur automatically, as if the thoughts just popped into one's head. Automatic thoughts are likely to be accepted as statements of fact rather than as opinions or habitual ways of interpreting events. Distorted thinking is not limited to particular cultures. Chinese researchers recently reported that among adolescents in Hunan Province, having a negative cognitive style (i.e., high levels of dysfunctional negative thinking) predicts greater depressive symptoms following negative life experiences (Abela et al., 2011).

Beck and his colleagues formulated a **cognitive-specificity hypothesis,** which proposes that different disorders are characterized by different types of automatic thoughts. Beck and his colleagues found some interesting differences in the types of automatic thoughts in people with depressive and anxiety disorders (Beck et al., 1987) (see Table 7.4). People with diagnosable depression more often reported automatic

---

TABLE 7.4

Automatic Thoughts Associated with Depression and Anxiety

Common Automatic Thoughts Associated with Depression	Common Automatic Thoughts Associated with Anxiety
1. I'm worthless.	1. What if I get sick and become an invalid?
2. I'm not worthy of other people's attention or affection.	2. I am going to be injured.
3. I'll never be as good as other people are.	3. What if no one reaches me in time to help?
4. I'm a social failure.	4. I might be trapped.
5. I don't deserve to be loved.	5. I am not a healthy person.
6. People don't respect me anymore.	6. I'm going to have an accident.
7. I will never overcome my problems.	7. Something will happen that will ruin my appearance.
8. I've lost the only friends I've had.	8. I am going to have a heart attack.
9. Life isn't worth living.	9. Something awful is going to happen.
10. I'm worse off than they are.	10. Something will happen to someone I care about.
11. There's no one left to help me.	11. I'm losing my mind.
12. No one cares whether I live or die.	
13. Nothing ever works out for me anymore.	
14. I have become physically unattractive.	

Source: Adapted from Beck & Young, 1985; Beck et al., 1979.

thoughts concerning themes of loss, self-deprecation, and pessimism. People with anxiety disorders more often reported automatic thoughts concerning physical danger and other threats.

RESEARCH EVIDENCE ON COGNITIONS AND DEPRESSION Research studies demonstrate support of Beck's model in finding that depressed patients tend to show more distorted or dysfunctional thinking than do nondepressed controls (e.g., Beevers, Wells, & Miller, 2007; Carson, Hollon, & Shelton, 2010; Riso et al., 2003). People with bipolar disorder also tend to show higher levels of dysfunctional thinking than do nonpatient controls (Goldberg et al., 2008).

Other evidence supports the basic tenets of the cognitive-specificity hypothesis that certain types of negative thoughts—those relating to themes of loss and failure—are strongly associated with depression, whereas negative thoughts relating to social threats of rejection or criticism are more strongly tied to anxiety symptoms (Schniering & Rapee, 2004).

But investigators need to consider causal linkages. Although dysfunctional cognitions (negative, distorted, or pessimistic thoughts) tend to be more common among people who are depressed, underlying causal pathways remain unclear. Negative or distorted thinking may cause depression or depression may cause negative, distorted thinking. Some evidence actually points to depression causing negative thinking rather than the reverse (LaGrange et al., 2011). However, other research suggests that distorted, negative thinking often precedes emotional distress and may indeed play a causal role in its development (Baer et al., 2012). Clearly, more research is needed to disentangle causes and effects.

We should also recognize that causal linkages may work both ways. In other words, thoughts may affect moods, and moods may affect thoughts. For example, depressed mood may induce negative, distorted thinking. The more negative and distorted depressed individuals' thinking becomes, the more depressed individuals may feel, and the more depressed they feel, the more dysfunctional their thinking becomes. However, it is equally possible that dysfunctional thinking comes first in the cycle, perhaps in response to a disappointing life experience, which then leads to a downcast mood. This in turn may accentuate negative thinking, and so on. Investigators are still faced with the old "chicken or egg" dilemma of determining which comes first in the causal sequence: distorted thinking or depressed mood. In all likelihood, distorted cognitions and negative moods interact in the complex web of factors leading to depression.

Learned Helplessness (Attributional) Theory

The **learned helplessness** model proposes that people may become depressed because they learn to view themselves as helpless to change their lives for the better. The originator of the learned helplessness concept, Martin Seligman (1973, 1975), suggests that people learn to perceive themselves as helpless because of their experiences. The learned helplessness model therefore straddles the behavioral and the cognitive: Situational factors foster attitudes that lead to depression.

Seligman and his colleagues based the learned helplessness model on early laboratory studies of animals. In these studies, dogs exposed to an inescapable electric shock showed the *learned helplessness effect* by failing to learn to escape when escape became possible (Overmier & Seligman, 1967; Seligman & Maier, 1967). Exposure to uncontrollable forces apparently taught the animals that they were helpless to change the situation (Forgeard et al., 2011). Animals that developed learned helplessness showed behaviors similar to those of depressed people, including lethargy, lack of motivation, and difficulty acquiring new skills (Maier & Seligman, 1976).

Seligman (1975, 1991) proposed that some forms of depression in humans might result from exposure to apparently uncontrollable situations. Such experiences can instill the expectation that future outcomes are beyond one's ability to control ("Why try? I'll only wind up failing again"). A cruel vicious cycle may come into play in cases of depression. A few failures may produce feelings of helplessness and expectations of further failure. Perhaps you know people who have failed certain subjects, such as mathematics. They may come to believe themselves incapable of succeeding in math. They may thus decide that studying for the quantitative section of the Graduate Record Exam is a waste of time. They then perform poorly, completing the self-fulfilling prophecy, which further intensifies feelings of helplessness, leading to lowered expectations, and so on, in a vicious cycle.

Although it stimulated much interest, Seligman's model failed to account for the low self-esteem typical of people who are depressed. Nor did it explain why depression persists in some people but not in others. Seligman and his colleagues (Abramson, Seligman, & Teasdale, 1978) offered a reformulation of the theory to meet such shortcomings. The revised theory held that perception of lack of control over future rewards or reinforcers did not by itself explain the persistence and severity of depression. It was also necessary to consider cognitive factors, especially ways in which people explain their failures and disappointments to themselves.

Seligman and his colleagues recast helplessness theory in terms of the social psychology concept of *attributional style*. An attributional style is a personal style of explanation. When disappointments or failures occur, we may explain them in various characteristic ways. We may blame ourselves (an internal attribution), or we may blame the circumstances we face (an external attribution). We may see bad experiences as typical events (a stable attribution) or as isolated events (an unstable attribution). We may see them as evidence of broader problems (a global attribution) or as evidence of precise and limited shortcomings (a specific attribution). The reformulated helplessness theory holds that people who explain the causes of negative events (such as failure in work, school, or romantic relationships) according to the following three types of attributions are most vulnerable to depression:

1. *Internal factors*, or beliefs that failures reflect their personal inadequacies, rather than external factors, or beliefs that failures are caused by environmental factors
2. *Global factors*, or beliefs that failures reflect sweeping flaws in personality rather than specific factors, or beliefs that failures reflect limited areas of functioning
3. *Stable factors*, or beliefs that failures reflect fixed personality factors rather than unstable factors, or beliefs that the factors leading to failures are changeable

Let's illustrate this attributional style with the example of a college student who goes on a disastrous date. Afterward, he shakes his head in wonder and tries to make sense of his experience. An internal attribution for the calamity is characterized by self-blame, as in "I really messed it up." An external attribution would place the blame elsewhere, as in "Some couples just don't hit it off," or "She must have been in a bad mood." A stable attribution would suggest a problem that cannot be changed, as in "It's my personality." An unstable attribution, on the other hand, would suggest a transient condition, as in "It was probably the head cold." A global attribution for failure magnifies the extent of the problem, as in "I really have no idea what I'm doing when I'm with people." A specific attribution, in contrast, chops the problem down to size, as in "My problem is how to make small talk to get a relationship going."

The revised theory holds that each attributional dimension makes a specific contribution to feelings of helplessness. Internal attributions for negative events are linked to lower self-esteem. Stable attributions help explain the persistence—or, in medical terms, the chronicity—of helplessness cognitions. Global attributions are associated with the generality or pervasiveness of feelings of helplessness following negative events. The adoption of a negative attributional style (i.e., attributing negative life events to internal, stable, and global factors) is not only a recognized risk factor for depression but is also connected to an increased risk of anxiety disorders (Riso et al., 2003; Safford, 2008).

"Is it me?" According to reformulated helplessness theory, the kinds of attributions we make concerning negative events can make us more or less vulnerable to depression. Responding to the breakup of a relationship by internalizing ("It's me"), globalizing ("I'm totally worthless"), and stabilizing ("Things are always going to turn out badly for me") can lead to depression.

7.7 Describe biological factors in depression.

Biological Factors

A large and growing body of evidence points to important roles for biological factors, especially genetics and neurotransmitter functioning, in the development of depressive disorders.

GENETIC FACTORS Genetic factors play a significant role in determining a person's risk of developing depressive disorders (e.g., Duric et al., 2010; Malhotra et al., 2011; Nes et al., 2012). Researchers are making progress drilling down to particular genes linked to depression (e.g., Kohli et al., 2011; Pinacho et al., 2011; Spijker et al., 2011; Zou et al., 2012). An emerging model in the field focuses on interactions of genetic and environmental factors in major depression and other mood disorders (Jokela et al., 2007). Underscoring the importance of interactions between biological and psychosocial factors, investigators find that variation of particular genes involved in regulating serotonin is linked to greater risk of depression in the face of life stress (Karg et al., 2011; NIMH, 2003). Serotonin is the neurotransmitter targeted by antidepressants such as Prozac and Zoloft, so it is not surprising it may play a role in proneness to depression.

What we have come to understand is that the effects of life stressors on the development of depression are greater in people at high genetic risk (Lau & Eley, 2010). Developing a better understanding of the role that particular genes play in depression may lead to the use of gene therapy in treating depression by means of directly influencing the functioning of targeted genes (Alexander et al., 2010).

Let's look more closely at evidence supporting the role of genetic factors in major depression. Not only does major depression tend to run in families, but the closer the genetic relationship people share, the more likely they are to share a depressive disorder. Yet, families share environmental as well as genetic similarities. To tease out the effects of genetic factors, investigators have turned to studies of twins. They examine the relative percentages of cases in which MZ, or identical, twins share a common trait or disorder, as compared with DZ, or fraternal, twins. The percentage of cases in which the twin of a person who is identified as having a given trait or disorder also has the trait or disorder is called the concordance (agreement) rate. Because MZ twins have 100% of genes in common, as compared with the 50% among DZ twins, evidence of a higher concordance rate among MZ twins provides strong support for a genetic contribution.

Ground-breaking research along these lines showed more than double the concordance rate for major depression among MZ twins than among DZ twins (Kendler et al., 1992b, 1993). This evidence provided strong support for a genetic component, but it was well short of the 100% concordance one would expect if genetics were solely responsible for these disorders. Although heredity appears to play an important role in major depression, it isn't the only determinant and may not even be the most important determinant. Environmental factors, as well as the interactions of genetic and environmental influences, may be even more important contributors to the development of major depression (Kendler et al., 1999).

Before going further, we should note that different psychological disorders may share common genetic links. A breakthrough study reported in 2013 showed that five separate disorders—major depression, bipolar disorder, schizophrenia, autism, and attention deficit hyperactivity disorder—all share certain genetic variations in common (Cross-Disorder Group of the Psychiatric Genomics Consortium, 2013). Two people may share the same genetic risk factor but develop very different disorders depending on their particular life experiences or other factors (Kolata, 2013). Developing a better understanding of the common genetic risk factors that cut across various psychological disorders may lead to new ways of classifying disorders that take into account underlying genetic patterns as well as differences in symptom presentation.

BIOCHEMICAL FACTORS AND BRAIN ABNORMALITIES Research on the biological underpinnings of mood disorders has largely focused on abnormalities in neurotransmitter activity in the brain. Early research, more than 50 years ago, showed that drugs we now call *antidepressants,* which increase levels of the neurotransmitters norepinephrine and serotonin in the brain, often helped relieve depression. Might depression be caused simply by a lack of key neurotransmitters in the brain? Investigators discount this view, in part because antidepressants boost levels of neurotransmitters in the brain within a few days or even hours of use, but it usually takes weeks or months before the full therapeutic effects are achieved (Cyan & O'Leary, 2010). Also, evidence fails to show a lack of norepinephrine and serotonin in people with major depression (Belmaker & Agam, 2008). Consequently, it is unlikely that depression is caused by a mere deficiency in serotonin or that antidepressants work simply by boosting levels of neurotransmitters in the brain.

More complex views of the role of neurotransmitters in depression are emerging. Among the intriguing possibilities is that depression may involve irregularities in the numbers of receptors on receiving neurons where neurotransmitters dock (having too many or too few), abnormalities in the sensitivity of these receptors to particular neurotransmitters, or irregularities in how these chemicals bind to receptors (Oquendo et al., 2007; Sharp, 2006). It is conceivable that antidepressants work to relieve depression by altering the number or density of these receptors or their sensitivity to neurotransmitters, a process that takes time to unfold (hence the several weeks' lag time before the effects of antidepressants occur). Although irregularities in how serotonin is used in the brain appear to be linked to depression (Carver, Johnson, & Joormann, 2008, 2009), investigators still don't have a final answer about the exact role that serotonin or other neurotransmitters play in depression or about the mechanisms explaining the therapeutic effects of antidepressants.

Another avenue of research into the biological underpinnings of mood disorders focuses on abnormalities in the brain. Brain-imaging studies show reduced size and lower metabolic activity in mood disorder patients in areas of the brain involved in regulating thinking processes and mood, including the prefrontal cortex and the limbic system (e.g., Duman & Aghajanian, 2012; Kieseppä et al., 2010; Lorenzetti et al., 2010; Wang et al., 2012). The prefrontal cortex lies in the frontal lobes of the cerebral cortex and is the area of the brain responsible for higher mental functions, such as thinking, problem solving and decision making, and organizing thoughts and behaviors. Parts of the limbic system are involved in forming new memories. The neurotransmitters serotonin and norepinephrine play important roles in regulating nerve impulses in the prefrontal cortex, so it is not surprising that evidence points to irregularities in this region of the brain.

As research using brain-imaging techniques continues, investigators will likely develop a clearer picture of how the brain of people with mood disorders differ from that of healthy individuals and perhaps even discover ways of better diagnosing these disorders and treating them. Other systems in the body, such as the endocrine system, may also play a role in the development of mood disorders in ways that future research may help clarify. As in other complex forms of abnormal behavior, such as anxiety disorders and schizophrenia, the underlying causes of depression in all likelihood involve multiple factors (Belmaker & Agam, 2008).

Causal Factors in Bipolar Disorders

7.8 Describe causal factors in bipolar disorders.

Many investigators believe that multiple causes acting together contribute to the development of bipolar disorders. Evidence points to cognitive deficits in people with bipolar disorder in recognizing facial cues of emotions in others—deficiencies that appear tied to abnormalities in the workings of the brain's prefrontal cortex and limbic system (Izard et al., 2009; McClure-Tone, 2009). Brain-imaging studies find supporting evidence of abnormalities in many regions of the brain, especially those involved in processing emotions (Degabriele & Lagopoulos, 2009; Henin et al., 2009).

Something Fishy About This

You may have heard that high concentrations of certain types of fish oil, especially *omega-3 fatty acids*, in the diet are linked to lower rates of cardiovascular disease. But you may not know that high dietary levels of fish oil are also linked to reduced risk of major depression and bipolar disorder (Yager, 2003). Omega-3 fatty acids are essential nutrients that the brain may need to function optimally. Although more research is needed, an increasing body of evidence points to the value of including omega-3 fatty acids in treating depression (e.g., Carney

Go fish. Might fish oil help combat mood disorders? We don't have a definitive answer, but some evidence suggests there may be a value in adding to the diet certain types of fish oil, especially omega-3 fatty acids, in treating depression.

et al., 2009; Lin et al, 2012; Martins et al., 2012; Montgomery & Richardson, 2008). Presently, omega-3 fatty acid supplements may be best suited as an adjunct to regular care, but not as a stand-alone treatment (Walsh, 2011).

We also have evidence from cross-national studies showing a link between high consumption of seafood, which is rich in omega-3 fatty acids, and low rates of mood disorders (Parker et al., 2006). In one cross-national study, the country consuming the most seafood, Iceland, showed low rates of bipolar disorder, whereas countries with lower levels of seafood consumption, such as Germany, Switzerland, Italy, and Israel, showed higher rates (Noaghiul & Hibbeln, 2003). **T / F**

truth OR fiction

High levels of fish oil in the diet are linked to increased risk of bipolar disorder.

☑ **FALSE**   Actually, evidence links high levels of dietary fish oil to lower rates of mood disorders.

We should caution that causal linkages cannot be ascertained from observed relationships between eating fish and lower risks of mood disorders. Nevertheless, these linkages encourage researchers to explore further whether a dietary supplement may indeed live up to its popular billing as good brain food. In the meantime, salmon anyone?

Genetic factors play a major role in bipolar disorder (Hyman, 2011). In a large population-based study in Finland, investigators found the concordance rate to be seven times greater among MZ twins than DZ twins (43% versus 6%, respectively) (Kieseppä et al., 2004). Genetics appears to play an even stronger role in bipolar disorder than it does in major depressive disorder (Belmaker & Agam, 2008).

Intriguing new findings reported in 2008 from Sweden showed a connection between higher risk of bipolar disorder and greater paternal age at birth, especially father's age 55 and older (Frans et al., 2008). We should note that maternal age was less clearly connected to bipolar disorder in offspring. A possible explanation for the paternal link is that genetic errors tend to be more frequent in the sperm of older men, so it is possible that such defects predispose their offspring to certain psychological disorders, including bipolar disorder.

Investigators are actively tracking down specific genes in bipolar disorder (Lee et al., 2013). However, genes don't tell the whole story. If bipolar disorder were caused entirely by genetics, then an identical twin of someone having the disorder would always develop the disorder, but this isn't the case. Consistent with the diathesis–stress model, stressful life changes and underlying biological influences may interact with a genetic predisposition to increase a person's vulnerability to bipolar disorder. Moreover, investigators have learned that stressful life events can trigger mood episodes in people with bipolar disorder (Miklowitz & Johnson, 2009). Negative life events (e.g., loss of a job, marital conflicts) may precede depressive episodes, whereas both negative and positive life events (e.g., getting a new job) may precede a hypomanic or manic episode (Alloy et al., 2009).

Investigators are also learning more about the role of psychosocial factors in bipolar disorder (Bender & Alloy, 2011). For example, social support from family members and friends can enhance the level of functioning of bipolar patients by providing them with a buffer against negative effects of stress. Moreover, the availability of social support appears to play a role in helping speed recovery from mood episodes and reducing the likelihood of recurrent episodes (Alloy et al., 2005).

Treatment of Mood Disorders

7.9 Identify and describe methods used to treat mood disorders.

Just as different theoretical perspectives point to many factors that may be involved in the development of mood disorders, these models have spawned different approaches to treatment. Here, we focus on the leading contemporary approaches.

Treating Depression

Depressive disorders are typically treated with psychotherapy, in the form of psychodynamic therapy, behavior therapy, or cognitive therapy, or with biomedical treatments, such as antidepressant medication or electroconvulsive therapy (ECT). Sometimes a combination of treatment approaches works best (Cuijpers et al., 2010; 2011b; Maina, Rosso, & Bogetto, 2009).

PSYCHODYNAMIC TREATMENT Traditional psychoanalysis aims to help depressed people understand underlying ambivalent (conflicting) feelings toward important people (objects) in their lives whom they have lost or whose loss was threatened. By working through feelings of anger toward these lost objects, people can turn anger outward—through verbal expression of feelings, for example—rather than leave it to fester and turn inward.

It can take years of traditional psychoanalysis to uncover and deal with unconscious conflicts. Modern psychoanalytic approaches also focus on unconscious conflicts, but they are more direct, relatively brief, and focus on present as well as past conflicted relationships (Rosso et al., 2012). Some psychodynamic therapists also use behavioral methods to help clients acquire the social skills needed to develop a broader social network. A recent meta-analysis of outcome studies supports the effectiveness of short-term psychodynamic therapy in treating depression (Driessen et al., 2010).

One form of psychodynamic treatment model receiving a good deal of research attention is *interpersonal psychotherapy* (IPT). This is a relatively brief therapy (usually lasting no more than 9 to 12 months) that emphasizes the role of interpersonal issues in depression and helps clients make healthy changes in their relationships (Weissman, Markowitz, & Klerman, 2000). IPT has emerged as an effective treatment for major depression and shows promise in treating other psychological disorders as well, including dysthymia, bulimia, and posttraumatic stress disorder (Markowitz et al., 2008; Rieger et al., 2010; Schramm et al., 2008; Weissman, 2007). Investigators also find IPT to be effective in treating depressed patients from other parts of the world, including sub-Saharan Africa (Bolton et al., 2003).

Although IPT shares some features with traditional psychodynamic approaches (principally the belief that early life experiences and rigid personality traits affect psychological adjustment), it differs from traditional psychodynamic therapy by focusing on the client's current relationships rather than on unconscious internal conflicts of childhood origin.

IPT helps clients deal with unresolved or delayed grief reactions following the death of a loved one as well as with role conflicts in present relationships. The therapist also helps clients identify areas of conflict in their present relationships, understand the underlying issues, and consider ways of resolving them. If the problems in a relationship are beyond repair, the therapist helps the client consider ways of ending it and establishing new relationships. Take the case of 31-year-old Sal D., whose depression was associated with marital conflict.

> ### → Interpersonal Psychotherapy in a Case of Depression
>
> *Sal began to explore his marital problems in the fifth therapy session, becoming tearful as he recounted his difficulty expressing his feelings to his wife because of feelings of being "numb." He felt that he had been "holding on" to his feelings, which was causing him to become estranged from his wife. The next session zeroed in on the similarities between him and his father, in particular how he was distancing himself from his wife in a similar way to how his father had kept a distance from him. By session 7, a turning point had been reached. Sal expressed how he and his wife had become "emotional" and closer to one another during the previous week and how he was able to talk more openly about his feelings, and how he and his wife had been able to make a joint decision concerning a financial matter that had been worrying them for some time. When later he was laid off from his job, he sought his wife's opinion, rather than picking a fight with her as a way of thrusting his job problems on her. To his surprise he found that his wife responded positively—not "violently," as he had expected—to times when he expressed his feelings. In his last therapy session (session 12), Sal expressed how therapy had led to a "reawakening" within himself with respect to the feelings he had been keeping to himself—an openness that he hoped to create in his relationship with his wife.*
>
> → *Adapted from Klerman et al., 1984, pp. 111–113*

BEHAVIOR THERAPY Behavior therapists generally focus on helping depressed patients develop more effective social or interpersonal skills and increasing their participation in pleasurable or rewarding activities. The most widely used behavioral treatment model, called *behavioral activation*, encourages patients to increase their frequency of rewarding or enjoyable activities (Chartier & Provencher, 2013; Kanter et al., 2010). Behavioral activation can produce substantial effects in treating depression (Carlbring et al., 2013; Dimidjian et al., 2011; Houghton, Curran, & Ekers, 2011; Hunnicutt-Ferguson, Hoxha, & Gollan, 2012). Behavioral approaches are often used along with cognitive therapy in a broader treatment model called cognitive-behavioral therapy (also called *cognitive behavior therapy*), which is perhaps the most widely used psychological treatment for depression today.

COGNITIVE-BEHAVIORAL THERAPY Cognitive-behavioral therapists believe that distorted thinking (cognitive distortions) plays a key role in the development of depression. Depressed people typically focus on how they are feeling rather than on the thoughts that may underlie their feeling states. That is, they usually pay more attention to how bad they feel than to the thoughts that may trigger or maintain their depressed moods. Aaron Beck and his colleagues (Beck et al., 1979) developed *cognitive therapy*, a leading form of cognitive-behavioral therapy (CBT), which focuses on helping people recognize and correct dysfunctional thought patterns. Table 7.5 shows some common examples of distorted, automatic thoughts, the types of cognitive distortions they represent, and rational alternative responses that can be used to replace them.

Cognitive therapy and other forms of cognitive-behavioral therapy are relatively brief, lasting perhaps 14 to 16 weekly sessions. Therapists use a combination of behavioral and cognitive techniques to help clients identify and change dysfunctional thoughts and

Interpersonal psychotherapy. IPT is usually a brief, psychodynamically oriented therapy that focuses on issues in the person's current interpersonal relationships. Like traditional psychodynamic approaches, IPT assumes that early life experiences are key issues in adjustment, but IPT focuses on the present—the here and now.

TABLE 7.5

Cognitive Distortions and Rational Responses

Automatic Thought	Kind of Cognitive Distortion	Rational Response
I'm all alone in the world.	All-or-nothing thinking	It may feel like I'm all alone, but there are some people who care about me.
Nothing will ever work out for me.	Overgeneralization	No one can look into the future. Concentrate on the present.
My looks are hopeless.	Magnification	I may not be perfect looking, but I'm far from hopeless.
I'm falling apart. I can't handle this.	Magnification	Sometimes, I just feel overwhelmed. But I've handled things like this before. I'll just take it a step at a time and I'll be okay.
I guess I'm just a born loser.	Labeling and mislabeling	Nobody is destined to be a loser. I need to stop talking myself down.
I've only lost 8 pounds on this diet. I should just forget it. I can't succeed.	Negative focusing/minimization/disqualifying the positive/jumping to conclusions/all-or-nothing thinking	Eight pounds is a good start. I didn't gain all this weight overnight, and I have to expect that it will take time to lose it.
I know things must really be bad for me to feel this awful.	Emotional reasoning	Feeling something doesn't make it so. If I'm not seeing things clearly, my emotions will be distorted too.
I know I'm going to flunk this course.	Fortune teller error	Just focus on getting through this course, not jumping to negative conclusions.
I know John's problems are really my fault.	Personalization	I need to stop blaming myself for everyone else's problems. There are many reasons why John's problems have nothing to do with me.
Someone my age should be doing better than I am.	Should statements	I need to stop comparing myself to others. All I can expect of myself is to do my best. What good does it do to compare myself to others? It only leads me to get down on myself rather than getting motivated.
I just don't have the brains for college.	Labeling and mislabeling	Stop calling myself names like "stupid." I can accomplish a lot more than I give myself credit for.
Everything is my fault.	Personalization	There I go again. Stop playing this game of pointing blame at myself. There's enough blame to go around. Better yet, forget placing blame and try to think through how to solve this problem.
It would be awful if Sue turns me down.	Magnification	It might be upsetting, but it needn't be awful unless I make it so.
If people really knew me, they would hate me.	Mind reader	What evidence is there for that? More people who get to know me like me than don't like me.
If something doesn't get better soon, I'll go crazy.	Jumping to conclusions/magnification	I've dealt with these problems this long without falling apart. I just have to hang in there. Things are not as bad as they seem.
I can't believe I have another pimple on my face. This is going to ruin my whole weekend.	Mental filter	Take it easy. A pimple is not the end of the world. It doesn't have to spoil my whole weekend. Other people get pimples and seem to have a good time.

Source: Adapted from Beck et al., 1987.

develop more adaptive behaviors. For example, they help clients connect thought patterns to negative moods by having them monitor the automatic negative thoughts they experience throughout the day using a thought diary or daily record. Clients note when and where negative thoughts occur and how they feel at the time. Then the therapist helps the client challenge the negative thoughts and replace them with more adaptive thoughts. The following case example shows how a cognitive therapist works with a client to challenge the validity of thoughts that reflect the cognitive distortion called *selective abstraction* (the tendency to judge oneself entirely on the basis of specific weaknesses or flaws in character). The client judged herself to be totally lacking in self-control because she ate a single piece of candy while she was on a diet.

CLIENT:	I don't have any self-control at all.
THERAPIST:	On what basis do you say that?
C:	Somebody offered me candy and I couldn't refuse it.
T:	Were you eating candy every day?
C:	No, I just ate it this once.
T:	Did you do anything constructive during the past week to adhere to your diet?
C:	Well, I didn't give in to the temptation to buy candy every time I saw it at the store. . . . Also, I did not eat any candy except that one time when it was offered to me and I felt I couldn't refuse it.
T:	If you counted up the number of times you controlled yourself versus the number of times you gave in, what ratio would you get?
C:	About 100 to 1.
T:	So if you controlled yourself 100 times and did not control yourself just once, would that be a sign that you are weak through and through?
C:	I guess not—not through and through (smiles).

Beck et al., 1979, p. 68

Cognitive-behavioral therapies, including Beck's cognitive therapy, have produced impressive results in treating major depression and reducing risks of recurrent episodes (e.g., Beck & Dozois, 2011; Hans & Hiller, 2013; Hollon & Ponniah, 2010; Rehm, 2010). The benefits of cognitive-behavioral therapy appear comparable to those of antidepressant medication in treating depression, even in treating moderate to severe depression (Beck & Dozois, 2011; Fournier et al., 2009; Siddique et al., 2012). However, the combination of psychological treatment and antidepressant medication in some cases may be more effective than either treatment alone (Cuijpers et al., 2009, 2010).

Biomedical Treatments

The most common biomedical approaches to treating mood disorders are the use of antidepressant drugs and electroconvulsive therapy for depression and lithium carbonate for bipolar disorder.

ANTIDEPRESSANT DRUGS The use of antidepressant drugs has skyrocketed in recent years in the United States, so much so that more than 1 in 10 adults is now taking them (Kuehn, 2011; Smith, 2012). Antidepressant use has mushroomed nearly 400% since 1988 (Hendrick, 2011). One statistic that seems to pop off the page is that nearly one in four (23%) American women in the 40- to 59-year age range are now taking antidepressants (Mukherjee, 2012). A significant consequence of the rising use of antidepressants is that fewer depressed patients today are receiving psychotherapy as compared with the 1990s (Dubovsky, 2012; Fullerton et al,. 2011). Although antidepressants are mostly used to treat depression, they are also employed to combat other psychological disorders, including anxiety disorders (see Chapter 5) and bulimia (see Chapter 9).

Antidepressants increase the availability of certain neurotransmitters in the brain, but they do so in different ways (see Figure 7.6). As noted in Chapter 2, there are four major classes of antidepressant drugs: (1) *tricyclics (TCAs);* (2) *monoamine oxidase (MAO) inhibitors;* (3) *selective serotonin-reuptake inhibitors (SSRIs);* and (4) *serotonin–norepinephrine reuptake inhibitors (SNRIs).*

The tricyclics, which include *imipramine* (Tofranil), *amitriptyline* (Elavil), *desipramine* (Norpramin), and *doxepin* (Sinequan), are so named because of their three-ringed molecular structure. They increase brain levels of the neurotransmitters norepinephrine and serotonin by interfering with the process of reuptake (reabsorption by the transmitting cell) of these chemical messengers.

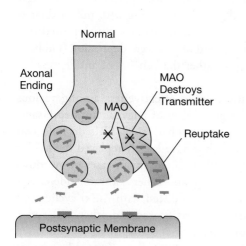

Normal

Axonal Ending

MAO

MAO Destroys Transmitter

Reuptake

Postsynaptic Membrane

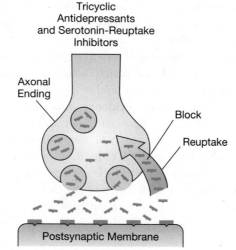

Tricyclic Antidepressants and Serotonin-Reuptake Inhibitors

Axonal Ending

Block

Reuptake

Postsynaptic Membrane

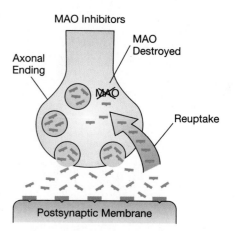

MAO Inhibitors

MAO Destroyed

Axonal Ending

MAO

Reuptake

Postsynaptic Membrane

FIGURE 7.5

The actions of various types of antidepressants at the synapse. Tricyclic antidepressants and selective reuptake inhibitors (SSRIs and NSRIs) increase the availability of neurotransmitters by preventing their reuptake by the presynaptic neuron. MAO inhibitors work by inhibiting the action of monoamine oxidase, an enzyme that normally breaks down neurotransmitters in the synaptic cleft.

Watch the Video *What's in It for Me? Your Brain on Drugs* on **MyPsychLab**

The MAO inhibitors, such as *phenelzine* (Nardil), increase the availability of neurotransmitters by inhibiting the action of monoamine oxidase, an enzyme that normally breaks down or degrades neurotransmitters in the synapse. MAO inhibitors are less widely used than other antidepressants because of potentially serious interactions with certain foods and alcoholic beverages.

The SSRIs, such as *fluoxetine* (Prozac) and *sertraline* (Zoloft), work in a similar fashion as the TCAs by interfering with reuptake of neurotransmitters, but they have more specific effects on serotonin. The SNRIs, such as *venlafaxine* (Effexor), selectively target reuptake of both norepinephrine and serotonin, which increases levels of these neurotransmitters in the brain. It is unclear whether this dual-targeting action produces any clinically meaningful improvement in treatment response over other antidepressants (Dubovsky, 2008a; Nemeroff et al., 2008).

Investigators understand how antidepressants affect neurotransmitter levels, but, as noted earlier, the underlying mechanisms explaining how they work to relieve depression remains unclear. Potential side effects of tricyclics and MAO inhibitors include dry mouth, a slowing down of motor responses, constipation, blurred vision, sexual dysfunction, and, less frequently, urinary retention, paralytic ileus (a paralysis of the intestines, which impairs the passage of intestinal contents), confusion, delirium, and cardiovascular complications, such as reduced blood pressure. Tricyclics are also highly toxic, which raises the prospect of suicidal overdoses if the drugs are used without close supervision.

Research evidence shows that antidepressants help relieve symptoms of major depression and dysthymia (Imel et al., 2008; Kennedy et al., 2009a,b; Wolf & Hopko, 2008). However, despite the dramatic effects touted in drug company commercials on television, full symptom relief (remission) in clinical trials typically occurs in only about one in three patients treated with a first round of antidepressants (e.g., Kennedy, Young, & Blier, 2011; Morehouse, MacQueen, & Kennedy, 2011; McClintock et al., 2011). Many patients continue to experience lingering symptoms such as insomnia, sadness, and problems with concentration. Moreover, investigators find that about two-thirds of the overall effects of antidepressants can be explained by placebo effects (Rief et al., 2009).

When one antidepressant doesn't bring about symptom relief, switching to another one or adding another antidepressant or psychiatric drug (such as Abilify) may bring about a more favorable response (Blier & Blondeau, 2011; Coryell, 2011; Nelson et al., 2010). Among patients in a recent study who failed to respond to one antidepressant, adding cognitive-behavioral therapy together with switching to a different drug was more effective than switching drugs alone (Brent et al., 2008).

The severity of depression also needs to be considered when evaluating the effectiveness of antidepressants. A review of six large-scale randomized controlled studies showed the relative benefits of antidepressants as compared with placebos (inert "sugar pills") were greater in treating severely depressed people than those with milder depression (Fournier et al., 2010). More recently, however, other investigators reported that antidepressants worked well in treating both milder and more severe depression (Gibbons et al., 2012). More research is needed to clarify whether the benefits of antidepressants depend on the person's level of depression.

Importantly, evidence shows little difference in effectiveness among various types of SSRIs or between SSRIs and the older generation of tricyclic antidepressants (Gartlehner et al., 2008; Serrano-Blanco et al., 2006). That said, SSRIs do hold two key advantages over the older drugs, which is why they have largely replaced them. The first advantage is that SSRIs are less toxic and thus less dangerous in cases of overdose. Secondly, they have fewer of the cardiovascular effects and other common side effects (such as dry mouth, constipation, and weight gain) associated with the tricyclics and MAO inhibitors. Still, they are not free of side effects, as Prozac and other SSRIs may lead to upset stomach, headaches, agitation, insomnia, lack of sexual drive, and impaired sexual responsiveness (see, for example, Nurnberg et al., 2008; Schweitzer, Maguire, & Ng, 2009). Antidepressants may actually worsen some associated features of depression, such as sleep problems (Morehouse, MacQueen, & Kennedy, 2011). Another, more significant concern is that use of antidepressants is associated with increased suicidal thinking in some children, adolescents, and young adults—an important issue we discuss further in Chapter 13.

Finally, another important concern with the use of antidepressant drugs is the high rate of relapse in patients when medication is withdrawn (Kellner et al., 2006; Mulder et al., 2009). Though relapses may occur even in patients who continue taking medication, the risk of relapse may be reduced when medication is continued for months after symptoms subside (Kim et al., 2011).

Cognitive-behavioral therapy (CBT) typically provides greater protection against relapse than antidepressant medication, perhaps because psychotherapy patients—unlike patients receiving only medication—learn skills in therapy they can later use to handle life stressors and disappointments (Beshai et al., 2011; Dobson et al., 2008; Spielmans, Berman, & Usitalo, 2011). CBT has been likened to a kind of psychological inoculation, providing continued protection long after the initial dose is given (Smith, 2009). Adding psychotherapy to drug therapy not only helps boost treatment effects, but it also reduces risks of relapse, even after psychiatric drugs are withdrawn (Friedman et al., 2004; Oestergaard & Møldrup, 2011).

Overall, about 50% to 70% of depressed patients treated in outpatient settings respond favorably to either psychotherapy or antidepressant medication (USDHHS, 1999). Some people who fail to respond to psychological approaches respond to antidepressants. The opposite is also true: Some people who fail to respond to drug therapy respond to psychological approaches.

ELECTROCONVULSIVE THERAPY *Electroconvulsive therapy (ECT),* more commonly called *shock therapy,* continues to evoke controversy. The idea of passing an electric current through someone's brain may seem barbaric. Yet, evidence supports ECT as a generally safe and effective treatment for severe depression and shows that it can help relieve major depression, even in cases in which drug treatments have failed (Bailine et al., 2010; Faedda et al., 2010; Kellner et al., 2012). Estimates are that about 100,000 Americans undergo ECT annually (Dahl, 2008).

In ECT, an electrical current of between 70 and 130 volts is applied to the head to induce a convulsion that is similar to a *grand mal* epileptic seizure. ECT is usually administered in a series of 6 to 12 treatments, given three times per week over several weeks. The patient is put to sleep with a brief-acting general anesthetic and given a muscle relaxant to avoid wild convulsions that might result in injury. As a result, spasms may be barely perceptible to onlookers. The patient awakens soon after the procedure and generally remembers nothing. Although ECT had earlier been used in the treatment of a wide variety of psychological disorders, including schizophrenia and bipolar disorder, the American Psychiatric Association recommends that ECT be used only to treat major depressive disorder in people who do not respond to antidepressant medication.

ECT leads to significant improvement in a majority of people with major depression who had failed to respond to antidepressant medication (Hampton, 2012; Medda et al., 2009; Reifler, 2006). It can also have dramatic effects on relieving suicidal thinking (Kellner et al., 2005). No one knows exactly how ECT works, but one possibility is that ECT helps normalize neurotransmitter activity in the brain.

Although ECT can be an effective short-term treatment of severe depression, it is no panacea. There is understandable concern among patients, relatives, and professionals about possible risks, especially memory loss for events occurring around the time of treatment (Meeter et al., 2011). Another nagging problem with ECT is a high rate of relapse following treatment (Sackeim et al., 2001). Many professionals view ECT as a treatment of last resort, to be considered only after other treatment approaches have been tried and failed.

All in all, effective psychological and pharmacological treatments are available for treating depressive disorders (Imel et al., 2008). Psychological treatment and drug therapies are generally comparable in their level of effectiveness (Wolf & Hopko, 2008). In some cases, however, a combination of psychological and drug therapy may be more effective than either therapy alone. More invasive treatment, such as ECT, is also available for people of severe depression who fail to respond to other approaches.

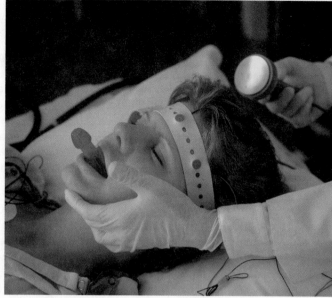

Electroconvulsive therapy. ECT is helpful for many people with severe or prolonged depression who do not respond to other forms of treatment. Still, its use remains controversial.

Treating Bipolar Disorder

Bipolar disorder is most commonly treated with drugs that aim to stabilize mood swings.

LITHIUM AND OTHER MOOD STABILIZERS It could be said that the ancient Greeks and Romans were among the first to use lithium as a form of chemotherapy. They prescribed mineral water that contained lithium for people with turbulent mood swings. Today, the drug *lithium carbonate,* a powdered form of the metallic element lithium, is widely used in treating bipolar disorder. **T / F**

Lithium helps reduce mania and stabilize moods in bipolar patients, and reduces the risk of relapse (Lichta, 2010; Shafti, 2010). People with bipolar disorder may be placed on lithium indefinitely to control their mood swings, just as diabetics may use insulin continuously to control their illness. Despite more than 40 years of use as a therapeutic drug, investigators still can't say with certainty how lithium works.

Despite its benefits, lithium is no panacea. Many patients either fail to respond to the drug or cannot tolerate it (Nierenberg et al., 2013). Lithium treatment must be closely monitored because of potential toxic effects and other side effects. Lithium can also lead to mild memory problems, which may lead people to stop taking it. Side effects may include weight gain, lethargy, and grogginess, as well as a general slowing down of motor functioning. Long-term use can produce gastrointestinal distress and lead to liver problems.

Although lithium is still widely used, the drug's limitations have prompted efforts to find alternative treatments. Anticonvulsant drugs used in the treatment of epilepsy can also help reduce manic symptoms and stabilize moods in people with bipolar disorder (Smith et al., 2010; van der Loos et al., 2009). These drugs include *carbamazepine* (Tegretol), *divalproex* (Depakote), and *lamotrigine* (Lamictal).

Anticonvulsant drugs may help people with bipolar disorder who fail to respond to lithium or cannot tolerate its side effects. Anticonvulsant drugs typically produce fewer or less severe side effects than lithium (Ceron-Litvoc et al., 2009). Because most manic patients do not respond adequately to any one drug, a combination of drugs that may include antipsychotic drugs used in the treatment of schizophrenia may improve the patient's response (The BALANCE Investigators, 2010; Suppes et al., 2009, 2010).

Mood disorders involve the interplay of multiple factors. Consistent with the *diathesis–stress model*, depression may reflect an interaction of biological factors (such as genetic factors, neurotransmitter irregularities, or brain abnormalities), psychological factors (such as cognitive distortions or learned helplessness), and social and environmental stressors (such as divorce or loss of a job).

Figure 7.6 illustrates a possible causal pathway on the basis of the diathesis–stress model. Let's break it down. Stressful life events, such as prolonged unemployment or a divorce, may have a depressing effect by reducing neurotransmitter activity in the brain. These biochemical effects may be more likely to occur or may be more pronounced in people with a genetic predisposition, or diathesis, for depression. However, a depressive disorder may not develop, or may develop in a milder form, in people with more effective coping resources for handling stressful situations. For example, people who receive emotional support from others may be better able to withstand the effects of stress than those who have to go it alone. The same is true for people who make active coping efforts to meet the challenges they face in life.

Sociocultural factors can become sources of stress that influence the development or recurrence of mood disorders. These factors include poverty; overcrowding; exposure to racism, sexism, and prejudice; violence in the home or community; disproportionately high stressful burdens placed on women; and family disintegration. Other sources of stress that can contribute to mood disorders include negative life events such as the loss of a job, the development of a serious illness, the breakup of a romantic relationship, and the loss of a loved one.

The diathesis for depression may take the form of a psychological vulnerability involving a depressive thinking style, one characterized by tendencies to exaggerate the consequences of negative events, to heap blame on oneself, and to perceive oneself as helpless to effect positive change. This cognitive diathesis may increase the risk of depression in the face of negative life events. These cognitive influences may also interact with a genetically based diathesis to further increase the risk of depression following stressful life events. The availability of social support from others may help bolster a person's resistance to stress during difficult times. People with more effective social skills may be better able to garner and maintain social reinforcement from others and thus be better able to resist depression than people lacking social skills. But biochemical changes in the brain might make it more difficult for people to cope effectively and bounce back from stressful life events. Lingering biochemical changes and feelings of depression may exacerbate feelings of helplessness, compounding the effects of the initial stressor.

Gender-related differences in coping styles may also come into play. According to Nolen-Hoeksema and colleagues (Nolen-Hoeksema, 2006, 2008; Nolen-Hoeksema, Morrow, & Fredrickson, 1993), women are more likely to ruminate when facing emotional problems, whereas men are more likely to abuse alcohol. These or other differences in coping styles may propel longer and more severe bouts of depression in women while setting the stage for the development of drinking problems in men. As you can see, a complex web of contributing factors is likely involved in the development of mood disorders.

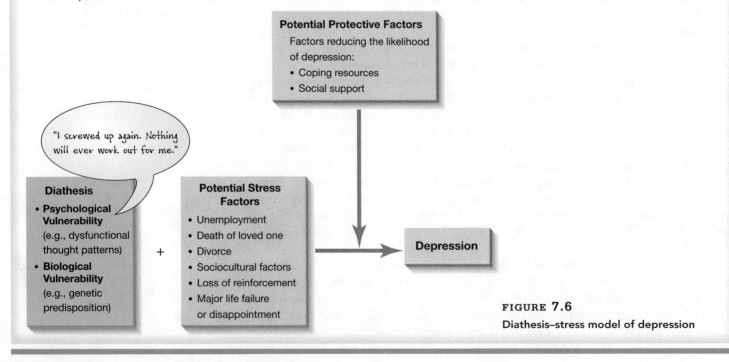

FIGURE **7.6**

Diathesis–stress model of depression

Magnetic Stimulation Therapy for Depression

Mesmer would be proud. Franz Friedrich Mesmer (1734–1815) was the 18th-century Austrian physician from whose name the term *mesmerism* is derived. (We still sometimes speak of people being "mesmerized" by things.) He believed that hysteria was caused by an underlying imbalance in the distribution of a magnetic fluid in the body—a problem he believed he could correct by prodding the body with metal rods. A scientific commission of the time debunked Mesmer's claims and attributed any cures he obtained to the effects of natural recovery or self-delusion (what we might today call the power of suggestion). The chairperson of the commission was none other than Benjamin Franklin, who served at the time as the ambassador to France from the newly independent United States. Although Mesmer's theories and practices were discredited, recent evidence into the therapeutic use of magnetism suggests that he might have been on to something.

Fast forward 200 years. Australian doctors identified 60 patients with major depression who had failed to respond to different types of antidepressants (Fitzgerald et al., 2003). In a double-blind controlled design, they treated these patients with either strong magnetic stimulation to the head (called *transcranial magnetic stimulation,* or TMS) or a fake treatment that had all the trappings of the active treatment except that the magnet was angled away to prevent magnetic stimulation of the brain. With TMS, a powerful electromagnet placed on the scalp generates a strong magnetic field that passes through the skull and affects the electrical activity of the brain.

After two weeks of treatment, patients receiving TMS showed clinical improvement in depression as opposed to the minimal change found in the control group. Improvement, however, was modest and did not occur in all patients. The investigators believe that longer treatment (at least four weeks) may be necessary to produce more meaningful therapeutic benefits. This study adds to a growing body of evidence supporting the antidepressant effects of TMS (e.g., Fitzgerald et al., 2012; George et al., 2010; Kennedy et al., 2009b; Peng et al., 2012; Raya et al., 2011). The specific form and intensity of TMS needed to produce therapeutic effects remains under study. We should also note that TMS carries some potential risks, such as the possibility of seizures. However, the risk of seizures may be reduced by using low-frequency stimulation.

In sum, TMS shows promise as a new form of treatment for moderate depression. Although it has been approved for medical use in Canada, it is still considered experimental in the United States. It also appears promising as an alternative to ECT for people with major depression who fail to respond to pharmacological treatment. TMS may be particularly helpful in treating

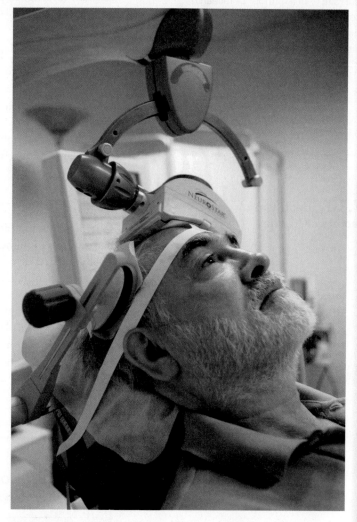

Transcranial magnetic stimulation therapy. TMS is a promising therapeutic approach in which powerful magnets are used to help relieve depression.
Source: NIH Photo Library. http://infocenter.nimh.nih.gov/il/public_il/searchresults.cfm

depression because the prefrontal cortex in the left cerebral hemisphere becomes less active in depressed patients, and this part of the brain can be directly affected by TMS (Henry, Pascual-Leone, & Cole, 2003). We should caution, however, that more evidence is needed to support its efficacy and safety, and to determine whether it is more effective than alternative treatments such as ECT, before it might be recommended for more general use in treating severe depression (Knapp et al., 2008). TMS may also have therapeutic benefits in treating other disorders, such as posttraumatic stress disorder (Cohen et al., 2004) and possibly a form of dementia in older adults (Jorge et al., 2008). **T / F**

Placing a powerful electromagnet on the scalp can help relieve depression.

☑ **TRUE** In a number of research studies, magnetic stimulation of the head has been shown to have antidepressant effects.

7.10 Identify risk factors in suicide.

However, because presently available drugs tend to produce only modest therapeutic gains, there remains a need to develop more effective treatments for mania (Calabrese & Kemp, 2008). More work also needs to be focused on treating the depressive phase of bipolar disorder, which is the more enduring phase of bipolar cycles and which is often resistant to drugs in present use (Frye, 2011; Nivoli et al., 2011; Suppes, 2011; Yatham, 2011).

PSYCHOLOGICAL TREATMENTS Large-scale investigations of the effects of psychological treatments for bipolar disorder are under way. Early studies suggest that psychosocial treatments, such as cognitive-behavioral therapy, interpersonal therapy, and family therapy, may be helpful when used along with drug therapy in the treatment of bipolar disorder (Alloy et al., 2005; Frank et al., 2005; González-Isasi et al., 2010; Miklowitz et al., 2007). Psychological treatment also helps boost adherence to a medication program in bipolar patients (Rougeta & Aubry, 2007).

Suicide

Suicidal thoughts are common enough. At times of great stress, many people have had fleeting thoughts of suicide. A nationally representative survey found that 13% of U.S. adults reported having experienced suicidal thoughts, and 4.6% reported making a suicide attempt (Kessler, Borges, & Walters, 1999). It is fortunate that most people who have suicidal thoughts do not act on them. Still, each year in the United States some 500,000 people are treated in hospital emergency rooms for attempted suicide, and more than 33,000 "succeed" in taking their lives (CDC, 2007; Mokdad et al., 2004). Suicide accounts for twice as many deaths as HIV/AIDS (NIMH, 2003). More than half of completed suicides involve the use of firearms (Miller & Hemenway, 2008). Suicide exacts a heavy toll on the nation, as you can see in statistics reported by the U.S. Surgeon General (see Table 7.6).

TABLE 7.6

U.S. Surgeon General's Report on Suicide: Cost to the Nation

- Every 17 minutes another life is lost to suicide. Every day, nearly 100 Americans take their own lives and over 1,500 attempt suicide.
- Suicide is now the eighth leading cause of death in Americans.
- For every two victims of homicide in the United States, there are three deaths from suicide.
- There are now twice as many deaths due to suicide than due to HIV/AIDS.
- Between 1952 and 1995, the incidence of suicide among adolescents and young adults nearly tripled.
- In the month prior to their suicide, 75% of elderly persons had visited a physician.
- Over half of all suicides occur in adult men, ages 25 to 65.
- Many who make suicide attempts never seek professional care immediately after the attempt.
- Men are four times more likely to commit suicide than are women.
- More teenagers and young adults die from suicide than from cancer, heart disease, AIDS, birth defects, stroke, pneumonia and influenza, and chronic lung disease combined.
- Suicide takes the lives of more than 30,000 Americans every year.

Source: Center for Mental Health Services, 2001.

Suicidal behavior is not a psychological disorder in itself. But it is often a feature or symptom of an underlying psychological disorder, usually a mood disorder (Bernal et al., 2007), which is why we discuss it in this chapter. Not surprisingly, suicide attempts are more likely in people with major depression during a major depressive episode than between episodes (Holma et al., 2010). Estimates are that about 60% of people who commit suicide suffer from a mood disorder (National Strategy for Suicide Prevention, 2001).

Who Commits Suicide?

What do you think is the second leading cause of death among college students, after motor vehicle accidents? Drugs? Homicide? The answer is suicide, with an estimated 1,000 suicides and 24,000 suicide attempts annually among college students aged 18 to 24 (Lamberg, 2006; Rawe & Kingsbury, 2006).

SUICIDE IN OLDER ADULTS Although attention is focused on the tragedy of young people and suicide, as well it should be, suicide rates are actually highest among adults aged 65 and older, especially older White males (CDC, 2009c; Mills et al., 2013; see Figure 7.7). (We discuss youth suicide further in Chapter 13.)

Despite life-extending advances in medical care, some older adults find the quality of their lives less than satisfactory. Older people are more susceptible to diseases such as cancer and Alzheimer's, which can leave them with feelings of helplessness and hopelessness that, in turn, can give rise to depression and suicidal thinking (Starkstein et al., 2005).

Many older adults also suffer a mounting accumulation of losses of friends and loved ones, leading to social isolation (Stroebe, Stroebe, & Abakoumkin, 2005). These losses, as well as the loss of good health and of a responsible role in the community, may wear down the will to live. Not surprisingly, the highest suicide rates in older men are among those who are widowed or socially isolated. Society's increased acceptance of suicide in older people may also play a part. Whatever the causes, suicide has become an increased risk for elderly people. Perhaps society should focus its attention on the quality of life that is afforded to our elderly, in addition to providing them the medical care that helps make longer life possible.

GENDER AND ETHNIC/RACIAL DIFFERENCES More women attempt suicide, but more men "succeed" (Hawton et al., 2013). For every female suicide, there are about four male suicides. More males succeed in large part because they tend to choose quicker-acting and more lethal means, such as handguns.

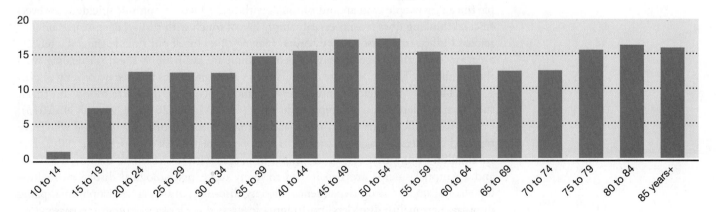

FIGURE 7.7

Suicide rates according to age. Although adolescent suicides may be more highly publicized, adults, especially older adults, have higher suicide rates. *Source:* U.S. Department of Health and Human Services, Centers for Disease Control and Prevention, National Center for Injury Prevention and Control, June 11, 2009.

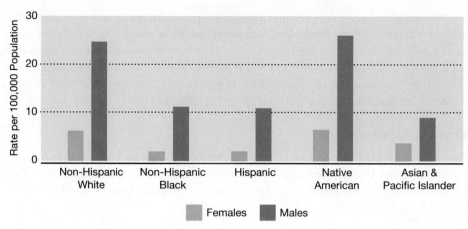

FIGURE 7.8

Ethnicity and suicide rates. Suicide rates are higher among males than females, and higher among non-Hispanic White Americans and Native Americans than other ethnicities. *Source: National Suicide Statistics at a Glance,* Centers for Disease Control, National Center for Injury Prevention and Control, 2009.

Suicides are more common among (non-Hispanic) White Americans and Native Americans than among African Americans, Asian Americans, or Hispanic Americans (Garlow, Purselle, & Heninger, 2005; Gone & Trimble, 2012) (see Figure 7.8). White Americans are more than twice as likely to take their own lives as African Americans (Joe et al., 2006). Yet the highest suicide rates in the nation are found among Native American adolescent and young adult males (Meyers, 2007).

Hopelessness and exposure to others who have attempted or committed suicide may contribute to the increased risk of suicide among Native American youth. Native American youth at greatest risk tend to be reared in communities that are largely isolated from U.S. society. They perceive themselves as having relatively few opportunities to gain the skills necessary to join the workforce in the larger society and are also relatively more prone to substance abuse, including alcohol abuse. Knowledge that peers have attempted or completed suicide renders suicide a highly visible escape from psychological pain.

Why Do People Commit Suicide?

To many lay observers, suicide seems so extreme an act that they believe only "insane" people (meaning people who are out of touch with reality) would commit suicide. However, suicidal thinking does not necessarily imply loss of touch with reality, deep-seated unconscious conflict, or a personality disorder. Having thoughts about suicide generally reflects a narrowing of the range of options people think are available to them for dealing with their problems. That is, they are discouraged by their problems and see no other way out.

The risk of suicide is much higher among people with severe mood disorders, such as major depression and bipolar disorder (Gonda et al., 2012; Hawton et al., 2013). People who suffer from more severe and chronic mood disorders and those who have repeated episodes of major depression are at even greater risk (Witte et al., 2009). But we shouldn't think that suicide is limited to people with severe mood disorders. Suicide and attempted suicide are also linked to many other psychological disorders, including alcoholism and drug dependence, anxiety disorders, anorexia, schizophrenia, panic disorder, personality disorders, posttraumatic stress disorder, and borderline personality disorder (e.g., Bolton et al., 2008; Ceskova, Prikryl, & Kasparek, 2011; Restifo, Harkvay-Friedman, & Shrout, 2009; Wilcox, Storr, & Breslau, 2009).

Past suicide attempts are an important predictor of later suicide attempts (Bolton et al., 2010; Hawton et al., 2013). Sadly, people who fail on a first attempt often succeed on a subsequent attempt. Those who survive an attempt but express to others that they wish they had died are more likely to go on to eventually complete suicide than are those who express ambivalence about the attempt (Henriques et al., 2005). Adolescents who have a history of attempted suicide stand a risk of a later completed suicide that is 14 times higher in females and 22 times higher in males as compared with the general adolescent population (Olfson et al., 2005).

Not all suicides are connected with psychological disorders. Some people suffering from intractable pain or terminal illness may seek to escape further suffering by taking their own lives. These suicides are sometimes labeled "rational suicides" in the belief that they are based on a rational decision that life is no longer worth living in light of continual suffering. However, in many of these cases, the person's judgment and reasoning ability may be colored by an underlying and potentially treatable psychological disorder, such as depression. Other suicides are motivated by deep-seated religious or political convictions, as in the case of people who sacrifice themselves in acts of protest against their governments or who kill themselves and others in suicide bombings in the belief that their acts will be rewarded in an afterlife.

Suicide attempts often occur in response to highly stressful life events, especially "exit events," such as the death of a spouse, close friend, or relative; divorce or separation; a family member's leaving home; or the loss of a close friend. Unemployment is also linked to higher risks of suicide (Barr et al., 2012). People who consider suicide in times of stress may lack problem-solving skills and may be unable to find alternative ways of coping with stressors.

Theoretical Perspectives on Suicide

7.11 Identify the major theoretical perspectives on suicide.

The classic psychodynamic model views depression as the turning inward of anger against the internal representation of a lost love object. Suicide then represents inward-directed anger that turns murderous. Suicidal people, then, do not seek to destroy themselves. Instead, they seek to vent their rage against the internalized representation of the love object. In so doing, they destroy themselves as well, of course. In his later writings, Freud speculated that suicide may be motivated by the "death instinct," a tendency to return to the tension-free state that preceded birth. Existential and humanistic theorists relate suicide to the perception that life has become meaningless, empty, and essentially hopeless.

In the 19th century, social thinker Emile Durkheim (1897/1958) noted that people who experienced *anomie*—who feel lost, without identity, rootless—are more likely to commit suicide. Sociocultural theorists likewise believe that alienation may play a role in suicide. In our modern, mobile society, people frequently move hundreds or thousands of miles to schools and jobs. Many people are socially isolated or cut off from their support groups. Moreover, city dwellers tend to limit or discourage informal social contacts because of crowding, overstimulation, and fear of crime. It is thus understandable that many people find few sources of support in times of crisis. In some cases, family support is available but not helpful. Family members may be perceived as part of the problem, not part of the solution.

Learning theorists focus largely on the lack of problem-solving skills for handling significant life stress. According to Shneidman (1985), those who attempt suicide wish to escape unbearable psychological pain and may perceive no other way out. People who threaten or attempt suicide may also receive sympathy and support from loved ones and others, perhaps making future—and more lethal—attempts more likely. This is not to suggest that suicide attempts or gestures should be ignored. People who threaten suicide are *not* merely seeking attention. Although those who threaten suicide may not carry out the act, they should be taken seriously. People who commit suicide often tell others of their intentions or provide clues. Moreover, many people make aborted suicide attempts before they go on to make actual suicide attempts.

Social-cognitive theorists suggest that suicide may be motivated by personal expectancies, such as beliefs that one will be missed by others or that survivors will feel guilty for having mistreated the person, or that suicide will solve one's own problems or even other people's problems (e.g., "He won't have to worry about me any longer") in one fell swoop.

Social-cognitive theorists also focus on the potential modeling effects of observing suicidal behavior in others, especially among teenagers who feel overwhelmed by

Starry, starry night. The famed artist Vincent van Gogh suffered from severe bouts of depression and eventually took his own life at the age of 37, dying of a self-inflicted gunshot wound. In this self-portrait, van Gogh strikes a melancholy pose that allows the viewer to sense the deep despair he had endured.

academic and social stressors. A *social contagion,* or spreading of suicide in a community, may occur in the wake of suicides that receive widespread publicity. Teenagers, who seem to be especially vulnerable to these modeling effects, may even romanticize the suicidal act as one of heroic courage. The incidence of suicide among teenagers sometimes rises markedly in the period following news reports about suicide. Copycat suicides may be more likely to occur when reports of suicides are sensationalized. Teenagers may come to expect their deaths will have a meaningful impact on their families and communities.

Biological factors are also implicated in suicide, including genetic factors and neurotransmitter imbalances involving the mood-regulating chemical serotonin (Crowell et al., 2008; Kohli et al., 2010; Uher & Perroud, 2010). Because serotonin is linked to depression, the relationship with suicide is not surprising. Yet serotonin also acts to curb or inhibit nervous system activity, so perhaps lowered serotonin activity leads to *disinhibition,* or release, of impulsive behavior that takes the form of a suicidal act in vulnerable individuals. Genes that affect the regulation of serotonin in the brain are also implicated in suicide (Crowell et al., 2008; Must et al., 2009).

Mood disorders in family members and parental suicide are also connected with suicide risk. But what are the causal connections? Do people who attempt suicide inherit vulnerabilities to mood disorders that are connected with suicide? Does the family atmosphere promote feelings of hopelessness? Does the suicide of one family member give others the idea of doing the same thing? Does one suicide create the impression that other family members are destined to kill themselves? These are all questions researchers need to address.

Suicide is often motivated by the desire to escape from unbearable emotional pain. Here, the celebrated actress Patty Duke, who rose to acclaim in childhood by playing the role of Helen Keller in the movie *The Miracle Worker* and who battled bipolar disorder throughout much of her life, expresses how the desire to escape pain motivated many of the suicide attempts she had made in her life.

> ## "I" "Please Make This Stop"
>
> I can't even remember how many times I tried to kill myself. Not all of them got as far as actually taking the pills or digesting the pills. And it was almost always pills, although I did make a show sometimes of trying to use razors. But I always chickened out. A couple of times I tried to jump out of a moving car. But I didn't seem willing to inflict physical pain on myself. Some of the attempts continued to be attention-getting devices. Others came out of so much pain. I just wanted it to stop. I wish I had a more colorful, more profound way to describe it, but the only thoughts that went through my head were "Please make this stop. Please make me brave enough to die so that this anguish will stop."
>
> Duke, P., & Hochman, G. (1992). A brilliant madness. New York: Bantam Dell.

Suicide involves a complex web of factors, and predicting it is not simple. Moreover, many myths about suicide abound (see Table 7.7). Yet, it is clear that many suicides could be prevented if people with suicidal feelings received treatment for underlying disorders, including depression, bipolar disorder, schizophrenia, and alcohol and substance abuse. We also need strategies that emphasize the maintenance of hope during times of severe stress.

Predicting Suicide

"I don't believe it. I just saw him last week and he looked fine."
"She sat here just the other day, laughing with the rest of us. How were we to know what was going on inside her?"
"I knew he was depressed, but I never thought he'd do something like this. I didn't have a clue."
"Why didn't she just call me?"

TABLE 7.7

Myths About Suicide

Myth	Fact
People who threaten suicide are only seeking attention.	Not so. Researchers report that most people who commit suicide gave prior indications of their intentions or consulted a health provider beforehand (Luoma, Martin, & Pearson, 2002). **T / F**
A person must be insane to attempt suicide.	Most people who attempt suicide may feel hopeless, but they are not insane (i.e., out of touch with reality).
Talking about suicide with a depressed person may prompt the person to attempt it.	An open discussion of suicide with a depressed person does not prompt the person to attempt it. In fact, extracting a promise that the person will not attempt suicide before calling or visiting a mental health worker may well *prevent* a suicide.
People who attempt suicide and fail aren't serious about killing themselves.	Most people who commit suicide have made previous unsuccessful attempts.
If someone threatens suicide, it is best to ignore it so as not to encourage repeated threats.	Although some people do manipulate others by making idle threats, it is prudent to treat every suicide threat as genuine and to take appropriate action.

Source: Adapted from Nevid, J. S. (2013). *Psychology: Concepts and applications,* (4th ed.). Belmont, CA: Cengage Learning. Reprinted by permission.

Friends and family members often respond to news of a suicide with disbelief or guilt that they failed to pick up signs of the impending act. Yet even trained professionals find it difficult to predict who is likely to commit suicide.

Evidence points to the pivotal role of hopelessness about the future in predicting suicidal thinking and suicide attempts (Kaslow et al., 2002; Hawton et al., 2013). But *when* does hopelessness lead to suicide?

People who commit suicide tend to signal their intentions, often quite explicitly, such as by telling others about their suicidal thoughts. Yet, some cloak their intentions. Behavioral clues may reveal suicidal intent. Edwin Shneidman, a leading researcher on suicide, found that 90% of the people who committed suicide had left clear clues, such as disposing of their possessions (Gelman, 1994). People contemplating suicide may also suddenly try to sort out their affairs, as in drafting a will or buying a cemetery plot. They may purchase a gun despite lack of prior interest in firearms. When troubled people decide to commit suicide, they may seem to be suddenly at peace; they feel relieved because they no longer have to contend with life problems. This sudden calm may be misinterpreted as a sign of hope. Other factors linked to increased suicidal risk include substance abuse, financial problems, a recent crisis, medical problems, and relationship problems (Logan, Hall, & Karch, 2011).

The prediction of suicide is not an exact science, even for experienced professionals. Many observable factors, such as hopelessness, seem to be connected with suicide, but we cannot accurately predict *when* a hopeless person will attempt suicide, if at all.

Suicide hotlines. Telephone hotlines provide emergency assistance and referral services to people experiencing suicidal thoughts or impulses. If you know someone experiencing suicidal thoughts or threatening suicide, speak to a mental health professional or call a suicide hotline in your community for advice.

7.12 Apply your knowledge of factors in suicide to steps you can take if someone you knew was experiencing suicidal thoughts.

a CLOSER look

Imagine yourself having an intimate conversation with a close campus friend, Chris. You know that things have not been good. Chris's grandfather died six weeks ago, and the two had been very close. Chris's grades have been going downhill, and Chris's romantic relationship also seems to be coming apart at the seams. Still, you are unprepared when Chris says very deliberately, "I just can't take it anymore. Life is just too painful. I don't feel like I want to live anymore. I've decided that the only thing I can do is to kill myself."

When somebody discloses that he or she is contemplating suicide, you may feel bewildered and frightened, as if a great burden has been placed on your shoulders. It has been. If someone confides suicidal thoughts to you, your goal should be to persuade him or her to see a professional, or to get the advice of a professional yourself as soon as you can. But if the suicidal person declines to talk to another person and you sense you can't break away for such a conference, here are some things you can do then and there:

1. *Draw the person out.* Shneidman advises framing questions such as "What's going on?" "Where do you hurt?" "What would you like to see happen?" (Schneidman 1985, p. 11). Such questions may prompt people to verbalize thwarted psychological needs and offer some relief. They also grant you the time to appraise the risk and contemplate your next move.

2. *Be sympathetic.* Show that you fathom how troubled the person is. Don't say something like, "You're just being silly. You don't really mean it."

3. *Suggest that means other than suicide can be discovered to work out the person's problems, even if they are not apparent at the time.* Shneidman (1985) notes that suicidal people can usually see only two solutions to their predicaments—suicide or some kind of magical resolution. Professionals try to help them see the available alternatives.

4. *Ask how the person expects to commit suicide.* People with explicit methods who also possess the means (e.g., a gun or drugs) are at greatest risk. Ask if you may hold on to the gun, drugs, or whatever, for a while. Sometimes the person agrees.

5. *Propose that the person accompany you to consult a professional right away.* Many campuses, towns, and cities have hotlines that you or the suicidal individual can call anonymously. Other possibilities include the emergency room of a general hospital, a campus health center or counseling center, or the campus or local police. If you are unable to maintain contact with the suicidal person, get professional assistance as soon as you separate.

6. *Don't say something like "You're talking crazy."* Such comments are degrading and injurious to the individual's self-esteem. Don't press the suicidal person to contact specific people, such as parents or a spouse. Conflict with these people may have given rise to the suicidal thoughts.

Above all, keep in mind that your primary goal is to confer with a helping professional. Don't go it alone any longer than you must.

7 summing up

Types of Mood Disorders

7.1 Define the term mood disorder and describe the key features of major depressive disorder.

Mood disorders are disturbances in mood that are unusually prolonged or severe and serious enough to impair daily functioning. Mood disorders are divided into two major types: (1) unipolar disorders (major depressive disorder, persistent depressive disorder, and premenstrual dysphoric disorder, all of which are characterized by a downward mood disturbance); and (2) bipolar disorders (bipolar disorder and cyclothymic disorder), which are characterized by mood swings.

In major depression, there is a profound change in mood that impairs the person's ability to function. The associated features of major depressive disorder include downcast mood; changes in appetite; difficulty sleeping; reduced sense of pleasure in formerly enjoyable activities; feelings of fatigue or loss of energy; sense of worthlessness; excessive or misplaced guilt; difficulties concentrating, thinking clearly, or making decisions; repeated thoughts of death or suicide; attempts at suicide; and even psychotic behaviors (hallucinations and delusions).

7.2 Evaluate factors that may account for the increased rates of depression among women.

Women are nearly twice as likely as men to suffer from major depression. The reasons are complex, but a number of factors may be involved, including the greater stress burden many women shoulder, hormonal influences, gender differences in coping styles (rumination versus distraction), greater influence in women of interpersonal relationships on self-esteem, and under-reporting of depression in men.

7.3 Describe the key features of persistent depressive disorder and premenstrual dysphoric disorder.

Persistent depressive disorder involves chronic forms of major depressive disorder or milder depression. These forms of depression vary in severity but both are associated with impaired functioning in social and occupational roles. Premenstrual dysphoric disorder is characterized by marked changes in mood during the woman's premenstrual period.

7.4 Describe the key features of bipolar disorder and cyclothymic disorder.

In bipolar disorder, people experience fluctuating mood states that interfere with their ability to function. Bipolar I disorder is identified by one or more manic episodes and, typically, by alternating episodes of major depression. Manic episodes are characterized by sudden elevation or expansion of mood and sense of self-importance, feelings of almost boundless energy, hyperactivity, and extreme sociability, which often takes a demanding and overbearing form. People in manic episodes tend to exhibit pressured or rapid speech, rapid "flight of ideas," and decreased need for sleep. Bipolar II disorder is characterized by the occurrence of at least one major depressive episode and one hypomanic episode, but without any full-blown manic episodes. Cyclothymic disorder is characterized by a chronic pattern of mild mood swings that sometimes progresses to bipolar disorder.

Causal Factors in Depressive Disorders

7.5 Evaluate the role of stress in depression.

Exposure to life stress is associated with an increased risk of development and recurrence of mood disorders, especially major depression. Yet some people are more resilient in the face of stress, perhaps because of psychosocial factors such as social support.

7.6 Describe the major psychological models of depression.

In classic psychodynamic theory, depression is viewed in terms of inward-directed anger. People who hold strongly ambivalent feelings toward people they have lost, or whose loss is threatened, may direct unresolved anger toward the inward representations of these people whom they have incorporated or introjected within themselves, producing self-loathing and depression. Bipolar disorder is understood within psychodynamic theory in terms of the shifting balances between the ego and superego. More recent psychodynamic models, such as the self-focusing model, incorporate both psychodynamic and cognitive aspects in explaining depression in terms of self-absorption with the lost love object.

Humanistic theorists view depression as reflecting a lack of meaning and authenticity in a person's life. Learning theorists explain depression by focusing on situational factors, such as changes in the level of reinforcement. When reinforcement is reduced, the person may feel unmotivated and depressed, which can occasion inactivity and further reduce opportunities for reinforcement. Coyne's interactional theory focuses on the negative family interactions that can lead the family members of people with depression to become less reinforcing toward them.

Beck's cognitive model focuses on the role of negative or distorted thinking in depression. Depression-prone people hold negative beliefs about themselves, the environment, and the future. This cognitive triad of depression leads to specific errors in thinking, or cognitive distortions, in response to negative events, which, in turn, lead to depression.

The learned helplessness model is based on the belief that people may become depressed when they come to view themselves as helpless to control the reinforcements in their environment or to change their lives for the better. A reformulated version of the theory holds that the ways in which people explain events—their attributions—determine their proneness toward depression in the face of negative events. The combination of internal, global, and stable attributions for negative events renders a person most vulnerable to depression.

7.7 Describe biological factors in depression.

Genetics appears to play a role in explaining major depressive disorder, as does imbalances in neurotransmitter activity in the brain. The diathesis–stress model is an explanatory framework that illustrates how biological or psychological diatheses may interact with stress in the development of mood disorders such as major depression.

Causal Factors In Bipolar Disorders

7.8 Describe causal factors in bipolar disorders.

Genetics appears to play an important role in bipolar disorder, but stressful life experiences also contribute. Bipolar disorders are perhaps best explained in terms of multiple causes acting together within a diathesis–stress framework. Social support may be important in speeding recovery from mood episodes and reducing the risks of recurrences.

Treatment of Mood Disorders

7.9 Identify and describe methods used to treat mood disorders.

Psychodynamic treatment of depression has traditionally focused on helping the depressed person uncover and work through ambivalent feelings toward the lost object, thereby lessening the anger directed inward. Modern psychodynamic approaches tend to be more direct and briefer and focus more on developing adaptive means of achieving self-worth and resolving interpersonal conflicts. Learning theory approaches have focused on helping people with depression increase the frequency of reinforcement in their lives through means such as increasing the rates of pleasant activities in which they participate. Cognitive therapists focus on helping people identify and correct distorted or dysfunctional thoughts and learn more adaptive behaviors. Biomedical treatments have focused on the use of antidepressant drugs and other biological treatments, such as electroconvulsive therapy. Antidepressant drugs may help normalize neurotransmitter functioning in the brain. Bipolar disorder is commonly treated with either lithium or anticonvulsant drugs.

Suicide

7.10 Identify risk factors in suicide.

Mood disorders are often linked to suicide. Although women are more likely to attempt suicide, more men actually succeed, probably because they select more lethal means. The elderly—not the young—are more likely to commit suicide. People who attempt suicide are often depressed, but they are generally in touch with reality. They may, however, lack effective problem-solving skills and see no other way of dealing with life stress than suicide. A sense of hopelessness also figures prominently in suicides.

7.11 Identify the major theoretical perspectives on suicide.

These draw on the classic psychodynamic model of anger turned inward; the role of social alienation; and learning, social-cognitive, and biologically based perspectives.

7.12 Apply your knowledge of factors in suicide to steps you can take if someone you knew was experiencing suicidal thoughts.

You should never ignore a person's threat to commit suicide. Although not all people who threaten suicide go on to commit the act, many do. People who commit suicide often signal their intentions, for example, by telling others about their suicidal thoughts. If someone you know is thinking about suicide, draw him or her out to talk about his or her feelings, be sympathetic, suggest means other than suicide of coping with the problems at hand, ask about his or her intentions, and most importantly, accompanying him or her to get professional help—now.

critical thinking questions

On the basis of your reading of this chapter, answer the following questions:

- "Women are just naturally more prone to depression than men." Do you agree or disagree? Explain your answer.

- Jonathan becomes clinically depressed after losing his job and his girlfriend. On the basis of your review of the different theoretical perspectives on depression, explain how these losses may have figured in Jonathan's depression.

- If you were to become clinically depressed, which course of treatment would you prefer—medication, psychotherapy, or a combination? Explain.

- Did your reading of the text change your ideas about how you might deal with a suicide threat by a friend or loved one? If so, how?

key terms

mood disorders 244
major depressive
   disorder 245
mania 245
hypomania 245

postpartum depression
   (PPD) 251
persistent depressive
   disorder 252
double depression 253

bipolar disorder 254
manic episode 256
cyclothymic disorder 257
cognitive triad of
   depression 262

cognitive-specificity
   hypothesis 265
learned helplessness 266

Substance-Related
and Addictive Disorders

8

learning objectives

8.1
Identify the major types of substance-related disorders in the *DSM-5* and describe their general features.

8.2
Describe nonchemical forms of addiction or compulsive behavior.

8.3
Explain the difference between physiological dependence and psychological dependence.

8.4
Identify common stages in the pathway to addiction.

8.5
Identify the major categories of psychoactive drugs and specific drugs in each category, and describe the effects of these drugs and the risks they pose.

8.6
Describe the major theoretical perspectives toward understanding substance use disorders

8.7
Explain how cocaine affects the brain.

8.8
Evaluate methods of treating substance use disorders.

8.9
Describe the basic features of gambling disorder and evaluate ways of treating it.

truth OR fiction

T☑ F☐ Legally available substances account for more deaths than all illegal substances combined. (p. 291)

T☑ F☐ You cannot become psychologically dependent on a drug without also becoming physically dependent on it. (p. 295)

T☑ F☐ More teenagers and young adults die from alcohol-related motor vehicle accidents than from any other cause. (p. 297)

T☐ F☐ It is safe to let someone who has passed out from drinking just sleep it off. (p. 301)

T☐ F☐ Even moderate use of alcohol increases the risk of heart attacks. (p. 303)

T☑ F☐ Coca-Cola originally contained cocaine. (p. 306)

T☐ F☐ More teens today use marijuana than either alcohol or tobacco (p. 310)

T☐ F☐ People who can "hold their liquor" better than most stand a lower risk of becoming problem drinkers. (p. 312)

T☐ F☐ A widely used treatment for heroin addiction involves substituting one addictive drug for another. (p. 320)

"I" "Nothing and Nobody Comes Before My Coke"

She had just caught me with cocaine again after I had managed to convince her that I hadn't used in over a month. Of course I had been tooting (snorting) almost every day, but I had managed to cover my tracks a little better than usual. So she said to me that I was going to have to make a choice—either cocaine or her. Before she finished the sentence, I knew what was coming, so I told her to think carefully about what she was going to say. It was clear to me that there wasn't a choice. I love my wife, but I'm not going to choose anything over cocaine. It's sick, but that's what things have come to. Nothing and nobody comes before my coke.

From Weiss & Mirin, 1987, p. 55

These comments from Eugene, a 41-year-old architect, underscore the powerful effects that drugs like cocaine can have on people's lives. Our society is flooded with psychoactive substances that alter the mood and twist perceptions—substances that lift you up, calm you down, and turn you upside down. Many young people start using these substances because of peer pressure or because their parents and other authority figures tell them not to. For many others who become addicted to drugs, like Eugene, the pursuit and use of drugs take center stage in their lives and becomes even more important than family, work, or their own welfare.

In this chapter, we examine the physiological and psychological effects of the major classes of drugs. We explore how mental health professionals classify substance-related disorders and where they draw the line between use and abuse. We then examine contemporary understandings of the origins of these disorders and how mental health professionals help people who struggle to combat them.

Classification of Substance-Related and Addictive Disorders

The use of psychoactive substances that affect a person's mental state is normal, at least as gauged by statistical frequency and social standards. In this sense, it is normal to start the day with caffeine in our coffee or tea, to consume wine or coffee with meals, to meet friends for a drink after work, and to end the day with a nightcap. Each of these substances affects our mental state, making us more alert, in the case of caffeine, or more relaxed, in the case of alcoholic beverages. Many of us take prescription drugs that calm us down or ease our pain. Flooding the bloodstream with nicotine through cigarette smoking is normal in the sense that about one in five Americans do it. However, use of some psychoactive substances, such as cocaine, marijuana, and heroin, is abnormal in the sense that it is illegal and therefore deviates from social standards. Ironically, two substances that are legally available to adults—tobacco and alcohol—cause more deaths through sickness and accidents than all illicit drugs combined. **T / F**

The classification of substance use disorders in the *DSM* system is not based on whether a drug is legal or not, but rather on how the use of a drug impairs the person's physiological and psychological functioning. *DSM-5* classifies substance-related disorders in terms of two major types: *substance-induced disorders* and *substance use disorders*.

Substance-induced disorders are patterns of abnormal behavior induced by use of psychoactive substances. Two of the major types are *substance intoxication* and *substance withdrawal*. Different substances have different effects, so some of these disorders may be induced by one, by a few, or by nearly all substances. In Chapter 14, we consider a substance-induced disorder called *Korsakoff's syndrome* that leads to irreversible memory loss after years of chronic alcohol abuse.

Substance intoxication is a substance-induced disorder involving a pattern of repeated episodes of intoxication, which is a state of drunkenness or being "high," brought about by use of a particular drug. The features of intoxication depend on which drug is ingested, the dose, the user's biological reactivity, and—to some degree—the user's expectations. Signs of intoxication often include confusion, belligerence, impaired judgment, inattention, and impaired motor and spatial skills.

It's important to note that overdoses of alcohol, cocaine, opioids (narcotics), and phencyclidine (PCP) can result in death (yes, you can die from alcohol overdoses), either because of the substance's biochemical effects or because of behavior patterns—such as suicide—that are connected with psychological pain or impaired judgment brought on by use of the drug. Accidental overdoses are the second-leading cause of accidental death (after motor vehicle accidents) in the United States, accounting for more than 27,000 deaths annually (Okie, 2010).

Substance withdrawal is a substance-induced disorder involving a cluster of symptoms that occur when a person abruptly stops using a particular substance following a period of prolonged and heavy use (or in the case of caffeine withdrawal, daily use) of the substance. Repeated use of a substance may alter the body's physiological reactions, leading to the development of physiological effects such as *tolerance* and a clearly defined *withdrawal syndrome* (also called an *abstinence syndrome*).

Tolerance is a state of physical habituation to a drug, resulting from frequent use, such that higher doses are needed to achieve the same effect. Withdrawal symptoms vary with the particular type of drug. Symptoms of alcohol withdrawal may include sweating or rapid pulse, tremors of the hand, fleeting hallucinations or illusions, insomnia, nausea or vomiting, agitated behavior, anxiety, and possible seizures. For caffeine withdrawal, the symptoms are generally milder and may include headache, significant drowsiness, depressed mood, problems with concentration, flu-like symptoms, nausea, and muscle stiffness or pain. People who experience a withdrawal syndrome often return to using the substance to relieve the discomfort associated with withdrawal, which thus serves to maintain the addictive pattern.

8.1 Identify the major types of substance-related disorders in the *DSM-5* and describe their general features.

truth OR fiction

Legally available substances account for more deaths than all illegal substances combined.

☑ **TRUE** Two legally available substances, alcohol and tobacco, cause far more deaths.

In some chronic, heavy users of alcohol, withdrawal produces a state of *delirium tremens,* or DTs. The DTs are usually limited to chronic, heavy users of alcohol who dramatically lower their intake of alcohol after many years of heavy drinking. DTs involve intense autonomic hyperactivity (profuse sweating and tachycardia) and *delirium*—a state of mental confusion characterized by incoherent speech, disorientation, and extreme restlessness. Terrifying hallucinations—frequently of creepy, crawling animals—may also be present.

Regular or prolonged use of certain substances may lead to a **withdrawal syndrome**, which is a cluster of psychological and physical symptoms following abrupt cessation of use of the substance. Psychoactive substances that can lead to withdrawal syndromes include alcohol, opioids (opiate drugs), stimulants such as cocaine and amphetamine, sedatives and sleep-inducing drugs (hypnotics), marijuana, and tobacco (which contains the stimulant nicotine). Because abrupt withdrawal from hallucinogens such as LSD and phencyclidine (PCP) and inhalants (e.g., glues or aerosols) does not produce clinically significant withdrawal effects, they are not recognized as producing identifiable withdrawal syndromes (APA, 2013).

Substance use disorders are patterns of maladaptive use of psychoactive substances that lead to significant levels of impaired functioning or personal distress. The term *substance use disorder* is a general diagnostic classification, but the specific diagnosis, such as *alcohol use disorder*, identifies the particular substance associated with problematic use. In addition to evidence of significant distress or impaired functioning resulting from problematic use of a psychoactive substance, the diagnosis of a substance use disorder requires two or more specific features or symptoms occurring during the preceding one-year period. The particular features vary with the type of drug. For example, alcohol use disorder is characterized by a range of features that include the following, although not all of these need be present:

- Spending an excessive amount of time seeking or using alcohol, or recovering from overuse.

- Having persistent problems cutting back or controlling alcohol use despite wanting to do so

- Using excessive amounts of alcohol beyond what the person intends

- Having difficulty fulfilling expectable roles as a student, employee, or family member because of alcohol use

- Continuing to use alcohol despite the social, interpersonal, psychological or medical problems it causes

- Developing tolerance or a withdrawal syndrome associated with alcohol use

- Using alcohol in situations that pose a risk to the person's safety or the safety of others, such as repeatedly drinking and driving

- Having strong, persistent urges or cravings for alcohol

- Withdrawing from usual activities because of alcohol use

The previous version of the *DSM* distinguished between two types of substance use disorders, a milder form called substance abuse disorder and a more severe form called substance dependence disorder. However, because the lines between the two categories of disorders were never clearly stipulated, the *DSM-5* combined the two types of disorders into a single category of substance use disorders. The *DSM-5* allows clinicians to designate the severity of the disorder by specifying whether it is mild, moderate, or severe.

People can develop substance use disorders involving a wide range of psychoactive substances, including alcohol, opioids (opiates such as heroin and morphine), sedatives and sleep-inducing or hypnotic drugs, stimulants such as cocaine and amphetamines, and tobacco. Yet the most widely used psychoactive drug, caffeine (the mild stimulant

Two of the many faces of alcohol use—and abuse. Alcohol is our most widely used—and abused—drug. Many people use alcohol to celebrate achievements and happy occasions, as in the photograph on the left. Unfortunately, like the man in the photograph on the right, some people use alcohol to drown their sorrows, which may only compound their problems. Where exactly does substance use end and abuse begin? Use becomes abuse when it leads to damaging consequences.

found in coffee, tea, colas, and even chocolate), is not identified with a recognized substance use disorder because it has not been reliably linked to problematic use leading to impaired functioning or personal distress. However, *DSM-5* lists caffeine use disorder in the Appendix of the diagnostic manual as a proposed diagnosis in need of further study. On the other hand, *DSM-5* recognizes that regular use of caffeine can lead to a substance withdrawal disorder following the abrupt cessation of caffeine intake after a prolonged period of daily use.

Not all nor even most of the associated features or symptoms of a substance use disorder need to be present for a diagnosis to be made. Consequently, not all persons with the same diagnosis fit the same symptom profile. For example, Henry may show clear signs of a withdrawal syndrome and have persistent difficulty curtailing use of alcohol despite multiple attempts. But Jessica's drinking may lead to recurrent problems at work or school and continue despite knowledge of these harmful consequences, even though she shows no evidence of a tolerance or of withdrawal symptoms when she goes without alcohol for a time.

Substance Use and Abuse

Where does the use of a drug or psychoactive substance end and substance abuse begin? The *DSM-5* draws the line at the point at which a pattern of substance use significantly impairs the person's occupational, social, or daily functioning or causes significant personal distress. Examples of impaired functioning include the following:

- Problems meeting one's role responsibilities as a student, worker, or parent
- Engaging in behavior that is physically dangerous (e.g., mixing driving and substance use)
- Repeated social or interpersonal problems (e.g., repeatedly getting into fights when drinking)

When people repeatedly miss school or work because they are drunk or "sleeping it off," their behavior may show signs of developing a substance use disorder. A single incident of excessive drinking at a friend's wedding would not qualify for a diagnosis.

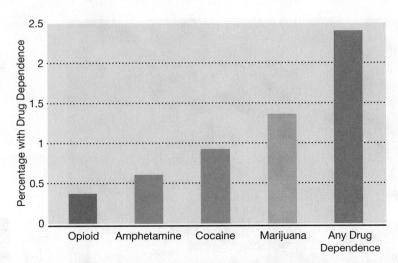

FIGURE 8.1 Lifetime prevalence of drug dependence by type of illicit drug. Drug dependence, which is characterized by impaired control over the use of a drug and physical dependence, affects nearly 2.5% of adults in the U.S. Under *DSM-5*, drug dependence is classified as a substance use disorder. Cannabis (marijuana) dependence is the most common type.

Source: Conway et al., 2006.

Nor would regular consumption of low to moderate amounts of alcohol be considered abusive so long as it is not connected with any impairment in functioning. Neither the amount nor the type of drug ingested, nor whether the drug is illicit, is the key to defining whether a substance use disorder is present. Rather, the determining feature of substance use disorder is whether a pattern of drug-using behavior continues although it causes significant problems in daily functioning or personal distress.

Unfortunately, substance use disorders are common in our society. About 1 in 10 adults (10.3%) in the United States develop substance use disorders involving an illicit (illegal) drug at some point in their lives (Compton, Conway, Stinson, Colliver, & Grant, 2005). Figure 8.1 shows the percentages of U.S. adults who develop substance use disorders involving dependence on illicit drugs. But the substances most commonly associated with drug dependence are legally available substances, alcohol and tobacco.

Although a popular stereotype exists that drug-related problems are more frequent among ethnic minorities, this belief is not supported by evidence. To the contrary, African Americans and Latinos have comparable or even lower rates of substance use disorders than do European Americans (non-Hispanic Whites) (Breslau, Kendler, Su, Gaxiola-Aguilar, & Kessler, 2005; Compton et al., 2005).

Nonchemical Addictions and Other Forms of Compulsive Behavior

8.2 Describe nonchemical forms of addiction or compulsive behavior.

The *DSM-5* introduced a new diagnostic category, Substance Use and Addictive Disorders, that includes both substance use disorders and *gambling disorder* (previously called *pathological gambling*), which is considered a nonchemical form of addiction. Pathological or compulsive gambling was previously classified in the *DSM-IV* in a diagnostic category called Impulse Control Disorders, which included other problem behaviors also characterized by difficulties controlling or restraining impulsive behavior, such as *kleptomania* (compulsive stealing) and *pyromania* (compulsive fire setting).

The change in diagnostic classification stems from the understanding that certain compulsive or addictive patterns of behavior share important features with drug-related problems. Compulsive gambling, compulsive shopping, and even compulsive Internet use share some hallmark features of drug addiction or dependence, such as impaired control over the behavior and the development of withdrawal symptoms like anxiety and depression if the substance use stops abruptly. Future versions of the *DSM-5* may incorporate other behavioral addictions such as compulsive shopping and compulsive Internet use as recognized disorders, but for now they are classified in a category of proposed disorders requiring further study.

Clarifying Terms

What is physical or chemical dependence? What do we mean by the term *drug addiction*? What is psychological dependence? There exists a confusing medley of terms used by professionals and laypeople to describe problem drug use. Let's take a moment to clarify how we use these terms in this text.

We use the term **physical dependence** (also called *chemical dependence* or *physiological dependence*) to refer to a pattern of drug-use behavior in which a person's body has changed as a result of regular use of the drug, such that the person now requires larger amounts of the drug to achieve the same effects (tolerance) or has troubling withdrawal symptoms upon cutting back or stopping use of the drug (a withdrawal syndrome).

But physical dependence is not the same thing as **addiction**. Scientists lack any universally accepted definition of *addiction*. For our purposes, we define *addiction* as compulsive use of a drug accompanied by signs of physical dependence. Addiction involves a loss of control over use of a drug despite knowledge of the harmful consequences it causes. People who are addicted to drugs have difficulty controlling how much or how often they use these drugs. They may have made many unsuccessful attempts to cut down or cut out their use of the drug or have a persistent desire to do so, but without following through.

The developers of the *DSM-5* decided to use the term *substance use disorder* for diagnostic purposes, rather than the term *addictive disorder*. They believed that the more neutral term *substance use disorder* is less stigmatizing and pejorative than the term *addiction*. They do use the term *addictive* to apply to nonchemical forms of compulsive behavior such as problem gambling. That said, the use of the term *addiction* is widespread among both professionals and laypeople alike.

People may become physically (or chemically) dependent on a drug but not become addicted. For example, people recuperating from surgery are often given narcotics derived from opium as painkillers. Some may develop signs of physiological dependence, such as tolerance and a withdrawal syndrome, but do not develop impaired control over the use of these drugs. They can stop when they no longer need the drug to control pain. You (and your authors as well) may become chemically dependent on caffeine if you regularly use the substance (say in your morning coffee) and feel "out of sorts" or have a headache if you go a day or two without it. But you have no difficulty controlling how much or how often you use the drug and can stop if you put your mind (and heart) to it.

Let's also consider people who develop a *nonchemical addiction,* such as compulsive gambling. They show impaired control over the problem behavior in a similar way that people with a chemical addiction have difficulty controlling their drug use. They may also show evidence of withdrawal symptoms if they cut back or stop performing the behavior. But their withdrawal symptoms are typically psychological (e.g., anxiety, irritability, or restlessness) rather than physiological (e.g., tremors, shaking hands, nausea) in nature.

Another pattern of problem drug use involves **psychological dependence** on a drug. People who become psychologically dependent use a drug compulsively to meet their psychological needs, such as relying on a drug to combat daily stress or anxiety. They may or may not be chemically or physiologically dependent or addicted to the drug. We can think of people who feel compelled to use marijuana (or caffeine or other drugs) to cope with the stresses of daily life, but do not require larger amounts of the substance to get high or experience distressing withdrawal symptoms when they cease using it. **T / F**

8.3 Explain the difference between physical and psychological dependence.

truth OR fiction

You cannot become psychologically dependent on a drug without also becoming physically dependent on it.

☑ **TRUE** You can become psychologically dependent on a drug without developing a physiological dependence.

Addiction. Although no one sets out to become addicted to drugs, routine drug use can lead to addiction when users feel powerless to control their use of drugs.

Pathways to Addiction

No one sets out to become addicted to drugs. What may have started off with experimentation can progress through a series of stages to drug dependence or addiction. Just as there are different routes to follow to arrive at the same destination, there are different pathways to addiction. Here we consider a common pathway in the road to addiction that involves three stages (Based on Weiss, R. D., & Mirin, S. M. (1987). Cocaine. Washington, DC: American Psychiatric Association.):

1. *Experimentation.* During the stage of experimentation, or occasional use, the drug temporarily makes users feel good, even euphoric. Users feel in control and believe they can stop at any time.

2. *Routine use.* During the next stage, a period of routine use, people begin to structure their lives around the pursuit and use of drugs. Denial plays a major role at this stage, as users mask the negative consequences of their behavior to themselves and others. Values change. What had formerly been important, such as family and work, comes to matter less than the drugs.

   A case example illustrates how denial can mask reality (Weiss & Mirin, 1987). A 48-year-old business owner was brought for a consultation by his wife. She complained that his once-successful business was jeopardized by his erratic behavior, that he was grouchy and moody, and had spent $7,000 in the previous month on cocaine. He also had missed more than a third of his workdays during the previous two months due to cocaine use. And yet he continued to deny that he had a problem with cocaine. telling the interviewer that missing so many days from work was not a big deal and that his company could run itself. When pressed further on the point, he still was unwilling to admit to his drug problem, but confessed that he just didn't want to think about it.

   As routine drug use continues, problems mount. Users devote more resources to drugs. They ravage family bank accounts, seek "temporary" loans from friends and family for trumped up reasons, and sell family heirlooms and jewelry for a fraction of their value. Lying and manipulation become a way of life to cover up the drug use. The husband sells the TV set and forces the front door open to make it look like a burglary. The wife claims to have been robbed at knifepoint to explain the disappearance of a gold chain or engagement ring. Family relationships become strained as the mask of denial shatters and the consequences of drug abuse become apparent: days lost from work, unexplained absences from home, rapid mood shifts, depletion of family finances, failure to pay bills, stealing from family members, and missing family gatherings or children's birthday parties.

3. *Addiction or dependence.* Routine use becomes addiction or dependence when users feel powerless to resist drugs, either because they want to experience their effects or to avoid the consequences of withdrawal. Little or nothing else matters at this stage, as we saw in the case of Eugene with which we opened the chapter.

Now let's examine the effects of different types of drugs of abuse and the consequences associated with their use and abuse.

Drugs of Abuse

Drugs of abuse are generally classified within three major groupings: (a) depressants, such as alcohol and opioids; (b) stimulants, such as amphetamines and cocaine; and (c) hallucinogens.

Depressants

A **depressant** is a drug that slows down or curbs the activity of the central nervous system. It reduces feelings of tension and anxiety, slows movement, and impairs cognitive processes. In high doses, depressants can arrest vital functions and cause death. The most widely used depressant, alcohol, can cause death when taken in large amounts because of its depressant effects on breathing. Other effects are specific to the particular kind of depressant. For example, some depressants, such as heroin, produce a "rush" of pleasure. Here, let's consider several major types of depressants.

ALCOHOL Alcohol is the most widely abused substance in the United States and worldwide. You might not think of alcohol as a drug, perhaps because it is so common, or perhaps because it is ingested by drinking rather than by smoking or injection. But alcoholic beverages—such as wine, beer, and hard liquor—contain a depressant drug called *ethyl alcohol* (or *ethanol*). The concentration of the drug varies with the type of beverage (wine and beer have less pure alcohol per ounce than distilled spirits such as rye, gin, or vodka). Alcohol is classified as a depressant because it has biochemical effects similar to those of a class of antianxiety agents or minor tranquilizers, the *benzodiazepines*, which includes the well-known drugs *diazepam* (Valium) and *chlordiazepoxide* (Librium). We can think of alcohol as an over-the-counter tranquilizer.

Most American adults drink alcohol at least occasionally and do so in moderation. But many people develop significant problems with alcohol. Many laypeople and professionals use the terms **alcoholism** and *alcohol dependence* interchangeably, as we will. We use either term to refer to a pattern of impaired control over the use of alcohol in someone who has become physiologically dependent on the drug. An estimated eight million U.S. adults suffer from alcoholism (Kranzler, 2006).

The most widely held view of alcoholism is the disease model, the belief that alcoholism is a medical illness or disease. From this perspective, once a person with alcoholism takes a drink, the biochemical effects of the drug on the brain create an irresistible physical craving for more. The disease model holds that alcoholism is a chronic, permanent condition. The peer-support group Alcoholics Anonymous (AA) subscribes to this view, which is expressed in their slogan, "Once an alcoholic, always an alcoholic." AA views people suffering from alcoholism as either drinking or "recovering," never "cured." Although some health care providers believe that at least some alcohol abusers can learn to drink responsibly without "falling off the wagon," the belief remains a source of controversy in the field.

The personal and social costs of alcoholism exceed those of all illicit drugs combined. Alcohol abuse is connected with lower productivity, loss of jobs, and downward movement in socioeconomic status. Alcohol plays a role in many violent crimes, including assaults and homicides, and more than 180,000 rapes and sexual attacks annually in the United States (Bartholow & Heinz, 2006; Buddie & Testa, 2005). About one in three suicides in the United States and about the same proportion of deaths due to unintentional injury (e.g., from motor vehicle accidents) are linked to alcohol use (Sher, 2005; Shneidman, 2005). More teenagers and young adults die from alcohol-related motor vehicle accidents than from any other cause. All told, about 85,000 people in the United States die from alcohol-related causes each year, with most of these deaths resulting from alcohol-related motor vehicle crashes and diseases (Kleiman, Caulkins, & Hawken, 2012; Lerner, 2011). **T / F**

questionnaire

Are You Hooked?

Are you dependent on alcohol? If you shake and shiver and undergo the tortures of "Hell" when you go without a drink for a while, the answer is clear enough. However, sometimes the clues are more subtle. For the following quiz, place a check mark in the Yes or No column for each item. Then check the key at the end of the chapter.

		Yes	No
1.	Do you skip meals when you are drinking or eat only junk food?		
2.	Do you feel down in the dumps after you've been drinking?		
3.	Do you drink more than most people you know?		
4.	Are you drinking more than usual?		
5.	Do you binge drink on occasion?		
6.	Are you sleeping it off in the morning after going out drinking the night before?		
7.	Have you missed work or school, or come in late, because of your drinking?		
8.	Have you been avoiding friends or family because you are embarrassed or feeling guilty about your drinking?		
9.	Do you find it difficult to go a day or two without drinking?		
10.	Do you need to drink more and more, just to get drunk?		
11.	Have you become more irritable because of your drinking?		
12.	Have you done things when you've been drinking that you later regretted?		

👁 **Watch the Video** *Chris: Alcoholism* on **MyPsychLab**

Despite the popular image of the person who develops alcoholism as a skid row drunk, only a small minority of people with alcoholism fit the stereotype. The great majority of people with alcoholism are quite ordinary—your neighbors, coworkers, friends, and members of your own family. They are found in all walks of life and every social and economic class. Many have families, hold good jobs, and live fairly comfortably. Yet alcoholism can have just as devastating an effect on the well-to-do as on the indigent, leading to wrecked careers and marriages, to motor vehicle and other accidents, and to severe, life-threatening physical disorders, as well as exacting an enormous emotional toll. Alcoholism is also linked to domestic violence and increased risk of divorce (Foran & O'Leary, 2008). 👁

No single drinking pattern is exclusively associated with alcoholism. Some people with alcoholism drink heavily every day; others binge only on weekends. Others can abstain for lengthy periods of time, but periodically go off the wagon and engage in episodes of binge drinking that last for weeks or months.

Alcohol, not cocaine or other drugs, is the drug of choice among young people today and the leading drug of abuse. Even though most college students are underage, drinking has become so integrated into college life that it is essentially normative, as much a part of the college experience as attending a weekend football or basketball game. Alcohol, not cocaine, heroin, or marijuana, is the BDOC—big drug on campus.

Drinking among college students tends to be limited to weekends and to be heavier early in the semester when academic demands are relatively light (Del Boca, Darkes, Greenbaum, & Goldman, 2004). College students tend to drink more than their peers who do not attend college (Slutske, 2005). Researchers describe a continuum of alcohol-related problems among college students, ranging from mild problems, such as missing class, to extreme problem behaviors, such as arrests resulting from drinking (Ham & Hope, 2003). In *A Closer Look*, we focus on binge drinking—a form of problem drinking that has become a leading problem on college campuses today.

Risk Factors for Alcoholism A number of factors place people at increased risk for developing alcoholism and alcohol-related problems. These include the following:

1. *Gender.* Men are more than twice as likely as women to develop alcoholism (Hasin et al., 2006). One possible reason for this gender difference is sociocultural; perhaps tighter cultural constraints are placed on women. Yet it may also be that alcohol hits women harder, and not only because women usually weigh less than men. Alcohol seems to "go to women's heads" more rapidly than to men's. One reason may be that women have less of an enzyme that metabolizes alcohol in the stomach than men do. Ounce for ounce, women absorb more alcohol into their bloodstreams than men do. As a result, they are likely to become inebriated on less alcohol than men. Consequently, women's bodies may put the brakes on excessive drinking more quickly than men's.

2. *Age.* The great majority of cases of alcohol dependence develop in young adulthood, typically between the ages 20 and 40. Although alcohol use disorders tend to develop somewhat later in women than in men, women who develop these problems experience similar health, social, and occupational problems by middle age as their male counterparts.

3. *Antisocial personality disorder.* Antisocial behavior in adolescence or adulthood increases the risk of later alcoholism. On the other hand, many people with alcoholism showed no antisocial tendencies in adolescence, and many antisocial adolescents do not abuse alcohol or other drugs as adults.

4. *Family history.* The best predictor of problem drinking in adulthood appears to be a family history of alcohol abuse. Family members who drink may act as models ("set a poor example"). Moreover, the biological relatives of people with alcohol dependence may also inherit a predisposition that makes them more likely to develop problems with alcohol.

5. *Sociodemographic factors.* Alcohol dependence is generally more common among people of lower income and educational levels, as well as among people living alone.

Ethnicity and Alcohol Use and Abuse Rates of alcohol use and alcoholism vary among American ethnic and racial groups. Some groups—Jews, Italians, Greeks, and Asians—have relatively low rates of alcoholism, largely as the result of tight social controls placed on excessive and underage drinking. Asian Americans, in general, drink less heavily than other population groups (Adelson, 2006). Not only do Asian families place strong cultural constraints on excessive drinking, but an underlying biological factor may be at work in curbing alcohol use. Asian Americans are more likely than other groups to show a *flushing* response to alcohol (Peng et al., 2010). Flushing is characterized by redness and feelings of warmth on the face, and, at higher doses, nausea, heart palpitations, dizziness, and headaches. Genes that control the metabolism of alcohol are believed to be responsible for regulating the flushing response (Luczak, Glatt, & Wall, 2006). Because people like to avoid these unpleasant experiences, flushing may serve as a natural defense against alcoholism by curbing excessive alcohol intake.

Hispanic American men and non-Hispanic White men have similar rates of alcohol consumption and alcohol-related physical problems. Hispanic American women, however, are much less likely to use alcohol and to develop alcohol use disorders than non-Hispanic White women. *Why?* An important factor may be cultural expectations. Traditional Hispanic American cultures place severe restrictions on the use of alcohol by women, especially heavy drinking. However, with increasing acculturation, Hispanic American women in the United States apparently are becoming more similar to European American women with respect to alcohol use and abuse.

Alcohol abuse is taking a heavy toll on African Americans. For example, the prevalence of *cirrhosis of the liver,* an alcohol-related, potentially fatal liver disease, is nearly twice as high in African Americans as in non-Hispanic White Americans. Yet African Americans show lower rates of alcohol abuse and dependence than do (non-Hispanic) White Americans. Why, then, do African Americans suffer more from alcohol-related problems?

Women and alcohol. Women are less likely to develop alcoholism, in part because of greater cultural constraints on excessive drinking by women, and perhaps because women absorb more pure alcohol into the bloodstream than men, making them more biologically sensitive to the effects of alcohol at the same level of intake as men.

Alcohol and ethnic diversity. The damaging effects of alcohol abuse appear to be taking the heaviest toll on African Americans and Native Americans. The prevalence of alcohol-related cirrhosis of the liver is nearly twice as high among African Americans as among White Americans, even though African Americans are less likely to develop alcohol abuse or dependence disorders. Jewish Americans have relatively low incidences of alcohol-related problems, perhaps because they tend to expose children to the ritual use of wine in childhood and impose strong cultural restraints on excessive drinking. Asian Americans tend to drink less heavily than most other Americans, in part because of cultural constraints and possibly because they have less biological tolerance for alcohol, as shown by a greater flushing response to alcohol.

Binge Drinking, a Dangerous College Pastime

A major drug problem on college campuses today is binge drinking. Binge drinking is generally defined as consuming five or more drinks (for men) or four or more drinks (for women) on a single occasion. More than two out of five college students reporting binge drinking episodes during the past month (Patrick & Schulenberg, 2011; Squeglia et al., 2012). Binge drinking is also reported by about one in four high school students (24%) (Johnston, Mash, Miller, & Ninowski, 2012). Overall, nearly one in five American adults (17%) reported a binge drinking episode during the past month (CDC, 2012a).

Concerns about binge drinking are well founded. Binge drinking is associated with a wide range of problems, including getting into trouble with the police, engaging in unprotected sexual activity, serious motor vehicle and other accidents, unintended pregnancies, violent behavior, getting poorer grades, and developing drug use problems (e.g., Hingson, Zha, & Weitzmanet, 2009; CDC, 2012a; Wechsler & Nelson, 2008). And things could get worse, as they did in the tragic case of Leslie, a young college student at the University of Virginia. An art major whose work her professors found promising, Leslie had maintained a 3.67 GPA and was completing her senior essay on a Polish-born sculptor (Winerip, 1998). But she never finished it, because one day, after binge drinking, she fell down a flight of stairs and died. We may hear more about the deaths of young people due to heroin or cocaine overdoses, but more than 1,000 college-age students, like Leslie, die each year from alcohol-related causes such as overdoses and alcohol-related accidents (Yaccino, 2012).

Binge drinking is quite common, even ritualized, in celebration of reaching the legal drinking age of 21 (Neighbors et al., 2012). A recent survey at the University of Missouri showed that about one-third of college men and about one-fourth of college women reported consuming at least 21 drinks or more on their 21st birthdays, which represents a level of severe intoxication that can result

in significant health risks, including coma and even death (Rutledge, Park, & Sher, 2008). The findings of the Missouri study most probably generalize to many college campuses.

In a review article, psychologists Lindsay Ham and Debra Hope (2003) identified two general subtypes of college students who appear most clearly at risk of becoming problem drinkers. The first type includes students who drink mostly for social or enjoyment purposes. They tend to be male, European American, and participate in Greek organizations or other social organizations in which heavy drinking is socially acceptable. The second type includes students who drink due to pressures to conform or who

Death by alcohol. Samantha Spady, a 19-year-old Colorado State University student, blacked out when drinking with her friends and never woke up. Samantha died of an alcohol overdose from heavy drinking. Would you recognize the signs of an alcohol overdose? What steps could you take—should you take—to help a friend or acquaintance who shows signs of an overdose?

Socioeconomic factors may help explain these differences. African Americans are more likely to encounter the stresses of unemployment and economic hardship, and stress may compound the damage to the body caused by heavy alcohol consumption. African Americans also tend to lack access to medical services and may be less likely to receive early treatment for the medical problems caused by alcohol abuse.

Rates of alcohol abuse and dependence vary from tribe to tribe, but Native Americans overall have higher rates of alcoholism and suffer from more alcohol-related problems than any other ethnic group—problems such as cirrhosis of the liver, fetal abnormalities, and automobile and other accident-related fatalities (Henry et al., 2011; Spillane & Smith, 2009). A recent national survey of adolescents found the highest rates of substance use and substance use disorders involving alcohol and drugs to be among Native American youth (Wu, Woody, Yang, Pan, & Blazer, 2011).

Many Native Americans believe the loss of their traditional culture is largely responsible for their high rates of drinking-related problems (Beauvais, 1998). The dis-

It is safe to let someone who has passed out from drinking just sleep it off.

☑ **FALSE**   Sadly, the person may never wake up. Passing out from drinking needs to be treated as a medical emergency.

use alcohol to soothe negative feelings. They more often tend to be female and to be troubled by problems with anxiety or depression. Generating these profiles may help counselors and health care providers identify young people at increased risk of developing problem drinking patterns.

Binge drinking and related drinking games (such as beer chugging) can place people at significant risk of death from alcohol overdose. Many students who play these games don't stop until they become too drunk or too sick to continue. What should you do if you see a friend or acquaintance become incapacitated or pass out from heavy drinking? Should you just let the person sleep it off? Can you tell whether a person has had too much to drink? Should you just mind your own business or turn to others for help?

You cannot tell simply by looking at a person whether the person has overdosed on alcohol. But a person who becomes unconscious or unresponsive is in need of immediate medical attention. Don't assume that the person will simply sleep it off: He or she may never wake up. Be aware of the signs of potential overdose, such as the following (adapted from Nevid & Rathus, 2013):

- Nonresponsive when talked to or shouted at
- Nonresponsive to being pinched, shaken, or poked
- Unable to stand up on his or her own
- Failure to wake up or gain consciousness
- Purplish color or clammy-feeling skin
- Rapid pulse rate or irregular heart rhythms, low blood pressure, or difficulty breathing

If you suspect an overdose, do not leave the person alone. Summon medical help or emergency assistance and remain with the person until help arrives. If possible, place the person on his or her side or have the person sit up with his or her head bowed. Do not give the person any food or drink or induce vomiting. If the person is responsive, find out if he or she had taken any medication or other drugs that might be interacting with the effects of the alcohol. Also, find out whether the person has an underlying illness that may contribute to the problem, such as diabetes or epilepsy. **T / F**

It may be easier to just pass by without taking action. But ask yourself what you would like someone else to do if you showed signs of overdosing on alcohol. Wouldn't you want one of your friends to intervene to save your life?

A dangerous pastime. Beer chugging and binge drinking can quickly lead to an alcohol overdose, a medical emergency that can have lethal consequences. Many college officials cite binge drinking as the major drug problem on campus.

ruption of traditional Native American culture caused by the appropriation of Indian lands and by attempts by European American society to sever Native Americans from their cultural traditions while denying them full access to the dominant culture resulted in severe cultural and social disorganization (Kahn, 1982). Beset by such problems, Native Americans are also prone to child abuse and neglect. Abuse and neglect contribute to feelings of hopelessness and depression among adolescents, who may seek escape from their feelings by using alcohol and other drugs.

Psychological Effects of Alcohol   The effects of alcohol or other drugs vary from person to person. By and large they reflect the interaction of (a) the physiological effects of the substances and (b) our interpretations of those effects. What do most people expect from alcohol? People frequently hold stereotypical expectations that alcohol will reduce tension, enhance pleasurable experiences, wash away worries, and enhance social skills. But what *does* alcohol actually do?

At a physiological level, alcohol appears to work like the benzodiazepines (a family of antianxiety drugs), by heightening activity of the neurotransmitter GABA (see Chapter 5). Because GABA is an inhibitory neurotransmitter (it tones down nervous system activity), increasing GABA activity produces feelings of relaxation. As people drink, their senses become clouded, and balance and coordination suffer. Still higher doses act on the parts of the brain that regulate involuntary vital functions, such as heart rate, respiration rate, and body temperature.

People may do many things when drinking that they would not do when sober, in part because of expectations concerning the drug and in part because of the drug's effects on the brain. For example, they may become more flirtatious or sexually aggressive or say or do things they later regret. Their behavior may reflect their expectation that alcohol has liberating effects and provides an external excuse for questionable behavior. Later, they can claim, "It was the alcohol, not me." The drug may also impair the brain's ability to curb impulsive, risk-taking, or violent behavior, perhaps by interfering with information-processing functions. Investigators find strong links between alcohol use and many forms of violent behavior, including domestic violence and sexual assaults (Abbey, Zawackia, Bucka, Clinton, & McAuslan, 2004; Fals-Stewart, 2003; Marshal, 2003).

Alcohol may lead people to feel more relaxed and self-confident, but it also impairs judgment, making it more difficult for people to weigh the consequences of their behavior. Under the influence of alcohol, people may make choices they might ordinarily reject, such as engaging in risky sexual behavior (Bersamin, Paschall, Saltz, & Zamboanga, 2012; Orchowski, Mastroleo, & Borsari, 2012; Ragsdale et al., 2012). Chronic alcohol abuse can impair cognitive abilities, such as memory, problem solving, and attention.

One of the lures of alcohol is that it induces short-term feelings of euphoria and elation that can drown self-doubts and self-criticism. Alcohol also makes people less capable of perceiving the unfortunate consequences of their behavior.

Alcohol use can dampen sexual arousal or excitement and impair sexual performance. As an intoxicant, alcohol also hampers coordination and motor ability. These effects help explain why alcohol use is implicated in about one in three accidental deaths in the United States.

Physical Health and Alcohol Chronic, heavy alcohol use affects virtually every organ and body system, either directly or indirectly. Heavy alcohol use is linked to increased risk of many serious health concerns, including liver disease, increased risk of some forms of cancer, coronary heart disease, and neurological disorders. Two of the major forms of alcohol-related liver disease are *alcoholic hepatitis,* a serious and potentially life-threatening inflammation of the liver, and cirrhosis of the liver, a potentially fatal disease in which healthy liver cells are replaced with scar tissue.

Habitual drinkers tend to be malnourished, which can put them at risk of complications arising from nutritional deficiencies. Chronic drinking is thus associated with nutritionally linked disorders such as cirrhosis of the liver (linked to protein deficiency) and *Korsakoff's syndrome* (connected with vitamin B deficiency), which is characterized by glaring confusion, disorientation, and memory loss for recent events (see Chapter 14).

Women who drink during pregnancy place their fetuses at risk for infant mortality, birth defects, central nervous system dysfunctions, and later academic problems. Children whose mothers drink during pregnancy may develop *fetal alcohol syndrome* (FAS), a syndrome characterized by facial features such as a flattened nose, widely spaced eyes, and an underdeveloped upper jaw, as well as mental retardation and social skills deficits (O'Connor & Paley, 2006). FAS affects from 1 to 3 of every 1,000 live births.

Although the risk is greater among women who drink heavily during pregnancy, FAS has been found among children of mothers who drank as little as a drink and a half per week (Carroll, 2003). As there is no established "safe" limit for alcohol use by pregnant women, the safest course for women who know or suspect they are pregnant is not to drink (Feldman et al., 2012; Stein, 2012). *Period.* The fact remains that FAS is an entirely preventable birth defect.

Moderate Drinking: Is There a Health Benefit? Despite this list of adverse effects associated with heavy drinking, correlational evidence links moderate use of alcohol (about one drink per day for women, about two drinks for men) to lower risks of heart attacks and strokes, as well as to lower death rates overall (Brien, Ronksley, Turner, Mukamal, & Ghali, 2011; King, Mainous, & Geesey, 2008; Ronksley, Brien, Turner, Mukamal, & Ghali, 2011). That said, we should point out that higher doses of alcohol used on a regular basis are associated with higher mortality (death) rates. **T / F**

Although it is possible that moderate alcohol use has a protective effect on the heart and circulatory system, public health officials have not endorsed use of alcohol for this reason, based largely on concerns that such an endorsement might increase risks of problem drinking. Also, investigators lack definitive evidence from experimental research that alcohol use is causally related to lower health risks (Rabin, 2009). We should also recognize that even moderate drinking has a modest effect on increasing the risk of breast cancer in women (Chen, Rosner, Hankinson, Colditz, & Willett, 2011; Kaunitz, 2011; Narod, 2011). Health promotion efforts might be better directed toward finding safer ways of achieving the health benefits associated with moderate drinking than by encouraging alcohol consumption, such as by quitting smoking, lowering dietary intake of fat and cholesterol, and exercising more regularly.

BARBITURATES About 1% of adult Americans develop a substance use disorder involving use of barbiturates, sleep medication (hypnotics), or antianxiety agents at some point in their lives. **Barbiturates** such as *amobarbital, pentobarbital, phenobarbital,* and *secobarbital* are depressants, or *sedatives.* These drugs have several medical uses, including easing anxiety and tension, dulling pain, and treating epilepsy and high blood pressure. Barbiturate use quickly leads to psychological and physiological dependence in the form of both tolerance and development of a withdrawal syndrome.

Barbiturates are also popular street drugs because they are relaxing and produce a mild state of euphoria, or high. High doses of barbiturates, like alcohol, produce drowsiness, slurred speech, motor impairment, irritability, and poor judgment—a particularly deadly combination of effects when their use is combined with operation of a motor vehicle. The effects of barbiturates last from three to six hours.

Because of synergistic effects, a mixture of barbiturates and alcohol is about four times as powerful as either drug used alone. A combination of barbiturates and alcohol was implicated in the deaths of the actresses Marilyn Monroe and Judy Garland. Even such widely used antianxiety drugs as Valium and Librium, which have a wide margin of safety when used alone, can be dangerous and lead to overdoses when combined with alcohol.

Physiologically dependent people need to be withdrawn carefully from sedatives, barbiturates, and antianxiety agents, and only under medical supervision. Abrupt withdrawal can produce states of delirium that may involve visual, tactile, or auditory hallucinations and disturbances in thought processes and consciousness. The longer the period of use and the higher the doses used, the greater the risk of severe withdrawal effects. Epileptic (grand mal) seizures and even death may occur if the individual undergoes untreated, abrupt withdrawal.

OPIOIDS Opioids are classified as **narcotics**—strongly addictive drugs that have pain-relieving and sleep-inducing properties. Opioids include both naturally occurring opiates (morphine, heroin, codeine) derived from the poppy plant and synthetic drugs (e.g., Demerol, Vicodin) that have opiate-like effects. The ancient Sumerians named the poppy plant *opium,* meaning "plant of joy."

Opioids produce a *rush,* or intense feelings of pleasure, which is the primary reason for their popularity as street drugs. They also dull awareness of one's personal problems, which is attractive to people seeking a mental escape from stress. Their pleasurable effects derive from their ability to directly stimulate the brain's pleasure circuits—the same brain networks responsible for feelings of sexual pleasure or pleasure from eating a satisfying meal.

Even moderate use of alcohol increases the risk of heart attacks.

☑ **FALSE** Findings from recent studies show that moderate intake of alcohol is associated with a lower risk of heart attacks and lower death rates.

The major medical application of opioids—natural or synthetic—is the relief of pain, or *analgesia*. Medical use of opioids, however, is carefully regulated because overdoses can lead to coma and even death. Street use of opioids is associated with many fatal overdoses and accidents. In a number of American cities, young men are more likely to die of a heroin overdose than in an automobile accident.

About 1.6 percent of Americans aged 12 or older report using heroin at some point in their lives and about 0.2% (2 in 1,000) report using the drug in the past year (SAMHSA, 2012). Once dependence sets in, it usually becomes chronic, relieved only by brief periods of abstinence. Adding to the problem is that prescription opioids, too, used medically for pain relief, can become drugs of abuse when they are used illicitly as street drugs (Friedman, 2006).

Two discoveries made in the 1970s show that the brain produces chemicals of its own that have opiate-like effects. One discovery was that neurons in the brain have receptor sites to which opiates fit like a key in a lock. The second was that the human body produces its own opiate-like substances that dock at the same receptor sites as opiates do. These natural substances, or **endorphins,** play important roles in regulating natural states of pleasure and pain. Opioids mimic the actions of endorphins by docking at receptor sites intended for endorphins, dulling pain and stimulating brain centers that produce pleasurable sensations. This helps explain why use of narcotic drugs produces feelings of pleasure (release of dopamine is yet another factor). Investigators have recently learned that drinking alcohol stimulates release of endorphins in the brain as well, which may help to account for why alcohol makes people feel good (Mitchell et al., 2012).

The withdrawal syndrome associated with opioids can be severe. It begins within four to six hours of the last dose. Flu-like symptoms are accompanied by anxiety, feelings of restlessness, irritability, and cravings for the drug. Within a few days, symptoms progress to rapid pulse, high blood pressure, cramps, tremors, hot and cold flashes, fever, vomiting, insomnia, and diarrhea, among others. Although these symptoms can be uncomfortable, they are usually not devastating, especially when other drugs are prescribed to relieve them. Moreover, unlike withdrawal from barbiturates, the withdrawal syndrome rarely results in death.

Morphine Morphine—which receives its name from Morpheus, the Greek god of dreams—was introduced at about the time of the American Civil War. Morphine, a powerful opium derivative, was used liberally to deaden pain from wounds. Physiological dependence on morphine became known as the "soldier's disease." There was little stigma attached to dependence until morphine became a restricted substance.

Heroin Heroin, the most widely used opiate, is a powerful depressant that can create a euphoric rush. Users of heroin claim that it is so pleasurable it can eradicate any thought of food or sex. Heroin was developed in 1875 during a search for a drug that would relieve pain as effectively as morphine, but without causing addiction. Chemist Heinrich Dreser transformed morphine into a drug believed to have "heroic" effects in relieving pain without addiction, which is why it was called *heroin*. Unfortunately, heroin does lead to a strong physiological dependence.

About four million Americans have used heroin at some point in their lives and some 300,000 are current users (SAMHSA, 2012). More than half of current users are addicted to heroin. Most heroin users are men over the age of 25 and the their average age of first use is about 22 years.

Heroin is usually injected either directly beneath the skin (skin popping) or into a vein (mainlining). The effects are

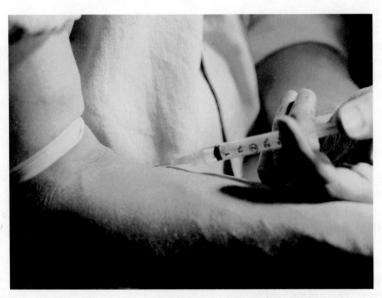

Shooting up. Heroin users often inject the substance directly into their veins. Heroin is a powerful depressant that provides a euphoric rush. Users often claim that heroin is so pleasurable that it obliterates any thought of food or sex.

immediate. There is a powerful rush that lasts from 5 to 15 minutes and a state of satisfaction, euphoria, and well-being that lasts from 3 to 5 hours. In this state, all positive drives seem satisfied. All negative feelings of guilt, tension, and anxiety disappear. With prolonged usage, addiction can develop. Many heroin dependent people support their habits through dealing (selling heroin), prostitution, or selling stolen goods. Heroin is a depressant, however, and its chemical effects do not directly stimulate criminal or aggressive behavior.

Stimulants

Stimulants are psychoactive substances that increase the activity of the central nervous system, which enhances states of alertness, and can produce feelings of pleasure or even euphoric highs. The effects vary with the particular drug.

AMPHETAMINES The **amphetamines** are a class of synthetic stimulants. Street names for stimulants include speed, uppers, bennies (for *amphetamine sulfate;* trade name Benzedrine), meth (for *methamphetamine;* trade name Methedrine), and dexies (for *dextroamphetamine;* trade name Dexedrine).

Amphetamines are used in high doses for their euphoric rush. They are often taken in pill form or smoked in a relatively pure form called ice or crystal meth. The most potent form of amphetamine, liquid methamphetamine, is injected directly into the veins and produces an intense and immediate rush. Some users inject methamphetamine for days on end to maintain an extended high. Eventually such highs come to an end. People who have been on extended highs sometimes "crash" and fall into a deep sleep or depression. Some people commit suicide on the way down. High doses can cause restlessness, irritability, hallucinations, paranoid delusions, loss of appetite, and insomnia.

In one study, about 5% of Americans aged 12 or older reported using meth at some point in their lives and about 0.3% (3 in 1,000) reported using the drug in the past year (SAMHSA, 2012). In all, more than 12 million Americans have used meth at some point in their lives (Jefferson, 2005). Physiological dependence can develop from using amphetamines, leading to an abstinence syndrome characterized by depression and fatigue, as well as by unpleasant, vivid dreams, insomnia or hypersomnia (excessive sleeping), increased appetite, and either a slowing down of motor behavior or agitation (APA, 2013). Psychological dependence is seen most often in people who use amphetamines as a way of coping with stress or depression.

Methamphetamine abuse can cause brain damage, producing deficits in learning and memory in addition to other effects (Thompson et al., 2004; Toomey et al., 2003). Chronic use is also associated with increased depression, aggressive behavior, and social isolation (Homer et al., 2008). Impulsive acts of violence may also occur, especially when the drug is smoked or injected intravenously. The hallucinations and delusions of **amphetamine psychosis** mimic those of paranoid schizophrenia, which has encouraged researchers to study the chemical changes induced by amphetamines as possible clues to the underlying causes of schizophrenia.

ECSTASY The drug *ecstasy,* or MDMA (3,4-methylenedioxymethamphetamine), is a **designer drug,** a chemical knockoff similar in chemical structure to amphetamine. It produces mild euphoria and hallucinations. Teen use of ecstasy dropped significantly in the early years of the new millennium, and then rose for a few years before declining significantly in 2012 (Johnston et al., 2012). Perhaps the message about the dangers of ecstasy is beginning to get across to young people.

Ecstasy can produce adverse psychological effects, including depression, anxiety, insomnia, and even paranoia and psychosis. The drug can cause brain damage that impairs cognitive performance on tasks involving attention, learning, and memory (Di Iorio et al., 2011; de Win et al., 2008). The greater the amount people use, the greater their risk of suffering long-lasting changes in the brain. Scientists suspect the drug kills or damages the neurons that produce the neurotransmitters dopamine and serotonin, key chemicals in the brain involved in regulating mood states and ability to reap pleasure in everyday life (Di Iorio et al., 2011; van Zessen et al., 2012). Physical side effects include higher heart rate and blood pressure, a tense or chattering jaw, and body warmth and/or chills. The drug can be lethal when taken in high doses.

COCAINE It might surprise you to learn that the original formula for Coca-Cola contained an extract of **cocaine.** In 1906, however, the company withdrew cocaine from its secret formula. The drink was originally described as a "brain tonic and intellectual beverage," in part because of its cocaine content. Cocaine is a natural stimulant extracted from the leaves of the coca plant—the plant from which the soft drink obtained its name. Coca-Cola is still flavored with an extract from the coca plant, but one that is not known to have psychoactive effects. **T / F**

It was long believed that cocaine was not physically addicting. However, the drug produces a tolerance effect and an identifiable withdrawal syndrome, which is characterized by depressed mood and disturbances in sleep and appetite. Intense cravings for the drug and loss of ability to experience pleasure may also be present. Withdrawal symptoms are usually brief in duration and may involve a crash, or period of intense depression and exhaustion, following abrupt withdrawal.

Cocaine is usually snorted in powder form or smoked in the form of **crack,** a hardened form of cocaine that may be more than 75% pure. Crack "rocks"—so called because they look like small white pebbles—are available in small, ready-to-smoke amounts and are considered to be the most habit-forming street drug available. Crack produces a prompt and potent rush that wears off in a few minutes. The rush from snorting powdered cocaine is milder and takes a while to develop, but it tends to linger longer than the rush of crack.

Freebasing also intensifies the effects of cocaine. In freebasing, cocaine in powder form is heated with ether, freeing the psychoactive chemical base of the drug, and then smoked. Ether, however, is highly flammable.

Next to marijuana, cocaine is the most widely used illicit drug in the United States. Nearly 15% of Americans aged 12 and older have used cocaine and about 2% have reported using it during the past year (SAMHSA, 2012).

Effects of Cocaine Like heroin, cocaine directly stimulates the brain's reward or pleasure circuits. It also produces a sudden rise in blood pressure and an accelerated heart rate that can cause potentially dangerous, even fatal, irregular heart rhythms. Overdoses can produce restlessness, insomnia, headaches, nausea, convulsions, tremors, hallucinations, delusions, and even sudden death due to respiratory or cardiovascular collapse. Regular snorting of cocaine can lead to serious nasal problems, including ulcers in the nostrils.

Repeated use and high-dose use of cocaine can lead to depression and anxiety. Depression may be severe enough to prompt suicidal behavior. Both initial and routine users report episodes of crashing (feelings of depression after a binge), although crashing is more common among long-term high-dose users. Psychotic behaviors, which can be induced by cocaine use as well as by use of amphetamines, tend to become more severe with continued use. Psychotic symptoms may include intense visual and auditory hallucinations and delusions of persecution.

NICOTINE Habitual smoking is not merely a bad habit: It is also a physical addiction to a stimulant drug, nicotine, found in tobacco products, including cigarettes, cigars, and smokeless tobacco. Smoking is also deadly, claiming nearly 450,000 lives each year in the United States alone, mostly from lung cancer and other lung diseases, as well as cardiovascular (heart and artery) disease (Tobacco Use, 2010). Smoking is recognized as the leading

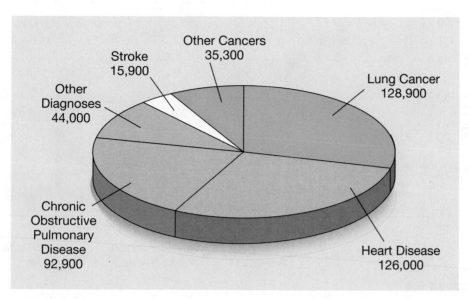

FIGURE 8.2

U.S. deaths attributable each year to cigarette smoking. Cigarette smoking claims the lives of nearly 450,000 Americans annually, mostly from lung cancer, heart disease, and chronic obstructive pulmonary disease. *Source:* Centers for Disease Control, 2008.

health risk in the United States and causes more premature deaths than any other cause, shaving about 10 years off the lifespan of the average smoker (Jha et al., 2013; Schroeder, 2013). Overall, smoking accounts for about one in five deaths of Americans and doubles the risk of dying before age 79 (Benowitz, 2010; Jha et al., 2013). Figure 8.2 shows the breakdown of causes of death in the United States attributable to cigarette smoking (CDC, 2009). The good news is that quitting smoking at any age greatly reduces—but does not eliminate—the increased risk of smoking-related death (Jha et al., 2013; Thun et al., 2013).

The World Health Organization estimates that one billion people worldwide smoke and more than three million die each year from smoking-related causes. The good news is that the percentage of Americans who smoke has declined markedly over the past 50 years, from 43% in the mid-1960s to about 19% today (CDC, 2011; Koh & Sebelius, 2012). Smoking among teens is also on the decline (Kuehn, 2013; Rattue, 2012). The bad news from a health perspective is that about one in five adult Americans still smoke and the rate of decline in smoking rates is actually slowing down (Koh & Sebelius, 2012).

It may surprise you to learn that more women die of lung cancer than any other type of cancer, including breast cancer. Although quitting smoking clearly has health benefits for women and men, it unfortunately does not reduce the risks to normal (nonsmoking) levels. The lesson is clear: If you don't smoke, don't start; if you do smoke, quit.

Ethnic differences in smoking rates are shown in Figure 8.3. With the exception of Native Americans (American Indian/Alaskan Native), women in each ethnic group are less likely to smoke than their male counterparts. Smoking is also becoming increasingly concentrated among people at lower income and educational levels (e.g., Blanco et al., 2008).

Nicotine is delivered to the body through the use of tobacco products. As a stimulant, it increases alertness but it can also give rise to cold, clammy skin, nausea and vomiting, dizziness and faintness, and diarrhea—all of which account for the discomforts of novice smokers. Nicotine also stimulates the release of epinephrine, a hormone

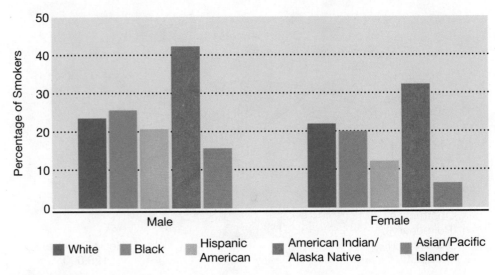

FIGURE 8.3

Ethnic and gender differences in rates of cigarette smoking among U.S. adults. Smoking rates are higher among men than women and among Native Americans (American Indian and Alaska Native) than other major racial/ethnic groups in the United States. *Source:* Centers for Disease Control, 2009.

that generates a rush of autonomic nervous system activity, including rapid heartbeat and release of stores of sugar into the blood. Nicotine quells the appetite and provides a psychological "kick." Nicotine also leads to the release of endorphins, the opiate-like hormones produced in the brain. This may account for the pleasurable feelings associated with tobacco use.

Habitual use of nicotine leads to physiological dependence on the drug. Nicotine dependence is associated with both tolerance (intake rises to a level of a pack or two a day before leveling off) and a characteristic withdrawal syndrome. The withdrawal syndrome for nicotine includes a wide range of features such as lack of energy, depressed mood, irritability, frustration, nervousness, impaired concentration, lightheadedness and dizziness, drowsiness, headaches, fatigue, insomnia, cramps, lowered heart rate, heart palpitations, increased appetite, weight gain, sweating, tremors, and strong craving for cigarettes. About 50% of tobacco users who quit for two or more days show evidence of tobacco withdrawal disorder (APA, 2013).

Smoking gives an almost instant "hit" of the stimulant nicotine. The nicotine in cigarette smoke begins to occupy nicotine receptors in the brain from the first several puffs.

Hallucinogens

Hallucinogens, also known as *psychedelics,* are a class of drugs that produce sensory distortions or hallucinations, including major alterations in color perception and hearing. Hallucinogens may also have other effects, such as relaxation and euphoria or, in some cases, panic.

Hallucinogens include lysergic acid diethylamide (LSD), psilocybin, and mescaline. Psychoactive substances that are similar in effect to psychedelic drugs are marijuana (*cannabis*) and *phencyclidine* (PCP). Mescaline is derived from the peyote cactus and has been used for centuries by Native Americans in the Southwest, Mexico, and Central America in religious ceremonies, as has been psilocybin, which is derived from certain mushrooms. LSD, PCP, and marijuana are the most commonly used hallucinogens in the United States.

Although tolerance to hallucinogens may develop, investigators lack evidence of a consistent or clinically significant withdrawal syndrome associated with their use (APA, 2013). However, cravings following withdrawal may occur.

LSD LSD is a synthetic hallucinogenic drug. In addition to the vivid parade of colors and visual distortions produced by LSD, users have claimed it "expands consciousness" and opens new worlds—as if they were looking into some reality beyond the usual reality. Sometimes they believe they have achieved great insights during the LSD "trip," but when it wears off, they usually cannot follow through or even summon up a memory of these discoveries.

The effects of LSD are unpredictable and depend on the amount taken as well as on the user's expectations, personality, mood, and surroundings. The user's prior experiences with the drug may also play a role, as users who have learned to handle the effects of the drug through past experience may be better prepared than new users.

Some users have unpleasant experiences with the drug, or "bad trips." Feelings of intense fear or panic may occur. Users may fear losing control or sanity. Some experience terrifying fears of death. Fatal accidents have sometimes occurred during LSD trips. *Flashbacks,* typically involving a reexperiencing of some of the perceptual distortions of the "trip," may occur days, weeks, or even years afterward. Flashbacks tend to occur suddenly and often without warning. Perceptual distortions may involve geometric forms, flashes of color, intensified colors, afterimages, or appearances of halos around objects, among others. They likely stem from chemical changes in the brain caused by the prior use of the drug. Triggers for flashbacks include entry into darkened environments, drug use, anxiety or fatigue, or stress. Psychological factors, such as underlying personality problems, may also explain why some users experience flashbacks. In some cases, a flashback may involve an imagined reenactment of the LSD experience.

PHENCYCLIDINE *Phencyclidine*—which is referred to as "angel dust" on the street—was developed as an anesthetic in the 1950s, but its use was discontinued when its hallucinatory side effects were discovered. A smokable form of PCP became popular as a street drug in the 1970s. However, its popularity has since waned, largely because of its unpredictable effects.

The effects of PCP, like most drugs, are dose related. In addition to causing hallucinations, PCP accelerates the heart rate and blood pressure and causes sweating, flushing, and numbness. PCP is classified as a *deliriant*—a drug capable of producing states of delirium. It also has dissociating effects, causing users to feel as if there is some sort of invisible barrier between them and their environment. Dissociation can be experienced as pleasant, engrossing, or frightening, depending on the user's expectations, mood, setting, and so on. Overdoses can give rise to drowsiness and a blank stare, convulsions, and, now and then, coma; paranoia and aggressive behavior; and tragic accidents resulting from perceptual distortion or impaired judgment during states of intoxication.

MARIJUANA Marijuana is derived from the *Cannabis sativa* plant. Marijuana is generally classified as a hallucinogen because it can produce perceptual distortions or mild hallucinations, especially in high doses or when used by susceptible individuals. The psychoactive substance in marijuana is *delta-9-tetrahydrocannabinol,* or THC for short. THC is found in branches and leaves of the plant but is highly concentrated in the resin of the female plant. *Hashish,* or hash, also derived from the resin, is more potent than marijuana but has similar effects.

Among Americans aged 12 or older, about 4 in 10 report having used marijuana or hashish at some point in their lives, and about 11.5% report using the drug during the past year (SAMHSA, 2012). About 1.5% of the U.S. adult population suffer from a cannabis (marijuana) use disorder in the current year (APA, 2013). Men are more likely than women to develop a marijuana use disorder, and rates of these disorders are greatest among people aged 18 to 30.

More teens today use marijuana than either alcohol or tobacco.

☑ **TRUE** Marijuana is more popular today among teens than either alcohol or cigarettes.

8.6 Describe the major theoretical perspectives toward understanding substance use disorders.

On the path to losing IQ points? Recent evidence shows that regular use of marijuana beginning in adolescence is linked to loss of IQ points by midlife.

Did you know that more teens today use marijuana than either alcohol or tobacco? Marijuana use among American youth has been rising for several years, although it stopped trending upward in 2012 (Johnston et al., 2012; Kuehn, 2011a, 2013; Wu et al., 2011). More than one in three 12th graders (36%) reported using marijuana during the previous year (Johnston et al., 2012; Kuehn, 2013). The increased use of marijuana stands in sharp contrast to continuing declines in youths in the use of cocaine. **T / F**

Low doses of the drug can produce relaxing feelings similar to those from drinking alcohol. Some users report that at low doses, the drug makes them feel more comfortable at social gatherings. Higher doses, however, often lead users to withdraw into themselves. Some users believe the drug increases their capacity for self-insight or creative thinking, although the insights achieved under its influence may not seem so insightful once the drug's effects have passed. People may turn to marijuana, and to other drugs as well, to help them cope with life problems or to help them function when they are under stress. Strongly intoxicated people perceive time as passing more slowly. A song of a few minutes may seem to last an hour. There is increased awareness of bodily sensations, such as heartbeat. Smokers also report that strong intoxication heightens sexual sensations. Visual hallucinations may occur.

Strong intoxication can cause smokers to become disoriented. If their moods are euphoric, disorientation may be construed as harmony with the universe. Yet some smokers find strong intoxication disturbing. An accelerated heart rate and sharpened awareness of bodily sensations cause some smokers to fear their hearts will "run away" with them. Some smokers are frightened by disorientation and the fear that they will not "come back." High levels of intoxication now and then induce nausea and vomiting.

Cannabis dependence is associated more with compulsive use or psychological dependence rather than with physiological dependence. Although tolerance to the drug may occur with chronic use, some users report reverse tolerance, or *sensitization,* making them more sensitive to the drug's effects with repeated use. Although a clear-cut withdrawal syndrome has not been reliably demonstrated, evidence does point to a definable withdrawal syndrome in long-term, heavy users who abruptly stop using the drug (Allsop et al., 2012; Mason et al., 2012). Moreover, regular marijuana use can lead to impairment in learning and memory, especially among heavier or more persistent users (Bossong et al., 2012; Han et al., 2012; Meier et al., 2012). Even more troubling is recent evidence that links persistent use of marijuana beginning in adolescence to loss of IQ points by midlife (Kuehn, 2012; Meier et al., 2012).

Evidence also links marijuana use to later use of harder drugs such as heroin and cocaine (Kandel, 2003). Whether marijuana use is a causal factor leading to use of harder drugs remains unclear. It is clear, however, that marijuana impairs perception and motor coordination and thus makes driving and the operation of other heavy machinery dangerous. Recent evidence shows that drivers who used marijuana within three hours of driving were nearly twice as likely to cause a crash as those who were unimpaired by drug use (Asbridge, Hayden, & Cartwright, 2012).

Although marijuana use induces positive mood changes in many users, some people report anxiety and confusion; there are also occasional reports of paranoia or psychotic reactions. Marijuana elevates heart rate and blood pressure and is linked to an increased risk of heart attacks in people with heart disease. And, like cigarettes, smoking marijuana can damage lung tissue and lead to serious respiratory diseases, such as chronic bronchitis, and may increase the risk of lung cancer (Singh et al., 2009; Zickler, 2006).

Theoretical Perspectives

People begin using psychoactive substances for various reasons. Some adolescents start using drugs because of peer pressure or because they believe drugs make them seem more sophisticated or grown up. Some use drugs as a way of rebelling against their parents or society at large. Regardless of why people get started with drugs, they continue to use them because drugs produce pleasurable effects or because they find it difficult to stop. Most adolescents, however, drink alcohol to get high, not to establish that they are adults. Many people smoke cigarettes for the pleasure they provide. Others smoke to help them relax when they are tense and, paradoxically, to give them a kick or a lift when they are tired. Many would like to quit but find it difficult to break their addiction.

People who are anxious about their jobs or social lives may be drawn to the calming effects of alcohol, marijuana (in certain doses), tranquilizers, and sedatives. People with low self-confidence and self-esteem may be drawn to the ego-bolstering effects of amphetamines and cocaine. Many poor young people attempt to escape the poverty, anguish, and tedium of inner-city life through use of heroin and similar drugs. More well-to-do adolescents may rely on drugs to manage the transition from dependence to independence and major life changes concerning jobs, college, and lifestyles. In the next sections, we consider several major theoretical perspectives on drug use and abuse.

Biological Perspectives

Investigators are beginning to learn much more about the biological underpinnings of drug use and addiction. Much of the recent research has focused on the roles of neurotransmitters, especially dopamine, and genetic factors.

NEUROTRANSMITTERS Many drugs of abuse, including nicotine, alcohol, heroin, marijuana, and especially cocaine and amphetamines, produce pleasurable effects by increasing the availability of the neurotransmitter dopamine, a key brain chemical involved in activation of the brain's reward or pleasure circuits—the networks of neurons that produce feelings of pleasure (Flagel et al., 2011; Voruganti & Awad, 2007; Whitten, 2009). When we eat because we are hungry or drink because we are thirsty, reward pathways in the brain become flooded with dopamine, producing feelings of pleasure associated with engaging in these life-sustaining activities. Neuroscientists find that in people with alcohol dependence, even the mere exposure to words associated with alcohol can activate reward pathways in the brain, the network of interconnected neurons that produce feelings of pleasure (see Figure 8.4).

The role of dopamine is yet more complex; it motivates us to pay attention to objects linked to rewarding behaviors and basic survival needs, such as food when we're hungry or threatening animals or other dangers (Angier, 2009). For addicts, the steady influx of dopamine from using drugs makes it difficult for them to focus on anything other than attaining and using drugs, even if the drugs no longer produce feelings of pleasure.

Over time, regular use of drugs such as cocaine, alcohol, and heroin may sap the brain's own production of dopamine. Consequently, the brain's natural reward system— the "feel good" circuitry that produces states of pleasure associated with the ordinarily rewarding activities of life, such as consuming a satisfying meal and engaging in pleasant activities—becomes blunted (Dubovsky, 2006). Evidence based on brain imaging shows lower levels of naturally produced dopamine in the brains of cocaine-dependent individuals (Martinez et al., 2009). An addict's brain may come to depend on having a supply of the drug available in order to produce any feelings of pleasure or satisfaction (Denizet-Lewis, 2006). Without drugs, life may not seem to be worth living.

Changes in the dopamine system may help explain the intense cravings and anxiety that accompany drug withdrawal and the difficulty people have in maintaining abstinence. But other neurotransmitters, including serotonin and endorphins, also appear to play important roles in drug abuse and dependence (Addolorato et al., 2005; Buchert et al., 2004).

Consider the role of endorphins, a class of neurotransmitters that have pain-blocking properties similar to those of opioids such as heroin. As we discussed earlier, endorphins and opiates dock at the same receptor sites in the brain. Normally, the brain produces a certain level of endorphins that maintains a psychological steady state of

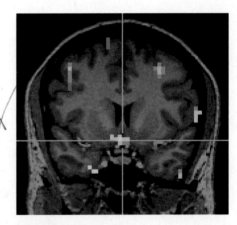

FIGURE 8.4

Your brain in response to alcohol words. In a recent fMRI study, a group of alcohol-dependent women showed greater levels of brain activation in parts of the limbic system and frontal lobes (indicated by yellow/orange colors) in response to alcohol cue words (e.g., *keg, binge*) than did a group of women who were light social drinkers. These parts of the brain are involved in reward pathways activated by use of alcohol and other drugs. These findings suggest that in people with alcohol dependence, the mere exposure to words associated with alcohol may produce similar effects in the brain as the drug itself. *Source:* Tapert, Brown, Baratta, & Brown, 2004.

comfort and potential to experience pleasure. However, when the body becomes habituated to a supply of opioids, it may stop producing endorphins. This makes the user dependent on opiates for comfort, relief from pain, and pleasure. When the habitual user stops using heroin or other opiates, feelings of discomfort and little aches and pains may be magnified until the body resumes adequate production of endorphins. This discomfort may account, at least in part, for the unpleasant withdrawal symptoms that people who are addicted to heroin or other opiates experience. However, this model remains speculative, and more research is needed to document direct relationships between endorphin production and withdrawal symptoms.

GENETIC FACTORS Evidence points to an important role for genetic factors in a range of substance use disorders involving alcohol, amphetamines, cocaine, heroin, and even tobacco (e.g., Ducci et al., 2011; Frahm et al., 2011; Hartz et al., 2012; Kendler et al., 2012; Ray, 2012). People who have a family history of substance use disorders stand a four to eight times greater chance of developing these disorders themselves (Urbanoski & Kelly, 2012). Environmental factors, such as family influences and peer pressure, appear to play a more important role in the initiation of drug use in early adolescence, whereas genetic factors play a prominent role in explaining continuation of drug use through early and middle adulthood (Kendler et al., 2008).

Investigators have begun to hunt for specific genes involved in alcohol and drug dependence or addiction (Ray et al., 2012; Sullivan et al., 2013). Our focus here is on the genetic underpinnings of alcohol dependence, because this has been the area of greatest research interest. However, it appears that some genes involved in alcoholism are also involved in other forms of addiction, such as addiction to cocaine, nicotine (regular smoking), and heroin (Ming & Burmeister, 2009).

Alcoholism tends to run in families. The closer the genetic relationship, the greater the risk. Familial patterns provide only suggestive evidence of genetic factors, because families share a common environment as well as common genes. More definitive evidence comes from twin and adoptee studies.

Monozygotic (MZ) twins have identical genes, whereas fraternal or dizygotic (DZ) twins share only half of their genes. If genetic factors are involved, we would expect MZ twins to have higher concordance (agreement) rates for alcoholism than DZ twins. We have converging evidence that points to an important genetic contribution to alcoholism (MacKillop, McGeary, & Ray, 2010). First, there is a large body of evidence showing higher concordance rates for alcoholism among MZ twins than among DZ twins, which is consistent with a genetic contribution to alcoholism. Second, among adopted children raised in nonalcoholic families, those having a family history of alcoholism are more prone to develop alcoholism themselves than are those without alcoholism in their families.

If problem drinking and alcoholism are influenced by genetic factors, what exactly is inherited? Some clues have emerged (e.g., Corbett et al., 2005; Radel et al., 2005). Alcoholism, nicotine dependence, and opioid addiction are linked to genes that determine the structure of dopamine receptors in the brain. As we've noted, dopamine is involved in regulating states of pleasure, so one possibility is that genetic factors enhance feelings of pleasure derived from alcohol.

The genetic vulnerability to alcoholism most probably involves a combination of factors, such as reaping greater pleasure from alcohol and a capacity for greater biological tolerance for the drug. People who can tolerate larger doses of alcohol without incurring upset stomachs, dizziness, and headaches may have difficulty knowing when to stop drinking. Thus, people who are better able to "hold their liquor" may be at greater risk of developing drinking problems. They may need to rely on other cues, such as counting their drinks, to limit their drinking. Other people whose bodies more readily "put the brakes" on excess drinking may be less likely to develop problems in moderating their drinking. T / F

Whatever role genetics may play in alcohol dependence and other forms of substance dependence, genes do not dictate behavior. Environment also plays a role, as do

---

8.7 Explain how cocaine affects the brain.

---

truth OR fiction

People who can "hold their liquor" better than most stand a lower risk of becoming problem drinkers.

☑ **FALSE** A high physical tolerance for liquor may lead a person to drink excessively, which may set the stage for problem drinking.

How Cocaine Affects the Brain

Cocaine works on the brain's use of dopamine (see Figure 8.5). Cocaine interferes with the process of *reuptake* by which excess molecules of dopamine are reabsorbed by the transmitting neuron. As a result, high levels of dopamine remain active in the synaptic gaps between neurons in brain networks that control feelings of pleasure, overstimulating neurons that produce states of pleasure, including the euphoric high associated with cocaine use. In effect, cocaine and other drugs such as heroin and alcohol that also affect dopamine feel good because of the effects they have on the availability of dopamine in the brain's reward or pleasure networks. However, regular use of cocaine over time makes the brain less capable of producing dopamine on its own. Consequently, cocaine abusers crash when they stop using the drug because the brain is stripped of its own supply of this pleasure-producing chemical.

1. Neurotransmitters, such as dopamine, are stored in synaptic vesicles in the sending neuron and released into the synaptic gap. Normally, excess molecules of neurotransmitters not taken up by receptor sites are absorbed by the sending neuron in a recycling process called *reuptake*.

2. Cocaine (orange circles in diagram) blocks the reuptake of dopamine by the sending neuron.

3. The accumulation of dopamine in the synapse overstimulates neurons in key reward pathways in the brain, producing a pleasurable "high." Over time, the brain becomes less capable of producing feelings of pleasure on its own, leading users to "crash" if they stop using the drug.

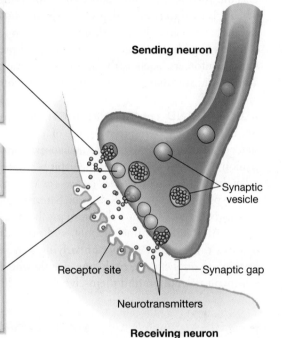

Sending neuron

Synaptic vesicle

Receptor site

Synaptic gap

Neurotransmitters

Receiving neuron

FIGURE 8.5

Cocaine's effects on the brain.

Source: Adapted from National Institute on Drug Abuse, U.S. Department of Health and Human Services, National Institutes of Health. Research Report Series: Cocaine Abuse and Addiction. NIH Publication Number 99-4342, revised November 2004. Reprinted from J.S. Nevid, Psychology: Concepts and Applications, 2009, with permission of Cengage Learning.

👁 **Watch** the **Video** *In the Real World: Neurotransmitters* on **MyPsychLab**

---

interactions of genetic and environmental factors. For example, investigators report that drug use among a sample of young people at heightened genetic risk of developing drug abuse problems was reduced for those who had highly supportive parents (Brody et al., 2009). Similarly, other investigators reported that being raised by parents free of alcoholism was associated with a lower risk of developing alcohol-related disorders in people at high genetic risk of alcohol-related problems (Jacob et al., 2003). In effect, good parenting can reduce the influence of bad genes. In sum, we can say that genetic factors act together with environmental and psychological factors in contributing to the development of substance use disorders.

Learning Perspectives

Learning theorists propose that substance use behaviors are largely learned and can, in principle, be unlearned. They focus on the roles of operant and classical conditioning and observational learning. Drug-related problems are not regarded as symptoms of disease but rather as problem habits. Although learning theorists do not deny that genetic or biological factors may increase susceptibility to substance abuse problems, they emphasize the role of learning in the development and maintenance of these problem behaviors. They also recognize that people who suffer from depression or anxiety may turn to alcohol as a way of relieving these troubling emotional states, however brief the relief may be. Emotional stress, such as anxiety or depression, often sets the stage for the development of drug-related problems.

Drug use may become habitual because it produces feelings of pleasure (positive reinforcement) or temporary relief (negative reinforcement) from negative emotions, such as anxiety and depression. With drugs like cocaine, which appear capable of directly stimulating pleasure mechanisms in the brain, the positive reinforcement is direct and powerful.

OPERANT CONDITIONING People may initially use a drug because of social influence, trial and error, or social observation. In the case of alcohol, they learn that the drug can produce reinforcing effects, such as feelings of euphoria, and reductions in anxiety and tension. Alcohol may also reduce behavioral inhibitions. Alcohol can thus be reinforcing when it is used to combat depression (by producing euphoric feelings, even if short lived), to combat tension (by functioning as a tranquilizer), or to help people sidestep moral conflicts (e.g., by dulling awareness of moral prohibitions). Drug abuse may also provide social reinforcers, such as the approval of drug-abusing companions and, in the cases of alcohol and stimulants, the (temporary) overcoming of social shyness.

ALCOHOL AND TENSION REDUCTION Learning theorists have long maintained that one of the primary reinforcers for use of alcohol is relief from states of tension or unpleasant states of arousal. According to the *tension-reduction theory,* the more often one drinks to reduce tension or anxiety, the stronger the habit becomes. We can think of these uses of alcohol and other drugs as forms of *self-medication*—as a means of using the pill or the bottle to temporarily ease psychological pain (Robinson, Sareen, Cox, & Bolton, 2009). We can see this pattern of negative reinforcement (relief from psychological pain) in the following case example.

Although nicotine, alcohol, and other drugs may temporarily alleviate emotional distress, they cannot resolve underlying personal or emotional problems. Rather than learning to resolve these problems, people who turn to alcohol or other drugs as forms of self-medication often find themselves facing additional substance use problems.

> ### "I" "Taking Away the Hurt I Feel"
>
> "I use them [the pills and alcohol] to take away the hurt I feel inside." Joceyln, a 36-year-old mother of two, was physically abused by her husband, Phil. "I have no self-esteem. I just don't feel I can do anything," she told her therapist. Joceyln had escaped from an abusive family background by getting married at age 17, hoping that marriage would offer her a better life. The first few years were free of abuse, but things changed when Phil lost his job and began to drink heavily. By then, Jocelyn had two young children and felt trapped. She blamed herself for her unhappy family life, for Phil's drinking, for her son's learning disability. "The only thing I can do is drink or do pills. At least then I don't have to think about things for a while." Although drug use temporarily dulled her emotional pain, it came with a greater long-term cost in terms of the burden of addiction.
>
> *From the Author's Files*

NEGATIVE REINFORCEMENT AND WITHDRAWAL Once people become physiologically dependent, negative reinforcement comes into play in maintaining the drug habit. In other words, people may resume using drugs to gain relief from unpleasant withdrawal symptoms. In operant conditioning terms, relief from unpleasant withdrawal symptoms is a negative reinforcer for resuming drug use (Higgins, Heil, & Lussier, 2004). For example, the addicted smoker who quits cold turkey may shortly return to smoking to fend off the discomfort of withdrawal.

THE CONDITIONING MODEL OF CRAVINGS Classical conditioning may help explain some forms of drug cravings. In some cases, cravings may represent a conditioned response to environmental cues associated with prior use of the substance (Kilts, Gross, Ely, & Drexler, 2004). In people with drug-related problems, exposure to cues such as the sight or aroma of an alcoholic beverage or the sight of a needle and syringe can become conditioned stimuli that elicit the conditioned response of strong drug cravings. For example, socializing with certain companions ("drinking buddies") or even passing a liquor store may elicit conditioned cravings for alcohol. In support of this theory, people who suffer from alcoholism show distinctive changes in brain activity in areas of the brain that regulate emotion, attention, and appetitive behavior when shown pictures of alcoholic beverages (George et al., 2001). Social drinkers, by comparison, do not show this pattern of brain activation.

Negative emotional states, such as anxiety and depression that have been paired with the use of alcohol or drugs in the past may also elicit cravings. The following case illustrates cravings conditioned to environmental cues.

Self-medication? People who turn to alcohol or other drugs to quell disturbing emotions can compound their problems by developing a substance use disorder.

A Case of Conditioned Drug Cravings

A 29-year-old man was hospitalized for the treatment of heroin addiction. After four weeks of treatment, he returned to his former job, which required him to ride the subway past the stop at which he had previously bought his drugs. Each day, when the subway doors opened at this location, [he] experienced enormous craving for heroin, accompanied by tearing, a runny nose, abdominal cramps, and gooseflesh. After the doors closed, his symptoms disappeared, and he went on to work.

From Weiss, R. D., & Mirin, S. M. (1987). Cocaine. Washington, DC: American Psychiatric Association.

Similarly, some people are primarily "stimulus smokers." They reach for a cigarette in the presence of smoking-related stimuli, such as seeing someone else smoke or smelling smoke. Smoking becomes a strongly conditioned habit because it is paired repeatedly with many situational cues—watching TV, finishing dinner, driving in the car, studying, drinking or socializing with friends, sex, and, for some, using the bathroom.

The conditioning model of craving is supported by early research showing that people with alcoholism tend to salivate more than others at the sight and smell of alcohol (Monti et al., 1987). Pavlov's classic experiment conditioned a salivation response in dogs by repeatedly pairing the sound of a bell (a conditioned stimulus) with the presentation of food powder (an unconditioned stimulus). Salivation among people who develop alcoholism can also be viewed as a conditioned response to alcohol-related cues. People with drinking problems who show the greatest salivary response to alcohol cues may be at highest risk of relapse. They may also profit from conditioning-based treatments designed to extinguish responses to alcohol-related cues.

In a form of treatment for alcoholism called *cue exposure training,* the person is seated in front of alcohol-related cues, such as open alcoholic beverages, but is prevented from imbibing (Dawe, Rees, Mattick, Sitharthan, Heather, 2002). The pairing of the cue (alcohol bottle) with nonreinforcement (by dint of preventing drinking) may lead to extinction of the conditioned cravings. However, cravings can return after treatment, and often do return when people go back to their usual environments (Havermans & Jansen, 2003).

OBSERVATIONAL LEARNING Modeling or observational learning plays an important role in determining risk of drug-related problems. Parents who model inappropriate or excessive drinking or use of illicit drugs may set the stage for maladaptive drug use in their children (Kirisci, Vanyukov, & Tarter, 2005). Evidence shows that adolescents who have a parent who smokes face a substantially higher risk of smoking than do their peers in families where neither parent smokes (Peterson et al., 2006). Other investigators find that having friends who smoke influences adolescents to begin smoking (Bricker et al., 2006).

Cognitive Perspectives

Evidence supports the role of cognitive factors in drug-related problems, especially the role of expectancies (Doran, Schweizer, & Myers, 2011). Holding positive expectancies about drug use, such as believing that drinking alcohol makes you more popular or outgoing, increases the likelihood of use of these substances (e.g., Cable & Sacker, 2007; Mitchell et al., 2006). Outcome expectancies in teens—what they expect a drug's effects will be—are strongly influenced by the beliefs held by others in their social environment, including friends and parents (e.g., Donovan, Molina, & Kelly, 2009; Gunn & Smith, 2010).

Alcohol or other drug use may also boost *self-efficacy expectations*—personal expectancies we hold about our ability to successfully perform tasks. If we believe we need a drink or two (or more) to "get out of our shell" and relate socially to others, we may come to depend on alcohol in social situations.

Expectancies may account for the "one-drink effect"—the tendency of chronic alcohol abusers to binge once they have a drink. The late psychologist G. Alan Marlatt (1978) explained the one-drink effect as a type of self-fulfilling prophecy. If people with alcohol-related problems believe that just one drink will cause a loss of control, they may perceive the outcome as predetermined when they drink. Having even one drink may thus escalate into a binge. This type of expectation is an example of what Aaron Beck calls *absolutist thinking*. When we insist on seeing the world in black and white rather than shades of gray—as either complete successes or complete failures—we may interpret one bite of dessert as proof that we are off our diets, or one cigarette as proof that we are hooked again. Rather than telling ourselves, "Okay, I goofed, but that's it. I don't have to have more," we encode our lapses as catastrophes and transform them into relapses. Still, alcohol-dependent people who believe they may go on a drinking binge if they have just one drink are well advised to abstain.

Psychodynamic Perspectives

According to traditional psychodynamic theory, alcoholism reflects an *oral-dependent personality*. Psychodynamic theory also associates excessive alcohol use with other oral traits, such as dependence and depression, and traces the origins of these traits to fixation in the oral stage of psychosexual development during infancy. Excessive drinking or smoking in adulthood symbolizes an individual's efforts to attain oral gratification.

Research support for these psychodynamic concepts is mixed. Although people who develop alcoholism often show dependent traits, it is unclear whether dependence contributes to or stems from problem drinking. Chronic drinking, for example, is connected with loss of employment and downward movement in social status, both of which would render drinkers more reliant on others for support. Moreover, an empirical connection between dependence and alcoholism does not establish that alcoholism represents an oral fixation that can be traced to infant development.

Then, too, many—but certainly not all—people who suffer from alcoholism have antisocial personalities characterized by independence-seeking as expressed through rebelliousness and rejection of social and legal codes. All in all, there doesn't appear to be any single alcoholic personality.

Sociocultural Perspectives

Drinking is determined, in part, by where we live, whom we worship with, and the social or cultural norms that regulate our behavior. Cultural attitudes can encourage or discourage problem drinking. As we have already seen, rates of alcohol abuse vary across ethnic

Subliminal Cues Trigger Brain Responses in Cocaine Abuse Patients

We've noted that exposure to drug-related cues, such as the sight of a bottle of Scotch whiskey or of a needle and syringe, can elicit drug cravings in people with drug-related problems. But a recent study with cocaine-abusing patients goes a step further. Investigators flashed cocaine-related images at blinding speeds that the patients could not consciously perceive (see Figure 8.6). Yet these "unseen" cues activated parts of the brain's *limbic system*, the interconnected parts of the inner brain involved in processing basic emotional responses, which is implicated in drug cravings and drug-seeking behavior (Childress et al., 2008) (see Figure 8.7). Dr. Nora Volkow, the director of the National Institute on Drug Abuse (NIDA), observed, "This is the first evidence that cues outside one's awareness can trigger rapid activation of the circuits driving drug-seeking behavior" (cited in "Subliminal Signals," 2008).

Activations

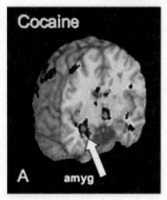
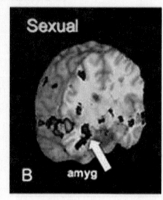

FIGURE 8.7

Limbic system response to "unseen" drug-related stimuli. Parts of the limbic system in the brain, including the amygdala (denoted here by *amyg*), become active in response to cocaine-related images flashed at such a high speed that they are not consciously perceived. A similar pattern of activation was found for "unseen" sexual cues, suggesting that drug-related cues activated similar reward pathways in the brain as sexual cues. Source: Childress et al., 2008.

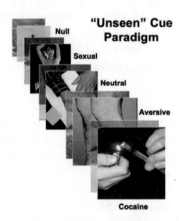

FIGURE 8.6

Visual stimuli used in subliminal cue study. These are examples of visual cues flashed to male cocaine patients to determine whether brain circuits involved in reward pathways of the brain would respond even if the stimuli themselves remained unseen. Source: Childress et al., 2008.

This research underscores the problems faced by patients with cocaine and other substance abuse problems. They may be exposed daily to images—even mere glimpses of images—that activate networks in the brain that prompt craving responses. As NIDA director Volkow puts it, "Patients often can't pinpoint when or why they start craving drugs. Understanding how the brain initiates that overwhelming desire for drugs is essential to treating addiction."

Compounding the problem further is that parts of the brain activated by drug-related subliminal cues are those that also become active in response to sexual images. Drug cravings may tap into the same reward systems as those involved in basic rewards such as sexual gratification and food consumption.

and religious groups. Let's note some other sociocultural factors. Church attendance, for example, is generally connected with abstinence from alcohol. Perhaps people who are more willing to engage in culturally sanctioned activities, such as churchgoing, are also more likely to adopt culturally sanctioned prohibitions against excessive drinking.

Peer pressure and exposure to a drug subculture are important influences in determining substance use among adolescents and young adults (Dishion & Owen, 2002; Hu, Davies, & Kandel, 2006). Children who start drinking before age 15 stand a five-fold higher risk of developing alcohol dependence in adulthood as compared with those who began drinking at a later age (Kluger, 2001). Yet studies of Hispanic and African American adolescents show that support from family members can reduce the negative influence of drug-using peers on the adolescent's use of tobacco and other drugs (Farrell & White, 1998; Frauenglass, Routh, Pantin, & Mason, 1997).

Treatment of Substance Use Disorders

There is a vast array of nonprofessional, biological, and psychological approaches to treating problems with substance abuse and dependence. However, treatment has often been a frustrating endeavor. In many, perhaps most, cases, drug-dependent people may not be ready or motivated to change their drug use behavior or may not seek treatment on their own. Substance abuse counselors may use techniques such as *motivational interviewing* to first increase their clients' readiness to make changes in their lives (Martins & McNeil, 2009; Miller & Rollnick, 2002). In a supportive rather than confrontational manner, counselors help clients recognize the problems caused by their drug use and the risks they face in continuing to use drugs. They then focus on raising clients' awareness of the differences between their present circumstances and how they want their lives to be and the steps they need to take to make these changes.

When drug-dependent people are ready to break free of drugs, the process of helping them through the withdrawal syndrome is an important first step. However, helping them pursue a life devoid of their preferred substances is more problematic. Treatment takes place in a setting—such as the therapist's office, a support group, a residential center, or a hospital—in which abstinence is valued and encouraged. Then the individual returns to the work, family, or street settings in which abuse and dependence were instigated and maintained. The problem of relapse can thus be more troublesome than the problems involved in initial treatment.

Another complication is that many people with drug-related problems have other psychological disorders as well. However, most clinics and treatment programs focus on the drug or alcohol problem, or the other psychological disorders, rather than treating all these problems simultaneously. This narrow focus results in poorer treatment outcomes, including more frequent rehospitalizations among those with these *dual diagnoses*.

Biological Approaches

An increasing range of biological approaches are being used in treating substance use disorders (Quenqua, 2012; Wessell & Edwards, 2010). For people with chemical dependencies, biological treatment typically begins with **detoxification**—that is, helping them through withdrawal from addictive substances.

DETOXIFICATION Detoxification is often more safely carried out in a hospital setting. In the case of addiction to alcohol or barbiturates, hospitalization allows medical personnel to monitor and treat potentially dangerous withdrawal symptoms such as convulsions. Antianxiety drugs, such as the benzodiazepines Librium and Valium, may help block severe withdrawal symptoms such as seizures and delirium tremens. Detoxification to alcohol takes about a week. Detoxification is an important step toward staying clean, but it is only a start. Approximately half of all drug abusers relapse within a year of detoxification (Cowley, 2001). Continuing support and structured therapy, such as behavioral counseling, plus possible use of therapeutic drugs, increase the chances of long-term success.

A number of therapeutic drugs are used in treating people with chemical dependencies, and more chemical compounds are in the testing stage. Here, we survey some of the major therapeutic drugs in use today.

DISULFIRAM The drug *disulfiram* (Antabuse) discourages alcohol consumption because the combination of the two—the drug and the alcohol—produces a violent response consisting of nausea, headache, heart palpitations, and vomiting. In some extreme cases, combining disulfiram and alcohol can produce such a dramatic drop in blood pressure that the individual goes into shock or even dies. Although disulfiram has been used widely in alcoholism treatment, its effectiveness is limited because many patients who want to continue drinking simply stop using the drug. Others stop taking the drug because they believe they can remain abstinent without it. Unfortunately, many return to uncontrolled drinking. Another drawback is that the drug has toxic effects in people with liver disease, a frequent ailment of people who suffer from alcoholism. Little evidence supports the efficacy of the drug in the long run.

ANTIDEPRESSANTS Antidepressants may help reduce cravings for cocaine following withdrawal. These drugs stimulate neural processes that promote feelings of pleasure derived from everyday experiences. If cocaine users can feel pleasure from non-drug-related activities, they may be less likely to return to using cocaine. However, antidepressants have yet to produce consistent results in reducing relapse rates for cocaine dependence, so it is best to withhold judgment concerning their efficacy. The antidepressant drug *bupropion* (Zyban) is used to blunt cravings for nicotine in much the same way that other antidepressants are being used to reduce cocaine cravings. The drug has a modest benefit in helping people quit smoking successfully (Croghan et al., 2007).

The drug *varenicline* (trade name Chantix) may be helpful in quitting smoking, but its effectiveness in scientific studies appears to be rather modest (e.g., Dubovsky, 2011; Garza et al., 2011). The drug works on the brain to blunt the pleasurable effects of nicotine while also helping to prevent cravings for nicotine following smoking cessation (Franklin et al., 2011). However, the drug is linked to serious complications, including increased risks of depression and suicidal behaviors as compared with other smoking-cessation treatments ("Chantix Unsuitable," 2011; Moore, Furberg, Glenmullen, Maltsberger, & Singh, 2011).

NICOTINE REPLACEMENT THERAPY Most regular smokers, perhaps the great majority, are nicotine dependent. The use of nicotine replacements in the form of prescription gum (Nicorette), transdermal (skin) patches, and nasal sprays can help smokers avoid unpleasant withdrawal symptoms and cravings for cigarettes (Strasser et al., 2005). After quitting smoking, ex-smokers can gradually wean themselves from the nicotine replacement. Evidence supports the therapeutic benefits of nicotine replacement therapy, although men seem to benefit more than women (e.g., Japuntich, Piper, Leventhal, Bolt, & Baker, 2011; Strasser et al., 2005).

Although nicotine replacement can help quell the physiological components of withdrawal, it has no effect on the behavioral patterns of addiction, such as the habit of smoking while drinking alcohol or socializing. As a result, nicotine replacement may be ineffective in promoting long-term changes unless it is combined with behavior therapy that focuses on fostering adaptive behavioral changes.

METHADONE MAINTENANCE PROGRAMS **Methadone** is a synthetic opiate that blunts cravings for heroin and helps curb the unpleasant symptoms that accompany withdrawal. Because methadone in normal doses does not produce a high or leave the user feeling drugged, it can help heroin addicts hold jobs and get their lives back on track (Schwartz et al., 2006). However, like other opioids, methadone is highly addictive. For this reason, people treated with methadone are, in effect, substituting dependence on one drug for dependence on another. Yet, because most methadone programs are publicly financed, they relieve people addicted to heroin of the need to resort to criminal activity to support their drug habit. Although methadone is safer than heroin, its use needs to be strictly monitored because overdoses can be lethal and it may become abused as a street drug (Veilleux, Colvin, Anderson, York, & Heinz, 2010).

Since the introduction of methadone treatment, the annual death rate from opioid dependence has declined significantly (Krantz & Mehler, 2004). One frequent criticism of methadone treatment is that many participants continue to take the drug indefinitely, potentially even for a lifetime, rather than be weaned from it. However, proponents of methadone treatment point out that the measure of success should be whether people are able to take care of themselves and their families and act responsibly, not how long they continue to receive treatment (Marion, 2005). Even so, not everyone succeeds in treatment. Some patients turn to other drugs, such as cocaine, to get a high or return to using heroin. Others drop out of methadone programs and resume using heroin.

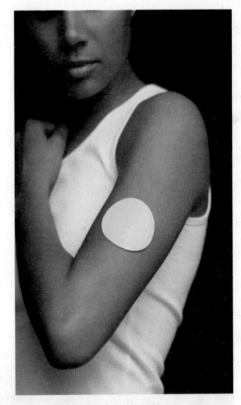

Is the path to abstinence from smoking skin deep? Forms of nicotine replacement therapy, such as the nicotine transdermal (skin) patch shown here and nicotine chewing gum, allow people to continue to take in nicotine when they quit smoking. Although nicotine replacement therapy is more effective than a placebo in helping people quit smoking, it does not address the behavioral components of addiction to nicotine, such as the habit of smoking while drinking alcohol. For this reason, nicotine replacement therapy may be more effective if it is combined with behavior therapy that focuses on changing smoking habits.

A widely used treatment for heroin
addiction involves substituting one
addictive drug for another.

☑ **TRUE** Methadone, a synthetic
narcotic, is widely used in treating
heroin addiction.

Buprenorphine, another synthetic opiate drug that is chemically similar to morphine, blocks withdrawal symptoms and cravings without producing a strong narcotic high (Ling et al., 2011; Veilleux et al., 2010). Many treatment providers prefer buprenorphine to methadone because it produces less of a sedative effective and can be taken in pill form only three times a week, whereas methadone is given in liquid form daily. *Levomethadyl,* another synthetic anti-opiate, also lasts longer than methadone and can be dispensed three times a week. The inclusion of psychosocial treatments, such as counseling and rehabilitation services, can help boost adherence to treatment with methadone or other therapeutic drugs (Veilleux et al., 2010). T / F

NALTREXONE **Naltrexone** is a drug that helps block the high or feelings of pleasure produced by alcohol, opioids such as heroin, and amphetamines. The drug doesn't prevent the person from taking a drink or using another drug, but seems to blunt cravings for these drugs (Anton, 2008; Myrick et al., 2008;). Blocking the pleasure produced by drugs may help break the vicious cycle in which one drink or ingestion of a drug creates a desire for more. However, evidence of the effectiveness of naltrexone and similar drugs in treating alcohol, opiate, and amphetamine dependence is mixed, with some studies showing benefits and others not (e.g., Anton et al., 2011; Jayaram-Lindström, Hammarberg, Beck, & Franck, 2008; Woody et al., 2008; Veilleux et al., 2010).

A nagging problem with drugs such as naltrexone, disulfiram, and methadone is that people who are suffering from drug addiction may drop out of treatment programs or simply stop using the drugs and soon return to their substance-abusing behavior. Nor do such drugs provide alternative sources of positive reinforcement that can replace the pleasurable states produced by drugs of abuse. These therapeutic drugs are effective only in the context of a broader treatment program consisting of psychological counseling and life skills components, such as job and stress management training. These treatments provide people with the skills they need to embark on a life in the mainstream culture and to find drug-free means for coping with stress (Fouquereau, Fernandez, Mullet, & Sorum, 2003).

Culturally Sensitive Treatment of Alcoholism

Members of ethnic minority groups may resist traditional treatment approaches because they feel excluded from full participation in society. Native American women, for example, tend to respond less favorably to traditional alcoholism counseling than White women (Rogan, 1986). Hurlburt and Gade (1984) attribute this difference to the resistance of Native American women to "White man's" authority, suggesting that Native American counselors might be more successful in overcoming this resistance.

THINKING CRITICALLY about abnormal psychology

@Issue: Should We Use Drugs to Treat Drug Abuse?

A variety of therapeutic drugs are used to treat drug addiction, including disulfiram for alcoholism, nicotine replacement for smoking dependence, antidepressants for cocaine dependence, and the most controversial of all, the opioid methadone to treat dependence on the opioid heroin. It may seem ironic, indeed paradoxical, to use drugs to treat problems with drugs.

In thinking critically about the issue of using therapeutic drugs to treat problems of drug abuse, answer the following questions:

- What drawbacks, if any, do you see in using therapeutic drugs to treat drug addiction?

- Should heroin addicts be given free opiates in the form of methadone by the government? Why or why not?

- Should there be limits placed on methadone treatment requiring people to be weaned from the drug after a certain period of time, or should they be permitted to take methadone as long as they feel they need it?

The use of counselors from the client's own ethnic group is an example of a *culturally sensitive treatment approach*. Culturally sensitive programs address all facets of the human being, including racial and cultural identity, that nurture pride and help people resist the temptation to cope with stress through chemicals. Culturally sensitive treatment approaches have been extended to other forms of drug dependence, including programs for smoking cessation (e.g., Nevid & Javier, 1997; Nevid, Javier, & Moulton, 1996).

Treatment providers may also be more successful if they recognize and incorporate indigenous forms of healing into treatment. For example, spirituality is an important aspect of traditional Native American culture, and spiritualists have played important roles as natural healers. Seeking the assistance of a spiritualist may improve the counseling relationship. Likewise, given the importance of the church in African American and Hispanic American cultures, counselors working with people with alcohol use disorders from these groups may be more successful when they draw on clergy and church members as resources.

Nonprofessional Support Groups

Despite the complexity of the factors contributing to drug abuse, drug treatment services are frequently provided by laypeople or nonprofessionals. Such people often have or had the same problems themselves. For example, self-help group meetings are sponsored by organizations such as Alcoholics Anonymous, Narcotics Anonymous, and Cocaine Anonymous. These groups promote abstinence and provide members an opportunity to discuss their feelings and experiences in a supportive group setting. More experienced group members (sponsors) support newer members during periods of crisis or potential relapse. The meetings are sustained by nominal voluntary contributions.

Culturally sensitive treatment. Culturally sensitive therapy or treatment addresses all aspects of the person, including ethnic factors and the nurturance of pride in one's cultural identity. Ethnic pride may help people resist the temptation to cope with stress through alcohol and other substances.

Alcoholics Anonymous, the most widely used nonprofessional program, is based on the belief that alcoholism is a disease, not a sin. The AA philosophy holds that people suffering from alcoholism will never be cured, regardless of how long they abstain from alcohol; rather, people with alcoholism who remain "clean and sober" are seen as "recovering alcoholics." It is also assumed that people who suffer from alcoholism cannot control their drinking and need help to stop drinking. AA has more than 50,000 chapters in North America. AA is so deeply embedded in the consciousness of helping professionals that many of them automatically refer newly detoxified people to AA as the follow-up agency. About half of AA members have problems with illicit drugs as well as alcohol.

The AA experience is in part spiritual, in part group supportive, in part cognitive. AA follows a 12-step approach that focuses on accepting one's powerlessness over alcohol and turning one's will and life over to a higher power. This spiritual component may be helpful to some participants but distasteful to others. (Other lay organizations, such as Rational Recovery, adopt a nonspiritual approach.) The later steps in AA's approach focus on examining one's character flaws, admitting one's wrongdoings, being open to a higher power for help to overcome one's character defects, making amends to others, and, in step 12, bringing the AA message to other people suffering from alcoholism. Members are urged to pray or meditate to help them get in touch with their higher power. The meetings themselves provide group support. So does the buddy, or sponsor, system, which encourages members to call each other for support when they feel tempted to drink.

The success rate of AA remains in question, in large part because AA does not keep records of its members, but also because of an inability to conduct randomized clinical trials in AA settings. However, evidence exists that participation in AA is linked to lower frequency and intensity of drinking (Ferri, Amato, & Davoli, 2006; Ilgen, Wilbourne, Moos, & Moos, 2008). However, many people drop out of AA, as well as from other treatment programs. People who are more likely to do well with AA tend to be those who make a commitment to abstinence, who express intentions to avoid high-risk situations associated with alcohol use, and who stay longer with the program (e.g., McKellar, Stewart, & Humphreys, 2003; Moos & Moos, 2004).

A path toward recovery. Self-help groups, such as Alcoholics Anonymous, provide support to people struggling with problems of alcohol and drug abuse.

Al-Anon, begun in 1951, is a spin-off of AA that supports the families and friends of people suffering from alcoholism. Another spin-off of AA, Alateen, provides support to children whose parents have alcoholism, helping them see that they are not to blame for their parents' drinking and are thus undeserving of the guilt they may feel.

Residential Approaches

A residential approach to treatment requires a stay in a hospital or therapeutic residence. Hospitalization is recommended when substance abusers cannot exercise self-control in their usual environments, cannot tolerate withdrawal symptoms, or behave self-destructively or dangerously. Less costly outpatient treatment is indicated when withdrawal symptoms are less severe, clients are committed to changing their behavior, and support systems, such as families, can help clients make the transition to a drug-free lifestyle. The great majority of alcohol-dependent patients are treated on an outpatient basis.

Most inpatient programs use an extended 28-day detoxification period. For the first few days, treatment focuses on helping clients with withdrawal symptoms. Then the emphasis shifts to counseling about the destructive effects of alcohol and combating distorted ideas or rationalizations. Consistent with the disease model, abstinence is the goal.

Most people with alcohol use disorders, however, do not require hospitalization. A classic review article showed that outpatient and inpatient programs achieved about the same relapse rates (Miller & Hester, 1986). However, because medical insurance does not always cover outpatient treatment, many people who might benefit from outpatient treatment admit themselves for inpatient treatment instead.

A number of residential therapeutic communities are also in use. Some have part- or full-time professional staffs. Others are run entirely by laypeople. Residents are expected to remain free of drugs and take responsibility for their actions. They are often challenged to take responsibility for themselves and to acknowledge the damage caused by their drug abuse. They share their life experiences to help one another develop productive ways of handling stress.

As with AA, there is a lack of evidence from controlled studies demonstrating the efficacy of residential treatment programs. Also like AA, therapeutic communities have high numbers of early dropouts. Moreover, many residents relapse upon returning to the world outside.

Psychodynamic Approaches

Psychoanalysts view alcohol and drug problems as symptoms of conflicts rooted in childhood experiences. The therapist attempts to resolve the underlying conflicts, assuming that abusive behavior will then subside as the client seeks more mature forms of gratification. Although there are many successful psychodynamic case studies of people with substance use problems, there is a dearth of controlled and replicable research studies. The effectiveness of psychodynamic methods for treating alcohol and drug-related problems thus remains unsubstantiated.

Behavioral Approaches

Behavioral approaches to treating alcohol and drug-related problems focus on modifying abusive and dependent behavior patterns. The key question for behaviorally oriented therapists is not whether alcohol- and drug-related problems are diseases but whether abusers can learn to change their behavior when they are faced with temptation.

Self-Control Strategies *Self-control training* helps abusers develop skills they can use to change their abusive behavior. Behavior therapists focus on three components—the ABCs—of substance abuse:

1. The *antecedent* cues or stimuli (As) that prompt or trigger abuse
2. The abusive *behaviors* (Bs) themselves
3. The reinforcing or punishing *consequences* (Cs) that maintain or discourage abuse

Table 8.1 shows the kinds of strategies used to modify the ABCs of substance abuse.

TABLE 8.1
Self-Control Strategies for Modifying the ABCs of Substance Abuse

1. Controlling the As (Antecedents) of Substance Abuse
People who abuse or become dependent on psychoactive substances become conditioned to a wide range of external (environmental) and internal (bodily states) stimuli. They may begin to break these stimulus–response connections by
- removing drinking and smoking paraphernalia from the home—including all alcoholic beverages, beer mugs, carafes, ashtrays, matches, cigarette packs, lighters, etc.
- restricting the stimulus environment in which drinking or smoking is permitted by using the substance only in a stimulus-deprived area of their homes, such as the garage, bathroom, or basement. All stimuli that might be connected to using the substance are removed from this area—e.g., there is no TV, reading material, radio, or telephone. In this way, substance abuse becomes detached from many controlling stimuli.
- not socializing with others with substance abuse problems, by avoiding situations linked to abuse—bars, the street, bowling alleys, etc.
- frequenting substance-free environments—lectures or concerts, a gym, museums, evening classes; and by socializing with nonabusers, eating in restaurants without liquor licenses.
- managing the internal triggers for abuse. This can be done by practicing self-relaxation or meditation and not taking the substance when tense; by expressing angry feelings by writing them down or self-assertion, not by taking the substance; by seeking counseling, not alcohol, pills, or cigarettes, for prolonged feelings of depression.

2. Controlling the Bs (Behaviors) of Substance Abuse
People can prevent and interrupt substance abuse by
- using response prevention—breaking abusive habits by physically preventing them from occurring or making them more difficult (e.g., by not bringing alcohol home or keeping cigarettes in the car).
- using competing responses when tempted; by being prepared to handle substance use situations with appropriate ammunition—mints, sugarless chewing gum, etc.; by taking a bath or shower, walking the dog, walking around the block, taking a drive, calling a friend, spending time in a substance-free environment, practicing meditation or relaxation, or exercising when tempted, rather than using the substance.
- making abuse more laborious—buying one can of beer at a time; storing matches, ashtrays, and cigarettes far apart; wrapping cigarettes in foil to make smoking more cumbersome; pausing for 10 minutes when struck by the urge to drink, smoke, or use another substance and asking oneself, "Do I really need *this* one?"

3. Controlling the Cs (Consequences) of Substance Abuse
Substance abuse has immediate positive consequences such as pleasure, relief from anxiety and withdrawal symptoms, and stimulation. People can counter these intrinsic rewards and alter the balance of power in favor of nonabuse by
- rewarding themselves for nonabuse and punishing themselves for abuse.
- switching to brands of beer and cigarettes they don't like.
- setting gradual substance reduction schedules and rewarding themselves for sticking to them.
- punishing themselves for failing to meet substance reduction goals. People with substance abuse problems can assess themselves, say, by setting aside a specific cash penalty for each slip and donating the cash to an unpalatable cause, such as a disliked brother-in-law's birthday present.
- rehearsing motivating thoughts or self-statements—such as writing reasons for quitting smoking on index cards, for example:
  - Each day I don't smoke adds another day to my life.
  - Quitting smoking will help me breathe deeply again.
  - Foods will smell and taste better when I quit smoking.
  - Think how much money I'll save by not smoking.
  - Think how much cleaner my teeth and fingers will be by not smoking.
  - I'll be proud to tell others that I kicked the habit.
  - My lungs will become clearer each and every day I don't smoke.
- Smokers can carry a list of 20 to 25 such statements and read several of them at various times throughout the day. They can become parts of one's daily routine, a constant reminder of one's goals.

CONTINGENCY MANAGEMENT PROGRAMS Learning theorists believe that our behavior is shaped by rewards and punishments. Consider how virtually everything you do, from attending class to stopping at red lights to working for a paycheck, is influenced by the flow of reinforcements or rewards (money, praise, approval) and punishments (traffic tickets, rebukes). *Contingency management* (CM) programs provide reinforcements (rewards) contingent on performing desirable behaviors, such as producing drug-negative urine samples (Petry, Alessi, Marx, Austin, & Tardif, 2005; Poling et al., 2006; Roll et al., 2006). In one example, a group of patients had the opportunity to draw from a bowl and win monetary rewards or prize money (rewards) ranging from $1 to $100 in value (Petry & Martin, 2002). The monetary reward was contingent on submitting clean urine samples for cocaine and opioids. On average, the contingency management (reward) group achieved longer periods of continual abstinence than the standard methadone treatment group. Investigators find that even modest rewards for abstinence can help improve therapeutic outcomes in treating substance abusers (Dutra et al., 2008; Higgins, 2006).

AVERSIVE CONDITIONING In *aversive conditioning,* painful or aversive stimuli are paired with substance abuse or abuse-related stimuli to condition a negative emotional response to drug-related stimuli. In the case of problem drinking, tasting alcoholic beverages is usually paired with drugs that cause nausea and vomiting or with electric shock. As a consequence, alcohol may come to elicit an unpleasant emotional or physical reaction. Unfortunately, aversive conditioning effects are often temporary and fail to generalize to real-life settings in which aversive stimuli are no longer administered. However, it may be useful as a treatment component in a broader-based treatment program.

SOCIAL SKILLS TRAINING Social skills training helps people develop effective interpersonal responses in social situations that prompt substance abuse. Assertiveness training, for example, may be used to train alcohol abusers to fend off social pressures to drink. Behavioral marital therapy seeks to improve marital communication and problem-solving skills with the goal of relieving marital stresses that can trigger abuse. Couples may learn how to use written behavioral contracts. For example, the person with a substance abuse problem might agree to abstain from drinking or to take Antabuse, while the spouse agrees to refrain from commenting on past drinking and the probability of future lapses.

CONTROLLED DRINKING: A VIABLE GOAL? According to the disease model of alcoholism, having even one drink causes people with alcoholism to lose control and go on a binge. Some professionals, however, argue that many people with alcohol abuse or dependence can develop self-control techniques that allow them to engage in *controlled drinking*—to have a drink or two without necessarily falling off the wagon (Sobell & Sobell, 1973a, 1973b, 1984). This contention, however, remains controversial. The proponents of the disease model of alcoholism strongly oppose attempts to teach controlled social drinking. However, controlled drinking programs may represent a pathway to abstinence for people who would not otherwise enter abstinence-only treatment programs (Tatarsky & Kellogg, 2010). That is, a controlled drinking program can be a first step toward giving up drinking completely. By offering moderation as a treatment goal, controlled drinking programs may reach many people who refuse to participate in abstinence-only treatment programs.

Relapse-Prevention Training

The word *relapse* derives from Latin roots meaning "to slide back." Because of the high rates of relapse in substance abuse treatment programs, cognitive-behavioral therapists have devised a number of methods referred to as *relapse-prevention training.* This training is designed to help substance abusers identify high-risk situations and learn effective coping skills for handling these situations without turning to alcohol or drugs (Witkiewicz & Marlatt, 2004). High-risk situations include negative mood states, such as depression, anger, or anxiety; interpersonal conflict, for example, marital problems or conflicts with employers; and socially conducive situations such as "the guys getting together" (Chung & Maisto,

2006). Participants learn to cope with these situations, for example, by learning relaxation skills to counter anxiety and by learning to resist social pressures to drink. They also learn to avoid practices that might prompt a relapse, such as keeping alcohol on hand for friends.

Relapse-prevention training also focuses on preventing *lapses* from turning into full-blown *relapses*. Clients learn about the importance of their *interpretations* of any lapses or slips that may occur, such as smoking a first cigarette or taking a first drink following quitting. They are taught not to overreact to a lapse by changing how they think about lapses. For example, they learn that people who lapse are more likely to relapse if they attribute their slip to personal weakness, and experience shame and guilt, than if they attribute the slip to an external or transient event. Consider a skater who slips on the ice (Marlatt & Gordon, 1985). Whether the skater gets back up and continues to perform depends largely on whether the skater sees the slip as an isolated and correctable event or as a sign of utter failure. Because lapses in ex-smokers often occur in response to withdrawal symptoms, it is important to help smokers develop ways of coping with these symptoms without resuming smoking (Piasecki, Jorenby, Smith, Fiore, & Baker, 2003). Participants in relapse-prevention training programs learn to view lapses as temporary setbacks that provide opportunities to learn what kinds of situations lead to temptation and to either avoid them or learn to cope with them. If they can learn to think, "Okay, I had a slip, but that doesn't mean all is lost unless I believe it is," they are less likely to relapse.

All in all, efforts to treat people with alcohol and drug problems have had mixed results at best. Many abusers really do not want to discontinue use of these substances, although they would prefer, if possible, to avoid their negative consequences. Yet many treatment approaches, including 12-step and cognitive-behavioral approaches, can work well when they are well delivered and when individuals desire change (DiClemente, 2011; Moos & Moos, 2005).

Effective treatment programs include multiple approaches that match the needs of substance abusers and the range of problems with which they often present, including co-occurring psychiatric problems, such as depression and personality disorders (Grant et al., 2004; Watkins et al., 2011). *Comorbidity* (co-occurrence) of substance use disorders and other psychological disorders, especially mood disorders, has become the rule in treatment facilities for substance abusers rather than the exception (Pettinati, O'Brien, & Dundon, 2013; Quello, Brady, & Sonne, 2005). Not surprisingly, drug abuse treatment is often complicated by the presence of other serious psychological problems. As noted in the following case example, the co-occurrence of substance abuse greatly complicates the treatment of other psychological disorders.

> ### "Surely They Can't Mean Beer!"
>
> A 30-year-old man who suffered from both bipolar disorder and alcoholism struggled with giving up alcohol, which he used to treat himself for symptoms of depression and mania. He later recounted how alcohol, especially beer, had become his best friend during those dark years when he was repeatedly hospitalized for recurrent manic episodes. It was during one of those hospital stays that he was told he needed to give up alcohol. He clearly remembered his response: "Surely they can't mean beer!" He was in complete denial about how alcohol was damaging his body and preventing him from benefiting from medication for bipolar disorder. It wasn't until his parents threatened to withdraw their emotional and financial support if his drinking contributed to yet another hospitalization that he finally decided to take action by participating in meetings of Alcoholics Anonymous. Over time, he eventually achieved abstinence, making it possible for his bipolar medication to work effectively. Stopping his use of alcohol, including beer, was an important step toward successful recovery, enabling him to work with his doctors to control his mood swings.
>
> *Source:* Adapted from a testimonial posted on an online support site, *NYC Voices*.

Although effective treatment programs are available, only a minority of people with alcohol dependence ever receive treatment, even when treatment is defined broadly enough to include AA (Kranzler, 2006). A Canadian study echoed these findings. In a sample of more than 1,000 people in Ontario, Canada, with alcohol abuse or dependence disorders, only about one in three had ever received any treatment for their disorder (Cunningham & Breslin, 2004). Clearly, more needs to be done in helping people with drug-related problems.

In the case of inner-city youth who have become trapped within a milieu of street drugs and hopelessness, culturally sensitive drug counseling and job training would be of considerable benefit in helping them to assume more productive social roles. The challenge is clear: to develop cost-effective ways of helping people recognize the negative effects of substances and forgo the powerful and immediate reinforcements they provide.

8.9 Describe the basic features of gambling disorder and evaluate ways of treating it.

Gambling Disorder

Gambling may never have been more popular in the United States than it is today. Legalized gambling encompasses many forms such as state lotteries, offtrack betting (OTB) parlors, casino nights sponsored by religious and fraternal organizations, and gambling meccas like Atlantic City and Las Vegas. There has been a proliferation of online gambling opportunities, including Internet betting on sports and horse races and online card games, in recent years, despite crackdowns by legal authorities (e.g., Hodgins, Stea, & Grant, 2011; King et al., 2013).

Most people who gamble are able to maintain self-control and can stop whenever they wish. Others, like the man in the case example on the following page, fall into a pattern of problem or compulsive gambling, which *DSM-5* classifies as a type of addictive disorder called **gambling disorder**.

Compulsive gambling can take many forms, from excessive wagering on horse races or in card games and casinos, to extravagant betting on sporting events, to chancy stock picks. Many compulsive gamblers seek treatment only during a financial or emotional crisis, such as a bankruptcy or divorce.

The first national survey of its kind on problem gambling showed that about 2% of young Americans aged 14 to 21 (some 750,000 people in total) engaged in problem gambling during the past year (Welte, Barnes, Tidwell, Hoffman, 2008). Problem gambling was represented by such behaviors as gambling more money than one had intended or stealing money to gamble. About 0.4% to 1.0% of the general population will develop a gambling disorder at some point in their lives (APA, 2013). Compulsive or problem gambling is on the rise, due in part to the increasing spread of legalized forms of gambling (Carlbring & Smit, 2008; Hodgins, Stea, & Grant, 2011). The question is, where should we draw the line between recreational gambling and compulsive gambling?

Compulsive or pathological gamblers often report they had experienced a big win, or a series of winnings, early in their gambling careers. Eventually, however, their losses begin to mount, and they feel driven to bet with increasing desperation to reverse their luck and recoup their losses. Losses sometimes begin with the first bet, and compulsive gamblers often become trapped in a negative spiral of betting yet more frequently to recover losses even as their losses—and

Gambling, American style. Gambling is big business in the United States. Although most gamblers can control their gambling behavior, compulsive gamblers are unable to resist impulses to gamble. Many compulsive gamblers seek help only when their losses throw them into financial or emotional crisis.

their debts—multiply. At some point, most compulsive gamblers hit rock bottom, a state of despair characterized by loss of control over gambling, financial ruin, suicide attempts, and shattered family relationships. They may attempt to reduce their mounting losses by gambling more frequently, hoping for the one "big score" that will put them "into the black." They may sometimes be bouncing with energy and overconfidence and at other times feel anxious and filled with despair. A compulsive gambler named Ed recounts, in his own words, how he sought the one big score to dig himself out of a financial whole. 👁

👁 **Watch** the **Video** *Ed: Gambling Disorder* on **MyPsychLab**

→ **"I"** **"The Big Hit"**

I looked at the amount of money I owed and thought there's no way I can go out and get a job and pay this off. I've got to have a big hit in order to do this. And you keep chasing and chasing not realizing you get further into a hole all the time. When gambling takes control of what you're doing rather than you controlling it, life became unmanageable. I was borrowing money. You shouldn't have to do that. I was lying about my gambling. You shouldn't have to do that. It [gambling] was taking away from other things in my life, my home life, my professional life, all those things were suffering because I was gambling.

Source: Excerpted from *Speaking Out: Videos in Abnormal Psychology*, Pearson Education, 2008. All rights reserved.

Many compulsive gamblers suffer from low self-esteem and were rejected or abused as children by their parents (Hodgins et al., 2010). Gambling may become a means of boosting their self-esteem by proving that they are winners. Far too often, however, winnings are elusive and losses mount. Losing only strengthens their negative self-image, which can lead to depression and even suicide. Here, Ed comments on how winning boosted his self-esteem and how losses were explained away:

→ **"I"** **"I Was Smarter Than Other People"**

There were a couple of things I know today were deficient in my character. I had failed as an athlete, I had failed as a student. I had failed in my original goal—I was going to be a priest. What was I going to be successful at? I was going to be successful as a handicapper (of greyhound dog races). I pursued that with a passion. I felt that [I] . . . would be successful and I would be an outstanding handicapper and make a lot of money at it.

The biggest rush of all was not so much winning fantastic sums of money or anything like that, but was being right. People would ask, how did you pick that? And it was my intelligence, that I was smarter than other people. I felt a definite sense of excitement, almost like a nervous anticipation . . . before the greyhounds were put in the box. While it's going on, you're almost in a nervous trance sensing what's going to happen and then depending on the final result, it was either one of ecstasy because you won or dejection because something had happened. It wasn't as if you made the wrong choice, but it was something that happened that impacted what would have gone your way. . . . I wanted people to look at me and say, "Wow, how did you do this, look at how smart you are." . . . They heard about my winnings, but they never heard about my losing's.

Source: Excerpted from *Speaking Out: Videos in Abnormal Psychology*, Pearson Education, 2008. All rights reserved.

Compulsive Gambling as a Nonchemical Addiction

We can think of compulsive gambling as a kind of nonchemical addiction. It shares with substance dependence (addiction) a loss of control over the behavior, a state of high arousal or pleasurable excitement experienced when the behavior is performed, and withdrawal symptoms, such as headaches, insomnia, and loss of appetite, when the person cuts back or stops the compulsive behavior.

Personality characteristics of compulsive gamblers and chemical abusers also overlap, with psychological test profiles of both groups showing traits such as impulsivity, self-centeredness, need for stimulation, emotional instability, low tolerance for frustration, and manipulativeness (e.g., Billieux et al., 2012; Clark, 2012; MacLaren, Best, Dixon, & Harrigan, 2011; Oleski et al., 2011). Compulsive gamblers and alcohol-dependent patients also share similar deficits on neuropsychological tests, suggestive of brain dysfunctions in the prefrontal cortex, the part of the brain responsible for controlling impulsive behavior (Goudriaan, Oosterlaan, de Beurs, & van den Brink, 2006). Investigators also find high rates of comorbidity (co-occurrence) between compulsive gambling and substance use disorders (e.g., Dannon, Lowengrub, Aizer, & Kotler, 2006). Like many forms of abnormal behavior, evidence also points to an important genetic component in compulsive gambling (Shaffer & Martin, 2011; Slutske, Zhu, Meier, & Martin, 2010, 2011).

Although *DSM-5* classifies gambling disorder within the category of Substance Related and Addictive Disorders, the addiction model may apply more directly to some compulsive gamblers than others. Some forms of compulsive gambling may be more closely aligned to mood disorders or obsessive–compulsive disorder than to addictive disorders.

Treatment of Compulsive Gambling

Treatment of compulsive gambling remains a challenge. Helping professionals face an uphill battle in working with compulsive gamblers who, like people with personality disorders and substance use disorders, make maladaptive choices and show little insight into the causes of their problems. They are reluctant to enter treatment and may resist efforts to help them. Successful treatment efforts are reported, however, including cognitive-behavioral programs that focus on helping gamblers correct cognitive biases (e.g., beliefs that they can control gambling outcomes that are actually governed by chance, and tendencies to credit themselves for their wins and explain away their losses) (e.g., Gooding & Tarrier, 2009; Okuda, Balán, Petry, Oquendo, & Blanco, 2009; Petry et al., 2008; Shaffer & Martin, 2011). Promising results are also reported from use of antidepressants and mood-stabilizing drugs, which suggests that compulsive gambling and mood disorders may share common features (e.g., Dannon et al., 2006; Grant, Williams, & Kim, 2006).

Many treatment programs involve peer support programs, like Gamblers Anonymous (GA), which models itself on Alcoholics Anonymous. This program emphasizes personal responsibility for one's behavior and ensures anonymity of group members so as to encourage participation and sharing of experiences. Within a supportive group setting, members gain insight into their self-destructive behaviors. In some cases, hospital-based or residential treatment programs may be used to sequester compulsive gamblers, so that they can help break away from their usual destructive routines. Upon release, they are encouraged to continue treatment by participating in GA or similar programs. To ensure anonymity, lay programs like GA do not keep records of participants, so it is difficult to appraise success. Still, it appears that GA can be helpful in many cases, but abstinence rates among attendees are unfortunately low (Petry et al., 2006; Tavares, 2012).

Some compulsive gamblers show improvement on their own; indeed, some become free of symptoms, even without receiving any formal treatment. The problem is that investigators don't know which problem gamblers are likely to improve on their own. An analysis of data from two nationally representative samples in the United States showed that about 4 out of 10 compulsive gamblers were symptom-free during the previous year (Slutske, 2006).

A Biopsychosocial Model of Substance Dependence

Substance use disorders involve maladaptive patterns of substance abuse and dependence and reflect the interplay of biological, psychological, and environmental factors. These problems are best understood by investigating the distinctive constellation of factors that apply to each individual case. No single model or set of factors will explain each case, which is why therapists need to understand each individual's unique characteristics and personal history and direct treatment accordingly. Figure 8.8 illustrates a biopsychosocial model of substance dependence, showing how these causal factors interact.

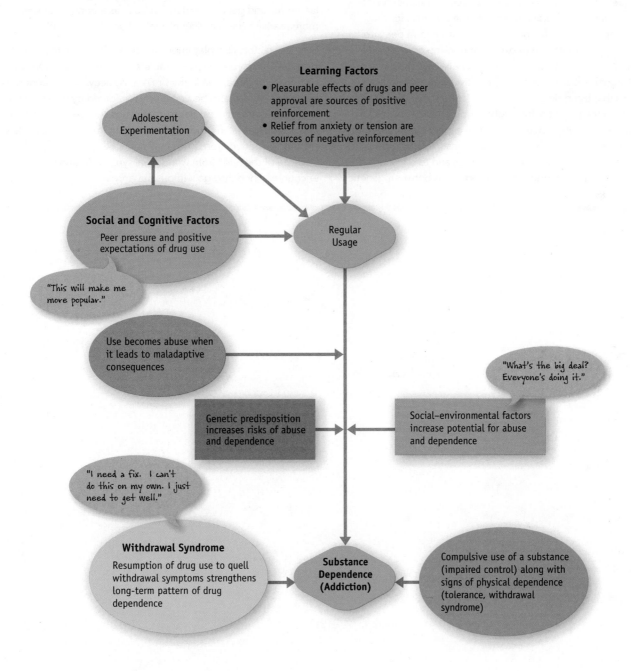

FIGURE 8.8

A biopsychosocial model of substance dependence.

As you can see in Figure 8.8, genetic factors can create a predisposition or diathesis for the development of drug-related problems (Young-Wolff, Enoch, & Prescott, 2011). Some people may be born with a greater tolerance for alcohol, which can make it difficult for them to regulate use of alcohol—to know "when to say when." Others have genetic tendencies that can lead them to become unusually tense or anxious. Perhaps they turn to alcohol or other drugs to quell their nervousness. Genetic predispositions can interact with environmental factors to increase the potential for drug abuse and dependence—factors such as pressure from peers to use drugs, parental modeling of excessive drinking or drug use, and family disruption that results in a lack of effective guidance or support. Cognitive factors, especially positive drug expectancies (e.g., beliefs that using drugs will enhance one's social skills or sexual prowess), raise the potential for alcohol or drug use problems. In adolescence and adulthood, these positive expectations, together with social pressures and a lack of cultural constraints, affect the young person's decision to begin using drugs and to continue to use them. Echoing the importance of interactions between genetic and environmental factors in explaining abnormal behavior patterns, investigators believe that genetic factors may increase the risk of people turning to alcohol or other drugs when they are under stress (Dong et al., 2011; Yager, 2011).

Sociocultural and biological factors are also included in this matrix of factors: the availability of alcohol and other drugs; the presence or absence of cultural constraints; the glamorizing of drug use in popular media; and genetic tendencies (such as among Asians) to flush more readily following alcohol intake (Luczak, et al., 2006).

Learning factors also play important roles. Drug use may be *positively* reinforced by pleasurable effects (mediated perhaps by release of dopamine in the brain or by activation of endorphin receptors). It may also be *negatively* reinforced by the reduction of tension and anxiety that depressant drugs such as alcohol, heroin, and tranquilizers can produce. In a sad but ironic twist, people who become dependent on drugs may continue to use them solely because of the relief from withdrawal symptoms and cravings they encounter when they go without the drugs.

8 summing up

Classification of Substance Use and Addictive Disorders

8.1 Identify the major types of substance-related disorders in the DSM-5 and describe their general features.

The *DSM-5* classifies substance related disorders in two major diagnostic categories, substance-induced disorders (repeated episodes of drug intoxication or development of a withdrawal syndrome), and substance use disorders (maladaptive use of a substance leading to psychological distress or impaired functioning).

8.2 Describe nonchemical forms of addiction or compulsive behavior.

Patterns of compulsive behavior, such as compulsive gambling and shopping, and perhaps even excessive Internet use, may represent nonchemical forms of addiction. These behavior patterns are associated with classic signs of drug dependence or addiction, including impaired control over the behavior and withdrawal symptoms such as anxiety or depression, upon abrupt cessation of use.

8.3 Explain the difference between physiological dependence and psychological dependence.

Physiological dependence involves changes in the body as the result of regular use of a substance, such as the development of tolerance and a withdrawal syndrome. Psychological dependence involves habitual use of a substance to meet a psychological need, either with or without physiological dependence.

8.4 Identify common stages in the pathway to drug dependence.

Three commonly identified stages in the pathway to drug dependence are (1) experimentation; (2) routine use; and (3) addiction or dependence.

Drugs of Abuse

8.5 Identify the major categories of psychoactive drugs and specific drugs in each category, and describe the effects of these drugs and the risks they pose.

Depressants are drugs that depress or slow down nervous system activity. They include alcohol, sedatives and minor tranquilizers, and opioids. Their effects include intoxication, impaired coordination, slurred speech, and impaired intellectual functioning. Chronic alcohol abuse is associated with health risks including Korsakoff's syndrome, cirrhosis of the liver, fetal alcohol syndrome, and other physical health problems. Barbiturates are depressants or sedatives that have been used medically for short-term relief of anxiety and treatment

of epilepsy, among other uses. Like alcohol, they can impair driving ability and also can be dangerous in overdose situations, especially when use of barbiturates is combined with alcohol. Opioids such as morphine and heroin are derived from the opium poppy. Others are synthesized. Opioids are used medically for relief of pain and are strongly addictive and can result in lethal overdoses.

Stimulants increase activity in the central nervous system. Amphetamines and cocaine are stimulants that increase the availability of neurotransmitters in the brain, leading to heightened states of arousal and pleasurable feelings. High doses can produce psychotic reactions that mimic features of paranoid schizophrenia. Habitual cocaine use can lead to a variety of health problems, and an overdose can cause sudden death. Repeated use of nicotine, a mild stimulant found in tobacco, leads to physiological dependence.

Hallucinogens are drugs that distort sensory perceptions and can induce hallucinations. They include LSD, psilocybin, and mescaline. Other drugs with similar effects are cannabis (marijuana) and phencyclidine, a deliriant that can induce a state of mental confusion or delirium. Although hallucinogens may not lead to physiological dependence, psychological dependence may occur. Concerns are also raised about the potential for brain damage affecting learning and memory ability in heavier users of marijuana.

Theoretical Perspectives

8.6 Describe the major theoretical perspectives toward understanding substance use disorders.

The biological perspective focuses on uncovering the biological pathways that may explain mechanisms of physiological dependence. The biological perspective spawns the disease model, which posits that alcoholism and other forms of substance dependence are disease processes. Learning perspectives view problems with substance abuse as learned patterns of behavior, with roles for classical and operant conditioning and observational learning. Cognitive perspectives focus on roles of attitudes, beliefs, and expectancies in accounting for substance use and abuse. Sociocultural perspectives emphasize the cultural, group, and social factors that underlie drug-use patterns, including the role of peer pressure in determining adolescent drug use. Psychodynamic theorists view problems of substance abuse, such as excessive drinking and habitual smoking, as signs of an oral fixation.

8.7 Explain how cocaine affects the brain.

Cocaine blocks the reuptake of dopamine by the transmitting neuron, which means that more dopamine remains in the synaptic gap, creating a euphoric high by overstimulating receiving neurons in brain networks that regulate feelings of pleasure.

Treatment of Substance Use Disorders

8.8 Describe methods of treating substance use disorders.

Biological approaches to substance use disorders include detoxification; the use of drugs such as disulfiram, methadone, naltrexone, and antidepressants; and nicotine replacement therapy.

Residential treatment approaches include hospitals and therapeutic residences. Nonprofessional support groups, such as Alcoholics Anonymous, promote abstinence within a supportive group setting. Psychodynamic therapists focus on uncovering the inner conflicts originating in childhood that they believe lie at the root of substance abuse problems. Behavior therapists who focus on helping people with substance use problems change problem behaviors through techniques such as self-control training, aversive conditioning, and skills training approaches. Regardless of the initial success of a treatment technique, relapse remains a pressing problem in treating people with substance abuse problems. Relapse-prevention training employs cognitive-behavioral techniques to help recovering substance abusers cope with high-risk situations and prevent lapses from becoming relapses by interpreting lapses in less damaging ways.

8.9 Describe the basic features of gambling disorder and evaluate ways of treating it.

Gambling disorder or compulsive gambling can be likened to a type of nonchemical addiction in which people experience a loss of control over the behavior, a state of high arousal or pleasurable excitement when the behavior is performed, and withdrawal symptoms when they stop gambling. People with the disorder frequently have comorbid conditions, especially substance use disorders and mood disorders. Promising treatment approaches for compulsive gambling have been developed, including antidepressants and mood-stabilizing drugs and cognitive-behavioral therapy, which is used to correct cognitive biases that may underlie compulsive gambling patterns. Many compulsive gamblers participate in peer support groups, such as Gamblers Anonymous, that help them gain insight into their self-defeating behavior and change their compulsive behavior patterns.

critical thinking questions

On the basis of your reading of this chapter, answer the following questions:

- What is the basis for determining when drug use becomes abuse or dependence? Have you or someone you've known crossed the line between use and abuse? On what evidence do you base this judgment?

- Do you or someone you know show evidence of nonchemical forms of addiction, such as compulsive shopping, gambling, or sexual behavior? How is this behavior affecting your (or his or her) life? What can you (or he or she) do about overcoming it?

- What do you think of the concept of using methadone, a narcotic drug, to treat addiction to another narcotic drug, heroin? What are the advantages and disadvantages of this approach? Do you believe the government should support methadone maintenance programs? Why or why not?

- Many teenagers today have parents who themselves smoked marijuana or used other drugs when they were younger. If you were one of those parents, what would you tell your children about drugs?

key terms

substance-induced disorders 291
substance intoxication 291
substance withdrawal 291
tolerance 291
withdrawal syndrome 292
substance use disorders 292
physical dependence 295
addiction 295
psychological dependence 295

depressant 296
alcoholism 297
barbiturates 303
narcotics 303
endorphins 304
morphine 304
heroin 304
stimulants 305
amphetamines 305

amphetamine psychosis 305
cocaine 306
crack 306
hallucinogens 308
marijuana 309
detoxification 318
methadone 319
naltrexone 320
gambling disorder 326

Scoring Key for "Are You Hooked?" Questionnaire

Any "yes" answer suggests that you may be dependent on alcohol. If you have answered any of these questions in the affirmative, we suggest you seriously examine what your drinking means to you and talk things over with a counselor or health care provider.

Eating Disorders and Sleep-Wake Disorders

9

9

learning objectives

9.1
Describe the key features of three types of eating disorders: anorexia nervosa, bulimia nervosa, and binge-eating disorder.

9.2
Describe causal factors involved in anorexia nervosa and bulimia nervosa.

9.3
Evaluate methods used to treat eating disorders.

9.4
Identify health risks associated with obesity.

9.5
Identify factors linked to obesity.

9.6
Identify and describe specific types of sleep-wake disorders.

9.7
Evaluate methods used to treat sleep-wake disorders.

9.8
Apply your knowledge of healthy sleeping habits to steps you can take to develop more adaptive sleep habits.

truth OR fiction

T ☑ / F ☐   Although others see them as extremely thin, young women with anorexia nervosa still see themselves as too fat. (p. 337)

T ☐ / F ☑   Although anorexia is a serious psychological disorder, women with anorexia are actually less likely to attempt suicide than are women in general. (p. 338)

T ☐ F ☑   Women with bulimia induce vomiting only after binges. (p. 342)

T ☑ F ☐   Obesity is one of the most common psychological disorders in the United States. (p. 346)

T ☐ F ☐   When people start losing significant amounts of weight, their bodies respond as though they were starving. (p. 347)

T ☑ F ☐   After Santa Claus, the most recognizable figure to children is Ronald McDonald. (p. 347)

T ☐ F ☐   Many people suffer from sleep attacks in which they suddenly fall asleep without any warning. (p. 355)

T ☐ F ☐   Some people literally gasp for breath hundreds of times during sleep without realizing it. (p. 356)

"I" "What's Up with That?"

Every night that I throw up I can't help but be afraid that my heart might stop or something else will happen. I just pray and hope I can stop this throwing up before it kills me. I hate this bulimia and I won't stop. It's hard for me to binge and throw up now (refrigerator is locked) and I just can't do it anymore. I just can't race through so much food so fast and then throw it up. I don't really want to. There are times that I do but not often. My new pattern is sure leaving me with an awful feeling in the morning. I eat dinner and kind of keep eating (snacking) afterwards to the point where I either feel too full or think (know) I've eaten too much, then I fall asleep (one hour or so) wake up and think I have to throw up. Half of me doesn't want to, the other half does and I always find myself throwing up. I try falling back asleep but it always seems like eventually sometime during the night I always throw up.

I feel crazy when I have a panic attack because someone I'm with is eating totally sugary foods, as though I'm afraid just being near it will somehow allow the food, or the fat, or the calories to attack me. Julie picked me up from class the other day, and she was eating dry sugar cookie mix from a bowl with a huge spoon. I panicked. I shook, perspired, had trouble taking full breaths, and couldn't focus or concentrate with all the thoughts rushing through my head. I wasn't eating it, but I could smell it and see it and heard the sugar crystals crunch as she chewed big mouthfuls of it. Then she started eating a cupcake. I couldn't handle it. She offered me some and I became severely nauseated by the mere thought of her offer. When she dropped me off, I raced into the house to gain control of this incredible binge. I was horrified and sick, saw myself gaining weight through my distorted vision, and immediately took laxatives to rid myself of all that forbidden food I felt inside, even though I hadn't eaten a thing.

After I calmed down, I realized the reality of the situation, and I felt stupid and crazy and like a total failure. Not only do I not need anyone else to abuse me, now I can do that myself. I don't even need a binge to have my purging cycle triggered to an intense degree. What's up with that?

Costin, 1997, pp. 62–63

The young woman who wrote this vignette has *bulimia nervosa,* an eating disorder characterized by repeated episodes of binge eating and purging. How can we explain eating disorders like *bulimia nervosa* or *anorexia nervosa,* a psychological disorder of self-starvation that can lead to serious medical consequences, even death? Eating disorders primarily affect young people of high school or college age, especially young women. Even if you don't know anyone with a diagnosable eating disorder, chances are you know people with disturbed eating behaviors such as occasional binge eating and excessive dieting. You probably also know people who suffer from obesity, a major health problem that affects increasing numbers of Americans.

This chapter explores the three major types of eating disorders: anorexia nervosa, bulimia nervosa, and binge-eating disorder. We also examine factors that contribute to obesity, a health problem that has reached epidemic proportions in our society. Our focus in this chapter also extends to another set of problems that commonly affects young adults: sleep-wake disorders. The most common form of sleep-wake disorder, insomnia disorder, affects many young people who are making their way in the world and tend to bring their worries and concerns to bed with them.

Eating Disorders

In a nation of plenty, some people literally starve themselves—sometimes to death. They are obsessed with their weight and desire to achieve an exaggerated image of thinness. Others engage in repeated cycles in which they binge on food and then attempt to purge their excess eating, for example, by inducing vomiting. These dysfunctional patterns are, respectively, the two major types of eating disorders, **anorexia nervosa** and **bulimia nervosa.**

Eating disorders involve disordered eating behaviors and maladaptive ways of controlling body weight. Eating disorders often occur together with other psychological disorders, such as depression, anxiety disorders, and substance abuse disorders (Jenkins et al., 2011). Table 9.1 provides an overview of the three types of eating disorders we examine in this chapter.

9.1 **Describe** the key features of three types of eating disorders: anorexia nervosa, bulimia nervosa, and binge-eating disorder.

TABLE 9.1
Overview of Eating Disorders

Type of Disorder	Lifetime Prevalence in Population (approx.)	Description	Associated Features
Anorexia Nervosa	0.9%, or 9 in 1,000 women; about 0.3%, or 3 in 1,000 men	Self-starvation, resulting in abnormally low body weight for one's age, gender, height, and physical health and developmental level	• Strong fears of gaining weight or becoming fat • Distorted self-image (perceiving oneself as fat despite extreme thinness) • Two general subtypes: binge eating/purging type and restricting type • Potentially serious, even fatal, medical complications • Typically affects young, European American women
Bulimia Nervosa	0.9% to 1.5% in women; 0.1% to 0.5% in men	Recurrent episodes of binge eating followed by purging	• Weight is usually maintained within a normal range • Overconcern about body shape and weight • Binge/purge episodes may result in serious medical complications • Typically affects young European American women
Binge-Eating Disorder	3.5% in women; 2% in men	Recurrent binge eating without compensatory purging	• Individuals with BED are frequently described as compulsive overeaters • Typically affects obese women who are older than those affected by anorexia or bulimia

Sources: Prevalence rates derived from Hudson et al., 2006, 2007; Smink, van Hoeken, & Hoek, 2012.

The great majority of cases of anorexia nervosa and bulimia nervosa occur among young women. Although eating disorders may develop in middle or even late adulthood, they typically begin during adolescence or early adulthood when the pressures to be thin are the strongest. As these social pressures have increased, so too have rates of eating disorders. Evidence from a large community-based survey indicates that anorexia nervosa affects about 0.9% of women (nearly 1 in 100) (Hudson et al., 2006). Bulimia nervosa is believed to affect about 0.9% to 1.5% of women (Smink, van Hoeken, & Hoek, 2012). There are also many cases of people with some anorexic or bulimic behaviors but not at a level that would warrant a diagnosis of an eating disorder.

Rates of anorexia nervosa and bulimia nervosa among men are estimated at about 0.3% (3 in 1,000) for anorexia and 0.1% to 0.5% (1 to 5 in 1,000) for bulimia (Hudson et al., 2006, 2007; Smink, van Hoeken, & Hoek, 2012). Many men with anorexia nervosa participate in sports, such as wrestling, that impose pressures on maintaining weight within a narrow range.

Anorexia Nervosa

→ Anorexia Nervosa: The Case of Karen

Karen was the 22-year-old daughter of a renowned English professor. She had begun her college career full of promise at the age of 17, but 2 years ago, after "social problems" occurred, she had returned to live at home and taken progressively lighter course loads at a local college. Karen had never been overweight, but about a year ago, her mother noticed that she seemed to be gradually "turning into a skeleton."

Karen spent literally hours every day shopping at the supermarket, butcher, and bakeries conjuring up gourmet treats for her parents and younger siblings. Arguments over her lifestyle and eating habits had divided the family into two camps. The camp led by her father called for patience; that headed by her mother demanded confrontation. Her mother feared that Karen's father would "protect her right into her grave" and wanted Karen placed in residential treatment "for her own good." The parents finally compromised on an outpatient evaluation.

At an even 5 feet, Karen looked like a prepubescent 11-year-old. Her nose and cheekbones protruded crisply. Her lips were full, but the redness of the lipstick was unnatural, as if too much paint had been dabbed on a corpse for the funeral. Karen weighed only 78 pounds, but she had dressed in a stylish silk blouse, scarf, and baggy pants so that not one inch of her body was revealed.

Karen vehemently denied that she had a problem. Her figure was "just about where I want it to be" and she engaged in aerobic exercise daily. A deal was struck in which outpatient treatment would be tried as long as Karen lost no more weight and showed steady gains back to at least 90 pounds. Treatment included a day hospital with group therapy and two meals a day. But word came back that Karen was artfully toying with her food—cutting it up, sort of licking it, and moving it about her plate— rather than eating it. After 3 weeks Karen had lost another pound. At that point, her parents were able to persuade her to enter a residential treatment program, where her eating behavior could be more carefully monitored.

→ From the Author's Files

The word *anorexia* derives from the Greek roots *an-*, meaning "without," and *orexis*, meaning "a desire for." *Anorexia* thus means "without desire for [food]," which is something of a misnomer, because people with anorexia nervosa rarely lose their appetite. However, they may be repelled by food and refuse to eat more than is absolutely necessary to maintain a minimal weight for their ages and heights. Often, they starve themselves to the point where they become dangerously emaciated. *Anorexia nervosa* (commonly referred to as *anorexia*) usually develops between the ages of 12 and 18, although earlier and later onsets are sometimes found.

The most prominent sign of anorexia nervosa is severe weight loss due to significant restriction of calorie intake or self-starvation. Other common features include the following:

- Excessive fears of gaining weight or becoming fat, despite being abnormally thin
- A distorted body image, as reflected in self-perception of one's body, or of parts of one's body, as fat, even though others perceive the person as thin
- Failure to recognize the risks posed by maintaining body weight at abnormally low levels

One common pattern of anorexia begins after menarche when the girl notices added weight and insists it must come off. The addition of body fat is normal in adolescent females: in an evolutionary sense, fat is added in preparation for childbearing and nursing. But women with anorexia seek to rid their bodies of any additional weight and so turn to extreme dieting and, often, excessive exercise. However, these efforts continue unabated after the initial weight loss goal is achieved, even after family and friends express concern. Another common pattern occurs when young women leave home to attend college and encounter difficulties adjusting to the demands of college life and independent living. Anorexia nervosa is also common among young women involved in ballet or modeling, both fields that place strong emphasis on maintaining an unrealistically thin body shape.

Adolescent girls and women with anorexia nervosa almost always deny that they are losing too much weight. They may argue that their ability to engage in stressful exercise demonstrates their fitness. Women with eating disorders are more likely than normal women to have a distorted body image. Other people may see them as nothing but "skin and bones," but women with anorexia still see themselves as too fat. Although they literally starve themselves, they may spend much of the day thinking and talking about food and even preparing elaborate meals for others. T / F

SUBTYPES OF ANOREXIA NERVOSA There are two general subtypes of the disorder, a binge eating/purging type and a restricting type. The binge eating/purging type is characterized by frequent episodes during the prior three-month period of binge eating or purging (such as by self-induced vomiting or overuse of laxatives, diuretics, or enemas); the restrictive type does not have bingeing or purging episodes. The distinction between the subtypes of anorexia nervosa is supported by differences in personality patterns. Individuals with the binge eating/purging type tend to have problems relating to impulse control, which in addition to binge-eating episodes may involve substance abuse or stealing. They tend to alternate between periods of rigid control and impulsive behavior. Those with the restrictive type tend to rigidly, even obsessively, control their diet and appearance.

MEDICAL COMPLICATIONS OF ANOREXIA NERVOSA Anorexia nervosa can lead to serious medical complications that in extreme cases can be fatal. Losses of as much as 35% of body weight may occur, and anemia may develop. Females suffering from anorexia nervosa are also likely to encounter dermatological problems such as dry, cracking skin; fine, downy hair; even a yellowish discoloration of the skin that may persist for years after weight is regained. Cardiovascular complications include heart irregularities, hypotension (low blood pressure), and associated dizziness upon standing, sometimes causing blackouts. Decreased food ingestion can cause gastrointestinal problems such as constipation, abdominal pain, and obstruction or paralysis of the bowels or intestines. Menstrual irregularities in women are common in cases of anorexia, as is amenorrhea (absence or suppression of menstruation). Muscular weakness and abnormal growth of bones may occur, causing loss of height and osteoporosis.

Then, sadly, there is an increased risk of death, which is pegged at 5% to 20% of cases of anorexia nervosa, due to either suicide or malnutrition due to starvation (Arcelus,

Watch the Video
Natasha: Anorexia
on **MyPsychLab**

truth OR fiction

Although others see them as extremely thin, young women with anorexia nervosa still see themselves as too fat.

☑ **TRUE**   Others may see them as nothing but "skin and bones," but anorexic women have a distorted body image and may still see themselves as too fat.

How do I see myself? A distorted body image is a common feature of eating disorders.

2011; Haynos, & Fruzzetti, 2011). Young women with anorexia nervosa are eight times more likely to commit suicide than are young women in the general population (Yager, 2008). In a study of several hundred people who had suffered from anorexia, or were suffering still—95% of whom were female—nearly one in five (17%) had made a suicide attempt (Bulik et al., 2008). **T / F**

Bulimia Nervosa

➤ Bulimia Nervosa: The Case of Nicole

Nicole has only opened her eyes, but already she wishes it was time for bed. She dreads going through the day, which threatens to turn out like so many other recent days. Each morning she wonders if this will be the day that she will be able to get by without being obsessed by thoughts of food. Or will she spend the day gorging herself? Today is the day she will get off to a new start, she promises herself. Today she will begin to live like a normal person. Yet she is not convinced that it is really up to her.

Nicole starts the day with eggs and toast. Then she goes to work on cookies; doughnuts; bagels smothered with butter, cream cheese, and jelly; granola; candy bars; and bowls of cereal and milk—all within 45 minutes. Then she cannot take in any more food and turns her attention to purging what she has eaten. She goes to the bathroom, ties back her hair, turns on the shower to mask any noise she will make, drinks a glass of water, and makes herself vomit. Afterward she vows, "Starting tomorrow, I'm going to change." But she suspects that tomorrow may be just another chapter of the same story.

➤ *Adapted from Boskind-White & White, 1983, p. 29*

Nicole suffers from *bulimia nervosa* (commonly referred to as *bulimia*). The word *bulimia* derives from the Greek roots *bous,* meaning "ox" or "cow," and *limos,* meaning "hunger." The unpretty picture inspired by the origin of the term is one of continuous eating, like a cow chewing its cud. Bulimia nervosa is an eating disorder characterized by recurrent episodes of gorging on large quantities of food, followed by use of inappropriate ways of compensating for overeating to prevent weight gain.

The defining feature of bulimia nervosa is the occurrence of frequent episodes of binge eating (gorging), followed by compensatory behaviors such as self-induced vomiting, abuse of laxatives, diuretics, or enemas, or fasting or excessive exercise. Other commonly occurring features of bulimia nervosa include the following:

- Feelings of lack of control over eating during binge eating episodes
- Excessive fear of gaining weight
- Excessive emphasis on body shape and body weight on self-image

A *DSM-5* diagnosis of bulimia nervosa nervosa requires that binge-eating episodes and the accompanying compensatory behaviors occur at an average frequency of at least once a week for three months (APA, 2013). A person with bulimia may use two or more strategies for purging, such as vomiting and laxatives. Although people with anorexia nervosa are extremely thin, those with bulimia nervosa are usually of normal weight. However, they have an excessive concern about their shape and weight.

People who suffer from bulimia nervosa typically gag themselves to induce vomiting. Most attempt to conceal their behavior. Fear of gaining weight is a constant factor. But people with bulimia nervosa do not pursue the extreme thinness characteristic of anorexia nervosa. Their ideal weights are similar to those of women who do not suffer from eating disorders.

Eating binges often occur in secret, typically during unstructured afternoon or evening hours. A binge may last from 30 to 60 minutes and involves consumption of forbidden foods that are generally sweet and rich in fat. Binge eaters typically feel a lack of control over their bingeing and may consume as many as 5,000 to 10,000 calories. One young woman described eating everything available in the refrigerator, even to the point of scooping out margarine from its container with her finger. The episode continues until the binger is spent or exhausted, suffers painful stomach distention, induces vomiting, or runs out of food. Drowsiness, guilt, and depression usually ensue, but bingeing is initially pleasant because of release from dietary constraints.

Bulimia nervosa typically affects women in late adolescence or early adulthood, when concerns about dieting and dissatisfaction with body shape or weight are at their height. Despite the widespread belief that eating disorders, especially anorexia nervosa, are most common among affluent people, the available evidence shows no strong linkage between socioeconomic status and eating disorders (Gibbons, 2001; Z. Wang et al., 2005). Beliefs that eating disorders are associated with high socioeconomic status may reflect the tendency for affluent patients to obtain treatment. Alternatively, it may be that the social pressures on young women to strive to achieve an ultrathin ideal have now generalized across all socioeconomic levels.

MEDICAL COMPLICATIONS OF BULIMIA NERVOSA Like anorexia nervosa, bulimia nervosa is associated with many medical complications. Many of these stem from repeated vomiting: skin irritation around the mouth due to frequent contact with stomach acid, blockage of salivary ducts, decay of tooth enamel, and dental cavities. The acid from the vomit may damage taste receptors on the palate, making the person less sensitive to the taste of vomit with repeated purging. Decreased sensitivity to the aversive taste of vomit may help maintain the purging behavior. Cycles of bingeing and vomiting may cause abdominal pain, hiatal hernia, and other abdominal complaints, as well as disturbed menstrual functioning. Stress on the pancreas may produce pancreatitis (inflammation of the pancreas), which is a medical emergency. Excessive use of laxatives may cause bloody diarrhea and laxative dependency, so the person cannot have normal bowel movements without laxatives. In extreme cases, the bowel can lose its reflexive eliminatory response to pressure from waste material. Bingeing on large quantities of salty food may cause convulsions and swelling. Repeated vomiting or abuse of laxatives can lead to potassium deficiency, producing muscular weakness, cardiac irregularities, and even sudden death—especially when diuretics are used. As with anorexia, menstruation may come to a halt. Also like patients with anorexia, those with bulimia have high rates of early deaths as compared to the general population, with deaths resulting from various causes such as suicide, substance abuse, and medical disorders (Crow et al., 2009b). Although patients with bulimia show a shockingly high rate of suicide attempts, estimated at 25% to 35%, it's not yet clear whether their rate of completed suicide is higher than average (Franko & Keel, 2006).

Causes of Anorexia Nervosa and Bulimia Nervosa

9.2 Describe causal factors involved in anorexia nervosa and bulimia nervosa.

Like other psychological disorders, anorexia nervosa and bulimia nervosa involve a complex interplay of factors. Perhaps most significant are social pressures that lead young women to base their self-worth on their physical appearance, especially their weight.

SOCIOCULTURAL FACTORS Sociocultural theorists point to social pressures and expectations placed on young women in our society as contributing factors in eating disorders (McKnight Investigators, 2003; Mendez, 2005). The drive for thinness and body dissatisfaction figure prominently in eating disorders (Brannan, & Petrie, 2011; Chernyak & Lowe, 2010). Comparing one's own body unfavorably to others in terms of appearance can lead to body dissatisfaction (Myers & Crowther, 2009). Young women begin measuring themselves against unrealistic standards of thinness—the "body perfect"— represented in media images of ultrathin models and performers, setting the stage for body dissatisfaction (Bell & Dittmar, 2011; Dalley, Buunk, & Umit, 2009; Rodgers, Salès, & Chabrol,

Body dissatisfaction starts early. Investigators find greater levels of body dissatisfaction in girls than boys as young as 8 years of age.

2010). Body dissatisfaction, in turn, may lead to excessive dieting and disturbed eating behaviors. Even in children as young as 8 years, investigators find that girls express more dissatisfaction with their bodies than boys do (Ricciardelli & McCabe, 2004). Pressures to achieve a thin ideal are underscored by findings from a college sample that one in seven (14%) women said they would feel embarrassed buying a single chocolate bar in a store (Rozin, Bauer, & Catanese, 2003). Peer pressure from friends to adhere to a thin body shape also emerges as a strong predictor of bulimic behavior in young women (Young, McFatter, & Clopton, 2001). Body dissatisfaction is also linked to eating disorders in young men (Olivardia et al., 2004).

The idealization of thinness in women can be illustrated in the changes in the **body mass index (BMI)** of winners of the Miss America pageant (Rubinstein & Caballero, 2000) (see Figure 9.1). BMI is a measure of height-adjusted weight. Notice the downward trend. What messages about feminine beauty might this be conveying to young women and young men?

The pressure to be thin is so prevalent that dieting has become the normative pattern of eating among young American women. Four out of five young women in the United States have gone on a diet by the time they reach their 18th birthdays. A recent survey of a sample of college women showed that regardless of how much they weighed, the great majority, about 80%, reported dieting (Malinauskas et al., 2006). Concerns about social pressures to be thin bring to light the idealized body images to which girls are exposed, including perhaps the most famous of all ultrathin ideals—Barbie (see *Thinking Critically About Abnormal Psychology* on page 344).

In support of the sociocultural model, evidence shows that eating disorders are much less common in non-Western countries that do not associate thinness with female beauty (Giddens, 2006). Yet even in non-Western cultures, such as those in East Africa, the level of exposure to Western media and travel in Western countries is associated with a higher rate of eating disorder symptoms in young women (Eddy, Hennessey, & Thompson-Brenner, 2007). Investigators also find high levels of both

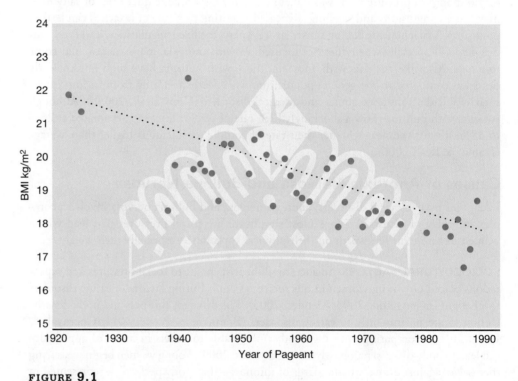

FIGURE 9.1

Thinner and thinner. Note the downward trend in the BMI levels of Miss America contest winners over time. What might these data suggest about changes in society's view of the ideal female form? *Source:* Rubinstein & Caballero (2000).

body dissatisfaction and disordered eating behaviors in male and female middle-school children in Korea (Jung, Forbes, & Lee, 2009). And in Taiwan, investigators find that body dissatisfaction among young women is predictive of intentions to lose weight (Lu & Hou, 2009).

Eating disorders in developing countries may be linked to factors other than obsessive concerns about weight. For example, among young women in the African country of Ghana, researchers found that extreme thinness was linked to fasting for religious reasons rather than for weight concerns (Bennett et al., 2004).

Rates of disordered eating behaviors and eating disorders also vary in the United States among ethnic groups, with higher rates found among Euro-American adolescents than among African American and other ethnic minority adolescents (Lamberg, 2003; Striegel-Moore et al., 2003). One likely reason for this discrepancy is that body image and body dissatisfaction are less closely tied to body weight among minority women (Angier, 2000b). That said, investigators expect that the prevalence of eating disorders in young women of color will rise with increased exposure to Eurocentric concepts of feminine beauty (Gilbert, 2003). Disturbed eating behaviors may also be more common among ethnic minority groups, including Native Americans, than is commonly believed (Shaw et al., 2004). Although anorexia nervosa is far more common in women than in men, an increasing number of young men are presenting with disturbed eating behavior, even anorexia nervosa. Factors associated with disturbed eating behavior in young men parallel those in young women, such as needs for perfection, perceived pressures from others to lose weight, and participation in sports that place a strong value on leanness (Ricciardelli & McCabe, 2004).

PSYCHOSOCIAL FACTORS Although cultural pressures to conform to an ultrathin female ideal play a major role in eating disorders, the great majority of young women exposed to these pressures do not develop eating disorders. Other factors must be involved. For one thing, a pattern of overly restricted dieting is common to women with bulimia nervosa and anorexia nervosa. Women with eating disorders typically adopt very rigid dietary rules and practices about what they can eat, how much they can eat, and how often they can eat. It's important to recognize, however, that eating disorders involve deeper emotional issues involving feelings of insecurity, body dissatisfaction, and use of food for emotional gratification, as illustrated in this woman's firsthand account.

"I" "My Voice, My Cry for Help"

I started dieting when I was 13. As I look back now, I can see that I had feelings of insecurity that were surfacing as I struggled with relationships, my identity, and my sexuality. Back then it just felt like I was too fat. As my body began to change from a normal undeveloped child to a rounder, curvier woman, I held on to the ideals I saw in the media of the very thin, tall, hard bodies that defined beauty. My body was wrong. All my emotional struggles and insecurities became placed on my body. The first day I put myself on a diet, I stopped listening to the wisdom and truth of my own body. I began instead the pattern of forcing myself to conform to cultural standards that were impossible for me to obtain. My soul was crying out for love, for reassurance, security, and emotional soothing during a very overwhelming, confusing period in my life. The only way I knew how to soothe myself was to eat. The only way I knew how to be accepted was to diet. My voice, my cry for help was buried under the obsession and compulsion of dieting and bingeing, bingeing and purging.

Source: Normandi & Rorak, 1998.

Bulimia nervosa is also linked to problems in interpersonal relationships. Women with bulimia tend to be shy and have few if any close friends. Enhancing the social skills of women with bulimia may increase the quality of their relationships and perhaps reduce their tendencies to use food in maladaptive ways.

EMOTIONAL FACTORS People with anorexia nervosa may restrict their food intake in a misguided attempt to relieve upsetting emotions by seeking mastery or control over their bodies (Merwin, 2011). Young women with bulimia nervosa often have more emotional problems and lower self-esteem than other dieters (Jacobi et al., 2004). Negative emotional states such as anxiety and depression can trigger episodes of binge eating (Reas & Grilo, 2007). Bulimia nervosa is often accompanied by other diagnosable disorders, such as depression, obsessive–compulsive disorder, and substance-related disorders. This suggests that some forms of binge eating represent attempts at coping with emotional distress. Unfortunately, cycles of bingeing and purging exacerbate emotional problems rather than relieve them. We also have learned that women with bulimia are more likely than other women to have experienced childhood sexual and physical abuse (Kent & Waller, 2000). In some cases, bulimia nervosa may develop as an ineffective means of coping with abuse. Binge eating may represent an attempt to manage or soothe negative feelings. Recent evidence links negative emotional states to binge eating episodes (Haedt-Matt & Keel, 2011).

LEARNING PERSPECTIVES From a learning perspective, we can conceptualize eating disorders as a type of weight phobia. In this model, relief from anxiety acts as negative reinforcement. Women with bulimia tend to have been slightly overweight before they developed bulimia, and the binge–purge cycle usually begins after a period of strict dieting to lose weight.

In a typical scenario, the rigid dietary controls fail, leading to a loss of inhibitions (disinhibition), which prompts a binge eating episode. The binge eating induces fear of weight gain, which in turn prompts self-induced vomiting or excessive exercise. Some people with bulimia even resort to vomiting after every meal. Purging is negatively reinforced because it produces relief, or at least partial relief, from anxiety over gaining weight. As in anorexia, food-rejecting behavior (and purging in cases of the binge eating/purging subtype) is negatively reinforced by relief from anxiety about weight gain. **T / F**

Dietary restraint appears to play a more prominent role in bulimia nervosa for women at high genetic risk of the disorder (Racine et al., 2011). This again illustrates the need to examine interactions of psychosocial factors (dietary restraint) and genetic factors in the development of psychological disorders.

COGNITIVE FACTORS Perfectionism and overconcern about making mistakes figure prominently in eating disorders (Deas et al., 2011; Wade & Tiggemann, 2013). People with eating disorders may impose perfectionistic pressures on themselves to achieve a "perfect body" and get down on themselves when they fail to meet their impossibly high standards. Their extreme dieting may give them a sense of control and independence that they feel they lack in other aspects of their lives. Here, a young woman with anorexia nervosa speaks about the feelings of power she experienced by deciding to go without food:

> **"I"** **"I Felt the Power"**
>
> I was constantly comparing myself to people . . . that was just the absolutely unavoidable thing . . . Just looking at everybody and thinking to myself, "Oh my gosh, do I look like that?" . . . I would only find the skinniest people . . . that's just where my eyes went, to the thinnest people and . . . that's where I would be like, "I want to be like them." I wasn't scared of gaining weight, I . . . just wanted to keep on losing weight and if I wasn't, then there was something wrong. Or if my jeans didn't fit just right or if they weren't baggy enough . . . or my thighs touched together—that was a big thing of mine—or my arms jiggling . . . But my idea of arms jiggling was my skin moving. . . . (And if your body jiggled, what did that mean?). . . That I was fat . . . if my body was moving, then that means I wouldn't eat for the day, or the night, or the weekend, whatever I decided, and that's where I felt the power that people talk about, the control, it's what I decided to do.
>
> *Source:* Excerpted from *Speaking Out: Videos in Abnormal Psychology*, Pearson Education, 2008. All rights reserved.

People who struggle with bulimia tend to think in dichotomous or "black or white" terms. Thus, they expect to adhere perfectly to their rigid dietary rules and judge themselves as complete failures when they deviate even slightly. They also judge themselves harshly for episodes of binge eating and purging. They may also hold exaggerated beliefs about the negative consequences of gaining weight, which further contributes to disordered eating. Investigators find that women with eating disorders tend to heap blame on themselves for negative events in general, and self-blame most probably contributes to maintaining their disordered eating behavior (Morrison, Waller, & Lawson, 2006).

Body dissatisfaction is also an important factor in eating disorders. Body dissatisfaction may lead to maladaptive attempts—through self-starvation and purging—to attain a desired body weight or shape. Women with eating disorders tend to be extremely concerned about their body weight and shape (Jacobi et al., 2004). Excessive weight-related concerns even affect many young children and may possibly set the stage for development of eating disorders in adolescence or early adulthood.

PSYCHODYNAMIC PERSPECTIVES Psychodynamic theorists suggest that girls with anorexia nervosa have difficulty separating from their families and consolidating separate, individuated identities (e.g., Bruch, 1973; Minuchin, Rosman, & Baker, 1978). Perhaps anorexia represents the girl's unconscious effort to remain a prepubescent child. By maintaining the veneer of childhood, pubescent girls may avoid dealing with adult issues such as increased independence and separation from their families, sexual maturation, and assumption of adult responsibilities.

FAMILY FACTORS Eating disorders frequently develop against a backdrop of family problems and conflicts. Some theorists focus on the brutal effect of self-starvation on parents. They suggest that some adolescents refuse to eat to punish their parents for feelings of loneliness and alienation they experience in the home.

Young women with eating disorders often come from dysfunctional family backgrounds characterized by high levels of family conflict and by parents who tend to be overprotective on the one hand but less nurturing and supportive on the other (e.g., Giordano, 2005; McGrane & Carr, 2002). Parents often seem less capable of promoting independence, or even permitting autonomy, in their daughters. Yet it remains uncertain whether these family patterns contribute to eating disorders or whether eating disorders disrupt family dynamics in these ways. The truth probably lies in an interaction between the two. Might binge eating, as suggested by Humphrey (1986), be a metaphoric effort to gain the nurturance and comfort through food that the daughter is lacking from the family?

From a systems perspective, families are systems that regulate themselves in ways that minimize the open expression of conflict and reduce the need for change. Within this perspective, girls who develop anorexia nervosa may be seen as helping maintain the shaky balances and harmonies found in dysfunctional families by displacing attention from family conflicts and marital tensions onto themselves. The girl may become the *identified patient,* although it is actually the family unit that is dysfunctional.

Regardless of the factors that initiate eating disorders, social reinforcers may maintain them. Children with eating disorders may quickly become the focus of attention in their families, receiving attention from their parents that is otherwise lacking.

BIOLOGICAL FACTORS Scientists suspect that abnormalities in brain mechanisms controlling hunger and satiety are involved in bulimia nervosa, most probably involving the brain chemical serotonin. Serotonin plays a key role in regulating mood and appetite, especially cravings for carbohydrates (Hildebrandt et al., 2010). Irregularities in the levels of serotonin or how it is used in the brain may contribute to binge-eating episodes. This line of thinking is buttressed by findings that antidepressants that specifically target serotonin, such as Prozac and Zoloft, help decrease binge eating episodes in bulimia (Walsh et al., 2004). We also know that many women with eating disorders are depressed or have a history of depression, and imbalances of serotonin are implicated in depressive disorders.

Death by starvation. A leading fashion model, Brazilian Ana Carolina Reston, was just 21 when she died in 2006 from complications due to anorexia. At the time of her death, the 5'7" Reston weighed only 88 pounds. Anorexia nervosa continues to be a widespread problem among fashion models today.

@Issue: Should Barbie Be Banned?

We're not suggesting that Barbie and her entourage be thrown overboard in some modern-day version of the Boston Tea Party, or that stores be prohibited from selling the popular toys. But by raising such a provocative question, we hope to encourage you to think critically about the effects that these anatomically incorrect figurines may have on the psyches of young women. Lest you think that Barbie, now more than 50 years old, is merely a quaint relic of an earlier generation, she is still the world's highest earning doll, accounting for some $1.2 billion in revenues annually (Towner, 2009).

As writer Laura Vanderkam (2003) notes in her article, "Barbie and Fat as a Feminist Issue," Barbie was designed to fit the

To be like Barbie. The Barbie doll has long represented a symbol of the buxom but thin feminine form that has become idealized in our culture. What message do you think the Barbie-doll figure conveys to young girls?

idealized male fantasy of a bosomy but impossibly thin female form, and then sold to girls who grew up wanting to look like her. Social worker Abigail Natenshon, author of *When Your Child Has an Eating Disorder*, argues that images of Barbie and ultrathin female models and actresses create expectations in the minds of young women about how they are supposed to look. Though many factors undoubtedly contribute to eating disorders, should parents keep Barbie at bay and not bring the doll into their homes? Or should they welcome Barbie but help their daughters see that her ultrathin form is not a female ideal, and help them understand that self-esteem should not be measured by a bathroom scale?

For that matter, should parents inform their sons that bulked-up wrestlers, muscularized movie heroes, and even action figures in video games are not exemplars of what they should aspire to? Even GI Joe–type action figures (i.e., dolls) appear more muscular today than in earlier versions.

Exposure to overly masculinized male images may create pressures on boys that can lead to disturbed eating behaviors. Evidence shows that many men express dissatisfaction with their bodies (Murray et al., 2013; Tiggemann, Martins, & Kirkbride, 2007). For both men and women, it appears that exposure to "perfect" bodies in the media and advertising reinforces the idea that "normal" bodies are not acceptable.

On the other hand, Vanderkam cautions us not to the throw the "Barbie" out with the bathwater (apologies for the pun). In light of the epidemic of obesity facing our society, perhaps we should champion the active, energetic lifestyle that Barbie embodies. What do you think?

In thinking critically about the issue, answer the following questions:

- Assume that you are a parent of a young boy or girl. Would you restrict the kinds of toys you buy based on considerations of appropriate body size and weight? Why or why not?

- What messages should parents convey to children regarding the overly slenderized and masculinized images that children regularly see?

Genetics appears to play an important role in the development of eating disorders (Baker et al., 2009; Kaye, 2009). We know that eating disorders tend to run in families, which is consistent with a genetic contribution (Hitti, 2006). We also have evidence of genetic factors from an important early study of more than 2,000 female twins (Kendler et al., 1991). The investigators found a much higher concordance rate for bulimia nervosa, 23% versus 9%, among monozygotic (MZ) twins than among dizygotic (DZ) twins. (Recall that concordance rate refers to the percentage of twins in which both twins have a given trait or disorder in common.) A greater concordance for anorexia nervosa is also found among MZ twins than among DZ twins, 50% versus 5% (Holland, Sicotte, &

Treasure, 1988). Nonetheless, genetic factors cannot fully account for the development of eating disorders. Consistent with the diathesis–stress model, a genetic predisposition affecting the regulation of neurotransmitter activity in the brain may interact with stress associated with social and family pressures to increase the risk of eating disorders.

Treatment of Anorexia Nervosa and Bulimia Nervosa

Anorexia and bulimia nervosa are often difficult to treat and outcomes remain less than satisfactory in many cases (Castellini et al., 2011; Haynos & Fruzzetti, 2011; Yager, 2011). Still, it's fair to say that progress is being made in treating these challenging disorders. Unfortunately, most people with these eating disorders do not receive appropriate medical or mental health treatment for their specific disorder (Hart et al., 2011; Labbe, 2011; Swanson et al., 2011).

Treatment of anorexia nervosa may involve hospitalization, especially in cases in which weight loss becomes severe or body weight falls rapidly. In the hospital, patients are usually placed on a closely monitored refeeding regimen. Behavioral therapy is commonly used, with rewards made contingent on adherence to the refeeding protocol. Commonly used reinforcers include ward privileges and social opportunities. However, relapses are common and upward of 50% of inpatients treated for anorexia nervosa are rehospitalized within a year of discharge (Haynos & Fruzzetti, 2011).

Psychodynamic therapy is sometimes combined with behavior therapy to probe for psychological conflicts. Family therapy may also be employed to help resolve underlying family conflicts. Continuing therapy following hospitalization, generally in the form of individual or family therapy, is recommended to provide continuing care.

Hospitalization may also be helpful in breaking the binge–purge cycle in bulimia nervosa, but it appears to be necessary only where eating behaviors are clearly out of control and outpatient treatment has failed, or where there are severe medical complications, suicidal thoughts or attempts, or substance abuse.

Research evidence supports the benefits of cognitive-behavioral therapy (CBT) in treating bulimia nervosa (Byrne et al., 2011; Crow et al., 2009a; Lampard et al., 2011; Masheb, Grilo, & Rolls, 2011). A recent large-scale study showed that CBT resulted in the elimination of bingeing episodes in about two of three eating disorder patients who presented with bingeing as a core symptom (Striegel-Moore et al., 2010).

CBT therapists help people with bulimia challenge self-defeating thoughts and beliefs, such as unrealistic, perfectionistic expectations regarding dieting and body weight. Another common dysfunctional thought pattern is dichotomous (all-or-nothing) thinking, which predisposes them to purge when they slip even a little from their rigid diets. CBT also challenges tendencies to overemphasize appearance in determining self-worth. To control self-induced vomiting, therapists may use the behavioral technique of *exposure with response prevention*, which was developed for treatment of people with obsessive–compulsive disorder. In this technique, the person with bulimia nervosa is exposed to eating forbidden foods while the therapist stands by to prevent vomiting until the urge to purge passes. Individuals with bulimia thus learn to tolerate violations of their rigid dietary rules without resorting to purging.

Interpersonal psychotherapy (IPT), a structured form of psychodynamic therapy, is also helpful in treating bulimia nervosa and may be useful in cases that fail to respond to CBT (Rieger et al., 2010). IPT focuses on resolving interpersonal problems based on the belief that more effective interpersonal functioning will lead to the adoption of healthier food habits and attitudes. Antidepressant drugs, such as Prozac, have demonstrated therapeutic benefits in treating bulimia nervosa (Walsh et al., 2004). These drugs decrease the urge to binge by normalizing levels of serotonin—the brain chemical involved in regulating appetite. However, tests of the effectiveness of antidepressant drugs have yielded mixed results in treating anorexia nervosa (Walsh et al., 2006).

In *A Closer Look*, we focus on a health problem closely identified with binge eating: **obesity.**

9.3 Evaluate methods used to treat eating disorders.

9.4 Identify health risks associated with obesity.

9.5 Identify factors linked to obesity.

Obesity: A National Epidemic

The problem of *obesity* once again brings into context the complex interrelationships between mind and body. Obesity is classified as a medical condition, not a psychological disorder, but psychological factors play important roles in its development and treatment, which is why it is the focus of our attention here. **T / F**

truth OR fiction

Obesity is one of the most common psychological disorders in the United States.

☑ **FALSE**   Obesity is a medical disorder, not a psychological disorder.

Obesity has reached epidemic proportions not only in the United States, but throughout the world. More Americans are overweight today than at any time since the government started tracking obesity in the 1960s. About one-third of Americans are obese and about another third are overweight (Bray, 2012; CDC, 2011; Flegal et al., 2012; Mitka, 2012). Assuming current trends continue, nearly 200 million American adults will be obese by the year 2030 (Gorman, 2012). Presently, about one in three children and teens in the United States is either overweight or obese (Tavernise, 2012; Weir, 2012).

Health officials are rightly concerned about obesity because it is a risk factor in many chronic and potentially life-threatening diseases, including heart disease, stroke, diabetes, respiratory disease, and some forms of cancer (Gorman, 2012; Khoo et al., 2011; Taubes, 2012). All told, obesity accounts for more than 160,000 excess deaths in the United States every year and shaves 6 or 7 years off the average person's life expectancy (Flegal et al., 2005; Fontaine et al., 2003; Freedman, 2011). But what about people who are overweight but not obese? The answer is not entirely clear, as recent findings indicate that overweight people who were not clinically obese actually have a lower risk of early death than people of normal weight (Flegal et al., 2013; Heymsfield & Cefalu, 2013).

Body weight is essentially a function of energy balance. When caloric intake exceeds energy output, the excess calories are stored in the body in the form of fat, leading to obesity (see

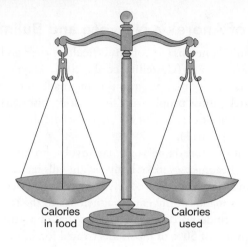

FIGURE 9.2

Weight: A balancing act. Body weight is determined by the balance between energy consumed in the form of food calories and energy used in the course of the day through physical activity and maintenance of bodily processes. When calories consumed in food exceed calories used, we gain weight. To lose weight, we need to take in fewer calories than we expend. Weight control involves a balance between calories consumed and calories used. *Source:* Physical Activity and Weight Control, National Institutes of Diabetes and Digestive and Kidney Diseases (NIDDK), http://win.niddk.nih.gov/publications/physical.htm.

Figure 9.2). Despite all the money and effort spent on weight-loss products and programs, our collective waistlines are getting larger—a result, health experts believe, of Americans consuming too many calories and exercising too little (Lamberg, 2006; Pollan, 2003). Americans today average 530 more calories per day than they did 30 years ago (Gorman, 2003). The reasons? A diet containing too much high-fat, high-calories, and supersized portions that are growing ever larger.

The key to preventing obesity is to bring energy expenditure in line with energy (caloric) intake. Unfortunately, this is easier said than done. Research suggests that a number of factors contribute to the imbalance between energy intake and expenditure that underlies obesity, including genetics, metabolic factors, lifestyle factors, psychological factors, and socioeconomic factors.

Genetic Factors

Obesity is a complex condition in which multiple causes are involved (Hamre, 2013). Evidence points to a role for genetics, but genes don't tell the whole story (Friedman, 2011; Small et al., 2011). Environmental factors (diet and exercise patterns) are also important contributors.

Metabolic Factors

Genetic differences in *metabolic rate* (the rate at which the body burns calories) may play an important role in determining risk of

Hazardous waist. Obesity is indeed a hazard to health and longevity.

obesity. Then too, when people start to lose significant amounts of weight, the body reacts as if it were starving by slowing the metabolic rate to preserve energy resources (Freedman, 2011). This makes it difficult to continue losing more weight or even to maintain weight that was lost. Mechanisms in the brain control the body's metabolism to keep body weight around a genetically influenced *set point*. The ability of the body to adjust the metabolic rate downward when calorie intake declines may have helped ancestral humans survive times of famine. However, this mechanism is a bane to people today who are trying to lose weight and keep it off. T / F

truth OR fiction

When people start losing significant amounts of weight, their bodies respond as though they were starving.

☑ **TRUE**   The body responds to slowing the metabolic rate, making it more difficult for dieters to lose additional weight or keep off the weight they lost.

People may be able to offset this metabolic adjustment by losing weight more gradually and by following a more vigorous exercise regimen. Vigorous exercise burns calories directly and may increase the metabolic rate by replacing fat tissue with muscle, especially if the exercise program involves weight-bearing activity. Also, ounce for ounce, muscle tissue burns more calories than fat tissue. Before starting an exercise regimen, check with your physician to determine which types of activity are best suited to your overall health condition.

Fat Cells

Fat cells, which are cells that store fat, comprise the fatty tissue in the body (also called *adipose tissue*). Obese people have more fat cells than people who are not obese. Severely obese people may have some 200 billion fat cells, as compared to 25 or 30 billion in normal-weight individuals. Why does this matter? As time passes after eating, the blood sugar level declines, drawing out fat from these cells to supply more nourishment to the body. The hypothalamus in the brain triggers hunger when it detects depletion of fat in these cells. Hunger is a drive that motivates eating, which thereby replenishes the fat cells. Unfortunately, even if we lose weight, we do not shed fat cells (Hopkin, 2008). In people who have more fatty tissue and hence higher numbers of fat cells, the body sends more signals of fat depletion to the brain than in people with fewer fat cells; as a result, they feel food deprived sooner, making it more difficult for them to lose weight or to maintain the weight they have lost.

Lifestyle Factors

Eating habits are changing, and not for the better. The constant bombardment of food-related cues in television commercials, print advertising, and the like can take a toll on our individual and collective waistlines. Restaurants today are competing with each other in terms of who can pile the most food on ever-larger dinner plates. Pizzerias are using larger pans and fast-food restaurants are supersizing meals—all of which takes a toll on the waistline. That "big gulp" 64-ounce soft drink packs an incredible 800 calories (T. K. Smith, 2003)! And guess which character, after Santa Claus, children recognize most often? The answer: Ronald McDonald (Parloff, 2003). T / F

truth OR fiction

After Santa Claus, the most recognizable figure to children is Ronald McDonald.

☑ **TRUE**   Ronald is the second-most recognizable figure among children. What might his popularity have to do with our fast-food-obsessed culture?

Another contributing factor to our expanding waistlines is America's growing suburbs and the car-dependent culture this entails (McKee, 2003). City dwellers may burn off some extra calories hiking around town, but suburbanites must rely on their cars to get from place to place in spread-out communities in the suburban sprawl.

Psychological Factors

According to psychodynamic theory, eating is the cardinal oral activity. Psychodynamic theorists believe that people who were fixated in the oral stage by conflicts concerning dependence and independence are likely to regress in times of stress to excessive oral activities such as overeating. Other psychological factors connected with overeating and obesity include low self-esteem, lack of self-efficacy expectancies, family conflicts, and negative emotions. Emotions such as anger, fear, and sadness can prompt excessive eating.

Socioeconomic Factors

Obesity is more prevalent among people of lower-income levels. Because people of color in our society are as a group lower in socioeconomic status than (non-Hispanic) White Americans, we should not be surprised that rates of obesity are higher among people of color, at least among women of color (see Figure 9.3).

Why are people on the lower rungs of the socioeconomic ladder at greater risk of obesity? For one thing, more affluent people have greater access to information about nutrition and health and are more likely to take health education courses. They also have greater

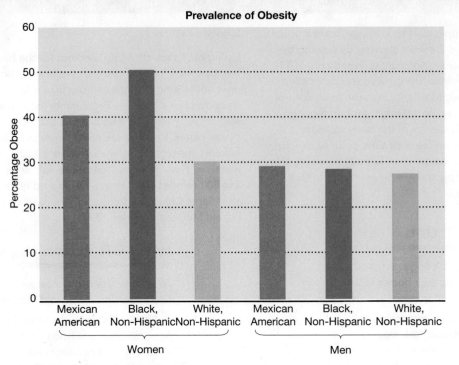

FIGURE 9.3

Rates of obesity (age 20 or higher). This figure shows the rates of obesity among U.S. adults in relation to race and ethnicity. *Source: Health, United States, 2003,* Centers for Disease Control and Prevention, National Center for Health Statistics, National Health and Nutrition Examination Survey.

access to health care providers. Poorer people also exercise less regularly than more affluent people do. More affluent people are more likely to have the time, the income, and the space to exercise. Many poor people in the inner city also turn to food as a way of coping with the stresses of poverty, discrimination, crowding, and crime.

Acculturation may also contribute to obesity, at least when it involves adopting the unhealthful dietary practices of the host culture. Consider that Japanese American men living in California and Hawaii eat a higher-fat diet than Japanese men do. Not surprisingly, the prevalence of obesity is two to three times higher among Japanese American men than among men living in Japan (Curb & Marcus, 1991).

Facing the Challenge of Obesity

Despite their appeal, quickie diets don't work. The great majority of people who diet, perhaps more than 9 out of 10 people, regain any weight they lose. Nor are antiobesity or diet drugs the answer, as they offer temporary benefits at best and can have significant side effects. Long-term success in the "battle of the bulge" requires a continuing commitment to following a sensible, lower-calorie, lower-fat diet combined with regular exercise (Bray, 2012; Freedman, 2011; Sacks et al., 2009). Even people whose heredity may work against them can control their weight within some broad limits through adopting a sensible diet, increasing activity and exercise levels, and developing healthier eating habits.

Although progress has been made in treating eating disorders, there is considerable room for improvement (Fairburn et al., 2009). Even CBT, which is recognized as the most effective form of treatment for bulimia, fails to succeed with a substantial proportion of patients (Wilson, Grilo, & Vitousek, 2007). Drug therapy sometimes proves helpful for patients with bulimia who fail to respond to cognitive-behavioral treatment

(Walsh et al., 2000). We can't yet say whether a combination CBT/medication approach is more effective than either component alone.

Eating disorders can be tenacious and enduring problems, especially when excessive fears about body weight and distortions in body image continue beyond active treatment (Fairburn et al., 2003). Though recovery from anorexia tends to be a long and uncertain process, we are encouraged by recent evidence that CBT can help delay or even prevent relapse (Carter et al., 2009).

Difficulties in treating eating disorders only affirm the need to develop effective prevention programs. Recent studies demonstrate reduced risks of eating disorders following participation in programs targeting disordered eating behaviors and attitudes (e.g., Becker et al., 2008; McMillan, W., Stice, E., & Rohde, 2011; Stice et al., 2011).

Binge-Eating Disorder

People with **binge-eating disorder (BED)** have repeated binge-eating episodes but unlike bulimia nervosa, there is no compensatory behavior afterward to reduce weight—no self-induced vomiting, excessive laxative use or exercise, for example. Binge-eating episodes in BED occur on an average of at least once a week for a period of three months (APA, 2013). These episodes are characterized by a lack of control over eating and by consuming far greater amounts of food than people typically eat in the same span of time. During a binge, the person may eat much more quickly than usual and continue eating despite feeling uncomfortably full. The person may binge alone because of embarrassment over excessive eating in front of others. Afterward, they may feel disgusted with themselves, be depressed, or be plagued by feelings of guilt.

BED is more common than either anorexia or bulimia, affecting about 3.5% of women and 2% of men at some point in their lives (Hudson et al., 2006). An estimated 8 million Americans struggle with BED (Ellin, 2012). People with BED tend to be older than those with anorexia or bulimia and the disorder tends to develop later in life, often in the person's 30s or 40s. Findings from a recent study showed that when compared to overweight individuals, people with BED tend to have higher levels of depression and more disturbed eating behaviors (Griet al., 2008).

Although people with bulimia nervosa typically fall within a normal weight range, many (but not all) BED patients are either overweight or obese (Bulik et al., 2012; Hudson et al., 2006). BED is also linked to depression and to a history of unsuccessful attempts at losing excess weight and keeping it off. Like other eating disorders, it occurs more often among women and may have a genetic component. But BED occurs more frequently among men than is the case with other eating disorders. Here, a 39-year-old man with BED relates his binge eating to negative feelings about himself: "Ultimately, it was about numbing out and self-loathing . . . There was this voice in my head that said, 'You're no good, worthless,' and I turned to food" (cited in Ellin, 2012).

BED may fall within a broader domain of compulsive behaviors characterized by impaired control over maladaptive behaviors, such as compulsive gambling and substance use disorders. A history of dieting may play a role in some cases of BED, but probably not to the extent that it does with bulimia.

CBT is helpful in treating BED and is recognized as the treatment of choice for the disorder (Griet et al., 2011; Grilo, Masheb, & Crosby, 2012; Munsch, Meyer, & Biedert, 2012; Striegel-Moore et al., 2010; Wilson et al., 2010). Antidepressants, especially SSRIs (selective serotonin reuptake inhibitors) such as Prozac, may also reduce binge-eating episodes by normalizing serotonin levels in the brain (Apopolinario et al., 2003). Serotonin is a neurotransmitter in brain networks that regulate appetite. However, CBT showed even better results than antidepressant medication at a follow-up evaluation 12 months after treatment (Griet et al., 2012).

Watch the Video
Stacy: Binge-Eating Disorder
on MyPsychLab

Eating Disorders

We can conceptualize eating disorders within a multifactorial framework in which psychosocial and biological influences interact in the development of disturbed eating behaviors. Figure 9.4 illustrates a potential causal pathway for explaining the development of bulimia nervosa. Note that negative reinforcement in the form of relief from anxiety about gaining weight plays a pivotal role in strengthening and maintaining maladaptive ways of controlling body weight through food-rejecting behavior in the case of anorexia nervosa and purging in the case of bulimia nervosa. Unfortunately, negative reinforcement is a powerful influence that contributes to maintaining these maladaptive behaviors.

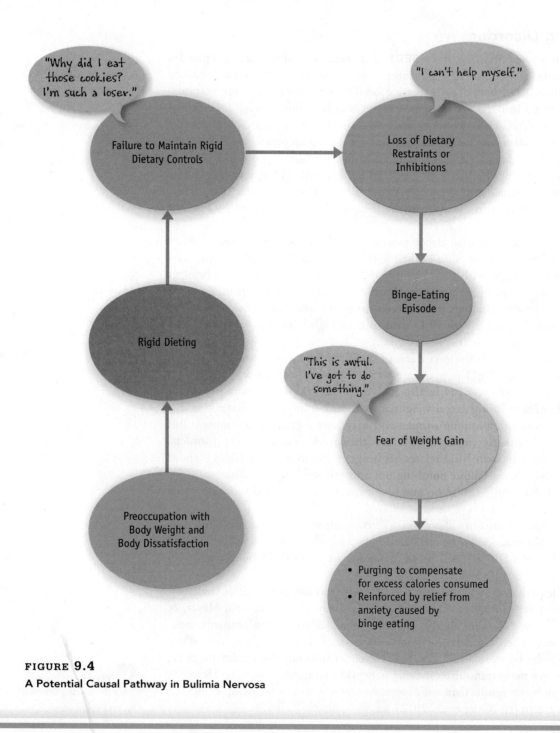

FIGURE 9.4

A Potential Causal Pathway in Bulimia Nervosa

Sleep-Wake Disorders

9.6 Identify and describe specific types of sleep-wake disorders.

Sleep is a biological function that remains in some ways a mystery. We know that sleep is restorative and that most of us need 7 or more hours of sleep a night to function at our best. Yet we cannot identify the specific biochemical changes occurring during sleep that account for its restorative function. We also know that many of us are troubled by sleep problems, although the causes of some of these problems remain obscure. Sleep problems of sufficient severity and frequency that they lead to significant personal distress or impaired functioning in social, occupational, or other roles are classified in the *DSM* system as **sleep-wake disorders.** The term *sleep-wake disorders* replaces the earlier diagnostic term, *sleep disorders*, so as to underscore the fact that these disorders involve problems occurring during sleep or at the threshold between sleep and wakefulness. Sleep-wake disorders also frequently occur together with other psychological disorders such as depression and with medical conditions such as cardiovascular problems, so that is important for people evaluated for sleep-wake problems to have a comprehensive psychological and medical evaluation.

Sleep problems have a major economic as well as psychological impact lost as the result of lower productivity and increased absences from work, including more than 250 million sick days among the nation's workers ("Sleep Problems," 2012). The estimated cost to American business for insomnia-related loss of productivity is some $63 billion (Weber, 2013). Table 9.2 provides an overview of the major types of sleep-wake disorders discussed in the chapter. There are a number of different types of sleep-wake disorders, including the major types we discuss here: insomnia disorder, hypersomnolence disorder, narcolepsy, breathing-related sleep disorders, circadian rhythm sleep-wake disorders, and parasomnias.

Highly specialized *sleep centers* have been established throughout the United States and Canada to provide more comprehensive assessment and diagnosis of sleep-related problems than is possible in a typical office setting. People with sleep-wake

---

TABLE 9.2
Overview of Major Sleep-Wake Disorders

Type of Disorder	Lifetime Prevalence in Population (approx.)	Description
Insomnia Disorder	6% to 10%	Persistent difficulty falling asleep, remaining asleep, or getting enough restful sleep
Hypersomnolence Disorder	1.5%	Persistent pattern of excessive daytime sleepiness
Narcolepsy	0.02% (2 in 10,000) to 0.04% (4 in 10,000) (with cataplexy)	Sudden attacks of sleep during the day
Breathing-Related Sleep Disorders	Varies with age, from 1%–2% in children to more than 20% in older adults	Sleep repeatedly interrupted due to difficulties breathing
Circadian Rhythm Sleep-Wake Disorders	1% or less in the general population, but more common in adolescents	Disruption of the internal sleep-wake cycle due to time changes in sleep patterns
Parasomnias		
Sleep Terrors	Unknown	Repeated experiences of sleep terrors resulting in sudden arousals
Sleepwalking	Estimated 1%–5% in children	Repeated episodes of sleepwalking
REM Sleep Behavior Disorder (RBD)	0.38%–0.5%	Vocalizing or thrashing about during REM sleep
Nightmare Disorder	Unknown	Repeated awakenings due to nightmares

Sources: Prevalence rates drawn from APA, 2013; Bootzin & Epstein, 2011; Ohayon, 1999; Ohayon, Dauvilliers, & Reynolds, 2012; Smith & Perlis, 2006.

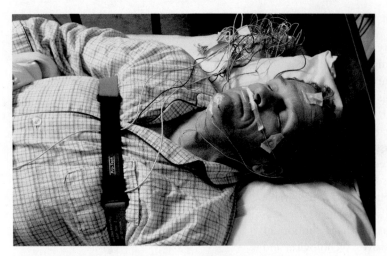

Sleep center. People with sleep-wake disorders are often evaluated in sleep centers, where their physiological responses can be monitored as they sleep.

disorders may spend a few nights at a sleep center, where they are wired to devices that track their physiological responses during sleep or attempted sleep—brain waves, heart and respiration rates, and so on. This form of assessment is termed *polysomnographic (PSG) recording* because it involves simultaneous measurement of diverse physiological response patterns, including brain waves, eye movements, muscle movements, and respiration. Information obtained from physiological monitoring of sleep patterns is combined with that obtained from medical and psychological evaluations, subjective reports of sleep disturbance, and sleep diaries (i.e., daily logs compiled by the problem sleeper that track the length of time between retiring to bed and falling asleep, number of hours slept, nightly awakenings, daytime naps, and so on). Multidisciplinary teams of physicians and psychologists sift through this information to arrive at a diagnosis and suggest treatment approaches to address the presenting problem.

INSOMNIA DISORDER The term **insomnia** derives from the Latin *in-,* meaning "not" or "without," and, of course, *somnus,* meaning "sleep." Occasional bouts of insomnia, especially during times of stress, are not abnormal. But persistent insomnia characterized by recurrent difficulty getting to sleep or remaining asleep is an abnormal behavior pattern (Harvey & Tang, 2012). An estimated 6% to 10% of U.S. adults suffer from the most commonly occurring sleep-wake disorder—**insomnia disorder** (formerly called *primary insomnia*) (Bootzin & Epstein, 2011; Smith & Perlis, 2006). A diagnosis of insomnia disorder requires that the problem has been present for at least three months and that it occurs at least three nights per week (APA, 2013) Chronic insomnia may also be a feature of an underlying physical problem or psychological disorder, such as depression, substance abuse, or physical illness. If the underlying problem is treated successfully, chances are that normal sleep patterns will be restored. Although problems with recurrent insomnia mostly affect people over age 40, many adolescents and young adults are also affected (Roberts, 2008). People with insomnia disorder complain about the amount or quality of their sleep. They have persistent difficulty falling asleep, remaining asleep, achieving restorative sleep (sleep that leaves the person feeling refreshed and alert), or waking up very early in the morning and being unable to get back to sleep. The disorder is accompanied by significant personal distress or impaired functioning in meeting daily responsibilities—complaints such as regularly feeling fatigued, feeling sleepy, or having low energy; having difficulty with memory or paying attention or concentrating at school or work; feeling down; or perhaps showing behavioral disturbance such as hyperactivity, impulsivity, or aggression. All in all, problems with insomnia can exact a significant toll on the quality of life.

Young people with insomnia disorder usually complain that it takes too long to get to sleep. Older people are more likely to complain of waking frequently during the night or of waking too early in the morning. Interestingly, many insomnia patients underestimate how much sleep they actually get—thinking they were lying awake when they actually had nodded off (Harvey & Tang, 2012).

There's a price to be paid for sleep deprivation associated with insomnia. Research evidence shows the sleep-deprived brain is less able to concentrate, pay attention, respond quickly, solve problems, and remember recently acquired information (Florian et al., 2011; Lim & Dinges, 2010). Chronic sleep deprivation—regularly getting too little sleep—is linked to a range of serious physical health problems, including poorer immune system functioning (Carpenter, 2013). The immune system protects the body against disease, so it is not surprising that researchers report that people who sleep less than 7 hours a night had a threefold higher risk of developing the common cold after exposure to cold viruses than those who sleep 8 or more hours nightly (Cohen et al., 2009; Reinberg, 2009).

If we miss a few hours of sleep, we may feel a little groggy the next day, but we will probably be able to muddle through. But over time, continued sleep deprivation takes a toll on our ability to function at our best, leading to daytime fatigue and creating difficulties performing our usual social, occupational, student, or other roles. Not surprisingly, people with the disorder often have other psychological problems as well, especially anxiety and depression.

Psychological factors contribute to primary insomnia. People troubled by insomnia tend to bring their anxieties and worries to bed with them, which raises their bodily arousal to a level that can prevent natural sleep. Another source of anxiety comes in the form of performance anxiety, or pressure felt from thinking one must get a full night's sleep to be able to function the next day (Sánchez-Ortuño & Edinger, 2010). People who are struggling with insomnia may try to force themselves to sleep, which typically backfires by creating more anxiety and tension, thus making sleep even less likely to occur. It's well worth recognizing that sleep cannot be forced. However, we can set the stage for sleep by going to bed when tired and relaxed and allowing sleep to occur naturally.

The principles of classical conditioning can help explain the development of chronic insomnia (Pollack, 2004b). After pairing a few anxious, sleepless nights with stimuli associated with the bedroom, simply entering the bedroom for the night may be sufficient to elicit bodily arousal that impairs sleep onset. Thus, states of heightened arousal become conditioned responses elicited by the conditioned stimuli of the bedroom—even the mere sight of bed.

HYPERSOMNOLENCE DISORDER The word *hypersomnolence* is derived from the Greek *hyper,* meaning "over" or "more than normal," and the Latin *somnus,* meaning "sleep." There are several major types of "more than normal sleep" or *hypersomnolence disorder* but they have in common complaints of excessive sleepiness or sudden sleep episodes during daytime hours.

Hypersomnolence disorder (formerly called *primary hypersomnia*), which is sometimes referred to as "sleep drunkenness," is a pattern of excessive sleepiness during daytime hours occurring at least three days a week for a period of at least three months (APA, 2013). People with hypersomnolence disorder may sleep 9 or more hours a night but still not feel refreshed upon awakening. They may have repeated episodes during the day of feeling an irresistible need to sleep, or napping repeatedly or falling asleep when they need to remain awake, or inadvertently dozing off while watching TV (Ohayon, Dauvilliers, & Reynolds, 2012). The daytime naps often last an hour or more, but the sleep does not leave the person feeling refreshed. The disorder cannot be accounted for by inadequate amounts of sleep during the night, by another psychological or physical disorder, or by drug or medication use.

Although many of us feel sleepy during the day from time to time, and may even drift off occasionally while reading or watching TV, people with hypersomnolence disorder have persistent periods of sleepiness that causes personal distress or difficulties in daily functioning, such as missing important meetings. About 1.5% of the general population meet the general criteria for hypersomnia (oversleeping), according to a recent estimate (Ohayon, Dauvilliers, & Reynolds, 2012).

The disorder may involve a defect in the sleep-wake mechanism in the brain and is often treated with stimulant medication to help the person maintain daytime wakefulness (M. Beck, 2012). A recent discovery suggests that in some cases of hypersomnia, a substance in the brain acts like a natural sleeping pill by increasing activity of GABA (gamma-aminobutyric acid), a neurotransmitter in the brain that induces feelings of drowsiness. GABA is the brain chemical affected by use of antianxiety drugs like Valium and Xanax (see Chapter 5) (Rye et al., 2012).

NARCOLEPSY The word **narcolepsy** derives from the Greek *narke,* meaning "stupor" and *lepsis,* meaning "an attack." People with narcolepsy experience an irresistible need to sleep or sudden sleep attacks or naps occurring at least three times a week for the past three months. During a sleep attack, the person suddenly falls asleep without warning and remains asleep for about 15 minutes. The person may be in the midst of a conversation at one moment and slump to the floor fast asleep a moment later.

Narcoleptic attacks are associated with an almost immediate transition from wakefulness to REM, or rapid eye movement, sleep—the stage of sleep primarily associated with dreaming. REM sleep is so named because the sleeper's eyes tend to dart about rapidly under the closed lids. Normally, a person who falls asleep transitions through other sleep stages before entering REM. The most common type of narcolepsy, called *narcolepsy/hypocretin deficiency syndrome,* involves a deficiency in the brain of *hypocretin* (also called *orexin*), a protein-like molecule produced by the hypothalamus that plays an important role in regulating the sleep-wake cycle.

Narcolepsy is often associated with **cataplexy,** a medical condition in which a person experiences a loss of muscle tone ranging from mild weakness in the legs to complete loss of muscle control, causing the person to collapse. Cataplexy most often (but not always) occurs in people with narcolepsy. It is triggered by strong emotional reactions such as joy, crying, anger, sudden terror, or intense laughter. Like narcolepsy, cataplexy involves deficiency of the brain chemical hypocretin. In a cataplectic episode, the person may slump to the floor and be unable to move for a period of seconds to perhaps a few minutes, but remain conscious. People experiencing cataplectic episodes experience blurry vision, but are able to hear and understand what is happening around them. In some cases, however, a person having a cataplectic episode may suddenly lapse into REM sleep. Mali, a woman who with long-standing narcolepsy, describes her cataplectic episodes:

"I" "Like a Marionette"

Cataplexy is the sudden loss of muscle tone in response to (strong) emotion. . . It's actually the same loss of muscle tone that everyone has when they are in REM sleep. It's almost like a marionette whose strings have been cut. You don't fall like a board . . . typically people won't hurt themselves, but it's more of a crumple, almost like somebody flipped the switch on the light switch and you lose all your muscle tone and it (then) comes back a few seconds, maybe a few minutes later. I hear absolutely everything that everyone says and can repeat everything when I come out of cataplexy, so it's an alert state, although (to) someone watching (a person) with cataplexy it seems like the person checked out and just went to sleep.

Source: Excerpted from *Speaking Out: Videos in Abnormal Psychology,* Pearson Education, 2010. All rights reserved.

People with narcolepsy may also experience **sleep paralysis,** a temporary state following awakening in which they feel incapable of moving or talking. They may also report **hypnagogic hallucinations,** which are often frightening hallucinations occurring just before the onset of sleep or shortly upon awakening. Here, Mali describes her experience with both sleep paralysis and hypnagogic hallucinations. 👁

Watch the Video
Mali: Narcolepsy
on **MyPsychLab**

"I" "A Normal Thing at an Abnormal Time"

Sleep paralysis is that same loss of muscle tone that's normal in REM sleep, but what's unusual in sleep paralysis is that you are conscious and awake but all of your muscles are paralyzed and you are unable to talk or move. . . . It became fairly normal for me, (but) it was still scary for me. For me, sleep paralysis often went hand in hand with the hypnagogic hallucinations, which again is a normal thing at an abnormal time. When (you) are in REM sleep, . . . you are unconscious and dreaming and if you (later) remember your dream it's a memory of the dream that you have. People with narcolepsy are sort of able to navigate these two worlds at the same time. So even though you're dreaming, there's a part of your brain that's conscious and awake, making the dream very, very realistic. And if you are having a negative or a scary dream, it can be kind of terrifying . . . For me, rather than having a lot of scary dreams I had a lot of dreams . . . that (left me wondering) whether I really had that conversation with someone . . . (or) did I really do that, did I really say that . . . I used to wake up in the morning and shake my head a bit and wondering what was real and what wasn't real.

Source: Excerpted from *Speaking Out: Videos in Abnormal Psychology*, Pearson Education, 2010. All rights reserved.

Affecting men and women about equally, narcolepsy with cataplexy affects an estimated 0.02% (2 in 10,000) to 0.04% (4 in 10,000) of the general adult population (APA, 2013). Unlike hypersomnia, in which daytime sleep episodes follow a period of increasing sleepiness, narcoleptic attacks occur abruptly, and the person awakes feeling refreshed. The attacks can be dangerous and frightening, especially if they occur when the person is driving or using heavy equipment or sharp implements. About two out of three people with narcolepsy have fallen asleep while driving, and four out of five have fallen asleep on the job (Aldrich, 1992). Not surprisingly, hypocretin, which the disorder is often associated with poor daily functioning. Household accidents resulting from falls are also common. The cause or causes of narcolepsy remain unknown, but suspicion focuses on genetic factors and loss of brain cells in the hypothalamus responsible for producing hypocretin, a brain chemical that helps maintain states of wakefulness (Goel et al., 2010; Hor et al., 2011). **T / F**

BREATHING-RELATED SLEEP DISORDERS People with **breathing-related sleep disorders** experience repeated disruptions of sleep due to respiratory problems. These frequent disruptions of sleep result in insomnia or excessive daytime sleepiness.

The subtypes of the disorder are distinguished in terms of the underlying causes of the breathing problem. The most common subtype, **obstructive sleep apnea hypopnea syndrome** (more commonly called *obstructive sleep apnea*), typically involves repeated episodes during sleep of snoring or gasping for breath, pauses of breath, or abnormally shallow breathing. (The word *apnea* derives from the Greek prefix *a-*, meaning "not" or "without," and *pneuma*, meaning "breath.") *Hypopnea* (literally "under breathing") refers to shallow or reduced breathing that is not as severe as full apnea.

Obstructive sleep apnea is generally accompanied by loud snoring and is a relatively common problem, affecting an estimated 28 million Americans (O'Connor, 2012). These breathing problems during sleep result from either complete or partial obstruction of breathing during sleep. The disorder also leads to excessive daytime sleepiness, fatigue, or complaints of unrefreshing sleep despite the opportunity to obtain sufficient sleep.

Obstructive sleep apnea is most common in middle age and affects men more frequently up to about the age of 50, at which point the rates are similar for men and women. The disorder occurs

Sleep apnea. Loud snoring may be a sign of obstructive sleep apnea, a breathing-related sleep disorder in which the person may temporarily stop breathing as many as 500 times during a night's sleep. Loud snoring, described by bed partners as reaching levels of industrial noise pollution, may alternate with momentary silences when breathing is interrupted or suspended.

Some people literally gasp for breath hundreds of times during sleep without realizing it.

☑ **TRUE** People with sleep apnea may gasp for breath hundreds of times during the night without realizing it.

more commonly among obese people, apparently because their upper airways tend to be narrowed due to an enlargement of soft tissue.

The breathing difficulty results from the blockage of airflow in the upper airways, which is often caused by a structural defect, such as an overly thick palate or enlarged tonsils or adenoids. In cases of complete obstruction, the sleeper may literally stop breathing for periods of 15 to 90 seconds as many as 500 times during the night! When these lapses of breathing occur, the sleeper may suddenly sit up, gasp for air, take a few deep breaths, and fall back asleep without awakening or realizing that breathing was interrupted. **T / F**

Although a biological reflex kicks in to force a gasping breath after these brief interruptions of breathing, the frequent disruptions of normal sleep resulting from apneas can leave people feeling sleepy the following day, making it difficult for them to function effectively.

Not surprisingly, people who have sleep apnea generally report an impaired quality of life. They also tend to have higher levels of depression than nonaffected individuals (Peppard et al., 2006). Sleep apnea is also a health concern because of its association with an increased risk of hypertension and of deaths due to cardiovascular problems (Campos-Rodriguez et al., 2012; Kapur & Weaver, 2012; Marin et al., 2012). Recent research points to yet another cause for concern: Repeated lapses of oxygen during episodes of apnea may lead to subtle forms of brain damage that affect psychological functioning, including thinking ability (Macey et al., 2008; Thorpy, 2008). Another concern is that people with sleep apnea also have higher risk of cancer (O'Connor, 2012). Unfortunately, about three out of four cases remain untreated (Minerd & Jasmer, 2006).

Another subtype of sleep-related breathing disorder is *central sleep apnea*, in which breathing problems during sleep are less dependent on respiratory resistance (blocked airways) and may involve heart-related problems or chronic use of opioid drugs. Another subtype, *sleep-related hypoventilation* (hypoventilation means "low breathing") is characterized by breathing problems that often trace to lung diseases or neuromuscular problems that affect lung functioning.

CIRCADIAN RHYTHM SLEEP-WAKE DISORDERS Most bodily functions follow a cycle or an internal rhythm—called a *circadian rhythm*—that lasts about 24 hours (Borgs et al., 2009). Even when people are relieved of scheduled activities and work duties and placed in environments where they are not aware of the time of day, they usually follow relatively normal sleep-wake schedules.

Circadian rhythm sleep-wake disorders involve a persistent disruption of the person's natural sleep-wake cycle. This disruption in normal sleep patterns can lead to insomnia or hypersomnolence and result in daytime sleepiness. The disorder causes significant levels of distress or impairs the person's ability to function in social, occupational, or other roles. The jet lag that accompanies travel between time zones does not qualify because it is usually temporary. However, frequent changes of time zones or frequent changes of work shifts (as encountered by nurses, for example) can induce more persistent or recurrent problems, resulting in a diagnosis of circadian rhythm sleep-wake disorder. Treatment may include a program of gradual adjustments in the sleep schedule to allow the person's circadian system to become aligned with changes in the sleep-wake schedule.

PARASOMNIAS Sleep typically runs in cycles of about 90 minutes each that progress in stages from light sleep to deep sleep and then to REM sleep, when most dreams occur. For some people, however, sleep is interrupted by partial or incomplete arousals during sleep. During these partials arousals, the person may appear confused, detached, or disconnected from the environment. The sleep may be unresponsive to attempts by other people to awaken them or comfort them. The sleeper typically gets up the next day without any memory of these episodes of partial arousal.

DSM-5 characterizes abnormal behavior patterns associated with partial or incomplete arousals as **parasomnias,** a category of sleep-wake disorders that is further divided into disorders associated with REM sleep and those associated with non-REM sleep. The word "parasomnia" literally means "around sleep" and signifies that abnormal behaviors involving partial or incomplete arousals occur around the boundary between wakefulness and sleep. As with other sleep-wake disorders, parasomnias cause significant levels of personal distress or interfere with the person's ability to perform expected social, occupational, or other important life roles. Here we consider the major types of parasomnias associated with non-REM sleep (*sleep terrors, sleepwalking*) and REM sleep (*rapid eye movement sleep behavior disorder* and *nightmare disorder*).

SLEEP TERRORS Sleep terrors are characterized by repeated episodes of terror-induced arousals that usually begin with a panicky scream (APA, 2013). The arousal typically begins with a loud, piercing cry or scream in the night. Even the most soundly sleeping parent will be summoned to the child's bedroom as if shot from a cannon. The child (most cases involve children) may be sitting up, appearing frightened and showing signs of extreme arousal—profuse sweating with rapid heartbeat and respiration. The child may start talking incoherently or thrashing about wildly but is not fully awake. If the child does awaken fully, he or she may not recognize the parent or may attempt to push the parent away. After a few minutes, the child falls back into a deep sleep and upon awakening in the morning remembers nothing of the experience. These terrifying attacks or *sleep terrors* are more intense than ordinary nightmares. Unlike nightmares, sleep terrors tend to occur during the first third of nightly sleep and during deep, non-REM sleep.

If awakening occurs during a sleep terror episode, the person will usually appear confused and disoriented for a few minutes. The person may feel a vague sense of terror and report some fragmentary dream images, but not the sort of detailed dreams typical of nightmares. Most of the time, the person falls back asleep and remembers nothing of the experience the following morning.

Children with sleep terror disorder typically outgrow the disorder during adolescence. More boys than girls are affected, but among adults, the gender ratio is about even. In adults, the disorder tends to follow a chronic course during which the frequency and intensity of the episodes wax and wane over time. Prevalence data on the disorder are lacking, but individual episodes of sleep terror are estimated to occur in about 37% of 18-month-old children, 20% of 30-month-old children, and about 2% of adults (APA, 2013). The cause of sleep terrors remains a mystery.

SLEEPWALKING In **sleepwalking,** people who are sleeping have repeated episodes in which they walk about the house while remaining asleep. During these episodes, the person is partially awake and can perform complex motor responses, such as getting out of bed and walking to another room. These motor behaviors are performed without conscious awareness and the person typically does not remember the incident upon fully awakening the following morning. Because these episodes tend to occur during the deeper (non-REM) stages of sleep in which there is an absence of dreaming, sleepwalking episodes do not seem to involve the enactment of a dream.

A sleepwalking disorder is most common in children, affecting 1% to 5% of children, according to some estimates (APA, 2013). Between 10% and 30% of children are believed to have had at least one episode of sleepwalking. The prevalence of the disorder among adults is unknown, as are its causes. Occasional episodes of sleepwalking are not unusual. About 4% of adults report experiencing a sleepwalking episode during the preceding year (Ohayon et al., 2012). But persistent or recurrent episodes may occasion a diagnosis of a sleepwalking disorder. Here, a man recounts an episode of sleepwalking from his childhood, which was one of many such incidents.

Sleep deprivation. Frequent changes in work shifts can disturb the body's natural sleep-wake cycle, resulting in a circadian rhythm sleep-wake disorder that can leave the person feeling sleep deprived.

We don't know what causes sleepwalking, but investigators believe that a combination of genetic and (unspecified) environmental factors are involved (Brooks & Kushida, 2002). Sleepwalkers tend to have a blank stare on their faces. Although they typically avoid walking into things, accidents do occasionally happen. Sleepwalkers are generally unresponsive to others and difficult to awaken. Upon awakening the following morning, they typically have little, if any, recall of their sleepwalking experience. If they are awakened during an episode, they may be disoriented or confused for a few minutes (as is the case with sleep terrors), but full alertness is soon restored. There is no basis to the belief that it is harmful to sleepwalkers to awaken them during episodes. Isolated incidents of violent behavior have been associated with sleepwalking, but these are rare and may well involve other forms of psychopathology.

RAPID EYE MOVEMENT SLEEP BEHAVIOR DISORDER (RBD) RBD involves repeated episodes of acting out one's dreams during REM sleep in the form of vocalizing parts of the dream or thrashing about. Normally, muscle activity is blocked during REM sleep to a point that the body's muscles, except those needed for breathing and other vital bodily functions, are essentially paralyzed. This is fortunate, since the muscle paralysis prevents injuries that might occur if the dreamer suddenly acts out the dream. But in cases of **REM sleep behavior disorder,** muscle paralysis is absent or incomplete and the person may suddenly kick or flail the arms during REM sleep, potentially causing injuries to the self or the bed partner.

RBD affects about 0.5% of the adult population and occurs most often among older adults, generally as the result of neurodegenerative disorders such as Parkinson's disease (Ohayon, 1999; Sixel-Döring et al., 2011). It may also be caused by withdrawal from alcohol or as an adverse consequence of certain drugs. In fact, RBD may be an early sign of the development of Parkinson's disease (Postuma et al., 2012). Medication may be used to help control RBD (Aurora et al., 2010).

NIGHTMARE DISORDER People with **nightmare disorder** have recurrent episodes of very disturbing and well-remembered nightmares during REM sleep. These nightmares are lengthy storylike dreams in which the dreamer attempts to avoid imminent threats or physical danger, such as in the case of being chased, attacked, or injured. The person usually recalls the nightmare vividly upon awakening. Although fear is the most common emotional effect, the disturbing dreams may occasion other negative reactions such as anger, sadness, frustration, guilt, disgust, or confusion. The dreamer may suddenly awaken during the nightmare, but have trouble getting back to sleep because of lingering feelings of fear resulting from the terrifying dream. These nightmarish dreams or the disruption of sleep they cause lead to significant personal distress or interfere with important areas of daily functioning.

Although many people have occasional nightmares, the percentage of people having the kind of intense, recurrent nightmares that lead to a diagnosis of nightmare disorder remains unknown. Nightmares are often associated with traumatic experiences and generally occur when the individual is under stress.

Nightmares generally occur during REM sleep, the stage of sleep in which most dreams occur. Periods of REM sleep tend to become longer and the dreams occurring during REM more intense in the latter half of nightly sleep, so nightmares usually occur late at night or toward morning. Although nightmares may involve a great deal of agitated movement in the dream itself, as in nightmares of fleeing from an assailant, dreamers show little muscle activity. The biological processes that activate dreams—including nightmares—inhibit body movement, causing a type of paralysis. This is indeed fortunate, as it prevents the dreamer from jumping out of bed and running into a dresser or a wall in the attempt to elude the pursuing assailants from the dream.

Treatment of Sleep-Wake Disorders

9.7 Evaluate methods used to treat sleep-wake disorders.

The most common method for treating sleep-wake disorders in the United States is the use of sleep medications. However, because of problems associated with these drugs, non-pharmacological treatment approaches, principally CBT, have come to the fore.

BIOLOGICAL APPROACHES Antianxiety drugs are often used to treat insomnia, including the class of antianxiety drugs called *benzodiazepines* (e.g., Valium and Ativan). (These psychiatric drugs are also widely used in the treatment of anxiety disorders, as we saw in Chapter 5.) Other sleep-inducing agents include the drug *zolpidem* (trade name Ambien), which is effective in both reducing the length of time it takes people with insomnia to fall asleep and increasing sleep duration (Roth et al., 2006).

When used for the short-term treatment of insomnia, sleep medications generally reduce the time it takes to get to sleep, increase total length of sleep, and reduce nightly awakenings. They work by reducing arousal and inducing feelings of calmness, thereby making the person more receptive to sleep. Sleep medications primarily work by increasing the activity of GABA, a neurotransmitter that dampens the activity of the central nervous system (see Chapter 5) (Pollack, 2004a).

Despite their benefits, sleep medications have significant drawbacks in treating insomnia. They tend to suppress REM sleep, which may interfere with some of the restorative functions of sleep. They can also lead to a carryover or "hangover" the following day, which is associated with daytime sleepiness and reduced performance. Rebound insomnia can also follow discontinuation of the drug, causing worse insomnia than was originally the case. Rebound insomnia may be lessened, however, by tapering off the drug rather than abruptly discontinuing it. These drugs quickly lose their effectiveness at a given dosage level, so progressively larger doses must be used to achieve the same effect. High doses can be dangerous, especially if they are mixed with alcoholic beverages at bedtime.

Sleep medications can also produce chemical dependence if used regularly over time and can lead to tolerance (Pollack, 2004a). Once dependence is established, people experience withdrawal symptoms when they stop using the drugs, including agitation, tremors, nausea, headaches, and, in severe cases, delusions or hallucinations.

Users can also become *psychologically* dependent on sleeping pills. That is, they can develop a psychological need for the medication and assume that they will not be able to get to sleep without it. Because worry heightens bodily arousal, such self-doubts are likely to become self-fulfilling prophecies. Moreover, users may attribute their success in falling asleep to the pill and not to themselves, which strengthens reliance on the drugs and makes it harder to forgo using them.

Reliance on sleeping pills does nothing to resolve the underlying cause of the problem or help the person learn more effective ways of coping. If they are used at all, sleep medications such as benzodiazepines should only be used for a brief period of time, a few weeks at most. The aim of treatment should be to provide a temporary respite so the therapist can help the client find more effective ways of handling sources of stress and anxiety that contribute to insomnia.

Antianxiety drugs of the benzodiazepine family and tricyclic antidepressants are also used to treat the deep-sleep disorders, such as sleep terrors and sleepwalking. They seem to have a beneficial effect of decreasing the length of time spent in deep sleep and reducing partial arousals between sleep stages. As with primary insomnia, use of sleep medications for these disorders incurs the risk of physiological and psychological dependence.

What's wrong with this picture? People who use their beds for many other activities besides sleeping, including eating, reading, and watching television, may find that lying in bed loses its value as a cue for sleeping. Behavior therapists use stimulus control techniques to help people with insomnia create a stimulus environment associated with sleeping.

9.8 Apply your knowledge of healthy sleeping habits to steps you can take to develop more adaptive sleep habits.

Therefore, sleep medications should be used only in severe cases and only as a temporary means of "breaking the cycle."

Stimulant drugs are often used to enhance wakefulness in people with narcolepsy and, as noted earlier, to combat daytime sleepiness in people suffering from hypersomnolence (Morgenthaler et al., 2007). Daily naps of 10 to 60 minutes and coping support from mental health professionals or self-help groups may also be helpful in treating narcolepsy.

The first-line treatment for sleep apnea is use of mechanical devices that help maintain breathing during sleep by keeping the upper airway passages open (Holley et al., 2011; Marin et al., 2012; Sawyer et al., 2011). Surgery may be used to widen the upper airways in some cases.

PSYCHOLOGICAL APPROACHES Psychological approaches have, by and large, been limited to treatment of primary insomnia. Cognitive-behavioral techniques are short term in emphasis and focus on lowering bodily arousal, establishing regular sleep habits, and replacing anxiety-producing thoughts with more adaptive thoughts. Cognitive-behavioral therapists typically use a combination of techniques, including stimulus control, adopting a regular sleep-wake cycle, relaxation training, and rational restructuring.

Stimulus control involves changing the environment associated with sleeping. We normally associate the bed and bedroom with sleep, so that exposure to these stimuli induces feelings of sleepiness. But when people use their beds for many other activities—such as eating, reading, planning the day's activities, and watching television—the bed loses its association with sleepiness. Moreover, when longer the person with insomnia lies in bed tossing and turning and worrying about not sleeping, the bed becomes a conditioned stimulus for anxiety and frustration.

Stimulus control techniques strengthen the connection between the bed and sleep by restricting as much as possible the activities in bed to sleeping. In other words, the bed should be reserved for sleep (and sex) to establish healthier sleep habits (Bootzin & Epstein, 2011). Typically, the person is instructed not to spend more than about 10 to 20 minutes in bed trying to fall asleep. If sleep does not occur during this time, the person should leave the bed and go to another room to regain a relaxed frame of mind before returning to bed—for example, by sitting quietly or reading, or practicing relaxation exercises.

Cognitive-behavioral therapists help clients program their bodies by establishing a consistent sleep-wake cycle. This involves going to bed and waking up at about the same time each day, including weekends and holidays. Relaxation techniques used before bedtime (such as the technique of progressive relaxation described in Chapter 6) help reduce states of physiological arousal to a level conducive to sleep.

Rational restructuring involves substituting rational alternatives for self-defeating, maladaptive thoughts or beliefs (see the following *A Closer Look*). The belief that failing to get a good night's sleep will lead to unfortunate, even disastrous, consequences the next day reduces the chances of falling asleep because it raises the level of anxiety. Most of us function reasonably well if we lose sleep or even miss a night of sleep.

CBT has become the treatment of choice for insomnia (Smith & Perlis, 2006). CBT yields substantial therapeutic benefits, as measured by reductions in the time it takes to get to sleep and by improved sleep quality (Bootzin & Epstein, 2011; Buysse et al., 2011; Harris et al., 2012; Schwartz & Carney, 2012; Vincent & Walsh, 2013). It also produces better results in the long term than sleep medications (Roy-Byrne, 2007; Wu et al., 2006). After all, taking a pill does not help people with insomnia learn more adaptive sleep habits. Sleep medication may produce faster results, but behavioral treatment tends to produce longer-lasting results (Pollack, 2004a, 2004b). However, adding sleep medication to CBT in the short term may increase the benefits of treatment over the use of CBT alone, but not if sleep medication is continued for months at a time (Morin et al., 2009).

To Sleep, Perchance to Dream

Many of us have difficulty from time to time falling asleep or remaining asleep. Although sleep is a natural function and cannot be forced, we can develop more adaptive sleep habits that help us become more receptive to sleep. However, if insomnia or other sleep-related problems persist or become associated with difficulties functioning during the day, it is worthwhile to have a professional evaluate the problem. Here are some steps you can take to develop healthier sleeping patterns:

1. *Establish a regular sleep-wake cycle.* Go to bed and wake up about the same time every day. Sleeping late to make up for lost sleep can throw off your body's internal clock. Set your alarm for the same time each morning and get up, regardless of how many hours you have slept.

2. *Limit your activities in bed as much as possible to sleeping.* Avoid watching TV or reading in bed.

3. *If after 10 to 20 minutes of lying in bed you are unable to fall asleep, get out of bed, go to another room, and put yourself in a relaxed mood by reading, listening to calming music, or practicing self-relaxation.*

4. *Avoid naps during the daytime.* You'll feel less sleepy at bedtime if you catch z's during the afternoon.

5. *Avoid ruminating in bed.* Don't focus on problems as you attempt to sleep. Tell yourself that you'll think about tomorrow, tomorrow. Help yourself enter a more sleepful frame of mind by engaging in a mental fantasy or mind trip, or just let all thoughts slip away from consciousness. If an important idea comes to you, don't rehearse it in your mind. Jot it down on a handy pad so you won't lose it. But if thoughts persist, get up and follow them elsewhere.

6. *Put yourself in a relaxed frame of mind before sleep.* Some people unwind before bed by reading; others prefer watching TV or just resting quietly. Do whatever you find most relaxing. You may find it helpful to incorporate within your regular bedtime routine the techniques for lowering your level of arousal discussed earlier in this text, such as meditation or progressive relaxation.

7. *Establish a regular daytime exercise schedule.* Regular exercise during the day (not directly before bedtime) can help induce sleepiness upon retiring.

8. *Avoid use of caffeinated beverages, such as coffee and tea, in the evening and late afternoon.* Also, avoid drinking alcoholic beverages. Alcohol can interfere with normal sleep patterns (reduced total sleep, REM sleep, and sleep efficiency), even when consumed upwards of 6 hours before bedtime.

9. *Practice rational restructuring.* Substitute rational alternatives for self-defeating thoughts. Here are some examples:

Self-Defeating Thoughts	Rational Alternatives
"I must fall asleep right now or I'll be a wreck tomorrow."	"I may feel tired, but I've been able to get by with little sleep before. I can make up for it tomorrow by getting to bed early."
"What's the matter with me that I can't seem to fall sleep?"	"I can't blame myself for not being able to fall asleep. I can't control sleep. I'll just let whatever happens, happen."
"If I don't get to sleep right now, I won't be able to concentrate on the exam (conference, meeting, etc.) tomorrow."	"My concentration may be off a bit, but I'm not going to fall apart. There's no point blowing things out of proportion. I might as well get up for a while and watch a little TV rather than lie here dwelling on this."

9 summing up

Eating Disorders

9.1 Describe the key features of three types of eating disorders: anorexia nervosa, bulimia nervosa, and binge-eating disorder.

Anorexia nervosa is characterized by self-starvation and failure to maintain normal body weight, intense fears of becoming overweight, and distorted body image. Bulimia nervosa involves preoccupation with weight control and body shape, repeated binges, and regular purging to keep weight down. Binge-eating disorder (BED) involves a recurrent pattern of binge eating that is not accompanied by compensatory behaviors such as purging. People with BED tend to be older than those with anorexia or bulimia and are more likely to be obese.

9.2 Describe causal factors involved in anorexia nervosa and bulimia nervosa.

Eating disorders typically begin in adolescence and affect more females than males. Anorexia nervosa and bulimia nervosa are linked to preoccupations with weight control and maladaptive ways of trying to keep weight down. Many other factors are implicated in their development, including social pressures on young women to adhere to unrealistic standards of thinness, issues of control, underlying psychological problems, and conflict within the family, especially over issues of autonomy.

9.3 Evaluate methods used to treat eating disorders.

Severe cases of anorexia are often treated in an inpatient setting where a refeeding regimen can be closely monitored. Behavior modification and other psychological interventions, including psychotherapy and family therapy, may also be helpful. Most cases of bulimia are treated on an outpatient basis, with evidence supporting the therapeutic benefits of cognitive-behavioral therapy (CBT), interpersonal psychotherapy, and antidepressant medication. CBT and antidepressant medication have been shown to be effective in treating BED.

9.4 Identify health risks associated with obesity.

Obesity is associated with many health risks, including cardiovascular disease, diabetes, respiratory disease, and some forms of cancer. It accounts for more than 160,000 excess deaths per year in the United States.

9.5 Identify factors linked to obesity.

Many factors are associated with obesity, including genetic factors, metabolic factors, fat cells, lifestyle factors, psychological factors, and socioeconomic factors such as income levels and acculturation.

Sleep-Wake Disorders

9.6 Identify and describe specific types of sleep-wake disorders.

Insomnia disorder is often associated with worry and anxiety, especially performance anxiety associated with overconcern about not getting enough sleep. Hypersomnolence disorder involves excessive daytime sleepiness, whereas narcolepsy involves the occurrence of abrupt sleep attacks during waking hours. Narcolepsy may involve genetic factors and loss of brain cells in the hypothalamus involved in producing a chemical that regulates wakefulness. Breathing-related sleep disorders involve recurrent episodes of momentary cessation of breathing during sleep and are often associated with daytime sleepiness. Obstructive sleep apnea hypopnea syndrome, the most common type of breathing-related sleep disorder, is typically caused by respiratory problems that interfere with normal breathing during sleep. Disorders of partial arousals include two disorders occurring during non-REM (rapid eye movement) sleep—sleep terrors (repeated episodes of sheer terror during sleep) and sleepwalking (repeatedly walking about in one's sleep)—and two disorders associated with sleep disturbances during REM sleep—REM sleep behavior disorder or RBD (nighttime thrashings or vocalizations during REM sleep) and nightmare disorder (persistent nightmares).

9.7 Evaluate methods used to treat sleep-wake disorders.

The most common form of treatment for sleep-wake disorders involves the use of antianxiety drugs. However, use of these drugs should be time limited because of the potential for psychological and/or physical dependence, among other problems. Cognitive-behavioral interventions have emerged as the treatment of choice for producing substantial benefits in helping people with chronic insomnia.

9.8 Apply your knowledge of healthy sleeping habits to steps you can take to develop more adaptive sleep habits.

Establish a regular sleep-wake cycle. Limit your activities in bed as much as possible to sleeping. Get out of bed after 10 to 20 minutes if you are unable to fall asleep and restore a restful state of mind. Avoid daytime naps and avoid ruminating in bed. Establish a regular daytime exercise schedule, and avoid use of caffeinated beverages in the evening and late afternoon. Practice rational restructuring of self-defeating thoughts.

critical thinking questions

Based on your reading of this chapter, answer the following questions:

- Why do you think people with anorexia nervosa and bulimia nervosa continue their self-defeating behaviors despite the medical complications of these conditions? Explain.

- What role do sociocultural factors play in eating disorders? How might we change societal attitudes and social pressures placed on young women that may lead to disordered eating habits?

- Do you believe that obesity results from a lack of willpower? Why or why not?

- Do your sleep habits help or hinder your sleep? Explain.

key terms

anorexia nervosa 335
bulimia nervosa 335
eating disorders 335
body mass index BMI 340
obesity 345
binge-eating disorder BED 349
sleep-wake disorders 351

insomnia 352
insomnia disorder 352
hypersomnolence disorder 353
narcolepsy 354
cataplexy 354
sleep paralysis 354
hypnagogic hallucinations 354

breathing-related sleep disorders 355
obstructive sleep apnea hypopnea syndrome 355
circadian rhythm sleep-wake disorders 356
parasomnias 357

sleep terrors 357
sleepwalking 357
REM sleep behavior disorder 358
nightmare disorder 358

Disorders Involving Gender and Sexuality

10

truth OR fiction

T☐ F☐ Gay males and lesbians have a gender identity of the opposite sex. (p. 368)

T☐ F☐ Orgasm is a reflex. (p. 373)

T☐ F☐ Walking at a brisk pace for two miles a day may cut the risk of erectile dysfunction in men by half. (p. 379)

T☐ F☐ Using antidepressants can interfere with a person's orgasmic response. (p. 379)

T☐ F☐ Wearing revealing bathing suits is a form of exhibitionism. (p. 386)

T☐ F☐ Some people cannot become sexually aroused unless they are subjected to pain or humiliation. (p. 390)

T☐ F☐ College women are more likely to be raped by strangers than by men they know. (p. 397)

T☐ F☐ Deep down, most women desire to be raped. (p. 399)

T☐ F☐ Rapists are mentally ill. (p. 399)

learning objectives

10.1
Describe the key features of gender dysphoria.

10.2
Explain the difference between gender dysphoria and homosexuality.

10.3
Describe the major theoretical perspectives on transgender identity.

10.4
Define the term sexual dysfunction and identify three major categories of sexual dysfunctions and specific disorders within each type.

10.5
Describe the causal factors involved in sexual dysfunctions.

10.6
Describe the methods used to treat sexual dysfunctions.

10.7
Define the term paraphilia and identify the major types of paraphilic disorders.

10.8
Describe the theoretical perspectives on paraphilias and the underlying causal factors.

10.9
Describe methods for treating paraphilic disorders.

10.10
Identify the major types of rape, describe the effects of rape, and identify the factors involved in rape.

Dr. Jayne Thomas taught psychology at Mission College in California until her death in 2002. Dr. Thomas was born a male and, until undergoing sex reassignment surgery, she had always felt that she was a female trapped in a man's body. She shared her perspectives on her remarkable personal journey with the authors, excerpted here:

"I" "I Know Something None of You Will Ever Know"

All of my life, I harbored the strongest conviction that I was inappropriately assigned to the wrong [sex]—that of a man—when inside I knew myself to be a woman. Even so. . . I continued a lifelong struggle with this deeply felt mistake. I was successful in school, became a national swimming champion, received my college degrees, married twice (fathering children in both marriages), and was respected as a competent and good man in the workplace. However, the persistently unrelenting wrongfulness of my life continued. Not until my fourth decade was I truly able to address my gender issue.

Jay Thomas, Ph.D., underwent sex reassignment and officially became Jayne Thomas, Ph.D., in November of 1985, and what has transpired in the ensuing years has been the most enlightening of glimpses into the plight of humankind. . . .

Iconoclastically, I try to challenge both the masculine and feminine. "I know something none of you women know or will ever know in your lifetime." I can provocatively address the females in my audiences as Jayne. "I once lived as a man and have been treated as an equal. You never have nor will you experience such equality." Or, when a male student once came to my assistance in a classroom, fixing an errant video playback device and then strutting peacock-like back to his seat as only a satisfied male can, I teasingly commented to a nearby female student, "I used to be able to do that."

Having once lived as a man and now as a woman, I can honestly state that I see profound differences in our social/psychological/biological being as man and woman. I have now experienced many of the ways in which women are treated as less than men. Jay worked as a consultant to a large banking firm in Los Angeles and continued in that capacity as a woman following her gender shift. Amazingly the world presented itself in a different perspective. As Jay, technical presentations to management had generally been received in a positive manner, and credit for my work fully acknowledged. Jayne now found management less accessible, credit for her efforts less forthcoming and, in general, found herself working harder to be well prepared for each meeting than she ever had as a male. As a man, her forceful and impassioned presentations were an asset; as a woman they definitely seemed a liability.

On one occasion, as Jayne, when I passionately asserted my position regarding what I felt to be an important issue, my emotion and disappointment in not getting my point across (my voice showed my frustration) was met with a nearby colleague (a man) reaching to touch my arm with words of reassurance, "There, there, take it easy, it will be all right." Believe me, that never happened to Jay. There was also an occasion when I had worked most diligently on a presentation to management only to find the company vice president more interested in the fragrance of my cologne than my technical agenda.

. . . Having lived as man and woman in the same lifetime, one personal truth seems clear. Rather than each gender attempting to change and convert the other to its own side, as I often see couples undertaking to accomplish (women need be more logical and men more sharing of their emotions), we might more productively come together in our relationships building upon our gender uniqueness and strengths. Men and women have different perspectives, which can be used successfully to address life's issues.

→ *Dr. Jayne Thomas, in her own words*

Dr. Jayne Thomas

Imagine what it must be like to be living in a body that feels alien to you by dint of the sex to which you were born. When children are born, even before fingers and toes are counted, the obstetrician will announce, "It's a girl" (or a boy). In this chapter, we explore a wide range of psychological disorders involving not only sexual identity, but also deviant or atypical patterns of sexual attraction and problems relating to lack of sexual interest or response. We will also consider a form of abnormal behavior that is not classified as a psychological disorder but that can have devastating emotional and physical effects on the people it victimizes: rape.

In sexual behavior, as in other types of behavior, the lines between the normal and the abnormal are not always agreed upon or precisely drawn. Sex, like eating, is a natural function. Also like eating, sexual behavior varies greatly among individuals and cultures. Our sexual behavior is profoundly affected by cultural, religious, and moral beliefs, custom, folklore, and superstition. In the realm of sexual behavior, our conceptions of what is normal or abnormal are influenced by cultural learning imparted through the family, school, and religious institutions.

Many patterns of sexual behavior, such as masturbation, premarital intercourse, and oral–genital sex, are normal in contemporary American society, if frequency of occurrence is any indication. But frequency is not the only yardstick of normal behavior. Behavior is frequently labeled abnormal when it deviates from the norms of a society. For example, kissing is highly popular in Western cultures but is considered deviant behavior in some preliterate societies in South America and Africa (Rathus, Nevid, & Fichner-Rathus, 2011). Members of the Thonga tribe of Africa were shocked when they first observed European visitors kissing. One man exclaimed, "Look at them—they eat each other's saliva and dirt." We will see that some sex-related activities are considered as abnormal in the eyes of mental health professionals as kissing seemed to the Thonga—for example, being more sexually aroused by articles of clothing than by one's partner, or losing interest in sex or being unable to become sexually aroused despite adequate stimulation.

We may also consider behavior to be abnormal when it is self-defeating, harms others, or causes personal distress. We shall see how psychological disorders discussed in this chapter meet one or more of these standards of abnormality. In exploring these disorders, we touch on questions that probe the boundaries between abnormality and normality. For example, is it abnormal to have difficulty becoming sexually aroused or reaching orgasm? How do mental health professionals define exhibitionism and voyeurism? When is it normal to watch another person disrobe, and when is it abnormal? Where do we draw the lines?

We begin with *gender dysphoria*, a diagnosable disorder that touches on the most basic part of our experience as sexual beings—our sense of being male or female.

Gender Dysphoria

Gender identity is the psychological sense of being male or female. For most people, gender identity is consistent with their physical or genetic sex. The diagnosis of **gender dysphoria** (previously called *gender identity disorder*) applies to people who experience significant personal distress or impaired functioning as a result of a conflict between their anatomic sex and their gender identity—their sense of maleness or femaleness. The word *dysphoria* (from the Greek *dysphoros*, meaning "difficult to bear") refers to feelings of dissatisfaction or discomfort, which in this case involves discomfort with one's designated gender. 👁

To clarify our terms, *gender* is a psychosocial concept distinguishing maleness from femaleness, as in *gender roles* (societal expectations of behaviors appropriate for men and women) and *gender identity*—our psychological sense of ourselves as females or males. The terms *sex* or *sexual* refer to the biological division between males and females of a species, as in *sexual organs* (not gender organs).

People with a **transgender identity** have the psychological sense of belonging to one gender while possessing the sexual organs of the other. Not all people with transgender identity have gender dysphoria or any other diagnosable disorder. The diagnosis of gender dysphoria only comes into play in cases of significant discomfort associated with having a transgender identity. These deep feelings of discomfort are accompanied by significant emotional distress or impaired functioning. The diagnosis of gender dysphoria is controversial, especially among transgender people who believe the mismatch between their gender identity and their anatomical sex is a mistake of nature and should not be treated as a mental health problem (see the nearby *Thinking Critically About Abnormal Psychology* feature).

The diagnosis of gender dysphoria may apply to children or adults, although it often begins in childhood. Children with gender dysphoria find their anatomical sex to be a source of persistent and intense distress. The diagnosis is not used simply to label "tomboyish" girls and "sissyish" boys. Rather, it is intended to apply to children who repudiate their biologic and associated characteristics in a number of ways, as described in Table 10.1.

We don't have reliable knowledge about how common gender dysphoria may be, but it is reasonable to assume that it is relatively uncommon. We do know that gender dysphoria can follow different paths. Gender dysphoria in childhood may end before adolescence, as children become more accepting of their biologic sex or come to terms with having a transgender identity. Or it may persist into adolescence or adulthood as they continue to struggle with their transgender identity. Many transgender people also suffer from depression as the result of living in a world in which they are stigmatized, mistreated, and discriminated against (Bockting et al., 2013).

10.1 Describe the key features of gender dysphoria.

 **Watch** the **Video** *Travis: Gender Dysphoria* on **MyPsychLab**

Chaz Bono. The daughter of famed entertainers Cher and Sony Bono, Chaz Bono always felt that he was a male. Chaz, who recently underwent female-to-male sex reassignment surgery, now says, "I feel like I'm living in my body for the first time, and it feels really good."

TABLE 10.1
Key Features of Gender Dysphoria in Childhood

- Strong desire to be a member of the other gender or strongly expressing the belief that one is a member of the other gender (or of some alternative gender)
- Strong preferences for playing with members of the other gender and for toys, games, and activities associated with the other gender
- Strong feelings of disgust and personal distress about one's sexual anatomy
- Strong desires to have physical characteristics (i.e., primary or secondary sexual characteristics) associated with one's experienced gender
- Strong preferences for assuming roles of the other gender in make believe or fantasy play
- Strong preferences for wearing clothing typically associated with the other gender and rejection of clothing associated with one's own gender

truth OR fiction

Gay males and lesbians have a gender identity of the opposite sex.

☑ **FALSE** Gender identity should not be confused with sexual orientation. Gay males and lesbians have erotic interest in members of their own gender, but their gender identity is consistent with their anatomic sex.

Gender identity should not be confused with sexual orientation. Gay males and lesbians have erotic interests in members of their own sex, but their gender identity (their sense of being male or female) is consistent with their anatomical sex. They do not desire to become members of the other sex nor despise their own genitals, as we typically find in people with gender dysphoria. **T / F**

Sex Reassignment Surgery

Not all people with gender dysphoria seek sex reassignment surgery. For those who do, surgeons attempt to construct external genital organs that closely resemble those of the opposite sex. Male-to-female surgery is generally more successful than female-to-male. Hormone treatments promote the development of secondary sex characteristics of the reassigned sex, such as growth of fatty tissue in the breasts in male-to-female cases and the growth of the beard and body hair in female-to-male cases.

People who undergo sex reassignment surgery can participate in sexual activity and even reach orgasm, but they cannot conceive or bear children because they lack the internal reproductive organs of their newly reconstructed sex. Investigators generally find positive effects on psychological adjustment and quality of life of transgender individuals (also called *transsexuals*) who undergo sex reassignment surgery (Parola et al., 2009; Wierck et al., 2011). A recent study of 32 patients who completed sex reassignment surgery showed that none regretted it and nearly all were generally satisfied with the results (Johansson et al., 2010).

Postoperative adjustment tends to be more favorable for female-to-male reassignment (Parola et al., 2009). One reason may be that society tends to be more accepting of women who desire to become men than the reverse (Smith et al., 2005). Female-to-male transgender individuals cases also may be better adjusted before surgery, so their superior postoperative adjustment may also represent a selection factor.

Dr. Jayne Thomas, whom we introduced at the beginning of the chapter, spoke about the psychological adjustment and shift in gender roles she experienced following sex reassignment surgery.

"I" "Everybody Is Born Unique, but Most of Us Die Copies"

. . . My parents had never realized that their eldest son was dealing with such a lifelong problem. Have they accepted or do they fully understand the magnitude of my issue? I fear not. After almost 15 years of having lived as a female, my father continues to call me by my male name. I do not doubt my parents' or children's love for me, but so uninformed are we of the true significance of gender identity that a clear understanding seems light-years away. Often I see my clients losing jobs, closeness with family members, visitation rights with children, and generally becoming relegated to the role of societal outcast. Someone once stated that "Everybody is born unique, but most of us die copies"—a great price my clients often pay for personal honesty and not living their lives as a version of how society deems they should.

Dr. Jayne Thomas

Men seeking sex reassignment outnumber women by about 3 to 1 (Spack, 2013). Most female-to-male individuals do not seek complete sex reassignment surgery. Instead, they may remove their internal sex organs (ovaries, fallopian tubes, and uterus) along with the fatty tissue in their breasts (Bockting & Fung, 2006). Testosterone (male sex hormone) treatments increase muscle mass and growth of the beard. But only a few female-to-male transgender individuals have the series of operations necessary to construct an artificial penis, largely because the constructed penises do not work very well, and the surgery is expensive. Therefore, most female-to-male transgender individuals limit their physical alteration to hysterectomies, mastectomies, and testosterone treatment (Bailey, 2003b).

THINKING CRITICALLY about abnormal psychology

@Issue: Are People With a Transgender Identity Suffering From a Mental Disorder?

One of the most controversial issues that has plagued the *DSM* system is whether to classify transgender identity as a mental disorder (Cohen-Kettenis & Pfäfflin, 2010). The previous edition of the DSM, the *DSM-IV*, diagnosed people with transgender identity as having *gender identity disorder* or GID if they experienced emotional distress or impaired functioning in their work life or social relationships. But many people, including many advocates in the transgender community, argue that "difference" should not be equated with "disease" and that the term *gender identity disorder* unfairly stigmatizes people whose identity is different than the norm by implying that they suffer from a mental disorder by dint of their gender identity.

As we noted, the term *gender identity disorder* was replaced in *DSM-5* with a new diagnostic term, *gender dysphoria,* to emphasize the intense discomfort or distress that transgender people may experience from the mismatch between their gender identity and their designated gender. This change underscores the view that gender identity itself is not a mental disorder. However, it remains unclear whether the use of the more neutral term, *gender dysphoria,* will quell the debate. Some people argue that whatever distress people with transgender identity experience may not reflect their personal struggles with their gender identity but rather the difficulties they face in adjusting to a society that stigmatizes and discredits them.

Let's consider the broader implications of perceiving gender identity through the lens of mental illness. Conceptions of gender differ both across and within cultures, and they also vary across time in a given culture. For example, there was a time when women in our society were barred from many Ph.D. programs because the higher echelons of education were perceived to be a privileged male domain. Today, however, women comprise a majority of students in many graduate and professional schools, including doctoral programs in psychology. Most assumptions we make about gender identity are based on the social construction of gender as a dichotomous, mutually exclusive category in which people are either male or female. Yet this assumption is challenged by studies of cultures that have a recognized social identity for persons who do not fit typical male or female roles or gender identities. These individuals have an accepted role in their societies and are not deemed to be disordered or undesirable.

For example, well into the late 1800s, the Plains Indians and many other Western tribes accepted young members of the tribe who adopted roles typically assigned to the opposite sex (Carocci, 2009; Tafoya, 1996; Wade & Tavris, 1994). In more than half of the surviving native languages, there are words to describe individuals who are assigned a third gender that is neither male nor female. Native tribal members believed that all human beings have both male and female elements. In many tribes, the term *two-spirit* was used for persons who embody a higher level of integration of their male and female spirits. Sometimes a two-spirit person was a biological male who took on the tribe's female gender roles but was not considered either a male or a female. On the other hand, a female could take on the role and behaviors associated with tribal males. She could be initiated into puberty as a male and could adopt male roles and activities, including marrying a female.

These cultural variations highlight the importance of taking cultural contexts into account when making judgments about disordered behavior. Given the malleability of gender roles and identities we observe across cultures, we may question the validity of conceptualizing a transgender identity as a type of psychological disorder.

People who are dissatisfied with their biologic sex may be atypical or different from the majority, but does that mean their behavior is a form of psychopathology? Perhaps, the emotional distress they experience is a result of the hostile treatment they receive in a society that insists that people fit into one of two arbitrarily designated categories and then treats harshly those who do not. Critics of the present diagnostic system contend that much of the distress that transgender children experience comes from difficulties getting along with other kids and being accepted by them, not from their gender identity per se (Hausman, 2003).

The plight of transgender individuals may be compared with that of lesbians and gay men. The distress that many lesbians and gay men experience in reference to their sexual orientation may be a function of the hostility and abuse they encounter in the broader society. From this perspective, their distress is not a direct consequence of inner conflicts over their sexual orientation, but is an understandable response to the negative treatment they receive from others, even their loved ones. Similarly, critics of the psychiatric diagnostic system contend that clinicians should not use dissatisfaction with one's biologic sex as a basis for diagnosing a psychological disorder. Rather, they argue that ill treatment of people with atypical patterns of gender identity creates emotional distress, not gender identity per se (Reid & Whitehead, 1992). Absent the social construction of mutually exclusive gender categories, the disorder would no longer exist. Just as beliefs about sexual orientation have changed over time, perhaps greater tolerance of transgender individuals and greater appreciation of the diversity of gender expression in human beings will lead us to conceptualize gender identity with greater flexibility. Until that happens, however, the medical/psychiatric and transgender communities may well continue to battle each other.

In thinking critically about the issue, answer the following questions:

- Do you believe that dissatisfaction with one's biologic sex should be considered abnormal behavior or a variation in gender expression? Explain your answer.
- Should the diagnosis of gender dysphoria be retained in the DSM system, changed (and if so, how?), or simply dropped? Explain.

What is normal and what is abnormal? The cultural context must be considered in defining what is normal and what is abnormal in the realm of sexual and sexually related behavior. The people in these photographs—and the ways in which they cloak or expose their bodies—would be quite out of place in one another's societies.

10.3 Describe the major theoretical perspectives on transgender identity.

Theoretical Perspectives on Transgender Identity

The origins of transgender identity remain unclear. Psychodynamic theorists point to extremely close mother–son relationships, empty relationships with parents, and fathers who were absent or detached (Stoller, 1969). These family circumstances may foster strong identification with the mother in young males, leading to a reversal of expected gender roles and identity. Girls with weak, ineffectual mothers and strong masculine fathers may overly identify with their fathers and develop a psychological sense of themselves as "little men."

Learning theorists similarly point to father absence in the case of boys—to the unavailability of a strong male role model. Children who were reared by parents who had wanted children of the other gender and who strongly encouraged cross-gender dressing and patterns of play may learn socialization patterns and develop a gender identity associated with the opposite sex.

Nonetheless, the great majority of people with the types of family histories described by psychodynamic and learning theorists do not develop a transgender identity. It may be the case that psychosocial influences interact with a biological predisposition in influencing the development of transgender identity. We know that many adults with a transgender identity showed cross-gender preferences in toys, games, and clothing very early in childhood (Drummond et al., 2008; Zucker, 2005a, 2005b). If critical early learning experiences play a part, they most probably occurred very early in life.

Some male transgender people recall that, as children, they preferred playing with dolls, enjoyed wearing frilly dresses, and disliked rough-and-tumble play. Some female transgender people report that, as children, they disliked dresses and acted like tomboys. They preferred playing "boys' games" and playing with boys. Female transgender individuals may have an easier time adjusting than their male counterparts, as "tomboys" generally find acceptance more easily than "sissy boys." Even in adulthood, it may be easier for a female transsexual to wear male clothes and "pass" as a slightly built man than it is for a brawny man to pass for a large woman.

The development of transgender identity may result from the effects of male sexual hormones on the developing brain during prenatal development (Diamond, 2011; Savic et al., 2010). Evidence links high levels of testosterone during prenatal development to more masculinized play in children (i.e., preference for rough-and-tumble games)

(Auyeung et al., 2009). We can speculate that a disturbance in the endocrine (hormonal) environment during gestation leads the brain to become differentiated with respect to gender identity in one direction while the genitals develop normally in the other direction. Investigators find differences in the brains of transgender people, but what these differences mean for the development of transgender identity remains to be determined (Luders et al., 2009; Veale, Clarke, & Lomax, 2010). Importantly, we continue to lack direct evidence of abnormal hormonal balances during prenatal development that could explain the development of transgender identity. Even if such hormonal factors were demonstrated, they are unlikely to be the sole cause.

In sum, a combination of genetic and hormonal influences may create a disposition that interacts with early life experiences in leading to the development of transgender identity (Glicksman, 2013). But explanations of the development of transgender identity do not directly teach us about factors that determine gender dysphoria. Many transgender individuals do not warrant a diagnosis of gender dysphoria, as they show no evidence of significant distress or impairment in daily functioning needed to meet diagnostic criteria. We presently lack the knowledge base needed to understand the developmental trajectory in transgender individuals that leads to gender dysphoria.

Sexual Dysfunctions

10.4 Define the term sexual dysfunction and identify three major categories of sexual dysfunctions and specific disorders within each type.

Sexual dysfunctions are persistent problems with sexual interest, arousal, or response. Table 10.2 provides an overview of the sexual dysfunctions reviewed in this chapter.

TABLE 10.2
Overview of Sexual Dysfunctions

Type of Disorder	Approximate Prevalence in Population	Description
Disorders Involving Lack of Sexual Interest or Lack of Sexual Excitement or Arousal		
Male Hypoactive Sexual Desire Disorder	Ranging from about 8% to about 25% across age ranges, with greater prevalence among older men	Deficiency or lack of sexual interest or desire for sexual activity
Female Sexual Interest/Arousal Disorder	About 10% to 55% across age ranges, with greater prevalence in older women	Deficiency or lack of sexual interest or drive and problems achieving or sustaining sexual arousal
Erectile Disorder	Varies widely with age; estimated at 1% to 10% under age 40, 20% to 40% in men in their 60s, and even higher among older men	Difficulty achieving or maintaining erection during sexual activity
Disorders Involving Impaired Orgasmic Response		
Female Orgasmic Disorder	10% to 42% across studies	Difficulty achieving orgasm in females
Delayed Ejaculation	Less than 1% to 10% across studies	Difficulty achieving orgasm or ejaculation in males
Premature (Early) Ejaculation	Upwards of 30% of men across studies report problems with rapid ejaculation, with about 1% to 2% reporting ejaculation within one minute of penetration	Climaxing (ejaculating) too early in males
Disorders Involving Pain During Intercourse or Penetration (in women)		
Genito-Pelvic Pain/Penetration Disorder	Varies across studies, but about 15% of women in North America report experiencing recurrent pain during intercourse	Pain during intercourse or attempts at penetration, or fear of pain associated with intercourse or penetration, or tensing or tightening of the pelvic muscles, making penetration difficult or painful.

Source: Prevalence rates derived from Lewis et al., 2010, based on most recent review of studies worldwide, and updated based on the *DSM-5* (APA, 2013)

Note: Prevalence rates reflect percentages of adults reporting problems and may not correspond to clinical diagnosis of sexual dysfunctions. Reports of sexual pain and climaxing too early were based on individuals who were sexually active during the past 12-month period.

Sexual dysfunctions. What are the different types of sexual dysfunctions? What treatments are available to help people with sexual problems?

Prevalence Rates of Sexual Dysfunctions

Reports of sexual problems are widespread. A recent worldwide review estimated that sexual dysfunctions affect 40% to 45% of adult women and 20% to 30% of adult men at some point in their lives (Lewis et al., 2010). Estimates of the prevalence of specific types of sexual problems are shown in Table 10.2.

Women more often report problems regarding painful sex, inability to attain orgasm, and lack of sexual desire. Men are more likely to report reaching orgasm too quickly (early or premature ejaculation). We should note that reports of sexual problems shown in the table mean that a significant problem was reported, and not that a diagnosable disorder is necessarily present. We continue to lack clear evidence of underlying rates of diagnosable sexual dysfunctions in the general community.

Sexual dysfunctions may be classified according to two general categories, lifelong versus acquired and situational versus generalized. Cases of sexual dysfunction that have existed for the individual's lifetime are called *lifelong dysfunctions. Acquired dysfunctions* begin following a period of normal functioning. In *situational dysfunctions,* the problems occur in some situations (e.g., with one's spouse), but not in others (e.g., with a lover or when masturbating), or at some times but not others. *Generalized dysfunctions* occur in all situations and every time the individual engages in sexual activity.

Despite the fact that sexual dysfunctions are believed to be widespread, relatively few people seek treatment for these problems. People may not know that effective treatments are available or where to obtain help, or they may avoid seeking help because of the long-standing stigma attached to admitting a sexual difficulty.

Types of Sexual Dysfunctions

As shown in Table 10.2, we can group sexual dysfunctions within three general categories:

1. Disorders involving problems with sexual interest, desire, or arousal
2. Disorders involving problems with orgasmic response
3. Problems involving pain during sexual intercourse or penetration (in women)

In making a diagnosis of a sexual dysfunction, the clinician must determine that the problem is not due to the use of drugs or medications, other medical conditions, severe relationship distress such as partner violence, or other serious stressors. The disorder must also cause significant levels of personal distress or impairment in daily functioning.

DISORDERS OF INTEREST AND AROUSAL These disorders involve deficiencies in either sexual interest or arousal. Men with **male hypoactive sexual desire disorder** (MHSDD) persistently have little, if any, desire for sexual activity or may lack sexual or erotic thoughts or fantasies. Lack of sexual desire is more common among women than men (Géonet, De Sutter, & Zech, 2012). Nevertheless, the belief that men are always eager for sex is a myth.

Women with **female sexual interest/arousal disorder** (FSIAD) experience either a lack of, or greatly reduced level of, sexual interest, drive, or arousal. Women with problems becoming sexually aroused may lack feelings of sexual pleasure or excitement that normally accompany sexual arousal. Or they may experience little or no sexual interest or pleasure. They may also have few if any genital sensations during sexual activity. A study of women with low levels of sexual interest or drive showed that they generally had a less active sex life and experienced less satisfaction with their sexual relationships than women without the disorder (Leiblum et al., 2006).

Clinicians do not necessarily agree on criteria for determining the level of sexual desire considered "normal." They may weigh various factors in reaching a diagnosis of FSIAD, such as the client's lifestyle (e.g., parents contending with the demands of young children may lack energy for interest in sex), sociocultural factors (culturally restrictive attitudes may restrain sexual desire or interest), the quality of the relationship (problems in a relationship may contribute to lack of interest in sex), and the client's age (desire normally declines with age) (McCarthy et al., 2006; West et al., 2008).

Sex researchers continue to debate how to define sexual dysfunctions, especially in women (Clay, 2009). For example, some researchers argue that labeling a lack of sexual desire in women as a dysfunction imposes on women a male model of what should be normal (Bean, 2002). Researchers also debate whether to diagnose female sexual dysfunction on the basis of a lack of desire or difficulty achieving orgasm or by the woman's perceptions of these experiences as causing distress (Clay, 2009). Keep in mind that lack of desire usually does not come to the health practitioner's attention unless one partner is more interested in sex than the other. That is when the less-interested partner may be labeled with a dysfunction. But questions remain about where to draw the line between "normal" and "abnormal" levels of sexual drive or interest.

Problems with sexual arousal in men typically takes the form of failure to achieve or maintain an erection sufficient to engage in sexual activity through completion. Almost all men have occasional difficulty achieving or maintaining erection during sex. But men with persistent erectile difficulties may be diagnosed with **erectile disorder** (ED) (also called *erectile dysfunction*). They may have difficulty achieving an erection or maintaining an erection to the completion of sexual activity, or have erections that lack the rigidity needed to perform effectively. The diagnosis requires the problem be present for a period of about six months or longer and that it occurs on all or almost all (approximately 75% to 100%) occasions of sexual activity.

Occasional problems in achieving or maintaining erection are common enough, due to factors such as fatigue, alcohol, or anxiety with a new partner. The more concerned the man becomes about his sexual ability, the more likely he is to suffer *performance anxiety*. As we will explore further, performance anxiety can contribute to repeated failure, and a vicious cycle of anxiety and failure may develop.

The risks of erectile disorder increase with age (Alderman, 2009). Approximately 50% of men in the 40- to 70-year age range experience some degree of erectile dysfunction (Saigal, 2004).

ORGASM DISORDERS Orgasm or sexual climax is an involuntary reflex that results in rhythmic contractions of the pelvic muscles and is usually accompanied by feelings of intense pleasure. In men, these contractions are accompanied by expulsion of semen. There are three types of disorders involving problems with achieving orgasm: **female orgasmic disorder, delayed ejaculation,** and **premature (early) ejaculation. T / F**

In *female orgasmic disorder* and *delayed ejaculation,* there is a marked delay in reaching orgasm (in women) or ejaculation (in men), or an infrequency or absence of orgasm or ejaculation. Diagnosis of these disorders requires that the problem be present for about six months or longer, that the symptoms cause a significant level of distress, and that the symptoms occur on all or almost all occasions of sexual activity (and for men, without a desire to delay ejaculation). The clinician needs to make a judgment about whether there is an "adequate" amount and type of stimulation needed to achieve orgasm, taking into account the wide variation that exists in normal sexual responsiveness (Ishak et al., 2010). Might a woman's difficulty achieving orgasm with her partner result from a lack of effective stimulation rather than an orgasmic disorder? Many women, for example, require direct clitoral stimulation (by their own hand or their partner's) to achieve orgasm during vaginal intercourse. This should not be considered abnormal because it is the *clitoris,* not the *vagina,* which is the woman's most erotically sensitive organ.

The *DSM-5* expanded the criteria for female orgasmic disorder to include cases in which women experience a sharp reduction in the intensity of orgasmic sensations. The

truth OR fiction

Orgasm is a reflex.

☑ **TRUE** People cannot will or force an orgasm. Nor can they will or force other sexual reflexes, such as erection and vaginal lubrication. Trying to force these responses generally backfires and only increases anxiety.

drafters of the *DSM-5* argue that orgasm is not an "all or nothing" experience and that some women have a diminished level of orgasmic intensity that may become a problem for them.

Delayed ejaculation has received little attention in the clinical literature. Men with this problem are generally able to ejaculate through masturbation but have difficulty achieving ejaculation during intercourse with a partner, or be unable to do so. Although the disorder may allow the man to prolong the sexual act, the experience is usually one of frustration for both partners (Althof, 2012).

Premature (early) ejaculation is characterized by a recurrent pattern of ejaculation occurring within about one minute of vaginal penetration and before the man desires it (APA, 2013). In some cases, rapid ejaculation occurs prior to penetration or following only a few penile thrusts. Occasional experiences of rapid ejaculation, such as when the man is with a new partner, has had infrequent sexual contacts, or is very highly aroused, are not considered abnormal. It is only when the problem becomes persistent and causes distress that a diagnosis is rendered.

GENITO-PELVIC PAIN/PENETRATION DISORDER This disorder applies to women who experience sexual pain and/or difficulty engaging in vaginal intercourse or penetration. In some cases, women experience genital or pelvic pain during vaginal intercourse or attempts at penetration. The pain cannot be explained by an underlying medical condition, and so is believed to have a psychological component. However, because many, if not most, cases of pain during intercourse are traceable to an underlying medical condition that may go undiagnosed, such as insufficient lubrication or a urinary tract infection, controversy persists over whether sexual pain during intercourse or penetration should be classified as a mental disorder (Binik, 2005; Spitzer, 2005; van Lankveld et al., 2010).

Some cases of **genito-pelvic pain/penetration disorder** involve **vaginismus,** a condition in which the muscles surrounding the vagina involuntarily contract whenever vaginal penetration is attempted, making sexual intercourse painful or impossible. Vaginismus is not a medical condition, but a conditioned response in which penile contact with the woman's genitals elicits an involuntary spasm of the vaginal musculature, preventing penetration or causing pain upon attempt penetration.

Theoretical Perspectives

10.5 Describe causal factors involved in sexual dysfunctions.

Many factors are implicated in the development of sexual dysfunctions, including factors representing psychological, biological, and sociocultural perspectives.

PSYCHOLOGICAL PERSPECTIVES The major contemporary psychological views of sexual dysfunctions emphasize the roles of anxiety, lack of sexual skills, irrational beliefs, perceived causes of events, and relationship problems. Here, we consider several potential causal pathways.

Physically or psychologically traumatic sexual experiences may lead to sexual contact producing anxiety rather than arousal or pleasure. Conditioned anxiety resulting from a history of sexual trauma or rape may lead to problems with sexual arousal or achieving orgasm or lead to pain in women during penetration (Colangelo & Keefe-Cooperman, 2012; Ishak et al., 2010). Women who have problems becoming sexually aroused may also harbor deep-seated anger and resentment toward their partners (Moore & Heiman, 2006). Underlying feelings of guilt about sex, and ineffective stimulation by one's partner, may also contribute to difficulties with sexual arousal.

Sexual trauma early in life may make it difficult for men or women to respond sexually when they develop intimate relationships. People with a history of sexual trauma may be flooded with feelings of helplessness, unresolved anger, or misplaced guilt. They may also experience flashbacks of the abusive experiences when they engage in sexual relations, preventing them from becoming sexually aroused or achieving orgasm. Other psychological problems, such as depression and anxiety, can also result in sexual dysfunctions involving impaired sexual interest, arousal, or response (Laurent & Simons, 2009).

Another principal form of anxiety in sexual dysfunctions is *performance anxiety,* which represents an excessive concern about the ability to perform successfully. Performance anxiety can develop when people experience problems performing sexually and begin to doubt their abilities. People troubled by performance anxiety become spectators during sex, rather than participants. Their attention is focused on how their bodies are responding (or not responding) to sexual stimulation. They are plagued by disruptive thoughts about the anticipated negative consequences of failing to perform adequately ("What will she think of me?") rather than focusing on their erotic experiences. Men with performance anxiety may have difficulty achieving or maintaining an erection or may ejaculate prematurely; women may fail to become adequately aroused or have difficulty achieving orgasm (Althof et al., 2010; Goldstein et al., 2006). A vicious cycle may ensue in which each failure experience instills deeper doubts, which leads to more anxiety during sexual encounters, which occasions repeated failure, and so on. This vicious cycle is illustrated in the accompanying figure (see Figure 10.1)

In Western cultures, there is a deeply ingrained connection between a man's sexual performance and his sense of manhood. The man who repeatedly fails to perform sexually may suffer a loss of self-esteem, become depressed, or feel he is no longer a man. He may see himself as a total failure, despite other accomplishments in life. Sexual opportunities are construed as tests of his manhood, and he may respond to them by bearing down and trying to will (force) an erection. Willing an erection may backfire because erection is a reflex that cannot be forced. With so much of his self-esteem on the line whenever he makes love, it is little wonder that performance anxiety may mount to a point that it inhibits erection. The erectile reflex is controlled by the parasympathetic branch of the autonomic nervous system. Activation of the sympathetic nervous system, which occurs when we are anxious or under stress, can block parasympathetic control, preventing the erectile reflex from occurring. Ejaculation, in contrast, is under sympathetic nervous system control, so heightened levels of arousal, as in the case of performance anxiety, can trigger rapid (premature) ejaculation (Hellstrom et al., 2006; Janssen & Bancroft, 2006). The relationship between performance anxiety and sexual dysfunction can become a vicious cycle:

One client who suffered from erectile dysfunction described his feelings of sexual inadequacy this way: I always felt inferior, like I was on probation, having to prove myself. I felt like I was up against the wall. You can't imagine how embarrassing this was. It's like you walk out in front of an audience that you think is a nudist convention and it turns out to be a tuxedo convention.

From the Author's Files

Another client described how performance anxiety led him to prepare for sexual relations as though he were psyching himself up for a big game.

"I" "Paralyzed with Anxiety"

At work, I have control over what I do. With sex, you don't have control over your sex organ. I know that my mind can control what my hands do. But the same is not true of my penis. I had begun to view sex as a basketball game. I used to play in college. When I would prepare for a game, I'd always be thinking, "Who was I guarding that night?" I'd try to psych myself up, sketching out in my mind how to play this guy, thinking through all possible moves and plays. I began to do the same thing with sex. If I were dating someone, I'd be thinking the whole evening about what might happen in bed. I'd always be preparing for the outcome. I'd sketch out in my mind how I was going to touch her, what I'd ask her to do. But all the time, right through dinner or the movies, I'd be worrying that I wouldn't get it up. I kept picturing her face and how disappointed she'd be. By the time we did go to bed, I was paralyzed with anxiety.

From the Author's Files

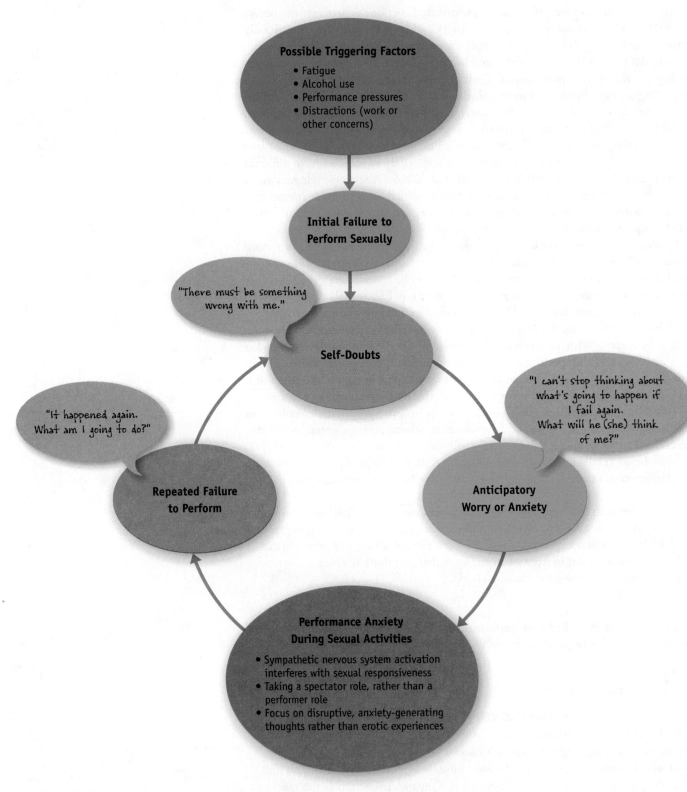

FIGURE **10.1**

Performance anxiety and sexual dysfunctions: a vicious cycle.

Women, too, may equate their self-esteem with their ability to reach frequent and intense orgasms. Yet, when men and women try to will arousal or lubrication, or to force an orgasm, they may find that the harder they try, the more these responses elude them. Several generations ago, the pressures concerning sex often revolved around the issue "Should I or shouldn't I?" Today, however, the pressures for both men and women are often based more on achieving performance goals relating to reaching orgasm and satisfying one's partner's sexual needs.

Sexual fulfillment is also based on learning sexual skills. Sexual skills or competencies, like other types of skills, are acquired through opportunities for new learning. We learn about how our own and our partner's bodies respond sexually in various ways, including trial and error with our partners, by learning about our own sexual response through self-exploration (as in masturbation), by reading about sexual techniques, and perhaps by talking to others or viewing sex films or videotapes. Yet, children who are raised to feel guilty or anxious about sex may have lacked opportunities to develop sexual knowledge and skills and so remain ignorant of the types of stimulation they need to achieve sexual gratification. They may also respond to sexual opportunities with feelings of anxiety and shame rather than arousal and pleasure.

Cognitive theorists, such as Albert Ellis (1977), point out that underlying irrational beliefs and attitudes can contribute to sexual dysfunctions. Consider two such irrational beliefs: (a) we must have the approval at all times of everyone who is important to us and (b) we must be thoroughly competent at everything we do. If we cannot accept the occasional disappointment of others, we may catastrophize the significance of a single frustrating sexual episode. If we insist that every sexual experience be perfect, we set the stage for inevitable failure.

How we appraise situations in terms of the perceived causes of events also plays a role. Attributing the cause for erectile difficulty to oneself ("What's wrong with me?") rather than to the situation ("It was the alcohol . . . ." "I was tired . . . .") can undermine future sexual functioning.

Relationship problems can also contribute to sexual dysfunctions, especially when they involve long-simmering resentments and conflicts (Fabrizi & Gambino, 2008; Moore & Heiman, 2006). The strain of a troubled relationship can take a toll on sexual desire, as can other stressful life events, such as job loss, family crisis, or serious illness (Heiman, 2008). The quality of sexual relations is usually no better than other facets of relationships or marriages. Couples who harbor resentments toward one another may choose the sexual arena for combat. Communication problems, moreover, are linked to general marital dissatisfaction. Couples who find it difficult to communicate their sexual desires may lack the means to help each other become more effective lovers.

The following case illustrates how sexual arousal disorder may be connected with problems in the relationship.

When a source of pleasure becomes a source of misery. Sexual dysfunctions can be a source of intense personal distress and lead to friction between partners. Lack of communication is a major contributor to the development and maintenance of sexual dysfunctions.

↦ The Case of Pete and Paula

After living together for 6 months, Pete and Paula are thinking seriously about getting married. But a problem has brought them to a sex therapy clinic. Paula explains to the therapist that for the past two months, Pete has been unable to sustain an erection during intercourse. Pete is 26 years old, a lawyer; Paula, 24, is a buyer for a large department store. They both grew up in middle-class, suburban families, were introduced through mutual friends and began having intercourse, without difficulty, a few months into their relationship. At Paula's urging, Pete moved into her apartment, although he wasn't sure he was ready for such a step. A week later, he began to have difficulty maintaining his erection during intercourse, although he felt strong desire for his partner. When his erection waned, he would try again, but would lose his desire and be unable to achieve another erection. After a few times like this, Paula would become so angry that she began striking Pete in the chest and screaming at him. Pete, who at 200 pounds weighed more than twice as much as Paula, would just walk away, which angered Paula even more. It became clear that sex was not the only trouble spot in their relationship. Paula complained that Pete preferred to spend time with his friends and go to baseball games rather than spending time with her. When together at home, he would become absorbed in watching sports events on television, and showed no interest in activities she enjoyed—attending the theater, visiting museums, and so on. Because there was no evidence that the sexual difficulty was due to either organic problems or depression, a diagnosis of male erectile disorder was given. Neither Pete nor Paula was willing to discuss their nonsexual problems with a therapist. Although the sexual problem was treated successfully with a form of sex therapy modeled after techniques developed by Masters and Johnson (as discussed later), and the couple later married, Pete's ambivalences continued, even well into their marriage, and there were future recurrences of sexual problems as well.

Adapted from Spitzer et al., 1994, pp. 198–200

BIOLOGICAL PERSPECTIVES Biological factors such as low testosterone levels and disease can dampen sexual desire and reduce responsiveness. Testosterone, the male sex hormone, plays a pivotal role in energizing sexual desire and sexual activity in both men and women (Braunstein, 2007; Davis et al., 2008). Both men and women produce testosterone in their bodies, although women produce smaller amounts. In men, a decline in testosterone production can lead to a loss of sexual interest and activity and difficulty achieving erections (Maggi, 2012; Montorsi et al., 2010). The adrenal glands and ovaries are the sites in the woman's body where testosterone is produced (Buvat et al., 2010). Women who have these organs surgically removed because of invasive disease no longer produce testosterone and may gradually lose sexual interest or develop a reduced capacity for sexual response (Davis & Braunstein, 2012; Wierman et al., 2010). We also have evidence linking low testosterone levels to some cases of depression in males, and depression may dampen sexual desire (Stephenson, 2008a). However, people with sexual dysfunctions typically have normal levels of sex hormone circulating in their bodies.

Cardiovascular problems involving impaired blood flow both to and through the penis can cause erectile disorder—a problem that becomes more common as men age (Miner et al., 2011). Erectile disorder may share common risk factors with cardiovascular disorders (heart and artery diseases), which should alert physicians that erectile dysfunction may be an early warning sign of underlying heart disease that should be medically evaluated (Alderman, 2009).

Erectile disorder is also linked to obesity in men (as are cardiovascular problems) and in men with prostate and urinary problems (Shabsigh et al., 2005; Tan et al., 2012). Obesity is associated with circulatory problems, so the connection to ED is not surprising. The good news is that obese men who lose weight and increase their activity levels may experience improved erectile functioning (Esposito et al., 2004).

Men with diabetes mellitus also stand an increased risk of ED (Eardley et al., 2010). Diabetes can damage blood vessels and nerves, including those serving the penis. Men with erectile disorder are more than twice as likely to have diabetes as men without erectile disorder (Sun et al., 2006).

Erectile disorder and delayed ejaculation may also result from multiple sclerosis (MS), a disease in which nerve cells lose the protective coatings that facilitate the smooth transmission of nerve impulses (Baranzini et al., 2010). Other forms of nerve damage, as well as chronic kidney disease, hypertension, cancer, and emphysema can also impair erectile response, as can endocrine disorders that suppress testosterone production (Buvat et al., 2010; Eardley et al., 2010; Koehler et al., 2012; Miner et al., 2011).

An important study of 2,000 men by Eric Rimm (2000) of the Harvard School of Public Health found that erectile dysfunction was associated with having a large waist, physical inactivity, and drinking too much alcohol (or not drinking at all). The common link among these factors may be high levels of cholesterol. Cholesterol can impede blood flow to the penis, just as it can impede blood flow to the heart. Exercise, weight loss, and moderate alcohol intake all help lower cholesterol levels, but we are not recommending that abstainers begin drinking to avert or treat erectile problems. However, the findings of the Massachusetts Male Aging Study suggest that regular exercise may reduce the risk of erectile dysfunction (Derby, 2000). In this study, men who burned 200 calories or more a day in physical activity, an amount that can be achieved by taking a daily walk at a brisk pace for two miles, had about half the risk of erectile dysfunction than did more sedentary men. Exercise may help prevent clogging of arteries, keeping them clear for the flow of blood into the penis. **T / F**

Women also develop vascular or nervous disorders that impair genital blood flow, reducing lubrication and sexual excitement, rendering intercourse painful, and reducing their ability to reach orgasm. As with men, these problems become more likely as women age.

Before we move on to discuss psychological factors, we need to note that prescription drugs and psychoactive drugs, including antidepressants and antipsychotics, can impair erectile functioning and cause orgasmic disorders (Olfson et al., 2005). About one in three women who use selective serotonin reuptake inhibitor (SSRI) antidepressants (such as Zoloft or Paxil) experience impaired orgasmic response or complete lack of orgasm (Ishak et al., 2010). Tranquilizers such as Valium and Xanax may cause orgasmic disorder in either men or women. Some medicinal drugs used to treat high blood pressure and high blood cholesterol levels can also interfere with erectile response. **T / F**

Depressant drugs such as alcohol, heroin, and morphine can reduce sexual desire and impair sexual arousal. Narcotics, such as heroin, also depress testosterone production, which can diminish sexual desire and lead to erectile failure. Regular use of cocaine can cause erectile disorder or delayed ejaculation and reduce sexual desire in both women and men. Some people report increased sexual pleasure from initial use of cocaine, but repeated use can lead to dependency on the drug for sexual arousal, and long-term use may lessen sexual pleasure.

SOCIOCULTURAL PERSPECTIVES At around the turn of the 20th century, an Englishwoman was quoted as saying she would "close her eyes and think of England" when her husband approached her to perform her marital duties. This old-fashioned stereotype suggests how sexual pleasure was once considered exclusively a male preserve—that sex, for women, was primarily a duty. Mothers usually informed their daughters of the conjugal duties before the wedding, and girls encoded sex as just one of the ways in which women serviced the needs of others. Women who harbor such stereotypical attitudes toward female sexuality are unlikely to become aware of their own sexual potential. In addition, sexual anxieties may transform negative expectations into self-fulfilling prophecies. Sexual dysfunctions in men, too, may be linked to extremely strict sociocultural beliefs and sexual taboos. Other negative beliefs about sexuality may interfere with sexual desire, such as the belief that sexual desire is not appropriate for older adults past childbearing age (Géonet, De Sutter, & Zech, 2012).

Our colleague, psychologist Rafael Javier (1993), takes note of the idealization within many Hispanic cultures of the *marianismo* stereotype, which derives its name from the Virgin Mary. From this sociocultural perspective, the ideal virtuous woman "suffers in silence" as she submerges her needs and desires to those of her husband and children. She is the provider of joy, even in the face of her own pain or frustration. It is not difficult to imagine that women who adopt these stereotypical expectations find it difficult to assert their own needs for sexual gratification and may express resistance to this cultural ideal by becoming sexually unresponsive.

Sociocultural factors play an important role in erectile dysfunction as well. Investigators find a greater incidence of erectile dysfunction in cultures with more restrictive sexual attitudes toward premarital sex among females, toward sex in marriage, and toward extramarital sex (Welch & Kartub, 1978). Men in these cultures may be prone to developing sexual anxiety or guilt that interferes with sexual performance.

In India, cultural beliefs that link the loss of semen to a draining of the man's life energy underlie the development of *dhat syndrome,* an irrational fear of loss of semen

Walking at a brisk pace for two miles a day may cut the risk of erectile dysfunction in men by about half.

☑ **TRUE** Results of a recent study showed that men who exercised regularly at a level comparable to taking a brisk walk for two miles a day had about half the risk of erectile dysfunction as sedentary men.

truth OR fiction

Using antidepressants can interfere with a person's orgasmic response.

☑ **TRUE** Use of SSRI-type antidepressants can impair orgasmic responsiveness.

(discussed in Chapter 6). Men with this condition sometimes develop erectile dysfunction because their fears about wasting precious seminal fluid interfere with their ability to perform sexually (Shukla & Singh, 2000).

10.6 Describe methods used to treat sexual dysfunctions.

Treatment of Sexual Dysfunctions

Until the groundbreaking research of the famed sex researchers William Masters and Virginia Johnson in the 1960s, there was no effective treatment for most sexual dysfunctions. Psychoanalytic therapy approached sexual dysfunctions indirectly. It was assumed that sexual dysfunctions represented underlying conflicts, and so treatment focused on resolving those conflicts through psychoanalysis. A lack of evidence about the efficacy of this approach led to development of methods that focus more directly on the sexual problems.

Most contemporary sex therapists assume that sexual dysfunctions can be treated by directly modifying the couple's sexual interactions. Pioneered by Masters and Johnson (1970), *sex therapy* uses cognitive-behavioral techniques in a brief therapy format to help individuals enhance their sexual competencies (sexual knowledge and skills) and relieve performance anxiety. Although therapists today may not strictly adhere to Masters and Johnson's techniques, they continue to incorporate many of their methods (Althof, 2010). When feasible, both partners are involved in therapy. In some cases, however, individual therapy may be preferable, as we shall see.

Before we turn to consider these specific methods, we should note that because sexual problems are often embedded in a context of troubled relationships, therapists may also use couple therapy to help couples share power in their relationships, improve communication skills, and negotiate differences (Coyle, 2006; McCarthy, Ginsberg, & Fucito, 2006).

Significant changes have occurred in the treatment of sexual dysfunctions in the past 25 years. Today, there is greater emphasis on biological or organic factors in the development of sexual problems and the use of medical treatments, such as the drug *sildenafil* (Viagra), to treat male erectile dysfunction. Erectile drugs have become so popular that they now represent a revenue source of $5 billion for drug makers and are used by tens of millions of men (Wilson, 2011). Let's survey some of the more common therapy techniques for particular types of disorders.

Masters & Johnson. Sex therapists William Masters and Virginia Johnson.

LOW SEXUAL DRIVE OR DESIRE Sex therapists may try to help people with low sexual desire kindle their sexual appetite through the use of self-stimulation (masturbation) exercises together with erotic fantasies. When working with couples, therapists prescribe mutual pleasuring exercises that the couple can perform at home or encourage them to expand their sexual repertoire to add novelty and excitement to their sex life. When a lack of sexual desire is connected with depression, the treatment focuses on treating the underlying depression. Couple therapy might be in order to resolve problems in the relationship that may be contributing to lack of sexual desire (Carvalho & Nobre, 2012). When problems of low sexual desire or interest appear to stem from deep-seated causes, some sex therapists use insight-oriented (psychodynamic) approaches to help uncover and resolve underlying issues.

Some cases of low sexual desire are associated with hormonal deficiencies, especially lack of the male sex hormone testosterone. The use of a testosterone gel patch attached to the skin for administering the hormone can increase sexual desire and improve sexual function in men with abnormally low levels of testosterone (Buvat et al., 2010; Granata et al., 2012; Montorsi et al., 2010). Testosterone treatments can have potentially serious complications, such as liver damage and possible prostate cancer, and so they should be undertaken cautiously. The long-term safety of testosterone treatment is not fully determined (Heiman, 2008).

Testosterone can also help boost sexual drive and interest in menopausal women with low sexual desire, but its effectiveness in premenopausal women remains unclear

(Brotto et al., 2010; Kingsberg, 2010). However, because the long-term effects of testosterone therapy on risks of breast cancer and other medical conditions in women are unknown, women seeking testosterone treatment need to consult with their medical care providers to weigh the potential risks and benefits. These hormonal treatments may also lead to growth of facial hair and acne.

DISORDERS OF SEXUAL AROUSAL Sexual arousal results in the pooling of blood in the genital region, causing erection in the male and vaginal lubrication in the female. These changes in blood flow occur as a reflexive response to sexual stimulation; they cannot be willed. Women who have difficulty becoming sexually aroused and men with erectile problems are first educated about the fact that they need not "do" anything to become aroused. As long as their problems are psychological, not organic, they need only expose themselves to sexual stimulation under relaxed, unpressured conditions, so that disruptive thoughts and anxiety do not inhibit reflexive responses.

Masters and Johnson have a couple counter performance anxiety by engaging in *sensate focus exercises*. These are nondemand sexual contacts—sensuous exercises that do not demand sexual arousal in the form of vaginal lubrication or erection. Partners begin by massaging one another without touching the genitals. The partners learn to "pleasure" each other and to "be pleasured" by following and giving verbal instructions and by guiding each other's hands. The method fosters both communication and sexual skills and countermands anxiety because there is no demand for sexual arousal. After several sessions, direct massage of the genitals is included in pleasuring. Even when obvious signs of sexual excitement are produced (lubrication or erection), the couple does not straightaway engage in intercourse, because intercourse might create performance demands. After excitement is achieved consistently, the couple engages in a relaxed sequence of other sexual activities, culminating eventually in intercourse.

Success rates in treating individual cases of erectile disorder with sex therapy techniques are variable, and we still lack methodologically sound studies that support the overall effectiveness of the technique (Binik & Meana, 2009; Leiblum & Rosen, 2000). The following case example illustrates sex therapy techniques for treating erectile dysfunction.

→ Victor: A Case of Erectile Dysfunction

Victor P., a 44-year-old concert violinist, was eager to show the therapist reviews of his concert tour. A solo violinist with a distinguished orchestra, Victor's life revolved around practice, performances, and reviews. He dazzled audiences with his technique and the energy of his performance. As a concert musician, Victor had exquisite control over his body, especially his hands. Yet he could not control his erectile response in the same way. Since his divorce seven years earlier, Victor had been troubled by recurrent episodes of erectile failure. Time and time again he had become involved in a new relationship, only to find himself unable to perform sexually. Fearing repetition, he would sever the relationship. He was unable to face an audience of only one. For a while he dated casually, but then he met Michelle.

Michelle was a writer who loved music. They were a perfect match because Victor, the musician, loved literature. Michelle, a 35-year-old divorcée, was exciting, earthy, sensual, and accepting. The couple soon grew inseparable. He would practice while she would write—poetry mostly, but also short magazine pieces. Unlike some women Victor met who did not know Bach from Bartok, Michelle held her own in conversations with Victor's friends and fellow musicians over late night dinner at Sardi's, a famous New York restaurant. They kept their own apartments; Victor needed his own space and solitude for practice.

In the nine months of their relationship, Victor was unable to perform on the stage that mattered most to him—his canopied bed. It was just so frustrating, he said. "I would become erect and then just as I approach her to penetrate, pow! It collapses on me." Victor's history of nocturnal erections and erections during light petting suggested that he was basically suffering from performance anxiety. He was bearing down to force an erection, much as he might try to learn the fingering of a difficult violin piece. Each night became a command performance in which Victor served as his own severest critic. Rather than focus on his partner, his attention was riveted on the size of his penis. As noted by the late great pianist Vladimir Horowitz, the worst thing a pianist can do is watch his fingers. Perhaps, the worst thing a man with erectile problems can do is watch his penis.

To break the vicious cycle of anxiety, erectile failure, and more anxiety, Victor and Michelle followed a sex therapy program (Rathus & Nevid, 1977) modeled after the Masters and Johnson treatment. The aim was to restore the pleasure of sexual activity, unfettered by anxiety. The couple was initially instructed to abstain from attempts at intercourse to free Victor from any pressure to perform. The couple progressed through a series of steps:

1. *Relaxing together in the nude without any touching, such as when reading or watching TV together.*
2. *Sensate focus exercises.*
3. *Genital stimulation of each other manually or orally to orgasm.*
4. *Nondemand intercourse (intercourse performed without any pressure on the man to satisfy his partner). The man may afterward help his partner achieve orgasm by using manual or oral stimulation.*
5. *Resumption of vigorous intercourse (intercourse involving more vigorous thrusting and use of alternative positions and techniques that focus on mutual satisfaction). The couple is instructed not to catastrophize occasional problems that may arise.*

The therapy program helped Victor overcome his erectile disorder. Victor was freed of the need to prove himself by achieving erection on command. He surrendered his post as critic. Once the spotlight was off the bed, he became a participant and not a spectator.

From the Author's Files

DISORDERS OF ORGASM Women with orgasmic disorder often harbor underlying beliefs that sex is dirty or sinful. They may have been taught not to touch themselves. They feel anxious about sex and have not learned, through trial and error, what kinds of sexual stimulation will arouse them and help them reach orgasm. Treatment in these cases includes modification of negative attitudes toward sex. When orgasmic disorder reflects the woman's feelings about or relationship with her partner, treatment also involves enhancing the relationship.

In either case, Masters and Johnson would prefer to work with the couple and first use sensate focus exercises to lessen performance anxiety, open channels of communication, and help the couple acquire sexual skills. The woman directs her partner to use caresses and techniques that stimulate her. By taking charge, the woman becomes psychologically freed from the stereotype of the passive, submissive female role.

Masters and Johnson preferred working with the couple in cases of female orgasmic dysfunction, but other sex therapists prefer to work with the woman individually by directing her to practice masturbation in private. Directed masturbation provides women opportunities to learn about their own bodies at their own pace and has a success rate of 70% to 90% (Leiblum & Rosen, 2000). It frees women of the need to rely on or please partners. Once women can reliably masturbate to orgasm, couple-oriented treatment may facilitate transfer of training to orgasm with a partner.

Delayed ejaculation has received little attention in the clinical literature, but may involve psychological factors such as fear, anxiety, hostility, and relationship difficulties (Rowland et al., 2010). The standard treatment, barring underlying organic problems, focuses on increasing sexual stimulation and reducing performance anxiety (Althof, 2012; Leiblum & Rosen, 2000).

The most widely used behavioral approach to treating premature (early) ejaculation, called the *stop-start* or *stop-and-go* technique, was introduced in 1956 by a urologist with the intriguing name of James Semans. The partners suspend sexual activity when the man is about to ejaculate and then resume stimulation when his sensations subside. Repeated practice enables him to regulate ejaculation by sensitizing him to the cues that precede the ejaculatory reflex, making him more aware of his "point of no return," the point at which the ejaculatory reflex is triggered. Therapists have reported high levels of success with the stop-start method, but relapse rates tend to be high (Segraves & Althof, 1998).

GENITAL PAIN DISORDERS Treatment of painful intercourse generally requires medical intervention to determine and treat any underlying physical problems, such as urinary tract infections, that might be causing pain (van Lankveld et al., 2010). In cases in which vaginismus contributes to pain, psychological treatment of vaginismus may help relieve pain.

Vaginismus is a conditioned reflex involving the involuntary constriction of the vaginal opening. It represents a psychologically based fear of penetration, rather than a medical problem. Treatment for vaginismus may include a combination of behavioral methods, including relaxation techniques and the gradual exposure method to desensitize the vaginal musculature to penetration by having the woman over the course of a few weeks insert fingers or plastic dilators of increasing sizes into the vagina while she remains relaxed (Reissing, 2012; ter Kuile et al., 2009). Although therapists often report good results with gradual exposure, we lack a sufficient body of evidence from controlled research trials testing its effectiveness (van Lankveld et al., 2010). Because many women with sexual pain or vaginismus have histories of rape or sexual abuse, psychotherapy may be part of the treatment program to deal with the psychological consequences of traumatic experiences.

BIOLOGICAL TREATMENTS OF SEXUAL DYSFUNCTION Erectile disorder frequently has organic causes, and so it is not surprising that treatment is becoming increasingly medicalized.

Sexual arousal in both men and women depends on engorgement of blood in the genitals. Drugs that increase blood flow to the penis, such as Viagra and Cialis, are safe and effective in helping men with ED achieve more reliable erections (Lue et al., 2010; Qaseem et al., 2009). However, evidence also indicates that combining psychotherapy with medications like Viagra can be more effective than medication alone (Aubin et al., 2009). When taking pills is ineffective, alternatives such as self-injection in the penis of a drug that increases penile blood flow, or use of a vacuum erection device that works like a penis pump, may prove more helpful (Alderman, 2009; Montorsi et al., 2010).

Investigators are exploring biomedical therapies for female sexual dysfunctions, including use of erectile dysfunction (ED) drugs such as Viagra. Research on the effectiveness of these drugs in treating female orgasmic dysfunction has yielded mixed results, but the drugs may be helpful in some cases (Ishak et al., 2010).

As noted, the male sex hormone testosterone may increase sexual drive in men and postmenopausal women with diminished sexual drive or interest. However, we shouldn't think that all cases of low sexual desire should be treated with hormones. As one leading sexual health expert put it, ". . . if someone is unhappy with her spouse, no amount of testosterone is going to fix that" (cited in Clay, 2009, p. 34). Problems of sexual desire should not be treated in isolation but in a larger context that takes into account psychological, cultural, and interpersonal contexts (Leiblum, 2010a). For example, lack of sexual desire may reflect problems in the relationship, in which case, couple therapy may be used to focus more on the relationship itself. As it stands, treatment of sexual desire problems is often more complex and less effective than treatment of other types of sexual dysfunction (LoPiccolo, 2011).

Surgery may be effective in rare cases in which blocked blood vessels prevent blood flow to the penis, or in which the penis is structurally defective. SSRIs, such as the antidepressants *fluoxetine* (Prozac), *paroxetine* (Paxil), and *sertraline* (Zoloft), work by increasing the action of the neurotransmitter serotonin. Increased availability of serotonin in the brain can have the side effect of delaying ejaculation, which can help men with early ejaculation problems (Mohee & Eardley, 2011; Rowland et al., 2010; Waldinger, 2011).

The medicalization of treatments for sexual dysfunctions holds great promise, but no pill or biomechanical device will enhance the quality of a relationship. If individuals have serious problems with their partners, popping a pill or applying a cream is unlikely to solve them. All in all, the success rates reported for treating sexual dysfunctions through psychological or biological approaches are quite encouraging, especially when we remember that only a few generations ago, there were no effective treatments.

Paraphilic Disorders

10.7 Define the term paraphilia and identify major types of paraphilic disorders.

The word *paraphilia* was coined from the Greek roots *para,* meaning "to the side of," and *philos,* meaning "loving." People with **paraphilias** have unusual or atypical patterns of sexual attraction that involve sexual arousal ("loving") in response to atypical stimuli ("to the side of" normally arousing stimuli). These atypical patterns of sexual arousal may be labeled by others as deviant, bizarre, or "kinky" (Lehne, 2009). Paraphilias involve strong and recurrent sexual arousal to atypical stimuli as evidenced by fantasies, urges, or behaviors (acting upon the urges) for a period of six months or longer. The range of atypical stimuli include nonhuman objects such as underwear, shoes, leather, or silk, to humiliation or experience of pain in oneself or one's partner, or children and other persons who do not or cannot grant consent (Fisher et al., 2011)

The *DSM-5* includes a class of mental disorders called *paraphilic disorders.* There is an important distinction between a paraphilia and a paraphilic disorder. Some forms of paraphilic behaviors, such as fetishism or transvestism (cross-dressing for sexual arousal), may not be associated with disturbing or distressing consequences to oneself or others and so are not classified as mental or psychological disorders. For a paraphilic disorder to be diagnosed, the paraphilia must cause personal distress or impairment in important areas of daily functioning, or (and this is different from other diagnostic categories) involve behaviors presently *or in the past* in which satisfaction of the sexual urge involved harm, or risk of harm, to other people (APA, 2013). Thus, the presence of paraphilia is a necessary but not a sufficient condition for a diagnosis of a paraphilic disorder.

For some individuals, engaging in paraphilic acts becomes the only means of achieving sexual gratification (Lehne, 2009). They cannot become sexually aroused unless these stimuli are used, in actuality or in fantasies. Others resort to these atypical or deviant stimuli occasionally or when under stress. Although the prevalence rates of paraphilias and paraphilic disorders are unknown, we do know that these behaviors are almost never diagnosed in women, with the exception of some cases of sexual masochism and some isolated cases of other disorders (Seligman & Hardenburg, 2000).

Types of Paraphilias

Some paraphilias are relatively harmless and victimless. Among these are fetishism and transvestic fetishism. Others, such as exhibitionism, pedophilia, and voyeurism have unwilling victims and so meet the diagnostic criteria for inflicting harm or risk of harm on others. A most harmful form of paraphilia is sexual sadism when acted out with a nonconsenting partner. Here, we focus on the paraphilias themselves, but bear in mind that the diagnosis of a paraphilic disorder requires that the paraphilia causes personal distress, impaired functioning, or harm or risk of harm to others either presently or in past episodes of paraphilic behavior.

EXHIBITIONISM The paraphilia of **exhibitionism** ("flashing") is characterized by strong and recurrent urges, fantasies, or behaviors of exposing of one's genitals to unsuspecting individuals for the purpose of sexual arousal. Typically, the person seeks to surprise, shock, or sexually arouse the victim. The person may masturbate while fantasizing about or actually exposing himself (almost all cases involve men). The victims are almost always women. Relatively few cases are reported to the police.

A national survey found that about 4% of men (and 2% of women) reported exposing their genitals for purposes of sexual arousal (Murphy & Page, 2008). The person diagnosed with exhibitionism usually does not seek sexual contact with the victim. Nevertheless, some people who expose their genitals progress to more serious crimes of sexual aggression (McLawsen et al., 2012). Whether or not the exhibitionist seeks physical contact, the victim may believe herself to be in danger and be traumatized by the act. Victims are probably best advised to show no reaction to a flasher, but to just continue on their way, if possible. It would be unwise to insult the exhibitionist, lest it provoke a violent reaction. Nor do we recommend an exaggerated show of shock or fear, which tends to reinforce the behavior.

Exhibitionism. Exhibitionism is a type of paraphilia that characterizes people who seek sexual arousal or gratification through exposing themselves to unsuspecting victims. People who expose themselves are usually not interested in actual sexual contact with their victims.

Men who engage in exhibitionistic acts do so as a means of indirectly expressing hostility toward women, perhaps because of perceptions of mistreatment (rejection) by women in the past. Men who perform exhibitionistic acts tend to be shy, lonely, dependent, and lacking in interpersonal skills and may have had difficulty relating to women or establishing relationships with women (Leue et al,. 2004; Murphy & Page, 2012). Some doubt their masculinity and harbor feelings of inferiority. Their victims' revulsion or fear boosts their sense of mastery of the situation and heightens their sexual arousal. Consider the following case example of exhibitionism.

→ Michael: A Case of Exhibitionism

Michael was a 26-year-old, handsome, boyish-looking married male with a 3-year-old daughter. He had spent about one-quarter of his life in reform schools and in prison. As an adolescent, he had been a fire-setter. As a young adult, he had begun to expose himself. He came to the clinic without his wife's knowledge because he was exposing himself more and more often—up to three times a day—and he was afraid that he would eventually be arrested and thrown into prison again.

Michael said he liked sex with his wife, but it wasn't as exciting as exposing himself. He couldn't prevent his exhibitionism, especially now, when he was between jobs and worried about where the family's next month's rent was coming from. He loved his daughter more than anything and couldn't stand the thought of being separated from her.

Michael's method of operation was as follows: He would look for slender adolescent females, usually near the junior high school and the senior high school. He would take his penis out of his pants and play with it while he drove up to a girl or a small group of girls. He would lower the car window, continuing to play with himself, and ask them for directions. Sometimes the girls didn't see his penis. That was okay. Sometimes they saw it and didn't react. That was okay, too. When they saw it and became flustered and afraid, that was best of all. He would start to masturbate harder, and now and then he managed to ejaculate before the girls had departed.

Michael's history was unsettled. His father had left home before he was born, and his mother had drunk heavily. He was in and out of foster homes throughout his childhood. Before he was 10 years old, he was involved in sexual activities with neighborhood boys. Now and then the boys also forced neighborhood girls into pet-ting, and Michael had mixed feelings when the girls got upset. He felt bad for them, but he also enjoyed it. A couple of times girls seemed horrified at the sight of his penis, and it made him "really feel like a man. To see that look, you know, with a girl, not a woman, but a girl—a slender girl, that's what I'm after."

From the Author's Files

Although some cases are reported among women, virtually all cases of exhibition-ism involve men (Hugh-Jones, Gough, & Littlewood, 2005). People who engage in exhi-bitionism are motivated by the wish to shock and dismay unsuspecting observers, not to show off the attractiveness of their bodies. Therefore, wearing skimpy bathing suits or other revealing clothing is not a form of exhibitionism in the clinical sense of the term. Nor do exotic dancers or strippers typically meet the clinical criteria for exhibition-ism. They are generally not motivated by the desire to expose themselves to unsuspecting strangers in order to arouse them or shock them. The chief motive of the exotic dancer is usually to earn a living (Philaretou, 2006). **T / F**

FETISHISM The French word *fétiche* is thought to derive from the Portuguese *feitico*, referring to a "magic charm." In this case, the "magic" lies in the object's ability to arouse sexually. The chief feature of **fetishism** is recurrent, powerful sexual urges, fantasies, or behaviors involving inanimate objects, such as an article of clothing (bras, panties, hosiery, boots, shoes, leather, silk, and the like) (Kafka, 2010). It is not abnormal for men to become sexually aroused by the sight, feel, and smell of their lovers' undergarments. Men with fetishism, however, may prefer the object to the person and may not be able to become sexually aroused without it. They often experience sexual gratification by mas-turbating while fondling the object, rubbing it, or smelling it or by having their partners wear it during sexual activity.

The origins of fetishism can be traced to early childhood in many cases. Most individuals with a rubber fetish in an early research sample were able to recall first experi-encing a fetishistic attraction to rubber sometime between the ages of 4 and 10 (Gosselin & Wilson, 1980).

TRANSVESTISM The paraphilia of **transvestism** (also called *transvestic fetishism*) refers to individuals who have recurrent and powerful urges, fantasies, or behaviors in which they become sexually aroused by cross-dressing. Although other men with fetishes can be satisfied by handling objects such as women's clothing while they masturbate, transvestite men want to wear them. They may wear full feminine attire and makeup or favor one particular article of clothing, such as women's stockings. Although some transvestite men are gay, transvestism is usually found among hetero-sexual men (Långström & Zucker, 2005; Taylor & Rupp, 2004). The man typically cross-dresses in private and imagines himself to be a woman whom he is stroking as he masturbates. Some frequent transvestite clubs or become involved in a transvestic subculture. Some transvestite men are sexually stimulated by fantasies that their own bodies are female (Bailey, 2003b).

Men with a transgender identity may cross-dress to "pass" as women or because they are not comfortable dressing in male clothing. Some gay men also cross-dress, perhaps to make a statement about overly rigid gender roles, but not because they seek to become sexually aroused. Because cross-dressing among gay men and transgender individuals is performed for reasons other than sexual arousal or gratification, their behavior is not clas-sified as transvestic fetishism. Nor are female impersonators who cross-dress for theatrical purposes considered to have a form of transvestism.

Most men with transvestism are married and engage in sexual activity with their wives, but they seek additional sexual gratification through dressing as women, as in the following case.

Archie was a 55-year-old plumber who had been cross-dressing for many years. There was a time when he would go out in public as a woman, but as his prominence in the community grew, he became more afraid of being discovered. His wife, Myrna, knew of his "peccadillo," especially because he borrowed many of her clothes, and she also encouraged him to stay at home, offering to help him with his "weirdness." For many years, his paraphilia had been restricted to the home.

The couple came to the clinic at the urging of the wife. Myrna described how Archie had imposed his will on her for 20 years. Archie would wear her undergarments and masturbate while she told him how disgusting he was. (The couple also regularly engaged in "normal" sexual intercourse, which Myrna enjoyed.) The cross-dressing situation had come to a head because a teenaged daughter had almost walked into the couple's bedroom while they were acting out Archie's fantasies.

With Myrna out of the consulting room, Archie explained that he grew up in a family with several older sisters. He described how underwear had been perpetually hanging all around the one bathroom to dry. As an adolescent, Archie experimented with rubbing against articles of underwear, then with trying them on. On one occasion, a sister walked in while he was modeling panties before the mirror. She told him he was a "dredge to society," and he straightaway experienced unparalleled sexual excitement. He masturbated when she left the room, and his orgasm was the strongest of his young life.

Archie did not think that there was anything wrong with wearing women's undergarments and masturbating. He was not about to give it up, regardless of whether his marriage was destroyed as a result. Myrna's main concern was finally separating herself from Archie's "sickness." She didn't care what he did anymore, so long as he did it by himself. "Enough is enough," she said.

That was the compromise the couple worked out in marital therapy. Archie would engage in his fantasies by himself. He would choose times when Myrna was not at home, and she would not be informed of his activities. He would also be very, very careful to choose times when the children were not around.

Six months later the couple were together and content. Archie had replaced Myrna's input into his fantasies with transvestic-sadomasochistic magazines. Myrna said, "I see no evil, hear no evil, smell no evil." They continued to have sexual intercourse. After a while, Myrna even forgot to check to see which underwear had been used.

→ From the Author's Files

VOYEURISM The paraphilia of **voyeurism** ("peeping") involves strong and recurrent sexual urges, fantasies, or behaviors in which the person becomes sexually aroused by watching unsuspecting people, generally strangers, who are naked, disrobing, or engaging in sexual activity. The person who engages in voyeurism does not typically seek sexual activity with the person or persons being observed, but becomes sexually aroused by the act of watching. Like exhibitionism, virtually all cases of voyeurism occur among men (Langstrom, 2010).

Are acts of watching your partner disrobe or viewing sexually explicit films forms of voyeurism? The answer is no. The people who are observed know they are being observed by their partners or will be observed by film audiences. Nor is attending a strip club for purposes of sexual stimulation considered abnormal, as it does not involve seeking sexual arousal by watching unsuspecting persons. People may also frequent strip clubs for reasons other than sexual gratification, such as bonding experiences with friends (Montemurro et al., 2003).

The voyeur usually masturbates while watching or while fantasizing about watching. Voyeurs are often lacking in sexual experiences and may harbor deep feelings of inferiority or inadequacy (Leue et al., 2004). Peeping may be the voyeur's only sexual outlet.

Some people engage in voyeuristic acts in which they place themselves in risky situations. The prospect of being discovered or injured apparently heightens their excitement.

FROTTEURISM The French word *frottage* refers to the artistic technique of making a drawing by rubbing against a raised object. The chief feature of the paraphilia of **frotteurism** is recurrent, powerful sexual urges, fantasies, or behaviors in which the person becomes sexually aroused by rubbing against or touching a nonconsenting person. Frotteurism, also called "mashing," often occurs in crowded places, such as subway cars, buses, or elevators. The rubbing or touching, not the coercive aspect of the act, sexually arouses the man. He may imagine himself enjoying an exclusive, affectionate sexual relationship with the victim. Because the physical contact is brief and furtive, people who perform acts of frotteurism stand only a small chance of being caught by authorities. Even victims may not realize at the time what has happened or register much protest. In the following case, a man victimized about 1,000 women over several years but was arrested only twice.

> ### Bumping on the Subway: A Case of Frotteurism
>
> *A 45-year-old man was seen by a psychiatrist following his second arrest for rubbing against a woman in the subway. He would select as his target a woman in her 20s as she entered the subway station. He would position himself behind her on the platform and wait for the train to enter the station. He would then follow her into the subway car and when the doors closed, would begin bumping against her buttocks, while fantasizing that they were enjoying having intercourse in a loving and consensual manner. About half of the time he would reach orgasm. He would then continue on his way to work. Sometimes when he hadn't reached orgasm, he would change trains and seek another victim. While he felt guilty for a time after each episode, he would soon become preoccupied with thoughts about his next encounter. He never gave any thought to the feelings his victims might have about what he had done to them. Although he was married to the same woman for 25 years, he appeared to be rather socially inept and unassertive, especially with women.*
>
> *Adapted from Spitzer et al., 1994, pp. 164–165*

What did he just do? Mashing, or unwelcome sexual rubbing or touching, occurs most often in tight crowded places, such as on subway car at rush hour.

PEDOPHILIA The word **pedophilia** derives from the Greek *paidos,* meaning "child." People with pedophilia have recurrent and powerful sexual urges or fantasies or behaviors involving sexual activity with children (typically 13 years old or younger). To be diagnosed with pedophilic disorder, the person must be at least 16 years of age and at least 5 years older than the child or children toward whom the person is sexually attracted or has victimized. However, the diagnosis does not apply to a person in late adolescence who has a continuing relationship with a 12 or 13 year old (APA, 2013) In some cases, the person with pedophilia is attracted only to children. In others, the person is attracted to both children and adults.

Although most cases of pedophilic disorder involve men who are sexually attracted to children, it is important to note that pedophilia may involve either men or women who seek sexual contact with either boys or girls. Some people with pedophilia restrict their deviant activities to looking at or undressing children, whereas others engage in exhibitionism, kissing, fondling, oral sex, and anal intercourse and, in the case of girls, vaginal intercourse. Not being worldly wise, children are often taken advantage of by molesters, who inform them they are "educating" them, "showing them something," or doing something they will "like."

Some pedophilic men limit their sexual activity with children to incestuous relations with family members; others only molest children outside the family. Sexual molestation of children is a criminal act and deservedly so. But not all child molesters have pedophilic disorder. The clinical definition of pedophilic disorder is brought to bear only when sexual attraction to prepubescent or early pubescent children is equal or greater than sexual attraction to mature individuals. Some child molesters experience pedophilic urges only occasionally or during times of opportunity and so would not warrant a diagnosis of pedophilic disorder.

Despite the stereotype, most cases of pedophilia do not involve "dirty old men" who hang around schoolyards in raincoats. Men with this disorder (virtually all cases involve men) are usually (otherwise) law-abiding, respected citizens in their 30s or 40s. Most are married or divorced and have children of their own. They are usually well acquainted with their victims, who are typically either relatives or friends of the family. Many cases of pedophilia are not isolated incidents. They often begin when children are very young and continue for years until they are discovered or the relationship is broken off.

The origins of pedophilia are complex and varied. Some cases fit the stereotype of the weak, shy, socially inept, and isolated man who is threatened by mature relationships and turns to children for sexual gratification because children are less critical and demanding. Evidence based on case studies shows that men with pedophilia tend to have fewer romantic relationships than other men, and the relationships they do have tend to be less satisfying (Seto, 2009). In some cases, childhood sexual experiences with other children may have been so enjoyable that the man, as an adult, attempts to recapture the excitement of earlier years. In some cases, men who were sexually abused in childhood reverse the situation in an effort to establish feelings of mastery.

EFFECTS OF SEXUAL ABUSE ON CHILDREN High profile cases in the news in recent years, such as the conviction of former Penn State assistant football coach Jerry Sandusky, have highlighted the problem of child sexual abuse. The occurrence of child sexual abuse is much more common than many people suspect.

A recent review of existing research showed that nearly 8% of adult males and nearly 20% of adult females reported some form of sexual abuse before the age of 18 (Pereda et al., 2009). Other recent estimates peg the frequency of sexual abuse during childhood at even higher levels—30% of girls and 15% of boys (Irish, Kobayashi, & Delahanty, 2010). The typical abuser is not the proverbial stranger lurking in the shadows, but a relative or step-relative of the child, a family friend, or a neighbor—someone who has held and then abused the child's trust.

Sexual abuse can inflict great psychological harm, whether it is perpetrated by a family member, an acquaintance, or a stranger. Abused children may suffer from a litany of psychological problems involving anger, anxiety, depression, eating disorders, inappropriate sexual behavior, aggressive behavior, drug abuse, suicide attempts, posttraumatic stress disorder, low self-esteem, sexual dysfunction, and feelings of detachment (e.g., Maniglio, 2011; Stoltenborgh et al., 2011). Adults who were sexually abused as children stand a higher risk of developing psychological disorders and significant physical health problems, as well as problems with memory and cognitive functioning (Gould et al., 2012; Irish, Kobayashi, & Delahanty, 2010). A U.K. study showed that people with a history of child sexual abuse were between 6 and 10 times more likely to engage in suicidal behavior (threatening suicide or making suicide attempts) in adulthood (Bebbington et al., 2009).

We should also note that psychological effects of sexual abuse on children are variable and that no one single pattern applies in all cases. Sexual abuse may also cause genital injuries and psychosomatic problems such as stomachaches and headaches.

Younger children sometimes react with tantrums or aggressive or antisocial behavior. Older children often develop substance abuse problems. Some abused children become socially withdrawn and retreat into fantasy or refuse to leave the house. Abused children may also show regressive behaviors, such as thumb sucking, fear of the dark, and fear of strangers. Many survivors of childhood sexual abuse develop posttraumatic stress disorder. They suffer flashbacks, nightmares, emotional numbing, and feel alienated from other people (Herrera & McCloskey, 2003).

The sexual development of abused children may veer off in dysfunctional directions. For example, abused children may become prematurely sexually active or promiscuous in adolescence and adulthood (Herrera & McCloskey, 2003). Adolescent girls who have been sexually abused tend to be more sexually active than their peers.

The effects of childhood sexual abuse tend to be similar in boys and girls (Maikovitch-Fong & Jaffee, 2010). Both tend to become fearful and have trouble sleeping, for example. However, some investigators report finding gender differences in the effects of abuse, with the most pronounced difference that boys more often externalize their problems, often through physical aggression. Girls more often internalize their difficulties, for example, by becoming depressed (Edwards et al., 2003).

Psychological problems may continue into adolescence and adulthood in the form of posttraumatic stress disorder, anxiety, depression, substance abuse, and relationship problems. Late adolescence and early adulthood are particularly difficult times for survivors of child sexual abuse, because unresolved feelings of anger and guilt and a deep sense of mistrust can prevent the development of intimate relationships. Evidence shows that women who blame themselves for the abuse experience relatively lower self-esteem and greater depression than those who do not (Edwards et al., 2003). Childhood sexual abuse is also linked to later development of borderline personality disorder, a psychological disorder discussed in Chapter 12.

SEXUAL MASOCHISM Sexual masochism derives its name from the Austrian novelist Ritter Leopold von Sacher Masoch (1835–1895), who wrote stories and novels about men who sought sexual gratification from women by inflicting pain on themselves, often in the form of flagellation (being beaten or whipped). Sexual masochism involves strong and recurrent sexual urges, fantasies, or behaviors in which the person becomes sexually aroused by being humiliated, bound, flogged, or made to suffer in other ways. In cases of sexual masochism disorder, the urges either are acted on or cause significant personal distress. In some cases of sexual masochism, the person cannot attain sexual gratification in the absence of pain or humiliation. Sexual masochism is the one form of paraphilia found with some frequency in women, although it is more common among men (Logan, 2008).

In some cases, sexual masochism involves binding or mutilating oneself during masturbation or sexual fantasies. In others, a partner is engaged to restrain (bondage), blindfold (sensory bondage), paddle, or whip the person. Some partners are prostitutes; others are consensual partners who are asked to perform the sadistic role. In some cases, the person may desire, for purposes of sexual gratification, to be urinated or defecated upon or subjected to verbal abuse. T / F

A most dangerous expression of sexual masochism is **hypoxyphilia,** in which participants become sexually aroused by being deprived of oxygen—for example, by using a noose, plastic bag, chemical, or pressure on the chest during a sexual act, such as masturbation. The oxygen deprivation is usually accompanied by fantasies of asphyxiating or being asphyxiated by a lover. People who engage in this activity generally discontinue it before they lose consciousness, but occasional deaths due to suffocation are reported.

SEXUAL SADISM Sexual sadism is named after the infamous Marquis de Sade, the 18th-century Frenchman who wrote stories about the pleasures of achieving sexual gratification by inflicting pain or humiliation on others. Sexual sadism is the flip side of sexual masochism. It is characterized by recurrent, powerful sexual urges, fantasies, or behaviors in which the person becomes sexually aroused by inflicting physical or psychological suffering or humiliation on another person.

People with sexually sadistic fantasies sometimes recruit consenting partners, who may be lovers or wives with masochistic interests, or prostitutes, who are paid to play a masochistic role. But some sexual sadists—a small minority—stalk and assault

truth OR fiction

Some people cannot become sexually aroused unless they are subjected to pain or humiliation.

☑ **TRUE** These people have a form of paraphilia called sexual masochism.

nonconsenting victims and become aroused by inflicting pain or suffering on them (Yates et al., 2008). Sadistic rapists fall into this last group. Laboratory evidence shows that sexual sadists tend to become genitally aroused by scenes of violence or injury to a victim in a sexual context (Seto et al., 2012). Let us note, however, that most rapists do not become sexually aroused by inflicting pain; many even lose sexual interest when they see their victims in pain.

Many people have occasional sadistic or masochistic fantasies or engage in sex play involving simulated or mild forms of **sadomasochism** with their partners. Sadomasochism refers to a practice of mutually gratifying sexual interactions involving both sadistic and masochistic acts. Stimulation may take the form of using a feather brush to "strike" one's partner, so that no actual pain is administered. This and other variations such as love bites, hair pulls, and mild scratching in the context of mutually consensual relationships are considered to fall within the normal spectrum of human sexual interactions (Laws & O'Donohue, 2012). Rituals such as the "master and slave" game are staged, as though they were scenes in a play. People who engage in sadomasochism frequently switch roles. The clinical diagnosis of *sexual masochism disorder* or *sexual sadism disorder* is not brought to bear unless these sexual behaviors, urges, or fantasies cause personal distress or negatively impact the person's ability to function in meeting social, occupational, or other roles or risked or caused harm to others. 👁

👁 **Watch** the **Video** *Jocelyn: Exploring Sadism and Masochism* on **MyPsychLab**

OTHER PARAPHILIAS There are many other paraphilias. These include making obscene phone calls (telephone scatologia), necrophilia (sexual urges or fantasies involving contact with corpses), partialism (sole focus on part of the body, such as the breasts), zoophilia (sexual urges or fantasies involving contact with animals), and sexual arousal associated with feces (coprophilia), enemas (klismaphilia), and urine (urophilia).

In the *Closer Look* feature on page 394, we discuss what may be a new psychological disorder—cybersex addiction.

Theoretical Perspectives

As in the case of so many psychological disorders, approaches to understanding the causes of paraphilias emphasize psychological and biological factors.

10.8 Describe theoretical perspectives on paraphilia and underlying causal factors.

PSYCHOLOGICAL PERSPECTIVES Psychodynamic theorists see many of the paraphilias as defenses against leftover castration anxiety from the phallic period of psychosexual development (see Chapter 2) (Friedman & Downey, 2008). In Freudian theory, the young boy develops a sexual desire for his mother and perceives his father as a rival. Castration anxiety—the unconscious fear that the father will retaliate by removing the organ that has become associated with sexual pleasure through masturbation—motivates the boy to give up his incestuous yearnings for his mother and identify with the aggressor, his father. But a failure to successfully resolve the conflict may lead to leftover castration anxiety in adulthood. The unconscious mind equates the disappearance of the penis during genital intercourse with adult women with the risk of castration. At an unconscious level, left-over castration anxiety prompts the man to displace his sexual arousal onto "safer" sexual activities, such as having sexual contact with women's undergarments, surreptitiously viewing others disrobing, or having sex with children he can easily control. In exposing his genitals, the exhibitionist may be unconsciously seeking reassurance that his penis is secure, as if were proclaiming, "Look! I have a penis!" Psychodynamic views of the origins of paraphilias remain speculative and controversial. We lack any direct evidence that men with paraphilias are handicapped by unresolved castration anxiety.

More recently, theorists speculated that paraphilias such as sexual masochism may represent a temporary escape from ordinary selfhood (Knoll & Hazelwood, 2009). Focusing on painful and pleasant sensations in the moment, and on the experience of

Role-playing or paraphilia? Sadomasochism is a form of sexual role-playing between consensual partners. When does this behavior cross the line and become a paraphilia?

being a sexual object, may provide a temporary reprieve from the responsibilities of maintaining a mature, responsible sense of self.

Learning theorists explain paraphilias in terms of conditioning and observational learning. Some object or activity becomes inadvertently associated with sexual arousal. The object or activity then gains the capacity to elicit sexual arousal. For example, sex researcher June Reinisch (1990) speculates that the earliest awareness of sexual arousal or response (such as erection) may have been connected with rubber pants or diapers. The person makes an association between the two, setting the stage for the development of a rubber fetish. Or a boy who glimpses his mother's stockings on the towel rack while he is masturbating goes on to develop a fetish for stockings (Breslow, 1989). Orgasm in the presence of the object reinforces the erotic connection, especially when it occurs repeatedly. Yet, if fetishes were acquired by mechanical association, we might expect people to develop fetishes to stimuli that are inadvertently and repeatedly connected with sexual activity, such as bed sheets, pillows, even ceilings. But they do not. The *meaning* of the stimulus plays a primary role. The development of fetishes may depend on eroticizing certain types of stimuli (like women's undergarments) by incorporating them within sexual fantasies and masturbation rituals.

Family relationships may play a role. Some transvestite men report a history of "petticoat punishment" during childhood. That is, they were humiliated by being dressed in girl's attire. Perhaps, the adult transvestite male is attempting psychologically to convert humiliation into mastery by achieving an erection and engaging in sexual activity despite being attired in female clothing.

BIOLOGICAL PERSPECTIVES Researchers are investigating the possible role of biological factors in paraphilic behavior. Investigators find evidence of higher-than-average sex drives in men with paraphilias, as evidenced by a higher frequency of sexual fantasies and urges and a shorter *refractory period* after orgasm by masturbation (i.e., length of time needed to become rearoused) (Haake et al., 2003; Jordan et al., 2011). Some professionals refer to the heightened sex drive that may apply to some cases of paraphilia as *hypersexual arousal disorder*—the opposite of hypoactive sexual desire disorder. In such cases, the person may have repeated difficulty controlling urges to engage in illegal or maladaptive behaviors, such as frequenting prostitutes, masturbating in public, or uncontrolled use of pornography (Levine, 2012).

Other investigators find differences between paraphilic men and male control subjects in brain wave patterns in response to paraphilic (fetishistic and sadomasochistic) images and control images (nude women, genital intercourse, oral sex) (Waismann et al., 2003). The meaning of these differences is not yet clear, but it is possible that in paraphilic men, the brain responds differently to different types of sexual stimuli than it does in other men. Recently, investigators found they could distinguish men with pedophilia from (nonpedophilic) healthy men with near 100% accuracy by examining brain responses, as measured by an fMRI scan, to images of nude children versus nude women (Ponseti et al., 2012). Other investigators find that pedophilic men show evidence of abnormal brain functioning in brain circuits that respond to sexual stimuli (Cantor et al., 2008). Although further research is needed, it is conceivable that disturbances in brain networks involved in sexual arousal may increase susceptibility to pedophilia in general or perhaps in men with a history of childhood trauma or abuse (Cowley, 2008).

With time, we can expect to learn more about the biological underpinnings of paraphilic behavior. Like other sexual patterns, paraphilias may have multiple biological, psychological, and sociocultural origins. Might our understanding of them thus be best approached from a theoretical framework that incorporates multiple perspectives? Sex researcher John Money (2000), for example, traced the origins of paraphilias to childhood. He suggested that childhood experiences etch a pattern in the brain, which he called a *lovemap*. A lovemap determines the types of stimuli and activities that become sexually arousing. In the paraphilias, lovemaps may become distorted or "vandalized" by early traumatic experiences. Evidence does tie early childhood emotional or sexual trauma to later development of paraphilias in many cases (Barbaree & Blanchard, 2008). As researcher Gregory Lehne notes, "A boy who is sexually abused may develop paraphilic fantasies involving sexual activity with a boy. . . . Being punished or embarrassed by being cross-dressed as a young boy may lead to some boys eroticizing the experience, which later is expressed as transvestism" (2009, p. 15).

Treatment of Paraphilic Disorders

A major problem with treating paraphilic disorders is that many people who engage in these behaviors are generally not motivated to change. They may not want to alter their behavior unless they believe that treatment will relieve them from serious punishment, such as imprisonment or loss of a family life. Consequently, they don't typically seek treatment on their own. They usually receive treatment in prison after they have been convicted of a sexual offense, such as exhibitionism, voyeurism, or child molestation. Or they are referred to a treatment provider by the courts. Under these circumstances, it is not surprising that sex offenders resist treatment. Therapists recognize that treatment may be futile when clients lack the motivation to change their behavior. Nonetheless, some forms of treatment, principally cognitive-behavioral therapy, may be helpful to sex offenders who seek to change their behavior (Abracen & Looman, 2004).

10.9 Describe methods of treating paraphilic disorders.

PSYCHOANALYSIS Psychoanalysts attempt to bring childhood sexual conflicts (typically of an Oedipal nature) into awareness so they can be resolved in light of the individual's adult personality (Laws & Marshall, 2003). Favorable results from individual case studies appear in the literature from time to time, but there is a dearth of controlled investigations to support the efficacy of psychodynamic treatment of paraphilias.

COGNITIVE-BEHAVIORAL THERAPY Traditional psychoanalysis involves a lengthy process of exploration of the childhood roots of the problem. Cognitive-behavioral therapy is briefer and focuses directly on changing the problem behavior. Cognitive-behavioral therapy includes a number of specific techniques, such as aversive conditioning, covert sensitization, and social skills training, to help eliminate paraphilic behaviors and strengthen appropriate sexual behaviors (Krueger & Kaplan, 2002). In many cases, a combination of methods is used.

The goal of aversive conditioning (also called *aversive therapy*) is to induce a negative emotional response to unacceptable stimuli or fantasies. Applying a conditioning model, sexual stimuli involving children are repeatedly paired with an aversive stimulus (e.g., an unpleasant smell such as ammonia) in the hope that the person will develop a conditioned aversion toward the paraphilic stimulus (Seto, 2009). Aversive conditioning can reduce sexual arousal in response to children as stimuli, but questions remain about how lasting these effects may be (Marshall & Laws, 2003; Seto, 2009).

Covert sensitization is a variation of aversion therapy in which paraphilic fantasies are paired with aversive stimuli in imagination. In a landmark study, men with pedophilia and men who had engaged in exhibitionism were first instructed to fantasize pedophilic or exhibitionistic scenes (Maletzky, 1980).Then,

> At a point . . . when sexual pleasure is aroused, aversive images are presented. . . . Examples might include a pedophiliac fellating a child, but discovering a festering sore on the boy's penis, an exhibitionist exposing to a woman but suddenly being discovered by his wife or the police, or a pedophiliac laying a young boy down in a field, only to lie next to him in a pile of dog feces. (Maletzky, 1980, p. 308)

In a 25-year follow-up study of 7,275 sex offenders who received similar treatment, Maletzky and Steinhauser (2002) found that benefits were maintained for many

"Cybersex Addiction"—A New Psychological Disorder?

Internet use has exploded in recent years, and cybersex is a major factor accounting for this growth. People are logging on to view adult sites on the Internet, engaging in online sex with people in Internet chat rooms, and sometimes progressing to real-life sexual encounters with people they meet online.

For some, the attraction to cybersex may be a relatively harmless recreational pursuit. But experts express concern that for others, easy access to cybersex is feeding a new type of psychological disorder called *cybersex addiction* (Green et al., 2012; Philaretou et al., 2005). An estimated 6% of adult users of the Internet show evidence of sexual compulsiveness in their online behavior, such as experiencing withdrawal symptoms when they are away from the Internet for a length of time (Bailey, 2003a).

People with cybersex compulsions can be likened to drug addicts, using the Internet for gratification in much the same way that a drug addict uses a drug of choice (Cooper et al., 2004; Schneider, 2005). Based on a survey of 9,265 men and women who admitted surfing the 'Net for sex, psychologist Al Cooper and his colleagues (2000) concluded that the 'Net is "the crack cocaine of sexual compulsivity," with at least 1% of respondents strongly addicted to online sex. Although some studies find that men who become addicted to online sex have ample sexual opportunities in the real world, other studies find them to be lonelier than other men (Yoder et al., 2005).

Physician Jennifer Schneider (2003, 2004) conducted a survey of 94 family members affected by cybersex addiction and found that it can arise even among people who are in good relationships and who have an abundance of sexual opportunities. "Sex on the 'Net is just so seductive and it's so easy to stumble upon it [that] people who are vulnerable can get hooked before they know it" (cited in Brody, 2000).

Schneider (2005) defends the view that cybersex addiction is a true addiction, characterized by "loss of control, continuation of the behavior despite significant adverse consequences, and preoccupation or obsession with obtaining the drug or pursuing the behavior." Although behavioral addictions do not involve taking drugs, they may cause changes in the brain, such as releasing endorphins—brain chemicals whose actions mimic those of the narcotic morphine—that maintain the behavior.

Sexual arousal and orgasm also reinforce the behavior. As researcher Mark Schwartz noted: "Intense orgasms from the minimal investment of a few keystrokes are powerfully reinforcing. Cybersex affords easy, inexpensive access to a

Cybersex addiction. Easy access to cybersex may be feeding a new psychological disorder called *cybersex addiction*. Many compulsive users of online sexual content deny that they have a problem, even though their behavior can seriously disrupt their work and home lives.

myriad of ritualized encounters with idealized partners" (cited in Brody, 2000).

As with other addictions, tolerance to cybersex stimulation can develop, prompting the person to take more and more risks to recapture the initial high. Online viewing that began as a harmless recreation can become all-consuming and even lead to real sexual encounters with people met online. People with cybersex compulsions sometimes ignore their partners and children and risk their jobs. Many companies monitor employees' online activities, and visits to sexual sites can cost employees their jobs. Schneider reports other adverse consequences, including broken relationships. Partners often report feeling betrayed, ignored, and unable to compete with the online fantasies.

A 34-year-old woman married 14 years wondered how she could possibly compete with all the anonymous women her husband brought into bed with her in his mind. She felt that her bed, which once had been a place of intimacy for them, was now crowded with all these faceless strangers (Brody, 2000).

Cybersex addiction is not yet recognized as an official diagnostic category. Nor can we clearly determine where recreational use of sexual material on the Internet ends and sexual compulsion begins. Yet, the problem of cybersex compulsion continues to grow, especially now that broadband availability allows for the streaming of explicit sexual video programming to computer screens around the world.

men with exhibitionism but few with pedophilia. However, fewer than 50% of the original participants could be contacted after this amount of time had elapsed.

Social skills training helps the individual improve his ability to develop and maintain relationships with adult partners. The therapist might first model a desired behavior, such as asking a woman out on a date or handling rejection. The client might then rehearse the behavior with the therapist playing the woman's role. The therapist provides feedback and additional guidance and modeling to help the client further improve his social skills.

Research on the effectiveness of cognitive-behavioral techniques is limited by the absence of untreated control groups (Seto, 2009). Consequently, we cannot discount the possibility that other factors, such as fears of legal consequences, influenced the outcomes.

BIOMEDICAL THERAPIES There is no magic pill or other medical cure for paraphilic disorders. Yet, progress is reported in treating exhibitionism, voyeurism, and fetishism with SSRI antidepressants, such as Prozac (Bradford, 2001; Thibaut, 2011) Why SSRIs? We noted in Chapter 5 that SSRIs are often helpful in treating obsessive–compulsive disorder, a psychological disorder characterized by recurrent obsessions and compulsions. Paraphilias appear to mirror these behavioral patterns, which suggests that they may fall within an obsessive–compulsive spectrum of behaviors. People with paraphilias often experience obsessive thoughts or images of the paraphilic object or stimulus, such as intrusive and recurrent mental images of young children. Many also feel compelled to repeatedly carry out the paraphilic acts.

Antiandrogen drugs reduce levels of testosterone in the bloodstream. Testosterone energizes sexual drives, so the use of antiandrogens may reduce sexual drives and urges, including urges to sexually offend and related fantasies, especially when they are used in combination with psychological treatment (Briken et al., 2011; Houts et al., 2011; Thibaut, 2011). However, antiandrogens do not completely eliminate paraphilac urges, nor do they change the types of erotic stimuli to which the client is attracted.

Before moving on, you may want to review Table 10.3, which provides an overview of paraphilias.

10.10 Identify the major types of rape, describe the effects of rape, and identify factors involved in rape.

Rape

Ann, a college student who met a young man at a party, offered the following account of a rape.

> **"I"** *"I Never Thought It Would Happen to Me"*
>
> I first met him at a party. He was really good looking and he had a great smile. I wanted to meet him but I wasn't sure how. I didn't want to appear too forward. Then he came over and introduced himself. We talked and found we had a lot in common. I really liked him. When he asked me over to his place for a drink, I thought it would be OK. He was such a good listener, and I wanted him to ask me out again.
>
> When we got to his room, the only place to sit was on the bed. I didn't want him to get the wrong idea, but what else could I do? We talked for a while and then he made his move. I was so startled. He started by kissing. I really liked him so the kissing was nice. But then he pushed me down on the bed. I tried to get up and I told him to stop. He was so much bigger and stronger. I got scared and I started to cry. I froze and he raped me.
>
> It took only a couple of minutes and it was terrible, he was so rough. When it was over he kept asking me what was wrong, like he didn't know. He had just forced himself on me and he thought that was OK. He drove me home and said he wanted to see me again. I'm so afraid to see him. I never thought it would happen to me.
>
> *From the Author's Files*

TABLE 10.3
Overview of Paraphilias

Major Types of Paraphilias: Atypical or deviant patterns of sexual gratification; excepting masochism, these disorders occur almost exclusively among males	
Exhibitionism	Sexual gratification from exposing one's genitals in public
Voyeurism	Sexual gratification from observing unsuspecting others who are naked, undressing, or engaging in sexual arousal
Sexual Masochism	Sexual gratification associated with the receipt of humiliation or pain
Fetishism	Sexual attraction to inanimate objects or particular body parts
Frotteurism	Sexual gratification associated with acts of bumping or rubbing against nonconsenting strangers
Sexual Sadism	Sexual gratification associated with inflicting humiliation or pain on others
Transvestic Fetishism	Sexual gratification associated with cross-dressing
Pedophilia	Sexual attraction to children
Causal Factors: Multiple causes may be involved	
Learning Perspective	• Atypical stimuli become conditioned stimuli for sexual arousal as the result of prior pairing with sexual activity • Atypical stimuli may become eroticized by incorporating them within erotic and masturbatory fantasies
Psychodynamic Perspective	• Unresolved castration anxiety from childhood leads to sexual arousal being displaced onto safer objects or activities
Multifactorial Perspective	• Sexual or physical abuse in childhood may corrupt normal sexual arousal patterns
Treatment Approaches: Results remain questionable	
Biomedical Treatment	• Drugs to help individuals control deviant sexual urges or reduce sexual drives
Cognitive-Behavioral Therapy	• Includes aversive conditioning (pairing deviant stimuli with aversive stimuli), covert sensitization (pairing the undesirable behavior with an aversive stimulus in imagination), and nonaversive methods such as social skills training that help individuals acquire more adaptive behaviors

Rape, especially date rape, is a pressing concern on college campuses, where thousands of women have been raped by dates or acquaintances. College men frequently perceive their dates' protests as part of an adversarial sex game. Consider the comments of Jim, the man who raped Ann.

"I" "Why Did She Put Up Such a Big Struggle?"

I first met her at a party. She looked really hot, wearing a sexy dress that showed off her great body. We started talking right away. I knew that she liked me by the way she kept smiling and touching my arm while she was speaking. She seemed pretty relaxed so I asked her back to my place for a drink. . . . When she said yes, I knew that I was going to be lucky!

When we got to my place, we sat on the bed kissing. At first, everything was great. Then, when I started to lay her down on the bed, she started twisting and saying she didn't want to. Most women don't like to appear too easy, so I knew that she was just going through the motions. When she stopped struggling, I knew that she would have to throw in some tears before we did it.

She was still very upset afterwards, and I just don't understand it! If she didn't want to have sex, why did she come back to the room with me? You could tell by the way she dressed and acted that she was no virgin, so why she had to put up such a big struggle I don't know.

From the Author's Files

Rape is not classified as a mental disorder in the *DSM* system, and rapists do not necessarily suffer from any diagnosable disorder. However, its violent nature and the often devastating effects it has on its victims place rape and other forms of sexual assault squarely within the framework of abnormal behavior. Moreover, rape survivors often experience a range of health problems, both psychological and physical.

Many rape survivors are traumatized by the experience (Bryant-Davis, 2011; Gannon et al., 2008; Kaczmarek, LeVine, & Segal, 2006). They may have trouble sleeping and cry frequently. They may report eating problems, cystitis, headaches, irritability, mood changes, anxiety and depression, and menstrual irregularity. Survivors may become withdrawn, sullen, and mistrustful. Women who are raped may at least partly blame themselves, which can lead to feelings of guilt and shame. Emotional distress tends to peak by about three weeks following the attack and generally remains high for a month or so, before beginning to decline (Duke et al., 2008; Littleton & Henderson, 2009). But many survivors encounter lasting problems. A study of women in the military who had survived rape and physical abuse found psychological and health-related problems a decade after the assault (Sadler et al., 2000). Some survivors suffer physical injuries and sexually transmitted infections, even HIV/AIDS.

The Federal Bureau of Investigation reports that nearly 90,000 forcible rapes occur annually in the United States (Rabin, 2011). However, these crime statistics greatly underreport the actual incidence of rape, because the great majority of rapes are not reported to authorities or prosecuted. Many women do not report rape because they fear being humiliated by the criminal justice system. Some fear reprisal from their families or from the rapist himself. Many women mistakenly believe that coercive sex is rape only when the rapist is a stranger or uses a weapon.

A recent national survey found that nearly one in five women reported being raped or experiencing an attempted rape (Rabin, 2011). Based on this survey, we can estimate the number of women who suffer rape or attempted rape at 1.3 million women annually. Other estimates suggest that about one in four women in the United States will suffer rape at some point in their lifetimes (Campbell & Wasco, 2005). Although women of all ages are at risk of being raped, two of three rapes involve young women between the ages of 11 and 24, and about 80% involve girls and young women under the age of 25 (CDC, 2011).

Types of Rape

The main types of rape include stranger rape, acquaintance rape, marital rape, and male rape. *Stranger rape* is committed by an assailant (or assailants) who is not acquainted with the victim. The stranger rapist tends to select targets who appear vulnerable— women who live alone, who are walking deserted or dimly lit streets, or who are asleep or drugged.

According to the U.S. Department of Justice (2006), more than four out of five rapes are *acquaintance rapes*—rapes committed by people known to the victim. Survivors of rape may not perceive sexual assaults by acquaintances as rapes. Even if a police report is filed, it may be treated as "misunderstanding" or "lovers' quarrel," rather than a violent crime. Only about one-quarter of the women in a large-scale national college survey who were sexually assaulted viewed themselves as victims of rape (Koss & Kilpatrick, 2001; Rozee & Koss, 2001). This bears repeating: Only about one in four college women labeled what happened to them when they were sexually assaulted as rape.

Figure 10.2 shows the relationship patterns of rapist and victim based on the same national survey of college women. This survey revealed a disturbingly high percentage of college women reporting they had experienced either rape (15.4%) or attempted rape. In nearly 90% of the rapes in the college sample, the woman was acquainted with the assailant. In any given year, about 3% of college women in the United States suffer rape or attempted rape (Fisher et al., 2003). **T / F**

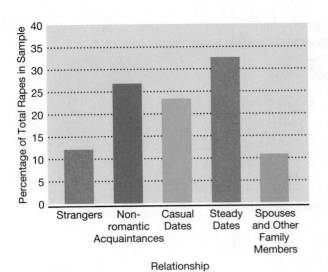

FIGURE 10.2

Relative percentages of stranger rapes and acquaintance rapes.

Date rape is a kind of acquaintance rape. Surveys show that as many as one college woman in four reports being forced into sexual intercourse by a date (McAnulty, 2012). Date rape is more likely to occur when the couple has been drinking and then park in the man's car or return to his room. Men tend to perceive a date's willingness to go home with him as a sign of willingness to have sexual relations. Most men who engage in date rape overcome the women's protests by force.

According to the national college survey, the great majority of rapes of college women were committed by men with whom the women were acquainted, including dates, nonromantic acquaintances, and family members (see Table 10.2).

Some date rapists mistakenly believe that acceptance of a date implies willingness to engage in sexual relations. They may believe that a woman they take out to dinner should pay with sex. Men may think that women who frequent singles bars and similar places are automatically willing to have sex. Some date rapists believe that women who resist advances are simply trying not to look "easy." These men misinterpret resistance as a ploy in the "battle of the sexes." Like Jim, who raped Ann in his dorm room, they may believe that when a woman says no, she means yes, especially when a sexual relationship had been established.

Investigators report that 10% to 14% of married women suffer marital rape (Martin, Taft, & Resick, 2007). A traditional-minded husband may think he is entitled to have sex with his wife whenever he wishes. He may see sex as his wife's duty, even when she is unwilling. But rape is rape, regardless of the woman's marital status. Men who are better educated and less accepting of traditional stereotypes about relationships between men and women are less likely to commit marital rape (Basile, 2002).

Gang rapists seek to exercise power over their victims and typically try to impress their friends by conforming to the stereotype of the tough "he-man." Consider the case of Kurt, who committed multiple rapes with his friend, Pete.

"I" *"I Couldn't Chicken Out"*

I always looked up to Pete and felt second-class to him. I felt I owed him and couldn't chicken out on the rapes. I worshiped him. He was the best fighter, lover, water-skier, motorcyclist I knew. Taking part in the sexual assaults made me feel equal to him. . . . I didn't have any friends and felt like a nobody. . . . He brought me into his bike club. He made me a somebody.

I'd go to a shopping center and find a victim. I'd approach her with a knife or a gun and then bring her to him. He'd rape her first and then I would. . . . We raped about eight girls together over a four-month period.

Groth & Birnbaum, 1979, p. 113

A commonly held myth is that men cannot be victims of rape (Peterson et al., 2010). Although women are much more likely to be raped, recent estimates indicate that some 1% to 3% of men at some point in their lives become victims of rape—defined as forced oral or anal penile penetration—(Rabin, 2012). Most men who engage in male rape are heterosexual. Their motives often include domination and control, revenge and retaliation, sadism and degradation, and—when the rape is carried out by a gang member—status and affiliation (Krahe, Waizenhofer, Moller, 2003). Sexual motives are often minimal or absent. As with women who are raped, male rape survivors often suffer serious physical and psychological effects (Peterson et al., 2010; Rabin, 2012).

Theoretical Perspectives

Many motives underlie rape. Feminists see rape as an expression of men's desire to dominate and degrade women, to establish unquestioned power and superiority over them. Other theorists argue that sexual motivation plays a key role in many kinds of rape, particularly acquaintance rape, date rape, and marital rape (Baumeister, Catanese, & Wallace, 2002; Bushman et al., 2003). In such cases, the motive may be largely sexual, but make no mistake—coerced sex in any form is an act of violence. Rape often occurs in a context of other forms of violent behavior (Gannon et al., 2008). For some rapists, violent cues appear to enhance sexual arousal, so they are motivated to combine sex with aggression. Some rapists who were abused as children may humiliate women as a way of expressing anger and power over women and of taking revenge.

Social attitudes and cultural myths also contribute to the high incidence of rape (Davies et al., 2012). Many people believe myths about rape, such as "Women say no when they mean yes." Yet another myth is that deep down inside, women want to be raped. Certainly, the popular media contribute to this belief when they portray a woman as first resisting a man's advances but then yielding to his overpowering masculinity. These myths have the effect of blaming the victim for the assault and legitimizing rape in the eyes of the public. Although both women and men believe some rape myths, researchers find that college men are more likely than college women to hold such beliefs (Maxwell, Robinson, & Post, 2003; Osman, 2003). The nearby questionnaire will afford you insight as to whether you believe in myths that have the effect of legitimizing rape. **T / F**

questionnaire

Beliefs That Create a Climate That Supports Rape

Indicate whether you believe each of the following statements is true or false by circling the letters T or F. Then use the scoring key at the end of the chapter to interpret your responses.

1. T F A woman who has a drink in a bar with a guy is just asking for sex.

2. T F Women cry rape when they can't admit to themselves that they wanted sex.

3. T F When a woman touches a man in a certain way, she should let him go all the way.

4. T F Women who dress seductively are basically just "asking for it."

5. T F Most women can prevent a man from taking advantage of them if they really wanted to.

6. T F When a woman says "no," it's generally because she doesn't want the man to think she is easy.

7. T F Women may have a hard time admitting it, but they really want a man to overpower them.

8. T F Date rape is basically a problem of miscommunication between a man and a woman.

9. T F Many women who say they really don't want sex are just not honest with themselves.

10. T F A woman wouldn't accompany a man back to his room after a date unless she really wanted to have intercourse.

Although some rapists show evidence of psychopathology on psychological tests, especially antisocial or psychopathic traits, many do not (Lalumière et al., 2005a). Psychological tests such as the Minnesota Multiphasic Personality Inventory (MMPI) (see Chapter 3) fail to identify any particular rapist profile based on personality traits (Gannon et al., 2008). The very normality of many rapists on psychological instruments suggests that socialization of young men plays an important role in creating a climate of sexual aggression. **T / F**

Perhaps, as some researchers contend, our society breeds rapists by socializing men into socially and sexually dominant roles (Malamuth, Huppin, & Paul, 2005; Steinfeldt & Steinfeldt, 2012). Men are often reinforced from childhood for aggressive and competitive behavior. They may learn to "score" at all costs, whether they are on the ball field or in the bedroom. Such socialization influences may also lead men to reject "feminine" traits such as tenderness and empathy that might restrain aggression. Adding alcohol to the mix further increases the risk of sexual assault (Cole, 2006). A rapist may be just like the boy next door; in fact, he may be the boy next door. We end with two questions that we hope will provoke some thoughtful discussion: What are we teaching our sons? How can we teach them differently?

truth OR fiction

Deep down, most women desire to be raped.

☑ **FALSE** This is an example of a rape myth. Holding such a belief can lead to blaming the victim and excusing perpetrators of sexual violence.

truth OR fiction

Rapists are mentally ill.

☑ **FALSE** Rape is a violent crime, not a symptom of a mental disorder. Many rapists do not show evidence of psychopathology. Rape is a form of social deviance, and rapists should be held accountable under the law for their violent acts.

summing up

Gender Dysphoria

10.1 Describe the key features of gender dysphoria.

People with gender dysphoria experience their biologic sex as a source of persistent and intense distress. People with the disorder may seek to change their sex organs to resemble those of the other sex, and many undergo hormone treatments and/or surgery to achieve this end.

10.2 Explain the difference between gender dysphoria and homosexuality.

In gender dysphoria, there is a mismatch between one's psychological sense of being male or female and one's anatomic sex that is associated with significant distress or discomfort. Sexual orientation relates to the direction of one's sexual attraction—toward members of one's own sex or the other sex. Unlike people with gender dysphoria, people with a gay male or lesbian sexual orientation have a gender identity that is consistent with their biologic sex.

10.3 Describe major theoretical perspectives on transgender identity.

Although the causes of transgender identity remain unknown, psychodynamic theorists emphasize the role of extremely close mother–son relationships and fathers who were absent or detached, whereas learning theorists focus on socialization patterns encouraging the development of cross-gender behavior. Biological explanations focus on genetic factors influencing the release of sex hormones in prenatal development involved in sculpting the brain along masculine or feminine lines. Biological factors operating during prenatal development may create a predisposition that interacts with early life experiences in leading to the development of transgender identity.

Sexual Dysfunctions

10.4 Define the term sexual dysfunction and identify three major categories of sexual dysfunctions and specific disorders within each type.

A sexual dysfunction is a persistent or recurrent pattern involving lack of sexual desire, problems in becoming sexually aroused, and/or problems in reaching orgasm. Sexual dysfunctions can be classified in three general categories: (1) disorders involving low sexual desire or impaired arousal (female sexual interest/arousal disorder, male hypoactive sexual desire disorder, erectile disorder); (2) disorders involving impaired orgasmic response (female orgasmic disorder, delayed ejaculation, and premature or early ejaculation); and (3) disorders involving sexual pain (genito-pelvic pain/penetration disorder).

10.5 Describe causal factors involved in sexual dysfunctions.

Sexual dysfunctions can stem from biological factors (such as fatigue, disease, the effects of aging, or the effects of alcohol and other drugs), psychological factors (such as performance anxiety, lack of sexual skills, disruptive cognitions, relationship problems), and sociocultural factors (such as sexually restrictive cultural learning).

10.6 Describe methods used to treat sexual dysfunctions.

Sex therapy is a cognitive-behavioral approach that helps people overcome sexual dysfunctions by enhancing self-efficacy expectancies, teaching sexual skills, improving communication, and reducing performance anxiety. Biomedical approaches include hormone treatments and most commonly, the use of drugs to facilitate blood flow to the genital region (Viagra and its chemical cousins) or to delay ejaculation (SSRIs).

Paraphilic Disorders

10.7 Define the term paraphilia and identify major types of paraphilia.

A paraphilia is a sexual deviation involving patterns of arousal to atypical stimuli such as nonhuman objects (e.g., shoes or clothes), humiliation or the experience of pain in oneself or one's partner, or children. Paraphilias include exhibitionism, fetishism, transvestic fetishism, voyeurism, frotteurism, pedophilia, sexual masochism, and sexual sadism. Although some paraphilias are essentially harmless (such as fetishism), others, such as pedophilia and sexual sadism with nonconsenting individuals, certainly do harm victims.

10.8 Describe theoretical perspectives on paraphilias and underlying causal factors.

Psychoanalysts see many paraphilias as defenses against castration anxiety. Learning theorists attribute paraphilias to early learning experiences. Biological factors may also be implicated, such as higher-than-normal sex drives and corrupted sexual arousal patterns in people with paraphilias.

10.9 Describe methods for treating paraphilic disorders.

Various treatment programs have been used with varying success, including psychoanalytic therapy, cognitive-behavioral therapy involving aversive conditioning, covert sensitization, and social skills training, and biological therapies, including use of SSRI antidepressants and antiandrogen drugs.

Rape

10.10 Identify the major types of rape, describe the effects of rape, and identify factors involved in rape.

The major types of rape include stranger rape, acquaintance rape, date rape, marital rape, and male rape. Many survivors of rape suffer physical and/or psychological trauma, such as posttraumatic stress disorder. They have trouble sleeping, cry frequently, may become sullen and mistrustful, and may blame themselves. There may be injuries to the genital organs and other parts of the body, and the victim may be infected with sexually transmitted diseases. Men rape women as a way of dominating them and as a way of coercing them into sexual activity. Cultural myths about rape have the effects of blaming the victim and creating a climate that legitimizes rape. For some rapists, sexual arousal and violence become fused together.

critical thinking questions

Based on your reading of this chapter, answer the following questions:

- What is the difference between transgender identity and a gay male or lesbian sexual orientation?

- Do you believe people who engage in exhibitionism, voyeurism, and sexual acts with children should be punished, treated, or both? Explain.

- Can you think of examples in your own life in which you have been affected by performance anxiety? What did you do about it?

- If you had a sexual dysfunction, would you be willing to seek help for it? Why or why not?

key terms

gender identity 367
gender dysphoria 367
transgender identity 367
sexual dysfunctions 371
male hypoactive sexual desire disorder 372
female sexual interest/arousal disorder 372

erectile disorder 373
female orgasmic disorder 373
delayed ejaculation 373
premature (early) ejaculation 373
genito-pelvic pain/penetration 374

vaginismus 374
paraphilias 384
exhibitionism 385
fetishism 386
transvestism 386
voyeurism 387
frotteurism 388
pedophilia 388

sexual masochism 390
hypoxyphilia 390
sexual sadism 390
sadomasochism 391
rape 397

Scoring Key for the Rape Beliefs Scale

This scale comprises a set of commonly held myths about rape. If you answered "true" to any of these items, you may wish to use your critical thinking skills to reexamine your beliefs. For example, the belief that women truly want to be overpowered by a man is a common rationalization rapists use to justify their behavior. How can a person possibly know what another person truly wants unless the other person expresses it? Rape myths are often used as self-serving justifications to explain away unacceptable behavior.

To be perfectly clear, when someone says "no" in a sexual context, it means "no." Not maybe, not perhaps, not in a few minutes, but simply, no. In addition, consenting to some forms of intimate contact, whether it be kissing, fondling, or oral sex does not imply consent to genital intercourse or other sexual activities. A person always retains the right at any time to say "no" or to place limits on what the person is willing to do.

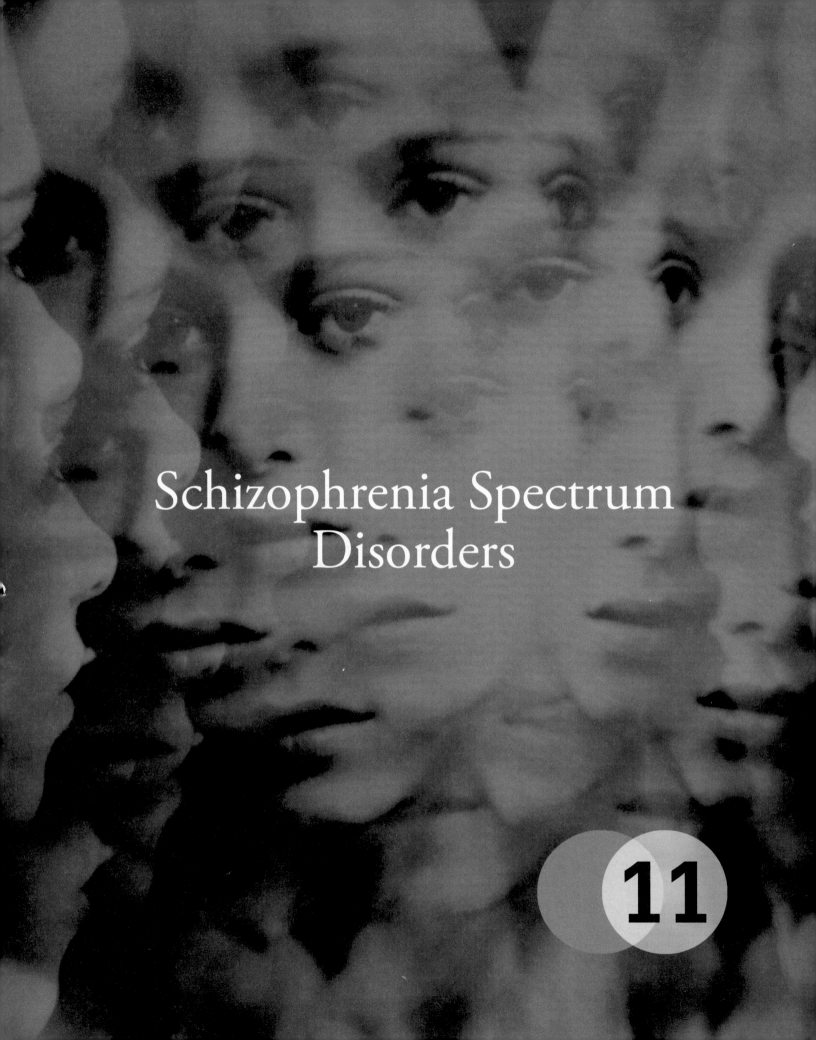

Schizophrenia Spectrum
Disorders

11

T □ F □   Visual hallucinations ("seeing things") are the most common type of hallucinations in people with schizophrenia. (p. 412)

T □ F □   It is normal for people to hallucinate nightly. (p. 413)

T □ F □   If you have both parents with schizophrenia, it's nearly certain that you will develop schizophrenia yourself. (p. 417)

T □ F □   If you are an adopted child raised by a parent with schizophrenia, you have about the same chance of developing schizophrenia as biological children of parents with schizophrenia. (p. 418)

T □ F □   Scientists believe that a defect on one particular gene causes schizophrenia, but they haven't yet been able to identify the defective gene. (p. 419)

T □ F □   Although schizophrenia is widely believed to be a brain disease, we still lack evidence of abnormal functioning in the brains of schizophrenia patients. (p. 421)

T □ F □   We now have drugs that not only treat schizophrenia but also can cure it in many cases. (p. 429)

T □ F □   Some people have delusions that they are loved by a famous person. (p. 434)

learning objectives

11.1
Define the term schizophrenia.

11.2
Describe the course of development of schizophrenia.

11.3
Describe the key features of schizophrenia.

11.4
Describe the psychodynamic and learning theory viewpoints on schizophrenia.

11.5
Describe the biological bases of schizophrenia.

11.6
Describe the role of family factors in schizophrenia.

11.7
Apply the diathesis–stress model to the development of schizophrenia.

11.8
Evaluate the methods used to treat schizophrenia.

11.9
Describe the general features of other disorders in the schizophrenia spectrum.

Schizophrenia typically develops in late adolescence or early adulthood, at the very time that young people are making their way from the family into the outside world (Dobbs, 2010; Tandon, Nasrallah, & Keshavan, 2009). For a young woman named Lori Schiller, the first *psychotic episode* or break with reality ("first break") came during her last year at summer camp.

"I" "I Hear Something You Can't Hear"

It was a hot night in August 1976, the summer of my seventeenth year, when, uninvited and unannounced, the Voices took over my life.

I was going into my senior year in high school, so this was to be my last year at summer camp. College, a job, adulthood, responsibility—they were all just around the corner. But for the moment I wasn't prepared for anything more than a summer of fun. I certainly wasn't prepared to have my life change forever… .

"You must die!" Other Voices joined in. "You must die! You will die!"

At first I didn't realize where I was. Was I at the lake? Was I asleep? Was I awake? Then I snapped back to the present. I was here at camp, alone. My summertime fling was long gone, two years gone. That long-ago scene was being played out in my mind, and in my mind alone. But as soon as I realized that I was in my bunk, and awake—and that my roommate was still sleeping peacefully—I knew I had to run. I had to get away from these terrible, evil Voices… .

Since that time, I have never been completely free of those Voices. At the beginning of that summer, I felt well, a happy, healthy girl—I thought—with a normal head and heart. By summer's end, I was sick, without any clear idea of what was happening to me or why. And as the Voices evolved into a full-scale illness, one that I only later learned was called schizophrenia, it snatched from me my tranquility, sometimes my self-possession, and very nearly my life.

Along the way I have lost many things: the career I might have pursued, the husband I might have married, the children I might have had. During the years when my friends were marrying, having their babies and moving into the houses I once dreamed of living in, I have been behind locked doors, battling the Voices who took over my life without even asking my permission.

→ *From Schiller & Bennett, 1994*

Schizophrenia is perhaps the most puzzling and disabling psychological disorder. It is the condition that best corresponds to popular conceptions of madness or lunacy. Although researchers are probing the psychological and biological foundations of schizophrenia, the disorder remains largely a mystery. In this chapter, we consider what we know about schizophrenia and what remains to be learned. Schizophrenia is not the only type of psychotic disorder in which a person experiences a break with reality. In this chapter, we also consider other psychotic disorders, including brief psychotic disorder, schizophreniform disorder, schizoaffective disorder, and delusional disorder. These disorders along with schizophrenia and a type of personality disorder called schizotypal personality disorder are classified in the *DSM-5* within a spectrum of schizophrenia-related disorders called Schizophrenia Spectrum and Other Psychotic Disorders. These disorders, excepting schizotypal personality disorder which is discussed in Chapter 12, are the focus of our study in this chapter, beginning with schizophrenia.

11.1 Define the term schizophrenia.

Schizophrenia

Schizophrenia is a chronic, debilitating disorder that touches every facet of the affected person's life. People who develop schizophrenia become increasingly disengaged from society. They fail to function in the expected roles of student, worker, or spouse, and their families and communities grow intolerant of their deviant behavior.

Acute episodes of schizophrenia involve a break with reality characterized by symptoms such as delusions, hallucinations, illogical thinking, incoherent speech, and bizarre behavior. Between acute episodes, people with schizophrenia may have lingering deficits, such as being unable to think clearly, speak only in a flat tone, have difficulty perceiving emotions in other people's voices or facial expressions, and may show little, if any, facial expressions of emotions themselves (Comparelli et al., 2013; Gold et al., 2012). Continuing impairment makes it difficult for schizophrenia patients to function in their daily lives, including holding a job. On a more positive note, 40% or more of schizophrenia patients have long periods of remission (i.e., no disturbing symptoms and ability to work in some capacity) lasting a year or longer (Jobe & Harrow, 2010). Some patients also remain free of disturbing symptoms for a number of years even when they are unmedicated (Jobe & Harrow, 2010; Harrow & Jobe, 2007).

Schizophrenia often elicits fear, misunderstanding, and condemnation rather than sympathy and concern. It strikes at the heart of the person, stripping the mind of the intimate connections between thoughts and emotions, and filling it with distorted perceptions, false ideas, and illogical conceptions, as in the following case example.

→ **Angela's "Hellsmen"**

Angela, 19, was brought to the emergency room by her boyfriend, Jaime, because she had cut her wrists. When she was questioned, her attention wandered. She seemed transfixed by creatures in the air, or by something she might be hearing. It seemed as if she had an invisible earphone.

Angela explained that she had slit her wrists at the command of the "hellsmen." Then she became terrified. Later she related that the hellsmen had cautioned her not to disclose their existence. Angela feared that the hellsmen would punish her for her indiscretion.

A beautiful mind. In the movie *A Beautiful Mind*, Russell Crowe portrayed Nobel Prize winner John Nash (shown here), a brilliant mathematician whose mind captured the beautiful intricacies of mathematical formulations but was also twisted by the delusions and hallucinations of schizophrenia.

Jaime related that Angela and he had been living together for nearly a year. They had initially shared a modest apartment in town. But Angela did not like being around other people and persuaded Jaime to rent a cottage in the country. There Angela spent much of her days making fantastic sketches of goblins and monsters. She occasionally became agitated and behaved as if invisible beings were issuing directions. Her words would become jumbled.

Jaime would try to persuade her to go for help, but she would resist. Then, about nine months ago, the wrist-cutting began. Jaime believed that he had made the bungalow secure by removing all knives and blades. But Angela always found a sharp object.

Then he would bring Angela to the hospital against her protests. Stitches would be put in, she would be held under observation for a while, and she would be medicated. She would recount that she cut her wrists because the hellsmen had informed her that she was bad and had to die. After a few days in the hospital, she would disavow hearing the hellsmen and insist on discharge.

Jaime would take her home. The pattern would repeat.

From the Author's Files

Course of Development

We noted that schizophrenia typically develops during late adolescence or early adulthood (Walker & Tessner, 2008). In some cases, the onset of the disorder is acute, as it was in the case of Lori Schiller. It occurs suddenly, within a few weeks or months. The individual may have been well adjusted and may have shown few signs of behavioral disturbance. Then a rapid transformation in personality and behavior leads to an acute psychotic episode.

In most cases, there is a slower, more gradual decline in functioning, as was the case with Ian Chovil, a young man who has been living with schizophrenia since the age of 17. He shares his story with the hope that the next generation of people affected by this debilitating disorder will be spared some of the experiences he has endured.

11.2 Describe the course of development of schizophrenia.

"I" "I and I, Dancing Fool, Challenge You the World to a Duel"

Insidious is an appropriate word to describe the onset of schizophrenia I experienced. I gradually lost all my human relationships, first my girlfriend, then my immediate family, then friends and coworkers. I experienced a lot of emotional turmoil and social anxiety. Somehow I graduated from Trent University in Peterborough, Ontario, Canada, but the last year I was smoking marijuana almost every day. I was creative but found it increasingly difficult to actually read anything. My career aspirations were to become a Rastafarian sociobiologist. I had become incapable of long-term romantic relationships after the demise of my first one. At graduate school in Halifax I was hospitalized for a couple of weeks, a nervous breakdown I thought. Although I was prescribed *chlorpromazine* and then *trifluoperazine* [two types of antipsychotic drugs], no one mentioned schizophrenia to me or my father, a family physician. I tried to complete my year, but some courses went unfinished and I was kicked out of graduate school.

Within two years I was one of the homeless in Calgary, sleeping in a city park or the single men's hostel, hungry because I didn't get to eat very often. A World War II hero wanted to hurt me because I had discovered the war was caused by the influenza of 1918. Tibetan Buddhists read my mind everywhere I went because I had caused the Mount Saint Helens eruption for them earlier that year with my natural tantric abilities. For 10 years I lived more or less like that, in abject poverty, without any friends, quite delusional. At first I was going to be a Buddhist saint, then I was a pawn in a secret war between the sexuals and the antisexuals that would determine the fate of humanity, then I realized I was in contact with aliens of the future. There was going to be a nuclear holocaust that would break up the continental plates, and the oceans would evaporate from the lava. The aliens had come to collect me and one woman. All life here was about to be destroyed. My future wife and I were going to become aliens and have eternal life.

My actual situation by then was a sharp contrast. I was living in a downtown Toronto rooming house with only cockroaches for friends, changing light bulbs as they burnt out in a large department store. It was a full time job I could do, but I hated it intensely. I worried about my enemies who were trying to turn me into a homosexual, and I was in constant telepathic conversation with my future wife, listening to rock and roll songs for messages from aliens in my spare time. I ran into trouble with the law one night after becoming furious with the aliens for not transferring my mind to another body. The judge sentenced me to 3 years of probation with the condition I see a psychiatrist for that time.

… I wrote a poem as an undergraduate that was published in the student newspaper. The first line was "I and I, dancing fool, challenge you the world to a duel." I intend to challenge the world to the best of my ability, until people like me have the quality of life possible with the most effective treatment strategies available.

From Chovil, 2000. Reprinted with permission of the National Institute of Mental Health.

As in this case, psychotic behaviors may emerge gradually over several years, although early signs of deterioration may be observed (Fusar-Poli et al., 2012; Mechelli et al., 2011; Walker et al., 2010; Ziermans et al., 2012). This period of gradual deterioration is called the **prodromal phase** or *prodrome.* It is characterized by subtle symptoms involving unusual thoughts or abnormal perceptions (but not outright delusions or hallucinations), as well as waning interest in social activities, difficulty meeting responsibilities of daily living, and impaired cognitive functioning involving problems with memory and attention, use of language, and ability to plan and organize one's activities.

One of the first signs of a prodrome is often a lack of attention to one's appearance. The person may fail to bathe regularly or wear the same clothes repeatedly. Over time, the person's behavior becomes increasingly odd. There are lapses in job performance or schoolwork. Speech becomes vague and rambling. These changes in personality may be so gradual that they raise little concern at first among friends and family. The changes may be attributed to "a phase" the person is passing through. But as behavior becomes more bizarre—such as hoarding food, collecting garbage, or talking to oneself on the street—the acute phase of the disorder begins. Frankly, psychotic symptoms then develop, such as wild hallucinations, delusions, and increasingly bizarre behavior.

Following acute episodes, some people with schizophrenia enter the **residual phase,** in which their behavior returns to the level of the prodromal phase. Flagrant psychotic behaviors are absent, but the person is still impaired by significant cognitive, social, and emotional deficits, such as a deep sense of apathy and difficulties in thinking or speaking clearly, and by harboring unusual ideas, such as beliefs in telepathy or clairvoyance. These cognitive and social deficits can make it difficult for schizophrenia patients to function effectively in their social and occupational roles (Harvey, 2010; Hooley, 2010). Here, in his first-person account, Ian Chovil observes that despite improvement following treatment with the antipsychotic drug *olanzapine*, his functioning was still impaired by these deficits—the "poverties" as he calls them.

"I" "The Poverties"

My life has been improving a little each year, and noticeably on *olanzapine*, but I am still quite unsure of myself. I still have what I call "the poverties," like poverty of thought, emotion, friends, and hard cash. My social life seems to be the slowest to improve. I have three or four recreational friends, only one without a mental illness, only one that I see fairly often. I lived for awhile with Rosemary, whom I still see often, in a two bedroom apartment until the government changed its regulations on cohabitation and we had to separate or lose almost $400 a month in income. Now I'm in a very nice subsidized apartment, fairly happy on my own for the first time thanks to *olanzapine* and my position at the Homewood, which brings me into contact with a lot of people.

From Chovil, 2000. Reprinted with permission of the National Institute of Mental Health.

Although schizophrenia is a chronic disorder, as many as one-half to two-thirds of schizophrenia patients improve significantly over time (USDHHS, 1999). Full return to normal behavior is uncommon but does occur in some cases. Typically, patients develop a chronic pattern characterized by occasional acute episodes and continued cognitive, emotional, and motivational impairment between psychotic episodes (Walker et al., 2004).

Prevalence of Schizophrenia

Schizophrenia affects about 1% of the U.S. population and about 0.3% to 0.7% of the global population (APA, 2013; Insel, 2010; Kapur, 2009; NIMH, 2009). Nearly 1 million people in the United States are treated for schizophrenia each year, with about a third of them requiring hospitalization. The World Health Organization (WHO) estimates that about 24 million people worldwide suffer from schizophrenia (Olson, 2001).

Men have a slightly higher risk of developing schizophrenia than women and also tend to develop the disorder at an earlier age (NCA, 2005; Tandon, Keshavan, & Nasrallah, 2008). The peak age at which psychotic symptoms first appear is in the early to middle twenties for men and the late twenties for women (APA, 2013). Women tend to have a higher level of functioning before the onset of the disorder and to have a less severe course of illness than men. Men with schizophrenia tend to have more cognitive impairment, greater behavioral deficits, and a poorer response to drug therapy than do women with the disorder. These gender differences have led researchers to speculate that men and women may tend to develop different forms of schizophrenia. Perhaps schizophrenia affects different areas of the brain in men and women, which may explain the differences in the form or features of the disorder.

Although schizophrenia likely occurs universally across cultures, the course of the disorder and its particular symptoms can vary from culture to culture. For example, visual hallucinations appear to be most common in some non-Western cultures (Ndetei & Singh, 1983). Moreover, the themes expressed in delusions or hallucinations, such as particular religious or racial themes, vary across cultures (Whaley & Hall, 2009).

Diagnostic Features

11.3 Describe the key features of schizophrenia.

Schizophrenia is a pervasive disorder that affects a wide range of psychological processes involving cognition, affect, and behavior. *DSM* criteria for schizophrenia require that psychotic behaviors be present at some point during the course of the disorder and that signs of the disorder be present for at least six months and must have been active and prominent for at least one month (if not treated successfully). People with briefer forms of psychosis receive other diagnoses, such as brief psychotic disorder (discussed later in the chapter).

Table 11.1 provides an overview of schizophrenia. The diagnostic features of schizophrenia are listed in the boxed feature on page 409. Note that the diagnosis of schizophrenia in the *DSM-5* requires that at least two features of the disorder be present (not just an isolated delusional belief or hallucination) and that at least one of these features must include the cardinal symptoms of delusions, hallucinations, or disorganized (loosely connected, incoherent, or bizarre) speech.

People with schizophrenia show a marked decline in occupational and social functioning (Ekinci et al., 2012; Kim et al., 2011). They may have difficulty

TABLE 11.1	
Types of Impairments Associated with Schizophrenia	
Disturbed thought processes	Delusions (fixed false ideas) and thought disorder (disorganized thinking and incoherent speech)
Attentional deficiencies	Difficulty attending to relevant stimuli and screening out irrelevant stimuli
Perceptual disturbances	Hallucinations (sensory perceptions in the absence of external stimulation)
Emotional disturbances	Flat (blunted) or inappropriate emotions
Other types of impairments	Confusion about personal identity, lack of volition, excitable behavior or states of stupor, odd gestures or bizarre facial expressions, impaired ability to relate to others, or possible catatonic behavior or gross disturbance in motor activity and orientation in which the person's behavior may slow to a stupor but abruptly shift to a highly agitated state

holding a conversation, forming friendships, holding a job, or taking care of their personal hygiene. Yet, no one behavior pattern is unique to schizophrenia. People with schizophrenia may exhibit delusions, problems with associative thinking, and hallucinations at one time or another, but not necessarily all at once. The diversity or heterogeneity of symptoms leads some investigators to suspect that what we call "schizophrenia" may actually involve a conglomeration of different disorders (Tandon, Nasrallah, & Keshavan, 2009).

Schizophrenia is associated with a wide range of abnormal behaviors that involve thinking, speech, attentional and perceptual processes, emotional processes, and voluntary behavior. One way of grouping the features of schizophrenia is to distinguish between positive and negative symptoms (Gold, 2011; Tandon, Nasrallah, & Keshavan, 2009):

- **Positive symptoms** involve a break with reality, as represented by the appearance of hallucinations and delusional thinking.

- **Negative symptoms** affect the person's ability to function in daily life and include such features as lack of emotions or emotional expression (maintaining a blank expression), loss of motivation, loss of pleasure in normally pleasant activities, social withdrawal or isolation, and limited output of speech ("poverty of speech") (Kring et al., 2013; Strauss et al., 2012). Negative symptoms tend to persist even when positive symptoms have abated and often have a greater effect on the person's functioning than positive symptoms (Barch, 2013; Rabinowitz et al., 2012). They are also less responsive than positive symptoms to treatment with antipsychotic drugs (Barch, 2013).

Here, we take a closer look at several key features or symptoms associated with schizophrenia.

DISTURBED THOUGHT AND SPEECH Schizophrenia is characterized by positive symptoms involving disturbances in thinking and expression of thoughts through coherent, meaningful speech. Aberrant thinking may be found in both the content and form of thought.

Aberrant Content of Thought Delusions represent disturbed content of thought. These are false beliefs that remain fixed in the person's mind despite their illogical bases and lack of evidence to support them. They tend to remain unshakable even in the face of disconfirming evidence. Delusions may take many forms. Some of the most common types are:

- *Delusions of persecution or paranoia* (e.g., "The CIA is out to get me")
- *Delusions of reference* ("People on the bus are talking about me," or "People on TV are making fun of me")

Course of development. Schizophrenia typically develops during late adolescence or early adulthood, a time of life when young people are beginning to make their way into the world.

A. Two (or more) of the following, each present for a significant portion of time during a 1-month period (or less if successfully treated). At least one of these must be (1), (2), or (3):
1. Delusions.
2. Hallucinations.
3. Disorganized speech (e.g., frequent derailment or incoherence).
4. Grossly disorganized or catatonic behavior.
5. Negative symptoms (i.e., diminished emotional expression or avolition).

B. For a significant portion of the time since the onset of the disturbance, level of functioning in one or more major areas, such as work, interpersonal relations, or self-care, is markedly below the level achieved prior to the onset (or when the onset is in childhood or adolescence, there is failure to achieve expected level of interpersonal, academic, or occupational functioning).

C. Continuous signs of the disturbance persist for at least 6 months. This 6-month period must include at least 1 month of symptoms (or less if successfully treated) that meet Criterion A (i.e., active-phase symptoms) and may include periods of prodromal or residual symptoms. During these prodromal or residual periods, the signs of the disturbance may be manifested by only negative symptoms or by two or more symptoms listed in Criterion A present in an attenuated form (e.g., odd beliefs, unusual perceptual experiences).

D. Schizoaffective disorder and depressive or bipolar disorder with psychotic features have been ruled out because either 1) no major depressive or manic episodes have occurred concurrently with the active-phase symptoms, or 2) if mood episodes have occurred during active-phase symptoms, they have been present for a minority of the total duration of the active and residual periods of the illness.

E. The disturbance is not attributable to the physiological effects of a substance (e.g., a drug of abuse, a medication) or another medical condition.

F. If there is a history of autism spectrum disorder or a communication disorder of childhood onset, the additional diagnosis of schizophrenia is made only if prominent delusions or hallucinations, in addition to the other required symptoms of schizophrenia, are also present for at least 1 month (or less if successfully treated).

Reprinted with permission from the Diagnostic and Statistical Manual of Mental Disorders, Fifth Edition, (Copyright 2013). American Psychiatric Association.

- *Delusions of being controlled* (believing that one's thoughts, feelings, impulses, or actions are controlled by external forces, such as agents of the devil)
- *Delusions of grandeur* (believing oneself to be Jesus or believing one is on a special mission, or having grand but illogical plans for saving the world)

Other delusions include beliefs that one has committed unpardonable sins, that one is rotting away from a horrible disease, that the world or oneself does not really exist, or, as in the following case, that one desperately needs to help people.

→ The Hospital at the North Pole: A Case of Schizophrenia

Although people with schizophrenia may feel hounded by demons or earthly conspiracies, Mario's delusions had a messianic quality. "I need to get out of here," he said to his psychiatrist. "Why do you need to leave?" the psychiatrist asked. Mario responded, "My hospital. I need to get back to my hospital." "Which hospital?" he was asked. "I have this hospital. It's all white and we find cures for everything wrong with people." Mario was asked where his hospital was located. "It's all the way up at the North Pole," he responded. His psychiatrist asked, "But how do you get there?" Mario responded, "I just get there. I don't know how. I just get there. I have to do my work. When will you let me go so I can help the people?"

→ *From the Author's Files*

Other commonly occurring delusions include *thought broadcasting* (believing one's thoughts are somehow transmitted to the external world so that others can overhear them), *thought insertion* (believing one's thoughts have been planted in one's mind by an external source), and *thought withdrawal* (believing that thoughts have been removed from one's mind). Mellor (1970) offers the following examples:

- *Thought broadcasting:* A 21-year-old student reported, "As I think, my thoughts leave my head on a type of mental ticker tape. Everyone around has only to pass the tape through their mind and they know my thoughts."

- *Thought insertion:* A 29-year-old housewife reported that when she looks out of the window, she thinks, "The garden looks nice and the grass looks cool, but the thoughts of [a man's name] come into my mind. There are no other thoughts there, only his... . He treats my mind like a screen and flashes his thoughts on it like you flash a picture."

- *Thought withdrawal:* A 22-year-old woman experienced the following: "I am thinking about my mother, and suddenly my thoughts are sucked out of my mind by a phrenological vacuum extractor, and there is nothing in my mind, it is empty."

Aberrant Forms of Thought Unless we are engaged in daydreaming or purposefully letting our thoughts wander, our thoughts tend to be tightly knit together. The connections (or associations) between our thoughts tend to be logical and coherent. In contrast, people with schizophrenia tend to think in a disorganized, illogical fashion. In schizophrenia, the form or structure of thought processes, as well as their content, is often disturbed. Clinicians label this type of disturbance a **thought disorder.**

Thought disorder is a positive symptom of schizophrenia involving a breakdown in the organization, processing, and control of thoughts. Looseness of associations is a cardinal sign of thought disorder. The speech pattern of people with schizophrenia is often disorganized or jumbled, with parts of words combined incoherently or words strung together to make meaningless rhymes. Their speech may jump disconnectedly from one topic to another. People with thought disorder are usually unaware that their thoughts and behavior appear abnormal. In severe cases, their speech may become completely incoherent or incomprehensible.

Another common sign of thought disorder is *poverty of speech* (speech that is coherent but so slow, limited in quantity, or vague that little information is conveyed). Less commonly occurring signs include *neologisms* (made-up words that have little or no meaning to others), *perseveration* (inappropriate but persistent repetition of the same words or train of thought), *clanging* (stringing together of words or sounds on the basis of rhyming, such as, "I know who I am but I don't know Sam"), and *blocking* (involuntary, abrupt interruption of speech or thought).

Many schizophrenia patients, but not all, show evidence of thought disorder. Some appear to think and speak coherently but have disordered content of thought, as seen by the presence of delusions. Nor is disordered thought unique to schizophrenia; it is even found in milder form among people without psychological disorders, especially when they are tired or under stress. Disordered thought is also found among other diagnostic groups, such as persons with mania. However, thought disorders in people experiencing a manic episode tend to be short lived and reversible. In people with schizophrenia, thought disorder tends to be more persistent or recurrent. Thought disorder occurs most often during acute episodes, but may linger into residual phases.

Schizophrenia patients tend to show other cognitive deficits, such as problems with memory, learning, reasoning, and attention. These deficits often emerge in childhood in people who go on to develop schizophrenia, long before the more flagrant symptoms of schizophrenia—the hallucinations, delusions, and thought disorder—first appear (Reichenberg et al., 2010). Recent research based on a long-term follow-up study in Denmark showed that even in early childhood, children who later developed schizophrenia showed delays in reaching certain developmental milestones, such as walking without

Watch the Video *Larry: Schizophrenia* on MyPsychLab

support (Sørensen et al., 2010). This suggests that schizophrenia involves developmental processes that may have roots in early childhood ("Team Finds Childhood Clues," 2010).

Attentional Deficiencies To read this book, you must screen out background noises and other environmental stimuli. Attention, the ability to focus on relevant stimuli and ignore irrelevant ones, is basic to learning and thinking. People with schizophrenia often have difficulty filtering out irrelevant stimuli, making it nearly impossible for them to focus their attention, organize their thoughts, and filter out unessential information. The mother of a son who had schizophrenia described her son's difficulties in filtering out extraneous sounds:

> His hearing is different when he's ill. One of the first things we notice when he's deteriorating is his heightened sense of hearing. He cannot filter out anything. He hears each and every sound around him with equal intensity. He hears the sounds from the street, in the yard, and in the house, and they are all much louder than normal.
>
> *Anonymous, as cited in Freedman et al., 1987, p. 670*

People with schizophrenia also appear to be *hypervigilant,* or acutely sensitive to extraneous sounds, especially during the early stages of the disorder. During acute episodes, they may become flooded by these stimuli, overwhelming their ability to make sense of their environments. Brain abnormalities associated with schizophrenia may lead to a deficit in the ability to filter out distracting sounds and other extraneous stimuli. Researchers believe that underlying genetic factors may explain the development of the sensory filtering deficit in people with schizophrenia (Hong et al., 2007).

Links between attentional deficits and schizophrenia are supported by various studies focusing on the psychophysiological aspects of attention. Here, we review some of this research.

Eye Movement Dysfunction Many schizophrenia patients have some form of *eye movement dysfunction,* such as difficulty tracking a slow-moving target across their field of vision ("Eye Movements," 2012). Rather than the eyes steadily tracking the target, they fall back and then catch up in a kind of jerky movement. Eye movement dysfunctions appear to involve defects in the brain's control of visual attention.

Eye movement dysfunctions are common in people with schizophrenia and in their first-degree relatives (parents, children, and siblings). This suggests it might be a genetically transmitted trait, or *biomarker,* associated with genes linked to schizophrenia (Keshavan et al., 2008). Recently, investigators reported 98% accuracy in discriminating people with schizophrenia from healthy control subjects based on a set of eye movement indicators (Benson et al., 2012). However, the role of eye movement dysfunction as a biological marker for schizophrenia is limited because it is not unique to schizophrenia. People with other psychological disorders, such as bipolar disorder, sometimes show the dysfunction. Nor do all people with schizophrenia or their family members show eye movement dysfunctions. What we're left with is the understanding that eye movement dysfunction may be a biomarker for one of the many different genetic pathways leading to schizophrenia.

Abnormal Event-Related Potentials Researchers have also studied brain wave patterns, called *event-related potentials,* or ERPs, that occur in

A painting by a man with schizophrenia. Paintings or drawings by schizophrenia patients often reflect the bizarre quality of their thought patterns and withdrawal into a private fantasy world.

Filtering out extraneous stimuli. You probably have little difficulty filtering out unimportant stimuli, such as street sounds. But people with schizophrenia may be distracted by irrelevant stimuli and be unable to filter them out. Consequently, they may have difficulty focusing their attention and organizing their thoughts.

response to external stimuli such as sounds and flashes of light. ERPs can be broken down into various components that emerge at different intervals following the presentation of a stimulus (Guillaume et al., 2012). Normally, a sensory gating mechanism in the brain inhibits or suppresses ERPs to a repeated stimulus occurring within the first hundredth of a second after a stimulus is presented. This gating mechanism allows the brain to disregard irrelevant stimuli, such as the sound of a ticking clock, but it doesn't seem to work effectively in cases of schizophrenia (Kéri, Beniczky, & Kelemen, 2010; Sánchez-Morla et al, 2013). As a result, schizophrenia patients may have greater difficulty filtering out distracting stimuli, leading to *sensory overload*, resulting in a jumbling of sensations.

Schizophrenia patients also show weaker ERPs occurring around 300 milliseconds (three-tenths of a second) after a sound or a flash of light is presented (e.g., Vohs et al., 2008; Xiong et al., 2010). These ERPs are involved in processes of focusing attention on a stimulus to extract meaningful information from it.

What we take away from these studies of ERPs is an understanding that many schizophrenia patients appear to be flooded with high levels of sensory information that impinge on their sensory organs but have great difficulty extracting useful information from these stimuli. As a result, they may become confused and find it difficult to filter out distracting stimuli.

Perceptual Disturbances

→ Voices, Devils, and Angels

Every so often during the interview, Sally would look over her right shoulder in the direction of the office door and smile gently. When asked why she kept looking at the door, she said that the voices were talking about the two of us just outside the door and she wanted to hear what they were saying. "Why the smile?" Sally was asked. "They were saying funny things," she replied, "like maybe you thought I was cute or something."

Tom was flailing his arms wildly in the hall of the psychiatric unit. Sweat seemed to pour from his brow, and his eyes darted about with agitation. He was subdued and injected with haloperidol (brand name Haldol) to reduce his agitation. When he was about to be injected, he started shouting, "Father, forgive them for they know not ... forgive them ... father ... ." His words became jumbled. Later, after he had calmed down, he reported that the ward attendants had looked to him like devils or evil angels. They were red and burning, and steam issued from their mouths.

→ *From the Author's Files*

HALLUCINATIONS The most common form of perceptual disturbance in schizophrenia is **hallucinations,** which are sensory perceptions experienced in the absence of external stimulation. They are difficult to distinguish from reality. For Sally, the voices coming from outside the consulting room were real enough, although no one was there. Hallucinations can involve various senses. A person may see things, feel things, hear things, and smell things that are not there. Auditory hallucinations ("hearing voices") are the most common form of hallucination, affecting about three of four schizophrenia patients (Goode, 2003b). Tactile hallucinations (such as tingling, electrical, or burning sensations) and somatic hallucinations (such as feeling like snakes are crawling inside one's belly) are also common. Visual hallucinations (seeing things that are not there), gustatory hallucinations (tasting things that are not present), and olfactory hallucinations (sensing odors that are not present) are rarer. **T / F**

People with schizophrenia may experience auditory hallucinations as female or male voices and as originating inside or outside their heads. Hallucinators may hear voices conversing about them in the third person, debating their virtues or faults. Some voices are experienced as supportive and friendly, but most are critical or even terrorizing.

truth OR fiction

Visual hallucinations ("seeing things") are the most common type of hallucinations in people with schizophrenia.

☑ **FALSE** Auditory, not visual, hallucinations are the most common type of hallucinations among people with schizophrenia.

Some people with schizophrenia experience *command hallucinations*, voices that instruct them to perform certain acts, such as harming themselves or others. Angela, for example, was instructed by the "hellsmen" to commit suicide. People with schizophrenia who experience command hallucinations are often hospitalized out of concern they may harm themselves or others. There is a good reason for this, as evidence shows that command hallucinations are linked to a higher risk of violent behavior (Shawyer et al., 2008). Some people who experience voices issuing commands to harm others do indeed act on them (Braham, Trower, & Birchwood, 2004). Yet, command hallucinations often go undetected by professionals, because patients deny them or are unwilling to discuss them.

Hallucinations are not unique to schizophrenia. People with major depression and mania sometimes experience hallucinations. It may surprise you to learn that hallucinations are occasionally experienced by people in the general population and are not necessarily a sign of psychopathology (Vellante et al., 2012). Hallucinations in people without psychiatric conditions are often associated with high fevers, states of bereavement (hearing the voice of the departed loved one), and unusually low levels of sensory stimulation, such as when lying in the dark in a soundproof room for an extended time or facing the monotony of driving through the desert or an empty road (Sacks et al., 2012). The experience of a "mirage" in people traveling through a desert is one such example. Unlike hallucinations in people with psychotic disorders, people who experience these types of fleeting hallucinations recognize that they are not real. **T / F**

People may sometimes experience hallucinations during the course of religious experiences or rituals. They may report fleeting trancelike states with visions or other strange perceptual experiences. Then too, we all hallucinate nightly during dreams in which we hear and see things in the theater of our minds without any external stimulation.

Hallucinations during waking states can also occur in response to hallucinogenic drugs, such as LSD. Drug-induced hallucinations tend to be visual and often involve abstract shapes such as circles, stars, or flashes of light. Schizophrenic hallucinations, in contrast, tend to be more fully formed and complex. Hallucinations (e.g., of bugs crawling on one's skin) may also arise during *delirium tremens* (the DTs), which often occur as part of the withdrawal syndrome of chronic alcoholism. Hallucinations may also occur as side effects of medications or in neurological disorders, such as Parkinson's disease.

Causes of Hallucinations The causes of psychotic hallucinations remain unknown, but speculations abound. Disturbances in brain chemistry are suspected. The neurotransmitter dopamine is implicated, largely because antipsychotic drugs that block dopamine activity also reduce hallucinations. Conversely, drugs that lead to increased production of dopamine, such as cocaine, can induce hallucinations. Because hallucinations resemble dreamlike states, they may be connected to a failure of brain mechanisms that normally prevent dream images from intruding on waking experiences.

Auditory hallucinations in schizophrenia patients may represent a type of inner speech (silent self-talk) (Jones & Fernyhough, 2007). Many of us, perhaps all of us, talk to ourselves from time to time, although we usually keep our mutterings under our breath (subvocal) and recognize the voice we "hear" as our own. Might auditory hallucinations in schizophrenia be a projection of the patient's own internal voice, or self-speech, onto external sources?

An intriguing possibility is that the brain may mistake inner speech for external sounds. Investigators find that the auditory cortex—the part of the brain that processes auditory stimulation—becomes active during auditory hallucinations in the absence of real sounds (Hunter et al., 2006). Auditory hallucinations may be a form of inner speech that for unknown reasons becomes attributed to external sources rather than to one's own thoughts (Arguedas, Stevenson, & Langdon, 2012; Jones & Fernyhough, 2007). This line of research has led to a form of treatment in which cognitive-behavioral

Hearing voices. Auditory hallucinations—hearing voices—is the most common form of hallucination in schizophrenia patients. Recent evidence suggests that auditory hallucinations may involve inner speech that becomes projected onto external sources.

therapists attempt to teach hallucinators to reattribute their voices to themselves and to change how they respond to the voices (Turkington & Morrison, 2012) (e.g., "My voices do not make me angry, it is how I think about the voices"). Patients are also trained to recognize the situational cues associated with their hallucinations. For example:

> one patient … recognized that her voices tended to become worse following family arguments. She became aware that the content of her voices reflected the things that she was feeling and thinking about her family but that she was unable to express. Specific targets and goals were then set to allow her to address these difficulties with her family, and techniques such as rehearsal, problem solving and cognitive restructuring were employed to help her work towards these goals.
>
> *Bentall, Haddock, & Slade, 1994, p. 58*

Cognitive-behavioral therapy is a useful addition to drug therapy to help control hallucinations and treat delusional thinking (e.g., Grant et al., 2012; Lincoln et al., 2012; Waller et al., 2012). But even if theories linking inner speech to auditory hallucinations stand up to further scientific inquiry, they cannot account for hallucinations in other sensory modalities, such as visual, tactile, or olfactory hallucinations.

The brain mechanisms responsible for hallucinations probably involve a number of interconnected systems. One intriguing possibility is that defects in deeper brain structures may lead the brain to create its own reality. This alternative reality goes unchecked because the higher thinking centers in the brain, located in the frontal lobes of the cerebral cortex, may fail to perform a "reality check" on these images to determine whether they are real, imagined, or hallucinated. Consequently, people may misattribute their own internally generated voices to outside sources. As we'll see later, evidence from brain-imaging studies points to abnormalities in the frontal lobes in people with schizophrenia.

EMOTIONAL DISTURBANCES Disturbed emotional response in schizophrenia may involve negative symptoms, such as loss of normal emotional expression, labeled as blunted affect or *flat affect*. In people showing flat affect, we observe an absence of emotional expression in the face and voice. People with schizophrenia may speak in a monotone and maintain an expressionless face, or "mask." They may not experience a normal range of emotional response to people and events. They may also display positive symptoms, which involve exaggerated or inappropriate affect. For example, they may laugh for no reason or giggle at bad news.

It is not clear, however, whether emotional blunting in people with schizophrenia is a disturbance in their ability to express emotions, to report the presence of emotions, or to actually experience emotions. Laboratory-based evidence shows that schizophrenia patients experience more intense negative emotions, but less intense positive emotions, than controls (Myin-Germeys, Delespaul, & deVries, 2000). In other words, schizophrenia patients may experience strong emotions (especially negative emotions), even if their experiences are not communicated to the world outside through their facial expressions or behavior. People with schizophrenia may lack the capacity to express their emotions outwardly.

OTHER TYPES OF IMPAIRMENTS People who suffer from schizophrenia may become confused about their personal identities—the cluster of attributes and characteristics that define themselves as individuals and give meaning and direction to their lives. They may fail to recognize themselves as unique individuals and be unclear about how much of what they experience is part of themselves. In psychodynamic terms, this phenomenon is sometimes referred to as loss of *ego boundaries*. They may also have difficulty adopting a third-party perspective: they fail to perceive their own behavior and verbalizations as socially inappropriate in a given situation because they cannot see things from another person's point of view (Carini & Nevid, 1992). They also have difficulty recognizing or perceiving emotions in others (Penn et al., 2000).

Disturbances of volition are most often seen in the residual or chronic state. These negative symptoms are characterized by loss of initiative to pursue goal-directed activities. People with schizophrenia may be unable to carry out plans and may lack interest or drive. Apparent ambivalence toward choosing courses of action may block goal-directed activities.

In some cases, schizophrenia patients show may show *catatonic behaviors,* which involve severely impaired cognitive and motor functioning. People with **catatonia** may become unaware of the environment and maintain a fixed or rigid posture—even bizarre, apparently strenuous positions for hours as their limbs become stiff or swollen (Daniels, 2009). They may exhibit odd gestures and bizarre facial expressions or become unresponsive and curtail spontaneous movement. They may show highly excited but seemingly purposeless behavior or slow down to a state of *stupor.* While catatonia was recognized as a separate subtype of schizophrenia in previous versions of the diagnostic manual, it is now used in the *DSM-5* as a type of specifier for further describing the psychiatric conditions in which it occurs (APA, 2013). It may also be used as a separate diagnosis when it occurs in the context of other (non-psychiatric) medical conditions.

A striking but less common feature of catatonia is *waxy flexibility,* which involves adopting a fixed posture into which they have been positioned by others. They will not respond to questions or comments during these periods, which can last for hours. Later, however, they may report that they heard what others were saying at the time.

A Case of Catatonia

A 24-year-old man had been brooding about his life. He professed that he did not feel well but could not explain his bad feelings. While hospitalized, he initially sought contact with people but a few days later, he was found in a statuesque position, his legs contorted awkwardly. He refused to talk to anyone and acted as if he couldn't see or hear. His face was an expressionless mask. A few days later, he began to talk, but in an echolalic or mimicking way. For example, he would respond to the question, "What is your name?" by saying, "What is your name?" He could not care for his needs and had to be fed.

Adapted from Arieti, 1974, p. 40

Catatonia is not unique to schizophrenia. It can occur in other disorders, including brain disorders, drug intoxication, and metabolic disorders. In fact, it is found more often in people with mood disorders than in those with schizophrenia (Taylor & Fink, 2003).

People with schizophrenia also show significant impairment in interpersonal relationships. They withdraw from social interactions and become absorbed in private thoughts and fantasies. Or they cling so desperately to others that they make them uncomfortable. They may become so dominated by their own fantasies that they essentially lose touch with the outside world. They also tend to be introverted and peculiar even before the appearance of psychotic behaviors. These early signs may be associated with a vulnerability to schizophrenia, at least in people with a genetic risk of developing the disorder.

Theoretical Perspectives

Schizophrenia has been approached from each of the major theoretical perspectives. Although the underlying causes of schizophrenia remain elusive, they are presumed to involve brain abnormalities in combination with psychological, social, and environmental influences (USDHHS, 1999). First, however, let's consider the viewpoints of psychodynamic and learning theories.

PSYCHODYNAMIC PERSPECTIVES Within the psychodynamic perspective, schizophrenia represents the overwhelming of the ego by primitive sexual or aggressive drives or impulses arising from the id. These impulses threaten the ego and give rise to intense intrapsychic conflict. Under such a threat, the person regresses to an early period in the oral

Catatonia. People in a catatonic state may remain in unusual, difficult positions that can last for hours, even though their limbs become stiff or swollen. They may seem oblivious to their environment during these episodes and fail to respond to people who are talking to them.

11.4 Describe the psychodynamic and learning theory viewpoints on schizophrenia.

stage, referred to as *primary narcissism*. In this period, the infant has not yet learned that the world is distinct from itself. Because the ego mediates the relationship between the self and the outer world, this breakdown in ego functioning accounts for the detachment from reality that is typical of schizophrenia. Input from the id causes fantasies to become mistaken for reality, giving rise to hallucinations and delusions. Primitive impulses may also carry more weight than social norms and be expressed in bizarre, socially inappropriate behavior.

Some of Freud's followers, such as Harry Stack Sullivan, placed more emphasis on interpersonal than on intrapsychic factors. Sullivan (1962), who devoted much of his life's work to schizophrenia, emphasized that impaired mother–child relationships can set the stage for gradual withdrawal from other people. In early childhood, anxious and hostile interactions between the child and the parent lead the child to take refuge in a private fantasy world. A vicious cycle ensues: The more the child withdraws, the less opportunity there is to develop a sense of trust in others and the social skills necessary to establish intimacy. Then the weak bonds between the child and others prompt social anxiety and further withdrawal. This cycle continues until young adulthood. Then, faced with increasing demands at school or work and in intimate relationships, the person becomes overwhelmed with anxiety and withdraws completely into a world of fantasy.

Critics of Freud's views point out that schizophrenic behavior and infantile behavior are different, so schizophrenia cannot be explained by regression. Critics of Freud and modern psychodynamic theorists note that psychodynamic explanations are post hoc, or retrospective. Early child–adult relationships are recalled from the vantage point of adulthood rather than observed longitudinally. Psychoanalysts have not been able to demonstrate that hypothesized early childhood experiences or family patterns lead to schizophrenia.

LEARNING PERSPECTIVES Although learning theory does not offer a complete explanation of schizophrenia, the development of some forms of schizophrenic behavior can be understood in terms of the principles of conditioning and observational learning. From this perspective, people with schizophrenia learn to exhibit certain bizarre behaviors when these are more likely to be reinforced than normal behaviors.

Consider a classic case study of operant conditioning. Haughton and Ayllon (1965) conditioned a 54-year-old woman with chronic schizophrenia to cling to a broom. A staff member first gave her the broom to hold, and when she did, another staff member gave her a cigarette (a reinforcement). This pattern was repeated several times. Soon the woman could not be parted from the broom. But the fact that reinforcement can influence people to engage in peculiar behavior does not demonstrate that the bizarre behaviors characteristic of schizophrenia are shaped by reinforcement.

Social-cognitive theorists suggest that modeling of schizophrenic behavior can occur within the mental hospital, where patients may begin to model themselves after fellow patients who act strangely. Hospital staff may also inadvertently reinforce schizophrenic behavior by paying more attention to patients who exhibit bizarre behavior. This understanding is consistent with the observation that schoolchildren who disrupt the class garner more attention from their teachers than well-behaved children do.

Perhaps some types of schizophrenic behaviors can be explained by the principles of modeling and reinforcement. However, many people display schizophrenic behavior patterns without prior exposure to other people with schizophrenia. In fact, the onset of schizophrenic behavior patterns is more likely to lead to hospitalization than to result from hospitalization.

11.5 Describe the biological bases of schizophrenia.

BIOLOGICAL PERSPECTIVES Although we still have much to learn about the biological underpinnings of schizophrenia, investigators recognize that biological factors play a key role in the development of the disorder.

Genetic Factors A wealth of evidence supports an important role for genetic factors in the development of schizophrenia (e.g., Brown & Patterson, 2012; Grant et al., 2012; Hyman, 2011; Keshavan, Nasrallah, & Tandon, 2011; Pogue-Geile & Yokley, 2010).

The closer the genetic relationship between schizophrenia patients and their family members, the greater the likelihood that their relatives will also have schizophrenia. Overall, first-degree relatives of people with schizophrenia (parents, children, or siblings) have about a tenfold greater risk of developing schizophrenia than do members of the general population (APA, 2000).

Figure 11.1 shows the pooled results of European studies conducted from 1920 to 1987 on family incidence of schizophrenia. However, the fact that families share common environments as well as common genes requires that we dig deeper to examine the genetic underpinnings of schizophrenia.

More direct evidence of a genetic factor in schizophrenia comes from twin studies showing *concordance rates* (percentage sharing the disorder) among identical or MZ twins of about 48%, or more than twice the rate found among fraternal or DZ twins (about 17%) (Gottesman, 1991; Pogue-Geile & Yokley, 2010). We should be careful, however, not to overinterpret the results of twin studies. MZ twins not only share 100% genetic similarity, but others may treat them more similarly than they would DZ twins. Consequently, environmental factors may contribute to the higher concordance rates found among MZ twins. **T / F**

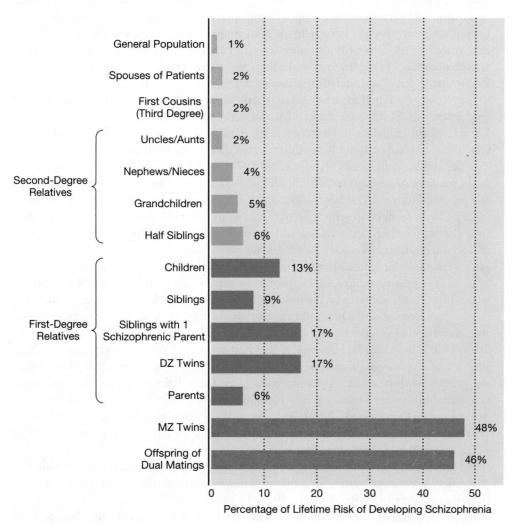

FIGURE 11.1

The familial risk of schizophrenia. Generally speaking, the more closely one is related to people who have developed schizophrenia, the greater the risk of developing schizophrenia oneself. Monozygotic (MZ) or identical twins, whose genetic heritages are identical, are much more likely than dizygotic (DZ) or fraternal twins, whose genes overlap by 50%, to be concordant for schizophrenia.

Source: Adapted from Gottesman et al., 1987.

If you are an adopted child raised by a parent with schizophrenia, you have about the same chance of developing schizophrenia as biological children of parents with schizophrenia.

☑ **FALSE** Among adopted children whose biological parents do not have schizophrenia, those raised by adoptive parents with schizophrenia stand no greater chance of developing schizophrenia than do those of nonschizophrenic adoptive parents.

To sort out environmental from genetic factors, investigators have turned to adoption studies in which high-risk children (of one or more biological parents with schizophrenia) were adopted shortly after birth and reared apart from their biological parents by adoptive parents who did not have schizophrenia (Wicks, Hjern, & Dalman, 2010). It turns out that the risk of schizophrenia was related to the presence of schizophrenia in the biological parents of the adopted children, not the adoptive parents (Tandon, Keshavan, & Nasrallah, 2008). Supporting the view that both genetics and environment play a part in schizophrenia, high-risk children who were adopted away but raised in economically disadvantaged homes (single parent homes or families with parental unemployment) stand a much higher risk than high-risk children raised in more comfortable circumstances (Wicks, Hjern, & Dalman, 2010). **T / F**

Other investigators have approached the question of heredity from the opposite direction. In a classic study, an American researcher, Seymour Kety, together with Danish colleagues (Kety et al., 1975, 1978) used official records in Denmark to find 33 index cases of children who had been adopted early in life and were later diagnosed with schizophrenia. They compared the rates of diagnosed schizophrenia in the biological and adoptive relatives of the index cases with those of the relatives of a matched reference group of adoptees with no psychiatric history. The results strongly supported the genetic explanation. The incidence of diagnosed schizophrenia was greater among biological relatives of adoptees who had schizophrenia than among biological relatives of control adoptees. Adoptive relatives of both index cases and control cases showed similar, *low* rates of schizophrenia. These findings and others show that family linkages in schizophrenia follow shared genes, not shared environments.

Another method for teasing out genetic from environmental influences, called the *cross-fostering study,* compares the incidence of schizophrenia among children whose biological parents either had or didn't have schizophrenia and who were reared by adoptive parents who either had or didn't have schizophrenia. In a classic study conducted in Denmark, Wender and his colleagues (Wender et al., 1974) found the risk of schizophrenia related to the presence of schizophrenia in the children's biological parents, but not in their adoptive parents. High-risk children (whose biological parents had schizophrenia) were almost twice as likely to develop schizophrenia as those of nonschizophrenic biological parents, regardless of whether they were reared by a parent with schizophrenia. It is also notable that adoptees whose biological parents did not suffer from schizophrenia were placed at no greater risk of developing schizophrenia by being reared by an adoptive parent with schizophrenia than by a nonschizophrenic parent. In sum, a genetic relationship with a person with schizophrenia seems to be the most prominent risk factor for developing the disorder.

Fast forward to the present. Investigators are zeroing in on particular genes linked to schizophrenia (e.g., Boot et al., 2012; Girgenti, LoTurco, & Maher, 2012; Guan et al., 2012; Hill & Bray, 2012). However, it is important to note that no single gene is responsible for schizophrenia (Walker et al., 2010). Rather, scientists believe that many different genes contribute to the development of brain abnormalities that interact with environmental influences in leading to schizophrenia (e.g., Hamilton, 2008; International Schizophrenia Consortium, 2009). Any one of these genes may have only a small effect individually, but when the effects of multiple genes are combined, the person stands a much greater risk of developing the disorder.

Increased vulnerability to schizophrenia may involve an unlucky combination of common variations of particular genes or perhaps genetic mutations or defects on a set of particular genes (Levinson et al., 2011; Li et al., 2011; McIlroy, 2010; Sigurdsson et al., 2010; Vacic et al., 2011). Scientists also find that offsprings of older fathers stand an increased risk of developing schizophrenia and autism, presumably because the sperm of older men are more prone to mutations (Kong et al., 2012). However, no increased risks of genetic mutations are found in older mothers (Carey, 2012b).

Before we move on, let us note that genetics alone does not fully determine a person's risk of developing schizophrenia. Environmental influences also play important roles. Consider the fact that many people at high genetic risk of developing schizophrenia do not develop the disorder. In fact, the rate of concordance among MZ twins, as we noted earlier, is well below 100%, even though identical twins carry identical genes. The prevailing view of schizophrenia today is represented by the diathesis–stress model (see the Tying It Together feature), which holds that some people inherit a predisposition or vulnerability to developing schizophrenia in the face of stressful life experiences. For example, a combination of genetic defects or variations in particular genes, together with stressful experiences early in life, may lead to abnormal brain development that increases the risk of later development of schizophrenia (Kim et al., 2012; Walker et al., 2010).

Let's now consider the roles of other biological factors in schizophrenia, including biochemical factors, possible viral infections, and brain abnormalities. **T / F**

Biochemical Factors Increasing evidence supports the view that schizophrenia involves irregularities in the use of dopamine in complex networks of neurons in the brain (Howes et al., 2012; Keshavan, Nasrallah, & Tandon, 2011). The leading biochemical model of schizophrenia, the **dopamine hypothesis,** posits that schizophrenia involves overactivity of dopamine transmission in the brain.

The major source of evidence for the dopamine model is found in the effects of antipsychotic drugs called *neuroleptics.* The most widely used neuroleptics belong to a class of drugs called *phenothiazines,* which includes drugs such as Thorazine, Mellaril, and Prolixin. Neuroleptic drugs block dopamine receptors, thereby reducing the level of dopamine activity. As a consequence, neuroleptics inhibit excessive transmission of neural impulses that may give rise to schizophrenic behavior.

Another source of evidence for the role of dopamine in schizophrenia is based on the actions of amphetamines, a class of stimulant drugs. These drugs increase the concentration of dopamine in the synaptic cleft by blocking its reuptake by presynaptic neurons. When given in large doses to normal people, these drugs cause symptoms that mimic paranoid schizophrenia.

Overall, the available evidence points to irregularities in neural pathways that utilize dopamine in the brains of schizophrenia patients—irregularities that may be genetically determined (Hirvonen et al., 2006; Huttunen et al., 2008). The specific nature of this abnormality remains under study. It doesn't appear that the brain of a schizophrenia patient has too much dopamine, but rather that the dopamine system in the brain is overactive or too responsive to stimulation of dopamine receptors (Grace, 2010; Valenti et al., 2011). Another possibility deserving further study is that overreactivity of dopamine receptors may be responsible for positive symptoms, whereas decreased dopamine reactivity may help explain the development of negative symptoms. We also have evidence pointing to roles for other neurotransmitters, including serotonin, acetylcholine, glutamate, and gamma-aminobutyric acid (GABA) (e.g., Dobbs, 2010; Rasmussen et al., 2010; Walker et al., 2010). The specific roles for these neurotransmitters in schizophrenia need to be explored further.

Viral Infections Is it possible that at least some forms of schizophrenia are caused by a slow-acting virus that attacks the developing brain of a fetus or newborn child? Prenatal rubella (German measles), a viral infection, is a cause of later mental retardation. Could another virus give rise to schizophrenia? The answer is that we don't yet know, but intriguing evidence points to possible links between prenatal infections and later development of schizophrenia (Brown et al., 2009). Investigators reported a sevenfold greater risk of schizophrenia in individuals exposed to the influenza virus (the "flu" virus) during the first three months of prenatal development (Brown et al., 2004). Moreover, the risk of schizophrenia is greater in people who are born in the winter and early spring months in the northern hemisphere, a time of the year associated with a greater risk of the flu (King, St-Hilaire, & Heidkamp, 2010). If this link is confirmed by other findings, it would suggest that viral agents may act on the developing brain in the early stages of prenatal development in ways that increase the risk of developing schizophrenia later in life. But even if a viral basis for schizophrenia were discovered, it would probably account for only a small fraction of cases.

Scientists believe that a defect on one particular gene causes schizophrenia, but they haven't yet been able to identify the defective gene.

☑ **FALSE** Scientists believe that many genes, not any one gene, are involved in complex processes that increase the likelihood that schizophrenia will develop.

11.6 Describe the role of family factors in schizophrenia.

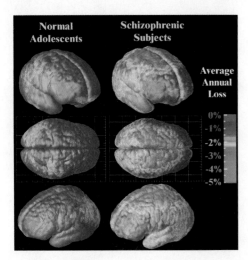

FIGURE 11.2

Loss of brain tissue in adolescents with early-onset schizophrenia. The brains of adolescents with early-onset schizophrenia (right image) show a substantial loss of gray matter. Some shrinkage of gray matter occurs normally during adolescence (left image), but the loss is more pronounced in adolescents with schizophrenia.

Source: Thompson et al. (2001).

Brain Abnormalities Brain scans of schizophrenia patients show abnormalities both in the physical structures of the brain and in brain functioning (e.g., Borgwardt, McGuire, & Fusar-Poli, 2011; Hulshoff Pol et al., 2012; Kubota et al., 2013; Schultz et al., 2010). The most prominent finding of structural abnormalities in the brains of many schizophrenia patients is loss of brain tissue (gray matter) as compared to the brains of normal controls (e.g., Arango et al., 2012; Keshavan, Nasrallah, & Tandon, 2011). In Figure 11.2, we see a visual representation of the brains of adolescents with early-onset (childhood) schizophrenia. The clearest sign of deterioration of brain tissue is the presence of abnormally enlarged ventricles, which are hollow spaces in the brain (see Figure 11.3) (Kempton et al., 2010).

In schizophrenia patients, the brain may have been damaged or failed to develop normally during prenatal development as the result of genetic factors or environmental influences (e.g., viral infections, inadequate fetal nutrition) or perhaps birth traumas or complications (King, St-Hilaire, & Heidkamp, 2010; Walker et al., 2010). One indication of possible prenatal complications is the finding of an association between low birth weight—a marker for problems in prenatal development—and later schizophrenia (Abel et al., 2010). We need to keep in mind, however, that not all cases of schizophrenia involve structural damage to brain tissue. There may be several forms of schizophrenia that have different causal processes.

The picture that is beginning to emerge from brain scans of schizophrenia patients shows abnormal functioning and loss of brain tissue in the *prefrontal cortex* of the brain (Kong et al., 2012; Mechelli et al., 2011; Ursu et al., 2011). The prefrontal cortex is the thinking, planning, and organizing center of the brain, which is why it is often called the brain's "executive center." The prefrontal cortex lies directly behind the forehead in the frontal lobes of the cerebral cortex and directly in front of the motor cortex (the part of the brain that controls voluntary body movements). The prefrontal cortex is responsible for many higher-order or executive-type functions of the brain, such as regulating attention, organizing thoughts and behavior, prioritizing information, and formulating goals—the very types of deficits often found in people with schizophrenia (Barch & Smith, 2008). Investigators believe that prefrontal abnormalities may largely have a genetic origin (Bakken et al., 2011).

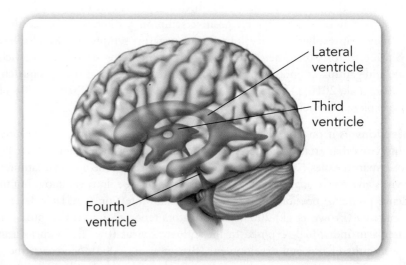

FIGURE 11.3

Brain ventricles. Individuals with schizophrenia typically have abnormally enlarged ventricles in the brain, which is a sign of deterioration or loss of brain tissue. Ventricles are hollow cavities containing a fluid that buffers or cushions the brain. Here we see the location of brain ventricles on the left side of the brain.

The prefrontal cortex serves as a kind of mental clipboard for holding information needed to guide and organize behavior. Prefrontal abnormalities may explain why people with schizophrenia often have difficulty with *working memory*—the memory system we use to hold information temporarily in mind and to work on that information (Hahn et al., 2012; Coleman et al., 2012; Mammarella et al., 2012). We regularly use our working memory to juggle information in our heads, such as when performing mental arithmetic or holding sounds in our minds just long enough to convert them into recognizable words in order to carry on a conversation. Impairment of working memory can lead to confusion and disorganized behavior of the type often seen in schizophrenia patients. Deficits in working memory often emerge before the first clinical symptoms of the disorder (Haenschel et al., 2007). **T / F**

Brain-imaging studies show lower levels of neural activity in parts of the prefrontal cortex in schizophrenia patients as compared to healthy controls—findings consistent with prefrontal abnormalities (e.g., Minzenberg et al., 2009). For example, schizophrenia patients show less prefrontal activation while performing arithmetic problems than do controls (Hugdahl et al., 2004). Reduced neural activity may reflect structural damage in the brain, perhaps as a result of loss of brain tissue. Investigators recently proposed yet another possibility, that the brains of schizophrenia patients may have relatively few pathways (think of them as roadways) in the prefrontal cortex for information to pass from one neuron to another (Cahill et al., 2009). As a result, messages may get bottled up in a veritable "traffic jam" in the brain (like drivers on an interstate needing to squeeze into a single lane because of construction). This, is turn, may result in confused and disorganized thinking ("Traffic Jam," 2009).

Evidence also points to abnormalities in brain circuitry connecting the prefrontal cortex and lower brain structures, including parts of the limbic system involved in regulating emotions and memory (e.g., Ferrarelli et al., 2012; Kubota et al, 2013; Woodward, Karbasforoushan, & Heckers, 2012). At a neurological level, there may be a disconnect between the "thinking parts" of the brain and other brain structures involved in regulating emotions and memory processes (Freedman, 2012; Park & Thakkar, 2010). These disturbances in neural networks may contribute to difficulties in focusing attention, thinking clearly, planning effectively, organizing activities, and processing emotions. In sum, evidence suggests that schizophrenia involves impairments in networks of neurons in different parts of the brain, rather than a defect or pathology in any one area (Guller et al., 2012; Shenton et al., 2009. We further explore the biological underpinnings of schizophrenia in the closer look section on page 425, "The Hunt for Endophenotypes in Schizophrenia."

Although evidence of the biological underpinnings of schizophrenia continues to mount, we should be aware of a divergent view long associated with a psychiatrist, Dr. Thomas Szasz, who argued against the very concept of mental illness. (see Thinking Critically About Abnormal Psychology).

FAMILY THEORIES What role does disturbed family relationships play in the development and course of schizophrenia? An early, but since discredited, theory focused on the role of the *schizophrenogenic mother* (Fromm-Reichmann, 1948, 1950). In what some feminists view as historic psychiatric sexism, the schizophrenogenic mother was described as cold, aloof, overprotective, and domineering. She was characterized as stripping her children of self-esteem, stifling their independence, and forcing them into dependency on her. Children reared by such mothers were believed to be at special risk for developing schizophrenia if their fathers were passive and failed to counteract the mother's pathogenic influences. Thankfully, the concept of the "schizophrenogenic mother" was discredited as investigators showed that mothers of people who develop schizophrenia do not fit this stereotypical pattern (e.g., Hirsch & Leff, 1975).

Today, investigators interested in family influences have turned to considering the effects of deviant patterns of communication within the family as well as intrusive, negative comments directed toward the schizophrenic family member.

truth OR fiction

Although schizophrenia is widely believed to be a brain disease, we still lack evidence of abnormal functioning in the brains of schizophrenia patients.

☑ **FALSE** Mounting evidence points to both structural and functional abnormalities in the brains of many schizophrenia patients.

@Issue: Is Mental Illness a Myth?

In 1961, the psychiatrist Thomas Szasz (1920–2012) shocked the psychiatric establishment by making a bold claim that mental illness does not exist. In his controversial book, *The Myth of Mental Illness*, Szasz, a long-time critic of the psychiatric establishment, argued that mental illness is a myth, a convenient fiction society uses to stigmatize and subjugate people whose behavior it finds to be deviant, odd, or bizarre (Szasz, 1961, 2008, 2011). To Szasz, the so-called mental illnesses are really "problems in living," not diseases in the same sense that influenza, hypertension, and cancer are diseases. Szasz did not dispute that the behavior of people diagnosed with schizophrenia or other mental disorders is peculiar or disturbed. Nor does he deny that these individuals suffer emotional problems or have difficulties adjusting to society. But he challenged the conventional view that strange or eccentric behavior is a product of an underlying disease. Szasz argued that treating problems as "diseases" empowers psychiatrists to put socially deviant people away in medical facilities. To Szasz, involuntary hospitalization is a form of tyranny disguised as therapy. It deprives people of human dignity and strips them of the most essential human right—liberty.

Are the myriad problems of people with schizophrenia—the deluded thoughts and hallucinations and incoherent speech—merely "problems in living," or are they symptoms of an underlying disease process? The belief that mental illness is a myth or a social construction is difficult to reconcile with a large body of evidence showing structural and functional differences in the brains of schizophrenia patients and of genetic factors that increase the risk of developing the disorder.

We've learned a great deal about the biological underpinnings of mental or psychological disorders since Szasz claimed that mental illness doesn't exist, although we still have much to learn. Our knowledge of the causes of many diseases, including cancer and Alzheimer's disease, is also incomplete, but a lack of knowledge does not make them any less of a disease. Many professionals believe that radical theorists like Szasz go too far in arguing that mental illness is merely a fabrication invented by society to stigmatize social deviants.

Evidence supports a prominent role for biological factors in many abnormal behavior patterns, including schizophrenia, mood disorders, and autism. But how far should we extend the disease model? Is antisocial personality disorder an illness? Or attention-deficit/hyperactivity disorder? Or specific phobias, such as fear of flying? What are the implications of treating abnormal behavioral patterns as diseases versus viewing them as problems in living?

The DSM itself does not take a position on which mental disorders, if any, are biologically based. It recognizes that the causes of most mental disorders remain uncertain: Some disorders may have purely biological causes. Some may have psychological causes. Still others, probably most, involve an interaction of biological, psychological, and social–environmental causes.

All in all, the views of Szasz and other critics of the mental health establishment have helped bring about much needed improvements in the protection of the rights of patients in psychiatric institutions. They have also directed our attention to the social and political implications of our responses to deviant behavior. Perhaps, most importantly, they have challenged us to examine our assumptions when we label and treat undesirable behaviors as signs of illness rather than as problems of adjustment.

In thinking critically about the issue, answer the following questions:

- What would it mean to say that schizophrenia is a problem of living rather than a disease? What would be the implications for treatment? In what way does society respond to people who behave in unusual ways?

- Based on knowledge that has accumulated since Szasz first wrote his book, which mental illnesses should be classified as problems of living? Which as diseases?

Thomas Szasz. Psychiatrist Thomas Szasz waged a long-standing battle with institutional psychiatry. Arguing that mental illness is a myth, Szasz believed that mental health problems are problems in living, not medical diseases.

Communication Deviance Communication deviance (CD) is a pattern of unclear, vague, disruptive, or fragmented communication that is often found among parents and family members of schizophrenia patients. CD is speech that is hard to follow and from which it is difficult to extract any shared meaning. High CD parents often have difficulty focusing on what their children are saying. They verbally attack their children rather than offer constructive criticism. They may also interrupt the child with intrusive, negative comments. They are prone to telling the child what she or he "really" thinks rather than allowing the child to formulate her or his own thoughts and feelings. Evidence shows that parents of schizophrenia patients tend to have higher levels of CD than parents in families without any schizophrenic member (Docherty et al., 2004).

We should note that the causal pathway between CD and schizophrenia may work in both directions. On the one hand, CD may increase the risk of schizophrenia in genetically vulnerable individuals. But CD may also be a parental reaction to the behavior of disturbed children. Parents may learn to use odd language as a way of coping with children who continually interrupt and confront them.

Expressed Emotion Another form of disturbed family communication, *expressed emotion* (EE), is a pattern of responding to the schizophrenic family member in hostile, critical, and unsupportive ways (A. Weisman et al., 2006). Schizophrenia patients living in a high EE family environment have more than twice the risk of suffering a relapse as those from low EE families (more supportive) families (Hooley, 2010).

High EE relatives typically show less empathy, tolerance, and flexibility than low EE relatives and tend to believe that schizophrenia patients can exercise greater control over their disturbed behavior (Weisman et al., 2000). EE in relatives is also associated with poorer outcomes in people with other psychological disorders, including major depression, eating disorders, and posttraumatic stress disorder (PTSD) (e.g., Barrowclough, Gregg, & Tarrier, 2008). Living with a high EE relative appears to impose greater stress on people who are challenged by mental disorders (Chambless et al., 2008).

Low EE families may actually protect, or buffer, the family member with schizophrenia from the adverse impact of outside stressors and help prevent recurrent episodes (see Figure 11.4). Yet, family interactions are a two-way street. Family members and patients influence each other and are influenced in turn. Disruptive behaviors by the family member with schizophrenia frustrate other members of the family, prompting them to respond to the person in a less supportive and more critical and hostile way. This, in turn, can exacerbate the schizophrenia patient's disruptive behavior.

We need to take a close look at cultural differences in both the frequency of EE in family members of schizophrenia patients and the effects these behaviors have on patients. Investigators find high EE families to be more common in industrialized countries, such as the United States and Canada, than in developing countries, such as India (Barrowclough & Hooley, 2003).

Cross-cultural evidence shows that Mexican American, Anglo American, and Chinese families with high levels of EE are more likely than low EE families to view the psychotic behavior of a family member with schizophrenia as within the person's control (Weisman et al., 1998; Yang et al., 2004). The anger and criticism of high EE family members may stem from the perception that patients can and should exert greater control over their aberrant behavior.

In a study of cultural differences in EE, investigators found that high levels of EE in family members were linked to more negative outcomes in schizophrenia patients among Anglo American families, but not among Mexican American families (Lopez et al., 2004). Rather, for Mexican American families, the degree of family warmth, not EE per se, was related to a more

11.7 Apply the diathesis–stress model to the development of schizophrenia.

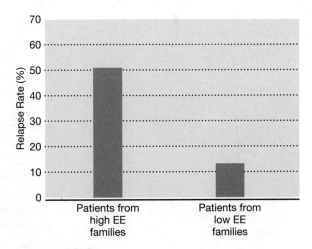

FIGURE 11.4

Relapse rates of people with schizophrenia in high and low EE families. People with schizophrenia whose families are high in EE are at greater risk of relapse than those whose families are low in EE. Whereas low EE families may help protect the family member with schizophrenia from environmental stressors, high EE families may impose additional stress.

Source: Adapted from King & Dixon, 1999.

What's in a name? Quite a lot, apparently. Many Mexican Americans perceive people with schizophrenia to be suffering from *nervios* ("nerves"). The label *nervios* carries less stigma and more positive expectations than the label of schizophrenia.

positive course of schizophrenia in the affected family members, whereas for Anglo American patients, family warmth did not relate to such outcomes. In another study, investigators reported that among African American patients, high levels of EE were actually associated with better outcomes (Rosenfarb, Bellack, & Aziz, 2006). What might be the reason for this apparent contradiction? The study investigators suggested that for African Americans, intrusive critical comments during family interactions may be perceived as signs of caring and concern rather than rejection. Other investigators concur, finding relationships between how much relatives criticize patients and patients' perceptions of their relatives' criticism only among White European and Latino patients, but not among African American patients (Weisman et al., 2006). These studies underscore the importance of looking at abnormal behavior patterns through a cultural lens.

Families of people with schizophrenia typically have little if any preparation for coping with the stress of caring for them. Rather than focusing so much attention on the negative influence of high EE family members, perhaps we should seek to help family members learn more constructive ways of relating to and supporting one another. Evidence shows that families can be helped to reduce their level of EE (Dixon, Adams, & Lucksted, 2000).

Family Factors in Schizophrenia: Causes or Sources of Stress? Evidence fails to support the belief that negative family interactions directly cause schizophrenia. Rather, people who have a genetic vulnerability to schizophrenia may be more likely to develop the disorder if they live in a family environment wracked by stressful family and social relationships (Reiss, 2005; Tienari et al., 2004).

How families conceptualize mental disorders has a bearing on how they relate to relatives who suffer from them. For example, the term *schizophrenia* carries a stigma in our society and comes with the expectation that the disorder is enduring (Jenkins & Karno, 1992). In contrast, to many Mexican Americans, a person with schizophrenia is perceived as suffering from *nervios* ("nerves"), a cultural label attached to a wide range of troubling behaviors, including anxiety, schizophrenia, and depression, and one that carries less stigma and more positive expectations than the label of *schizophrenia* (Jenkins & Karno, 1992). The label *nervios* may have the effect of destigmatizing family members with schizophrenia.

Family members may respond differently to relatives who have schizophrenia if they ascribe aspects of their behavior to a temporary or curable condition, which they believe can be altered by willpower, than if they believe the behavior is caused by a permanent brain abnormality. The degree to which relatives perceive family members with schizophrenia as having control over their disorders may be a critical factor in how they respond to them. Families may cope better with a family member with schizophrenia by taking a balanced view that while people with schizophrenia can maintain some control over their behavior, some of their odd or disruptive behavior is a product of their underlying disorder. It remains to be seen whether these different ways in which family members conceptualize schizophrenia are connected with differences in the rates of recurrence of the disorder among affected family members.

Treatment Approaches

There is no cure for schizophrenia. Treatment is generally multifaceted, incorporating pharmacological, psychological, and rehabilitative approaches. Most people treated for schizophrenia in organized mental health settings receive some form of antipsychotic medication, which is intended to control symptoms such as hallucinations and delusions and decrease the risk of recurrent episodes.

11.8 Evaluate the methods used to treat schizophrenia.

The Hunt for Endophenotypes in Schizophrenia

Although still in its infancy, the scientific search for **endophenotypes** has begun (Allen et al., 2009). An endophenotype is a measurable process or mechanism, unseen by the unaided human eye, which explains how genetic instructions encoded in an organism's DNA influence an observable characteristic of the organism, or *phenotype* (Gottesman & Gould, 2003). Phenotypes are outward expressions of traits, such as eye color or observed behavior. Think of endophenotypes as mechanisms or critical links by which genes become expressed in behavioral or physical traits or disorders.

Investigators are exploring possible endophenotypes in schizophrenia, including disturbances in brain circuitry, deficits in working memory, impaired attentional and cognitive processes, and abnormalities in neurotransmitter functioning (e.g., Greenwood et al., 2011; Hall et al., 2007; Martin et al., 2008; Zhao et al., 2011). One example involves disturbances in brain circuitry as a possible endophenotype. Brain circuits connecting the prefrontal cortex and lower brain regions, including the limbic system, are involved in organizing thoughts, perceptions, emotions, and attentional processes. Defects in this circuitry may lead to a breakdown in these processes, resulting in positive features of schizophrenia such as hallucinations, delusions, and thought disorder.

To better understand how schizophrenia develops, we need to dig under the surface to examine how genes affect underlying processes, and then account for how these processes lead to the disorder (Goldman, 2011). In research along these lines, investigators are now exploring the role of more than 20 genes involved in the kinds of memory and attentional deficits observed in schizophrenia patients, all of which influence the functioning of the prefrontal cortex (Greenwood et al., 2011).

Figure 11.5 shows a model representing links between candidate genes and possible endophenotypes,

leading to increased vulnerability to schizophrenia. While the search for these hidden mechanisms in schizophrenia is well under way, we should understand that scientists haven't found any one brain abnormality that is present in every schizophrenia patient. Perhaps it shouldn't surprise us that a "one size fits all" model doesn't apply. Schizophrenia is a complex disorder characterized by different subtypes and symptom complexes. Different causal processes in the brain may explain different forms of schizophrenia. What we now call *schizophrenia* may actually turn out to be more than one disorder.

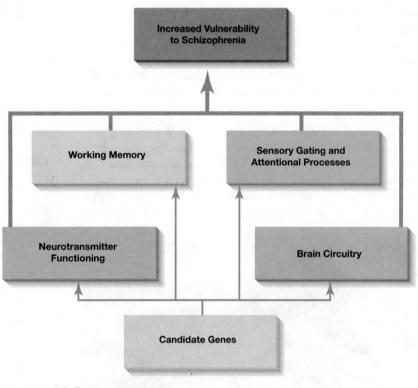

FIGURE 11.5

From genes to vulnerability.

Source: Adapted from Gottesman & Gould, 2003.

BIOLOGICAL APPROACHES The advent in the 1950s of antipsychotic drugs—also referred to as *major tranquilizers* or *neuroleptics*—revolutionized the treatment of schizophrenia and provided the impetus for large-scale releases of mental patients into the community (deinstitutionalization). Antipsychotic medication helps control the more flagrant behavior patterns of schizophrenia, such as delusional thinking and hallucinations, and reduces the need for long-term hospitalization.

For many patients with chronic schizophrenia, entering a hospital is like going through a revolving door: they are repeatedly admitted and discharged. Many are simply

The Diathesis–Stress Model

In 1962, psychologist Paul Meehl proposed an integrative model for schizophrenia that led to the development of the diathesis–stress model. Meehl suggested that certain people possess a genetic predisposition to schizophrenia that is expressed behaviorally only if they are reared in stressful environments (Meehl, 1962, 1972).

Later, Zubin and Spring (1977) formulated the diathesis–stress model, which views the development of schizophrenia in terms of an interaction or combination of a *diathesis*, or genetic predisposition to develop the disorder, and stressful life factors, especially environmental stress that exceeds the individual's stress threshold or coping resources (see Figure 11.6 for a representation of the diathesis–stress model of schizophrenia). Also note that the presence of protective factors may potentially buffer the effects of life stress, thereby reducing the likelihood that a genetic predisposition for schizophrenia will expressed in the development of the disorder.

Environmental stressors may include psychological factors, such as family conflict, child abuse, emotional deprivation, or loss of supportive figures, as well as physical environmental influences, such as early brain trauma or injury. On the other hand, if environmental stress remains below the person's stress

threshold, schizophrenia may never develop, even in persons at genetic risk.

Research Evidence Supporting the Diathesis–Stress Model

Several lines of evidence support the diathesis–stress model. One is the fact that schizophrenia tends to develop in late adolescence or early adulthood, around the time that young people typically face the increased stress associated with establishing independence and finding a role in life. Other evidence shows that psychosocial stress, such as EE (harping criticisms from family members), worsens symptoms in people with schizophrenia and increases risks of relapse. Other stressors, such as economic hardship and living in distressed neighborhoods, may also interact with genetic vulnerability in the causal matrix leading to schizophrenia. However, whether stress directly triggers the initial onset of schizophrenia in genetically vulnerable individuals remains an open question.

More direct support for the diathesis–stress model comes from longitudinal studies of high-risk children who are at increased genetic risk of developing the disorder by virtue of having one or both parents with schizophrenia. Longitudinal studies of high-risk children support the central tenet of the diathesis–stress model that heredity interacts with environmental influences in determining vulnerability to schizophrenia. Longitudinal studies track individuals over extended periods of time. Ideally, they begin before the emergence of the disorder or the behavior pattern in question and follow its course. In this way, investigators may identify early characteristics that predict the later development of a disorder. These studies require a commitment of many years and substantial cost. Because schizophrenia occurs in only about 1% of the general adult population, researchers have focused on high-risk children. Children with one parent with schizophrenia have about 10% to 25% chance of developing schizophrenia, and those with both parents with schizophrenia have about a 45% risk (Erlenmeyer-Kimling et al., 1997; Gottesman, 1991).

The best-known longitudinal study of high-risk children was undertaken by Sarnoff Mednick and his colleagues in Denmark. In 1962, the Mednick group identified 207 high-risk children (whose mothers had schizophrenia) and 104 reference subjects who were matched for factors such as gender, social class, age, and education but whose mothers did not have schizophrenia (Mednick, Parnas, & Schulsinger, 1987). The children from both groups ranged in age from 10 to 20 years, with a mean of 15 years. None showed signs of disturbance when first interviewed.

Five years later, at an average age of 20, the children were reexamined. By then 20 of the high-risk children were found to have demonstrated abnormal behavior, although not necessarily a

Protective factors in high-risk children. A supportive and nurturing environment may reduce the likelihood of developing schizophrenia among high-risk children.

schizophrenic episode (Mednick & Schulsinger, 1968). The children who showed abnormal behavior, referred to as the high-risk "sick" group, were then compared with a matched group of 20 high-risk children from the original sample who remained well functioning (a high-risk "well" group) and a matched group of 20 low-risk subjects. It turned out that the mothers of the high-risk "well" offspring had experienced easier pregnancies and deliveries than those of the high-risk "sick" group or the low-risk group. Seventy percent of the mothers of the high-risk "sick" children had serious complications during pregnancy or delivery. Perhaps, consistent with the diathesis–stress model, stressful factors such as complications during pregnancy, childbirth, or shortly after birth may cause brain damage that, in combination with a genetic vulnerability, leads to severe mental disorders later in life.

In another classic research, Finnish researchers also find links between fetal and postnatal abnormalities and the development of schizophrenia in adulthood (Jones et al., 1998). The low rate of complications during pregnancy and birth in the high-risk "well" group in the Danish study suggests that normal pregnancies and births may actually help protect high-risk children from developing abnormal behavior patterns (Mednick et al., 1987).

Again from Denmark, more recent evidence from tracking nearly 1.4 million births showed an interesting connection supporting the role of maternal stress during prenatal development. The offspring of mothers who experienced a highly stressful event—the death of a relative—during the first trimester showed higher than average rates of schizophrenia (Khashan et al., 2008). This evidence suggests that severe stressors during early pregnancy may adversely affect brain development in the fetus.

Positive environmental factors, such as good parenting, may help prevent the disorder in children who stand an increased genetic risk. In support of the role of early environmental influences, Mednick and his colleagues found that high-risk children who later developed schizophrenia had poorer relationships with their parents than did high-risk children who did not develop the disorder (Mednick et al., 1987). The presence of childhood behavior problems may also be a marker for the later development of schizophrenia-related disorders in high-risk children (Amminger et al., 1999).

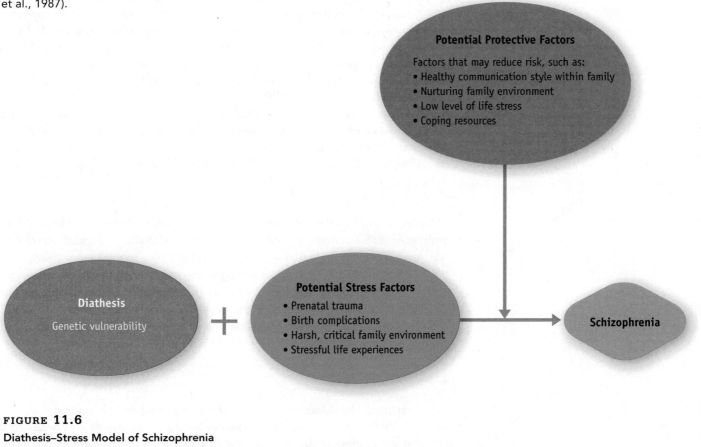

FIGURE 11.6
Diathesis–Stress Model of Schizophrenia

discharged to the streets once they are stabilized on medication and receive little, if any, follow-up care. This often leads to a pattern of chronic homelessness punctuated by brief stays in the hospital.

The first generation of antipsychotic drugs included the phenothiazines *chlorpromazine* (Thorazine), *thioridazine* (Mellaril), *trifluoperazine* (Stelazine), and *fluphenazine* (Prolixin). *Haloperidol* (Haldol), which is chemically distinct from the phenothiazines, produces similar effects.

Antipsychotic drugs block dopamine receptors in the brain, which reduces dopamine activity in the brain and helps quell the more obvious symptoms such as hallucinations and delusions. The effectiveness of antipsychotic drugs has been repeatedly demonstrated in double-blinded, placebo-controlled studies (Geddes, Stroup, & Lieberman, 2011; Nasrallah et al., 2009). Even so, these drugs don't help all schizophrenia patients and relapses can and do occur in patients, even in some patients who continue taking medication.

The major risk of long-term use of neuroleptics is a potentially disabling side effect called **tardive dyskinesia** (TD). TD can take different forms, the most common of which is frequent eye blinking. Common signs of the disorder include involuntary chewing and eye movements, lip smacking and puckering, facial grimacing, and involuntary movements of the limbs and trunk. In some cases, the movement disorder is so severe that patients have difficulty breathing, talking, or eating. In many cases, the disorder persists even when the neuroleptic medication is withdrawn.

TD is most common among older people and among women. Although TD tends to improve gradually or stabilize over a period of years, many people with TD remain persistently and severely disabled. We presently lack an effective and safe treatment for this very troubling side effect. The risk of this potentially disabling side effect requires physicians to carefully weigh the risks and benefits of long-term drug treatment.

A second generation of antipsychotic drugs, referred to as *atypical antipsychotics*, has largely replaced the earlier generation of antipsychotics (Friedman, 2012; Tandon, Nasrallah, & Keshavan, 2010). Atypical antipsychotics are at least as effective as the first-generation antipsychotics but have the advantage of carrying fewer neurological side effects and a lower risk of TD (Correll & Shenk, 2009; Crespo-Facorro et al., 2011; Friedman, 2012).

The more commonly used atypical antipsychotics include *clozapine* (brand name Clozaril), *risperidone* (brand name Risperdal), and *olanzapine* (brand name Zyprexa) (Hatta et al., 2009). For Lori Schiller, the woman who experienced her first psychotic break during summer camp, the voices became softer when she was treated with *clozapine*.

"I" The Voices Grow Softer

It was as if it [my brain] were draining out from the inside. My head had been filled with sticky stuff, like melted rubber or motor oil. Now all that sticky stuff was dripping out, leaving only my brain behind. Slowly I was beginning to think more clearly.

And the Voices? The Voices were growing softer. Were the Voices growing softer? They were growing softer! They began moving around, from outside my skull, to inside, to outside again. But their decibel level was definitely falling.

It was happening. I was being set free. I had prayed to find some peace, and my prayers were finally being answered.... I want to live. I want to live.

From Schiller & Bennett, 1994

Over time, the voices receded into the background and then disappeared. Lori needed to learn to live without the voices and to build a life for herself. She began venturing beyond the confines of the hospital. She entered a halfway house and began to move toward a more independent life. Lori spent three and a half years at a halfway house and is now living independently.

Antipsychotic drugs help control symptoms of schizophrenia, but they are not a cure (Walker & Tessner, 2008). People with chronic schizophrenia typically receive maintenance doses of antipsychotic drugs once their acute symptoms abate. However, many patients relapse even if they keep taking medication. The risk of relapse is even greater for patients who stop taking medication. Still, not all people with schizophrenia require antipsychotic medication to live independently (Jobe & Harrow, 2010). Unfortunately, we cannot yet predict which patients can manage effectively without continued medication. **T / F**

Atypical antipsychotics also carry risks of significant side effects, including such serious medical complications as sudden cardiac death, substantial weight gain, and metabolic disorders associated with increased risks of death due to heart disease and stroke (e.g., Abbott, 2010; Morrato et al., 2010; Stroup et al., 2011). In addition, the atypical antipsychotic drug *clozapine* carries a risk of a potentially lethal disorder in which the body produces inadequate supplies of white blood cells. Because of the seriousness of this risk, patients receiving the drug need to have their blood checked regularly. In sum, doctors face a difficult choice, having to balance the benefits of treatment with the attendant risks (Friedman, 2005; Zhao, 2008).

Whatever the benefits of antipsychotic medication may be, drugs alone cannot meet the multifaceted needs of people with schizophrenia. Psychiatric drugs may improve the more flagrant symptoms but have only a limited impact on the person's general social functioning, quality of life, and remediation of negative symptoms (Friedman, 2012; Turkington & Morrison, 2012; Tandon, Nasrallah, & Keshavan, 2009). Consequently, drug therapy needs to be supplemented with psychological treatment, rehabilitation, cognitive (memory and attention) training, social skills training (including focusing on perception of emotional expression in people's faces), and social services designed to help schizophrenia patients adjust to demands of community living (e.g., Guo et al., 2010; Hooker et al., 2012; LeVine, 2012; Patela et al., 2011; Wykes et al., 2011). A wide array of treatment components are needed within a comprehensive model of care, including the use of antipsychotic medication, medical care, psychological treatment, family therapy, social skills training, crisis intervention, rehabilitation services, and housing and other social services. Treatment programs must also ensure a continuity of care between the hospital and the community.

SOCIOCULTURAL FACTORS IN TREATMENT Investigators find that response to psychiatric medications and dosage levels varies with patient ethnicity (USDHHS, 1999). Asians and Hispanics, for example, may require lower doses of neuroleptics than European Americans do. Asians also tend to experience more side effects from the same dosage. But racial disparities also exist in how schizophrenia patients are treated. For example, African American patients in one study were less likely to receive the newer generation of atypical antipsychotics than were European American patients (Kuno & Rothbard, 2002).

Ethnicity may also play a role in the family's involvement in treatment. In a study of 26 Asian Americans and 26 non-Hispanic White Americans with schizophrenia, family members of the Asian American patients were more frequently involved in the treatment program (Lin et al., 1991). For example, family members were more likely to accompany the Asian American patients to their medication evaluation sessions. The greater family involvement among Asian Americans may reflect the relatively stronger sense of family responsibility in Asian cultures. Non-Hispanic White Americans are more likely to emphasize individualism and self-responsibility.

Maintaining connections between the person with schizophrenia and the family and larger community is part of the cultural tradition in many Asian cultures, as well as in other parts of the world, such as Africa. The seriously mentally ill of China, for instance, retain strong supportive links to their families and workplaces, which helps increase their chances of being reintegrated into community life (Liberman, 1994). In traditional healing centers for the treatment of schizophrenia in Africa, the strong support that patients receive from their family and community members, together with a community-centered lifestyle, are important elements of successful care (Peltzer & Machleidt, 1992).

We now have drugs that not only treat schizophrenia but also can cure it in many cases.

☑ **FALSE** Antipsychotic drugs help control the symptoms of schizophrenia but cannot cure the disorder.

PSYCHODYNAMIC THERAPY Freud did not believe that traditional psychoanalysis was well suited to the treatment of schizophrenia. The withdrawal into a fantasy world that typifies schizophrenia prevents the individual with schizophrenia from forming a meaningful relationship with the psychoanalyst. The techniques of classical psychoanalysis, Freud wrote, must "be replaced by others; and we do not know yet whether we shall succeed in finding a substitute" (as cited in Arieti, 1974, p. 532).

Other psychoanalysts, such as Harry Stack Sullivan and Frieda Fromm-Reichmann, adapted psychoanalytic techniques specifically for the treatment of schizophrenia. However, research has failed to demonstrate the effectiveness of psychoanalytic or psychodynamic therapy for treating schizophrenia. However, promising results are reported for a modified form of psychodynamic therapy, grounded in the diathesis–stress model, that helps patients cope with stress and build social skills, such as learning how to deal with criticism from others (Bustillo et al., 2001; Hogarty et al., 1997).

LEARNING-BASED THERAPIES Although few behavior therapists believe that faulty learning causes schizophrenia, learning-based interventions have proved to be effective in modifying schizophrenic behavior and in helping people with the disorder develop behaviors that can help them adjust more effectively to living in the community. Therapy methods include the following:

1. *Selective reinforcement of behavior,* such as providing attention for appropriate behavior and extinguishing bizarre verbalizations through withdrawal of attention;
2. *Token economy,* in which individuals on inpatient units are rewarded for appropriate behavior with tokens, such as plastic chips, that can be exchanged for tangible reinforcers such as desirable goods or privileges;
3. *Social skills training,* in which clients are taught conversational skills and other appropriate social behaviors through coaching, modeling, behavior rehearsal, and feedback.

Although token economies can help increase desirable behaviors of psychiatric inpatients, they have largely fallen out of favor in mental hospitals in recent years (Dickerson, Tenhula, & Green-Paden, 2005). Part of the problem is that they are time- and staff-intensive. To be successful, they must have strong administrative support, skilled treatment leaders, extensive staff training, and continuous quality control, all of which can limit their practicality.

Social skills training programs help individuals acquire a range of social and vocational skills. People with schizophrenia are often deficient in basic social skills needed for community living, such as assertiveness, interviewing skills, and general conversational skills. Social skills training can help them improve their social skills and general level of social functioning (Addington, Piskulic, & Marshall, 2010; Hooley, 2010; Kurtz & Mueser, 2008). However, social skills training has only a modest effect on reducing relapse rates once patients leave the hospital.

The basic model for social skills training incorporates role-playing exercises within a group format. Participants practice skills such as starting or maintaining conversations with new acquaintances and receive feedback and reinforcement from the therapist and other group members. The first step might be a dry run in which the participant role-plays the targeted behavior, such as asking strangers for bus directions. The therapist and other group members then praise the effort and provide constructive feedback. Role-playing is augmented by techniques such as modeling (observation of the therapist or other group members enacting the desired behavior), direct instruction (specific directions for enacting the desired behavior), shaping (reinforcement for successive approximations to the target behavior), and coaching (use of verbal or nonverbal prompts to elicit a particular desired behavior in the role-play). Participants are given homework assignments to practice the behaviors in the settings in which they live, such as in the hospital ward or in the community. The aim is to generalize the training or transfer it to other settings. Training sessions may also be run in stores, restaurants, schools, and other real-life settings.

Another learning-based approach coming into wider practice in treating schizophrenia as an adjunct to drug therapy is cognitive-behavioral therapy (Rector & Beck, 2012). A large and growing body of evidence backs up the effectiveness of cognitive-behavioral therapy not only for reducing hallucinations (as discussed earlier) but also for reducing delusional thinking (by offering alternative explanations to delusional beliefs) and negative symptoms, such as lack of motivation and apathy, the kinds of problem behaviors that make it difficult for patients to adjust to the demands of community living (e.g., Coltheart, Langdon, & McKay, 2011; Grant et al., 2012; Keuhn, 2011b; Lincoln et al., 2012; Ruddle, Mason, & Wykes, 2011; Sivec & Montesano, 2012; Snavely & Chessick, 2011; Turkington & Morrison, 2012). This focus on cognitive-behavioral therapy treatment in helping schizophrenia patients develop adaptive skills of living brings us to consider the role of psychosocial rehabilitation as part of a multifaceted treatment approach.

Building skills: Social skills training groups help schizophrenia patients develop the social and vocational skills they need to adapt to more independent life in the community.

PSYCHOSOCIAL REHABILITATION People with schizophrenia typically have difficulties functioning in social and occupational roles and performing work that depends on basic cognitive abilities involving attention and memory. These problems limit their ability to adjust to community life, even in the absence of overt psychotic behavior. Recently, promising results were reported for cognitive rehabilitation training to help schizophrenia patients strengthen basic cognitive skills such as attention and memory (Minzenberg & Carter, 2012; Moritz et al., 2011; Wykes et al., 2011).

A number of self-help clubs (commonly called clubhouses) and rehabilitation centers have sprung up to help people with schizophrenia find a place in society. Many centers were launched by nonprofessionals or by people with schizophrenia themselves, largely because mental health agencies often failed to provide comparable services. A "clubhouse" is not a home; rather, it serves as a self-contained community that provides members with social support and help in finding educational opportunities and paid employment.

Multiservice rehabilitation centers typically offer housing as well as job and educational opportunities. These centers often make use of skills training approaches to help clients learn how to handle money, resolve disputes with family members, develop friendships, take buses, cook their own meals, shop, and so on.

FAMILY INTERVENTION PROGRAMS Family conflicts and negative family interactions can heap stress on family members with schizophrenia, increasing the risk of recurrent episodes. Researchers and clinicians have worked with families of people with schizophrenia to help them cope with the burdens of care and to assist them in developing more cooperative, less confrontational ways of relating to others. The specific components of family interventions vary, but they usually share some common features, such as a focus on the practical aspects of everyday living, educating family members about schizophrenia, teaching them how to relate in a less hostile way to family members with schizophrenia, improving communication, and fostering effective problem-solving and coping skills. Structured family intervention programs can reduce friction in the family, improve social functioning in schizophrenia patients, and even reduce relapse rates (Addington, Piskulic, & Marshall, 2010; Guo et al., 2010; Patterson & Leeuwenkamp, 2008). However, the benefits appear to be relatively modest, and questions remain about whether relapses are prevented or merely delayed.

In sum, no single treatment approach meets all the needs of people with schizophrenia. The conceptualization of schizophrenia as a lifelong disability underscores the need for long-term treatment interventions that incorporate antipsychotic medication, family therapy, supportive or cognitive-behavioral forms of therapy, vocational training, and housing and other social support services. To help the individual reach maximal social adjustment, these interventions should be coordinated and integrated within a comprehensive model of treatment.

Other Schizophrenia Spectrum Disorders

11.9 Describe the general features of other disorders in the schizophrenia spectrum.

The *DSM-5* classifies a range of psychological disorders within the schizophrenia spectrum of disorders. They range from milder forms of disorganized or unusual thinking and difficulties relating to others associated with schizotypal personal disorder (discussed in Chapter 12) to frankly psychotic disorders, including brief psychotic disorder, schizophreniform disorder, delusional disorder, and schizoaffective disorder, as well as schizophrenia itself.

Brief Psychotic Disorder

Some brief psychotic episodes do not progress to schizophrenia. The diagnostic category of **brief psychotic disorder** applies to a psychotic disorder that lasts from a day to a month and is characterized by at least one of the following features: delusions, hallucinations, disorganized speech, or grossly disorganized or catatonic behavior. Eventually, there is a full return to the individual's prior level of functioning. Brief psychotic disorder is often linked to a significant stressor or stressors, such as the loss of a loved one or exposure to brutal traumas in wartime. Women sometimes experience the disorder after childbirth.

Schizophreniform Disorder

Schizophreniform disorder consists of abnormal behaviors identical to those in schizophrenia that have persisted for at least one month but less than six months. They thus do not yet justify the diagnosis of schizophrenia. Although some cases have good outcomes, in others, the disorder persists beyond six months and may be reclassified as schizophrenia or perhaps another form of psychotic disorder, such as schizoaffective disorder. However, questions remain about the validity of the diagnosis. It may be more appropriate to diagnose people who show psychotic features of recent origin with a classification that does not specify a specific type of psychotic disorder until additional information clearly indicates which specific disorder applies.

Delusional Disorder

Many of us, perhaps even most of us, feel suspicious of other people's motives at times. We may feel that others have it in for us or believe that others are talking about us behind our backs. For most of us, however, paranoid thinking does not take the form of outright delusions. The diagnosis of **delusional disorder** applies to people who hold persistent, clearly delusional beliefs, often involving paranoid themes (Sammons, 2005b). Delusional disorder is rare, affecting an estimated 20 people in 10,000 during their lifetimes (APA, 2013).

In delusional disorder, the delusional beliefs may be bizarre (e.g., believing that aliens have implanted electrodes in the person's head) or may fall within a range of seeming plausibility, such as unfounded beliefs concerning the infidelity of a spouse, persecution by others, or attracting the love of a famous person. The apparent plausibility of some of these beliefs may lead other people to take them seriously and check them out before concluding that they are unfounded. Apart from the delusion, the individual's behavior may not show evidence of obviously bizarre or odd behavior, as we see in the following case example.

Hit Men: A Case of Delusional Disorder

A married 42-year-old postal worker was brought to the hospital by his wife because he had been insisting that there was a contract out on his life. He told the doctors that the problem started about four months ago when his supervisor accused him of tampering with a package, an offense that could have cost him his job. Though the supervisor was exonerated at a formal hearing, he was furious and felt publicly humiliated. The man went on to say that his coworkers soon began avoiding him, turning away from him when he walked by, as if they didn't want to see him. He began to think that they were talking about him behind his back, although he could never clearly make out what they were saying. He gradually became convinced that his coworkers were avoiding him because his boss had put a contract on his life. He said he had noticed several large white cars cruising up and down the street where he lived. He believed there were hit men in these cars and refused to leave his home without a companion. Other than reporting that his life was in danger, his thinking and behavior appeared entirely normal on interview. He denied any hallucinations and excepting his unusual beliefs about his life being in danger, he showed no other signs of psychotic behavior. The diagnosis of Delusional Disorder, Persecutory type, seemed the most appropriate, because there was no evidence that a contract had been taken on his life (hence, it was deemed a persecutory delusion) and there were no other clear signs of psychosis that might support a diagnosis of schizophrenia.

Adapted from Spitzer et al., 1994, pp. 177–179

Is someone out to get you? People with delusional disorder often weave paranoid fantasies in their minds that they confuse with reality.

The Love Delusion

Erotomania, or the love delusion, is a rare delusional disorder in which the individual believes that he or she is loved by someone else, usually someone famous or of high social status. In reality, the individual has only a passing or nonexistent relationship with the alleged lover. People with erotomania are often unemployed and socially isolated (Kennedy et al., 2002). Although the love delusion was once thought to be predominantly a female disorder, recent reports suggest it may not be a rarity among men. Although women with erotomania may have a potential for violence when their attentions are rebuffed, men with this condition appear more likely to threaten or commit acts of violence in the pursuit of the objects of their unrequited desires (Goldstein, 1986). Antipsychotic medications may reduce the intensity of the delusion but do not appear to eliminate it (Kelly, Kennedy, & Shanley, 2000). Nor do we have evidence that psychotherapy helps people with erotomania. The prognosis is thus bleak, and people with erotomania may harass their love objects for many years. Mental health professionals need to be aware of the potential for violence in the management of people who possess these delusions of love. The following cases provide some examples of the love delusion. **T / F**

truth or fiction

Some people have delusions that they are loved by a famous person.

☑ **TRUE** Some people do suffer from the delusion that they are loved by a famous person. They are said to have a delusional disorder, erotomanic type.

➤ Three Cases of Erotomania

Mr. A., a 35-year-old man, was described as a "love-struck" suitor of a daughter of a former president of the United States. He was arrested for repeatedly harassing the woman in an attempt to win her love, although they were actually perfect strangers. Refusing to adhere to the judge's warnings to stop pestering the woman, he placed numerous phone calls to her from prison and was later transferred to a psychiatric facility, still declaring they were very much in love.

Mr. B. was arrested for breaching a court order to stop pestering a famous pop singer. A 44-year-old farmer, Mr. B. had followed his love interest across the country, constantly bombarding her with romantic overtures. He was committed to a psychiatric hospital, but maintained the belief that she'd always wait for him.

Then there was Mr. C., a 32-year-old businessman, who believed a well-known woman lawyer had fallen in love with him following a casual meeting. He constantly called and sent flowers and letters, declaring his love. While she repeatedly rejected his advances and eventually filed criminal charges for harassment, he felt tha t she was only testing his love by placing obstacles in his path. He abandoned his wife and business and his functioning declined. When the woman continued to reject him, he began sending her threatening letters and was committed to a psychiatric facility.

➤ *Adapted from Goldstein, 1986, p. 802*

Mr. Polsen's delusional belief that "hit teams" were pursuing him was treated with antipsychotic medication in the hospital and faded in about three weeks. His belief that he had been the subject of an attempted "hit" stuck in his mind, however. A month following admission, he stated, "I guess my boss has called off the contract. He couldn't get away with it now without publicity" (Spitzer et al., 1994, p. 179).

Although delusions frequently occur in schizophrenia, delusional disorder is believed to be distinct from schizophrenia. Persons with delusional disorder do not exhibit confused or jumbled thinking. Hallucinations, when they occur, are not as prominent. Delusions in schizophrenia are embedded within a larger array of disturbed thoughts, perceptions, and behaviors. In delusional disorders, the delusion itself may be the only clear sign of abnormality.

Various types of delusional disorders in the *DSM-5* are described in Table 11.2. Like other forms of psychosis, delusional disorders often respond to antipsychotic medication (Morimoto et al., 2002; Sammons, 2005b). However, once the delusion is established, it may persevere, although the individual's concern about it may wax and wane over the years. In other cases, the delusion may disappear entirely for periods of time and then recur. Sometimes the disorder permanently disappears.

TABLE 11.2	
Types of Delusional Disorders	
Type	Description
Erotomanic type	Delusional beliefs that someone else, usually a person of higher social status such as a movie star or a political figure, is in love with you; also called *erotomania*.
Grandiose type	Inflated beliefs about one's own worth, importance, power, knowledge, or identity, or beliefs that one has a special relationship to a deity or to a famous person. Cult leaders who believe they have special mystical powers of enlightenment may have delusional disorders of this type.
Jealous type	Delusions of jealousy in which the person may become convinced, without due cause, of the infidelity of his or her partner. The delusional person may misinterpret certain clues as signs of unfaithfulness, such as spots on the bed sheets.
Persecutory type	The most common type of delusional disorder, persecutory delusions, involve themes of being conspired against, followed, cheated, spied on, poisoned or drugged, or otherwise maligned or mistreated. People with these delusions may repeatedly bring legal actions against those whom they perceived to be responsible for their mistreatment, or may even commit acts of violence against them.
Somatic type	Delusions involving the person's physical or medical condition. People with these delusions may believe that foul odors are emanating from their bodies or that internal parasites are eating away at them.
Mixed type	Delusions typify more than one of the other types with no single predominant theme.

Schizoaffective Disorder

Schizoaffective disorder is sometimes referred to as a "mixed bag" of symptoms because it includes psychotic behaviors associated with schizophrenia (e.g., hallucinations and delusions) occurring at the same time as a major mood disorder (major depressive episode or manic episode). At some point in the course of the disorder, however, delusions or hallucinations must have occurred for a period of at least two weeks without the presence of a major mood disorder (so as to distinguish the disorder from a mood disorder with psychotic features). The lifetime prevalence of the disorder is estimated to be 0.3% of the general population (APA, 2013).

Like schizophrenia, schizoaffective disorder tends to follow a chronic course that is characterized by persistent difficulties adjusting to the demands of adult life. Also like schizophrenia, the psychotic features of schizoaffective disorder often respond to antipsychotic drugs (Glick et al., 2009; Díaz-Marsá et al., 2009). Schizoaffective disorder and schizophrenia appear to share a genetic link (Bramon & Sham, 2001). We need to discover why this common genetic substrate or predisposition leads to one disorder and not the other.

11 summing up

Schizophrenia

11.1 Define the term *schizophrenia*.

Schizophrenia is a chronic psychotic disorder characterized by acute episodes involving a break with reality, as manifested by features such as delusions, hallucinations, illogical thinking, incoherent speech, and bizarre behavior. Schizophrenia is believed to affect about 1% of the adult population.

11.2 Describe the course of development of schizophrenia.

Schizophrenia usually develops in late adolescence or early adulthood. Its onset may be abrupt or gradual. Gradual onset involves a prodromal phase, a period of gradual deterioration that precedes the onset of acute symptoms. Acute episodes, which may occur periodically throughout life, are typified by clear psychotic symptoms, such as hallucinations and delusions. Between acute episodes, the disorder is characterized by a residual phase in which the person's level of functioning is similar to that which was present during the prodromal phase, but deficits still remain in cognitive, emotional, and social areas of functioning.

11.3 Describe the key features of schizophrenia.

Among the more prominent features of schizophrenia are disorders in the content of thought (delusions) and the form of thought (thought disorder), as well as the presence of often severe perceptual distortions (hallucinations) and emotional disturbances (flattened or inappropriate affect). There are also dysfunctions in brain processes regulating attention to stimuli from the external world.

11.4 Describe psychodynamic and learning theory viewpoints on schizophrenia.

In the traditional psychodynamic model, schizophrenia represents a regression to a psychological state corresponding to early infancy in which the prodding of the id produces bizarre, socially deviant behavior and gives rise to hallucinations and delusions. Learning theorists propose that some forms of schizophrenic behavior may result from lack of social reinforcement, which leads to gradual detachment from the social environment and increased attention to an inner world of fantasy. Modeling and selective reinforcement of bizarre behavior may explain some schizophrenic behaviors in the hospital setting. Evidence based on psychodynamic and learning-based models of schizophrenia have limited value in explaining the development of schizophrenia.

11.5 Describe the biological bases of schizophrenia.

Compelling evidence for a strong genetic component in schizophrenia comes from studies of family patterns of schizophrenia, twin studies, and adoption studies. The mode of genetic transmission remains unknown. Most researchers believe the neurotransmitter dopamine plays a role in schizophrenia, especially in the more flagrant features of the disorder. Viral factors may also be involved, but definite proof of viral involvement is lacking. Evidence also demonstrates that schizophrenia involves both structural and functional abnormalities in the brain.

11.6 Describe the role of family factors in schizophrenia.

Family factors such as CD and EE may act as sources of stress that increase the risk of development or recurrence of schizophrenia among people with a genetic predisposition to the disorder.

11.7 Apply the diathesis–stress model to the development of schizophrenia.

The diathesis–stress model posits that schizophrenia results from an interaction of a genetic predisposition (the diathesis) and environmental stressors (e.g., family conflict, child abuse, emotional deprivation, loss of supportive figures, and early brain trauma).

11.8 Evaluate methods used to treat schizophrenia.

Contemporary treatment approaches tend to be multifaceted, incorporating pharmacological and psychosocial approaches. Antipsychotic medication is not a cure, but it can help control the more flagrant features of the disorder and reduce the need for hospitalization and the risk of recurrent episodes. Psychosocial interventions such as token economy systems and social skills training can help increase adaptive behaviors of schizophrenia patients. Psychosocial rehabilitation approaches help people with schizophrenia adapt more successfully to occupational and social roles in the community. Family intervention programs help families cope with the burdens of care, communicate more clearly, and learn more helpful ways of relating to the patient.

Other Schizophrenia Spectrum Disorders

11.9 Describe the general features of other disorders in the schizophrenia spectrum.

These include schizotypal personality disorder (a personality disorder discussed in Chapter 12), brief psychotic disorder (a psychotic disorder lasting less than a month that may be reactive to a significant stressor), schizophreniform disorder (symptoms identical to those of schizophrenia but lasting for a month to less than six months), schizoaffective disorder (a combination of psychotic symptoms and significant mood disturbance), and delusional disorder (denoted by delusions that may be the only sign of disturbed thinking or behavior).

critical thinking questions

Based on your reading of this chapter, answer the following questions:

- Schizophrenia is perhaps the most disabling type of mental or psychological disorder. What makes it so?

- Have you known anyone who was diagnosed with schizophrenia? What information do you have about the person's family history, family relationships, and stressful life events that might shed light on the development of the disorder?

- How does the diathesis–stress model attempt to account for the development of schizophrenia? What evidence supports the model?

- What are the relative risks and benefits of antipsychotic medication? Why is medication alone not sufficient to treat schizophrenia? Do you believe that people with schizophrenia should be treated indefinitely with antipsychotic drugs? Why or why not?

key terms

schizophrenia 404
prodromal phase 406
residual phase 406
positive symptoms 408

negative symptoms 408
thought disorder 410
hallucinations 412
catatonia 415

dopamine hypothesis 419
endophenotypes 425
tardive dyskinesia 428
brief psychotic disorder 432

schizophreniform disorder 432
delusional disorder 432
erotomania 434
schizoaffective disorder 435

Personality Disorders
and Impulse-Control Disorders

12

truth OR fiction

T ☐ F ☐ People with schizoid personalities may have deeper feelings for animals than they do for people. (p. 443)

T ☐ F ☐ People we call psychopaths are psychotic. (p. 445)

T ☐ F ☐ People with antisocial personalities inevitably run afoul of the law. (p. 445)

T ☐ F ☐ Recent research findings support the popular image of psychopathic murderers as "cold-blooded" killers. (p. 448)

T ☐ F ☐ Many notable figures in history, from Lawrence of Arabia to Adolf Hitler and even Marilyn Monroe, showed signs of borderline personality. (p. 449)

T ☐ F ☐ Men with borderline personalities tend to be self-directed in their aggressive behavior, whereas women are more likely to show outward aggression. (p. 450)

T ☐ F ☐ People with dependent personality disorder have so much difficulty making independent decisions that they may allow their parents to decide whom they will marry. (p. 455)

T ☐ F ☐ Despite years of trying, we still lack evidence that psychotherapy can help people with borderline personality disorder. (p. 470)

T ☐ F ☐ Kleptomania, or compulsive stealing, is usually motivated by poverty. (p. 473)

learning objectives

12.1
Define the concept of personality disorders.

12.2
Identify the three major categories of personality disorders.

12.3
Describe the key features of personality disorders characterized by odd or eccentric behavior.

12.4
Describe the key features of personality disorders characterized by dramatic, emotional, or erratic behavior.

12.5
Describe the key features of personality disorders characterized by anxious or fearful behavior.

12.6
Evaluate the problems associated with the classification of personality disorders.

12.7
Describe the major theoretical perspectives on understanding personality disorders—the psychodynamic, learning, cognitive, family, biological, and sociocultural perspectives.

12.8
Evaluate methods used to treat personality disorders.

12.9
Define the concept of impulse-control disorders and describe the features of several major types.

"I" "My Dark Place"

She wrote about herself on an online bulletin board, sharing her personal anguish with strangers, wanting others to know just how deeply she had suffered. She wrote there were times when she entered a "dark place" in which she would experience an urge to cut herself at different places on her body, mostly on her arms and legs. She later learned that her self-mutilation or cutting was a symptom of borderline personality disorder or BPD. She could not run or hide from these urges to cut herself and felt powerless to control them. She recounted how she had battled depression since she was a young girl and had began cutting herself at the age of 8. The cutting would bring a momentary sense of relief, blotting out the negative feelings. Strangely, it became a way in which she could comfort herself and block the deeper pain she felt inside. Now as a young adult she realizes she must find other ways of relieving her emotional pain, but recognizes it will be a long process that will take a great deal of work and therapy.

Source: Adapted from an anonymous posting on an online support site, *New York City Voices*

Like this person, people with borderline personality disorder are often severely depressed and turn to self-mutilation in a twisted attempt to escape from emotional pain. But their problems lie deeper than depression. They involve the kinds of rigid, inflexible, and maladaptive behavior patterns that clinicians classify as *personality disorders*. These behavior patterns involve maladaptive expressions of personality traits, which have far-reaching consequences for the person's psychological adjustment and relationships with others.

All of us have particular styles of behavior and ways of relating to others. Some of us are orderly, others sloppy. Some of us prefer solitary pursuits; others are more social. Some of us are followers; others are leaders. Some of us seem immune to rejection by others, whereas others avoid social initiatives for fear of getting shot down. When behavior patterns become so inflexible or maladaptive that they cause significant personal distress or impair people's social or occupational functioning, they may be classified as personality disorders.

Later in the chapter, we discuss another class of disorders, called impulse-control disorders, which are also characterized by maladaptive patterns of behavior. With impulse-control disorders, such as kleptomania and intermittent explosive disorder, the maladaptive behaviors take the form of failure to resist impulses that lead to harmful consequences. Another feature that personality disorders and impulse disorders have in common is that people diagnosed with these disorders often fail to see how their own behaviors are seriously disrupting their lives.

As an historical note, gambling was recognized in earlier editions of the *DSM* as a type of impulse-control disorder (called *pathological gambling*), as it is characterized by difficulty controlling an impulse to gamble. However, the close relationships between compulsive gambling and addictive disorders led to its reclassification as a type of addictive disorder in *DSM-5* that is called *gambling disorder* (see Chapter 8).

Types of Personality Disorders

In most of us by the age of thirty, the character has set like plaster, and will never soften again.

—*William James*

Personality disorders are characterized by overly rigid and maladaptive patterns of behavior and ways of relating to others that reflect extreme variations on underlying personality traits, such as undue suspiciousness, excessive emotionality, and impulsivity (Clark, 2009). These problem traits become evident by adolescence or early adulthood. They continue through much of adult life and become so deeply ingrained that they are often highly resistant to change. The warning signs of personality disorders may emerge in childhood based on problem behaviors involving disturbed conduct, depression, anxiety, and immaturity. An estimated 6% to 10% of the general population are believed to have personality disorders (Samuels, 2011).

People with personality disorders often fail to see how their own behaviors are seriously disrupting their lives. They may blame others for the problems they have, rather than take a long, hard look in the mirror. Take a moment to think about the person who stares back at you in the bathroom mirror. What is that person like? How would you describe that person's traits or behavioral characteristics? How do these attributes influence the person's behavior and ways of relating to others? Is the person shy or outgoing? Reliable and conscientious, or lax and undependable? Anxious or calm? What makes this person unique? What accounts for the consistency in the person's behavior from place to place and time to time?

Let's first define what we mean by the term *personality*. Psychologists use the term *personality* to describe the set of distinctive psychological traits and behavioral characteristics that make each of us unique and help account for the consistency of our behavior. No two people are completely alike, not even identical twins. We each have our own distinctive ways of relating to others and interacting with the world at large. But people with personality disorders have exaggerated or excessive personality traits that lead to personal distress or significantly interfere with the person's ability to function effectively in their home, school, or work environments and the communities in which they live.

Despite the self-defeating consequences of their behavior, people with personality disorders typically don't believe they need to change. Using psychodynamic terms, the *DSM* notes that people with personality disorders tend to perceive their traits as **ego syntonic**—as natural parts of themselves. Consequently, people with personality disorders are more likely to be brought to the attention of mental health professionals by others than to seek services themselves. In contrast, people with anxiety disorders (Chapter 5) or mood disorders (Chapter 7) tend to view their disturbed behaviors as **ego dystonic.** They do not see their behaviors as parts of their self-identities and are thus more likely to seek help to relieve the distress caused by these behaviors. Although personality traits may not be as hardened after the age of 30 as the famed early psychologist William James held, the extreme variations of personality traits that we find in personality disorders tend to be stable over time.

The *DSM* groups personality disorders into three clusters:

Cluster A: People who are perceived as odd or eccentric. This cluster includes paranoid, schizoid, and schizotypal personality disorders.

Cluster B: People whose behavior is overly dramatic, emotional, or erratic. This grouping consists of antisocial, borderline, histrionic, and narcissistic personality disorders.

Cluster C: People who often appear anxious or fearful. This cluster includes avoidant, dependent, and obsessive–compulsive personality disorders.

Table 12.1 provides an overview of the personality disorders discussed in this chapter. We should also note that people with personality disorders often have other diagnosable psychological disorders. For example, a person may be diagnosed with major depression, as well as with a personality disorder such as borderline personality disorder.

12.2 **Identify** the three major categories of personality disorders.

Personality Disorders Characterized by Odd or Eccentric Behavior

This group of personality disorders includes paranoid, schizoid, and schizotypal disorders. People with these disorders often have difficulty relating to others or show little or no interest in developing social relationships. Here we consider paranoid and schizoid personality disorders.

12.3 **Describe** the key features of personality disorders characterized by odd or eccentric behavior.

TABLE 12.1
Overview of Personality Disorders

Disorder	Lifetime Prevalence in Population (approx.)	Description
Personality Disorders Characterized by Odd or Eccentric Behavior		
Paranoid Personality Disorder	2.3% to 4.4% across samples	Pervasive suspiciousness of the motives of others but without outright paranoid delusions
Schizoid Personality Disorder	3.1% to 4.9% across samples	Social aloofness and shallow or blunted emotions
Schizotypal Personality Disorder	4.6% (based on U.S. sample)	Persistent difficulty forming close social relationships and odd or peculiar beliefs and behaviors without clear psychotic features
Personality Disorders Characterized by Dramatic, Emotional, or Erratic Behavior		
Antisocial Personality Disorder	Upward of 6% in men, 1% in women	Chronic antisocial behavior, callous treatment of others, irresponsible behavior, and lack of remorse for wrongdoing
Borderline Personality Disorder	1.6% to 5.9%	Tumultuous moods and stormy relationships with others, unstable self-image, and lack of impulse control
Histrionic Personality Disorder	1.8%	Overly dramatic and emotional behavior; demands to be the center of attention; excessive needs for reassurance, praise, and approval
Narcissistic Personality Disorder	Under 1% to 6.2% across samples	Grandiose sense of self; extreme needs for admiration
Personality Disorders Characterized by Anxious or Fearful Behavior		
Avoidant Personality Disorder	About 2.4%	Chronic pattern of avoiding social relationships due to fears of rejection
Dependent Personality Disorder	Less than 1%	Excessive dependence on others and difficulty making independent decisions
Obsessive–Compulsive Personality Disorder	2.1% to 7.9% across samples	Excessive needs for orderliness and perfectionism, excessive attention to detail, rigid ways of relating to others

Sources: Prevalence rates derived from APA, 2013; Cale & Lilienfeld, 2002; Kessler et al., 1994.

PARANOID PERSONALITY DISORDER The defining trait of the **paranoid personality disorder** is pervasive suspiciousness—the tendency to interpret other people's behavior as deliberately threatening or demeaning. People with the disorder are excessively mistrustful of others, and their relationships suffer for it. Although they may be suspicious of coworkers and supervisors, they can generally maintain employment.

The following case illustrates the unwarranted suspicion and reluctance to confide in others that typifies people with paranoid personalities.

> ### → A Case of Paranoid Personality Disorder
>
> An 85-year-old retired businessman was interviewed by a social worker to determine health care needs for himself and his wife. The man had no history of treatment for a mental disorder. He appeared to be in good health and mentally alert. He and his wife had been married for 60 years, and it appeared that his wife was the only person he'd ever really trusted. He had always been suspicious of others. He would not reveal personal information to anyone but his wife, believing that others were out to take advantage of him. He had refused offers of help from other acquaintances because he suspected their motives. When called on the telephone, he would refuse to give out his name until he determined the nature of the caller's business. He'd always involved himself in "useful work" to occupy his time, even during his 20 years of retirement. He spent a good deal of time monitoring his investments and had altercations with his stockbroker when errors on his monthly statement prompted suspicion that his broker was attempting to cover up fraudulent transactions.
>
> → *Adapted from Spitzer et al., 1994, pp. 211–213*

People who have paranoid personality disorder tend to be overly sensitive to criticism, whether real or imagined. They take offense at the smallest slight. They are readily angered and hold grudges when they think they have been mistreated. They are unlikely to confide in others because they believe that personal information may be used against them. They question the sincerity and trustworthiness of friends and associates. A smile or a glance may be viewed with suspicion. As a result, they have few friends and intimate relationships. When they do form an intimate relationship, they may suspect infidelity, even without evidence. They tend to remain hypervigilant, as if they must be on the lookout against harm. They deny blame for misdeeds, even when warranted, and are perceived by others as cold, aloof, scheming, devious, and humorless. They tend to be argumentative and may launch repeated lawsuits against those who they believe have mistreated them.

Clinicians need to weigh cultural and sociopolitical factors when arriving at a diagnosis of paranoid personality disorder. For example, members of immigrant or ethnic minority groups, political refugees, or people from other cultures may seem guarded or defensive, but this behavior may reflect unfamiliarity with the language, customs, or rules and regulations of the majority culture or cultural mistrust arising from a history of neglect or oppression. Such behavior should not be confused with paranoid personality disorder.

Although people with paranoid personality disorder harbor exaggerated and unwarranted suspicions, they do not have the outright paranoid delusions that characterize the thought patterns of people with paranoid schizophrenia (e.g., believing the FBI is out to get them). People who have paranoid personalities are unlikely to seek treatment; they see others as causing their problems. The reported prevalence of paranoid personality disorder in the general population ranges from 2.3% to 4.4% across samples (APA, 2013). The disorder is diagnosed more often in men than in women among people receiving mental health treatment.

SCHIZOID PERSONALITY DISORDER Social isolation is the cardinal feature of **schizoid personality disorder.** Often described as a loner or an eccentric, the person with a schizoid personality lacks interest in social relationships. The person's emotions usually appear shallow or blunted, but not to the degree found in schizophrenia (see Chapter 11). People with this disorder rarely, if ever, experience strong anger, joy, or sadness. They may appear distant from others or aloof. Their faces tend to show no emotional expression, and they rarely exchange social smiles or nods. They seem indifferent to criticism or praise and appear to be wrapped up in abstract ideas rather than in thoughts about people. Although they prefer to remain distant from others, they maintain better contact with reality than people with schizophrenia do. The prevalence of the disorder in the general population remains unknown. Men with this disorder rarely date or marry. Women with the disorder are more likely to accept romantic advances passively and to marry, but they seldom initiate relationships or develop strong attachments to their partners.

We may find inconsistencies between the outer appearances and the inner lives of people with schizoid personalities (Akhtar, 2003). For example, they may appear to have little appetite for sex, but harbor voyeuristic wishes or become absorbed with pornography. However, the apparent social distance and aloofness of people with schizoid personalities may be somewhat superficial. They may harbor exquisite sensitivity, deep curiosities about people, and wishes for love that they cannot express. In some cases, sensitivity is expressed in deep feelings for animals rather than people. **T / F**

Schizoid personality. It is normal to be reserved about displaying one's feelings, especially when one is among strangers, but people with schizoid personalities rarely express emotions and are distant and aloof. Yet the emotions of people with schizoid personalities are not as shallow or blunted as those of people with schizophrenia.

Schizotypal Personality Disorder

People with **schizotypal personality disorder** have persistent difficulties in forming close relationships with others and display behaviors, mannerisms, and thought patterns that seem peculiar or odd, but not disturbed enough (not a "break with reality") to merit a diagnosis of schizophrenia.

People with schizotypal personality disorder lack a coherent sense of self. They may have a distorted self-concept or lack self-direction (e.g., not knowing where they are going in life). They also lack the capacity for empathy, showing a lack of understanding for how their own behavior affects others or misinterpreting other people's behaviors or motives. They may be especially anxious in social situations, even when interacting with familiar people. They have difficulty forming close relationships, or even any relationships, a finding also reported in other cultures, such as in a Chinese population in Singapore (Guoa et al., 2010). The social anxiety of schizotypal patients is often linked to paranoid thinking (e.g., fears that others mean them harm) rather than to concerns about being rejected or evaluated negatively by others. People with schizotypal personality disorder often have other co-occurring emotional disorders, such as major depression and anxiety disorders, as well as an increased risk of suicidal behavior (Lentz et al., 2010).

People with schizotypal personality disorder may experience unusual perceptions or illusions, such as feeling the presence of a deceased family member in the room. They realize, however, that the person is not actually there. They may become unduly suspicious of others or paranoid in their thinking. They may develop *ideas of reference*, such as the believing that others are talking about them behind their backs. They may engage in *magical thinking*, such as believing they possess a "sixth sense" (i.e., can foretell the future) or that others can sense their feelings. They may attach unusual meanings to words. Their own speech may be vague or unusually abstract, but it is not incoherent or filled with the loose associations that characterize schizophrenia. They may appear unkempt, display unusual mannerisms, and engage in unusual behaviors, such as talking to themselves in the presence of others. Their thought processes also appear odd and are marked by vague, metaphorical, or stereotyped thinking. Their faces may register little emotion. They may fail to exchange smiles with, or nod at, others. Or they may appear silly and smile and laugh at the wrong times. They tend to be socially withdrawn and aloof, with few, if any,

12.4 Describe the key features of personality disorders characterized by dramatic, emotional, or erratic behavior.

close friends or confidants. They seem to be especially anxious around unfamiliar people. We can see evidence of the social aloofness and illusions that are often associated with schizotypal personality disorder in the following case example:

> **Jonathan: A Case of Schizotypal Personality Disorder**
> Jonathan, a 27-year-old auto mechanic, had few friends and preferred reading science fiction novels to socializing with other people. He seldom joined in conversations. At times, he seemed to be lost in his thoughts, and his coworkers would have to whistle to get his attention when he was working on a car. He often showed a "queer" expression on his face. Perhaps the most unusual feature of his behavior was his reported intermittent experience of "feeling" his deceased mother standing nearby. These illusions were reassuring to him, and he looked forward to their occurrence. Jonathan realized they were not real. He never tried to reach out to touch the apparition, knowing it would disappear as soon as he drew closer. It was enough, he said, to feel her presence.
>
> *From the Author's Files*

Schizotypal personality disorder may be slightly more common in males than in females and is believed to affect about 4.6% of the general population (APA, 2013). Investigators also find higher rates of the disorder among African Americans than among Caucasians or Hispanic Americans (Chavira et al., 2003). However, clinicians need to be careful not to label as schizotypal certain behavior patterns that reflect culturally determined beliefs or religious rituals, such as beliefs in voodoo and other magical beliefs.

As discussed in Chapter 11, schizotypal personality disorder is conceptualized by *DSM-5* as part of the schizophrenia spectrum of disorders. Schizophrenia and schizotypal personality disorder appear to share a common genetic basis (Chemerinski et al., 2012). Moreover, evidence from a brain-imaging study also shows that brain abnormalities in patients with schizotypal personality disorder are similar to those found in schizophrenia patients (Dickey et al., 2006, 2007). We can speculate that the emergence of schizophrenia in people with this shared genetic predisposition may be determined by the presence of other factors such as stressful life experiences. However, it's important to point out that relatively few people diagnosed with schizotypal personality disorder eventually develop schizophrenia or other psychotic disorders (APA, 2013).

Antisocial personality. Serial killer Ted Bundy, shown here shortly before his execution, killed without feeling or remorse but also displayed some of the superficial charm seen in some people with antisocial personality disorder.

Personality Disorders Characterized by Dramatic, Emotional, or Erratic Behavior

This cluster of personality disorders includes the antisocial, borderline, histrionic, and narcissistic types. People with these disorders exhibit behavior patterns that are excessive, unpredictable, or self-centered; they also have difficulty forming and maintaining relationships and show antisocial behavior.

ANTISOCIAL PERSONALITY DISORDER People with **antisocial personality disorder** are *antisocial* in the sense that they often violate the rights of others, disregard social norms and conventions, and, in some cases, break the law. They show a lack of concern or callous indifference about violating the rights of others and using other people for their own gain. We should note they are not "antisocial" in the colloquial sense of seeking to avoid people.

People with antisocial personalities tend to be impulsive and fail to live up to their commitments to others (Swann et al., 2009). Yet they often show a superficial charm and possess at least average intelligence. They frequently have little, if any, anxiety when faced with threatening situations and lack feelings of guilt or remorse following wrongdoing (Goldstein et al., 2006; Kiehl, 2006). Punishment may have little or no effect on their behavior. Although parents and others have usually punished them for their misdeeds, they persist in leading irresponsible and impulsive lives.

Antisocial personality disorder occurs more commonly in men than in women, with prevalence rates based on community samples ranging from about 1% in women to nearly 6% in men (Cale & Lilienfeld, 2002; Kessler et al., 1994; see Figure 12.1). The diagnosis is limited to people 18 years of age or older. However, the pattern of antisocial behavior that characterizes antisocial personality disorder begins in childhood or adolescence and extends into adulthood (e.g., Blonigen et al., 2006; Lahey et al., 2005). Antisocial behaviors emerge before the age of 15 in the form of *conduct disorder* (discussed further in Chapter 13). These early forms of antisocial behavior may include truancy, running away, initiating physical fights, use of weapons, forcing someone into sexual activities, physical cruelty to people or animals, deliberate destruction of property or fire setting, lying, stealing, robbery, and assaulting others.

Clinicians once used terms such as *psychopath* and *sociopath* to refer to people who today are classified as having antisocial personalities—people whose behavior is amoral, asocial, and impulsive, and who lack remorse and shame. Some clinicians continue to use these terms interchangeably with *antisocial personality*. The roots of the word *psychopath* focus on the idea that there is something amiss (pathological) in the individual's psychological functioning. The roots of *sociopath* center on the person's social deviance. **T / F**

Over time, antisocial and criminal behavior associated with the disorder tends to decline with age and may disappear by the time the person reaches the age of 40, but not so for the underlying personality traits associated with the disorder—traits such as egocentricity; manipulativeness; lack of empathy, guilt, or remorse; and callousness toward others. These appear to be relatively stable even with increasing age (Harpur & Hare, 1994).

Much of our attention in this chapter focuses on antisocial personality disorder. Historically, this is the personality disorder that has been most extensively studied by scholars and researchers.

SOCIOCULTURAL FACTORS AND ANTISOCIAL PERSONALITY DISORDER Antisocial personality disorder cuts across all racial and ethnic groups. The disorder is most common, however, among people in lower socioeconomic groups. One explanation is that people with antisocial personality disorder drift downward occupationally, perhaps because their antisocial behavior makes it difficult for them to hold steady jobs or to progress upward. People from lower socioeconomic levels may also be more likely to have parents who modeled antisocial behavior. However, the diagnosis may also be misapplied to people living in hard-pressed communities who engage in seemingly antisocial behaviors as a survival strategy (APA, 2013).

Antisocial Behavior and Criminality

We tend to think of antisocial behavior as synonymous with criminal behavior. Although antisocial personality disorder is associated with an increased risk of criminality (Kosson, Lorenz, & Newman, 2006), not all criminals have antisocial personalities, nor do all people with antisocial personality disorder become criminals. Many people with antisocial personality disorders are law abiding and successful in their careers, even though they may treat others in a callous and insensitive manner. **T / F**

Investigators have begun to view antisocial personality as composed of two somewhat independent dimensions. The first is a *personality dimension*. It consists of traits such as superficial charm, selfishness, lack of empathy, callous and remorseless use of

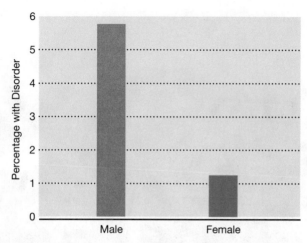

FIGURE 12.1

Lifetime prevalences of antisocial personality disorder by gender. Antisocial personality disorder is more than five times as common among men as among women. However, the prevalence of the disorder has been rising more rapidly among women in recent years.

Source: National Comorbidity Survey (Kessler et al., 1994).

truth OR fiction

People we call psychopaths are psychotic.

☑ **FALSE**   People we call psychopaths have psychopathic personalities. They may be diagnosed with antisocial personality disorder, but do not suffer from psychosis (manifested by a break with reality, as in schizophrenia).

truth OR fiction

People with antisocial personalities inevitably run afoul of the law.

☑ **FALSE**   Not all criminals show signs of psychopathy and not all people with psychopathic personalities become criminals.

Criminality or antisocial personality disorder? It is likely that many prison inmates could be diagnosed with antisocial personality disorder; however, people may become criminals or delinquents not because of a disordered personality but because they were raised in environments or exposed to subcultures that both encouraged and rewarded criminal behavior.

others, and disregard for others' feelings and welfare. This type of psychopathic personality applies to people who have these kinds of psychopathic traits but don't become lawbreakers.

The second dimension is a *behavioral dimension.* It is characterized by the adoption of a generally unstable and antisocial lifestyle, including frequent problems with the law, poor employment history, and unstable relationships. These two dimensions are not entirely separate; many antisocial individuals show evidence of both sets of traits.

We should also note that some people do not become criminals or delinquents because of a disordered personality but because they were reared in environments or subcultures that rewarded criminal behavior. Although criminal behavior is deviant to society at large, it is normal by the standards of the subculture. Also, lack of remorse, which is a cardinal feature of antisocial personality disorder, does not characterize all criminals. Some criminals regret their crimes, and judges and parole boards consider evidence of remorse when passing sentence or recommending a prisoner for parole.

Despite the popular impression that criminals are all psychopaths, and vice versa, only about half of prison inmates could be diagnosed with antisocial personality disorder (Robins, Locke, & Reiger, 1991). Moreover, only a minority of people diagnosed with antisocial personality disorder run afoul of the law. Many fewer (thankfully!) fit the stereotype of the psychopathic killer popularized in films such as *The Silence of the Lambs.*

Profile of the Antisocial Personality Antisocial personality or psychopathy is associated with a wide range of traits, including failure to conform to social norms, irresponsibility, aimlessness and lack of long-term goals or plans, impulsive behavior, outright lawlessness, violence, chronic unemployment, marital problems, lack of remorse or empathy, substance abuse or alcoholism, and a disregard for the truth and for the feelings and needs of others. In a classic work in the field originally published in 1941, Hervey Cleckley (1976) argued that the characteristics that define the psychopathic or antisocial personality—self-centeredness, irresponsibility, impulsivity, and insensitivity to the needs of others—exist not only among criminals but also among many respected members of the community, including doctors, lawyers, politicians, and business executives.

More recent work on measuring psychopathic traits shows they can be grouped in terms of four basic factors or dimensions (Neumann & Hare, 2008): (1) an *interpersonal factor* characterized by superficiality, grandiosity, and deceitfulness; (2) an *affective factor* characterized by lack of remorse and empathy and a failure to accept responsibility for misbehavior; (3) a *lifestyle factor* characterized by impulsivity and lack of goals; and (4) an *antisocial factor* characterized by poor behavioral control and antisocial behavior.

Irresponsibility, a common trait among people with antisocial personalities, may be seen in a personal history dotted by repeated, unexplained absences from work, abandonment of jobs without having other job opportunities to fall back on, or long stretches of unemployment. Irresponsibility often extends to financial matters, where there may be repeated failure to repay debts, to pay child support, or to meet other financial responsibilities to one's family and dependents. The key clinical features of antisocial personality disorder are shown in Table 12.2. Not all of these behaviors need to be present in every case. The following case represents a number of these antisocial characteristics.

"Twisted Sister": A Case of Antisocial Behavior

The 19-year-old male is brought by ambulance to the hospital emergency room in a state of cocaine intoxication. He's wearing a T-shirt with the imprint "Twisted Sister" on the front, and he sports a punk-style haircut. His mother is called and sounds groggy and confused on the phone; the doctors must coax her to come to the hospital. She later tells the doctors that her son has arrests for shoplifting and for driving while intoxicated. She suspects that he takes drugs, although she has no direct evidence. She believes that he is performing fairly well at school and has been a star member of the basketball team.

It turns out that her son has been lying to her. In actuality, he never completed high school and never played on the basketball team. A day later, his head cleared, the patient tells his doctors, almost boastfully, that his drug and alcohol use started at the age of 13, and that by the time he was 17, he was regularly using a variety of psychoactive substances, including alcohol, speed, marijuana, and cocaine. Lately, however, he has preferred cocaine. He and his friends frequently participate in drug and alcohol binges. At times, they each drink a case of beer in a day along with downing other drugs. He steals car radios from parked cars and money from his mother to support his drug habit, which he justifies by adopting a (partial) "Robin Hood" attitude—that is, taking money only from people who have lots of it.

Adapted from Spitzer et al., 1994, pp. 81–83

TABLE 12.2
Key Features of Antisocial Personality Disorder

Features	Examples
Failure to adhere to social rules, social norms, or legal codes	Engaging in criminal behavior that may result in arrest, such as destruction of property, engaging in unlawful occupations, stealing, or harassing others
Aggressive or hostile behavior	Repeatedly getting into physical confrontations and fights with others or assaulting others, even one's own children or spouse
Lack of responsible behavior	Failure to maintain regular employment due to chronic absences or lateness or failure to seek gainful employment when it is available; failure to honor financial obligations, such as failing to meet child support responsibilities or defaulting on debts; failure to establish or maintain a stable monogamous relationship
Impulsive behavior	Acting on impulse and failing to plan ahead or consider consequences; traveling around without any clear employment opportunities or goals
Lack of truthfulness	Repeatedly lying, conning others, or using aliases for personal gain or pleasure
Reckless behavior	Taking undue risks to one's safety or the safety of others, such as by driving at unsafe speeds or driving while intoxicated
Lack of remorse for misdeeds	Lack of concern or remorse for the harm done to others by one's behavior, or rationalizing harm to others

"In Cold Blood": Peering into the Minds of Psychopathic Murderers

The popular image we hold of the psychopathic murderer is of a "cold-blooded" killer, someone motivated by external goals in carrying out calculating, premeditated murder. But is this image supported by hard evidence?

Canadian researchers compared homicides committed by psychopathic offenders with those committed by nonpsychopathic offenders in a sample of 125 incarcerated murderers (Woodworth & Porter, 2002). They expected that homicides committed by the psychopathic offenders would fit the profile of a cold-blooded killing, whereas those committed by nonpsychopathic offenders would be "crimes of passion" (impulsive, "hot-headed," angry reactions to provocative situations).

The sample was drawn from two Canadian federal institutions, one in British Columbia and the other in Nova Scotia. The investigators administered a widely used and well-validated measure of psychopathy to classify offenders as psychopathic. The results supported the hypothesis that psychopathic offenders were more likely to have committed cold-blooded homicides—intentional acts motivated by goals such as obtaining drugs, money, sex, or revenge but without any emotional trigger. More than 90% (93%) of the homicides committed by the psychopathic offenders fit this profile, as compared to 48% of the murders committed by offenders who were not psychopathic.

Interestingly, the image of the "cold-blooded" psychopathic killer does not square with the long-recognized belief that

psychopathic personalities often engage in impulsive, acting-out behavior. The investigators suggest that psychopathic offenders may engage in *selective impulsivity* by constraining their impulses to perform such an extreme act as murder. With such high stakes involved (e.g., lifetime incarceration if convicted), the psychopathic offender may adopt a more calculated role when carrying out these acts.

However chilling the results of this study, they help us to better understand the psychological aspects of homicide. In that respect, they may help homicide investigators narrow the scope of their investigations by focusing on personality profiles of offenders who are likely to commit particular types of crimes. T / F

truth OR fiction

Recent research findings support the popular image of psychopathic murderers as "cold-blooded" killers.

☑ **TRUE** Canadian researchers found that psychopathic murderers incarcerated for homicide were more likely than other incarcerated murderers to have committed cold-blooded homicides.

Although this case is suggestive of antisocial personality disorder, the diagnosis was maintained as provisional because the interviewer could not determine whether the deviant behavior (lying, stealing, skipping school) began before the age of 15.

BORDERLINE PERSONALITY DISORDER **Borderline personality disorder (BPD)** is characterized by features such as a deep sense of emptiness, an unstable self-image, a history of turbulent and unstable relationships, dramatic mood changes, impulsivity, difficulty regulating negative emotions, self-injurious behavior, and recurrent suicidal behaviors (Gratz et al., 2010; Krause-Utz et al., 2013; Salzer et al., 2013; Soloff & Chiappetta, 2012).

People with borderline personality disorder tend to be uncertain about their personal identities—their values, goals, careers, perhaps even their sexual orientations. This instability in self-image or personal identity leaves them with nagging feelings of emptiness and boredom. They cannot tolerate being alone and make desperate attempts to avoid feelings of abandonment. Fear of abandonment leads them to become clinging and demanding in their personal relationships, but their clinging often pushes away the very people on whom they depend. Rejection may enrage them, putting further strain on their relationships. Their feelings toward others are intense and shifting. They alternate between extremes of adulation (when their needs are met)

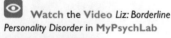

Watch the Video *Liz: Borderline Personality Disorder* in **MyPsychLab**

and loathing (when they feel scorned). They tend to view other people as either all good or all bad and abruptly shift in their appraisals of others from one extreme to the other. As a result, they may flit from partner to partner in a series of brief and stormy relationships. People they had idealized are treated with contempt when relationships end or when they feel that other people fail to meet their needs.

Borderline personality disorder is believed to affect about 1.6% to 5.9% of the general adult population (APA, 2013; Kernberg & Michels, 2009; Paris, 2010). Although women more frequently receive the diagnosis than men, it remains undetermined whether this gender difference reflects diagnostic practices or underlying differences in the prevalence rates of the disorder for men and women. The disorder appears to be more common among Latino Americans than White European Americans and African Americans (Chavira et al., 2003). The factors accounting for these ethnic differences require further investigation. Many notable figures have been described as having personality features associated with borderline personality disorder, including Marilyn Monroe, Lawrence of Arabia, Adolf Hitler, and the philosopher Sören Kierkegaard. **T / F**

The term *borderline personality* was originally used to refer to individuals whose behavior appeared to be on the border between neuroses and psychoses. People with borderline personality disorder generally maintain better contact with reality than people with psychoses, although they may show fleeting psychotic behaviors during times of stress. Generally speaking, they are more severely impaired than most people with neuroses but not as dysfunctional as those with psychotic disorders.

One of the central features of borderline personality disorder is difficulty regulating emotions (Baer et al., 2012). People with borderline personality disorder have mood changes that run the gamut from anger and irritability to depression and anxiety (Weissman, 2011). They tend to be troubled by intense emotional pain and chronic feelings of anger, which often gives rise to angry outbursts (Ferraz et al., 2009). Feelings of emptiness and shame are common, together with a long-standing negative self-image (Gunderson, 2011). They often lack the ability to thoughtfully plan their actions in advance and will act impulsively without considering the consequences (Gvirts et al., 2012; Millon, 2011). They may be prone to fighting others or smashing things. They may fly into a rage at the slightest sign of rejection or for little or no reason at all, as this woman recounts about her husband:

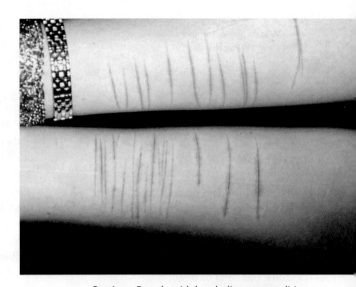

Cutting. People with borderline personalities may engage in impulsive acts of self-mutilation, such as cutting themselves, perhaps as a means of temporarily blocking or escaping from deep, emotional pain.

truth OR fiction

Many notable figures in history, from Lawrence of Arabia to Adolf Hitler and even Marilyn Monroe, showed signs of borderline personality.

☑ **TRUE** Many notable public figures have shown personality traits associated with borderline personality disorder.

"I" Walking on Eggshells

They may fly into a rage at the slightest sign of rejection or for little or no reason at all.

Living with a borderline person, as one women put it, is like "walking on eggshells" (Mason & Kreger, 1998). She described her borderline husband as having two personalities, a "Jovial Jekyll" and a "Horrible Hyde." Living with him, she said, was heaven one minute but hell the next. He would often explode at a moment's notice, sometimes because she spoke too quickly or too soon, or in the wrong tone of voice, or even with the wrong facial expression. Just about anything would set him off an emotional tirade. We should recognize that rage in borderline personalities masks deeper emotional pain. It may cover up deep-seated fears of abandonment or rejection or a need to hurt others because they themselves have been hurt or abused by others.

Watch the Video *Mary: Non-Suicidal Self-Injury* in **MyPsychLab**

truth OR fiction

Men with borderline personalities tend to be self-directed in their aggressive behavior, whereas women are more likely to show outward aggression.

☑ **FALSE** Men with borderline personalities tend to direct their aggressive impulses toward themselves, whereas women are generally more outwardly directed in their aggressive behavior

People with borderline personalities often act on impulse, such as eloping with someone they have just met. Impulsive and unpredictable behavior is often self-destructive, involving self-mutilation (for example, cutting) and suicidal gestures or actual attempts, especially when underlying fears of abandonment are kindled (Gunderson, 2011; Leichsenring et al., 2011; Welch et al., 2008). Maladaptive behaviors such as cutting, substance use, and lashing out in anger may be attempts at controlling intense negative feelings (Baer et al., 2012). About three out of four people with borderline personality disorder make suicide attempts and about one in ten eventually commits suicide.

Women with borderline personality disorder tend to show more inwardly directed aggression, such as cutting or other forms of self-mutilation. Men with borderline personality disorder tend to show more outward expressions of aggression (Schmahl & Bremner, 2006). Suicide attempts and nonsuicidal self-injuries may be motivated by the desire to escape from troubling emotions. 👁 **T / F**

Borderline personality disorder is usually diagnosed in early adulthood, although signs of the disorder are often seen in adolescence (Gunderson, 2011). Impulsive behavior may include spending sprees, gambling, drug abuse, unsafe sexual activity, reckless driving, binge eating, or shoplifting. Impulsive acts of self-mutilation, such as the self-inflicted cutting described at the opening of this chapter, may also involve scratching the wrists or even touching burning cigarettes on the arms. The following dialogue illustrates this type of behavior.

CLIENT: I've got such repressed anger in me; what happens is . . . I can't *feel* it; I get anxiety attacks. I get very nervous, smoke too many cigarettes. So what happens to me is I tend to *explode.* Into tears or hurting myself or whatever . . . because I don't know how to contend with all those mixed up feelings.

INTERVIEWER: What was the more recent example of such an "explosion"?

CLIENT: I was alone at home a few months ago; I was frightened! I was trying to get in touch with my boyfriend and I couldn't. . . . He was nowhere to be found. All my friends seemed to be busy that night and I had no one to talk to. . . . I just got more and more nervous and more and more agitated. Finally, *bang!* . . . I took out a cigarette and lit it and stuck it into my forearm. I don't know why I did it because I didn't really care for him all that much. I guess I felt I had to do something dramatic. . . .

—*Adapted from Stone, 1980, p. 400*

Self-mutilation is sometimes an expression of anger or a means of manipulating others. Such acts may be intended to counteract self-reported feelings of "numbness," particularly in times of stress. Individuals with borderline personality disorder often have very troubled relationships with their families and others (Gratz et al., 2008; Johnson et al., 2006). They often had troubling childhood experiences, such as parental losses or separations, harsh punishment or maltreatment, parental neglect or lack of nurturing, or witnessing violence. They tend to view their relationships as rife with hostility and to perceive others as rejecting and abandoning. They also tend to be difficult to work with in psychotherapy (Silk, 2008). They tend to demand a great deal of support from therapists, calling them at all hours or acting suicidal to elicit support, or dropping out of therapy prematurely. Their feelings toward therapists, as toward other people, undergo rapid alterations between idealization and outrage. Psychoanalysts interpret these abrupt shifts in feelings as signs of **splitting,** or inability to reconcile the positive and negative aspects of one's experience of oneself and others.

People with borderline personality disorder may cling desperately to others whom they first idealize, but then shift abruptly to utter contempt when they perceive the other person—a therapist, lover, family member, close friend—as rejecting them or failing to meet their emotional needs. The unfortunate irony is that their desperate attempts to obtain emotional support places unreasonable demands on others, which can result in pushing others away, leading to perceptions of rejection and a belief that the other person never truly was "there for them." Perceptions of rejection are thus linked to rage (Berenson et al., 2011).

A saving grace is that many features of borderline personality, including suicidal thinking, turbulent emotions, self-harm, and impulsivity, tend to improve over a period of years (Bateman, 2012; Gunderson et al., 2011). Investigators also comment that impulsivity tends to "burn out" with increasing age (Stevenson, Meares, & Comerford, 2003).

HISTRIONIC PERSONALITY DISORDER **Histrionic personality disorder** is characterized by excessive emotionality and an overwhelming need to be the center of attention. The term is derived from the Latin *histrio*, which means "actor." People with histrionic personality disorder tend to be dramatic and emotional, but their emotions seem shallow, exaggerated, and volatile. The disorder was formerly called *hysterical personality*. The following case example illustrates the excessively dramatic behaviors typical of someone with histrionic personality disorder.

Over the top? Not all people who dress outrageously or flamboyantly have histrionic personalities. What other personality features characterize people with histrionic personality disorder?

> ### Marcella: A Case of Histrionic Personality Disorder
>
> Marcella was a 36-year-old, attractive, but overly made up woman who was dressed in tight pants and high heels. Her hair was in a bird's nest of the type that had been popular when she was a teenager. Her social life seemed to bounce from relationship to relationship, from crisis to crisis. Marcella sought help from the psychologist at this time because her 17-year-old daughter, Nancy, had just been hospitalized for cutting her wrists. Nancy lived with Marcella and Marcella's current boyfriend, Morris, and there were constant arguments in the apartment. Marcella recounted the disputes that took place with high drama, waving her hands, clanging the bangles that hung from her bracelets, and then clutching her breast. It was difficult having Nancy live at home because Nancy had expensive tastes, was "always looking for attention," and flirted with Morris as a way of "flaunting her youth." Marcella saw herself as a doting mother and denied any possibility that she was in competition with her daughter.
>
> Marcella came for a handful of sessions, during which she basically ventilated her feelings and was encouraged to make decisions that might lead to a reduction of some of the pressures on herself and her daughter. At the end of each session she said, "I feel so much better" and thanked the psychologist profusely. At termination of "therapy," she took the psychologist's hand and squeezed it endearingly. "Thank you so much, Doctor," she said and made her exit.
>
> *From the Author's Files*

The supplanting of *hysterical* with *histrionic* and the associated exchange of the roots *hystera* (meaning "uterus") and *histrio* allow professionals to distance themselves from the notion that the disorder is intricately bound up with being female. The disorder is diagnosed more frequently in women than in men (Fowler, 2007), although some studies using structured interview methods find similar rates of occurrence among men and women (APA, 2013). Whether the gender discrepancy in clinical practice reflects true differences in the underlying rates of the disorder, diagnostic biases, or unseen factors remains an open question.

People with histrionic personalities may become unusually upset by news of a sad event and exude exaggerated delight at a pleasant occurrence. They may faint at the sight of blood or blush at a slight faux pas. They tend to demand that others meet their needs for attention and play the victim when others fall short. They also tend to be self-centered and intolerant of delays of gratification: They want what they want when they want it. They grow quickly restless with routine and crave novelty and stimulation. They are drawn to fads. Others may see them as putting on airs or playacting, although they may evince a certain charm. They tend to be flirtatious and seductive but are too wrapped up in themselves to develop intimate relationships or have deep feelings toward others. As a result, their associations tend to be stormy and ultimately ungratifying. They tend to use their physical appearance as a means of drawing attention to themselves. Men with the disorder may act and dress in an overly "macho" way, and women may choose very frilly, feminine clothing. Glitter supersedes substance.

People with histrionic personalities may be attracted to professions like modeling or acting, where they can hog the spotlight. Despite outward successes, they lack self-esteem and strive to impress others to boost their self-worth. If they suffer setbacks or lose their place in the limelight, depressing inner doubts may emerge.

NARCISSISTIC PERSONALITY DISORDER *Narkissos* was a handsome youth who, according to Greek myth, fell in love with his reflection in a spring. Because of his excessive self-love, the gods transformed him into the flower we know as the narcissus.

People with **narcissistic personality disorder** have an inflated or grandiose sense of themselves and an extreme need for admiration. They brag about their accomplishments and expect others to shower them with praise. They expect others to notice their special qualities, even when their accomplishments are ordinary, and they enjoy basking in the light of adulation. They are self-absorbed and lack empathy for others. Although they share certain features with histrionic personalities, such as demanding to be the center of attention, they have a much more inflated view of themselves and are less melodramatic than people with histrionic personality disorder. As compared to people with borderline personality disorder, those with narcissistic personality disorder are generally better able to organize their thoughts and actions. They tend to be more successful in their careers and are better able to rise to positions of status and power. Their relationships also tend to be more stable than those of people with borderline personality disorder.

Although more than half of the people diagnosed with narcissistic personality disorder are men, we cannot say whether there is an underlying gender difference in prevalence rates in the general population. A certain degree of narcissism may represent a healthful adjustment to insecurity, a shield from criticism and failure, or a motive for achievement. Excessive narcissistic qualities can become unhealthful, especially when the cravings for adulation are insatiable. Up to a point, self-interest fosters success and happiness. In more extreme cases, as with narcissism, it can compromise relationships and careers.

People with narcissistic personalities tend to be preoccupied with fantasies of success and power, ideal love, or recognition for brilliance or beauty. Like people with histrionic personalities, they may gravitate toward careers in modeling, acting, or politics. Although they tend to exaggerate their accomplishments and abilities, many people with narcissistic personalities are quite successful in their occupations. But they envy those who achieve even greater success. Insatiable ambition may prompt them to devote themselves tirelessly to work. They are driven to succeed, not so much for money as for the adulation that comes with success.

People with narcissistic personalities are extremely sensitive to the slightest hint of rejection or criticism. These *narcissistic injuries,* as they are called, hurt so deeply because they reopen very old psychological wounds. Even a seemingly trivial comment can throw the person into a tailspin, as in the following example of a woman, Stephanie, whose husband's criticism exposed old wounds of inadequacy. Moreover, instead of making the pain go away, his mild rebuke added insult to injury.

"I" Rubbing Salt into a Wound

"Watch the ball," she told herself [during a game of tennis], "get sideways, hit through, finish up." . . . For a few precious moments, she was in that "zone" that athletes cherish when everything comes together and there are no mistakes.

She was smiling secretly, enjoying an illicit high, wondering if her husband, Doug, had also noticed how well she was hitting today, when a heavily underspun return angled into her backhand. She lunged, stabbed, and caught the ball on her racquet rim, sending it flying out of the court. "You never read that spin," Doug scolded from the far court. "Never," Stephanie echoed, suddenly feeling as though she had just blown an internal tire. Pain washed over her and settled in the middle of her chest. . . . "I'll never be any good at this game," she thought miserably, smashing the next three balls into the net. The elation of only moments before had evaporated, replaced by a hopeless feeling of ineptitude. Stephanie swallowed the tears rising in her throat and gave herself a mental kick in the backside. "You're such a baby," she muttered to herself as she prepared to pack up and go home. "You wimping out on me again?" Doug called out. He was only teasing, trying to goad her back into the drill, but his words were like salt on a fresh abrasion. There would be no more tennis this day.

Source: Hotchkiss, 2002.

Interpersonal relationships are invariably strained by the demands that people with narcissistic personality impose on others and by their lack of empathy with, and concern for, other people. They seek the company of flatterers and, although they are often superficially charming and friendly, their interest in people is one-sided: They seek people who will serve their interests and nourish their sense of self-importance. They have feelings of entitlement that lead them to exploit others. They tend to adopt a game-playing style in romantic relationships rather than seeking true intimacy, apparently because of their needs for power and autonomy (Campbell, Foster, & Finkel, 2002). They treat sex partners as devices for their own pleasure or to brace their self-esteem, as in the case of Bill.

Bill: A Case of Narcissistic Personality Disorder

Most people agreed that Bill, a 35-year-old investment banker, had a certain charm. He was bright, articulate, and attractive. He possessed a keen sense of humor that drew people to him at social gatherings. He would always position himself in the middle of the room, where he could be the center of attention. The topics of conversation invariably focused on his "deals," the "rich and famous" people he had met, and his outmaneuvering of opponents. His next project was always bigger and more daring than the last. Bill loved an audience. His face would light up when others responded to him with praise or admiration for his business successes, which were always inflated beyond their true measure. But when the conversation shifted to other people, he would lose interest and excuse himself to make a drink or to call his answering machine. When hosting a party, he would urge guests to stay late and feel hurt if they had to leave early; he showed no sensitivity to, or awareness of, the needs of his friends.

The few friends he had maintained over the years had come to accept Bill on his own terms. They recognized that he needed to have his ego fed or that he would become cool and detached.

Bill had also had a series of romantic relationships with women who were willing to play the adoring admirer and make the sacrifices that he demanded—for a time. But they are inevitably tired of the one-sided relationship or grew frustrated by Bill's inability to make a commitment or feel deeply toward them. Lacking empathy, Bill was unable to recognize other people's feelings and needs. His demands for constant attention from willing admirers did not derive from selfishness, but from a need to ward off underlying feelings of inadequacy and diminished self-esteem. It was sad, his friends thought, that Bill needed so much attention and adulation from others and that his many achievements were never enough to calm his inner doubts.

From the Author's Files

12.5 **Describe** the key features of personality disorders characterized by anxious or fearful behavior.

Personality Disorders Characterized by Anxious or Fearful Behavior

This cluster of personality disorders includes the avoidant, dependent, and obsessive–compulsive types. Although the features of these disorders differ, they share a component of fear or anxiety.

AVOIDANT PERSONALITY DISORDER People with **avoidant personality disorder** are so terrified of rejection and criticism that they are generally unwilling to enter into relationships without ardent reassurances of acceptance. As a result, they may have few close relationships outside their immediate families. They also tend to avoid group occupational or recreational activities for fear of rejection. They prefer to lunch alone at their desks. They shun company picnics and parties, unless they are perfectly sure of acceptance. Avoidant personality disorder, which appears to be equally common in men and women, is believed to affect about 2.4% of the general population (APA, 2013).

Unlike people with schizoid qualities, with whom they share the feature of social withdrawal, individuals with avoidant personalities have interest in, and feelings of warmth toward, other people. However, fear of rejection prevents them from striving to meet their needs for affection and acceptance. In social situations, they tend to hug the walls and avoid conversing with others. They fear public embarrassment, the thought that others might see them blush, cry, or act nervously. They tend to stick to their routines and exaggerate the risks or effort involved in trying new things. They may refuse to attend a party that is an hour away on the pretext that the late drive home would be too taxing. Consider the following case example.

An avoidant personality? People with avoidant personalities often keep to themselves because of fear of rejection.

→ Harold: A Case of Avoidant Personality Disorder

Harold, a 24-year-old accounting clerk, had dated but a few women, and he had met them through family introductions. He never felt confident enough to approach a woman on his own. Perhaps it was his shyness that first attracted Stacy, a 22-year-old secretary who worked alongside Harold and asked him if he would like to get together sometime after work. At first Harold declined, claiming some excuse, but when Stacy asked again a week later, Harold agreed, thinking she must really like him if she was willing to pursue him. The relationship developed quickly, and soon they were dating virtually every night. The relationship was strained, however. Harold interpreted any slight hesitation in her voice as a lack of interest. He repeatedly requested reassurance that she cared about him, and he evaluated every word and gesture for evidence of her feelings. If Stacy said that she could not see him because of fatigue or illness, he assumed she was rejecting him and sought further reassurance. After several months, Stacy decided she could no longer accept Harold's nagging, and the relationship ended. Harold assumed that Stacy had never truly cared for him.

→ *From the Author's Files*

Avoidant personality disorder is often comorbid (co-occurring) with social anxiety disorder (Friborg et al., 2013). The overlap between the two disorders suggests they may share common genetic factors (Reichborn-Kjennerud et al., 2008). It may well turn out that avoidant personality disorder is a more severe form of social anxiety disorder, not a distinct diagnosis. If that is the case, then perhaps people with avoidant personality disorder might best be treated with techniques proven to be effective in treating social anxiety disorder, such as cognitive-behavior therapy (Cowley, 2008). That said, the *DSM* classifies the two disorders as distinct diagnoses.

DEPENDENT PERSONALITY DISORDER **Dependent personality disorder** describes people who have an excessive need to be taken care of by others. This leads them to be overly submissive and clinging in their relationships and extremely fearful of separation. People with this disorder find it very difficult to do things on their own. They seek advice in making even the smallest decision. Children or adolescents with the problem may look to their parents to select their clothes, diets, schools or colleges, even their friends. Adults with the disorder allow others to make important decisions for them. Sometimes they are so dependent on others that they allow their parents to determine whom they will marry, as in the case of Matthew.

> ### → Matthew: A Case of Dependent Personality Disorder
>
> Matthew, a 34-year-old single accountant who lives with his mother, sought treatment when his relationship with his girlfriend came to an end. His mother had objected to marriage because his girlfriend was of a different religion, and—because "blood is thicker than water"—Matthew acceded to his mother's wishes and ended the relationship. Yet he is angry with himself and at his mother because he feels that she is too possessive to ever grant him permission to get married. He describes his mother as a domineering woman who "wears the pants" in the family and is accustomed to having things her way. Matthew alternates between resenting his mother and thinking that perhaps she knows what's best for him.
>
> Matthew's position at work is several levels below what would be expected of someone of his talent and educational level. Several times he has declined promotions in order to avoid increased responsibilities that would require him to supervise others and make independent decisions. He has maintained close relationships with two friends since early childhood and has lunch with one of them on every working day. On days his friend calls in sick, Matthew feels lost. Matthew has lived his whole life at home, except for one year away at college. He returned home because of homesickness.
>
> → *Adapted from Spitzer et al., 1994, pp. 179–180*

After marriage, people with dependent personality disorder may rely on their spouses to make decisions such as where they should live, which neighbors they should cultivate, how they should discipline the children, what jobs they should take, how they should budget money, and where they should vacation. Like Matthew, individuals with dependent personality disorder avoid positions of responsibility. They turn down challenges and promotions and work beneath their potential. They tend to be overly sensitive to criticism and preoccupied with fears of rejection and abandonment. They may be

People with dependent personality disorder have so much difficulty making independent decisions that they may allow their parents to decide whom they will marry.

☑ **TRUE** People with dependent personality disorder in our culture may be so dependent on others for making decisions that they allow their parents to determine whom they will marry.

devastated by the end of a close relationship or by the prospect of living on their own. Because of fear of rejection, they often subordinate their wants and needs to those of others. They may agree with outlandish statements about themselves and do degrading things to please others. **T / F**

Before going further, we should note that dependence needs to be examined through the lens of culture. Arranged marriages are the norm in some traditional cultures, so people from those cultures who let their parents decide whom they will marry would not be classified as having dependent personality disorder. Similarly, in strongly patriarchal cultures, women may be expected to defer to their fathers and husbands in making many life decisions, even small everyday decisions.

But we needn't look beyond our own society to consider the role of culture. Evidence shows that dependent personality disorder in our culture is diagnosed more frequently in women than in men (APA, 2013). The diagnosis is often applied to women who, for fear of abandonment, tolerate husbands who openly cheat on them, abuse them, or gamble away the family's resources. Underlying feelings of inadequacy and helplessness discourage them from taking effective action. In a vicious cycle, their passivity encourages further abuse, leading them to feel yet more inadequate and helpless. Applying the diagnosis to women with this pattern is controversial and may be seen as unfairly "blaming the victim," because women in our society are often socialized to dependent roles. Women typically encounter greater stress than men in contemporary life as well as greater social pressures to be passive, demure, or deferential. Therefore, dependent behaviors in women may reflect cultural influences rather than an underlying personality disorder.

Dependent personality disorder is linked to other psychological disorders, including mood disorders and social phobia, as well as to physical problems such as hypertension, cardiovascular disorder, and gastrointestinal disorders like ulcers and colitis (Bornstein, 1999; Samuels, 2011; Schuster et al., 2010). There also appears to be a link between dependent personality and what psychodynamic theorists refer to as "oral" behavior problems, such as smoking, eating disorders, and alcoholism (Bornstein, 1999). Psychodynamic theorists trace dependent behaviors to the utter dependence of the newborn baby and the baby's seeking of nourishment through oral means (suckling). Food may come to symbolize love, and people with dependent personalities may overeat to ingest love symbolically. People with dependent personalities often attribute their problems to physical rather than emotional causes and seek support and advice from medical experts rather than psychologists or counselors.

OBSESSIVE–COMPULSIVE PERSONALITY DISORDER The defining features of **obsessive–compulsive personality disorder** include excessive orderliness, perfectionism, rigidity, difficulty coping with ambiguity, difficulty expressing feelings, and meticulousness in work habits. Estimates of the prevalence of the disorder vary from 2.1% to 7.9% of the population (APA, 2013). The disorder is about twice as common in men as in women. Unlike obsessive–compulsive anxiety disorder, people with obsessive–compulsive personality disorder do not necessarily experience outright obsessions or compulsions. If they do, both diagnoses may be deemed appropriate.

People with obsessive–compulsive personality disorder are so preoccupied with the need for perfection that they cannot complete work on time. Their efforts inevitably fall short of their expectations, so they redo their work. Or they ruminate about how to prioritize their work and never seem to start working. They focus on details that others perceive as trivial. As the saying goes, they fail to see the forest for the trees. Their rigidity impairs their social relationships; they insist on doing things their way rather than compromising. Their zeal for work keeps them from participating in, or enjoying, social and leisure activities. They tend to be stingy with money. They find it difficult to make decisions and postpone or avoid them for fear of making the wrong choice. They tend to be inflexible and overly rigid in issues of morality and ethics, to be overly formal in relationships, and to find it difficult to express feelings. It is hard for them to relax and enjoy pleasant activities; they worry about the costs of such diversions. Consider the following case example.

> ### Jerry: A Case of Obsessive–Compulsive Personality Disorder

Jerry, a 34-year-old systems analyst, was perfectionistic, overly concerned with details, and rigid in his behavior. Jerry was married to Marcia, a graphic artist. He insisted on scheduling their free time hour by hour and became unnerved when they deviated from his agenda. He would circle a parking lot repeatedly in search of just the right parking spot to ensure that another car would not scrape his car. He refused to have the apartment painted for over a year because he couldn't decide on the color. He had arranged all the books in their bookshelf alphabetically and insisted that every book be placed in its proper position.

Jerry never seemed to relax. Even on vacation, he was bothered by thoughts of work that he had left behind and by fears that he might lose his job. He couldn't understand how people could lie on the beach and let all their worries evaporate in the summer air. Something can always go wrong, he figured, so how can people let themselves go?

> *From the Author's Files*

Problems with the Classification of Personality Disorders

Questions remain about the classification of personality disorders in the *DSM* system and the criteria used to diagnose them. Here, we focus on major concerns that clinicians and researchers have raised about how these patterns of behavior are classified and diagnosed.

PERSONALITY DISORDERS—CATEGORIES OR DIMENSIONS? Are personality disorders best understood as distinct categories of psychological disorders marked by particular symptoms or behavioral features? Or should we think of them as extreme variations of common personality dimensions found in the general population? The *DSM* adopts a categorical model for classifying abnormal behavior patterns into specific diagnostic categories based on particular diagnostic criteria.

Let's use antisocial personality disorder as an example. To warrant a diagnosis of antisocial personality disorder, a person must show a range of clinical features similar to those outlined in Table 12.2. But just how many of the seven features listed in the table need to be present for a diagnosis of antisocial personality disorder? Three of them, four of them, or perhaps all of them? The answer, according to the diagnostic manual, is that three or more of these criteria need to be present. Why *three*? Basically, this determination represents a consensus of the authors of the *DSM*. A person may exhibit two of these features in abundance, but still not be diagnosed with antisocial personality disorder, whereas someone showing three of the features in a milder form would merit a diagnosis. The problem of where to draw the line when applying diagnostic categories ripples throughout the *DSM* system, raising concerns of many critics that the system relies too heavily on an arbitrary set of cutoffs or diagnostic criteria.

Another concern with the categorical model is that many of the features associated with personality disorders and with many other diagnostic categories (e.g., mood disorders, anxiety disorders) are found to some degree in the general population. Thus, it may be difficult to distinguish between normal variations of these features (or traits) and abnormal variations (Skodol & Bender, 2009). People with antisocial personality disorder, for example, may fail to plan ahead, show impulsive behavior, or lie for personal gain. But so do many people without antisocial personality disorder.

The dimensional model of personality disorders offers an alternative to the traditional categorical model of the *DSM* (e.g., Ferraz et al., 2009; Widiger, Livesley, &

"A place for everything, and everything in its place"? People with obsessive–compulsive personalities may have invented this maxim. Many such people have excessive needs for orderliness in their environments, as suggested by this Laurie Simmons photograph, Red Library #2.

12.6 Evaluate problems associated with the classification of personality disorders.

Clark, 2009). The dimensional model depicts personality disorders as maladaptive and extreme variations along a continuum of personality traits found within the general population.

You may recall that psychologist Thomas Widiger discussed the dimensional approach to the diagnosis of personality disorder in Chapter 3. Widiger and his colleagues propose that personality disorders can be represented as extreme variations of the following five basic traits of personality that comprise the Five-Factor Model of personality (the so-called "Big Five"): (1) *neuroticism* or emotional instability, (2) *extraversion*, (3) *openness to experience*, (4) *agreeableness* or friendliness, and (5) *conscientiousness* (Widiger, 2008; Widiger & Mullins-Sweatt, 2009). In the dimensional model, a disorder like antisocial personality disorder might be characterized in part by extremely low levels of conscientiousness and agreeableness (Lowe & Widiger, 2008). People with this combination of traits are often described as aimless and unreliable, as well as manipulative and exploitive of others. In a similar way, other personality disorders can be mapped onto extreme ends of the Big Five dimensions. A growing body of evidence shows links between the dimensions underlying personality disorders and the Big Five personality traits (e.g., Miller et al., 2012; Samuel & Widiger, 2008; Tackett et al., 2008). One limitation of the dimensional model is that we lack clear guidelines for setting cut-off scores on personality scales to determine just how extreme a trait needs to be for it to be deemed clinically meaningful (Skodol, 2012).

The developers of the *DSM-5* are currently reviewing just how best to diagnose personality in preparation for the next version of the *DSM-5*, to be called *DSM-5.1*. Several alternative models are under consideration, including a hybrid dimensional-categorical model that is part categorical and part dimensional. The dimensional model is based on the Big Five personality traits. Under the proposed plan, a diagnosis of a personality disorder would be based on meeting specified criteria for particular disorders (the categorical approach) together with ratings of extreme or pathological traits (the dimensional approach). This hybrid model is consistent with methods used to diagnose medical illnesses, which rely on both specific criteria (e.g., findings of cancerous cells on biopsies, symptoms of infectious diseases) and extreme measures on continuous dimensions (e.g., a diagnosis of hypertension based on high blood pressure readings). An advantage of the dimensional component in assessment and diagnosis is that it allows the examiner to make a judgment of the severity of the problem based on the degree of extremity of pathological traits, as opposed to merely a yes/no or dichotomous judgment of whether a particular disorder is present or not.

Many proponents of the dimensional model believe the proposed hybrid model does not go far enough in representing dysfunctional personality in a dimensional framework. They claim that it continues to endorse an overriding categorical model. We hope that as the debate continues to unfold about whether the *DSM* should be categorical, dimensional, or a kind of hybrid of the two models, it will be informed by evidence pertaining to the utility and validity of different models of classification.

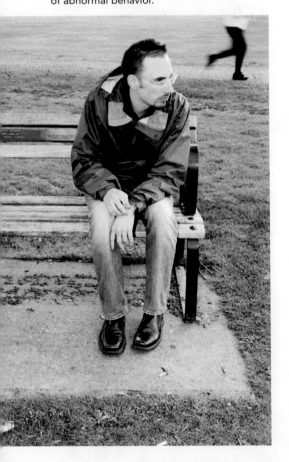

Dimensions or categories? A major point of controversy is whether personality disorders should be conceptualized as extreme variations of personality traits found in the general population or as discrete categories of abnormal behavior.

PROBLEMS DISTINGUISHING PERSONALITY DISORDERS FROM OTHER CLINICAL SYNDROMES One nagging question is whether personality disorders can be reliably differentiated from other clinical syndromes. For example, clinicians often have difficulty distinguishing between obsessive–compulsive disorder and obsessive–compulsive personality disorder. Clinical syndromes are believed to be variable over time, whereas personality disorders are held to be generally more enduring patterns of disturbance. Yet the features of personality disorders may vary over time with changes in circumstances, while some other clinical syndromes (e.g., dysthymia) follow a more or less chronic course.

OVERLAP AMONG DISORDERS A high degree of overlap exists among the personality disorders. Most people receiving a diagnosis of a personality disorder meet criteria for more than one (Skodol, 2012; Zimmerman et al., 2005). Although some personality disorders have distinct features, many share common traits, such as problems in interpersonal relationships. For example, a person may have traits suggestive of both antisocial personality disorder and borderline personality disorder (e.g., impulsivity, unstable relationship patterns). People may also have traits suggestive of both dependent personality disorder (inability to make decisions or initiate activities independently) and avoidant personality disorder (extreme social anxiety and heightened sensitivity to criticism).

Co-occurrence (called *comorbidity*) of different personality disorders is quite common (Grant et al., 2005b). This suggests that the specific types of personality disorders in the *DSM* system may not be clearly distinct from each other. Some personality disorders may not actually be distinct disorders, but rather subtypes or variations of other personality disorders.

DIFFICULTY IN DISTINGUISHING BETWEEN NORMAL AND ABNORMAL BEHAVIOR Another problem with the diagnosis of personality disorders is that they involve personality traits, which, in lesser degrees, describe the behavior of most normal individuals (Warner et al., 2004). Feeling suspicious now and then does not mean you have a paranoid personality disorder. The tendency to exaggerate your own importance does not mean you are narcissistic. You may avoid social interactions for fear of embarrassment or rejection without having an avoidant personality disorder, and you may be especially conscientious in your work without having an obsessive–compulsive personality disorder. Because the defining attributes of these disorders are common personality traits, clinicians should only apply these diagnostic labels when the patterns are so pervasive that they interfere with the individual's functioning or cause significant personal distress. We still lack the evidence we need to determine the particular points at which personality traits become maladaptive and to justify a diagnosis of a personality disorder.

CONFUSING LABELS WITH EXPLANATIONS It may seem obvious that we should not confuse diagnostic labels with explanations, but in practice, the distinction is sometimes clouded. If we confuse labeling with explanation, we may fall into the trap of circular reasoning. For example, what is wrong with the logic of the following statements?

1. John's behavior is antisocial.
2. Therefore, John has antisocial personality disorder.
3. John's behavior is antisocial because he has antisocial personality disorder.

The statements demonstrate circular reasoning because they (a) use behavior to make a diagnosis, and then (b) use the diagnosis as an explanation for the behavior. We may be guilty of circular reasoning in our everyday speech. Consider the following statements: "John never gets his work in on time; therefore, he is lazy. John doesn't get his work in because he's lazy." The label may be acceptable in everyday conversation, but it lacks scientific rigor. For a construct such as *laziness* to have scientific rigor, we need to understand the causes of laziness and the factors that help maintain it. We should not confuse the label we attach to a behavior with the cause of the behavior.

Moreover, labeling people with disturbing behavior as having personality disorders overlooks the social and environmental contexts of the behavior. The impact of traumatic life events, which may occur with a greater range or intensity among members of a particular gender or cultural groups, is an important underlying factor in maladaptive behavior. However, the conceptual underpinnings of the personality disorders do not consider cultural differences, social inequalities, or power differences between genders or cultural groups. For example, many women diagnosed with personality disorders have a history of childhood physical and sexual abuse. The ways in which people cope with abuse may come to be viewed as flaws in their character rather than as reflections of the dysfunctional societal factors that underlie abusive relationships.

Personality disorders are convenient labels for identifying common patterns of ineffective and self-defeating behavior, but labels do not explain the behaviors they name. Still, the development of an accurate descriptive system is an important step toward scientific explanation. The establishment of reliable diagnostic categories sets the stage for valid research into causation and treatment.

SEXIST BIASES The construction of certain personality disorders may have sexist underpinnings. The diagnostic criteria seem to label stereotypical feminine behaviors as pathological with greater frequency than stereotypical masculine behaviors. Take the example of histrionic personality, which seems a caricature of the traditional stereotype of the feminine personality: flighty, emotional, shallow, seductive, attention-seeking.

But if the feminine stereotype corresponds to a diagnosable mental disorder, shouldn't we also have a diagnostic category that reflects the masculine stereotype of the "macho male"? We might argue that overly masculinized traits can be associated with significant distress or impairment in social or occupational functioning in certain males. For example, highly masculinized males may get into fights and experience difficulties working for female bosses. Yet there is presently no personality disorder corresponding to the "macho male" stereotype.

Does the diagnosis of dependent personality disorder unfairly stigmatize women who have been socialized into dependent roles by attaching to them a label of a personality disorder? Women may be at greater risk of receiving diagnoses of histrionic or dependent personality disorders simply because clinicians perceive these patterns as common among women or because women are more likely than men to be socialized into these behavior patterns.

Are some personality disorders more likely to be diagnosed in men or in women because of societal expectations rather than underlying pathology? Clinicians tend to show a bias in favor of perceiving women as having histrionic personality disorder and men as having antisocial personality disorder, even when they demonstrate the same symptoms (Garb, 1997). Additional evidence of gender bias is found in a study that examined diagnoses of borderline personality disorder. Researchers presented a hypothetical case example to 311 psychologists, social workers, and psychiatrists (Becker & Lamb, 1994). Half of the sample was presented with a case identified as a female; the other half read the identical case, except that the person was identified as male. Clinicians more often diagnosed the case identified as female as having borderline personality disorder.

Is the *DSM* classification of personality disorders gender biased or gender free? Should it be more evenly balanced in its characterizations of disordered personality? What do you think? Consider your own attitudes: Have you ever assumed that women are "just dependent or hysterical" or that men are "just narcissists or antisocial"?

Theoretical Perspectives

12.7 Describe the major theoretical perspectives on understanding personality disorders—the psychodynamic, learning, cognitive, family, biological, and sociocultural perspectives.

In this section, we consider theoretical perspectives on the personality disorders. Many theoretical accounts of disturbed personality derive from the psychodynamic model. We thus begin with a review of traditional and modern psychodynamic models.

Psychodynamic Perspectives

Traditional Freudian theory focused on problems arising from the Oedipus complex as the foundation for abnormal behaviors, including personality disorders. Freud believed that children normally resolve the Oedipus complex by forsaking incestuous wishes for the parent of the opposite gender and identifying with the parent of the same gender. As a result, they incorporate the parent's moral principles in the form of a personality structure called the *superego*. Many factors may interfere with appropriate identification and sidetrack the normal developmental process, preventing children from developing moral constraints and the feelings of guilt or remorse that normally follow antisocial behavior. Freud's account of moral development focused mainly on the development of males. He has been criticized for failing to account for the moral development of females.

More recent psychodynamic theories have generally focused on the earlier, pre-Oedipal period of about 18 months to 3 years, during which infants begin to develop identities separate from those of their parents. These theories focus on the development of the sense of self in explaining disorders such as narcissistic and borderline personality disorders.

HANS KOHUT One of the principal shapers of modern psychodynamic concepts is Hans Kohut, whose theory is labeled *self psychology* because of its emphasis on processes in the development of a cohesive sense of self. Freud believed that the resolution of the Oedipus complex was central to the development of the adult personality. Kohut disagreed, arguing that what matters most is how the self develops—whether the person is able to develop self-esteem, values, and a cohesive and realistic sense of self as opposed to an inflated, narcissistic personality (Anderson, 2003; Goldberg, 2003).

Kohut (1966) believed that people with narcissistic personalities mount a facade of self-importance to cover up deep feelings of inadequacy. The narcissist's self-esteem is like a reservoir that needs to be constantly replenished with a steady stream of praise and attention lest it run dry. A sense of grandiosity helps people with a narcissistic personality mask their underlying feelings of worthlessness. Failures or disappointments threaten to expose these feelings and drive the person into a state of depression, and so as a defense against despair, the person attempts to diminish the importance of disappointments or failures.

People with narcissistic personalities may become enraged by others whom they perceive have failed to protect them from disappointment or have declined to shower them with reassurance, praise, and admiration. They may become infuriated by even the slightest criticism, no matter how well intentioned. They may mask feelings of rage and humiliation by adopting a facade of cool indifference. They can make difficult psychotherapy clients because they may become enraged when therapists puncture their inflated self-images to help them develop more realistic self-concepts.

To Kohut, early childhood involves a normal stage of *healthy narcissism*. Infants feel powerful, as though the world revolves around them. Infants also normally perceive their parents as idealized towers of strength and wish to be one with them and to share their power. Empathic parents reflect their child's inflated perceptions by making them feel that anything is possible and by nourishing their self-esteem (e.g., telling them how terrific and precious they are). Even empathic parents are critical from time to time, however, and puncture their children's grandiose sense of self. Or they fail to measure up to their children's idealized views of them. Gradually, unrealistic expectations dissolve and are replaced by more realistic appraisals of oneself and others. In adolescence, childhood idealization is transformed into realistic admiration for parents, teachers, and friends. In adulthood, these ideas develop into a set of internal ideals, values, and goals.

Lack of parental empathy and support, however, sets the stage for *pathological narcissism*. Children who are not prized by their parents fail to develop a sturdy sense of self-esteem. They develop damaged self-concepts and feel incapable of being loved and admired. Pathological narcissism involves the construction of a grandiose facade of self-perfection that cloaks perceived inadequacies. The facade is always on the brink of crumbling, however, and must be shored up by a constant flow of reassurance that one is special and unique. This leaves the person vulnerable to painful blows to self-esteem following failure to achieve social or occupational goals.

Kohut's approach to therapy provides clients who have a narcissistic personality with an initial opportunity to express their grandiose self-images and to idealize the therapist. Over time, however, the therapist helps them explore the childhood roots of their narcissism and gently points out imperfections in both client and therapist to encourage clients to form more realistic images of the self and others.

OTTO KERNBERG Otto Kernberg (1975), a leading psychodynamic theorist, views borderline personality in terms of a failure in early childhood to develop a sense of constancy and unity in one's image of oneself and others. From this perspective, borderline individuals cannot synthesize contradictory (positive and negative) elements of themselves and others into complete, stable wholes. Rather than viewing important people in their lives as sometimes loving and sometimes rejecting, they shift back and forth between pure idealization and utter hatred. This rapid shifting back and forth between viewing others as either "all good" or "all bad" is referred to as *splitting*.

Kernberg tells of a woman in her 30s whose attitude toward him vacillated in such a way. The woman would respond to him in one session as the most wonderful therapist and feel that all her problems were solved. But several sessions later she would turn against him and accuse him of being unfeeling and manipulative, become dissatisfied with treatment, and threaten to drop out (cited in Sass, 1982).

In Kernberg's view, parents, even excellent parents, invariably fail to meet all their children's needs. Infants, therefore, face the early developmental challenge of reconciling images of the nurturing, comforting "good mother" with those of the withholding, frustrating "bad mother." Failure to reconcile these opposing images into a realistic, unified, and stable parental image may have the effect of psychologically fixating the child in the pre-Oedipal period of psychosexual development. Consequently, as an adult, the person may continue to have rapidly shifting attitudes toward therapists and others, idealizing them one moment and rejecting them the next.

MARGARET MAHLER Margaret Mahler, another influential modern psychodynamic theorist, explained borderline personality disorder in terms of childhood separation from the mother figure. Mahler and her colleagues (Mahler & Kaplan, 1977; Mahler, Pine, & Bergman, 1975) believed that during the first year, infants develop a symbiotic attachment to their mothers. *Symbiosis,* or interdependence, is a biological term derived from Greek roots meaning "to live together." In psychology, symbiosis is a state of oneness in which the child's identity is fused with the mother's. Normally, children gradually differentiate their own identities or senses of self from that of their mothers. The process, *separation-individuation*, is the development of a separate psychological and biological identity from the mother (separation) and recognition of personal characteristics that define one's self-identity (individuation). Separation-individuation may be a stormy process. Children may vacillate between seeking greater independence and moving closer to, or "shadowing," the mother, which is seen as a wish for reunion. The mother may disrupt normal separation-individuation by refusing to let go of the child or by too quickly pushing the child toward independence. The tendencies of people with borderline personalities to react to others with ambivalence and to alternate between love and hate are suggestive of earlier ambivalences during the separation-individuation process. Borderline personality disorder may arise from the failure to master this developmental challenge.

Psychodynamic theory provides ways of understanding the development of several types of personality disorders. But a limitation of the theory is that it is based largely on inferences drawn from behavior and retrospective accounts of adults rather than on observations of children. We may also question whether it is valid to compare normal childhood experiences with abnormal behaviors in adulthood. For example, the ambivalences that characterize the adult borderline personality may bear only a superficial relationship, if any, to children's vacillations between closeness and separation during separation-individuation.

Links between abuse in childhood and later development of personality disorders suggest that failure to form close bonding relationships with parental caretakers in childhood plays a critical role in the development of personality disorders. We will explore the links between abuse and personality disorders later in this chapter.

Separation-individuation. According to the influential psychodynamic theorist Margaret Mahler, young children undergo a process of separation-individuation by which they learn to differentiate their own identities from those of their mothers. She believed that a failure to successfully master this developmental challenge may lead to the development of a borderline personality.

Learning Perspectives

Learning theorists focus on maladaptive behaviors rather than disorders of personality. They are interested in identifying the learning histories and environmental factors that give rise to maladaptive behaviors associated with diagnoses of personality disorders and the reinforcers that maintain them.

Learning theorists suggest that childhood experiences shape the pattern of maladaptive habits of relating to others that constitute personality disorders. For example, children who are regularly discouraged from speaking their minds or exploring their environments may develop a dependent behavior pattern. Excessive parental discipline may lead to obsessive–compulsive behaviors. Psychologist Theodore Millon (1981) suggests that children whose behavior is rigidly controlled and punished by parents, even for slight transgressions, may develop inflexible, perfectionistic standards. As these children mature, they strive to develop themselves in an area in which they excel, such as schoolwork or athletics, as a way of avoiding parental criticism or punishment. But because of overattention to a single area of development, they do not become well rounded. Thus, they squelch expressions of spontaneity and avoid risks. They may also place perfectionistic demands on themselves to avoid punishment or rebuke, or develop other behaviors associated with the obsessive–compulsive personality pattern.

Millon suggests that histrionic personality disorder may be rooted in childhood experiences in which social reinforcers, such as parental attention, are connected to the child's appearance and willingness to perform for others, especially when reinforcers are dispensed inconsistently. Inconsistent attention teaches children not to take approval for granted and to strive for it continually. People with histrionic personalities may also identify with parents who are dramatic, emotional, and attention-seeking. Extreme sibling rivalry would further heighten motivation to perform for attention from others.

Social-cognitive theories emphasize the role of reinforcement in explaining the origins of antisocial behaviors. In an early influential work, Ullmann and Krasner (1975) proposed that people with antisocial personalities failed to learn to respond to other people as potential reinforcers. Most children learn to treat others as reinforcing agents because others reinforce them with praise for good behavior and punishment for bad. Reinforcement and punishment provide feedback that helps children modify their behavior to maximize the chances of future rewards and minimize the risks of future punishments. As a consequence, children become sensitive to the demands of powerful others, usually parents and teachers, and learn to regulate their behavior accordingly. They thus adapt to social expectations. They learn what to do and what to say, how to dress and how to act to obtain praise and approval (social reinforcement) from others.

People with antisocial personalities, by contrast, may not have become socialized in this way because their early learning experiences lacked consistency and predictability. Perhaps they were sometimes rewarded for doing the "right thing," but just as often not. They may have borne the brunt of harsh physical punishments, delivered at random. As adults, they do not place much value on what other people expect, because as children, they saw no connection between their own behavior and reinforcement. Although Ullmann and Krasner's views may account for some features of antisocial personality disorder, they may not adequately address the development of the "charming" type of antisocial personality; people in this group are skillful at reading the social cues of others and using them for personal advantage. Some people with psychopathy are remarkably successful in their lines of

What are the origins of antisocial personality disorder? Are youth who develop antisocial personalities largely "unsocialized" because their early learning experiences lack the consistency and predictability that help other children connect their behavior with rewards and punishments? Or are they very "socialized," but socialized to imitate the behavior of other antisocial youth? To what extent does criminal behavior or membership in gangs overlap with antisocial personality disorder?

work and appear to be more conscientious and reliable in their work habits than other psychopathic personalities (Mullins-Sweatt et al., 2010) But, as pointed out by psychologists Paul Babiak and David Hare in their recent book, *Snakes in Suits*, the numbers of psychopathic personalities who attain executive positions in business where they can control others and where they use guile, manipulation, and charm to cause damage to others far exceed the numbers in prisons or in society at large (Babiak & Hare, 2006).

Social-cognitive theorist Albert Bandura has studied the role of observational learning in aggressive behavior, a common component of antisocial behavior. In a classic study, he and his colleagues (e.g., Bandura, Ross, & Ross, 1963) showed that children acquire skills, including aggressive skills, by observing the behavior of others. Exposure to aggression may come from watching violent television programs or observing parents who behave violently. Bandura, however, does not believe that children and adults display aggressive behaviors in a mechanical way. Rather, people usually do not imitate aggressive behavior unless they are provoked and believe they are more likely to be rewarded than punished for it. Children are most likely to imitate violent role models who get their way with others by acting aggressively. Children may also acquire antisocial behaviors such as cheating, bullying, or lying by direct reinforcement if they find that those behaviors help them avoid blame or manipulate others.

Social-cognitive psychologists have also shown that the ways in which people with personality disorders interpret their social experiences influences their behavior. Evidence shows that antisocial (psychopathic) individuals often have difficulty "reading" emotions in other people's faces (Kosson et al., 2002) and even picking out emotions in people's speech or vocal expressions, especially the emotion of fear (Blair et al., 2002). Antisocial adolescents tend to have hostile cognitive biases—they incorrectly interpret other people's behavior as threatening (Dodge et al., 2002). Often, perhaps because of their family and community experiences, they presume that others intend them ill when they do not. A method of therapy called *problem-solving therapy* helps aggressive, antisocial children and adolescents reconceptualize conflict situations as problems to be solved rather than as threats to be responded to aggressively (Kazdin & Whitley, 2003). Children learn to generate nonviolent solutions to social confrontations and, like scientists, to test the most promising ones. In the section on biological perspectives, we also see that there may be a physiological basis explaining why people with antisocial personalities may fail to learn from punishing experiences.

All in all, learning approaches to personality disorders, like the psychodynamic approaches, have their limitations. They are grounded in theory rather than in observations of family interactions that presage the development of personality disorders. Research is needed to determine whether childhood experiences proposed by psychodynamic and learning theorists actually lead to the development of particular personality disorders as hypothesized.

Family Perspectives

Many theorists have argued that disturbances in family relationships underlie the development of personality disorders. Consistent with psychodynamic formulations, researchers find that people with borderline personality disorder remember their parents as having been more controlling and less caring than reference subjects with other psychological disorders do (Zweig-Frank & Paris, 1991). When people with borderline personality disorder recall their earliest memories, they are more likely than other people to paint significant others as malevolent or evil. They portray their parents and others close to them as likely to injure them or as failing to protect them (Nigg et al., 1992).

Researchers link childhood physical or sexual abuse or neglect to the development of personality disorders, including borderline personality disorder (e.g., Golier et al., 2003; McLean & Gallop, 2003). Perhaps the "splitting" observed in people with the disorder is a function of having learned to cope with unpredictable and harsh behavior from parental figures or other caregivers.

Also consistent with psychodynamic theory, family factors such as parental over-protection and authoritarianism (a "do what I said because I said so" style of parenting) are implicated in the development of dependent personality traits (Bornstein, 1992). Extreme fears of abandonment may also be involved, perhaps resulting from a failure to develop secure bonds with parental attachment figures in childhood due to parental neglect, rejection, or death. Subsequently, these individuals develop a chronic fear of abandonment by significant others, leading to the clinginess that typifies dependent personality disorder. Theorists also suggest that obsessive–compulsive personality disorder may emerge within a strongly moralistic and rigid family environment, which does not permit even minor deviations from expected roles or behavior (e.g., Oldham, 1994).

As with borderline personality disorder, researchers find that childhood abuse, parental neglect, or lack of parental nurturing are important risk factors in the development of antisocial personality disorder in adulthood (Johnson et al., 2006; Lobbestael & Arntz, 2009). In an early but influential view that straddled the psychodynamic and learning theories, the McCords (McCord & McCord, 1964) focused on the role of parental rejection or neglect in the development of antisocial personality disorder. They suggest that children normally learn to associate parental approval with conformity to parental practices and values and disapproval with disobedience. When tempted to transgress, children feel anxious about losing parental love. Anxiety signals the child to inhibit antisocial behavior. Eventually, the child identifies with parents and internalizes these social controls in the form of a conscience. When parents do not show love for their children, this identification does not occur. Children do not fear loss of love, because they have never had it. The anxiety that might have served to restrain antisocial and criminal behavior is absent.

Children who are rejected or neglected by their parents may not develop warm feelings of attachment to others. They may lack the ability to empathize with the feelings and needs of others, developing instead an attitude of indifference. Or perhaps they retain a wish to develop loving relationships but lack the ability to experience genuine feelings.

Although family factors may be implicated in some cases of antisocial personality disorder, many neglected children do not later show antisocial or other abnormal behaviors. We are left to develop other explanations to predict which deprived children will develop antisocial personalities or other abnormal behaviors, and which will not.

Biological Perspectives

Much remains to be learned about the biological underpinnings of personality disorders. Most of the attention in the research community has centered on antisocial personality disorder and the personality traits that underlie the disorder, which is the focus of much of our discussion.

GENETIC FACTORS Evidence points to genetic factors playing a role in the development of several types of personality disorders, including antisocial, narcissistic, paranoid, and borderline types (Gunderson, 2011; Kendler et al., 2008; Meier et al., 2011; Raine, 2008). Parents and siblings of people with personality disorders, such as antisocial, schizotypal, and borderline types, are more likely to be diagnosed with these disorders themselves than are members of the general population (APA, 2013; Battaglia et al., 1995). Genetic factors also appear to be involved in the development of personality traits that underlie the psychopathic personality, such as callousness, antisocial behavior, impulsivity, and irresponsibility (Larsson, Andershed, & Lichtenstein, 2006; Van Hulle et al., 2009). Investigators also report finding genetic indicators in a particular chromosome linking to features of borderline personality disorder (Distel et al., 2008a,b).

Although we have evidence of genetic contributions to personality traits associated with personality disorders, it is important to recognize that environmental factors also play an important contributing role (Hopwood et al., 2011). For example, exposure to environmental influences, such as being raised in a dysfunctional or troubled family, may predispose individuals to develop personality disorders, such as antisocial or borderline personality disorders.

Child maltreatment. Child abuse and neglect figure prominently in cases of people with personality disorders, including borderline personality disorder. What are some of the emotional consequences associated with childhood abuse and neglect?

We should also note that personality traits associated with particular personality disorders may represent interactions of genetic factors and life experiences (Gabbard, 2005). Along these lines, investigators found that a variant of a particular gene was associated with antisocial behavior in adult men, but only in those who were maltreated in childhood (Caspi et al., 2002).

LACK OF EMOTIONAL RESPONSIVENESS According to a leading theorist, Hervey Cleckley (1976), people with antisocial personalities can maintain their composure in stressful situations that would induce anxiety in most people. Lack of anxiety in response to threatening situations may help explain the failure of punishment to induce antisocial people to relinquish antisocial behavior. For most of us, the fear of getting caught and being punished is sufficient to inhibit antisocial impulses. People with antisocial personalities, however, often fail to inhibit behavior that has led to punishment in the past, perhaps because they experience little, if any, fear or anticipatory anxiety about being caught and punished.

When people get anxious, their palms tend to sweat. This skin response, called the *galvanic skin response* (GSR), is a sign of activation of the sympathetic branch of the autonomic nervous system (ANS). In an early study, Hare (1965) showed that people with antisocial personalities had lower GSR levels when they were expecting painful stimuli than normal controls did. Apparently, the people with antisocial personalities experienced little anxiety in anticipation of impending pain.

Hare's findings of a weaker GSR response in people with antisocial personalities has been replicated a number of times in studies showing lower levels of physiological responsiveness in people with psychopathic or antisocial personalities (e.g., Fung et al., 2005; Lorber, 2004). This lack of emotionality may help explain why the threat of punishment seems to have so little effect on deterring their antisocial behavior. It is conceivable that the ANS of people with antisocial personalities is underresponsive to threatening stimuli.

THE CRAVING-FOR-STIMULATION MODEL Other investigators have attempted to explain the antisocial personality's lack of emotional response in terms of the levels of stimulation necessary to maintain an optimum level of arousal. Your optimum level of arousal is the degree of arousal at which you feel best and function most efficiently.

People with antisocial or psychopathic personalities appear to have exaggerated cravings for stimulation (Arnett et al., 1997). Perhaps they require a higher-than-normal threshold of stimulation to maintain an optimum state of arousal. In other words, they may need more stimulation than other people to maintain interest and function normally.

A need for higher levels of stimulation may explain why people with antisocial personality traits tend to become bored easily and gravitate to stimulating but potentially dangerous activities, like the use of intoxicants such as drugs or alcohol, motorcycling, skydiving, high-stakes gambling, or high-risk sexual adventures. A higher-than-normal threshold for stimulation would not directly cause antisocial or criminal behavior; after all, astronauts, soldiers, police officers, and firefighters must also exhibit this trait to some respect. However, the threat of boredom and the inability to tolerate monotony may influence some sensation seekers to drift into crime or reckless behavior.

BRAIN ABNORMALITIES Brain imaging links borderline personality disorder and antisocial personality disorder to dysfunctions in parts of the brain involved in regulating emotions and restraining impulsive behaviors, especially aggressive behaviors (Calzada-Reyes et al., 2012; Carrasco et al., 2012; Gunderson, 2011; Siegle, 2008).

Areas of the brain most directly implicated are the *prefrontal cortex* (located in the front or anterior part of the frontal lobes) and deeper brain structures in the limbic system. The prefrontal cortex is involved in controlling impulsive behavior, weighing consequences of actions, and solving problems. It serves as a kind of "emergency brake" to keep impulses from becoming expressed in violent or aggressive behavior (Raine, 2008). The limbic system is involved in processing emotional responses and forming new memories.

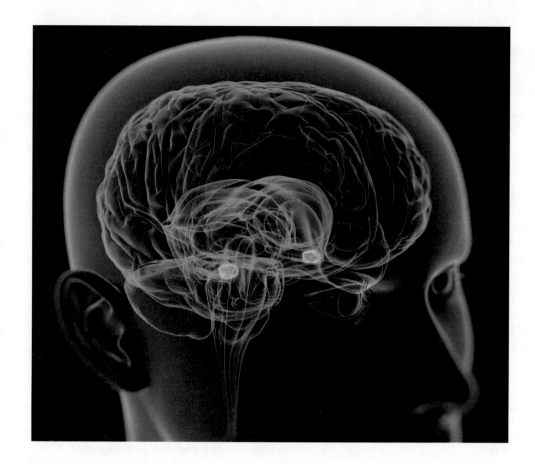

Brain Circuitry. Abnormalities in brain circuitry between the prefrontal cortex, the brain's thinking center, and the limbic system, may contribute to impulse control problems in people with borderline and antisocial personality disorders. The limbic system is a primitive part of the brain involved in regulating emotional processing and memory formation. The amygdala, a part of the limbic system involved in triggering fear, is highlighted here (one on each side of the brain).

A developing area of research involves attempts to identify neural networks in the brain that may underlie personality disorders, which may give us a better understanding of these disorders and possibly lead to more effective treatments. Recent studies using brain imaging techniques show differences in the brains of people with antisocial personalities involving brain circuitry that connects the amygdala, the fear-generating center in the limbic system, with the prefrontal cortex, the part of the brain responsible for weighing the consequences of behavior (Craig et al., 2009; Motzkin et al., 2011). These abnormalities may help explain difficulties with impulse control problems that we see in many people with borderline personality and antisocial personality disorders. In the case of borderline personality disorder, an intriguing possibility is that the prefrontal cortex fails to inhibit or restrain impulsive behaviors in the face of strong negative emotions (Silbersweig et al., 2008).

Sociocultural Perspectives

Social conditions may contribute to the development of personality disorders. Because antisocial personality disorder is reported most frequently among people from lower socioeconomic classes, the kinds of stressors encountered by disadvantaged families may contribute to antisocial behavior patterns. Many inner-city neighborhoods are beset with social problems such as alcohol and drug abuse, teenage pregnancy, and disorganized and disintegrating families. These stressors are associated with an increased likelihood of child abuse and neglect, which may in turn contribute to lower self-esteem and breed feelings of anger and resentment in children. Neglect and abuse may become translated into a lack of empathy and a callous disregard for the welfare of others that are associated with antisocial personalities.

Children reared in poverty are also more likely to be exposed to deviant role models, such as neighborhood drug dealers. Maladjustment in school may lead to alienation and frustration with the larger society, leading to antisocial behavior. Addressing the

The Sensation-Seeking Scale

Do you crave stimulation or seek sensation? Are you satisfied by reading or by watching television, or must you ride the big wave or bounce your motorbike over desert dunes? Psychologist Marvin Zuckerman (2007) uses the term *sensation seeker* to describe people with a high need for arousal and constant stimulation. They have a strong need to pursue thrill and adventure and are easily bored by routine. Although some sensation seekers abuse drugs or get into trouble with the law, many limit their sensation-seeking behaviors to sanctioned activities. Thus, sensation seeking should not be interpreted as criminal or antisocial in itself.

The following questionnaire can help you assess whether you are a sensation seeker. For each of the following items, select the choice, A or B, that best describes you. Then compare your responses to those in the key at the end of the chapter.

1. _____ a. I prefer to go out on the town to all hours of the night.
or _____ b. I prefer spending a quiet evening at home.

2. _____ a. I like scary amusement park rides.
or _____ b. I avoid scary amusement park rides.

3. _____ a. I am the type of person who craves thrilling experiences.
or _____ b. I'm the type of person who likes quiet, relaxing activities.

4. _____ a. I have been skydiving or would like to go skydiving.
or _____ b. Skydiving is not for me.

5. _____ a. Every so often I like to stir up a little excitement in my life.
or _____ b. I prefer keeping things calm and mellow.

6. _____ a. When traveling, I prefer to follow a planned itinerary.
or _____ b. When traveling, I like going places without any definite plans.

7. _____ a. I'm basically a creature of habit.
or _____ b. I get bored easily with routines.

8. _____ a. I would do practically anything on a dare.
or _____ b. I avoid risky situations if at all possible.

9. _____ a. I enjoy loud parties.
or _____ b. I prefer to relax at home or going out with friends.

10. _____ a. I believe you should live life to the max.
or _____ b. I prefer things to be slow and steady.

11. _____ a. I love going out in really cold, brisk weather just for the feel of it against my skin.
or _____ b. I prefer staying indoors when it gets really cold.

12. _____ a. I'm the kind of person that prefers peace and tranquility.
or _____ b. I'm the kind of person that needs a high level of stimulation to feel alive.

problem of antisocial personality may thus require attempts at a societal level to redress social injustice and improve social conditions.

Little information is available about the rates of personality disorders in other cultures. One initiative in this direction involved a joint program sponsored by the World Health Organization (WHO) and the U.S. Alcohol, Drug Abuse, and Mental Health Administration (ADAMHA). The goal of the program was to develop and standardize diagnostic instruments that could be used to arrive at psychiatric diagnoses worldwide. One result of this effort was the development of the International Personality Disorder Examination (IPDE), a semistructured interview protocol for diagnosing personality disorders (Loranger et al., 1994). The IPDE was pilot-tested by psychiatrists and clinical psychologists in 11 countries (India, Switzerland, the Netherlands, Great Britain, Luxembourg, Germany, Kenya, Norway, Japan, Austria, and the United States). The interview protocol diagnoses personality disorders reasonably reliably among the different languages and cultures that were sampled. Although more research is needed to determine the rates of particular personality disorders in other countries, investigators found the borderline and avoidant types to be the most frequently diagnosed. Perhaps the characteristics associated with these personality disorders reflect some dimensions of personality disturbance that are common throughout the world.

TYING it Together

A Multifactorial Pathway in the Development of Antisocial Personality Disorder

Throughout the text, we've endorsed the value of a multifactorial model of abnormal behavior, the view that psychological disorders result from a complex web of psychological, sociocultural, and biological factors. Our understanding of personality disorders is no exception. A history of childhood abuse, neglectful or punitive parents, and learning experiences that breed fear of social interactions rather than self-confidence may underlie the development of personality disorders, such as antisocial personality disorder. Social-cognitive factors, such as the effects of modeling aggressive behavior and cognitive biases that predispose people to misconstrue other people's behavior as threatening, also influence the development of maladaptive ways of relating to others that become identified with personality disorders. Genetic factors also contribute to the matrix of causal factors.

Other biological factors implicated specifically in antisocial personality disorder include a lack of emotional responsiveness to threatening cues, excessive need for stimulation, and underlying brain abnormalities. Sociocultural factors, such as social stressors associated with poverty and living in a disintegrating, crime-ridden neighborhood, are linked to a greater likelihood of child abuse and neglect, which in turn sets the stage for lingering resentments and lack of empathy for others that typify the antisocial personality.

How are these factors linked together? Typically, we find common themes in the development of specific personality disorders, such as harsh or punitive parenting in the case of antisocial personality. However, we need to allow for different combinations of factors and causal pathways to come into play. For example, some people with antisocial personality disorder were raised in economically deprived conditions and lacked consistent parenting. Others were raised in middle-class families but experienced neglectful or harsh parenting. Clinicians need to evaluate how each person's developmental history may have shaped his or her way of relating to others.

Figure 12.2 illustrates a potential causal pathway leading to the development of antisocial personality disorder based on a multifactorial model. This is but one of many possible causal pathways leading to the same outcome. In this causal pathway, poor parenting and modeling influences in the family lead to poor socialization in the child, but whether the child goes on to develop antisocial personality disorder may depend on the presence of particular vulnerability risk factors that increase the risk potential for the disorder.

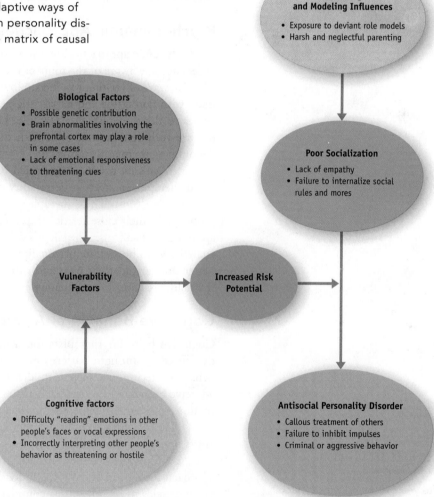

FIGURE 12.2

A multifactorial model of antisocial personality disorder.

Treatment of Personality Disorders

We began the chapter with a quote from the eminent psychologist William James, who suggested that people's personalities seem to be "set in plaster" by a certain age. James's view is applicable to many people with personality disorders, who are typically highly resistant to change.

People with personality disorders usually see their behaviors, even maladaptive, self-defeating behaviors, as natural parts of themselves. Even when unhappy and distressed, they are unlikely to perceive their own behavior as causative. Like Marcella, whom we described as showing features of a histrionic personality disorder, they may condemn others for their problems and believe that others, not they, need to change. Thus, they usually do not seek help on their own. Or they begrudgingly acquiesce to treatment at the urging of others but drop out or fail to cooperate with the therapist. Even if they go for help, they commonly feel overwhelmed by anxiety or depression and terminate treatment as soon as they find some relief, rather than probing more deeply for the underlying causes of their problems. Despite these obstacles, evidence supports the effectiveness of psychotherapy in treating personality disorders, and some of these treatment approaches are described in the following sections (e.g., Abbass et al., 2008; Muran et al., 2010; Paris, 2012).

Psychodynamic Approaches

Psychodynamic approaches are often used to help people diagnosed with personality disorders become aware of the roots of their self-defeating behavior patterns and learn more adaptive ways of relating to others. However, people with personality disorders, especially those with borderline and narcissistic personality disorders, often present particular challenges to the therapist. For example, people with borderline personality disorder tend to have turbulent relationships with therapists, sometimes idealizing them, sometimes denouncing them as uncaring.

Promising results are reported using structured forms of psychodynamically oriented therapies in treating personality disorders (e.g., Clarkin et al., 2007; Gunderson, 2011; Paris, 2008). These therapies raise clients' awareness of how their behaviors cause problems in their close relationships. The therapist takes a more direct, confrontational approach that addresses the client's defenses than would be the case in traditional psychoanalysis. With borderline personality disorder, the psychodynamic therapist helps clients better understand their own and other people's emotional responses in the context of their close relationships (Bateman & Fonagy, 2009).

Cognitive-Behavioral Approaches

Cognitive behavior therapists focus on changing clients' maladaptive behaviors and dysfunctional thought patterns rather than their personality structures. They may use behavioral techniques such as modeling and reinforcement to help clients develop more adaptive behaviors. For example, when clients are taught behaviors that are likely to be reinforced by other people, the new behaviors may well be maintained.

Despite difficulties in treating borderline personality disorder, two groups of therapists headed by Aaron Beck (e.g., Beck et al., 2003) and Marsha Linehan (e.g., Linehan et al., 2006) report treatment benefits from using cognitive-behavioral techniques. Beck's approach focuses on helping the individual identify and correct distorted thinking, such as tendencies to see oneself as completely defective, bad, and helpless. Linehan's technique, called *dialectical behavior therapy* (DBT), is specifically designed to treat borderline personality disorder. DBT combines cognitive-behavioral therapy and Buddhist mindfulness meditation (discussed in Chapter 6) to help people with borderline personality disorder accept and tolerate strong negative emotions and learn more adaptive ways of relating to others. DBT has consistently shown therapeutic benefits in treating people with borderline personality disorder (e.g., Kliem, Kröger, & Kosfelder, 2010; Neacsiu, Rizvi, & Linehan, 2011; Pasieczny & Connor, 2011; Pistorello et al., 2012). **T / F**

The word *dialectic* is drawn from classical philosophy and applies to a form of reasoning in which you consider both sides of an argument, an argument and a counter-argument, and try to reconcile them through rational discussion. As applied to DBT, the dialectical approach involves the attempt to reconcile the opposites or contradictions of *acceptance* and *change*. DBT therapists recognize the need to show acceptance of people with borderline personalities by validating their feelings while also gently encouraging them to make adaptive changes in their behavior. Therapists help patients to recognize how their feelings and behaviors cause problems in their lives, enable them to learn to regulate their emotions through cognitive-behavioral and mindfulness techniques, and encourage them to identify alternative ways of relating to others. The tension between acceptance and mild encouragement of change constitutes the dialectical approach.

DBT incorporates behavioral techniques to help clients improve their relationships with others, develop problem-solving skills, and learn more adaptive ways of handling confusing feelings. It also involves cognitive-behavioral techniques focused on helping people learn to regulate their emotions and mindfulness techniques (see Chapter 4) intended to help people accept and tolerate their disturbing emotions. Because people with borderline personality disorder tend to be overly sensitive to even the slightest cues of rejection, therapists offer acceptance and support, even when clients become manipulative or overly demanding.

Some antisocial adolescents have been placed, often by court order, in residential and foster-care programs that contain numerous behavioral treatment components. These programs have concrete rules and clear rewards for obeying them. Some residential programs rely on *token economies*, in which prosocial behaviors are rewarded with tokens such as plastic chips that can be exchanged for privileges. Although participants in such programs often show improved behavior, it remains unclear whether such programs reduce the risk that adolescent antisocial behavior will continue into adulthood.

"I" "I Cannot Die a Coward"

In 2011 at the age of 68, the renowned psychologist Marsha Linehan, developer of one of the leading treatments for borderline personality disorder, dialectical behavior therapy (DBT), stood before a group of friends, family, and fellow professionals to reveal a dark secret—that she too had suffered from borderline personality disorder. She began by explaining her reason for finally coming out: "So many people have begged me to come forward, and I just thought —well, I have to do this. I owe it to them. I cannot die a coward" (cited in Carey, 2011).

The faded burns, cuts, and welts on her arms attested to the personal pain she carried with her from her youth, from her psychiatric hospitalization at age 17, where she was placed in seclusion and repeatedly inflicted herself with cigarette burns on her wrists, banging her head, and cutting her arms and other parts of her body. She received electroshock therapy, but nothing seemed to work to relieve her deep inner pain. She was hospitalized for 26 months and was one of the most disturbed patients in the hospital. Looking back, she told a reporter, "I was in hell . . . And I made a vow: when I get out, I'm going to come back and get others out of here." It wasn't an easy road to follow. There were later suicide attempts and another hospitalization. She eventually turned to her Catholic faith, finding the inner strength to put her life on track, getting a job in an insurance company, taking college classes, and eventually completing a doctoral program in clinical psychology and from there to a long, distinguished career as a leading researcher and clinician, and through her development of DBT, providing help to a great many people struggling with suicidal thinking and the inner anguish of BPD. Looking back on her life, she told the interviewer that she is a very happy person now. She went on to say that, yes, she still has her ups and downs, ". . . but I think no more than anyone else."

Biological Approaches

Drug therapy does not directly treat personality disorders. However, antidepressant and antianxiety drugs are sometimes used to treat depression and anxiety in people with personality disorders. Neurotransmitter activity is also implicated in aggressive behavior of the type seen in individuals with borderline personality disorder. The neurotransmitter serotonin helps put the brakes on impulsive behaviors, including acts of impulsive aggression (Carver, Johnson, & Joormann, 2008; Seo, Patrick, & Kennealy, 2008). Antidepressants of the selective serotonin reuptake inhibitor (SSRI) class (e.g., Prozac) increase the availability of serotonin in synaptic connections between neurons and can help temper feelings of anger and rage. However, we've yet to see antidepressant medication produce any substantial benefits relative to placebo in treating borderline personality disorder (Gunderson, 2011). Atypical antipsychotics (discussed in Chapter 11) may have benefits in controlling aggressive and self-destructive behavior in people with borderline personality disorder, but the effects are modest and the drugs carry serious potential side effects (Gunderson, 2011). Moreover, drugs alone do not target long-standing patterns of maladaptive behavior that are the defining features of personality disorders.

Much remains to be learned about working with people who have personality disorders. The major challenges involve recruiting people who do not see themselves as being disordered into treatment and prompting them to develop insight into their self-defeating or injurious behaviors. Current efforts to help such people are too often reminiscent of the old couplet:

He that complies against his will,
Is of his own opinion still.

—Samuel Butler, *Hudibras*

Impulse-Control Disorders

12.9 Define the concept of impulse-control disorders and **describe** the features of several major types.

People with borderline personalities often have difficulty controlling their impulses. But problems with impulse control are not limited to people with personality disorders. The *DSM* includes a category of mental disorders called **impulse-control disorders** that are characterized by difficulties in controlling or restraining impulsive behavior.

Have you ever blown your budget on a sale item? Have you ever made a bet you could not afford? Have you ever lost it and screamed at someone, even though you knew you should be keeping your cool? Most of us keep our impulses under control most of the time. Although we may sometimes surrender to a tempting dessert or occasionally blurt out an obscenity in anger, we generally hold our impulsive behaviors in check. People with impulse-control disorders, however, have persistent difficulty resisting harmful impulses, temptations, or drives. They experience a rising level of tension or arousal just prior to the impulsive act, followed by a sense of relief or release after the act is completed. They often have other psychological disorders, especially mood disorders, a fact that leads investigators to question whether these disorders should be classified within a broader spectrum of mood disorders.

Impulse-control disorders in *DSM-5* are grouped in a broader category of disruptive, impulse-control, and conduct disorders that also includes conduct disorder and oppositional defiant disorder. Other impulse control problems such as compulsive Internet use and compulsive shopping are presently under consideration for inclusion in later versions of the diagnostic manual. Our focus here is on three types of impulse-control disorders: *kleptomania*, *intermittent explosive disorder*, and *pyromania*.

Kleptomania

Kleptomania, which derives from the Greek *kleptes*, meaning thief, and *mania*, meaning "madness" or "frenzy," is characterized by repeated acts of compulsive stealing. The stolen objects are typically of little value or use to the person. The person may give them away, return them secretly, discard them, or just keep them hidden at home. In most cases, people with kleptomania can easily afford the items they steal. Even wealthy people have been known to be compulsive shoplifters. The thefts are apparently unmotivated by anger or vengeance. These crimes typically result from a momentary impulse, are poorly planned, and sometimes lead to arrests.

Although shoplifting is common, kleptomania is a recurring pattern of compulsive stealing. Kleptomania is considered a rare condition, affecting less than 1% of the general population, but occurring more frequently in women by a ratio of about 3 to 1 (APA, 2013; Shoenfeld & Dannon, 2012). We have little scientific evidence on kleptomania to guide our understanding of the disorder. The presence of an irresistible, repetitive pattern in kleptomania suggests common features with obsessive–compulsive disorder. However, there is an important distinction. People with obsessive–compulsive anxiety disorder experience only temporary relief from anxiety when they perform compulsive acts; by contrast, people with kleptomania experience pleasurable excitement or gratification when they engage in compulsive stealing. Another difference is that kleptomania appears to be an end in itself, whereas compulsions in obsessive–compulsive anxiety disorder are performed to avoid potential unfortunate events (like repeatedly checking the gas jets to prevent a gas explosion). **T / F**

All in all, some forms of kleptomania may be like obsessive–compulsive anxiety disorder, whereas others forms may have more in common with substance use or mood disorders (Grant, 2006). Perhaps the thrill of theft is a way in which some people attempt to fend off feelings of depression. By coming to better understand the subtypes, we may learn to be better equipped to tailor more effective treatment approaches. As it stands, the few isolated treatment studies are limited to a few cases.

Traditional psychodynamic formulations viewed kleptomania as a defense against unconscious penis envy in women and castration anxiety in men. The classic psychodynamic belief is that people with kleptomania are motivated to steal phallic objects (symbols of the penis) as a magical way of protecting themselves against the apparent loss (in females) or threatened loss (in males) of the penis (Fenichel, 1945). Whether this theoretical speculation has merit remains uncertain, as we lack any supportive evidence of these unconscious processes.

There is little formal research on the treatment of kleptomania (Grant, 2006; Kohn & Antonuccio, 2002). In the following case example, we describe a behavioral approach to treating kleptomania.

"Baby Shoes": A Case of Kleptomania

The client was a 56-year-old woman, who has shoplifted every day of the preceding 14 years. Her compulsive urges to steal fit the clinical criteria that may distinguish kleptomania from other types of shoplifting, although her booty had no apparent meaning to her. Typical loot consisted of a pair of baby shoes, although there was no baby in her family to whom she could give the shoes. The compulsion to steal was so strong that she felt powerless to resist it. She told her therapist that she wished she could be "chained to a wall" (Glover, 1985, p. 213) in order to prevent her from acting out. She expressed anger that it was so easy to steal from a supermarket, in effect blaming the store for her own misconduct.

Her treatment, called covert sensitization, involved the pairing in imagination of an aversive stimulus with the undesired behavior. The therapist directed the woman to imagine feeling nauseous and vomiting while stealing. She was instructed to picture herself in the supermarket, approaching an object she intends to steal, and becoming nauseated and vomiting as she attempts to remove it, which draws the scowling attention of other shoppers. She is then directed to imagine herself replacing the object and consequently feeling relief from the nausea.

In a subsequent session, she imagined the nausea starting as she approached the object, but the nausea disappeared when she turned away rather than removing it. She was also asked to practice the imaginal scenes on her own throughout the week, as homework assignments. She reported a decline in stealing behavior during the treatment program. She reported only one instance of shoplifting between the completion of treatment and a 19-month follow-up evaluation.

Adapted from Glover, 1985

Was the treatment effective? Perhaps. But then again, uncontrolled case studies cannot ascertain cause-and-effect relationships. For example, we cannot know whether the treatment itself or other factors, such as the client's motivation to change her life, were responsible for the changes in her behavior. Controlled studies are needed to evaluate the effectiveness of treatment.

Intermittent Explosive Disorder

RAGE. It is the very first word of the *Iliad*, Homer's epic poem about the Trojan War, establishing a theme for the entire work. Homer's poem, believed to have been written about 750 B.C.E, chronicles the tragic consequences that unfold as unrestrained rage leads to war, killing, and destruction.

People have been concerned about the human capacity for rage and the violent behavior it often provokes for time immemorial. Rage is not a criterion used to diagnose mental or psychological disorders in the *DSM*. But rage is often a feature of **intermittent explosive disorder,** or IED, a type of impulse-control disorder characterized by repeated episodes of impulsive, uncontrollable aggression in which people strike out at others or destroy property (Kessler et al., 2012). The core feature of IED is impulsive aggression, the tendency to lose control of aggressive impulses (Coccaro, 2010).

People with IED have episodes of violent rage in which they suddenly lose control and hit or try to hit other people or smash objects. One man with IED had episodes of explosive rage in which he would smash anything he could lay his hands on, including cell phones, keyboards, remote controls, tables, and even drywall. Even minor provocations or perceived insults can lead to aggressive outbursts that are grossly out of proportion to the situation. People with IED typically experience a state of tension before their violent outbursts and a sense of relief afterwards. Typically, people with IED attempt to justify their behavior, but they also feel genuine remorse or regret because of the harm their behavior causes. Incidents of road rage and domestic violence often occur in cases of IED. Early studies suggested that IED may be a rare condition, but more recent work indicates it may be as common as many other psychiatric disorders (Coccaro, 2012; Tamam, Eroğlu, & Paltacı, 2011).

Recent research on IED has largely focused on its biological underpinnings, and particularly on the possible role of the neurotransmitter serotonin. You'll recall earlier in the chapter that serotonin serves to put the brakes on impulsive behaviors, including acts of impulsive aggression associated with IED. Research in this area is preliminary, but it is pointing toward possible irregularities in serotonin transmission in the brains of people with IED (Coccaro, Lee, & Kavoussi, 2010). Supporting this view is evidence that treatment with antidepressant drugs that boost serotonin availability, such as Prozac, has shown promise in treating impulsive aggression associated with IED (Coccaro & McCloskey, 2010). Functioning of the prefrontal cortex, the part of the brain that curbs impulsive behavior, may also be impaired. Psychological treatment in the form of anger management training may be used to help individuals with IED develop better control over anger outbursts that lead to impulsive acts of aggression and learn to stop and think before they act.

Anger and rage are often a feature of psychological disorders, but the *DSM* does not include a category of anger disorders. In the *Thinking Critically About Abnormal Psychology* section, a leading researcher, Jerry Deffenbacher of Colorado State University, takes up the controversial question of whether the *DSM* should include a category of anger disorders.

Pyromania

Pyromania, from the Latin roots p*yr*, meaning "fire" and the Greek word *mania*, meaning "madness" or "frenzy," is characterized by repeated acts of compulsive fire setting in response to irresistible urges. Only a small percentage of arsonists are diagnosed with pyromania. The most common motives for fire setting appear to be anger and revenge,

THINKING CRITICALLY about abnormal psychology

@Issue: Anger Disorders and the DSM: Where Has All the Anger Gone?—Jerry Deffenbacher

As you may recall from Chapter 4, evidence links chronic anger to serious health problems, including coronary heart disease. Anger also contributes to a range of problem behaviors such as abusive parenting, aggressive behaviors including intimate partner violence and aggressive (as well as risky) driving, problems at work, and negative feelings about oneself (e.g., Dahlen, Edwards, Tubre, & Zyphur, 2012; Shorey, Cornelius, & Idema, 2011; Spector, 2011). Anger also serves as a "red flag" in predicting both poorer outcomes in psychotherapy and a greater risk of relapse after successful treatment of substance abuse (Patterson et al., 2008). However, anger is not necessarily problematic. When it is mild or moderate in degree and expressed constructively, anger can lead to positive outcomes such as standing up for oneself, setting appropriate limits, and mobilizing one's efforts to resolve problems in personal relationships. Problems occur when anger becomes too strong or is expressed inappropriately, leading to many negative outcomes such as states of personal distress (e.g., embarrassment, guilt, self-recrimination), negative physical outcomes (e.g., injury to self and others), legal and financial problems (e.g., arrests for assault or disturbing the peace, legal bills, and property damage), educational problems (e.g., dismissal from college), vocational problems (e.g., losing a job), interpersonal problems (e.g., damaged or terminated relationships), and impaired role behaviors (e.g., abusive or dysfunctional parenting). The personal suffering and costs associated with excessive or inappropriate anger more than meet the threshold for maladaptive or dysfunctional behavior.

With so many negative consequences linked to anger, one might think that anger figures prominently in the classification of abnormal behavior patterns, but this is not the case. It is true that anger is often part of the clinical profile we find in certain psychological disorders, including major depressive disorder, bipolar disorder, posttraumatic stress disorder, and personality disorders such as antisocial and borderline personality disorders. However, anger is not a necessary diagnostic feature of these disorders. Some people with these diagnoses show problems with anger, but many do not. People who display impulsive acts of aggression toward others that result in serious personal harm or destruction of property may receive a diagnosis of IED. IED is a type of impulse-control disorder in which a person shows impaired ability to control impulses. In IED, acts of uncontrolled aggression are grossly out of proportion to any provocation or precipitating stressors. Although intense anger is often associated with IED, the diagnosis is based on failure to control aggressive impulses, not on anger per se. Moreover, IED is not prevalent enough to account for most anger-related mental health problems clinicians see in their practices.

Simply put, there are no anger-based disorders in the *DSM* system (i.e., disorders in which anger is the cardinal feature and must be present to make a diagnosis). Compare the absence of anger disorders to the wide range of disorders that involve two other major negative emotions—anxiety and depression. Anxiety, or course, is the chief feature of anxiety disorders such as panic disorder, phobias, obsessive–compulsive anxiety disorder, and generalized anxiety disorder. Depression is the keynote feature of various mood disorders such as major depressive disorder and dysthymia. The absence of anger disorders in the *DSM* system does not mean such problems do not exist. People do suffer from anger-related problems, and, in some cases, these problems bring considerable suffering to others.

I have argued (e.g., Deffenbacher, 2003) along with others in the field that anger disorders should be included in the *DSM* system. In the scheme I proposed, dysfunctional anger may be conceptualized in terms of four types of triggering events: (a) a specific situation, such as driving; (b) many different types of situations, such as problems at work and at home; (c) an identifiable psychosocial stressor, such as the break-up of a relationship; or (d) unclear triggers in which anger wells up quickly and intensely. We can then use this scheme to classify four types of corresponding anger disorders: (a) situational anger disorder, (b) generalized anger disorder, (c) adjustment disorder with anger, and (d) anger attacks. (Recall that adjustment disorders involve maladaptive reactions to an identifiable stressor.) Because maladaptive anger may be associated with aggressive behavior, we could also elaborate each of these anger disorders in terms of the presence of significant aggression that is likely in need of attention. This diagnostic scheme might help legitimize the pain and suffering of people with anger-related problems and provide the basis for insurance reimbursement of clinical services to treat these problems and funds for much needed research on their causes and treatments (Fernandez, in press).

Not every professional agrees that the diagnostic system should be expanded to include anger disorders. Some argue that including these disorders in the *DSM* system may excuse aggressive or violent behaviors committed in anger by labeling them as forms of mental illness and that bringing these behaviors under the umbrella of the diagnostic system will lead to cases in which people who commit violent acts are not held fully accountable for their behavior. A related concern is that diagnosing anger disorders might undermine efforts to reduce intimate partner violence. As things stand, the *DSM-5* does not include anger disorders, despite how anger negatively impacts the lives of many people. It remains to be seen if the diagnostic manual will be expanded to include anger-related disorders in future editions.

In thinking critically about the issue, answer the following questions:

- Do you know someone who has a serious anger problem? Should his or her behavior be considered abnormal? What are the legal, moral, and ethical consequences of diagnosing these problems as types of mental or psychological disorders?

- If a person with anger-related problems entered therapy for anger reduction, should insurance companies be required to reimburse treatment at a rate comparable to that of treatment for anxiety or depression? If yes, why? If no, why not?

- Should a person who acts out violently against someone else in a state of anger be held fully responsible for his or her behavior? Why or why not?

Jerry L. Deffenbacher, Ph.D., ABPP, is professor laureate and former director of clinical training in the Department of Psychology at Colorado State University. He routinely teaches large undergraduate classes in abnormal psychology. In discussing how he became interested in anger-related problems, he noted that he essentially stumbled into it more than 25 years ago during clinical supervision. Graduate students wanted help in treating angry clients, but he recognized he knew little about the treatment of anger. When he and students searched the scientific literature, they found very little guidance. He then became curious about helping people with anger problems and has been involved in the study of problematic anger ever since.

rather than a psychiatric disorder (Grant & Odlaug, 2011). Other instances of arson may be motivated by financial incentives, as in cases of owners of failing business who arrange to have their premises torched in order to illicitly collect insurance settlements. Intentional fire setting also occurs among some youths with *conduct disorder* (a psychological disorder affecting children and adolescents, as discussed in Chapter 13). Fire setting associated with conduct disorder is part of a larger pattern of antisocial and intentionally cruel or harmful behavior.

Pyromania is considered a rare disorder, which may help explain why it remains so poorly understood. People with pyromania feel a sense of release or psychological relief when setting fires and perhaps feelings of empowerment as the result of prompting firefighters to rush to the scene of the blaze, along with the heavy firefighting equipment they bring. The fire setter may also experience pleasurable excitement by watching or even participating in the firefighting effort. The origins of pyromania remain obscure, but there does appear to have been a morbid fascination with fire from an early age (Lejoyeux & Germain, 2012). Here a female college student who was committed to a mental hospital for compulsive fire-setting recounts her experiences:

"I" "A Part of My Vocabulary"

Fire became a part of my vocabulary in preschool days. . . .Each summer, I would look forward to the beginning of fire season as well as the fall. . . I may feel abandoned, lonely, or bored, which triggers feelings of anxiety or emotional arousal before the fire. . . I want to see the chaos as well as the destruction that I or others have caused. . . [After the fire is out] I feel sadness and anguish and the desire to set another fire.

Source: Wheaton, 2001, as quoted in Lejoyeux & Germain, 2012, p. 139

Treatment of pyromania may involve cognitive-behavioral therapy focused on helping the person identify thoughts and situational cues that prompt fire-setting urges and practice in using coping responses to resist them. But here again we lack controlled studies of treatment effectiveness.

12 summing up

Types of Personality Disorders

12.1 Define the concept of personality disorders.

Personality disorders are maladaptive or rigid behavior patterns or personality traits associated with states of personal distress that impair the person's ability to function in social or occupational roles. People with personality disorders do not generally recognize the need to change themselves.

12.2 Identify the three major categories of personality disorders.

The three major clusters of personality disorders are categorized on the basis of the following characteristics: (1) odd or eccentric behavior, (2) dramatic, emotional, or erratic behavior, and (3) anxious or fearful behavior.

12.3 Describe the key features of personality disorders characterized by odd or eccentric behavior.

Personality disorders involving odd or eccentric behavior include paranoid personality disorder, schizoid personality disorders, and schizotypal personality disorder. People with paranoid personality disorder are unduly suspicious and mistrustful of others, to the point that their relationships suffer. But they do not hold the more flagrant paranoid delusions typical of schizophrenia. Schizoid personality disorder describes people who have little, if any, interest in social relationships, show a restricted range of emotional expression, and appear distant and aloof. People with schizotypal personalities appear odd or eccentric in their thoughts, mannerisms, and behavior, but not to the degree found in schizophrenia.

12.4 Describe the key features of personality disorders characterized by dramatic, emotional, or erratic behavior.

Personality disorders involving dramatic, emotional, or erratic behavior include antisocial personality disorder, borderline personality disorder, narcissistic personality disorder, and histrionic personality disorder. Antisocial personality disorder describes people who persistently engage in behavior that violates social norms and the rights of others and who tend to show no remorse for their misdeeds. Borderline personality disorder is defined in terms of instability in self-image, relationships, and mood. People with borderline personality disorder often engage in impulsive acts, which are frequently self-destructive. People with histrionic personality disorder tend to be highly dramatic and emotional in their behavior, whereas people diagnosed with narcissistic personality disorder have an inflated or grandiose sense of self, and like those with histrionic personalities, they demand to be the center of attention.

12.5 Describe the key features of personality disorders characterized by anxious or fearful behavior.

Personality disorders involving anxious or fearful behavior include avoidant personality disorder, dependent personality disorder, and obsessive–compulsive personality disorder. Avoidant personality disorder describes people who are so terrified of rejection and criticism that they are generally unwilling to enter relationships without unusually strong reassurances of acceptance. People with dependent personality disorder are overly dependent on others and have extreme difficulty acting independently or making even the smallest decisions on their own. People with obsessive–compulsive personality disorder have various traits such as orderliness, perfectionism, rigidity, and overattention to detail, but are without the true obsessions and compulsions associated with obsessive–compulsive (anxiety) disorder.

12.6 Evaluate problems associated with the classification of personality disorders.

Various controversies and problems attend the classification of personality disorders, including overlap among the categories, difficulty in distinguishing between variations in normal behavior and abnormal behavior, confusion of labels with explanations, and possible underlying sexist biases.

Theoretical Perspectives

12.7 Describe the major theoretical perspectives on understanding personality disorders—the psychodynamic, learning, cognitive, family, biological, and sociocultural perspectives.

Earlier Freudian theory focused on unresolved Oedipal conflicts in explaining normal and abnormal personality development. More recent psychodynamic theorists have focused on the pre-Oedipal period in explaining the development of personality disorders such as narcissistic and borderline personality. Learning theorists view personality disorders in terms of maladaptive patterns of behavior rather than personality traits. Learning theorists seek to identify the early learning experiences and present reinforcement patterns that explain the development and maintenance of personality disorders. Antisocial adolescents are more likely to interpret social cues as provocations or intentions of ill will. This cognitive bias may lead them to be confrontational in their relationships with peers.

Many theorists argue that disturbed family relationships play formative roles in the development of personality disorders. For example, theorists connect antisocial personality to parental rejection or neglect and parental modeling of antisocial behavior. Biological explanations of antisocial personality focus on the possible role of lack of emotional responsiveness to physically threatening stimuli and reduced levels of ANS reactivity and the need for higher levels of stimulation to maintain optimal levels of arousal in people with antisocial personalities. Sociocultural theorists focus on the roles of poverty, urban blight, and drug abuse in leading to family disorganization and disintegration that makes it less likely that children will receive the nurturance and support they need to develop more socially adaptive personalities. Sociocultural theorists believe that such factors may underlie the development of personality disorders, especially antisocial personality disorder.

Treatment of Personality Disorders

12.8 Evaluate methods used to treat personality disorders.
Therapists help people with personality disorders become aware of their self-defeating behavior patterns and learn more adaptive ways of relating to others. Despite difficulties in working therapeutically with people with personality disorders, promising results have emerged from the use of relatively short-term psychodynamic therapy and cognitive-behavioral treatment approaches, including DBT and cognitive therapy.

Impulse-Control Disorders

12.9 Define the concept of impulse-control disorders and describe the features of several major types.
Impulse-control disorders are psychological disorders characterized by a pattern of repeated failure to resist impulses to perform acts that lead to harmful consequences to self or others. People affected by these disorders experience a rising level of tension or arousal just before the act, then a sense of relief or release when the act is committed. Kleptomania is characterized by a compulsion to steal, usually involving items of little value to the person. Intermittent explosive disorder (IED) involves acts of impulsive aggression and may involve irregularities in serotonin transmission in the brain. Pyromania, or compulsive fire-setting, is poorly understood but may be motivated in part by the desire to control the response of fire fighters and even assist them in their work.

critical thinking questions

Based on your reading of this chapter, answer the following questions:

- How is psychopathic behavior different from psychotic behavior? How is this distinction sometimes confused in the movies or on television shows?

- Are some personality disorders more likely to be diagnosed in men or in women because of gender-based societal expectations? Have you ever assumed that women are "just dependent or hysterical" or that men are "just narcissists or antisocial"? What kinds of problems do underlying assumptions like these pose for clinicians and researchers?

- Have you known people whose personality traits or behaviors caused significant difficulties in their personal relationships? In what ways? Do you think that any of the personality disorders discussed in this chapter might apply to this person or persons? Explain your answer. Did the person ever seek help from a mental health professional? If so, what was the outcome? If not, why not?

- What factors make it difficult for therapists to treat people with personality disorders? If you were a therapist, how might you attempt to overcome these difficulties?

key terms

personality
  disorders 440
ego syntonic 440
ego dystonic 440
paranoid personality
  disorder 442
schizoid personality
  disorder 442

schizotypal personality
  disorder 443
antisocial personality
  disorder 444
borderline personality
  disorder (BPD) 448
splitting 450

histrionic personality
  disorder 451
narcissistic personality
  disorder 452
avoidant personality
  disorder 454
dependent personality
  disorder 455

obsessive–compulsive
  personality disorder 456
impulse-control
  disorders 472
kleptomania 472
intermittent explosive
  disorder 474
pyromania 474

Key for Sensation-Seeking Scale

Although we don't have any applicable norms, answers that agree with the following key are suggestive of sensation seeking. The more answers keyed in this direction, the stronger your sensation-seeking needs are likely to be.

1. A **2.** A **3.** A **4.** A **5.** A **6.** B

7. B **8.** A **9.** A **10.** A **11.** A **12.** B

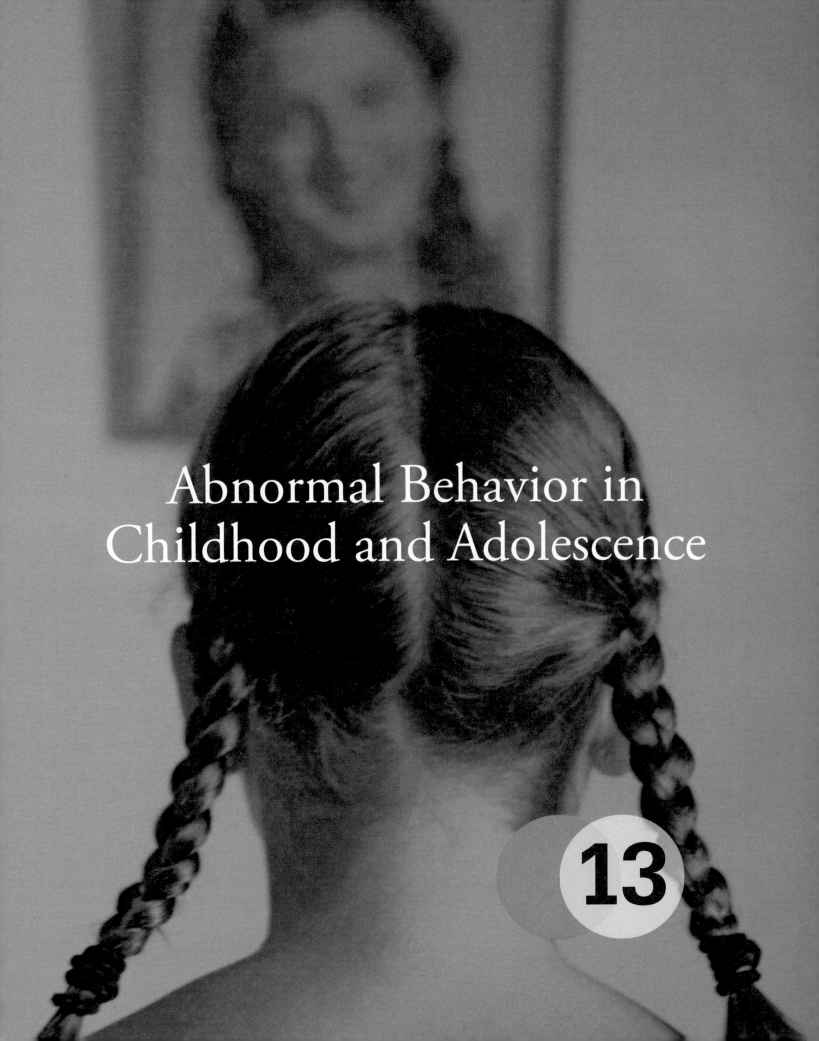

Abnormal Behavior in Childhood and Adolescence

13

13

learning objectives

13.1
Explain the differences between normal and abnormal behavior in childhood and adolescence and the role of cultural beliefs in determining abnormality.

13.2
Describe the effects of child abuse.

13.3
Describe key features of autism spectrum disorder and ways of understanding and treating it.

13.4
Describe the key features and causes of intellectual disability.

13.5
Identify the types of deficits associated with learning disorders and describe ways of understanding and treating learning disorders.

13.6
Define the concept of communication disorders and identify specific types.

13.7
Describe the key features of attention-deficit hyperactivity disorder, oppositional defiant disorder, and conduct disorder.

13.8
Describe causal factors in ADHD and evaluate treatment methods.

13.9
Describe the key features of anxiety and depression in children and adolescents.

13.10
Identify risk factors for suicide among adolescents.

13.11
Describe the key features of elimination disorders and evaluate methods of treating bed-wetting.

truth OR fiction

T ☐ F ☐ Many behavior patterns considered normal for children would be considered abnormal in adults. (p. 481)

T ☐ F ☐ Boys are more likely to develop anxiety and mood disorders than girls are. (p. 483)

T ☐ F ☐ When it comes to child maltreatment, it's not just "sticks and stones" that do damage. (p. 483)

T ☐ F ☐ Childhood vaccines cause autism. (p. 487)

T ☐ F ☐ A former vice president of the United States had such difficulty with arithmetic that he could never balance a checkbook. (p. 496)

T ☐ F ☐ Children who are hyperactive are often given depressants to help calm them down. (p. 505)

T ☐ F ☐ Difficulties at school, problem behaviors, and physical complaints may actually be signs of depression in children. (p. 512)

T ☐ F ☐ Suicide is unfortunately quite common among young teens around the time of puberty. (p. 513)

T ☐ F ☐ Principles of classical conditioning can be applied to treat bed-wetting in children. (p. 518)

An autistic woman, Donna Williams, reflects on what it is like to be an autistic child. In this excerpt from her memoir *Nobody Nowhere*, she speaks about her need to keep the world out. She was about 3 years old when her parents took her to a doctor out of concern that she appeared malnourished.

"I" "A World of My Own Creation"

"My parents thought I had leukemia and took me for a blood test. The doctor took some blood from my earlobe. I cooperated. I was intrigued by a multicolored cardboard wheel the doctor had given me. I also had hearing tests because, although I mimicked everything, it appeared that I was deaf. My parents would stand behind me and make sudden loud noises without my so much as blinking in response. 'The world' simply wasn't getting in. . . . The more I became aware of the world around me, the more I became afraid. Other people were my enemies, and reaching out to me was their weapon, with only a few exceptions—my grandparents, my father, and my Aunty Linda. . . ."

Donna also recalled how, for her, people became things and things existed to offer her protection and shield her from a fear of vulnerability:

"I collected scraps of colored wool and crocheted bits and would put my fingers through the holes so that I could fall asleep securely. For me, the people I liked were things, and those things (or things like them) were my protection from the things I didn't like—other people.

The habits I adopted of keeping and manipulating these symbols were my equivalent of magic spells cast against the nasties who could invade me if I lost my cherished objects or had them taken away. My strategies were not the result of insanity or hallucination, but simply harmless imagination made potent by my overwhelming fear of vulnerability. . . .

People were forever saying that I had no friends. In fact my world was full of them. They were far more magical, reliable, predictable, and real than other children, and they came with guarantees. It was a world of my own creation where I didn't need to control myself or the objects, animals, and nature, which were simply being in my presence."

→ *Williams, 1992, pp. 5, 6, 9*

Psychological disorders of childhood and adolescence often have a special poignancy, perhaps none more than autism. These disorders affect children at ages when they have little capacity to cope. Some of these problems, such as autism and intellectual disability (formerly called *mental retardation*), prevent children from fulfilling their developmental potentials. Some psychological problems in children and adolescents mirror those found in adults—problems such as mood disorders and anxiety disorders. In some cases, the problems are unique to childhood, such as separation anxiety; in others, such as ADHD, or attention-deficit/hyperactivity disorder, the problem manifests itself differently in childhood than in adulthood.

Normal and Abnormal Behavior in Childhood and Adolescence

Determining whether a child's behavior is abnormal depends on our expectations about what is normal for a child of a given age in a given culture. We need to consider whether a child's behavior falls outside the range of developmental and cultural norms. For example, determining that 7-year-old Jimmy is hyperactive depends on the types of behaviors deemed reasonable for children of the same age and cultural background (Drabick & Kendall, 2010; Kendall & Drabick, 2010).

Many problems are first identified when the child enters school. Although these problems may have existed earlier, they may have been tolerated or not seen as "problems" in the home. Sometimes the stress of starting school contributes to their onset. Keep in mind, however, that what is socially acceptable at a particular age, such as intense fear of strangers at about 9 months, may be socially unacceptable at more advanced ages.

Many behavior patterns we might consider abnormal among adults—such as intense fear of strangers and lack of bladder control—are perfectly normal for children at certain ages. Many children are misdiagnosed when clinicians fail to take developmental expectations into account. Researchers estimate that nearly one million American children may have been misdiagnosed with ADHD in kindergarten and treated with medication simply because they were the youngest (and hence least mature) children in their classes ("Nearly One Million," 2010). As the lead researcher, Todd Edler, told a reporter, "If a child is behaving poorly, if he's inattentive, if he can't sit still, it may simply be because he's 5 and the other kids are 6." **T / F**

Many of the psychological disorders affecting children and adolescents are classified in the *DSM-5* category of **neurodevelopmental disorders.** These disorders involve an impairment of brain functioning or development that affects the child's psychological, cognitive, social, or emotional development. This category of mental disorders includes the following types of disorders we discuss in this chapter:

- Autism spectrum disorder
- Intellectual disability
- Specific learning disorder
- Communication disorders
- Attention-deficit/hyperactivity disorder

In this chapter, we also review these and other disorders affecting children and adolescents, including disruptive behavior disorders (oppositional defiant disorder and conduct disorder), problems relating to anxiety and depression, and elimination disorders.

13.1 **Explain** the differences between normal and abnormal behavior in childhood and adolescence and the role of cultural beliefs in determining abnormality.

truth OR fiction

Many behavior patterns considered normal for children would be considered abnormal in adults.

☑ **TRUE** Many behavior patterns that would be considered abnormal among adults—such as intense fear of strangers and lack of bladder control—are perfectly normal for children at certain ages.

How serious is this problem? Thai parents might judge the aggressive behaviors shown by these children to be less serious than American parents would. Thai-Buddhist values tolerate broad variations in children's behavior and assume that it will change for the better over time.

Cultural Beliefs About What Is Normal and Abnormal

Cultural beliefs help determine whether people view behavior as normal or abnormal. Because children rarely label their own behavior as abnormal, definitions of *normality* depend largely on how a child's behavior is filtered through a cultural lens (Callanan & Waxman, 2013; Norbury & Sparks, 2013). Cultures vary with respect to the types of behaviors they classify as unacceptable or abnormal as well as the threshold for labeling child behaviors as deviant. In an illustrative study, groups of American and Thai parents were presented with vignettes depicting two children, one with problems of "overcontrol" (e.g., shyness and fears) and one with problems of "undercontrol" (e.g., disobedience and fighting). Thai parents rated both types of problems as less serious and worrisome than American parents did (Weisz et al., 1988). Thai parents also rated the children in the vignettes as more likely to improve over time, even without treatment. These viewpoints are embedded within traditional Thai-Buddhist beliefs and values, which tolerate broad variations in children's behavior and assume that change is inevitable.

Like definitions of *abnormality*, methods of treatment differ for children. Children may not have the verbal skills to express their feelings through speech or the attention span required to sit through a typical therapy session. Therapy methods must be tailored to the level of the child's cognitive, physical, social, and emotional development. For example, psychodynamic therapists have developed techniques of *play therapy* in which children enact family conflicts symbolically through their play activities, such as by play-acting with dolls or puppets. Or they might be given drawing materials and asked to draw pictures, in the belief that their drawings will reflect their underlying feelings.

As with other forms of therapy, child therapy needs to be offered in a culturally sensitive framework. Therapists need to tailor their interventions to the cultural backgrounds and social and linguistic needs of children in order to establish effective therapeutic relationships.

Prevalence of Mental Health Problems in Children and Adolescents

Just how common are mental health problems among America's children and adolescents? Unfortunately, quite common. Approximately four of ten adolescents (40.3%) have experienced a diagnosable mental disorder during the past year (Kessler et al., 2012). About one in four (23.4%) are presently affected. About one in ten children suffer from a mental disorder severe enough to impair development ("A Children's Mental Illness 'Crisis,'" 2001). Many psychological disorders in adults first appeared in childhood (Cohen, 2011).

In children 6 to 17 years of age, the most commonly diagnosed psychological disorders are learning disorders (11.5%) and attention-deficit/hyperactivity disorder (8.8%) (Blanchard, Gurka, & Blackman, 2006). If we limit our scope to adolescents, anxiety disorders top the list of the most commonly diagnosed disorders (Kessler et al., 2012). Depression too is all too common, as seen in results of a telephone survey that was based on a national probability sample of American youth ages 12 to 17. The survey found that 7% of the boys and 14% of the girls had suffered from major depression in the preceding six-month period of time (Kilpatrick et al., 2003).

Despite the prevalence of childhood psychological disorders, the great majority of children with psychological disorders fail to get the treatment they need. A recent study showed that only about one-third of adolescents with diagnosable mental disorders received treatment (Merikangas et al., 2011). Even a majority of adolescents with severe mental disorders fail to receive treatment ("Majority of US adolescents," 2011). Children who have *internalized* problems, especially anxiety and depression, are at higher

"Pop, am I experiencing a normal childhood?"

Source: © Lee Lorenz/The New Yorker Collection/www.cartoonbank.com

13.2 Describe the effects of child abuse.

risk of going untreated than children with *externalized* problems (problems involving acting out or aggressive behavior) that are disruptive or annoying to others.

Risk Factors for Childhood Disorders

Many factors contribute to increased risk of developmental disorders, including genetic susceptibility, environmental stressors (such as living in decaying neighborhoods), and family factors (such as inconsistent or harsh discipline, neglect, or physical or sexual abuse) (e.g., Goodnight et al., 2012). Children of depressed parents also stand a higher risk of developing psychological disorders, perhaps because parental depression contributes to greater levels of family stress (Essex et al., 2006; Weissman et al., 2006).

Ethnicity and gender are other discriminating factors. For reasons that remain unclear, ethnic minority children stand a higher risk of developing problems such as ADHD and anxiety and depressive disorders (Anderson & Mayes, 2010; Miller, Nigg, & Miller, 2009). Boys are at greater risk for developing many childhood disorders, ranging from autism to hyperactivity to elimination disorders. Problems of anxiety and depression also affect boys proportionally more often than girls. In adolescence, however, anxiety and mood disorders become more common in girls and remain so throughout adulthood (USDHHS, 1999). T / F

Physical and sexual abuse and neglect are linked to a wide range of psychological disorders in childhood and adulthood, such as depression, substance abuse, anxiety disorders, ADHD, posttraumatic stress disorder (PTSD), and conduct disorder (e.g., Arseneault et al., 2011; Cannon et al., 2011; Nanni, Uher, & Danese, 2012; Nauert, 2011a; Sugaya et al., 2012). (Effects of childhood sexual abuse are discussed in Chapter 10.) Even milder forms of physical punishment that may not rise to the level of physical abuse or neglect, such as spanking, smacking, and pushing, increase the risk of anxiety and mood disorders in adulthood (Afifi et al., 2012).

Physically abused or neglected children often have difficulty forming healthy peer relationships and healthy attachments to others. They may lack the capacity for empathy or fail to develop a sense of conscience or concern about the welfare of others. They may act out in ways that mirror the cruelty they've experienced in their lives, such as by torturing or killing animals, setting fires, or picking on smaller, more vulnerable children. Other common psychological effects of neglect and abuse include lowered self-esteem, depression, immature behaviors such as bed-wetting or thumb-sucking, suicide attempts and suicidal thinking, poor school performance, behavior problems, and failure to venture beyond the home to explore the outside world. The behavioral and emotional consequences of child abuse often extend into adulthood (Miller-Perrin et al., 2009).

Child sexual and physical abuse is hardly an isolated problem. A recent international study of data drawn from the United States and 21 other countries showed that about 8% of men and 20% of women had suffered sexual abuse before the age of 18 (Pereda et al., 2009). Moreover, more than 1.5 million children in the United States each year are victims of child abuse or neglect (Gershater-Molkoa, Lutzker, & Sherman, 2002). And tragically, between 1,000 and 2,000 children in the United States die each year as the result of abuse or neglect, more than twice the rate (adjusted for population size) of Great Britain, France, Canada, or Japan (Koch, 2009). As horrific as these numbers are, they greatly understate the problem, as most incidents of child maltreatment are never publicly identified.

Concerns about physical abuse are understandable, but we should not lose sight of the emotional consequences of verbal abuse, of parents harshly scolding, belittling, and swearing at their children. Yes, "sticks and stones" can break bones, but words can do extensive emotional harm (Teicher et al., 2006). Moreover, exposure to domestic violence or spousal abuse in the home is also associated with higher levels of behavioral and emotional problems in children (Evans, Davies, & DiLillo, 2008). T / F

Play therapy. In play therapy, children may enact scenes with dolls or puppets that symbolically represent conflicts occurring within their own families.

truth OR fiction

Boys are more likely to develop anxiety and mood disorders than girls are.

☑ **TRUE** However, anxiety and mood disorders become more common among women beginning in adolescence.

truth OR fiction

When it comes to child maltreatment, it's not just "sticks and stones" that do damage.

☑ **TRUE** Verbal abuse can lead to extensive emotional harm.

We now consider the specific types of psychological disorders in childhood and adolescence. We will examine the features of these disorders, their causes, and the treatments used to help children who suffer from them. First, you may wish to review Table 13.1, which provides an overview of these disorders.

TABLE 13.1

Overview of Psychological Disorders in Childhood and Adolescence

Types of Disorders	Description	Major Types/Estimated Prevalence Rates, If Known	Features
Autism Spectrum Disorder	A spectrum of autism-related disorders varying in level of severity	• 1% to 2%	• Impaired functioning; marked deficits relating to others; impaired language and cognitive functioning; restricted range of activities and interests
Intellectual Disability (Intellectual Developmental Disorder)	A broad-based delay in the development of cognitive and social functioning	• Deficits vary with level of severity from mild to profound (about 1% overall)	• Diagnosed on the basis of low IQ score and poor adaptive functioning
Specific Learning Disorder	Deficiencies in specific learning abilities in the context of at least average intelligence and exposure to learning opportunities	• May involve deficiencies in mathematics, writing, reading, or executive functions; for deficiencies in reading, writing, and mathematics, 5% to 15% of school-age children	• For mathematics deficiencies , difficulties understanding basic mathematical or arithmetical operations • For writing deficiencies, grossly deficient writing skills • For reading deficiencies, difficulties recognizing words or comprehending written text • For executive function deficiencies, difficulties with planning and organizing skills
Communication Disorders	Difficulties in understanding or using language	• Language Disorder • Speech Sound disorder (formerly phonological disorder) • Childhood-Onset Fluency Disorder (stuttering) (1%) • Social (Pragmatic) Communication Disorder	• Difficulty understanding or using spoken language • Difficulty articulating sounds of speech • Difficulty speaking fluently without interruption • Problems communicating with others in conversations or social contexts
Attention-Deficit/ Hyperactivity and Disruptive Behavior Disorders	Patterns of disturbed behavior that are generally disruptive to others and to adaptable social functioning	• Attention-Deficit/Hyperactivity Disorder (7%–9%) • Conduct Disorder (12% males; 7% females) • Oppositional Defiant Disorder (1% –11%)	• ADHD: Problems of impulsivity, inattention, and hyperactivity • Conduct disorder: Antisocial behavior that violates social norms and the rights of others • Oppositional defiant disorder: Pattern of noncompliant, negativistic, or oppositional behavior
Anxiety and Mood Disorders	Emotional disorders affecting children and adolescents	• Separation Anxiety Disorder (4%–5%) • Specific Phobia • Social Phobia • Generalized Anxiety Disorder • Major Depressive Disorder (5% in children to upward of 20% in adolescents) • Bipolar Disorder	• Anxiety and depression often have similar features in children as in adults, but some differences exist • Children may suffer from school phobia as a form of separation anxiety • Depressed children may fail to label their feelings as depression or may show behaviors, such as conduct problems and physical complaints, that mask depression
Elimination Disorders	Persistent problems with controlling urination or defecation that cannot be explained by organic causes	• Enuresis (lack of control over urination) (5% – 10% among 5-year-olds) • Encopresis (lack of control over defecation) (1% of 5-year-olds)	• Enuresis: Nighttime-only enuresis (bed-wetting) is the most common type • Encopresis: Occurs most often during daytime hours

Sources: Prevalence rates derived from APA, 2013; CDC, 2009, 2012; Frick & Silverthorn, 2001; Galanter, 2013; Kaper, Alderson, & Hude, 2012; Loeber et al., 2009; Masi, Mucci, & Millipiedi, 2001; Nock et al., 2006; Rhode et al., 2013; Shear et al., 2006; Wingert, 2000; Yeargin-Allsopp et al., 2003.

Autism and Autism Spectrum Disorder

Autism is one of the most severe behavioral disorders of childhood. It is a chronic, life-long condition. Children with autism, like Peter, seem utterly alone in the world, despite parental efforts to bridge the gulf that divides them.

13.3 Describe key features of autism spectrum disorder and ways of understanding and treating it.

→ A Case of Autism

Peter nursed eagerly, sat and walked at the expected ages. Yet some of his behavior made us vaguely uneasy. He never put anything in his mouth. Not his fingers nor his toys—nothing. . . .

More troubling was the fact that Peter didn't look at us, or smile, and wouldn't play the games that seemed as much a part of babyhood as diapers. He rarely laughed, and when he did, it was at things that didn't seem funny to us. He didn't cuddle, but sat upright in my lap, even when I rocked him. But children differ and we were content to let Peter be himself. We thought it hilarious when my brother, visiting us when Peter was 8 months old, observed that "That kid has no social instincts, what-soever." Although Peter was a first child, he was not isolated. I frequently put him in his playpen in front of the house, where the schoolchildren stopped to play with him as they passed. He ignored them, too.

It was Kitty, a personality kid, born two years later, whose responsiveness emphasized the degree of Peter's difference. When I went into her room for the late feeding, her little head bobbed up and she greeted me with a smile that reached from her head to her toes. And the realization of that difference chilled me more than the wintry bedroom.

Peter's babbling had not turned into speech by the time he was 3. His play was solitary and repetitive. He tore paper into long thin strips, bushel baskets of it every day. He spun the lids from my canning jars and became upset if we tried to divert him. Only rarely could I catch his eye, and then saw his focus change from me to the reflection in my glasses. . . .

[Peter's] adventures into our suburban neighborhood had been unhappy. He had disregarded the universal rule that sand is to be kept in sandboxes, and the children themselves had punished him. He walked around a sad and solitary figure, always carrying a toy airplane, a toy he never played with. At that time, I had not heard the word that was to dominate our lives, to hover over every conversation, to sit through every meal beside us. That word was autism.

→ *Adapted from Eberhardy, 1967*

The word *autism* derives from the Greek *autos*, meaning "self." The term was first used in 1906 by the Swiss psychiatrist Eugen Bleuler to refer to a peculiar style of thinking among people with schizophrenia. Autistic thinking is the tendency to view oneself as the center of the universe, to believe that external events somehow refer to oneself. In 1943, another psychiatrist, Leo Kanner, applied the diagnosis "early infantile autism" to a group of disturbed children who seemed unable to relate to others, as if they lived in their own private worlds. Unlike children with intellectual disability, these children seemed to shut out any input from the outside world, creating a kind of "autistic aloneness" (Kanner, 1943).

The *DSM-5* places autism (previously called *autistic disorder*) in a broader diagnostic category called **autism spectrum disorder,** or ASD, that includes a range of autism-related disorders that vary in severity. *DSM-5* identifies ASD on the basis of a common set of behaviors representing persistent deficits in communication and social interactions and restricted or fixated interests and repetitive behaviors (see DSM-5 box). Clinicians need to rate the severity of ASD as severe, moderate, or mild. The more severe the disorder, the greater the level of support that is needed.

Watch the **Video** *Xavier: Autism* in **MyPsychLab**

A. Persistent deficits in social communication and social interaction across multiple contexts, as manifested by the following, currently or by history (examples are illustrative, not exhaustive; see text):

1. Deficits in social-emotional reciprocity, ranging, for example, from abnormal social approach and failure of normal back-and-forth conversation; to reduced sharing of interests, emotions, or affect; to failure to initiate or respond to social interactions.

2. Deficits in nonverbal communicative behaviors used for social interaction, ranging, for example, from poorly integrated verbal and nonverbal communication; to abnormalities in eye contact and body language or deficits in understanding and use of gestures; to a total lack of facial expressions and nonverbal communication.

3. Deficits in developing, maintaining, and understanding relationships, ranging, for example, from difficulties adjusting behavior to suit various social contexts; to difficulties in sharing imaginative play or in making friends; to absence of interest in peers.

B. Restricted, repetitive patterns of behavior, interests, or activities, as manifested by at least two of the following, currently or by history (examples are illustrative, not exhaustive; see text):

1. Stereotyped or repetitive motor movements, use of objects, or speech (e.g., simple motor stereotypies, lining up toys or flipping objects, echolalia, idiosyncratic phrases).

2. Insistence on sameness, inflexible adherence to routines, or ritualized patterns of verbal or nonverbal behavior (e.g., extreme distress at small changes, difficulties with transitions, rigid thinking patterns, greeting rituals, need to take same route or eat same food every day).

3. Highly restricted, fixated interests that are abnormal in intensity or focus (e.g., strong attachment to or preoccupation with unusual objects, excessively circumscribed or perseverative interests).

4. Hyper- or hyporeactivity to sensory input or unusual interest in sensory aspects of the environment (e.g., apparent indifference to pain/temperature, adverse response to specific sounds or textures, excessive smelling or touching of objects, visual fascination with lights or movement).

C. Symptoms must be present in the early developmental period (but may not become fully manifest until social demands exceed limited capacities, or may be masked by learned strategies in later life).

D. Symptoms cause clinically significant impairment in social, occupational, or other important areas of current functioning,

E. These disturbances are not better explained by intellectual disability (intellectual developmental disorder) or global developmental delay. Intellectual disability and autism spectrum disorder frequently co-occur; to make comorbid diagnoses of autism spectrum disorder and intellectual disability, social communication should be below that expected for general developmental level.

Note: Individuals with a well-established DSM-IV diagnosis of autistic disorder, Asperger's disorder, or pervasive developmental disorder not otherwise specified should be given the diagnosis of autism spectrum disorder. Individuals who have marked deficits in social communication, but whose symptoms do not otherwise meet criteria for autism spectrum disorder, should be evaluated for social (pragmatic) communication disorder.

Reprinted with permission from the Diagnostic and Statistical Manual of Mental Disorders, Fifth Edition, (Copyright 2013). American Psychiatric Association.

Watch the **Video** David: Asperger's in MyPsychLab

The diagnostic terms *Asperger's disorder* and *childhood disintegrative disorder* were used in the previous edition of the *DSM* to describe distinct disorders within the autism spectrum, but are now classified as forms of autism spectrum disorder if diagnostic criteria for ASD are met. Asperger's disorder refers to a pattern of abnormal behavior involving social awkwardness and stereotyped or repetitive behaviors but without the significant language or cognitive deficits associated with more severe forms of autistic spectrum disorder (Rausch, Johnson, & Casanova, 2008). Children with Asperger's don't show the profound deficits in intellectual, verbal, and self-care skills we find in children with the classic form of autism (Harmon, 2012). They may have remarkable verbal skills, such as reading newspapers at age 5 or 6, and may develop an obsessive interest in, and body of knowledge about, an obscure or narrow range of topics, like the interstate highway system, or, as in one case, vacuum cleaners (Osborne, 2002; Wallis, 2009).

Childhood disintegrative disorder was used in the previous version of the *DSM* to apply to children who show a significant loss (disintegration) of previously acquired skills in areas such as understanding or using language, social or adaptive functioning, bowel or bladder control, play, or motor skills. The child also shows impaired social interactions or communication and narrow, stereotyped, and repetitive behaviors, interests, or activities. It is a rare condition appearing more commonly in boys.

How Common Is Autism Spectrum Disorder?

The reported prevalence of ASD has been rising steadily over the past twenty years. In 2013, government researchers estimated that 1in 50 children (2%) in the United States—more than 1 million children in total—were affected by some form of autism spectrum disorder, up from 1 in 86 reported in 2007 (Blumberg et al., 2013; "U.S. Autism," 2013). The estimate is based on a nationwide phone survey of parents, not on careful diagnosis of cases. However, government officials believe the estimate reflects the proportion of American families struggling with some form of autism.

Autism. Children with autism lack the ability to relate to others and seem to live in their own private worlds.

What might have caused this jump in cases remains unclear, but experts suspect that better diagnostic practices and greater awareness of the disorder among health care professionals in the community largely contribute to the increase (Kim et al., 2011; Kuehn, 2012). In addition, much of the rise in cases of autism and related disorders may be accounted for by a sharp increase in the numbers of cases of Asperger's disorder and other milder forms of autism spectrum disorder (Charman, 2011). It remains to be seen whether the introduction of new diagnostic criteria for ASD in *DSM-5* will affect the reported rates of autism (Carey, 2012b). Some parents of children with Asperger's worry that their children may not qualify for the *DSM-5* diagnosis of ASD and perhaps not receive the treatment services they need or be eligible for reimbursement for these services (Carey, 2012b; Mestel, 2012).

Scientists are investigating whether other factors, perhaps prenatal or childhood infections or environmental factors such as exposure to environmental toxins, may be contributing to increased rates of autism (Newman, 2011; Weintraub, 2011). As reported in Chapter 11, investigators linked increased risk of both autism and schizophrenia in children with older fathers (but, curiously, not with older mothers) (Kong et al., 2012). The link is explained by a greater prevalence of random genetic mutations in the sperm of older men, which may be contributing to a true increase in the rates of autism because couples today are more likely to postpone having children than those in earlier generations (Carey, 2012). Still, the risks remain relatively low in offspring of older men, about 2% for fathers in their 40s or older.

One source of concern about the risk of autism is the widespread suspicion among parents of affected children regarding possible contamination from a chemical preservative in the widely used MMR (measles, mumps, rubella) vaccine. However, investigators have consistently failed to find links between autism and use of childhood vaccines (Fombonne, 2008; Weintraub, 2011). **T / F**

Autism is nearly five times as common in boys as girls (CDC, 2012). Signs of the disorder (lack of nonverbal communication) may first be observed at around 12 to 18 months of age (Ingersoll, 2011; Norton, 2012). Children with autism are often described by their parents as having been "good babies" early in infancy. This generally means they were not demanding. As they develop, however, they begin to reject physical affection, such as cuddling, hugging, and kissing. Their speech development begins to fall behind the norm. Signs of social detachment often begin during the first year of life, such as failure to look at other people's faces. The disorder can be diagnosed reliably by around age 2 or 3, but the average autistic child doesn't receive a diagnosis until about age 6. Delays in diagnosis can be detrimental, because the earlier children with autism are diagnosed and treated, the better they generally do.

truth OR fiction

Childhood vaccines cause autism.

☑ **FALSE** Investigators find no links between autism and childhood vaccines.

Features of Autism

Perhaps the most poignant feature of autism is the child's utter aloneness. Other features include profound deficits in social skills, language, and communication and ritualistic or stereotyped behavior. The child may also be mute, or if some language skills are present, they may be characterized by peculiar usage, as in *echolalia* (parroting back what the child has heard in a high-pitched monotone); pronoun reversals (using "you" or "he" instead of "I"); use of words that have meaning only to those who have intimate knowledge of the child; and tendencies to raise the voice at the end of sentences, as if asking a question. Nonverbal communication may also be impaired or absent. For example, autistic children may avoid eye contact and show an absence of any facial expressions. They are also slow to respond to adults who try to grab their attention, if they respond at all. Although they may be unresponsive to others, they display strong emotions, especially strong negative emotions, such as anger, sadness, and fear.

One of the primary features of autism is repetitive, purposeless, stereotyped movements—interminably twirling, flapping the hands, or rocking back and forth with the arms around the knees (Leekam, Prior, & Uljarevic, 2011). Some children with autism mutilate themselves, even as they cry out in pain. They may bang their heads, slap their faces, bite their hands and shoulders, or pull out their hair. They may also throw sudden tantrums or panics. Another feature of autism is aversion to environmental changes—a feature termed *preservation of sameness*. When familiar objects are moved even slightly from their usual places, children with autism may throw tantrums or cry continually. Children with autism may insist on eating the same food every day.

Children with autism are bound by ritual. The teacher of a 5-year-old girl with autism learned to greet her every morning by saying, "Good morning, Lily, I am very, very glad to see you" (Diamond, Baldwin, & Diamond, 1963). Although Lily would not respond to the greeting, she would shriek if the teacher omitted even one of the *verys*.

Like Donna Williams, the woman whose childhood experiences opened this chapter, autistic children often view people as a threat. Reflecting back on his childhood, a high-functioning autistic young man speaks about his needs for sameness and for performing repetitive, stereotyped behaviors. For this young man, people were a threat because they were not always the same and were made up of pieces that didn't quite fit together:

"I" "I Didn't Know What They Were For"

I loved repetition. Every time I turned on a light I knew what would happen. When I flipped the switch, the light went on. It gave me a wonderful feeling of security because it was exactly the same each time. Sometimes there were two switches on one plate, and I liked those even better; I really liked wondering which light would go on from which switch. Even when I knew, it was thrilling to do it over and over. It was always the same.

People bothered me. I didn't know what they were for or what they would do to me. They were not always the same and I had no security with them at all. Even a person who was always nice to me might be different sometimes. Things didn't fit together to me with people. Even when I saw them a lot, they were still in pieces, and I couldn't connect them to anything. . . .

From Barron & Barron, 2002, pp. 20–21

Autistic children appear to lack a differentiated self-concept, a sense of themselves as distinct individuals. Despite their unusual behavior, they are often quite attractive and have an "intelligent look" about them. However, as measured by scores on standardized tests, their intellectual development tends to lag well below the norm (Matson & Shoemaker, 2009). Though some autistic children have normal IQs, many show evidence of intellectual disability (Mefford, Batshaw, & Hoffman, 2012). Even those without intellectual impairment have difficulty acquiring the ability to symbolize, such as recognizing emotions, engaging in symbolic play, and solving problems conceptually. They also display difficulty in performing tasks that require interaction with other people. The relationship between autism and intelligence is clouded, however, by difficulties in administering standardized IQ tests to these children. Testing requires cooperation, a skill that is dramatically lacking in children with autism. At best, we can only estimate their intellectual ability.

Establishing contact. One of the principal therapeutic tasks in working with children with autism is the establishment of interpersonal contact. Behavioral therapists use reinforcers to increase adaptive social behaviors, such as paying attention to the therapist and playing with other children. Behavioral therapists may also use punishments to suppress self-mutilative behavior.

Theoretical Perspectives on Autism

An early and now discredited belief held that the autistic child's aloofness was a reaction to parents who were cold and detached—"emotional refrigerators" who lacked the ability to establish warm relationships with their children.

Psychologist O. Ivar Lovaas and his colleagues (1979) offered a cognitive learning perspective on autism. They suggest that children with autism have perceptual deficits that limit them to processing only one stimulus at a time. As a result, they are slow to learn by means of classical conditioning (association of stimuli). From the learning theory perspective, children become attached to their primary caregivers through associations with primary reinforcers such as food and hugging. Autistic children, however, attend either to the food or to the cuddling and do not connect it with the parent.

Autistic children often have difficulties integrating information from various senses (Russo et al., 2010). At times, they seem unduly sensitive to stimulation. At other times, they become so insensitive that an observer might wonder whether they are deaf. Perceptual and cognitive deficits seem to diminish their capacity to make use of information—to comprehend and apply social rules.

We don't yet know what causes autism, but mounting evidence points to a neurological basis involving brain abnormalities, perhaps involving prenatal influences leading to abnormal wiring in the circuitry of the developing brain (Norton, 2012; Russo et al., 2010; Valasquez-Manoff, 2012; Weintraub, 2011; Wolff et al., 2012). Evidence of brain abnormalities comes more directly from brain-imaging studies showing malfunctions in complex circuitry in networks of brain cells and structural damage involving loss of brain tissue (e.g., Cortese et al., 2012; Ecker et al., 2013; Hazlett et al., 2011; Uddin et al., 2011).

Scientists suspect that the brain of the child with autism develops abnormally due to a combination of genetic factors and (presently unknown) environmental influences, possibly involving exposure to certain toxins or viruses or prenatal influences (Dawson, 2013; Halmayer et al., 2011; Szatmari et al., 2011). Even before symptoms emerge, we see evidence of abnormal brain development in infant children who go on to develop autism (Wolff et al., 2012). Recent evidence links a greater risk of ASDs to certain prenatal risk factors, including influenza infection or prolonged fevers in the mother during pregnancy (Atladóttir et al., 2012). These factors may adversely affect the developing brain in the fetus.

We also have recent evidence suggesting in children with autism, parts of the brain responsible for language and social behavior grow much more slowly than in other children (Hua et al., 2011). Lead researcher, Xua Hua, explained, "Because the brain of a child with autism develops more slowly during this critical period of life, these children may have an especially difficult time struggling to establish personal identity, develop social interactions and refine emotional skills" ("Autistic Brains Develop More Slowly," 2011). Delays in brain development may continue into adolescence.

Multiple genes are involved in determining susceptibility to autism, not just any one individual gene (Nauert, 2011; State et al., 2011). Work is proceeding in research laboratories across the world to track down the responsible genes (e.g., Dennis et al., 2012; Michaelson et al., 2012; Sakai et al., 2011; Santini et al., 2012). Scientists are beginning to make headway identifying autism-related genes and the effects they have on brain functioning (e.g., Leblond et al., 2012; Neale et al., 2012; O'Roak et al., 2012). For example, one group of researchers discovered mutations on three genes linked to at least some cases of autism (Carey, 2012; Sanders et al., 2012).

Treatment of Autism

Although there is no cure for autism, early, intensive behavioral programs that apply learning principles in the child's environment can significantly improve learning and language skills and socially adaptive behavior in autistic children (Eikeseth et al., 2012; Ingersoll, 2011; Reichow et al., 2011). These learning-based approaches are generally called *applied behavior analysis* or ABA treatment models. No other treatment approach has produced comparable results. Using operant conditioning methods, therapists and parents engage in the painstaking work, systematically using rewards and mild punishments to increase the child's ability to attend to others, play with other children, develop academic skills, and reduce or eliminate self-mutilation.

The most widely used behavioral treatment programs are highly intensive and structured, offering a great deal of individual, one-to-one instruction. In a classic study, psychologist O. Ivar Lovaas of UCLA (University of California, Los Angeles) demonstrated impressive gains in autistic children who received more than 40 hours of one-to-one behavioral treatment each week for at least two years (Lovaas, 1987). Subsequent research shows favorable gains in autistic children treated with long-term, intensive behavioral treatment with respect to language development, intellectual functioning, and social functioning and other adaptive behaviors (Eikeseth et al., 2012; Virués-Ortega, 2010). The earlier the treatment is started (before age 5) and the more intensive the treatment, the better the results tend to be (Vismara & Rogers, 2010).

Autistic toddlers also benefit from early training that focuses on building imitation skills, helping lay the foundation for social interactions (Kuehn, 2011; Landa et al., 2011). Unfortunately, intensive one-to-one treatment is very expensive, and parents seeking publically subsidized programs can expect to deal with long waiting lists.

Biomedical treatments are limited largely to the use of antipsychotic drugs to control disruptive behavior, such as tantrums, aggression, self-injurious behavior, and stereotyped behavior in autistic children (McDougle et al., 2005). Recently, investigators found that antispychotic drugs work better when treatment includes parents in a training program that teaches them how to respond to the child's disruptive behavior (Scahill et al., 2012). Although drugs do not produce consistent improvement in cognitive and language development in autistic children, drugs may have a role to play in fostering language development (Beversdorf et al., 2011).

Autistic traits generally continue into adulthood to one degree or another. Yet some autistic children go on to earn college degrees and function independently. Others need continuing treatment throughout their lives, even institutionalized care. There appears to be a small subset of autistic children who can overcome the disorder. A 2013 study showed that a small but significant minority of children with previously diagnosed autism had no symptoms of the disorder when evaluated in later childhood or adolescence (Carey, 2013; Fein et al., 2013). Although these findings offer hope to autistic children and their families, we should caution that only a small minority of autistic children show this level of improvement.

Helping Autistic Children Communicate: We've Got an App for That

There are phone apps today for virtually anything, including, as it turns out, helping autistic children communicate. One example, iMean™, is the brainchild of Michael Bergmann, whose son Daniel suffers from autism ("iPad App Helps Autistic," 2010). The app converts the iPhone into a large-button keyboard with a word prediction feature. Many autistic children lack the fine motor control needed to type on a regular keyboard or phone display. The app's large letter display allows the user to point at particular letters and see predictions of the full word on the display screen. The autistic child can work independently to gradually build communication skills. A later version of the app includes speech recognition capabilities.

iPads offer another means for autistic children to communicate with the outside world and to access educational programming. A parent of a 9-year-old autistic body was amazed by his son's reaction to the iPad (Kendrick, 2010). His son immediately took to working with the device and with only a little training began using a wide range of educational tools, such as spelling and counting games and features. Electronic devices like the iPad herald potentially revolutionary new ways of reaching and teaching autistic children.

Yes, There's an App for That The creator of the iMean™, Michael Bergmann, holding an iPad displaying the app, shown here with his son Daniel, who uses the letterboard to work with abstract thoughts.

Intellectual Disability

About 1% of the general population is affected by **intellectual disability** or ID (also called *intellectual developmental disorder* or *IDD*). The primary feature of ID is a general deficit in intellectual development. Formerly called *mental retardation,* intellectual disability is the diagnostic term applying to individuals who have significant and broad-ranging limitations or deficits in intellectual functioning and adaptive behaviors (e.g., lack of basic conceptual, social, and practical skills of daily living). Children with ID tend to have deficits in reasoning and problem-solving ability, abstract thinking skills, judgment, and school performance.

Intellectual disability begins before the age of 18 during child development and follows a lifelong course. However, many children with ID improve over time, especially if they receive support, guidance, and enriched educational opportunities. Those who are reared in impoverished environments may fail to improve or may deteriorate further.

Intellectual disability is diagnosed on the basis of a low IQ score and impaired adaptive functioning occurring before the age of 18 that results in significant impairments in meeting expected standards of independent functioning and social responsibility. These impairments may involve difficulty performing common tasks of daily life expected of someone of the same age in a given cultural setting in three domains: (1) conceptual (skills relating to use of language, reading, writing, math, reasoning, memory, and problem solving), (2) social (skills relating to awareness of other people's experiences, ability to communicate effectively with others, and ability to form friendships, among

13.4 Describe the key features and causes of intellectual disability.

others), and (3) practical (ability to meet personal care needs, fulfill job responsibilities, manage money, and organize school and work tasks, among others). Although earlier versions of the *DSM* required an IQ score of less than 70 (100 is the average score) for a diagnosis of mental retardation, *DSM-5* does not set any particular IQ score for the diagnosis of ID.

The level of severity depends upon the child's adaptive functioning, or ability to meet the expectable demands children face at school and in the home. Most children with ID (about 85%) fall into the mild range. These children are generally capable of meeting basic academic demands, such as learning to read simple passages. As adults, they are generally capable of independent functioning, although they may require some guidance and support. Table 13.2 provides a description of the deficits and abilities associated with various degrees of ID.

Causes of Intellectual Disability

The causes of ID include biological factors, psychosocial factors, or a combination of these factors. Biological causes include chromosomal and genetic disorders, infectious diseases, and maternal alcohol use during pregnancy. Psychosocial causes include exposure to an impoverished home environment marked by the lack of intellectually stimulating activities during childhood.

TABLE 13.2

Levels of Intellectual Disability (formerly called Mental Retardation), Typical Ranges of IQ Scores, and Types of Adaptive Behaviors

Severity/Approximate IQ Score Range	Preschool Age (0–5) Maturation and Development	School Age (6–21) Training and Education	Adult (21 and Over) Social and Vocational Adequacy
Mild/50–70	Often not noticed as intellectually disabled by casual observer, but is slower to walk, feed self, and talk than most children.	Can acquire practical skills and useful reading and arithmetic to a 3rd- to 6th-grade level with special education. Can be guided toward social conformity.	Can usually achieve social and vocational skills adequate to self-maintenance; may need occasional guidance and support when under unusual social or economic stress.
Moderate/35–49	Noticeable delays in motor development, especially in speech; responds to training in various self-help activities.	Can learn simple communication, elementary health and safety habits, and simple manual skills; does not progress in functional reading or arithmetic.	Can perform simple tasks under sheltered conditions; participates in simple recreation; travels alone in familiar places; usually incapable of self-maintenance.
Severe/20–34	Marked delay in motor development; little or no communication skill; may respond to training in elementary self-help—e.g., self-feeding.	Usually walks, barring specific disability; has some understanding of speech and some response; can profit from systematic habit training.	Can conform to daily routines and repetitive activities; needs continuing direction and supervision in protective environment.
Profound/Below 20	Gross intellectual disability; minimal capacity for functioning in sensorimotor areas; needs nursing care.	Obvious delays in all areas of development; shows basic emotional responses; may respond to skillful training in use of legs, hands, and jaws; needs close supervision.	May walk, may need nursing care, may have primitive speech; will usually benefit from regular physical activity; incapable of self-maintenance.

Source: Adapted from *Essentials of Psychology* (6th ed.) by S. A. Rathus. Copyright © 2001. Reprinted with permission of Brooks/Cole, an imprint of the Wadsworth Group, a division of Thomson Learning, now Cengage Learning.

DOWN SYNDROME AND OTHER CHROMOSOMAL ABNORMALITIES The most frequently identified cause of ID is **Down syndrome** (formerly called Down's syndrome), which is characterized by an extra chromosome on the 21st pair of chromosomes, resulting in 47 chromosomes rather than the normal complement of 46 (Einfeld & Brown, 2010; Mefford, Batshaw, & Hoffman, 2012). Down syndrome occurs in about 1 in 800 births. It usually occurs when the 21st pair of chromosomes in either the egg or the sperm fails to divide normally, resulting in an extra chromosome. Chromosomal abnormalities become more likely as parents age, so expectant couples in their mid-30s or older often undergo prenatal genetic tests to detect Down syndrome and other genetic abnormalities. Down syndrome can be traced to the mother's egg cell in about 90% of cases, with about 10% attributable to the father's sperm (Genetic Science Learning Center, 2012).

People with Down syndrome are recognizable by distinctive physical features: a round face, broad, flat nose, and small, downward-sloping folds of skin at the inside corners of the eyes, which give the impression of slanted eyes. A protruding tongue; small, squarish hands and short fingers; a curved fifth finger; and disproportionately small arms and legs in relation to their bodies also characterize children with Down syndrome. Nearly all of these children have ID and many suffer from physical problems, such as malformations of the heart and respiratory difficulties. Sadly, the average life expectancy of Down syndrome patients is only 49 years (Yang, Rasmussen, & Friedman, 2002). In their later years, people with Down syndrome tend to suffer memory losses and experience childish emotions that represent a form of dementia. Unfortunately, we don't have a treatment for Down syndrome, but scientists are hopeful that learning more about the affected genes on chromosome 21 may lead to ways of regulating them to improve brain functioning (Einfeld & Brown, 2010).

Children with Down syndrome suffer various deficits in learning and development (Sanchez et al., 2012). They tend to be uncoordinated and to lack proper muscle tone, which makes it difficult for them to carry out physical tasks and play like other children. Down syndrome children suffer memory deficits, especially for information presented verbally, which makes it difficult for them to learn in school. They also have difficulty following instructions from teachers and expressing their thoughts or needs clearly in speech. Despite their disabilities, most can learn to read, write, and perform simple arithmetic, if they receive appropriate schooling and encouragement.

Although less common than Down syndrome, chromosomal abnormalities on the sex chromosome may also result in intellectual disabilities, such as in Klinefelter's syndrome and Turner's syndrome. *Klinefelter's syndrome,* which only occurs among males, is characterized by the presence of an extra X chromosome, resulting in an XXY chromosomal pattern rather than the normal XY pattern. Estimates of the prevalence of Klinefelter's syndrome are one to two cases per 1,000 male births (Morris et al., 2008). These men fail to develop appropriate secondary sex characteristics, resulting in small, underdeveloped testes, low sperm production, enlarged breasts, poor muscular development, and infertility. ID and learning disorders (also called *learning disabilities*) are also common. Men with Klinefelter's syndrome often don't discover they have the condition until they undergo tests for infertility.

Turner's syndrome occurs only in females and is characterized by the presence of a single X chromosome instead of the normal two (or only a partial second X chromosome) (Hong, Dunkin, & Reiss, 2011). Girls with Turner's develop normal external genitals, but their ovaries remain poorly developed, producing reduced amounts of estrogen. As women, they are

Striving to achieve. Most children with Down syndrome can learn basic academic skills if they are afforded opportunities to learn and are provided with encouragement.

generally of short stature, are infertile, and have endocrine and cardiovascular problems. They also tend to show evidence of mild intellectual disability, especially in skills relating to math and science.

FRAGILE X SYNDROME AND OTHER GENETIC ABNORMALITIES Scientists have identified several genetic causes of ID (formerly mental retardation). The most commonly identified genetic cause is **Fragile X syndrome,** which affects about 1 out of 1,000 to 1,500 males and about 1 out of 2,000 to 2,500 females (Hall et al., 2008; Maher, 2007). The syndrome is the second most common form of ID overall, after Down syndrome. The disorder is caused by a mutation on a single gene in an area of the X chromosome that appears fragile, hence the name (Kim et al., 2011; Muddashetty et al., 2011; Seltzer et al., 2012).

The effects of Fragile X syndrome range from mild learning disorders to ID so profound that those affected can hardly speak or function. Females normally have two X chromosomes, whereas males have only one. For females, having two X chromosomes seems to provide some protection against the disorder if the defective gene turns up on one of the two chromosomes, which generally results in a milder form of intellectual disability. This may explain why the disorder usually has more profound effects on males than on females. Yet the mutation does not always manifest itself. Many males and females carry the fragile X mutation without showing any clinical signs. Such carriers can still pass the syndrome to their offspring.

A genetic test can detect the genetic defect that causes fragile X syndrome. Although there is currently no treatment for the syndrome, genetic research focused on identifying the molecular cause of the disorder may someday lead to effective treatments (Bar-Nur, Caspi, & Benvenisty, 2012; Healy, Rush, & Ocain, 2011; Jacquemont et al., 2011).

Phenylketonuria (PKU) is a genetic disorder that occurs in about 1 in 10,000 to 15,000 births (Widaman, 2009). It is caused by a recessive gene that prevents the child from metabolizing the amino acid phenylalanine, which is found in many foods. Consequently, phenylalanine and its derivative, phenylpyruvic acid, accumulate in the body, causing damage to the central nervous system, resulting in severe intellectual disability. PKU can be detected in newborns by analyzing blood or urine samples. Although there is no cure for PKU, children with the disorder may suffer less damage or develop normally if they are placed on a diet low in phenylalanine soon after birth. These children receive protein supplements that compensate for their nutritional loss.

Today, various prenatal tests can detect chromosomal abnormalities and genetic disorders. In *amniocentesis,* which is usually conducted about 14 to 15 weeks following conception, a sample of amniotic fluid is drawn with a syringe from the amniotic sac that contains the fetus. Cells from the fetus can then be separated from the fluid, allowed to grow in a culture, and examined for abnormalities, including Down syndrome. Blood tests are used to detect carriers of other disorders.

PRENATAL FACTORS Some cases of ID are caused by maternal infections or substance abuse during pregnancy. Rubella (German measles) in the mother, for example, can be passed along to the unborn child, causing brain damage resulting in intellectual disability. It may also play a role in autism. Although the mother may experience mild symptoms or none at all, the effects on the fetus can be tragic. Other maternal infections that may cause retardation in the child include syphilis, cytomegalovirus, and genital herpes.

Widespread programs that immunize women against rubella before pregnancy and tests for syphilis during pregnancy have reduced the risk of transmission of these infections to children. Most children who contract genital herpes from their mothers do so during delivery by coming into contact with the herpes simplex virus in the birth canal. Therefore, delivery by caesarean section (C-section) can prevent viral transmission during childbirth.

Drugs that the mother ingests during pregnancy may pass through the placenta to the child. Some can cause severe birth deformities and ID. Children whose mothers take alcohol during pregnancy are often born with *fetal alcohol syndrome* (described in Chapter 8), one of the most prominent causes of ID.

Birth complications, such as oxygen deprivation or head injuries, place children at increased risk for neurological disorders, including ID. Prematurity also places children at risk of intellectual disability and other developmental problems. Brain infections, such as encephalitis and meningitis, or traumas during infancy and early childhood, can result in ID and other health problems. Children who ingest toxins, such as paint chips containing lead, may also suffer brain damage that leads to ID.

CULTURAL–FAMILIAL CAUSES Most cases of ID fall in the mild range of severity and have no apparent biological cause or distinguishing physical feature. These cases typically have cultural–familial roots, such as being raised in an impoverished home or social or cultural environment lacking in intellectually stimulating activities or wracked by neglect or abuse.

Children in impoverished families may lack toys, books, or opportunities to interact with adults in intellectually stimulating ways. Consequently, they may not develop appropriate language skills or acquire any motivation to learn. Economic burdens, such as the need to hold multiple jobs, may prevent their parents from spending time reading to them, talking to them at length, and exposing them to creative play or activities. The children may spend most of their days glued to the TV set. The parents, most of whom were also reared in poverty, may lack the reading or communication skills to help their children develop these skills. A vicious cycle of poverty and impoverished intellectual development is repeated from generation to generation.

Children with this form of intellectual disability may respond dramatically when provided with enriched learning experiences, especially at an early age. Social programs, such as Head Start, have helped many children at risk of cultural–familial intellectual disability to function within the normal range of mental ability.

Interventions

The services that children with ID need depend on the level of severity and type of retardation. With appropriate training, children with mild forms of intellectual disability may approach a sixth-grade level of competence. They can acquire vocational skills and support themselves minimally through meaningful work. Many such children can be mainstreamed in regular classes. At the other extreme, children with severe or profound ID may need institutional care or placement in a residential care facility in the community, such as a group home. Placement in an institution is often based on the need to control destructive or aggressive behavior, not because of the severity of the individual's intellectual impairment. Consider the case of a child with moderate level of intellectual disability.

> **A Case of Intellectual Disability (Moderate Severity)**
> The mother pleaded with the emergency room physician to admit her 15-year-old son, claiming that she couldn't take it anymore. Her son, a Down syndrome patient with an IQ of 45, had alternated since the age of 8 between living in institutions and at home. Each visiting day he pleaded with his mother to take him home, and after about a year at each placement, she would bring him home but find herself unable to control his behavior. During temper tantrums, he would break dishes and destroy furniture and had recently become physically assaultive toward his mother, hitting her on the arm and shoulder during a recent scuffle when she attempted to stop him from repeatedly banging a broom on the floor.
>
> *Adapted from Spitzer et al., 1989, pp. 338–340*

Educators sometimes disagree about whether children with ID should be mainstreamed in regular classes or placed in special education classes. Although some children with mild intellectual disability achieve better when they are mainstreamed, others do not. They may find these classes overwhelming and withdraw from their schoolmates. There has also been a trend toward deinstitutionalization of people with more severe ID, motivated in large part by public outrage over the appalling conditions that formerly existed in many institutions serving this population. The Developmentally Disabled Assistance and Bill of Rights Act, which Congress passed in 1975, provided that people with mental retardation (now labeled ID) have the right to receive appropriate treatment in the least-restrictive treatment setting. Nationwide, the population of institutions for people with ID shrank by nearly two-thirds in the years following the legislation. People with ID who are capable of functioning in the community have the right to receive less restrictive care than is provided in large institutions. Many are capable of living outside the institution and have been placed in supervised group homes. Residents typically share household responsibilities and are encouraged to participate in meaningful daily activities, such as training programs or sheltered workshops. Others live with their families and attend structured day programs. Intellectually disabled adults often work in outside jobs and live in their own apartments or share apartments with other people with mild intellectual disability. Although the large-scale dumping of mental patients into the community from psychiatric institutions resulted in massive social problems and swelled the ranks of America's homeless population, deinstitutionalization of people with ID has largely been a success story that has been achieved with rare dignity (Hemmings, 2010; Lemay, 2009).

People with ID stand a high risk of developing other psychiatric disorders, such as anxiety and depression, as well as behavioral problems (McGillivray & Kershaw, 2013; Rojahn et al., 2012). Unfortunately, the emotional life of people with ID has received little attention in the literature (e.g., Lucas-Carrasco & Salvador-Carulla, 2012; Vos et al., 2012). Many professionals even assumed (wrongly) that people with ID are somehow immune from psychological problems or that they lack the verbal skills needed to benefit from psychotherapy. However, evidence shows that people with ID can benefit from psychological treatment for depression and other emotional problems (McGillivray & Kershaw, 2013; Prout & Browning, 2011).

People with ID often need psychological help dealing with adjustment to life in the community (McKenzie, 2011). Many have difficulty making friends and become socially isolated. Problems with self-esteem are also common, especially because people who have ID are often demeaned and ridiculed. Psychological counseling may be supplemented with behavioral techniques that help people acquire skills in areas such as personal hygiene, work, and social relationships. Structured behavioral approaches are used to teach people with more severe intellectual disability to master basic hygienic behaviors such as tooth-brushing, self-dressing, and hair combing. Other behavioral treatment techniques include social skills training, which focuses on increasing the individual's ability to relate effectively to others, and anger management training to help individuals develop effective ways of handling conflicts without acting out.

13.5 Identify the types of deficits associated with learning disorders and **describe** ways of understanding and treating learning disorders.

truth OR fiction

A former vice president of the United States had such difficulty with arithmetic that he could never balance a checkbook.

☑ **FALSE** Nelson Rockefeller, vice president during the Ford administration in the 1970s, suffered from dyslexia and struggled with reading, not arithmetic.

Learning Disorders

Nelson Rockefeller was a governor of New York State and a vice president of the United States. He was brilliant and well educated. However, despite the best of tutors, he always had trouble reading. Rockefeller suffered from **dyslexia,** a condition whose name is derived from the Greek roots *dys-*, meaning "bad," and *lexikon*, meaning "of words." Dyslexia is the most common type of **learning disorder** (also called *learning disability*), accounting for perhaps 80% of cases. People with dyslexia have trouble reading despite the fact that they possess at least average intelligence **T / F**

Learning disorders are typically chronic disorders that affect development well into adulthood. Children with learning disorders tend to perform poorly in school in relation to their level of intelligence and age. Their teachers and families often view them as failures. It is not surprising that children with learning disorders often have other psychological problems, such as low self-esteem. They also stand a higher risk of developing ADHD.

The *DSM-5* applies a single diagnosis of *specific learning disorder* to encompass various types of learning disorders or disabilities involving significant deficits in skills involved in reading, writing, arithmetic and math, and executive functions. These deficits significantly impact academic performance. They emerge during the grade-school years, but may not be recognized until academic demands exceed the individual's abilities, such as when timed tests are introduced. The diagnosis also requires that learning deficits cannot be better explained by a generalized delay in intellectual development (i.e., ID) or by underlying neurological or other medical conditions. The examiner needs to specify the particular learning deficit that interferes with academic, social or occupational functioning, or, as commonly is the case, by a combination of specific deficits.

PROBLEMS WITH READING Children with specific learning disorder involving reading difficulties have persistent problems with basic reading skills. Although *DSM-5* does not use the term *dyslexia,* the term remains in widespread use among teachers, clinicians, and researchers to describe significant deficits in reading skills.

Children with dyslexia may struggle to understand or recognize basic words or comprehend what they read, or they may read unusually slowly or in a halting manner. Dyslexia affects about 4% of school-age children and is much more common in boys than in girls (Rutter et al., 2004). Boys with dyslexia are also more likely than girls to show disruptive behavior in class and so are more likely to be referred for evaluation.

Children with dyslexia may read slowly and with great difficulty and may distort, omit, or substitute words when reading aloud. They have trouble decoding letters and letter combinations and translating them into the appropriate sounds (Meyler et al., 2008). They may also misperceive letters as upside down (e.g., confusing *w* for *m*) or in reversed images (*b* for *d*). Dyslexia is usually apparent by the age of 7, coinciding with the second grade, although it is sometimes recognized in 6-year-olds. Children and adolescents with dyslexia are prone to problems such as depression, low self-worth, and ADHD.

Rates of dyslexia vary with respect to native language. Rates are higher in English-speaking and French-speaking countries, where the language contains a large number of ways of spelling words containing the same meaningful sounds (e.g., the same "o" sound in the words "toe" and "tow"). They are low in Italy, where the language has a smaller ratio of sounds to letter combinations (Paulesu et al., 2001).

PROBLEMS WITH WRITING This deficiency is characterized by errors in spelling, grammar, or punctuation; by problems with legibility or fluent handwriting; or by difficulty composing clear, well-organized sentences and paragraphs. Severe writing difficulties generally become apparent by age 7 (second grade), although milder cases may not be recognized until the age of 10 (fifth grade) or later.

PROBLEMS WITH ARITHMETIC AND MATHEMATIC REASONING SKILLS Children may have problems understanding basic arithmetic facts, such as addition or subtraction operations, or performing calculations or learning multiplication tables or solving math reasoning problems. The problem may become apparent as early as the first grade (age 6) but is not generally recognized until about the second or third grade.

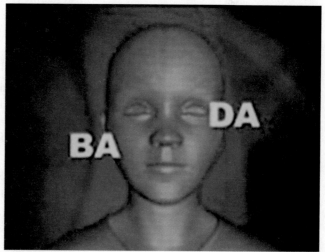

Distinguishing speech sounds. Dyslexic children appear to have difficulty distinguishing basic speech sounds, such as "ba" and "da" and connecting these sounds to particular letters in the alphabet.

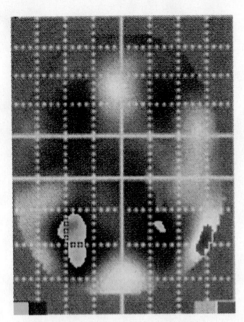

Brain-imaging study of dyslexic adults. Brain scans taken during a reading task show that stronger activation of the reading systems in the left hemisphere (shown here by areas tinted in yellow) is associated with better reading skills in nondyslexic readers. By contrast, more competent dyslexic readers rely more on the right hemisphere (as shown by blue-tinted areas). More capable dyslexic readers seem to rely on different neural pathways than normal readers. By examining differences in activation of particular areas of the brain, scientists hope to learn more about the neurological underpinnings of dyslexia.

13.6 Define the concept of communication disorders and **identify** specific types.

PROBLEMS WITH EXECUTIVE FUNCTIONS Executive function skills are a set of higher mental abilities involved in organizing, planning, and coordinating tasks needed to manage one's task or assignments. Though many children struggle with these types of challenges, children with executive function deficits have marked and sustained difficulties organizing and coordinating their school-related activities. They may frequently fall behind in school work, fail to keep track of homework assignments, or fail to plan ahead in order to complete assignments on time.

Understanding and Treating Learning Disorders

Much of the research on learning disorders focuses on dyslexia, with mounting evidence pointing to brain abnormalities that affect how visual and auditory information is processed (Golden, 2008; Nicolson & Fawcett, 2008). People with dyslexia have difficulty connecting the sounds that correspond to particular letters (e.g., seeing an *f* or a *ph* or a *gh* and saying or hearing in their minds an *f* sound). They also have trouble distinguishing speech sounds, such as the sounds "ba" and "da." Evidence points to a genetic influence in the development of these difficulties (Gabrieli, 2009; Paracchini et al., 2008).

Investigators speculate that dyslexia may take two general forms, one more genetically influenced and one more environmentally influenced (Morris, 2003; Shaywitz et al., 2003). The genetic form appears to involve defects in the neural circuitry in the brain that readers use to process speech sounds (Shaywitz, Mody, & Shaywitz, 2006). Dyslexic children with this genetic form of the disorder learn to compensate for these defects by relying on other brain capabilities, although they continue to read slowly. In the environmentally influenced form, neural circuitry is intact but people rely more on memory than on decoding strategies to understand written words. This second type may be more prevalent in children from disadvantaged educational backgrounds and is associated with more persistent reading disability (Kersting, 2003).

Linking learning disorders to defects in brain circuitry responsible for processing sensory (visual and auditory) information may point toward the development of treatment programs that help children adjust to their sensory capabilities. Therapists need to design strategies tailored to each child's particular type of disability and educational needs. For example, a child who can work better with auditory information than with visual information might be taught verbally, for example, by using recordings rather than written materials. Other intervention approaches focus on evaluating children's learning competencies and designing strategies to help them acquire skills needed to perform basic academic tasks, such as arithmetic and reading skills (Solis et al., 2012). In addition, language specialists can help dyslexic children grasp the structure and use of words.

Communication Disorders

Communication disorders are persistent difficulties in understanding or using language or speaking clearly and fluently. Because of the primacy of speech and language in daily life, these disorders can greatly interfere with the person's ability to succeed in school, the workplace, or in social situations. Here we consider the major types of communication disorders.

Language Disorder

Language disorder involves impairments in the ability to produce or understand spoken language. There may be specific impairments, such as slow vocabulary development, errors in tenses, difficulties recalling words, and problems producing sentences of appropriate length and complexity for the individual's age. Affected children may also have a speech sound (articulation) disorder, compounding their speech problems.

Children with language disorder may also have difficulties understanding words or sentences. In some cases, they struggle with understanding certain word types (such as words expressing differences in quantity—*large, big,* or *huge*), spatial terms (such as *near*

The Savant Syndrome

Got a minute? Try the following:

1. Without referring to a calendar, calculate the day of the week that March 15, 2079, will fall on.

2. List the prime numbers between 1 and 1 billion. (Hint: The list starts 1, 2, 3, 5, 7, 11, 13, 17. . . .)

3. Repeat verbatim the newspaper stories you read over coffee this morning.

4. Sing accurately every note played by the first violin in Beethoven's *Ninth Symphony*.

Give up? Don't feel bad about yourself, because very few people can perform such mental feats. Ironically, the people most likely to be able to accomplish these tasks suffer from autism, intellectual disability, or both. Clinicians use the label *savant syndrome* to refer to someone with severe mental deficiencies who possesses some remarkable mental abilities. Commonly, these people are called *savants* (the term *savant* is derived from the French *savoir*, meaning "to know"). People with savant syndrome have shown remarkable though circumscribed mental skills, such as calendar calculating and rare musical talents, which stand in contrast to their limited general intellectual abilities. Some people with the syndrome engage in lightning calculations, such as calendar calculating. One young man could tell you in a few seconds the day of the week of any given date—for example, what day of the week October 23, 1996, was (Thioux et al., 2006). Another savant could make extraordinary drawings as a child, even though could barely speak (Selfe, 2011).

There have also been cases of savants who were blind but could play back any musical piece, no matter how complex, or repeat long passages of foreign languages without losing a syllable. Others could make exact estimates of elapsed time. One could reportedly repeat verbatim the contents of a newspaper he had just read; another could repeat backward what he had just read (Tradgold, 1914, cited in Treffert, 1988).

The savant syndrome phenomenon occurs more frequently in males by a ratio of about 6 to 1. The special skills of people with the savant syndrome tend to appear out of the blue and may disappear as suddenly.

Many theories have been proposed to explain the savant syndrome, but scientists have yet to reach a consensus. One theory is that people with savant syndrome may inherit two sets of hereditary factors, one for intellectual disability and the other for special memory abilities. Other theorists speculate that the brains of savants are wired with specialized circuitry that allows them to perform concrete and narrowly defined tasks, such as perceiving number relationships (Treffert, 1988). An environment that reinforces savant abilities and provides opportunities for practice and concentration would give further impetus to the development of these unusual abilities. Still, the savant syndrome remains a mystery.

Savant syndrome. Leslie Lemke, a blind autistic savant musician, played music he heard verbatim and composed his own music, even though he had no music education. One day when he was about 14, he played flawlessly the entirety of Tchaikovsky's Piano Concerto No. 1 after having heard it once the night before.

or *far*), or sentence types (such as sentences that begin with the word *unlike*). Other cases are marked by difficulties understanding simple words or sentences.

Problems with Speech

Children may also have problems producing clear and fluent speech. In **speech sound disorder** (formerly called *phonological disorder*), there is persistent difficulty articulating the sounds of speech in the absence of defects in the oral speech mechanism or neurological impairment. Children with the disorder may omit, substitute, or mispronounce certain sounds—especially *ch, f, l, r, sh,* and *th*, which most children articulate properly by the time they reach the early school years. It may sound as if they are uttering "baby talk."

Training the Brain in Dyslexic Children

Recent research evidence shows improved brain functioning in dyslexic children as the result of remedial reading instruction (Meyler et al., 2008). Before training, the parts of the cerebral cortex responsible for decoding the sounds of written letters and assembling them into words and sentences were less active in these children than in nondyslexic controls (Meyler et al., 2008). But after just 100 hours of intensive remedial instruction, these brain regions showed increased levels of neural activity. These gains in neural activity further strengthened over the next year, to a point that differences in brain activation between dyslexic and control children virtually disappeared (see Figure 13.1).

One of the investigators, Marcel Just of Carnegie Mellon University, points out that we can see actual evidence of how remedial training changes brain functioning. He elaborated by saying, "Any kind of education is a matter of training the brain. When poor readers are learning to read, a particular brain area is not performing as well as it might, and remedial instruction helps to shape that area up." As Professor Just puts it, these findings suggest that "poor readers can be helped to develop buff brains" (cited in "Remedial Instruction," 2008).

Good > Poor at Phase 1 (Pre-remediation)

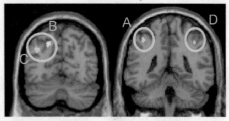

Good > Poor at Phase 3 (One-year Follow-up)

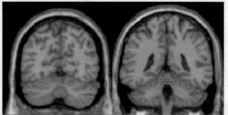

**A = left inferior parietal, B = left superior parietal,
C = left angular gyrus, D = right inferior parietal**

FIGURE 13.1

Differences in brain activation of dyslexic and nondyslexic children. Here we see areas of the brain showing greater activation in good readers versus poor readers (shown in yellow). The right side of the brain is depicted on the left side of the figure and the left side of the brain is depicted on the right side. These differences virtually disappeared after remedial reading instruction (post-remediation) and at a one-year follow-up evaluation.

Source: Image courtesy of Marcel Just of Carnegie Mellon University.

Children with more severe cases have problems articulating sounds usually mastered during the preschool years: *b, m, t, d, n,* and *h.* Speech therapy is often helpful, and mild cases often resolve themselves by the age of 8.

Persistent stuttering, which is characterized by impaired fluency of speech, is classified in *DSM-5* as a type of communication disorder called **childhood-onset fluency disorder.** People who stutter have difficulty speaking fluently with the appropriate timing of speech sounds. Stuttering usually begins between 2 and 7 years of age (APA, 2013). The disorder is characterized by one or more of the following characteristics: (a) repetitions of sounds and syllables; (b) prolongations of certain sounds; (c) interjections of inappropriate sounds; (d) broken words, such as pauses occurring within a spoken word; (e) blocking of speech; (f) circumlocutions (substitutions of alternative words to avoid problematic words); (g) displaying an excess of physical tension when emitting words; and (h) repetitions of monosyllabic whole words (e.g., "I-I-I-I am glad to meet you").

Stuttering occurs in three times as many males as females. The good news is that most children who stutter, upward of 80%, overcome the problem without any treatment, typically before age 16.

Although the specific causes of stuttering remain under study, genetic factors play an important role, perhaps involving genes that influence the control of the muscles involved in producing speech (Fibiger et al., 2010). Scientists recently reported discovering a mutation on a particular gene linked to persistent stuttering (Kang et al., 2010).

Stuttering also has an emotional component. Children who stutter tend to be more emotionally reactive than nonstutterers—when faced with stressful or challenging situations, they become more upset or excited (Karrass et al., 2006). They also tend to be troubled by social anxiety stemming from overconcern about how others evaluate them (Kraaimaat, Vanryckeghem, & Van Dam-Baggen, 2002). Stuttering is often accompanied by anxiety about speaking or avoidance of speaking situations, arising from embarrassment.

Social (Pragmatic) Communication Disorder

Social (pragmatic) communication disorder is a newly recognized disorder in *DSM-5*. The diagnosis applies to children who have continuing and profound difficulties communicating verbally and nonverbally with other people in their natural contexts—in school, at home, or in play. These children have difficulty carrying on conversations and may fall silent when in a group of children. They have difficulty acquiring and using both spoken and written language. Yet they do not show a general low level of language or mental abilities that might explain their difficulties communicating with others. Their communication deficits make it difficult for them to participate fully in social interactions and adversely affects their school or work performance.

Treatment of communication disorders is generally approached with specialized speech and language therapy or with fluency training, which involves learning to speak more slowly and to regulate one's breathing and progressing from simpler to more complex words and sentences (NIDCD, 2010). Stuttering treatment may also include psychological counseling for the anxiety in speaking situations that is often experienced by people who struggle with stuttering.

Behavior Problems: Attention-Deficit/Hyperactivity Disorder, Oppositional Defiant Disorder, and Conduct Disorder

13.7 Describe the key features of attention-deficit/hyperactivity disorder, oppositional defiant disorder, and conduct disorder.

In the previous diagnostic manual, the *DSM-IV*, these three disorders were grouped in a category of disruptive behavior disorders. Although the *DSM-5* now separates them into different diagnostic categories, we find it useful to link them together because they all involve problem behaviors that can seriously interfere with the child's functioning in school, at home, and in the playground. These disorders are socially disruptive and are usually more upsetting to other people than to the children who are diagnosed with these problems. The rate of comorbidity (co-occurrence) among these disorders is very high (Beauchaine et al., 2010).

Attention-Deficit/Hyperactivity Disorder

Many parents believe that their children are not attentive toward them—that they run around on a whim and do things their own way. Some inattention, especially in early childhood, is normal enough. In **attention-deficit/hyperactivity** (ADHD), however, children display impulsivity, inattention, and hyperactivity that are inappropriate to their developmental levels. 👁

👁 **Watch** the Video *Jimmy: Attention-Deficit/Hyperactivity Disorder* in **MyPsychLab**

Attention-deficit/hyperactivity disorder (ADHD). ADHD is more common in boys than girls and is characterized by attentional difficulties, restlessness, impulsivity, excessive motor behavior (continuous running around or climbing), and temper tantrums.

ADHD affects between 7% and 9% of children and adolescents in the U.S. according to recent estimates (Galanter, 2013; Kasper, Alderson, & Hude, 2012; Smith, 2011). Diagnosed cases of ADHD have been rising rapidly in recent years, mostly as the result of increased diagnoses of children with mild inattentive or hyperactive systems. Today, more than 6 million children ages 4 through 17 in the U.S. are diagnosed with ADHD (Schwarz & Cohen, 2013). The rise in diagnosed cases of ADHD raises concerns that too many children are receiving ADHD medication (see *Thinking Critically About Abnormal Psychology* on page 514). About two-thirds of children diagnosed with ADHD presently take prescribed medication, generally stimulant drugs that help them focus their attention (Aleccia, 2011; Kratochvil, 2012)

ADHD is diagnosed two to nine times more often in boys than in girls. Black and Hispanic children are less likely to receive the diagnosis than Euro-American children (Schneider & Eisenberg, 2006). The disorder is usually first diagnosed during elementary school, when problems with attention or hyperactivity–impulsivity make it difficult for the child to adjust to school. However, the inattentive or hyperactive and impulsive features of ADHD may arise at any time before the age of 12. ADHD frequently occurs together with other disorders, especially learning disabilities, conduct disorder, anxiety and depressive disorders, and communication disorders (Bauchner, 2011; Larson et al., 2011; Stein, 2011).

In addition to inattention, associated problems in ADHD include inability to sit still for more than a few minutes, bullying, temper tantrums, stubbornness, and failure to respond to punishment. In some cases of ADHD, the problem is basically limited to attentional problems, whereas other cases predominantly involve hyperactive or impulsive behaviors, and still others involve a combination of attentional and hyperactive/impulsive problem behaviors.

Children with ADHD have great difficulty in school. They seem incapable of sitting still. They fidget and squirm in their seats, butt into other children's games, have outbursts of temper, and may engage in dangerous behavior, such as running into the street without looking. All in all, they can drive parents and teachers to despair.

Where does "normal" age-appropriate overactivity end and hyperactivity begin? Assessment of the degree of hyperactive behavior is crucial, because many normal children are called "hyper" from time to time. Some critics of the ADHD diagnosis argue that it merely labels children who are difficult to control as mentally disordered or sick. Most children, especially boys, are highly active during the early school years. Proponents of the diagnosis counter that there is a difference in quality between normal overactivity and ADHD. Normally overactive children are usually goal directed and can exert voluntary control over their behavior. But children with ADHD appear hyperactive without reason and seem unable to conform their behavior to the demands of teachers and parents. Put another way: Most children can sit still and concentrate for a while when they want to; children who are hyperactive seemingly cannot.

Children with ADHD tend to be of average or above-average intelligence, but they tend to underachieve in school. They are frequently disruptive in the classroom and tend to get into fights (especially the boys). They may fail to follow or remember instructions or complete assignments. Compared to children not diagnosed with ADHD, they are more likely to have learning disabilities, to repeat grades, and to be placed in special education classes. Inattention in elementary school tracks to poorer educational outcomes in adolescence and early adulthood, including increased risk of failing to complete high school by early adulthood (Gau, 2011; Pingault et al., 2011). Children with ADHD tend to have problems with *working memory* (holding information in mind in order to work on it), which makes it more difficult to keep one's mind on a task at hand (Kasper, Alderson, & Hudec, 2012).

TABLE 13.3
Key Features of Attention-Deficit/Hyperactivity Disorder (ADHD)

Problem Behaviors	Specific Behavior Pattern
Lack of attention	Fails to attend to details or makes careless errors in schoolwork
	Has difficulty sustaining attention in schoolwork or play
	Doesn't appear to pay attention to what is being said
	Fails to follow through on instructions or to finish work
	Has trouble organizing work and other activities
	Avoids work or activities that require sustained attention
	Loses work tools (e.g., pencils, books, assignments, toys)
	Becomes readily distracted
	Is forgetful in daily activities
Hyperactivity	Fidgets with hands or feet or squirms in his or her seat
	Leaves seat in situations such as the classroom in which remaining seated is required
	Is constantly running around or climbing on things
	Has difficulty playing quietly
Impulsivity	Frequently "calls out" in class
	Fails to wait his/her turn in line, games, etc.

Children with ADHD are also more likely to have mood disorders, anxiety disorders, and problems getting along with family members. Investigators find that boys with ADHD tend to lack empathy, or awareness of other people's feelings (Braaten & Rosén, 2000). Not surprisingly, children with ADHD tend to be less well liked by their classmates and more likely to be rejected than other children (Hoza et al., 2005). Compared to their peers, children with ADHD are more likely in adolescence and early adulthood to have problems with drugs; have difficulty holding a job and attaining higher educational levels; show more delinquent and antisocial behavior; and develop mood disorders, anxiety disorders, and, in young women, eating disorders (Biederman et al., 2010, 2010b; Klein et al., 2012; Kuriyan et al., 2013; Lee et al., 2011; Sibley et al., 2011).

ADHD symptoms tend to decline with age, but the disorder often persists in milder form into adolescence and adulthood. ADHD affects about 4% of U.S. adults at some point in their lives (Kessler et al., 2006). ADHD in adulthood usually takes the form of inattention, problems with working memory, and distractibility rather than hyperactivity—racing thoughts rather than racing around the room (Finke et al., 2011; Gonzalez-Gadea et al., 2013; Smith, 2012).

THEORETICAL PERSPECTIVES Increasing evidence points to an important role for genetics in the development of ADHD (Beauchaine et al., 2010; Chang et al., 2013; Stergiakouli et al., 2012; Williams et al., 2012). Consistent with a genetic contribution to the disorder, investigators find higher concordance rates for ADHD among monozygotic twins than among dizygotic twins (Burt, 2009; Waldman & Gizera, 2006).

Genes do not operate in a vacuum; we need to consider the role of environmental influences and interactions of genetic and environmental factors in the development of ADHD. Environmental factors linked to ADHD include maternal smoking and emotional stress during pregnancy, high levels of family conflict, and poor parenting skills in handling children's misbehavior. Recently, investigators linked lead exposure in children to ADHD symptoms (hyperactivity and inattention) (Goodlad, Marcus, & Fulton, 2013). Scientists are also seeking to track down the specific genes involved in ADHD and how environmental factors interact with genetic susceptibility (Pennington et al., 2009).

13.8 Describe causal factors in ADHD and evaluate treatment methods.

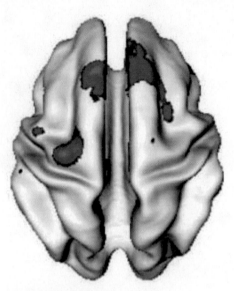

FIGURE 13.2

Here we see parts of the brain, shown in blue/purple and based on MRI imaging, where children with ADHD have a thinner prefrontal cortex as compared to other children. These regions of the brain regulate processes of attention and motor activity that are often affected in children with ADHD. Note that the front of the brain is at top of this image.

Source: National Institute of Mental Health, Image Library. http://infocenter.nimh.nih. gov/il/public_il/image_details.cfm?id=291

For example, we recently learned that certain genetic variations increased vulnerability to ADHD, but only in families with inconsistent parenting (Martel et al., 2011).

The emerging view among researchers today is that ADHD may be attributable to a breakdown in executive control functions of the brain, involving processes of attention and restraint of impulsive behaviors needed to organize and follow through on goal-directed behaviors (Casey & Durston, 2006; Winstanley, Eagle, & Robbins, 2006). This viewpoint is supported by mounting evidence from brain-imaging studies showing abnormalities or delayed maturation in parts of the brain in children with ADHD, especially in the prefrontal cortex, the part of the brain responsible for regulating attention and controlling impulsive behavior (e.g., Hart et al., 2013; Ivanov et al., 2010; Klein, 2011; Nakao et al., 2011; Shaw et al., 2011) (see Figure 13.2). Investigators also find signs of abnormal brain development in preschool children with ADHD (Mahone et al., 2011). These brain abnormalities may set the stage for the development of attentional and learning problems these children later encounter in school.

TREATMENT At first glance, it may seem odd that many of the drugs used to help ADHD children calm down and attend better in school are actually stimulants. Examples include the widely used stimulant drug Ritalin and a longer-acting stimulant called Concerta, which is a one-dose-a-day drug. However, it's not odd that these drugs are effective if we consider the fact that stimulant drugs activate the prefrontal cortex, the part of the brain that regulates attentional processes and control of impulsive, acting-out behaviors associated with ADHD. **T / F**

Stimulant drugs reduce disruptive, hyperactive behavior and also improve attention spans of children with ADHD (Chronis, Jones, & Raggi, 2006; Van der Oord et al., 2008). Stimulant drugs are even being used with preschoolers as young as 3 to 5 years of age. Although use of stimulants is not without critics, these drugs help many children with ADHD calm down and concentrate better on tasks and schoolwork, perhaps for the first time in their lives.

Although stimulant medication helps reduce restlessness and increases attention in school, it remains unclear whether these gains translate into improved academic performance (Stein et al., 2003). We should also note that a common problem with stimulant medication, as with other psychiatric drugs, is a high rate of relapse after the person stops taking the medication. Also, the range of effectiveness is limited, as in the following case example.

> ### Eddie Hardly Ever Sits Still: A Case of ADHD
>
> Nine-year-old Eddie is a problem in class. His teacher complains that he is so restless and fidgety that the rest of the class cannot concentrate on their work. He hardly ever sits still. He is in constant motion, roaming the classroom and talking to other children while they are working. He has been suspended repeatedly for outrageous behavior, most recently swinging from a fluorescent light fixture and being unable to get himself down.
>
> His mother reports that Eddie has been a problem since he was a toddler. He has never needed much sleep and always awakened before anyone else in the family, making his way downstairs and wrecking things in the living room and kitchen. He was continually restless and demanding. Once, at the age of 4, he unlocked the front door and wandered into traffic, but was rescued by a passerby.
>
> Psychological testing shows Eddie to be average in academic ability but to have a "virtually nonexistent" attention span. He shows no interest in television or in games or toys that require concentration. He is unpopular with peers and prefers to ride his bike alone or to play with his dog. He has become disobedient at home and at school and has stolen small amounts of money from his parents and classmates.

> Eddie has been treated with low doses of methylphenidate (Ritalin), but it was discontinued because it had no effect on his disobedience and stealing. However, it seemed to reduce his restlessness and increase his attention span at school.
>
> ⟶ *Adapted from Spitzer et al., 1989, pp. 315–317*

Then there's the matter of side effects. Although short-term side effects (e.g., loss of appetite or insomnia) usually subside within a few weeks or may be eliminated by lowering the dose, use of stimulant drugs may lead to other effects, including a slowdown of physical growth (DeNoon, 2006). Fortunately, children taking stimulant medication eventually catch up to their peers in physical stature.

The first nonstimulant drug approved for use in treating ADHD was Strattera (generic name *atomoxetine*). Strattera works differently from stimulant medication. It is a *selective norepinephrine reuptake inhibitor,* which means that it increases the availability of the neurotransmitter norepinephrine in the brain by interfering with the reuptake of the chemical by transmitting neurons. Although we don't know precisely how the drug works on ADHD, the increased availability of norepinephrine may enhance the brain's ability to regulate impulsive behavior and attention. Like the stimulant drug Ritalin, Strattera appears to be more effective than placebo drugs in treating ADHD, although it is perhaps not as effective as Ritalin (Newcorn et al., 2008).

Whatever the benefits of ADHD medication may be, drugs cannot teach new skills, so psychological interventions are needed to help the child develop more adaptive behaviors. For example, behavior modification programs to train parents and teachers to use contingent reinforcement for appropriate behaviors (e.g., a teacher praising the child for sitting quietly) may be combined with cognitive modification (e.g., training the child to silently talk him- or herself through the steps involved in solving challenging academic problems). Cognitive-behavioral therapists help ADHD children learn to "stop and think" before expressing angry impulses and acting out aggressively. Evidence backs up the effectiveness of cognitive-behavioral interventions in treating ADHD, although the effects may not be as strong as those of stimulant medication (Fabiano et al., 2009; Toplak et al., 2008).

Some children may do well with therapeutic drugs alone, others with cognitive-behavioral therapy (CBT) alone, and still others with a combination of both treatments (Pelham et al., 2005). Adults who are treated with medication for ADHD may also benefit from including CBT in their treatment program (Safren et al., 2010). Recently, investigators reported therapeutic benefits in treating adults with ADHD with a form of cognitive training that focused on building organizational, planning, and time management skills (Solanto et al., 2010).

Conduct Disorder

Although it also involves disruptive behavior, **conduct disorder** (CD) differs in important ways from ADHD. Whereas children with ADHD seem literally incapable of controlling their behavior, children with CD purposefully engage in antisocial behavior that violates social norms and the rights of others. Whereas children with ADHD throw temper tantrums, children diagnosed as conduct disordered are intentionally aggressive and cruel. They are frequently aggressive toward others, bullying or threatening other children or starting physical altercations. Like antisocial adults, many conduct-disordered children are callous and apparently do not experience guilt or remorse for their misdeeds. They may lie or con others to obtain what they want, steal or destroy property, start fires, break into other people's houses, and, as they get older, commit serious crimes such as rape, armed robbery, or even homicide. They may cheat in school—when they bother to attend—and lie to cover their tracks. They frequently engage in substance abuse and early sexual activity.

Conduct disorder is a surprisingly common problem, affecting about 12% of males and 7% of females (9.5% overall) (Nock et al., 2006). The disorder is not only

Children who are hyperactive are often given depressants to help calm them down.

☑ **FALSE** Children with ADHD are often given stimulant drugs, such as Ritalin, not depressants. These stimulants have a paradoxical effect of calming them down and increasing their attention spans.

Oppositional defiant disorder (ODD). Children with ODD show negativistic and oppositional behavior in response to directives from parents, teachers, or other authority figures. They may act spitefully or vindictively toward others, but do not typically show the cruelty, aggressivity, and delinquent behavior associated with conduct disorder.

more common among boys than among girls, but it also takes somewhat different forms. In boys, CD is more likely to be exhibited in stealing, fighting, vandalism, or disciplinary problems at school, whereas in girls, it is more likely to involve lying, truancy, running away, substance use, and prostitution. Children with CD often present with other disorders, including ADHD, major depression, and substance use disorders (Conner & Lochman, 2010). CD in childhood is also linked to antisocial behavior and development of antisocial personality disorder in adulthood (Burke, Waldman, & Lahey, 2010; Olino, Seeley, & Lewinsohn, 2010).

The average (median) age of onset of CD is 11.6 years, although it can develop at younger or older ages (Nock et al., 2006). CD is typically a chronic or persistent disorder. Although CD is closely linked to antisocial behavior, other commonly found traits include callousness (being uncaring, mean, and cruel) and an unemotional way of relating to others.

Oppositional Defiant Disorder

Conduct disorder and **oppositional defiant disorder** (ODD) are often combined under the general heading of "conduct problems." Though the disorders may be related, ODD is a separate diagnostic category, not merely a milder form of CD. ODD involves more nondelinquent (negativistic or oppositional) forms of conduct disturbance, whereas CD involves more outright delinquent behavior, such as truancy, stealing, lying, and aggression. Yet ODD, which typically develops earlier than CD, may lead to the development of CD at later ages. That said, only a minority of children with ODD go on to develop CD (Burke & Loeber, 2010).

Children with ODD tend to be overly negativistic or oppositional. They defy authority by frequently arguing with parents and teachers and refusing to follow requests or directives. They may deliberately annoy other people, become easily angered or lose their temper, become touchy or easily annoyed, blame others for their mistakes or misbehavior, feel resentful toward others, or act in spiteful or vindictive ways toward others. They tend to easily lose their temper and often display an angry or irritable mood. They also act in a spiteful or vindictive manner towards others they feel have wronged them. The disorder typically begins before 8 years of age and develops gradually over a period of months or years. It typically starts in the home environment but may extend to other settings, such as school.

ODD is one of the most common diagnoses among children. The disorder is estimated to affect from 1% to 11% of children and adolescents (APA, 2013). ODD is more common among boys than girls before age 12, but it i is unclear whether there is a gender difference among adolescents and adults (APA, 2013). By contrast, most studies find CD to be more common in boys than in girls across all age groups.

THEORETICAL PERSPECTIVES ON ODD AND CD The causal factors in ODD remain obscure. Some theorists believe that oppositionality is an expression of an underlying temperament described as the "difficult-child" type (Rey, 1993). Others believe that unresolved parent–child conflicts or overly strict parental control lie at the root of the disorder. Psychodynamic theorists look at ODD as a sign of fixation at the anal stage of psychosexual development, when conflicts between the parent and child emerge over toilet training. Leftover conflicts may later become expressed in the form of rebelliousness against parental wishes.

Learning theorists view oppositional behaviors as arising from parental use of inappropriate reinforcement strategies. In this view, parents may inappropriately reinforce oppositional behavior by giving in when the child refuses to comply with their wishes, which can become a pattern.

Family factors are also implicated in the development of CD. The disorder often develops in the context of negative parenting, such as failure to positively reinforce or praise the child for appropriate behavior and use of harsh and inconsistent discipline following misbehavior (Berkout, Young, & Gross, 2011). Family interactions of families of conduct-disordered children are often characterized by negative, coercive interactions. Conduct-disordered children are often very demanding and noncompliant with their parents and other family members. Family members often reciprocate by using inappropriate or harsh behaviors, such as threatening or yelling at the child or using physical means of coercion. Parental aggression against children with conduct behavior problems commonly includes pushing, grabbing, slapping, spanking, hitting, or kicking. It's not too much of a stretch to speculate that parental modeling of antisocial behaviors can lead to antisocial conduct in children. Some conduct-disordered children go on to develop antisocial personality disorder in adulthood (Burke, Waldman, & Lahey, 2010).

Conduct disorder often occurs in a context of parental distress, such as marital conflict. Coercive parental discipline and poor parental monitoring are also linked to increased risk of CD (Kilgore et al., 2000). Poor parenting behaviors, such as harsh discipline and lack of monitoring, may foster the lack of empathy for others and the poor control over disruptive behavior we find in conduct-disordered children.

Children with disruptive behavior disorders such as CD or ODD also tend to show biased ways of processing social information (Crozier et al., 2008). For example, they may wrongly assume that others intend them ill. They are often quick to blame others for the scrapes they get into. They tend to view others as treating them unfairly regardless of the evidence. They may also show other cognitive deficits, such as an inability to generate alternative, nonviolent responses to social conflicts.

As with many psychological disorders, evidence points to a genetic contribution interacting with environmental influences in the development of CD (Jian et al., 2011; Kendler, Aggen, & Patrick, 2013; Lahey et al., 2011). For example, evidence shows that early experiences of physical abuse and harsh parenting increase the risk of CD, but only in children with a certain genetic profile (Dodge, 2009). Genetic factors may also be involved in the development of ODD.

TREATMENT APPROACHES Behaviorally based parent-training programs are often used to help parents reduce children's aggressive, disruptive, and oppositional behavior and increase their adaptive behavior. Treatment targets several goals, including helping parents use more consistent and clearer rules and effective discipline strategies, increase positive reinforcement (use of rewards and praise for desirable behaviors of the child), and increase positive interactions with the child (Rajwan, Chacko, & Moeller, 2012). Thus, parents must learn not only how to alter disruptive behaviors of their children but also to pay attention to their children and reward them when they act appropriately. Anger control training may also be of value in treating children with anger problems and aggressive behavior (Sukhodolsky et al., 2005).

The following example illustrates the involvement of the parents in the behavioral treatment of a child with ODD:

→ **Billy: A Case of Oppositional Defiant Disorder**

Billy was a 7-year-old second grader referred by his parents. The family was relocated frequently because the father was in the Navy. Billy usually behaved when his father was taking care of him, but he was noncompliant with his mother and yelled at her when she gave him instructions. His mother was incurring great stress in the effort to control Billy, especially when her husband was at sea.

Billy had become a problem at home and in school during the first grade. He ignored and violated rules in both settings. Billy failed to carry out his chores and frequently yelled at and hit his younger brother. When he acted up, his parents would restrict him to his room or the yard, take away privileges and toys, and spank him. But all of these measures were used inconsistently. He also played on the railroad tracks near his home, and twice the police brought him home after he had thrown rocks at cars.

A home observation showed that Billy's mother often gave him inappropriate commands. She interacted with him as little as possible and showed no verbal praise, physical closeness, smiles, or positive facial expressions or gestures. She paid attention to him only when he misbehaved. When Billy was noncompliant, she would yell back at him and then try to catch him to force him to comply. Billy would then laugh and run from her.

Billy's parents were informed that the child's behavior was a product of inappropriate cueing techniques (poor directions), a lack of reinforcement for appropriate behavior, and lack of consistent sanctions for misbehavior. They were taught the appropriate use of reinforcement, punishment, and time out. The parents then charted Billy's problem behaviors to gain a clearer idea of what triggered and maintained them. They were shown how to reinforce acceptable behavior and use time out as a contingent punishment for misbehavior. Billy's mother was also taught relaxation training to help desensitize her to Billy's disruptions. Biofeedback was used to enhance the relaxation response.

During a 15-day baseline period, Billy behaved in a noncompliant manner about four times per day. When treatment was begun, Billy showed an immediate drop to about one instance of noncompliance every two days. Follow-up data showed that instances of noncompliance were maintained at a bearable level of about one per day. Fewer behavioral problems in school were also reported, even though they had not been addressed directly.

Adapted from Kaplan, 1986, pp. 227–230

Conduct-disordered children are sometimes placed in residential treatment programs that establish explicit rules with clear rewards and mild punishments (e.g., withdrawal of privileges). Many conduct-disordered children, especially boys, display aggressive behavior and have problems controlling their anger. Many can benefit from programs designed to help them develop skills to manage conflict without resorting to aggressive behavior (Webster-Stratton, Reid, & Hammond, 2001).

Cognitive-behavioral therapy (CBT) is also used to teach aggressive children to reconceptualize social provocations as problems to be solved rather than as challenges to answer with violence. These children learn to use calming self-talk to inhibit impulsive behavior and control anger and to find and use nonviolent solutions to social conflicts.

13.9 **Describe** the key features of anxiety disorders and depression in children and adolescents.

Childhood Anxiety and Depression

Anxieties and fears are a normal feature of childhood, just as they are a normal feature of adult life. Childhood fears—of the dark or of small animals—are common, and most children outgrow them naturally. Anxiety is abnormal, however, when it is excessive and interferes with normal academic or social functioning or becomes troubling or persistent. Like adults, children may suffer from anxiety-related problems, including phobic disorders and generalized anxiety disorder (GAD), obsessive–compulsive disorder (OCD) and posttraumatic stress disorder (PTSD).

Anxiety disorders are the most common type of psychological disorder affecting adolescents (Kessler et al., 2012). They are often comorbid (co-occurring) with depressive disorders (Garber & Weersing, 2010). Anxiety disorders and depressive disorders also occur more frequently among ethnic minority children, which alerts us to the need to examine the kinds of stressors that may put minority children at greater risk for these problems (Anderson & Mayes, 2010).

Problems involving anxiety in childhood often go unrecognized and undertreated, in part because helping professionals may have difficulty distinguishing developmentally appropriate fears, worries, and shyness in children from the more extreme forms of these problems associated with anxiety disorders (Emslie, 2008). Another problem with proper diagnosis is that many anxious children report only physical symptoms, such as headache and stomachache. They may be unable to express in words feeling states such as "worry" and "fear." Or their symptoms may be masked because they tend to avoid the objects or situations they fear. The socially phobic child, for instance, may avoid opportunities to socially interact with other children. The failure to detect anxiety disorders is unfortunate, in part because effective treatments are available and in part because undetected anxiety disorders in childhood increase the risk of anxiety disorders, depression, and substance abuse in later life (Emslie, 2008). In the next section, we focus on a specific anxiety disorder that typically develops during early childhood: separation anxiety disorder.

Separation Anxiety Disorder

It is normal for young children to show anxiety when they are separated from their caregivers. Famed attachment researcher Mary Ainsworth (1989) chronicled the development of attachment behaviors and found that separation anxiety normally begins during the first year. The sense of security normally provided by bonds of attachment apparently encourages children to explore their environments and become progressively independent of their caregivers. Having a strong attachment to the mother may help buffer the effects of later stressful life experiences. Compared to more securely attached infants, those who show insecure attachments are more prone to develop problem behaviors, such as anxiety, in later childhood in the face of negative life events experienced by the family (Dallaire & Weinraub, 2007).

Separation anxiety disorder in children is diagnosed when the level of fear or anxiety associated with separation from a caregiver or attachment figure is persistent and excessive or inappropriate for the child's developmental level. That is, 3-year-olds ought to be able to attend preschool without nausea and vomiting brought on by anxiety. Similarly, 6-year-olds ought to be able to attend first grade without persistent dread that something awful will happen to them or their parents. Children with separation anxiety disorder tend to cling to their parents and follow them around the house. They may voice concerns about death and dying and insist that someone stay with them while they are falling asleep. Other features of the disorder include nightmares, stomachaches, nausea and vomiting when separation is anticipated (as on school days), pleading with parents not to leave, or throwing tantrums when parents are about to depart. Children may refuse to attend school for fear that something will happen to their parents while they are away.

Separation anxiety disorder affects an estimated 4% to 5% of children and is the most common anxiety disorder affecting children under the age of 12 (APA, 2013; Shear et al., 2006). The disorder occurs most often in girls and is often associated with school refusal. It also frequently occurs together with social anxiety (Ferdinand et al., 2006). The disorder may persist into adulthood, leading to an exaggerated concern about the well-being of one's children and spouse and difficulty tolerating any separation from them.

In the past, separation anxiety disorder was usually referred to as *school phobia*. However, separation anxiety disorder may occur at preschool ages. In young children, refusal to attend school is usually viewed as separation anxiety. In adolescents, however, refusal to attend school is frequently connected with academic and social concerns, so the label of *separation anxiety disorder* would not apply.

The development of separation anxiety disorder frequently follows a stressful life event, such as illness, the death of a relative or pet, or a change of school or home. In the following example, Alison's problems followed the death of her grandmother.

Social anxiety. Socially anxious children tend to be excessively shy and withdrawn and have difficulty interacting with other children.

→ Alison's Fear of Death

Alison's grandmother died when Alison was 7 years old. Her parents decided to permit her request to view her grandmother in the open coffin. Alison took a tentative glance from her father's arms across the room, then asked to be taken out of the room. Her 5-year-old sister took a leisurely close-up look, with no apparent distress.

Alison had been concerned about death for two or three years by this time, but her grandmother's passing brought on a new flurry of questions: "Will I die?," "Does everybody die?," and so on. Her parents tried to reassure her by saying, "Grandma was very, very old, and she also had a heart condition. You are very young and in perfect health. You have many, many years before you have to start thinking about death."

Alison could not be alone in any room in her house. She pulled one of her parents or her sister along with her everywhere she went. She also reported nightmares about her grandmother and, within a couple of days, insisted on sleeping in the same room with her parents. Fortunately, Alison's fears did not extend to school. Her teacher reported that Alison spent some time talking about her grandmother, but her academic performance was apparently unimpaired.

Alison's parents decided to allow Alison time to "get over" the loss. Alison gradually talked less and less about death, and by the time three months had passed, she was able to go into any room in her house by herself. She wanted to continue to sleep in her parents' bedroom, however. So her parents "made a deal" with her. They would put off the return to her own bedroom until the school year ended (a month away), if Alison would agree to return to her own bed at that time. As a further incentive, a parent would remain with her until she fell asleep for the first month. Alison overcame the anxiety problem in this fashion with no additional delays.

From the Author's Files

Understanding and Treating Childhood Anxiety

Theoretical perspectives on anxiety in children parallel to some degree explanations of anxiety disorders in adults. Psychoanalytic theorists argue that childhood anxieties and fears, like their adult counterparts, symbolize unconscious conflicts. Cognitive theorists focus on the role of cognitive biases. Anxious children tend to show the types of cognitive distortions found in adults with anxiety disorders, including interpreting social situations as threatening and expecting bad things to happen (Eldar et al., 2012; Micco et al., 2013; Muris & Field, 2013). They also tend to engage in negative self-talk (Kendall & Treadwell, 2007). Expecting the worst, combined with having low self-confidence, encourages avoidance of feared activities—with friends, in school, and elsewhere. Negative expectations also heighten feelings of anxiety to the point where they impair performance in the classroom or the athletic field.

Learning theorists suggest that generalized anxiety may arise from fears of rejection or failure that carry across situations. Underlying fears of rejection or feelings of inadequacy generalize to most areas of social interaction and achievement. Genetic factors also appear to contribute to the development of anxiety disorders in children, including separation anxiety and specific phobias (Bolton et al., 2006).

Whatever the causes of anxiety disorders may be, anxious children can benefit from the same cognitive-behavioral techniques for treating anxiety as adults, such as gradual exposure to phobic stimuli and relaxation training (Rapee, Schniering, & Hudson, 2009) (see Chapter 5). Cognitive techniques can help children identify anxiety-generating thoughts and replace them with calming alternative thoughts. CBT has shown good results in treating various anxiety disorders in children and adolescents (e.g., Chorpita et al., 2011; Franklin et al., 2011, 2012; Lebowitz & Omer, 2013; Manassis, 2013; Reynolds et al., 2012).

Antidepressants of the class of selective serotonin reuptake inhibitors (SSRIs), such as *fluvoxamine* (brand name Luvox), *sertraline* (Zoloft), and *fluoxetine* (Prozac), work well in treating anxious children and adolescents (Beidel et al., 2007). In a recent large-scale study, 488 children with diagnoses of separation anxiety disorder, GAD, or social phobia were randomly assigned to treatment conditions in which they received CBT, antidepressant medication (Zoloft), a combination of CBT and antidepressant medication, or a placebo drug. The investigators found superior effects for both CBT and medication as compared to the placebo, but greater effects still for the combination of CBT and antidepressant medication (Walkup et al., 2008). However, children receiving CBT reported less insomnia, fatigue, sedation, and restlessness than those receiving medication. Because of such side effects, parents may be reluctant to have their children treated with antidepressants.

Childhood Depression

We may think of childhood as the happiest time of life. Most children are protected by their parents and are unencumbered by adult responsibilities. From the perspective of aging adults, their bodies seem made of rubber and free of aches. They have apparently boundless energy. However, many children and adolescents suffer from diagnosable mood disorders, including major depression and bipolar disorder. Major depression is the most common of these disorders, affecting about 5% of children age 5 to 12.9 years and upward of 20% of adolescents from 13 to 17.9 years of age (Rohde et al., 2013). Major depression even occurs among preschoolers, although it is rare. Girls are more likely to experience a first episode of major depression during childhood or adolescence, but there does not appear to be a gender difference in the likelihood of having a recurrent episode (Rohde et al., 2013).

Like depressed adults, depressed children and adolescents typically have feelings of hopelessness; distorted thinking patterns and tendencies to blame themselves for negative events; and lower self-esteem, self-confidence, and perceptions of competence. They report episodes of sadness and crying, feelings of apathy, as well as insomnia, and fatigue. They may experience loss of appetite or weight loss, but do not typically show weight gain or increased appetite (Cole et al., 2012). They may also experience suicidal thoughts or even attempt suicide.

Depression in children is also associated with some distinctive features, such as refusal to attend school, fears of parents' dying, and clinging to parents. Depression may also be masked by behaviors that appear unrelated. Conduct and academic problems, physical complaints, and hyperactivity may stem from unrecognized depression. Among adolescents, aggressive and sexual acting out may also be signs of depression.

Depressed children or adolescents may not label what they are feeling as depression. They may not report feeling sad even though they appear sad to others. Part of the problem is cognitive–developmental. Children are not usually capable of recognizing internal feeling states until about the age of 7 years. They may not be able to identify negative feeling states, such as depression, in themselves. Some children appear bored or irritable rather than sad, at least in the early stages of depression. **T / F**

Children with relatively few friends are at increased risk of depression (Schwartz et al., 2008). Becoming isolated from friendship groups in late childhood or cliques predicts the development of depression in early adolescence (Witvliet et al., 2010). Depressed children often lack academic and athletic skills, as well as social skills needed to form friendships. Depressed children may find it hard to concentrate in school and may suffer from impaired memory, making it difficult for them to keep their grades up. They often keep their feelings to themselves, which may prevent their parents from recognizing the problem and seeking help. Children may express negative feelings in the form of anger, sullenness, or impatience, leading to conflicts with parents that in turn can accentuate and prolong depression.

Major depressive episode in childhood or adolescence may last upward of a year or longer and may reoccur later in life. Yet childhood depression rarely occurs by itself. Depressed children often have other significant psychological problems, including anxiety disorders, CD or ODD, and among adolescent girls, eating disorders (e.g., Small et al., 2000). A sizable percentage of depressed adolescents (between 20% and 40%) also develop bipolar disorder later (USDHHS, 1999).

Is this child too young to be depressed? Although we tend to think of childhood as the happiest and most carefree time of life, depression is actually quite common among older children and adolescents. Depressed children may report feelings of sadness and lack of interest in previously enjoyable activities. Many, however, do not report or are not aware of feelings of depression, even though they may look depressed to observers. Depression may also be masked by other problems, such as conduct or school-related problems, physical complaints, and overactivity.

Difficulties at school, problem behaviors, and physical complaints may actually be signs of depression in children.

☑ **TRUE** Children may not label what they are feeling as depression or be able to put into words how they feel. Depression is often masked by conduct problems, academic problems, and physical complaints.

Understanding and Treating Childhood Depression

Depression and suicidal behavior in childhood are frequently related to family problems and conflicts. Children and adolescents exposed to stressful life events affecting the family, such as parental conflict or unemployment, stand an increased risk of depression (Rudolph, Kurlakowsky, & Conley, 2001). Stressful life events, such as romantic breakups or strained friendships, diminish a person's sense of self-worth, competence, and desirability and can trigger depressive episodes in vulnerable adolescents (Hammen, 2009). In girls, disturbed eating behaviors and body dissatisfaction after puberty often predict the development of major depression during adolescence (Stice et al., 2000).

Negative thinking styles begin to enter the picture as children mature and their cognitive abilities develop (Garber, Keiley, & Martin, 2002). Like adults, depressed children and adolescents tend to show distorted patterns of thinking such as the following:

- Expecting the worst (pessimism)
- Catastrophizing the consequences of negative events
- Blaming themselves for disappointments and negative outcomes, even when this is unwarranted
- Minimizing their accomplishments and focusing only on negative aspects of events

Investigators also find distorted thinking patterns in depressed children in other cultures. For example, a study of 582 Chinese children in secondary schools in Hong Kong linked feelings of depression to distorted thinking patterns involving tendencies to minimize accomplishments and blow failures and shortcomings out of proportion (Leung & Poon, 2001). European researchers linked several thinking patterns to depression in young people, including blaming oneself for things that were not one's fault, ruminating about one's problems (mulling them over again and again in one's mind), and blowing problems out of proportion (Garnefski, Kraaij, & Spinhoven, 2001).

Although there are links between cognitive factors and depression, we do not know which comes first; that is, whether children become depressed because of a depressive mindset or whether depression leads to distorted, negative thoughts. Quite possibly, the relationship is reciprocal, with depression affecting thinking patterns and thinking patterns affecting emotional states.

Adolescent girls tend to show greater levels of depressive symptoms than adolescent boys do, a finding that mirrors the gender gap in depression among adults (Stewart et al., 2004). Girls who adopt a passive, ruminative coping style (e.g., brooding and obsessing about their problems) may be at greater risk of developing depression.

Evidence supports the effectiveness of CBT in treating depression in children and adolescents (Brunwasser, Gillham, & Kim, 2009; Chorpita et al., 2011). In one recent study, 75% of depressed youths treated with CBT no longer showed signs of depression by the end of treatment (Weisz et al., 2009). CBT typically involves social skills training (e.g., learning how to start a conversation and make friends), training in problem-solving skills, increasing frequency of rewarding activities, and countering depressive thoughts. In addition, family therapy may help families resolve underlying conflicts and reorganize their relationships so that members can become more supportive of each other.

Lithium can be used to treat and prevent manic episodes in bipolar children, but questions remain about its effectiveness with children (NIMH, 2008). SSRI-type antidepressant drugs such as *fluoxetine* (brand name Prozac) show therapeutic benefits in treating depression in children and adolescents (March et al, 2004). The combination of CBT and antidepressants may be used to boost the effectiveness of either treatment alone (March & Vitiello, 2009). However, concerns have been raised that psychiatric drugs, including stimulants and antidepressants, are being prescribed much too widely in treating children with psychological problems, as we examine in *Thinking Critically About Abnormal Psychology* on page 514.

Suicide in Children and Adolescents

Suicide is rare in childhood and early adolescence but becomes more common in late adolescence and early adulthood (Pelkonen & Marttunen, 2003). Among college students, suicide is the second leading cause of death, after motor vehicle accidents (Rawe & Kingsbury, 2006). Among young people overall in the 15- to 24-year-old age group, suicide is the third most common cause of death, after accidents and homicides (NIMH, 2003; Winerman, 2004). Approximately 1 person per 10,000 (0.01%) in this age range commits suicide. Official statistics only account for reported suicides; some apparent accidental deaths, such as those due to falling from a window, may be suicides as well. **T / F**

Despite the commonly held view that children and adolescents who talk about suicide are only venting their feelings, most young people who kill themselves send out signals beforehand (Bongar, 2002). In fact, those who discuss their plans are the ones most likely to carry them out. Unfortunately, parents tend not to take their children's suicidal talk seriously.

In addition to increasing age, other factors associated with heightened risk of suicide in children and adolescents include the following (e.g., Dervic, Brent & Oquendo, 2008; Fergusson & Woodward, 2002; NIMH, 2003; Pelkonen & Marttunen, 2003):

- *Gender*. Girls, like women, are three times more likely than boys to attempt suicide. However, boys, like men, are more likely to succeed, perhaps because boys, like men, are more apt to use lethal means, such as guns.

- *Geography*. Adolescents in less-populated areas are more likely to commit suicide. Adolescents in the rural western regions of the United States have the highest suicide rate.

- *Ethnicity*. The suicide rates for African American, Asian American, and Hispanic American youth are about 30% to 60% lower than that of (non-Hispanic) White youth. Yet, as noted in Chapter 7, the highest suicide rates in the United States are among Native American adolescent and young adult males (Meyers, 2007).

- *Depression and hopelessness*. Depression figures as prominently in youth suicide as it does in adult suicide, especially when it is combined with feelings of hopelessness and low self-esteem.

- *Previous suicidal behavior*. One-quarter of adolescents who attempt suicide are repeaters. More than 80% of adolescents who take their lives have talked about it before doing so. Suicidal teenagers may carry lethal weapons, talk about death, make suicide plans, or engage in risky or dangerous behavior.

- *Prior sexual abuse*. In an Australian sample, young people with a history of childhood sexual abuse had rates of suicide more than 10 times higher than the national average (Plunkett et al., 2001). Moreover, about one-third of young people who had been abused had attempted suicide, compared to none in a nonabused control group.

- *Family problems*. Family problems contribute to an increased risk of suicide attempts and actual suicides. These problems include family instability and conflict, physical or sexual abuse, loss of a parent due to death or separation, and poor parent–child communication.

- *Stressful life events*. Many suicides among young people are directly preceded by stressful or traumatic events, such as breaking up with a girlfriend or boyfriend, having an unwanted pregnancy, getting arrested, having problems at school, moving to a new school, or having to take an important test.

- *Substance abuse*. Addiction in the adolescent's family, or substance abuse by the adolescent, is a factor.

- *Social contagion*. Adolescent suicides sometimes occur in clusters, especially when a suicide or a group of suicides receives widespread publicity. Adolescents may

13.10 Identify risk factors for suicide among adolescents.

truth OR fiction

Suicide is unfortunately quite common among young teens around the time of puberty.

☑ **FALSE** Actually, suicide is rare among children and young adolescents. But the risks increase with age into late adolescence and early adulthood.

@Issue: Are We Overmedicating Our Kids?

The rising use of psychiatric drugs in recent years to treat ADHD, depression, and other psychological disorders in children has been nothing short of explosive.

Roughly three million children in the United States receive psychiatric medication for emotional or behavioral problems (Simpson et al., 2008). The great majority of medicated children, about 90%, are prescribed stimulants or other drugs to control ADHD. The use of stimulant drugs for ADHD has increased dramatically in recent years—up about twentyfold since the 1980s (Sroufe, 2012). Today, about 5% of American children and adolescents are treated with stimulant medications (Smith, 2012; Zuvekas & Vitiello, 2012).

Among adolescents, use of antidepressants nearly matches that ADHD medication. About 5% of 12- to 19-year olds are receiving antidepressants, with another 6% receiving ADHD drugs, primarily stimulant medication (Sharpe, 2012). Antidepressants are used to treat teens with depression, panic disorder, and eating disorders. Increasing numbers of young people are also receiving other psychiatric drugs, including mood stabilizers (anticonvulsants), anti-anxiety drugs, sleep medications, and even powerful antipsychotic drugs (Olfson et al., 2012).

Two flashpoints in the controversy concern the use of powerful antipsychotic drugs and the use of Ritalin and other stimulant drugs to control hyperactivity. Antipsychotic drugs such as Risperdal and Zyprexa (discussed in Chapter 11) used to treat schizophrenia in adults have become more widely used in treating ADHD, even though these drugs are not approved for that purpose. These drugs carry risks of serious side effects, including serious metabolic disorders and potentially irreversible tic disorders, such as *tardive dyskinesia* (also discussed in Chapter 11). These potent antipsychotic drugs are also used to treat other problem behaviors in children and teens, including aggressive behavior and bipolar disorder (Olfson et al., 2012). (See further discussion in "The Bipolar Kid" on page 516).

With so many children receiving powerful psychiatric drugs, critics claim we are too ready to seek a "quick fix" for problem behavior rather than examining contributing factors, such as family conflicts, that may take more effort and time to treat. One pediatrician expressed these concerns in 1996 in a way that still resonates today: "It takes time for parents and teachers to sit down and talk to kids. . . . It takes less time to get a child a pill" (Hancock, 1996, p. 52). If a child is not sitting quietly at his or desk doing schoolwork, there is pressure to find a chemical solution. Young people who become accustomed to using powerful psychiatric drugs to control negative feelings may be discouraged from finding other ways of managing them (Sharpe, 2012).

The two sides of the debate are clearly drawn. Critics contend that we are overusing psychiatric drugs, especially Ritalin. They point to the risk of potentially troubling side effects, such as weight loss

and sleeplessness from Ritalin, and express concerns that we just don't know how stimulants and other powerful psychiatric drugs affect still-developing brains (e.g., Geller, 2006; Stambor, 2006). Nor can we rule out that ADHD drugs cause cardiovascular problems in children and adolescents (Kratochvil, 2012; Vitiello et al., 2012).

The effects of stimulant drugs are also limited, very limited. They may enhance the child's ability to concentrate for a short time, but become less effective over time and do not lead to general improvements in grades or academic performance (Sroufe, 2012). A leading researcher on ADHD, psychologist L. Alan Sroufe, commented that the fixation on finding a pill to fix behavior problems in children is short-sighted: "The illusion that children's behavior problems can be cured with drugs prevents us as a society from seeking the more complex solution that will be necessary" (cited in Sroufe, 2012, p. 6). As Sroufe points out, we cannot expect to solve all of the problems we face in life with a pill. Critics contend that while alternative treatments, such as CBT, are available to treat many of these problems, they remain underused in comparison with the prescription pad.

On the other side of the debate, proponents of drug therapy point to the therapeutic benefits of using drugs to treat disorders such as ADHD and depression. Stimulant drugs can help calm down hyperactive children and improve concentration, and antidepressants can combat anxiety and depression. However, we still lack evidence of the long-term effectiveness and safety of using psychiatric drugs with youths.

Clouding the picture further are warnings issued by the Food and Drug Administration (FDA) about a small increased risk of suicidal symptoms in youths and young adults treated with antidepressant medication. This increased risk seems to apply only to young people under the age of 25 (Stone et al., 2009). However small the increased risk may be, providers and family members need to carefully watch for warning signs of suicidal behavior in young patients (Reeves & Ladner, 2009). Clinicians also need to be aware of factors that may raise the risk of self-harm in adolescents treated with antidepressants, such as the presence of suicidal thinking, family conflict, and drug use (Brent et al., 2009). The FDA warnings are having an effect, as the numbers of prescriptions for antidepressants for adolescents declined since the warnings went into effect (Clarke et al., 2012).

Not only are millions of children taking psychiatric drugs, but an estimated 1.6 million are taking two or more drugs, sometimes even three or more, at a time. For example, many kids are taking stimulants for ADHD and antidepressants or mood stabilizers for mood disorders. However, we have only minimal evidence to support the use of taking two psychiatric drugs at the same time and no evidence at all to support the use of three or more drugs (Harris, 2006). As psychiatrist Daniel Safer, a leading authority on the use of psychiatric drugs in children, put it, "No one has been able to show that the benefits of these combinations outweigh the risks in children" (cited in Harris, 2006, p. A28.)

One thing on which both sides seem to agree is that drug therapy alone is not sufficient to treat psychological problems in children and adolescents. The child with academic difficulties, problems at home, and low self-esteem needs more than a pill (or a combination of pills). Any use of therapeutic drugs needs to be supplemented by psychological interventions to help troubled children develop more adaptive behaviors. Perhaps drug therapy should be considered a second-line treatment when nonpharmacological approaches prove ineffective. Sometimes a combination approach works best.

In thinking critically about the issue, answer the following questions:

- Why is the prescription of stimulant drugs and antidepressants in treating childhood disorders controversial?

- In many comparable countries, drugs are prescribed much less frequently for childhood disorders than they are in the United States. What does this suggest?

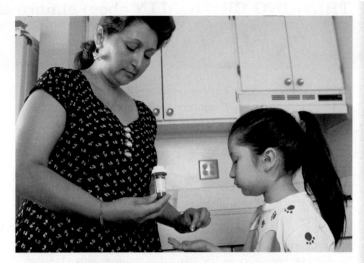

Should this child be medicated? The use of psychiatric drugs in children has skyrocketed in recent years. Do you know any children who have benefited from psychiatric drugs? What concerns does the use of these drugs pose? What alternatives are available?

romanticize suicide as a heroic act of defiance. There are often suicides or attempts among the siblings, friends, parents, or adult relatives of suicidal adolescents. Perhaps the suicide of a family member or schoolmate renders suicide a more "real" option for managing stress or punishing others. Perhaps the other person's suicide gives the adolescent the impression that he or she is "doomed" to commit suicide. Adolescent suicides may occur in bunches in a community, especially when adolescents are subjected to mounting academic pressures, such as competing for admission to college. Note the case of Pam.

Pam, Kim, and Brian

Pam was an exceptionally attractive 17-year-old who was hospitalized after cutting her wrists. "Before we moved to [an upper-middle-class town in suburban New York]," she told the psychologist, "I was the brightest girl in the class. Teachers loved me. If we had a yearbook, I'd have been the most likely to succeed. Then we moved, and suddenly I was hit with it. Everybody was bright, or tried to be. Suddenly I was just another ordinary student planning to go to college.

"Teachers were good to me, but I was no longer special, and that hurt. Then we all applied to college. Do you know that 90 percent of the kids in the high school go on to college? I mean four-year colleges? And we all knew—or suspected—that the good schools had quotas on kids from here. I mean you can't have 30 kids from our senior class going to Yale or Princeton or Wellesley, can you? You're better off applying from Utah.

"Then Kim got her early-acceptance rejection from Brown. Kim was number-one in the class. Nobody could believe it. Her father had gone to Brown and Kim had almost 1,500 SATs. Kim was out of commission for a few days—I mean she didn't come to school or anything—and then, boom, she was gone. She offed herself, kaput, no more, the end. Then Brian was rejected from Cornell. A few days later, he was gone, too. And I'm like, 'These kids were better than me.' I mean their grades and their SATs were higher than mine, and I *was going to apply to Brown and Cornell. I'm like, 'What chance do I have? Why bother?'"

→ *From the Author's Files*

@Issue: The Bipolar Kid

There was a knock at her bedroom door. Six-year-old Claire had been happily watching goofy videos on her favorite Website, *jibjab* (Egan, 2008). She had barricaded the door, using her toy chest and then piling on toys and other weighty objects. "If it's my brother," she said to a visiting journalist, "don't open it." She then said that she didn't care if she was being mean, but she couldn't trust her brother. Her brother, Claire said, always jumps out in a bad, scary way.

Her brother, 10-year-old James, had been diagnosed with bipolar disorder two years earlier. Like other children with a bipolar diagnosis, James had a history of aggressive behavior and episodes of explosive rage. There were times he would reach out to his mother, craving attention, but then suddenly explode into a rage, storming away from her, but later returning, seeking to connect, cuddle, and even cling to her. A decade or so ago, a child like James might have been diagnosed with ADHD or ODD. But in the 1990s, many professionals began diagnosing children like James with bipolar disorder, a diagnosis that previously had rarely been applied to children. As the diagnosis of childhood-onset bipolar disorder exploded in recent years, so too did the use of powerful drugs such as antipsychotics, anticonvulsives, and lithium that are used in treating adult forms of bipolar disorder.

By the early 2000s, as many as 1% of children and adolescents in the United States had received a bipolar disorder diagnosis, a rate that had jumped some fortyfold compared to the early 1990s (Holden, 2008; Moreno et al., 2007). Critics claim there is no real increase in the underlying rates of the disorder, but rather a tendency for mental health providers to relabel children who previously would have received another diagnosis, such as ADHD or CD (Holtmann, Bölte, & Poustka, 2008).

Underscoring concerns about overdiagnosis are findings from the National Institute of Mental Health study that showed the great majority of children (80%) receiving a bipolar disorder diagnosis did not meet diagnostic criteria for the disorder (Carey, 2012; Egan, 2008). On the other side of the debate are those who argue that bipolar disorder is more common in children than many mental health professionals suspect and that practitioners are only now recognizing a disorder that has been overlooked for many years.

Critics also claim that the pharmaceutical industry, which stands to profit enormously from medications used to treat bipolar disorder, has spurred overdiagnosis of the disorder by encouraging physicians to prescribe the latest drugs (Holden, 2008). As University of Washington psychiatrist Jack McClellan put it, "The treatment of bipolar disorder is meds first, meds second and meds third . . . whereas if these kids have a behavior disorder,

then behavioral treatment should be considered the primary treatment" (cited in Carey, 2010, p. A17).

Bipolar disorder is characterized by clear-cut episodes of mania and depression, so professionals need to verify that children show both ends of the mood spectrum before reaching a diagnosis. Concerns about overdiagnosis of bipolar disorder in children and adolescents prompted changes in *DSM-5* to limit the diagnosis to children with clear signs of bipolar disorder. A new diagnosis of *disruptive mood dysregulation disorder* (DMDD) was introduced in *DSM-5* to apply to children with extreme irritability and severe and frequent temper outbursts (like those in the case of James described earlier), but who do not show mood changes, inflated self-esteem, pressured speech, or other features of mania associated with bipolar disorder.

Children diagnosed with DMDD tend to fly off the handle, showing intense and prolonged rage reactions. Their frequent outbursts are greatly out of proportion to the situation and are accompanied by physical aggression against people or property or by verbal expressions of rage (Axelson, 2013). The diagnosis requires evidence of frequent behavior outbursts occurring at least three or more times a week for at least a year.

DMDD is a controversial diagnosis in large part because of concerns that it may medicalize or pathologize common behavior problems in children, such as frequent temper tantrums. Such concerns may be overstated, as recent research shows that only about 1% of school-age children meet all criteria for the disorder (Copeland et al., 2013). However, we should recognize that explosive rage may be a sign of other disorders, such as ADHD, CD, and ODD, or even bipolar disorder. All in all, how the new DMDD disorder will play out in practice remains to be seen (Carey, 2012b).

Why does it matter whether children are diagnosed with bipolar disorder or another disorder like ADHD? The main reason is that diagnosis is used to guide treatment. Drugs used to treat ADHD, especially stimulant drugs like Ritalin, can trigger or exacerbate manic episodes, whereas bipolar drugs like lithium would be inappropriate and potentially harmful if used to treat ADHD.

Controversy also swirls around potential risks of treating young children with powerful antipsychotic drugs often used with bipolar adults. Although atypical antipsychotics like Risperdal (generic name *risperidone*) can blunt anger and explosive rage, they are also associated with risk of significant weight gain (typically about 7% or more) and metabolic changes that may lead to diabetes and heart disease (Correll et al., 2009; Varley & McClellan, 2009). Other drugs, like lithium and anticonvulsive drugs used to treat epilepsy, also carry risks of significant side effects and complications. No one knows for certain what the long-term effects of these drugs may be on the developing brain of the child or adolescent (Kumra et al., 2008).

Another question is whether children who show frequent temper tantrums will now be medicated because a new diagnosis is rendered—*DMDD*. Many professionals believe the DMDD diagnosis will only exacerbate the overmedication of children, by focusing efforts on finding drugs that control disruptive behaviors rather than helping children learn to regulate their negative emotions and using behavioral techniques to help children learn more adaptive behaviors.

Clearly, children who receive a bipolar diagnosis have serious behavioral problems that can cause enormous difficulties for them and their families. As research continues, we hope to learn more about the best ways of conceptualizing and treating "bipolar kids."

In thinking critically about the issue, answer the following questions:

- What do you believe accounts for the surge in diagnoses of bipolar disorder in children in recent years?

- Should children with the types of behavior problems that lead to a bipolar diagnosis be treated with powerful psychiatric drugs or by other forms of treatment? Explain.

You can see how catastrophizing thoughts play a role in such tragic cases. Consistent with the literature on suicide among adults, young people who attempt suicide do not use active problem-solving strategies in handling stressful situations. They may see no other way out of their perceived failures or stresses. As with adults, one approach to working with suicidal children helps them to challenge distorted thinking and generate alternative strategies for handling problems and stressors. Promising prevention programs, including school-based skills training programs, have been developed, but evidence supporting their effectiveness remains to be gathered (Gould et al., 2003).

Elimination Disorders

Fetuses and newborn children eliminate waste products reflexively. As children develop and undergo toilet training, they develop the ability to inhibit the natural reflexes that govern urination and bowel movements. For some children, however, problems with controlling elimination persist in the form of *enuresis* and *encopresis,* disorders of elimination that are not due to organic causes.

13.11 Describe the key features of elimination disorders and **evaluate** methods of treating bed-wetting.

Enuresis

The term *enuresis* derives from the Greek roots *en-,* meaning "in," and *ouron,* meaning "urine." **Enuresis** is failure to control urination after one has reached the "normal" age for attaining such control. Conceptions of what age is normal for achieving control vary among clinicians.

To be diagnosed with enuresis according to the *DSM,* the child must be at least 5 years of age or at an equivalent developmental level and meet the following criteria:

- Repeatedly wetting bedding or clothes (whether intentionally or involuntarily)

- Wetting occurs at least twice a week for three months or causes significant distress or impairment in functioning

- There is no medical or organic basis to the disorder; nor is it caused by use of a drug or medication

Enuresis, like so many other developmental disorders, is more common among boys. Bed-wetting affects upward of seven million children age 6 years and over in the United States (Lim, 2003). An estimated five to ten percent of children meet diagnostic criteria for enuresis at age 5 (APA, 2013). The disorder usually resolves itself by adolescence, if not earlier, although in about 1% of cases, the problem continues into adulthood.

As you might suspect, enuresis can be extremely distressing, especially to the older child (Butler, 2004). Wetting may occur during nighttime sleep only, during waking hours only, or during both nighttime sleep and waking hours. Nighttime-only enuresis is the most common type, and accidents occurring during sleep are referred to as *bed-wetting*. Achieving bladder control at night is more difficult than achieving daytime control. When asleep at night, children must learn to wake up when they feel the pressure of a full bladder and then go to the bathroom to relieve themselves. The younger the "trained" child is, the more likely she or he is to wet the bed at night. It is perfectly normal for children who have acquired daytime control over their bladders to have nighttime accidents for a year or more. Bed-wetting usually occurs during the deepest stage of sleep and may reflect immaturity of the nervous system. The diagnosis of enuresis applies in cases of repeated bed-wetting or daytime wetting of clothes by children of at least 5 years of age.

THEORETICAL PERSPECTIVES Psychodynamic explanations of enuresis suggest that it represents the expression of hostility toward children's parents because of harsh toilet training. It may represent regression in response to the birth of a sibling or some other stressor or life change, such as starting school or suffering the death of a parent or relative. Learning theorists point out that enuresis occurs most commonly in children whose parents attempted to train them early. Early failures may have connected anxiety with efforts to control the bladder. Conditioned anxiety, then, induces rather than curbs urination.

Primary enuresis, the most prevalent form of the disorder, characterizes children with persistent nocturnal bed-wetting who have never established urinary control through the night. It is due to maturational delays that have genetic underpinnings (Mast & Smith, 2012; Wei et al., 2010). We don't yet understand the genetic mechanism in enuresis, but one possibility implicates the genes that regulate the rate of development of motor control over eliminatory reflexes by the cerebral cortex. Although genetic factors appear to be involved in the transmission of primary enuresis, it is likely that environmental and behavioral factors also come into play in determining the development and course of the disorder. The other type of enuresis, *secondary enuresis,* is apparently not genetically influenced and characterizes children with occasional bed-wetting who developed the problem after having established urinary control.

TREATMENT Enuresis usually resolves itself as children mature. Behavioral methods have been shown to be helpful when enuresis endures or causes parents or children great distress, however. These methods condition children to wake up when their bladders are full. One dependable example is the use of a urine alarm method, a variation on a technique introduced by psychologist O. Hobart Mowrer in the 1930s.

The problem in bed-wetting is that children with enuresis continue to sleep despite bladder tension that awakens most other children (Butler, 2004). As a consequence, they reflexively urinate in bed. Mowrer pioneered the use of the urine alarm, which in its present form involves a moisture-activated alarm that is placed beneath the sleeping child. A sensor sounds the alarm when the child wets the bed, which awakens the child (Lim, 2003). After several repetitions, most children learn to awaken in response to bladder tension—*before* the alarm is sounded. The technique is usually explained through principles of classical conditioning. Tension in children's bladders is paired repeatedly with a stimulus (an alarm) that wakes them up when they wet the bed. The bladder tension (a conditioned stimulus) elicits the same response (waking up—the conditioned response) that is elicited by the alarm (the unconditioned stimulus). **T / F**

Treatment for enuresis, generally involving the urine alarm technique or drug therapy, is often helpful (Houts, 2010). Certain psychiatric drugs can also be helpful, such as *fluvoxamine* (brand name Luvox), an SSRI-type

Urine alarm. The urine alarm method is widely used in the treatment of nighttime enuresis. How does the method illustrate the principles of classical conditioning?

antidepressant that works on brain systems that control urination. However, the urine alarm technique has the highest cure rates and the lowest relapse rates among available treatments (Glazener, Evans, & Peto, 2000; Thiedke, 2003). The higher relapse rates associated with drug treatment underscores the fact that therapeutic drugs by themselves do not teach any new skills or adaptive behaviors that can be retained beyond the active treatment period.

Encopresis

The term *encopresis* derives from the Greek roots *en-* and *kopros,* meaning "feces." **Encopresis** is lack of control over bowel movements that is not caused by an organic problem. The child must have a chronological age of at least 4 years, or in children with intellectual impairment, a mental age of at least 4 years. About 1% of 5-year-olds have encopresis (APA, 2013). Like enuresis, this condition is most common among boys. Soiling may be voluntary or involuntary and is not caused by an organic problem, except in cases in which constipation is involved. Among the possible predisposing factors are inconsistent or incomplete toilet training and psychosocial stressors, such as the birth of a sibling or beginning school.

Soiling, unlike enuresis, is more likely to happen during the day than at night. It can thus be keenly embarrassing to the child. Classmates often avoid or ridicule soilers. Because feces have a strong odor, teachers may find it hard to act as though nothing has happened. Parents, too, are eventually galled by recurrent soiling and may increase their demands for self-control and employ powerful punishments for failure. As a result, children may hide soiled underwear, distance themselves from classmates, or feign sickness to stay at home. Their levels of anxiety concerning soiling increase. Because anxiety, which involves arousal of the sympathetic branch of the autonomic nervous system, promotes bowel movements, control may become yet more elusive. Not surprisingly, children who soil have more emotional and behavioral problems than those who do not soil (Joinson et al., 2006).

When soiling is involuntary, it is often associated with constipation, impaction, or retention that results in subsequent overflow. Constipation may be related to psychological factors, such as fears associated with defecating in a particular place or with a more general pattern of negativistic or oppositional behavior. Or constipation may be related to physiological factors, such as complications from an illness or from medication. Much less frequently, encopresis is deliberate or intentional.

Soiling often appears to follow harsh punishment for an accident or two, particularly in children who are already highly stressed or anxious. Harsh punishment may rivet children's attention on soiling. They may then ruminate about soiling, raising their level of anxiety so that self-control is impaired.

Behavior therapy techniques are helpful in treating encopresis (Loening-Baucke, 2002). Treatment generally involves the parents rewarding (by praise and other means) successful attempts at self-control and using mild punishments for continued accidents (e.g., gentle reminders to attend more closely to bowel tension and having the child clean her or his own underwear). When encopresis persists, thorough medical and psychological evaluation is recommended to determine possible causes and appropriate treatments.

13 summing up

Normal and Abnormal Behavior in Childhood and Adolescence

13.1 Explain the differences between normal and abnormal behavior in childhood and adolescence and the role of cultural beliefs in determining abnormality.

In addition to the criteria described in Chapter 1 in distinguishing between normal and abnormal behavior in general, we need to take into account the child's age and cultural background in determining whether a child's or adolescent's behavior is abnormal with respect to deviating from developmental and normative standards. We also need to consider cultural norms in determining whether behavior in a given culture is deemed abnormal.

13.2 Describe the effects of child abuse.

The effects of child abuse range from physical injuries, even death, to emotional consequences, such as difficulties forming healthy attachments, low self-esteem, suicidal thinking, depression, and failure to explore the outside world, among other problems. The emotional and behavioral consequences of child abuse and neglect often extend into adulthood.

Autism and Autism Spectrum Disorder

13.3 Describe key features of autism spectrum disorder and ways of understanding and treating it.

Children with autism spectrum disorder seem detached from others or utterly alone and show deficits in social interactions and ability to develop and maintain relationships, repetitive or restricted movements or behaviors, restricted or fixated interests, attempts to preserve sameness and routines, and peculiar speech habits such as repetitive speech, echolalia, pronoun reversals, and idiosyncratic speech. The causes of autism remain unknown, but increasing evidence points to roles of genetic factors and brain abnormalities, perhaps in combination with as yet unspecified environmental influences. Gains in academic and social functioning have been obtained through the use of intensive behavior therapy.

Intellectual Disability

13.4 Describe the key features and causes of intellectual disability.

Intellectual disability (ID) is characterized by major impairment of intellectual and adaptive abilities. It is assessed by intelligence tests and measures of functional ability. Most cases fall in the mild range. ID is caused by chromosomal abnormalities, such as Down syndrome; genetic disorders, such as Fragile X syndrome and phenylketonuria; prenatal factors, such as maternal diseases and alcohol use; and familial–cultural factors associated with intellectually impoverished home or social environments.

Learning Disorder

13.5 Identify the types of deficits associated with learning disorders and describe ways of understanding and treating learning disorders.

Learning disorders (also called learning disabilities) are specific deficits in the development of reading, writing, math, or executive function skills. The causes remain under study but probably involve underlying brain dysfunctions that make it difficult to process or decode visual and auditory information. Intervention focuses mainly on attempts to remediate specific skill deficits.

Communication Disorders

13.6 Define the concept of communication disorders and identify specific types.

These disorders are characterized by impaired understanding or use of language. The specific types of communication disorders include language disorder, speech sound disorder, childhood-onset fluency disorder (stuttering), and social (pragmatic) communication disorder.

Problem Behaviors: Attention-Deficit/Hyperactivity Disorder, Oppositional Defiant Disorder, and Conduct Disorder

13.7 Describe the key features of attention-deficit/hyperactivity disorder, oppositional defiant disorder, and conduct disorder.

Attention-deficit/hyperactivity disorder (ADHD) is characterized by impulsivity, inattention, and hyperactivity. Children with conduct disorder intentionally engage in antisocial behavior. Children with oppositional defiant disorder (ODD) show negativistic or oppositional behavior but not the outright delinquent or antisocial behavior characteristic of conduct disorder. However, ODD may lead to the development of conduct disorder.

13.8 Describe causal factors in ADHD and evaluate treatment methods.

Causal factors in ADHD focus on an interaction of genetic and environmental factors, such as inconsistent or poor parenting behaviors, affecting the executive control functions of the brain. Stimulant medication is generally effective in reducing hyperactivity and increasing attention in ADHD children, but it has not led to general academic gains. Behavior therapy may help ADHD children adapt better to school. Behavior therapy can also be helpful in modifying behaviors of children with conduct disorders and oppositional defiant disorder.

Childhood Anxiety and Depression

13.9 Describe the key features of anxiety disorders and depression in children and adolescents.

Anxiety disorders in children and adolescents commonly include specific phobias, social phobia, and GAD. Children may also show separation anxiety disorder, which involves excessive anxiety at times when they are separated from their parents. Cognitive biases, such as expecting negative outcomes, negative self-talk, and interpreting ambiguous situations as threatening, figure prominently in anxiety disorders in children and adolescents, as they often do in adults.

Depressed children, especially younger children, may not report or be aware of feeling depressed. Depression may also be masked by seemingly unrelated behaviors, such as conduct disorders. Depressed children also tend to show cognitive biases associated with depression in adulthood, such as adoption of a pessimistic explanatory style and distorted thinking. Although rare, suicide in children does occur and threats should be taken seriously.

13.10 Identify risk factors for suicide among adolescents.
Risk factors for adolescent suicide include gender, age, geography, race, depression, past suicidal behavior, strained family relationships, stress, substance abuse, and social contagion.

Elimination Disorders

13.11 Describe the key features of elimination disorders and evaluate methods of treating bed-wetting.
Elimination disorders involve problems of impaired control over urination (enuresis) or bowel movements (encopresis) that cannot be accounted for by organic causes. Both disorders are more common in boys. The best established method for treating bed-wetting is the urine alarm method, a technique that conditions children with enuresis to respond to bladder tension by awakening before urinating.

critical thinking questions

Based on your reading of this chapter, answer the following questions:

- Do you believe children with intellectual disability should be mainstreamed within regular classes? Why or why not?

- Do you believe people with learning disorders should be given special consideration, such as extra time, when taking standardized tests like the Scholastic Aptitude Test (SAT)? Why or why not?

- If you had a child with ADHD, would you consider using stimulant drugs like Ritalin? Why or why not?

- Do you know children who were treated for a psychological disorder? What treatments did they receive? What were the outcomes?

key terms

neurodevelopmenetal disorders 481
autism spectrum disorder 485
intellectual disability 491
Down syndrome 493
Fragile X syndrome 494
phenylketonuria (PKU) 494

dyslexia 496
learning disorder 496
communication disorders 498
language disorder 498
speech sound disorder 499
childhood-onset fluency disorder 500

social (pragmatic) communication disorder 501
attention-deficit/hyperactivity disorder 501
conduct disorder 505
oppositional defiant disorder 506

separation anxiety disorder 509
enuresis 517
encopresis 519

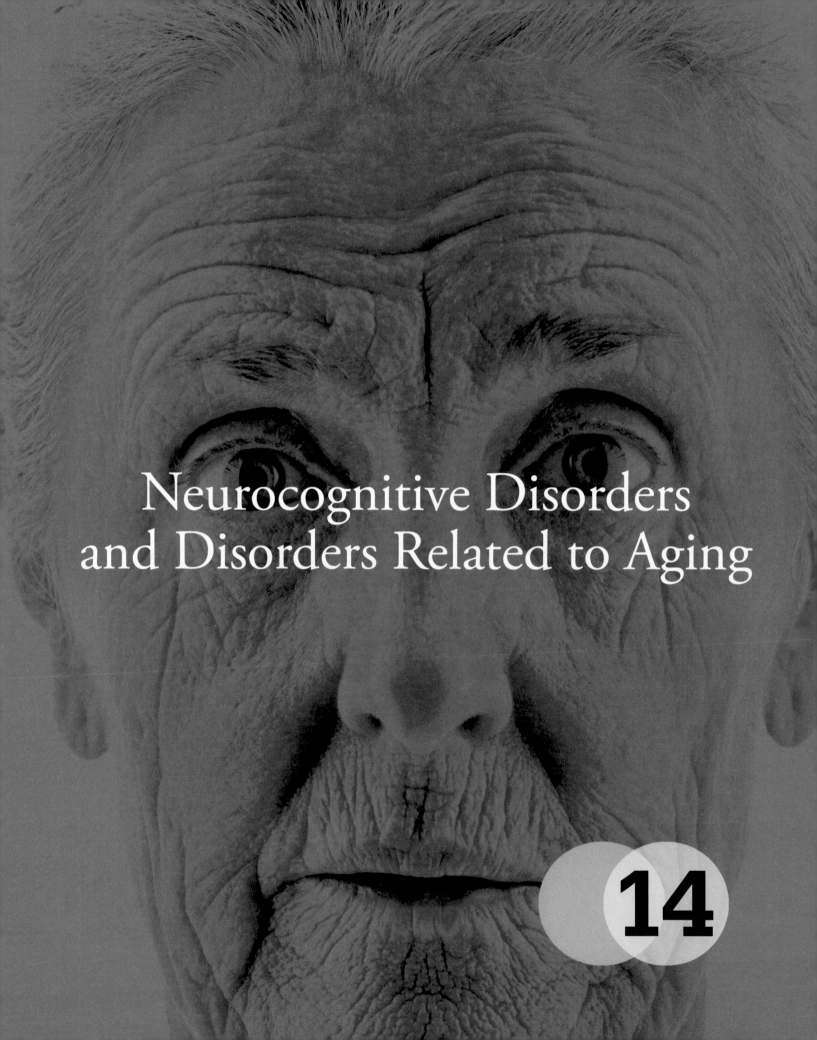

Neurocognitive Disorders and Disorders Related to Aging

14

truth OR fiction

T☐ F☐   Dementia is a normal part of the aging process. (p. 529)

T☐ F☐   Most older adults who develop mild cognitive impairment (MCI) go on to develop Alzheimer's disease within 5 to 10 years. (p. 530)

T☐ F☐   People who become occasionally forgetful as they age are probably suffering from the early stages of Alzheimer's disease. (p. 530)

T☐ F☐   Fortunately, we now have drugs that can halt the progression of Alzheimer's disease or even cure it in some cases. (p. 534)

T☐ F☐   After a motorcycle accident, a medical student failed to recognize the woman he had married a few weeks earlier. (p. 538)

T☐ F☐   A famous folksinger and songwriter was misdiagnosed with alcoholism and spent several years in mental hospitals until the correct diagnosis was made. (p. 541)

T☐ F☐   A form of dementia is linked to mad-cow disease. (p. 543)

T☐ F☐   Anxiety disorders are the most common psychological disorders among older adults, even more common than depression. (p. 544)

learning objectives

14.1
Define the concept of neurocognitive disorder and identify three major types.

14.2
Describe the key features and causes of delirium.

14.3
Describe the key features and causes of major neurocognitive disorder.

14.4
Describe the key features of mild neurocognitive disorder.

14.5
Describe the key features and causes of Alzheimer's disease and evaluate current treatments.

14.6
Identify and describe other types of neurocognitive disorders.

14.7
Identify other psychological disorders related to aging.

"You should pray for a sound mind in a sound body."

—Juvenal, Roman poet, 55–127 B.C.E.

"I" "Now Is the Last Best Time"

The disease [Alzheimer's disease] works slowly, destroying the mind, stealing life in a tedious, silent dance of death. Slowly the memory is impaired, and then you wander in a world without certainty and names. Yesterdays disappear, except those long ago. Eventually there is a descent into silence and a dependence on caretakers. Hands other than yours feed and bathe you. A cipher takes your place amid the tubes and tragedy. By the end, Alzheimer's leaves its victims silent, quivering in their flesh, awaiting the last rites. Some common illness often takes credit on the death certificate. . . .

I am alone and I can hear water running somewhere in the house. I don't remember going to the bathroom. Who else turned on the water?

Writing sometimes becomes difficult. Words vanish before they reach the page. Most of the time the biggest drawback is my plummeting typing accuracy. So far there are few words the spell checker cannot correct. . . .

I do not want to succumb to this illness, but I am powerless in its clutches. Words come when I sit down to write, but they dance away seductively, and meaning and substance disappear quickly. Of course, this is not new; such things happen many times, but before they were retrievable and now they are not. . . .

There are many days of tears now. Some mornings I wake and my eyes are wet. I cry, choked with emotion I cannot express. I am having trouble reading the writing I do with a pencil or pen. It used to be clear and sharp; now it wobbles and is full of uncertainty. The words come normally but the letters are sometimes not in the proper order. I spend valuable time deciphering the meaning in each letter of the alphabet until the word's meaning becomes clear. Progress is slow and I am losing time. A few months ago I had no trouble writing. I have to be careful to spell correctly but sometimes. . . .

I am aware of the loss of language more than ever before. I am afraid to write because watching the words come out distorted is painful and it reveals the destructive power of the disease over which I have no control.

Now is the last best time.

From DeBaggio, 2002

Having a "sound mind in a sound body" is an ancient prescription for a healthy and happy life. However, brain diseases and injuries can make us unsound in both body and mind. When damage to the brain results from an injury or stroke, the deterioration in cognitive, social, and occupational functioning can be rapid and severe. In the case of a more gradual but progressive form of deterioration, such as in Alzheimer's disease (AD), the decline of mental functioning is more gradual but leads eventually to a state of virtual helplessness. Sadly, people with Alzheimer's may come to realize that each day is their last best time.

In this chapter, we focus on the class of psychological disorders called neurocognitive disorders. These disorders arise from injuries or diseases that affect the brain. Some of these diseases, including AD, primarily affect older adults. Other neurocognitive disorders affect people of different age groups, not just older adults (Ganguli et al., 2012). We begin by discussing the various types of neurocognitive disorders and then focus on other psychological disorders that tend to affect people in late adulthood.

14.1 **Define** the concept of neurocognitive disorder and **identify** three major types.

Neurocognitive Disorders

Neurocognitive disorders are diagnosed based on deficits in cognitive functioning that represent a marked change from the individual's prior level of functioning. These disorders were formerly called *cognitive disorders* in earlier versions of the *DSM*, but the nomenclature was broadened in *DSM-5* to better reflect the fact that cognitive functions such as thinking, memory, and attention are closely linked to particular brain regions and neural pathways or networks in the brain (Ganguli et al., 2012). Neurocognitive disorders are not psychologically based; they are caused by physical or medical diseases or drug use or withdrawal that affect the functioning of the brain. In some cases, the specific cause of the neurocognitive disorder can be pinpointed; in others, it cannot. Although these disorders are biologically based, psychological and environmental factors play key roles in determining the impact and range of disabling symptoms as well as the individual's ability to cope with them.

Our ability to perform cognitive functions—to think, reason, store, and recall information—depends on the functioning of the brain. Neurocognitive disorders arise when the brain is either damaged or impaired in its ability to function due to injury, illness, exposure to toxins, or use or abuse of psychoactive drugs. The more widespread the damage to the brain, the greater and more extensive the impairment in functioning. The extent and location of brain damage largely determine the range and severity of impairment. The location of the damage is also critical because many brain structures or regions perform specialized functions. Damage to the temporal lobe, for example, is associated with defects in memory and attention, whereas damage to the occipital lobe may result in visual–spatial deficits, as in the famous case of Dr. P., a distinguished musician and teacher who lost the ability to visually recognize objects, including faces.

In *The Man Who Mistook His Wife for a Hat,* the neurologist Oliver Sacks (1985) recounts how Dr. P. failed to recognize the faces of his students at the music school. When a student spoke, however, Dr. P. immediately recognized his or her voice. Not only did the professor fail to discriminate faces visually, but sometimes he perceived faces where none existed. He patted the heads of fire hydrants and parking meters, which he took to be children. He warmly addressed the rounded knobs on furniture. Dr. P. and his colleagues generally dismissed these peculiarities as jokes—after all, Dr. P. was well known for his oddball humor and jests. His music remained as accomplished as ever, and his general health seemed fine, so these misperceptions seemed little to be concerned about.

Not until three years later did Dr. P. seek a neurological evaluation. His ophthalmologist had found that although Dr. P.'s eyes were healthy, he had problems interpreting visual stimulation. So he made the referral to Dr. Sacks, a neurologist. When Dr. Sacks engaged Dr. P. in conversation, Dr. P.'s eyes fixated oddly on miscellaneous features of Dr. Sacks's face—his nose, then his right ear, then his chin, sensing parts of his face but apparently not connecting them in a meaningful pattern. When Dr. P. sought to put on his shoe after a physical examination, he confused his foot with the shoe. When preparing to leave, Dr. P. looked around for his hat, and then . . .

[Dr. P.] reached out his hand, and took hold of his wife's head, tried to lift it off, to put it on. He had apparently mistaken his wife for a hat! His wife looked as if she was used to such things. (Sacks, 1985, p. 10)

Dr. P.'s peculiar behavior may seem amusing to some, but his loss of visual perception was tragic. Although Dr. P. could identify abstract forms and shapes—a cube, for example—he no longer recognized the faces of his family, or his own. Some features of particular faces would strike a chord of recognition. For example, he could recognize a picture of Einstein from the distinctive hair and mustache and a picture of his own brother from the square jaw and big teeth. But he was responding to isolated features, not grasping the facial patterns as wholes.

Sacks recounts a final test:

It was still a cold day, in early spring, and I had thrown my coat and gloves on the sofa.
"What is this?" I asked, holding up a glove.
"May I examine it?" he asked, and, taking it from me, he proceeded to examine it as he had examined the geometrical shapes.
"A continuous surface," he announced at last, "infolded on itself. It appears to have"—he hesitated—"five outpouchings, if this is the word."
"Yes," I said cautiously. "You have given me a description. Now tell me what it is."
"A container of some sort?"
"Yes," I said, "and what would it contain?"
"It would contain its contents!" said Dr. P., with a laugh. "There are many possibilities. It could be a change-purse, for example, for coins of five sizes. It could . . .."
I interrupted the blarney flow. "Does it not look familiar? Do you think it might contain, might fit, a part of your body?"
No light of recognition dawned on his face.
No child would have the power to see and speak of "a continuous surface . . . infolded on itself," but any child, any infant, would immediately know a glove as a glove, see it as familiar, as going with a hand. Dr. P. didn't. He saw nothing as familiar. Visually, he was lost in a world of lifeless abstractions. (Sacks, 1985, p. 13)

Later, we might add, Dr. P. accidentally put the glove on his hand, exclaiming, "My God, it's a glove!" (Sacks, 1985, p. 13). His brain immediately seized the pattern of tactile information, although his visual brain centers were powerless to interpret the shape as a whole. That is, Dr. P. showed lack of visual knowledge—a symptom referred to as visual **agnosia,** derived from Greek roots meaning "without knowledge." Still, Dr. P.'s musical abilities and verbal skills remained intact. He was able to function, to dress himself, take a shower, and eat his meals, by singing various songs to himself—for example, eating songs and dressing songs—that helped him coordinate his actions. However, if his dressing song was interrupted while he was dressing himself, he would lose his train of thought and be unable to recognize not only the clothes his wife had laid out but also his own body. When the music stopped, so did his ability to make sense of the world. Sacks later learned that Dr. P. had a massive tumor in the area of the brain that processes visual information. Dr. P. was apparently unaware of his deficits, having filled his visually empty world with music to function and imbue his life with meaning and purpose.

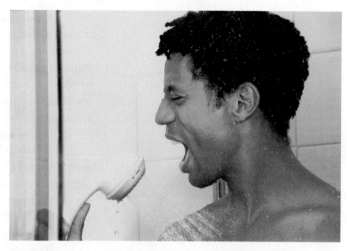

Does this man's singing help him coordinate his actions? In a celebrated case study, Dr. Oliver Sacks discussed the case of "Dr. P.," who was discovered to be suffering from a brain tumor that impaired his ability to process visual cues. Yet he could still eat meals and wash and dress himself so long as he could sing to himself.

Dr. P.'s case is unusual in the peculiarity of his symptoms, but it illustrates the universal dependence of psychological functioning on an intact brain. The case also shows how some people adjust—sometimes so gradually that the changes are all but imperceptible—to developing physical or organic problems. Dr. P.'s visual problems might have been relatively more debilitating in a person who was less talented or who had less social support to draw on. The tragic case of Dr. P. illustrates how psychological and environmental factors determine the impact and range of disabling symptoms as well as the individual's ability to cope with them.

People who suffer from neurocognitive disorders may become completely dependent on others to meet basic needs in feeding, toileting, and grooming. In other cases, although some assistance in meeting the demands of daily living may be required, people are able to function at a level that permits them to live semi-independently. The cognitive deficit that Dr. P. developed, *agnosia*, is often a feature of *dementia*, a severe neurocognitive disorder in which there is general deterioration of mental functioning.

The *DSM-5* restructured the "playing field" for classifying disorders of cognitive functioning, organizing them into three types of disorders: delirium, major neurocognitive disorder, and mild neurocognitive disorder. Table 14.1 provides an overview of these three major types of neurocognitive disorders in the *DSM* system.

Delirium

14.2 Describe the key features and causes of delirium.

The word *delirium* derives from the Latin roots *de-*, meaning "from," and *lira,* meaning "line" or "furrow." It means straying from the line or the norm, in perception, cognition, and behavior. **Delirium** is a state of extreme mental confusion in which people have difficulty focusing their attention, speaking clearly and coherently, and orienting themselves to the environment (see Table 14.2). People suffering from delirium may find it difficult to tune out irrelevant stimuli or to shift their attention to new tasks. They may speak excitedly, but their speech conveys little—if any—meaning. Disorientation as to time (not knowing the current date, day of the week, or time) and place (not knowing where one is) is common. Disorientation to person (the identities of oneself and others) is not. People in a state of delirium may experience terrifying hallucinations, especially visual hallucinations. The severity of symptoms tends to fluctuate during the course of the day (APA, 2013).

Disturbances in perceptions often occur, such as misinterpretations of sensory stimuli (e.g., confusing an alarm clock for a fire bell) or illusions (e.g., feeling as if the bed has an electrical charge passing through it). There can be a dramatic slowing down of movement into a state resembling catatonia. There may be rapid fluctuations between restlessness and stupor. Restlessness is characterized by insomnia, agitated, aimless movements, even bolting out of bed or striking out at nonexistent objects. This may alternate with periods in which the person has to struggle to stay awake.

There are many causes of delirium, including head trauma; metabolic disorders, such as hypoglycemia (low blood sugar); underlying medical conditions such as severe infections or heart failure; drug abuse or withdrawal; fluid or electrolyte imbalances; seizure disorders (epilepsy); deficiencies of the B vitamin thiamine; brain lesions; stroke and diseases affecting the central nervous system, including Parkinson's disease, AD, viral encephalitis (a type of brain infection), liver disease, and kidney disease (e.g., Oldenbeuving et al., 2011; Torpy, Burke, & Glass, 2010).

The prevalence of delirium is estimated at about 1% to 2% in the general community, but rises to 14% among people over the age of 85 (Inouye, 2006). Delirium most often affects hospitalized patients, especially elderly hospitalized patients following surgical operations (Choi et al., 2012; Day et al., 2012). Between 15% and 50% of elderly patients experience delirium following major surgery (Marcantonio, 2012).

Delirium may also occur due to exposure to toxic substances (such as eating certain poisonous mushrooms), as a side effect of using certain medications, or during states of drug or alcohol intoxication. Among young people, delirium is most commonly the result of abrupt withdrawal from psychoactive drugs, especially alcohol. However, among older patients, it is often a sign of a life-threatening medical condition (Inouye, 2006).

TABLE 14.1

Overview of Neurocognitive Disorders

Type of Disorder	Subtypes or Specifiers	Approximate Lifetime Prevalence in Population	Description	Associated Features
Delirium	• Delirium due to a general medical condition • Substance intoxication delirium • Substance withdrawal delirium • Medication-induced delirium	Estimated to be 1% to 2% overall, but higher among older adults	States of extreme mental confusion interfering with concentration and ability to speak coherently	• Difficulty filtering out irrelevant stimuli or shifting attention; excited speech that conveys little meaning • Disorientation as to time and place; frightening hallucinations or other perceptual distortions • Motor behavior may slow to a stupor or fluctuate between states of restlessness and stupor • Mental states may fluctuate between lucid intervals and periods of confusion
Major Neurocognitive Disorder	(specified below)	Estimated to be !% to 2% at age 65, rising to as high as 30% by age 80	Profound deterioration of mental functioning	• Most forms, such as dementia due to Alzheimer's disease, are irreversible and progressive • Significant declines in cognitive abilities
Mild Neurocognitive Disorder	(specified below)	Estimated to be 2% to 10% at age 65 and between 5% and 25% by age 85	Mild or modest decline in cognitive impairment over time; also called mild cognitive impairment or MCI	• Complaints about cognitive declines must be supported by formal tests of cognitive functioning • People with the disorder can function independently but find it more difficult to perform mental tasks they were accustomed to performing easily • Some cases, but not most, eventually progress to Alzheimer's disease

Subtypes of Major and Mild Neurocognitive Disorders	• Neurocognitive disorder due to:
	  o Alzheimer's disease
	  o Traumatic brain injury
	  o Parkinson's disease
	  o HIV infection
	  o Huntington's disease
	  o Prion disease
	• Vascular neurocognitive disorder
	• Frontotemporal neurocognitive disorder
	• Substance/medication-induced neurocognitive disorder
	• Neurocognitive disorder with Lewy bodies
		Varies with underlying condition	Cognitive impairment caused by a variety of underlying physical diseases or disorders that affect brain functioning	• Level of cognitive impairment can range from mild to severe (major)
				• Treatment depends on the underlying cause of brain dysfunction

Sources: Prevalence rates derived from APA, 2000, 2013; Hebert et al., 2003.

People with chronic alcoholism who abruptly stop drinking may experience a form of delirium called *delirium tremens,* or DTs. During an acute episode of the DTs, the person may be terrorized by wild and frightening hallucinations, such as "bugs crawling down walls" or on the skin. The DTs can last for a week or more and are best treated in a hospital, where the patient can be carefully monitored and the symptoms treated with mild tranquilizers and environmental support. Although there are many known causes of delirium, in many cases, the specific cause cannot be identified.

Whatever the cause may be, delirium involves a widespread disruption of brain activity, possibly resulting from imbalances in the levels of certain neurotransmitters (Inouye, 2006). As a result, the person may be unable to process incoming

TABLE 14.2

Features of Delirium

Domain	Level of Severity		
	Mild	Moderate	Severe
Emotion	Apprehension	Fear	Panic
Cognition and perception	Confusion, racing thoughts	Disorientation, delusions	Meaningless mumbling, vivid hallucinations
Behavior	Tremors	Muscle spasms	Seizures
Autonomic activity	Abnormally fast heartbeat (tachycardia)	Perspiration	Fever

Source: Adapted from Freemon (1981), p. 82.

information, leading to a state of general confusion. The person may not be able to speak or think clearly or to make sense of his or her surroundings. States of delirium may occur abruptly, as in cases resulting from seizures or head injuries, or gradually over hours or days, as in cases involving infections, fever, or metabolic disorders. During the course of delirium, the person's mental state often fluctuates between periods of clarity ("lucid intervals"), which are most common in the morning, and periods of confusion and disorientation. Delirium is generally worse in the dark and following sleepless nights.

Unlike dementia or other forms of major neurocognitive disorder (discussed below) in which there is a gradual deterioration of mental functioning, delirium develops rapidly, generally in a few hours to a few days and involves more clearly disturbed processes of attention and awareness (Wong et al., 2010). Also unlike dementia, which typically follows a chronic and progressive course, delirium tends to clear up spontaneously when the underlying medical or drug-related cause is resolved. Psychiatric medication may be used to reduce the symptoms (Torpy, Burke, & Glass, 2010). However, if the underlying cause persists or leads to further deterioration, delirium may progress to disability, coma, and even death (Inouye, 2006).

14.3 Describe the key features and causes of major neurocognitive disorder.

Major Neurocognitive Disorder

Major neurocognitive disorder (commonly called *dementia*) represents a profound decline or deterioration in mental functioning characterized by significant impairment of memory, thinking processes, attention, and judgment and by specific cognitive deficits such as those listed in Table 14.3. There are many causes of major neurocognitive disorder or dementia, but the most frequent cause is the disabling and degenerative brain disease called Alzheimer's disease (AD). Other causes include brain diseases, such as Pick's disease, and infections or disorders affecting the functioning of the brain, such as meningitis, HIV infection, and encephalitis. In some cases, major neurocognitive disorder or dementia can be halted or reversed, especially if it is caused by certain types of tumors, or by seizures, metabolic disturbances, or treatable infections, or when it results from depression or substance abuse. But sadly, the great majority of cases, including the most common form, dementia due to AD, follow a progressive and irreversible course.

A form of dementia caused by a bacterium had historical significance in the development of the medical model of mental disorders. This form of dementia was called **general paresis** (from the Greek *parienai,* meaning "to relax") or "relaxation" of the brain in its most negative connotation. The dementia resulted from *neurosyphilis,* a form of later-stage syphilis, a sexually transmitted disease caused by the bacterium *Treponema pallidum.* In neurosyphilis, the bacterium directly attacks the brain, resulting in dementia. The 19th-century discovery of the connection between this form of dementia and a concrete physical illness, syphilis, strengthened the medical model and held out the promise that organic causes would eventually be found for other abnormal behavior patterns.

TABLE 14.3

Cognitive Deficits Associated with Dementia

Type of Cognitive Deficit	Description	Further Information
Aphasia	Impaired ability to comprehend and/or produce speech	There are several types of aphasia. In sensory or receptive aphasia, people have difficulty understanding written or spoken language, but retain the ability to express themselves through speech. In motor aphasia, the ability to express thoughts through speech is impaired, but the person can understand spoken language. A person with a motor aphasia may not be able to summon up the names of familiar objects or may scramble the normal order of words.
Apraxia	Impaired ability to perform purposeful movements despite an absence of any defect in motor functioning	There may be an inability to tie a shoelace or button a shirt, although the person can describe how these activities should be performed and despite the fact that there is nothing wrong with the person's arm or hand. The person may have difficulty pantomiming the use of an object (e.g., combing one's hair).
Agnosia	Inability to recognize objects despite an intact sensory system	Agnosias may be limited to specific sensory channels. A person with a visual agnosia may not be able to identify a fork when shown a picture of the object, although he or she has an intact visual system and may be able to identify the object if allowed to touch it and manipulate it by hand. Auditory agnosia is marked by impairment in the ability to recognize sounds; in tactile agnosia, people are unable to identify objects (such as coins or keys) by holding them or touching them.
Disturbance in Executive Functioning	Deficits in planning, organizing, or sequencing activities or in engaging in abstract thinking	An office manager who formerly handled budgets and scheduling loses the ability to manage the flow of work in the office or adapt to new demands. An English teacher loses the ability to extract meaning from a poem or story.

General paresis once accounted for upwards of 30% of admissions to psychiatric hospitals. However, advances in detection and the development of antibiotics that cure the infection have greatly reduced the incidence of late-stage syphilis and the development of general paresis. The effectiveness of treatment depends on when antibiotics are introduced and the extent of brain damage. In cases where extensive tissue damage has occurred, antibiotics can stem the infection and prevent further damage, producing some improvement in intellectual performance; however, they cannot restore people to their original levels of functioning.

Impaired memory is the major feature of dementia due to AD, but other major neurocognitive disorders may entail different kinds of cognitive impairments such as profound deficits in language use. The particular deficits depend largely on the part of the brain affected by the underlying condition. Although the term *dementia* is no longer used as a diagnostic label, it continues to be used widely in describing cognitive impairments in older adults. Yet, it has limited applicability to younger patients suffering from different forms of cognitive impairment. The developers of the *DSM-5* also believe it is a pejorative term that carries an unfortunate stigma. Consequently, they decided to replace it in the diagnostic manual with a more descriptive term, major neurocognitive disorder, just as they did with another pejorative term, *mental retardation* (now labeled *intellectual disability*). Because dementia continues to be widely used to describe some forms of cognitive impairment, especially in older adults, we continue to use the term where it applies.

Dementias usually occur in people over the age of 80. Those that begin after age 65 are called late-onset or **senile dementias.** Those that begin at age 65 or earlier are termed early-onset or **presenile dementias.** Although the risk of dementia is g reater in later life, dementia is not a consequence of normal aging. It is a sign of a degenerative brain disease, such as AD. T / F

truth OR fiction

Dementia is a normal part of the aging process.

☑ **FALSE** Dementia is not a normal part of aging. It is caused by an underlying disease affecting brain functioning.

Mild Neurocognitive Disorder

Mild neurocognitive disorder is a newly recognized disorder in *DSM-5* that applies to people who suffer a mild or modest decline in cognitive functioning from their prior level. The decline is not of sufficient magnitude to justify a diagnosis of major neurocognitive disorder. Concerns about the person's cognitive functioning must be recognized by either the person, by someone knowledgeable about the person, or by a professional, but these concerns must be confirmed by formal tests of cognitive functioning on skills such as memory, attention, and problem solving.

Mild neurocognitive disorder is a new name for a clinical syndrome widely identified as *mild cognitive impairment* (MCI). People with mild neurocognitive disorder or MCI are able to function independently and complete tasks of daily living at home and on the job, but they need to apply more effort in completing tasks that used to come more easily. Or they may compensate in some ways to maintain their independence, such as shifting job responsibilities to others or using electronic devices to supplement their lagging memory. But clinicians struggle with determining the thresholds to use to distinguish MCI from normal age-related changes in cognitive abilities, especially memory for names and mental arithmetic.

truth OR fiction

Most older adults who develop mild cognitive impairment (MCI) go on to develop Alzheimer's disease within 5 to 10 years.

☑ **FALSE** Sadly, some do, but most do not progress to Alzheimer's.

Mild impairment of cognitive functioning frequently occurs in the early stages of neurogenerative diseases like AD and other conditions affecting the brain, such as traumatic brain injury, HIV infection, substance-use-related brain disorders, and diabetes. For example, AD typically develops gradually over time, with most cases showing evidence of memory problems associated with MCI for years before full-fledged symptoms of Alzheimer's appear (Buchhave et al., 2012; Malek-Ahmadi et al., 2012; Sperling et al., 2011; Steenhuysen, 2011). However, we should note that the majority of people with MCI do not develop AD. **T / F**

The inclusion of a new diagnosis of mild neurocognitive disorder in *DSM-5* is important for several reasons. Firstly, it highlights the need to identity cases of MCI that can be targeted for early intervention before more serious deficits emerge. Early intervention may involve treatment with drugs or cognitive retraining that is not effective once more severe levels of cognitive impairment develop. Secondly, diagnosing the disorder enables researchers to identify groups of possible research participants who may be willing to participate in research trials focusing on finding ways of preventing the progression from mild to severe forms of cognitive impairment.

Subtypes of Major and Mild Neurocognitive Disorders

Here we focus on specific subtypes of neurocognitive disorders in which the level of cognitive impairment may range from mild in the case of mild neurocognitive disorders to severe in the case of major neurocognitive disorders. Our focus is primarily on AD because it is the most prominent cause of significant cognitive impairment.

truth OR fiction

People who become occasionally forgetful as they age are probably suffering from the early stages of Alzheimer's disease.

☑ **FALSE** Occasional memory loss or forgetfulness is a normal consequence of the aging process.

Neurocognitive Disorder Due to Alzheimer's Disease

Alzheimer's disease (AD) is a degenerative brain disease that leads to progressive and irreversible dementia, characterized by memory loss and deterioration of other cognitive functions, including judgment and ability to reason. The risk of AD increases dramatically with advancing age (Querfurth & LaFerla, 2010). More than 99% of cases occur in people over the age of 65 (Alzheimer's Society, 2008). The disease affects about 1 in 8 people age 65 or older and more than 1 in 3 people over the age of 85—about 4.7 million Americans in total (Hebert et al., 2013). As the U.S. population continues to age, the prevalence rate in the U.S. is expected to more than double to 13.8 million people by the year 2050 (Hebert et al., 2013). AD accounts for more than half of the cases of dementia in the general population. AD that strikes earlier in life appears to involve a more severe form of the disease. **T / F**

The great majority of cases of AD occur in people over the age of 65, most typically in those in their late 70s and 80s (see Figure 14.1). Women are at higher risk of developing the disease than men, although this may be because women tend to live longer. Yet, it is important to note again that although AD is strongly connected with aging, it is a degenerative brain disease and not a consequence of normal aging.

Dementia associated with AD takes the form of progressive deterioration or loss of mental abilities involving memory, language, and problem solving. Occasional memory loss or forgetfulness in middle life (e.g., forgetting where one put one's glasses) is normal and not a sign of the early stages of AD. People in later life (and some of us not quite that advanced in years) complain of not remembering names as well as they used to or of forgetting names that were once well known to them.

Forgetting where you put your keys is a normal occurrence; forgetting where you live is not. Here, a woman with early-onset Alzheimer's recounts how her memory began slipping away. She relates an experience that happened to her one day as she was driving home from her husband's office.

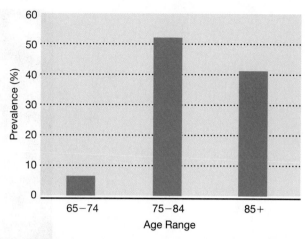

FIGURE 14.1

Prevalence of Alzheimer's disease among older adults. Among older adults, the risk of Alzheimer's disease is much greater among people over the age of 75 than among those aged 65–74.

Source: Hebert et al., 2003.

→ "Living in the Labyrinth"

I was hopelessly lost, and had no idea how to get home. . . . My body was shaking with fear and uncontrollable sobs. What was happening?

A few yards ahead, there was a park ranger building. Trembling, I wiped my eyes, and breathing deeply, tried to calm myself. . . . The guard smiled and inquired how he could assist me.

"I appear to be lost," I began. . . .

"Where do you need to go?" the guard asked politely.

A cold chill enveloped me as I realized I could not remember the name of my street. Tears began to flow down my cheeks. I did not know where I wanted to go. . . .

I felt panic wash over me anew as I searched my memory and found it blank. Suddenly, I remembered bringing my grandchildren to this park. That must mean I lived relatively nearby, surely.

"What is the closest subdivision?" I quavered.

The guard scratched his head thoughtfully.

"The closest Orlando subdivision would be Pine Hills, maybe," he ventured.

"That's right!" I exclaimed gratefully. The name of my subdivision had rung a bell. . . .

I drove carefully in the exact direction he advised and searched each intersection. . . . Finally, . . . I recognized the entrance to the subdivision. . . .

Once home, a wave of relief brought more tears. . . . I took refuge in the darkened master bedroom, and sat, curled up on my bed, my arms wrapped tightly around myself.

Source: From McGowin, 1993.

Suspicions of AD are raised when cognitive impairment is more severe and pervasive, affecting the individual's ability to meet the ordinary responsibilities of daily work and social roles. Over the course of the illness, people with AD may get lost in parking lots or in stores, or even in their own homes. The wife of an AD patient describes how AD affected her husband: "With no cure, Alzheimer's robs the person of who he is. It is painful to see Richard walk around the car several times because he can't find the door" (Morrow, 1998). Agitation, wandering behavior, depression, and aggressive behavior are common as the disease progresses.

People with AD may become depressed, confused, or even delusional when they sense that their mental ability is slipping away but do not understand why. They may

Alzheimer's disease (AD). AD has struck a number of notable people, including former President Ronald Reagan, shown here with his wife, Nancy, at his first public appearance after being diagnosed with AD. Reagan died of the disease in June 2004.

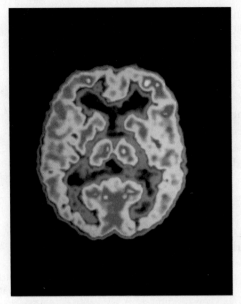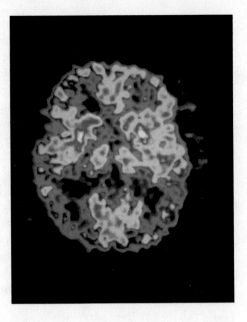

FIGURE 14.2

PET scans of brains from a healthy aged adult (left) and a patient with Alzheimer's disease (right). The excess of dark shading in the photo to the right suggests how the neurological changes associated with Alzheimer's disease impair brain activity.

Source: Friedland, R. P., Case Western Reserve University, courtesy of *Clinical Neuroimaging.* Copyright ©1988 by John Wiley and Sons, Inc.

experience hallucinations and other psychotic features. Bewilderment and fear may lead to paranoid delusions or beliefs that their loved ones have betrayed them, robbed them, or don't care about them. They may forget the names of their loved ones or fail to recognize them. They may even forget their own names.

AD was first described in 1907 by the German physician Alois Alzheimer (1864–1915). During an autopsy of a 56-year-old woman who had suffered from severe dementia, he found two brain abnormalities now regarded as characteristic signs of the disease: plaques (deposits of fibrous protein fragments composed of a material called *beta amyloid*) and neurofibrillary tangles (twisted bundles of fibers of a protein called *tau*) (Carrillo et al., 2012; Han et al., 2012) (see Figure 14.2). The darkly shaded areas in the photo to the right in Figure 14.2 show the diminished brain activity associated with AD.

DIAGNOSIS Various medical and psychological conditions sometimes mimic symptoms of AD, such as severe depression resulting in memory loss. Consequently, misdiagnoses may occur, especially in the early stages of the disease, and so doctors need to be careful in making a diagnosis of this dreadful disease. In 2012, a new brain scanning technology became available, allowing doctors for the first time to diagnose AD based on brain scans showing plaques associated with the disease together with clinical evidence of memory loss (Kolata, 2012). Brain scanning techniques may soon be available to predict which patients with MCI are likely to progress to AD (Bohnen et al., 2011; Chen et al., 2011; Jack et al., 2011; McEvoy et al., 2011).

SYMPTOMS OF ALZHEIMER'S DISEASE The early stages of AD are marked by limited memory problems and subtle personality changes. People may at first have trouble managing their finances; remembering recent events or basic information such as telephone numbers, area codes, zip codes, and the names of their grandchildren; and performing numerical computations. A business executive who once managed millions of dollars may become unable to perform simple arithmetic. There may be subtle personality changes, such as signs of withdrawal in people who had been outgoing or irritability in people who had been gentle. In these early stages, people with AD generally appear neat and well groomed and are generally cooperative and socially appropriate.

Some people with AD are not aware of their deficits. Others deny them. At first, they may attribute their problems to other causes, such as stress or fatigue. Denial may protect people with AD in the early or mild stages of the disease from recognizing that their intellectual abilities are declining. Or the recognition that their mental abilities are slipping away may lead to depression.

In moderately severe AD, people require assistance in managing everyday tasks. At this stage, Alzheimer's patients may be unable to select appropriate clothes or recall their addresses or names of family members. When they drive, they begin making mistakes, such as failing to stop at stop signs or accelerating when they should be braking. They may encounter difficulties in toileting and bathing themselves. They often make mistakes in recognizing themselves in mirrors. They may no longer be able to speak in full sentences. Verbal responses may become limited to a few words. 👁

Movement and coordination functions deteriorate further. People with AD at the moderately severe level may begin walking in shorter, slower steps. They may no longer be able to sign their names, even when assisted by others. They may have difficulty handling a knife and fork. Agitation becomes a prominent feature at this stage, and patients may act out in response to the threat of having to contend with an environment that no longer seems controllable. They may pace or fidget or display aggressive behavior such as yelling, throwing, or hitting. Patients may wander off because of restlessness and be unable to find their way back.

People with advanced AD may start talking to themselves or experience visual hallucinations or paranoid delusions. They may believe that someone is attempting to harm them or is stealing their possessions or that their spouses are unfaithful to them. They may even believe that their spouses are actually other people.

At the most severe stage, cognitive functions decline to the point where people become essentially helpless. They may lose the ability to speak or control body movement. They become incontinent; are unable to communicate, walk, or even sit up; and require assistance in toileting and feeding. In the end state, seizures, coma, and death result.

👁 **Watch** the **Video** *Alvin: Dementia (Alzheimer's Type)* on **MyPsychLab**

Do you know my name? Alzheimer's disease can devastate patients' families. Spouses usually provide the bulk of daily care. This man has been caring for his wife for several years, and he believes that his hugs and kisses sometimes prompt his wife to murmur his name.

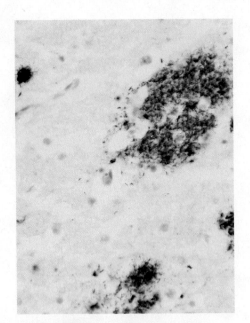

Plaques linked to Alzheimer's disease. In Alzheimer's disease, nerve tissue in the brain degenerates, forming steel-wool-like clumps or plaques composed of beta-amyloid protein fragments shown here as blue-stained areas in a section of the cerebral cortex.

truth OR fiction

Fortunately, we now have drugs that can halt the progression of Alzheimer's disease or even cure it in some cases.

☑ **FALSE** Although active research efforts are under way to develop such drugs, we lack drugs that can curb the progression of the disease or offer hope of a cure. At best, presently available drugs may slow the rate of cognitive decline.

AD wreaks havoc not only on the affected person but also on the entire family. Families who helplessly watch their loved ones slowly deteriorate have been described as attending a "funeral that never ends" (Aronson, 1988). The symptoms of advanced AD, such as wandering away, aggressiveness, destructiveness, incontinence, screaming, and remaining awake at night, impose high levels of stress on caregivers. Living with a person with advanced AD may seem like living with a stranger—so profound are the changes in personality and behavior. Not surprisingly, caregivers tend to experience more health-related problems and higher levels of stress hormones than do noncaregivers (Vitaliano, Zhang, & Scanlan, 2003). Typically, the caretaking burden falls disproportionately on the adult daughters in the family, who are often middle-aged women feeling "sandwiched" between their responsibilities to their children and to their affected parents.

CAUSAL FACTORS We don't yet know what causes AD, but clues may lie in understanding the process by which steel-wool-like plaques and tangled nerve fibers form in the brain in AD patients. We don't yet know whether the accumulation of plaques and tangles accounts for memory loss and other symptoms in AD or is merely a symptom of the disease ("Alzheimer's Disease," 2011; Herrup, 2010).

Scientists are drilling down to the underlying processes involved in AD, focusing on the loss of synapses in the brain—the tiny gaps between neurons through which neurons communicate (Hongpaisan, Sun, & Alkon, 2011; "Gene Linked, 2013"). The hope is that a better understanding of the biological bases of AD may lead to specific therapies to treat or perhaps even prevent the disease ("New Therapies," 2011; Orešič et al., 2011).

Scientists have identified a number of genes linked to AD, raising hopes that we may one day find ways of counteracting their adverse effects (e.g., Braskie et al., 2011; Naj et al., 2011; Pottier et al., 2012; Ramanan et al., 2012). Different combinations of genes may be involved in different forms of the disease. Some forms of AD are associated with particular genes linked to the production of beta amyloid or to abnormal buildup of amyloid plaques and neurofibrillary tangles associated with AD (Bookheimer & Burggren, 2009; Harold et al., 2009). People with a genetic variant called the *ApoE4* gene stand a much higher risk of developing AD, perhaps as much as three times greater risk than average ("Alzheimer's Risk Gene," 2011).

Environmental factors may also be involved in the development of AD (Sotiropoulos et al., 2011; "Stress May Increase," 2011). We don't yet know which environmental factors may be involved, but stress is a possible culprit. Scientists are working to develop a better understanding of how genes and environmental factors interact in the development of the disease.

TREATMENT AND PREVENTION Presently available drugs for AD offer at best only modest benefits in slowing cognitive decline and boosting cognitive functioning. None is a cure. One widely used drug *donepezil* (brand name Aricept) increases levels of the neurotransmitter acetylcholine (ACh). AD patients show lower levels of ACh, possibly because of the death of brain cells in ACh-producing areas of the brain. However, the drug produces only small or modest improvements in cognitive functioning in people with moderate to severe AD (Howard et al., 2012; Kuehn, 2012). Another drug *memantine* (brand name Axura) blocks the neurotransmitter glutamate, a brain chemical found in abnormally high concentrations in AD patients (Rettner, 2011). High levels of glutamate may damage brain cells. Unfortunately, recent evidence fails to support the benefits of the drug over a placebo in treating milder forms of AD (Schneider et al., 2011). Antipsychotic medication may also be used to help control the aggressive or agitated behavior of dementia patients, but these drugs carry significant safety risks (Corbett & Ballard, 2012; Devanand et al., 2012). **T / F**

Taking a Page From Facebook: Neuroscientists Examine Brain Networks in Alzheimer's Patients

Facebook, the popular social networking site, builds friendship networks based on connecting individuals to each other through common friends or interests. The common links between people are called *hubs* ("Hey, I see we share a dog groomer together. Want to join our dog-walking group?"). In this example, the dog groomer is a hub that connects two or more people together. You might eventually meet other customers of the same dog groomer, but Facebook hubs makes communication faster and more reliable.

Neuroscientists at Stanford University School of Medicine compared networks of interconnected neurons or "hubs" in the brains of patients with AD with those in healthy people (Conger, 2008a, 2008b; Supekar et al., 2008). Functional magnetic imaging (fMRI) scans showed less well-connected neural networks in the brains of the Alzheimer's patients. In effect, the brains of Alzheimer's patients had fewer working hubs. A breakdown of hubs or connecting stations in the brain may help explain some of the memory loss and confusion of Alzheimer's patients (see Figure 14.3). Consequently, it becomes more difficult for neurons in the brain to communicate with each other because they are not as closely linked in active networks.

Analysis of these neural networks allowed investigators to correctly identify Alzheimer's patients and healthy controls about 75% of the time. This research may be a first step toward developing a new diagnostic tool that can distinguish early-stage AD from other brain disorders.

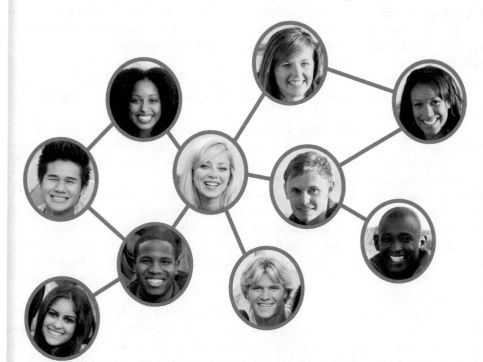

FIGURE 14.3

Your brain on Facebook. Facebook connects people through common links or hubs based on shared acquaintances or interest patterns. Neuroscientists find that the brains of Alzheimer's patients have less well-developed "hubs" or networks of interconnected neurons, which may help to explain cognitive impairments in memory and thinking processes.

Source: www.thetechbrief.com/. . ./facebook _network_31.jpg.

Inflammation in the brain appears to play a key role in the development of AD. Hence, investigators are evaluating the potential preventive effects of anti-inflammatory drugs, such as the common pain reliever *ibuprofen* (brand name Advil). Medical experts caution against widespread use of these drugs until it becomes clear whether they can reduce the risk of AD or delay its onset (Rogers, 2009). Unfortunately, we lack any drugs that can prevent or delay the development of AD (Kolata, 2010). Scientists suspect that the biological process involved in AD may begin more than 20 years before dementia develops (Bateman et al., 2012). Consequently, investigators are calling for greater attention to developing drugs that target the early stages of the disease rather than its end stage (Buchhave et al., 2012; Selkoe, 2012; Sperling et al., 2011b).

Engaging in stimulating cognitive activities—solving puzzles, reading newspapers, playing word games, etc.—can help boost cognitive performance in people with mild to moderate AD (Woods et al., 2012). AD patients may also benefit from memory training programs to help them make optimal use of their remaining abilities. Hopes for the future lie in the development of an effective vaccine to prevent this devastating disease (Michaud et al., 2013; Winblad et al., 2012). On the prevention front, there is some evidence that lifestyle factors such as maintaining a regular exercise program and following a healthy diet low in animal fat and rich in vegetables and fish can reduce the risk of AD (Buchman et al., 2012; Nisbett et al., 2012; Walsh, 2011). That said, links between lifestyle factors such as diet and exercise and the risk of AD need to be more fully tested. Encouraging findings along these lines reported in 2013 showed that physical fitness in middle adulthood was associated with a lower risk of dementia in later adulthood (DeFina et al., 2013). This study was based on observational methods that cannot demonstrate cause and effect relationships, but it does suggest that physical fitness programs may help prevent dementia. We also need other research to test whether regular mental exercises of the type involved in completing mentally challenging tasks can delay or perhaps even prevent the development of AD.

14.6 Identify and describe other types of neurocognitive disorders.

Vascular Neurocognitive Disorder

The brain, like other living tissues, depends on the bloodstream to supply it with oxygen and glucose and to carry away its metabolic wastes. A stroke, also called a **cerebrovascular accident (CVA)**, occurs when part of the brain becomes damaged because of a disruption in its blood supply, usually as the result of a blood clot that becomes lodged in an artery that services the brain and obstructs circulation (Adler, 2004). Areas of the brain may be damaged or destroyed, leaving the victim with disabilities in motor, speech, and cognitive functions. Death may also occur.

Vascular neurocognitive disorder (formerly called vascular dementia or *multi-infarct dementia*) is a form of major or mild neurocognitive disorder resulting from cerebrovascular events (strokes) affecting the brain (Staekenborg et al., 2009). Vascular dementia, the second most common form of dementia after AD, most often affects people in later life but at somewhat earlier ages than dementia due to AD. The disease affects more men than women and accounts for about one in five cases of dementia. Although any individual stroke may produce gross cognitive impairments, such as **aphasia,** they do not typically cause the more generalized cognitive declines associated with dementia. Vascular forms of dementia generally result from multiple strokes occurring at different times that have cumulative effects on a wide range of mental abilities.

The symptoms of vascular neurocognitive disorder are similar to those of dementia due to Alzheimer's, including impaired memory and language ability, agitation and emotional instability, and loss of ability to care for one's own basic needs. However, AD is characterized by an insidious onset and a gradual decline of mental functioning, whereas vascular dementia typically occurs abruptly and follows a stepwise course of deterioration involving rapid declines in cognitive functioning that are believed to reflect the effects of additional strokes. Some cognitive functions in people with vascular dementia remain relatively intact in the early course of the disorder, leading to a pattern of patchy deterioration in which islands of mental competence remain while other abilities suffer gross impairment, depending on the particular areas of the brain that have been damaged by multiple strokes.

Frontotemporal Neurocognitive Disorder

This neurocognitive disorder is characterized by deterioration (thinning or shrinkage) of brain tissue in the frontal and temporal lobes of the cerebral cortex. This typically takes the form of progressive dementia symptomatically similar to AD. Symptoms include memory loss and social inappropriateness, such as a loss of modesty or the display of flagrant sexual

Examining Your Attitudes Toward Aging

What are your assumptions about late adulthood? Do you see older people as basically different from the young in their behavior patterns and their outlooks, or just as more mature?

To evaluate the accuracy of your attitudes toward aging, mark each of the following items true or false. Then turn to the answer key at the end of the chapter.

	TRUE	FALSE
1. By age 60 most couples have lost their capacity for satisfying sexual relations.	____	____
2. Older people cannot wait to retire.	____	____
3. With advancing age, people become more externally oriented, less concerned with the self.	____	____
4. As individuals age, they become less able to adapt satisfactorily to a changing environment.	____	____
5. General satisfaction with life tends to decrease as people become older.	____	____
6. As people age, they tend to become more homogeneous—that is, all old people tend to be alike in many ways.	____	____
7. For the older person, having a stable intimate relationship is no longer highly important.	____	____

	TRUE	FALSE
8. The aged are susceptible to a wider variety of psychological disorders than young and middle-aged adults.	____	____
9. Most older people are depressed much of the time.	____	____
10. Church attendance increases with age.	____	____
11. The occupational performance of the older worker is typically less effective than that of the younger adult.	____	____
12. Most older people are just not able to learn new skills.	____	____
13. Compared to younger people, older people tend to think more about the past than about the present or the future.	____	____
14. Most people in later life are unable to live independently and reside in nursing homes or similar institutions.	____	____

Source: Adapted from Nevid & Rathus (2013). *Psychology and the challenges of life: Adjustment and modern life* (12th ed.), p. 484. Hoboken, NJ: John Wiley and Sons. Reprinted with permission

behavior. This form of dementia was originally known as **Pick's disease,** after the doctor who discovered abnormal structures, is now called Pick's bodies in the brains of some dementia patients. Diagnosis is confirmed only upon autopsy by the *absence* of the neurofibrillary tangles and plaques that are found in AD and by the presence of Pick's bodies in nerve cells. Pick's disease is believed to account for about 6% to 12% of all dementias (Kertesz, 2006). Unlike AD, the disease usually begins in middle age rather than late adulthood, but it occasionally affects young adults in their 20s (Love & Spillantini, 2011). The risk declines with advancing age after 70. Men are more likely than women to suffer from Pick's disease. Pick's disease often runs in families and evidence points to a genetic component (Kertesz, 2006; Love & Spillantini, 2011).

Neurocognitive Disorder Due to Traumatic Brain Injury

Head trauma resulting from jarring, banging, or cutting brain tissues, usually because of accident or assault, can injure the brain, sometimes severely so. Progressive dementia due to traumatic brain injury is more likely to result from multiple head traumas (as in the case of boxers who receive multiple blows to the head during their careers) than from a single blow or head trauma (McCrea et al., 2003). Football players stand a heightened risk of immediate and long-term brain damage because of the repetitive head injuries on

Headed toward dementia? A National Football League (NFL) study showed that former professional football players said they were diagnosed with Alzheimer's or other memory-related diseases at a much higher than average rate. Multiple blows to the head on the playing field may lead to dementia and other types of cognitive impairment.

truth OR fiction

After a motorcycle accident, a medical student failed to recognize the woman he had married a few weeks earlier.

☑ **TRUE**   After the accident, the student failed to recognize his wife of a few weeks, although he remembered his parents.

the field. A widely cited study by the National Football League (NFL) in 2009 showed reports of dementia and significant memory problems among retired football players to be much higher than the rate found in the general population (Schwarz, 2009). More recently, preliminary results of a small study of brain images of five retired NFL players by UCLA researchers showed evidence of abnormal brain proteins associated with AD (Small et al., 2013).

Although risks of brain damage are greater with multiple head injuries, even a single head trauma can have psychological effects, leading to neurocognitive disorder. If severe enough, a traumatic brain injury can lead to physical disability or death. Specific changes in personality following traumatic injury to the brain vary with the site and extent of the injury, among other factors. Damage to the frontal lobe, for example, is associated with a range of emotional changes involving alterations of mood and personality.

Amnesia (memory loss) frequently follows a traumatic event, such as a blow to the head, an electric shock, or a major surgical operation. A head injury may prevent people from remembering events that occurred shortly before the accident. An automobile accident victim may not remember anything that transpired after getting into the car. A football player who develops amnesia from a blow to the head during the game may not remember anything after leaving the locker room. In some cases, people retain memories of the remote past but lose those of recent events. For example, people with amnesia may be more likely to remember events from their childhood than last evening's dinner. Consider the following case.

→ Who Is She? A Case of Amnesia

A medical student was rushed to the hospital after he was thrown from a motorcycle. His parents were with him in his hospital room when he awakened. As his parents were explaining what had happened to him, the door suddenly flew open and his flustered wife, whom he had married a few weeks earlier, rushed into the room, leaped onto his bed, began to caress him, and expressed her great relief that he was not seriously injured. After several minutes of expressing her love and reassurance, his wife departed and the flustered student looked at his mother and asked, "Who is she?" **T / F**

→ *Adapted from Freemon, 1981, p. 96*

The medical student's long-term memory loss included memories dating not only to the accident but also farther back to the time before he was married or had met his wife. Like most victims of posttraumatic amnesia, the medical student recovered his memory fully.

There are two general types of amnesia—**retrograde amnesia** (loss of memory of past events and personal information) and **anterograde amnesia** (inability or difficulty forming or storing new memories). A football player who does not remember anything after leaving the locker room has retrograde amnesia, but some cases are reported in the medical annals of people for whom information literally "goes in one ear and out the other" because they are unable to form new memories. These patients are experiencing anterograde amnesia. Problems with forming new memories may be revealed by an inability to remember the names of, or to recognize, people whom the person met 5 or 10 minutes earlier. Immediate memory, as measured by ability to repeat back a series of numbers, seems to be unimpaired in states of amnesia. The person is unlikely to remember the number series later, no matter how often it is rehearsed.

In a famous medical case, an epileptic patient known by the initials H.M. developed anterograde amnesia as a complication of surgery performed to control his seizures (Carey, 2009). After the surgery, he became unable to learn any new information. Every time he would visit a store, it would be as if it were the first time. He would meet a new acquaintance time after time but would never recall having met the person before. He was quoted as saying, "Every day is alone by itself, whatever enjoyment I have had, whatever sorrow I have had."

People with amnesia may experience disorientation, more commonly involving disorientation to place (not knowing where one is at the time) and time (not knowing the day, month, and year) than disorientation as to self (not knowing one's own name). They may not be aware of their memory loss or may attempt to deny or mask their memory deficits even when evidence of their impairment is presented to them. They may attempt to fill the gaps in their memories with imaginary events. Or they may admit they have a memory problem but appear apathetic about it, showing a kind of emotional blandness.

Although amnesia patients may suffer profound memory losses, their general intelligence tends to remain within a normal range. In contrast, in progressive dementias such as AD, both memory and intellectual functioning deteriorate. Early detection and diagnosis of the causes of memory problems are critical because they are often curable if the underlying cause is treated successfully.

In addition to brain trauma, other causes of amnesia include brain surgery; **hypoxia,** or sudden loss of oxygen to the brain; brain infection or disease; **infarction,** or blockage of the blood vessels supplying the brain; and chronic, heavy use of certain psychoactive substances, most commonly alcohol.

Substance/Medication-Induced Neurocognitive Disorder

The use of, or withdrawal from, psychoactive substances or medications can impair brain functioning in many ways, leading to minor or major neurocognitive disorder. The most common example is **Korsakoff's syndrome,** which involves irreversible memory loss due to brain damage resulting from deficiency of vitamin B1 (thiamine). The disorder is associated with chronic alcoholism because alcohol abusers tend to take poor care of their nutritional needs and may not follow a diet rich enough in vitamin B1, or their alcohol-soaked livers may not be able to metabolize the vitamin efficiently. The memory deficits persist even years after the person stops drinking. However, Korsakoff's syndrome is not limited to people with chronic alcoholism. It has been reported in other groups that experience thiamine deficiencies during times of deprivation, such as prisoners of war.

People with Korsakoff's syndrome have major gaps in their memory of past experiences and significant difficulty learning new information. Despite their memory losses, patients with Korsakoff's syndrome may retain their general level of intelligence. They are often described as being superficially friendly but lacking in insight, unable to discriminate between actual events and wild stories they invent to fill the gaps in their memories. They sometimes become grossly disoriented and confused and require custodial care.

Korsakoff's syndrome often follows an acute attack of **Wernicke's disease,** another brain disorder caused by thiamine deficiency that occurs most often among people with alcoholism (Charness, 2009). Wernicke's disease is marked by confusion and disorientation, **ataxia** or difficulty maintaining balance while walking, and paralysis of the muscles that control eye movements. These symptoms may pass, but the person is often left with Korsakoff's syndrome and enduring memory impairment. If, however, Wernicke's disease is treated promptly with major doses of vitamin B1, Korsakoff's syndrome may not develop.

Neurocognitive Disorder With Lewy Bodies

Neurocognitive disorder with Lewy bodies is among the most common types of progressive dementia (NINDS, 2012). It accounts for about 10% of dementias in older adults. The disease has features of both AD and Parkinson's. **Lewy bodies** are abnormal protein deposits that form within the nucleus of cells in parts of the brain, disrupting brain processes that control memory and motor control. The distinguishing features of the disorder, in addition to profound cognitive decline similar to that of AD, is the appearance of fluctuating alertness and attention, marked by frequent periods of drowsiness and staring into space, as well as recurrent visual hallucinations and rigid body movements and stiff muscles typical of Parkinson's disease. People with Lewy body dementia may also suffer from depression. The disease usually develops between the ages of 50 and 85, and unfortunately there is no cure. Nor do scientists know why Lewy bodies accumulate in brain cells in some people.

Neurocognitive Disorder Due to Parkinson's Disease

Parkinson's disease is a slowly progressing neurological disease of unknown cause affecting 500,000 to 1 million people in the United States, including such notable figures as former heavyweight champion Muhammad Ali and actor Michael J. Fox. The disease affects men and women about equally, most often strikes between the ages of 50 and 69, and affects more than 1% of people over 65 years. Dementia often occurs in Parkinson's disease, with estimates indicating that nearly 80% of Parkinson's disease patients will eventually develop dementia over the course of the illness (Shulman, 2010).

Parkinson's disease is characterized by uncontrollable shaking or tremors, rigidity, disturbances in posture (leaning forward), and lack of control over body movements. People with Parkinson's disease may be able to control their shaking or tremors, but only briefly. Some cannot walk at all. Others walk laboriously, in a crouch. Some execute voluntary body movements with difficulty, have poor control over fine motor movements, such as finger control, and have sluggish reflexes. They may look expressionless, as if they were wearing masks, a symptom that apparently reflects the degeneration of brain tissue that controls facial muscles. It is particularly difficult for patients to engage in sequences of complex movements, such as those required to sign their names. People with Parkinson's disease may be unable to coordinate two movements at the same time, as seen in this description of a Parkinson's patient who had difficulty walking and reaching for his wallet at the same time.

> **→ Motor Impairment in a Case of Parkinson's Disease**
>
> *A 58-year-old man was walking across the hotel lobby in order to pay his bill. He reached into his inside jacket pocket for his wallet. He stopped walking instantly as he did so and stood immobile in the lobby in front of strangers. He became aware of his suspended locomotion and resumed his stroll to the cashier; however, his hand remained rooted in his inside pocket, as though he were carrying a weapon he might display once he arrived at the cashier.*
>
> → *Adapted from Knight, Godfrey, & Shelton (1988)*

Despite the severity of motor disability, cognitive functions seem to remain intact during the early stages of the disease. Dementia is more common in the later stages or among those with more severe forms of the disease. The form of dementia associated with Parkinson's disease typically involves a slowing down of thinking processes, impaired ability to think abstractly or to plan or organize a series of actions, and difficulty in retrieving memories. Overall, the cognitive impairments associated with Parkinson's disease tend to be more subtle than those associated with AD. Parkinson's patients often become socially withdrawn and depressed, perhaps because of the demands of coping with the disease or possibly due to underlying disturbances in the brain associated with the disease.

Parkinson's disease involves destruction of dopamine-producing nerve cells in the *substantia nigra* ("black substance"), an area of the brain that helps regulate body movement (Sahin & Kirik, 2012). The underlying causes of the disease remain unknown, but scientists today suspect an interaction between genetic influences and environmental factors, perhaps involving exposure to certain toxins (Dai et al., 2012; Yang et al., 2009). According to one expert, "Dopamine is like the oil in the engine of a car. . . . If the oil is there, the car runs smoothly. If not, it seizes up" (cited in Carroll, 2004, p. F5).

Whatever the underlying cause, the symptoms of the disease—the uncontrollable tremors, shaking, rigid muscles, and difficulty in walking—are tied to deficiencies in the amount of dopamine in the

Battling Parkinson's disease. Actor Michael J. Fox has been waging a personal battle against Parkinson's disease and has brought national attention to the need to fund research efforts to develop more effective treatments for this degenerative brain disease.

brain (Sahin & Kirik, 2012). The drug L-dopa, which increases dopamine levels, brought hope to Parkinson's patients when it was introduced in the 1970s. L-dopa is converted in the brain into dopamine (Devos, Moreau, & Destée, 2009).

Parkinson's remains an incurable and progressive disease, but L-dopa can help control the symptoms of the disease and slow its progress. After a few years of treatment, L-dopa begins to lose its effectiveness, and the disease continues to progress. Several other drugs are in the experimental stage, offering hope for further advances in treatment. Other sources of hope come from genetic studies that may one day lead to an effective gene therapy for Parkinson's disease and from experimental use of electrical stimulation of deep brain structures (Rezai et al., 2011; Weaver et al., 2009). Investigators report that deep brain electrical stimulation help block tremors in some Parkinson patients (Schuepbach et al., 2013; Tanner, 2013).

Neurocognitive Disorder Due to Huntington's Disease

Huntington's disease, also known as *Huntington's chorea,* was first recognized by the neurologist George Huntington in 1872. In Huntington's disease, there is progressive deterioration of the basal ganglia, a part of the brain that helps regulate body movement and posture.

The most prominent physical symptoms of the disease are involuntary, jerky movements of the face (grimaces), neck, limbs, and trunk—in contrast to the poverty of movement that typifies Parkinson's disease. These twitches carry the label of *choreiform,* a word that derives from the Greek root *choreia,* meaning "dance." Unstable moods, alternating with states of apathy, anxiety, and depression, are common in the early stages of the disease. As the disease progresses, paranoia may develop, and people may become "suicidally" depressed. Difficulties retrieving memories in the early course of the disease may later develop into dementia. Eventually, there is loss of control of bodily functions, leading to death occurring typically within 15 to 20 years after the onset of the disease ("Huntington's Disease Advance," 2011).

Huntington's disease afflicts about 1 in 10,000 people in the United States or about 30,000 in total ("A Step Toward Controlling," 2011). The disease typically begins in the prime of adulthood, between the ages of 30 and 45. One of the victims of the disease was the famed folksinger Woody Guthrie, who gave us the beloved song "This Land Is Your Land," among many others. He died of Huntington's disease in 1967, after 22 years of battling the malady. Because of the odd, jerky movements associated with the disease, Guthrie, like many other Huntington's victims, was misdiagnosed as suffering from alcoholism. He spent several years in mental hospitals before the correct diagnosis was made. **T / F**

Huntington's disease is caused by a genetic defect on a single gene (Chung et al., 2011). The defective gene produces abnormal protein deposits in nerve cells in the brain (Biglan et al., 2012; Tsunemi et al., 2012). The disease is transmitted genetically from either parent to children of either gender. People who have a parent with Huntington's disease stand a 50% chance of inheriting the gene. People who inherit the gene eventually contract the disease. Although there is no cure or effective treatment, scientists are attempting to block or counteract the effects of the defective gene, raising hopes for a potential breakthrough treatment (Aronin & Moore, 2012; Olson et al., 2011; Song et al., 2011; Zwilling et al., 2011).

A genetic test can determine whether a person carries the defective gene that causes Huntington's disease. Whether or not a person who has a parent with Huntington's undergoes genetic testing is a controversial and personally poignant question, as we explore in the *Thinking Critically About Abnormal Psychology* feature on page 542.

Neurocognitive Disorder Due to HIV Infection

The human immunodeficiency virus (HIV), which causes AIDS, can invade the central nervous system and cause a minor or major neurocognitive disorder. The major cognitive effects of HIV infection include forgetfulness, impaired concentration, and

truth OR fiction

A famous folksinger and songwriter was misdiagnosed with alcoholism and spent several years in mental hospitals until the correct diagnosis was made.

☑ **TRUE** The folksinger and songwriter was Woody Guthrie, whose Huntington's disease went misdiagnosed for years.

@Issue: The Danger Lurking Within—Would You Want to Know?

Until recently, children of patients with Huntington's disease had to wait until they developed symptoms themselves—usually in midlife—to know whether they had inherited the disease. A genetic test is now available that can detect carriers of the defective gene, those who will eventually develop the disease should they live long enough. Eventually, perhaps, genetic engineering may provide a means of modifying the defective gene or its effects. Because researchers have not yet developed ways to cure or control Huntington's disease, some potential carriers prefer not to know whether they have inherited the gene. A famous example is folksinger Arlo Guthrie, son of the famed folksinger Woody Guthrie, who had died from the disease. Arlo preferred not to know and never underwent testing. Fortunately, he escaped his father's fate.

If you were in Arlo's position, would you want to know if you have inherited Huntington's?" Or would you prefer keeping yourself in the dark and living your life as best you could?

What about AD? Would you want to know if you have AD or are carrying genes that put you at heightened risk? New brain scanning technology makes it possible to diagnose the disease, but the effects of learning that you have Alzheimer's can be emotionally devastating. Without any effective treatment or means of slowing it down, is it worth knowing? People with positive brain scans for Alzheimer's also stand the risk of being denied long-term care insurance (Kolata, 2012). But proponents of testing argue that providing information can help remove uncertainty, help people prepare as best they can, and identify candidates for experimental treatment programs that may lead to advances in treatment or prevention. When asked, most people in a recent study said they would prefer not knowing whether AD is imprinted in their genes (Miller, 2012).

In thinking critically about these questions, you may wish to challenge some common assumptions, such as that knowledge is necessarily better than ignorance. Gaining knowledge is valuable when it can help stave off or limit the impact of disease. But what if the knowledge carried no health benefits? Might ignorance be better than knowledge? Deciding on genetic testing for defective genes is a personal choice. But controversy arises over whether people who may be potential carriers of genetic diseases have an ethical or moral responsibility to determine their genetic risk before deciding whether or not to bear children. We pose the question to encourage you to examine the issue critically. Do you believe that people at genetic risk have an obligation to determine their genetic risk before becoming parents? Going further, should people who discover they are carrying a potentially lethal or disabling gene be morally (or perhaps legally) obliged not to bear children? How

Would you want to know? Folksinger Arlo Guthrie decided no. What do you think you would do if you had been in Arlo's place?

might you look at this question differently if you were a fundamentalist Christian, an orthodox Jew, or a practicing Buddhist or Muslim?

Genetics plays an important role in many diseases discussed in this chapter, such as Parkinson's disease and AD. Genes are also implicated in many physical conditions, such as Tay-Sachs disease, sickle-cell disease, and cystic fibrosis. As we gain more knowledge and the ability to determine whether people carry many different conditions, insurance companies might require expectant parents to undergo genetic testing. Knowledge about the genetic causes of devastating disease has deep ramifications for society.

In thinking critically about the issue, answer the following questions:

- Should people be required to be tested for genetic defects?
- Should we be required to reveal our relative risk of developing a wide range of diseases as a condition for obtaining health insurance or for getting a job? What are the effects of requiring such disclosure? Of not requiring it?

problem-solving ability. Dementia is rare in people with HIV who have not yet developed full-blown AIDS. Common behavioral features of dementia associated with HIV disease are apathy and social withdrawal. As AIDS progresses, the dementia grows more severe, taking the form of delusions, disorientation, further impairments in memory and thinking processes, and perhaps even delirium. In its later stages, the dementia may resemble the profound deficiencies found among people with advanced AD (Clifford et al., 2009).

Neurocognitive Disorder Due to Prion Disease

Prions are protein molecules found normally in body cells. But in the case of prion disease, abnormal clusters of prions form and become infectious, converting other prion molecules to assume an abnormal, infectious form. Prion disease can cause brain damage when clusters of abnormal prion molecules spread within the brain. The best known example of prion disease is *Creutzfeldt-Jakob disease,* a rare but fatal brain disease. It is characterized by the formation of small cavities in the brain that resemble the holes in a sponge. The disease causes brain damage, which commonly results in dementia (major neurocognitive disorder). Symptoms of the disease usually begin in the late 50s. There are no treatments for the disease, and death usually results within months of the onset of symptoms. Most forms of Creutzfeldt-Jakob disease occur without any apparent cause, but in rare cases a genetic cause (inheriting an abnormal prion from a parent) is suspected. A variant of Creutzfeldt-Jakob disease is related to *mad-cow disease,* a fatal illness spread by eating infected beef. **T / F**

Psychological Disorders Related to Aging

Many physical changes occur with aging. Changes in calcium metabolism cause the bones to grow brittle and heighten the risk of breaks from falls. The skin grows less elastic, creating wrinkles and folds. The senses become less keen, so older people see and hear less acutely. Older people need more time (called *reaction time*) to respond to stimuli, whether they are driving or taking intelligence tests. For example, older drivers require more time to react to traffic signals and other cars. The immune system functions less effectively with increasing age, so people become more vulnerable to illness.

14.7   **Identify** other psychological disorders related to aging.

Cognitive changes occur as well. It is normal for people in later life to experience some decline in memory functioning and general cognitive ability, as measured by tests of intelligence, or IQ tests. The decline is sharpest on timed items, such as the performance subtests of the Wechsler Adult Intelligence Scale (discussed in Chapter 3). Some abilities, such as vocabulary and accumulated store of knowledge, hold up well and may actually improve over time. However, people typically experience some reduction in memory as they age, especially memory for names or recent events. But apart from the occasional social embarrassment resulting from forgetting a person's name, in most cases cognitive declines do not significantly interfere with the person's ability to meet social or occupational responsibilities. Declines in cognitive functioning may also be offset to a certain extent by increased knowledge and life experience.

The important point here is that dementia, or senility, is not the result of normal aging. Rather, it is a sign of degenerative brain disease. Screening and testing for neurological and neuropsychological deficits can help distinguish dementias from normal aging processes. Generally speaking, the decline in intellectual functioning in dementia is more rapid and severe.

All told, about one in five older adults suffers from a mental disorder, including dementia as well as anxiety and mood disorders (Karel, Gatz, & Smyer, 2012). Here we focus on several of these disorders, beginning with anxiety disorders, the most commonly experienced type of psychological disorder affecting older adults.

What changes take place as we age? How do they affect our moods? Although some declines in cognitive and physical functioning are connected with aging, older adults who remain active and engage in rewarding activities can be highly satisfied with their lives.

Anxiety Disorders and Aging

Although anxiety disorders may develop at any point in life, they tend to be less prevalent among older adults than among their younger counterparts. Still, anxiety disorders are the most commonly occurring psychological disorder among older adults, even more common than depression. Approximately 1 in 10 adults over the age of 55 suffer from a diagnosable anxiety disorder (USDHHS, 1999). Older women are more likely than older men to be affected by anxiety disorders (Bryant, Jackson, & Ames, 2008). **T / F**

The most frequently occurring anxiety disorders among older adults are generalized anxiety disorder (GAD) and phobic disorders. Although less common, panic disorder occurs in about 1 in 100 older adults (Chou, 2010). Most cases of agoraphobia affecting older adults tend to be of recent origin and may involve the loss of social support systems due to the death of a spouse or close friends. Then again, some older individuals who are frail may have realistic fears of falling on the street and may be misdiagnosed as agoraphobic if they refuse to leave the house alone. Generalized anxiety disorder may arise from the perception that one lacks control over one's life, which may be the case for older people contending with infirmity, loss of friends and loved ones, and lessened economic opportunities. Social anxiety disorder (also called social phobia) affects about 2% to 5% of older adults but does not appear to have a significant impact on the quality of late adulthood (Chou, 2009).

Antianxiety drugs, such as the *benzodiazepines* (Valium is one), are commonly used to quell anxiety in older adults. Psychological interventions, such as cognitive-behavioral therapy, show therapeutic benefits in treating anxiety in older adults and do not carry the risks of the drug's side effects or potential dependence (Mohlman, 2012; Stanley et al., 2009; Zou et al., 2012).

Depression and Aging

Depression is a common problem affecting many older adults, especially those with a prior history of depression (Reppermund et al., 2011). For many older adults, late-life depression often involves a continuation of a lifelong pattern.

Estimates are that between 1% and 5% of older adults are currently suffering from a diagnosable major depressive episode (Fiske, Wetherell, & Gatz, 2009; Luijendijk et al., 2008). A much higher proportion of older adults, estimated to be as many as one in three, currently suffer from depressive symptoms that may not warrant a diagnosis but are significant enough to interfere with their quality of life (Meeks et al., 2011). Depression is higher among some groups of older adults, such as residents of nursing homes. Despite the fact that fewer older adults suffer from major depression than do younger adults, suicide is more frequent among older adults, especially among older white males (Bruce et al., 2004; Eddleston, 2006).

Older people of color often carry an especially heavy stress burden. In one study, a sample of 127 elderly African Americans recruited from senior citizens' programs in two large urban centers in the northeastern United States were administered measures of race-related stress, satisfaction with life, and health concerns (Utsey et al., 2002). The investigators found that men reported experiencing higher levels of institutional and collective forms of racism than women did. The investigators commented that they weren't surprised by these findings, as African American men have traditionally been subjected to harsher experiences of societal racism and oppression. Going further, the investigators reported that institutional race-related stress was associated with poorer psychological well-being. Many of the elderly men in this sample had experienced institutional racism (i.e., government-sanctioned discrimination in housing, education, employment, health care, and public policy) during their early and middle lives. This study contributes to a growing body of literature showing links between race-related stress and mental health functioning of African Americans.

Agoraphobia or a need for support? Some older adults may refuse to venture away from home on their own because of realistic fears of falling in the street. They may be in need of social support, not therapy.

Other investigators have examined the role of acculturative stress in older adults from immigrant groups. A study of Mexican American older adults showed that those who were minimally acculturated to U.S. society had higher rates of depression than either highly acculturated or bicultural individuals (Zamanian et al., 1992).

Depressive disorders often occur in people suffering from brain disorders, such as AD, Parkinson's disease, and stroke, which disproportionately affect older people (e.g., Even & Weintraub, 2012; Jasinska-Myga et al., 2010; Richard et al., 2012). In the case of Parkinson's disease, depression may result not only from coping with the disease but also from neurobiological changes in the brain caused by the disease.

Social support can help buffer the effects of stress, bereavement, and illness, thereby reducing the risk of depression. Social support is especially important to older people who are challenged because of physical disability. Participation in volunteer or religious organizations may also provide a sense of meaning and purpose as well as a needed social outlet.

Older people may be especially vulnerable to depression because of the stress of coping with life changes—retirement; physical illness or incapacitation; placement in a residential facility or nursing home; the deaths of a spouse, siblings, lifetime friends, and acquaintances; or the need to care for a spouse whose health is declining. Retirement, whether voluntary or forced, may lead to a loss of role identity. Deaths of relatives and friends induce grief and remind older people of their own advanced age as well as reduce the availability of social support. Older adults may feel incapable of forming new friendships or finding new goals in life. The chronic strain of coping with a family member with AD can lead to depression in the caregiver, even without any prior vulnerability to depression (Mittelman et al., 2004).

Despite the prevalence of depression in older people, physicians often fail to recognize it or to treat it appropriately. Health care providers may be less likely to recognize depression in older people than in middle-aged or young people, in part because they tend to focus more on the older patient's physical complaints and because depression in older people is often masked by physical complaints and sleeping problems.

The good news about geriatric depression is that effective treatment is available, including antidepressant medication, cognitive-behavioral therapy, and interpersonal psychotherapy (e.g. Calati et al., 2013; Reynolds et al., 2011; Sheline et al., 2012; Scogin & Shah, 2012; Unützer & Park, 2012). Evidence of treatment effectiveness should put to rest the erroneous belief that psychotherapy or psychiatric medication is not appropriate for people in late adulthood. Moreover, memory impairment that often accompanies late-life depression may lift when the underlying depression is resolved.

Sleep Problems and Aging

Sleep problems, especially insomnia, are common among older people. Upward of 50% of older adults report sleep problems (Vitiello, 2009). Insomnia in late adulthood is actually more prevalent than depression. Sleep problems in older adults are often linked to other psychological disorders, such as depression, dementia, and anxiety disorders, as well as medical illness. Psychosocial factors, such as loneliness and the related difficulty of sleeping alone after the loss of a spouse, are also implicated in many cases. Dysfunctional thoughts, such as excessive concerns about lack of sleep and perceptions of hopelessness and helplessness about controlling sleep, are another contributor to sleep problems in later life.

Sleep medications are often used in treating late-life insomnia, but long-term use can cause dependence and withdrawal symptoms as they can in younger adults. Fortunately, behavioral approaches, similar to those described in Chapter 9, are effective in treating insomnia in later life and produce therapeutic benefits that are as good as, if not better than, those of sleep medications, without risks of side effects or drug dependence (Bélanger, LeBlanc, & Morin, 2011; Bootzin & Epstein, 2011; Buysse et al., 2011). Moreover, older adults are as capable of benefiting from behavioral treatment as younger adults are.

Late-life depression. Many older adults struggle with clinical depression. What factors contribute to depression in late adulthood?

14 summing up

Neurocognitive Disorders

14.1 Define the concept of neurocognitive disorders and identify three major types.

Neurocognitive disorders are disturbances of thinking or memory that represent a marked decline in cognitive functioning. They are caused by physical or medical conditions or drug use or withdrawal affecting the functioning of the brain. The three major types identified in *DSM-5* are delirium, major neurocognitive disorder, and mild neurocognitive disorder.

14.2 Describe the key features and causes of delirium.

Delirium is a state of mental confusion characterized by symptoms such as impaired attention, disorientation, disorganized thinking and rambling speech, reduced level of consciousness, and perceptual disturbances. Delirium is most commonly caused by alcohol withdrawal, as in the form of DTs, but may also occur in hospitalized patients, especially after major surgery.

14.3 Describe the key features and causes of major neurocognitive disorder.

Major neurocognitive disorder (dementia) is a significant cognitive deterioration or impairment, as evidenced by memory deficits, impaired judgment, personality changes, and disorders of higher cognitive functions such as problem-solving ability and abstract thinking. Dementia is not a normal consequence of aging; rather, it is a sign of a degenerative brain disorder. There are various causes of major neurocognitive disorder, including Alzheimer's disease (AD) and Pick's disease, and brain infections and disorders.

14.4 Describe the key features of mild neurocognitive disorder.

Formerly called mild cognitive impairment (MCI), mild neurocognitive disorder refers to a milder decline in cognitive functioning. The person with the disorder is able to function but needs to expend greater effort or to use compensatory strategies to compensate for cognitive declines.

14.5 Describe the key features and causes of AD and evaluate current treatments.

AD is a progressive brain disease characterized by progressive loss of memory and cognitive ability, as well as deterioration in personality functioning and self-care skills. There is neither cure nor effective treatment for AD. Currently available drug treatments offer only modest effects at best. Research into the causes of the disease points to roles for genetic factors and possible imbalances in neurotransmitters in the brain, especially acetylcholine.

14.6 Identify other subtypes of neurocognitive disorders.

Other medical conditions can lead to neurocognitive disorders, including vascular disease, Pick's disease, Parkinson's disease, Huntington's disease, prion disease, HIV infection, and head trauma.

Psychological Disorders Related to Aging

14.7 Identify other psychological disorders related to aging.

Generalized anxiety disorder and phobic disorders are the most commonly occurring anxiety disorders among older people. Depression to varying degrees is common among people in later life and may be associated with memory deficits that may lift as the depression clears. It involves irreversible and progressive memory impairment. Sleep problems such as insomnia, are also common among older people.

critical thinking questions

Based on your reading of this chapter, answer the following questions:

- Do you expect people to become senile as they age? If so, what is the basis of your opinion?

- Why do you think depression is so common among older people? In what ways might depression be related to lowered role expectations placed on older people in our society? In what ways might society provide more meaningful social roles for people as they age?

- Should children be permitted to play physical contact sports that may lead to concussions or other head injuries? Why or why not? What precautions should be taken to protect children who participate in these sports?

- Have you known someone who was affected by AD? How was their behavior affected? What was done to help the person and the family? Do you think more could have been done or should have been done? Explain.

key terms

Scoring Key for Attitudes Toward Aging Scale

1. False. Most healthy couples continue to engage in satisfying sexual activities into their 70s and 80s.

2. False. This is too general a statement. Those who find their work satisfying are less anxious to retire.

3. False. In late adulthood, people tend to become more concerned with internal matters—their physical functioning and their emotions.

4. False. Adaptability remains reasonably stable throughout adulthood.

5. False. Age itself is not linked to noticeable declines in life satisfaction. Of course, people may respond negatively to disease and losses, such as the death of a spouse.

6. False. Although we can predict some general trends for older adults, we can also do so for younger adults. Older adults, like their younger counterparts, are heterogeneous in personality and behavior patterns.

7. False. Older adults with stable intimate relationships are more satisfied.

8. False. People are susceptible to a wide variety of psychological disorders at all ages.

9. False. Only a minority are depressed.

10. False. Actually, church attendance declines, but not verbally expressed religious beliefs.

11. False. Although reaction time may increase and general learning ability may undergo a slight decline, older adults usually have little or no difficulty at familiar work tasks. In most jobs, experience and motivation are more important than age.

12. False. Learning may just take a bit longer.

13. False. Older adults do not direct a higher proportion of thoughts toward the past than do younger people. Regardless of age, people may spend more time daydreaming if they have more time on their hands.

14. False. Fewer than 10% of older adults require some form of institutional care.

Abnormal Psychology and the Law

15

truth OR fiction

T☐ F☐ People can be committed to psychiatric facilities because of odd or eccentric behavior. (p. 551)

T☐ F☐ Most people who are diagnosed with mental disorders commit violent crimes. (p. 552)

T☐ F☐ Patients in mental hospitals may be required to perform general house-keeping duties in a facility. (p. 558)

T☐ F☐ Therapists may not breach patient confidentiality even when a patient makes a death threat against a specific person. (p. 560)

T☐ F☐ An attempt to assassinate the president of the United States was seen by millions of television viewers, but the would-be assassin was found not guilty by a court of law. (p. 562)

T☐ F☐ The insanity defense is used in a large number of trials, usually successfully. (p. 563)

T☐ F☐ People who are found not guilty of a crime by reason of insanity may be confined to a mental hospital for many years longer than they would have been sentenced to prison, had they been found guilty. (p. 566)

T☐ F☐ A defendant may be held competent to stand trial but still be judged not guilty of a crime by reason of insanity. (p. 568)

learning objectives

15.1
Explain the difference between civil commitment and criminal commitment.

15.2
Evaluate the ability of mental health professionals to predict dangerousness.

15.3
Identify major court cases establishing the rights of mental patients.

15.4
Define the duty to warn and evaluate the dilemma it poses for therapists.

15.5
Describe the history of the insanity defense, citing specific court cases.

15.6
Describe the guidelines proposed by the American Law Institute for determining the legal basis of insanity.

15.7
Describe the legal basis for determining length of criminal commitment.

15.8
Describe the legal basis for determining competency to stand trial.

"I" "Point-Blank Range"

Congresswoman Gabrielle (Gabby) Giffords of Arizona was greeting constituents outside a supermarket on a sunny day in January 2011. A lone gunman approached from the rear. She had no warning and never saw the assailant. Shot through the head at point-blank range, Giffords was critically injured, but miraculously survived. Tragically, 6 bystanders were killed in the shooting and 13 others wounded. After her stay in a critical care facility, Giffords entered a rehabilitation facility, beginning a long and arduous process of recovery that is still ongoing. Yet she was able to return to the House of Representatives to receive well wishes of her colleagues and even led the Pledge of Allegiance at the 2012 Democratic National Convention. She later resigned from Congress to concentrate on her recovery, but promised to return to public service at some point in the future.

But what of the alleged shooter, 22-year-old Jared Loughner? A fellow student at the community college Loughner attended described him as a "troubled young man" whom no one wanted to sit next to in class (Lipton, Savage, & Shane, 2011). His behavior was so disturbing that his classmate wondered if he was taking hallucinogens. The portrait of Loughner that emerged in media reports was of an angry and deeply troubled young man who had become increasingly alienated from society and who displayed odd and even bizarre thoughts and behaviors. A series of short videos apparently posted on social media sites by Loughner were rambling and incoherent. The videos spoke of him becoming "treasurer of a new currency" and controlling "English grammar structure." There were mentions of brainwashing and belief that he had powers of mind control.

Appearing before a U.S. district court, Loughner was held to be incompetent to stand trial and remanded to a federal facility for further evaluation of his mental competency. Even his own attorneys described him as a "gravely mentally ill man" ("Ariz. Shooting Spree Suspect," 2011). We never had a formal determination of Loughner's mental status at the time of the shooting because he later pled guilty to the charges.

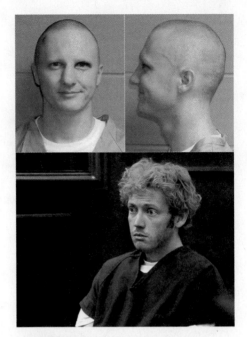

Jared Loughner (top) and James Holmes (bottom). Punishment or treatment? Or both? What should society do about someone who is severely disturbed but commits a horrible crime?

And what of James Holmes, the 24-year-old alleged shooter in the movie theater massacre in 2012 in Aurora, Colorado, that left 12 people dead and 58 others wounded? Holmes reportedly had received treatment from a University of Colorado psychiatrist while attending the university. In his first court appearance after the shooting, he appeared dazed and sported flaming orange hair. His mental status remained undetermined at the time of this writing.

The tragic events in Arizona and Colorado (and in other tragic cases, such as the mass killings at Virginia Tech University and at Sandy Hook Elementary School in Newtown, Connecticut) highlight the interface between abnormal behavior and the law. What should society do with someone accused of a violent crime, even a heinous crime, if the person's behavior suggests a lack of mental competence to even understand the proceedings? What if the defendant can understand the proceedings and mount a credible defense, but the alleged criminal behavior is deemed to have been a product of mental defect or disease? Should someone who has committed grievous acts be judged to be "not guilty by reason of insanity"? How should society treat mentally disturbed individuals who commit crimes? Should they be punished by confinement in prison or treated in a mental institution?

In this chapter, we will discuss the insanity defense, its history in U.S. law, and the legal and moral arguments that underlie its use. We will also examine the legal rights of mental patients and the legal responsibility that falls on mental health care providers to warn third parties of threats made by patients. We will address questions that touch on the general issue of how to balance the rights of the individual with the rights of society. Do people who are obviously mentally disturbed have the right to refuse treatment? Do psychiatric institutions have the right to administer antipsychotic and other drugs to patients against their will? Should mental patients with a history of disruptive or violent behavior be hospitalized indefinitely or permitted to live in supervised residences in the community once their conditions are stabilized? When severely disturbed people break the law, should society respond to them with the criminal justice system or with the mental health system?

We begin with the concept of civil or psychiatric commitment, the process by which individuals are involuntarily confined in mental hospitals because they are deemed to be mentally ill and a danger to either themselves or others. Civil commitment brings into focus the interface between the rights of individuals and the rights of society.

15.1 Explain the difference between civil commitment and criminal commitment.

Civil Commitment and Patients' Rights

Legal placement of people in psychiatric institutions against their will is called **civil commitment** (also called *psychiatric commitment*). Through civil commitment, individuals who are judged to be mentally ill and a threat to themselves or others can be involuntarily confined to psychiatric institutions to provide them with treatment and help ensure their own safety and that of others.

Civil commitment should be distinguished from *voluntary hospitalization*, in which an individual voluntarily seeks treatment in a psychiatric institution and can, with adequate notice, leave the institution when she or he so desires. Even in such cases, however, when the hospital staff believes that a voluntary patient presents a threat to her or his own welfare or to others, they may petition the court to change the patient's legal status from voluntary to involuntary.

We also need to distinguish civil commitment from **criminal commitment,** in which an individual who is acquitted of a crime by reason of insanity is placed in a psychiatric institution for treatment. In criminal commitment, a defendant's unlawful act is judged by a court of law to result from a mental disorder or defect, and the defendant is committed to a psychiatric hospital where treatment can be provided rather than incarcerated in a prison.

Civil commitment in a psychiatric hospital usually requires that a relative or professional file a petition with the court, which empowers psychiatric examiners to evaluate the person. Finally, a judge hears the psychiatric testimony and decides whether or not to commit the individual. In the event of commitment, the law usually requires periodic legal review and recertification of the patient's involuntary status. The legal process is intended to ensure that people are not indefinitely "warehoused" in psychiatric hospitals. Hospital staff must demonstrate the need for continued inpatient treatment.

Legal safeguards protect people's civil rights in commitment proceedings. Defendants have the right to due process and to be assisted by an attorney, for example. But when individuals are deemed to present a clear and imminent threat to themselves or others, the court may order immediate hospitalization until a formal commitment hearing can be held. Such emergency powers are usually limited to a specific period, usually 72 hours (Failer, 2002; Strachen, 2008). If a formal commitment petition is not filed with the court during this time, the individual has a right to be discharged.

Standards for psychiatric commitment have been tightened over the past generation, and the rights of individuals who are subject to commitment proceedings are more strictly protected. In the past, psychiatric abuses were more common. People were often committed without clear evidence that they posed a threat. Not until 1979, in fact, did the U.S. Supreme Court rule, in *Addington* v. *Texas,* that in order for individuals to be hospitalized involuntarily, they must be judged both to be mentally ill and to present a clear and present danger to themselves or others. Thus, people cannot be committed because of their odd behavior or eccentricity. **T / F**

Few would argue that contemporary tightening of civil commitment laws protects the rights of the individual. Even so, some critics of the psychiatric system have called for the abolition of psychiatric commitment on the grounds that commitment deprives the individual of liberty in the name of therapy, and that such a loss of liberty cannot be justified in a free society. Perhaps the most vocal and persistent critic of the civil commitment statutes was the psychiatrist Thomas Szasz, who died in 2012 (Szasz, 1970, 2003a, 2003b, 2007). Szasz argued that the label of *mental illness* is a societal invention that transforms social deviance into medical illness. In Szasz's view, people should not be deprived of their liberty because their behavior is perceived to be socially deviant or disruptive. Szasz likens involuntary hospitalization to institutional slavery (Szasz, 2003b). According to Szasz, people who violate the law should be prosecuted for criminal behavior, not confined to a psychiatric hospital. Although psychiatric commitment may prevent some individuals from acting violently, it does violence to many people who are innocent of any crime by depriving them of the fundamental right of liberty:

> The mental patient, we say, *may be* dangerous: he may harm himself or someone else. But we, society, *are* dangerous: we rob him of his good name and of his liberty, and subject him to tortures called "treatments."
>
> —*From Szasz, 1970*

> It is a fundamental principle of English and American law that only persons charged with and convicted of certain crimes are subject to imprisonment. Persons who respect other people's rights to life, liberty, and property have an inalienable right to their own life, liberty, and property.
>
> —*From Szasz, 2003a*

Szasz's strident opposition to institutional psychiatry and his condemnation of psychiatric commitment focused attention on abuses in the mental health system. Many people who have experienced psychiatric commitment rail against the practice.

Szasz was effective in persuading many professionals to question the legal, ethical, and moral bases of coercive psychiatric treatment in the forms of involuntary

People can be committed to psychiatric facilities because of odd or eccentric behavior.

☑ **FALSE** People cannot be committed because they are eccentric. The U.S. Supreme Court has determined that people must be judged mentally ill and present a clear and present danger to themselves or others to be committed to a psychiatric facility.

hospitalization and forced medication. Many caring and concerned professionals draw the line at abolishing psychiatric commitment, however. They argue that people may not be acting in their considered best interests when they threaten suicide or harm to others, or when their behavior becomes so disorganized that they cannot meet their basic needs (McMillan, 2003; Sayers, 2003). Most countries, including the United States and Canada, have laws that permit commitment of dangerous, mentally ill people (Appelbaum, 2003). Yet, the issue of psychiatric commitment continues to rouse debate, as we discuss in *Thinking Critically About Abnormal Psychology* (see page 554).

15.2 Evaluate the ability of mental health professionals to predict dangerousness.

truth OR fiction

Most people who are diagnosed with mental disorders commit violent crimes.

☑ **FALSE**   Actually, only a small minority of people with mental disorders commit violent crimes.

Predicting Dangerousness

Mental health professionals are often called on to judge whether patients are a danger to themselves or others as part of the legal proceedings to determine whether people should be involuntarily hospitalized or maintained involuntarily in the hospital. But how accurate are the judgments of professionals when predicting dangerousness? Do professionals have special skills or clinical wisdom that renders their predictions accurate, or are their predictions no more accurate than those of laypeople? **T / F**

Unfortunately, psychologists and other mental health professionals who rely on their clinical judgments are not very accurate when it comes to predicting the dangerousness of the people they treat. Mental health professionals tend to overpredict dangerousness—that is, to label many individuals as dangerous when they are not. Clinicians tend to err on the side of caution in predicting the potential for dangerous behavior, perhaps because they believe that failure to predict violence may have more serious consequences than overprediction. However, overprediction of dangerousness does deprive many people of liberty. According to Szasz and other critics, the commitment of the many to prevent the violence of the few is a form of preventive detention that violates basic constitutional principles (Szasz, 2007).

The leading professional organizations, the American Psychological Association (1978) and the American Psychiatric Association (1998), have both gone on record as stating that neither psychologists nor psychiatrists, respectively, can reliably predict violent behavior. As a leading authority in the field, John Monahan of the University of Virginia, said, "When it comes to predicting violence, our crystal balls are terribly cloudy" (Rosenthal, 1993).

Clinician predictions are generally also less accurate than predictions based on evidence of past violent behavior (Odeh, Zeiss, & Huss, 2006). Basically, clinicians do not possess any special knowledge or ability for predicting violence beyond that of the average person. In fact, a layperson supplied with information concerning an individual's past violent behavior may predict the individual's potential for future violence more accurately than the clinician, who bases a prediction solely on a clinical interview (Mossman, 1994). Unfortunately, although past violent behavior is the best predictor of future violence, hospital staff may not be permitted access to criminal records or may lack the time or resources to track down these records. The prediction problem has been cited by some as grounds for abandoning dangerousness as a criterion for civil commitment.

Why is predicting dangerousness so difficult? Investigators have identified a number of factors that lead to inaccurate predictions, including the following.

Predicting dangerousness. Should mental health professionals or school administrators have recognized signs of impending violence by Seung-Hui Cho, the man who went on a killing rampage at Virginia Tech in 2007? It is always easier after the fact to piece together fragments of a person's prior behaviors as signs of impending violent behavior in 2007. Predicting a violent act before it occurs is a much more difficult task, however, even for professionals.

THE POST HOC PROBLEM   Recognizing violent tendencies after a violent incident occurs (post hoc) is easier than predicting it beforehand. It is often said that hindsight is 20/20. Like Monday morning quarterbacking, it is easier to piece together fragments of people's prior behaviors as evidence of violent tendencies *after* they have committed acts of violence. Predicting a violent act before the fact is a more difficult task, however.

THE PROBLEM IN LEAPING FROM THE GENERAL TO THE SPECIFIC Generalized perceptions of violent tendencies may not predict specific acts of violence. Most people who have "general tendencies" toward violence never act on them. Nor is a diagnosis associated with aggressive or dangerous behavior, such as antisocial personality disorder, a sufficient basis for predicting specific violent acts by individuals.

PROBLEMS IN DEFINING DANGEROUSNESS One difficulty in predicting dangerousness is the lack of agreement over what types of behavior are violent or dangerous. Most people would agree that crimes such as murder, rape, and assault are acts of violence. There is less agreement, even among authorities, for labeling other acts— for example, driving recklessly, harshly criticizing one's spouse or children, destroying property, selling drugs, shoving into people at a tavern, or stealing cars—as violent or dangerous. Consider, also, the behavior of business owners and corporate executives who produce and market cigarettes despite widespread knowledge of the death and disease these substances cause. Clearly, the determination of which behaviors are regarded as dangerous involves moral and political judgments within a given social context.

BASE-RATE PROBLEMS The prediction of dangerousness is complicated by the fact that violent acts such as murder, assault, or suicide are infrequent within the general population, even if newspaper headlines sensationalize them regularly. Other rare events—such as earthquakes—are also difficult to predict with any degree of certainty concerning when or where they will strike.

The relative difficulty of making predictions about infrequent or rare events is known as the *base-rate problem*. Consider as an example the problem of suicide prediction. If the suicide rate in a given year has a low base rate of about 1% of a clinical population, the likelihood of accurately predicting that any given person in this population will commit suicide is very small. If you predicted that any given individual in this population would *not* commit suicide in a given year, you would be correct 99% of the time. But if you predict the nonoccurrence of suicide in every case, you would fail to predict the relatively few cases in which suicide does occur, even though virtually all your predictions would likely be correct. Therefore, predicting the one likely occurrence of suicide among those 100 people is likely to be tricky. When clinicians make predictions, they weigh the relative risks of a *false negative*—predicting that a violent behavior will not occur but it does—and a *false positive*—predicting that a violent behavior will occur but it does not. Clinicians often deliberately err on the side of the false positive and overpredict dangerousness. From their perspective, erring on the side of caution might seem like a no-lose situation. However, such a prediction practice results in many people being committed to an institution when they would not actually have acted violently against themselves or others, thereby denying them their liberty.

THE UNLIKELIHOOD OF DISCLOSURE OF DIRECT THREATS OF VIOLENCE How likely is it that truly dangerous people will disclose their violent intentions to a health professional who is evaluating them or to their own therapist? The client in therapy is not likely to inform a therapist of a clear threat, such as "I'm going to kill ____ next Wednesday morning." Threats are more likely to be vague and nonspecific, as in "I'm so sick of ____; I could kill her" or "I swear he's driving me to murder." In such cases, therapists must infer dangerousness from hostile gestures and veiled threats. Vague, indirect threats of violence are less reliable indicators of dangerousness than specific, direct threats.

THE DIFFICULTY OF PREDICTING BEHAVIOR IN THE COMMUNITY FROM BEHAVIOR IN THE HOSPITAL Mental health professionals fall well short of the mark when making long-term predictions of dangerousness. They are often wrong when predicting whether patients will become dangerous following release from the hospital.

THINKING CRITICALLY about abnormal psychology

@Issue: What Should We Do About the "Wild Man of West 96th Street"?

The case of Larry Hogue touches on the problem of how society deals with the psychiatric homeless population. We first learned about Hogue—the "wild man of West 96th Street"—back in the early 1990s. Hogue was a homeless Vietnam War veteran who inhabited the alleyways and doorways of Manhattan's affluent Upper West Side. He went barefoot in winter, ate from garbage cans, and muttered to himself. He was described in newspaper reports as terrorizing the neighborhood, becoming especially violent when he smoked crack. Once, he was arrested for pushing a schoolgirl in front of a school bus (Shapiro, 1992). (Miraculously, she escaped injury.)

Hogue was shuttled in and out of state psychiatric hospitals and prisons more than 40 times. He popped up in the news again in 2009, having escaped from a Queens mental hospital and made his way back to West 96th Street in Manhattan, again frightening residents by his mere presence. As one resident told a reporter, "People called each other . . . saying, 'He's back.' Nobody, after 17 years, had to ask who" ("Wild Man," 2009).

For Hogue, the criminal justice, social services, and mental health systems were nothing but revolving doors. Typically, Hogue would improve during a brief hospital stay and be released, only to return to using crack instead of his psychiatric medication. His behavior would then deteriorate. For many people, Larry Hogue became a national symbol of the many cracks in the system.

In 2008, the public spotlight focused again on the cracks in the mental health system in the wake of a vicious murder ("Queen's Man Arraigned," 2008). It happened in New York, but it could have happened anywhere. The victim, Dr. Kathryn Faughey, a Manhattan psychologist, was found butchered to death in her office. She had been stabbed 15 times with a meat cleaver and a 9-inch knife. A suspect, David Tarloff, age 39, was soon arrested

and held for trial. Tarloff appeared agitated and disturbed during his arraignment hearing. The police supplied a motive. Tarloff apparently came to the office to rob an office mate of the slain psychologist, another psychologist who had been treating him over the years. Tarloff told police he hadn't intended to harm Dr. Faughey and didn't realize at first that she was in the office. Later, the suspect's brother provided some background. The family, he told a reporter, had tried to get his brother help for many years. He had been hospitalized and released many times over the years. A neighbor of Tarloff described him as a "cuckoo" who had ". . . some weird reactions from time to time."

Doesn't society have a right to protect itself from the likes of people like Hogue and Tarloff? And what of those whose behavior may appear disturbed or deviant but who have not threatened or harmed others, such as people who sleep in the darkened corners of alleyways and over sidewalk heating vents, mumbling incoherently to themselves, but refusing psychiatric treatment?

Society certainly has a right to protect itself from people whose disturbed behavior causes physical harm to others or threatens harm. It may seem just as obvious that a humane society has the responsibility to provide care to people who seem unable to care for themselves. But critics of the mental health system, such as Thomas Szasz, argue that by the very nature of a free society, people should be free to make their own decisions, even when those decisions are not in the best interests of their own health or welfare. Szasz argues that if they cause harm to others, or threaten harm, they should be subject to the criminal justice system, not psychiatric commitment.

Now let's extend the argument: If society has an obligation to protect individuals from themselves, as in the case of someone

One reason is that they often base their predictions on patients' behavior in the hospital. But violent or dangerous behavior may be situation specific. A model patient who is able to adapt to a structured environment like that of a psychiatric hospital may be unable to cope with the pressures of independent community life. We can expect clinicians to be more accurate when they base their predictions on the patient's previous behavior in the community than in the controlled setting of a mental hospital.

Overall, although clinician predictions of dangerousness are significantly better than predictions based on chance alone, they are still often inaccurate (Kaplan, 2000). Although their crystal balls may be cloudy, mental health professionals who work in institutional settings continue to be called on to make predictions—deciding whom to commit and whom to discharge largely on the basis of how they judge the potential for violence (McNiel, Gregory, Lam, Binder, & Sullivan, 2003). Rather than expecting clinicians to rely only on their clinical judgment, investigators are developing better decision-making tools, such as more objective screening methods and violence rating scales to help guide assessment of violence risk (e.g., McNiel et al., 2003; Yang, Wong, & Coid, 2010).

threatening suicide, does it not have a similar obligation to protect people whose behavior is harmful in other ways, such as those who smoke cigarettes, drink alcohol to excess, or become obese? Where would you draw that line?

And what about mental patients who commit violent crimes? Such cases, thankfully, are relatively uncommon, as only a small minority of people with mental disorders commit violent crimes. Later in the chapter, we consider the important question about whether mentally disturbed people who commit crimes should be held accountable. Here, let us discuss the more general issue of how to balance the rights of the individual with the rights of society and offer several questions that challenge us to think critically about these issues.

In thinking critically about the issue, answer the following questions:

- Do people in a free society have the right to live on the streets under unsanitary conditions?

- Do people who are obviously mentally disturbed have the right to refuse treatment?

- Should mental patients with a history of disruptive or violent behavior be hospitalized indefinitely or, once their conditions have stabilized, be permitted to live in supervised residences in the community?

- Do mentally ill people have a right to be left alone, so long as they do not break any laws? Or do you agree with psychiatrist E. Fuller Torrey and attorney Mary Zdanowicz (1999) that ". . . for individuals whose brain is impaired by severe mental illness, defending their right to remain mentally ill is mindless"?

- When severely mentally disturbed people do break the law, should society respond to them with the criminal justice system or with the mental health system?

"The wild man of West 96th Street." Larry Hogue, the so-called wild man of West 96th Street in New York City, has become a symbol of the cracks in the mental health, criminal justice, and social services systems.

These efforts are helping to improve the ability of clinicians to predict the likelihood of violent behavior, at least with respect to short-term predictions (McNiel et al., 2003; Mills, Kroner & Morgan, 2011). Clinicians may be more successful in predicting violence by basing predictions on a composite of factors, including evidence of past violent behavior, than on any single factor. Still, it's fair to say that predicting future violent behavior is difficult and presently available methods are far from perfect (Yang et al., 2010). Not surprisingly, the accuracy of clinician predictions of violence is generally greater when clinicians agree with one another than when they disagree (McNiel, Lam, & Binder, 2000). Accuracy also tends to be better when clinicians make shorter-term predictions of dangerousness (Mills et al., 2011).

VIOLENCE AND SEVERE MENTAL DISORDERS The importance of developing tools to predict dangerousness is underscored by evidence of an increased risk of violence among people with severe mental disorders, such as schizophrenia, as compared to that in the general population (e.g., Douglas, Guy, & Hart, 2009; Fazel et al., 2009). However, we should also note that people with severe mental disorders account for but a relatively small proportion of violent crimes in society, about 4% overall (Appelbaum, 2006; Carey & Hartocollis, 2013). The general public's perception of the mentally ill as dangerous is exaggerated by the disproportionate attention given to a few highly publicized cases in the media. Media reports of a few cases of violence by people with severe mental disorders reinforce stereotypes and further contribute to stigmatization of mental patients in general (Kuehn, 2012).

Digging deeper into the evidence reveals certain factors associated with an increased risk of violent behavior among schizophrenia patients (Elbogen & Johnson, 2009). For one thing, the risk of violent crime is much higher, perhaps four or more times higher, among schizophrenia patients who also abuse alcohol or other drugs as compared to that in the general population (Fazel et al., 2009; Volavka & Swanson, 2010). For another, certain symptoms are associated with a greater risk of violence among schizophrenia patients—symptoms such as delusions of persecution and antisocial behavior (Bo, Abu-Akel, Kongerslev, Haahrc, & Simonsen, 2011; Harris & Lurigio, 2007; Swanson et al., 2006). That said, only a small number of patients with severe psychiatric disorders, even those who are untreated, commit violent acts (Torrey, 2011).

The risk of violent behavior among schizophrenia patients is greater among those with command hallucinations—voices commanding them to harm themselves or others (McNiel et al., 2000). The risk potential for violence is also greater among patients with severe mental illness who are living in economically distressed neighborhoods (Appelbaum, 2006). Having noted these increased risks of mental patients acting violently, let us also point out that people with severe psychiatric disorders actually stand a greater chance of becoming a victim of violent crimes than people in the general population do (Teplin, McClelland, Abram, & Weiner, 2005).

As we explore in *A Closer Look,* the problem of predicting dangerousness also arises when therapists need to evaluate the seriousness of threats made by their patients against others. Do therapists have a *duty to warn*—a legal obligation to warn the intended targets of these threats? The duty to warn is one of many legal issues arising from society's response to problems of abnormal behavior. In the following sections, we discuss major legal issues such as patients' rights, the insanity defense, and the right of mental patients to refuse treatment. Table 15.1 lists landmark court cases that underpin our discussion of these issues.

TABLE 15.1
Mental Health and the Law

Case	Issue
Durham v. *United States,* 1954	Insanity defense
Wyatt v. *Stickney,* 1972	Minimum standard of care
O'Connor v. *Donaldson,* 1975	Patients' rights
Jackson v. *Indiana,* 1972	Competency to stand trial
Tarasoff v. *the Regents of the University of California,* 1976	Duty to warn
Rogers v. *Okin,* 1979	Right to refuse treatment
Youngberg v. *Romeo,* 1982	Right to confinement in less-restrictive conditions
Jones v. *United States,* 1983	Length of criminal commitment
Medina v. *California,* 1992	Burden of proof for determining mental competency
Sell v. *United States,* 2003	Forced medication of mentally ill defendants

Patients' Rights

We have considered issues regarding society's right to hospitalize involuntarily people who are judged to be mentally ill and to pose a threat to themselves or others. But what happens after commitment? Do involuntarily committed patients have the right to receive or demand treatment? Or can society just warehouse them in psychiatric facilities indefinitely without treating them? Consider the opposite side of the coin as well: May people who are involuntarily committed refuse treatment? Such issues—which have been brought into public light by landmark court cases—fall under the umbrella of *patients' rights*. Generally speaking, the history of abuses in the mental health system, as highlighted in popular books and movies such as *One Flew Over the Cuckoo's Nest,* has led to a tightening of standards of care and adoption of legal guarantees to protect patients' rights.

RIGHT TO TREATMENT We might assume that mental health institutions that accept people for treatment would provide them with treatment. Not until the 1972 landmark federal court case of *Wyatt* v. *Stickney,* however, did a federal court establish a minimum standard of care to be provided by hospitals. The case was a class action suit against Stickney, the commissioner of mental health for the state of Alabama, brought on behalf of Ricky Wyatt, a mentally retarded young man, and other patients at a state hospital and school in Tuscaloosa.

The federal district court in Alabama held both that the hospital had failed to provide treatment to Wyatt and others and that living conditions at the hospital were inadequate and dehumanizing. The court described the hospital dormitories as "barnlike structures" that afforded no privacy to the residents. The bathrooms had no partitions between stalls, the patients were outfitted with shoddy clothes, the wards were filthy and crowded, the kitchens were unsanitary, and the food was substandard. In addition, the staff was inadequate in number and poorly trained. The case of *Wyatt* v. *Stickney* established certain patient rights, including the right not to be required to perform work that is performed for the sake of maintaining the facility. The court held that mental hospitals must, at a minimum, provide the following (*Wyatt* v. *Stickney,* 1972):

1. A humane psychological and physical environment
2. Qualified staff in numbers sufficient to administer adequate treatment
3. Individualized treatment plans T / F

The court established that the state was obliged to provide adequate treatment for people who were involuntarily confined to psychiatric hospitals. The court further ruled that to commit people to hospitals for treatment involuntarily and then not to provide treatment violated their rights to due process under the law.

Table 15.2 lists some of the rights granted to institutionalized patients under the court's ruling. Although the ruling of the court was limited to Alabama, many other states have revised their mental hospital standards to ensure that involuntarily committed patients are not denied basic rights. Other court cases have further clarified patients' rights.

O'Connor v. Donaldson The 1975 case of Kenneth Donaldson is another landmark in patients' rights. Donaldson, a former patient at a state hospital in Florida, sued two hospital doctors on the grounds that he had been involuntarily confined without receiving treatment for 14 years, although he posed no serious threat to himself or others. Donaldson had been originally committed on the basis of a petition filed by his father, who had perceived him as delusional. Although Donaldson received no treatment during his

What are the rights of mental patients? Popular books and films, such as *One Flew Over the Cuckoo's Nest* starring Jack Nicholson, have highlighted many of the abuses occurring in mental hospitals. In recent years, a tightening of standards of care and the adoption of legal safeguards have led to better protection of the rights of patients in mental hospitals.

15.3 Identify major court cases establishing the rights of mental patients.

Kenneth Donaldson. Donaldson points to the U.S. Supreme Court decision that ruled that people who are considered mentally ill but not dangerous cannot be confined against their will if they can be maintained safely in the community.

Patients in mental hospitals may be required to perform general housekeeping duties in a facility.

☑ **FALSE** The Alabama case of *Wyatt* v. *Stickney* established certain patient rights, including the right not to be required to perform work for the sake of maintaining the psychiatric hospital.

TABLE 15.2

Partial Listing of the Patient's Bill of Rights Under *Wyatt* v. *Stickney*

1. Patients have rights to privacy and to be treated with dignity.
2. Patients shall be treated under the least restrictive conditions that can be provided to meet the purposes that commitment was intended to serve.
3. Patients shall have rights to visitation and telephone privileges unless special restrictions apply.
4. Patients have the right to refuse excessive or unnecessary medication. In addition, medication may not be used as a form of punishment.
5. Patients shall not be kept in restraints or isolation except in emergency conditions in which their behavior is likely to pose a threat to themselves or others and less-restrictive restraints are not feasible.
6. Patients shall not be subject to experimental research unless their rights to informed consent are protected.
7. Patients have the right to refuse potentially hazardous or unusual treatments, such as lobotomy, electroconvulsive shock, or aversive behavioral treatments.
8. Unless it is dangerous or inappropriate to the treatment program, patients shall have the right to wear their own clothing and keep possessions.
9. Patients have rights to regular exercise and to opportunities to spend time outdoors.
10. Patients have rights to suitable opportunities to interact with the opposite gender.
11. Patients have rights to humane and decent living conditions.
12. No more than six patients shall be housed in a room, and screens or curtains must be provided to afford a sense of privacy.
13. No more than eight patients shall share one toilet facility, with separate stalls provided for privacy.
14. Patients have a right to nutritionally balanced diets.
15. Patients shall not be required to perform work that is performed for the sake of maintenance of the facility.

---

confinement and was denied grounds privileges and occupational training, his repeated requests for discharge were denied as well. He was finally released when he threatened to sue the hospital. Once discharged, Donaldson did sue his doctors and was awarded damages of $38,500 from O'Connor, the superintendent of the hospital. The case was eventually argued before the U.S. Supreme Court.

Court testimony established that although the hospital staff had not perceived Donaldson to be dangerous, they had refused to release him. The hospital doctors argued that continued hospitalization had been necessary because they had believed Donaldson was unlikely to adapt successfully to community living. The doctors had prescribed antipsychotic medications, but Donaldson had refused to take them because of his Christian Science beliefs. As a result, he received only custodial care.

In 1975, the Supreme Court held in *O'Connor* v. *Donaldson* that "mental illness [alone] cannot justify a State's locking a person up against his will and keeping him indefinitely in simple custodial confinement." There is no constitutional basis for confining such persons involuntarily if they are dangerous to no one and can live safely in freedom. The ruling addressed mentally ill patients who are not considered dangerous. It is not yet clear whether the same constitutional rights would be applied to committed patients who are judged to be dangerous.

In its ruling in *O'Connor* v. *Donaldson*, the Supreme Court did not deal with the larger issue of the rights of patients to receive treatment. The ruling does not directly obligate state institutions to treat involuntarily committed, nondangerous people because the institutions may elect to release them instead.

The Supreme Court did touch on the larger issue of society's rights to protect itself from individuals who are perceived as offensive. In delivering the opinion of the Court, Justice Potter Stewart wrote,

> May the State fence in the harmless mentally ill solely to save its citizens from exposure to those whose ways are different? One might as well ask if the State, to avoid public uneasiness, could incarcerate all who are physically unattractive or socially eccentric. Mere public intolerance or animosity cannot constitutionally justify the deprivation of a person's physical liberty.

Youngberg v. Romeo In a 1982 case, *Youngberg* v. *Romeo,* the U.S. Supreme Court more directly addressed the issue of the patient's right to treatment. Even so, it seemed to retreat somewhat from the patients' rights standards established in *Wyatt* v. *Stickney.* Nicholas Romeo, a 33-year-old man with profound retardation who was unable to talk or care for himself, had been institutionalized in a state hospital and school in Pennsylvania. While in the state facility, he had a history of injuring himself through his violent behavior and was often kept in restraints. The case was brought by the patient's mother, who alleged that the hospital was negligent in not preventing his injuries and in routinely using physical restraints for prolonged periods while not providing adequate treatment.

The Supreme Court ruled that involuntarily committed patients, such as Nicholas, have a right to be confined in less-restrictive conditions, such as being freed from physical restraints whenever it is reasonable to do so. The Supreme Court ruling also included a limited recognition of the committed patient's right to treatment. The Court held that institutionalized patients have a right to minimally adequate training to help them function free of physical restraints, but only to the extent that such training can be provided in reasonable safety. Reasonableness, the Court held, should be determined on the basis of the judgment of qualified professionals. The federal courts should not interfere with the internal operations of the facility, the Court held, because "there's no reason to think judges or juries are better qualified than appropriate professionals in making such decisions." The courts should only second guess the judgments of qualified professionals when such judgments depart from professional standards of practice. But the Supreme Court did not address the broader issues of the rights of committed patients to receive training that might eventually enable them to function independently outside the hospital.

The related issue of whether people with severe psychological disorders who reside in the community have a constitutional right to receive mental health services (and whether states are obligated to provide these services) continues to be argued in the courts at both the state and federal levels.

RIGHT TO REFUSE TREATMENT Consider the following scenario. A person, John Citizen, is involuntarily committed to a mental hospital for treatment. The hospital staff determines that John suffers from a psychotic disorder, paranoid schizophrenia, and should be treated with antipsychotic medication. John, however, decides not to comply with treatment. He claims that the hospital has no right to treat him against his will. The hospital staff seeks a court order to mandate treatment, arguing that it makes little sense to commit people involuntarily unless the hospital is empowered to treat them as the staff deems fit.

Does an involuntary patient, such as John, have the right to refuse treatment? If so, does this right conflict with states' rights to involuntarily commit people to mental institutions to receive treatment? One might also wonder whether people who are judged in need of involuntary hospitalization are competent to make decisions about which treatments are in their best interests.

The right of committed patients to refuse psychotropic medications was tested in a 1979 case, *Rogers* v. *Okin,* in which a Massachusetts federal district court imposed an injunction on a Boston state hospital prohibiting the forced medication of committed

15.4 Define the duty to warn and **evaluate** the dilemma it poses for therapists.

One of the most difficult dilemmas a therapist faces is whether to disclose confidential information that may protect third parties from harm. Part of the difficulty lies in determining whether the client has made a bona fide threat. The other part is that information a client discloses in psychotherapy is generally protected as privileged communication, which carries a right to confidentiality. But this right is not absolute. State courts have determined that a therapist is obligated to breach confidentiality under certain conditions, such as when there is clear and compelling evidence that an individual poses a serious threat to others.

A 1976 court ruling in California in *Tarasoff* v. *the Regents of the University of California* established the legal basis for the therapist's **duty to warn** (Jones, 2003). In 1969, a graduate student at the University of California at Berkeley, Prosenjit Poddar, a native of India, became depressed when his romantic overtures toward a young woman, Tatiana Tarasoff, were rebuffed. Poddar entered psychotherapy with a psychologist at a student health facility and informed the psychologist that he intended to kill Tatiana when she returned from her summer vacation. The psychologist, concerned about Poddar's potential for violence, first consulted with his colleagues and then notified the campus police that Poddar was dangerous, recommending that he be taken to a facility for psychiatric treatment.

The campus police interviewed Poddar. They believed he was rational and released him after he promised to keep away from Tatiana. Poddar then terminated treatment with the psychologist and shortly afterward killed Tatiana. Poddar was found guilty of the lesser sentence of voluntary manslaughter rather than murder, on the basis of testimony of three psychiatrists that he suffered from diminished mental capacity and paranoid schizophrenia. Under California law, his diminished capacity prevented the finding of malice that was necessary for a murder conviction. Following a prison term, Poddar returned to India, where he reportedly made a new life for himself (Schwitzgebel & Schwitzgebel, 1980).

Tatiana's parents, however, sued the university. They claimed that the university health center had failed in its responsibility to warn Tatiana of the threat made against her by Poddar. The California Supreme Court agreed with the parents. The Court ruled that a therapist who has reason to believe that a client poses a serious threat to another person is obligated to warn the potential victim, not merely to notify police. This ruling imposed on therapists a duty-to-warn obligation when their clients show the potential for violence by making threats against others. **T / F**

The ruling recognized that the rights of the intended victim outweigh the rights of confidentiality. Under *Tarasoff*, the therapist does not merely have a *right* to breach confidentiality and warn potential victims of danger, but is *obligated* by law to divulge such confidences to the potential victim.

The duty-to-warn provision poses ethical and practical dilemmas for clinicians. Under *Tarasoff*, therapists may feel obliged to protect their personal interests and those of others by breaching confidentiality on the mere suspicion that their clients harbor violent intentions. Because clients' threats are seldom carried out, the *Tarasoff* ruling may deny many clients their rights to confidentiality to prevent such rare instances. Although some clinicians may "overreact" to *Tarasoff* and breach confidentiality without sufficient cause, it can be argued that the interests of the few potential victims outweigh the interests of the many who may suffer a loss of confidentiality.

Another problem with applying the *Tarasoff* standard is the lack of any special ability on the therapist's part to predict dangerousness. Nevertheless, the *Tarasoff* ruling obliges therapists to judge whether or not their clients' disclosures indicate an imminent intent to harm others (VanderCreek & Knapp, 2001). In *Tarasoff*, the threat was obvious. In most cases, however, threats are not so clear-cut. There are no

truth OR fiction

Therapists may not breach patient confidentiality even when a patient makes a death threat against a specific person.

☑ **FALSE**   Therapists are actually obligated under some state laws to breach client confidentiality to warn people when threats of violence are made against them by their clients.

patients except in emergency situations—for example, when patients' behaviors posed a significant threat to themselves or others. The court recognized that a patient may be unwise to refuse medication, but it held that a patient with or without a mental disorder has the right to exercise bad judgment so long as the effects of the "error" do not impose "a danger of physical harm to himself, fellow patients, or hospital staff."

clear criteria for determining whether a therapist "should have known" that a client was dangerous before a violent act occurs. In the absence of guidelines that specify the criteria therapists should use to fulfill their duty to warn, they must rely on their best clinical judgment.

The ethical issues become even murkier when therapists treat HIV-infected patients who put their sexual partners at risk by concealing their HIV status. Therapists must balance their duty-to-warn obligations with their ethical responsibility to protect patient confidentiality. Presently, psychologists lack a clear set of professional standards that therapists can follow to resolve these dilemmas (Huprich, Fuller, & Schneider, 2003). Psychologists must follow the laws of the states in which they practice regarding the requirements for maintaining confidentiality of their clients' HIV status and become aware of any exceptions that might exist for breaching confidentiality (Barnett, 2010).

The *Tarasoff* ruling and state laws implemented in its wake that mandate a duty to warn raise many concerns among clinicians who are trying to meet their legal responsibilities under *Tarasoff* provisions and their clinical responsibilities to their clients. Although the intent of the *Tarasoff* decision was to protect potential victims, it may inadvertently increase the risks of violence when applied to clinical practice, as in the following situations (Weiner, 2003):

1. *Clients may be less willing to confide in their therapists,* making it more difficult for therapists to help them diffuse violent feelings.
2. *Potentially violent people may be less likely to enter therapy,* fearing that disclosures made to a therapist will be revealed.
3. *Therapists may be less likely to probe violent tendencies,* seeking to avoid legal complications. Therapists may avoid asking clients about potential violence or may avoid treating patients who are believed to have violent tendencies.

The *Tarasoff* case was brought in California, and the decision applied only in that state. Other states have different statutes (Pabian, Welfel, & Beebe, 2009). As mentioned, therapists must be aware of the duty-to-warn laws in the particular states in which they practice. Some states permit therapists to breach confidentiality to warn third parties, but do not impose an obligation on therapists to do so. But most states impose a duty to warn on therapists (or what is sometimes called a *duty to protect*) in some situations, such as when a client threatens a particular person and the threat of violence is imminent (American Psychological Association, 2012). In other states, however, a duty to warn is legally obligated even when there is no clearly identifiable victim, as when a client threatens to kill people at random or makes a threat to harm someone but does not identify the targeted person (American Psychological Association, 2011). Laws in different states also specify how the duty to warn needs to be met, such as filing a report with the police or taking steps to prevent potential acts of violence, such as by hospitalizing the client.

Although therapists are under a legal obligation to follow the laws in the states in which they practice, they must also not lose sight of the primary therapeutic responsibility to their clients when legal issues arise. They must balance the obligation to meet their responsibilities under duty-to-warn provisions with the need to help their clients resolve the feelings of rage and anger that give rise to violent threats.

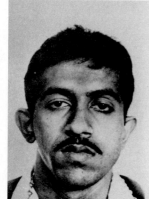

Tatiana Tarasoff and Prosenjit Poddar. Poddar, Tatiana's killer, was a rejected suitor who had made threats against her to his therapist at a university health center. Poddar was subsequently convicted of voluntary manslaughter. A suit brought by Tatiana's parents against the university led to a landmark court ruling that established an obligation for therapists to warn third parties of threats made against them by their clients.

Although statutes and regulations vary from state to state, cases in which hospitalized patients refuse medications are often first brought before an independent review panel. If the panel rules against the patient, the case may then be brought before a judge, who makes the final decision about whether the patient is to be forcibly medicated (Rolon & Jones, 2008). In practice, relatively few patients, perhaps only about 10%, refuse medication.

Furthermore, the great majority of refusals that reach the review process are eventually overridden. Our discussion of legal issues and abnormal behavior now turns to the controversy concerning the insanity defense.

15.5 **Discuss** the history of the insanity defense, citing specific court cases.

truth OR fiction

An attempt to assassinate the president of the United States was seen by millions of television viewers, but the would-be assassin was found not guilty by a court of law.

☑ **TRUE** John Hinkley, who was seen by millions of TV viewers attempting to assassinate President Reagan, was found "not guilty by reason of insanity" by a court of law.

The Insanity Defense

The 2011 shooting of Representative Gabby Giffords recalls another high-profile shooting in which the president of the United States, Ronald Reagan, was shot outside a hotel in Washington, D.C., in March 1981. Millions of Americans witnessed the shooting on their television screens, but the assailant, John Hinckley, a 25-year-old drifter, was found not guilty by reason of insanity and confined to a mental hospital, where he remains as of this writing, more than 30 years after the shooting. **T / F**

When gunshots rang out that cold day in March, Secret Service agents formed a human shield around the president; one shoved him into a waiting limousine, which sped to a hospital. The president was wounded, but fortunately recovered. James Brady, his press secretary, was hit by a stray bullet that shattered his spine and left him partially paralyzed. Federal agents seized the gunman, John Hinckley.

A letter Hinckley left in his hotel room, parts of which are reproduced below, revealed his hope that his assassination of the president would impress a young actress, Jodie Foster. Hinckley had never met Foster but had a crush on her.

At Hinckley's trial, there was never any question whether Hinckley had fired the wounding bullets, but the prosecutor was burdened to demonstrate beyond a reasonable doubt that Hinckley had the capacity to control his behavior and appreciate its wrongfulness. The defense presented testimony that portrayed Hinckley as an incompetent schizophrenic who suffered under the delusion that he would achieve a "magic union" with Foster as a result of killing the president. The jury sided with the defense and found Hinckley *not guilty by reason of insanity*. He was remanded to a federal psychiatric facility, St. Elizabeth's Hospital in Washington, D.C., where he has remained ever since.

Fast-forward to 2005: a federal judge ruled that the Hinckley, then 50 years old, was permitted home visits to be supervised by his parents for three or four nights at a time. By 2009, a federal court permitted him to extend his home visits to nine days at a time and gave him greater opportunity to spend time outside the hospital and even to obtain a driver's license. By the time this book reaches your hands, Hinckley may well have been granted a full release. His doctors assert that his psychiatric condition (a combination of psychosis and depression) is now "in full remission."

The idea that Hinckley or others found not guilty of heinous crimes by reason of insanity might one day be granted full release is unsettling to many people. Shouldn't he have been imprisoned rather than treated in a mental hospital? How should society treat mentally disturbed individuals who commit crimes? Then again, had Hinckley been convicted of a crime, might he have already been set free or at least paroled?

→ **"I"** *"Please Look Into Your Heart"*

Dear Jodie,

There is a definite possibility that I will be killed in my attempt to get Reagan. It is for this very reason that I am writing you this letter now.

As you well know by now I love you very much. Over the past seven months I've left you dozens of poems, letters and love messages in the faint hope that you could develop an interest in me. . . .

Jodie, I would abandon this idea of getting Reagan in a second if I could only win your heart and live out the rest of my life with you, whether it be in total obscurity or whatever.

I will admit to you that the reason I'm going ahead with this attempt now is because I just cannot wait any longer to impress you. I've got to do something now to make you understand, in no uncertain terms, that I am doing all of this for your sake!

By sacrificing my freedom and possibly my life, I hope to change your mind about me. This letter is being written only an hour before I leave for the Hilton Hotel. Jodie, I'm asking you to please look into your heart and at least give me the chance, with this historical deed, to gain your respect and love.

Source: Linder, 2004, "The John Hinckley Trial."

→ *John Hinckley's letter to actress Jodie Foster, written on March 31, 1981, shortly before he attempted to assassinate President Ronald Reagan*

Perceptions of the use of the **insanity defense** tend to stray far from the facts. Contrary to the common perception that the insanity defense is widely and often successfully used, it is in fact used rarely and is usually unsuccessful. In actuality, it is applied in about 1% of felony cases and succeeds in acquittals in a fraction of these cases, perhaps only 15 to 25% (Lilienfeld & Arkowitz, 2011). Thus, the use of the insanity defense is rare, and acquittals are rarer still. T / F

The public also overestimates the proportion of defendants acquitted on the basis of insanity who are set free rather than confined to mental health institutions and underestimates the length of hospitalization of those who are confined (Silver, Cirincione, & Steadman, 1994). People found not guilty of a crime on the basis of insanity are often confined to mental hospitals for longer periods of time than they would have otherwise served in prison (Lymburner & Roesch, 1999). The net result is that although changes in the insanity defense, or its abolition, might prevent a few flagrant cases of abuse, they would not afford the public much broader protection.

The Aftermath of the Hinckley Case

The Hinckley verdict led to a public outcry, with many calling for the abolition of the insanity defense. One objection focused on the fact that once the defense presented evidence to support a plea of insanity, the federal prosecutor had the responsibility of proving *beyond a reasonable doubt* that the defendant was sane. It can be difficult enough to demonstrate that someone is sane or insane in the present, so imagine the problems that attend proving someone was sane at the time a criminal act was committed.

In the aftermath of the Hinckley verdict, the federal government and many states changed their statutes to shift the burden of proof to the defense to prove insanity. Even the American Psychiatric Association went on record stating that psychiatric expert witnesses should not be called on to render opinions about whether defendants can control their behavior. In the opinion of the association, these are not medical judgments that psychiatrists are trained to provide.

In the wake of the Hinckley acquittal, a number of states adopted a new type of verdict, the *guilty-but-mentally-ill* (GBMI) verdict. The GBMI verdict offers juries the option of finding that a defendant is mentally ill but that the mental illness did not cause the defendant to commit the crime. People convicted under a GBMI statute go to prison but receive treatment while incarcerated.

The GBMI verdict has sparked considerable controversy. Although it was intended to reduce the number of NGRI (not guilty by reason of insanity) verdicts, it has failed to do so (Melville & Naimark, 2002; Slovenko, 2009). All in all, the GBMI verdict is widely seen as a social experiment that has failed to prove its usefulness (Palmer & Hazelrigg, 2000). Critics argue that the verdict merely stigmatizes defendants who are found guilty as also being mentally ill. Fewer than half of the states today permit a GMBI verdict (Kutys & Esterman, 2009).

Legal Bases of the Insanity Defense

Although the public outrage over the Hinckley and other celebrated insanity verdicts led to a reexamination of the insanity defense, society has long held to the doctrine of free will as a basis for determining responsibility for wrongdoing. The doctrine of free will, as applied to criminal responsibility, requires that people can be held guilty of a crime only

Not guilty by reason of insanity. Was he insane when he shot the president? John Hinckley Jr. attempted to assassinate President Ronald Reagan in 1981 but was found not guilty by reason of insanity. The public outrage over the Hinckley verdict led to a reexamination of the insanity plea in many states.

if they are judged to have been in control of their actions at the time. Not only must a court of law determine, beyond a reasonable doubt, that a defendant had committed a crime, but it must also consider the individual's state of mind in determining guilt. The court must thus rule not only on whether a crime was committed but also on whether the defendant is morally responsible and deserving of punishment. The insanity defense is based on the belief that when a criminal act derives from a distorted state of mind, and not from the exercise of free will, the individual should not be punished but rather treated for the underlying mental disorder. The insanity defense has a long legal history.

Three major modern court rulings bear on the insanity defense. The first was an 1834 case in Ohio in which it was ruled that people could not be held responsible if they are compelled to commit criminal actions because of impulses they are unable to resist.

The second major legal test of the insanity defense is referred to as the M'Naghten rule, based on a case in England in 1843 of a Scotsman, Daniel M'Naghten, who had intended to assassinate the prime minister of England, Sir Robert Peel. Instead, he killed Peel's secretary, whom he had mistaken for the prime minister. M'Naghten claimed that the voice of God had commanded him to kill Peel. The English court acquitted M'Naghten on the basis of insanity, finding that the defendant had been "labouring under such a defect of reason, from disease of the mind, as not to know the nature and quality of the act he was doing; or, if he did know it, that he did not know he was doing what was wrong." The M'Naghten rule holds that people do not bear criminal responsibility if, by reason of a mental disease or defect, they either have no knowledge of their actions or are unable to tell right from wrong.

The third major case that helped lay the foundation for the modern insanity defense was *Durham* v. *United States,* 1954. The verdict in this case held that the "accused [person] is not criminally responsible if his unlawful act was the product of mental disease or mental defect." Under the *Durham* rule, juries were expected to decide not only whether the accused suffered from a mental disease or defect but also whether this mental condition was causally connected to the criminal act. The U.S. Court of Appeals Court recognized that criminal intent is a precondition of criminal responsibility:

> The legal and moral traditions of the western world require that those who, of their own free will and with evil intent . . . commit acts which violate the law, shall be criminally responsible for those acts. Our traditions also require that where such acts stem from and are the product of a mental disease or defect . . . moral blame shall not attach, and hence there will not be criminal responsibility.

The intent of the *Durham* rule was to reject as outmoded the two earlier standards of legal insanity, the irresistible impulse rule and the *right–wrong* principle. The Court argued that the right–wrong test was outmoded because the concept of mental disease is broader than the ability to recognize right from wrong. The legal basis of insanity should thus not be judged on just one feature of a mental disorder, such as deficient reasoning ability. The irresistible impulse test was denied because the Court recognized that in certain cases, criminal acts arising from "mental disease or defect" might occur in a cool and calculating manner rather than in the manner of a sudden, irresistible impulse. Defendants may have known they were committing criminal acts, but were not driven to do so by an irresistible impulse (Sokolove, 2003).

The *Durham* rule, however, has proved to be unworkable for several reasons, such as a lack of precise definitions of terms such as *mental disease* or *mental defect.* Courts were confused, for example, about whether a personality disorder (e.g., antisocial personality disorder) constituted a "disease." Also, juries found it difficult to draw conclusions about whether an individual's "mental disease" was causally connected to the criminal act. Without clear or precise definitions of terms, juries have come to rely on expert psychiatric testimony. In many cases, verdicts simply endorsed the testimony of expert witnesses.

By 1972, the *Durham* rule was replaced in many jurisdictions by legal guidelines formulated by the American Law Institute (ALI) to define the legal basis of insanity

15.6 Describe the guidelines proposed by the American Law Institute for determining the legal basis of insanity.

(Van Susteren, 2002). These guidelines, which essentially combine the M'Naghten principle with the irresistible impulse principle, include the following provisions (American Law Institute, 1962):

1. A person is not responsible for criminal conduct if at the time of such conduct as a result of mental disease or defect he lacks substantial capacity either to appreciate the criminality (wrongfulness) of his conduct or to conform his conduct to the requirements of law.
2. . . . The terms "mental disease or defect" do not include an abnormality manifested only by repeated criminal or otherwise antisocial conduct.

The first guideline incorporates aspects of the M'Naghten test (being unable to appreciate right from wrong) and the irresistible impulse test (being unable to conform one's behavior to the requirements of law) of insanity. The second guideline asserts that repeated criminal behavior (such as a pattern of drug dealing) is not sufficient in itself to establish a mental disease or defect that might relieve the individual of criminal responsibility. Although many legal authorities believe the ALI guidelines are an improvement over earlier tests, questions remain as to whether a jury composed of ordinary citizens can be expected to make complex judgments about the defendant's state of mind, even on the basis of expert testimony, especially in cases in which experts disagree with each other (Sadoff, 2011). Under the ALI guidelines, juries must determine whether defendants lack substantial capacity to be aware of, or capable of, conforming their behavior to the law. By adding the term *substantial capacity* to the legal test, the ALI guidelines broaden the legal basis of the insanity defense, implying that defendants need not be completely incapable of controlling their actions to meet the legal test of not guilty by reason of insanity.

Under the U.S. system of justice, juries must struggle with the complex question of determining criminal responsibility, not merely criminal actions. But what of those individuals who successfully plead not guilty by reason of insanity? Should they be committed to a mental institution for a fixed sentence, as they might have been had they been incarcerated in a penal institution? Or should their commitments be of an indeterminate term and their release dependent on their mental status? The legal basis for answering such questions was decided in the case of a man named Michael Jones.

Determining the Length of Criminal Commitment

The issue of determinate versus indeterminate commitment was addressed in the case of Michael Jones (*Jones* v. *United States*), who was arrested in 1975 and charged with petty larceny for attempting to steal a jacket from a Washington, D.C., department store. Jones was first committed to a public mental hospital, St. Elizabeth's Hospital (the same hospital where John Hinckley remains committed as of this writing). Jones was diagnosed as suffering from paranoid schizophrenia and was kept hospitalized until he was judged competent to stand trial, about six months later. Jones offered a plea of not guilty by reason of insanity, which the court accepted without challenge, remanding him to St. Elizabeth's. Although Jones's crime carried a maximum sentence of one year in prison, Jones's repeated attempts to obtain release were denied in subsequent court hearings.

The U.S. Supreme Court eventually heard his appeal seven years after Jones was hospitalized and reached its decision in 1983. It ruled against Jones's appeal and affirmed the decision of the lower courts that he was to remain in the hospital. The Supreme Court thereby established a principle that individuals who are acquitted by reason of insanity "constitute a special class that should be treated differently" from civilly committed individuals (Morris, 2002). They may be committed for an indefinite period to a mental institution under criteria that require a less stringent level of proof of dangerousness than is ordinarily applied in cases of civil commitment. Thus, people found not guilty by reason of insanity may remain confined to a mental hospital for many years longer than they would have been sentenced to prison had they been found guilty. **T / F**

15.7 Describe the legal basis for determining the length of criminal commitment.

People who are found not guilty of a crime by reason of insanity may be confined to a mental hospital for many years longer than they would have been sentenced to prison, had they been found guilty.

☑ **TRUE** People who are found not guilty of a crime by reason of insanity may remain confined in a mental hospital for many years longer than they would have served a prison term.

Among other things, the Supreme Court ruling in *Jones* v. *United States* provides that the usual and customary sentences that the law provides for particular crimes have no bearing on criminal commitment. In the words of the Supreme Court,

> . . . different considerations underlie commitment of an insanity acquittee. As he was not convicted, he may not be punished. His confinement rests on his continuing illness and dangerousness. There simply is no necessary correlation between severity of the offense and length of time necessary for recovery.

The Supreme Court ruling held that a person who is criminally committed may be confined "to a mental institution until such time as he has regained his sanity or is no longer a danger to society." As in the case of Michael Jones, people who are acquitted on the basis of insanity may remain confined for much longer periods of time than they would have been sentenced to prison. They may also be released earlier than they might have been released from prison, if their "mental condition" improves. However, public outrage over a speedy release, especially for a major crime, might prevent rapid release.

The indeterminateness of criminal commitment raises various questions. Is it reasonable to deny people such as Michael Jones their liberty for an indefinite and possibly lifelong term for a relatively minor crime, such as petty larceny? On the other hand, is justice served by acquitting perpetrators of heinous crimes by reason of insanity and then releasing them early if they are deemed by professionals to be able to rejoin society?

The Supreme Court's ruling in *Jones* v. *United States* seems to imply that we must separate the notion of legal sentencing from that of legal or criminal commitment. Legal sentencing rests on the principle that the punishment should fit the crime: The more serious the crime, the longer the punishment. In criminal commitment, however, persons acquitted of their crimes by reason of insanity are guiltless in the eyes of the law, and their length of confinement is determined by their mental state.

Perspectives on the Insanity Defense

The insanity defense places special burdens on juries. In assessing criminal responsibility, the jury must determine not only that the accused committed a crime but also the defendant's state of mind at the time. In rejecting the *Durham* decision, courts have relieved psychiatrists and other expert witnesses from responsibility for determining whether the defendant's behavior is a product of a *mental disease or defect*. But is it reasonable to assume that juries are better able to assess defendants' states of mind than mental health professionals? In particular, how can a jury evaluate the testimony of conflicting expert witnesses? The jury's task is made even more difficult by the mandate to decide whether the defendant was mentally incapacitated *at the time of the crime*. The defendant's courtroom behavior may bear little resemblance to his or her behavior during the crime.

Thomas Szasz and others who deny the existence of mental illness have raised another challenge to the insanity defense. If mental illness does not exist, then the insanity defense becomes groundless. Szasz argues that the insanity defense is ultimately degrading because it strips people of personal responsibility for their behavior. People who break laws are criminals, Szasz argues, and should be prosecuted and sentenced accordingly. Acquittal of defendants by reason of insanity treats them as nonpersons, as unfortunates who are not deemed to possess the basic human qualities of free choice, self-determination, and personal responsibility. We are each responsible for our behavior, Szasz contends, and we should each be held accountable for our misdeeds.

Szasz argues that the insanity defense has historically been invoked in crimes that were particularly heinous or perpetrated against persons of high social rank. When persons of low social rank commit crimes against persons of higher status, Szasz argues, the insanity defense directs attention away from the social ills that may have motivated the crime. Despite Szasz's contention, the insanity defense is invoked in many cases of less shocking crimes or in cases involving people from similar social classes.

How, then, are we to evaluate the insanity defense? To abolish it would reverse hundreds of years of legal tradition that recognizes that people are not to be held responsible for their criminal behavior when their ability to control themselves is impaired by a mental disorder or defect.

Consider a hypothetical example. John Citizen commits a crime, say a heinous crime such as murder, while acting on a delusional belief that the victim was intent on assassinating him. The accused claims that voices from his TV set informed him of the identity of the would-be assassin and commanded him to kill the person to save himself and other potential victims. Cases like this are thankfully rare. Few mentally disturbed people, even few people with psychotic features, commit violent crimes, and even fewer commit murder.

In reaching a judgment on the insanity plea, juries need to consider whether the law should apply special standards in cases such as John Citizen's, or whether one standard of criminal responsibility should apply to all. If lawmakers assert the legitimacy of the insanity defense in some cases, they still need a standard of insanity that can be interpreted and applied by juries of ordinary citizens. The furor over the Hinckley verdict suggests that issues concerning the insanity plea remain unsettled and are likely to continue to be so for a long period of time.

Competency to Stand Trial

There is a basic rule of law that those who stand accused of crimes must be able to understand the charges and proceedings brought against them and be able to participate in their own defense. The concept of **competency to stand trial** should not be confused with the insanity defense. A defendant can be held competent to stand trial but still be judged not guilty of a crime by reason of insanity. A clearly delusional person, for example, may understand the court proceedings and be able to confer with defense counsel but still be acquitted by reason of insanity. On the other hand, a person may be incapable of standing trial at a particular time but be tried at a later time when competency is restored (Zapf & Roesch, 2011). Defendants who suffer from psychotic disorders, those who are unemployed, and those who have had a history of psychiatric hospitalization are more likely than those without these characteristics to be judged incompetent (Pirelli, Gottdiener, & Zapf, 2011). **T / F**

People are much more likely to be confined to mental institutions on the basis of the lack of mental competence to stand trial than on the basis of the insanity verdict (Roesch, Zapf, & Hart, 2010). People who are declared incompetent to stand trial are generally confined to a mental institution until they are deemed competent or until it is determined that they are unlikely to regain competency. Abuses may occur, however, if the accused are kept incarcerated for indefinite periods awaiting trial. In 1972, the U.S. Supreme Court ruled, in the case of *Jackson* v. *Indiana,* that a person could not be kept in a mental hospital awaiting trial longer than it would take to determine whether treatment was likely to restore competency. Under *Jackson,* psychiatric examiners must determine whether there exists a substantial probability that the defendant would regain competency through treatment within the foreseeable future (Hubbard, Zapf, & Ronan, 2003). If it does not seem the person would ever become competent, even with treatment, the individual must either be released or committed under the procedures for civil commitment. However, compliance with the *Jackson* standard has been inconsistent, with some states imposing a minimum length of treatment (e.g., five years) before acknowledging that a defendant is deemed permanently incompetent (Morris, 2002).

15.8 Describe the legal basis for determining competency to stand trial.

Not Competent to Stand Trial Jason Rodriguez, right, who was charged with one count of first-degree murder and five counts of attempted murder in an Orlando, Florida, office shooting is shown here consulting with his public defender during a competency hearing. After hearing from three psychiatrists and a psychologist who testified that Rodriguez was currently incompetent to stand trial, the judge ordered him to a state mental hospital for treatment

A defendant may be held competent to stand trial but still be judged not guilty of a crime by reason of insanity.

☑ **TRUE** Yes, a defendant can be held competent to stand trial but then be found not guilty of a crime by reason of insanity at trial.

A 1992 ruling by the U.S. Supreme Court, in the case of *Medina* v. *California,* held that the burden of proof for determining competency to stand trial lies with the defendant, not the state. Then, in 2003, the U.S. Supreme Court held in the case of *Sell* v. *United States* that mentally ill defendants could be forcibly medicated to render them competent to stand trial, at least under some limited circumstances (Bassman, 2005). The decision allows a defendant to be involuntarily medicated if it is deemed medically appropriate and would not cause side effects that would compromise the fairness of the trial (Heilbrun & Kramer, 2005). The effect of the *Sell* decision may be to bring to trial many defendants whose trials were delayed because of a lack of mental competence.

We opened this book by noting that despite the popular impression that abnormal behavior affects only a few of us, it actually affects every one of us in one way or another. Let us close by suggesting that if we all work together to foster research into the causes, treatment, and prevention of abnormal behavior, perhaps we can meet the multifaceted challenges that abnormal behavior poses to our society at large.

summing up

Civil Commitment and Patients' Rights

15.1 Explain the difference between civil commitment and criminal commitment.

The legal process by which people are placed in psychiatric institutions against their will is called *civil* or *psychiatric commitment*. Civil commitment is intended to provide treatment to people who are deemed to suffer from mental disorders and to pose a threat to themselves or others. Criminal commitment, by comparison, involves the placement of a person in a psychiatric institution for treatment who has been acquitted of a crime by reason of insanity. In voluntary hospitalization, people voluntarily seek treatment in a psychiatric facility and can leave of their own accord unless a court rules otherwise.

15.2 Evaluate the ability of mental health professionals to predict dangerousness.

Although people must be judged dangerous to be placed involuntarily in a psychiatric facility, mental health professionals have not demonstrated any special ability to predict dangerousness. Factors that may account for the failure to predict dangerousness include the following: (a) recognizing violent tendencies post hoc is easier than predicting them; (b) generalized perceptions of violent tendencies may not predict specific acts of violence; (c) there is lack of agreement in defining *violence* or *dangerousness*; (d) base-rate problems make it difficult to predict rare events; (e) it is unlikely that potential offenders would directly disclose their violent intentions; and (f) predictions based on hospital behavior may not generalize to community settings.

15.3 Identify major court cases establishing the rights of mental patients.

In *Wyatt* v. *Stickney,* a court in Alabama imposed a minimum standard of care. In *O'Connor* v. *Donaldson,* the U.S. Supreme Court ruled that nondangerous mentally ill people could not be held in psychiatric facilities against their will if such people could be maintained safely in the community. In *Youngberg* v. *Romeo,* the Supreme Court ruled that involuntarily confined patients have a right to less-restrictive types of treatment and to receive training to help them function well. Court rulings, such as that of *Rogers* v. *Okin* in Massachusetts, have established that patients have a right to refuse medication, except in case of emergency.

15.4 Define the duty to warn and evaluate the dilemma it poses for therapists.

Although information disclosed by a client to a therapist generally carries a right to confidentiality, the *Tarasoff* ruling held that therapists have a duty or obligation to warn third parties of threats made against them by their clients. It poses ethical and practical dilemmas for therapists who need to determine whether to breach confidentiality on the basis of their judgment that patients have hostile intentions toward others and are likely to carry them out, even though therapists have no special ability to predict future dangerousness.

The Insanity Defense

15.5 Describe the history of the insanity defense, citing specific court cases.

Three court cases established legal precedents for the insanity defense. In 1834, a court in Ohio applied a principle of irresistible impulse as the basis of an insanity defense. The M'Naghten rule, based on a case in England in 1843, treated the failure to appreciate the wrongfulness of one's action as the basis of legal insanity. The Durham rule was based on a case in the United States in 1954, in which it was held that people did not bear criminal responsibility if their criminal behavior was the product of "mental disease or mental defect."

15.6 Describe the guidelines proposed by the American Law Institute for determining the legal basis of insanity.

These guidelines are a set of standards developed by the American Law Institute that combines the M'Naghten principle of inability to ascertain the difference between right and wrong and the irresistible impulse principle of being unable to conform one's behavior to the requirements of law due to mental disease or defect.

15.7 Describe the legal basis for determining length of criminal commitment.

The legal basis for determining length of criminal commitment holds that people who are criminally committed may be hospitalized for an indefinite period of time, with their eventual release dependent on a determination of their mental status.

15.8 Describe the legal basis for determining competency to stand trial.

People who are accused of crimes but are incapable of understanding the charges against them or of assisting in their own defense can be found incompetent to stand trial and remanded to a psychiatric facility. In the case of *Jackson* v. *Indiana,* the U.S. Supreme Court placed restrictions on the length of time a person judged incompetent to stand trial could be held in a psychiatric facility.

critical thinking questions

Based on your reading of this chapter, answer the following questions:

- Do you believe that psychiatric patients who wander city streets mumbling to themselves and living in cardboard boxes should be hospitalized against their will? Why or why not?

- If you were called on to evaluate whether an individual posed a danger to him- or herself, or to others, on what criteria would you base your judgment? What evidence would you need to make your determination?

- Do you believe therapists should be obligated to breach confidentiality when their clients make threats against others? Why or why not? What concerns have therapists raised about the duty to warn? Do you believe their concerns are warranted?

- Do you believe the insanity verdict should be abolished or replaced with another type of verdict, like the guilty-but-mentally-ill verdict? Why or why not?

key terms

civil commitment 550
criminal commitment 550
duty to warn 560

insanity defense 563
competency to stand trial 567

A

Abnormal psychology. The branch of psychology that deals with the description, causes, and treatment of abnormal behavior patterns.

Acculturative stress. Pressure to adjust to a host or mainstream culture.

Acute stress disorder. A traumatic stress reaction occurring during the month following exposure to a traumatic event.

Addiction. Impaired control over the use of a chemical substance despite the harmful consequences it causes.

Adjustment disorder. A maladaptive reaction to an identified stressor, characterized by impaired functioning or emotional distress that exceeds what would normally be expected.

Adoptee studies. Studies that compare the traits and behavior patterns of adopted children to those of their biological parents and their adoptive parents.

Agnosia. A disturbance of sensory perception, usually affecting visual perception.

Agoraphobia. Excessive, irrational fear of open or public places.

Alarm reaction. The first stage of the GAS, characterized by heightened sympathetic nervous system activity.

Alcoholism. Alcohol addiction or dependence resulting in serious personal, social, occupational, or health problems.

Alzheimer's disease (AD). A progressive brain disease characterized by gradual loss of memory and intellectual functioning, personality changes, and eventual loss of ability to care for oneself.

Amnesia. Memory loss that frequently follows a traumatic event, such as a blow to the head, an electric shock, or a major surgical operation.

Amphetamine psychosis. A psychotic state characterized by hallucinations and delusions, induced by ingestion of amphetamines.

Amphetamines. A class of synthetic stimulants that activate the central nervous system, producing heightened states of arousal and feelings of pleasure.

Anorexia nervosa. An eating disorder characterized by maintenance of an abnormally low body weight, a distorted body image, and intense fears of gaining weight.

Anterograde amnesia. Loss or impairment of ability to form or store new memories.

Antianxiety drugs. Drugs that combat anxiety and reduce states of muscle tension.

Antidepressants. Drugs used to treat depression that affect the availability of neurotransmitters in the brain.

Antipsychotic drugs. Drugs used to treat schizophrenia or other psychotic disorders.

Antisocial personality disorder. A personality disorder characterized by antisocial and irresponsible behavior and lack of remorse for misdeeds.

Anxiety. An emotional state characterized by physiological arousal, unpleasant feelings of tension, and a sense of apprehension or foreboding.

Anxiety disorder. A class of psychological disorders characterized by excessive or maladaptive anxiety reactions.

Aphasia. Impaired ability to understand or express speech.

Archetypes. Primitive images or concepts that reside in the collective unconscious.

Ataxia. Loss of muscle coordination.

Attention-deficit/hyperactivity disorder (ADHD). A behavior disorder characterized by excessive motor activity and inability to focus one's attention.

Autism spectrum disorder. A developmental disorder characterized by significant deficits in communication and social interaction, as well as development of restricted or fixated interests and repetitive behaviors.

Autonomic nervous system. The division of the peripheral nervous system that regulates the activities of the glands and involuntary functions.

Avoidant personality disorder. A personality disorder characterized by avoidance of social relationships due to fears of rejection.

Axon. The long, thin part of a neuron along which nerve impulses travel.

B

Barbiturates. Sedative drugs that are depressants with high addictive potential.

Basal ganglia. An assemblage of neurons at the base of the forebrain involved in regulating postural movements and coordination.

Behavior therapy. The therapeutic application of learning-based techniques to resolve psychological disorders.

Behavioral assessment. The approach to clinical assessment that focuses on the objective recording and description of problem behavior.

Behaviorism. The school of psychology that defines psychology as the study of observable behavior and that focuses on the role of learning in explaining behavior.

Binge-eating disorder (BED). An eating disorder characterized by recurrent eating binges without subsequent purging.

Biofeedback training (BFT). A method of giving an individual information (feedback) about bodily functions so that the person can gain some degree of control over them.

Biopsychosocial model. An integrative model for explaining abnormal behavior in terms of the interactions of biological, psychological, and sociocultural factors.

Bipolar disorder. A psychological disorder characterized by mood swings between states of extreme elation and depression.

Blind. A state of being unaware of whether one has received an experimental treatment or a placebo.

Body dysmorphic disorder (BDD). A psychological disorder characterized by preoccupation with an imagined or exaggerated physical defect in appearance.

Body mass index (BMI). A standard measure that takes both body weight and height into account.

Borderline personality disorder (BPD). A personality disorder characterized by abrupt shifts in mood, lack of a coherent sense of self, and unpredictable, impulsive behavior.

Breathing-related sleep disorders. Sleep disorder in which sleep is repeatedly disrupted by difficulty with breathing normally.

Brief psychotic disorder. A psychotic disorder lasting from a day to a month that may follow exposure to a major stressor.

Bulimia nervosa. An eating disorder characterized by recurrent binge eating followed by self-induced purging, accompanied by overconcern with body weight and shape.

C

Cardiovascular disease. A disease or disorder of the cardiovascular system, such as coronary heart disease or hypertension.

Case study. A carefully drawn biography based on clinical interviews, observations, and psychological tests.

Cataplexy. A physical condition triggered by a strong emotional reaction that involves loss of muscle tone and voluntary muscle control, which may result in the person slumping or collapsing to the floor.

Catatonia. Gross disturbances in motor activity and cognitive functioning, as in a catatonic state or stupor.

Central nervous system. The brain and spinal cord.

Cerebellum. A structure in the hindbrain involved in coordination and balance.

Cerebral cortex. The wrinkled surface area of the cerebrum responsible for processing sensory stimuli and controlling higher mental functions, such as thinking and use of language.

Cerebrovascular accident (CVA). A stroke or brain damage resulting from a rupture or blockage of a blood vessel supplying oxygen to the brain.

Cerebrum. The large mass of the forebrain, consisting of the two cerebral hemispheres.

Childhood disintegrative disorder. Now diagnosed as autistic spectrum disorder, the disorder is characterized by loss of previously acquired skills and abnormal functioning following a period of apparently normal development during the first two years of life.

Childhood-onset fluency disorder. Persistent stuttering, which is characterized by impaired fluency of speech.

Circadian rhythm sleep-wake disorders. Sleep-wake disorders characterized by a mismatch between the body's normal sleep-wake cycle and the demands of the environment.

Civil commitment. The legal process of placing a person in a mental institution, even against his or her will.

Classical conditioning. A form of learning in which a response to one stimulus can be made to occur in response to another stimulus by pairing or associating the two stimuli.

Cocaine. A stimulant derived from the leaves of the coca plant.

Cognitive assessment. Measurement of thoughts, beliefs, and attitudes that may be associated with emotional problems.

Cognitive restructuring. A cognitive therapy method that involves replacing irrational thoughts with rational alternatives.

Cognitive therapy. A form of therapy that helps clients identify and correct faulty cognitions (thoughts, beliefs, and attitudes) believed to underlie their emotional problems and maladaptive behavior.

Cognitive triad of depression. The view that depression derives from adopting negative views of oneself, the environment or world at large, and the future.

Cognitive-behavioral therapy. A learning-based approach to therapy incorporating cognitive and behavioral techniques.

Cognitive-specificity hypothesis. The belief that different emotional disorders are linked to particular kinds of automatic thoughts.

Communication disorders. A class of psychological disorders characterized by difficulties in understanding or using language.

Competency to stand trial. The ability of criminal defendants to understand the charges and proceedings brought against them and to participate in their own defense.

Compulsion. A repetitive or ritualistic behavior that the person feels compelled to perform.

Conditional positive regard. Valuing other people on the basis of whether their behavior meets one's approval.

Conditioned response. In classical conditioning, a learned response to a previously neutral stimulus.

Conditioned stimulus. A previously neutral stimulus that evokes a conditioned response after repeated pairings with an unconditioned stimulus that had previously evoked that response.

Conduct disorder. A psychological disorder in childhood and adolescence characterized by disruptive, antisocial behavior.

Confidentiality. Protection of research participants by keeping records secure and not disclosing their identities.

Congruence. The coherence or fit among one's thoughts, behaviors, and feelings.

Conscious. To Freud, the part of the mind that corresponds to our present awareness.

Construct validity. The degree to which treatment effects can be accounted for by the theoretical mechanisms (constructs) represented in the independent variables.

Construct validity. The degree to which a test measures the hypothetical construct that it purports to measure.

Content validity. The degree to which the content of a test or measure represents the the traits it purports to measure.

Control group. In an experiment, a group that does not receive the experimental treatment.

Conversion disorder. A somatoform disorder characterized by loss or impairment of physical function in the absence of any apparent organic cause.

Correlation coefficient. A statistical measure of the strength of the relationship between two variables expressed along a continuum that ranges between –1.00 and +1.00.

Correlational method. A scientific method of study that examines the relationships between factors or variables expressed in statistical terms.

Countertransference. In psychoanalysis, the transfer of the analyst's feelings or attitudes toward other persons in her or his life onto the client.

Couple therapy. A form of therapy that focuses on resolving conflicts in distressed couples.

Crack. The hardened, smokable form of cocaine.

Criminal commitment. The legal process of confining a person found not guilty by reason of insanity in a mental institution.

Criterion validity. The degree to which a test correlates with an independent, external criterion or standard.

Critical thinking. Adoption of a questioning attitude and careful scrutiny of claims and arguments in light of evidence.

Culture-bound syndromes. Patterns of abnormal behavior found predominantly in only one or a few cultures.

Cyclothymic disorder. A mood disorder characterized by a chronic pattern of less severe mood swings than are found in bipolar disorder.

D

Defense mechanisms. The reality-distorting strategies used by the ego to shield the self from awareness of anxiety-provoking impulses.

Deinstitutionalization. The policy of shifting care for patients with severe or chronic mental health problems from inpatient facilities to community-based facilities.

Delayed ejaculation. Persistent or recurrent delay in achieving orgasm or inability to achieve orgasm despite a normal level of sexual interest and arousal. Formerly called male orgasmic disorder.

Delirium. A state of mental confusion, disorientation, and inability to focus attention.

Delusional disorder. A type of psychosis characterized by persistent delusions, often of a paranoid nature, that do not have the bizarre quality of the type found in paranoid schizophrenia.

Dementia praecox. The term given by Kraepelin to the disorder now called schizophrenia.

Dendrites. The rootlike structures at the ends of neurons that receive nerve impulses from other neurons.

Dependent personality disorder. A personality disorder characterized by difficulty making independent decisions and overly dependent behavior.

Dependent variables. Factors that are observed in order to determine the effects of manipulating an independent variable.

Depersonalization-derealization disorder. A dissociative disorder characterized by persistent or recurrent episodes of depersonalization and/or derealization.

Depersonalization. Feelings of unreality or detachment from one's self or one's body.

Depressant. A drug that lowers the level of activity of the central nervous system.

Derealization. A sense of unreality about the outside world.

Detoxification. The process of ridding the system of alcohol or other drugs under supervised conditions.

Dhat syndrome. A culture-bound disorder, found primarily among Asian Indian males, characterized by excessive fears over the loss of seminal fluid.

Diathesis. A vulnerability or predisposition to a particular disorder.

Diathesis–stress model. A model that posits that abnormal behavior problems involve the interaction of a vulnerability or predisposition and stressful life events or experiences.

Dissociative amnesia. A dissociative disorder in which a person experiences memory loss without any identifiable organic cause.

Dissociative disorder. A disorder characterized by disruption, or dissociation, of identity, memory, or consciousness.

Dissociative identity disorder. A dissociative disorder in which a person has two or more distinct, or alter, personalities.

Dopamine hypothesis. The prediction that schizophrenia involves overactivity of dopamine transmission in the brain.

Double depression. Concurrent major depressive disorder and dysthymia.

Down syndrome. A condition caused by the presence of an extra chromosome on the 21st pair and characterized by intellectual developmental disorder and various physical anomalies.

Downward drift hypothesis. A theory that attempts to explain the link between low socioeconomic status and behavior problems by suggesting that problem behaviors lead people to drift downward in social status.

Duty to warn. The therapist's obligation to warn third parties of threats made against them by clients.

Dyslexia. A learning disorder characterized by impaired reading ability.

E

Eating disorders. Psychological disorders characterized by disturbed patterns of eating and maladaptive ways of controlling body weight.

Eclectic therapy. An approach to psychotherapy that incorporates principles or techniques from various systems or theories.

Ego. The psychic structure that corresponds to the concept of the self, governed by the reality principle and characterized by the ability to tolerate frustration.

Ego dystonic. Referring to behaviors or feelings that are perceived to be alien to one's self-identity.

Ego psychology. Modern psychodynamic approach that focuses more on the conscious strivings of the ego than on the hypothesized unconscious functions of the id.

Ego syntonic. Referring to behaviors or feelings that are perceived as natural parts of the self.

Electroconvulsive therapy (ECT). A method of treating severe depression by administering electrical shock to the head.

Emotion-focused coping. A coping style that involves reducing the impact of a stressor by ignoring or escaping it rather than dealing with it directly.

Empathy. The ability to understand someone's experiences and feelings from that person's point of view.

Encopresis. Lack of control over bowel movements that is not caused by an organic problem in a child who is at least 4 years old.

Endocrine system. The system of ductless glands that secrete hormones directly into the bloodstream.

Endophenotypes. Measurable processes or mechanisms not apparent to the naked eye that explain how an organism's genetic code influences its observable characteristics or phenotypes.

Endorphins. Natural substances that function as neurotransmitters in the brain and are similar in their effects to opioids.

Enuresis. Failure to control urination after one has reached the expected age for attaining such control.

Epidemiological studies. Research studies that track rates of occurrence of particular disorders among different population groups.

Epigenetics. The study of heritable changes in processes affecting gene expression that occur without changes in the DNA itself, the chemical material that houses the genetic code.

Erectile disorder. A sexual dysfunction in males characterized by difficulty achieving or maintaining erection during sexual activity.

Erotomania. A delusional disorder characterized by the belief that one is loved by someone of high social status.

Exhaustion stage. The third stage of the GAS, characterized by lowered resistance, increased parasympathetic nervous system activity, and eventual physical deterioration.

Exhibitionism. A type of paraphilia almost exclusively occurring in males, in which the man experiences persistent and recurrent sexual urges and sexually arousing fantasies involving the exposure of his genitals to unsuspecting strangers.

Expectancies. Beliefs about expected outcomes.

Experimental group. In an experiment, a group that receives the experimental treatment.

Experimental method. A scientific method that aims to discover cause-and-effect relationships by manipulating independent variables and observing the effects on the dependent variables.

External validity. The degree to which experimental results can be generalized to other settings and conditions.

Eye movement desensitization and reprocessing (EMDR). A controversial form of therapy for PTSD that involves the client's eye tracking of a visual target while holding images of the traumatic experience in mind.

F

Factitious disorder. A disorder characterized by intentional fabrication of psychological or physical symptoms for no apparent gain.

Family therapy. A form of therapy in which the family, not the individual, is the unit of treatment.

Fear-stimulus hierarchy. An ordered series of increasingly fearful stimuli.

Female orgasmic disorder. A type of sexual dysfunction involving persistent difficulty achieving orgasm despite adequate stimulation.

Female sexual interest/arousal disorder. A type of sexual dysfunction in women involving difficulty becoming sexually aroused or lack of sexual excitement or pleasure during sexual activity.

Fetishism. A type of paraphilia in which a person uses an inanimate object as a focus of sexual interest and as a source of arousal.

Fight-or-flight reaction. The inborn tendency to respond to a threat by either fighting or fleeing.

Fixation. In Freudian theory, a constellation of personality traits associated with a particular stage of psychosexual development, resulting from either too much or too little gratification at that stage.

Flooding. A behavior therapy technique for overcoming fears by means of exposure to high levels of fear-inducing stimuli.

Fragile X syndrome. An inherited form of intellectual developmental disorder caused by a mutated gene on the X chromosome.

Free association. The method of verbalizing thoughts as they occur without a conscious attempt to edit or censor them.

Frotteurism. A type of paraphilia involving sexual urges or sexually arousing fantasies about bumping and rubbing against nonconsenting persons for sexual gratification.

G

Gambling disorder. An addictive disorder characterized by a pattern of habitual gambling and impaired control over the behavior.

Gender dysphoria. A psychological disorder characterized by strong and persistent discomfort or distress about one's biologic or anatomic sex.

Gender identity. One's psychological sense of being female or being male.

General adaptation syndrome (GAS). The body's three-stage response to prolonged or intense stress.

General paresis. A form of dementia resulting from neurosyphilis.

Generalized anxiety disorder (GAD). A type of anxiety disorder characterized by general feelings of dread and foreboding and heightened states of bodily arousal.

Genito-pelvic pain/penetration disorder. Persistent or recurrent pain experienced during vaginal intercourse or penetration attempts.

Genotype. The set of traits specified by an individual's genetic code.

Genuineness. The ability to recognize and express one's true feelings.

Gradual exposure. A behavior therapy technique for overcoming fears through direct exposure to increasingly fearful stimuli.

Gradual exposure. In behavior therapy, a method of overcoming fears through a stepwise process of exposure to increasingly fearful stimuli in imagination or in real-life situations.

Group therapy. A form of therapy in which a group of clients with similar problems meets together with a therapist.

H

Hallucinations. Perceptions occurring in the absence of external stimuli that become confused with reality.

Hallucinogens. Substances that cause hallucinations.

Health psychologist. A psychologist who studies the interrelationships between psychological factors and physical health.

Heroin. A narcotic derived from morphine that has strong addictive properties.

Histrionic personality disorder. A personality disorder characterized by excessive need for attention, praise, reassurance, and approval.

Hoarding disorder. A psychological disorder characterized by strong needs to acquire and resistance to discarding large collections of seemingly useless or unneeded possessions.

Hormones. Substances secreted by endocrine glands that regulate body functions and promote growth and development.

Humors. According to the ancient Hippocratic belief system, the vital bodily fluids (phlegm, black bile, blood, yellow bile).

Huntington's disease. An inherited degenerative disease that is characterized by jerking and twisting movements, paranoia, and mental deterioration.

Hypersomnolence disorder. Persistent pattern of excessive sleepiness during the day.

Hypnagogic hallucinations. Hallucinations occurring at the threshold between wakefulness and sleep onset or shortly upon awakening.

Hypochondriasis. A pattern of abnormal behavior characterized by misinterpretation of physical symptoms as signs of underlying serious disease, now classified as a form of either somatic symptom disorder or illness anxiety disorder.

Hypomania. A relatively mild state of mania.

Hypothalamus. A structure in the forebrain involved in regulating body temperature, emotion, and motivation.

Hypothesis. A prediction that is tested through experimentation.

Hypoxia. Decreased supply of oxygen to the brain or other organs.

Hypoxyphilia. A paraphilia in which a person seeks sexual gratification by being deprived of oxygen by means of a noose, plastic bag, chemical, or pressure on the chest.

I

Id. The unconscious psychic structure, present at birth, that contains primitive instincts and is regulated by the pleasure principle.

Illness anxiety disorder. A somatic symptom disorder characterized by unduly high levels of anxiety or concerns about having a serious illness, even though physical symptoms are either absent or minor.

Immune system. The body's system of defense against disease.

Impulse control disorders. Psychological disorders characterized by failure to control impulses, temptations, or drives, resulting in harm to oneself or others.

Incidence. The number of new cases of a disorder that occurs within a specific period of time.

Independent variables. Factors that are manipulated in experiments.

Infarction. The development of an infarct, or area of dead or dying tissue, resulting from the blocking of blood vessels normally supplying the tissue.

Informed consent. The principle that research participants should receive enough information about an experiment beforehand to decide freely whether to participate.

Insanity defense. A legal defense in which a defendant in a criminal case pleads not guilty on the basis of insanity.

Insomnia disorder. A sleep-wake disorder characterized by chronic or persistent insomnia not caused by another psychological or physical disorder or by the effects of drugs or medications.

Insomnia. Difficulties falling asleep, remaining asleep, or achieving restorative sleep.

Intellectual disability (ID). A generalized delay or impairment in the development of intellectual and adaptive abilities.

Intermittent explosive disorder. A type of impulse-control disorder characterized by impulsive aggression.

Internal validity. The degree to which manipulation of the independent variables can be causally related to changes in the dependent variables.

K

Kleptomania. A type of impulse control disorder characterized by compulsive stealing.

Koro syndrome. A culture-bound disorder, found primarily in China, in which people fear that their genitals are shrinking and retracting into their bodies.

Korsakoff's syndrome. A syndrome associated with chronic alcoholism that is characterized by memory loss and disorientation.

L

Language disorder. A type of communication disorder characterized by difficulties understanding or using language.

Learned helplessness. A behavior pattern characterized by passivity and perceptions of lack of control.

Learning disorder. A deficiency in a specific learning ability in the context of normal intelligence and exposure to learning opportunities.

Lewy bodies. Abnormal protein deposits in brain cells that cause a form of dementia.

Limbic system. A group of forebrain structures involved in emotional processing; memory; basic drives such as hunger, thirst, and aggression.

Longitudinal study. A research study in which subjects are followed over time.

M

Major depressive disorder. A severe mood disorder characterized by major depressive episodes.

Major neurocognitive disorder. Profound deterioration of cognitive functioning, characterized by deficits in memory, thinking, judgment, and language use. Formerly called *dementia* in earlier versions of the *DSM*.

Male hypoactive sexual desire disorder. Persistent or recurrent lack of sexual interest or sexual fantasies in men.

Malingering. Faking illness to avoid work or duty.

Mania. A state of unusual elation, energy, and activity.

Manic episode. A period of unrealistically heightened euphoria, extreme restlessness, and excessive activity characterized by disorganized behavior and impaired judgment.

Marijuana. A hallucinogenic drug derived from the leaves and stems of the plant Cannabis sativa.

Medical model. A biological perspective in which abnormal behavior is viewed as symptomatic of underlying illness.

Medulla. An area of the hindbrain involved in regulation of heartbeat, respiration, and blood pressure.

Methadone. A synthetic opiate that does not produce a pleasurable high when used properly, but which can avert withdrawal symptoms in people with heroin addiction when they stop using heroin.

Mild neurocognitive disorder. Mild deterioration of cognitive functioning in which the person is able to perform tasks of daily living, but needs to put in greater effort or compensate in other ways to maintain independent functioning.

Modeling. A behavior therapy technique for helping an individual acquire a target behavior by observing a therapist or another individual demonstrate the target behavior and then imitating it.

Modeling. Learning by observing and imitating the behavior of others.

Mood disorders. Psychological disorders characterized by unusually severe or prolonged disturbances of mood.

Morphine. A strongly addictive narcotic derived from the opium poppy that relieves pain and induces feelings of well-being.

Münchausen syndrome. A type of factitious disorder characterized by the fabrication of medical symptoms.

Myelin sheath. The insulating layer or protective coating of the axon that helps speed transmission of nerve impulses.

N

Naltrexone. A drug that blocks the high from alcohol as well as from opiates.

Narcissistic personality disorder. A personality disorder characterized by an inflated self-image and extreme needs for attention and admiration.

Narcolepsy. A sleep disorder characterized by sudden, irresistible episodes of sleep.

Narcotics. Drugs that are used medically for pain relief but that have strong addictive potential.

Naturalistic observation method. A research method in which behavior is observed and measured in its natural environment.

Negative reinforcers. Reinforcers that, when removed, increase the frequency of the preceding behavior.

Negative symptoms. Behavioral deficiencies associated with schizophrenia, such as social skills deficits, social withdrawal, flattened affect, poverty of speech and thought, psychomotor retardation, and failure to experience pleasure.

Neurocognitive disorders. A class of psychological disorders characterized by impairments in cognitive abilities and daily functioning that involve underlying brain disorders or abnormalities.

Neurodevelopmental disorders. A category of mental disorders in the *DSM-5* affecting children and adolescents that involve impaired brain functioning or development.

Neurons. Nerve cells.

Neuropsychological assessment. Measurement of behavior or performance that may be indicative of underlying brain damage or defects.

Neurotransmitters. Chemical substances that transmit messages from one neuron to another.

Nightmare disorder. A sleep-wake disorder characterized by recurrent awakenings due to frightening nightmares.

Nonspecific treatment factors. Factors not specific to any one form of psychotherapy, such as therapist attention and support and creating positive expectancies of change.

O

Obesity. A condition of excess body fat; generally defined by a BMI of 30 or higher.

Objective tests. Self-report personality tests that can be scored objectively and that are based on a research foundation.

Object-relations theory. The psychodynamic viewpoint that focuses on the influences of internalized representations of the personalities of parents and other strong attachment figures (called "objects").

Obsession. A recurring thought, image, or urge that the individual cannot control.

Obsessive–compulsive disorder (OCD). A type of anxiety disorder characterized by recurrent obsessions, compulsions, or both.

Obsessive–compulsive personality disorder. A personality disorder characterized by rigid ways of relating to others, perfectionistic tendencies, lack of spontaneity, and excessive attention to detail.

Obstructive sleep apnea hypopnea syndrome. A subtype of breathing-related sleep disorders, more commonly called obstructive sleep apnea. It typically involves repeated episodes during sleep of snorting or gasping for breath, pauses of breath, or abnormally shallow breathing.

Operant conditioning. A form of learning in which behavior is acquired and strengthened when it is reinforced.

Oppositional defiant disorder (ODD). A psychological disorder in childhood and adolescence characterized by excessive oppositionality or tendencies to refuse requests from parents and others.

P

Panic disorder. A type of anxiety disorder characterized by repeated episodes of intense anxiety or panic.

Paranoid personality disorder. A personality disorder characterized by undue suspiciousness of others' motives, but not to the point of delusion.

Paraphilias. Atypical patterns of sexual attraction in which one experiences recurrent sexual urges and sexually arousing fantasies involving nonhuman objects (such as articles of clothing), inappropriate or nonconsenting partners (e.g., children), or situations producing humiliation or pain to oneself or one's partner.

Parasomnias. Sleep-wake disorders involving abnormal behavior patterns associated with partial or incomplete arousals.

Parasympathetic nervous system. The division of the autonomic nervous system whose activity reduces states of arousal and regulates bodily processes that replenish energy reserves.

Parkinson's disease. A progressive disease characterized by muscle tremor and shakiness, rigidity, difficulty walking, poor control of fine motor movements, lack of facial muscle tone, and in some cases, cognitive impairment.

Pedophilia. A type of paraphilia involving sexual attraction to children.

Peripheral nervous system. The somatic and autonomic nervous systems.

Persistent depressive disorder. A mild but chronic type of depressive disorder. Also called *dysthymia.*

Personality disorders. Excessively rigid behavior patterns, or ways of relating to others, that ultimately become self-defeating.

Person-centered therapy. The establishment of a warm, accepting therapeutic relationship that frees clients to engage in self-exploration and achieve self-acceptance.

Phenotype. An individual's actual or expressed traits.

Phenylketonuria (PKU). A genetic disorder that prevents the metabolization of phenylpyruvic acid, leading to intellectual developmental disorder unless the diet is strictly controlled.

Phobia. An excessive, irrational fear.

Physical dependence. Bodily changes resulting from regular use of a drug, as denoted by the development of tolerance and/or a withdrawal syndrome (also called chemical dependence).

Physiological assessment. Measurement of physiological responses that may be associated with abnormal behavior.

Pick's disease. A form of dementia, similar to Alzheimer's disease, but distinguished by specific abnormalities (Pick's bodies) in nerve cells and the absence of neurofibrillary tangles and plaques.

Placebo. An inert medication or bogus treatment that is intended to control for expectancy effects.

Pleasure principle. The governing principle of the id, involving demands for immediate gratification of needs.

Pons. A structure in the hindbrain involved in body movements, attention, sleep, and respiration.

Positive psychology. A growing contemporary movement within psychology that focuses on the positive attributes of human behavior.

Positive reinforcers. Reinforcers that, when introduced, increase the frequency of the preceding behavior.

Positive symptoms. Flagrant symptoms of schizophrenia, such as hallucinations, delusions, bizarre behavior, and thought disorder.

Postpartum depression (PPD). Persistent and severe mood changes that occur after childbirth.

Posttraumatic stress disorder (PTSD). A prolonged maladaptive reaction to a traumatic event.

Preconscious. To Freud, the part of the mind whose contents lie outside present awareness but can be brought into awareness by focusing on them.

Premature (early) ejaculation. A type of sexual dysfunction involving a pattern of unwanted rapid ejaculation during sexual activity.

Presenile dementias. Forms of dementia that begin at or before age 65.

Prevalence. The overall number of cases of a disorder in a population within a specific period of time.

Proband. The case first diagnosed with a given disorder.

Problem-focused coping. A coping style that involves confronting a stressor directly.

Prodromal phase. In schizophrenia, the period of decline in functioning that precedes the first acute psychotic episode.

Projective tests. Psychological tests that present ambiguous stimuli onto which the examinee is thought to project his or her personality and unconscious motives.

Psychoanalysis. The method of psychotherapy developed by Sigmund Freud.

Psychoanalytic theory. The theoretical model of personality developed by Sigmund Freud, based on the belief that psychological problems are rooted in unconscious motives and conflicts from childhood; also called psychoanalysis.

Psychodynamic model. The theoretical model of Freud and his followers, in which abnormal behavior is viewed as the product of clashing forces within the personality.

Psychodynamic therapy. Therapy that helps individuals gain insight into, and resolve, deep-seated conflicts in the unconscious mind.

Psychological dependence. Compulsive use of a substance to meet a psychological need.

Psychological disorder. Abnormal behavior pattern that involves impairment of psychological functioning or behavior.

Psychological hardiness. A cluster of stress-buffering traits characterized by commitment, challenge, and control.

Psychopharmacology. The field of study that examines the effects of therapeutic or psychiatric drugs.

Psychosis. A severe form of disturbed behavior characterized by impaired ability to interpret reality and difficulty meeting the demands of daily life.

Psychosomatic. Pertaining to a physical disorder in which psychological factors play a causal or contributing role.

Psychotherapy. A structured form of treatment derived from a psychological framework that consists of one or more verbal interactions or treatment sessions between a client and a therapist.

Punishment. Application of aversive or painful stimuli that reduces the frequency of the behavior it follows.

Pyromania. A type of impulse-control disorder characterized by compulsive fire-setting.

R

Random assignment. A method of assigning research subjects at random to experimental or control groups to balance the characteristics of people who comprise them.

Random sample. A sample that is drawn in such a way that every member of a population has an equal chance of being included.

Rape. Forced penetration of the vagina or anus by any body part or object, or of the mouth by a sexual organ [Prior to 2012, the definition of rape used by law enforcement officials authorities was limited to forced sexual intercourse].

Rapid eye movement sleep behavior disorder (RBD). A sleep-wake disorder characterized by vocalizing parts of a dream or thrashing about during a dream.

Rational emotive behavior therapy. A therapeutic approach that focuses on helping clients replace irrational, maladaptive beliefs with alternative, more adaptive beliefs.

Reality principle. The governing principle of the ego, which involves considerations of social acceptability and practicality.

Reality testing. The ability to perceive the world accurately and to distinguish reality from fantasy.

Rebound anxiety. The experiencing of strong anxiety following withdrawal from a tranquilizer.

Receptor site. A part of a dendrite on a receiving neuron that is structured to receive a neurotransmitter.

Reinforcement. A stimulus or event that increases the frequency of the response that it follows.

Reliability. In psychological assessment, the consistency of a measure or diagnostic instrument or system.

REM sleep behavior disorder. The disorder when muscle paralysis is absent or incomplete and a person may suddenly kick or flail the arms during REM sleep, potentially causing injuries to the self or the bed partner.

Residual phase. In schizophrenia, the phase that follows an acute phase, characterized by a return to the level of functioning of the prodromal phase.

Resistance stage. The second stage of the GAS, involving the body's attempt to withstand prolonged stress and preserve resources.

Reticular activating system. Brain structure involved in processes of attention, sleep, and arousal.

Retrograde amnesia. Loss or impairment of ability to recall past events.

Reversal design. An experimental design that consists of repeated measurement of a subject's behavior through a sequence of alternating baseline and treatment phases.

S

Sadomasochism. Sexual activities between partners involving that attainment of gratification by means of inflicting and receiving pain and humiliation.

Sanism. The negative stereotyping of people who are identified as mentally ill.

Schizoaffective disorder. A type of psychotic disorder in which individuals experience both severe mood disturbance and features associated with schizophrenia.

Schizoid personality disorder. A personality disorder characterized by persistent lack of interest in social relationships, flattened affect, and social withdrawal.

Schizophrenia. A chronic psychotic disorder characterized by severely disturbed behavior, thinking, emotions, and perceptions.

Schizophreniform disorder. A psychotic disorder lasting less than 6 months in duration, with features that resemble schizophrenia.

Schizotypal personality disorder. A personality disorder characterized by lack of close personal relationships and eccentricities of thought and behavior, but without clearly psychotic features.

Scientific method. A systematic method of conducting scientific research in which theories or assumptions are examined in light of evidence.

Selection factor. A type of bias in which differences between experimental and control groups result from differences in the types of participants in the group, not from the influence of the independent variable.

Self-actualization. In humanistic psychology, the tendency to strive to become all that one is capable of being; the motive that drives one to reach one's full potential and express one's unique capabilities.

Self-efficacy expectancies. Beliefs in one's ability to cope with challenges and to accomplish particular tasks.

Self-monitoring. The process of observing or recording one's own behaviors, thoughts, or emotions.

Semistructured interview. A clinical interview in which the clinician follows a general outline of questions designed to gather essential information but is free to ask them in any order and to branch off in other directions.

Senile dementias. Forms of dementia that begin after age 65.

Separation anxiety disorder. A childhood disorder characterized by extreme fear of separation from parents or other caretakers.

Sexual dysfunctions. Persistent or recurrent problems with sexual interest, arousal, or response.

Sexual masochism. A type of paraphilia characterized by sexual urges and sexually arousing fantasies about receiving humiliation or pain.

Sexual sadism. A type of paraphilia or sexual deviation characterized by recurrent sexual urges and sexually arousing fantasies about inflicting humiliation or physical pain on sex partners.

Single-case experimental design. A type of case study in which the subject is used as his or her own control.

Sleep paralysis. A temporary state of muscle paralysis upon awakening.

Sleep terrors. A sleep-wake disorder characterized by recurrent episodes of terror-induced arousals during sleep.

Sleepwalking. A sleep-wake disorder involving repeated episodes of sleepwalking.

Sleep-wake disorders. Persistent or recurrent sleep-related problems that cause distress or impaired functioning.

Social (pragmatic) communication disorder. A type of communication disorder characterized by difficulties communicating with others in social contexts.

Social anxiety disorder. Excessive fear of social interactions or situations. Also called *social phobia*.

Social causation model. A belief that social stressors, such as poverty, account for the greater risk of severe psychological disorders among people of lower socioeconomic status.

Social-cognitive theory. A learning-based theory that emphasizes observational learning and incorporates roles for cognitive variables in determining behavior.

Somatic nervous system. The division of the peripheral nervous system that relays information from the sense organs to the brain and transmits messages from the brain to the skeletal muscles.

Somatic symptom and related disorders. A category of psychological disorders characterized by persistent emotional or behavioral problems relating to physical symptoms.

Somatic symptom disorder. A psychological disorder characterized by excessive concerns about one's physical symptoms.

Specific phobia. A phobia that is specific to a particular object or situation.

Speech fluency disorder (stuttering). A type of communication disorder characterized by difficulties with speech fluency.

Speech sound disorder. A type of communication disorder characterized by difficulties in articulating speech.

Splitting. An inability to reconcile the positive and negative aspects of the self and others, resulting in sudden shifts between positive and negative feelings toward others.

Stimulants. Psychoactive substances that increase the activity of the central nervous system.

Stress. A demand made on an organism to adapt or adjust.

Stressor. A source of stress.

Structured interview. A clinical interview that follows a preset series of questions in a particular order.

Substance intoxication. A type of substance-induced disorder characterized by repeated episodes of intoxication.

Substance use disorders. Substance-related disorders characterized by maladaptive use of psychoactive substances, leading to significant impairment of functioning or personal distress.

Substance withdrawal. A type of substance-induced disorder characterized by a cluster of symptoms following the sudden reduction or cessation of use of a psychoactive substance after physical dependence has developed.

Substance-induced disorders. A category of substance-related disorders induced by using psychoactive substance.

Superego. The psychic structure that incorporates the values of our parents and important others and functions as a moral conscience.

Survey method. A research method in which large samples of people are questioned by means of a survey instrument.

Sympathetic nervous system. The division of the autonomic nervous system whose activity leads to heightened states of arousal.

Synapse. The junction between one neuron and another through which nerve impulses pass.

Systematic desensitization. A behavior therapy technique for overcoming phobias by means of exposure to progressively more fearful stimuli (in imagination or by viewing slides) while remaining deeply relaxed.

T

Tardive dyskinesia (TD). A disorder characterized by involuntary movements of the face, mouth, neck, trunk, or extremities caused by long-term use of antipsychotic medication.

Terminals. The small branching structures at the tips of axons.

Thalamus. A structure in the forebrain involved in relaying sensory information to the cortex and in regulating sleep and attention.

Theory. A formulation of the relationships underlying observed events.

Thought disorder. A disturbance in thinking characterized by the breakdown of logical associations between thoughts.

Token economy. A behavioral treatment program in which a controlled environment is created in which desirable behaviors are reinforced by dispensing tokens that may be exchanged for desired rewards.

Tolerance. Physical habituation to a drug in which frequent use leads to higher doses being needed to achieve the same effects.

Transference relationship. In psychoanalysis, the client's transfer or generalization to the analyst of feelings and attitudes the client holds toward important figures in his or her life.

Transgender identity. A type of gender identity in which one's psychological experience of oneself as male or female is opposite to one's physical or genetic sex.

Transvestic fetishism. A type of paraphilia characterized by sexual urges and fantasies involving cross-dressing. Also termed *transvestism.*

Trephination. A harsh, prehistoric practice of cutting a hole in a person's skull, possibly in an attempt to release demons.

Two-factor model. A theoretical model that accounts for the development of phobic reactions on the basis of classical and operant conditioning.

Type A behavior pattern (TABP). A behavior pattern characterized by a sense of time urgency, competitiveness, and hostility.

U

Unconditional positive regard. Valuing other people as having basic worth regardless of their behavior at a particular time.

Unconditioned response. An unlearned response.

Unconditioned stimulus. A stimulus that elicits an unlearned response.

Unconscious. To Freud, the part of the mind that lies outside the range of ordinary awareness and that contains instinctual urges.

Unstructured interview. A clinical interview in which the clinician adopts his or her own style of questioning rather than following any standard format.

V

Vaginismus. The involuntary spasm of the muscles surrounding the vagina when vaginal penetration is attempted, making sexual intercourse difficult or impossible.

Validity. The degree to which a test or diagnostic system measures the traits or constructs it purports to measure.

Vascular neurocognitive disorder. Dementia resulting from repeated strokes that cause damage in the brain.

Virtual reality therapy. A form of exposure therapy involving the presentation of phobic stimuli in a virtual reality environment.

Voyeurism. A type of paraphilia involving sexual urges and sexually arousing fantasies focused on acts of watching unsuspecting others who are naked, in the act of undressing, or engaging in sexual activity.

W

Wernicke's disease. A brain disorder, associated with chronic alcoholism, characterized by confusion, disorientation, and difficulty maintaining balance while walking.

Withdrawal syndrome. A cluster of physical and psychological symptoms arising following abrupt withdrawal from use of a psychoactive substance.

A

A children's mental illness "crisis": Report: 1 in 10 children suffers enough to impair development. (2001, January 3). *MSNBC.com*. Retrieved from http://www.msnbc.com/news/510934.asp

A step toward controlling Huntington's disease? Potential new way of blocking activity of gene that causes HD. (2011, June 23). *ScienceDaily*. Retrieved from http://www.sciencedaily.com

Abbey, A., Zawackia, T., Bucka, O., Clinton, A. M., & McAuslan, P. (2004). Sexual assault and alcohol consumption: What do we know about their relationship and what types of research are still needed? *Aggression and Violent Behavior, 9,* 271–303. doi:10.1016/S1359-1789(03) 00011-9

Abela, J. R. Z., Stolow, D., Mineka, S., Yao, S., Zhu, X. Z., & Hankin, B. L. (2011). Cognitive vulnerability to depressive symptoms in adolescents in urban and rural Hunan, China: A multiwave longitudinal study. *Journal of Abnormal Psychology, 120,* 765–778. doi:10.1037/a0025295escents

Abraham, K. (1948). The first pregenital stage of the libido. In D. Bryan & A. Strachey (Eds.), *Selected papers of Karl Abraham, M.D.* London: The Hogarth Press. (Original work published 1916.)

Abramowitz, J. S. (2008). Cognitive-behavioral therapy for OCD. *Clinical Psychology Review, 21,* 683–703.

Abramowitz, J. S., & Braddock, A. E. (2008). *Psychological treatment of health anxiety and hypochondriasis: A biopsychosocial approach.* Toronto, CA: Hogrefe & Huber.

Abramowitz, J. S., & Braddock, A. E. (2011). *Hypochondriasis and health anxiety. Advances in psychotherapy—evidence-based practice.* Cambridge, MA: Hogrefe Publishing.

Abramowitz, J. S., Olatunji, B. O., & Deacon, B. J. (2008). Health anxiety, hypochondriasis, and the anxiety disorders. *Behavior Therapy, 38,* 86–94. doi:10.1016/j.beth.2006.05.001

Abramson, L. T., Seligman, M. E. P., & Teasdale, J. D. (1978). Learned helplessness in humans: Critique and reformulation. *Journal of Abnormal Psychology, 87,* 49–74.

Achenbach, T. M., & Dumenci, L. (2001). Levent advances in empirically based assessment: Revised cross-informant syndromes and new DSM-oriented scales for the CBCL, YSR, and TRF: Comment on Lengua, Sadowski, Friedrich, and Fisher (2001). *Journal of Consulting and Clinical Psychology, 69,* 699–702. doi:10.1037/0022-006X.69.4.699

Adam, M. B., McGuire, J. K., Walsh, M., Basta, J., & LeCroy, C. (2005). Acculturation as a predictor of the onset of sexual intercourse among Hispanic and white teens. *Archives of Pediatrics & Adolescent Medicine, 159,* 261–265.

Addington, J., Piskulic, D., & Marshall, C. (2010). Psychosocial treatments for schizophrenia. *Current Directions in Psychological Science, 19,* 260–263. doi:10.1177/0963721410377743

Addis, M. E. (2008). Gender and depression in men. *Clinical Psychology: Science and Practice, 15,* 153–168. doi:10.1111/j.1468-2850.2008.00125.x

Addolorato, G., Leggio, L., Abenavoli, L., Gasbarrini, G., & on behalf of the Alcoholism Treatment Study Group. (2005). Neurobiochemical and clinical aspects of craving in alcohol addiction: A review. *Addictive Behaviors, 30,* 1209–1224. doi:10.1016/j.addbeh.2004.12.011

Adelson, R. (2006, January). Cultural factors in alcohol abuse. *Monitor on Psychology, 37*(1), 32.

Adler, J. (2004, March 8). The war on strokes. *Newsweek,* 42–48.

Adriano, F., Spoletini, I., Caltagirone, C., & Spalletta, G. (2010). Updated meta-analyses reveal thalamus volume reduction in patients with first-episode and chronic schizophrenia. *Schizophrenia Research, 123,* 1–14.

Afifi, T. O., Asmundson, G. J. G., Taylor, S., & Jang, K. L. (2010). The role of genes and environment on trauma exposure and posttraumatic stress disorder symptoms: A review of twin studies. *Clinical Psychology Review, 30,* 101–112. doi:10.1016/j.cpr.2009.10.002

Afifi, T. O., Mota, N. P., Dasiewicz, P., MacMillan, H. L., & Sareen, J. (2012). Physical punishment and mental disorders: Results from a nationally representative US sample. *Pediatrics,* published online ahead of print July 2, 2012, doi:10.1542/peds.2011-2947 doi: 10.1542/peds.2011-2947

Agren, T., Engman, J., Frick, A., Björkstrand, J., Larsson, E.-M., Furmark, T., & Fredrikson, M. (2012). Disruption of reconsolidation erases a fear memory trace in the human amygdala. *Science, 337,* 1550. doi:http://dx.doi.org/10.1126/science.1223006

Aguilera, A., & Muñoz, R. F. (2011). Text messaging as an adjunct to CBT in low-income populations: A usability and feasibility pilot study. *Professional Psychology: Research and Practice, 42,* 472–478. doi: 10.1037/a0025499

Ainsworth, M. D. S. (1989). Attachments beyond infancy. *American Psychologist, 44,* 709–716.

Akhtar, S. (1988). Four culture-bound psychiatric syndromes in India. *The International Journal of Social Psychiatry, 34,* 70–74.

Akiskal, H. S., & Benazzi, F. (2006). The *DSM-IV* and *ICD-10* categories of recurrent [major] depressive and bipolar II disorders: Evidence that they lie on a dimensional spectrum. *Journal of Affective Disorders, 92,* 45–54.

Alarcón, R. D., Becker, A. E., Lewis-Fernández, R., Like, R. C., Desai, P., Foulks, E., et al. (2009). Issues for *DSM-V:* The role of culture in psychiatric diagnosis. *The Journal of Nervous and Mental Disease, 197,* 559–660. doi:10.1097/NMD.0b013e3181b0cbff

Albarracín, D., Durantini, M. R., & Ear, A. (2006). Empirical and theoretical conclusions of an analysis of outcomes of HIV-prevention interventions. *Current Directions in Psychological Science, 15,* 73–78.

Albert, M. S., Dickson, D., Dubois, B., Feldman, H. H., Fox, N. C., Gamst, A., . . . Phelps, C. H. (2011). The diagnosis of mild cognitive impairment due to Alzheimer's disease: Recommendations from the National Institute on Aging and Alzheimer's Association workgroup. *Alzheimers Dementia, 7,* 70.

Aldrich, M. S. (1992). Narcolepsy. *Neurology, 42* (7, Suppl. 6), 34–43.

Aleccia, J. (2011, December 17). Lingering shortage of ADHD drugs unravels lives. *MSNBC.com*. Retrieved from http://vitals.msnbc.msn.com/_news/2011/12/15/9472468-lingering-shortage-of-adhd-drugs-unravels-lives

Alexander, B., Warner-Schmidt, J., Eriksson, T., Tamminga, C., Arango-Llievano, M., Ghose, S., . . . Kaplitt, M. G. (2010). Reversal of depressed behaviors in mice by p11 gene therapy in the nucleus accumbens. *Science Translational Medicine, 2,* 54ra76. doi:1s0.1126/scitranslmed.3001079

Alexander, G. C., Gallagher, S. A., Mascola, A., Moloney, R. M., & Stafford, R. S. (2011). Increasing off-label use of antipsychotic medications in the United States, 1995–2008. *Pharmacoepidemiology and Drug Safety, 173,* 271. doi:10.1002/pds.2082

Ali, M., Farooq, N., Bhatti, M. A., & Kuroiwa, C. (2012). Assessment of prevalence and determinants of posttraumatic stress disorder in survivors of earthquake in Pakistan using Davidson Trauma Scale. *Journal of Affective Disorders, 136,* 238–243.

Allderidge, P. (1979). Hospitals, madhouses and asylums: Cycles in the care of the insane. *British Journal of Psychiatry, 134,* 1476–1478.

Allen, D. N., Thaler, N. S., Ringdahl, E. N., Barney, S. J., & Mayfield, J. (2011). Comprehensive trail making test performance in children and adolescents with traumatic brain injury. *Psychological Assessment,* in press. doi:10.1037/a0026263

Allen, D. N.,Thaler, N. S., Ringdahl, E. N., Barney, S. J., & Mayfield, J. (2011). Comprehensive trail making test performance in children and adolescents with traumatic brain injury. *Psychological Assessment, 24,* 556–564. doi: 10.1037/a0026263

Allgulander, C., Dahl, A. A., Austin, C., Morris, P. L. P., Sogaard, J. A., Fayyad, R., . . . Clary, C. M. (2004). Efficacy of sertraline in a 12-week trial for generalized anxiety disorder. *American Journal of Psychiatry, 161,* 1642–1649.

Alloy, L. B., Abramson, L. Y., Urosevic, S., Bender, R. E., & Wagner, C. A. (2009). Longitudinal predictors of bipolar spectrum disorders: A behavioral approach system perspective. *Clinical Psychology: Science and Practice, 16,* 206–226. doi:10.1111/j.1468-2850.2009.01160.x

Alloy, L. B., Abramson, L. Y., Urosevic, S., Walshaw, P. D., Nusslock, R., & Neeren, A. M. (2005). The psychosocial context of bipolar disorder: Environmental, cognitive, and developmental risk factors. *Clinical Psychology Review, 25,* 1043–1075.

Allsop, D. J., Copeland, J., Norberg, M. M., Fu, S., Molnar, A., Lewis, J., & Budney, A. J. (2012). Quantifying the clinical significance of cannabis withdrawal. *PLoS ONE, 7*(9), e44864. doi:10.1371/journal.pone.0044864

Althof, S. E. (2012). Psychological interventions for delayed ejaculation/orgasm. *International Journal of Impotence Research, 24,* 131–136. doi:10.1038/ijir.2012.2.

Althof, S. E., Berner, M. M., Goldstein, I., Claes, H. I. M., Cappelleri, J. C., Bushmakin, A. G., . . . Schnetzler, G. (2010). Interrelationship of sildenafil treatment effects on the physiological and psychosocial aspects of erectile dysfunction of mixed or organic etiology. *Journal of Sexual Medicine, 7,* 3170–3178.

Althouse, R. (2010). Jails are nation's largest institutions for mentally ill. *National Psychologist, 19*(6), 1, 5.

Alvarez, P., Puente, V. M., Blasco, M. J., Salgado, P., Merino, A., & Bulbena, A. (2012). Concurrent Koro and Cotard syndromes in a Spanish male patient with a psychotic depression and cerebrovascular disease. *Psychopathology, 45,* 126–129. doi: 10.1159/000329739

Alzheimer's Disease: Are plaques and tangles a symptom, not the cause? (2011, January 11). *ScienceDaily*. Retrieved from http://www.sciencedaily.com/releases/2010/12/101214181932.htm.

Alzheimer's risk gene disrupts brain's wiring 50 years before disease hits. (2011, May 16). *ScienceDaily*. Retrieved from http://www.sciencedaily.com.

Alzheimer's Society (2008, October). *Genetics and dementia.* Retrieved from http://alzheimers.org.uk/site/scripts/documents_info.php?documentID=

American Heart Association. (2009). Heart disease and stroke statistics 2009 update: A report from the American Heart Association Statistics Committee and Stroke Statistics Subcommittee. *Circulation, 119,* e21–e181. doi:10.1161/CIRCULATIONAHA.108.191261

American Law Institute. (1962). *Model penal code: Proposed official draft.* Philadelphia, PA: Author.

American Psychiatric Association. (1998). *Fact sheet: Violence and mental illness.* Washington, DC: Author.

American Psychiatric Association. (2000). *DSM-IV-TR: Diagnostic and statistical manual of mental disorders* (4th ed., Text Revision). Washington, DC: Author.

American Psychiatric Association. (2013). *DSM-5: Diagnostic and statistical manual of mental disorders* (5th ed.). Washington, DC: Author.

American Psychological Association (2010). *Stress in America 2011: Executive summary.* Retrieved from http://www.apa.org/news/press/releases/stress-exec-summary.pdf. Page 8.

American Psychological Association (2012, Winter). Dealing with threatening client encounters. *Good practice.* Retrieved from www.apa.org.

American Psychological Association. (1978). Report of the task force on the role of psychology in the criminal justice system. *American Psychologist, 33,* 1099–1113.

American Psychological Association. (2002). Ethical principles of psychologists and code of conduct. *American Psychologist, 57,* 1060–1073.

American Psychological Association. (2007a, October 24). *Stress in America Survey.* Retrieved from http://74.125.45.104/search?q=cache:UAeL3kDHQdoJ:apahelpcenter.mediaroom.com/file.php/138/Stress%2Bin%2BAmerica%2BREPORT%2BFINAL.doc+Stress+in+America+Survey&hl=en&ct=clnk&cd=1&gl=us

American Psychological Association. (2007b, October 25). *Stress a major health problem in the U.S., warns APA.* Retrieved from http://www.apa.org/releases/stressproblem.html

American Psychological Association. (2010). *Stress in America 2011: Executive summary.* Retrieved from http://www.apa.org/news/press/releases/stress-exec-summary.pdf. Page 8.

American Psychological Association. (2011). *A matter of law: Psychologists' duty to protect.* http://www.apapracticecentral.org/business/legal/professional/secure/duty-protect.aspx

American Psychological Association. (2012, Winter). Dealing with threatening client encounters. *Good practice.* Retrieved from www.apa.org

Amir, N., Beard, C., Burns, M., & Bomyea, J. (2009). Attention modification program in individuals with generalized anxiety disorder. *Journal of Abnormal Psychology, 118,* 28–33. doi:10.1037/a0012589

Amstadter, A. B., Broman-Fulks, J., Zinzowa, H., Ruggiero, K. J., & Cercone, J. (2009). Internet-based interventions for traumatic stress-related mental health problems: A review and suggestion for future research. *Clinical Psychology Review, 29,* 410–420. doi:10.1016/j.cpr.2009.04.001

Andero, R., Heldt, S. A., Ye, K., Liu, X., Armario, A., & Ressler, K. J. (2011). Effect of 7,8-Dihydroxyflavone, a small-molecule TrkB agonist, on emotional learning. *American Journal of Psychiatry, 168,* 163–172. doi:10.1176/appi.ajp.2010.10030326

Anderson, E. M., & Lambert, M. J. (2001). A survival analysis of clinically significant change in outpatient psychotherapy. *Journal of Clinical Psychology, 57,* 875–888.

Anderson, E. R., & Mayes, L. C. (2010). Race/ethnicity and internalizing disorders in youth: A review. *Clinical Psychology Review, 30,* 338–348. doi: 10.1016/j.cpr.2009.12.008

Anderson, J. W., Liu, C., & Kryscio, R. J. (2008). Blood pressure response to transcendental meditation: A meta-analysis. *American Journal of Hypertension, 21,* 310–316.

Anderson, S. W., & Booker, M. B., Jr. (2006). Cognitive behavioral therapy versus psychosurgery for refractory obsessive-compulsive disorder. *Journal of Neuropsychiatry & Clinical Neurosciences, 18,* 129.

Andersson, E., Enander, J., Andrén, P., Hedman, E., Ljótsson, B., Hursti, T., et al. . . . Rück, C. (2012). Internet-based cognitive behaviour therapy for obsessive–compulsive disorder: A randomized controlled trial. *Psychological Medicine, 11,* 1–11.

Ang, R. P., Rescorla, L. A., Achenbach, T. M., Ooi, Y. P., Fung, D. S. S., & Woo, B. (2011). Examining the Criterion validity of CBCL and TRF problem scales and items in a large Singapore Sample. *Child Psychiatry & Human Development, 43,* 70–86. doi: 10.1007/s10578-011-0253-2

Angier, N. (2009, October 26). A molecule of motivation, dopamine excels at its task. *The New York Times.* Retrieved from www.nytimes.com

Anson, M., Veale, D., & de Silva, P. (2012). Social-evaluative versus self-evaluative appearance concerns in body dysmorphic disorder. *Behaviour Research and Therapy, 50,* 753–760.

Anton, R. F. (2008). Naltrexone for the management of alcohol dependence. *New England Journal of Medicine, 359,* 715–721.

Anton, R. F., Myrick, H., Wright, T. M., Latham, P. K., Baros, A. M., Waid, L. R., . . . Randall, P. K. (2011). Gabapentin combined with naltrexone for the treatment of alcohol dependence. *American Journal of Psychiatry, 168,* 709–717.

Antoni, M. H. (2012). Psychosocial intervention effects on adaptation, disease course and biobehavioral processes in cancer. *Brain, Behavior, and Immunity,* May 22. Epub ahead of print.

Antoni, M. H. (in press). Psychosocial intervention effects on adaptation, disease course and biobehavioral processes in cancer. *Brain, Behavior, and Immunity.*

Antony, M. M., Ledley, D. R., Liss, A., & Swinson, R. P. (2006). Responses to symptom induction exercises in panic disorder. *Behaviour Research and Therapy, 44,* 85–98.

Antunez, C., Boada, M., Gonzalez-Perez, A., Gayan, J., Ramirez-Lorca, R., Marín, J., ... Ruiz, A. (2011). The membrane-spanning 4-domains, subfamily A (MS4A) gene cluster contains a common variant associated with Alzheimer's disease. *Genome Medicine, 31,* 33.

APA Task Force on Evidence-Based Practice. (2006). Evidence-based practice in psychology. *American Psychologist, 61,* 271–285.

Apopolinario, J. C., Bacaltchuk, J., Sichieri, R., Claudino, A. M., Godoy-Matos, A., Morgan, C., et al. (2003). A randomized, double-blind, placebo-controlled study of sibutramine in the treatment of binge-eating disorder. *Archives of General Psychiatry, 60,* 1109–1116.

Appelbaum, P. S. (2003). Dangerous persons, moral panic, and the uses of psychiatry. *Psychiatric Services, 54,* 441–442.

Appelbaum, P. S. (2006). Violence and mental disorders: Data and public policy. *American Journal of Psychiatry, 163,* 1319–1321.

Arango, C., Rapado-Castro, M., Reig, S., Castro-Fornieles, J., González-Pinto, A., Otero, S., . . . Desco, M. (2012). Progressive brain changes in children and adolescents with first-episode psychosis. *Archives of General Psychiatry, 69,* 16–26. doi:10.1001/archgenpsychiatry.2011.150

Arbisi, P. A., Ben-Porath, Y., S., & McNulty, J. A. (2002). A comparison of MMPI-2 validity in African American and Caucasian psychiatric inpatients. *Psychological Assessment, 14,* 3–15.

Arcelus, J., Mitchell, A. J., Wales, J., & Nielsen, S. 2011). Mortality rates in patients with anorexia nervosa and other eating disorders: A meta-analysis of 36 studies. *Archives of General Psychiatry, 68,* 724.

Arch, J. J., Ayers, C. R., Baker, A., Almklov, E., Dean, D. J., & Craske, M. G. (2013). Randomized clinical trial of adapted mindfulness based stress reduction versus group cognitive behavioral therapy for heterogeneous anxiety disorders. *Behaviour Research and Therapy, 51,* 185–196.

Arguedas, D., Stevenson, R., J., & Langdon, R. (2012). Source monitoring and olfactory hallucinations in schizophrenia. *Journal of Abnormal Psychology, 121,* 936–943. doi: 10.1037/a0027174

Ariz. shooting spree suspect incompetent for trial. (2011, May 25). *MSNBC.com.* Retrieved from http://www.msnbc.msn.com/id/43165830/ns/us_news-crime_and_courts/

Armfield, J. M. (2006). Cognitive vulnerability: A model of the etiology of fear. *Clinical Psychology Review, 26,* 746–768.

Arnold, P. D., Sicard, T., Burroughs, E., Richter, M. A., & Kennedy, J. L. (2006). Glutamate transporter gene slc1a1 associated with obsessive-compulsive disorder. *Archives of General Psychiatry, 63,* 769–776.

Aronin, N., & Moore, M. (2012). Hunting down Huntingtin. *New England Journal of Medicine, 367,* 1753–1754. doi:10.1056/NEJMcibr1209595

Aronson, M. K. (1988). Patients and families: Impact and long-term-management implications. In M. K. Aronson (Ed.), *Understanding Alzheimer's disease* (pp. 74–78). New York: Charles Scribners and Sons.

Arseneault, L., Cannon, M., Fisher, H. L., Polanczyk, G., Moffitt, T. E., & Caspi, A. (2011). Childhood trauma and children's emerging psychotic symptoms: a genetically sensitive longitudinal cohort study. *American Journal of Psychiatry, 168,* 65–72.

As Valentine's Day approaches. (2012, February 7). *ScienceDaily.* Retrieved from http://www.sciencedaily.com/releases/2012/02/120207121928.htm

Asbridge, M., Hayden, J. A., & Cartwright, J. L. (2012). Acute cannabis consumption and motor vehicle collision risk: Systematic review of observational studies and meta-analysis. *British Medical Journal, 344,* e536.

Atladóttir, H. O., Henriksen, T. B., Schendel, D. E., & Parner, E. T. (2012). Autism after infection, febrile episodes, and antibiotic use during pregnancy: An exploratory study. *Pediatrics,* doi:10.1542/peds.2012-1107

Aurora, R. N., Zak, R. S., Maganti, R. K., Auerbach, S. H., Casey, K. R., Chowdhuri, S., . . . Standards of Practice Committee, American Academy of Sleep Medicine (2010). Best practice guide for the treatment of REM sleep behavior disorder (RBD). *Journal of Clinical Sleep Medicine, 6,* 85–95.

Autistic brains develop more slowly than healthy brains, researchers say. (2011, October 20). *ScienceDaily.* Retrieved from www.sciencedaily.com

Autistic brains develop more slowly than healthy brains, researchers say. (2011, October 20). ScienceDaily. Retrieved from *ScienceDaily,* 000

Axelson, D. (2013). Taking disruptive mood dysregulation disorder out for a test drive. *American Journal of Psychiatry,170,* 136–139. 10.1176/appi.ajp.2012.12111434

Ayers, J. W., Hofstetter, C. R., Usita, P., Irvin, V. L., Kang, S., Hovell, M. F. (2009). Sorting out the competing effects of acculturation, immigrant stress, and social support on depression: A report on Korean women in California. *The Journal of Nervous and Mental Disease, 197,* 742–747. doi:10.1097/NMD.0b013e3181b96e9e

Azrin, N. H., & Peterson, A. L. (1989). Reduction of an eye tick by controlled blinking. *Behavior Therapy, 20,* 467–473.

B

Bäckström T., Andreen, L., Birzniece, V., Björn, I., Johansson, I. M., Nordenstam-Haghjo, M., Nyberg, S., . . . Zhu, D. (2003). The role of hormones and hormonal treatments in premenstrual syndrome. *CNS Drugs, 17*(5), 325–342.

Baer, L., & Blais, M. A. (2010). *Handbook of clinical rating scales and assessment in psychiatry and mental health* (3rd ed.). Totowa, NJ: Human Press.

Baer, R. A., Peters, J. R., Eisenlohr-Moula, T. A., Geiger, P. J., & Sauer, S. E. (2012). Emotion-related cognitive processes in borderline personality disorder: A review of the empirical literature. *Clinical Psychology Review, 32* (5), 359–369.

Baer, R. A., Peters, J. R., Eisenlohr-Moula, T. A., Geiger, P. J., & Sauer, S. E. (2012). Emotion-related cognitive processes in borderline personality disorder: A review of the empirical literature. *Clinical Psychology Review, 32,* 359–369. doi: 10.1016/j.cpr.2012.03.00

Baer, R. A., Peters, J. R., Eisenlohr-Moula, T. A., Geiger, P. J., & Sauer, S. E. (2012). Emotion-related cognitive processes in borderline personality disorder: A review of the empirical literature. *Clinical Psychology Review,* in press

Bailar, J. C., III. (2001). The powerful placebo and the wizard of Oz. *New England Journal of Medicine, 344,* 1630–1632.

Bailey, D. S. (2003, November). The "Sylvia Plath" effect. *Monitor on Psychology, 34* (10), 42–43.

Bailey, J. M. (1999). Homosexuality and mental illness. *Archives of General Psychiatry, 56,* 883–884.

Bailine, S., Fink, M., Knapp, R., Petrides G., Husain, M. M., Rasmussen, K., . . . Kellner, C. H. (2010). Electroconvulsive therapy is equally effective in unipolar and bipolar depression. *Acta Psychiatrica Scandinavica, 121,* 431–436.

Baker, J. H., Maes, H. H., Lissner, L., Aggen, S. H., Lichtenstein, P., & Kendler, K. S. (2009). Genetic risk factors for disordered eating in adolescent males and females.

Journal of Abnormal Psychology, 118, 576–578. doi: 10.1037/a0016314

Baller, E. B., Wei, S.-M., Kohn, P. D., Rubinow, D. R., Alarcón, G., Schmidt, P. J., . . . Berman, K. F. (2013). Abnormalities of dorsolateral prefrontal function in women with premenstrual dysphoric disorder: A multimodal neuroimaging study. *American Journal of Psychiatry, 170,* 305.

Ballie, R. (2002, January). Kay Redfield Jamison receives $500,000 "genius award." *Monitor on Psychology.* Retrieved from http://www.apa.org/monitor/jan02/redfield.html

Bandura, A. (1986). *Social foundations of thought and action: A social-cognitive theory.* Englewood Cliffs, NJ: Prentice Hall.

Bandura, A. (2004). Swimming against the mainstream: The early years from chilly tributary to transformative mainstream. *Behaviour Research and Therapy, 42,* 613–630.

Bandura, A. (2006). Toward a psychology of human agency. *Perspectives on Psychological Science, 1,* 164–180.

Bandura, A., Taylor, C. B., Williams, S. L., Medford, I. N., & Barchas, J. D. (1985). Catecholamine secretion as a function of perceived coping self-efficacy. *Journal of Consulting and Clinical Psychology, 53,* 406–414.

Baranzini, S. E., Mudge, J., van Velkinburgh, J C., Khankhanian, P., Khrebtukova, I., Miller, N. A., . . . Kingsmore, S. F. (2010). Genome, epigenome and RNA sequences of monozygotic twins discordant for multiple sclerosis. *Nature, 464,* 1351. doi:10.1038/nature08990

Barbaree, H. E., & Blanchard, R. (2008) Sexual deviance over the lifespan. In D. R. Laws & W. T. O'Donohue (Eds.), *Sexual deviance: Theory, assessment, and treatment* (pp. 37–60). New York: Guilford Press.

Barch, D. M. (2013). The CAINS: Theoretical and practical advances in the assessment of negative symptoms in schizophrenia. *American Journal of Psychiatry, 170,* 133–135. 0.1176/appi.ajp.2012.12101329

Barnett, J. (2010, August 12). *Is there a duty to warn when working with HIV-positive clients?* (American Psychological Association, Division of Psychotherapy, Div. 29). Retrieved from http://www.divisionofpsychotherapy.org/ask-the-ethicist-hiv/

Bar-Nur, O., Caspi, I., & Benvenisty, N. (2012). Molecular analysis of FMR1 reactivation in fragile-X induced pluripotent stem cells and their neuronal derivatives. *Journal of Molecular Cell Biology, 4,* 180–183. doi: 10.1093/jmcb/mjs007

Barr, B., Taylor-Robinson, D., Scott-Samuel, A., McKee, M., & Stuckler, D. (2012). Suicides associated with the 2008-10 economic recession in England: Time trend analysis. *British Medical Journal, 345,* e5142. doi: 10.1136/bmj.e5142.

Barron, J., & Barron, S. (2002). *There's a boy in here.* Arlington, TX: Future Horizons.

Barsky, A. J., & Ahern, D. K. (2004). Cognitive behavior therapy for hypochondriasis: A randomized controlled trial. *Journal of the American Medical Association, 291,* 1464–1470.

Barsky, A. J., Ahern, D. K., Bailey, E. D., Saintfort, R., Liu, E. B., & Peekna, H. M. (2001). Hypochondriacal patients' appraisal of health and physical risks. *American Journal of Psychiatry, 158,* 783–787.

Barsky, A. J., Orav, E. J., & Bates, D. W. (2005). Somatization increases medical utilization and costs independent of psychiatric and medical comorbidity. *Archives of General Psychiatry, 62,* 903–910.

Barsky, A. J., Wool, C., Barnett, M. C., & Cleary, P. D. (1994). Histories of childhood trauma in adult hypochondriacal patients. *American Journal of Psychiatry, 151,* 397–401.

Bartholow, B. D., & Heinz, A. (2006). Alcohol and aggression without consumption alcohol cues, aggressive thoughts, and hostile perception bias. *Psychological Science, 17,* 30–37.

Bassett, A. S., Scherer, S. W., & Brzustowicz, L. M. (2010). Copy number variations in schizophrenia: Critical review and new perspectives on concepts of genetics and disease. *American Journal of Psychiatry, 167,* 899–914. *doi: 10.1176/appi.ajp.2009.09071016*

Bassman, R. (2005). Mental illness and the freedom to refuse treatment: Privilege or right. *Professional Psychology: Research and Practice, 36,* 488–497.

Bateman, A. W. (2012). Treating borderline personality disorder in clinical practice. *American Journal of Psychiatry, 169,* 560–563. 10.1176/appi.ajp.2012.12030341

Bateman, R. J., Xiong, C., Benzinger, T. L. S., Fagan, A. M., Goate, A., Fox, N. C., . . . John C. Morris, J. C. (2012). Clinical and biomarker changes in dominantly inherited Alzheimer's disease. *New England Journal of Medicine, 367,* 795–804. doi.org/10.1056/NEJMoa1202753

Bauchner, H. (2011). A snapshot of children with ADHD. *Journal Watch Medicine.* Retrieved from http://general-medicine.jwatch.org/cgi/content/full/2011/317/4?q=etoc_jwgenmed

Baucoma, K. J. W., Sevier, M., Eldridge, K. A., Doss, B. D., & Christensen, A. (2011). Observed communication in couples two years after integrative and traditional behavioral couple therapy: outcome and link with five-year follow-up. *Journal of Consulting and Clinical Psychology, 79*, 565–576. doi:10.1037/a0025121

Bauer, S., Okon, E., Meermann, R., & Kordy, H. (2012). Technology-enhanced maintenance of treatment gains in eating disorders: Efficacy of an intervention delivered via text messaging. *Journal of Consulting and Clinical Psychology, 80*, 700–706. doi: 10.1037/a0028030

Baxter, L. R., Jr. (2003). Basal ganglia systems in ritualistic social displays: Reptiles and humans; function and illness. *Physiology and Behavior, 79*, 451–460.

Beals, J., Novins, D. K., Whitesell, N. R., Spicer, P., Mitchell, C. M., & Manson, S. M. (2005). Prevalence of mental disorders and utilization of mental health services in two American Indian reservation populations: Mental health disparities in a national context. *American Journal of Psychiatry, 162*, 1723–1732.

Beard, C., Weisberg, R. B., & Amir, N. (2011). Combined cognitive bias modification treatment for social anxiety disorder: A pilot trial. *Depression and Anxiety, 28*, 981–988. doi: 10.1002/da.20873

Beauchaine, T. P. Hinshaw, S. P., & Pang, K. L. (2010). Comorbidity of attention-deficit/hyperactivity disorder and early-onset conduct disorder: biological, environmental, and developmental mechanisms. *Clinical Psychology: Science and Practice, 17*, 327–336. doi: 10.1111/j.1468-2850.2010.01224.x

Beauvais, F. (1998). American Indians and alcohol. *Alcohol Health and Research World, 22*, 253–259.

Beck, A. T. (2005). The current state of cognitive therapy: A 40-year retrospective. *Archives of General Psychiatry, 62*, 953–959

Beck, A. T. (2005). The current state of cognitive therapy: A 40-year retrospective. *Archives of General PsychiatryArch. Gen. Psychiatry, 62*,: 953–959. [CrossRef]

Beck, A. T., & Alford, B. A. (2009). *Depression: Causes and treatment* (2nd ed.). Baltimore: University of Pennsylvania Press.

Beck, A. T., Brown, G., Steer, R. A., Eidelson, J. I., & Riskind, J. H. (1987). Differentiating anxiety and depression: A test of the cognitive content-specificity hypothesis. *Journal of Abnormal Psychology, 96*, 179–183.

Beck, A. T., & Dozois, D. J. A. (2011). Cognitive therapy: Current status and future directions. *Annual Review of Medicine, 62*, 397–409. doi:10.1146/annurev-med-052209-100032

Beck, A. T., Rush, A. J., Shaw, B. F., & Emery, G. (1979). *Cognitive therapy of depression*. New York: Guilford Press.

Beck A. T., & Weishaar, M. E. (2011). Cognitive therapy. In R. J. Corsini & D. Wedding (Eds.) (9th ed.), *Current psychotherapies*. Belmont, CA: Brooks/Cole.

Beck, A. T., & Young, J. E. (1985). Depression. In D. H.Barlow (Ed.), *Clinical handbook of psychological disorders* (pp. 206–244). New York: Guilford Press.

Becker, B., Scheele, D., Moessner, R., Maier, W., & Hurlemann, R. (2013). deciphering the neural signature of conversion blindness. *American Journal of Psychiatry, 170*, 121–122. 10.1176/appi.ajp.2012.12070905

Becker, C. B., Bull, S., Schaumberg, K., Cauble, A., & Franco, A. (2008). Effectiveness of peer-led eating disorders prevention: A replication trial. *Journal of Consulting and Clinical Psychology, 76*, 347–354.

Beck, M. (2012, December 11). Scientists try to unravel the riddle of too much sleep. *Wall Street Journal*, pp. D1, D2.

Beesdo, K., Lau, J. Y. F., Guyer, A. E., McClure-Tone, E. B., Monk, C. S., Nelson, E. E., . . . Pine, D. S. (2009). Common and distinct amygdala-function perturbations in depressed vs. anxious adolescents. *Archives of General Psychiatry, 66*, 275–285.

Beevers, C. G., Wells, T. T., & Miller, I. W. (2007). Predicting response to depression treatment: The role of negative cognition. *Journal of Consulting and Clinical Psychology, 75*, 422–431.

Behrman, A. (2002). *Electroboy: A memoir of mania*. New York: Random House.

Beidel, D. C., Turner, S. M., Sallee, F. R., Ammerman, R. T., Crosby, L. A., & Pathak, S. (2007). SET-C versus fluoxetine in the treatment of childhood social phobia. *Journal of American Academy of Child and Adolescent Psychiatry, 46*, 1622–1632.

Beitman, B. D., Goldfried, M. R., & Norcross, J. C. (1989). The movement toward integrating the psychotherapies: An overview. *American Journal of Psychiatry, 146*, 138–147.

Bélanger, L., LeBlanc, M., & Morin, C. M. (2011). Cognitive behavioral therapy for insomnia in older adults. *Cognitive and Behavioral Practice, 68*, 991–998. doi:10.1016/j.cbpra.2010.10.003

Belkin, L. (2005, May 22). Can you catch obsessive-compulsive disorder? *The New York Times*. Retrieved from http://www.nytimes.com

Bell, B. T., & Dittmar, H. (2011). Does media type matter? The role of identification in adolescent girls' media consumption and the impact of different thin-ideal media on body image. *Sex Roles, 65*, 478–490. doi: 10.1007/s11199-011-9964-x

Belluck, P. (2010, December 15). With Alzheimer's patients growing in number, Congress endorses a national plan. *The New York Times*, p. A2

Belmaker, R. H., & Agam, G. (2008). Major depressive disorder. *New England Journal of Medicine, 35*, 55–68.

Benazon, N. R. (2000). Predicting negative spousal attitudes toward depressed persons: A test of Coyne's interpersonal model. *Journal of Abnormal Psychology, 109*, 500–554.

Bender, R. E., & Alloy, L. B. (2011). Life stress and kindling in bipolar disorder: Review of the evidence and Integration with emerging biopsychosocial theories. *Clinical Psychology Review, 31*, 383–398. doi:10.1016/j.cpr.2011.01.004

Bennett, D. (1985). Rogers: More intuition in therapy. *APA Monitor, 16*, 3.

Bennett, D., Sharpe, M., Freeman, C., & Carson, A. (2004). Anorexia nervosa among female secondary school students in Ghana. *British Journal of Psychiatry, 185*, 312–317.

Benowitz, N. L. Nicotine addiction. (2010). *New England Journal of Medicine, 362*, 2295–2303.

Benson, P. J., Beedie, S. A., Shephard, E., Giegling, I., Rujescu, D., & St. Clair, D. (2012). Simple viewing tests can detect eye movement abnormalities that distinguish schizophrenia cases from controls with exceptional accuracy. *Biological Psychiatry, 72*, 716. doi: 10.1016/j.biopsych.2012.04.019

Berenson, K., R., Downey, G., Rafaeli, E., Coifman, K. G., & Paquin, N. L. (2011). The rejection–rage contingency in borderline personality disorder. *Journal of Abnormal Psychology, 120*, 681–690. doi: 10.1037/a0023335

Berkel, S., Marshall, C. R., Weiss, B., Howe, J., Roeth, R., Moog, U., Endris, V., . . . Rappold, G. A. (2010). Mutations in the SHANK2 synaptic scaffolding gene in autism spectrum disorder and mental retardation. *Nature, 42*, 489–491. doi:10.1038/ng.589 DOI: 10.1038/ng.589

Berkout, O. V., Young, J. N, & Gross, A. M. (2011). Mean girls and bad boys: Recent research on gender differences in conduct disorder. *Aggression and Violent Behavior*, 16, 503–511. doi:10.1016/j.avb.2011.06.001

Berle, D., Starcevic, V., Hannan, A., Milicevica, D., Lamplugh, C., & Fenech, P. (2008). Cognitive factors in panic disorder, agoraphobic avoidance and agoraphobia. *Behaviour Research and Therapy, 46*, 282–291.

Bernal, M., Haro, J. M., Bernert, S., Brugha, T., de Graaf, R., Bruffaerts, R., . . . Alonso, J . (2007). Risk factors for suicidality in Europe: Results from the ESEMED study. *Journal of Affective Disorders, 101*, 27–34.

Bernstein, D. M., & Loftus, E. F. (2009). The consequences of false memories for food preferences and choices. *Perspectives on Psychological Science, 4*, 135–139. doi:10.1111/j.1745-6924.2009.01113

Bernstein, E. M., & Putnam, F. W. (1986). Development, reliability, and validity of a dissociation scale. *Journal of Nervous and Mental Disease,174*, 727–735.

Bersamin, M. M., Paschall, M. J., Saltz, R. F., & Zamboanga, B. L. (2012). Young adults and casual sex: the relevance of college drinking settings. *Journal of Sex Research*, 49, 274–281. doi: 10.1080/00224499.2010.548012

Beshai, S., Dobson, K. S., Bockting, C. L. H., & Quigley, L. (2011). Relapse and recurrence prevention in depression: Current research and future prospects. *Clinical Psychology Review, 31*, 1349–1360.

Beversdorf, D. Q., Saklayen, S., Higgins, K. F., Bodner, K. E., Kanne, S. M., & Christ, S. E. (2011). Effect of propranolol on word fluency in autism. *Cognitive and Behavioral Neurology, 24*, 11–17. doi: 10.1097/WNN.0b013e318204d20e

Bhatia, M. S., Jhanjee, A., & Kumar, P. (2011). Culture bound syndromes- a cross-sectional study from India. *European Psychiatry, 26*, 448.

Biederman, J., Petty, C. R., Monuteaux, M. C., Fried, R., Byrne, D., Mirto, T.,Faraone, S. V. (2010). Adult psychiatric outcomes of girls with attention deficit hyperactivity disorder: 11-year follow-up in a longitudinal case-control study. *American Journal of Psychiatry, 167*, 409–417. doi: 10.1176/ appi.ajp.2009.09050736

Biederman, J., Petty, C. R., Monuteaux, M. C., Fried, R., Byrne, D., Mirto, T., & Faraone, S.V. (2010b). Adult psychiatric outcomes of girls with attention deficit hyperactivity disorder: 11-year follow-up in a longitudinal case-control study. *Archives of General Psychiatry, 167*, 409–417.

Bien-Ly, N., Gillespie, A., K., Walker, D., Yoon, S. Y., & Huang, Y. (2012).Reducing human apolipoprotein e levels attenuates age-dependent Aβ Accumulation in mutant human amyloid precursor protein transgenic mice. *The Journal of Neuroscience, 32*, 4803–4811. doi:10.1523/JNEUROSCI.0033-12.2012

Bigal, M. E., Serrano, D., Reed, M., & Lipton, R. B. (2008). Chronic migraine in the population: Burden, diagnosis, and satisfaction with treatment. *Neurology, 71*, 559.

Biglan, K. M., Dorsey, E. R., Evans, R. V. V. , Ross, C. A., Hersch, S., . . . Kieburtz, K. (2012). Plasma 8-hydroxy-2'-deoxyguanosine levels in Huntington Disease and healthy controls treated with coenzyme Q10. *Journal of Huntington's Disease*, in press. doi:10.3233/JHD-2012-120007

Billieux, J., Lagrange, G., Van der Linden, M., Lançon, C., Adida, M., & Jeanningros, R. (2012). Investigation of impulsivity in a sample of treatment-seeking pathological gamblers: A multidimensional perspective. *Psychiatry Research, 198*(2), 291–296.

Billieux, J., Lagrange, G., Van der Linden, M., Lançon, C., Adida, M., & Jeanningros, R. (2012). Investigation of impulsivity in a sample of treatment-seeking pathological gamblers: A multidimensional perspective. *Psychiatry Research*, in press.

Birnbaum, M. H., Martin, H., & Thomann, K. (1996). Visual function in multiple personality disorder. *Journal of the American Optometric Association, 67*, 327–334.

Bjornsson, A., Dyck, I., Moitra, E., Stout, R. L., Weisberg, R. B.,Keller, M. B., & Phillips, K. A. (2011). The clinical course of body dysmorphic disorder in the Harvard/Brown Anxiety Research Project (HARP). *Journal of Nervous & Mental Disease, 199*, 55–57. doi: 10.1097/NMD.0b013e31820448f7

Bjornsson, A. S. (2011). Beyond the "psychological placebo": Specifying the nonspecific in psychotherapy. *Clinical Psychology: Science and Practice, 18*, 113–118. doi: 10.1111/j.1468-2850.2011.01242.x

Blair, K., Geraci, M., Devido, J., McCaffrey, D., Chen, G., Ng, M. V. P., Hollon, N., . . . Pine, D. S. (2008). Neural response to self- and other referential praise and criticism in generalized social phobia. *Archives of General Psychiatry, 165*, 1176–1184.

Blais, M. A., Holdwick, D. J., Jr., McLean, R. Y., Otto, M. W., Pollack, M. H., & Hilsenroth, M. J. (2003). Exploring the psychometric properties and construct validity of the MCMI-III anxiety and avoidant personality scales. *Journal of Personality Assessment, 81*, 237–241.

Blanchard, E. B., & Hickling, E. J. (2004). *After the crash: Psychological assessment and treatment of survivors of motor vehicle accidents* (2nd ed.). Washington, DC: American Psychological Association.

Blanchard, L. T., Gurka, M. J., & Blackman, J. A. (2006). Emotional, developmental, and behavioral health of American children and their families: A report from the 2003 National Survey of Children's Health. *Pediatrics, 117*, 1202–1212.

Blanco, C., Heimberg, R. G., Schneier, F. R., Fresco, D. M., Chen, H., Turk, C. L., Liebowitz, M. R. (2010). A placebo-controlled trial of phenelzine, cognitive behavioral group therapy, and their combination for social anxiety disorder. *Archives of General Psychiatry, 7*, 286–295.

Blanco, C., Okuda, M., Wright, C., Hasin, D. S., Grant, B. F., Liu, S. M., & Olfson, M. (2008). Mental health of college students and their non–college-attending peers: Results from the National Epidemiologic Study on Alcohol and Related Conditions. *Archives of General Psychiatry, 65*, 1429–1437.

Blankers, M., Koeter, M. W. J., & Schippers, G. M. (2011). Internet therapy versus internet self-help versus no treatment for problematic alcohol use: A randomized controlled trial. *Journal of Consulting and Clinical Psychology, 79*, 330–341. doi:10.1037/a0023498

Blatt, S. J., Zuroff, D. C., Bondi, C. M., Sanislow, C. A., & Pilkonis, P. (1998). When and how perfectionism impedes the brief treatment of depression: Further analyses of the National Institute of Mental Health Treatment of Depression Collaborative Research Program. *Journal of Consulting and Clinical Psychology, 66*, 423–428.

Blier, P., & Blondeau, C. (2011). Neurobiological bases and clinical aspects of the use of aripiprazole in treatment-resistant major depressive disorder. *Journal of Affective Disorders, 128,* S3-S10. doi:10.1016/S0165-0327(11)70003-9

Blomsted, P., Sjöberg, R. L., Hansson, M., Bodlund, O., & Hariz, M. I. (2011). Deep brain stimulation in the treatment of depression. *Acta Psychiatrica Scandinavica, 123,* 4–11. doi:10.1111/j.1600-0447.2010.01625.x

Blum, H. P. (2010). Object relations in clinical psychoanalysis. *International Journal of Psychoanalysis, 91,* 973–976.

Bohnen, N. I., Djang, D. S. W., Herholz, K., Anzai, Y., & Minoshima, S. (2011). Effectiveness and safety of 18F-FDG PET in the evaluation of dementia: A review of the recent literature. *Journal of Nuclear Medicine, 53,* 59. doi: 10.2967/jnumed.111.096578

Bolton, D., Eley, T. C., O'Connor, T. G., Perrin, S., Rabe-Hesketh, S., Rijsdijk, F., et al. (2006). Prevalence and genetic and environmental influences on anxiety disorders in 6-year-old twins. *Psychological Medicine, 36,* 335–344.

Bolton, J. M., Cox, B. J., Afifi, T. O., Enns, M. W., Bienvenu, O. J., & Sareen, J. (2008). Anxiety disorders and risk for suicide attempts: Findings from the Baltimore Epidemiologic Catchment Area follow-up study. *Depression and Anxiety, 25,* 477.

Bolton, J. M., Pagura, J., Enns, M. W., Grant, B., & Sareen, J. (2010). A population-based longitudinal study of risk factors for suicide attempts in major depressive disorder. *Journal of Psychiatric Research.* Retrieved from http://www.ncbi.nlm.nih.gov/pubmed/20122697

Bolton, P., Bass, J., Neugebauer, R., Verdeli, H., Clougherty, K. F., Wickramaratne, P., Speelman, L., . . . Weissman, M. (2003). Group interpersonal psychotherapy for depression in rural Uganda: A randomized controlled trial. *Journal of the American Medical Association, 289,* 3117–3124.

Bonanno, G. A., Galea, S., Bucciarelli, A., & Vlahov, D. (2006). Psychological resilience after disaster: New York City in the aftermath of the September 11th terrorist attack. *Psychological Science, 17,* 181–186.

Bongaarts, J., Pelletier, F., & Gerland, P. (2010a). How many more AIDS deaths? *The Lancet, 375,* 103–104. doi:10.1016/S0140-6736(09)61756-6

Bongar, B. (2002). *The suicidal patient: Clinical and legal standards of care* (2nd ed.). Washington, DC: American Psychological Association.

Boodman, S. G. (2012). *Docs: Antipsychotics often prescribed for 'problems of living.'* Retrieved from http://vitals.msnbc.msn.com/_news/2012/03/18/10724080-docs-antipsychotics-often-prescribed-for-problems-of-living

Bookheimer, S., & Burggren, A. (2009). APOE-4 genotype and neurophysiological vulnerability to Alzheimer's and cognitive aging. *Annual Review of Clinical Psychology, 5,* 343–362.

Boot, E., Kant, S. G., Otter, M., Cohen, D., Nabanizadeh, A., & Baas, R. W. J. (2012). Overexpression of Chromosome 15q11-q13 gene products: a risk factor for schizophrenia and associated Psychoses? *American Journal of Psychiatry, 169,* 96–97. 10.1176/appi.ajp.2011.11091382

Bootzin, R. R., & Epstein, D. R. (2011). Understanding and treating insomnia. *Annual Review of Clinical Psychology, 7,* 435–458. doi: 10.1146/annurev.clinpsy.3.022806.091516

Borgs, L., Beukelaers, P., Vandenbosch, R., Belachew, S., Nguyen, L., & Malgrange, B. (2009). Cell "circadian" cycle: New role for mammalian core clock genes. *Cell Cycle, 8* (6), 832–837.

Borgwardt, S., McGuire, P., & Fusar-Poli, P. (2011). Gray matters! — Mapping the transition to psychosis. *Schizophrenia Research, 133,* 63–67.

Borjesson, M., & Dahlof, B. (2005). Physical activity has a key role in hypertension therapy. *Lakartidningen, 102,* 123–124, 126, 128–129.

Borkovec, T. D., Newman, M. G., Pincus, A. L., & Lytle, R. (2002). A component analysis of cognitive-behavioral therapy for generalized anxiety disorder and role of interpersonal problems. *Journal of Consulting and Clinical Psychology, 70,* 288–298.

Bo, S., Abu-Akel, A., Kongerslev, M., Haahrc, U. H., & Simonsen, E. (2011). Risk factors for violence among patients with schizophrenia. *Clinical Psychology Review, 31,* 711–726. doi:10.1016/j.cpr.2011.03.002

Boskind-White, M., & White, W. C. (1983). *Bulimarexia: The binge–purge cycle.* New York: W. W. Norton.

Bossong, M. G., Jansma, J. M., van Hell, H. H., Jager, G., Oudman, E., Saliasi, E., . . . Ramsey, N. F. (2012). Effects of 9-tetrahydrocannabinol on human working memory function. *Biological Psychiatry, 71,* 693.

Bousman, C. A., Twamley, E. W., Vella, L., Gale, M., Norman, S. B., Judd, B., . . Heaton, R. K. (2011). Homelessness and neuropsychological impairment: Preliminary analysis

of adults entering outpatient psychiatric treatment. *Journal of Nervous & Mental Disease, 198,* 790–794. doi: 10.1097/NMD.0b013e3181f97dff

Braaten, E. B., & Rosén, L. E. (2000). Self-regulation of affect in attention deficit–hyperactivity disorder (ADHD) and non-ADHD boys: Differences in empathic responding. *Journal of Consulting and Clinical Psychology, 68,* 313–321.

Bradford, A., & Meston, C. M. (2010). Behavior and symptom change among women treated with placebo for sexual dysfunction. *The Journal of Sexual Medicine, 8,* 191–201. doi: 10.1111/j.1743-6109.2010.02007.x

Bradshaw, J. (2010, May/June). Oregon governor vetoes RxP. *The National Psychologist,* p. 6.

Brain imaging study of preschoolers with ADHD detects brain differences linked to symptoms. (2011, June 10). *ScienceDaily.* Retrieved from http://www.sciencedaily.com/

Brain scans show meditation changes minds, increases attention. (2007, June 25). *University of Wisconsin-Madison News.* Retrieved from http://www.news.wisc.edu/13890

Brand, B. L., Classen, C. C., McNary, S. W., & Zaveri, P. (2009). A review of dissociative disorders treatment studies: Collapse box. *The Journal of Nervous and Mental Disease, 197,* 646–654. doi:10.1097/NMD.0b013e3181b3afaa

Brand, B. L., Lanius, R., Vermetten, E., Loewenstein, R. J., & Spiegel, D. (2012a). Where are we going? an update on assessment, treatment, and neurobiological research in dissociative disorders as we move toward the DSM-5. *Journal of Trauma & Dissociation, 13,* 9–31. doi:10.1080/15299732.2011.620687

Brand, B. L., Myrick, A. C., Loewenstein, R. J., Classen, C. C., Lanius, R., McNary, S. W., . . . Putnam, F. (2012b). A survey of practices and recommended treatment interventions among expert therapists treating patients with dissociative identity disorder and dissociative disorder not otherwise specified. *Psychological Trauma: Theory, Research, Practice, and Policy, 4,* 490–500. doi:10.1037/a0026487

Brannan, M. E., & Petrie, T. A. (2011). Psychological well-being and the body dissatisfaction- bulimic symptomatology relationship: An examination of moderators. *Eating Behaviors, 12,* 233–241. doi:10.1016/j.eatbeh.2011.06.002

Brannigan, G. G., & Decker, S. L. (2006). The Bender-Gestalt II. *American Journal of Orthopsychiatry, 76,* 10–12.

Braskie, M. N., Jahanshad, N., Stein, J. L., Barysheva, M., McMahon, K. L, de Zubicaray, G. I., . . . Thompson, P. M. (2011). Common Alzheimer's disease risk variant within the CLU gene affects white matter microstructure in young adults. *Journal of Neuroscience, 31,* 6764. doi: 10.1523/JNEUROSCI.5794-10.2011

Bray, G. A. (2012). Diet and exercise for weight loss. *Journal of the American Medical Association, 307,* 2641–2642. doi:10.1001/jama.2012.7263

Brefczynski-Lewis, J. A., Lutz, A., Schaefer, H. S., Levinson, D. B., & Davidson, R. J. (2007). Neural correlates of attentional expertise in long-term meditation practitioners. *Proceedings of the National Academy of Sciences, 104,* 11483–11488.

Brent, D. A., Emslie, G. J., Clarke, G. N., Asarnow, J., Spirito, A., Ritz, L., et al. (2009). Predictors of spontaneous and systematically assessed suicidal adverse events in the Treatment of SSRI-Resistant Depression in Adolescents (TORDIA) Study. *American Journal of Psychiatry, 166,* 418–426. doi: 10.1176/appi.ajp.2008.08070976

Brent, D., Emslie, G., Clarke, G., Wagner, K. D., Asarnow, J. R., Keller, M., . . . Zelazny, J. (2008). Switching to another SSRI or to venlafaxine with or without cognitive behavioral therapy for adolescents with SSRI-resistant depression: The TORDIA randomized controlled trial. *Journal of the American Medical Association, 299,* 901–913.

Breslau, J., Aguilar-Gaxiola, S., Kendler, K. S., Su, M., Williams, D., & Kessler, R. C. (2006). Specifying race-ethnic differences in risk for psychiatric disorder in a USA national sample. *Psychological Medicine, 36,* 57–68.

Breslau, J., Kendler, K. S., Su, M., Gaxiola-Aguilar, S., & Kessler, R. C. (2005). Lifetime risk and persistence of psychiatric disorders across ethnic groups in the United States. *Psychological Medicine, 35,* 317–327.

Bricker, J. B., Peterson, A. V., Jr., Andersen, M. R., Rajana, K. B., Leroux, B. G., & Sarasona, I. G. (2006). Childhood friends who smoke: Do they influence adolescents to make smoking transitions? *Addictive Behaviors, 31,* 889–900.

Brien, S. E., Ronksley, P. E., Turner, B. J., Mukamal, K. J., & Ghali, W. A. (2011). Effect of alcohol consumption on biological markers associated with risk of coronary heart disease: Systematic review and meta-analysis of interventional studies. *British Medical Journal, 342,* d636. doi:10.1136/bmj.d636

Briken, P., Hill, A., & Berner, W. (2011). Pharmacotherapy of sexual offenders and men who are at risk of sexual offending. In D. P. Boer et al. (Eds.). *International Perspectives on the Assessment and Treatment of Sexual Offenders: Theory, Practice, and Research* (pp. 419–431). Hoboken, NJ: Wiley.

Briken, P., Hill, A., & Berner, W. (2011). Pharmacotherapy of sexual offenders and men who are at risk of sexual offending. In D. P. Boer, R., Eher, L. A. Craig, M. H. Miner, & P. Pfafflin (Eds.). *International perspectives on the assessment and treatment of sexual offenders: Theory, practice, and research* (pp. 419–431). Hoboken, NJ: Wiley.

Britton, J. C., Gold, A. L., Feczko, E. J., Rauch, S. L., Williams, D., & Wright, C. I. (2007). D-cycloserine inhibits amygdala responses during repeated presentations of faces. *CNS Spectrum, 12,* 600–605.

Brody, G. H., Beach, S. R. H., Philibert, R. A., Chen, Y.-F., Lei, M.-K., Murry, V. M., & Brown, A. C.. (2009). Parenting moderates a genetic vulnerability factor in longitudinal increases in youths' substance use. *Journal of Consulting and Clinical Psychology, 77,* 1–11. doi:2283, 35400018793225.0010

Brody, J. E. (2009, November 3). A breathing technique offers help for people with asthma. *The New York Times,* p. D7.

Brooks, S., & Kushida, C. (2002). Behavioral parasomnias. *Current Psychiatric Reports, 4,* 363–368.

Brothers, B. M., Yang, H.-C., Strunk, D. R., & Andersen, B. L. (2011). Cancer patients with major depressive disorder: Testing a biobehavioral/cognitive behavior intervention. *Journal of Consulting and Clinical Psychology.* Advance online publication. doi:10.1037/a0022566

Brown, A. S., & Patterson, P. H. (2012). (Eds.). *The origins of schizophrenia.* New York: Columbia University.

Brown, M. J. (2006). Hypertension and ethnic group. *British Medical Journal, 332,* 833–836.

Bruce, M. L., Ten Have, T. R., Reynolds, C. F., III, Katz, I. I., Schulberg, H. C., Mulsant, B. H., Brown, G. K., et al. (2004). Reducing suicidal ideation and depressive symptoms in depressed older primary care patients: A randomized controlled trial. Journal of the American Medical Association, 291, 1081–1091.

Bruch, H. (1973). *Eating disorders: Obesity, anorexia and the person within.* New York: Basic Books.

Brunet, A., Orr, S. P., Tremblay, J., Robertson, K., Nader, K., & Pitman R. K. (2007). Effect of post-retrieval propranolol on psychophysiologic responding during subsequent script-driven traumatic imagery in post-traumatic stress disorder. *Journal of Psychiatric Research, 42,* 503–506.

Brunwasser, S. M., Gillham, J. E., & Kim, E. S. A. (2009). A meta-analytic review of the Penn Resiliency Program's effect on depressive symptoms. *Journal of Consulting and Clinical Psychology, 77,* 1042–1054.

Bryant, C., Jackson, H., & Ames, D. (2008). The prevalence of anxiety in older adults: Methodological issues and a review of the literature. *Journal of Affective Disorders, 109,* 233–250.

Bryant, R. A., Moulds, M. L., Guthrie, R. M., Dang, S. T., & Nixon, R. D. V. (2003). Imaginal exposure alone and imaginal exposure with cognitive restructuring in treatment of posttraumatic stress disorder. *Journal of Consulting and Clinical Psychology, 71,* 706–712.

Bryant, R., & Das, P. (2012). The neural circuitry of conversion disorder and its recovery. *Journal of Abnormal Psychology, 121,* 289–296. doi:10.1037/a0025076

Buchert, R., Thomasius, R., Wilke, F., Petersen, K., Nebeling, B., Obrocki, J., . . . Clausen, M. (2004). A voxel-based PET investigation of the long-term effects of "ecstasy" consumption on brain serotonin transporters. *American Journal of Psychiatry, 161,* 1181–1189.

Buchhave, P., Minthon, L., Zetterberg, H., Wallin, A. K., Blennow, K., & Hansson, O. (2012). Cerebrospinal fluid levels of b-Amyloid 1–42, but not of tau, are fully changed already 5 to 10 years before the onset of Alzheimer dementia. *Archives of General Psychiatry, 69,* 98–106. doi:10.1001/archgenpsychiatry.2011.155

Buchman, A. S., Boyle, P. A., Yu, L., Shah, R. C., Wilson, R., S., & Bennett, D. A. (2012). Total daily physical activity and the risk of AD and cognitive decline in older adults. *Neurology,* in press. doi: 10.1212/WNL.0b013e3182535d35

Buddie, A. M., & Testa, M. (2005). Rates and predictors of sexual aggression among students and nonstudents. *Journal of Interpersonal Violence, 20,* 713–724.

Buhlmann, U., Marques, L. M., & Wilhelm, S. (2012). Traumatic experiences in individuals with body dysmorphic disorder. *Journal of Nervous and Mental Disease, 200,* 95–98. doi: 10.1097/NMD.0b013e31823f6775

Building a better antipsychotic drug by treating schizophrenia's cause: How drugs act on dopamine-producing neurons.

(2011, August 27). *ScienceDaily*. Retrieved from http://www.sciencedaily.com/

Bulik, C. M., Marcus, M. D., Zerwas, S., Levine, M. D., & La Via, M. (2012). The changing "weightscape" of bulimia nervosa. *American Journal of Psychiatry, 169*, 1031–1036. 10.1176/appi.ajp.2012.12010147

Bulik, C. M.,Thornton, L., Poyastro, Pinheiro A., Plotnicov, K., Klump, K. L., Brandt, H., et al. (2008). Suicide attempts in anorexia nervosa. *Psychosomatic Medicine, 70*, 378.

Bullmore, E. (2012). The future of functional MRI in clinical medicine. *NeuroImage, 62*, 1267–1271. doi: 10.1016/j.neuroimage.2012.01.026

Bulmash, E. L., Moller, H. J., Kayumov, L., Shen, J., Wang, X., & Shapiro, C. M. (2006). Psychomotor disturbance in depression: Assessment using a driving simulator paradigm. *Journal of Affective Disorders, 93*, 213–218.

Bunde, J., & Suls, J. (2006). A quantitative analysis of the relationship between the Cook-Medley Hostility Scale and traditional coronary artery disease risk factors. *Health Psychology, 25*, 493–500.

Burcusa, S. L., & Iacono, W. G. (2007). Risk for recurrence in depression. *Clinical Psychology Review, 27*, 959–985.

Buriel, R., Calzada, S., & Vasquez, R. (1982). The relationship of traditional Mexican American culture to adjustment and delinquency among three generations of Mexican American male adolescents. *Hispanic Journal of Behavioral Science, 4*, 41–55.

Burke, J. D., Waldman, I., & Lahey, B. B. (2010). Predictive validity of childhood oppositional defiant disorder and conduct disorder: Implications for the DSM-V. *Journal of Abnormal Psychology, 119*, 739–751. doi: 10.1037/a0019708

Burke, J. & Loeber, R. (2010). Oppositional defiant disorder and the explanation of the comorbidity between behavioral disorders and depression. *Clinical Psychology: Science and Practice, 17*, 319–326. doi: 10.1111/j.1468

Burns, D. D. (1980). *Feeling good: The new mood therapy.* New York: Morris.

Burrow-Sanchez, J. J, & Wrona, M. (2012). Comparing culturally accommodated versus standard group CBT for Latino adolescents with substance use disorders: A pilot study. *Cultural Diversity and Ethnic Minority Psychology, 18*, 373–383. doi: 10.1037/a0029439

Burrow-Sanchez, J. J., & Wrona, M. (2012). Comparing culturally accommodated versus standard group CBT for Latino adolescents with substance use disorders: A pilot study. *Cultural Diversity and Ethnic Minority Psychology, 18*, 373–383. doi: 10.1037/a0029439

Burt, A. (2009). Rethinking environmental contributions to child and adolescent psychopathology: A meta-analysis of shared environmental influences. *Psychological Bulletin, 135*, 608–637. doi: 10.1037/a0015702

Burton, N., & Lane, R. C. (2001). The relational treatment of dissociative identity disorder. *Clinical Psychology Review, 21*, 301–320.

Busscher, B., Spinhoven, P., van Gerwen, L. J., & de Geus, E. J. C. (2013).Anxiety sensitivity moderates the relationship of changes in physiological arousal with flight anxiety during in vivo exposure therapy. *Behaviour Research and Therapy, 51*, 98–105

Busscher et al., 2013; Ho et al., 2011; Naragon-Gainey, 2010; Wheaton et al., 2012 (Author to add complete citation)

Butcher, J. N. (2011). *A beginner's guide to the MMPI-2* (3rd ed.). Washington, DC: American Psychological Association.

Butler, A. C., Chapman, J. E., Forman, E. M., & Beck, A. T. (2006). The empirical status of cognitive-behavioral therapy: A review of meta-analyses. *Clinical Psychology Review, 26*, 17–33.

Butler, L. D., Duran, R. E. F., Jasiukaitus, P., Koopman, C., & Spiegel, D. (1996). Hypnotizability and traumatic experience: A diathesis-stress model of dissociative symptomatology. *American Journal of Psychiatry, 153*(Suppl. 7), 42–63.

Butler, R. J. (2004). Childhood nocturnal enuresis: Developing a conceptual framework. *Clinical Psychology Review, 24*, 909–931.

Buvat, J., et al. (2010). Endocrine aspects of male sexual dysfunctions. *Journal of Sexual Medicine, 7*, 1627–1656.

Colangelo, J. J., & Keefe-Cooperman, K. (2012). Understanding the impact of childhood sexual abuse on women's sexuality. *Journal of Mental Health Counseling, 34*, 14–37.

Buvat, J., Maggi, M., Gooren, L., Guay, A.T., Kaufman, J., Morgentaler, A., . . . Zitzmann, M. (2010). Endocrine aspects of male sexual dysfunctions. *Journal of Sexual Medicine, 7*, 1627–1656.

Buysse, D. J., Germain, A., Moul, D. E., Franzen, P. L., Brar, L. K., Fletcher, M. E., . . . Monk, T. H.. (2011). Efficacy of brief behavioral treatment for chronic insomnia in older adults. *Archives of Internal Medicine, 171*, 887–895.

Buysse, D. J., Germain, A., Moul, D. E., Franzen, P. L., Brar, L. K., Fletcher, M. E., . . Monk, T. H. (2011). Efficacy of brief behavioral treatment for chronic insomnia in older adults. *Archives of Internal Medicine*. Retrieved from http://dx.doi.org/10.1001/archinternmed.2010.535)

Byrne, S. M., Fursland, A., Allen, K. L., & Watson, H. (2011). The effectiveness of enhanced cognitive behavioural therapy for eating disorders: An open trial. *Behaviour Research and Therapy, 49*, 219–226. doi:10.1016/j.brat.2011.01.006 |

C

Cable, N., & Sacker, A. (2007). The role of adolescent social disinhibition expectancies in moderating the relationship between psychological distress and alcohol use and misuse. *Addictive Behaviors, 32*, 282–295.

Caetano, R. (1987). Acculturation and drinking patterns among U.S. Hispanics. *British Journal of Addiction, 82*, 789–799.

Cai, D., Pearce, K, Chen, S., & Glanzman.D. L. (2011). Protein kinase M maintains long-term sensitization and long-term facilitation in aplysia. *Journal of Neuroscience, 31*, 6421–6431. doi:10.1523/JNEUROSCI.4744-10.2011

Cain, S. (2011, June 25). Shyness: Evolutionary tactic? *The New York Times*. Retrieved from http://www.nytimes.com

Calabrese, J. R., & Kemp, D. E. (2008). Bipolar drug development: Are we getting closer to the real world? *Archives of General Psychiatry, 165*, 1234–1236.

Calati, R., Signorelli, M. S., Balestri, M., Marsano, A., De Ronchi, D., Aguglia, E., & Serretti, A. (2013). Antidepressants in elderly: Metaregression of double-blind, randomized clinical trials. *Journal of Affective Disorders, 147*, 1–8.

Callanan, M., & Waxman, S. (2013). Commentary on special section: Deficit or difference? Interpreting diverse developmental paths. *Developmental Psychology, 49*, 80–83. doi: 10.1037/a0029741.

Calzada-Reyes, A., Alvarez-Amador, A., Galán-García, L., Valdés-Sosa, M. (2012). Electroencephalographic abnormalities in antisocial personality disorder. *Journal of Forensic and Legal Medicine, 19*, 29–34. doi:10.1016/j.jflm.2011.10.002

Cambron, M. J., Acitelli, L. K., & Pettit, J. W. (2009). Explaining gender differences in depression: An interpersonal contingent self-esteem perspective. *Sex Roles, 61*, 751–894. doi:10.1007/s11199-009-9616-6

Cameron, N. (1963). *Personality development and psychopathology: A dynamic approach.* Boston: Houghton Mifflin.

Campbell, T. (2000). First person account: Falling on the pavement. *Schizophrenia Bulletin, 26*, 507–509.

Campos-Rodriguez, F., et al. (2012). Cardiovascular mortality in women with obstructive sleep apnea with or without continuous positive airway pressure treatment: A cohort study. *Annals of Internal Medicine, 156*, 115.

Campos-Rodriguez, F., Martinez-Garcia, M. A., de la Cruz-Moron, I., Almeida-Gonzalez, C. Catalan-Serra, P., & Montserrat, J. M. (2012). Cardiovascular mortality in women with obstructive sleep apnea with or without continuous positive airway pressure treatment: A cohort study. *Annals of Internal Medicine, 156*, 115.

Can traumatic memories be erased? (2011, April 28). *ScienceDaily*. Retrieved from http://www.sciencedaily.com/releases/2011/04/110427154315.htm

Cannon, C. P. (2011). High-density lipoprotein cholesterol as the Holy Grail. *Journal of the American Medical Association, 306*, 2153–2155. doi:10.1001/jama.2011.1687

Cannon, M., Fisher, H. L., Polanczyk, G., Moffitt, T. E., & Caspi, A. (2011). Childhood trauma and children's emerging psychotic symptoms: A genetically sensitive longitudinal cohort study. *American Journal of Psychiatry, 168*, 65–72.

Cardeña, E., & Carlson, E. (2011). Acute stress disorder revisited. *Annual Review of Clinical Psychology, 7*, 245–267. doi:10.1146/annurev-clinpsy-032210-104502

Carey, B. (2005, October 18). Can brain scans see depression? *The New York Times*. Retrieved from http://www.nytimes.com

Carey, B. (2009, December 3). Dissection begins on famous brain. *The New York Times*, A27.

Carey, B. (2009, November 26). Surgery for mental ills offers both hope and risk. *The New York Times*. Retrieved from http://www.nytimes.com/2009/11/27/health/

research/27brain.html?_r=1&scp=1&sq=psychosurgery&st=cse

Carey, B. (2010, February 10). Revising book on disorders of the mind. *The New York Times*. Retrieved from www.nytimes.com

Carey, B. (2011). Expert on mental illness reveals her own fight. *The New York Times*, pp. A1, A17.

Carey, B. (2012, April 4). Scientists link gene mutation to autism risk. *The New York Times*. Retrieved from nytimes.com

Carey, B. (2012, December 11). A tense compromise on defining disorders. *The New York Times*, pp. D1, D6.

Carey, B. (2012a, January 19). New autism definition may exclude many, study suggests. *The New York Times*. Retrieved from www.nytimes.com

Carey, B. (2012b, August 23). Study finds risk of autsim linked to older fathers. *The New York Times*. Retrieved from www.nytimes.com

Carey, B. (2013, January 16). Some with autism diagnosis can overcome symptoms, study finds. *The New York Times*. Retrieved from nytimes.com

Carey, B., & Hartocollis, A. (2013, January 16). Warning signs of violent acts often unclear. *The New York Times*, pp. A1, A15.

Carey, M. P., Carey, K. B., Maisto, S. A., Gordon, C. M., Schroder, K. E. E., & Vanable, P. A. (2004). Reducing HIV-risk behavior among adults receiving outpatient psychiatric treatment: Results from a randomized controlled trial. *Journal of Consulting and Clinical Psychology, 72*, 252–268.

Carey, T. A. (2011). Exposure and reorganization: The what and how of effective psychotherapy. *Clinical Psychology Review, 31*, 236–248.doi:10.1016/j.cpr.2010.04.004

Carlbring, P., & Smit, F. (2008). Randomized trial of internet-delivered self-help with telephone support for pathological gamblers. *Journal of Consulting and Clinical Psychology, 76*, 1090–1094.

Carlbring, P., Hägglund, M., Luthström, A., Dahlin, M., Kadowaki, A., Vernmark, K., & Andersson, G. (2013). Internet-based behavioral activation and acceptance-based treatment for depression: A randomized controlled trial. *Journal of Affective Disorders*, in press

Carlbring, P., Maurin, L, Törngren, C., Linna, E., Eriksson, T., Sparthan, E., . . . Andersson, G. (2011). Individually-tailored, Internet-based treatment for anxiety disorders: A randomized controlled trial. *Behaviour Research and Therapy, 49*, 18–24. doi:10.1016/j.brat.2010.10.002

Carney, R. M., Freedland, K. E., Rubin, E. H., Rich, M. W., Steinmeyer, B. C., & Harris, W. S. (2009). Omega-3 augmentation of sertraline in treatment of depression in patients with coronary heart disease: A randomized controlled trial. *Journal of the American Medical Association, 302*, 1651–1657. Retrieved from http://jama.ama-assn.org/cgi/content/abstract/302/15/1651

Carpenter, S. (2013, January). Awakening to sleep. *Monitor on Psychology, 44*, pp. 40–45.

Carrasco, J. L., Tajima-Pozo, K., Díaz-Marsá, M., Casado, A., López-Ibor, J. J, Arrazola, J. Yus, M. (2012). Microstructural white matter damage at orbitofrontal areas in borderline personality disorder. *Journal of Affective Disorders, 139*, 149–153. http://dx.doi.org/10.1016/j.jad.2011.12.019

Carrillo, M. C., Blennow, K., Soares, H., Lewczuk, P., Mattsson, N., Oberoi, P., Umek, R., . . . Zetterberg, H. (2012). Global standardization measurement of cerebral spinal fluid for Alzheimer's disease: An update from the Alzheimer's Association Global Biomarkers Consortium. *Alzheimer's & Dementia*, in press. doi: 10.1016/j.jalz.2012.11.003

Carroll, L. (2003, November 4). Fetal brains suffer badly from effects of alcohol. *The New York Times Online*. Retrieved from http://www.nytimes.com

Carroll., L. (2004, February 10). Parkinson's research focuses on links to genes and toxins. *The New York Times, p. F5*.

Carson, R. C., Hollon. S. D., & Shelton, R. C. (2010). Depressive realism and clinical depression. *Behaviour Research and Therapy, 48*, 257–265. doi:10.1016/j.brat.2009.11.011

Carter, J. C., McFarlane, T. L., Bewell, C., Olmsted, M. P., Woodside, D. B., Kaplan, A. S., Crosby, R. D. (2009). Maintenance treatment for anorexia nervosa: A comparison of cognitive behavior therapy and treatment as usual. *International Journal of Eating Disorders, 42*, 202–207. doi: 10.1002/eat.20591

Carter, J. S., & Garber, J. (2011). Predictors of the first onset of a major depressive episode and changes in depressive symptoms across adolescence: Stress and negative cognitions. *Journal of Abnormal Psychology, 120*, 779–796. doi:10.1037/a0025441

Carvalho, J., & Nobre, P. (2010). Gender issues and sexual desire: The role of emotional and relationship variables. *Journal of Sexual Medicine, 7,* 2469–2478.
Carver, C. S., Johnson, S. L., & Joormann, J. (2008). Serotonergic function, two-mode models of self-regulation, and vulnerability to depression: What depression has in common with impulsive aggression. *Psychological Bulletin, 134,* 912–943.
Carver, C. S., Johnson, S. L., & Joormann, J. (2009). Two-mode models of self-regulation as a tool for conceptualizing effects of the serotonin system in normal behavior and diverse disorders. *Current Directions in Psychological Science, 18,* 195–199. doi:10.1111/j.1467-8721.2009.01635.x
Carver, C. S., Scheier, M. F., & Segerstrom, S. C. (2010). Optimism. Clinical Psychology Review, 30, 879–889. doi:10.1016/j.cpr.2010.01.006
Casey, B. J., & Durston, S. (2006). From behavior to cognition to the brain and back: What have we learned from functional imaging studies of attention deficit hyperactivity disorder? *American Journal of Psychiatry, 163,* 957–960.
Casey, L. M., Oei, T. P. S., & Newcombe, P. A. (2004). An integrated cognitive model of panic disorder: The role of positive and negative cognitions. *Clinical Psychology Review 24,* 529–555.
Casey, P., Maracy, M., Kelly, B. D., Lehtinend, V., Ayuso-Mateose, J.-L., Dalgard, O. S., & Dowrick, C. (2006). Can adjustment disorder and depressive episode be distinguished? Results from ODIN. *Journal of Affective Disorders, 92,* 291–297.
Castellini, G., Lo Sauro, C., Mannucci, E., Ravaldi, C., Rotella, C. M., Faravelli, C., . . . Ricca, V. (2011). Diagnostic crossover and outcome predictors in eating disorders according to DSM-IV and DSM-V proposed criteria: A 6-year follow-up study. *Psychosomatic Medicine, 73,* 270–279. http://dx.doi.org/10.1097/PSY.0b013e31820a1838)
Centers for Disease Control. (2008). Smoking-attributable mortality, years of potential life lost, and productivity losses—United States, 2000–2004. *Morbidity and Mortality Weekly Report, 57*(45), 1226–1228.
Centers for Disease Control. (2009). Obesity and overweight. *FastStats.* Retrieved from http://www.cdc.gov/nchs/fastats/overwt.htm
Centers for Disease Control. (2009). *Suicide: Facts at a glance, summer 2009.* National Center for Injury Prevention and Control. Retrieved from www.cdc.gov/injury/wisqars/index.html
Centers for Disease Control and Prevention (CDC). (2009a). Cigarette smoking among adults and trends in smoking cessation: United States, 2008. *Morbidity and Mortality Weekly Report, 58,* 1227–1232.
Centers for Disease Control and Prevention. (2011) Vital signs: Prevalence, treatment, and control of hypertension—United States, 1999–2002 and 2005–2008. *Morbidity and Mortality Weekly Report, Journal of the American Medical Association, 305,* 1531–1534.
Centers for Disease Control and Prevention (2011, December 14). Centers for Disease Control and Prevention. The National Intimate Partner and Sexual Violence Survey (NISVS). Retrieved from//www.cdc.gov/ViolencePrevention/NISVS/index.html (Accessed July 16, 2012).
Centers for Disease Control and Prevention (CDC). (2011, July). Overweight and obese. Retrieved from http://www.cdc.gov/obesity/data/adult.html
Centers for Disease Control and Prevention (CDCP). (2011a). Prevalence of coronary heart disease —United States, 2006–2010. *Morbidity and Mortality Weekly Report, Journal of the American Medical Association, 306,* 2084–2086.
Centers for Disease Control and Prevention (CDC). (2011b). Vital signs: current cigarette smoking among adults aged ≥18 years—United States, 2005–2010. *Morbidity and Mortality Weekly Report, 60,* 1207–1212.
Centers for Disease Control and Prevention (2012, March 29). *CDC estimates 1 in 88 children in United States has been identified as having an autism spectrum disorder.* Retrieved from http://www.cdc.gov/media/releases/2012/p0329_autism_disorder.html
Centers for Diseaase Control and Prevention (CDC). (2012a). Vital signs: Binge drinking prevalence, frequency, and intensity among adults—United States, 2010. *Morbidity and Mortality Weekly Report, Journal of the American Medical Association, 307,* 908–910.
Ceron-Litvoc, D., Soares, B. G., Geddes, J., Litvoc, J., & de Lima, M. S. (2009). Comparison of carbamazepine and lithium in treatment of bipolar disorder: A systematic review of randomized controlled trials. *Human Psychopharmacology: Clinical and Experimental Human, 24,* 19–28. doi:10.1002/hup.990
Ceskova, E., Prikryl, R., & Kasparek, T. (2011). Suicides in males after the first episode of schizophrenia. *Journal of Nervous & Mental Disease, 199,* 62–64. doi: 10.1097/NMD.0b013e31820448e4
Chang, Z., Lichtenstein, P., Asherson, P. J., & Larsson, H. (2013). Developmental twin study of attention problems: High heritabilities throughout development. *JAMA Psychiatry,70,* 311–318. doi:10.1001/jamapsychiatry.2013.287.
Chantix unsuitable for first-line smoking cessation use, study finds. (2011, November 2). *ScienceDaily.* Retrieved from http://www.sciencedaily.com/
Charman, T. (2011). The highs and lows of counting autism. *American Journal of Psychiatry,* 168, 873–875. doi: 10.1176/appi.ajp.2011.11060897
Charness, M. E. (2009). Functional connectivity in Wernicke encephalopathy. *JournalWatch Neurology.* Retrieved from http://neurology.jwatch.org/cgi/content/full/2009/623/4?q=etoc_jwneuro
Chartier, I. S., & Provencher, M. D. (2013). Behavioural activation for depression: Efficacy, effectiveness and dissemination. *Journal of Affective Disorders, 145,* 292–299
Chasson, G. S., Buhlmann, U., Tolin, D. F., Rao, S. R., Reese, H. E., Rowley, T., . . . Wilhelm, S. (2010). Need for speed: Evaluating slopes of OCD recovery in behavior therapy enhanced with d-cycloserine. *Behaviour Research and Therapy, 48,* 675–679. doi:10.1016/j.brat.2010.03.007
Chemerinski, E., Byne, W., Kolaitis, J. C., Glanton, C. F., Canfield, E. L., Newmark, R. E. . . . Hazlett, E. A. (2012). Larger putamen size in antipsychotic-naïve individuals with schizotypal personality disorder. *Schizophrenia Research, 43,* 158–164. doi: 10.1016/j.schres.2012.11.00
Chemerinski, E., Byne, W., Kolaitis, J. C., Glanton, C. F., Canfield, E. L., Newmark, R. E. . . . Hazlett, E. A. (2012). Larger putamen size in antipsychotic-naïve individuals with schizotypal personality disorder. *Schizophrenia Research,* in press.
Chen, J., Rathore, S. S., Radford, M. J., Wang, Y., & Krumholz, H. M. (2001). Racial differences in the use of cardiac catheterization after acute myocardial infarction. *The New England Journal of Medicine, 344,* 1443–1449.
Chen, W. Y., Rosner, B., Hankinson, S. E., Colditz, G. A., & Willett, W. C. (2011). Moderate alcohol consumption during adult life, drinking patterns, and breast cancer risk. *Journal of the American Medical Association, 306,* 1884–1890.
Chen, Y.,Wolk, D. A., Reddin, J. S., Korczykowski, M., Martinez, P. M., Musiek, E. S., . . . Detre, J. A. (2011). Voxel-level comparison of arterial spin-labeled perfusion MRI and FDG-PET in Alzheimer disease. *Neurology, 77,* 1977–1985. doi: 10.1212/WNL.0b013e31823a0ef7
Chernyak, Y., & Lowe, M. R. (2010). Motivations for dieting: Drive for thinness is different from drive for objective thinness. *Journal of Abnormal Psychology, 119,* 276–281. doi: 10.1037/a0018398
Cheung, F. M. (1991). The use of mental health services by ethnic minorities. In H. F. Myers et al. (Eds.), *Ethnic minority perspectives on clinical training and services in psychology* (pp. 23–31). Washington, DC: American Psychological Association.
Cheung, F. M., Kwong, J. Y. Y., & Zhang, J. (2003). Clinical validation of the Chinese Personality Assessment Inventory. *Psychological Assessment, 15,* 89–100.
Chida, Y., & Steptoe, A. (2009). The association of anger and hostility with future coronary heart disease: A meta-analytic review of prospective evidence. *Journal of the American College of Cardiology 53,* 936–946. doi:10.1016/j.jacc.2008.11.044
Chiesa, A., & Serretti, A. (2011). Mindfulness based cognitive therapy for psychiatric disorders: A systematic review and meta-analysis. *Psychiatry Research, 187,* 441–453.
Childress, A. R., Ehrman, R. N., Wang, Z., Li, Y., Sciortino, N., Hakun, J., . . . O'Brien, C. P. (2008). Prelude to passion: Limbic activation by "unseen" drug and sexual cues. *PLoS ONE, 3*(1), e1506. Retrieved from http://www.plosone.org/article/info:doi/10.1371/journal.pone.0001506
Chioqueta, A.P., & Stiles, T.C. (2007). Dimensions of the Dysfunctional Attitude Scale and the Automatic Thoughts Questionnaire as cognitive vulnerability factors in the development of suicide ideation. *Behavioral and Cognitive Psychotherapy, 35,* 579–589.
Choi, I., Zou, J., Titov, N., Dar, B. F., Li, S., Johnston, L., . . . Hunt, C. (2012). Culturally attuned Internet treatment for depression amongst Chinese Australians: A randomised controlled trial. *Journal of Affective Disorders, 136,* 459–468.
Choi, S.-H., Lee, H., Chung, T.-S., Park, K.-M., Jung, Y. C., Kim, S. I., . . . Kim, J.-J. (2012). Neural network functional connectivity during and after an episode of delirium. *American Journal of Psychiatry, 169,* 498–507. 10.1176/appi.ajp.2012.1106097
Chorpita, B. F., Daleiden, E. L., Ebesutani, C., Young, J., Becker, K. D., Nakamura, B. J., . . . Starace, N. (2011). Evidence-based treatments for children and adolescents: An updated review of indicators of efficacy and effectiveness. *Clinical Psychology: Science and Practice, 18,* 154–172. doi: 10.1111/j.1468-2850.2011.01247.x
Chou, K.-L. (2009). Social anxiety disorder in older adults: Evidence from the National Epidemiologic Survey on Alcohol and Related Conditions. *Journal of Affective Disorders, 119,* 76–83.
Chou, K.-L. (2010). Panic disorder in older adults: Evidence from the National Epidemiologic Survey on Alcohol and Related Conditions. *International Journal of Geriatric Psychiatry,* in press. doi: 10.1002/gps.2424
Chou, T., Asnaani, A., & Hofmann, S. G. (2012). Perception of racial discrimination and psychopathology across three U.S. ethnic minority groups. *Cultural Diversity and Ethnic Minority Psychology, 18,* 74–81. doi: 10.1037/a0025432
Choy, Y., Fyer, A. J., & Lipsitz, J. D. (2007). Treatment of specific phobia in adults. *Clinical Psychology Review, 27,* 266–286.
Chronis, A. M., Jones, H. A., & Raggi, V. L. (2006). Evidence-based psychosocial treatments for children and adolescents with attention-deficit/hyperactivity disorder. *Clinical Psychology Review, 26,* 486–502.
Chu, J. A. (2011a). *Falling apart: dissociation and the dissociative disorders. Rebuilding shattered lives: Treating complex PTSD and dissociative disorders* (2nd ed). Hoboken: John Wiley & Sons.
Chu, J. A. (2011a). Falling apart: Dissociation and the dissociative disorders. In J. A. Chu (Ed.), *Rebuilding shattered lives: Treating complex PTSD and dissociative disorders* (2nd ed., pp. 41–64). Hoboken: John Wiley & Sons.
Chu, J. A. (2011b). *The rational treatment of dissociative identity disorder. Rebuilding shattered lives: Treating complex PTSD and dissociative disorders* (2nd ed). Hoboken: John Wiley & Sons.
Chu, J. A. (2011b). The rational treatment of dissociative identity disorder. In J. A. Chu (Ed.), *Rebuilding shattered lives: Treating complex PTSD and dissociative disorders* (2nd ed., pp. 205–227). Hoboken: John Wiley & Sons.
Chung, D. W., Rudnicki, D. D., Yu, L., & Margolis, R. L. (2011). A natural antisense transcript at the Huntington's disease repeat locus regulates HTT expression. *Human Molecular Genetics, 20,* 3467–3477. doi: 10.1093/hmg/ddr263
Chung, R. - H., Ma, D., Wang, K., Hedges, D. J., Jaworski, M. M., Gilbert, J. R., . . . Martin, E. R. (2011). An X-chromosome-wide association study in autism families identifies TBL1X as a novel autism spectrum disorder candidate gene in males. *Molecular Autism, 4,* 18.
Chung, T., & Maisto, S. A. (2006). Relapse to alcohol and other drug use in treated adolescents: Review and reconsideration of relapse as a change point in clinical course. *Clinical Psychology Review, 26,* 149–161.
Clark, D. M. (1986). A cognitive approach to panic. *Behaviour Research and Therapy, 24,* 461–470.
Clark, L. (2012). Epidemiology and phenomenology of pathological gambling. In J. E. Grant & M. N. Potenza (Eds.), *The Oxford handbook of impulse control disorders* (pp. 94–116). New York: Oxford University Press.
Clark, R. (2006). Perceived racism and vascular reactivity in Black college women: Moderating effects of seeking social support. *Health Psychology, 25,* 20–25.
Clarke., G., Dickerson, J., Gullion, C. M., & Debar, L. L. (2012). Trends in youth antidepressant dispensing and refill limits, 2000 through 2009. *Journal of Child and Adolescent Psychopharmacology, 22,* 11–20.
Clay, R. A. (2001, January). Bringing psychology to cardiac care. *Monitor on Psychology, 32*(1), 46–49.
Clay, R. A. (2012, February). Improving disorder classification, worldwide. *Monitor on Psychology, 43*(2), 40
Clifford, D. B., Fagan, A. M., Holtzman, D. M., Morris J. C., Teshome M., Shah, A. R., Kauwe, J. S., et al. (2009). CSF biomarkers of Alzheimer disease in HIV-associated neurologic disease. *Neurology, 73,* 1982. *Clinical and Health Psychology, 10,* 5–21.
Cloud, J. (2010, January 6). Why your DNA isn't your destiny. *Time Magazine.* Retrieved from http://www.time.com/time/magazine/article/0,9171,1952313-1,00.html

Clough, B. A., & Casey, L. M. (2011). Technological adjuncts to enhance current psychotherapy practices: A review. *Clinical Psychology Review, 31*, 279–292. doi:10.1016/j.cpr.2010.12.008

Coccaro, E. F. (2010). A family history study of intermittent explosive disorder. *Journal of Psychiatric Research, 44*, 1101–1105.

Coccaro, E. F. (2012). Intermittent explosive disorder as a disorder of impulsive aggression for DSM-5. *American Journal of Psychiatry, 169*, 577–588. 10.1176/appi.ajp.2012.11081259

Coccaro, E. F., & McCloskey, M. S. (2010). Intermittent explosive disorder: Clinical aspects. In E. Aboujaoude & L. M. Koran (Eds.), *Impulse control disorders* (pp. 221–232). Cambridge, UK: Cambridge University Press.

Coccaro, E. F., Lee, R., & Kavoussi, R. J. (2010). Aggression, suicidality, and intermittent explosive disorder: Serotonergic correlates in personality disorder and healthy control subjects. *Neuropsychopharmacology, 35*, 435–444. doi:10.1038/npp.2009.148

Cochran, S. D., Sullivan, J. G., & Mays, V. M. (2003). Prevalence of mental disorders, psychological distress, and mental health services use among lesbian, gay, and bisexual adults in the United States. *Journal of Consulting and Clinical Psychology, 71*, 53–61.

Cochran, S. V., & Rabinowitz, F. E. (2003). Gender-sensitive recommendations for assessment and treatment of depression in men. *Professional Psychology: Research and Practice, 34*, 132–140.

Coelho, C. M., Waters, A. M., Hine, T. J., & Wallis, G. (2009). The use of virtual reality in acrophobia research and treatment. *Journal of Anxiety Disorders, 23*, 563–574. doi:10.1016/j.janxdis.2009.01.014

Coffey, S. F., Schumacher, J. A., Baschnagel, J. S., Hawk, L. W., & Holloman, G. (2011). Impulsivity and risk-taking in borderline personality disorder with and without substance use disorders. *Personality Disorders: Theory, Research, and Treatment, 2*, 128–141. doi:10.1037/a0020574

Cohen, H., Kaplan, Z., Kotler, M., Kouperman, I., Moisa, R., & Grisaru, N. (2004). Repetitive transcranial magnetic stimulation of the right dorsolateral prefrontal cortex in posttraumatic stress disorder: A double-blind, placebo-controlled study. *American Journal of Psychiatry, 161*, 515–524.

Cohen, J. (2012). The many states of HIV in America. *Science, 6091*, 168–171. doi: 10.1126/science.337.6091.168

Cohen, P. (2011). Abuse in childhood and the risk for psychotic symptoms in later life. *American Journal of Psychiatry, 168*, 7–8. doi:10.1176/appi.ajp.2010.10101513

Cohen, S., Doyle, W. J., Alper, C. M., Janicki-Deverts, D., & Turner, R. B. (2009). Sleep habits and susceptibility to the common cold. *Archives of Internal Medicine, 169*, 62–66. doi:10.1001/archinternmed.2008.505

Cohen, S., Doyle, W. J., Turner, R., Alper, C. M., & Skoner, D. P. (2003). Sociability and susceptibility to the common cold. *Psychological Science, 14*, 389–395.

Cohen, S., Janicki-Deverts, D., & Miller, G. E. (2007). Psychological stress and disease. *Journal of the American Medical Association, 298*, 1685–1687. doi:10.1001/jama.298.14.1685.

Cohen, S., Janicki-Deverts, D., Doyle, W. J., Miller, G. E., Frank, E., Rabin, B. S., . . . Turner, R. B. (2012). Chronic stress, glucocorticoid receptor resistance, inflammation, and disease risk. *PNAS, 109*, 5995–5999. doi: 10.1073/pnas.1118355109

Cohen, S., Janicki-Deverts, D., Doyle, W. J., Miller, G. E., Frank, E., Rabin, B. S., . . . Turner, R. B. (2012). Chronic stress, glucocorticoid receptor resistance, inflammation, and disease risk. *Proceedings of the National Academy of Sciences of the United States of America.109*, 5995–5999. doi:10.1073/pnas.1118355109

Cohen, S., Kozlovsky, N ., Matar, M. A., Kaplan, Z., Zohar, J., & Cohen, H. (2012). Post-exposure sleep deprivation facilitates correctly timed interactions between glucocorticoid and adrenergic systems, which attenuate traumatic stress responses. *Neuropsychopharmacology, 37*, 2388–2404. doi:10.1038/npp.2012.94

Coila, B. (2009). *What is epigenetics?* Retrieved from http://bridget-coila.suite101.com/what-is-epigenetics-a104553

Colangelo, J. J., & Keefe-Cooperman, K. (2012). Understanding the impact of childhood sexual abuse on women's sexuality. *Journal of Mental Health Counseling, 34*, 14–37.

Colditz, G. A., Wolin, K. Y., & Gehlert, S. (2012). Applying what we know to accelerate cancer prevention. *Science Translational Medicine, 4*, 127. doi: 10.1126/scitranslmed.3003218

Coldwell, C. M., & Bender, W. S. (2007). The effectiveness of assertive community treatment for homeless populations with severe mental illness: A meta-analysis. *American Journal of Psychiatry, 164*, 393–399.

Cole, D. A., Cho, S.-J., Martin, N. C., Youngstrom, E. A., March, J. S., Findling, R. L., . . . Maxwell, M. A. (2012). Are increased weight and appetite useful indicators of depression in children and adolescents? *Journal of Abnormal Psychology, 121*, 838–851. doi: 10.1037/a0028175

Coleman, M. J., Krastoshevsky, O., Tu, X., Mendell, N. R., & Levy, D. L. (2012). The effects of perceptual encoding on the magnitude of object working memory impairment in schizophrenia. *Schizophrenia Research, 139*, 60–65. doi: 10.1016/j.schres.2012.05.003 in press.

Coltheart, M., Langdon, R., & McKay, R. (2011). Delusional belief. *Annual Review of Psychology, 62*, 271–298. doi: 10.1146/annurev.psych.121208.131622

Comas-Diaz, L. (2011a). Multicultural psychotherapies. In R. J. Corsini & D. Wedding (Eds.) (9th ed.), *Current psychotherapies* (pp. 536–567). Belmont, CA: Brooks/Cole.

Comas-Diaz, L. (2011b). *Multicultural care: A clinician's guide to cultural competence.* Washington, D.C.: American Psychological Association.

Comparelli, A., Corigliano, V., De Carolis, A., Mancinelli, I., Trovini, G., Ottavi, G., . . . Girardi, P. (2013).Emotion recognition impairment is present early and is stable throughout the course of schizophrenia. *Schizophrenia Research, 143*, 65–69.

Compton, W. M., Grant, B. F., Colliver, J. D., Glantz, M. D., & Stinson, F. S. (2004). Prevalence of marijuana use disorders in the United States: 1991–1992 and 2001–2002. *Journal of the American Medical Association, 291*, 2114–2121.

Compton, W., Conway, K. P., Stinson, F. S., Colliver, J. D., & Grant, B. F. (2005). Prevalence and comorbidity of DSM-IV antisocial syndromes and specific drug use disorders in the United States: Results from the National Epidemiologic Survey on Alcohol and Related Conditions. *Journal of Clinical Psychiatry, 66*, 676–685.

Conger, K. (2008a, June 26). Facebook concepts indicate brains of Alzheimer's patients aren't as networked, Stanford study shows. *Stanford University School of Medicine News Release.* Retrieved from http://med.stanford.edu/news_releases/2008/june/alzheimers21.html

Conger, K. (2008b, July 9). Taking a page from Facebook: Researchers track brain networks in Alzheimer's. *Stanford University School of Medicine News Release.* Retrieved from http://med.stanford.edu/mcr/2008/alzheimers-0709.html

Conner, B. T., & Lochman, J. E. (2010). Comorbid conduct disorder and substance use disorders. *Clinical Psychology: Science and Practice, 17*, 337–349. doi: 10.1111/j.1468-2850.2010.01225.x

Conway, K. P., Compton, W., Stinson, F. S., & Grant, B. F. (2006). Lifetime comorbidity of DSM-IV mood and anxiety disorders and specific drug use disorders: Results from the National Epidemiologic Survey on Alcohol and Related Conditions. *Journal of Clinical Psychiatry, 67*, 247–257.

Cook, J. M., Biyanova, T., & Coyne, J. C. (2009). Comparative case study of diffusion of eye movement desensitization and reprocessing in two clinical settings: Empirically supported treatment status is not enough. *Journal of Consulting and Clinical Psychology, 40*, 518–524. doi:10.1037/a0015144

Coons, P. M. (1986). Treatment progress in 20 patients with multiple personality disorder. *The Journal of Nervous and Mental Disease, 174*, 715–721.

Cooper, A., Scherer, C. R., Boies, S. C., & Gordon, B. L. (1999). Sexuality on the Internet: From sexual exploration to pathological expression. *Professional Psychology: Research & Practice, 30* (2), 154–164.

Copeland, W. E., Angold, A., Costello, E. J., & Egger, H. (2013). Prevalence, comorbidity, and correlates of DSM-5 proposed disruptive mood dysregulation disorder. *American Journal of Psychiatry, 170*, 173–179.

Corbett, A., & Ballard, C. (2012). Antipsychotics and mortality in dementia. *American Journal of Psychiatry, 169*, 7–9. doi: 10.1176/appi.ajp.2011.11101488

Corbett, J., Saccone, N. L., Foroud, T., Goate, A., Edenberg, H., Nurnberger, J., . . . Rice, J. P. (2005). Sex adjusted and age adjusted genome screen for nested alcohol dependence diagnoses. *Psychiatric Genetics, 15*, 25–30.

Coronado, S. F., & Peake, T. H. (1992). Culturally sensitive therapy: Sensitive principles. *Journal of College Student Psychotherapy, 7*, 63–72.

Cororve, M. B., & Gleaves, D. H. (2001). Body dysmorphic disorder: A review of conceptualizations, assessment, and treatment strategies. *Clinical Psychology Review, 21*, 949–970.

Correll, C. U., Manu, P., Olshanskiy, V., Napolitano, B., Kane, J. M., & Malhotra, A. K. (2009). Cardiometabolic risk of second-generation antipsychotic medications during first-time use in children and adolescents. *Journal of the American Medical Association, 302*, 1765–1773. doi: 10.1001/jama.2009.1549

Cortese, S., Kelly, C., Chabernaud, C., Proal, E., Di Martino, A., Milham, M. P., & Castellanos, F. X. (2012). Toward systems neuroscience of ADHD: A meta-analysis of 55 fMRI studies. *American Journal of Psychiatry, 169*, 1038–1055. 10.1176/appi.ajp.2012.11101521

Cortina, L. M., & Kubiak, S. P. (2006). Gender and posttraumatic stress: Sexual violence as an explanation for women's increased risk. *Journal of Abnormal Psychology, 115*, 753–759.

Coryell, W. (2011). The search for improved antidepressant strategies: Is bigger better? *American Journal of Psychiatry, 168*, 664–666. doi: 10.1176/appi.ajp.2011.11030510

Coryell, W., Pine, D., Fyer, A., & Klein, D. (2006). Anxiety responses to CO_2 inhalation in subjects at high risk for panic disorder. *Journal of Affective Disorders, 92*, 63–70.

Costello, D. M., Swendsen, J., Rose, J. S., & Dierkera, L. C. (2008). Risk and protective factors associated with trajectories of depressed mood from adolescence to early adulthood. *Journal of Consulting and Clinical Psychology, 76*, 173–183.

Costello, E. J., Compton, S. N., Keele, G., & Angold, A. (2003). Relationships between poverty and psychopathology: A natural experiment. *Journal of the American Medical Association, 290*, 2023–2029.

Costin, C. (1997). *Your dieting daughter: Is she dying for attention?* New York: Brunner/Mazel.

Cowley, G. (2001, February 12). New ways to stay clean. *Newsweek*, pp. 45–47.

Cox, B. J., MacPherson, P. S., & Enns, M. W. (2005). Psychiatric correlates of childhood shyness in a nationally representative sample. Behavior Research and Therapy, 43, 1019–1027.

Coyne, J. C. (1976). Toward an interactional description of depression. *Psychiatry, 39*, 14–27.

Cramer, P. (2000). Defense mechanisms in psychology today: Further processes for adaptation. *American Psychologist, 55*, 637–646.

Craske, M. G., Roy-Byrne, P. P., Stein, M. B., Sullivan, G., Sherbourne, C., & Bystritsky, A. (2009). Treatment for anxiety disorders: Efficacy to effectiveness to implementation. *Behaviour Research and Therapy, 47*, 931–937. doi:10.1016/j.brat.2009.07.012

Creed, F., & Barsky, A. (2004). A systematic review of the epidemiology of somatisation disorder and hypochondriasis. *Journal of Psychosomatic Research, 56*, 391–408.

Crespo-Facorro, B ., Pérez-Iglesias, R-O., Mata, I., Ramirez-Bonilla, M., Martínez-Garcia, O., Pardo-Garcia, G. . . . Vázquez-Barquero, J. L. (2011). Effectiveness of haloperidol, risperidone and olanzapine in the treatment of first-episode non-affective psychosis: results of a randomized, flexible-dose, open-label 1-year follow-up comparison. *Journal of Psychopharmacology, 219*, 225–233. doi: 10.1177/0269881110388332

Critic calls American Psychiatric Association approval of DSM-V "a sad day for psychiatry." (2012, December 3). Retrieved from healthnewsreview.org

Crits-Christoph, P., Gibbons, M. B. C., Hamilton, J., Ring-Kurtz, S., & Gallop, R. (2011). The dependability of alliance assessments: The alliance–outcome correlation is larger than you might think. *Journal of Consulting and Clinical Psychology, 79*, 267–278. doi: 10.1037/a0023668

Croghan, I. T., Hurt, R. D., Dakhil, S. R., Croghan, G. A., Sloan, J. A., Novotny, P. J., . . . Loprinzi, C. L. (2007). Randomized comparison of a nicotine inhaler and bupropion for smoking cessation and relapse prevention. *Mayo Clinic Proceedings, 82*, 186–195.

Cross-Disorder Group of the Psychiatric Genomics Consortium (2013, February 28). Identification of risk loci with shared effects on five major psychiatric disorders: a genome-wide analysis. *The Lancet, Early Online Publication.* Retrieved from http://press.thelancet.com/psychiatricdisorders.pdf

Crouse, K., & Pennington, B. (2012, November 13). Panic attack leads to hospital on way to golfer's first victory. *The New York Times*, pp. A1, A3.

Crow, S. J., Mitchell, J. E., Crosby, R. D., Swanson, S. A., Wonderlich, S., & Lancaster, K. (2009a). The cost effectiveness of cognitive behavioral therapy for bulimia nervosa delivered via telemedicine versus face-to-face. *Behaviour Research and Therapy, 47,* 451–453. doi: 10.1016/j.brat.2009.02.006

Crow, S. J., Peterson, C. B., Swanson, S. A., Raymond, N. C., Specker, S., Eckert, E. D., & Mitchell, J. E. (2009b). Increased mortality in bulimia nervosa and other eating disorders. *American Journal of Psychiatry, 166,* 1342–1346. doi:10.1176/appi.ajp.2009.09020247

Crowell, S. E., Beauchaine, T. P., McCauley, E., Smith, C. V., Vasilev, C. A., & Stevens, A. (2008). Parent-child interactions, peripheral serotonin, and self-inflicted injury in adolescents. *Journal of Consulting and Clinical Psychology, 76,* 15–21.

Crozier, J. C., Dodge, K. A., Fontaine, R. G., Lansford, J. E., Bates, J. E., Pettit, G. S., et al. (2008). Social information processing and cardiac predictors of adolescent antisocial behavior. *Journal of Abnormal Psychology, 117,* 253–267.

Cryan, J. F., & O'Leary, O. F. (2010). A glutamate pathway to faster-acting antidepressants? *Science, 329,* 913–914. doi: 10.1126/science.1194313

Csordas, T. J., Storck, M. J., & Strauss, M. (2008). Diagnosis and distress in Navajo healing. *Journal of Mental and Nervous Disease, 196,* 585–596.

Cuijpers, P., Clignet, F., van Meijel, B., van Straten, A., Lid, J., & Andersson, G. (2011). Psychological treatment of depression in inpatients: A systematic review and meta-analysis. *Clinical Psychology Review, 31,* 353–360. doi:10.1016/j.cpr.2011.01.002

Cuijpers, P., Li, J., Hofmann, S. J., & Andersson, G. (2010). Self-reported versus clinician-rated symptoms of depression as outcome measures in psychotherapy research on depression: A meta-analysis. *Clinical Psychology Review, 30,* 768–778.

Cuijpers, P., Muñoz, R. F, Clarke, G. N., & Lewinsohn, P M. (2009). Psychoeducational treatment and prevention of depression: The "Coping with Depression" course thirty years later. *Clinical Psychology Review, 29,* 449–458. doi:10.1016/j.cpr.2009.04.005

Cuijpers, P., van Straten, A., Schuurmans, J., van Oppen, P., Hollon, S. D., & Andersson, G. (2010). Psychotherapy for chronic major depression and dysthymia: A meta-analysis. *Clinical Psychology Review, 30,* 51–62. doi:10.1016/j.cpr.2009.09.003

Cukor, J., Spitalnick, J., Difede, J., Rizzo, A., & Rothbaum, B. O. (2009). Emerging treatments for PTSD. *Clinical Psychology Review, 29,* 715–726.

Cunningham, J. A., & Breslin, F. C. (2004). Only one in three people with alcohol abuse or dependence ever seek treatment. *Addictive Behaviors, 29,* 221–223.

Curb, J. D., & Marcus, E. B. (1991). Body fat and obesity in Japanese-Americans. *American Journal of Clinical Nutrition, 53,* 1552S–1555S.

Cuttler, C., & Grafa, P. (2009). Checking-in on the memory deficit and meta-memory deficit theories of compulsive checking. *Clinical Psychology Review, 29,* 393–409.

D

Dahl, M. (2008, August 6). *Shock therapy makes a quiet comeback.* Retrieved from http://www.msnbc.msn.com/id/26044935/

Dahlen, E. R., Edwards, B. D., Tubre, T., Zyphur, M. J., & Warren, C. (2012). Taking a look behind the wheel: An investigation into personality predictors of aggressive driving. *Accident Analysis and Prevention, 45,* 1–9

Dai, Y.B., Tan, X.J., Wu, W.F., Warner, M., & Gustafsson, J.A. (2012). Liver X receptor protects dopaminergic neurons in a mouse model of Parkinson disease. *Proceedings of the National Academy of Sciences, 109,* 13112. doi:10.1073/pnas.1210833109

Dale, K. Y., Berg, R., Elden, A., Ødegård, A., & Holte A. (2009). Testing the diagnosis of dissociative identity disorder through measures of dissociation, absorption, hypnotizability and PTSD: A Norwegian pilot study. *Journal of Trauma and Dissociation, 10,* 102–112. doi:10.1080/15299730802488478

Dalenberg, C. J., Brand, B. L., Gleaves, D. H., Dorahy, M. J., Loewenstein, R. J., Cardeña, E., . . . Spiegel, D. (2012). Evaluation of the evidence for the trauma and fantasy models of dissociation. *Psychological Bulletin, 138,* 550–588. doi:10.1037/a0027447

Dallaire, D. H., & Weinraub, M. (2007). Infant-mother attachment security and children's anxiety and aggression at first grade. *Journal of Applied Developmental Psychology, 28,* 477–492.

Dalley, S. E., Buunk, A. P., & Umit, T. (2009). Female body dissatisfaction after exposure to overweight and thin media images: The role of body mass index and neuroticism. *Personality and Individual Differences, 45,* 47–51. doi: 10.1016/j.paid.2009.01.044

Dannon, P. N., Lowengrub, K., Aizer, A., & Kotler, M. (2006). Pathological gambling: Comorbid psychiatric diagnoses in patients and their families. *Israel Journal of Psychiatry and Related Sciences, 43,* 88–92.

Dao, T. K., & Prevatt, F. (2006). A psychometric evaluation of the Rorschach Comprehensive System's Perceptual Thinking Index. *Journal of Personality Assessment, 86,* 180–189.

Dauvilliers, Y., Arnulf, I., & Mignot, E. (2007). Narcolepsy with cataplexy. *The Lancet, 369,* 499–511.

David, D., & Szentagotaia, A. (2006). Cognitions in cognitive-behavioral psychotherapies: Toward an integrative model. *Clinical Psychology Review, 26,* 284–298.

Davies, M., Gilston, J., & Rogers, P. (2012). Examining the relationship between male rape myth acceptance, female rape myth acceptance, victim blame, homophobia, gender roles, and ambivalent sexism. *Journal of Interpersonal Violence*, 27, 2807–2823.

Davis, M., Ressler, K., Rothbaum, B. O., & Richardson, R. (2006). Effects of D-cycloserine on extinction: Translation from preclinical to clinical work. *Biological Psychiatry, 60,* 369–375.

Davis, S. R., & Braunstein, G. D. (2012). Efficacy and safety of testosterone in the management of hypoactive sexual desire disorder in menopausal women. *The Journal of Sexual Medicine, 9,* 1134–1148

Davis, S. R., Davison, S. L., Donath, S., & Bell, R. J. (2005). Circulating androgen levels and self-reported sexual function in women. *Journal of the American Medical Association, 294,* 91–96.

Davis, S. R., Moreau, M., Kroll, R., Bouchard, C., Panay, N., Gass, M., . . . the APHRODITE Study Team (2008). Testosterone for low libido in postmenopausal women not taking estrogen. *New England Journal of Medicine,* 359, 2005–2017.

Davis, T. E. III, May, A., & Whiting, S. E. (2011). Evidence-based treatment of anxiety and phobia in children and adolescents: current status and effects on the emotional response. *Clinical Psychology Review, 31,* 592–602. doi:10.1016/j.cpr.2011.01.001

Dawe, S., Rees, V. W., Mattick, R., Sitharthan, T., & Heather, N. (2002). Efficacy of moderation-oriented cue exposure for problem drinkers: A randomized controlled trial. *Journal of Consulting and Clinical Psychology, 70,* 1045–1050.

Dawson, G. (2013). Dramatic increase in autism prevalence parallels explosion of research into its biology and causes. *JAMA Psychiatry, 70,* 9. doi:10.1001/jamapsychiatry.2013.488.

Day, H. R., Perencevich, E. N., Harris, A. D., Gruber-Baldini, A. L., Himelhoch, S. S., Brown, C. H., . . Morgan, D. J. (2012). The association between contact precautions and delirium at a tertiary care center. *Infection Control and Hospital Epidemiology, 33,* 34–39.

de Gonzalez, A. B., Hartge, P., Cerhan, J. R., Flint, A. R., Hannan, L., MacInnis, R. J., . . . Thun, M. J. (2011). Mass index and mortality among 1.46 million white adults. *New England Journal of Medicine, 363,* 2211–2219.

de Kleine, R. A., Hendriks, G.-J., Kusters, W. J. C., Broekman, T. G., & van Minnen, A. (2012). A randomized placebo-controlled trial of d-cycloserine to enhance exposure therapy for posttraumatic stress disorder. *Biological Psychiatry, 71,* 962–968. doi: 10.1016/j.biopsych.2012.02.033Volume

De La Cancela, V., & Guzman, L. P. (1991). Latino mental health service needs: Implications for training psychologists. In H. F. Myers et al. (Eds.), *Ethnic minority perspectives on clinical training and services in psychology* (pp. 59–64). Washington, DC: American Psychological Association.

De Leon, P. (2012, March/April). An impressive evolution. *The National Psychologist,* p. 5.

de Win, M. M. L., Jager, G., Booij, J., Reneman, L., Schilt, T., Lavini, C., . . . van den Brink, W. (2008). Sustained effects of ecstasy on the human brain: A prospective neuroimaging study in novel users. *Brain, 131,* 2936.

DeAngelis, T. (2012a, March). Practicing distance therapy, legally and ethically. *Monitor on Psychology, 43*(3), 52.

DeAngelis, T. (2012b). A second life for practice? *Monitor on Psychology, 43*(3), 48.

Dear, B. F., Titov, N., Schwencke, G., Andrews, G., Johnston, L., Craske, M. G., & McEvoy, P. (2011). An open trial of a brief transdiagnostic internet treatment for anxiety and depression. *Behaviour Research and Therapy, 49,* 830–837. doi:10.1016/j.brat.2011.09.007 |

Deas, S., Power, K., Collin, P., Yellowlees, A., & Grierson, D. (2011). The relationship between disordered eating, perceived parenting, and perfectionistic schemas. *Cognitive Therapy and Research, 35,* 414–424. doi: 10.1007/s10608-010-9319-x

DeBaggio, T. (2002). *Losing my mind. An intimate look at life with Alzheimer's.* New York: The Free Press.

DeFina, L. F., Willis, B. L., Radford, N. B., Gao, A., Leonard, D., Haskell, W. L., . . . Berry, J. D. (2013). The association between midlife cardiorespiratory fitness levels and later-life dementia: A cohort study. *Annals of Internal Medicine, 158,* 162-16

Degabriele, R., & Lagopoulos, J. (2009). A review of EEG and ERP studies in bipolar disorder. *Acta Neuropsychiatrica, 21,* 58–66. doi:10.1111/j.1601-5215.2009.00359.x

Del Boca, F. K., Darkes, J., Greenbaum, P. E., & Goldman, M. S. (2004). Up close and personal: Temporal variability in the drinking of individual college students during their first year. *Journal of Consulting and Clinical Psychology, 72,* 155–164.

Delahanty, D. L. (2011a). Toward the predeployment detection of risk for PTSD. *American Journal of Psychiatry, 168,* 9–11. doi: 10.1176/appi.ajp.2010.10101519

Delahanty, D .L. (2011b, November). Injury severity and posttraumatic stress. *Clinician's Research Digest*, p. 3.

Delgado, M. Y., Updegraff, K. A., Roosa, M. W., & Umaña-Taylor, A. J. (2010). Discrimination and Mexican-origin adolescents' adjustment: the moderating roles of adolescents', mothers', and fathers' cultural orientations and values. *Journal of Youth and Adolescence, 40,* 125–139. doi: 10.1007/s10964-009-9467-z

Dempster, E. L., Pidsley, R., Schalkwyk, L. C., Owens, S., Georgiades, A., Kane, F., ... Mill, J. (2011). Disease-associated epigenetic changes in monozygotic twins discordant for schizophrenia and bipolar disorder. *Human Molecular Genetics, 43,* 969–976. doi: 10.1093/hmg/ddr416

Denizet-Lewis, B. (2006, June 25). An anti-addiction pill? *The New York Times Magazine,* pp. 48–53.

Dennis, E. L., Jahanshad, N., Rudie, J. D., Brown, J. A., Johnson, K., McMahon, K. . . . Thompson, P. (2012). Altered structural brain connectivity in healthy carriers of the autism risk gene, CNTNAP2. *Brain Connectivity, 1,* 447–459. doi: 10.1089/brain.2011.0064

Denollet, J., & Pedersen, S. S. (2009). Anger, depression, and anxiety in cardiac patients: The complexity of individual differences in psychological risk. *Journal of the American College of Cardiology, 53,* 947–949. doi:10.1016/j.jacc.2008.12.006

DeNoon, D. (2006, May 1). Do ADHD drugs stunt kids' growth? *WebMD Medical News.* Retrieved from http://www.webmd.com/content/article/121/114370Reviewed

Denson, T. F., Spanovic, M., & Miller, N. (2009). Cognitive appraisals and emotions predict cortisol and immune responses: A meta-analysis of acute laboratory social stressors and emotion inductions. *Psychological Bulletin, 135,* 823–853. doi:10.1037/a0016909

Denys, D., Mantione, M., Figee, M., van den Munckhof, P., Koerselman, F., Westenberg, H., . . . Schuurman, R. (2010). Deep brain stimulation of the nucleus accumbens for treatment-refractory obsessive-compulsive disorder. *Archives of General Psychiatry, 67,* 1061–1068. doi:10.1001/archgenpsychiatry.2010.122

Depression ups risk of complications following heart attack, study suggests. *ScienceDaily*. Retrieved from http://www.sciencedaily.com/releases/2008/07/080701194736.htm

Dervic, K., Brent, D. A., & Oquendo, M. A. (2008). Completed suicide in childhood. *Psychiatric Clinics of North America, 31,* 271–291.

Devan, G. S. (1987). Koro and schizophrenia in Singapore. *British Journal of Psychiatry, 150,* 106–107.

Devanand, D. P., Mintzer, J., Schultz, S. K., Andrews, H. F., Sultzer, D. L., de la Pena, D., Gupta, S, . . . Levin, B. (2012). Relapse risk after discontinuation of risperidone in Alzheimer's disease. *New England Journal of Medicine, 367,* 1497.

Devos, D., Moreau, C., & Destée, A. (2009). Levodopa for Parkinson's disease. *New England Journal of Medicine, 360,* 935–936.

Di Iorio, C. R., Watkins, T. J., Dietrich, M. S., Cao, A., Blackford, J. U., Rogers, B., . . . Cowan, R. L. (2011). Evidence for chronically altered serotonin function in the cerebral cortex of female 3,4-methylenedioxymethamphetamine polydrug users. *Archives of General Psychiatry, 69,* 399–409. doi:10.1001/archgenpsychiatry.2011.156

Diamond, M. (2011). Developmental, sexual and reproductive neuroendocrinology: Historical, clinical and ethical considerations. *Frontiers in Neuroendocrinology, 32,* 255–263.

Diamond, S., Baldwin, R., & Diamond, R. (1963). *Inhibition and choice.* New York: Harper & Row.

Dick, D. M. (2011). Gene-environment interaction in psychological traits and disorders. *Annual Review of Clinical Psychology, 7,* 383–409. doi: 10.1146/annurev-clinpsy-032210-104518

Dickel, D. E., Veenstra-VanderWeele, J., Cox, N. J., Wu, A., Fischer, D. J., Van Etten-Lee, M., Himle, J. A., . . . Hanna, G. L. (2006). Association testing of the positional and functional candidate gene SLC1A1/EAAC1 in early-onset obsessive-compulsive disorder. *Archives of General Psychiatry, 63,* 778–785.

DiClemente, C. (2011). Project MATCH. In J. C. Norcross, G. R. VandenBos, & D. K. Freedheim (Eds.) (2011). *History of psychotherapy: Continuity and change* (2nd ed.). (pp. 395–401). Washington, DC: American Psychological Association.

DiMauro, J., Domingues, J., Fernandez, G., & Tolina, D. F. (2012). Long-term effectiveness of CBT for anxiety disorders in an adult outpatient clinic sample: A follow-up study. *Behaviour Research and Therapy, 51,* 82–86. doi: 10.1016/j.brat.2012.10.00

Dimeff, L.A., Paves, A. P., Skutch J.M., & Woodcock E.A. (2011). Shifting paradigms in clinical psychology: How innovative technologies are shaping treatment delivery. In D. H. Barlow (Ed.), *The Oxford handbook of clinical psychology* (pp. 618–648). New York: Oxford University Press.

Dimidjian, S., Barrera, M. Jr., Martell, C., Muñoz, R. F., & Lewinsohn, P. M. (2011). The origins and current status of behavioral activation treatments for depression. *Annual Review of Clinical Psychology, 7,* 1–38. doi:10.1146/annurev-clinpsy-032210-104535

Dishion, T. J., & Owen, L. D. (2002). A longitudinal analysis of friendships and substance use: Bidirectional influence from adolescence to adulthood. *Developmental Psychology, 38,* 480–491.

Dixon-Gordon, K. L., Chapman, A. L., Lovasz, N., & Walters, K. (2011). Too upset to think: The interplay of borderline personality features, negative emotions, and social problem solving in the laboratory. *Personality Disorders: Theory, Research, and Treatment, 2,* 243–260. doi:10.1037/a0021799

Djoussé, L., Driver, J. A., & Gaziano, J. M. (2009). Relation between modifiable lifestyle factors and lifetime risk of heart failure. *Journal of the American Medical Association, 302,* 394–400.

Dobbs, D. (2010). Schizophrenia appears during adolescence. But where does one begin and the other end? *Nature, 468,* 154–156. doi:10.1038/468154a

Dobson, K. S., Hollon, S. D., Dimidjian, S., Schmaling, K. B., Kohlenberg, R. J., Gallop, R. J., . . . Jacobson, N. S. (2008). Randomized trial of behavioral activation, cognitive therapy, and antidepressant medication in the prevention of relapse and recurrence in major depression. *Journal of Consulting and Clinical Psychology, 76,* 468–477. doi:10.1037/ 0022-006X.76.3.468

Dodge, K. A. (2009). Mechanisms of gene–environment interaction effects in the development of conduct disorder. *Perspectives on Psychological Science, 4,* 408–414. doi: 10.1111/j.1745-6924.2009.01147.x

Dodick, D. W., & Gargus, J. J. (2008). Why migraines strike. *Scientific American.* Retrieved from http://www.sciam.com/article.cfm?id=whymigraines-strike&page=5

Dohrenwend, B. P. (2006). Inventorying stressful life events as risk factors for psychopathology: Toward resolution of the problem of intracategory variability. *Psychological Bulletin, 132,* 477–495.

Dohrenwend, B. P., Turner, J. B., Turse, N. A., Adams, B. G., Koenen, K. C., & Marshall, R. (2006). The psychological risks of Vietnam for U.S. veterans: A revisit with new data and methods. *Science, 313,* 979–982.

Dolan, D. C., Taylor, D. J., Bramoweth, A. D., & Rosenthal, L. D. (2010). Cognitive behavioral therapy of insomnia: A clinical case series study of patients with comorbid disorders and using hypnotic medications. *Behavior Research and Therapy, 48,* 321–327. doi:10.1016/j.brat.2009.12.004

Donaldson, S. I., Csikszentmihalyi, M., & Nakamura, J. (Eds.). (2011). *Applied positive psychology: Improving everyday life, health, schools, work, and society. Series in applied psychology.* New York: Routledge/Taylor & Francis Group.

Donegan, E., & Dugas, M. J. (2012). Generalized anxiety disorder: A comparison of symptom change in adults receiving cognitive-behavioral therapy or applied relaxation. *Journal of Consulting and Clinical Psychology, 80,* 490–496. doi: 10.1037/a0028132

Dong, L., Bilbao, A., Laucht, M., Henriksson, R., Yakovlev, T., Ridinger, M., . . . Schuman, G. (2011). Effects of the circadian rhythm gene period 1 (Per1) on psychosocial stress–induced alcohol drinking. *American Journal of Psychiatry, 168,* 1090–1098. doi:org/10.1176/appi.ajp.2011.10111579

Dong, L., Bilbao, A., Laucht, M., Henriksson, R., Yakovlev, T., Ridinger, M., Desrivieres, S., . . . Schuman, G. (2011). Effects of the circadian rhythm gene period 1 (Per1) on psychosocial stress–induced alcohol drinking. *American Journal of Psychiatry, 168,* 1090–1098. doi: org/10.1176/appi.ajp.2011.10111579

Donovan, J. E., Molina, B. S. G., & Kelly, T. M. (2009). Alcohol outcome expectancies as socially shared and socialized beliefs. *Psychology of Addictive Behaviors, 23,* 248–259. doi:10.1037/a0015061

Doran, N., Schweizer, C. A., & Myers, M. G. (2011). Do expectancies for reinforcement from smoking change after smoking initiation? *Psychology of Addictive Behaviors, 25,* 101–107. doi: 10.1037/a0020361

Dougall, A. L., & Baum, A. (2001). Stress, health, and illness. In A. Baum, T. A. Revenson, & J. E. Singer (Eds.), *Handbook of health psychology* (pp. 339–348). Mahwah, NJ: Erlbaum.

Douglas, K. S., Guy, L. S., & Hart, S. D. (2009). Psychosis as a risk factor for violence to others: A meta-analysis. *Psychological Bulletin, 135,* 679–706. doi:10.1037/a0016311

Drabick, D. A. G. (2009). Can a developmental psychopathology perspective facilitate a paradigm shift toward a mixed categorical-dimensional classification system? *Clinical Psychology: Science and Practice, 16,* 41–49. doi:10.1111/j.1468-2850.2009.01141.x

Drabick, D. A. G., & Kendall, P. C. (2010). Developmental psychopathology and the diagnosis of mental health problems among youth. *Clinical Psychology: Science and Practice, 17,* 272–280. doi: 10.1111/j.1468-2850.2010.01219.x

Drieling, T., van Calker, D., & Hecht, H. (2006). Stress, personality and depressive symptoms in a 6.5 year follow-up of subjects at familial risk for affective disorders and controls. *Journal of Affective Disorders, 91,* 195–203.

Driessen, E., Cuijpers, P., de Maat, S. C. M., Abbass, A. A., de Jonghe, F., & Dekker, J. J. M. (2010). The efficacy of short-term psychodynamic psychotherapy for depression: A meta-analysis. *Clinical Psychology Review, 30,* 25–36. doi:10.1016/j.cpr.2009.08.010

Dubovsky, S. (2006, February 12). An update on the neurobiology of addiction. *Journal Watch Psychiatry.* Retrieved from http://psychiatry.jwatch.org/cgi/content/full/2006/222/7?q=etoc

Dubovsky, S. (2008, March 24). Venlafaxine vs. SSRIs: A meta-analysis. *Journal Watch Psychiatry.* Retrieved from http://psychiatry.jwatch.org/cgi/content/full/2008/324/2

Dubovsky, S. (2010, October 18). Epigenetics — A mechanism for the impact of experience on inheritance? *Journal Watch Psychiatry.* Retrieved from http://psychiatry.jwatch.org/cgi/content/full/2010/1018/1

Dubovsky, S. (2011, June 13). Varenicline: No harm, but little benefit. *Journal Watch Psychiatry.* Retrieved from http://psychiatry.jwatch.org/cgi/content/full/2011/613/5

Dubovsky, S. (2012, January 13). How well are we treating depression? *Journal Watch Psychiatry.* Retrieved from http://psychiatry.jwatch.org/cgi/content/full/2012/113/2?q=etoc_jwpsych

Ducci, F., Kaakinen, M., Pouta, A., Hartikainen, A.-L., Veijola, J., Isohanni, M., . . . Ekelund, J. (2011). TTC12-ANKK1-DRD2 and CHRNA5-CHRNA3-CHRNB4 influence different pathways leading to smoking behavior from adolescence to mid-adulthood. *Biological Psychiatry, 69,* 650–660. doi: 10.1016/j.biopsych.2010.09.055

Duke, L. A., Allen, R. N., Rozee, P., & Bommaritto, M. (2008). The sensitivity and specificity of flashbacks and nightmares to trauma. *Journal of Anxiety Disorders, 22,* 319–327.

Duke, P., & Hochman, G. (1992). *A brilliant madness.* New York: Bantam Dell.

Duman, R. S., & Aghajanian, G. K. (2012). Synaptic dysfunction in depression: Potential therapeutic targets. *Science, 338* (6103), 68–72.

Duran, B., Oetzel, J., Lucero, J., Jiang, Y., Novins, D. K., Manson, S., et alBeals, J. (2005). Obstacles for rural American Indians seeking alcohol, drug, or mental health treatment. *Journal of Consulting and Clinical Psychology, 73,* 819–829.

Durham, R. C., Higgins, C., Chambers, J. A., Swan, J. S., & Dow, M. G. T. (2012). Long-term outcome of eight clinical trials of CBT for anxiety disorders: Symptom profile of sustained recovery and treatment-resistant groups. *Journal of Affective Disorders, 136,* 875–881.

Duric, V., Banasr, M., Licznerski, P., Schmidt, H. D., Stockmeier, C. A., Simen, A. S., Newton, S. S., & Duman, R. S. (2010). A negative regulator of MAP kinase causes depressive behavior. *Nature Medicine, 16,* 1328–1332.doi: 10.1038/nm.2219

Durkheim, E. (1958). *Suicide.* (J. A. Spaulding & G. Simpson, Trans.). New York: Free Press. (Original work published 1897.)

Dutra, L., Stathopoulou, G., Basden, S. L., Leyro, T. M., Powers, M. B., & Otto, M. W. (2008). A meta-analytic review of psychosocial interventions for substance use disorders. *American Journal of Psychiatry, 165,* 179–187.

Dzokoto, V. A., & Adams, G. (2005). Understanding genital-shrinking epidemics in West Africa: Koro, juju, or mass psychogenic illness? *Culture, Medicine and Psychiatry, 29,* 53–78.

E

Eagly, A. H., Eaton, A., Rose, S. M., Riger, S., & McHugh, M. C. (2012). Feminism and psychology: Analysis of a half-century of research on women and gender. *American Psychologist, 67,* 211–230. doi: 10.1037/a0027260

Eardley, I., Donatucci, C., Corbin, J., El-Meliegy, A, Hatzimouratidis, K., McVary, K., . . . Lee, S. W. (2011). Pharmacotherapy for erectile dysfunction. *Journal of Sexual Medicine, 7,* 524–540.

Eaton, W. W., Shao, H., Nestadt, G., Lee, B. H., Bienvenu, O. J., & Zandi, P. (2008). Population-based study of first onset and chronicity in major depressive disorder. *Archives of General Psychiatry, 65,* 513–520.

Eberhardy, F. (1967). The view from "the couch." *Journal of Child Psychological Psychiatry, 8,* 257–263.

Ebmeier, K. P., Donaghey, C., & Steele, J. D. (2006). Recent developments and current controversies in depression. *The Lancet, 367,* 153–167.

Ecker, C., Ginestet, C., Feng, Y., Johnston, P., Lombardo, M. V., Lai, M.-C., . . . MRC AIMS Consortium. (2013). Brain surface anatomy in adults with autism: the relationship between surface area, cortical thickness, and autistic symptoms. *JAMA Psychiatry, 70,* 59–70. doi:10.1001/jamapsychiatry.2013.265.

Eddleston, M. (2006). Physical vulnerability and fatal self-harm in the elderly. *British Journal of Psychiatry, 189,* 278–279.

Eddy, K. T., Hennessey, M., & Thompson-Brenner, H. (2007). Eating pathology in East African women: The role of media exposure and globalization. *The Journal of Nervous and Mental Disease, 195,* 196–202.

Edman, J. L., & Johnson, R. C. (1999). Filipino American and Caucasian American beliefs about the causes and treatment of mental problems. *Cultural Diversity and Ethnic Minority Psychology, 5,* 380–386.

Egan, J. (2008, September 14). The bipolar puzzle. *The New York Times Magazine,* pp. 66, 75, 94–97.

Ehlers, A., Bisson, J., Clark, D. M., Creamer, M., Pilling, S., Richards, D., Yule, W. (2010). Do all psychological treatments really work the same in posttraumatic stress disorder? *Clinical Psychology Review, 30,* 269–276. doi:10.1016/j.cpr.2009.12.001

Ehlkes, T., Michie, P. T., & Schall, U. (2012). Brain imaging correlates of emerging schizophrenia. *Neuropsychiatry, 2,* 147–154. doi:10.2217/npy.12.13

Ehrenreich, B., Righter, B., Rocke, D.A., Dixon, L., & Himelhoch, S. (2011). Are mobile phones and handheld computers being used to enhance delivery of psychiatric treatment? A systematic review. *Journal of Nervous and Mental Disease, 199,* 886–891. doi: 10.1097/NMD.0b013e3182349e90

Eichstedt, J. A., & Arnold, S. L. (2001). Childhood-onset obsessive-compulsive disorder. A tic-related subtype of OCD? *Clinical Psychology Review, 21,* 137–157.

Eikeseth, S., Klintwall, L., Jahr, E., & Karlsson, P. (2012). Outcome for children with autism receiving early and intensive behavioral intervention in mainstream preschool and kindergarten settings. *Research in Autism Spectrum Disorders, 6,* 829–835. doi:10.1016/j.rasd.2011.09.002

Einfeld, S. L,. & Brown, R. (2010). Down syndrome—new prospects for an ancient disorder. *Journal of the American Medical Association, 303,* 2525–2526.

Ekinci, O., Albayrak, Y., & Ekinci, A. (2012). Cognitive insight and its relationship with symptoms in deficit and nondeficit schizophrenia. *Journal of Nervous and Mental Disease, 200, 44–50.* doi: 10.1097/NMD.0b013e31823e66af

Elbogen, E. B., & Johnson, S. C. (2009). The intricate link between violence and mental disorder: Results from the National Epidemiologic Survey on Alcohol and Related Conditions. *Archives of General Psychiatry, 66,* 152–161.

Eldar, S., Apter, A., Lotan, D., Edgar, K. P., Naim, R., Fox, N. A . . . Bar-Haim, Y. (2012). Attention bias modification treatment for pediatric anxiety disorders: A randomized controlled trial. *American Journal of Psychiatry, 169,* 213–230. doi: 10.1176/appi.ajp.2011.11060886

Elder, T. E. (2010). The importance of relative standards in ADHD diagnoses: Evidence based on exact birth dates. *Journal of Health Economics, 29,* 641–656. doi: 10.1016/j.jhealeco.2010.06.003

Ellason, J. W., & Ross, C. A. (1997). Two-year follow-up of inpatients with dissociative identity disorder. *American Journal of Psychiatry, 154,* 832–839.

Ellin, A. (2012, August 13). Binge eating among men steps out of the shadows. *The New York Times.* Retrieved from www.nytimes.com

Ellis, A. (1977). The basic clinical theory of rational-emotive therapy. In A. Ellis & R. Grieger (Eds.), *Handbook of rational-emotive therapy* (pp. 3–34). New York: Springer.

Ellis, A. (1993). Reflections on rational-emotive therapy. *Journal of Consulting and Clinical Psychology, 61,* 199–201.

Ellis, A. (2001). *Overcoming destructive beliefs, feelings, and behaviors: New directions for rational emotive behavior therapy.* Amherst, NY: Prometheus Books.

Ellis, A. (2011). Rational emotive behavior therapy. In R. J. Corsini & D. Wedding (Eds.), (9th ed.), *Current psychotherapies* (pp. 196–234). Belmont, CA: Brooks/Cole.

Ellis, A., & Ellis, D. J. (2011). *Rational emotive behavior therapy. Theories of psychotherapy.* Washington, DC: American Psychological Association.

Elwood, L. S., Hahn, K. S., Olatunji, B. O., & Williams, N. L. (2009). Cognitive vulnerabilities to the development of PTSD: A review of four vulnerabilities and the proposal of an integrative vulnerability model. *Clinical Psychology Review, 29,* 87–100. doi:10.1016/j.cpr.2008.10.002

Emslie, G. J. (2008). Pediatric anxiety—underrecognized and undertreated. *New England Journal of Medicine, 359,* 2835–2836.

Eonta, A., M., Christon, L. M., Hourigan, S. E., Ravindran, N., Vrana, S. R., & Southam-Gerow, M. (2011). Using everyday technology to enhance evidence-based treatments. *Professional Psychology: Research and Practice, 42,* 513–520. doi: 10.1037/a0025825

Epperson, C. N. (2013). Premenstrual dysphoric disorder and the brain. *American Journal of Psychiatry, 170,* 248–252. 10.1176/appi.ajp.2012.1212155

Epping-Jordan, J. E., Compas, B. E., & Howell, D. C. (1994). Predictors of cancer progression in young adult men and women. *Health Psychology, 13,* 539–547.

Erdleyi, M. H. (2010). The ups and downs of memory. *American Psychologist, 65,* 622–633. doi:10.1037/a0020440

Esman, A. H. (2011). Charcot, Freud, and the treatment of "nervous disorders." *Journal of Nervous & Mental Disease, 199,* 828–829. doi: 10.1097/NMD.0b013e3182348cf9

Essau, C. A., Lewinsohn, P. M., Seeley, J. R., & Sasagawa, S. (2010). Gender differences in the developmental course of depression. *Journal of Affective Disorders, 127,* 185–190 doi:10.1016/j.jad.2010.05.016 |

Essex, M. J., Kraemer, H. C., Armstrong, J. M., Boyce, W. T., Goldsmith, H. H., Klein, M. H., et al. (2006). Exploring risk factors for the emergence of children's mental health problems. *Archives of General Psychiatry, 63,* 1246–1256.

Etkin, A., Prater, K. E., Schatzberg, A. F., Menon, V., & Greicius, M. D. (2009). Disrupted amygdalar subregion functional connectivity and evidence of a compensatory network in generalized anxiety disorder. *Archives of General Psychiatry, 66,* 1361–1372.

Evans, S. E., Davies, C., & DiLillo, D. (2008). Exposure to domestic violence: A meta-analysis of child and adolescent outcomes. *Aggression and Violent Behavior, 13,* 131–140.

Even, C., & Weintraub, D. (2012). Is depression in Parkinson's Disease (PD) a specific entity? *Journal of Affective Disorders, 139,* 103–112. http://dx.doi.org/10.1016/j.jad.2011.07.002

Evraire, L. E., & Dozois, D. J. A. (2011). An integrative model of excessive reassurance seeking and negative feedback seeking in the development and maintenance of depression. *Clinical Psychology Review, 31,* 1291–1303. doi:10.1016/j.cpr.2011.07.014 |

Exner, J. E., Jr. (2002). Early development of the Rorschach test. *Academy of Clinical Psychology Bulletin, 8,* 9–24.

Eye movements and the search for biomarkers for schizophrenia. (2012, October 29). *ScienceDaily.* Retrieved from http://www.sciencedaily.com/releases/2012/10/121029081833.htm

F

Fabiano, G. A., Pelham, W. E., Jr., Coles, E. K., Gnagy, E. M., Chronis-Tuscano, A., & O'Connor, B. C. (2009). A meta-analysis of behavioral treatments for attention-deficit/hyperactivity disorder. *Clinical Psychology Review, 29,* 129–140. doi:10.1016/j.cpr.2008.11.001

Fabrega, H., Jr. (1990). Hispanic mental health research: A case for cultural psychiatry. *Journal of Behavioral Sciences, 12,* 339–365.

Faedda, G. L., Becker, I., Baroni, A., Tondo, L., Aspland, E., & Koukopoulos, A. (2009). The origins of electroconvulsive therapy: Prof. Bini's first report on ECT. *Journal of Affective Disorders, 120,* 12–15. doi: 10.1016/j.jad.2009.01.023

Failer, J. L. (2002). *Who qualifies for rights? Homelessness, mental illness, and civil commitment.* Ithaca, NY: Cornell University Press.

Fairburn, C. G., Cooper, Z., Doll, H. A., O'Connor, M. E., Bohn, K., Hawker, D. M., et al. (2009). Transdiagnostic cognitive-behavioral therapy for patients with eating disorders: A two-site trial with 60-week follow-up. *American Journal of Psychiatry, 166,* 311–319. doi:10.1176/appi.ajp.2008. 08040608

Fairburn, C. G., Stice, E., Cooper, Z., Doll, H. A., Norman, P. A., & O'Connor, E. E. (2003). Understanding persistence in bulimia nervosa: A 5-year naturalistic study. *Journal of Consulting and Clinical Psychology, 71,* 103–109.

Fals-Stewart, W. (2003). The occurrence of partner physical aggression on days of alcohol consumption: A longitudinal diary study. *Journal of Consulting and Clinical Psychology, 71,* 41–52.

Fan, Y., Tang, Y., Lu, Q., Feng, S., Yu, Q., Sui, D., . . . Song, L. (2009). Dynamic changes in salivary cortisol and secretory immunoglobulin A response to acute stress. *Stress and Health, 25,* 189–194. doi:10.1002/smi.1239

Farr, C. B. (1994). Benjamin Rush and American psychiatry. *American Journal of Psychiatry, 151* (Suppl.), 65–73.

Farrell, A. D., & White, K. S. (1998). Peer influences and drug use among urban adolescents: Family structure and parent/adolescent relationship as protective factors. *Journal of Consulting and Clinical Psychology, 66,* 248–258.

Fazel, S., Långström, N., Hjern, A., Grann, M., & Lichtenstein, P. (2009). Schizophrenia, substance abuse, and violent crime. *Journal of the American Medical Association, 301,* 2016–2023.

Fein, D., Barton, M., Eigsti, I.-M., Kelley, E., Naigles, L, Schultz, R. T., . . . Tyson, K. (2013). Optimal outcome in individuals with a history of autism. *Journal of Child Psychology and Psychiatry, 54,* 195–205.

Feldman, H. S., Jones, K. L., Lindsay, S., Slymen, D., Klonoff-Cohen, H., Kao, K., . . . Chambers, C. (2012). Prenatal alcohol exposure patterns and alcohol-related birth defects and growth deficiencies: A prospective study. *Alcoholism: Clinical and Experimental Research, 36,* 670–676. doi: 10.1111/j.1530-0277.2011.01664.x

Feldman, M. D. (2003). Foreword. In J. Gregory (Ed.), *Sickened: The memoir of a Munchausen by proxy childhood* (pp. v–ix). New York: Bantam.

Ferdinand, K. C., & Ferdinand, D. P. (2009). Cardiovascular disease disparities: Racial/ethnic factors and potential solutions. *Current Cardiovascular Risk Reports, 3,* 187–193. doi:10.1007/s12170-009-0030-y

Ferdinand, R. F., Bongersa, I. L., van der Ende, J., van Gastela, W., Tick, N., Utens, E., et al. (2006). Distinctions between separation anxiety and social anxiety in children and adolescents. *Behaviour Research and Therapy, 44,* 1523–1535.

Fergusson, D. M., & Woodward, L. J. (2002). Mental health, educational, and social role outcomes of adolescents with depression. *Archives of General Psychiatry, 59,* 225–231.

Fernandez, E. (2013). *Treatments for anger in specific populations: Theory, application, and outcome.* New York: Oxford University Press.

Ferrarelli, F., Sarasso, S., Guller, Y., Riedner, B. A., Peterson, M. J., Bellesi, M., . . . Tononi, G. (2012). Reduced natural oscillatory frequency of frontal thalamocortical circuits in schizophrenia. *Archives of General Psychiatry, 69,* 766–774. doi:10.1001/archgenpsychiatry.2012.147

Ferri, M., Amato, L., & Davoli, M. (2006). Alcoholics Anonymous and other 12-step programmes for alcohol dependence. *The Cochrane Database of Systematic Reviews, 3.* Retrieved from http://dx.doi.org/10.1002/14651858.CD005032.pub2

Feusner, J. D., Townsend, J., Bystritsky, A., & Bookheimer, S. (2007). Visual information processing of faces in body dysmorphic disorder. *Archives of General Psychiatry, 64,* 1417–1425.

Fibiger, S., Hjelmborg, V. B., Fagnani, C., &, Skytthe, A. (2010). Genetic epidemiological relations between stuttering, cluttering and specific language impairment. *Proceedings. 6th World Congress On Fluency Disorders, 5th–8th August, 2009, Rio de Janeiro, Brazil.* Retrieved from http://www.theifa.org/IFA2009

Fichter, M. M., Quadflieg, N., Nisslmüller, K., Lindner, S., Osen, B., Huber, T., & Wünsch-Leiteritz, W. (2012). Does iinternet-based prevention reduce the risk of relapse for anorexia nervosa? *Behaviour Research and Therapy, 50,* 180–190,

Field, A. P. (2006). Is conditioning a useful framework for understanding the development and treatment of phobias? *Clinical Psychology Review, 26,* 857–875.

Fieve, R. R. (1975). *Moodswings: The third revolution in psychiatry.* New York: Morrow.

Finke, K., Schwarzkopf, W., Müller, U., Frodl, T., Müller, H. J., Schneider, W. X., . . . Hennig-Fast, K. (2011). Disentangling the adult attention-deficit hyperactivity disorder endophenotype: Parametric measurement of attention. *Journal of Abnormal Psychology, 120,* 890–901. doi: 10.1037/a0024944

First, M. (2006). Beyond clinical utility: Broadening the *DSM-V* research appendix to include alternative diagnostic constructs. *American Journal of Psychiatry, 163,* 1679–1681.

Fisher, A. D., Bandini, E., Casale, H., & Maggi, M. (2011). Paraphilic disorders: Diagnosis and treatment. In M. Maggi (Ed.). *Hormonal therapy for male sexual dysfunction* (pp. 94–110). Hoboken, NJ: Wiley.

Fisher, H. L., Cohen-Woods, S., Hosang, G. M., Korszun, A., Owen, M., Craddock, N., Craig, I. W., ... Uher, R. (2013). Interaction between specific forms of childhood maltreatment and the serotonin transporter gene (5-HTT) in recurrent depressive disorder. *Journal of Affective Disorders, 145,* 136–141.

Fisher, P. L., & Wells, A. (2005). How effective are cognitive and behavioral treatments for obsessive–compulsive disorder? A clinical significance analysis. *Behaviour Research and Therapy, 43,* 1543–1558.

Fiske, A., Wetherell, J. L, & Gatz, M. (2009). Depression in older adults. *Annual Review of Clinical Psychology, 5,* 363–389. doi:10.1146/annurev.clinpsy.032408.153621

Fitzgerald, P. B., Brown, T. L., Marston, N. A. U., Daskalakis, J., de Castella, A., & Kulkarni, J. (2003). Transcranial magnetic stimulation in the treatment of depression: A double-blind, placebo-controlled trial. *Archives of General Psychiatry, 60,* 1002–1008.

Fitzgerald, P. B., Hoy, K. E., Herring, S. E., McQueen, S., Peachey, A. V. J., Segrave, R. A., Maller, J . . . Daskalakis, Z. J. (2012). A double blind randomized trial of unilateral left and bilateral prefrontal cortex transcranial magnetic stimulation in treatment resistant major depression. *Journal of Affective Disorders, 139,* 193–198. Retrieved from http://dx.doi.org/10.1016/j.jad.2012.02.017

Flagel, S. B., Clark, J. J., Robinson, T. E., Mayo, L., Czuj, A., Willuhn, I., . . . Akil, H. (2011). A selective role for dopamine in stimulus–reward learning. *Nature, 469,* 53–57. doi:10.1038/nature09588

Flegal, K. M., Carroll, M. D., Kit, B. K., & Ogden, C. L. (2012). Prevalence of obesity and trends in the distribution of body mass index among US adults, 1999–2010. *Journal of the American Medical Association, 307,* 491–497. doi: 10.1001/jama.2012.39

Flegal, K. M., Carroll, M. D., Kit, B. K., & Ogden, C. L. (2012). Prevalence of obesity and trends in the distribution of body mass index among US Adults, 1999–2010. *Journal of the American Medical Association,* in press. doi: 10.1001/jama.2012.39

Flegal, K. M., Graubard, B.I., Williamson, D. F., & Gail, M. H. (2005). Excess deaths associated with underweight, overweight, and obesity. *Journal of the American Medical Association, 293,* 1861–1867.

Flegal, K. M., Kit, B., Orpana, H., & Graubard, B. I. (2013). Association of all-cause mortality with overweight and obesity using standard body mass index categories:

A systematic review and meta-analysis. *Journal of the American Medical Association, 309*, 71–82. doi:10.1001/jama.2012.113905.

Florian, C., Vecsey, C. G., Halassa, M. M., Haydon, P. G., & Abel, T. (2011). Astrocyte-derived adenosine and a1 receptor activity contribute to sleep loss-induced deficits in hippocampal synaptic plasticity and memory in mice. *Journal of Neuroscience, 31*, 6956.

Foley, E., Baillie, A., Huxter, M., Price, M., & Sinclair, E. (2010). Mindfulness-based cognitive therapy for individuals whose lives have been affected by cancer: A randomized controlled trial. *Journal of Consulting and Clinical Psychology, 78*, 72–79. doi:10.1037/a0017566

Folsom, D. P., Hawthorne, W., Lindamer, L., Gilmer, T., Bailey, A., Golshan, S., Garcia, P., et al. (2005). Prevalence and risk factors for homelessness and utilization of mental health services among 10,340 patients with serious mental illness in a large public mental health system. *American Journal of Psychiatry, 162*, 370–376.

Fombonne, E. (2008). Thimerosal disappears but autism remains. *Archives of General Psychiatry, 65*, 15–16.

Fontaine, K. R., Redden, D. T., Wang, C., Westfall, A. O., & Allison, D. B. (2003). Years of life lost due to obesity. *Journal of the American Medical Association, 289*, 187–193.

Foote, B., Smolin, Y., Kaplan, M., Legatt, M. E., & Lipschitz, D. (2005). Prevalence of dissociative disorders in psychiatric outpatients.*American Journal of Psychiatry, 163*, 623–629.

Foote, B., Smolin, Y., Neft, D. I., & Lipschitz, D. (2008). Dissociative disorders and suicidality in psychiatric outpatients. *American Journal of Psychiatry, 163*, 23–629.

Foran, H. M., & O'Leary, K. D. (2008). Alcohol and intimate partner violence: A meta-analytic review. *Clinical Psychology Review, 28*, 1222–1234.

Forgas, J. P. (2008). Affect and cognition. *Perspectives on Psychological Science, 3*(2), 94–101.

Forgeard, M. J. C., & Seligman, M. E. P. (2012). Seeing the glass half full: A review of the causes and consequences of optimism. *Pratiques Psychologiques, 18*, 107–120. http://dx.doi.org/10.1016/j.prps.2012.02.002

Forgeard, M. J. C., & Seligman, M. E. P. (2012). Seeing the glass half full: A review of the causes and consequences of optimism. *Pratiques Psychologiques, 18*, 107–120. doi:10.1016/j.prps.2012.02.002

Forgeard, M. J. C., Haigh, E. A. P., Beck, A. T., Davidson, R. J., Henn, F. A., Maier, S. F., . . . Seligman, M. (2012). Beyond depression: Toward a process-based approach to research, diagnosis, and treatment. *Clinical Psychology: Science and Practice, 18*, 275–299. doI; 10.1111/j.1468-2850.2011.01259.x

Forman, E. M., Chapman, J. E., Herbert, J. D., Goetter, E. M., Yuen, E. K., & Moitra, E. M. (2012). Using session by session measurement to compare mechanisms of action for acceptance and commitment therapy and cognitive therapy. *Behavior Therapy, 43*, 341-54.

Fouquereau, E., Fernandez, A., Mullet, E., & Sorum, P. C. (2003). Stress and the urge to drink. *Addictive Behaviors, 28*, 669–685.

Fournier, J. C., DeRubeis, R. J., Hollon, S. D., Dimidjian, S., Amsterdam, J. D., Shelton, R. C., & Fawcett, J. (2010). Antidepressant drug effects and depression severity: A patient-level meta-analysis. *Journal of the American Medical Association, 303*, 47–53.

Fournier, J. C., DeRubeis, R. J., Shelton, R. C., Hollon, S. D., Amsterdam, J. D., & Gallop, R. (2009). Prediction of response to medication and cognitive therapy in the treatment of moderate to severe depression. *Journal of Consulting and Clinical Psychology, 77*, 775–787. doi:10.1037/a0015401

Fowler, K. A., O'Donohue, W., & Lillienfeld, S. O. (2007). Introduction: Personality disorders in perspective. In W. O'Donohue, W., & Lillienfeld, S. O. (Eds.), *Personality disorders: Toward the DSM-V.* Los Angeles: Sage Publications.

Foxhall, K. (2001, March). Study finds marital stress can triple women's risk of recurrent coronary event. *Monitor on Psychology, 32*(3), 14.

Frahm, S., Ślimak, M. A., Ferrarese, L., Santos-Torres, J., Antolin-Fontes, B., Auer,S ., . . . Ibañez-Tallon, I. (2011). Aversion to nicotine is regulated by the balanced activity of b4 and a5 nicotinic receptor subunits in the medial habenula. *Neuron, 70*, 522–535. doi: 10.1016/j.neuron.2011.04.013

Frances, A. J., & Widiger, T. (2012). Psychiatric diagnosis: Lessons from the DSM-IV Past and cautions for the DSM-5 Future. *Annual Review of Clinical Psychology, 8*, 109–130. doi: 10.1146/annurev-clinpsy-032511-143102

Frank E., Kupfer, D. J., Thase, M. E., Mallinger, A. G., Swartz, H. A., Fagiolini, A. M. (2005). Two-year outcomes for interpersonal and social rhythm therapy in individuals with bipolar I disorder. *Archives of General Psychiatry, 62*, 996–1004.

Frank, E., & Kupfer, D. J. (2003). Progress in therapy of mood disorders: Scientific support. *American Journal of Psychiatry, 160*, 1207–1208.

Frank, R. G., & Glied, S. A. (2006). *Better but not well: Mental health policy in the United States since 1950.* Baltimore, MD: Johns Hopkins University Press.

Franklin, M. E., & Foa, E. B. (2011). Treatment of obsessive compulsive disorder. *Annual Review of Clinical Psychology, 7*, 229–243. doi:10.1146/annurev-clinpsy-032210-104533x

Franklin, M. E., Abramowitz, J. S., Bux, D. A., Jr., Zoellner, L. A., & Feeny, N. C. (2002). Cognitive–behavioral therapy with and without medication in the treatment of obsessive–compulsive disorder. *Professional Psychology: Research and Practice, 33*, 162–168.

Franklin, M. E., Freeman, J. B., & March, J. S. (2012). Cognitive behavior therapy for pediatric obsessive-compulsive disorder—reply. JAMA. 2012;307(6):560–561. doi: 10.1001/jama.2012.109

Franklin, M. E., Sapyta, J, Freeman, J. B., Khanna, M., Compton, S, Almirall, D., . . . March, J. S. (2011). Cognitive behavior therapy augmentation of pharmacotherapy in pediatric obsessive-compulsive disorder: The Pediatric OCD Treatment Study II (POTS II) Randomized Controlled Trial. *The Journal of the American Medical Association, 306*, 1224. doi: 10.1001/jama.2011.1344

Franklin, T. B., Russig, H., Weiss, I. C., Gräff, J., Linder, N., Michalon, A., . . . Mansuy, I. M. (2011). Epigenetic transmission of the impact of early stress across generations. *Biological Psychiatry, 68*, 408–415.

Franklin, T., Wang, Z., Suh, J. J., Hazan, R., Cruz, J., Li, Y., Goldman, M., . . . Childress, A. R. (2011). Effects of varenicline on smoking cue–triggered neural and craving responses. *Archives of General Psychiatry, 68*, 516–526. doi:10.1001/archgenpsychiatry.2010.190

Franko, D. L., & Keel, P. K. (2006). Suicidality in eating disorders: Occurrence, correlates, and clinical implications. *Clinical Psychology Review, 26*, 769–782.

Franko, D. L., Thompson-Brenner, H., Thompson, D. R., Boisseau, C., Davis, A., Forbush, K., . . . Wilson, G. T. (2012). Racial/ethnic differences in adults in randomized clinical trials of binge eating disorder. *Journal of Consulting and Clinical Psychology, 80*, 186–195.

Frans, E. M., Sandin, S., Reichenberg, A., Lichtenstein, P., Långström, N., Hultman, C., M. (2008). Advancing paternal age and bipolar disorder. *Archives of General Psychiatry, 65*, 1034–1040.

Frattaroli, J. (2006). Experimental disclosure and its moderators: A meta-analysis. *Psychological Bulletin, 132*, 823–865.

Frauenglass, S., Routh, D. K., Pantin, H. M., & Mason, C. A. (1997). Family support decreases influence of deviant peers on Hispanic adolescents' substance use. *Journal of Clinical Child Psychology, 26*, 15–23.

Fredrickson, B. L., Tugade, M. M., Waugh, C. E., & Larkin, G. R. (2003). What good are positive emotions in crises? A prospective study of resilience and emotions following the terrorist attacks on the United States on September 11th, 2001. *Journal of Personality and Social Psychology, 84*, 365–376.

Free, C., Robertson, S., Whittaker, R., Edwards, P., Zhou, W., Rodgers, A., . . . Roberts, I. (2011). Smoking cessation support delivered via mobile phone text messaging (txt2stop): A single-blind, randomised trial. *Lancet, 378*, 49–55. doi: http://dx.doi.org/10.1016/S0140-6736(11)60701-0

Freedman, D. H. (2011, February). How to fix the obesity crisis. *Scientific American*. Retrieved from http://www.scientificamerican.com/article.cfm?id=how-to-fix-the-obesity-crisis

Freedman, R. (2012). Brain development and schizophrenia *American Journal of Psychiatry, 169*, 1019–1021. 10.1176/appi.ajp.2012.12081017

Freeman, M. P. (2011, December 21). The menstrual cycle and mood: Premenstrual dysphoric disorder. *Journal Watch Women's Health*. Retrieved from http://womens-health.jwatch.org/cgi/content/full/2011/1221/1?q=etoc_jwwomen

Freemon, F. R. (1981). *Organic mental disease*. Jamaica, NY: Spectrum.

Freud, S. (1957). Mourning and melancholia. In J. Rickman (Ed.), *A general selection from the works of Sigmund Freud.* Garden City, NY: Doubleday. (Original work published 1917.)

Freud, S. (1964). New introductory lectures. In *Standard edition of the complete psychological works of Sigmund Freud* (Vol. 22). London: Hogarth Press. (Original work published 1933)

Friborg, O., Martinussen, M., Kaiser, S., Øvergårda, K. T., & Rosenvinge, J. H. (2013). Comorbidity of personality disorders in anxiety disorders: A meta-analysis of 30 years of research. *Journal of Affective Disorders, 45*, 143–155.

Frick, P. J., & Silverthorn, P. (2001). Psychopathology in children and adolescents. In H. E. Adams (Ed.), *Comprehensive handbook of psychopathology* (3rd ed., pp. 879–919). New York: Plenum Press.

Friedman, BR. A. (2012, September 25). A call for caution on antipsychotic drugs. *The New York Times, Science Times*, p. D6.

Friedman, M. A., Detweiler-Bedell, J. B., Leventhal, H. E., Horne, R., Keitner, G. I., & Miller, I. W. (2004). Combined psychotherapy and pharmacotherapy for the treatment of major depressive disorder. *Clinical Psychology: Science and Practice, 11*, 47–68.

Friedman, R. A. (2006). The changing face of teenage drug abuse—the trend toward prescription drugs. *New England Journal of Medicine, 354*, 1448–1450.

Friedman, R. C., & Downey, J. I. (2008) Sexual differentiation of behavior: The foundation of a developmental model of psychosexuality. *Journal of the American Psychoanalytic Association, 56*(1), 147–175.

Friedman, S. H. (2009). Postpartum mood disorders: Genetic progress and treatment paradigms. *American Journal of Psychiatry, 166*, 1201–1204. doi:10.1176/appi.ajp.2009.09081185

Friedmann, P. D. (2013). Alcohol use in adults. *New England Journal of Medicine, 368*, 365–373. doi: 10.1056/NEJMcp1204714

From Hagen & Carouba, 2002 (to be added by author)

Frost, R. O., Steketee, G., & Tolin, D. F. (2012). Diagnosis and assessment of hoarding disorder. *Annual Review of Clinical Psychology, 8*, 219–242.

Frye, M. A. (2011). Bipolar disorder—A focus on depression. *New England Journal of Medicine, 364*, 51–59.

Fuertes, J. N., & Brobst, K. (2002). Clients' ratings of counselor multicultural competency. *Cultural Diversity and Ethnic Minority Psychology, 8*, 214–223.

Fullerton, C. A., Busch, A. B., Normand, S. L., McGuire, T. G., & Epstein, A. M.. (2011). Ten-year trends in quality of care and spending for depression: 1996 through 2005. *Archives of General Psychiatry, 68*, 1218–1226.

Fulton, J. J., Marcus, D. K., & Merkey, T. (2011). Irrational health beliefs and health anxiety. *Journal of Clinical Psychology, 67*, 527–538. doi: 10.1002/jclp.20769

Furr, J. M., Comer, J. S., Edmunds, J. M., & Kendall, P. C. (2010). Disasters and youth: A meta-analytic examination of posttraumatic stress. *Journal of Consulting and Clinical Psychology, 78*, 765–780. doi: 10.1037/a0021482

Fusar-Poli, P., Deste, G., Smieskova, R., Barlati, S., Yung, A. R., Howes, O., Stieglitz, R.-D . . . Borgwardt, S. (2012). Cognitive functioning in prodromal psychosis: A meta-analysis. *Archives of General Psychiatry, 69*, 562–571. doi:10.1001/archgenpsychiatry.2011.1592

G

Géonet, M., De Sutter, P., Zech, E. (2012). Cognitive factors in women hypoactive sexual desire disorder. *Sexologies*, in press.

Gabb, J., Sonderegger, L., Scherrer, S., & Ehlert, U. (2006). Psychoneuroendocrine effects of cognitive-behavioral stress management in a naturalistic setting—A randomized controlled trial. *Psychoneuroendocrinology, 31*, 428–438.

Gabbard, G. O. (2012). Clinical challenges in the Internet era. *American Journal of Psychiatry, 169*, 460–463. doi:10.1176/appi.ajp.2011.11101591

Gabert-Quillen, C. A., Fallon, W., & Delahanty, D. L. (2011). PTSD after traumatic injury: An investigation of the impact of injury severity and peritraumatic moderators. *Journal of Health Psychology, 16*, 678–687.

Gabrieli, J. D. E. (2009). Dyslexia: A new synergy between education and cognitive neuroscience. *Science, 325*, 280–283. doi: 10.1126/science.1171999

Galanter,C. A., (2013). Limited support for the efficacy of nonpharmacological treatments for the core symptoms of ADHD. *American Journal of Psychiatry*, 170, 241–244. 10.1176/appi.ajp.2012.12121561

Galea, S., Nandi, A., & Vlahov, D. (2005). The epidemiology of post-traumatic stress disorder after disasters. *Epidemiologic Reviews, 27*, 78–91.

Galliher, R. V., Jones, M. D., & Dahl, A. (2011). Concurrent and longitudinal effects of ethnic identity and experiences of discrimination on psychosocial adjustment of Navajo adolescents. *Developmental Psychology, 47*, 509–526. doi:10.1037/a0021061

Ganguli, M., Blacker, D., Blazer, D. G., Grant, I., Jeste, D. V., Paulsen, J. S., . . . The Neurocognitive Disorders Work Group of the American Psychiatric Association's (APA) DSM5 Task Force (2012). Classification of neurocognitive disorders in DSM-5: A work in progress. *American Journal of Geriatric Psychiatry,19*, 205–210.

Garb, H. N. (2007). Computer-administered interviews and rating scales. *Psychological Assessment, 19*, 4–13.

Garb, H. N., Wood, J. M., Lilienfeld, S. O, & Nezworski, M. T. (2005). Roots of the Rorschach controversy. *Clinical Psychology Review, 25*, 97–118.

Garb, H. N., Wood, J. M., Lilienfeld, S. O., & Nezworski, M.T. (2002). Effective use of projective techniques in clinical practice: Let the data help with selection and interpretation. *Professional Psychology: Research and Practice, 33*, 454–463.

Garber, J. & Weersing, V. R. (2010). Comorbidity of anxiety and depression in youth: Implications for treatment and prevention. *Clinical Psychology: Science and Practice, 17*, 293–306. doi:10.1111/j.1468-2850.2010.01221.x

Garber, J., Keiley, M. K., & Martin, N. C. (2002). Developmental trajectories of adolescents' depressive symptoms: Predictors of change. *Journal of Consulting & Clinical Psychology, 70*, 79–95.

Garlow, S. J., Purselle, D., & Heninger, M. (2005). Ethnic differences in patterns of suicide across the life cycle. *American Journal of Psychiatry, 162*, 319–323.

Garnefski, N., Kraaij, V., & Spinhoven, P. (2001). De relatie tussen cognitieve copingstrategieen en symptomen van depressie, angst en suiecidaliteit. *Gedrag & Gezondheid: Tijdschrift voor Psychologie & Gezondheid, 29*, 148–158.

Gartlehner, G., Gaynes, B. N., Hansen, R. A., Thieda, P., DeVeaugh-Geiss, A., Krebs, E. E., . . . Lohr, K. N. (2008). Comparative benefits and harms of second-generation antidepressants: Background paper for the American College of Physicians. *Annals of Internal Medicine, 149*, 734–750.

Garza, D., Murphy, M., Tseng, L. J., Riordan, H. J., & Chatterjee, A. (2011). A double-blind randomized placebo-controlled pilot study of neuropsychiatric adverse events in abstinent smokers treated with varenicline or placebo. *Biological Psychiatry, 69*, 1075–1082.

Gau, S., S.-F. (2011). Childhood trajectories of inattention symptoms predicting educational attainment in young adults. *American Journal of Psychiatry*, *168*, 1131–1133. doi: 10.1176/appi.ajp.2011.11091328

Geddes, J.R.,Stroup,S., & Lieberman, J.A. (2011). Comparative efficacy and effectiveness in the drug treatment of schizophrenia. In D. R. Weinberg & P. Harrison (Eds.), *Schizophrenia* (pp. 525–539). Hoboken, NJ: Wiley-Blackwell.

Gehar, D. R. (2009). *Mastering competencies in family therapy.* Belmont, CA: Brooks/Cole.

Geipert, N. (2007, January). Don't be mad: More research links hostility to coronary risk. *Monitor on Psychology, 38*(1), 50–51.

Geller, B. (2006, October 16). Early use of methylphenidate: The jury on neuronal effects is still out. *Journal Watch Psychiatry*. Retrieved from http://psychiatry.jwatch.org/cgi/content/full/2006/1016/2

Gelman, D. (1994, April 18). The mystery of suicide. *Newsweek*, pp. 44–49.

Gene linked to Alzheimer's. (2013). *Nature, 493*, 454–455. doi:10.1038/493454d

Genetic Science Learning Center, University of Utah (2012). *Down syndrome.* Retrieved from http://learn.genetics.utah.edu/content/disorders/whataregd/down

George, M. S., Anton, R. F., Bloomer, C., Teneback, C., Drobes, D. J., Lorberbaum, J. P., . . . Vincent, D. J.. (2001). Activation of prefrontal cortex and anterior thalamus in alcoholic subjects on exposure to alcohol-specific cues. *Archives of General Psychiatry, 58*, 345–352.

George, M. S., Lisanby, S. H., Avery, D., McDonald, W. M., Durkalski,V., Pavlicova, M., Anderson, B., . . Sackeim, H. A. (2010). Daily left prefrontal transcranial magnetic stimulation therapy for major depressive disorder: A sham-controlled randomized trial. *Archives of General Psychiatry, 67*, 507–516.

Gershater-Molkoa, R. M., Lutzker, J. R., & Sherman, J. A. (2002). Intervention in child neglect: An applied behavioral perspective. *Aggression and Violent Behavior, 7*, 103–124.

Gershon, E. S., & Rieder, R. O. (1992). Major disorders of mind and brain. *Scientific American, 267*(3), 128.

Gibbons, M. B. C, Crits-Christoph, P., Barber, J. P., Wiltsey Stirman, S., Gallop, R., Goldstein, L. A., Ring-Kurtz, S. (2009). Unique and common mechanisms of change across cognitive and dynamic psychotherapies. *Journal of Consulting and Clinical Psychology, 94*, 801–813. doi: 10.1037/a0016596

Gibbons, P. (2001). The relationship between eating disorder and socioeconomic status: It's not what you think. *Nutrition Noteworthy, 4* (1), 1–5.

Gibbons, R. D., Hur, K., Brown, C. H., Davis, J. M., & Mann, J. J. (2012). Benefits from antidepressants: Synthesis of 6-week patient-level outcomes from double-blind placebo-controlled randomized trials of fluoxetine and venlafaxine. *Archives of General Psychiatry, 69*, 572–579. doi:10.1001/archgenpsychiatry.2011.2044

Giddens, A. (2006). *Sociology* (5th ed.). Cambridge, UK: Polity.

Gil, K. M., Williams, D. A., Keefe, F. J., & Beckham, J. C. (1990). The relationship of negative thoughts to pain and psychological distress. *Behavior Therapy, 21*, 349–362.

Gilbert, S. C. (2003). Eating disorders in women of color. *Clinical Psychology: Science and Practice, 10*, 444–455.

Giordano, S. (2005). *Understanding eating disorders: Conceptual and ethical issues in the treatment of anorexia and bulimia nervosa.* Melbourne, Australia: Oxford University Press.

Girgenti, M. J., LoTurco, J. J., & Maher, B. J. (2012). 1ZNF804a regulates expression of the schizophrenia-associated genes PRSS16, COMT, PDE4B, and DRD2. *PLoS ONE*, e32404. doi:10.1371/journal.pone.0032404

Glaser, R., Kiecolt-Glaser, J. K., Speicher, C. E., & Holliday, J. E. (1985). Stress, loneliness, and changes in herpes virus latency. *Journal of Behavioral Medicine, 8*, 249–260.

Glassman, A. H., Bigger, T., Jr., & Gaffney, M. (2009). Psychiatric characteristics associated with long-term mortality among 361 patients having an acute coronary syndrome and major depression: Seven-year follow-up of SADHART participants. *Archives of General Psychiatry, 66*, 1022.

Glazener, C. M., Evans, J. H., & Peto, R. E. (2000). Tricyclic and related drugs for nocturnal enuresis in children. *Cochrane Database Systems Review, 3*, CD002117.

Gleaves, D. H. (1996). The sociocognitive model of dissociative identity disorder: A reexamination of the evidence. *Psychological Bulletin, 120*, 42–59.

Gleaves, D. H., Smith, S. M., Butler, L. D., & Spiegel, D. (2004). False and recovered memories in the laboratory and clinic: A review of experimental and clinical evidence. *Clinical Psychology: Science and Practice, 11*, 3–28.

Gloster, A. T., Wittchen, H.-U., Einsle, F., Lang, T., Helbig-Lang, S., Fydrich, T., . . . Aroltn,V. (2011). Psychological treatment for panic disorder with agoraphobia: a randomized controlled trial to examine the role of therapist-guided exposure in situ in CBT. *Journal of Consulting and Clinical Psychology, 79*, 406–420. doi:10.1037/a0023584

Goddard, A. W., Mason, G. F., Almai, A., Rothman, D. L., Behar, K. L., . . . Krystal, J. H. (2001). Reductions in occipital cortex GABA levels in panic disorder detected with 1h-magnetic spectroscopy. *Archives of General Psychiatry, 58*, 556–561.

Goel, N., Banks, S., Mignot, E., & Dinges, D. R. (2010). DQB1*0602 predicts interindividual differences in physiologic sleep, sleepiness, and fatigue. *Neurology, 75*, 1509–1519.

Goenjian, A. K., Noble, E. P., Walling, D. P., Goenjian, H. A., Karayan, I. S., Ritchie, T., & Bailey, J. N. (2008). Heritabilities of symptoms of posttraumatic stress disorder, anxiety, and depression in earthquake exposed Armenian families. *Psychiatric Genetics, 18*, 261–266.

Gold, J. M. (2011). Imaging emotion in schizophrenia: Not finding feelings in all the right places. *American Journal of Psychiatry, 168*, 237–239.

Gold, R., Butler, P., Revheim, N., Leitman, D. I., Hansen, J. A., Gur, R. C., . . . Javitt, D. C. (2012). Auditory emotion recognition impairments in schizophrenia: Relationship to acoustic features and cognition. *American Journal of Psychiatry, 169*, 424–432. 10.1176/appi.ajp.2011.11081230

Goldberg, J. F., Gerstein, R. K., Wenze, S. J., Welker, T. M., & Beck, A. T. (2008). Dysfunctional attitudes and cognitive schemas in bipolar manic and unipolar depressed outpatients: Implications for cognitively based psychotherapeutics. *The Journal of Nervous and Mental Disease, 196*, 207–210.

Golden, G. S. (2008). Review of "Dyslexia, learning, and the brain." *New England Journal of Medicine, 359*, 2737.

Goldfried, M. R. (2012). On entering and remaining in psychotherapy. *Clinical Psychology: Science and Practice, 19*, 125–128. doi: 10.1111/j.1468-2850.2012.01278.x

Goldman, D., (2011). Molecular etiologies of schizophrenia: Are we almost there yet? *American Journal of Psychiatry, 168*, 879–881. doi: 10.1176/appi.ajp.2011.11050694

Goleman, D. (1995, June 21). "Virtual reality" conquers fear of heights. *The New York Times*, p. C11.

Gonda, X., Pompili, M., Serafini, G., Montebovi, F., Campi, S., Dome, P., . . . Rihmer, Z. (2012). Suicidal behavior in bipolar disorder: Epidemiology, characteristics and major risk factors. *Journal of Affective Disorders, 143*, 16–26.

Gone, J. P., & Trimble, J. E. (2012). American Indian and Alaska Native mental health: Diverse perspectives on enduring disparities. *Annual Review of Clinical Psychology, 8*, 131–160.

González, H. M., Vega, W. A., Williams, D. R., Tarraf, W., West, B. T., & Neighbors, H. W. (2010). Depression care in the United States: Too little for too few. *Archives of General Psychiatry, 67*, 37–46.

González-Isasi, A., Echeburúa, E., Mosquera, F., Ibáñez, B., Aizpuru, F., & González-Pinto, A. (2010). Long-term efficacy of a psychological intervention program for patients with refractory bipolar disorder: A pilot study. *Psychiatry Research, 176*, 161–165.

Gonzales, N. A., Dumka, L. E., Millsap, R. E., Gottschall, A., McClain, D. B., Wong, J. J., . . .Yeong. S. (2012). Randomized trial of a broad preventive intervention for Mexican American adolescents. *Journal of Consulting and Clinical Psychology, 80*, 1–16. doi: 10.1037/a0026063

Gonzalez-Gadea, M. L., Baez, S., Torralva, T., Castellanos, F. X., Rattazzi, A., Bein, V., . . . Ibanez, A. (2013). Cognitive variability in adults with ADHD and AS: Disentangling the roles of executive functions and social cognition. *Research in Developmental Disabilities, 34*, 817–830.

Gooding, P., & Tarrier, N. (2009). A systematic review and meta-analysis of cognitive-behavioural interventions to reduce problem gambling: Hedging our bets? *Behaviour Research and Therapy, 47*, 592–560. doi:10.1016/j.brat.2009.04.002

Goodlad, J. K., Marcus, D. K., & Fulton, J. J. (2013). Lead and attention-deficit/hyperactivity disorder (ADHD) symptoms: a meta-analysis. *Clinical Psychology Review*, in press

Goodnight, J. A., Lahey, B. B., Van Hulle, C. A., Rodgers, J. L., Rathouz, P. J., Waldman, I. D., & D'Onofrio, B. M. (2012). A quasi-experimental analysis of the influence of neighborhood disadvantage on child and adolescent conduct problems. *Journal of Abnormal Psychology, 121*, 95–108. doi: 10.1037/a0025078

Gordon, J. L., Ditto, B., Lavoie, K. L., Pelletier, R., Campbell, T. S., Arsenault, A., . . . Bacon, S. L. (2011). The effect of major depression on postexercise cardiovascular recovery. *Psychophysiology, 48*, 1605–1610. doi: 10.1111/j.1469-8986.2011.01232.x.

Gormally, J., Sipps, G., Raphael, R., Edwin, D., & Varvil-Weld, D. (1981). The relationship between maladaptive cognitions and social anxiety. *Journal of Consulting and Clinical Psychology, 49*, 300–301.

Gorman, C. (2003, October 20). How to eat smarter. *Time*, pp. 48–59.

Gorman, C. (2012, January). Five hidden dangers of obesity: Excess weight can harm health in ways that may come as a surprise. *Scientific American*. Retrieved from https://www.scientificamerican.com/article.cfm?id=five-hidden-dangers-of-obesity

Gothold, J. J. (2009). Peeling the onion: Understanding layers of treatment. *Annals of the New York Academy of Sciences, 1159*, 301–312.

Gottesman, I. I., Laursen, T. M., Bertelsen, A., & Mortensen, P. B. (2010). Severe mental disorders in offspring with 2 psychiatrically ill parents. *Archives of General Psychiatry, 67*, 252–257.

Gottlieb, J. D., Romeo, K. H., Penn, D. L., Mueser, K. T., & Chiko, B. P. (2013). Web-based cognitive–behavioral therapy for auditory hallucinations in persons with psychosis: A pilot study. *Schizophrenia Research, 145*, 82–87.

Goudriaan, A. E., Oosterlaan, J., de Beurs, E., & van den Brink, W. (2006). Neurocognitive functions in pathological gambling: A comparison with alcohol dependence, Tourette syndrome and normal controls. *Addiction, 101*, 534–547.

Gouin, J.-P., Glaser, R., Malarkey, W. B., Beversdorf, D., & Kiecolt-Glaser, J. (2012). Chronic stress, daily stressors, and circulating inflammatory markers. *Health Psychology, 31*, 264–268. doi: 10.1037/a0025536

Gould, F., Clarke, J., Heim, C., Harvey, P. D., Majer, M., & Nemeroff, C. B. (2012). The effects of child abuse and neglect on cognitive functioning in adulthood. *Journal of Psychiatric Research, 46*, 500–506.

Gould, M. S., Greenberg, T., Velting, D. M., & Shaffer, D. (2003). Youth suicide risk and preventive interventions: A review of the past 10 years. *Journal of the American Academy of Child and Adolescent Psychiatry, 42*, 386–405.

Grace, A. A. (2010). Ventral hippocampus, interneurons, and schizophrenia: A new understanding of the pathophysiology of schizophrenia and its implications for treatment and prevention. *Current Directions in Psychological Science, 19,* 232–237. doi: 10.1177/0963721410378032

Graham, J. R. (2011). *MMPI-2: Assessing personality and psychopathology* (5th ed.). New York: Oxford University Press.

Granata, A. R., Pugni, V., Rochira, V., Zirilli, L., & Carani, C. (2012). Hormonal regulation of male sexual desire: The role of testosterone, estrogen, prolactin, oxytocin, and others. In M. Maggi (Ed.). *Hormonal therapy for male sexual dysfunction* (pp. 72–82). Hoboken, NJ: Wiley.

Grant, A., Fathalli, G,. Rouleau, G., Joober, R., Flores, C. (2012). Association between schizophrenia and genetic variation in DCC: A case–control study. *Schizophrenia Research, 137,* 26–31.

Grant, B. F., Harford, T. C., Muthen, B. O., Yi, H. Y., Hasin, D. S., & Stinson, F. S. (2006). *DSM-IV* alcohol dependence and abuse: Further evidence of validity in the general population. *Drug and Alcohol Dependence, 86,* 154–166.

Grant, B. F., Hasin, D. S., Blanco, C., Stinson, F. S., Chou, S. P., Goldstein, R. B., . . . Huang, B. (2006a). The epidemiology of social anxiety disorder in the United States: Results from the National Epidemiologic Survey on Alcohol and Related Conditions. *Journal of Clinical Psychiatry, 66,* 1351–1361.

Grant, B. F., Hasin, D. S., Stinson, F. S., Dawson, D. A., Goldstein, R. B., Smith, S., . . . Saha, T. D. (2006b). The epidemiology of DSM-IV panic disorder and agoraphobia in the United States: Results from the National Epidemiologic Survey on Alcohol and Related Conditions. *Journal of Clinical Psychiatry, 67,* 363–374.

Grant, B. F., Hasin, D. S., Stinson, F. S., Dawson, D. A., Ruan, W.J., Goldstein, R. B., et al. (2005). Prevalence, correlates, co-morbidity, and comparative disability of DSM-IV generalized anxiety disorder in the USA: results from the National Epidemiologic Survey on Alcohol and Related Conditions. *Psychological Medicine, 35,* 1747–1759.

Grant, B. F., Stinson, F. S., Dawson, D. A., Chou, P., Ruan, W. J., & Pickering, R. P. (2004). Co-occurrence of 12-month alcohol and drug use disorders and personality disorders in the United States: Results from the National Epidemiologic Survey on Alcohol and Related Conditions. *Archives of General Psychiatry, 61,* 361–368.

Grant, J. E., & Odlaug, B. L. (2009). Asessment and treatment of pyromania. In J. E. Grant & M. N. Potenza (Eds.), *The Oxford handbook of impulse control disorders* (pp. 353–359). Oxford, UK: Oxford University Press.

Grant, J. E., Odlaug, B. L., & Kim, S. W. (2012). Assessment and treatment of kleptomnia. In J. E. Grant & M. N. Potenza (Eds.), *The Oxford handbook of impulse control disorders* (pp. 334–343). New York: Oxford University Press.

Grant, J. E., Williams, K. A., & Kim, S. W. (2006). Update on pathological gambling. *Current Psychiatry Reports, 8,* 53–58.

Grant, P. M., Huh, G. A., Perivoliotis, D., Stolar, N. M., & Beck, A. T. (2012). Randomized trial to evaluate the efficacy of cognitive therapy for low-functioning patients with schizophrenia. *Archives of General Psychiatry, 69,* 121–127. doi:10.1001/archgenpsychiatry.2011.129

Gray, M. J., & Acierno, R. (2002) Posttraumatic stress disorder. In M. Hersen (Ed.), *Clinical behavior therapy: Adults and children* (pp. 106–124). New York: John Wiley & Sons.

Gray-Little, B., & Hafdahl, A. R. (2000). Factors influencing racial comparisons of self-esteem: A quantitative review. *Psychological Bulletin, 126,* 26–54.

Green, B. A., Carnes, S., & Carnes, P. J. (2012). Cybersex addiction patterns in a clinical sample of homosexual, heterosexual, and bisexual men and women. *Sexual Addiction and Compulsivity, 19*(1–2), 77–98.

Green, M. F., & Horan, W. P. (2010). Social cognition in schizophrenia. *Current Directions in Psychological Science, 19,* 243–248. doi:10.1177/0963721410377600

Greene, B. (2009). The use and abuse of religious beliefs in dividing and conquering between socially marginalized groups: The same sex marriage debate. *American Psychologist, 64* (8), 698–709.

Greene, B. A. (1990). Sturdy bridges: The role of African American mothers in the socialization of African American children. *Women & Therapy, 10,* 205–225.

Greene, B. A. (1993a). African American women. In L. Comas-Diaz & B. Greene (Eds.), *Women of color and mental health* (pp. 13–25). New York: Guilford Press.

Greene, B. A. (1993b, Spring). Psychotherapy with African American women: The integration of feminist and psychodynamic approaches. *Journal of Training and Practice in Professional Psychology, 7,* 49–66.

Greene, R. L., Robin, R. W., Albaugh, B., Caldwell, A., & Goldman, D. (2003). Use of the MMPI-2 in American Indians: II. Empirical correlates. *Psychological Assessment, 5,* 360–369.

Greenwood, A. (2006, April 25). Natural killer cells power immune system response to cancer. *NCI Cancer Bulletin, 3* (17). Retrieved from http://www.cancer.gov/ncicancerbulletin/NCI_Cancer_Bulletin_042506/page4

Greenwood, T. A., Lazzeroni, L. C., Murray, S. S., Cadenhead, K. S., Calkins, M. E., Dobie, D. J., Braff, D. L. (2011). Analysis of 94 candidate genes and 12 endophenotypes for schizophrenia from the consortium on the genetics of schizophrenia. *American Journal of Psychiatry, 168,* 930–946.

Gregory, J. (2003). *Sickened: The memoir of a Münchausen by proxy childhood.* New York: Bantam.

Grilo, C. M., Crosby, R. D., Wilson, G. T., & Masheb, R. (2012). 12-month follow-up of fluoxetine and cognitive behavioral therapy for binge eating disorder. *Journal of Consulting and Clinical Psychology, 80,* 1108–1113. doi: 10.1037/a0030061

Grilo, C. M., Hrabosky, J. I., White, M. A., Allison, K. C., Stunkard, A. J., & Masheb, R. M. (2008). Overvaluation of shape and weight in binge eating disorder and overweight controls: Refinement of a diagnostic construct. *Journal of Abnormal Psychology, 117,* 414–419.

Grilo, C. M., Masheb, R. M., & Crosby, R. D. (2012). Predictors and moderators of response to cognitive behavioral therapy and medication for the treatment of binge eating disorder. *Journal of Consulting and Clinical Psychology, 80,* 897–906. doi: 10.1037/a0027001

Grilo, C. M., Masheb, R. M., Wilson, G. T., Gueorguieva, R., & White, M. A. (2011). A cognitive–behavioral therapy, behavioral weight loss, and sequential treatment for obese patients with binge-eating disorder: A randomized controlled trial. *Journal of Consulting and Clinical Psychology, 79,* 675–685. doi: 10.1037/a0025049

Grob, G. N. (1983). *Mental illness and American society, 1875–1940.* Princeton, NJ: Princeton University Press.

Grob, G. N. (1994). *The mad among us: A history of the care of America's mentally ill.* New York: Free Press.

Grob, G. N. (2009). *Mental institutions in America: Social policy to 1875*: Piscataway, NJ: Transaction Publishers Rutgers—The State University of New Jersey

Gropalis, M., Bleichhardt, G., Witthöft, M., & Hiller, W. (2012). Hypochondriasis, somatoform disorders, and anxiety disorders: Sociodemographic variables, general psychopathology, and naturalistic treatment effects. *Journal of Nervous & Mental Disease, 200,* 406–412.

Grossman, L. (2003, January 20). Can Freud get his job back? *Time,* pp. 48–51.

Grothe, K. B., Dutton, G. R., Jones, G. N., Bodenlos, J., Ancona, M., & Brantley, P. J. (2005). Validation of the Beck Depression Inventory-II in a low-income African American sample of medical outpatients. *Psychological Assessment, 17,* 110–114.

Guan, F., Wei, W., Feng, J., Zhang, C., Xing, B., Zhang, H., . . . Li, S. (2012).Association study of a new schizophrenia susceptibility locus of 10q24.32–33 in a Han Chinese population. *Schizophrenia Research, 138,* 63–68.

Guastella, A. J., Richardson, R., Lovibond, P. F., Rapee, R. M., Gaston, J. E., Mitchell, P., & Dadds, M. R. (2008). A randomised controlled trial of D-cycloserine enhancement of exposure therapy for social anxiety disorder. *Biological Psychiatry, 63,* 544–549.

Guillaume, F., Guillem, F., Tiberghien, G., & Stip. E. (2012). ERP investigation of study-test background mismatch during face recognition in schizophrenia. *Schizophrenia Research, 134,* 101–109.

Guller, Y., Ferrarelli, F., Shackman, A. J., Sarasso, S., Peterson, M. J.., Langheim, F. J., . . . Postle, B. R. (2012). Probing thalamic integrity in schizophrenia using concurrent transcranial magnetic stimulation and functional magnetic resonance imaging. *Archives of General Psychiatry, 69,* 662–671. doi:10.1001/archgenpsychiatry.2012.23

Gunderson, J. G. (2011). Borderline personality disorder. *New England Journal of Medicine, 364,* 2037–2042.

Gunderson, J. G., Stout, R. L., McGlashan, T. H., Shea, M. T., Morey, L. C., Grilo, C. M, . . Skodol, A. E. (2012). Ten-year course of borderline personality disorder: psychopathology and function from the Collaborative Longitudinal Personality Disorders Study. *Archives of General Psychiatry, 68,* 827–837.

Gunn, R. L., & Smith, G. T. (2010). Risk factors for elementary school drinking: Pubertal status, personality, and alcohol expectancies concurrently predict fifth grade alcohol consumption. *Psychology of Addictive Behaviors, 24,* 617–627. doi:10.1037/a0020334

Gunter, R. W., & Whittal, M. L. (2010). Dissemination of cognitive-behavioral treatments for anxiety disorders: Overcoming barriers and improving patient access. *Clinical Psychology Review, 30,* 194–202. doi:10.1016/j.cpr.2009.11.001

Guo, X., Zhai, J., Liu, Z., Fang, M., Wang, B., Wang, C., . . . Zhao, J. (2010). Effect of antipsychotic medication alone vs combined with psychosocial intervention on outcomes of early-stage schizophrenia: A randomized, 1-year study. *Archives of General Psychiatry, 67,* 895–904. doi:10.1001/archgenpsychiatry.2010.105

Guoa, M. E., Collinson, S. L., Subramaniam, M., & Chong. S. A (2010). Gender differences in schizotypal personality in a Chinese population. *Personality and Individual Differences, 50,* 404–408. doi:10.1016/j.paid.2010.11.005

Gvirts, H. Z., Harari, H., Braw, Y., Shefet, D., Shamay-Tsoory, S. G. & Levkovitz, Y. (2012). Executive functioning among patients with borderline personality disorder (BPD) and their relatives. *Journal of Affective Disorders, 143,* 261–264.

H

Hölzel, L, Härter,. M, Reese, C., & Kriston, L. (2011). Risk factors for chronic depression—A systematic review. *Journal of Affective Disorders, 129,* 1–13.

Hadjistavropoulos, H. D.,Thompson, M., Ivanov, M., Drost, C., Butz, C., Klein, B., . . . Austin, D. W. (2011). Considerations in the development of a therapist-assisted internet cognitive behavior therapy service. *Professional Psychology: Research and Practice, 42,* 463–471. doi: 10.1037/a0026176

Haedt-Matt, A. A., & Keel, P. K. (2011). Revisiting the affect regulation model of binge eating: A meta-analysis of studies using ecological momentary assessment. *Psychological Bulletin, 137,* 660–681. doi: 10.1037/a0023660

Hagen, S., & Carouba, M.(2002). Women at Ground Zero: Stories of courage and compassion. Indianapolis, IN: Alpha.

Hahn, B., Hollingworth, A., Robinson, B. M., Kaiser, S. T., Leonard, C. J., Beck, V. M., . . . Gold, J. M. (2012). Control of working memory content in schizophrenia. *Schizophrenia Research, 134,* 70–75.

Halbreich, U., O'Brien, S., Eriksson, E., Bäckström, T., Yonkers, K.A., & Freeman, E.W. (2006). Are there differential symptom profiles that improve in response to different pharmacological treatments of premenstrual syndrome/premenstrual dysphoric disorder? *CNS Drugs, 20,* 523–547.

Hall, G. C. N., Hong, J. J., Zane, N. W. S., & Meyer, O. L. (2011). Culturally competent treatments for Asian Americans: The relevance of mindfulness and acceptance-based psychotherapies. *Clinical Psychology: Science and Practice, 18,* 215–231. doi:10.1111/j.1468-2850.2011.01253.x

Hall, H. I., Song, R., Rhodes, P., Prejean, J., An, Q., Lee, L. M., et al. (2008). Estimation of HIV incidence in the United States. *Journal of the American Medical Association, 300,* 520–529.

Hallmayer, J., Cleveland, S., Torres, A., Phillips, J., Cohen, B., Torigoe, T., . . . Risch, N. (2011). Genetic heritability and shared environmental factors among twin pairs with autism. *Archives of General Psychiatry, 68,* 1095–1102. doi:10.1001/archgenpsychiatry.2011.76

Ham, L. S., & Hope, D. A. (2003). College students and problematic drinking: A review of the literature. *Clinical Psychology Review, 23,* 719–759.

Hamel, M., Shafer, T. W., & Erdberg, P. (2003). A study of nonpatient preadolescent Rorschach protocols. *Journal of Personality Assessment, 75,* 280–294.

Hamilton, K. E., Wershler, J. L., Macrodimitris, S. D., Backs-Dermott, B. J., Ching, L. E., & Mothersill, K. J. (2012). Exploring the effectiveness of a mixed-diagnosis group cognitive behavioral therapy intervention across diverse populations. *Cognitive and Behavioral Practice, 19,* 472–482.

Hamilton, S. P. (2008). Schizophrenia candidate genes: Are we really coming up blank? *American Journal of Psychiatry, 165,* 420–423.

Hammen, C. (2009). Adolescent depression: Stressful interpersonal contexts and risk for recurrence. *Current Directions in Psychological Science, 18,* 200–204. doi: 10.1111/j.1467-8721.2009.01636.x

Hampton, T. (2012). Effects of ECT. *Journal of the American Medical Association, 307,* 1790–1790. doi:10.1001/jama.2012.3723

Hamre, K. (2013). Obesity: Multiple factors contribute. *Nature, 493,* 480. doi:10.1038/493480c

Han, J., Kesner, P., Metna-Laurent, M., Duan, T., Xu, L., Georges, G., Koehl, M., . . . Ren, W. (2012). Acute cannabinoids impair working memory through astroglial CB1 receptor modulation of hippocampal LTD. *Cell, 148*(5), 1039–1050. doi:10.1016/j.cell.2012.01.037

Han, J.-H., Kushner, S. A., Yiu, A. P., Hsiang, H.-L., Buch, T., Waisman, A., et al. (2009). Selective erasure of a fear memory. *Science, 323*, 1492–1496. doi: 10.1126/science.1164139

Han, S. D., Gruhl, J., Beckett, L., Dodge, H. H., Stricker, H. H., . . . Mungas, D. (2012). Beta amyloid, tau, neuroimaging, and cognition: sequence modeling of biomarkers for Alzheimer's Disease. *Brain Imaging and Behavior, 6*, 610–620.

Hancock, L. (1996, March 18). Mother's little helper. *Newsweek*, pp. 51–56.

Hans, E., & Hiller, W. (2013). Effectiveness of and dropout from outpatient cognitive behavioral therapy for adult unipolar depression: A meta-analysis of nonrandomized effectiveness studies. *Journal of Consulting and Clinical Psychology, 81*, 75–88. doi: 10.1037/a0031080

Hansen, N. B., Lambert, M. J., & Forman, E. M. (2002). The psychotherapy dose-response effect and its implications for treatment delivery services. *Clinical Psychology: Science and Practice, 9*, 329–343.

Hansen, N. D., Randazzo, K. V., Schwartz, A., Marshall, M., Kalis, D., Frazier, ER., . . . Norvig, G. et al. (2006). Do we practice what we preach? An exploratory survey of multicultural psychotherapy competencies. *Professional Psychology: Research and Practice, 37*, 66–74.

Hardy, J., & Low, N. C. (2011). Genes and environment in psychiatry: Winner's curse or cure? *Archives of General Psychiatry, 68*, 455–456.

Hariri, A. R., Mattay, V. S., Tessitore, A., Kolachana, B., Fera, F., Goldman, D. (2002). Serotonin transporter genetic variation and the response of the human amygdala. *Science, 19*, 400–403.

Harkin, B., & Kessler, K. (2011). The role of working memory in compulsive checking and OCD: A systematic classification of 58 experimental findings. *Clinical Psychology Review, 31*, 1004–1021. doi:10.1016/j.cpr.2011.06.004

Harkness, K. L., Alavi, N., Monroe, S. M., Slavich, G. M., Gotlib, I. H., & Bagby, R. M. (2010). Gender differences in life events prior to onset of major depressive disorder: The moderating effect of age. *Journal of Abnormal Psychology, 119*, 791–803. doi: 10.1037/a0020629

Harmon, A. (2012, April 8). The autism wars. *The New York Times*, p. SR3.

Harold, D., Abraham, R., Hollingworth, P., Sims, R., Gerrish, A., Hamshere, M. L., et al. (2009). Genome-wide association study identifies variants at CLU and PICALM associated with Alzheimer's disease. *Nature Genetics*. Retrieved from http://www.nature.com/ng/journal/vaop/ncurrent/abs/ng.440.html

Harris, A., & Lurigio, A. J. (2007). Mental illness and violence: A brief review of research and assessment strategies. *Aggression and Violent Behavior, 12*, 542–551.

Harris, E., & Younggren, J. N. (2011). Risk management in the digital world. *Professional Psychology: Research and Practice, 42*, 412–418. doi: 10.1037/a0025139

Harris, G. (2006, November 23). Proof is scant on psychiatric drug mix for young. *The New York Times*, pp. A1, A28.

Harris, J. et al. (2012). A randomized controlled trial of intensive sleep retraining (ISR): A brief conditioning treatment for chronic insomnia. *Sleep*, in press, *35*, 49.

Harris, J., Lack, L., Kemp, K., Wright, H., & Bootzin, R. (2012). A randomized controlled trial of intensive sleep retraining (ISR): A brief conditioning treatment for chronic insomnia. *Sleep, 35*, 49–60. doi: 10.5665/sleep.1584

Harrison, B. J., Soriano-Mas, C., Pujol, J., Ortiz, H., Lopez-Sola, M., Hernandez-Ribas, Deus, J., Cardoner, N. (2009). Altered corticostriatal functional connectivity in obsessive-compulsive disorder. *Archives of General Psychiatry, 66*, 1189–1200.

Harrow, M., & Jobe T. (2007). Factors involved in outcome and recovery in schizophrenia patients not on antipsychotic medications: A 15-year multi-follow-up study. *Journal of Nervous and Mental Disease, 195*, 406–414.

Hart, H., Radua, J., Nakao, T., Mataix-Cols, D., & Rubia, K. (2013). Meta-analysis of functional magnetic resonance imaging studies of inhibition and attention in attention-deficit/hyperactivity disorder. *JAMA Psychiatry, 70*, 185–198. doi:10.1001/jamapsychiatry.2013.277.

Hart, L. M., Granillo, M. T., Jorm, A. F., & Paxton, S. J. (2011). Unmet need for treatment in the eating disorders: A systematic review of eating disorder specific treatment seeking among community cases. *Clinical Psychology Review, 31*, 727–735. doi:10.1016/j.cpr.2011.03.004

Hartz, S. M., Short, S. E., Saccone, N. L., Culverhouse, R., Chen, L, Schwantes-An, T.-H., . . . Bierut, L. J. (2012). Increased genetic vulnerability to smoking at CHRNA5 in early-onset smokers. *Archives of General Psychiatry, 69*, 854–860. doi:10.1001/archgenpsychiatry.2012.124

Harvey, A. G., & Tang, N. K. Y (2012). (Mis)perception of sleep in insomnia: A puzzle and a resolution. *Psychological Bulletin, 138*, 77–101. doi: 10.1037/a0025730

Harvey, P. D. (2010). Cognitive functioning and disability in schizophrenia. *Current Directions in Psychological Science, 19*, 249–254. doi:10.1177/0963721410378033

Hasin, D. S., Goodwin, R. D., Stinson, F. S., & Grant, B. F. (2005). Epidemiology of major depressive disorder: Results from the National Epidemiologic Survey on Alcoholism and Related Conditions. *Archives of General Psychiatry, 62*, 1097–1106.

Hasin, D., Hatzenbuehler, M. L., Keyes, K., & Ogburn, E. (2006). Substance use disorders: *Diagnostic and Statistical Manual of Mental Disorders*, fourth edition (DSM-IV) and *International Classification of Diseases*, tenth edition (ICD-10). *Addiction, 101* (Suppl. 1), 59–75.

Hassija, C. M., & Gray, M. J. (2010). Are cognitive techniques and interventions necessary? A case for the utility of cognitive approaches in the treatment of PTSD. *Clinical Psychology: Science and Practice, 17*, 112–127. doi:10.1111/j.1468-2850.2010.01201.x

Havermans, R. C., & Jansen, A. T. M. (2003). Increasing the efficacy of cue exposure treatment in preventing relapse of addictive behavior. *Addictive Behaviors, 28*, 989–994.

Hawton, K., Casañas i Comabella, C., Haw, C., & Saunders, K. (2013). Risk factors for suicide in individuals with depression: A systematic *review. Journal of Affective Disorders, 47*, 17–28.

Hayes, B. (2001). *Sleep demons: An insomniac's memoir*. New York: Washington Square Press.

Hayes, S. C., Muto, T., & Masuda, A. (2011). Seeking cultural competence from the ground up. *Clinical Psychology: Science and Practice, 18*, 232–237. doi: 10.1111/j.1468-2850.2011.01254.x

Haynos, A. F., & Fruzzetti, A. E. (2011). Anorexia nervosa as a disorder of emotion dysregulation: Evidence and treatment implications. *Clinical Psychology: Science and Practice, 18*, 183–202. doi: 10.1111/j.1468-2850.2011.01250.x

Hays, P. A. (2009). Integrating evidenced-based practice, cognitive–behavior therapy, and multicultural therapy: Ten steps for culturally competent practice. *Professional Psychology: Research and Practice, 40*, 354–360.

Hazlett, H. C., Poe, M. D., Gerig, G., Styner, M., Chappell, C., Gimpel Smith, R., . . . Piven, J. (2011). Early brain overgrowth in autism associated with an increase in cortical surface area before age 2 years. *Archives of General Psychiatry, 68*, 467–476. doi:10.1001/archgenpsychiatry.2011.39

Healy, A., Rush, R., & Ocain, T. (2011). Fragile X syndrome: An update on developing treatment modalities. *ACS Chemical Neuroscience, 2*, 402–410. doi: 10.1021/cn200019zdoi : 10.1021/cn200019z.

Hebert, L. E., Scherr, P. A., Bienias, J. L., Bennett, D. A., & Evans, D. A. (2003). Alzheimer's disease in the U.S. population: Prevalence estimates using the 2000 census. *Archives of Neurology, 60*, 1119–1122.

Heilbrun, K., & Kramer, G. M. (2005). Involuntary medication, trial competence, and clinical dilemmas: Implications of Sell v. United States for psychological practice. *Professional Psychology: Research and Practice, 36*, 459–466.

Heinemann, L. A. J., Minh, T. D., Filonenko, A., & Uhl-Hochgräber, K. (2010). Explorative evaluation of the impact of severe premenstrual disorders on work absenteeism and productivity. *Women's Health Issues, 20*, 58–65. doi:10.1016/j.whi.2009.09.005

Heinrichs, M., Wagner, D., Schoch, W., Soravia, L. M., Hellhammer, D. H., & Ehlert, U. (2005). Predicting posttraumatic stress symptoms from pretraumatic risk factors: A 2-year prospective follow-up study in firefighters. *American Journal of Psychiatry, 162*, 2276–2286.

Hemmings, C. (2010). Service use and outcomes. In N. Bouras (Ed.), *Mental health services for adults with intellectual disability: Strategies and solutions* (pp. 75–88). New York: Psychology Press.

Hendrick, B. (2011), Use of antidepressants on the rise in the U.S.. (2011, October 19). *WebMD Health*. Retrieved from http://www.webmd.com/depression/news/20111019/use-of-antidepressants-on-the-rise-in-the-us

Hendrick, B. (2011, October 19). Use of antidepressants on the rise in the U.S. *WebMD Health*. Retrieved from http://www.webmd.com/depression/news/20111019/use-of-antidepressants-on-the-rise-in-the-us

Henig, R. M. (2012, September 30). Valium's contribution to our new normal. *The New York Times Sunday Review*, p. 9.

Henin, A., Micco, J. A., Wozniak, J., Briesch, J. M., Narayan, A. J., & Hirshfeld-Becker, D. R. (2009). Neurocognitive functioning in bipolar disorder. *Clinical Psychology: Science and Practice, 16*, 231–250. doi:10.1111/j.1468-2850.2009.01162.x

Henriques, G., Wenzel, A., Brown, G. K., & Beck, A. T. (2005). Suicide attempters' reaction to survival as a risk factor for eventual suicide. *American Journal of Psychiatry, 162*, 2180–2182.

Henry, K. L., McDonald, J. N., Oetting, E. R., Silk Walker, P., Walker, R. D., & Beauvais, F. (2011). Age of onset of first alcohol intoxication and subsequent alcohol use among urban American Indian adolescents. *Psychology of Addictive Behaviors, 25*, 48–56. doi: 10.1037/a0021710

Henry, M., Pascual-Leone, A., & Cole, J. (2003). *Electromagnetic stimulation shows promise for treatment-resistant depression*. Retrieved from http://www.healthyplace.com/communities/depression/treatment/tms/index.asp

Henslee, A. M., & Coffey, S. F. (2010). Exposure therapy for posttraumatic stress disorder in a residential substance use treatment facility. *Professional Psychology: Research and Practice, 41*, 34–40.

Herbst, N., Voderholzer, U., Stelzer, N., Knaevelsrud, C., Hertenstein, E., Schlegl, S., . . . Külza, A. K. (2012). The potential of telemental health applications for obsessive-compulsive disorder. *Clinical Psychology Review, 32*, 454–466.

Herrup, K. (2010). Reimagining Alzheimer's Disease—an age-based hypothesis. *Journal of Neuroscience, 30*, 16755-16762. doi: 10.1523/jneurosci.4521-10.2010

Heymsfield, S., B., & Cefalu, W. T. (2013). Does body mass index adequately convey a patient's mortality risk? *Journal of the American Medical Association, 309*, 87–88. doi:10.1001/jama.2012.185445.

Higgins, S. T. (2006). Extending contingency management to the treatment of methamphetamine use disorders. *American Journal of Psychiatry, 163*, 1870–1872.

Higgins, S. T., Heil, S. H., & Lussier, J. P. (2004). Clinical implications of reinforcement as a determinant of substance use disorders. *Annual Review of Psychology, 55*, 431–461.

Hildebrandt, T., Alfano, L., Tricamo, M., & Pfaff, D. W. (2010). Conceptualizing the role of estrogens and serotonin in the development and maintenance of bulimia nervosa. *Clinical Psychology Review, 30*, 655–668. doi: 0.1016/j.cpr.2010.04.011

Hill, M., J., & Bray, N. J. (2012).Evidence that schizophrenia risk variation in the ZNF804A gene exerts its effects during fetal brain development. *American Journal of Psychiatry, 169*, 1301–1308. 10.1176/appi.ajp.2012.11121845

Hingson, R. W., Zha, W., & Weitzmanet, E. R. (2009). Magnitude of and trends in alcohol-related mortality and morbidity among U.S. college students ages 18 to 24, 1998–2005. *Journal of Studies on Alcohol and Drugs, 16*, 12–20. doi:10.1146/annurev.publhealth.26.021304.144652

Hinton, D. E., Park, L., Hsia, C., Hofmann, S., & Pollack, M. H. (2009). Anxiety disorder presentations in Asian populations: A review. *CNS Neuroscience & Therapeutics, 15*, 295–303. doi: 10.1111/j.1755-5949.2009.00095.x

Hirschfeld, R. M. A. (2011). Deep brain stimulation for treatment-resistant depression. *American Journal of Psychiatry, 168*, 455–456. doi: 10.1176/appi.ajp.2011.11020231

Hirshfeld-Becker, D. R., Masek, B., Henin, A., Blakely, L. R., Pollock-Wurman, R., McQuade, J., . . . Biederman, J. (2010). Cognitive behavioral therapy for 4- to 7-year-old children with anxiety disorders: A randomized clinical trial. *Journal of Consulting and Clinical Psychology, 78*, 498–510. doi: 10.1037/a0019055

Hitti, M. (2006, March 6). Eating disorders may run in families. Retrieved from http://psychologytoday.webmd.com/content/article/119/113378?src=rss_psychtoday

Ho, M.-H R., Auerbach, R. P., Jun, H. L., Abela, J. R. Z., Zhu, X., & Yao, S. (2011). Understanding anxiety sensitivity in the development of anxious and depressive symptoms. *Cognitive Therapy and Research, 35*, 232–240. doi: 10.1007/s10608-009-9280-8

Hodgins, D. C., Schopflocher, D. P., el-Guebaly, N., Casey, D. M., Smith, G. J., . . . Wood, R. T. (2010). The association between childhood maltreatment and gambling problems in a community sample of adult men and women. *Psychology of Addictive Behaviors, 24*, 548–554. doi: 10.1037/a0019946

Hodgins, D. C., Schopflocher, D. P., el-Guebaly, N., Casey, D. M., Smith, G. J., Williams, R. J.,& Wood, R. T. (2010). The association between childhood maltreatment and gambling problems in a community sample of adult men and women. *Psychology of Addictive Behaviors, 24*, 548–554. doi:10.1037/a0019946

Hodgins, D., C., Stea, J. N., & Grant, J. E. (2011). Gambling disorders. *The Lancet, 378*, 1874–1884. doi: 10.1016/S0140-6736(10)62185-X

Hoeft, F., Walter, E., Lightbody, A. A., Hazlett, H. C., Chang, C., Piven, J., . . . Reiss, A. L. (2011). Neuroanatomical differences in toddler boys with Fragile X Syndrome and idiopathic autism. *Archives of General Psychiatry, 68,* 295–305. doi:10.1001/archgenpsychiatry.2010.153

Hoffmann et al., 2004

Hofmann, S. G. (2008). Cognitive processes during fear acquisition and extinction in animals and humans: Implications for exposure therapy of anxiety disorders. *Clinical Psychology Review, 28,* 200–211.

Hofmann, S. G., Asmundson, G. J. G., & Beck, A. T. (2011). The science of cognitive therapy. *Behavior Therapy*, in press.

Hofmann, S. G., Asnaani, A., Vonk, I. J. J., Sawyer, A. T., & Fang, A. (2012). The efficacy of cognitive behavioral therapy: a review of meta-analyses. *Cognitive Therapy and Research, 36*,, 427–440. doi: 10.1007/s10608-012-9476-1

Hofmann, S. G., Meuret, A. E., Smits, J. A. J., Simon, N. M., Pollack, M. H., Eisenmenger, K., . . . Otto, M. W. (2006). Augmentation of exposure therapy with D-cycloserine for social anxiety disorder. *Archives of General Psychiatry, 63,* 298–304.

Hofmann, S. G., Moscovitch, D. A., Kim, H. J., & Taylor, A. N. (2004). Changes in self-perception during treatment of social phobia. *Journal of Consulting and Clinical Psychology, 72,* 588–596.

Holahan, C. J., Moos, R. H., Holahan, C. K., Brennan, P. L., & Schutte, K. K. (2005). Stress generation, avoidance coping, and depressive symptoms: A 10-year model. *Journal of Consulting and Clinical Psychology, 73,* 658–666.

Holbrook, T. L., Galarneau, M. R., Dye, J. L., Quinn, K., & Dougherty, A. L. (2010). Morphine use after combat injury in Iraq and post-traumatic stress disorder. *New England Journal of Medicine, 362,* 110–117.

Holden, C. (2008a). Bipolar disorder: Poles apart. *Science, 321,* 193–195.

Holder-Perkins, V., & Wise, T. N. (2002). Somatization disorder. In K. A. Phillips (Ed.), *Somatoform and factitious disorders. Review of Psychiatry* (Vol. 20, pp. 1–26). Washington, DC: American Psychiatric Association.

Holland, A. J., Sicotte, N., & Treasure, J. (1988). Anorexia nervosa: Evidence of a genetic basis. *Journal of Psychosomatic Research, 32,* 561–571.

Holley, A. B., et al. (2011). Efficacy of an adjustable oral appliance and comparison with continuous positive airway pressure for the treatment of obstructive sleep apnea syndrome. *Chest, 140,* 1511.

Holley, A. B., Lettieri, C. J., & Shah, A. A. (2011). Efficacy of an adjustable oral appliance and comparison with continuous positive airway pressure for the treatment of obstructive sleep apnea syndrome. *Chest, 140,* 1511.

Hollingshead, A. B., & Redlich, F. C. (1958). *Social class and mental illness: Community study.* New York: Wiley.

Hollingworth, P., Harold, D., Sims, R., Gerrish, A., Lambert, J.-C., Carrasquillo, M. M., . . . Williams J. (2011). Common variants at ABCA7, MS4A6A/MS4A4E, EPHA1, CD33 and CD2AP are associated with Alzheimer's disease. *Nature Genetics, 43,* 429.

Hollon, S. D., & Ponniah, K. (2010). A review of empirically supported psychological therapies for mood disorders in adults. *Depression and Anxiety, 27,* 891–932.

Hollon, S.D., Kendall, P.C. (1980), Cognitive self-statements in depression: Development of an automatic thoughts questionnaire. *Cognitive Therapy and Research, 4,* 383–395.

Holma, K. M., Melartin, T. K., Haukka, J., Holma, I. A. K., Sokero, T. P., & Isometsä, E. T. (2010). Incidence and predictors of suicide attempts in DSM–IV major depressive disorder: A five-year prospective study. *American Journal of Psychiatry, 167,* 801–808.

Holroyd, K. A. (2002). Assessment and psychological management of recurrent headache disorders. *Journal of Consulting and Clinical Psychology, 70,* 656–677.

Holtgraves, T. (2009). Gambling, gambling activities, and problem gambling. *Psychology of Addictive Behaviors, 23,* 295–302. doi:10.1037/a0014181

Holtmann, M., Bölte, S., & Poustka, F. (2008). Rapid increase in rates of bipolar diagnosis in youth: "True" bipolarity or misdiagnosed severe disruptive behavior disorders? *Archives of General Psychiatry, 65,* 477.

Holtz, J. L. (2011). *Applied clinical neuropsychology.* New York: Springer.

Holtzheimer, P. E., Kelley, M. E., Gross, R. E., Filkowski, M. M., Garlow, S. J., Barrocas, A., . . . Mayberg, H. S. (2012). Subcallosal cingulate deep brain stimulation for treatment-resistant unipolar and bipolar depression. *Archives of General Psychiatry, 69,* 150–158. doi:10.1001/archgenpsychiatry.2011.1456

Homer, B. D., Solomon, T. M., Moeller, R. W., Mascia, A., DeRaleau, L., & Halkitis, P. N. (2008). Methamphetamine abuse and impairment of social functioning: A review of the underlying neurophysiological causes and behavioral implications. *Psychological Bulletin, 134,* 301–310.

Hong, D. S., Dunkin, B., & Reiss, A. L. (2011). Psychosocial functioning and social cognitive processing in girls with Turner syndrome. *Journal of Developmental & Behavioral Pediatrics, 7,* 512–520.

Hongpaisan, J., Sun, M.-K., & Alkon, D. L. (2011). PKC ε activation prevents synaptic loss, Aβ elevation, and cognitive deficits in Alzheimer's Disease transgenic mice. *Journal of Neuroscience, 31,* 630–643. doi: 10.1523/JNEUROSCI.5209-10.2011

Hooker, C. I., Bruce, L., Fisher, M., Verosky, S. C., Miyakawa, A., & Vinogradov, S. (2012). Neural activity during emotion recognition after combined cognitive plus social cognitive training in schizophrenia. *Schizophrenia Research, 39,* 53–59. doi: 10.1016/j.schres.2012.05.009

Hooley, J. M. (2010). Social factors in schizophrenia. *Current Directions in Psychological Science, 19,* 238–242. doi:10.1177/0963721410377597

Hopkin, M. (2008, May 5). Fat cell numbers stay constant through adult life. *Nature News.* doi:10.1038/ news.2008.800

Hopko, D. R., Armento, M. E. A., Robertson, S. M. C., Ryba, M. M., Carvalho, J. P., Colman, L. K., . . . Lejuez, C. W. (2011). Brief behavioral activation and problem-solving therapy for depressed breast cancer patients: Randomized trial. *Journal of Consulting and Clinical Psychology, 79,* 834–849. doi:10.1037/a0025450

Hopwood, C. J., Donnellan, M. B., Blonigen, D. M., Krueger, R. F., McGue, M., Iacono, W. G., & Burt, S. A. (2011). Genetic and environmental influences on personality trait stability and growth during the transition to adulthood: A three-wave longitudinal study. *Journal of Personality and Social Psychology, 100,* 545–556. doi: 10.1037/a0022409.

Hor, H., Bartesaghi, L., Kutalik, Z., Vicário, J. L., de Andrés, C., Pfister, C., . . . & Peraita-Adrados, R. (2011). A missense mutation in myelin oligodendrocyte glycoprotein as a cause of familial narcolepsy with cataplexy. *American Journal of Human Genetics, 89,* 474–479. doi: 10.1016/j.ajhg.2011.08.007

Houghton, S., Curran, J., & Ekers, D. (2011). Behavioural activation in the treatment of depression. *Mental Health Practice, 14,* 18–23.

Houry, D. (2004). Suicidal patients in the emergency department: Who is at greatest risk? *Annals of Emergency Medicine, 43,* 731–732.

Houts, A. C. (2010). Behavioral treatment for enuresis. In J. R. Weisz & A. E. Kazdin (Eds.) (2nd ed), *Evidence-based psychotherapies for children and adolescents* (pp. 359–374). New York: Guilford Press.

Houts, F. W., Taller, I., Tucker, D. E., & Berlin, F. S. (2011). Sexual dysfunction. In R. Balon (Ed.). *Beyond the brain-body connection. Advances in Psychosomatic Medicine, Vol. 31,* 149–163. Basel: Karger.

Howard, R., McShane, R., Lindesay, J., Ritchie, C., Baldwin, A., Barber, R., . . . Phillips, P. (2012). Donepezil and memantine for moderate-to-severe Alzheimer's Disease. *New England Journal of Medicine, 66,* 893–903.

Howell, E. F. (2011). *Understanding and treating dissociative identity disorder: A rational approach.* New York: Routledge/Taylor & Francis.

Howes, O. D., Kambeitz, J., Kim, E., Stahl, D., Slifstein, M., Abi-Dargham, A., & Kapur, S. (2012). The nature of dopamine dysfunction in schizophrenia and what this means for treatment: Meta-analysis of imaging studies. *Archives of General Psychiatry, 69,* 776–786. doi:10.1001/archgenpsychiatry.2012.169

Hoza, B., Mrug, S., Gerdes, A. C., Hinshaw, S. P., Bukowski, W. M., Gold, J. A., et al. (2005). What aspects of peer relationships are impaired in children with attention-deficit/hyperactivity disorder? *Journal of Consulting and Clinical Psychology, 73,* 411–423.

Hrobjartsson, A., & Gotzsche, P. C. (2001). Is the placebo powerless? An analysis of clinical trials comparing placebo with no treatment. *New England Journal of Medicine, 344,* 1594–1602.

Hu, M.-C., Davies, M., & Kandel, D. B. (2006). Epidemiology and correlates of daily smoking and nicotine dependence among young adults in the United States. *American Journal of Public Health, 96,* 299–308.

Hua, X., Thompson, P. M., Leow, A. D., Madsen, S. K., Caplan, R., Alger, J. R., . . Levitt, J. G. (2011). Brain growth rate abnormalities visualized in adolescents with autism. *Human Brain Mapping.* Retrieved from http://onlinelibrary.wiley.com/doi/10.1002/hbm.21441/abstract

Hubbard, K. L., Zapf, P. A., & Ronan, K. A. (2003). Competency restoration: An examination of the differences between defendants predicted restorable and not restorable to competency. *Law and Human Behavior, 27,* 127–139.

Hudson, J. I., Lalonde, J. K., Berry, J. M., Pindyck, L. J., Bulik, C. M., Crow, S. J., et al. (2006). Binge-eating disorder as a distinct familial phenotype in obese individuals. *Archives of General Psychiatry, 63,* 313–319.

Huffman, J. C., Smith, F. A., Blais, M. A., Taylor, A. M., Januzzi, J. L., & Fricchione, G. L. (2008). Pre-existing major depression predicts in-hospital cardiac complications after acute myocardial infarction. *Psychosomatics, 49,* 309–316. doi:10.1176/appi.psy.49.4.309

Hulshoff Pol, H. E., van Baal, G. C., M., Schnack, H. G., Brans, R. G. H., van der Schot, A C., Brouwer, R. M., . . . Kahn, R. S. (2012). Overlapping and segregating structural brain abnormalities in twins with schizophrenia or bipolar disorder. *Archives of General Psychiatry, 69,* 349–359. doi:10.1001/archgenpsychiatry.2011.1615

Humphrey, L. L. (1986). Family dynamics in bulimia. In S. C. Feinstein et al. (Eds.), *Adolescent psychiatry* (pp. 315–332). Chicago: University of Chicago Press.

Hunnicutt-Ferguson, K., Hoxha, D., & Gollan, J. (2012). Exploring sudden gains in behavioral activation therapy for Major Depressive Disorder. *Behaviour Research and Therapy, 50,* 223–230.

Hunsley, J., & Bailey, J. M. (2001). Whither the Rorschach? An analysis of the evidence. *Psychological Assessment, 13,* 472–485.

Hunter, E. C. M., Phillips, M. L., Chalder, T., Sierra, M., & David, A. S. (2003). Depersonalisation disorder: A cognitive– behavioural conceptualization. *Behaviour Research and Therapy, 41,* 1451–1467.

Huntington's Disease advance: Overactive protein triggers a chain reaction that causes brain nerve cells to die. (2011, February 23). *ScienceDaily.* Retrieved from http://www.sciencedaily.com/

Huprich, S. K., Fuller, K. M., & Schneider, R. B. (2003). Divergent ethical perspectives on the duty-to-warn principle with HIV patients. *Ethics & Behavior, 13,* 263–278.

Hurlburt, G., & Gade, E. (1984). Personality differences between Native American and Caucasian women alcoholics: Implications for alcoholism counseling. *White Cloud Journal, 3,* 35–39.

Huynh, Q.-L., Devos, T., & Dunbar, C. M. (2012). The psychological costs of painless but recurring experiences of racial discrimination. *Cultural Diversity and Ethnic Minority Psychology, 18,* 26–34. doi: 10.1037/a0026601

Hwang, W.-C. (2006). The psychotherapy adaptation and modification framework: Application to Asian Americans. *American Psychologist, 61,* 702–715.

Hwang, W.-C. (2011). Cultural adaptations: A complex interplay between clinical and cultural issues. *Clinical Psychology: Science and Practice, 18,* 238–241. doi: 10.1111/j.1468-2850.2011.01255.

Hyde, J. S., Mezulis, A. H., & Abramson, L. Y. (2008). The ABCs of depression: Integrating affective, biological, and cognitive models to explain the emergence of the gender difference in depression. *Psychological Review, 115,* 291–313.

Hyman, S. E. (2011). The meaning of the Human Genome Project for neuropsychiatric disorders. *Science, 331,* 1026. doi: 10.1126/science.1203544

I

I. D. R. Laws & W. T. O'Donohue (Eds.). *Sexual deviance: Theory, assessment, and treatment* (pp. 61–75). New York: Guilford Press.

Ibarra-Rovillard, M. S., & Kuiper, N. A. (2011). Social support and social negativity findings in depression: perceived responsiveness to basic psychological needs. *Clinical Psychology Review, 31,* 342–352. doi:10.1016/j.cpr.2011.01.005 in El Salvador.

Ilgen, M. A., Wilbourne, P. L., Moos, B. S., & Moos, R. H. (2008). Problem-free drinking over 16 years among individuals with alcohol use disorders. *Drug and Alcohol Dependence, 92,* 116.

Imel, Z. E., Malterer, M. B., McKay, K. M., & Wampold, B. E. (2008). A meta-analysis of psychotherapy and medication in unipolar depression and dysthymia. *Journal of Affective Disorders, 110,* 197–206.

Ingersoll, B. (2011). Recent advances in early identification and treatment of autism. *Current Directions in Psychological Science, 20,* 335–339. doi: 10.1177/0963721411418470

Ingram, R. E., & Siegle, G. J. (2001). Cognition and clinical science: From revolution to evolution. In K. S. Dobson (Ed.), *Handbook of cognitive-behavioral therapies* (2nd ed., pp. 111–137). New York: Guilford Press.

Inouye, S. K. (2006). Delirium in older persons. *New England Journal of Medicine, 354,* 1157–1165.

Insel, T.R. (2010). Rethinking schizophrenia. *Nature, 468,* 187–193.

iPad App helps autistic teen communicate. (2010, April 7). *Globe Newswire.* Retrieved from http://www.globenewswire.com/newsroom/news.html?d=188282

Irish, L., Kobayashi, I., & Delahanty, D. L. (2010). Long-term physical consequences of childhood sexual abuse: A meta-analytic review. *Journal of Pediatric Psychology, 35,* 450–461.

Ishak, W. w., Bokarius, A., Jeffrey, J. K., Davis, M. C., & Bakhta, Y. (2010). Disorders of orgasm in women: A literature review of etiology and current treatments. *Journal of Sexual Medicine, 7,* 3254–3268. doi: 10.1111/j.1743-6109.2010.01928.x.

Ivanov, I., Bansal, R., Hao, X., Zhu, H., Kellendonk, C., Miller, L. . . . Peterson, B. S. (2010). Morphological abnormalities of the thalamus in youths with attention deficit hyperactivity disorder. *American Journal of Psychiatry, 167,* 397–408.

Izard, C. E., Krauthamer-Ewing, S., Woodburn, E. M., Finlon, K. J., & Rosen, J. (2009). Emotion–cognition interplay in motivating and guiding plans and actions: Commentary on McClure-Tone's socioemotional functioning in bipolar disorder. *Clinical Psychology: Science and Practice, 16,* 114–120. doi:10.1111/j.1468-2850.2009.01151.x

J

Jablensky, A. V., Morgan, V., Zubrick, S. R., Bower, C., & Yellachich, L.-A. (2005). Pregnancy, delivery, and neonatal complications in a population cohort of women with schizophrenia and major affective disorders. *American Journal of Psychiatry, 162,* 79–91.

Jablensky, A., Sartorius, N., Ernberg, G., & Anker, M. (1992). Schizophrenia: Manifestations, incidence and course in different cultures: A World Health Organization ten-country study. *Psychological Medicine, 20* (Monograph Suppl.), 1–97.

Jack, C. R., Jr., Albert, M. S., Knopman, D. S., McKhann, G. M., Sperling, R. A., Carrillo, M. C., . . . Phelps, C. H. (2011). Introduction to the recommendations from the National Institute on Aging and the Alzheimer's Association workgroup on diagnostic guidelines for Alzheimer's disease. *Alzheimers Dementia, 7,* 257–262.

Jackson, L. C., & Greene, B. A. (Eds.). (2000). *Psychotherapy with African American women: Innovations in psychodynamic perspectives and practice.* New York: Guilford Press.

Jacob, T., Waterman, B., Heath, A., True, W., Bucholz, K. K., Haber, R., . . . Fu, Q. (2003). Genetic and environmental effects on offspring alcoholism: New insights using an offspring-of-twins design. *Archives of General Psychiatry, 60,* 1265–1272.

Jacobi, C., Hayward, C., de Zwaan, M., Kraemer, H. C., & Agras, W. S. (2004). Coming to terms with risk factors for eating disorders: Application of risk terminology and suggestions for a general taxonomy. *Psychological Bulletin, 130,* 19–65.

Jacquemont, S., Curie, A., des Portes, V., Torrioli, M. G., Berry-Kravis, E., Hagerman, R. J., . . . Gomez-Mancilla, B. (2011). Epigenetic modification of the FMR1 Gene in Fragile X Syndrome is associated with differential response to the mGluR5 antagonist AFQ056. *Science Translational Medicine, 3,* 64. doi: 10.1126/scitranslmed.3001708

Jamison, K. R. (1995). *An unquiet mind.* New York: Knopf.

Japuntich, S. J., Piper, M. E., Leventhal, A. M., Bolt, D. M., & Baker, T. B. (2011). The effect of five smoking cessation pharmacotherapies on smoking cessation milestones. *Journal of Consulting and Clinical Psychology, 79,* 34–42. doi: 10.1037/a0022154

Jasinska-Myga, B., et al. (2010). Depression in Parkinson's disease. *Canadian Journal of Neurological Sciences, 37,* 61.

Jayaram-Lindström, N., Hammarberg, A., Beck, O., & Franck, J. (2008). Naltrexone for the treatment of amphetamine dependence: A randomized, placebo-controlled trial. *American Journal of Psychiatry, 165,* 1442–1448.

Jefferson, D. J. (2005, August 8). America's most dangerous drug. *Newsweek,* pp. 41–48.

Jemal, A., Siegel, R., Ward, E., Murray, T., Xu, J., & Thun, M. J. (2007). Cancer statistics, 2007. *CA: A Cancer Journal for Clinicians, 57,* 43–66.

Jemmott, J. B., Borysenko, J. Z., Borysenko, M., McClelland, D. C., Chapman, R., Meyer, D., & Benson, H. (1983). Academic stress, power motivation, and decrease in secretion rate of salivary secretory immunoglobulin A. *Lancet, 1,* 1400–1402.

Jenkins, C. D. (1988). Epidemiology of cardiovascular diseases. *Journal of Consulting and Clinical Psychology, 56,* 324–332.

Jenkins, P. E., Hoste, R. R., Meyer, C., & Blissett, M. M. (2011). Eating disorders and quality of life: A review of the literature. *Clinical Psychology Review, 31,* 113–121. doi:10.1016/j.cpr.2010.08.003

Jha, P., Ramasundarahettige, C., Landsman, V., Rostron, B., Thun, M., Anderson, R. N., McAfee, T., & Peto, R. (2013). 21st-century hazards of smoking and benefits of cessation in the United States. *New England Journal of Medicine, 368,* 341–350. doi:10.1056/NEJMsa1211128

Jia, Z., Huang, X., Wu, Q., Zhang, T., Lui, S., Zhang, J., Amatya, N., . . . Gong, Q. (2010). High-field magnetic resonance imaging of suicidality in patients with major depressive disorder. *American Journal of Psychiatry, 167,* 1381–1390. doi: 10.1176/appi.ajp.2010.09101513)

Jian, X.-Q., Wang, K.-S., Wu, T.-J., Hillhouse, J. J., & Mullersman, J. E. (2011). Association of ADAM10 and CAMK2A polymorphisms with conduct disorder: Evidence from family-based studies. *Journal of Abnormal Child Psychology, 39,* 773–782. doi:10.1007/s10802-011-9524-4

Jiang, H., & Chess, L. (2006). Regulation of immune responses by T cells. *New England Journal of Medicine, 354,* 1166–1176.

Jobe, T. H., & Harrow, M. (2010). Schizophrenia course, long-term outcome, recovery, and prognosis. *Current Directions in Psychological Science, 19,* 220–225. doi: 10.1177/0963721410378034

Joe, S., Baser, E., Breeden, G., Neighbors, H. W., & Jackson, J. S. (2006). Prevalence of and risk factors for lifetime suicide attempts among Blacks in the United States. *Journal of the American Medical Association, 296,* 2112–2123.

Johansson, A., Sundbom, E., Höjerback, T., & Bodlund, O. (2010). A five-year follow-up study of Swedish adults with gender identity disorder. *Archives of Sexual Behavior, 39,* 1429–1437. doi: 10.1007/s10508-009-9551-1

Johnson, D. B., Oyama, N., LeMarchand, L., & Wilkens, L. (2004). Native Hawaiians mortality, morbidity, and lifestyle: Comparing data from 1982, 1990, and 2000. *Pacific Health Dialog, 11,* 120–130.

Johnson, S. L., Murray, G., Fredrickson, B., Youngstrom, E. A., Hinshaw, S., Bass, J. M., . . . Salloum, I. (2011). Creativity and bipolar disorder: Touched by fire or burning with questions? *Clinical Psychology Review, 32,* 1–12. doi:10.1016/j.cpr.2011.10.001

Johnston, C., Mash, E. J., Miller, N., & Ninowski, J. E. (2012). Parenting in adults with attention-deficit/hyperactivity disorder (ADHD*). Clinical Psychology Review, 32,* 215–228.

Johnston, L. D., O'Malley, P. M., Bachman, J. G., & Schulenberg, J. E. (2010a). *Marijuana use is rising; ecstasy use is beginning to rise; and alcohol use is declining among U.S. Teens.* University of Michigan News Service: Ann Arbor, MI. Retrieved from http://www.monitoringthefuture.org.

Johnston, L. D., O'Malley, P. M., Bachman, J. G., & Schulenberg, J. E. (December 19, 2012). *The rise in teen marijuana use stalls, synthetic marijuana use levels, and use of 'bath salts' is very low.* University of Michigan News Service: Ann Arbor, MI. Retrieved from http://www.monitoringthefuture.org.

Joiner, T. E., Conwell, Y., Fitzpatrick, K. K., Witte, T. K., Schmidt, N. B., Berlim, M. T., . . . Rudd, M. D. (2005). Four studies on how past and current suicidality relate even when "everything but the kitchen sink" is covaried. *Journal of Abnormal Psychology, 114,* 291–303.

Joinson, C., Heron, J., Butler, U., von Gontard, A., & the Avon Longitudinal Study of Parents and Children Study Team. (2006). Psychological differences between children with and without soiling problems. *Pediatrics, 117,* 1575–1584.

Jokela, M., Keltikangas-Jarvinen, L., Kivimaki, M., Puttonen, S., Elovainio, M., Rontu R., & Lehtimaki, T. (2007). Serotonin receptor 2A gene and the influence of childhood maternal nurturance on adulthood depressive symptoms. *Archives of General Psychiatry, 64,* 356–360.

Jones, C. (2003). Tightropes and tragedies: 25 years of Tarasoff. *Medicine, Science, and the Law, 43,* 13–22.

Jones, E. (1953). *The life and work of Sigmund Freud.* New York: Basic Books.

Jones, M. P. (2006). The role of psychosocial factors in peptic ulcer disease: Beyond Helicobacter pylori and NSAIDs. *Journal of Psychosomatic Research, 60,* 407–412.

Joormann, J., & Levens, S. M., & Gotlib, I. H. (2011). Depression and rumination are associated with difficulties manipulating emotional material in working memory. *Psychological Science, 22,* 979–983. doi: 10.1177/0956797611415539

Jordan, K., Fromberger, P., Stolpmann, G., & Muller, J. L. (2011). The role of testosterone in sexuality and paraphilia—A neurobiological approach. *Sexual Medicine, 8*(11), 3008–3029.

Jorge, R. E., Moser, D. J., Acion, L., & Robinson, R. G. (2008). Treatment of vascular depression using repetitive transcranial magnetic stimulation. *Archives of General Psychiatry, 65,* 268–276.

Jung, J., Forbes, G. B., & Lee, Y.-J. (2009). Body dissatisfaction and disordered eating among early adolescents from Korea and the US. *Sex Roles, 61,* 42–54. doi: 10.1007/s11199-009-9609-5

Just, N., Abramson, L. Y., & Alloy, L. B. (2001). Remitted depression studies as tests of the cognitive vulnerability hypotheses of depression onset: A critique and conceptual analysis. *Clinical Psychology Review, 21,* 63–83.

K

Kafka, M. P. (2010). The DSM diagnostic criteria for fetishism. *Archives of Sexual Behavior,* DOI: 10.1007/s10508-009-9558-7.

Kahn, M. W. (1982). Cultural clash and psychopathology in three aboriginal cultures. *Academic Psychology Bulletin, 4,* 553–561.

Kaiser Family Foundation (2012). HIV/AIDS: The state of the epidemic after 3 decades: *Journal of the American Medical Association, 308,* 330–330. doi:10.1001/jama.2012.8700

Kalibatseva, Z., & Leong, F. T. L. (2011). Depression among Asian Americans: Review and Recommendations. *Depression Research and Treatment.* Retrieved from http://www.hindawi.com/journals/drt/2011/320902/

Kamphuis, J. H., & Noordhof, A. (2009). On categorical diagnoses in *DSM-V:* Cutting dimensions at useful points? *Psychological Assessment, 21,* 294–301. doi:10.1037/a0016697

Kandel, D. B. (2003). Does marijuana use cause the use of other drugs? *Journal of the American Medical Association, 289,* 482–483.

Kang, C., Riazuddin, S., Mundorff, J., Krasnewich, D., Friedman, P., Mullikin, J. C., & Drayna, D. (2010). Mutations in the lysosomal enzyme–targeting pathway and persistent stuttering. *New England Journal of Medicine, 362,* 677–685. doi: 10.1056/NEJMoa0902630

Kangas, M., Henry, J. L, & Bryant, R. A. (2005). The relationship between acute stress disorder and posttraumatic stress disorder following cancer. *Journal of Consulting and Clinical Psychology, 73,* 360–364.

Kanner, L. (1943). Autistic disturbances of affective content. *Nervous Child, 2,* 217–240.

Kanter, J. W., Manos, R. C, Bowe, W. M, Baruch, D. E, Busch, A. M., & Rusch, L. C. (2010). What is behavioral activation?: A review of the empirical literature. *Clinical Psychology Review, 30,* 608–620. doi:10.1016/j.cpr.2010.04.001

Kaplan, R. M. (2000). Two pathways to prevention. *American Psychologist, 55,* 382–396.

Kaplan, S. J. (1986). *The private practice of behavior therapy: A guide for behavioral practitioners.* New York: Plenum Press.

Kapur S. (2009). Schizophrenia. *Lancet, 374,* 635–645. doi:10.1016/S0140-6736(09)60995-8., T.R. (2010). Rethinking schizophrenia. *Nature, 468,* 187–193.

Kapur, V., K., & Weaver, E. M. (2012). Filling in the pieces of the sleep apnea–hypertension puzzle. *Journal of the American Medical Association, 307,* 2197–2198. doi:10.1001/jama.2012.5039 [Editorial].

Kapur, V., K., & Weaver, E. M. (2012). Filling in the pieces of the sleep apnea–hypertension puzzle. *Journal of the American Medical Association, 307,* 2197–2198. doi:10.1001/jama.2012.5039 [Editorial]

Karatzias, T., Power, K., Brown, K., McGoldrick, T., Begum, M., Young, J., . . . Adams, S., (2011). A controlled comparison of the effectiveness and efficiency of two psychological therapies for posttraumatic stress disorder: Eye movement desensitization and reprocessing vs. emotional freedom techniques. *Journal of Nervous & Mental Disease, 199,* 372–378. doi: 10.1097/NMD.0b013e31821cd262

Karel, M. J., Gatz, M., & Smyer, M. A. (2012). Aging and mental health in the decade ahead: What psychologists need to know. *American Psychologist, 67,* 184–198. doi: 10.1037/a0025393

Karg, K., Burmeister, M., Shedden, K., & Sen, S. (2011). The serotonin transporter promoter variant (5-httlpr), stress, and depression meta-analysis revisited: Evidence of genetic moderation. *Archives of General Psychiatry, 68,* 444–454. doi:10.1001/archgenpsychiatry.2010.189

Karlsgodt, K. H., Sun, D., & Cannon, T. D. (2010). Structural and functional brain abnormalities in schizophrenia. *Current Directions in Psychological Science, 19*, 226–231.

Karrass, J., Walden, T. A., Conturea, E. G., Graham, C. G., Arnold, H. S., Hartfield, K. N., et al. (2006). Relation of emotional reactivity and regulation to childhood stuttering. *Journal of Communication Disorders, 39*, 402–423.

Karver, M. S., Handelsman, J. B., Fields, S., & Bickman, L. (2006). Meta-analysis of therapeutic relationship variables in youth and family therapy: The evidence for different relationship variables in the child and adolescent treatment outcome literature. *Clinical Psychology Review, 26*, 50–65.

Kaslow, N. J., Thompson, M. P., Okun, A., Price, A., Young, S., Bender, M., . . . Parker, R. (2002). Risk and protective factors for suicidal behavior in abused African American women. *Journal of Consulting and Clinical Psychology, 70*, 311–319.

Kasper, L. J., Alderson, R. M., & Hude, K. L. (2012). Moderators of working memory deficits in children with attention-deficit/hyperactivity disorder (ADHD): A meta-analytic review. *Clinical Psychology Review, 32*, 605–617. doi: 10.1016/j.cpr.2012.07.001

Kasper, L. J., Alderson, R. M., & Hude, K. L. (2012). Moderators of working memory deficits in children with attention-deficit/hyperactivity disorder (ADHD): A meta-analytic review. Clinical Psychology Review, in press http://dx.doi.org/10.1016/j.cpr.2012.07.001

Kasper, L. J., Alderson, R. M., & Hudec, K. L. (2012). Moderators of working memory deficits in children with attention-deficit/hyperactivity disorder (ADHD): A meta-analytic review. *Clinical Psychology Review, 32*, 605–617.

Katon, W. J. (2006). Panic disorder. *New England Journal of Medicine, 354*, 2360–2367.

Katsiaficas, D., Suárez-Orozco, C., Sirin, S. R., & Gupta, T. (2013). Mediators of the relationship between acculturative stress and internalization symptoms for immigrant origin youth. *Cultural Diversity and Ethnic Minority Psychology, 19*, 27–37. doi: 10.1037/a0031094

Kaunitz, A. M. (2011, November 3). Alcohol and breast cancer risk. *Journal Watch Women's Health.* Retrieved from http://womens-health.jwatch.org/cgi/content/full/2011/1103/1?q=etoc_jwwomen

Kay, A. B. (2006). Natural killer T cells and asthma. *New England Journal of Medicine, 354*, 1186–1188.

Kaye, W., (2009). Eating disorders: Hope despite mortal risk. *American Journal of Psychiatry, 166*, 139–1311. doi: 10.1176/appi.ajp.2009.09101424

Kazdin, A. E. (2003). *Research design in clinical psychology* (4th ed.). Boston: Allyn & Bacon.

Kazdin, A. E., & Blasé, S. L. (2011). Rebooting psychotherapy research and practice to reduce the burden of mental illness. *Perspectives on Psychological Science, 6*, 21–37. doi: 10.1177/1745691610393527

Keeley, J. W., DeLao, C. S., & Kirk, C. L. (2013). The commutative property in comorbid diagnosis. Does A + B = B + A? *Clinical Psychological Science, 1*, 16–29. doi: 10.1177/2167702612455742

Keeley, M. L., Storch, E. A., Merlo, L. J., & Geffken, G. R. (2008). Clinical predictors of response to cognitive-behavioral therapy for obsessive-compulsive disorder. *Clinical Psychology Review, 28*, 118–130.

Kellner, C. H., Fink, M., Knapp, R., Petrides, G., Husain, M., Rummans, T., . . . Malur, C. (2005). Relief of expressed suicidal intent by ECT: A Consortium for Research in ECT Study. *American Journal of Psychiatry, 162*, 977–982.

Kellner, C. H., Greenberg, R. M., Murrough, J. W., Bryson, E. O., Briggs, M. C. & Pasculli, R. M. (2012). ECT in treatment-resistant depression. *American Journal of Psychiatry, 169*, 1238–1244. doi:10.1176/appi.ajp.2012.12050648

Kellner, C. H., Knapp, R. G., Petrides, G., Rummans, T. A., Husain, M. M., Rasmussen, K., . . . Fink, M. (2006). Continuation electroconvulsive therapy vs. pharmacotherapy for relapse prevention in major depression. *Archives of General Psychiatry, 63*, 1337–1344.

Kemeny, M. E. (2003). The psychobiology of stress. *Current Directions in Psychological Science, 12*, 124–129.

Kempton, M. J., Stahl, D., Williams, S. C. R., & DeLisi, L. E. (2010). Progressive lateral ventricular enlargement in schizophrenia: A meta-analysis of longitudinal MRI studies. *Schizophrenia Research, 120*, 54–62.

Kendall, P. C., & Drabick, D. A. G. (2010). Problems for the book of problems? Diagnosing mental health disorders among youth. *Clinical Psychology: Science and Practice, 17*, 265–271. doi:10.1111/j.1468-2850.2010.01218.x

Kendall, P. C., & Treadwell, K. (2007). The role of self-statements as a mediator in treatment for anxiety-disordered youth. *Journal of Consulting and Clinical Psychology, 75*, 380–389.

Kendler, K. S. (2005). "A gene for. . .": The nature of gene action in psychiatric disorders. *American Journal of Psychiatry, 162*, 1243–1252.

Kendler, K. S. (2010). Advances in our understanding of genetic risk factors for autism spectrum disorders. *American Journal of Psychiatry, 167*, 1291–1293. doi: 10.1176/appi.ajp.2010.10081160

Kendler, K. S., & Gardner, C. O. (2010). Dependent stressful life events and prior depressive episodes in the prediction of major depression: The problem of causal inference in psychiatric epidemiology. *Archives of General Psychiatry, 67*, 1120–1127. doi:10.1001/archgenpsychiatry.2010.136

Kendler, K. S., & Prescott, C. A. (1999). A population-based twin study of lifetime major depression in men and women. *Archives of General Psychiatry, 56*, 39–44.

Kendler, K. S., Aggen, S. H., & Patrick, C. J. (2013). Familial influences on conduct disorder reflect 2 genetic factors and 1 shared environmental factor. *JAMA Psychiatry, 70*, 78–86. doi:10.1001/jamapsychiatry.2013.267.

Kendler, K. S., Aggen, S. H., Czajkowski, N., Røysamb, E., Tambs, K., Torgersen, S., . . . Reichborn-Kjennerud, T. (2008). The structure of genetic and environmental risk factors for DSM-V personality disorders: A multivariate twin study. *Archives of General Psychiatry, 65*, 1438–1446.

Kendler, K. S., Aggen, S. H., Knudsen, G. P., Røysamb, E., Neale, M. C., & Reichborn-Kjennerud, T. (2011ab). The structure of genetic and environmental risk factors for syndromal and subsyndromal common DSM-IV Aaxis I and Aall Aaxis II Disorders. *American Journal of Psychiatry, 168*, 29–34.

Kendler, K. S., Aggen, S. H., Knudsen, G. P., Røysamb, E., Neale, M. C., & Reichborn-Kjennerud, T. (2011b). The structure of genetic and environmental risk factors for syndromal and subsyndromal common DSM-IV Axis I and All Axis II Disorders. *American Journal of Psychiatry, 168*, 29–34.

Kendler, K. S., Eaves, L. J., Loken, E. K., Pedersen, N. L., Middeldorp, C. M., Reynolds, C., . . . Gardner, C. O. (2011a). The impact of environmental experiences on symptoms of anxiety and depression across the life span. *Psychological Science, 22*, 1343–1352. doi: 10.1177/0956797611417255

Kendler, K. S., et al. (1991). The genetic epidemiology of bulimia nervosa. *American Journal of Psychiatry, 148*, 1627–1637.

Kendler, K. S., Hettema, J. M., Butera, F., Gardner, C. O., & Prescott, C. A. (2003). Life event dimensions of loss, humiliation, entrapment, and danger in the prediction of onsets of major depression and generalized anxiety. *Archives of General Psychiatry, 60*, 789–796.

Kendler, K. S., Kuhn, J., & Prescott, C. A. (2004). The interrelationship of neuroticism, sex, and stressful life events in the prediction of episodes of major depression. *American Journal of Psychiatry, 161*, 631–636.

Kendler, K. S., Myers, J., & Reichborn-Kjennerud, T. (2011). Borderline personality disorder traits and their relationship with dimensions of normative personality: A web-based cohort and twin study. *Acta Psychiatrica Scandinavica, 123*, 349–359.

Kendler, K. S., Neale, M. C., Kessler, R. C., Heath, A. C., & Eaves, L. J. (1993). The lifetime history of major depression in women: Reliability of diagnosis and heritability. *Archives of General Psychiatry, 50*, 863–870.

Kendler, K. S., Sundquist, K., Ohlsson, H., Palmér, K., Maes, H., Winkleby, M. A.,& Sundquist, J. (2012). Genetic and familial environmental influences on the risk for drug abuse: A National Swedish Adoption Study. *Archives of General Psychiatry, 69*, 690–697. doi:10.1001/archgenpsychiatry.2011.2112

Kendrick, J. (2010, August 12). *iPad may help communication for autistic children.* Retrieved from http://gigaom.com/mobile/ipad-is-reaching-autistic-children/

Kenga, S.-L., Smoski, M. J., & Robins, C. J. (2011). Effects of mindfulness on psychological health: A review of empirical studies. *Clinical Psychology Review, 31*, 1041–1056. doi:10.1016/j.cpr.2011.04.006

Kennedy, S. H, Lam, R. W., Parikh, S. V., Patten, S. B., & Ravindran, A. V. (2009). Introduction: Canadian Network for Mood and Anxiety Treatments (CANMAT) Clinical guidelines for the management of major depressive disorder in adults. *Journal of Affective Disorders, 117* (Suppl. 1), S1–S2. doi:10.1016/j.jad.2009.06.043

Kennedy, S. H., Giacobbe, P., Rizvi, S. J., Placenza, F. M., Nishikawa, Y., Mayberg, H.S., . . . Lozano, A. M. (2011). Deep brain stimulation for treatment-resistant depression: Follow-up after 3 to 6 years. *American Journal of Psychiatry, 168*, 502–510. doi: 10.1176/appi.ajp.2010.10081187

Kennedy, S. H., Milev, R., Giacobbe, P., Ramasubbu, R., Lam, R. W., Parikh, S. V., . . . Ravindran, A. V. (2009). Canadian Network for Mood and Anxiety Treatments (CANMAT) clinical guidelines for the management of major depressive disorder in adults: IV. Neurostimulation therapies. *Journal of Affective Disorders, 117* (Suppl. 1), S44–S53. doi:10.1016/j.jad.2009.06.039

Kennedy, S. H., Young, A. H., & Blier, P. (2011). Strategies to achieve clinical effectiveness: Refining existing therapies and pursuing emerging targets. *Journal of Affective Disorders, 132*, S21–S28. doi:10.1016/j.jad.2011.03.048

Kent, A., & Waller, G. (2000). Childhood emotional abuse and eating psychopathology. *Clinical Psychology Review, 20*, 887–903.

Kéri, S., Beniczky, S., & Kelemen, O. (2010). Suppression of the P50 evoked response and Neuregulin 1-Induced AKT phosphorylation in first-episode schizophrenia. *American Journal of Psychiatry,167*, 444–450. doi: 10.1176/appi.ajp.2009.09050723

Kersting, K. (2003, November). Study shows two types of reading disability. *Monitor on Psychology.* Retrieved from http://www.apa.org/monitor/nov03/study.html

Kertesz, A. (2006). Progress in clinical neurosciences: Frontotemporal dementia-Pick's disease. *Canadian Journal of Neurological Sciences, 33*, 143–148.

Keshavan, M. S., Nasrallah, H. A., & Tandon, R. (2011). Schizophrenia, "Just the Facts" 6. Moving ahead with the schizophrenia concept: From the elephant to the mouse. *Schizophrenia Research, 127*, 3–13

Keshtkar, M., Ghanizadeh, A., & Firoozabadi, A. (2012). Repetitive transcranial magnetic stimulation versus electroconvulsive therapy for the treatment of major depressive disorder, a randomized controlled clinical trial. *Journal of ECT, 27*, 310.

Kessler, R. C., Adler, L., Barkley, R., Biederman, J., Conners, C. K., . . . Zaslavsky, A. M . (2006). The prevalence and correlates of adult ADHD in the United States: Results from the National Comorbidity Survey Replication. *American Journal of Psychiatry, 163*, 716–723.

Kessler, R. C., Aguilar-Gaxiola, S., Alonso, J., Chatterji, S., Lee, S., Ormel, J., . . . Wang, S. (2009). The global burden of mental disorders: An update from the WHO World Mental Health (WMH) surveys. *Epidemiologia e Psichiatria Sociale 18*, 23–33.

Kessler, R. C., Avenevoli, S., Costello, E. J., Georgiades, K., Green, J. G., Gruber, M. J., . . . Merikangas, K. R. (2012). Prevalence, persistence, and sociodemographic correlates of DSM-IV disorders in the National Comorbidity Survey Replication Adolescent Supplement. *Archives of General Psychiatry, 69*, 372–380. doi:10.1001/archgenpsychiatry.2011.160

Kessler, R. C., Berglund, P. A., Demler, O., Jin, R., & Walters, E. E. (2005). Lifetime prevalence and age-of-onset distributions of DSM-IV disorders in the National Comorbidity Survey Replication (NCS-R). *Archives of General Psychiatry, 62*, 593–602.

Kessler, R. C., Borges, G., & Walters, E. E. (1999). Prevalence of and risk factors for lifetime suicide attempts in the National Comorbidity Survey. *Archives of General Psychiatry, 56*, 617–626.

Kessler, R. C., Chiu, W. T., Demler, O., & Walters, E. E. (2005). Prevalence, severity, and comorbidity of 12-month DSM-IV disorders in the National Comorbidity Survey Replication. *Archives of General Psychiatry, 62*, 617–627.

Kessler, R. C., Coccaro, E. F., Fava, M., & McLaughlin, K. A. (2012). The phenomenology and epidemiology of intermittent explosive disorder. In J. E. Grant & M. N. Potenza, *The Oxford handbook of impulse control disorders* (pp. 149–164). New York: Oxford University Press.

Kessler, R. C., Demler O., Frank, R. G., Olfson, M., Pincus, H. A., Walters, E. E., . . . Zaslavsky, A. M.et al. (2005). Prevalence and treatment of mental disorders, 1990 to 2003. *New England Journal of Medicine, 352*, 2515–2523.

Kessler, R. C., Sonnega, A., Bromet, E., Hughes, M., & Nelson, C. B. (1995). Posttraumatic stress disorder in the National Comorbidity Survey. *Archives of General Psychiatry, 52*, 1048–1060.

Khanna, M. S., & Kendall, P. C. (2010). Computer-assisted cognitive behavioral therapy for child anxiety: Results of a randomized clinical trial. *Journal of Consulting and Clinical Psychology, 78,* 737–745. doi: 10.1037/a0019739

Khoo, J., Piantadosi, C., Duncan, R., Worthley, S. G., Jenkins, A., Noakes, M., . . . Wittert, G. A. (2011). Comparing effects of a low-energy diet and a high-protein low-fat diet on sexual and endothelial function, urinary tract symptoms, and inflammation in obese diabetic men. *The Journal of Sexual Medicine, 8,* 2868–2875.

Kiecolt-Glaser, J. K. (2009). Psychoneuroimmunology: Psychology's gateway to the biomedical future. *Perspectives on Psychological Science, 4,* 367–369. doi:10.1111/j.1745-6924.2009.01139.x

Kiecolt-Glaser, J. K., McGuire, L., Robles, T. F., & Glaser, R. (2002). Psychoneuroimmunology and psychosomatic medicine: Back to the future. *Psychosomatic Medicine, 64,* 15–28.

Kiecolt-Glaser, J. K., Speicher, C. E., Holliday, J. E., & Glaser, R. (1984). Stress and the transformation of lymphocytes in Epstein-Barr virus. *Journal of Behavioral Medicine, 7,* 1–12.

Kieseppä, T., Eerola, M., Mäntylä, R., Neuvonen, T., Poutanen, V.-P., Luoma, K., . . . Isometsä, E. (2010). Major depressive disorder and white matter abnormalities: A diffusion tensor imaging study with tract-based spatial statistics. *Journal of Affective Disorders, 120,* 240–244. doi:10.1016/j.jad.2009.04.023

Kieseppä, T., Partonen, T., Haukka, J., Kaprio, J., & Lönnqvist, J. (2004). High concordance of bipolar I disorder in a nationwide sample of twins. *American Journal of Psychiatry, 161,* 1814–1821.

Kiesner, J. (2009). Physical characteristics of the menstrual cycle and premenstrual depressive symptoms. *Psychological Science, 20,* 763–770.

Kilgore, K., Snyder, J., & Lentz, C. (2000). The contribution of parental discipline, parental monitoring, and school risk to early-onset conduct problems in African American boys and girls. *Developmental Psychology, 36,* 835–845.

Kilpatrick, D. G., Ruggiero, K. J., Acierno, R., Saunders, B. E., Resnick, H. S., & Best, C. L. (2003). Violence and risk of PTSD, major depression, substance abuse/dependence, and comorbidity: Results from the National Survey of Adolescents. *Journal of Consulting & Clinical Psychology, 71,* 692–700.

Kilts, C. D., Gross, R. E., Ely, T. D., & Drexler, K. P. G. (2004). The neural correlates of cue-induced craving in cocaine-dependent women. *American Journal of Psychiatry, 161,* 233–241.

Kim, J. Y., Liu, C. Y., Zhang, F., Duan, X., Wen, Z., Song, J., . . Ming, G.-L. (2012). Interplay between DISC1 and GABA signaling regulates neurogenesis in mice and risk for schizophrenia. *Cell, 148,* 1051. doi: 10.1016/j.cell.2011.12.037

Kim, J., Park, S., & Blake, R. (2011). Perception of biological motion in schizophrenia and healthy individuals: A behavioral and fMRI study. *PLoS ONE, 6,* e19971. doi: 10.1371/journal.pone.0019971

Kim, K.-H., Lee, S.-M., Paik, J.-W., & Kim, N.-S. (2011). The effects of continuous antidepressant treatment during the first 6 months on relapse or recurrence of depression. *Journal of Affective Disorders, 132,* 121–129.

Kim, Y. S., Leventhal, B. L., Koh, Y.-J., Fombonne, E., Laska, E., Lim, E.-C., . . . Grinker, R. R. (2011). Prevalence of autism spectrum disorders in a total population sample. *American Journal of Psychiatry, 168,* 904–912.

Kindt, M., Soeter, M., & Vervliet, B. (2009). Beyond extinction: Erasing human fear responses and preventing the return of fear. *Nature Neuroscience, 12,* 256–258. doi:10.1038/nn.2271

Kinetz, E. (2006, September 26). Is hysteria real? Brain images say yes. *The New York Times,* pp. F1, F4.

King, D. E., Mainous, A. G., III, & Geesey, M. E. (2008). Adopting moderate alcohol consumption in middle age: Subsequent cardiovascular events. *American Journal of Medicine, 121,* 201–206.

King, D. L., Haagsma, M. C., Delfabbro, P. H., Gradisar, M., & Griffiths, M. D. (2013). Toward a consensus definition of pathological video-gaming: A systematic review of psychometric assessment tools. *Clinical Psychology Review, 33,* 331–342

King, M. (2008). A systematic review of mental disorder, suicide, and deliberate self harm inlesbian, gay and bisexual people. *BMC Psychiatry, 8.* Retrieved from http://www.biomedcentral.com/1471-244X/8/70.

King, S., St-Hilaire, A., & Heidkamp, D. (2010). Prenatal factors in schizophrenia. *Current Directions in Psychological Science, 19,* 209–213. doi: 10.1177/0963721410378360

Kingsberg, S. (2010). Hypoactive sexual desire disorder: When is low sexual desire a disorder? *Journal of Sexual Medicine, 7,* 2907–2908.

Kinoshita, Y., Chen, J., Rapee, R. M., Bogels, S., Schneier, F. R., Choy, Y., et al. (2008). Cross-cultural study of conviction subtype taijin kyofu: Proposal and reliability of Nagoya-Osaka diagnostic criteria for social anxiety disorder. *The Journal of Nervous and Mental Disease, 196,* 307–313.

Kirisci, L., Vanyukov, M., & Tarter, R. (2005). Detection of youth at high risk for substance use disorders: A longitudinal study. *Psychology of Addictive Behaviors, 19,* 243–252.

Kirkbride, J. B., Jones, P. B., Ullrich, S., & Coid, J. W. (2012). Social deprivation, inequality, and the neighborhood-level incidence of psychotic syndromes in East London. *Schizophrenia Bulletin,* in press. doi: 10.1093/schbul/sbs151

Kleiman, M. A. R., Caulkins, J. P., & Hawken, A. (2012, April 21–22). Rethinking the war on drugs. *The Wall Street Journal,* p. C1.

Klein, D. F. (1994). "Klein's suffocation theory of panic": Reply. *Archives of General Psychiatry, 51,* 506.

Klein, R. G. (2011). Thinning of the cerebral cortex during development: A dimension of ADHD. *American Journal of Psychiatry, 168,* 111–113. doi: 10.1176/appi.ajp.2010.10111679

Klein, R. G., Mannuzza, S., Olazagasti, M. A. R., Roizen, E., Hutchison, J. A., Lashua, E. C., & Castellanos, F. X. (2012). Clinical and functional outcome of childhood attention-deficit/hyperactivity disorder 33 years later. *Archives of General Psychiatry,69,*1295-1303. doi:10.1001/archgenpsychiatry.2012.271

Kleinman, A. (1987). Anthropology and psychiatry: The role of culture in cross-cultural research on illness. *British Journal of Psychiatry, 151,* 447–454.

Kliem, S., Kröger, C., & Kosfelder, J. (2010). Dialectical behavior therapy for borderline personality disorder: A meta-analysis using mixed-effects modeling. *Journal of Consulting and Clinical Psychology, 78,* 936–951. doi: 10.1037/a0021015

Kluger, J. (2001, June 18). How to manage teen drinking (the smart way). *Time,* pp. 42–44.

Knapp, M., Romeo, R., Mogg, A., Eranti, S., Pluck, G., Purvis, R., . . . McLoughlin, D. M. (2008). Cost-effectiveness of transcranial magnetic stimulation vs. electroconvulsive therapy for severe depression: A multi-centre randomised controlled trial. *Journal of Affective Disorders, 109,* 273–285.

Knekt, P., Lindfors, O., Laaksonen, M. A., Renlund, C., Haaramo, P., Härkänen, T., . . . the Helsinki Psychotherapy Study Group. (2011). Quasi-experimental study on the effectiveness of psychoanalysis, long-term and short-term psychotherapy on psychiatric symptoms, work ability and functional capacity during a 5-year follow-up. *Journal of Affective Disorders, 132,* 37–47. doi:10.1016/j.jad.2011.01.014

Knight, R. G., Godfrey, H. P. D., & Shelton, E. J. (1988). The psychological deficits associated with Parkinson's disease. *Clinical Psychology Review, 8,* 391–410.

Knoblauch, S. (2009). From self psychology to selves in relationship: A radical process of micro and macro expansion in conceptual experience. In W. Coburn & N. Vanderhide (Eds.), *Self and systems: Annals of the New York Academy of Sciences, 1159,* 262–278.

Knoll, J. L., & Hazelwood, R. R. (2009). Becoming the victim: Beyond sadism in serial sexual murderers. *Aggression and Violent Behavior, 14,* 106–114.

Kobasa, S. C. (1979). Stressful life events, personality, and health: An inquiry into hardiness. *Journal of Personality and Social Psychology, 37,* 1–11.

Kobasa, S. C., Maddi, S. R., & Kahn, S. (1982). Hardiness and health: A prospective study. *Journal of Personality and Social Psychology, 42,* 168–177.

Koch, W. (2009, October 20). Abuse report: 10,440 kids died 2001–2007. *USA Today,* p. 3A.

Koehler, N., Holze, S., Gansera, L., Rebmann, U., Roth, S., Scholz, H. J., . . . Braehler, E. (2012). Erectile dysfunction after radical prostatectomy: the impact of nerve-sparing status and surgical approach. *International Journal of Impotence Research,* doi:10.1038/ijir.2012.8.

Koenen, K. C., Stellman, J. M., & Stellman, S. D. (2003). Risk factors for course of posttraumatic stress disorder among Vietnam veterans: A 14-year follow-up of American Legionnaires. *Journal of Consulting and Clinical Psychology, 71,* 980–986.

Koh, H. K., & Sebelius, K. G. (2012). Ending the tobacco epidemic. *Journal of the American Medical Association, 308,* 767–768. doi:10.1001/jama.2012.9741

Kohli, M. A., Lucae, S., Saemann, P. G., Schmidt, M. V., Demirkan, A., Hek, K., . . . Ripke, S. (2011). The neuronal transporter gene SLC6A15 confers risk to major depression. *Neuron, 70,* 252–265. doi: 10.1016/j.neuron.2011.04.005

Kohli, M. A., Salyakina, D., Pfennig, A., Lucae, S., Horstmann, S., Menke, A., . . . Binder, E. B. (2010). Association of genetic variants in the neurotrophic receptor–encoding gene NTRK2 and a lifetime history of suicide attempts in depressed patients. *Archives of General Psychiatry, 67,* 348–359.

Kok, B. C., Herrell, R. K., Thomas, J. L., & Hoge, C. (2012). Posttraumatic stress disorder associated with combat service in Iraq or Afghanistan: Reconciling prevalence differences between studies. *Journal of Nervous & Mental Disease, 200,* 444–450. doi: 10.1097/NMD.0b013e3182532312

Kolata, G. (2010, August 28). Years later, no magic bullet against Alzheimer's Disease. *The New York Times.* Retrieved from http://www.nytimes.com/2010/08/29/health/research/29prevent.html?pagewanted=2&_r=

Kolata, G. (2012, November 16). For Alzheimer's patients, detection advances outpace treatment options. *The New York Times,* pp. A1, A24.

Kolata, G. (2013, March 1). 5 disorders share genetic risk factors, study finds. *The New York Times,* p. A11.

Kõlves, K., Ide, N., & De Leo, D. (2010). Suicidal ideation and behaviour in the aftermath of marital separation: Gender differences. *Journal of Affective Disorders, 120,* 48–53. doi:10.1016/j.jad.2009.04.019

Kong, A., Frigge, M. L., Masson, G., Besenbacher, S., Sulem, P., Magnusson, G., . . Stefansson, K. (2012). Rate of de novo mutations and the importance of father's age to disease risk. *Nature, 488,* 471–475. doi:10.1038/nature11396

Kong, L., Bachmann, S., Thomann, P. A., Essig, M., & Schröder, J. (2012). Neurological soft signs and gray matter changes: A longitudinal analysis in first-episode schizophrenia. *Schizophrenia Research, 134,* 27–32.

Kornfeld, B. D., Bair-Merritt, M. H., Frosch, E., & Solomon, B. S. (2012). Postpartum depression and intimate partner violence in urban mothers: Co-occurrence and child health care utilization. *The Journal of Pediatrics, 161* (2), 348–353.

Kornfeld, B. D., Bair-Merritt, M. H., Frosch, E., & Solomon, B. S. (2012). Postpartum depression and intimate partner violence in urban mothers: Co-occurrence and child health care utilization. *The Journal of Pediatrics, 161,* 348–353. doi: 10.1016/j.jpeds.2012.01.047

Koster, E. H. W., De Lissnyder, E., Derakshan, N., & De Raedt, R. (2011). Understanding depressive rumination from a cognitive science perspective: The impaired disengagement hypothesis. *Clinical Psychology Review, 31,*138–145. doi:10.1016/j.cpr.2010.08.005

Kouyoumdjian, H., Zamboanga, B. L., & Hansen, D. J. (2003). Barriers to community mental health services for Latinos: Treatment considerations. *Clinical Psychology: Science and Practice, 10,* 394–422.

Kraaimaat, F. W., Vanryckeghem, M., & Van Dam-Baggen, R. (2002). Stuttering and social anxiety. *Journal of Fluency Disorders, 27,* 319–330.

Krakauer, S. Y. (2001). *Treating dissociative identity disorder: The power of the collective heart.* Philadelphia: Brunner-Routledge.

Krantz, D. S., Contrada, R. J., Hills, D. R., & Friedler, E. (1988). Environmental stress and bio-behavioral antecedents of coronary heart disease. *Journal of Consulting and Clinical Psychology, 56,* 333–341.

Krantz, M. J., & Mehler, P. S. (2004). Treating opioid dependence: Growing implications for primary care. *Archives of Internal Medicine, 164,* 277–288.

Kranzler, H. R. (2006). Evidence-based treatments for alcohol dependence: New results and new questions. *Journal of the American Medical Association, 295,* 2075–2076.

Kratochvil, C. J. (2012). ADHD pharmacotherapy: rates of stimulant use and cardiovascular risk. *American Journal of Psychiatry, 169,* 112–114. doi: 10.1176/appi.ajp.2011.11111703

Krause-Utz, A., Sobanski, E., Alm, B., Valerius, G., Kleindienst, N., Bohus, M., . . Schmahl, D. (2013). Impulsivity in relation to stress in patients with borderline personality disorder with and without co-occurring attention-deficit/hyperactivity disorder: an exploratory study. *Journal of Nervous & Mental Disease, 201,* 116–123. doi: 10.1097/NMD.0b013e31827f6462

Kring, A. M., & Caponigro, J. M. (2010). Emotion in schizophrenia: Where feeling meets thinking. *Current Directions in Psychological Science, 19,* 255–259. doi:10.1177/0963721410377599

Kring, A. M., Gur, R. E., Blanchard, J. J., Horan, W. P., & Reise, S. P. (2013). The Clinical Assessment Interview for Negative Symptoms (CAINS): Final development and

validation. *American Journal of Psychiatry,170,* 165–172. 10.1176/appi.ajp.2012.12010109
Kroenke, K. (2009). Efficacy of treatment for somatoform disorders: A review of randomized controlled trials. *Psychosomatic Medicine, 69,* 881–888.
Kronmüller, K.-T., Backenstrass, M., Victor, D., Postelnicu, L., Schenkenbach, C., Joesta, K., . . . Mundt, C. (2011). Quality of marital relationship and depression: Results of a 10-year prospective follow-up study. *Journal of Affective Disorders, 128,* 64–71. doi:10.1016/j.jad.2010.06.026
Kronmüller, K.-T., Backenstrass, M., Victor, D., Postelnicu, L., Schenkenbach, C., Joesta, K., Fiedler, P., & Mundt, C. (2011). Quality of marital relationship and depression: Results of a 10-year prospective follow-up study. *Journal of Affective Disorders, 128,* 64–71. doi:10.1016/j.jad.2010.06.026
Kubiszyn, T., Tom, W., Meyer, G. J., Finn, S. E., Eyde, L. D., Kay, G. G., et al. (2000). Empirical support for psychological assessment in clinical health care settings. *Professional Psychology: Research and Practice, 31,* 119–130.
Kubota, M., Miyata, J., Sasamoto, A., Sugihara, G., Yoshida, H., Kawada, R., . . Murai, T. (2013). Thalamocortical disconnection in the orbitofrontal region associated with cortical thinning in schizophrenia. *JAMA Psychiatry, 70,* 12–21. doi:10.1001/archgenpsychiatry.2012.1023
Kuehn, B. M. (2011). Antidepressant use increases. *Journal of the American Medical Association, 306,* 2207. doi: 10.1001/jama.2011.1697
Kuehn, B. M. (2011). Autism intervention. *Journal of the American Medical Association, 305,* 348. doi: 10.1001/jama.2010.1963
Kuehn, B. M. (2011b). Cognitive therapy may aid patients with schizophrenia. *Journal of the American Medical Association, 306,* 1749. doi: 10.1001/jama.2011.1553
Kuehn, B. M. (2011b). Mobile PTSD care. *Journal of the American Medical Association, 306,* 815. doi: 10.1001/jama.2011.1198
Kuehn, B. M. (2012). Data on autism prevalence, trajectories illuminate socioeconomic disparities. *Journal of the American Medical Association, 307,* 2137–2138. doi:10.1001/jama.2012.3916
Kuehn, B. M. (2012). Evidence suggests complex links between violence and schizophrenia. *Journal of the American Medical Association, 308,* 658–659. doi:10.1001/jama.2012.9364
Kuehn, B. M. (2012). Marijuana use starting in youth linked to IQ loss. *Journal of the American Medical Association, 308,*1196. doi:10.1001/2012.jama.12205.
Kuehn, B. M. (2012).Challenge to Alzheimer drug. *Journal of the American Medical Association, 308,* 2557. doi:10.1001/jama.2012.156122.
Kuehn, B. M. (2013). Teen perceptions of marijuana risks shift: Use of alcohol, illicit drugs, and tobacco declines. *Journal of the American Medical Association,* 309, 429–430. doi:10.1001/jama.2012.211240.
Kumra, S., Oberstar, J. V., Sikich, L., Findling, R. L., McClellan, J. M., et al. (2008). Efficacy and tolerability of second-generation antipsychotics in children and adolescents with schizophrenia. *Schizophrenia Bulletin, 34,* 60–71.
Kuriyan, A. B., Pelham Jr., W. E., Molina, B. S. G., Waschbusch, D. A., Gnagy, E. M., Sibley, M. H., . . . Yu, J. (2013). Young adult educational and vocational outcomes of children diagnosed with ADHD. *Journal of Abnormal Child Psychology, 41,* 27–41.
Kutys, J., & Esterman, J. (2009, November). Guilty but Mentally Ill (GBMI) vs. Not Guilty by Reason of Insanity (NGRI): An annotated bibliography. *The Jury Expert, 21*(6). Retrieved from http://www.astcweb.org/public/publication/article.cfm/1/21/6/An-annotated-bibliography-of-theGBMI-&-NGRI-pleas

L

López, I., Rivera, R., Ramirez, R., Guarnaccia, P. J., Canino, G., & Bird, H. R. (2009). Ataques de nervios and their psychiatric correlates in Puerto Rican children from two different contexts. *The Journal of Nervous and Mental Disease, 297,* 923–929. doi: 10.1097/NMD.0b013e3181c2997d
López, S. R., Barrio, C., Kopelowicz, A., & Vega, W. A. (2012). From documenting to eliminating disparities in mental health care for Latinos. *American Psychologist, 67,* 511–523. doi: 10.1037/a0029737
Labbe, C. (2011, March 7). Most teens with eating disorders go without treatment. *NIMH Science Update.* Retrieved from http://www.nimh.nih.gov/science-news/2011/most-teens-with-eating-disorders-go-without-treatment.shtml?WT.mc_id=rss
Labonté, B., Suderman, M., Maussion, G., Navaro, L., Yerko, V., Mahar, I., . . . Turecki, G. (2012). Genome-wide epigenetic regulation by early-life trauma. *Archives of General Psychiatry, 69,* 722–731. doi:10.1001/archgenpsychiatry.2011.2287
LaFromboise, T. D., Albright, K., & Harris, A. (2010) Patterns of hopelessness among American Indian adolescents: relationships by levels of acculturation and residence. Cultural Diversity and Ethnic Minority Psychology, 16, 68–76. doi: 10.1037/a0016181.
LaGrange, B., Cole, D. A., Jacquez, F., Ciesla, J., Dallaire, D., Pineda, A., . . . Felton, J. (2011). Disentangling the prospective relations between maladaptive cognitions and depressive symptoms. *Journal of Abnormal Psychology, 120,* 511–527. doi:10.1037/a0024685
LaGrange, B., Cole, D. A., Jacquez, F., Ciesla, J., Dallaire, D., Pineda, A., Truss, A., . . . Felton, J. (2011). Disentangling the prospective relations between maladaptive cognitions and depressive symptoms. *Journal of Abnormal Psychology, 120,* 511–527. doi: 10.1037/a0024685
Lahey, B. B., Rathouz, P. J., Lee, S. S., Chronis-Tuscano, A., Pelham, W. E., Waldman, I.D., Irwin D., . . . Cook, E. H. (2011). Interactions between early parenting and a polymorphism of the child's dopamine transporter gene in predicting future child conduct disorder symptoms. *Journal of Abnormal Psychology, 120,* 33–45. doi: 10.1037/a0021133
Lam, R. W., Levitt, A. J., Levitan, R. D., Enns, M. W., Morehouse, R., Michalak, E. E., & Tam, E. M. (2006). The Can-SAD Study: A randomized controlled trial of the effectiveness of light therapy and fluoxetine in patients with winter seasonal affective disorder. *American Journal of Psychiatry, 163,* 805–811.
Lamberg, L. (2003). Advances in eating disorders offer food for thought. *Journal of the American Medical Association, 290,* 1437–1442.
Lamberg, L. (2006). Rx for obesity: Eat less, exercise more, and–maybe–get more sleep. *Journal of the American Medical Association, 295,* 2341–2344.
Lampard, A. M., Byrne, S. M., McLean, N, & Fursland, A. (2011) An evaluation of the enhanced cognitive-behavioural model of bulimia nervosa. *Behaviour Research and Therapy, 49,* 529–535. doi:10.1016/j.brat.2011.06.002 |
Lancee, J., van den Bout, J., van Straten, A., & Spoormaker, V. I. (2012). Internet-delivered or mailed self-help treatment for insomnia? A randomized waiting-list controlled trial. *Behaviour Research and Therapy, 50,* 22–29.
Landa, R. J., Holman, K. C., O'Neill, A. H., & Stuart, E. A. (2011). Intervention targeting development of socially synchronous engagement in toddlers with autism spectrum disorder: a randomized controlled trial. *Journal of Child Psychology and Psychiatry, 52,* 13–21. doi: 10.1111/j.1469-7610.2010.02288.x
Lane, R. F., Raines, S. M., Steele, J. W., Ehrlich, M. E., Lah, J. A., Small, S., A., . . . Gandy S. (2010). Diabetes-associated SorCS1 regulates Alzheimer's amyloid-β metabolism: Evidence for involvement of SorL1 and the Retromer Complex. *Journal of Neuroscience, 30,* 39. doi: 10.1523/JNEUROSCI.3872-10.2010
Lange, N., DuBray, M. B., Lee, J. E., Froimowitz, M. P., Froehlich, A., Adluru, N. . . Lainhart, J. E. (2010). Atypical diffusion tensor hemispheric asymmetry in autism. *Autism Research, 3,* 350–358. doi: 10.1002/aur.162
Langstrom, N. (2010). The DSM diagnostic criteria for exhibitionism, voyeurism, and frotteurism. *Archives of Sexual Behavior, 39,* 317–324. doi: 10.1007/s10508-009-9577-4.
Langstrom, N. (2010). The DSM diagnostic criteria for exhibitionism, voyeurism, and frotteurism. *Archives of Sexual Behavior.* doi: 10.1007/s10508-009-9577-4.
Larson, K., Russ, S. A., Kahn, R. S., & Halfon, N. (2011). Patterns of comorbidity, functioning, and service use for US children with ADHD, 2007. *Pediatrics, 127,* 462–470.
Lau, J. Y. F., & Eley, T. C. (2010). The genetics of mood disorders. *Annual Review of Clinical Psychology, 6,* 313–337. doi 10.1146/annurev.clinpsy.121208.131308
Lauzon, N. M., Bechard, M., Ahmad, T., & Laviolette, S. R. (2012). Supra-normal stimulation of dopamine D1 receptors in the prelimbic cortex blocks behavioral expression of both aversive and rewarding associative memories through a cyclic-AMP-dependent signaling pathway. *Neuropharmacology, 67,*104. doi:10.1016/j.neuropharm.2012.10.029
Lazarus, R. S., & Folkman, S. (1984). *Stress, appraisal, and coping.* New York: Springer.
Le Meyer, O., Zane, N., Cho, Y., II, & Takeuchi, D. T. (2009). Use of specialty mental health services by Asian Americans with psychiatric disorders. *Journal of Consulting and Clinical Psychology, 94,* 1000–1005. doi: 10.1037/a0017065
Lear, M. S. (1988, July 3). Mad malady. *The New York Times,* pp. 21–22.
Leblond, C. S., Heinrich, J., Delorme, R., Proepper, C., Betancur, C., Huguet, G., . . . Bourgeron, T. (2012). Genetic and functional analyses of SHANK2 mutations suggest a multiple hit model of autism spectrum disorders. *PLoS Genetics,* 8, e1002521. doi: 10.1371/journal.pgen.1002521
Lebowitz, E. R., & Omer, H. (2013). *Treating childhood and adolescent anxiety: A guide for caregivers.* Hoboken, NJ: John Wiley
Lee, B., K., Glass, T. A., James, B., D., Bandeen-Roche, K., & Schwartz, B. S. (2011). Neighborhood psychosocial environment, Apolipoprotein E genotype, and cognitive function in older adults. *Archives of General Psychiatry, 68,* 314–321. doi:10.1001/archgenpsychiatry.2011.6
Lee, D. T. S., Yip, A., Chiu, H., Leung, T., & Chung, T. (2001). A psychiatric epidemiological study of postpartum Chinese women. *American Journal of Psychiatry, 158,* 220–226.
Lee, H.-J., Woo, H. G., Greenwood, T. A., Kripke, D. F., & Kelsoe, J. R. (2013). A genome-wide association study of seasonal pattern mania identifies NF1A as a possible susceptibility gene for bipolar disorder. *Journal of Affective Disorders, 145,* 200–207.
Lee, J., & Hahm, H. C. (2010). Acculturation and sexual risk behaviors among Latina adolescents transitioning to young adulthood. *Journal of Youth and Adolescence, 39,* 1573–6601.
Lee, S. S., Humphreys, K. L., Flory, K., Liu, R, & Glass, K. (2011). Prospective association of childhood attention-deficit/hyperactivity disorder (ADHD) and substance use and abuse/dependence: A meta-analytic review. *Clinical Psychology Review, 31,* 328–341. doi:10.1016/j.cpr.2011.01.006
Leekam, S. R., Prior, M. R., & Uljarevic, M. (2011). Restricted and repetitive behaviors in autism spectrum disorders: A review of research in the last decade. *Psychological Bulletin, 137,* 562–593. doi: 10.1037/a0023341
Lefley, H. P. (1990). Culture and chronic mental illness. *Hospital and Community Psychiatry, 41,* 277–286.
Lehmann, M.I., & Herkenham, M. (2011). Environmental enrichment confers stress resiliency to social defeat through an infralimbic cortex-dependent neuroanatomical pathway. *Journal of Neuroscience, 31,* 6159–6173.
Lehne, G. K. (2009). Phenomenology of paraphilia: Lovemap theory. In F. M. Saleh et al.(Eds.), *Sex offenders: Identification, risk assessment, treatment, and legal issue* (pp. 12– 26). New York: Oxford University Press.
Leibenluft, E., & Yonkers, K. A. (2010). The ties that bind: Maternal-infant interactions and the neural circuitry of postpartum depression. *American Journal of Psychiatry, 167,* 1294–1296. doi:10.1176/appi.ajp.2010.10081159
Leiblum, S. R. (2010b). Introduction and overview: clinical perspectives on and treatment for sexual desire disorders. In S. R. Leiblum (Ed.), *Treating sexual desire disorders: A clinical casebook.* New York: Guilford Press.
Leiblum, S. R. (Ed.) (2010a). *Treating sexual desire disorders: A clinical casebook.* New York: Guilford Press.
Leichsenring, F. Leibling, E., Kruse, J., New, A. S., & Leweke, F. (2011). Borderline personality disorder. *Lancet, 377,* 74–84.
Leichsenring, F., & Rabung, S. (2008). Effectiveness of long-term psychodynamic psychotherapy. *Journal of the American Medical Association, 300,* 1551.
Leiner, A. S., Kearns, M. C., Jackson, J. L., Astin, M. C., & Rothbaum, B. O. (2012). Avoidant coping and treatment outcome in rape-related posttraumatic stress disorder. *Journal of Consulting and Clinical Psychology, 80,* 317–321. doi: 10.1037/a0026814
Lejoyeux, M. & Germain, C. (2012). Pyromania: Phenomenology and epidemiology. In J. E. Grant & M. N. Potenza, *The Oxford handbook of impulse control disorders* (pp. 135–148). New York: Oxford University Press.
Lemay, R. A. (2009). Deinstitutionalization of people with developmental disabilities: A review of the literature. *Canadian Journal of Community Mental Health, 28*(1), 000.
Lentz, V., Robinson, J., & Bolton, J. M. (2010). Childhood adversity, mental disorder comorbidity, and suicidal behavior in schizotypal personality disorder. *Journal of*

Nervous and Mental Disease, 198, 795–801. doi: 10.1097/NMD.0b013e3181f9804c

Leocani, L., Locatelli, M., Bellodi, L., Fornara, C., Hénin, M., Magnani, G., . . . Comi, G. (2001). Abnormal pattern of cortical activation associated with voluntary movement in obsessive-compulsive disorder: An EEG study. *American Journal of Psychiatry, 158*, 140–142.

Leong, F. T. L., & Kalibatseva, Z. (2011). Effective psychotherapy for Asian Americans: From cultural accommodation to cultural congruence. *Clinical Psychology: Science and Practice, 18*, 242–245, doi: 10.1111/j.1468-2850.2011.01256.x

Lerner, B. H. (2011). Drunk driving, distracted driving, moralism, and public health. *New England Journal of Medicine.* Retrieved from http://healthpolicyandreform.nejm.org/?p=15251&query=home

Lester, K., Resick, P. A., Young-Xu, Y., & Artz, C. (2010). Impact of race on early treatment termination and outcomes in posttraumatic stress disorder treatment. *Journal of Consulting and Clinical Psychology, 78*, 480–489. doi.org/10.1037/a0019551

Leue, A., Borchard, B., & Hoyer, J. (2004). Mental disorders in a forensic sample of sexual offenders. *European Psychiatry, 19*, 123–130.

Leung, P. W. L., & Poon, M. W. L. (2001). Dysfunctional schemas and cognitive distortions in psychopathology: A test of the specificity hypothesis. *Journal of Child Psychology & Psychiatry & Allied Disciplines, 42*, 755–765.

LeVine, E. S. (2012). Facilitating recovery for people with serious mental illness employing a psychobiosocial model of care. *Professional Psychology: Research and Practice, 43*, 58–64. doi: 10.1037/a0026889

Levine, E. S., & Schmelkin, L. P. (2006). The move to prescribe: A change in paradigm? *Professional Psychology: Research and Practice, 37*, 205–209.

Levine, S. B. (2012). Problematic sexual excesses. *Neuropsychiatry, 2*(1), 69–79.

Levinson, D. F., Duan, J., Oh, S., Wang, K., Sanders, A. R., Shi, J., Zhang, N., . . . Gejman, P. V. (2011). Copy number variants in schizophrenia: confirmation of five previous findings and new evidence for 3q29 microdeletions and VIPR2 duplications. *American Journal of Psychiatry, 168*, 302–316. doi: 10.1176/appi.ajp.2010.10060876

Levy, D. (2012). Combating the epidemic of heart disease. *Journal of the American Medical Association, 308*, 2624–2625. doi:10.1001/jama.2012.164971.

Levy, K. N., & Scala, J. W. (2012). Transference, transference interpretations, and transference-focused psychotherapies. *Psychotherapy, 49*, 391–403.

Lewinsohn, P. M. (1974). A behavioral approach to depression. In R. J. Friedman & M. M. Katz (Eds.), *The psychology of depression: Contemporary theory and research.* Washington, DC: Winston-Wiley.

Lewis, R. W., Fugl-Meyer, K. S., Corona, G., Hayes, R. D., Laumann, E. O., Moreira, E. D., Jr., . . . Segraves, T. (2010). Definitions/epidemiology/risk factors for sexual dysfunction. *Journal of Sexual Medicine, 7*, 1598–1607.

Li, D., Morris, J. S., Liu, J., Hassan, M. M., Day, R. S., Bondy, M. L., & Abbruzzese, J. L. (2009). Body mass index and risk, age of onset, and survival in patients with pancreatic cancer. *Journal of the American Medical Association, 301*, 2553–2562.

Li, J., Zhou, G., Ji, W., Feng, G., Zhao, Q., Liu, J., . . . Shi, Y. (2011). Common variants in the BCL9 gene conferring risk of schizophrenia. *Archives of General Psychiatry, 68*, 232–240. doi:10.1001/archgenpsychiatry.2011.1

Lichta, R. W. (2010). A new BALANCE in bipolar I disorder. *The Lancet, 375*, 350–352. doi:10.1016/S0140-6736(09)61970-X

Lichtenstein, P., Carlström, E., Råstam, M., Gillberg, C., & Anckarsäter, H. (2010). The genetics of autism spectrum disorders and related neuropsychiatric disorders in childhood. *American Journal of Psychiatry, 167*, 1357–1363.

Lichtman, J. H., Bigger, J. T., Jr., Blumenthal, J. A., Frasure-Smith, N., Kaufmann, P. G., Lespérance, F., . . . Froelicher, E. S. (2008). Depression and coronary heart disease. Recommendations for screening, referral, and treatment. *Circulation, 118*, 1–8.

Lieberman, J. S. A. (2010). Psychiatric care shortage: What the future holds. *Medscape Psychiatry and Mental Health.* Retrieved from www.medscape.com

Liebowitz, M. R., Gelenberg, A. J., & Munjack, D. (2005). Venlafaxine extended release vs. placebo and paroxetine in social anxiety disorder. *Archives of General Psychiatry, 62*, 190–198.

Liebowitz, M. R., Stein, M. B., Tancer, M., Carpenter, D., Oakes, R., & Pitts, C. D. (2002). A randomized, double-blind, fixed-dose comparison of paroxetine and placebo in treatment of generalized social anxiety disorder. *Journal of Clinical Psychiatry, 63*, 66–74.

Lilienfeld, S. O., Fowler, K. A., & Lohr, J. M. (2003). And the band played on: Science, pseudoscience, and the Rorschach Inkblot Method. *The Clinical Psychologist, 56* (1), 6–7.

Lilienfeld, S., & Arkowitz, H. (2011, Jan/Feb). The insanity verdict on trial. *Scientific American Mind, 6*, 64–65.

Lim, J., & Dinges, D. F. (2010). A meta-analysis of the impact of short-term sleep deprivation on cognitive variables. *Psychological Bulletin, 136*, 375–389. doi: 10.1037/a0018883

Lim, S. (2003, September 2). *Beating the bed-wetting blues.* Retrieved from http://www.msnbc.com/news/954846.asp

Lin, P.-Y., Mischoulon, D., Freeman, M. P., Matsuoka, Y., Hibbeln, J., Belmaker, R. H., & Su,K.-P. (2012). Are omega-3 fatty acids antidepressants or just mood-improving agents? The effect depends upon diagnosis, supplement preparation, and severity of depression. *Molecular Psychiatry, 17*, 1161.

Lincoln, A. (1841/1953). To John T. Stuart. In R. P. Basler, M. D. Pratt, & L. A. Dunlap (Eds.), *The collected works of Abraham Lincoln* (Vol. 1, p. 230). New Brunswick, NJ: Rutgers University Press.

Lincoln, T. M., Ziegler, M., Mehl, S., Kesting, M.-L., Lüllmann, E., Westermann, S., . . . Rief, W. (2012). Moving from efficacy to effectiveness in cognitive behavioral therapy for psychosis: A randomized clinical practice trial. *Journal of Consulting and Clinical Psychology, 80*, 674–686. doi: 10.1037/a0028665

Linder, D. (2004). *The John Hinckley trial* [Hinckley's communications with Jodie Foster]. Retrieved from http://www.law.umkc.edu/faculty/projects/ftrials/hinckley/hinckleytrial.html

Ling, W., Casadonte, P., Bigelow, G., Kampman, K. M., Patkar, A., Bailey, G. L., . . . Beebe, K. L. (2011). Buprenorphine implants for treatment of opioid dependence: A randomized controlled trial. *Journal of the American Medical Association, 304*, 1576–1583.

Lipsman, N., Neimat, J. S., & Lozano, A. M. (2007). Deep brain stimulation for treatment-refractory obsessive-compulsive disorder: The search for a valid target. *Neurosurgery, 61*, 1–13.

Lipton, E., Savage, C., & Shane, S. (2011, January 9). Arizona suspect's recent acts offer hints of alienation. *The New York Times.* Retrieved from http://www.nytimes.com/2011/01/09/us/politics/09shooter.html?pagewanted=all

Liu, R. T., & Alloy, L B. (2010). Stress generation in depression: A systematic review of the empirical literature and recommendations for future study. *Clinical Psychology Review, 30*, 582–593.

Lo, C. S. L, Ho, S. M. Y., & Hollon, S. D. (2008). The effects of rumination and negative cognitive styles on depression: A mediation analysis. *Behaviour Research and Therapy, 46*, 487–495.

Loeber, R., Burke, J. D., Lahey, B. B., Winters, A., & Zera, M. (2000). Oppositional defiant and conduct disorder: A review of the past 10 years. *Journal of the American Academy of Child and Adolescent Psychiatry, 39*, 1468–1484.

Loening-Baucke, V. (2002). Encopresis. *Current Opinions in Pediatrics, 14*, 570–575.

Loftus, E. F. (1996). The myth of repressed memory and the realities of science. *Clinical Psychology: Science and Practice, 3*, 356–365.

Logan, J., Hall, J., & Karch, D. (2011). Suicide categories by patterns of known risk factors: A latent class analysis. *Archives of General Psychiatry, 68*, 935–941. doi:10.1001/archgenpsychiatry.2011.85

Lohr, J. M, Lilienfeld, S. O., & Rosen, G. M. (2012). Anxiety and its treatment: Promoting science–based practice. *Journal of Anxiety Disorders, 26*, 719–727. doi: 10.1016/j.janxdis.2012.06.007 in press

Lohr, J. M, Lilienfeld, S. O., & Rosen, G. M. (2012). Anxiety and its treatment: Promoting science–based practice. *Journal of Anxiety Disorders. 26*, 719–727. doi:10.1016/j.janxdis.2012.06.007. Epub 2012 Jul 13.

Lohr, J. M. (2011). What is (and what is not) the meaning of evidence-based psychosocial intervention? *Clinical Psychology: Science and Practice, 18*, 100–104. doi: 10.1111/j.1468-2850.2011.01240.x

Lonsdorf, T. B., Weike, A. I., Nikamo, P., Schalling, M., Hamm, A. O., & Öhman, A. (2009). Genetic gating of human fear learning and extinction: Possible implications for gene-environment interaction in anxiety disorder. *Psychological Science, 20*, 198–206. doi:10.1111/j.1467-9280.2009.02280.x

LoPiccolo, J. (2011). Most difficult to treat: Sexual desire disorders. *PsycCRITIQUES, 56*, in press.

Lorenzetti, V., Allen, N. B., Whittle, S., & Yücel, M. (2010). Amygdala volumes in a sample of current depressed and remitted depressed patients and healthy controls. *Journal of Affective Disorders, 120*, 112–119. doi:10.1016/j.jad.2009.04.021

Lothane, Z. (2006). Freud's legacy—is it still with us? *Psychoanalytic Psychology, 23*, 285–301.

Lovaas, O. I. (1987). Behavioral treatment and normal educational and intellectual functioning in young autistic children. *Journal of Consulting and Clinical Psychology, 55*, 3–9.

Lovaas, O. I., Koegel, R. L., & Schreibman, L. (1979). Stimulus overselectivity in autism: A review of the research. *Psychological Bulletin, 86*, 1236–1254.

Love, S., & Spillantini, M. G. (2011). Unpicking frontotemporal lobar degeneration. *Brain, 134*, 2453–2455. doi: 10.1093/brain/awr176

Low, C. A., Stanton, A. L., & Danoff-Burg, S. (2006). Expressive disclosure and benefit finding among breast cancer patients: Mechanisms for positive health effects. *Health Psychology, 25*, 181–189.

Lowe, S. R., Chan, C. S., & Rhodes, J. E. (2010). Pre-hurricane perceived social support protects against psychological distress: A longitudinal analysis of low-income mothers. *Journal of Consulting and Clinical Psychology, 78*, 551–560. doi: 10.1037/a0018317

Lu, H.-Y., & Hou, H.-Y. (2009). Testing a model of the predictors and consequences of body dissatisfaction. *Body Image, 6*, 19–23.

Lubell, S. (2004, February 19). On therapist's couch, a jolt of virtual reality. *The New York Times*, p. G5.

Lucas-Carrasco, R., & Salvador-Carulla, L. (2012). Life satisfaction in persons with intellectual disabilities. *Research in Developmental Disabilities, 33*, 1103–1109.

Luczak, S. E., Glatt, S. J., & Wall, T. J. (2006). Meta-analyses of ALDH2 and ADH1B with alcohol dependence in Asians. *Psychological Bulletin, 132*, 607–621.

Lue, T. F., Giuliano, F., Montorsi, F., Rosen, R. C., Andersson, K. E., Althof, S., . . . Wagner, G (2010). Summary of the recommendations on sexual dysfunctions in men. *Journal of Sexual Medicine, 7*, 6–23.

Luijendijk, H. J., van den Berg, J. F., Marieke, J. H. J., Dekker, M. D., van Tuijl, H. R., Otte, W., et al. (2008). Incidence and recurrence of late-life depression. Archives of General Psychiatry, 65, 1394–1401.

Luppa, M., Sikorski, C., Luck, T., Ehreke, L., Konnopka, A., Wiese, B., . . .Riedel-Heller, S. G. (2012). Age- and gender-specific prevalence of depression in latest-life – Systematic review and meta-analysis. *Journal of Affective Disorders, 136*, 212–221.

Lupski, J. R. (2007). Structural variation in the human genome. *New England Journal of Medicine, 356*, 1169–1171.

Lymburner, J. A., & Roech, R. (1999). The insanity defense: Five years of research (1993–1997). *International Journal of Law and Psychiatry, 22*, 213–240.

Lynch, F. L., Dickerson, J. F., Clarke, G., Vitiello, B., Porta, G., Wagner, K. D., . . . Brent, D. (2011). Incremental cost-effectiveness of combined therapy vs medication only for youth with selective serotonin reuptake inhibitor–resistant depression: Treatment of SSRI-l. *Archives of General Psychiatry, 68*, 253–262. doi:10.1001/archgenpsychiatry.2011.9

M

Macey, P. M., Kumar, R., Woo, M. A., Valladares, E. M., Yan-Go, F. L., & Harper, R. M. (2008). Brain structural changes in obstructive sleep apnea. *Sleep, 31*, 967.

MacKillop, J., McGeary, J. E., & Ray, L. A. (2010). Genetic influences on addiction: Alcoholism as an exemplar. In D. Ross, P. Collins, & D. Spurrett (Eds.), *What is addiction?* (pp. 53–98).Cambridge, MA: MIT Press.

MacLaren, V. V., Best, L. A., Dixon, M. J., & Harrigan, K. A. (2011). Problem gambling and the five factor model in university students. *Personality and Individual Differences, 50*, 335–338. doi:10.1016/j.paid.2010.10.011

MacLaren, V. V., Fugelsang, J. A., Harrigan, K. A., & Dixon, M. J. (2011). The personality of pathological gamblers: A meta-analysis. *Clinical Psychology Review, 31*, 1057–1067. doi:10.1016/j.cpr.2011.02.002

Madsen, H.Ø., Dam, H., & Hageman I. (2011). Seasonal affective disorder. *Ugeskr Laeger, 173*, 3013–3016.

Maggi, M. (2012). *Hormonal therapy for male sexual dysfunction.* Hoboken, NJ: Wiley.

Maher, B. (2007). Fragile X fixed in mice. *Nature News.* Retrieved from http://www.nature.com/news/2007/191207/full/news.2007.386.html

Maher, W. B., & Maher, B. A. (1985). Psychopathology. I. From ancient times to the eighteenth century. In G. A. Kimble & K. Schlesinger (Eds.), *Topics in the history of psychology* (Vol. 2, pp. 251–294). Hillsdale, NJ: Erlbaum.

Mahon, P. B., Payne, J. L., MacKinnon, D. F., Mondimore, F. M., Goes, F. S., Schweizer, B., . . . Potash, J. B. (2009). Genome-wide linkage and follow-up association study of postpartum mood symptoms. *American Journal of Psychiatry, 166*, 1229–1237. doi:10.1176/appi.ajp.2009 .09030417

Mahone, E., M., Crocetti, D., Ranta, M. E., Gaddis, A., Cataldo, M., Slifer, K. J., . . . Mostofsky, H. (2011). A preliminary neuroimaging study of preschool children with ADHD. *The Clinical Neuropsychologist, 25*, 1009–1028. doi: 10.1080/13854046.2011.580784

Maier, S. F., & Seligman, M. E. P. (1976). Learned helplessness: Theory and evidence. *Journal of Experimental Psychology (General), 105*, 3–46.

Maikovich-Fong, A. K., & Jaffee, S. R. (2010). Sex differences in childhood sexual abuse characteristics and victims' emotional and behavioral problems: findings from a national sample of youth. *Child Abuse and Neglect, 34*, 429–437.

Maina, G., Rosso, G., & Bogetto, F. (2009). Brief dynamic therapy combined with pharmacotherapy in the treatment of major depressive disorder: Long-term results. *Journal of Affective Disorders, 114*, 200–207. doi:10.1016/ j.jad.2008.07.010

Majority of US adolescents with severe mental disorders have never received treatment for their conditions, study finds. (2011, January 18). *ScienceDaily*. Retrieved from http://www. sciencedaily.com-/

Maldonado, J. R., Butler, L. D., & Spiegel, D. (1998). Treatments for dissociative disorders. In P. E. Nathan & J. M. Gorman (Eds.), *A guide to treatments that work* (pp. 423–446). New York: Oxford University Press.

Male eating disorders on rise, experts say. (2004, May 12). Retrieved from http://www.cnn.com/2004/HEALTH/diet. fitness/05/12/male.eating.disorder.ap/index.html

Malek-Ahmadi, M., Davis, K., Belden, C., Jacobson, S., & Sabbagh, M. N. (2012). Informant-reported cognitive symptoms that predict amnestic mild cognitive impairment. *BMC Geriatrics, 12*, 3.

Malhotra, D., McCarthy, S., Michaelson, J. J., Vacic, V., Burdick, K. E., Yoon, S., . . . Sebat, J. (2011). High frequencies of de novo CNVs in bipolar disorder and schizophrenia. *Neuron, 72*, 951. doi: 10.1016/j. neuron.2011.11.007

Malinauskas, B. M., Raedeke, T. D., Aeby, V. G., Smith, J. L., & Dallas, M. B. (2006). Dieting practices, weight perceptions, and body composition: A comparison of normal weight, overweight, and obese college females. *Nutrition Journal, 5*, 11.

Mammarella, N., Fairfield, B., De Leonardis, V., Carretti, B., Borella, E., Frisullo, E., & Di Domenico, A. (2012). Is there an affective working memory deficit in patients with chronic schizophrenia? *Schizophrenia Research, 138*, 99–101.

Manassis, K. (2013). Empirically supported psychosocial treatments. In C. A. Essau & T. H. Ollendick (Eds.), *The Wiley-Blackwell handbook of the treatment of childhood and adolescent anxiety* (pp. 207–228). Hoboken, NJ: John Wiley.

Manicavasgar, V., Parker, G., & Perich, T. (2011). Mindfulness-based cognitive therapy vs cognitive behaviour therapy as a treatment for non-melancholic depression. *Journal of Affective Disorders, 130*, 138–144. doi:10.1016/j. jad.2010.09.027

Manicavasgar, V., Parker, G., & Perich, T. (2011). Mindfulness-based cognitive therapy vs cognitive behaviour therapy as a treatment for non-melancholic depression. *Journal of Affective Disorders, 130*, 138–144. doi:10.1016/j. jad.2010.09

Manne, S., Winkel, G., Zaider, T., Rubin, S., Hernandez, E., & Bergman, C. (2010). Therapy processes and outcomes of psychological interventions for women diagnosed with gynecological cancers: A test of the generic process model of psychotherapy. *Journal of Consulting and Clinical Psychology, 78*, 236–248. doi: 10.1037/a0018223

Marcantonio, E. R. (2012). Postoperative delirium: A 76-year-old woman with delirium following surgery. *Journal of the American Medical Association, 308*, 73–81. doi:10.1001/ jama.2012.6857

March, J. S., & Vitiello, B. (2009). Clinical messages from the Treatment for Adolescents with Depression Study (TADS). *American Journal of Psychiatry, 166*, 1118–1123. doi:10.1176/ appi.ajp.2009.08101606

March, J., Silva, S., Petrycki, S., Curry, J., Wells, K., Fairbank, J. . . . Treatment for Adolescents with Depression Study (TADS) team. (2009). Fluoxetine, cognitive-behavioral therapy, and their combination for adolescents with depression: Treatment for Adolescents with Depression Study (TADS) randomized controlled trial. *Journal of the American Medical Association, 292*, 807–820.

Marin, J. M., Agusti, A., Villar, I., Forner, M., Nieto, D., Carrizo, S. J., . . . Jelic, S. (2012). Association between treated and untreated obstructive sleep apnea and risk of hypertension. *Journal of the American Medical Association, 307*, 2169–2176. doi:10.1001/jama.2012.

Marion, I. J. (2005, December). The neurobiology of cocaine addiction. *Science Practice Perspectives, National Institute on Drug Abuse, 3*(1), 25–31.

Markowitz, J. C., Kocsis, J. H., Christos, P., Bleiberg, K., & Carlin, A. (2008). Pilot study of interpersonal psychotherapy versus supportive psychotherapy for dysthymic patients with secondary alcohol abuse or dependence. *The Journal of Nervous and Mental Disease, 196*, 468–474.

Marlatt, G. A. (1978). Craving for alcohol, loss of control, and relapse: A cognitive-behavioral analysis. In P. E. Nathan, G. A. Marlatt, & T. Loberg (Eds.), *Alcoholism: New directions in behavioral research and treatment* (pp. 271–314). New York: Plenum Press.

Marlatt, G. A., & Gordon, J. R. (1985). *Relapse prevention: Maintenance strategies in the treatment of addictive behaviors*. New York: Guilford Press.

Marques, L., LeBlanc, N., Weingarden, H., Greenberg, J. L, Traeger, L. N., Keshaviah, A., & Wilhelm, S. (2011). Body dysmorphic symptoms: Phenomenology and ethnicity. *Body Image, 8*, 1673–1678.

Marshal, M. P. (2003). For better or for worse? The effects of alcohol use on marital functioning. *Clinical Psychology Review, 23*, 959–997.

Mart, E. G. (2003). Munchausen's syndrome by proxy reconsidered. *Child Maltreatment: Journal of the American Professional Society of the Abuse of Children, 8*, 72–73.

Martel, M. M., Nikolas, M., Jernigan, K., Friderici, K., Waldman, I., & Nigg, J. T. (2011). The Dopamine receptor D4 gene (DRD4) moderates family environmental effects on ADHD. *Journal Of Abnormal Child Psychology, 39*, 1–10. doi: 10.1007/s10802-010-9439-5

Martin, J. P. (1998, February 27). The insanity defense: A closer look. *The Washington Post*. Retrieved from http://www. washingtonpost.com/wp-srv/local/longterm/aron/qa227.htm

Martinez, D., Greene, K., Broft, A., Kumar, D., Liu, F., Narendran, R., . . . Kleber, H. D. (2009). Lower level of endogenous dopamine in patients with cocaine dependence: Findings from pet imaging of D2/D3 receptors following acute dopamine depletion export. *American Journal of Psychiatry, 166*, 1170–1177. doi:10.1176/appi. ajp.2009.08121801

Martins, J. G., Bentsen, H., & Puri, B. K. (2012). Eicosapentaenoic acid appears to be the key omega-3 fatty acid component associated with efficacy in major depressive disorder: A critique of Bloch and Hannestad and updated meta-analysis. *Molecular Psychiatry, 17*, 1144.

Martins, R. K., & McNeil, D. W. (2009). Review of motivational interviewing in promoting health behaviors. *Clinical Psychology Review, 29*, 283–293. doi:10.1016/j. cpr.2009.02.001

Marx, R. F., & Didziulis, V. (2009, March 1). A life, interrupted. *The New York Times*, pp. CY1, CY7.

Maser, J. D., Normal, S. B., Zisook, S., Everall, I. P., Stein, M. R., Schettler, P. J., et al. (2009). Psychiatry nosology is ready for a paradigm shift in *DSM-V*. *Clinical Psychology: Science and Practice, 16*, 24–40. doi:10.1111 /j.1468-2850.2009.01140

Masheb, R. M., Grilo, C. M., & Rolls, B. J. (2011). A randomized controlled trial for obesity and binge eating disorder: Low-energy-density dietary counseling and cognitive-behavioral therapy. *Behaviour Research and Therapy, 49*, 821–829. doi:10.1016/j.brat.2011.09.006

Masi, G., Mucci, M., & Millepiedi, S. (2001). Separation anxiety disorder in children and adolescents: Epidemiology, diagnosis, and management. *CNS Drugs, 15* (2), 93–104.

Mason, B. J., Crean, R., Goodell, V., Light, J. M., Quello, S., Shadan, F., . . . Rao, S. (2012). A proof-of-concept randomized controlled study of gabapentin: Effects on cannabis use, withdrawal and executive function deficits in cannabis-dependent adults. *Neuropsychopharmacology, 37*, 1689–1698. doi: 10.1038/npp.2012.37:1689.

Mason, B. J., et al. (2012). . A proof-of-concept randomized controlled study of gabapentin: Effects on cannabis use, withdrawal and executive function deficits in cannabis-dependent adults. *Neuropsychopharmacology*, in press, 37:1689.

Mast, R. C., & Smith, A. B. (2012). Elimination disorders: Enuresis and encopresis. In W. M. Klykyo, & J. K. (Eds.), *Clinical child psychiatry* (pp. 305–328). New York: Wiley Interscience.

Mata, J., Thompson, R. J., Jaeggi, S. M., Buschkuehl, M., Jonides, J., & Gotlib, I. H. (2012). Walk on the bright side: Physical activity and affect in major depressive disorder. *Journal of Abnormal Psychology, 121*, 297–308. doi:10.1037/ a0023533

Mata, J., Thompson, R. J., Jaeggi, S. M., Buschkuehl, M., Jonides, J., & Gotlib, I. H. (2012). Walk on the bright side: Physical activity and affect in major depressive disorder. *Journal of Abnormal Psychology, 121*, 297–308. doi: 10.1037/ a0023533

Mataix-Cols, D., Frost, R. O., Pertusa, A., Clark, L. A., Saxena, S., Leckman, J. F.,. . . Wilhelm, S. (2010). Hoarding disorder: a new diagnosis for DSM-V? *Depression and Anxiety, 27*, 556–572. doi:10.1002/da.20693

Matson, J. J., & Shoemaker, M. (2009). Intellectual disability and its relationship to autism spectrum disorders. *Research in Developmental Disabilities, 30*, 1107–1114. doi: 10.1016/j. ridd.2009.06.003

Mauri, L. (2012). Why we still need randomized trials to compare effectiveness. *New England Journal of Medicine, 366*, 1538–1540. [Editorial]

McAnulty, R. D. (Ed.). (2012). *Sex in college: The things they don't write home about* (pp. 263–288). Santa Barbara, CA: ABC-CLIO.

McCain, N. L., Gray, D. P., Elswick, R. K., Jr., Robins, J. W., Tuck, I., Walter, J. M., . . . Ketchum, J. M.(2008). A randomized clinical trial of alternative stress management interventions in persons with HIV infection. *Journal of Consulting and Clinical Psychology, 76*, 431–441.

McClellan, J., & King, M.-C. (2010). Genomic analysis of mental illness: A changing landscape. *Journal of the American Medical Association, 303*, 2523–2524.

McClintock, S. M., Husain, M. M., Wisniewski, S. R., Nierenberg, A. A., Stewart, J. W., Trivedi, M. H., . . . Rush, J. (2011). Residual symptoms in depressed outpatients who respond by 50% but do not remit to antidepressant medication. *Journal of Clinical Psychopharmacology, 31*, 180. doi:10.1097/JCP.0b013e31820ebd2c

McClure-Tone, E. B. (2009). Socioemotional functioning in bipolar disorder versus typical development: Behavioral and neural differences. *Clinical Psychology: Science and Practice, 16*, 98–113. doi:10.1111/j.1468-2850.2009.01150.x

McCord, C. E., Elliott, T. R., Wendel, M. L., Brossart, D. F., Cano, M. A., Gonzalez, G., . . . Burdine, J. (2011). Community capacity and teleconference counseling in rural Texas. *Professional Psychology: Research and Practice, 42*, 521–527. doi: 10.1037/a0025296

McCrea, M., Guskiewicz, K. M., Marshall, S. W., Barr, W., Randolph, C., Cantu, R. C. et al. (2003). Acute effects and recovery time following concussion in collegiate football players: The NCAA Concussion Study. *Journal of the American Medical Association, 290*, 2556–2563

McDermott, J. F. (2001). Emily Dickinson revisited: A study of periodicity in her work. *American Journal of Psychiatry, 158*, 686–690.

McDougle, C. J., Scahill, L., Aman, M. G., McCracken, J. T., Tierney, E., Davies, M., et al. (2005). Risperidone for the core symptom domains of autism. *American Journal of Psychiatry, 162*, 1142–1148.

McEvoy, L. K., Holland, D., Hagler, D. J., Fennema-Notestine, C., Brewer, J. B., & Dale, A. M. (2011). Mild Cognitive impairment: Baseline and longitudinal structural MR imaging measures improve predictive prognosis. *Radiology, 43*, 561–564. doi: 10.1148/radiol.11101975

McEvoy, P. M, Nathan, P., Rapee, R. M., & Campbell, B. N. C. (2012). Cognitive behavioural group therapy for social phobia: Evidence of transportability to community clinics. *Behaviour Research and Therapy, 50*, 258–265.

McEvoy, P. M. (2008). Effectiveness of cognitive behavioural group therapy for social phobia in a community clinic: A benchmarking study. *Behaviour Research and Therapy, 45*, 3030–3040.

McGillivray, J. A., & Kershaw, M. M. (2013). The impact of staff initiated referral and intervention protocols on symptoms of depression in people with mild intellectual disability. *Research in Developmental Disabilities, 34*,730–738.

McGowin, D. F. (1993). *Living in the Labyrinth: A personal journey through the maze of Alzheimer's.* New York: Dell.
McGrane, D., & Carr, A. (2002). Young women at risk for eating disorders: Perceived family dysfunction and parental psychological problems. *Journal of Contemporary Family Therapy, 24,* 385–395.
McGrath, R. E. (2010). Prescriptive authority for psychologists. *Annual Review of Clinical Psychology, 6,* 21–47. doi:10.1146/annurev-clinpsy-090209-151448
McIlroy, A. (2010, September 6). Scientists link genetic 'typos' to schizophrenia. *Globe and Mail.* http://www.theglobeandmail.com/life/health/scientists-link-genetic-typos-to-schizophrenia/article1687069/
McIntyre, R. S., Liauw, S., & Taylor, V. H. (2011). Aripiprazole in the treatment of anxiety, major depressive disorder, and bipolar depression/disorder. *Journal of Affective Disorders, 128,* S29–S36.
McKee, B. (2003, September 4). As suburbs grow, so do waistlines. *The New York Times,* pp. F1, F 13.
McKellar, J., Stewart, E., & Humphreys, K. (2003). Alcoholics Anonymous involvement and positive alcohol-related outcomes: Cause, consequence, or just a correlate? A prospective 2-year study of 2,319 alcohol-dependent men. *Journal of Consulting and Clinical Psychology, 71,* 302–308.
McKenzie, K. (2011). Providing services in the United Kingdom to people with an intellectual disability who present behaviour which challenges: A review of the literature. *Research in Developmental Disabilities, 32,* 395–403. doi:10.1016/j.ridd.2010.12.001
McLawsen, J. E., Scalora, M. J., & Darrow, C. (2012). Civilly committed sex offenders: A description and interstate comparison of populations. *Psychology, Public Policy, and Law, 18,* 453–476. doi: 10.1037/a0026116
McLean, C. P., & Anderson, E. R. (2009). Brave men and timid women? A review of the gender differences in fear and anxiety. *Clinical Psychology Review, 29,* 496–505. doi:10.1016/j.cpr.2009.05.003
McMillan, J. R. (2003). Dangerousness, mental disorder, and responsibility. *Journal of Medical Ethics, 29,* 232–235.
McMillan, W., Stice, E., & Rohde, P. (2011). High- and low-level dissonance-based eating disorder prevention programs with young women with body image concerns: An experimental trial. *Journal of Consulting and Clinical Psychology, 79,* 129–134. doi: 10.1037/a0022143
McNally, R. J., & Geraerts, E. (2009). A new solution to the recovered memory debate. *Perspectives on Psychological Science, 4,* 126–134. doi:10.1111/j.1745-6924.2009.01112.x
McNiel, D. E., Gregory, A. L., Lam, J. N., Binder, R. L., & Sullivan, G. R. (2003). Utility of decision support tools for assessing acute risk of violence. *Journal of Consulting and Clinical Psychology, 71,* 945–953.
McNiel, D. E., Lam, J. N., & Binder, R. L. (2000). Relevance of interrater agreement to violence risk assessment. *Journal of Consulting and Clinical Psychology, 68,* 1111–1115.
McNulty, J. K., & Fincham, F. D. (2012). Beyond positive psychology? Toward a contextual view of psychological processes and well-being. *American Psychologist, 67,* 101–110.
Mead, M. (1935). *Sex and temperament in three primitive societies.* New York: Dell.
Mechelli, A., Riecher-Rössler, A., Meisenzahl, E. M., Tognin, S., Wood, S. J., Borgwardt, S. J., . . . McGuire, P. (2011). Neuroanatomical abnormalities that predate the onset of psychosis: A multicenter study. *Archives of General Psychiatry, 68,* 489–495. doi:10.1001/archgenpsychiatry.2011.42
Medda, P., Perugi, G., Zanello, S., Ciuffa, M., & Cassano, G. B. (2009). Response to ECT in bipolar I, bipolar II and unipolar depression. *Journal of Affective Disorders, 118,* 55–59. doi:10.1111/j.1399-5618.2009.00702.x
Meeks, T. W., Vahia, I. V., Lavretsky, H., Kulkarni, G., & Jeste, D. V. (2011). A tune in "a minor" can "b major": A review of epidemiology, illness course, and public health implications of subthreshold depression in older adults. *Journal of Affective Disorders, 129,* 126.
Meeter, M., Murre, J. M. J., Janssen, S. M. J., Birkenhager, T., & van den Broek, W. W. (2011). Retrograde amnesia after electroconvulsive therapy: A temporary effect? *Journal of Affective Disorders, 132,* 216–222. doi:10.1016/j.jad.2011.02.026
Meeter, M., Murre, J. M. J., Janssen, S. M. J., Birkenhager, T., & van den Broek, W.W.(2011). Retrograde amnesia after electroconvulsive therapy: A temporary effect? *Journal of Affective Disorders, 132,* 216–222. doi:10.1016/j.jad.2011.02.026
Mefford, H. C., Batshaw, M. L., & Hoffman, E. P. (2012). Genomics, intellectual disability, and autism. *New England Journal of Medicine, 366,* 733–743.
Mehta, D., Gonik, M., Klengel, T., Rex-Haffner, M., Menke, A., Rubelt, J., ...Binder, E. B. (2011). Using polymorphisms in FKBP5 to define biologically distinct subtypes of posttraumatic stress disorder: Evidence from endocrine and gene expression studies. *Archives of General Psychiatry, 68,* 901.
Mehta, V., De, A., & Balachandran, C. (2009). Dhat syndrome: a reappraisal. *Indian Journal of Dermatology, 54,* 89–90.
Meier, M. H., Caspi, A., Ambler, A., Harrington, H., Houts, R., Keefe, S. J., . . . Moffitt, T. E.. (2012). Persistent cannabis users show neuropsychological decline from childhood to midlife. *Proceedings of the National Academy of Sciences, 109*(40), E2657–E2664..
Meier, M. H., Caspi,A., Ambler, A., Harrington, H., Houts, R., Keefe, R. S., E., . . . Moffitt, T. E. (2012). Persistent cannabis users show neuropsychological decline from childhood to midlife. *Proceedings of the National Academy of Sciences, 109,* E2657-E2664.
Meier, M. H., Slutske, W. S., Heath, A. C., & Martin, N. G. (2011). Sex differences in the genetic and environmental influences on childhood conduct disorder and adult antisocial behavior. *Journal of Abnormal Psychology, 120,* 377–388. doi: 10.1037/a0022303
Melas, P. A., Rogdaki, M., Osby, U., Schalling, M., Lavebratt, C., & Ekstrom, T. J. (2012). Epigenetic aberrations in leukocytes of patients with schizophrenia: aAssociation of global DNA methylation with antipsychotic drug treatment and disease onset. *The FASEB Journal, 6,* 2712–2718 . doi: 10.1096/fj.11-202069
Melville, J. D., & Naimark, D. (2002). Punishing the insane: The verdict of guilty but mentally ill. *Journal of the American Academy of Psychiatry and the Law, 30,* 553–555.
Mendez, J. L. (2005). Conceptualizing sociocultural factors within clinical and research contexts. *Clinical Psychology: Science and Practice, 12,* 434–437.
Menon, C. V., & Harter, S. L. (2012). Examining the impact of acculturative stress on body image disturbance among Hispanic college students. *Cultural Diversity and Ethnic Minority Psychology, 18,* 239–246. doi: 10.1037/a0028638
Mercer, K. B., Orcutt, H. K., Quinn, J. F., Fitzgerald, C. A., Conneely, K. N., Barfield, R. T. . . . Ressler, K. J. (2012). Acute and posttraumatic stress symptoms in a prospective gene x environment study of a university campus shooting. *Archives of General Psychiatry, 69*(1), 89–97. Retrieved from http://dx.doi.org/10.1001/archgenpsychiatry.2011.109
Mercer, K. B., Orcutt, H. K., Quinn, J. F., Fitzgerald, C. A., Conneely, K. N., Barfield, R. T., . . . Ressler, K. J. (2011). Acute and posttraumatic stress symptoms in a prospective gene x environment study of a university campus shooting. *Archives of General Psychiatry, 69,* 89–97. doi: 10.1001/archgenpsychiatry.2011.109
Merckelbach, H., Arntz, A., & de Jong, P. (1991). Conditioning experiences in spider phobics. *Behaviour Research and Therapy, 29,* 301–304.
Merckelbach, H., de Jong, P. J., Muris, P., & van den Hout, M. A. (1996). The etiology of specific phobias: A review. *Clinical Psychology Review, 16,* 337–361.
Merikangas, K. R., & Pato, M. (2009). Recent developments in the epidemiology of bipolar disorder in adults and children: Magnitude, correlates, and future directions. *Clinical Psychology: Science and Practice, 16,* 121–133. doi:10.1111/j.1468-2850.2009.01152.x
Merikangas, K. R., Akiskal, H. S., Angst, J., Greenberg, P. E., Hirschfeld, R. M. A. , Petukhova, M., &. Kessler, R. C. (2007). Lifetime and 12-month prevalence of bipolar spectrum disorder in the National Comorbidity Survey Replication *Archives of General Psychiatry,* 64, 543–552. doi:10.1001/archpsyc.64.5.543.
Merikangas, K. R., He, J.-P., Burstein, M., Swendsen, J., Avenevoli, S., Case, B.,. . . Olfson, M. (2011). Service utilization for lifetime mental disorders in U.S. adolescents: Results of the National Comorbidity Survey–Adolescent Supplement (NCS-A). *Journal of the American Academy of Child & Adolescent Psychiatry, 50,* 32–45. doi: 10.1016/j.jaac.2010.10.006
Merikangas, K. R., Jin, R., He, J.-P., Kessler, R. C., Lee, S., Sampson, N. A., . . . Zarkov, Z. (2011). Prevalence and correlates of bipolar spectrum disorder in the World Mental Health Survey Initiative. *Archives of General Psychiatry, 68,* 241–251. doi:10.1001/archgenpsychiatry.2011.
Merrick, E. L., & Reif, S. (2010). Services in an era of managed care. In B. L. Levin & . A. Becker (Eds.), *A public health perspective of women's mental health.* New York: Springer.
Merwin, R. M. (2011). Anorexia nervosa as a disorder of emotion regulation: theory, evidence, and treatment implications. *Clinical Psychology: Science and Practice, 18,* 208–214. doi: 10.1111/j.1468-2850.2011.01252.
Messer, S. B. (2001). Empirically supported treatments: What's a nonbehaviorist to do? In B. D. Slife & R. N. Williams (Eds.), *Critical issues in psychotherapy: Translating new ideas into practice* (pp. 3–19). Thousand Oaks, CA: Sage.
Mestel, R. (2012, December 9). *Changes to the psychiatrists' bible, DSM: Some reactions.* Retrieved from latimes.com
Meuret, A. E., Rosenfield, D., Wilhelm, F. H., Zhou, E., Conrad, A., Ritza, T., & Roth, W. T. (2011). Do unexpected panic attacks occur spontaneously? *Biological Psychiatry, 70,* 985–991. doi: 10.1016/j.biopsych.2011.05.027
Meyer, G. J. (2001). To the final special section in the special series on the utility of the Rorschach for clinical assessment. *Psychological Assessment, 13,* 419–422.
Meyer, G. J., Finn, S. E., Eyde, L. D., Kay, G. F., Moreland, K. L., Dies, R. R., et al. (2001). Psychological testing and psychological assessment: A review of evidence and issues. *American Psychologist, 56,* 128–165.
Meyer, I. H. (2003). Prejudice, social stress, and mental health in lesbian, gay, and bisexual populations: Conceptual issues and research evidence. *Psychological Bulletin, 129,* 674–697.
Meyers, L (2007, February). "A struggle for hope." *Monitor on Psychology, 38*(2), 30–31.
Meyler, A., Keller, T. A., Cherkassky, V. L., Gabrieli, J. D. E., & Just, M. A. (2008). Modifying the brain activation of poor readers during sentence comprehension with extended remedial instruction: A longitudinal study of neuroplasticity. *Neuropsychologia, 46,* 2580–2592.
Micco, J. A., Hirshfeld-Becker, D. R., Henin, A., & Ehrenreich-May, J. (2013). Content specificity of threat interpretation in anxious and non-clinical children. *Cognitive Therapy and Research, 37,* 78–88.
Michaelson, J. J., Shi, Y., Gujral, M., Zheng, H., Malhotra, D., Jin, X., Jian, M., . . . Sebat, J. (2012). Whole-genome sequencing in autism identifies hot spots for de novo germline mutation. *Cell,151,* 1431. doi:10.1016/j.cell.2012.11.019
Michal, M., Wiltink, J., Subic-Wrana, C., Zwerenz, R., Tuin, I., Lichy, M., . . . Beutel, M. E. (2009). Prevalence, correlates, and predictors of depersonalization experiences in the German general population. *The Journal of Nervous and Mental Disease, 197,* 499–506. doi:10.1097/NMD.0b013e3181aacd94
Michaud, J.-P., Hallé, M., Lampron, A., Thériault, P., Préfontaine, P., Filali, M., . . . Rivest, S. (2013). Toll-like receptor 4 stimulation with the detoxified ligand monophosphoryl lipid A improves Alzheimer's disease-related pathology. *PNAS,* in press. doi: 10.1073/pnas.1215165110
Miklowitz, D. J., & Johnson, S. L. (2009). Social and familial factors in the course of bipolar disorder: Basic processes and relevant interventions. *Clinical Psychology: Science and Practice, 16,* 281–296. doi:10.1111/j.1468-2850.2009.01166.x
Miklowitz, D. J., Otto, M. W., Frank, E., Reilly-Harrington, N. A., Wisniewski, S. R., Kogan, J. N., . . . Sachs, G. S. (2007). Psychosocial treatments for bipolar depression: A 1-year randomized trial from the systematic treatment enhancement program. *Archives of General Psychiatry, 64,* 419–426.
Milad, R. R., & Quirk, G. J. (2002). Neurons in medial prefrontal cortex signal memory for fear extinction. *Nature 420,* 70–74.
Miller, E. (1987). Hysteria: Its nature and explanation. *British Journal of Clinical Psychology, 26,* 163–173.
Miller, G. (2011). Predicting the psychological risks of war. *Science, 333,* 520–521. doi: 10.1126/science.333.6042.520
Miller, G. (2012). How to talk about Alzheimer's risk. *Science, 792.* Retrieved from http://www.sciencemag.org/content/337/6096/792.summary
Miller, J. D., Morse, J. Q., Nolf, K., Stepp, S. D., & Pilkonis, P. A. (2012). Can DSM-IV borderline personality disorder be diagnosed via dimensional personality traits? Implications for the DSM-5 personality disorder proposal. *Journal of Abnormal Psychology, 121,* 944–950. doi: 10.1037/a0027410
Miller, M., & Hemenway, D. (2008). Guns and suicide in the United States. *New England Journal of Medicine, 359,* 989–991.

Miller, M., Azrael, D., & Hemenway, D. (2004). The epidemiology of case fatality rates for suicide in the northeast. *Annals of Emergency Medicine, 43,* 723–730.

Miller, T. W., Nigg, J. T., & Miller, R. L (2009). Attention deficit hyperactivity disorder in African American children: What can be concluded from the past ten years? *Clinical Psychology Review, 29,* 77–86. doi: 10.1016/j.cpr.2008.10.001

Miller, W. R., & Hester, R. K. (1986). Inpatient alcoholism treatment: Who benefits? *American Psychologist, 41,* 794–805.

Miller, W. R., & Rollnick, S. (2002). *Motivational interviewing: Preparing people to change.* New York: Guilford Press.

Miller-Perrin, C. L., Perrin, R. D., & Kocur, K. L. (2009). Parental physical and psychological aggression: Psychological symptoms in young adults. *Child Abuse & Neglect, 33,* 1–11. doi: 10.1016/S0145-2134(97)00009-4

Millon, T. (1982). *Millon Clinical Multiaxial Inventory manual* (3rd ed.). Minneapolis: National Computer Systems.

Millon, T. (2011). *Disorders of personality: Introducing a DSM/ICD spectrum from normal to abnormal* (3rd ed.). Hoboken, NJ: Wiley.

Mills, J. F., Kroner, D. F., & Morgan, R. (2011). *Clinician's guide to violence risk assessment.* New York: Guilford Press.

Mills, K. L., Teesson, M., Back, S. E., Brady, K. T., Baker, A. L., Hopwood, S. . . . Ewer, P. L. (2012). Integrated exposure-based therapy for co-occurring posttraumatic stress disorder and substance dependence: A randomized controlled trial. *Journal of the American Medical Association, 308,* 690–699. doi:10.1001/jama.2012.9071

Mills, P. D., Watts, B. V., Huh, T. J. W., Boar, S., & Kemp, J. (2013). Helping elderly patients to avoid suicide: A review of case reports from a national veterans affairs database. *Journal of Nervous & Mental Disease, 201,* 12–16. doi: 10.1097/NMD.0b013e31827ab29c

Milrod, B., Leon, A. C., Busch, F., Rudden, M., Schwalberg, M., Clarkin, J., Aronson, A., . . . Shear, M. K. (2007). A randomized controlled clinical trial of psychoanalytic psychotherapy for panic disorder. *American Journal of Psychiatry, 164,* 265–272.

Minarik, M. L., & Ahrens, A. H. (1996). Relations of eating and symptoms of depression and anxiety to the dimensions of perfectionism among undergraduate women. *Cognitive Research & Therapy, 20,* 155–169.

Miner, M. M. (2011). Erectile dysfunction and cardiovascular disease: A harbinger for cardiovascular events. *Journal of Sexual Medicine,* Virtual Issue Number 2.

Minerd, J., & Jasmer, R. (2006, April). *Forty winks or more to make a healthier America.* Retrieved from http://www.medpagetoday.com/PrimaryCare/SleepDisorders/tb/3009

Ming, D. L., & Burmeister, M. (2009). New insights into the genetics of addiction. *Nature Reviews Genetics, 10,* 225–231. doi:10.1038/nrg2536

Minuchin, S., Rosman, B. L., & Baker, L. (1978). *Psychosomatic families: Anorexia nervosa in context.* Cambridge, MA: Harvard University Press.

Minzenberg, M., J., & Carter, C. S. (2012). Developing treatments for impaired cognition in schizophrenia. *Trends in Cognitivey Sciences, 16,* 35–42. doi:10.1016/j.tics.2011.11.017

Miranda, R., Reynolds, E., Ray, L., Justus, A., Knopik, V. S., McGeary, J., & Meyerson, L. A. (2012). Preliminary evidence for a gene-environment interaction in predicting alcohol use disorders in adolescents. *Alcoholism: Clinical and Experimental Research, 37,* 325–331. doi: 10.1111/j.1530-0277.2012.01897

Mischel, W., & Brooks, D. (2011). The news from psychological science: A conversation between David Brooks and Walter Mischel. *Perspectives on Psychological Science, 6,* 515–520, doi:10.1177/1745691611425013

Mitchell, C. M., Beals, J., & The Pathways of Choice Team. (2006). The development of alcohol use and outcome expectancies among American Indian young adults: A growth mixture model. *Addictive Behaviors, 31,* 1–14.

Mitchell, J. M., O'Neil, J. P., Janabi, M., Marks, S. M., Jagust, W. J., & Fields, H. L. (2012). Alcohol consumption induces endogenous opioid release in the human orbitofrontal cortex and nucleus accumbens. *Science Translational Medicine, 4,* 116ra6. doi: 10.1126/scitranslmed.3002902

Mitchell, S. L., Teno, J. M., Kiely, D. K., Shaffer, M. L., Jones, R. N., Prigerson, H. G., Hamel, M. B. (2009). The clinical course of advanced dementia. *New England Journal of Medicine, 361,* 1529–1531.

Mitka, M. (2011). Strategies sought for reducing cost, improving efficiency of clinical research. *Journal of the American Medical Association, 306,* 364–365. doi: 10.1001/jama.2011.1018

Mitka, M. (2012). Heart disease and stroke deaths fall, but some fear a reverse in the trend. *Journal of the American Medical Association, 307,* 550–552. doi: 10.1001/jama.2012.86

Mitte, K. (2005). Meta-analysis of cognitive-behavioral treatments for generalized anxiety disorder: A comparison with pharmacotherapy. *Psychological Bulletin, 131,* 785–795.

Mittelman, M. S., Roth, D. L., Coon, D. W., & Haley, W. E. (2004). Sustained benefit of supportive intervention for depressive symptoms in caregivers of patients with Alzheimer's disease. *American Journal of Psychiatry, 161,* 850–856.

MMWR. Prevalence of obesity among persons aged 20–79 years, by sex—Canada, 2007–2009, and United States, 2007–2008. (2011b). *Morbidity and Mortality Weekly Report, 60,* 1135.

Modestin, J. (1992). Multiple personality disorder in Switzerland. *American Journal of Psychiatry, 149,* 88–92.

Moerman, D. E. (2011). Meaningful placebos—controlling the uncontrollable. *New England Journal of Medicine, 365,* 171–172.

Moffitt, T. E., Caspi, A., & Rutter, M. (2006). Measured gene-environment interactions in psychopathology concepts, research strategies, and implications for research, intervention, and public understanding of genetics. *Perspectives on Psychological Science, 1,* 5–27.

Mohee, A., & Eardley, I. (2011). Medical therapy for premature ejaculation. *Therapeutic Advances in Urology, 3,* 211–222.

Mohlman, J. (2012). A community based survey of older adults' preferences for treatment of anxiety. *Psychology and Aging, 27,* 1182–1190. doi:10.1037/a0023126

Mokdad, A. H., Marks, J. S., Stroup, D. F., & Gerberding, J. L. (2004). Actual causes of death in the United States, 2000. *Journal of the American Medical Association, 291,* 1238, 1241.

Monk, C. S., Telzer, E. H., Mogg, K., Bradley, B. P., Mai, X., Louro, H. M. C., Chen, G., . . . Pine, D. S. (2008). Amygdala and ventrolateral prefrontal cortex activation to masked angry faces in children and adolescents with generalized anxiety disorder. *Archives of General Psychiatry, 65,* 568–576.

Monroe, S. M., & Reid, M. W. (2008). Gene-environment interactions in depression research: Genetic polymorphisms and life-stress polyprocedures. *Psychological Science, 19,* 947–956.

Monroe, S. M., & Reid, M. W. (2009). Life stress and major depression. *Current Directions in Psychological Science, 18,* 68–72. doi:10.1111/j.1467-8721.2009.01611.x

Monroe, S. M., Slavich, G. M., Torres, L. D., & Gotlib, I. H. (2007). Major life events and major chronic difficulties are differentially associated with history of major depressive episodes. *Journal of Abnormal Psychology, 116,* 116–124.

Montgomery, P., & Richardson, A. J. (2008). Omega-3 fatty acids for bipolar disorder. *Cochrane Database of Systematic Reviews, 2.* doi:10.1002/14651858.CD005169.pub2

Monti, P. M., Binkoff, J. A., Abrams, D. B., Zwick, W. R., Nirenberg, T. D., & Liepman, M. R. (1987). Reactivity of alcoholics and nonalcoholics to drinking cues. *Journal of Abnormal Psychology, 96,* 122–126.

Montorsi, F., Adaikan, G., Becher, E., Giuliano, F., Khoury, S., Lue, T. F., . . . Wasserman M. (2010). Summary of the recommendations on sexual dysfunctions in men. *Journal of Sexual Medicine, 7,* 572–588. doi: 10.1111/j.1743-6109.2010.02062.x.

Monuteaux, M. C., Mick, E., Faraone, S. V., & Biederman, J. (2010). The influence of sex on the course and psychiatric correlates of ADHD from childhood to adolescence: A longitudinal study. *Journal of Child Psychology and Psychiatry, 51,* 233–241. doi: 10.1111/j.1469-7610.2009.02152.x

Mooney, M., White, T., & Hatsukami, D. (2004). The blind spot in the nicotine replacement therapy literature: Assessment of the double-blind in clinical trials. *Addictive Behaviors, 29,* 673–684.

Moore, T. J., Furberg, C. D., Glenmullen, J., Maltsberger, J. T, & Singh, S. (2011). Suicidal behavior and depression in smoking cessation treatments. *PLoS ONE, 6,* e27016. doi: 10.1371/journal.pone.0027016and

Moos, R. H., & Moos, B. S. (2004). Long-term influence of duration and frequency of participation in Alcoholics Anonymous on individuals with alcohol use disorders. *Journal of Consulting and Clinical Psychology, 72,* 81–90.

Moos, R. H., & Moos, B. S. (2005). Paths of entry into Alcoholics Anonymous: Consequences for participation and remission. *Alcoholism: Clinical and Experimental Research, 29,* 1858–1868.

Mor, N., & Winquist, J. (2002). Self-focused attention and negative affect: A meta-analysis. *Psychological Bulletin, 128,* 638–662.

Mora, L. E., Nevid, J., & Chaplin, W. T. (2008). Psychologist treatment recommendations for Internet-based therapeutic interventions. *Computers in Human Behavior, 24,* 3052–3062.

Moran, M. (2013). DSM-5 updates: Depressive, anxiety, and OCD criteria. *Psychiatric News, 48*(4), 22–43. doi:10.1176/appi.pn.2013.2b39

Morbidity and Mortality Weekly Report. (2012a). Vital Signs: Binge drinking prevalence, frequency, and intensity among adults—United States, 2010. *Journal of the American Medical Association, 307,* 908–910.

More than 3,000 survivors of the World Trade Center attacks experience long-term post-traumatic stress disorder. (2011, January 7). *ScienceDaily.* Retrieved from http://www.sciencedaily.com-/

Morehouse, R., MacQueen, G., & Kennedy, S. H. (2011). Barriers to achieving treatment goals: A focus on sleep disturbance and sexual dysfunction. *Journal of Affective Disorders, 132* (Suppl. 1), S14–S20. doi:10.1016/j.jad.2011.03.047

Moreno, C., Laje, G., Blanco, C., Jiang, H., Schmidt, A. B., & Olfson, M. (2007). National trends in the outpatient diagnosis and treatment of bipolar disorder in youth. *Archives of General Psychiatry, 64,* 1032–1039.

Moretz, M. W., & McKay, D. (2009). The role of perfectionism in obsessive–compulsive symptoms: "Not just right" experiences and checking compulsions. *Journal of Anxiety Disorders, 23,* 640–644. doi:10.1016/j.janxdis.2009.01.015

Morey, R. A., Gold, A. L., LaBar, K. S., Beall, S. K., Brown, V. M., Haswell, C., C., . . . for the Mid-Atlantic MIRECC Workgroup. (2012). Amygdala volume changes in posttraumatic stress disorder in a large case-controlled veterans group. Archives of General Psychiatry, 69, 1169–1178 doi: 10.1001/archgenpsychiatry.2012.50

Morgenthaler, T. I., Kapur, V. K., Brown, T., Swick, T. J., Alessi, C., Aurora, N., et al. (2007). Practice parameters for the treatment of narcolepsy and other hypersomnias of central origin. *Sleep, 30,* 1705.

Morin, C. M., Vallières, A., Guay, B., Ivers, H., Savard, J., Mérette, C., et al. (2009). Cognitive behavioral therapy, singly and combined with medication, for persistent insomnia: A randomized controlled trial. *Journal of the American Medical Association, 301,* 2005–2015.

Moritz, S.,. Kerstan, A., Veckenstedt, R., Randjbar, S., Vitzthum, F., Schmidt, C., Heise, M., & Woodward, T. S. (2011). Further evidence for the effectiveness of a metacognitive group training in schizophrenia. *Behaviour Research and Therapy, 49,* 151–157. doi:10.1016/j.brat.2010.11.010 | How

Morley, T. E., & Moran, G. (2011). The origins of cognitive vulnerability in early childhood: Mechanisms linking early attachment to later depression. *Clinical Psychology Review, 31,* 1071–1082. doi:10.1016/j.cpr.2011.06.006

Morris M.E., Kathawala Q., Leen T.K., Gorenstein E.E., Guilak F., Labhard M., Deleeuw W. (2010). Mobile therapy: Case study evaluations of a cell phone application for emotional self-awareness. *Journal of Medical Internet Research, 12,* e10.

Morris, B. R. (2003, July 8). Two types of brain problems are found to cause dyslexia. *The New York Times,* p. F5.

Morris, G. H. (2002). Commentary: Punishing the unpunishable—the abuse of psychiatry to confine those we love to hate. *Journal of the American Academy of Psychiatry and the Law, 30,* 556–562.

Morris, J. K., Alberman, E., Scott, C., & Jacobs, P. (2008). Is the prevalence of Klinefelter syndrome increasing? *European Journal of Human Genetics, 16,* 163.

Morris, M. C., Ciesla, J. A., & Garber, J. (2008). A prospective study of the cognitive-stress model of depressive symptoms in adolescents. *Journal of Abnormal Psychology, 117,* 719–734.

Morrison, T., Waller, G., & Lawson, R. A. (2006). Attributional style in the eating disorders. *The Journal of Nervous and Mental Disease, 194,* 303–305.

Morrow, D. J. (1998, March 5). Stumble on the road to market. *The New York Times,* p. D1, D4.

Mossman, D. (1994). Assessing predictions of violence: Being accurate about accuracy. *Journal of Consulting and Clinical Psychology, 62,* 783–792.

Motzkin, J. C., Newman, J. P., Kiehl, K. A., & Koenigs, M. (2011). Reduced prefrontal connectivity in psychopathy.

Journal of Neuroscience, 31, 17348-17357. doi: 10.1523/JNEUROSCI.4215-11.2011
Moulds, M. L., & Nixon, R. D. (2006). In vivo flooding for anxiety disorders: Proposing its utility in the treatment of posttraumatic stress disorder. *Journal of Anxiety Disorder, 20*, 498–509.
Mowrer, O. H. (1960). *Learning theory and behavior.* New York: Wiley.
Muñoz, R. F., Beardslee, W. R., & Leykin, Y. (2012). Major depression can be prevented. *American Psychologist, 67*, 285–295. doi: 10.1037/a0027666
Muddashetty, R. S., Nalavadi, V. C., Gross, C., Yao, X., Xing, L., Laur, O., . . . Bassell, G. (2011). Reversible inhibition of PSD-95 mRNA translation by miR-125a, FMRP phosphorylation and mGluR signaling. *Molecular Cell, 42*, 673–688. doi: 10.1016/j.molcel.2011.05.00
Mueller, K., Jech, R., & Schroeter, M. L. (2013). Deep-brain stimulation for Parkinson's disease. *New England Journal of Medicine, 368*, 482–484. doi:10.1056/NEJMc1214078
Mukherjee, S. (2012, April 22). Post-Prozac nation. *The New York Times*, pp. 48–54.
Mulder, R. T., Frampton, C. M. A., Luty, S. E., & Joyce, P. R. (2009). Eighteen months of drug treatment for depression: Predicting relapse and recovery. *Journal of Affective Disorders, 114*, 263–270.
Mullins-Sweatt, S. N., Glover, N. G., Derefinko, K. J., Miller, J. D., & Widiger, T. A. (2010). The search for the successful psychopath. *Journal of Research in Personality, 44*, 554–558. doi:10.1016/j.jrp.2010.05.010
Munsch, S., Meyer, A. H., & Biedert, E. (2012). Efficacy and predictors of long-term treatment success for cognitive-behavioral treatment and behavioral weight-loss-treatment in overweight individuals with binge eating disorder. *Behaviour Research and Therapy, 50*, 775–785.
Muran, J. C., Eubanks-Carter, C., & Safran, J. D. (2010). A relational approach the treatment of personality dysfunction. In J. J. Magnavita (Ed.), *Evidence-based treatment of personality dysfunction: Principles, methods, and processes* (pp. 167–192). Washington, DC: American Psychological Association.
Muraven, M. (2005). Self-focused attention and the self-regulation of attention: Implications for personality and pathology. *Journal of Social and Clinical Psychology, 24*, 382–400.
Muris, P., & Field, A. (2013). Information processing biases. In C. A. Essau & T. H. Ollendick (Eds.), *The Wiley-Blackwell handbook of the treatment of childhood and adolescent anxiety* (pp. 141–156). Hoboken, NJ: John Wiley
Murphy, M. L. M., Slavich, G. M., Rohleder, N., & Miller, G. E. (2013). Targeted rejection triggers differential pro- and anti-inflammatory gene expression in adolescents as a function of social status. *Clinical Psychological Science, 1*, 30–40. doi: 10.1177/2167702612455743
Murphy, W. D., & Page, I. J. (2012). Exhibitionism: Psychopathology and theory. I. D. R. Laws & W. T. O'Donohue (Eds.). *Sexual deviance: Theory, assessment, and treatment* (pp. 61–75). New York: Guilford Press.
Murray, S. B., Rieger, E., Karlov, L. , & Touyz, S. W. (2013). Masculinity and femininity in the divergence of male body image concerns. *Journal of Eating Disorders, 1*, 11. doi: 10.1186/2050-2974-1-11
Must, A., Kõks, S., Vasar, E., Tasa, G., Lang, A., Maron, E., and Väli, M. (2009). Common variations in 4p locus are related to male completed suicide. *NeuroMolecular Medicine, 11*, 13–19. doi:10.1007/s12017-008-8056-8
Myers, N.L. (2011). Update: Schizophrenia across cultures. *Current Psychiatry Reports, 13*, 305–311.
Myers, T. A., & Crowther, J. H. (2009). Social comparison as a predictor of body dissatisfaction: A meta-analytic review. *Journal of Abnormal Psychology, 118*, 683–698.
Myrick, H., Anton, R. F., Li, X., Henderson, S., Randall, P. K., & Voronin, K. (2008). Effect of naltrexone and ondansetron on alcohol cue–induced activation of the ventral striatum in alcohol-dependent people. *Archives of General Psychiatry, 65*, 466–475.

N

Naggiar, S. (2012, September 24). *'Broken heart' syndrome can be triggered by stress, grief.* Retrieved from http://vitals.nbcnews.com/_news/2012/09/24/14072649-broken-heart-syndrome-can-be-triggered-by-stress-grief?lite
Naggiar, S. (2012, September 24). Broken heart syndrome, is not like a heart attack. Retrieved from http://vitals.nbcnews.com/_news/2012/09/24/14072649-broken-heart-syndrome-can-be-triggered-by-stress-grief?lite
Naglieri, J. A., Drasgow, F., Schmit, M., Handler, L., Prifitera, A., Margolis, A., Velasquez, R. (2004). Psychological testing on the Internet: New problems, old issues. *American Psychologist, 59*, 150–162.
Naj, A. C., Jun, G., Beecham, G. W., Wang, L. S., Vardarajan, B. N., Buros, J., Gallins, P. J., . . . Schellenberg, G. D. (2011). Common variants at MS4A4/MS4A6E, CD2AP, CD33 and EPHA1 are associated with late-onset Alzheimer's disease. *Nature Genetics, 43*, 436–441. doi: 10.1038/ng.801
Nakao, T., Radua, J., Rubia, K., & Mataix-Cols, D. (2011). Gray matter volume abnormalities in ADHD: Voxel-based meta-analysis exploring the effects of age and stimulant medication. *American Journal of Psychiatry, 16*8, 1154–1163. doi: 10.1176/appi.ajp.2011.11020281
Nanni, V., Uher, R., & Danese, A. (2012). Childhood maltreatment predicts unfavorable course of illness and treatment outcome in depression: a meta-analysis. *American Journal of Psychiatry, 169*, 141–151. doi: 10.1176/appi.ajp.2011.11020335
Naragon-Gainey, K. (2010). Meta-analysis of the relations of anxiety sensitivity to the depressive and anxiety disorders. *Psychological Bulletin, 136*, 128–150. doi: 10.1037/a0018055.
Narod, S. A. (2011). Alcohol and risk of breast cancer. *Journal of the American Medical Association, 306*, 1920–1921. doi: 10.1001/jama.2011.1589
National Center for Health Statistics. (2012a). *Health, United States, 2012: In brief.* Hyattsville, MD.
National Center for Health Statistics. (2012b). *Health, United States, 2011: With special feature on socioeconomic status and health.* Hyattsville, MD.
National Institute of Mental Health (NIMH). (2003b, December 23). *Suicide facts.* Retrieved from http://www.nimh.nih.gov/research/suifact.cfm
National Institute of Mental Health (NIMH). (2008). *Bipolar disorder in children and teens: A parent's guide.* U.S. Department of Health and Human Services. NIH Publication 08-3679. Bethesda, MD: Author.
National Institute of Mental Health (NIMH). (2008, October 22). *Social phobia patients have heightened reactions to negative comments.* Retrieved from http://www.nimh.nih.gov/science-news/2008/social-phobiapatients-have-heightened-reactions-to-negative-comments.shtml
National Institute of Mental Health (NIMH). (2009). *Schizophrenia.* Bethesda, MD: Author.
National Institute of Neurological Disorders and Stroke (NINDS). (2012, May 16*).NINDS Dementia With Lewy Bodies information page.* Retrieved from http://www.ninds.nih.gov/disorders/dementiawithlewybodies/dementiawithlewybodies.htm
National Institute on Deafness and Other Communication Disorders (NIDCD). (2010). *Stuttering.* Retrieved from http://www.nidcd.nih.gov/health/voice/pages/stutter.aspx
National Institutes of Health (NIH). (2002). Mimicking brain's "all clear" quells fear in rats. *NIH News Release.* Retrieved from http://www.nimh.nih.gov/science-news/2002/mimicking-brains-all-clear-quells-fear-in-rats.shtml
National Institutes of Health (NIH). (2003). *HIV/AIDS, severe mental illness and homelessness.* Retrieved from http://grants.nih.gov/grants/guide/pa-files/PA-04–024.html.
National Institutes of Health (NIH). (2011, June 9). *Stress-defeating effects of exercise traced to emotional brain circuit* (2011, June 9). Retrieved from http://www.nimh.nih.gov/science-news/2011/stress-defeating-effects-of-exercise-traced-to-emotional-brain-circuit.shtml?WT.mc_id=rss
National Strategy for Suicide Prevention. (2001, May). *National strategy for suicide prevention: Goals and objectives for action: Summary. A joint effort of SAMHS, CDC, NIH, and HRSA.* Washington, DC: Author.
Nauert, R. (2011a). Childhood exposure to trauma ups physical, mental health risks. *PsychCentral.* Retrieved from http://psychcentral.com/news/2011/06/09/childhood-exposure-to-trauma-ups-physical-mental-health-risks/26799.html
Nauert, R. (2011b, June 11). Numerous genetic factors tied to autism. *PsychCentral.* Retrieved from http://psychcentral.com/news/2011/06/09/numerous-genetic-factors-tied-to-autism/26801.html
Navarro, P., García-Estevea, L., Ascaso, C., Aguado, J., Gelabert, E., & Martín-Santos, R. (2008). Non-psychotic psychiatric disorders after childbirth: Prevalence and comorbidity in a community sample. *Journal of Affective Disorders, 109*, 171–176.
Neacsiu, A. D., Rizvi, S. L., & Linehan, M. M. (2010). Dialectical behavior therapy skills use as a mediator and outcome of treatment for borderline personality disorder. *Behaviour Research and Therapy, 48*, 832–839. doi:10.1016/j.brat.2010.05.017
Neale, B. M., Kou, Y., Liu, L., Ma'ayan, A., Samocha, K. E., Sabo, A., . . . Daly, M. J. (2012). Patterns and rates of exonic de novo mutations in autism spectrum disorders. *Nature, 485*, 242–245. doi: 10.1038/nature11011. press. doi: 10.1038/nature11011
Nearly one million children in U.S. potentially misdiagnosed with ADHD, study finds. (2010, August 17). *ScienceDaily.* Retrieved from www.sciencedaily.
Negy, C. & Woods, D. J. (1993). Mexican- and Anglo-American differences on the Psychological Screening Inventory. *Journal of Personality Assessment, 60*, 543–555.
Negy, C. (under review). Psychosocial adjustment of U.S. – deported Salvadorans transitioning to life in El Salvador.
Negy, C., & Snyder, D. K. (1997). Ethnicity and acculturation: Assessing Mexican American couples' relationships using the Marital Satisfaction Inventory—Revised. *Psychological Assessment, 9*, 414–421.
Negy, C., & Snyder, D. K. (2004). A research note on male chauvinism and Mexican Americans. *Psychology and Education, 41*, 22–27.
Negy, C., & Woods, D. J. (1992). A note on the relationship between acculturation and socioeconomic status. *Hispanic Journal of Behavioral Sciences, 14*, 248–251.
Negy, C., & Woods, D. J. (1992). Mexican Americans' performance on the Psychological Screening Inventory as a function of acculturation. *Journal of Clinical Psychology, 48*, 315–319.
Negy, C., & Woods, D. J. (1992). The importance of acculturation in understanding research with Hispanic-Americans. *Hispanic Journal of Behavioral Sciences, 14*, 224–247.
Negy, C., & Woods, D. J. (1992a). Mexican Americans' performance on the Psychological Screening Inventory as a function of acculturation. *Journal of Clinical Psychology, 48*, 315–319.
Negy, C., & Woods, D. J. (1992b). A note on the relationship between acculturation and socioeconomic status. *Hispanic Journal of Behavioral Sciences, 14*, 248–251.
Negy, C., & Woods, D. J. (1993). Mexican- and Anglo-American differences on the Psychological Screening Inventory. *Journal of Personality Assessment, 60*, 543–555.
Negy, C., Hammons, M. E., Reig-Ferrer, A., & Carper, T. M. (2010). The importance of addressing acculturative stress in marital therapy with Hispanic immigrant women. *International Journal of Clinical and Health Psychology, 10*, 5–21.
Negy, C., Schwartz, S., & Reig-Ferrer, A. (2009). Violated expectations and acculturative stress among U.S. Hispanic immigrants. *Cultural Diversity and Ethnic Minority Psychology, 15*, 255–264. doi:10.1037/a0015109
Negy, C., Snyder, D. K., & Diaz-Loving, R. (2004). A cross-national comparison of Mexican and Mexican American couples using the Marital Satisfaction Inventory-Revised (Spanish Version). *Assessment, 11*, 49–56.
Neighbors, C., Lee, C. M., Atkins, D. C., Lewis, M. A., Kaysen, D., Mittmann, A., . . . Larimer, M. A. (2012). A randomized controlled trial of event-specific prevention strategies for reducing problematic drinking associated with 21st birthday celebrations. *Journal of Consulting and Clinical Psychology, 80*, 850–862. doi: 10.1037/a0029480
Neighbors, H. W., Caldwell, C., Williams, D. R., Nesse, R., Taylor, R. J., Bullard, K. M., . . . Jackson, J. S.et al. (2007). Race, ethnicity, and the use of services for mental disorders: Results from the National Survey of American Life. *Archives of General Psychiatry, 64*, 485–494.
Nelson, J. C., Mankoski, R., Baker, R. A., Carlson, B. X., Eudicone, J., M. Pikalov, A., Berman, R. M. (2010). Effects of aripiprazole adjunctive to standard antidepressant treatment on the core symptoms of depression: A post-hoc, pooled analysis of two large, placebo-controlled studies. *Journal of Affective Disorders, 120*, 133–140. doi:10.1016/j.jad.2009.06.026
Nemeroff, C., Entsuah, R., Benattia, I., Demitrack, M., Sloan, D., & Thase, M. (2008). Comprehensive analysis

of remission (COMPARE) with venlafaxine versus SSRIs. *Biological Psychiatry, 63*, 424–434.

Nes, R. B., Czajkowski, N. O., Røysamb, E., Ørstavik, R. E., Tambs, K., & Reichborn-Kjennerud, T. (2012). Major depression and life satisfaction: A population-based twin study. *Journal of Affective Disorders, 144* (1–2), 51–58. doi:10.1016/j.jad.2012.05.060

Nestler, E. J. (2011, December 1). Epigenetics offers new clues to mental illness. (2011, December 1). *Scientific American*. Retrieved from http://www.scientificamerican.com/article.cfm?id=hidden-switches-in-the-mind

Nestoriuc, Y., & Martin, A. (2007). Efficacy of biofeedback for migraine: A meta-analysis. *Radiology Source, 128*, 111–127.

Nettle, D. (2001). *Strong imagination: Madness, creativity, and human nature*. New York: Oxford University Press.

Neugebauer, R. (1979). Medieval and early modern theories of mental illness. *Archives of General Psychiatry, 36*, 477–484.

Nevid, J. S., & Javier, R. A. (1997). Preliminary investigation of a culturally specific smoking cessation intervention for Hispanic smokers. *American Journal of Health Promotion, 11*, 198–207.

Nevid, J. S., & Rathus, S. A. (2013). *Psychology and the challenges of life: Adjustment and growth* (12th ed.). New York: Wiley.

Nevid, J. S., Javier, R. A., & Moulton, J. (1996). Factors predicting participant attrition in a community-based culturally specific smoking cessation program for Hispanic smokers. *Health Psychology, 15*, 226–229.

New therapies for prevention and treatment of Alzheimer's Disease identified. (2011, January 11). *ScienceDaily*. Retrieved from http://www.sciencedaily.com

Newcorn, J. H., Kratochvil, C. J., Allen, A. J., Casat, C. D., Ruff, D. D., Moore, R. J., Michelson, D., et al. (2008). Atomoxetine and osmotically released methylphenidate for the treatment of attention deficit hyperactivity disorder: Acute comparison and differential response. *American Journal of Psychiatry, 165*, 721–730. doi: 10.1176/appi.ajp.2007.05091676

Newman, D. (2011). Special issue on neuroscience: The autism enigma. *Nature, 479*, 21. doi:10.1038/479021a

Newman, M. G., & Llera, S. J. (2011). A novel theory of experiential avoidance in generalized anxiety disorder: A review and synthesis of research supporting a contrast avoidance model of worry. *Clinical Psychology Review, 31*, 371–382. doi:10.1016/j.cpr.2011.01.008

Newman, M. G., Castonguay, L. F., Borkovec, T. D., Fisher, A. J., Boswell, J. F., Szkodny, L. E., . . . Nordberg, S. S. (2011). Randomized controlled trial of cognitive-behavioral therapy for generalized anxiety disorder with integrated techniques from emotion-focused and interpersonal therapies. *Journal of Consulting and Clinical Psychology, 79*, 171–181. doi:10.1037/a0022489

Newman, M. G., Szkodny, L. E., Llera, S. J., & Przeworski, A. (2011b). A review of technology-assisted self-help and minimal contact therapies for drug and alcohol abuse and smoking addiction: Is human contact necessary for therapeutic efficacy? *Clinical Psychology Review, 31*, 178–186. doi:10.1016/j.cpr.2010.10.002

Newman, M. G., Szkodny, L. E., Llera, S. J., & Przeworski, A. (2011ba). A review of technology-assisted self-help and minimal contact therapies for anxiety and depression: Is human contact necessary for therapeutic efficacy? *Clinical Psychology Review, 31*, 89–103.

Nicolson, R. I., & Fawcett, A. J. (2008). *Dyslexia, learning, and the brain*. Cambridge, MA: MIT Press.

Nielsen, S. F., Hjorthøj, C. R., Erlangsen, A., & Nordentoft, M. (2011). Psychiatric disorders and mortality among people in homeless shelters in Denmark: A nationwide register-based cohort study. *The Lancet, 377*, 2205–2214. doi:10.1016/S0140-6736(11)60747-2.

Nierenberg, A. A., Friedman, E. S., Bowden, C. L., Sylvia, L. G., Thase, M. E., . . . Calabrese, J. R. (2013). Lithium Treatment Moderate-Dose Use Study (LiTMUS) for bipolar disorder: a randomized comparative effectiveness trial of optimized personalized treatment with and without lithium. *American Journal of Psychiatry, 170*, 102–110. 10.1176/appi.ajp.2012.12060751

Nisbett, R. E., Aronson, J., Blair, C., Dickens, W., Flynn, J., Halpern, D. E., & Turkheimer, E. (2012). Intelligence: New findings and theoretical developments. *American Psychologist, 67*, 130–159. doi: 10.1037/a0026699

Nitschke, J. B., Sarinopoulos, I., Oathes, D. J., Johnstone, T., Whalen, P. J., Davidson, R. J., & Kalin, N. H. (2009). Anticipatory activation in the amygdala and anterior cingulate in generalized anxiety disorder and prediction of treatment response. *American Journal of Psychiatry, 166*, 302–310. doi:10.1176/appi.ajp.2008.0710168

Nivoli, A. M. A., Colom, F., Murru, A., Pacchiarotti, I., Castro-Loli, P., González-Pinto, A., . . . Vieta, E. (2011). New treatment guidelines for acute bipolar depression: A systematic review. *Journal of Affective Disorders, 129*, 14–26. doi:10.1016/j.jad.2010.05.018

Noaghiul, S., & Hibbeln, J. R. (2003). Cross-national comparisons of seafood consumption and rates of bipolar disorders. *American Journal of Psychiatry, 160*, 2222–2227.

Nock, M. K., Kazdin, A. E., Hiripi, E., & Kessler, R. C. (2006). Prevalence, subtypes, and correlates of DSM-IV conduct disorder in the National Comorbidity Survey Replication. *Psychological Medicine, 36*, 699–710.

Nolen-Hoeksema, S. (2008). It is not what you have; it is what you do with it: Support for Addis's gendered responding framework. *Clinical Psychology: Science and Practice, 15*, 178–181.

Nolen-Hoeksema, S. (2012). Emotion regulation and psychopathology: The role of gender. *Annual Review of Clinical Psychology, 8*, 161–187. doi: 10.1146/annurev-clinpsy-032511-143109

Nolen-Hoeksema, S., Morrow, J., & Fredrickson, B. L. (1993). Response styles and the duration of episodes of depressed mood. *Journal of Abnormal Psychology, 102*, 20–28.

Nolen-Hoeksema, S., Wisco, B. E., & Lyubomirsky, S. (2008). Rethinking rumination. *Perspectives on Psychological Science, 3*, 400–424.

Norbury, C. R., & Sparks, A. (2013). Difference or disorder? Cultural issues in understanding neurodevelopmental disorders. *Developmental Psychology, 49*, 45–58. doi: 10.1037/a0027446

Norcross, J. C., & Beutler, L. (2011). Integrative psychotherapies. In R. J. Corsini & D. Wedding (Eds.) (9th ed.), *Current psychotherapies* (9th ed., (pp. 502–535). Belmont, CA: Brooks/Cole.

Norcross, J. C., & Karpiak, C. P. (2012). Clinical psychologists in the 2010s: 50 years of the APA Division of Clinical Psychology. *Clinical Psychology: Science and Practice, 19*, 1–12. doi:10.1111/j.1468-2850.2012.01269

Norcross, J.C., & Beutler,L. (2011). Integrative psychotherapies. In R. J. Corsini & D. Wedding (Eds.) (9th ed.), *Current psychotherapies*. Belmont, CA: Brooks/Cole.

Normandi, E. E., & Roark, L. (1998). *It's not about food: Change your mind; change your life; end your obsession with food and weight*. New York: Berkley.

Norris, F. N., Murphy, A. D., Baker, C. K., Perilla, J. L., Rodriguez, F. G., & Rodriguez, J. D. J. G. (2003). Epidemiology of trauma and posttraumatic stress disorder in Mexico. *Journal of Abnormal Psychology, 112*, 646–656.

North, C. S., Oliver, J., & Pandya, A. (2012). Examining a comprehensive model of disaster-related posttraumatic stress disorder in systematically studied survivors of 10 disasters. *American Journal of Public Health, 102*, e40.

Norton, E. (2012). Rewiring the autistic brain. *Science*. Retrieved from http://news.sciencemag.org/sciencenow/2012/09/rewiring-the-autistic-brain.html?ref=hp

Ntouros, E., Ntoumanis, A., Bozikas, V. P., Donias, S., Giouzepas, I., & Garyfalos, G. (2010). Koro-like symptoms in two Greek men. *BMJ Case Reports*. Retrieved from http://casereports.bmj.com/content/2010/bcr.08.2008.0679.abstract

Nurnberg, H. G., Hensley, P. L., Heiman, J. R., Croft, H. A., Debattista, C., & Paine, S. (2008). Sildenafil treatment of women with antidepressant-associated sexual dysfunction: A randomized controlled trial. *Journal of the American Medical Association, 300*, 395–404.

Nusslock, R., Harmon-Jones, E., Alloy, L. B., Urosevic, S., Goldstein, K., & Abramson, L. Y. (2012). Elevated left mid-frontal cortical activity prospectively predicts conversion to bipolar I disorder. *Journal of Abnormal Psychology, 121*, 592–601. doi: 10.1037/a0028973

O

O'Connor, A. (2011, December 15). Regular marijuana use by high school students hits new peak, report finds. *The New York Times*, p.A20.

O'Connor, M. J.,& Paley, B. (2006). The relationship of prenatal alcohol exposure and the postnatal environment to child depressive symptoms. *Journal of Pediatric Psychology, 31*, 50–64.

O'Connor, A. (2012). Sleep apnea is linked to a higher risk of cancer. *The New York Times*, pp. D5.

O'Roak, B. J., Vives, L., Girirajan, S., Karakoc, E., Krumm, N., Coe, B. P. . . . Eichler, E. E. (2012). Sporadic autism exomes reveal a highly interconnected protein network of de novo mutations. *Nature*, 246–250. doi: 10.1038/nature10989.

O. Hobart Mowrer (1960)

Odeh, M. S., Zeiss, R. A., & Huss, M. T. (2006). Cues they use: Clinicians' endorsement of risk cues in predictions of dangerousness. *Behavioral Sciences & the Law, 24*, 147–156.

Oestergaard, S., & Møldrup, C. (2011). Optimal duration of combined psychotherapy and pharmacotherapy for patients with moderate and severe depression: A meta-analysis. *Journal of Affective Disorders, 131*, 24–36. doi:10.1016/j.jad.2010.08.014

Ohayon M.M., & Schenck, C. H. (1997). Violent behaviour during sleep. *Journal of Clinical Psychiatry, 58*, 369–376.

Ohayon, M. M., Dauvilliers, Y., & Reynolds, C. F. (2012). Operational definitions and algorithms for excessive sleepiness in the general population: Implications for DSM-5 NOSOLOGY. *Archives of General Psychiatry, 69*, 71–79. doi:10.1001/archgenpsychiatry.2011.1240.

Ohayon, M. M., Mahowald, M. W., Dauvilliers, Y., Krystal, A. D., & Leger, D. (2012). Prevalence and comorbidity of nocturnal wandering in the US adult general population. *Neurology, 78*, 1583. doi: 10.1212/WNL.0b013e3182563

Okie, S. (2010). A flood of opioids, a rising tide of deaths. *New England Journal of Medicine, 363*, 1981–1985.

Okuda, M., Balán, I., Petry, N. M., Oquendo, M., & Blanco, C. (2009). Cognitive-behavioral therapy for pathological gambling: Cultural considerations. *American Journal of Psychiatry, 166*, 1325–1330.

Oldenbeuving, A. W., de Kort, P. L., Jansen, B. P., Algra, A., Kappelle, L. J., & Roks G. (2011). Delirium in the acute phase after stroke: Incidence, risk factors, and outcome. *Neurology, 76*, 993–999.

Olff, M., Langeland, W., Draijer, N., & Gersons, B. P. R. (2007). Gender differences in posttraumatic stress disorder. *Psychological Bulletin, 133*, 183–204.

Olfson, M., & Marcus, S. C. (2010). National trends in outpatient psychotherapy. *American Journal of Psychiatry, 167*, 1456–1463. doi: 10.1176/appi.ajp.2010.10040570

Olfson, M., Blanco, C., Liu, S.-M., Wang, S., & Correll, C. U. (2012). National trends in the office-based treatment of children, adolescents, and adults with antipsychotics. *Archives of General Psychiatry, 69*, 1247–1256. doi:10.1001/archgenpsychiatry.2012.647

Olfson, M., Gameroff, M. J., Marcus, S. C., Greenberg T., & Shaffer, D. (2005). Emergency treatment of young people following deliberate self-harm. *Archives of General Psychiatry, 62*, 1122–1128.

Olino, T. M., Seeley, J. R., & Lewinsohn, P. M. (2010). Conduct disorder and psychosocial outcomes at age 30: Early adult psychopathology as a potential mediator. *Journal of Abnormal Child Psychology, 38*, 1139–1149. doi: 10.1007/s10802-010-9427-9

Olivardia, R., Pope, H. G., Jr., Borowiecki, J. J., III, & Cohane, G. H. (2004). Biceps and body image: The relationship between muscularity and self-esteem, depression, and eating disorder symptoms. *Psychology of Men & Masculinity, 5*, 112–120.

Ollendick, T., Allen, B., Benoit, K., & Cowart, M. (2011). The tripartite model of fear in children with specific phobias: Assessing concordance and discordance using the behavioral approach test. *Behaviour Research and Therapy, 49*, 459–465. doi:10.1016/j.brat.2011.04.00

Olson, M. B., Krantz, D. S., Kelsey, S. F., Pepine, C. J., Sopko, G., Handberg, E., . . . Merz, C. N. B. (2006). Hostility scores are associated with increased risk of cardiovascular events in women undergoing coronary angiography: A report from the NHLBI-sponsored WISE Study. *Psychosomatic Medicine, 67*, 546–552.

Olson, S. D., Kambal, A., Pollock, K., Mitchell, G.-M., Stewart, H., Kalomoiris, S., Cary,W., . . . Nolta, J. A. (2011). Examination of mesenchymal stem cell-mediated RNAi transfer to Huntington's disease affected neuronal cells for reduction of huntingtin. *Molecular and Cellular Neuroscience, 49*, 271–281. n press. doi: 10.1016/j.mcn.2011.12.001

Olson, S. E. (1997). *Becoming one: A story of triumph over multiple personality disorder*. Pasadena, CA: Trilogy Books.

Oquendo, M. A., Hastings, R. S., Huang, Y., Simpson, N., Ogden, R. T., Hu, X.-Z.,. . . Parsey, R. V. (2007). Brain serotonin transporter binding in depressed patients with bipolar disorder using positron emission tomography. *Archives of General Psychiatry, 64*, 201–208.

Orchowski, L. M., Mastroleo, N. R., & Borsari, B. (2012). Correlates of alcohol-related sex among college students. *Psychology of Addictive Behaviors, 26*, 782-90. doi: 10.1037/a0027840.

Orešič, M., Hyötyläinen, T., Herukka, S.-K., Sysi-Aho, M., Mattila, I., Seppänan-Laakso, T., Julkunen, V., . . . Soininen, H. (2011). Metabolome in progression to Alzheimer's disease. *Translational Psychiatry, 1*, e57.

Oren, E., & Solomon, R. (2012). EMDR therapy: An overview of its development and mechanisms of action. *European Review of Applied Psychology. 62*, 197–203.

O'Roak, B. J., Vives, L., Girirajan, S., Karakoc, E., Krumm, N., Coe, B. Pâ€¦. Eichler, E. E. (2012). Sporadic autism exomes reveal a highly interconnected protein network of de novo mutations. *Nature*, 246–250. doi: 10.1038/nature10989.

Ortega, A. N., Rosenheck, R., Alegría, M., & Desai, R. A. (2000). Acculturation and the lifetime risk of psychiatric and substance use disorders among Hispanics. *Journal of Nervous & Mental Disease, 188*, 728–735.

Orth-Gomér, K., Wamala, S. P., Horsten, M., Schenck-Gustafsson, K., Schneiderman, N., & Mittleman, M. A. (2000). Marital stress worsens prognosis in women with coronary heart disease: The Stockholm Female Coronary Risk Study. *Journal of the American Medical Association, 284*, 3008–3014.

Osborn, I. (1998). *The hidden epidemic of obsessive-compulsive disorder.* New York: Random House.

Osborne, L. (2002). *American normal: The hidden world of Asperger syndrome.* Katlenburg-Lindau, Germany: Copernicus Books.

Ota, V., K., Gadelha, A., Assunção, I. B., Santoro, M. L., Christofolini, D. M., Bellucco, T. T. . .. Jackowski, A. P. (2013). ZDHHC8 gene may play a role in cortical volumes of patients with schizophrenia. *Schizophrenia Research, 145*, 33–35.

Öst, L. G. (2008). Efficacy of the third wave of behavioral therapies: A systematic review and meta-analysis. *Behaviour Research and Therapy, 46*, 296–321.

Otto, M. W. (2006, September 1). Three types of treatment for depression: A comparison. *Journal Watch Psychiatry*. Retrieved from http://psychiatry.jwatch.org/cgi/content/full/2006/901/2

Otto, M. W., & Deveney C. (2005). Cognitive-behavioral therapy and the treatment of panic disorder: Efficacy and strategies. *Journal of Clinical Psychiatry, 66*(Suppl. 4), 28–32.

Overmier, J. B. L., & Seligman, M. E. P. (1967). Effect of inescapable shock upon subsequent escape and avoidance learning. *Journal of Comparative and Physiological Psychology, 63*, 28–33.

Oyserman, D. (2008). Racial-ethnic self-schemas: Multidimensional identity-based motivation. *Journal of Research in Personality, 42*, 1186–1198.

Ozer, E. J., & Weiss, D. S. (2004). Who develops posttraumatic stress disorder? *Current Directions in Psychological Science, 13*, 169–172.

Ozer, E. J., Best, S. R., Lipsey, T. L., & Weiss, D. S. (2003). Predictors of posttraumatic stress disorder and symptoms in adults: A meta-analysis. *Psychological Bulletin, 129*, 52–73.

P

Pabian, Y. L., Welfel, E., & Beebe, R. S. (2009). Psychologists' knowledge of their states' laws pertaining to Tarasoff-type situations. *Professional Psychology, 40*, 8–14. doi:10.1037/a0014784

Pacemaker for brain may ease mental illness. (2008, November 12). Retrieved from http://www.msnbc.msn.com/id/27684083/

Palmer, C. A., & Hazelrigg, M. (2000). The guilty but mentally ill verdict: A review and conceptual analysis of intent and impact. *Journal of the American Academy of Psychiatry and the Law, 28*, 47–54.

Pampaloni, I., Sivakumaran, T., Hawley, C. J., Al Allaq, A., Farrow, J., Nelson, S., & Fineberg, N. A. (2009). High-dose selective serotonin reuptake inhibitors in OCD: A systematic retrospective case notes survey. *Journal of Psychopharmacology.* Retrieved from http://jop.sagepub.com/cgi/content/abstract/0269881109104850v1

Pan, D., Huey, S. J., Jr., & Hernandez, D. (2011). Culturally adapted versus standard exposure treatment for phobic Asian Americans: Treatment efficacy, moderators, and predictors. *Cultural Diversity and Ethnic Minority Psychology, 17*, 11–22. doi: 10.1037/a0022534

Panek, R. (2002, November 24). Hmm, what did you mean by all that, Dr. Freud? *The New York Times*, p. AR36.

Paracchini, S., Steer, C. D., Buckingham, L.-L., Morris, A. P., Ring, S., Scerri, T., et al. (2008). Association of the KIAA0319 dyslexia susceptibility gene with reading skills in the general population. *American Journal of Psychiatry, 165*, 1576–1584.

Paris, J. (2010). Estimating the prevalence of personality disorders in the community. *Journal of Personality Disorders, 24*, 405–411.

Paris, J. (2012). The outcome of borderline personality disorder: Good for most but not all patients. *American Journal of Psychiatry, 169*, 445–446. 10.1176/appi.ajp.2012.12010092

Parish, B.S., & Yutsy, S. H. (2011). Somatoform disorders. In R.E. Hales, S. C. Yudofksy, & G.O. Gabbard, *Essentials of psychiatry* (3rd ed., pp. 229–254). Arlington, VA: American Psychiatric Publishing.

Parker, G., Gibson, N. A., Brotchie, H., Heruc, G., Rees, A.-M., & Hadzi-Pavlovic, D. (2006). Omega-3 fatty acids and mood disorders. *American Journal of Psychiatry, 163*, 969–978.

Parloff, R. (2003, February 3). Is fat the next tobacco? *Fortune*, pp. 51–54.

Parmet, S, Lynm, C., & Golub, R. M. (2011). Obsessive-compulsive disorder. *Journal of the American Medical Association, 305*, 1926. doi:10.1001/jama.305.18.1926

Parsons, T. D., & Rizzo, A. A. (2008). Affective outcomes of virtual reality exposure therapy for anxiety and specific phobias: A meta-analysis. *Journal of Behavior Therapy and Experimental Psychiatry, 39*, 250–261.

Parto, J. A., Evans, M. K., & Zonderman, A. B. (2011). Symptoms of posttraumatic stress disorder among urban residents. *Journal of Nervous and Mental Disease, 199*, 436–439. doi: 10.1097/NMD.0b013e3182214154

Pasieczny, N., & Connor, J. (2011). The effectiveness of dialectical behaviour therapy in routine public mental health settings: An Australian controlled trial. *Behaviour Research and Therapy, 49*, 4–10. doi:10.1016/j.brat.2010.09.006

Patela, A., Knapp, M., Romeo, R., Reeder, C., Matthiasson, P., Everitt, B., . . Wykes, T. (2011). Cognitive remediation therapy in schizophrenia: Cost-effectiveness analysis. *Schizophrenia Research, 120*, 217–224.

Patrick, M. E., & Schulenberg, J. E. (2011). How trajectories of reasons for alcohol use relate to trajectories of binge drinking: National panel data spanning late adolescence to early adulthood. *Developmental Psychology, 47*, 311–317.

Paulesu, E., Demonet, J. F., Fazio, F., McCrory, E., Chanoine, V., Brunswick, N., et al. (2001). Dyslexia: Cultural diversity and biological unity. *Science, 291*, 2165–2167.

Payne, J. L. (2007). Antidepressant use in the postpartum period: Practical considerations. *American Journal of Psychiatry, 164*, 1329–1332. doi:10.1176/ appi.ajp.2007.07030390

Pelham, W. E., Burrows-MacLean, L., Gnagy, E. M., Fabiano, G. A., Coles, E. K., Tresco, K. E., et al. (2005). Transdermal methylphenidate, behavioral, and combined treatment for children with ADHD. *Experimental and Clinical Psychopharmacology, 13*, 111–126.

Pelkonen, M., & Marttunen, M. (2003). Child and adolescent suicide: Epidemiology, risk factors, and approaches to prevention. *Paediatric Drugs, 5*, 243–265.

Peng, H., Zheng, H., Li, L., Liu, J., Zhang, Y., Shan, B., Zhang, L., . . . Zhang, Z. (2012). High-frequency rTMS treatment increases white matter FA in the left middle frontal gyrus in young patients with treatment-resistant depression. *Journal of Affective Disorders, 136*, 249–257.

Peng, Y., Hong, S., Qi, X., Xiao, C., Zhong, H., Ma, R. Z., & Su, B. (2010). The ADH1B Arg47His polymorphism in East Asian populations and expansion of rice domestication in history. *BMC Evolutionary Biology, 10*, 15.

Peng, Y., Hong, S., Qi, X., Xiao, C., Zhong, H., Ma, R. Z., & Su, B. (2010). The ADH1B Arg47His polymorphism in East Asian populations and expansion of rice domestication in history. *BMC Evolutionary Biology, 10*, 15. doi: 10.1186/1471-2148-10-15

Pengilly, J. W., & Dowd, E. T. (2000). Hardiness and social support as moderators of stress. *Journal of Clinical Psychology, 56*, 813–820.

Pennington, B. F., McGrath, L. M., Rosenberg, J., Barnard, H., Smith, S. D., Willcutt, E., et al. (2009). Gene environment interactions in reading disability and attention-deficit/hyperactivity disorder. *Developmental Psychology, 45*, 77–89. doi: 10.1037/a0014549

Pennington, B. F., McGrath, L. M., Rosenberg, J., Barnard, H., Smith, S. D., Willcutt, E., et al.. . Olson, R. K. (2009). Gene environment interactions in reading disability and attention-deficit/hyperactivity disorder. *Developmental Psychology, 45*, 77–89. doi: 10.1037/a0014549

Penninx, B. W. J. H., Beekman, A. T. F., Honig, A., Deeg, D. J. H., Schoevers, R. A., van Eijk, J. T. M., & van Tilburg, W. (2000). Depression and cardiac mortality. *Archives of General Psychiatry, 58*, 221–227.

People with depression get stuck on bad thoughts, unable to turn their attention away, study suggests. (2011, June 3). *ScienceDaily*. Retrieved from http://www.sciencedaily.com/releases/2011/06/110602162828.htm

Peppard, P. E., Szklo-Coxe, M., Hla, K. M., & Young, T. (2006). Longitudinal association of sleep-related breathing disorder and depression. *Archives of Internal Medicine, 166*, 1709–1715.

Pereda, N., Guilera, G., Forns, M., & Gómez-Benito, J. (2009). The prevalence of child sexual abuse in community and student samples: A meta-analysis. *Clinical Psychology Review, 29*, 328–338. doi: 10.1016/j.cpr.2009.02.007

Perle, J. G., Langsam, L. C., & Nierenberg, B. (2011). Controversy clarified: An updated review of clinical psychology and tele-health. *Clinical Psychology Review, 31*, 1247–1258. doi:10.1016/j.cpr.2011.08.003

Perlin, M. L. (2002-2003). Things have changed: looking at non-institutional mental disability law through the sanism filter. *New York Law School Review, 535*,539 .

Perlis, R. H., Ostacher, M., Fava, M., Nierenberg, A. A., Sachs, G. S., & Rosenbaum, J. F. (2010). Assuring that double-blind is blind. *American Journal of Psychiatry, 167*, 250–252. doi:10.1176/ appi.ajp.2009.09060820.

Peterson, A. V., Jr., Leroux, B. G., Bricker, J., Kealey, K. A., Marek, P. M., Sarason, I. G., & Andersen, M. R. (2006). Nine-year prediction of adolescent smoking by number of smoking parents. *Addictive Behaviors, 31*, 788–801.

Peterson, E., & Yancy, C. W. (2009). Eliminating racial and ethnic disparities in cardiac care. *New England Journal of Medicine, 360*, 1172–1174. doi:10.1056/NEJMp0810121

Peterson, Z. D., Voller, E. K., Polusny, M. A., & Murdoch, M. (2010). Prevalence and consequences of adult sexual assault of men: Review of empirical findings and state of the literature. *Clinical Psychology Review*, *31*, 1–24. doi:10.1016/j.cpr.2010.08.

Petry, N. M., & Martin, B. (2002). Low-cost contingency management for treating cocaine- and opioid-abusing methadone patients. *Journal of Consulting and Clinical Psychology, 70*, 398–405.

Petry, N. M., Alessi, S. M., Marx, J., Austin, M., & Tardif, M. (2005). Vouchers versus prizes: Contingency management treatment of substance abusers in community settings. *Journal of Consulting and Clinical Psychology, 73*, 1005–1014.

Petry, N. M., Ammerman, Y., Bohl, J., Doersch, A., Gay, H., Kadden, R., . . . Steinberg, K. (2006). Cognitive-behavioral therapy for pathological gamblers. *Journal of Consulting and Clinical Psychology, 74*, 555–567.

Petry, N. M., Weinstock, J., Ledgerwood, D. M., & Morasco, B. (2008). A randomized trial of brief interventions for problem and pathological gamblers. *Journal of Consulting and Clinical Psychology, 76*, 318–328.

Pettinati, H. M., O'Brien, C. P., & Dundon, W. D. (2013). Current status of co-occurring mood and substance use disorders: A new therapeutic target. *American Journal of Psychiatry, 170*, 23–30. 10.1176/appi.ajp.2012:12010112

Phillips, J., & Sharpe, S. M., Matthey, S., & Charles, M. (2010). Subtypes of postnatal depression? A comparison of women with recurrent and de novo postnatal depression. *Journal of Affective Disorders, 120*, 67–75. doi:10.1016/j.jad.2009.04.011

Phillips, K. A., & Menard, W. (2006). Suicidality in body dysmorphic disorder: A prospective study. *American Journal of Psychiatry, 163*, 1280–1282.

Phillips, K. A., Albertini, R. S., & Rasmussen, S. A. (2002). A randomized placebo-controlled trial of fluoxetine in body dysmorphic disorder. *Archives of General Psychiatry, 59*, 381–388.

Phillips, K. A., Pagano, M. E., Menard, W., & Stout, R. L. (2006). A 12-month follow-up study of the course of body dysmorphic disorder. *American Journal of Psychiatry, 163*, 907–912.

Phillips, K.A., & Rogers, J. (2011). Cognitive-behavioral therapy for youth with body dysmorphic disorder: Current status and future directions. *Child and Adolescent Psychiatric Clinics of North America, 20*, 287–304.

Piasecki, T. M., Jorenby, D. E., Smith, S. S., Fiore, M. C., & Baker, T. B. (2003). Smoking withdrawal dynamics: I. Abstinence distress in lapsers and abstainers. *Journal of Consulting and Clinical Psychology, 112*, 3–13.

Piet, J., Würtzen, H., & Zachariae, R. (2012). The effect of mindfulness-based therapy on symptoms of anxiety and depression in adult cancer patients and survivors: A systematic review and meta-analysis. *Journal of Consulting and Clinical Psychology, 80,* 1007–1020. doi: 10.1037/a0028329

Pinacho, R., Villalmanzo, N., Lalonde, J., Haro, J. M., Meana, J. J., Gill, G., . . . Ramos, B. (2011). The transcription factor SP4 is reduced in postmortem cerebellum of bipolar disorder subjects: control by depolarization and lithium. *Bipolar Disorders, 13,* 474. doi:10.1111/j.1399-5618.2011.00941.x

Pingault, J. B., Tremblay, R. E., Vitaro, F., Carbonneau, R., Genolini, C., Falissard, B., . . Côté, S. M. (2011). Childhood trajectories of inattention and hyperactivity and prediction of educational attainment in early adulthood: A 16-year longitudinal population-based study. *American Journal of Psychiatry, 168,* 1164–1170.

Pirelli, G., Gottdiener, W. H., & Zapf, P. (2011). A meta-analytic review of competency to stand trial research. *Psychology, Public Policy, & Law, 17,* 1–53. doi: 10.1037/a0021713.

Pistorello, J., Fruzzetti, A. E., & MacLane, C., Gallop, R., & Iverson, K. M. (2012). Dialectical behavior therapy (DBT) applied to college students: A randomized clinical trial. *Journal of Consulting and Clinical Psychology, 80,* 982–994. doi:10.1037/

Pitman, R. K. (2006). Combat effects on mental health: The more things change, the more they remain the same. *Archives of General Psychiatry, 63,* 127–128.

Plunkett, A., O'Toole, B., Swanston, H., Oates, R. K., Shrimpton, S., & Parkinson, P. (2001). Suicide risk following child sexual abuse. *Ambulatory Pediatrics, 5,* 262–266.

PMDD proposed as new category in DSM-5 (2012, May 25). *PsychiatricNews Alert.* Retrieved from http://alert.psychiatricnews.org/2012/05/pmdd-proposed-as-new-category-in-dsm-5.html

Pogue-Geile, M. F., & Yokley, J. L. (2010). Current research on the genetic contributors to schizophrenia. *Current Directions in Psychological Science, 19,* 214–219. doi: 10.1177/0963721410378490).

Polanczyk, G., Caspi, A., Williams, B., Price, T. S., Danese, A., Sugden, K., Uher, R., Moffitt, T. E. (2009). Protective effect of CRHR1 gene variants on the development of adult depression following childhood maltreatment: Replication and extension. *Archives of General Psychiatry, 66,* 978–985. doi: 10.1001/archgenpsychiatry.2009.114

Pole, N., Best, S. R., Metzler, T., & Marmar, C. R. (2005). Why are Hispanics at greater risk for PTSD? *Cultural Diversity and Ethnic Minority Psychology, 11,* 144–161.

Poling, J., Oliveto, A., Petry, N., Sofuoglu, M., Gonsai, K., Gonzalez, G., . . . Kosten, T. R. (2006). Six-month trial of bupropion with contingency management for cocaine dependence in a methadone-maintained population. *Archives of General Psychiatry, 63,* 219–228.

Pollack, A. (2004a, January 13). Sleep experts debate root of insomnia: Body, mind or a little of each. *The New York Times,* p. F8.

Pollack, A. (2004b, January 13). Putting a price on a good night's sleep. *The New York Times,* pp. F1, F8.

Pollan, M. (2003, October 12). The (agri)cultural contradictions of obesity. *The New York Times Magazine,* pp. 41, 48.

Polusny, M. A., Kehle, S. M., Nelson, N. W., Erbes, C. R., Arbisi, P. A., & Thuras, P. (2011). Longitudinal effects of mild traumatic brain injury and posttraumatic stress disorder comorbidity on postdeployment outcomes in national guard soldiers deployed to Iraq. *Archives of General Psychiatry, 68,* 79–89. doi:10.1001/archgenpsychiatry.2010.172

Ponseti, J., Granert, O., Jansen, O., Wolff, S., Beier, K., Neutze, J., . . . Bosinski, H. (2012). Assessment of pedophilia using hemodynamic brain response to sexual stimuli. *Archives of General Psychiatry, 69,* 187–194. doi:10.1001/archgenpsychiatry.2011.130

Postuma, R. B., Lang, A. E., Gagnon, J. F., Pelletier, A., & Montplaisir, J. Y. (2012). How does parkinsonism start? Prodromal parkinsonism motor changes in idiopathic REM sleep behaviour disorder. *Brain, 135,* 1860–1870.

Potkin, S. G., Guffanti, G., Lakatos, A., Turner, J. A., Kruggel, F., Fallon, J. H., . . . Alzheimer's Disease Neuroimaging Initiative. (2009, August 7). Hippocampal atrophy as a quantitative trait in a genome-wide association study identifying novel susceptibility genes for Alzheimer's Disease. *PLos One.* Retrieved from http://www.plosone.org/article/info:doi/10.1371/journal.pone.0006501;jsessionid=8C9F392B696757818A7FF8EC8D7016EE

Pottier, C., Hannequin, D., Coutant, S., Rovelet-Lecrux, A., Wallon, D., Rousseau, S., . . . Campion, D. (2012). High frequency of potentially pathogenic SORL1 mutations in autosomal dominant early-onset Alzheimer disease. *Molecular Psychiatry, 17,* 875–879. doi: 10.1038/mp.2012.15

Powers, M. P., Halpern, J. M, Ferenschak, M. P., Gillihan, S. J., & Foa, E. B. (2010). A meta-analytic review of prolonged exposure for posttraumatic stress disorder. *Clinical Psychology Review, 30,* 635–641, doi:10.1016/j.cpr.2010.04.007

Powers, M., & Emmelkamp, P. M. G. (2008). Virtual reality exposure therapy for anxiety disorders: A meta-analysis. *Journal of Anxiety Disorders, 22,* 561–569.

Pratt, L. A., & Brody, D. J. (2008, September). Depression in the United States household population, 2005–2006. *NCHS Data Brief, Number 7.* Retrieved from http://www.cdc.gov/nchs/data/databriefs/db07.htm

Pressman, S. D., & Cohen, S. (2005). Does positive affect influence health? *Psychological Bulletin, 131,* 925–971.

Price, M. (2009, December). More than shelter. *Monitor on Psychology, 40*(11), 59–62.

Prochaska, J. O., & Norcross, J. C. (2010). *Systems of psychotherapy* (7th ed.). Belmont, CA: Brooks/Cole.

Prout, H. T., & Browning, B. K. (2011). Psychotherapy with persons with intellectual disabilities: a review of effectiveness research. *Advances in Mental Health and Intellectual Disabilities, 5,* 53–59. doi: 59.910.1108/20441281111180673

Psychiatric GWAS Consortium Bipolar Disorder Working Group. (2011). Large-scale genome-wide association analysis of bipolar disorder identifies a new susceptibility locus near ODZ4. *Nature Genetics, 43,* 977–983. doi: 10.1038/ng.943

Pulkki-Raback, L., Kivimaki, M., Ahola, K., Joutsenniemi, K., Elovainio, M., Rossi, H., . . . Virtanen, M. (2012). Living alone and antidepressant medication use: A prospective study in a working-age population. *BMC Public Health, 12,* 236. doi:10.1186/1471-2458-12-236

Pumariega, A. J. (1986). Acculturation and eating attitudes in adolescent girls. *Journal of the American Academy of Child Psychiatry, 25,* 276–279.

Purkis, H. M., Lester, K. J., & Field, A. P. (2011). But what about the Empress of Racnoss? The allocation of attention to spiders and doctor who in a visual search task is predicted by fear and expertise. *Emotion, 11,* 1484–1488.

Pyszczynski, T., & Greenberg, J. (1987). Self-regulatory preservation and the depressive self-focusing style: A self-awareness theory of reactive depression. *Psychological Bulletin, 102,* 122–138.

Q

Quan, M., Lee, S.-H., Kubicki, M., Kikinis, Z., Rathi, Y., Seidman, L. J., Mesholam-Gately, R. I., ... Levitt,J. J. (2013). White matter tract abnormalities between rostral middle frontal gyrus, inferior frontal gyrus and striatum in first-episode schizophrenia. *Schizophrenia Research, 145,* 1–10.

Queen's man arraigned in therapist's slaying. (2008, February 17). MSNBC.com. =Retrieved from http://www.msnbc.msn.com/id/23199458/ns/us_news-crime_and_courts/t/queens-man-arraigned-therapists-killing/#.UPctQyeoOpU

Quello, S. B., Brady, K. T., & Sonne, S. C. (2005). Mood disorders and substance abuse disorders: A complex comorbidity. *Science & Practice Perspectives, 3,* 13–24.

Quenqua, D. (2012, May 22). Drugs help tailor alcoholism. treatment. *The New York Times,* pp. D1, D 6.

Querfurth, H. W., & LaFerla, F. M. (2010). Alzheimer's Disease. *New England Journal of Medicine, 362,* 329–344.

Quinn, S. (1987). *A mind of her own: The life of Karen Horney.* New York: Summit Books.

R

Rabasca, L. (2000, March). Listening instead of preaching. *Monitor on Psychology, 31* (3), pp. 50–51.

Rabin, R. C. (2009, June 16). Alcohol's good for you? Some scientists doubt it. *The New York Times,* pp. D1, D6.

Rabin, R. C. (2011, December 15). Nearly 1 in 5 women in U.S. survey say they have been sexually assaulted. *The New York Times,* p. A32.

Rabinowitz, J., Levine, S. Z., Garibaldi, G., Bugarski-Kirola, D., Berardo, C. G., & Kapur, S. (2012). Negative symptoms have greater impact on functioning than positive symptoms in schizophrenia: Analysis of CATIE data. *Schizophrenia Research, 137,* 147–150.

Rachman, S., & DeSilva, P. (2009). *Obsessive-compulsive disorder* (4th ed.). Oxford, UK: Oxford University Press.

Rachman, S. (2000). Joseph Wolpe (1915–1997). *American Psychologist, 55,* 431.

Rachman, S. (2009). Psychological treatment of anxiety: The evolution of behavior therapy and cognitive behavior

therapy. *Annual Review of Clinical Psychology, 5,* 97–119. doi:10.1146/annurev.clinpsy.032408.153635

Racine, S. E., Burt, S. A., Iacono, W. G., McGue, M., & Klump, K. L. (2011). Dietary restraint moderates genetic risk for binge eating. *Journal of Abnormal Psychology, 120,* 119–128. doi: 10.1037/a0020895

Radel, M., Vallejo, R. L., Iwata, N., Aragon, R., Long, J. C., Virkkunen, M., & Goldman, D. (2005). Haplotype based localization of an alcohol dependence gene to the 5q34{gamma} aminobutyric acid type A gene cluster. *Archives of General Psychiatry, 62,* 47–55.

Ragsdale, K., Porter, J. R., Zamboanga, B. L., St. Lawrence, J. S., Read-Wahidi, R., & White, A. (2012). High-risk drinking among female college drinkers at two reporting intervals: Comparing Spring Break to the 30 days prior. *Sexuality Research and Social Policy, 9*(1), 31–40.

Rajwan, E., Chacko, A., & Moeller, M. (2012). Nonpharmacological interventions for preschool ADHD: State of the evidence and implications for practice. *Professional Psychology: Research and Practice, 43,* 520–526. doi: 10.1037/a0028812

Ramanan, V. K., Kim, S., Holohan, K., Shen, L., Nho, K., Risacher, S. L., . . . Aisen, P. S. (2012). Genome-wide pathway analysis of memory impairment in the Alzheimer's Disease Neuroimaging Initiative (ADNI) cohort implicates gene candidates, canonical pathways, and networks. *Brain Imaging and Behavior, 6,* 634–648.

Rapee, R. M., Gaston, J. E., & Abbott, M. J. (2009). Testing the efficacy of theoretically derived improvements in the treatment of social phobia. *Journal of Consulting and Clinical Psychology, 77,* 317–327. doi:10.1037/a0014800

Rapee, R. M., Kennedy, S. J., Ingram, M., Edwards, S. L., & Sweeney, L. (2010). Altering the trajectory of anxiety in at-risk young children. *American Journal of Psychiatry, 167,* 1518–1525.

Rapee, R. M., Schniering, C. A., & Hudson, J. L. (2009). Anxiety disorders during childhood and adolescence: Origins and treatment. *Annual Review of Clinical Psychology, 5,* 311–341. doi: 10.1146/annurev. clinpsy.032408 .153628

Rapgay, L., Bystritsky, A., Dafter, R. E., & Spearman, M. (2011). New strategies for combining mindfulness with integrative CBT for the treatment of GAD. *Journal of Rational-Emotive & Cognitive-Behavior Therapy, 29,* 92–119.

Raskin, N. J., Rogers, C. R., & Witty, M. C. (2011). Person-centered therapy. In R. J. Corsini & D. Wedding (Eds.) (9th ed.), *Current psychotherapies* (pp. 148–195). Belmont, CA: Brooks/Cole.

Rasmussen, K. M., Negy, C., Carlson, R., & Burns, J. M. (1997). Suicide ideation and acculturation among low socioeconomic status Mexican American adolescents. *Journal of Early Adolescence, 17,* 390–407.

Rate of patients in psychiatric hospitals has fallen to level of 1850. (2012, December 8). *Allgov.com.* Retrieved from http://www.allgov.com/news/controversies/rate-of-patients-in-psychiatric-hospitals-has-fallen-to-level-of-1850-121228?news=846605

Rathus, S. A. (2001). *Essentials of psychology* (6th ed.). Belmont, CA: Wadsworth.

Rattue, P. (2012, May 21). Adolescents are still smoking, but percentages have dropped. *Medical News Today.* Retrieved from www.medicalnewstoday.com/articles/245646.php

Rausch, J. L., Johnson, M. E., & Casanova. M. F. (2008). *Asperger's disorder.* New York: Informa Healthcare.

Rawe, J., & Kingsbury, K. (2006, May 22). When colleges go on suicide watch. *Time,* pp. 62–63.

Ray, R. A. (2012). Clinical neuroscience of addiction: Applications to psychological science and practice. *Clinical Psychology: Science and Practice, 19,* 154–166. doi:10.1111/j.1468-2850.2012.01280.

Raya, S., Nizamie, S. H., Akhtar, S., Praharaj, S. K., Mishra, B. R., & Zia-ul-Haq, M. (2011). Efficacy of adjunctive high frequency repetitive transcranial magnetic stimulation of left prefrontal cortex in depression: A randomized sham controlled study. *Journal of Affective Disorders, 128,* 153–159.

Reas, D. L., & Grilo, C. M. (2007). Timing and sequence of the onset of overweight, dieting, and binge eating in overweight patients with binge eating disorder. *International Journal of Eating Disorders, 40,* 165–170.

Reck, C., Stehle, E., Reinig, K., & Mundt, C. (2009). Maternity blues as a predictor of DSM-IV depression and anxiety disorders in the first three months postpartum. *Journal of Affective Disorders, 113,* 77–87. doi:10.1016/j.jad.2008.05.003

Rector, N. A., & Beck, A. T. (2012). Cognitive behavioral therapy for schizophrenia: An empirical review. *New England Journal of Medicine, 189*, 278–287.
Redd, W. H., & Jacobsen, P. (2001). Behavioral intervention in comprehensive cancer care. In A. Baum, T. A. Revenson, & J. E. Singer (Eds.), *Handbook of health psychology* (pp. 757–776). Mahwah, NJ: Erlbaum.
Reeves, G. M., Nijjar, G. V., Langenberg, P., Johnson, M. A., Khabazghazvini, B., Sleemi, A., . . . Postolache, T. T. (2012). Improvement in depression scores after 1 hour of light therapy treatment in patients with seasonal affective disorder. *Journal of Nervous and Mental Disease, 200*, 51–55. doi: 10.1097/NMD.0b013e31823e56ca
Reeves, R. R., & Ladner, M. E. (2009). Antidepressant-induced suicidality: Implications for clinical practice. *Southern Medical Journal, 102*, 713–718. doi: 10.1097/SMJ.0b013e3181a918bd
Reger, G. M., Holloway, K. M, Candy, C., Rothbaum, B. O. Difede, J., Rizzo, A. A., & Gahm, G. A. (2011). Effectiveness of virtual reality exposure therapy for active duty soldiers in a military mental health clinic. *Journal of Traumatic Stress, 24*, 93–96.
Rehm, L. P. (2008). How far have we come in teletherapy? Comment on "telephone-administered psychotherapy." *Clinical Psychology: Science and Practice, 15*, 259–261.
Rehm, L. P. (2010). *Depression: Advances in psychotherapy—Evidence-based practice*. Cambridge, MA: Hogrefe Publishing.
Rehman, U. S., Gollan, J., & Mortimer, A. R. (2008). The marital context of depression: Research, limitations, and new directions. *Clinical Psychology Review, 28*, 179–198.
Reichow, B., Doehring, P.,Cicchetti, D. V., & Volkmar, F. R. (Eds.). (2011). *Evidence-based practices and treatments for children with autism*. New York: Springer.
Reifler, B. V. (2006). Play it again, Sam—Depression is recurring. *New England Journal of Medicine, 354*, 1189–1190.
Reinberg, S. (2009, January 12). Lack of sleep linked to common cold. *WashingtonPost.com*. Retrieved from http://www.washingtonpost.com/wp-dyn/content/article/2009/01/12/AR2009011202090.html
Reisner, A. D. (1994). Multiple personality disorder diagnosis: A house of cards? *American Journal of Psychiatry, 151*, 629.
Reitan, R. M., & Wolfson, D. (2012). Detection of malingering and invalid test results using the Halstead–Reitan Battery. In C. R. Reynolds & A. M. Horton, *Detection of malingering during head injury litigation* (pp. 241–272). New York: Springer.
Reitan, R. M., & Wolfson, D. (2012). Detection of malingering and invalid test results using the Halstead–Reitan Battery. In C. R. Reynolds & A. M. Horton, *Detection of malingering during head injury litigation* (pp. 241–272). New York: Springer.
Remedial instruction rewires dyslexic brains, provides lasting results, study shows. (2008, August 7). *ScienceDaily*. Retrieved from http://www.sciencedaily.com/releases/2008/08/080805124056.htm
Remington, G., Agid, O., Foussias, G., Hahn, M., Rao, N., & Sinyor, M. (2013). Clozapine's role in the treatment of first-episode schizophrenia. *American Journal of Psychiatry, 170*, 146–151. 10.1176/appi.ajp.2012.12060778
Renfrey, G. S. (1992). Cognitive-behavior therapy and the Native American client. *Behavior Therapy, 23*, 321–340.
Reppermund, S,. Brodaty, H., Crawford, J. D., Kochan, N. A., Slavin, M. J., Trollor, J. N., Draper, B., & Sachdev, P. S. (2011). The relationship of current depressive symptoms and past depression with cognitive impairment and instrumental activities of daily living in an elderly population: The Sydney Memory and Ageing Study. *Journal of Psychiatric Research, 45*, 1600–1607. doi:10.1016/j.jpsychires.2011.08.001
Resick, P. A., Williams, L. F., Suvak, M. K., Monson, C. M., & Gradus, J. L. (2012). Long-term outcomes of cognitive–behavioral treatments for posttraumatic stress disorder among female rape survivors. *Journal of Consulting and Clinical Psychology, 80*, 201–210. doi: 10.1037/a0026602
Restifo, K., Harkavy-Friedman, J. M., & Shrout, P. E. (2009). Suicidal behavior in schizophrenia: A test of the demoralization hypothesis. *The Journal of Nervous and Mental Disease, 197*, 147–153. doi:10.1097/NMD.0b013e318199f452
Rettner, R. (2011, April 10). Popular drug for mild Alzheimer's largely a flop. *MSNBC.com*. Retrieved from http://www.msnbc.msn.com/id/42540787/ns/health-alzheimers_disease/
Reuven-Magril, O., Dar, R., & Liberman, N. (2008). Illusion of control and behavioral control attempts in obsessive-compulsive disorder. *Journal of Abnormal Psychology, 117*, 334–341.
Rey, J. M. (1993). Oppositional defiant disorder. *American Journal of Psychiatry, 150*, 1769–1778.
Reynolds, C. F., III, Butters, M. A., Lopez, O., Pollock, B. G., Dew, M. A., Mulsant, B. H., . . . DeKosky, S. T. (2011). Maintenance treatment of depression in old age: a randomized, double-blind, placebo-controlled evaluation of the efficacy and safety of donepezil combined with antidepressant pharmacotherapy. *Archives of General Psychiatry, 68*, 51–60. doi:10.1001/archgenpsychiatry.2010.184
Reynolds, E. H. (2012). Hysteria, conversion and functional disorders: a neurological contribution to classification issues. *British Journal of Psychiatry, 201*, 253–254.
Reynolds, S., Wilson, C., Austin, J., & Hooper, L. (2012). Effects of psychotherapy for anxiety in children and adolescents: A meta analytic review. *Clinical Psychology Review, 32*, 251–262. doi: 10.1016/j.cpr.2012.01.005
Rezai, A. R., Leehey, M. A., Ojemann, S. G., Flaherty, A. W., Eskandar, E. N., Kostyk, S. K., . . . Feigin. A. (2011). AAV2-GAD gene therapy for advanced Parkinson's disease: A double-blind, sham-surgery controlled, randomised trial. *Lancet Neurology, 10*, 309–319. doi:10.1016/S1474-4422(11)70039-4
Ribisl, K. M., Cruz, T. B., Rohrbach, L. A., Ribisl, K. M., Baezconde-Garbanati, L., Chen, X. . . . Johnson, C. A. (2000). English language use as a risk factor for smoking initiation among Hispanic and Asian American adolescents: Evidence for mediation by tobacco-related beliefs and social norms. *Health Psychology, 19*, 403–410.
Ricciardelli, L. A., & McCabe, M. P. (2004). A biopsychosocial model of disordered eating and the pursuit of muscularity in adolescent boys. *Psychological Bulletin, 130*, 179–205.
Richard, E., Reitz, C., Honig, L.H., Schupf, N., Tang, M.X., Manly, J. J., . . Luchsinger, J. A.. (2012). Late-life depression, mild cognitive impairment, and dementia. *Archives of Neurology*, in press.
Richards, D. (2011). Prevalence and clinical course of depression: A review. *Clinical Psychology Review, 31*, 1117–11125. doi:10.1016/j.cpr.2011.07.004
Richards, D., & Richardson, T. (2012). Computer-based psychological treatments for depression: A systematic review and meta-analysis. *Clinical Psychology Review, 32*, 329–342.
Rief, W., & Sharpe, M. (2004). Somatoform disorders—new approaches to classification, conceptualization, and treatment. *Journal of Psychosomatic Research, 56*, 387–390.
Rief, W., Nestoriuc, Y., Weiss, S., Welzel, E., Barsky, A. J., & Hofmann, S. G. (2009). Meta-analysis of the placebo response in antidepressant trials. *Journal of Affective Disorders, 118*, 1–8. doi:10.1016/j.jad.2009.01.029
Rieger, E., Van Buren, D. J., Bishop, M., Tanofsky-Kraff, M., Welch, R., & Wilfley, D. E. (2010). An eating disorder-specific model of interpersonal psychotherapy (IPT-ED): Causal pathways and treatment implications. *Clinical Psychology Review, 30*(4), 400–410. doi: 10.1016/j.cpr.2010.02.001
Risch, N., Herrell, R., Lehner, T., Liang, K.-Y., Eaves, L., Hoh, J., . . . Merikangas, K. R. (2009). Interaction between the serotonin transporter gene (5-httlpr), stressful life events, and risk of depression: A meta-analysis. *Journal of the American Medical Association, 301*, 2462–2471.
Riso, L. P., duToit, P. L., Blandino, J. A., Penna, S., Dacey, S., Duin, J. S., . . . Ulmer, C. S. (2003). Cognitive aspects of chronic depression. *Journal of Abnormal Psychology, 112*, 72–80.
Roberts, R. E. (2008). Persistence and change in symptoms of insomnia among adolescents. *Sleep, 31*, 177.
Robin, R. W., Greene, R. L., Albaugh, B., Caldwell, A., & Goldman, D. (2003). Use of the MMPI-2 in American Indians: I. Comparability of the MMPI-2 between two tribes and with the MMPI-2 normative group. *Psychological Assessment, 15*, 351–359.
Robinson, J. A., Sareen, J., Cox, B. J., & Bolton, J. M. (2009). Correlates of self-medication for anxiety disorders: Results from the National Epidemiologic Survey on Alcohol and Related Conditions. *The Journal of Nervous and Mental Disease, 297*, 873–878. doi:10.1097/NMD.0b013e3181c299c2
Rodgers, R. F., Salès, P., & Chabrol, H. (2010). Psychological functioning, media pressure and body dissatisfaction among college women. *European Review of Applied Psychology, 60*(2), 89–95. doi: 10.1016/j.erap.2009.10.001
Rodriguez, J., Umaña-Taylor, A., Smith, E. P., & Johnson, D. J. (2009). Cultural processes in parenting and youth outcomes: Examining a model of racial-ethnic socialization and identity in diverse populations. *Cultural Diversity and Ethnic Minority Psychology, 15*, 106–111. doi:10.1037/a0015510
Roesch, R., Zapf, P. A., & Hart, S. D. (2010). *Forensic psychology and law*. Hoboken, NJ: Wiley.
Rogan, A. (1986, Fall). Recovery from alcoholism: Issues for black and Native American alcoholics. *Alcohol Health and Research World, 10*, 42–44.
Roger, V. L. (2009). Lifestyle and cardiovascular health: Individual and societal choices. *Journal of the American Medical Association, 302*, 437–439.
Rogers, J. (2009, August 5). Alzheimer disease and inflammation: More epidemiology, more questions. *JournalWatch Neurology*. Retrieved from http://neurology.jwatch.org/cgi/content/full/2009/804/3?q=etoc_jwneuro
Rohan, K. J., Sigmon, S. T., & Dorhofer, D. M. (2003). Cognitive–behavioral factors in seasonal affective disorder. *Journal of Consulting and Clinical Psychology, 71*, 22–30.
Rohde, P., Lewinsohn, P. M., Klein, D. N., Seeley, J. R., & Gau, J. M. (2013). Key characteristics of major depressive disorder occurring in childhood, adolescence, emerging adulthood, and adulthood. *Clinical Psychological Science*, in press, doi: 10.1177/2167702612457599
Rojahn, J., Zaja, R. H., Turygin, N., Moore, L., & van Ingen, D. J. (2012). Functions of maladaptive behavior in intellectual and developmental disabilities: Behavior categories and topographies. *Research in Developmental Disabilities, 33*, 2020–2027.
Roll, J. M., Petry, N. M., Stitzer, M. L., Brecht, M. L., Peirce, J. M., McCann, M. J., . . . Kellogg, S. (2006). Contingency management for the treatment of methamphetamine use disorders. *American Journal of Psychiatry, 163*, 1993–1999.
Rolon, Y. M., & Jones, J. C. W. (2008). Right to refuse treatment. *Journal of the American Academy of Psychiatry and the Law, 36*, 252–255.
Ronksley, P. E., Brien, S. E., Turner, B. J., Mukamal, K. J., & Ghali, W. A. (2011). Association of alcohol consumption with selected cardiovascular disease outcomes: A systematic review and meta-analysis. *British Medical Journal, 342*, 671. doi:10.1136/bmj.d671
Rosenberg, T. (2012, September 30). A sruge in new treatment for veterans' trauma. *The New York Times Sunday Review*, p. 7.
Rosenheck, R. (2012). Homelessness, housing, and mental illness. *American Journal of Psychiatry, 169*, 225–226. doi:10.1176/appi.ajp.2011.11081217.
Rosenthal, E. (1993, April 9). Who will turn violent? Hospitals have to guess. *The New York Times*, pp. A1, C12.
Ross, C. A., & Ness, L. (2010). Symptom patterns in dissociative identity disorder patients and the general population. *Journal of Trauma & Dissociation, 11*, 458–468.
Ross, C. A., Miller, S. D., Reagor, P., Bjornson, L., Fraser, G. A., & Anderson, G. (1990). Structured interview data on 102 cases of multiple personality disorder from four centers. *American Journal of Psychiatry, 147*, 596–601.
Ross, C. A., Norton, G. R., & Wozney, K. (1989). Multiple personality disorder: An analysis of 236 cases. *Canadian Journal of Psychiatry, 34*, 413–418.
Rosso, G., Martini, B., & Maina, G. (2012). Brief dynamic therapy and depression severity: A single-blind, randomized study. *Journal of Affective Disorders*, 19, S0165-0327. doi: 10.1016/j.jad.2012.10.017.
Roth, T., Soubrane, C., & Titeux, L., & Walsh, J. K., on behalf of the Zoladult Study Group (2006). Efficacy and safety of zolpidem-MR: A double-blind, placebo-controlled study in adults with primary insomnia. *Sleep Medicine, 7*, 397–406.
Rothbaum, B. O., Hodges, L., Anderson, P. L., Price, L., & Smith, S. (2002). Twelve-month follow-up of virtual reality and standard exposure therapies for the fear of flying. *Journal of Consulting and Clinical Psychology, 70*, 428–432.
Rotter, J. B. (1966). Generalized expectancies for internal vs. external control of reinforcement. *Psychological Monographs, 1*, 210–609.
Rougeta, B. W., & Aubry, J.-M. (2007). Efficacy of psychoeducational approaches on bipolar disorders: A review of the literature. *Journal of Affective Disorders, 98*, 11–27.
Rowland, D., McMahon, C. G., Abdo, C., Chen, J., Jannini, E., Waldinger, M. D., & Ahn, T. Y. (2010). Disorders of orgasm and ejaculation in men. *Journal of Sexual Medicine*, 7,1668–1686.
Roy-Byrne, P. (2007, January 2). Behavioral treatment for chronic insomnia. Retrieved from http://psychiatry.jwatch.org/cgi/content/full/2006/1229/3?qetoc
Roy-Byrne, P., Craske, M. G., Sullivan, G., Rose, R. D., Edlund, M. J., Lang, A. J., . . . Sherbourne, C. D. (2010). Delivery of evidence-based treatment for multiple anxiety disorders in primary care: A randomized controlled trial. *Journal of the American Medical Association, 303*, 1921–1928.
Rozin, P., Bauer, R., & Catanese, D. (2003). Food and life, pleasure and worry, among American college students:

Gender differences and regional similarities. *Journal of Personality and Social Psychology, 85,* 132–141.

Rubinstein, S., & Caballero, B. (2000). Is Miss America an undernourished role model? *Journal of the American Medical Association, 283,* 1569.

Ruddle, A, Mason, O., & Wykes, T. (2011). A review of hearing voices groups: Evidence and mechanisms of change. *Clinical Psychology Review, 31,* 757–766. doi:10.1016/j.cpr.2011.03.010

Rudolph, K. D., Kurlakowsky, K. D., & Conley, C. S. (2001). Developmental and social-contextual origins of depressive control-related beliefs and behavior. *Cognitive Therapy & Research, 25,* 447–475.

Rush, A. J., Trivedi, M. H., Stewart, J. W., Nierenberg, A. A., Fava, M., Kurian, B. T. . . . Wisniewski, S. R. (2011). Combining medications to enhance depression outcomes (CO-MED): acute and long-term outcomes of a single-blind randomized study. *American Journal of Psychiatry, 168,* 689–701.

Russo, N., Foxe, J. J., Brandwein, A. B., Altschuler, T., Gomes, H., & Molholm, S. (2010). Multisensory processing in children with autism: High-density electrical mapping of auditory-somatosensory integration. *Autism Research, 3,* 253–267.

Rutledge, P. C., Park, A., & Sher, K. J. (2008). 21st birthday drinking: Extremely extreme. *Journal of Consulting and Clinical Psychology, 76,* 517–523.

Rutter, M., Caspi, A., Fergusson, D., Horwood, L. J., Goodman, R., Maughan, B., et al. (2004). Sex differences in developmental reading disability: New findings from 4 epidemiological studies. *Journal of the American Medical Association, 291,* 2007–2012.

Ryder, A. G., Yang, J., Zhu, X., Yao, S., Yi, J., Heine, S. J., et al. (2008). The cultural shaping of depression: Somatic symptoms in China, psychological symptoms in North America? *Journal of Abnormal Psychology, 117,* 300–313.

Rye, D. B., Bliwise, D. L., Parker, K., Trotti, L. M., Saini, P., Fairley, J., . . . Jenkins, A. (2012). Modulation of vigilance in the primary hypersomnias by endogenous enhancement of GABAA receptors. *Science Translational Medicine, 4,* 161ra151. doi: 10.1126/scitranslmed.3004685

Rylands, A. J., McKie, S., Elliott, R., Deakin, J. F. W., & Tarrier, N. (2011). A functional magnetic resonance imaging paradigm of expressed emotion in schizophrenia. *Journal of Nervous & Mental Disease, 199,* 25–29. doi: 10.1097/NMD.0b013e3182043b87

S

Sánchez-Morla, E. M., Santos, J. L., Aparicio, A., García-Jiménez, M. A, Soria, C., Arango, C. (2013). Neuropsychological correlates of P50 sensory gating in patients with schizophrenia. Schizophrenia Research, 143, 102–106

Sánchez-Ortuño, M. M., & Edinger, J. D. (2010). A penny for your thoughts: Patterns of sleep-related beliefs, insomnia symptoms and treatment outcome. *Behavior Research and Therapy, 48,* 125–133. doi: 10.1016/j.brat.2009.10.003

Séguin, M., Boyer, R., Lesage, A., McGirr, A., Suissa, A., Tousignant, M., & Turecki, G. (2010). Suicide and gambling: Psychopathology and treatment-seeking. *Psychology of Addictive Behaviors, 24,* 541–547. doi: 10.1037/a0019041

Sackeim, H. A., Haskett, R. F., Mulsant, B. H., Thase, M. E., Mann, J. J., Pettinati, H. M., . . . Prudic, J. (2001). Continuation pharmacotherapy in the prevention of relapse following electroconvulsive therapy. *Journal of the American Medical Association, 285,* 1299–1307.

Sacks, F. M., Bray, G. A., Carey, V. J., Smith, S. R., Ryan, D. H., Anton, S. D., McManus, K., et al. (2009). Comparison of weight-loss diets with different compositions of fat, protein, and carbohydrates. *New England Journal of Medicine, 360,* 859–873.

Sacks, O. (1985). *The man who mistook his wife for a hat and other clinical tales.* New York: Summit.

Sadoff, R. L. (2011). Expert psychiatric testimony. In R. L. Sadoff, J. A. Baird, S. M. Bertoglia, E. Valenti, & D. L. Vanderpool (Eds.), *Ethical issues in forensic psychiatry: Minimizing harm* (pp. 97–110). Hoboken, NJ: Wiley-Blackwell.

Safford, S. M. (2008). Gender and depression in men: Extending beyond depression and extending beyond gender. *Clinical Psychology: Science and Practice, 15,* 169–173.

Safren, S. A., Sprich, S., Mimiaga, M. J., Surman, C., Knouse, L., Groves, M., . . . Otto, M. W. (2010). Cognitive behavioral therapy vs relaxation with educational support

for medication-treated adults with ADHD and persistent symptoms: A randomized controlled trial. *Journal of the American Medical Association, 304,* 875–880. doi:10.1001/jama.2010.1192

Sahin, G., & Kirik, D. (2012). Efficacy of L-DOPA therapy in Parkinson's disease. In J. P. F. D'Mello (Ed.), *Amino acids in human nutrition and health* (pp. 454–463). Oxfordshire, UK: Cabi.

Sakai, Y., Shaw, C. A., Dawson, B. C., Dugas, D. V., Al-Mohtaseb, Z., Hill, D. E., . . . Zoghbi, H. Y. (2011). Protein interactome reveals converging molecular pathways among autism disorders. *Science Translational Medicine, 3,* 86. doi: 10.1126/scitranslmed.3002166

Salekin, R. T., Ziegler, T. A., Larrea, M. A., Anthony, V. L., et al. (2003). Predicting dangerousness with two Millon Adolescent Clinical Inventory psychopathy scales: The importance of egocentric and callous traits. *Journal of Personality Assessment, 80,* 154–163.

Salgado de Snyder, V. N. (1987). Factors associated with acculturative stress and depressive symptomatology among married Mexican immigrant women. *Psychology of Women Quarterly, 11,* 475–488.

Salgado de Snyder, V. N., Cervantes, R. C., & Padilla, A. M. (1990). Gender and ethnic differences in psychosocial stress and generalized distress among Hispanics. *Sex Roles, 22,* 441–453.

Salkovskis, P. M., & Clark, D. M. (1993). Panic disorder and hypochondriasis. Special issue: Panic, cognitions and sensations. *Advances in Behaviour Research and Therapy, 15,* 23–48.

Salkovskis, P. M., Thorpe, S. J., Wahl, K., Wroe, A. L., & Forrester, E. (2003). Neutralizing increases discomfort associated with obsessional thoughts: An experimental study with obsessional patients. *Journal of Abnormal Psychology, 112,* 709–715.

Salzer, S., Streeck, U., Jaeger, U., Masuhr, O., Warwas, J., Leichsenring, F., . . . Leibing, E. (2013). Patterns of interpersonal problems in borderline personality disorder. *Journal of Nervous & Mental Disease, 201,* 94–98. doi: 10.1097/NMD.0b013e3182532b59

Samuels, J. (2011). Personality disorders: Epidemiology and public health issues. *International Journal of Psychiatry, 23,* 223–233. doi:10.3109/09540261.2011.588200

Sanchez, M. M., Heyn, S. N., Das, D., Moghadam, S., Martin, K. J., & Salehi, A. (2012). Neurobiological elements of cognitive dysfunction in Down Syndrome: Exploring the role of APP. *Biological Psychiatry, 71,* 403. doi:10.1016/j.biopsych.2011.08.016

Sanchez-Hucles, J. (2000). *The first session with African Americans: A step by step guide.* San Francisco: Jossey Bass.

Sanders Thompson, V. L., Bazile, A., & Akbar, M. (2004). African Americans' perceptions of psychotherapy and psychotherapists. *Professional Psychology: Research and Practice, 35,* 19–26.

Sanders, B., & Green, J. A. (1995). The factor structure of the Dissociative Experiences Scale in college students. *Progress in the Dissociative Disorders, 7,* 23–27.

Sanders, L. (2006, June 18). Heartache. *The New York Times,* pp. 27–28.

Sanders, S. J., Ercan-Sencicek, A. g., Hus, V., Luo, R., Murtha, M. T., Moreno-De-Luca, D., . . . State, M. W. (2011). Multiple recurrent de novo cnvs, including duplications of the 7q11.23 Williams Syndrome region, are strongly associated with autism. *Neuron, 70,* 863–885. doi: 10.1016/j.neuron.2011.05.002

Sanders, S. J., Murtha, M. T., Gupta, A. R., Murdoch, J. D., Raubeson, M. J., Willsey, A. J., . . . State, M. W. (2012). De novo mutations revealed by whole-exome sequencing are strongly associated with autism. *Nature, 485,* 237–241. doi: 10.1038/nature10945

Santini, E., Huynh, T. N., MacAskill, A. F., Carter, A. G., Pierre, P., Ruggero, D., . . . Klann, E. (2012). Exaggerated translation causes synaptic and behavioural aberrations associated with autism. *Nature, 493,* 411–415. doi: 10.1038/nature11782

Sar, V., Yargic, L. I., & Tutkun, H. (1996). Structured interview data on 35 cases of dissociative identity disorder in Turkey. *American Journal of Psychiatry, 153,* 1329–1333.

Sareen, J., Afifi, T. O., McMillan, K. A., & Asmundson, G. J. G. (2011). Relationship between household income and mental disorders: Findings from a population-based longitudinal study. *Archives of General Psychiatry, 68,* 419. doi: 10.1001/archgenpsychiatry.2011.15

Satcher, D. (2000). Mental health: A report of the Surgeon General—executive summary. *Professional Psychology: Research and Practice, 31,* 5–13.

Saulny, S. (2011, March 24). Census data presents rise in multiracial population of youths. *The New York Times.* Retrieved from nytimes.com.

Saulsmana, L. M. (2011).Depression, Anxiety, and the MCMI–III: Construct validity and diagnostic efficiency. *Journal of Personality Assessment, 93,* 76–83. doi:10.1080/00223891.2010.528481

Savage, C. (2012, January 7). U.S. to expand its definition of rape in statistics. *The New York Times.* Retrieved from www.nytimes.com

Savic, I., Garcia-Falgueras, A., & Swaab, D. F. (2010). Sexual differentiation of the human brain in relation to gender identity and sexual orientation. In I. Savic (Ed.). *Sex differences in the human brain, Their underpinnings and implications: Progress in Brain Research, 186* (pp. 41–64). New York: Elsevier.

Sawyer, A. M., Gooneratne, N. S., Marcus, C. L., Ofer, D., Richards, K. C., & Weaver, T. E. (2011). A systematic review of CPAP adherence across age groups: Clinical and empiric insights for developing CPAP adherence interventions. *Sleep Medicine Reviews, 15,* 343. doi: 10.1016/j.smrv.2011.01.003

Sayers, G. M. (2003). Psychiatry and the control of dangerousness: A comment. *Journal of Medical Ethics, 29,* 235–236.

Scahill, L., McDougle, C. J., Aman, M. G., Johnson, C., Handen, B., Bearss, K., . . . Vitiello, B. (2012). Effects of risperidone and parent training on adaptive functioning in children with pervasive developmental disorders and serious behavioral problems. *Journal of the American Academy of Child & Adolescent Psychiatry, 51,* 136. doi: 10.1016/j.jaac.2011.11.010

Scheier, M. F., & Carver, C. S. (1985). Optimism, coping, and health: Assessment and implications of generalized outcome expectancies. *Health Psychology, 4,* 219–247.

Schizophrenia Psychiatric Genome-Wide Association Study (GWAS) Consortium. (2011). Genome-wide association study identifies five new schizophrenia loci. *Nature Genetics, 43,* 969–976. doi: 10.1038/ng.940.

Schmidt, N. B., & Keough, M. E. (2010). Treatment of panic. *Annual Review of Clinical Psychology, 6,* 241–256. doi:10.1146/annurev.clinpsy.121208.131317

Schmidt, N. B., Richey, J. A., Buckner, J. D., & Timpano, K. R. (2009). Attention training for generalized social anxiety disorder. *Journal of Abnormal Psychology, 118,* 5–14. doi:10.1037/a0013643

Schneck, C. D., Miklowitz, D. J., Calabrese, J. R., Allen, M. H., Thomas, M. R., Wisniewski, S. R., . . . Sachs, G. S. (2004). Phenomenology of rapid-cycling bipolar disorder: Data from the first 500 participants in the systematic treatment enhancement program. *American Journal of Psychiatry, 161,* 1902–1908.

Schneck, C. D., Miklowitz, D. J., Miyahara, S., Araga, M., Wisniewski, S., Gyulai, L., . . . Sachs, G. S. (2008). The prospective course of rapid-cycling bipolar disorder: Findings from the STEP-BD. *American Journal of Psychiatry, 165,* 370–377.

Schneider, H., & Eisenberg, D. (2006). Who receives a diagnosis of attention-deficit/ hyperactivity disorder in the United States elementary school population? *Pediatrics, 117,* e601–e609.

Schneider, L. S., Dagerman, K. S., Higgins, J.P., & McShane, R. (2011). Lack of evidence for the efficacy of memantine in mild Alzheimer disease. *Archives of Neurology, 68,* 991–998.

Schneider, R. H., Grim, C. E., Rainforth, M. V., Kotchen, T., Nidich, S. I., Gaylord-King, C., . . . Alexander, C. N. (in press). Stress reduction in the secondary prevention of cardiovascular disease: randomized, controlled trial of transcendental meditation and health education in Blacks. *Circulation: Cardiovascular Quality and Outcomes.* doi:10.1161/CIRCOUTCOMES.112.967406

Schneider, R. H., Grim, C. E., Rainforth, M. V., Kotchen, T., Nidich, S. I., Gaylord-King, C., . . . Alexander, C. N. (2012). Stress reduction in the secondary prevention of cardiovascular disease: Randomized, controlled trial of transcendental meditation and health education in Blacks. *Circulation: Cardiovascular Quality and Outcomes, 5,* 750–758. doi: 10.1161/CIRCOUTCOMES.112.967406.

Schneier, F. R. (2006). Social anxiety disorder. *New England Journal of Medicine, 355,* 1029–1036.

Schneier, F. R., Neria, Y., Pavlicova, M., Hembree, E., Suh, E. J., Amsel, L., . . . Marshall, R. D. (2012). Combined prolonged exposure therapy and paroxetine for PTSD related to the World Trade Center attack: A randomized controlled trial. *American Journal of Psychiatry, 169,* 80–88. doi:10.1176/appi.ajp.2011.11020321

Schniering, C. A., & Rapee, R. M. (2004). The relationship between automatic thoughts and negative emotions in children and adolescents: A test of the cognitive content-specificity hypothesis. *Journal of Abnormal Psychology, 113,* 464–470.

Schoenman, T. J. (1984). The mentally ill witch in textbooks of abnormal psychology: Current status and implications of a fallacy. *Professional Psychiatry, 15,* 299–314.

Schreier, H. M. C., & Chen, E. (2008). Prospective associations between coping and health among youth with asthma. *Journal of Consulting and Clinical Psychology, 76,* 790–798.

Schreier, H., & Ricci, L. R. (2002). Follow-up of a case of Münchausen by proxy syndrome. *Journal of the American Academy of Child and Adolescent Psychiatry, 41,* 1395–1396.

Schroeder, S. A. (2013). New evidence that cigarette smoking remains the most important health hazard. *New England Journal of Medicine, 368,* 389–390. doi: 10.1056/NEJMe1213751

Schuepbach, W.M.M., Rau, J., Knudsen, K., Volkmann, J., Krack, P., Timmermann, L., Hälbig, T. D., . . . EARLYSTIM Study Group. Neurostimulation for Parkinson's Disease with early motor complications. *New England Journal of Medicine, 368,* 610–622. doi:10.1056/NEJMoa1205158

Schultz, L. T., & Heimberg, R. G. (2008). Attentional focus in social anxiety disorder: Potential for interactive processes. *Clinical Psychology Review, 28,* 1206–1221.

Schulze, T. G., Ohlraun, S., Czerski, P. M., Schumacher, J., Kassem, L., Deschner, M., . . . Rietschel, M. (2005). Genotype-phenotype studies in bipolar disorder showing association between the DAOA/G30 locus and persecutory delusions: A first step toward a molecular genetic classification of psychiatric phenotypes. *American Journal of Psychiatry, 162,* 2101–2108.

Schwartz, D. R., & Carney, C. E. (2012). Mediators of cognitive-behavioral therapy for insomnia: A review of randomized controlled trials and secondary analysis studies. *Clinical Psychology Review, 32,* 664–675. http://dx.doi.org/10.1016/j.cpr.2012.06.006

Schwartz, D., Gorman, A. H., Duong, M. T., & Nakamoto, J. (2008). Peer relationships and academic achievement as interacting predictors of depressive symptoms during middle childhood. *Journal of Abnormal Psychology, 117,* 289–299.

Schwartz, R. P., Highfield, D. A., Jaffe, J. H., Brady, J. V., Butler, C. B., Rouse, C. A., . . . Battjes, R. J. . (2006). A randomized controlled trial of interim methadone maintenance. *Archives of General Psychiatry, 63,* 102–109.

Schwarz, A. (2009, October 23). N.F.L. data reinforces dementia links. Retrieved from www.nytimes.com

Schwarz, A., & Cohen, S. (2013, April 1). More diagnoses of hyperactivity in new C.D.C. data. *The New York Times,* pp. A1 A 11.

Schweitzer, I., Maguire, K., & Ng, C. (2009). Sexual side-effects of contemporary antidepressants: Review. *Australian and New Zealand Journal of Psychiatry, 43,* 795–808. doi:10.1080/00048670903107575

Schwitzgebel, R. L., & Schwitzgebel, R. K. (1980). *Law and psychological practice.* New York: Wiley.

ScienceDaily, 2011 (AU to add complete citation)

Scientists discover migraine gene. (2003, January 21). Retrieved from http://www.msnbc.comScott-Sheldon, L. A., Kalichman, S. C., Carey, M. P., & Fielder, R. L. (2008). Stress management interventions for HIV+ adults: A meta-analysis of randomized controlled trials, 1989 to 2006. *Health Psychology, 27,* 129–139.

Scogin, F., & Shah, A. (Eds.). (2012). *Making evidence-based psychological treatments work with older adults.* Washington, DC: American Psychological Association.

Scroppo, J. C., Drob, S. L., Weinberger, J. L., & Eagle, P. (1998). Identifying dissociative identity disorder: A self-report and projective study. *Journal of Abnormal Psychology, 107,* 272–284.

Sedlmeier, P., Eberth, J., Schwarz, M., Zimmermann, D., Haarig, F., Jaeger, S., . . . Kunze, S. (2012). The psychological effects of meditation: A meta-analysis. *Psychological Bulletin, 138,* 1139–1171. doi:10.1037/a0028168

Seedat, S., Scott, K. M., Angermeyer, M. C., Berglund, P., Bromet, E. J., Brugha, T. S., . . . Kessler, R. C. (2009). Cross-national associations between gender and mental disorders in the World Health Organization World Mental Health Surveys. *Archives of General Psychiatry, 66,* 785–795.

Segal, Z. V., Bieling, P., Young, T., MacQueen, G., Cooke, R. Martin, L., . . . Levitan, R. D. (2010). Antidepressant monotherapy vs sequential pharmacotherapy and mindfulness-based cognitive therapy, or placebo, for relapse prophylaxis in recurrent depression. *Archives of General Psychiatry, 67,* 1256–1264.

Segerstrom, S. C., & Miller, G. E. (2004). Psychological stress and the human immune system: A meta-analytic study of 30 years of inquiry. *Psychological Bulletin, 130,* 601–630.

Selfe, L. (2011). *Nadia revisited: A longitudinal study of an autistic savant. Essays in developmental psychology series.* New York, NY: Psychology Press.

Seligman, M. E. P. (1973). Fall into helplessness. *Psychology Today, 7,* 43–48.

Seligman, M. E. P. (1975). *Helplessness: On depression, development, and death.* San Francisco: Freeman.

Seligman, M. E. P. (1991). *Learned optimism.* New York: Knopf.

Seligman, M. E. P., & Maier, S. F. (1967). Failure to escape traumatic shock. *Journal of Experimental Psychology, 74,* 1–9.

Seligman, M. E. P., Steen, T. A., Park, N., & Peterson, C. (2005). Positive psychology progress: Empirical validation of interventions. *American Psychologist, 60,* 410–421.

Selkoe, D. J. (2012). Preventing Alzheimer's Disease. *Science, 337,* 1488–1492 doi: 10.1126/science.1228541

Seltzer, M. M., Baker, M. W., Hong, J. Maenner, M., Greenberg, J., & Mandel, D. (2012). Prevalence of CGG expansions of the FMR1 gene in a US population-based sample. *American Journal of Medical Genetics Part B: Neuropsychiatric Genetics, 159B,* 589. doi:10.1002/ajmg.b.32065

Selye, H. (1976). *The stress of life* (Rev. ed.). New York: McGraw-Hill.

Serrano-Blanco, A., Gabarron, E., Garcia-Bayo, I., Soler-Vila, M., Caramés, E., Peñarrubia-Maria, M. T., . . . Haro, J. M. (2006). Effectiveness and cost-effectiveness of antidepressant treatment in primary health care: A six-month randomised study comparing fluoxetine to imipramine. *Journal of Affective Disorders, 91,* 153–163.

Serretti, A., & Mandelli, L. (2008). The genetics of bipolar disorder: Genome "hot regions," genes, new potential candidates and future directions. *Molecular Psychiatry, 13,* 742.

Seshadri, S., Fitzpatrick, A. L., Ikram, A., DeStefano, A. L., Gudnason, V., Boada, M., . . . EADI1 Consortium. (2010). Genome-wide analysis of genetic loci associated with Alzheimer Disease. *Journal of the American Medical Association, 303,* 1832–1840.

Seto, M. C., Lalumière, M L., Harris, G. T., & Chivers, M. (2012). The sexual responses of sexual sadists. *Journal of Abnormal Psychology, 121,* 739–753. doi: 10.1037/a0028714

Settles, I . H., Navarrete, C. D., Pagano, S. J., Abdou, C. M., & Sidanius, J. (2010). Racial identity and depression among African American women. *Cultural Diversity and Ethnic Minority Psychology, 16,* 248–255. doi:10.1037/a0016442

Shadish, W. R., Matt, G. E., Navarro, A. M., & Phillips, G. (2000). The effects of psychological therapies under clinically representative conditions: A meta-analysis. *Psychological Bulletin, 126,* 512–529.

Shaffer, H. J., & Martin, R. (2011). Disordered gambling: Etiology, trajectory, and clinical considerations. *Annual Review of Clinical Psychology, 7,* 483–510. doi:10.1146/annurev-clinpsy-040510-143928

Shafti, S S. (2010). Olanzapine vs. lithium in management of acute mania. *Journal of Affective Disorders, 122,* 273–276. doi:10.1016/j.jad.2009.08.013

Shalev, A. Y., & Freedman, S. (2005). PTSD following terrorist attacks. *American Journal of Psychiatry, 162,* 1188–1191.

Shapiro, E. (1992, August 22). Fear returns to sidewalks of West 96th Street. *The New York Times,* pp. B3–B4.

Shapiro, F. (2001). *Eye movement desensitization and reprocessing: Basic principles, protocols and procedures* (2nd ed.). New York: Guilford Press.

Shapiro, J. R., C. Bauer, S., Andrews, E., Pisetsky, E., Bulik-Sullivan, B., Hamer, R. M., & Bulik, C. M. (2010). Mobile therapy: Use of text-messaging in the treatment of bulimia nervosa. *International Journal of Eating Disorders, 43,* 513–519.

Sharp, T. A. (2006). New molecule to brighten the mood. *Science, 311,* 45–46.

Sharpe, K. (2012, June 300-July 1). The medication generation. *Wall Street Journal,* pp. C1, C2.

Sharpless, B. A., & Barber, J. P. (2011). A clinician's guide to PTSD treatments for returning veterans. *Professional Psychology: Research and Practice, 42,* 8–15. doi:10.1037/a0022351

Shaw, H., Ramirez, L., Trost, A., Randall, P., & Stice, E. (2004). Body image and eating disturbances across ethnic groups: More similarities than differences. *Psychology of Addictive Behaviors, 18,* 12–18.

Shaw, P., Gilliam, M., Liverpool, M., Weddle, C., Malek, M., Sharp, W., . . . Giedd, J. (2011). Cortical development in typically developing children with symptoms of hyperactivity and impulsivity: support for a dimensional view of attention deficit hyperactivity disorder. *American Journal of Psychiatry, 168,* 143–151.

Shaw, R., Cohen, F., Doyle, B., & Pelesky, J. (1985). The impact of denial and repressive style on information gain and rehabilitation outcomes in myocardial infarction patients. *Psychosomatic Medicine, 47,* 262–275.

Shaywitz, S. E., Shaywitz, B. A., Fulbright, R. K., Skudlarski, P., Mencl, W. E., et al. (2003). Neural systems for compensation and persistence: Young adult outcome of childhood reading disability. *Biological Psychiatry, 54,* 25–33.

Shear, K., Jin, R., Ruscio, A. M., Walters, E. E., & Kessler, R. C. (2006). Prevalence and correlates of estimated DSM-IV child and adult separation anxiety disorder in the National Comorbidity Survey Replication. *American Journal of Psychiatry 163,* 1074–1083.

Shedler, J. (2010). The efficacy of psychodynamic psychotherapy. *American Psychologist,* 65, 98–109. doi: 10.1037/a0018378.

Shedler, J., Beck, A., Fonagy, P., Gabbard, G. O., Gunderson, J. G., . . . Westen, D. (2010). Personality disorders in *DSM-5. American Journal of Psychiatry, 167,* 1027–1028.

Shedler, J., Beck, A., Fonagy, P., Gabbard, G. O., Gunderson, J. G., . . .(2010). Personality disorders in DSM-5. *American Journal of Psychiatry,*167, 1027–1028.

Sheehan, D. V., & Mao, C. G. (2003). Paroxetine treatment of generalized anxiety disorder. *Psychopharmacology Bulletin, 37*(Suppl. 1), 64–75.

Sheline, Y. I., Disabato, B. M., Hranilovich, J., Morris, C., D'Angelo, G., Pieper, C., . . . Doraiswamy, P. M., (2012). Treatment course with antidepressant therapy in late-life depression. *American Journal of Psychiatry, 169,* 1185–1193. doi: 10.1176/appi.ajp.2012.12010122.

Sher, L. (2005). Suicide and alcoholism. *Nordic Journal of Psychiatry, 59,* 152.

Sheridan, M. S. (2003). The deceit continues: An updated literature review of Münchausen syndrome by proxy. *Child Abuse and Neglect, 27,* 431–451.

Shields, A. E., Lerman, C., & Sullivan, P. (2005). The use of race variables in genetic studies of complex traits and the goal of reducing health disparities: A transdisciplinary perspective. *American Psychologist, 60,* 77–103.

Shields, D. C., Asaad, W., Eskandar, E. N., Jain, F. A., Cosgrove, G. R., Flaherty, A. W., et al.. . . Dougherty, D. D. (2008). Prospective assessment of stereotactic ablative surgery for intractable major depression. *Biological Psychiatry, 64,* 449.

Shinozaki, G., Romanowicz, M., Passov, V., Rundell, J., Mrazek, D., & Kung, S. (2013). State dependent gene–environment interaction: Serotonin transporter gene–child abuse interaction associated with suicide attempt history among depressed psychiatric inpatients. *Journal of Affective Disorders, 147,* 373–378.

Shneidman, E. (1985). *Definition of suicide.* New York: Wiley.

Shneidman, E. (2005). Prediction of suicide revisited: A brief methodological note. *Suicide & Life-Threatening Behavior, 35,* 1–2.

Shoenfeld, N., & Dannon, P. N. (2012). Phenomenology and epidemiology of kleptomania. In J. E. Grant & M. N. Potenza, *The Oxford handbook of impulse control disorders* (pp. 135–134). New York: Oxford University Press.

Shore, J. H., Savin, D., Orton, H., Beals, J., & Manson, S. M. (2007). Diagnostic reliability of telepsychiatry in American Indian veterans. *American Journal of Psychiatry, 164,* 115–118.

Shorey, R., Cornelius, T. L., & Idema, C. (2011). Trait anger as a mediator of difficulties with emotion regulation and female-perpetrated psychological aggression. *Violence and Victims, 26,* 271–282.

Shulman, J. M. (2010, March 3). Incidence and risk for dementia in Parkinson disease. *JournalWatch Psychiatry.* Retrieved from http://neurology.jwatch.org/cgi/content/full/2010/302/2?q=etoc_jwneuro

Shute, N., Locy, T., & Pasternak, D. (2000, March 6). The perils of pills. *U.S. News & World Report,* pp. 44–50.

Sibley, M. H., Pelham, W. E., Molina, B. S., G., Gnagy, E. M., Waschbusch, D. A., Biswas, A., Karch, K.M.(2011). The delinquency outcomes of boys with ADHD with and without comorbidity. *Journal of Abnormal Child Psychology, 39,* 21–32. doi: 10.1007/s10802-010-9443-9.

Siddique, J., Chung, J. Y., Brown, C. H., & Miranda, J. (2012). Comparative effectiveness of medication versus cognitive-behavioral therapy in a randomized controlled trial of low-income young minority women with depression. *Journal of Consulting and Clinical Psychology, 80,* 995–1006. doi:10.1037/a0030452

Siegel, J. M. (2004). Hypocretin (orexin): Role in normal behavior and neuropathology. *Annual Review of Psychology, 55,* 125–148.
Sierra, M., Gomez, J., Molina, J. J., Luque, R., Munoz, J. F., & David, A. S. (2006). Depersonalization in psychiatric patients: A transcultural study. *The Journal of Nervous and Mental Disease, 194,* 356–361.
Sierra, M., Medford, N, Wyatt, G., & Davis, A. S. (2012). Depersonalization disorder and anxiety: A special relationship? *Psychiatry Research, 197,* 123–127.
Silver, E., Cirincione, C., & Steadman, H. J. (1994). Demythologizing inaccurate perceptions of the insanity defense. *Law and Human Behavior, 18,* 63–70.
Simeon, D., Guralnik, O., Hazlett, E. A., Spiegel-Cohen, J., Hollander, E., & Buchsbaum, M. S. (2000). Feeling unreal: A PET study of depersonalization disorder. *American Journal of Psychiatry, 157,* 1782–1788.
Simeon, D., Guralnik, O., Schmeidler, J., &, Knutelska, M. (2004). Fluoxetine therapy in depersonalisation disorder: Randomised controlled trial. *British Journal of Psychiatry, 185,* 31–36.
Simon, G. E., Fleck, M., Lucas, R., & Bushnell, D. M. (2004). Prevalence and predictors of depression treatment in an international primary care study. *American Journal of Psychiatry, 161,* 1626–1634.
Simpson, G. A., Cohen, R. A., Pastor, P. N., & Reuben, C. A. (2008). Use of mental health services in the past 12 months by children aged 4–17 years: United States, 2005–2006. *CHS Data Brief,* Number 8. Retrieved from http://www.cdc.gov/nchs/data/datab
Simpson, H. B., Foa, E. B., Liebowitz, M. R., Ledley, D. R., Huppert, J. D., & Cahill, S. (2008). A randomized, controlled trial of cognitive-behavioral therapy for augmenting pharmacotherapy in obsessive-compulsive disorder. *American Journal of Psychiatry, 165,* 621–630.
Singh, G. (1985). Dhat syndrome revisited. *Indian Journal of Psychiatry, 27,* 119–122.
Singh, R., Sandhu, J., Kaur, B., Juren, T., Steward, W. P., Segerbäck, D., & Farmer, P. B. (2009). Evaluation of the DNA damaging potential of cannabis cigarette smoke by the determination of acetaldehyde derived n2-ethyl-2-deoxyguanosine adducts. *Chemical Research in Toxicology, 22,* 1181–1188. doi:10.1021/tx900106y
Sivec, H. J., & Montesano, V. L. (2012). Cognitive behavioral therapy for psychosis in clinical practice. *Psychotherapy, 49,* 258–270. doi: 10.1037/a0028256.
Sixel-Döring, F., Trautmann, E., Mollenhauer, B., & Trenkwalder, C. (2011). Associated factors for REM sleep behavior disorder in Parkinson disease. *Neurology, 77,* 1048–1054.
Skodol, A. E.(2012).Personality disorders in DSM-5. *Annual Review of Clinical Psychology, 8,* 317–344. doi:10.1146/annurev-clinpsy-032511-143131.
Skoog, G., & Skoog, I. (1999). A 40-year follow-up of patients with obsessive-compulsive disorder. *Archives of General Psychiatry, 56,* 121–127.
Skritskaya, N. A., Carson-Woing, A. R., Moeller, J. R., Shen, S., Barsky, A. J., & Fallo, B. A. (2012). A clinician-administered severity rating scale for illness anxiety: Development, reliability and validity of the H-YBOCS-M. *Depression and Anxiety, 29,* 652–664.
Sleep problems cost billions. (2012, November 1). *ScienceDaily.com.* Retrieved from http://www.sciencedaily.com/releases/2012/11/121101110514.htm.
Sloan, D. M., Marx, B. P., & Epstein, E. M. (2005). Further examination of the exposure model underlying the efficacy of written emotional disclosure. *Journal of Consulting and Clinical Psychology, 73,* 549–554.
Sloan, D. M., Marx, B. P., Epstein, E. M., & Lexington, J. M. (2007). Does altering the writing instructions influence outcome associated with written disclosure? *Behavior Therapy, 38,* 155–168.
Slovenko, R. (2009). *Psychiatry in law/Law in psychiatry* (2nd ed.). New York: Routledge /Taylor & Francis Group.
Slutske, W. S. (2005). Alcohol use disorders among US college students and their non-college-attending peers. *Archives of General Psychiatry, 62,* 321–327.
Slutske, W. S., Zhu, G., Meier, M. H., & Martin, N. G. (2010). Genetic and environmental influences on disordered gambling in men and women. *Archives of General Psychiatry, 67,* 624–630.
Slutske, W. S., Zhu, G., Meier, M. H., & Martin, N. G. (2011). Disordered gambling as defined by the Diagnostic and Statistical Manual of Mental Disorders and the South Oaks Gambling Screen: Evidence for a common etiologic structure. *Journal of Abnormal Psychology, 120,* 743–751. doi:10.1037/a0022879
Slutske, W.S. (2006). Natural recovery and treatment-seeking in pathological gambling: Results of two US national surveys. *American Journal of Psychiatry, 163,* 297–302. See abstract in PubMed
Small, D. M., Simons, A. D., Yovanoff, P., Silva, S. G., Lewis, C. C., Murakami, J. L., et al. (2008). Depressed adolescents and comorbid psychiatric disorders: Are there differences in the presentation of depression? *Journal of Abnormal Child Psychology, 36,* 1015–1028.
Small, G. W., Kepe, V., Siddarth, P., Ercoli, L. M., Merrill, D. A., Donoghue, N., . . . Barrio, J. R. (2013). PET scanning of brain tau in retired National Football League Players: Preliminary findings. *The American Journal of Geriatric Psychiatry, 21,* 138–144.
Small, K. S., Hedman, A. K., Grundberg, E., Nica, A. C., Thorleifsson, G., Kong, A., . . . McCarthy, M. I. (2011). Identification of an imprinted master trans regulator at the KLF14 locus related to multiple metabolic phenotypes. *Nature Genetics, 43,* 561–564. doi : 10.1038/ng.833.
Smink, F. R., E., van Hoeken, D., & Hoek, H. W. (2012). Epidemiology of eating disorders: Incidence, prevalence and mortality rates. *Current Psychiatry Reports, 14,* 406–414. doi: 10.1007/s11920-012-0282-y.
Smith, A. E. M., Msetfi, R. M., & Golding, L. (2010). Client self rated adult attachment patterns and the therapeutic alliance: A systematic review. *Clinical Psychology Review, 30,* 326–337. doi: 10.1016/ j.cpr.2009.12.007
Smith, B. J. (2012, June). Inappropriate prescribing. *Monitor on Psychology, 43,* 36–40.
Smith, B. L. (2011,July/August). ADHD among preschoolers. *Monitor on Psychology,* pp. 50–52.
Smith, B. L. (2012, March). Bringing life into focus *Monitor on Psychology, 43,* 62.
Smith, C. O, Levine, D. W., Smith, E. P., Dumas, J., & Prinz, R. J. (2009). A developmental perspective of the relationship of racial–ethnic identity to self-construct, achievement, and behavior in African American children. *Cultural Diversity and Ethnic Minority Psychology, 15,* 145–157. doi: 10.1037/a0015538
Smith, D. B. (2009, Autumn). The doctor is in. *The American Scholar.* Retrieved from http://www.theamericanscholar.org/the-doctor-is-in
Smith, G. N., Ehmann, T. S., Flynn, S. W., MacEwan, G. W., Tee, K., Kopala, L. C., . . . Honer, W. G. (2011). The Assessment of Symptom Severity and Functional Impairment with *DSM-IV* Axis V. Psychiatric Services 2011. doi:10.1176/appi.ps.62.4.411
Smith, G. T. (2005). On construct validity: Issues of method and measurement. *Psychological Assessment, 17,* 396–408.
Smith, L. A., Cornelius, V. R., Azorin, J. M., Perugic, G., Vietad, E., Younge, A. H., & Bowden, C. L. (2010). Valproate for the treatment of acute bipolar depression: Systematic review and meta-analysis. *Journal of Affective Disorders, 122,* 1–9. doi:10.1016/j.jad.2009.10.033
Smith, M. L., & Glass, G. V. (1977). Meta-analysis of psychotherapy outcome studies. *American Psychologist, 32,* 752–760.
Smith, M. L., Glass, G. V., & Miller, T. I. (1980). *The benefits of psychotherapy.* Baltimore: Johns Hopkins University Press.
Smith, M. T., & Perlis, M. L. (2006). Who is a candidate for cognitive-behavioral therapy for insomnia? *Health Psychology, 25,* 15–19.
Smith, T. K. (2003, February). We've got to stop eating like this. *Fortune,* pp. 58–70.
Smoller, E. S. (1997). *I can't remember: Family stories of Alzheimer's disease.* Philadelphia, PA: Temple University Press.
Smoller, J. W., Paulus, M. P., Fagerness, J. A., Purcell, S., Yamaki, L. H., Hirshfeld-Becker, D., . . . Stein, M. B. (2008). Influence of RGS2 on anxiety-related temperament, personality, and brain function. *Archives of General Psychiatry, 65,* 298–308.
Snavely, A., & Chessick, C. (2011). CBT for psychosis: a symptom-based approach. *American Journal of Psychiatry, 168,* 1226–1227. 10.1176/appi.ajp.2011.11050682
Snowden, L. (2012, October). Health and mental health policies' role in better understanding and closing African American-White American disparities in treatment access and quality of care. *American Psychologist, 67,* 524–531.
Snowden, L. R. (2012). Health and mental health policies' role in better understanding and closing African American–White American disparities in treatment access and quality of care. *American Psychologist, 67,* 524–531. doi:10.1037/a0030054
Snyder, C. R., & Lopez, S. J. (2007). *Positive psychology: The science and practical explorations of human strength.* Thousand Oaks, CA: Sage Publications.
Sobell, M. B., & Sobell, L. C. (1973a). Alcoholics treated by individualized behavior therapy: One-year treatment outcome. *Behaviour Research and Therapy, 11,* 599–618.
Sobell, M. B., & Sobell, L. C. (1973b). Individualized behavior therapy for alcoholics. *Behavior Therapy, 4,* 49–72.
Sobell, M. B., & Sobell, L. C. (1984). The aftermath of heresy: A response to Pendery et al.'s (1982) critique of "Individualized behavior therapy for alcoholics." *Behaviour Research and Therapy, 22,* 413–440.
Sobot, V., Ivanovic-Kovacevic, S., Markovic, J., Misic-Pavkov, G., & Novovic, Z. (2012). Role of sexual abuse in development of conversion disorder: Case report. *European Review for Medical and Pharmacological Sciences,16,* 276–279.
Sockol, L. E., Epperson, C. N., & Barber, J. P. (2011). A meta-analysis of treatments for perinatal depression. *Clinical Psychology Review, 31,* 839–849. doi:10.1016/j.cpr.2011.03.009
Sokolove, M. (2003, November 16). Should John Hinckley go free? *The New York Times Magazine,* 54–57.
Solanto, M. V., Marks, D. J., Wasserstein, J., Mitchell, K., Abikoff, H., Ma, J., . . . Kofman, M. D. (2010). Efficacy of meta-cognitive therapy for adult ADHD. *American Journal of Psychiatry, 167,* 958–968.
Solis, M., Ciullo, S., Vaughn, S., Pyle, N., Hassaram, B., & Leroux, A. (2012). Reading comprehension interventions for middle school students with learning disabilities: A synthesis of 30 years of research. *Journal of Learning Disabilities, 45,* 327–340. doi: 10.1177/0022219411402691
Soloff, P. H., & Chiappetta, L. (2012). Prospective predictors of suicidal behavior in borderline personality disorder at 6-year follow-up. *American Journal of Psychiatry, 169,* 484–490. 10.1176/appi.ajp.2011.11091378
Solomon, D. A., Keller, M. B., Leon, A. C., Mueller, T. I., Lavori, P. W., Shea, M. T., . . . Endicott, J. (2000). Multiple recurrences of major depressive disorder. *American Journal of Psychiatry, 157,* 229–233.
Song, W., Chen, J., Petrilli, A., Liot, G. , Klinglmayr, E., Zhou, Y., . . . Bossy-Wetzel, E. (2011). Mutant huntingtin binds the mitochondrial fission GTPase dynamin-related protein-1 and increases its enzymatic activity. *Nature Medicine, 17,* 377–382. doi: 10.1038/nm.231
Sotiropoulos, I., Catania, C., Pinto, L. G., Silva, R., Pollerberg, G. E., Takashima, A., . . . Almeida, O. F. X. (2011). Stress acts cumulatively to precipitate Alzheimer's Disease-like tau pathology and cognitive deficits. *Journal of Neuroscience, 31,* 7840–7847. doi: 10.1523/JNEUROSCI.0730-11.2011
Spack, N. P. (2013). Management of transgenderism. *Journal of the American Medical Association,* 309, 478–484. doi:10.1001/jama.2012.165234.
Spanos, N. P. (1994). Multiple identity enactments and multiple personality disorder: A sociocognitive perspective. *Psychological Bulletin, 116,* 143–165.
Spatola, C. M. A., Scaini, S., Pesenti-Gritti, P., Medland, S. E., Moruzzi, S., Ogliari, A., . . . Battaglia, M. (2011). Gene–environment interactions in panic disorder and CO2 sensitivity: Effects of events occurring early in life. *American Journal of Medical Genetics Part B: Neuropsychiatric Genetics, 156,* 79–88. doi:10.1002/ajmg.b.31144
Spector, P. (2011). The relationship of personality to counterproductive work behavior (CWB): An integration of perspectives. *Human Resource Management Review, 21,* 342–352
Spence, S. H., Donovan, C. L., March, S., Gamble, A., Anderson, R. E., Prosser, S., . . Kenardy, J. (2011). A randomized controlled trial of online versus clinic-based CBT for adolescent anxiety. *Journal of Consulting and Clinical Psychology, 79,* 629–642. doi: 10.1037/a0024512
Spencer, D. J. (1983). Psychiatric dilemmas in Australian aborigines. *International Journal of Social Psychiatry, 29,* 208–214.
Sperling, R. A., Aisen, P. S., Beckett, L. A., Bennett, D. A., Craft, S., Fagan, A. M., . . . Phelps, C. H. (2011). Toward defining the preclinical stages of Alzheimer's disease: Recommendations from the National Institute on Aging and the Alzheimer's Association workgroup. *Alzheimers Dementia, 7,* 280.
Sperling, R. A., Jack, C. R., Jr., & Aisen, P. S. (2011b). Testing the right target and right drug at the right stage. *Science Translational Medicine, 3,* 111. doi: 10.1126/scitranslmed.3002609
Spiegel, D. (2006). Recognizing traumatic dissociation. *American Journal of Psychiatry, 163,* 566–568.
Spiegel, D. (2009). Coming apart: Trauma and the fragmentation of the self. In D. Gordon (Ed.), *Cerebrum 2009: Emerging ideas in brain science* (pp. 111). Washington, DC: Dana Press.

Spielmans, G.I., Berman, M. I.& Usitalo, A. N. (2011). Psychotherapy versus second-generation antidepressants in the treatment of depression: a meta-analysis. *Journal of Nervous and Mental Disease, 199,* 142–149. doi: 10.1097/NMD.0b013e31820caefb

Spijker, S., Van Zanten, J. S., De Jong, S., Penninx, B. W., van Dyck, R., Zitman, F. G., Smit, J. H., . . . Hoogendijk, W. J. (2011). Stimulated gene expression profiles as a blood marker of major depressive disorder. *Biological Psychiatry, 68,* 179–186.

Spillane, N. S., & Smith, G. T. (2009). On the pursuit of sound science for the betterment of the American Indian community: Reply to Beals et al. (2009). *Psychological Bulletin, 135,* 344–346. doi:10.1037/a0014997

Spitzer, R. L., et al. (1994). *DSM-IV case book* (4th ed.). Washington, DC: American Psychiatric Press.

Spitzer, R. L., Gibbon, M., Skodol, A. E., Williams, J. B. W., & First, M. B. (1989). *DSM-III-R casebook.* Washington, DC: American Psychiatric Press.

Spitzer, R. L., Gibbon, M., Skodol, A. E., Williams, J. B. W., & First, M. B. (1994). *DSM-IV case book* (4th ed.). Washington, DC: American Psychiatric Press.

Sprenger, T. (2011, April 5). Weather and migraine. *Journal Watch Neurology.* Retrieved from http://neurology.jwatch.org/

Squeglia, L. M., Sorg, S. F., Schweinsburg, A. D., Wetherill, R. R., Pulido, C., & Tapert, S. F. (2012). Binge drinking differentially affects adolescent male and female brain morphometry. *Psychopharmacology, 220,* 529–539

Sroufe, L. A. (2012, January 28). Ritalin gone wrong. *The New York Times Review.* Retrieved from www.nytimes.com

Staddon, J. E. R., & Cerutti, D. T. (2003). Operant conditioning. *Annual Review of Psychology, 4,* 115–144.

Staekenborg, S. S., Su, T., van Straaten, E. C. W., Lane, R., Scheltens, P., Barkhof, F., van der Flier, W. M. (2009). Behavioural and psychological symptoms in vascular dementia: Differences between small and large vessel disease. *Journal of Neurology, Neurosurgery & Psychiatry,* in press. doi: 10.1136/jnnp.2009.187500

Stambor, (2006, October). Psychologist calls for more research on adolescents' brains. *Monitor on Psychology, 37* (9), 16.

Stanley, M. A., Wilson, N. L., Novy, D. M., Rhoades, H. M., Wagener, P. D., Greisinger, A. J. (2009). Cognitive behavior therapy for generalized anxiety disorder among older adults in primary care: A randomized clinical trial. *Journal of the American Medical Association, 301,* 1460–1467.

Starcevic, V., Portman, M., & Beck, A. T. (2012). Generalized anxiety disorder: Between neglect and an epidemic. *Journal of Nervous and Mental Disease, 200,* 664–667. doi:10.1097/NMD.0b013e318263f947

Starkman, M. N. (2006). The terrorist attack of September 11 2001 as psychological toxin: Increase in suicide attempts. *Journal of Nervous and Mental Disease, 194,* 547–550.

Starkstein, S. E., Jorge, R., Mizrahi, R., & Robinson, R. G. (2005).The construct of minor and major depression in Alzheimer's disease. *American Journal of Psychiatry, 62,* 2086–2093.

Starr, L. R., & Davila, J. (2008). Excessive reassurance seeking, depression, and interpersonal rejection: A meta-analytic review. *Journal of Abnormal Psychology, 117,* 762–775.

State, M. W., et al. (2011). Multiple recurrent de novo cnvs, including duplications of the 7q11.23 Williams Syndrome region, are strongly associated with autism. *Neuron, 70,* 863–885. doi: 10.1016/j.neuron.2011.05.002

Steele J. D., Christmas, D., Eljamel, M. S., & Matthews, K. (2008). Anterior cingulotomy for major depression: Clinical outcome and relationship to lesion characteristics. *Biological Psychiatry, 63,* 670.

Steenhuysen, J. (2011, April 19). New Alzheimer's guidelines tap precursors to the disease. *MSNBC.com.* Retrieved from http://www.msnbc.msn.com/id/42653936/ns/health-alzheimers_disease/

Stein, A. L., Trana, G. Q., Lund, L. M., Haji, U., Dashevsky, B. A., & Baker, D. G. (2005). Correlates for posttraumatic stress disorder in Gulf War veterans: A retrospective study of main and moderating effects. *Journal of Anxiety Disorders, 19,* 861–876.

Stein, M. A., Sarampote, C. S., Waldman, I. D., Robb, A. S., Conlon, C., Pearl, P. L., et al. (2003). A dose-response study of OROS methylphenidate in children with attention-deficit/hyperactivity disorder. *Pediatrics, 112,* 404–413.

Stein, M. B., & Stein, D. J. (2008). Social anxiety disorder. *The Lancet, 371,* 1115–1125.

Stein, M. T. (2011, March 23). Most ADHD is complex. *Journal Watch Pediatrics and Adolescent Medicine.* Retrieved from http://pediatrics.jwatch.org/

Stein, M. T. (2012). No safe pattern of alcohol consumption during pregnancy. *Journal Watch Pediatrics and Adolescent Medicine.* Retrieved from http://pediatrics.jwatch.org/cgi/content/full/2012/229/2?q=etoc_jwpeds

Steinfeldt, M., & Steinfeldt, J. A. (2012). Athletic identity and conformity to masculine norms among college football players. *Journal of Applied Sport Psychology, 24,* 115–128.

Steketee, R.O. Frost, D.F., Tolin, J. Rasmussen, & T.A. Brown, (2010). Waitlist-controlled trial of cognitive behavior therapy for hoarding disorder. *Depression and Anxiety, 27,* 476–484.

Stergiakouli, E., Hamshere, M., Holmans, P., Langley, K., Zaharieva, I., Hawi, Z., . . . Thapar, A. (2012). Investigating the contribution of common genetic variants to the risk and pathogenesis of ADHD. *American Journal of Psychiatry, 169,* 186–194. doi: 10.1176/appi.ajp.2011.11040551

Stewart, R. E., & Chambless, D. L. (2009). Cognitive–behavioral therapy for adult anxiety disorders in clinical practice: A meta-analysis of effectiveness studies. *Journal of Consulting and Clinical Psychology, 77,* 595–606. doi: 10.1037/a0016032

Stewart, S. E., Platko, J., Fagerness, J., Birns, J., Jenike, E., Smoller, J. W., . . . Pauls, D. L. (2007). A genetic family-based association study of olig2 in obsessive-compulsive disorder. *Archives of General Psychiatry, 64,* 209–214.

Stewart, S. M., Kennard, B. D., Lee, P. W. H., Hughes, C. W., Mayes, T. L., Emslie, G. J., et al. (2004). A cross-cultural investigation of cognitions and depressive symptoms in adolescents. *Journal of Abnormal Psychology, 113,* 248–257.

Stewart, W. F., Ricci, J. A., Chee, E., Hahn, S. R., & Morganstein, D. (2003). Cost of lost productive work time among US workers with depression. *Journal of the American Medical Association, 289,* 3135–3141.

Stice, E., et al. (2000). Body-image and eating disturbances predict onset of depression among female adolescents: A longitudinal study. *Journal of Abnormal Psychology, 109,* 438–444.

Stice, E., Presnell, K., Gau, J., & Shaw, H. (2007). Testing mediators of intervention effects in randomized controlled trials: An evaluation of two eating disorder prevention programs. *Journal of Consulting and Clinical Psychology, 75,* 20–32.

Stice, E., Rohde, P., Gau, J. M., & Wade, E. (2010). Efficacy trial of a brief cognitive–behavioral depression prevention program for high-risk adolescents: Effects at 1- and 2-year follow-up. *Journal of Consulting and Clinical Psychology, 78,* 856–867. doi: 10.1037/a0020544

Stice, E., Rohde, P., Gau, J., & Shaw, H. (2009). An effectiveness trial of a dissonance-based eating disorder prevention program for high-risk adolescent girls. *Journal of Consulting and Clinical Psychology, 94,* 825–834. doi: 10.1037/a0016132

Stice, E., Rohde, P., Shaw, H., & Gau, J. (2011). An effectiveness trial of a selected dissonance-based eating disorder prevention program for female high school students: Long-term effects. *Journal of Consulting and Clinical Psychology, 79,* 500–508. doi: 10.1037/a0024351

Stoltenborgh, M., van IJzendoorn, M. H., Euser, E. M., & Bakermans-Kranenburg, M. J. (2011). A global perspective on child sexual abuse: meta-analysis of prevalence around the world. *Child Maltreatment, 16,* 79–101. doi: 10.1177/1077559511403920

Stone J., Smyth R., Carson, A., Lewis, S., Prescott, R., Warlow, C., & Sharpe, M. (2006). La belle indifférence in conversion symptoms and hysteria: Systematic review. *British Journal of Psychiatry, 188,* 204–209.

Stone, J., Smyth, R., Carson, A., Lewis, S., Prescott, R., Warlow, C., & Sharpe, M. (2005). Systematic review of misdiagnosis of conversion symptoms and "hysteria." *British Medical Journal, 331,* 989.

Stone, M., Laughren, T., Jones, M. L., Levenson, M., Holland, P. C., Hughes, A., et al. (2009). Risk of suicidality in clinical trials of antidepressants in adults: Analysis of proprietary data submitted to US Food and Drug Administration. *British Medical Journal, 339,* 2880. doi: 10.1136/bmj.b2880

Stout-Shaffer, S., & Page, G. (2008). Effects of relaxation training on physiological and psychological measures of distress and quality of life in HIV-seropositive subjects. *Brain, Behavior, and Immunity, 22*(4, Suppl. 1), 8.

Strachen, E. (2008). Civil commitment evaluations. In R. Jackson (Ed.), *Learning forensic assessment* (pp. 509–535). New York: Routledge/Taylor & Francis Group.

Strasser, A. A., Kaufmann, V., Jepson, C., Perkins, K. A., Pickworth, W. B., & Wileyto, E. P. (2005). Effects of different nicotine replacement therapies on postcessation psychological responses. *Addictive Behaviors, 30,* 9–17.

Strauss, G. P., Sandt, A. T., Catalano, L. T., & Allen, D. N. (2012). Negative symptoms and depression predict lower psychological well-being in individuals with schizophrenia. *Comprehensive Psychiatry, 53,*1137-44. doi: 10.1016/j.comppsych.2012.05.009.

Stress may increase risk for Alzheimer's disease. (2011, May 26). *ScienceDaily.* Retrieved from http://www.sciencedaily.com-/

Stricker, G. (2003). Is this the right book at the wrong time? *Contemporary Psychology, 48,* 726–728.

Striegel-Moore, R. H., Dohm, F. A., Kraemer, H. C., Taylor, C. B., Daniels, S. D., Crawford, P. B., et al. (2003). Eating disorders in white and black women. *American Journal of Psychiatry, 160,* 1326–1331.

Striegel-Moore, R. H., Wilson, G. T., DeBar, L., Perrin, N., Lynch, F., Rosselli, F., . . Kraemer, H. (2010). Cognitive behavioral guided self-help for the treatment of recurrent binge eating. *Journal of Consulting and Clinical Psychology, 78,* 312–321.

Strike, P. C., Magid, K., Whitehead, D. L., Brydon, L., Bhattacharyya, M. R., & Steptoe, A. (2006). Pathophysiological processes underlying emotional triggering of acute cardiac events. *Proceedings of the National Academy of Sciences.* Retrieved from http://www.pnas.org/cgi/content/abstract/103/11/4322

Strobbe, M. (2010, November 10). 1 in 10 kids in U.S. has ADHD, new study says. *MSNBC.com.* Retrieved from http://today.msnbc.msn.com/id/44190936/ns/today-today_health/t/us-kids-has-adhd-study-finds/

Stroebe, M., Stroebe, W., & Abakoumkin, G. (2005). The broken heart: Suicidal ideation in bereavement. *American Journal of Psychiatry, 162,* 2178–2180.

Stroud, C. B., Davila, J., & Moyer, A. (2008). The relationship between stress and depression in first onsets versus recurrences: A meta-analytic review. *Journal of Abnormal Psychology, 117,* 206–213.

Stroup, T. S., McEvoy, J. P., Ring, K. D., Hamer, R. H., LaVange, L. M., Swartz, M. S., . . . Schizophrenia Trials Network. (2011). A randomized trial examining the effectiveness of switching from olanzapine, quetiapine, or risperidone to aripiprazole to reduce metabolic risk: comparison of antipsychotics for metabolic problems (CAMP). *American Journal of Psychiatry, 168,* 947–956. doi: 10.1176/Appi.Ajp.2011.10111609

Stuart, R. B. (2004). Twelve practical suggestions for achieving multicultural competence. *Professional Psychology: Research and Practice, 35,* 3–9.

Substance Abuse and Mental Health Services Administration (SAMHSA) (2012). *National Survey on Drug Use and Health, 2010 and 2011.* Center for Behavioral Health Statistics and Quality Retrieved from www.samhsa.gov

Substance Abuse and Mental Health Services Administration (SAMHSA) Office of Applied Studies. (2007). *Results from the 2007 National Survey on Drug Use and Health: National findings.* Rockville, MD: SAMHSA Office of Applied Studies.

Substance Abuse and Mental Health Services Administration (SAMSHA). (2010a). *Results from the 2008 National Survey on Drug Use and Health: National Findings, Updated 2010.* Retrieved from http://oas.samhsa.gov/NSDUH/2K8NSDUH/tabs/toc.htm

Substance Abuse and Mental Health Services Administration. (SAMHSA) (2010b). *Results from the 2009 National Survey on Drug Use And Health: National Findings* (Office of Applied Studies, NSDUH Series H-38A, HHS Publication No. SMA 10-4586). Rockville, MD: Author.

Sudak, D. M. (2011). Combining CBT and medication: An evidence-based approach. Hoboken, NJ: John Wiley & Sons Inc.

Sue, D. W. (2010). *Microaggressions in everyday life: Race, gender and sexual orientation.* New York: John Wiley and Sons.

Sue, S., Yan Cheng, J. K., Saad, C. S., & Chu, J. P. (2012). Asian American mental health: A call to action. *American Psychologist, 67,* 532–544. doi:10.1037/a0028900

Sue, S., Zane, N., Hall, G. C. N., & Berger, L. K. (2009). The case for cultural competency in psychotherapeutic interventions. *Annual Review of Psychology, 60,* 525–548.

Sugaya, L., Hasin, D. S., Olfson, M., Lin, K. H., Grant, B. F., & Blanco, C. (2012). Child physical abuse and adult mental health: A national study. *Journal of Traumatic Stress, 25,* 384–392. doi: 10.1002/jts.21719.

Suinn, R. M. (2001). The terrible twos—anger and anxiety: Hazardous to your health. *American Psychologist, 56,* 27–36.

Sukhodolsky, D. G., Golub, A., Stone, E. C., & Orban, L. (2005). Dismantling anger control training for children: A randomized pilot study of social problem-solving versus social skills training components. *Behavior Therapy, 36,* 15–23.

Sullivan, D., Pinsonneault, J. K., Papp, A. C., Zhu, H., Lemeshow, S., Mash, D.C., & Sadee, W. (2013). Dopamine transporter DAT and receptor DRD2 variants affect risk of

lethal cocaine abuse: a gene–gene–environment interaction. *Translational Psychiatry, 3*, e222. doi: 10.1038/tp.2012.146
Sulloway, F. (1983). *Freud: Biologist of the mind*. New York: Basic Books.
Sunderland, M., Wong, N., Hilvert-Bruce, Z., & Andrews, G. (2012). Investigating trajectories of change in psychological distress amongst patients with depression and generalised anxiety disorder treated with internet cognitive behavioural therapy. *Behaviour Research and Therapy, 50*, 374–380.
Supekar, K., Menon, V., Rubin, D., Musen, M., & Greicius, M. D. (2008). Network analysis of intrinsic functional brain connectivity in Alzheimer's disease. *PLoS Computational Biology, 4* (6), e1000100. doi: 10.1371/ journal.pcbi.1000100
Suppes, T. (2011). Is there a role for antidepressants in the treatment of Bipolar II depression? *American Journal of Psychiatry, 167*, 738–740. doi:10.1176/appi.ajp.2010.10040590
Suppes, T., Datto, C., Minkwitz, M., Nordenhem, A., Walker, C., & Darko, D. (2010). Effectiveness of the extended release formulation of quetiapine as monotherapy for the treatment of acute bipolar depression. *Journal of Affective Disorders, 121*, 106–115. doi:10.1016/j.jad.2009.10.007
Suppes, T., Vieta, E., Liu, S., Brecher, M., & Paulsson, B. (2009). Maintenance treatment for patients with bipolar I disorder: Results from a North American study of quetiapine in combination with lithium or divalproex (Trial 127). *American Journal of Psychiatry, 166*, 476–488. doi:10.1176/appi.ajp.2008.08020189
Sutker, P. B., Davis, J., M., Uddo, M., & Ditta, S. R. (1995). War zone stress, personal resources, and PTSD in Persian Gulf War returnees. *Journal of Abnormal Psychology, 104*, 444–452.
Swann, A. C., Lafer, B., Perugi, G., Frye, M. A., Bauer, M., Bahk, W.-M., . . Suppes, T. (2013). Bipolar mixed states: An International Society for Bipolar Disorders Task Force Report of Symptom Structure, Course of Illness, and Diagnosis. *American Journal of Psychiatry, 170*, 31–42. 10.1176/appi.ajp.2012.12030301
Swanson, J. W., Swartz, M. S., Van Dorn, R. A., Elbogen, E. B., Wagner, R., Rosenheck, R. A. . . . Lieberman, J. A. (2006). A national study of violent behavior in persons with schizophrenia. *Archives of General Psychiatry, 63*, 490–499.
Swanson, S. A., Crow, S. J., LeGrange, D., Swendsen, J., & Merikangas, K. R. (2011). Prevalence and correlates of eating disorders in adolescents: Results from the National Comorbidity Survey Replication Adolescent Supplement. *Archives of General Psychiatry.* Online ahead of print March 7, 2011.
Swendsen, J., Ben-Zeev, D., & Granholm, E. (2010). Real-time electronic ambulatory monitoring of substance use and symptom expression in schizophrenia. *American Journal of Psychiatry, 168*, 202–209. doi:10.1176/appi.ajp.2010.10030463
Szasz, T. (1970). *Ideology and insanity: Essays on the psychiatric dehumanization of man*. New York: Doubleday Anchor.
Szasz, T. (2003a). Psychiatry and the control of dangerousness: On the apotropaic function of the term "mental illness." *Journal of Medical Ethics, 29*, 227–230.
Szasz, T. (2003b). Response to: "Comments on psychiatry and the control of dangerousness: On the apotropaic function of the term 'mental illness.'" *Journal of Medical Ethics, 29*, 237.
Szasz, T. (2007). *Coercion as cure: A critical history of psychiatry*. New Brunswick, NJ: Transaction.
Szasz, T. S. (2011). *The myth of mental illness: Foundations of a theory of personal conduct*. New York: HarperCollins.
Szatmari, P. (2011). Is autism, at least in part, a disorder of fetal programming? *Archives of General Psychiatry, 68*, 1091–1092. doi:10.1001/archgenpsychiatry.2011.99
Szeszko, P. R., Christian, C., MacMaster, F., Lencz, T., Mirza, Y., Taormina, P., Easter, P., . . . Rosenberg, D. R. (2008). Gray matter structural alterations in psychotropic drug-naive pediatric obsessive-compulsive disorder: An optimized voxel-based morphometry study. *American Journal of Psychiatry, 16*, 1299–1307.

T

Taft, C. T., Watkins, L. E., Stafford, J., Street, A. E., & Monson, C. M. (2011). Posttraumatic stress disorder and intimate relationship problems: A meta-analysis. *Journal of Consulting and Clinical Psychology, 79*, 22–33. doi:10.1037/a0022196
Tamam, L., Eroğlu, M. Z., & Paltacı, O. (2011). Intermittent explosive disorder. *Current Approaches in Psychiatry*, 3, 387–425doi: 10.5455/cap.20110318
Tamminga, C. A. (2011). When is polypharmacy an advantage? *American Journal of Psychiatry, 68*, 663. doi: 10.1176/appi.ajp.2011.11050695
Tan, H. M., Tong, S. F., & Ho, C. C. K. (2012). Men's health: Sexual dysfunction, physical, and psychological health—Is there a link? *Journal of Sexual Medicine, 9*, 663–671.
Tandon, R., Nasrallah, H. A., & Keshavan, M. S. (2010). Schizophrenia, "just the facts": 5. Treatment and prevention. past, present, and future. *Schizophrenia Research, 122*, 1–23. doi:10.1016/j.schres.2010.05.025
Tanguay, P. E. (2011). Autism in *DSM-5*. *American Journal of Psychiatry, 168*, 1142–1144. doi:10.1176/appi.ajp.2011.11071024
Tanner, C. M. (2013). A second honeymoon for Parkinson's Disease? *New England Journal of Medicine, 368*, 675–676. doi 10.1056/NEJMe121491313
Tapert, S. F., Brown, G. G., Baratta, M. V., & Brown, S. A. (2004). fMRI BOLD response to alcohol stimuli in alcohol dependent young women. *Addictive Behaviors, 29*, 33–50.
Tarquinio, C., Rydberg, J. A., & Oren, E. U. (2012). Recent advances in EMDR research and practice (Eye movement desensitization and reprocessing therapy). *European Review of Applied Psychology, 62*, 191.
Tarquinio, C., Rydberg, J. A., & Oren, E. U. (in press). Recent advances in EMDR research and practice (Eye movement desensitization and reprocessing therapy). *European Review of Applied Psychology. 62*, 191.
Tatarsky, A., & Kellogg, S. (2010). Integrative harm reduction psychotherapy: A case of substance use, multiple trauma, and suicidality. *Journal of Clinical Psychology, Special Issue: Harm Reduction in Psychotherapy, 66*, 123–135. doi:10.1002/jclp.20666
Tauber, E., Miller-Fleming, L., Mason, R. P., Kwan, W., Clapp, J., Butler, N. J., . . . Giorgini, F. (2010). Functional gene expression profiling in yeast implicates translational dysfunction in mutant Huntingtin toxicity. *Journal of Biological Chemistry, 286*, 410. doi: 10.1074/jbc.M110.101527
Taubes, G. (2012). Unraveling the obesity-cancer connection. *Science, 335*, 28–32. doi: 10.1126/science.335.6064.28
Tavares, H. (2012). Assessment and treatment of pathological gambling. In J. E. Grant & M. N. Potenza (Eds.), *The Oxford handbook of impulse control disorders* (pp. 279–312). New York: Oxford University Press.
Tavernise, S. (2012, December 11).Obesity in young is seen as falling in several cities. *The New York Times*. Retrieved from nytimes.com.
Taylor, C. B., & Luce, K. H. (2003). Computer- and Internet-based psychotherapy interventions. *Current Directions in Psychological Science, 12*, 18–22.
Taylor, K. L., Lamdan, R. M., Siegel, J. E., Shelby, R., Moran-Klimi, K., & Hrywna, M. (2003). Psychological adjustment among African American breast cancer patients: One-year follow-up results of a randomized psychoeducational group intervention. *Health Psychology, 22*, 316–323.
Taylor, M. K., Pietrobon, R., Taverniers, J., Leon, M. R., & Fern, B. F. (2013). Relationships of hardiness to physical and mental health status in military men: a test of mediated effects, *Journal of Behavioral Medicine, 36*, 1–9.
Taylor, S. (2011). Etiology of obsessions and compulsions: A meta-analysis and narrative review of twin studies. *Clinical Psychology Review, 31*, 1361–1372. doi:10.1016/j.cpr.2011.09.008
Taylor, S., & Jang, K. L. (2011). Biopsychosocial etiology of obsessions and compulsions: An integrated behavioral–genetic and cognitive–behavioral analysis. *Journal of Abnormal Psychology, 120*, 174–186. doi:10.1037/a0021403
Teachman, B. A., Marker, C. D., & Clerkin, E. M. (2010). Catastrophic misinterpretations as a predictor of symptom change during treatment for panic disorder. *Journal of Consulting and Clinical Psychology, 78*, 964–973. doi:10.1037/a0021067
Teicher, M. H., Samson, J. A., Polcari, A., & McGreenery, C. E. (2006). Sticks, stones, and hurtful words: Relative effects of various forms of childhood maltreatment. *American Journal of Psychiatry, 163*, 993–1000.
Teplin, L. A., McClelland, G. M., Abram, K. M., & Weiner, D. A. (2005). Crime victimization in adults with severe mental illness: Comparison with the National Crime Victimization Survey. *Archives of General Psychiatry, 62*, 911–921.
The McKnight Investigators. (2003). Risk factors for the onset of eating disorders in adolescent girls: Results of the McKnight Longitudinal Risk Factor Study. *American Journal of Psychiatry, 160*, 248–254.
The National Center For Health Statistics. Prevalence of current depression among persons aged ≥12 years, by age group and sex—United States, National Health and Nutrition Examination Survey, 2007–2010. *Journal of the American Medical Association, 307*, 1576.
Therapy and hypochondriacs often make poor mix, study says. (2004, March 25). *The New York Times*, p. A19.
Thibaut, F. (2011). Pharmacological treatment of sex offenders. *Sexologies, 20*, 166–168. doi:10.1016/j.sexol.2011.02.003
Thiedke, C. C. (2003). Nocturnal enuresis. *American Family Physician, 67*, 1509–1510.
Thioux, M., Stark, D. E., Klaiman, C., & Schultz, R. (2006). The day of the week when you were born in 700 ms: Calendar computation in an autistic savant. *Journal of Experimental Psychology: Human Perception and Performance, 32*, 1155–1168.
Thompson, M. A., Aberg, J. A., Hoy, J. E., Telenti, A., Benson, C., Cahn, P., . . . Volberding, P. A. (2012). Antiretroviral treatment of adult HIV infection: 2012 recommendations of the International Antiviral Society–USA Panel. *Journal of the American Medical Association, 308*, 387–402. doi:10.1001/jama.2012.7961
Thompson, P. M., Hayashi, K. M., Simon, S. L., Geaga, J. A., Hong, M. S., Sui, Y., . . . London, E. D. (2004). Structural abnormalities in the brains of human subjects who use methamphetamine. *Journal of Neuroscience, 30*, 6028–6036.
Thompson, T. (1995). *The beast: A journey through depression*. New York: Putnam.
Thomson, A. B., & Page, L. A. (2007). Psychotherapies for hypochondriasis. *Cochrane Database System Review, 4*, 1–35.
Thorpy, M. (2008). Brain structure in obstructive sleep apnea. *Journal Watch Neurology*. Retrieved from http://neurology.jwatch.org/cgi/content/full/2008/1007/4
Thun, M. J., Carter, B. D., Feskanich, D., Freedman, N. D., Prentice, R., Lopez, A. D., . . . Gapstur, S. M. (2013). 50-year trends in smoking-related mortality in the United States. *New England Journal of Medicine, 368*, 351–364. doi: 10.1056/NEJMsa1211127
Tiggemann, M., Martins, Y., & Kirkbride, A. (2007). Oh to be lean and muscular: Body image ideals in gay and heterosexual men. *Psychology of Men & Masculinity, 8*, 15–24.
Tindle, H. A., Chang, Y.-F., Kuller, L. H., Manson, J. E., Robinson, J. G., Rosal, M. C., . . . Matthews, K. A. (2009). Optimism, cynical hostility, and incident coronary heart disease and mortality in the women's health initiative. *Circulation, 120*, 656–662. doi:10.1161/CIRCULATIONAHA.108.82
Tobacco use in the USA. (2010, September 18). *The Lancet, 376*, 930. doi:10.1016/S0140-6736(10)61433-
Tohen, M., Zarate, C. A., Hennen, J., Khalsa, H.-M. K., Strakowski, S. M., Gebre-Medhin, P., . . . Baldessarini, R. J. (2003). The McLean-Harvard First-Episode Mania Study: Prediction of recovery and first recurrence. *American Journal of Psychiatry, 160*, 2099–2107.
Tolin, D. F., & Foa, E. B. (2006). Sex differences in trauma and posttraumatic stress disorder: A quantitative review of 25 years of research. *Psychological Bulletin, 132*, 959–992.
Tolin, D. F., (2010). Is cognitive–behavioral therapy more effective than other therapies? A meta-analytic review. *Clinical Psychology Review, 30*, 710–720. doi:10.1016/j.cpr.2010.05.003
Tolin, D. F, Stevens, M. C., Nave, A., Villavicencio, A. L., & Morrison, S. (2012). Neural mechanisms of cognitive behavioral therapy response in hoarding disorder: A pilot study. *Journal of Obsessive-Compulsive and Related Disorders, 1*, 180–188.
Tomb, E., Rafanelli, C., Grandi, S., Guidi, J. & Fava. G .A. (2012). Clinical configuration of cyclothymic disturbances. *Journal of Affective Disorders, 139*, 244–249. http://dx.doi.org/10.1016/j.jad.2012.01.014
Toomey, R., Lyons, M. J., Eisen, S. A., Xian, H., Chantarujikapong, S., Seidman, L. J., . . . Tsuang, M. T. (2003). A twin study of the neuropsychological consequences of stimulant abuse. *Archives of General Psychiatry, 60*, 303–310.
Toplak, M. E., Connors, L., Shuster, J., Knezevic, B., & Parks, S. (2008). Review of cognitive, cognitive-behavioral, and neural-based interventions for attention-deficit/hyperactivity disorder (ADHD). *Clinical Psychology Review, 28*, 801–820.
Torpy, J. M., Burke, A., E., & Golub, R. M. (2011). Generalized anxiety disorder. *Journal of the American Medical Association, 305*, 522. doi:10.1001/jama.305.5.522
Torres, L, Driscoll, M. W., & Voell, M. (2012). Discrimination, acculturation, acculturative stress, and Latino psychological distress: A moderated mediational model. *Cultural Diversity and Ethnic Minority Psychology, 18*, 17–25. doi:10.1037/a0026710
Torrey, E. F. (2011). The association of stigma with violence [Letter]. *American Journal of Psychiatry, 168*, 325. doi:10.1176/appi.ajp.2011.10121710.

Torrey, E. F. (2011). The association of stigma with violence. *American Journal of Psychiatry, 168,* 325. [Letter] doi: 10.1176/appi.ajp.2011.10121710

Torrey, E. F., & Zdanowicz, M. (1999, May 28). A right to mental illness? *PsychLaws.Org.* Retrieved from http://www.psychlaws.org/GeneralResources/article14.htm

Town, J. M., Diener, M. J., Abbass, A., Leichsenring, F., Driessen, E., & Rabung, S. (2012). A meta-analysis of psychodynamic psychotherapy outcomes: Evaluating the effects of research-specific procedures. *Psychotherapy, 49,* 276–290. doi: 10.1037/a0029564

Towner, B. (2009, March). 50 and still a doll. *AARP Bulletin, 50,* p. 35.

Treanor, M. (2011). The potential impact of mindfulness on exposure and extinction learning in anxiety disorders. *Clinical Psychology Review, 31,* 617–625. doi:10.1016/j.cpr.2011.02.003

Treffert, D. A. (1988). The idiot savant: A review of the syndrome. *American Journal of Psychiatry, 145,* 563–572.

Trimble, J. E. (1991). The mental health service and training needs of American Indians. In H. F. Myers et al. (Eds.), *Ethnic minority perspectives on clinical training and services in psychology* (pp. 43–48). Washington, DC: American Psychological Association.

Tseng, W., Mo, K. M., Li, L. S., Chen, G. Q., Ou, L. W., & Zheng, H. B. (1992). Koro epidemics in Guangdong, China: A questionnaire survey. *The Journal of Nervous and Mental Disease, 180,* 117–123.

Tsunemi, T., Ashe, T. D., Morrison, B. E., Soriano, K. R., Au, J., Vázquez Roque, R. A., . . La Spada, A. R. (2012). PGC-1α rescues Huntington's Disease proteotoxicity by preventing oxidative stress and promoting TFEB function. *Science Translational Medicine, 4,* 142ra97. doi: 10.1126/scitranslmed.3003799.

Turkington, D., & Morrison, A. P. (2012). Cognitive therapy for negative symptoms of schizophrenia. *Archives of General Psychiatry,69,* 119–120. doi:10.1001/archgenpsychiatry.2011.141

Turner, S. M., & Beidel, D. C. (1989). Social phobia: Clinical syndrome, diagnosis, and comorbidity. *Clinical Psychology Review, 9,* 3–18.

U

U.S. Department of Health and Human Services, Substance Abuse and Mental Health Services Administration, Center for Mental Health Services, National Institutes of Health, National Institute of Mental Health. (1999). *Mental Health: A Report of the Surgeon General.* Rockville, MD: Author.

U.S. Department of Health and Human Services, Substance Abuse and Mental Health Services Administration, Center for Mental Health Services, National Institutes of Health, National Institute of Mental Health. (2001). *Mental health: Culture, race, and ethnicity: A supplement to mental health: A report of the Surgeon General—Executive summary.* Rockville, MD: Author.

Uddin, L. Q., Menon, V., Young, C. B., Ryali, S., Chen, T., Khouzam, A., . . . Hardan A. Y. (2011). Multivariate searchlight classification of structural magnetic resonance imaging in children and adolescents with autism. *Biological Psychiatry, 70,* 833–841. doi: 10.1016/j.biopsych.2011.07.014

Uher, R., & Perroud, N. (2010). Probing the genome to understand suicide. *American Journal of Psychiatry, 167,* 1425–1427. doi:10.1176/appi.ajp.2010.10081227

Uhl, G. R., & Grow, R. W. (2004). The burden of complex genetics in brain disorders. *Archives of General Psychiatry, 61,* 223–229.

UK ECT Review Group. (2003). Efficacy and safety of electroconvulsive therapy in depressive disorders: A systematic review and meta-analysis. *Lancet, 361,* 799–808.

Uliaszek, A. A., Zinbarg, R. E., Mineka, S., Craske, M. G., Griffith, J. W., Sutton, J. M., . . . Hammen, C. (2012). A longitudinal examination of stress generation in depressive and anxiety disorders. *Journal of Abnormal Psychology, 121,* 4–15. doi:10.1037/a0025835

Unützer, J., & Park, M. (2012). Older adults with severe, treatment-resistant depression. *Journal of the American Medical Association, 308,* 909–918. doi:10.1001/2012.jama.10690

Urbanoski, K. A., & Kelly, J. F. (2012). Understanding genetic risk for substance use and addiction: A guide for non-geneticists. *Clinical Psychology Review, 32,* 60–70. doi:10.1016/j.cpr.2011.11.002 |

Ursu, S., Kring, A. M., Gard, M. G., Minzenberg, M. J., Yoon, J. H., Ragland, J. D., . . Carter, C. S. (2011). Prefrontal cortical deficits and impaired cognition-emotion interactions in schizophrenia. *American Journal of Psychiatry, 168,* 276–285

Utsey, S. O., Chae, M. H., Brown, C. F., & Kelly, D. (2002). Effect of ethnic group membership on ethnic identity, race-related stress, and quality of life. *Cultural Diversity and Ethnic Minority Psychology, 8,* 366–377.

V

Vázquez, F. L., Torres, A., Blanco, V., Díaz, O., & Otero, P., & Hermida, E. (2012). Comparison of relaxation training with a cognitive-behavioural intervention for indicated prevention of depression in university students: A randomized controlled trial. *Journal of Psychiatric Research, in press.*

Vázquez, F. L., Torres, A., Blanco, V., Díaz, O., & Otero, P., & Hermida, E. (2012). Comparison of relaxation training with a cognitive-behavioural intervention for indicated prevention of depression in university students: A randomized controlled trial. *Journal of Psychiatric Research, 46,* 1456–1463. doi: 10.1016/j.jpsychires.2012.08.007

Vøllestad, J., Sivertsen, B., & Nielsen, G. H. (2011). Mindfulness-based mindfulness-based stress reduction for patients with anxiety disorders: Evaluation in a randomized controlled trial. *Behaviour Research and Therapy, 49,* 281–288. doi:10.1016/j.brat.2011.01.007

Vacic, V., McCarthy, S., Malhotra, D., Murray, F., Chou, H.-H., Peoples, A., . . . Sebat, J. (2011). Duplications of the neuropeptide receptor gene VIPR2 confer significant risk for schizophrenia. *Nature, 471,* 499–503. doi: 10.1038/nature0988

Valasquez-Manoff, M. (2012, August 26). An immune disorder at the root of autism. *The New York Times, Sunday Review,* pp. 1, 12.

Valenti, O., Cifelli, P., Gill, K. M, & Grace, A. A. (2011). Antipsychotic drugs rapidly induce dopamine neuron depolarization block in a developmental rat model of schizophrenia. *Journal of Neuroscience, 31,* 12330-12338. doi: 10.1523/JNEUROSCI.2808-11.2011

Van Allen, J., & Roberts, M. C. (2011). Critical incidents in the marriage of psychology and technology: A discussion of potential ethical issues in practice, education, and policy. *Professional Psychology: Research and Practice, 42,* 433–439. doi: 10.1037/a0025278

van den Hout, M. A., Engelhard, I. M., Rijkeboer, M. M., Koekebakker, J., Hornsveld, H., Leer, A. . . . Aksea, N. (2011). EMDR: Eye movements superior to beeps in taxing working memory and reducing vividness of recollections. *Behaviour Research and Therapy, 49,* 92–98. doi:10.1016/j.brat.2010.11.00

van der Kloet, D., Giesbrecht, T., Lynn, S. J., Merckelbach, H., & de Zutter, A. (2012). Sleep normalization and decrease in dissociative experiences: Evaluation in an inpatient sample. *Journal of Abnormal Psychology, 12,* 140–150. doi:10.1037/a0024781

van der Loos, M. L. M., Mulder, P. G., Hartong, E. G., Blom, M. B., Vergouwen, A. C., de Keyzer, H. J., . . . Nolen, W. A. (2009). Efficacy and safety of lamotrigine as add-on treatment to lithium in bipolar depression: A multicenter, double-blind, placebo-controlled trial. *Clinical Psychiatry, 70,* 223–231.

Van der Oord, S., Prins, P. J. M., Oosterlaan, J., & Emmelkamp, P. M. G. (2008). Efficacy of methylphenidate, psychosocial treatments and their combination in school-aged children with ADHD: A meta-analysis. *Clinical Psychology Review, 28,* 783–800.

van der Waerden, J. E., B., Hoefnagels, C., & Hosman, C. M. (2011). Psychosocial preventive interventions to reduce depressive symptoms in low-SES women at risk: A meta-analysis. *Journal of Affective Disorders, 128,* 10–23. doi:10.1016/j.jad.2010.02.137

van Lankveld, J. J., Granot, M., Willibrord, C. M., Schultz, W., Binik, Y. M., Wesselmann, U. , . . Achtrari, C. (2010). Women's sexual pain disorders. *Journal of Sexual Medicine, 7,* 615–631.

van Lankveld, J. J., Granot, M., Weijmar Schultz, W. C., Binik, Y. M., Wesselmann, U., Pukall, C. F., . . . Achtrari, C. (2010). Women's sexual pain disorders. *Journal of Sexual Medicine, 7,* 615–631. doi: 10.1111/j.1743-6109.2009.01631.x.

Van Meter, A. R., Youngstrom, E. A., & Findling, R. L. (2012). Cyclothymic disorder: A critical review, in press. *Clinical Psychology Review, 32,* 229–243. doi: 10.1016/j.cpr.2012.02.001

Van Meter, A. R., Youngstrom, E. A., & Findling, R. L. (2012). Cyclothymic disorder: A critical review. *Clinical Psychology Review, 32*(4), 229–243.

Van Susteren, L. (2002). The insanity defense, continued [Editorial]. *The Journal of the American Academy of Psychiatry and the Law, 30,* 474–475.

van Tol, M.-J., van der Wee, N. J. A., van den Heuvel, O. A., Nielen, M. M. A., Demenescu, L. R., Aleman, A., . . . Veltman, D. J. (2010). Regional brain volume in depression and anxiety disorders. *Archives of General Psychiatry, 67,* 1002–1011. doi:10.1001/archgenpsychiatry.2010.121

van Veelen, N. M., J., Vink, M., Ramsey, N. F. , & Kahn, R. S. (2010). Left dorsolateral prefrontal cortex dysfunction in medication-naive schizophrenia. *Schizophrenia Research, 123,* 22–29.

van Zessen, R., Phillips, J. L., Budygin, E. A., & Stuber, G. D. (2012). Activation of VTA GABA neurons disrupts reward consumption. *Neuron, 73,* 1184–1194. doi:10.1016/j.neuron.2012.02.016

VanderCreek, L., & Knapp, S. (2001). *Tarasoff and beyond: Legal and clinical considerations in the treatment of life-endangering patients.* Sarasota, FL: Professional Resource Press.

Vanderkam, L. (2003). *Barbie and fat as a feminist issue.* Retrieved from http://www.shethinks.org/articles/an00208.cfm

Varley, C. K., & McClellan, J. (2009). Implications of marked weight gain associated with atypical antipsychotic medications in children and adolescents. *Journal of the American Medical Association, 302,* 1811.

Vasey, M. W., Vilensky, M. R., Heath, J. H., Harbaugh, C. N., Buffington, A. G., & Fazio, R. H. (2012). It was as big as my head, I swear! *Journal of Anxiety Disorders, 26,* 20. doi:10.1016/j.janxdis.2011.08.009

Vaziri-Bozorg, S. M ., Ghasemi-Esfe, A.R., Khalilzadeh, O., Sotoudeh, H., Rokni-Yazdi, H.,. . . Shakiba, M. (2012). Antidepressant effects of magnetic resonance imaging—based stimulation on major depressive disorder: a double-blind randomized clinical trial. *Brain Imaging and Behavior, 6,* 70–76. doi: 10.1007/s11682-011-9143-2

Vega, W. A., Kolody, B., Aguilar-Gaxiola, S., Alderete, E., Catalano, R., Caraveo-Anduaga, J. (1998). Lifetime prevalence of DSM-III-R psychiatric disorders among urban and rural Mexican Americans in California. *Archives of General Psychiatry, 55,* 771–778.

Vega, W. A., Rodriguez, M. A., & Ang, A. (2010). Addressing stigma of depression in Latino primary care patients. *General Hospital Psychiatry, 32*(2), 182–191. doi: 10.1016/j.genhosppsych.2009.10.008

Veilleux, J. C., Colvin, P. J., Anderson, J., York, C., & Heinz, A. J. (2010). A review of opioid dependence treatment: Pharmacological and psychosocial interventions to treat opioid addiction. *Clinical Psychology Review, 30,* 155–166. doi:10.1016/j.cpr.2009.10.006

Vellante, M., Larøi, F., Cella, M., Raballo, A., Petretto, D. R., & Preti, A. (2012). Hallucination-like experiences in the nonclinical population. *Journal of Nervous and Mental Disease, 200,* 310–315. doi: 10.1097/NMD.0b013e31824cb2ba

Venner, K. L., Greenfield, B. L., Vicuña, B., Muñoz, R., Bhatt, S., & O'Keefe, V. (2012). "I'm not one of them": Barriers to help-seeking among American Indians with alcohol dependence. *Cultural Diversity and Ethnic Minority Psychology, 18,* 352–362. doi: 10.1037/a0029757

Vermetten E., Schmah, C., Lindner, S., Loewenstein, R. J., & Bremner, J. D. (2006). Hippocampal and amygdalar volumes in dissociative identity disorder. *American Journal of Psychiatry, 163,* 630–636.

Vickers, K., & McNallly, R. J. (2005). Respiratory symptoms and panic in the National Comorbidity Survey: A test of Klein's suffocation false alarm theory. *Behaviour Research and Therapy, 43,* 1011–1018.

Viguera, A. C., Tondo, L., Koukopoulos, A. E., Reginaldi, D., Lepri, B., & Baldessarini, R. J. (2011). Episodes of mood disorders in 2,252 pregnancies and postpartum periods. *American Journal of Psychiatry, 168,* 1179–1185. doi:10.1176/appi.ajp.2011.11010148

Vincent, N., & Walsh, K. (2013). Hyperarousal, sleep scheduling, and time awake in bed as mediators of outcome in computerized cognitive-behavioral therapy (cCBT) for insomnia. *Behaviour Research and Therapy,* 5, 161–166. doi: 10.1016/j.brat.2012.12.003.

Virués-Ortega, J. (2010). Applied behavior analytic intervention for autism in early childhood: Meta-analysis, meta-regression and dose–response meta-analysis of multiple outcomes. *Clinical Psychology Review, 30,* 387–399. doi: 10.1016/j.cpr.2010.01.008

Vismara, L. A., & Rogers, S. J. (2010). Behavioral treatments in autism spectrum disorder: what do we know? *Annual Review of Clinical Psychology, 6*, 447–468. doi: 10.1146/annurev.clinpsy.121208.131151

Visser, S. N., Bitsko, R. H., Danielson, M. L, & Perou, R. (2010). Increasing prevalence of parent-reported attention-deficit/hyperactivity disorder among children —United States, 2003 and 2007. *Morbidity and Mortality Weekly (MMWR), 59*, 1439–1443.

Vital signs: Binge drinking among high school students and adults—United States, 2009. (2010). *Morbidity and Mortality Weekly Report, Journal of the American Medical Association, 304*, 2474–2478.

Vitaliano, P. P., Zhang, J., & Scanlan, J. M. (2003). Is caregiving hazardous to one's physical health? A meta-analysis. *Psychological Bulletin, 129*, 946–972.

Vitiello, B., Elliott, G. R., Swanson, J. M., Arnold, L. E., Hechtman, L., Abikoff, H., . . Gibbons, R. (2012). Blood pressure and heart rate over 10 years in the multimodal treatment study of children with ADHD. *American Journal of Psychiatry, 169*, 167–177. 10.1176/appi.ajp.2011.10111705

Vitiello, M. V. (2009). Recent advances in understanding sleep and sleep disturbances in older adults: Growing older does not mean sleeping poorly. *Current Directions in Psychological Science, 18*, 316–320. doi: 10.1111/ j.1467-8721.2009.01659.x

Voelker, R. (2012). Asthma forecast: Why heat, humidity trigger symptoms. *Journal of the American Medical Association, 308*, 20–20. doi:10.1001/jama.2012.7533 Text Size

Voineagu, I., Wang, X., Johnston, J., Lowe, J. K., Tian, Y., Horvath, S., . . . Geschwind, D. H. (2011). Transcriptomic analysis of autistic brain reveals convergent molecular pathology. *Nature, 474*, 380–384. doi:10.1038/nature10110

Volavka, J. & Swanson, J. (2010). Violent behavior in mental illness: The role of substance abuse. *Journal of the American Medical Association, 304*, 563–564. doi:10.1001/jama.2010.1097

Volkow, N. D. (2006). Map of human genome opens new opportunities for drug abuse research. *NIDA Notes, 20(4)*, 3.

Vorstenbosch, V., Antony, M. M., Koerner, N., & Boivin, M. (2011). Assessing dog fear: Evaluating the psychometric properties of the Dog Phobia Questionnaire. *Journal of Behavior Therapy and Experimental Psychiatry, 43*, 780–786.

Voruganti, L. N. P., & Awad, A. G. (2007). Role of dopamine in pleasure, reward and subjective responses to drugs. In M. S. Ritsner & A. G. Awad (Eds.), *Quality of life impairment in schizophrenia, mood and anxiety disorders* (pp. 21–31). Netherlands: Springer.

Vos, P., De Cock, P., Munde, V., Petry, K., Van Den Noortgate, W., & Maes, B. (2012). The tell-tale: What do heart rate; skin temperature and skin conductance reveal about emotions of people with severe and profound intellectual disabilities? *Research in Developmental Disabilities, 33*, 1117–1127.

W

Wade, T. D., & Tiggemann, M. (2013). The role of perfectionism in body dissatisfaction. *Journal of Eating Disorders, 1*, 2. doi: 10.1186/2050-2974-1-2

Wadsworth, M. E., & Achenbach, T. M. (2005). Explaining the link between low socioeconomic status and psychopathology: Testing two mechanisms of the social causation hypothesis. *Journal of Consulting and Clinical Psychology, 73*, 1146–1153.

Wagner, B, Schulz, W., & Knaevelsrud, C. (2011). Efficacy of an Internet-based intervention for posttraumatic stress disorder in Iraq: A pilot study. *Psychiatry Research, 195*, 85–88. doi:10.1016/j.psychres.2011.07.026

Wainwright, N. W. J., & Surtees, P. G. (2002). Childhood adversity, gender and depression over the life-course. *Journal of Affective Disorders, 72*, 33–44.

Waldinger, M. D. (2011). The management of premature ejaculation. *Current Clinical Urology, Part 5*, 709–720.

Waldman, I. D., & Gizera, I. R. (2006). The genetics of attention deficit hyperactivity disorder. *Clinical Psychology Review, 26*, 396–432.

Walker, E., Shapiro, D., Esterberg, M. & Trotman, H. (2010). Neurodevelopment and schizophrenia: Broadening the focus. *Psychological Science, 19*, 204–208. doi: 10.1177/0963721410377744

Walkup, J. T., Albano, A. M., Piacentini, J., Birmaher, B., Compton, S. N., Sherrill, J. T., et al. (2008). Cognitive behavioral therapy, sertraline, or a combination in childhood anxiety. *New England Journal of Medicine, 359*, 2753–2766.

Waller, H., Garety, P. A., Jolley, S., Fornells-Ambrojo, M., Kuipers, E., Onwumere, J., Emsley, T. C., . . . Craig, T. (2012). Low intensity cognitive behavioural therapy for psychosis: A pilot study. *Journal of Behavior Therapy and Experimental Psychiatry, 44*, 98–104. doi: 10.1016/j.jbtep.2012.07.013

Waller, N. G., & Ross, C. A. (1997). The prevalence of biometric structure of pathological dissociation in the general population: Taxometric and behavior genetic findings. *Journal of Abnormal Psychology, 106*, 499–510.

Wallis, C. (2009, November 3). A powerful identity, a vanishing diagnosis. *The New York Times*, pp. D1, D4.

Walsh, B. T., et al. (2000). Fluoxetine for bulimia nervosa following poor response to psychotherapy. *American Journal of Psychiatry, 157*, 1332–1334.

Walsh, B. T., Fairburn, C. G., Mickley, D., Sysko, R., & Parides, M. K. (2004). Treatment of bulimia nervosa in a primary care setting. *American Journal of Psychiatry, 161*, 556–561.

Walsh, B. T., Kaplan, A. S., Attia, E., Olmsted, M., Parides, M., Carter, J. C., et al. (2006). Fluoxetine after weight restoration in anorexia nervosa: A randomized controlled trial. *Journal of the American Medical Association, 295*, 2605–2612.

Walsh, R. (2011). Lifestyle and mental health. *American Psychologist, 66*, 579–592. doi:10.1037/a0021769

Walters, J. T., R., Corvin, A., Owen, M. J., Williams, H., Dragovic, M., . . . Donohoe, G., Psychosis susceptibility gene ZNF804A and cognitive performance in schizophrenia. *Archives of General Psychiatry, 67*, 692–700. doi:10.1001/archgenpsychiatry.2010.81

Wampold, B. E. (2001). *The great psychotherapy debate: Models, methods, and findings.* Mahwah, NJ: Erlbaum.

Wampold, B. E., Stephanie, L. B., Laska, K. M., Del Re, A. C., Baardseth, T. P., Flűckiger,C., Minamic, T., . . . Gunn, W. (2011). Evidence-based treatments for depression and anxiety versus treatment-as-usual: A meta-analysis of direct comparisons. *Clinical Psychology Review, 31*, 1304–1312. doi:10.1016/j.cpr.2011.07.012

Wang, L., Hermens, D.F., Hickie, I.B., & Lagopoulos J. (2012).. A systematic review of resting-state functional-MRI studies in major depression. *Journal of Affective Disorders, 142*, 6–12.

Wang, P. S., Lane, M., Olfson, M., Pincus, H. A., Wells, K. B., & Kessler, R. C. (2005). Twelve-month use of mental health services in the United States: Results from the National Comorbidity Survey Replication. *Archives of General Psychiatry, 62*, 590–592.

Wang, S. S. (2011, April 19). New guidelines for spotting Alzheimer's. *The Wall Street Journal*, p. D4.

Wang, Z., Byrne, N. M., Kenardy, J. A., & Hills, A. P. (2005). Corresponding influences of ethnicity and socioeconomic status on the body dissatisfaction and eating behaviour of Australian children and adolescents. *Eating Behaviors, 6*, 23–33.

Wartik, N. (2000, June 25). Depression comes out of hiding. *The New York Times*, pp. MH1, MH4.

Watkins, K. E., Hunter, S. B., Hepner, K. A., Paddock, S. M., de la Cruz, E., Zhou, A. J., & Gilmore, J. (2011). An effectiveness trial of group cognitive behavioral therapy for patients with persistent depressive symptoms in substance abuse treatment. *American Journal of Psychiatry, 68*, 577–584. doi:10.1001/archgenpsychiatry.2011.53

Watson, J. B., & Rayner, R. (1920). Conditioned emotional reactions. *Journal of Experimental Psychology, 3*, 1–14.

Weaver, F. W., Follett, K., Stern, M., Hur, K., Harris, C., Marks, W. J., Jr., et al. (2009). Bilateral deep brain stimulation vs. best medical therapy for patients with advanced Parkinson disease: A randomized controlled trial. *Journal of the American Medical Association, 301*, 63–73.

Weber, L. (2013, January 23). Go ahead, hit the snooze button. *Wall Street Journal*, pp. B1, B8.

Webster-Stratton, C., Reid, J., & Hammond, M. (2001). Social skills and problem-solving training for children with early-onset conduct problems: Who benefits? *Journal of Child Psychology & Psychiatry & Allied Disciplines, 42*, 943–952.

Wechsler, D. (1975). Intelligence defined and undefined: A relativistic appraisal. *American Psychologist, 30*, 135–139.

Wechsler, H., & Nelson, T. F. (2008). What we have learned from the Harvard School of Public Health College Alcohol Study: Focusing attention on college student alcohol consumption and the environmental conditions that promote it. *Journal of Studies on Alcohol and Drugs, 69*, 481.

Weck, F., Bleichhardt, G., Witthöft, M., & Hiller, W. (2011). Explicit and implicit anxiety: Differences between patients with hypochondriasis, patients with anxiety disorders, and healthy controls. *Cognitive Therapy and Research, 35*, 317–325. doi:10.1007/s10608-010-9303-5

Weed, W. S. (2003, December 14). Questions for Raymond Damadian: Scanscam? *The New York Times.* Retrieved from www.nytimes.com

Weems, C. F., Hayward, C., Killen, J., & Taylor, C. B. (2002). A longitudinal investigation of anxiety sensitivity in adolescence. *Journal of Abnormal Psychology, 111*, 471–477.

Weems, C. F., Pina, A. A., Costa, N. M., Watts, S. E., Taylor, L. K., & Cannon, M. F. (2007). Predisaster trait anxiety and negative affect predict posttraumatic stress in youths after Hurricane Katrina. *Journal of Consulting and Clinical Psychology, 75*, 154–159.

Wei, C.-C., Wan, L., Lin, W.-Y., & Tsai, F.-J. (2010). Rs 6313 polymorphism in 5-hydroxytryptamine receptor 2A gene association with polysymptomatic primary nocturnal enuresis. *Journal of Clinical Laboratory Analysis, 24*, 371–375. doi: 10.1002/jcla.20386

Weiner, I. B., Spielberger, C. D., & Abeles, N. (2003). Once more around the park: Correcting misinformation about Rorschach assessment. *The Clinical Psychologist, 56*, 8–9.

Weiner, J. R. (2003). Tarasoff warnings resulting in criminal charges: Two case reports. *The Journal of the American Academy of Psychiatry and the Law, 31*, 239–241.

Weintraub, K. (2011). The prevalence puzzle: Autism counts. *Nature, 479*, 22–24. doi:10.1038/479022a

Weir, K. (2012, December). Big kids. *Monitor on Psychology, 43*, pp.58–63

Weir, K. (2012, June). The roots of mental illness. *Monitor on Psychology, 43*, 30–33.

Weiss, R. D., & Mirin, S. M. (1987). *Cocaine.* Washington, DC: American Psychiatric Press.

Weissman, A. N., & Beck, A. T. (1978). *Development and validation of the Dysfunctional Attitudes Scale: A preliminary investigation.* Paper Presented at the Annual Meeting of the American Educational Research Association, Toronto, Ontario, CA.

Weissman, M. M. (2007). Cognitive therapy and interpersonal psychotherapy: 30 years later. *American Journal of Psychiatry, 164*, 693–696.

Weissman, M. M. (2011). Can epidemiology translate into understanding major depression with borderline personality disorder? *American Journal of Psychiatry, 168*, 231–233. doi: 10.1176/appi.ajp.2010.10121737

Weissman, M. M., Bruce, M. L., Leaf, P. J., Florio, L. P., & Holzer, C. (1991). Affective disorders. In L. N. Robins & D. A. Regier (Eds.), *Psychiatric disorders in America: The Epidemiologic Catchment Area Study* (pp. 53–80). New York: Free Press.

Weissman, M. M., Markowitz, J. C., & Klerman, G. L. (2000). *Comprehensive guide to interpersonal psychotherapy.* New York: Basic Books.

Weissman, M. M., Pilowsky, D. J., Wickramaratne, P. J., Talati, A., Wisniewski, S. R., Fava, C.W., et al. (2006). Remissions in maternal depression and child psychopathology: A STAR*D-child report. *Journal of the American Medical Association, 295*, 1389–1398.

Weisstaub, N. V., Zhou, M., Lira, A., Lambe, E., González-Maeso, J., Hornung, J. P., . . . Gingrich, J. A. (2006). Cortical 5-HT2A receptor signaling modulates anxiety-like behaviors in mice. *Science, 313*, 536–540.

Weisz, J. R., Southam-Gerow, M. A., Gordis, E. B., Connor-Smith, J. K., Chu, B. C., Langer, D. A., et al. (2009). Cognitive–behavioral therapy versus usual clinical care for youth depression: An initial test of transportability to community clinics and clinicians. *Journal of Consulting and Clinical Psychology, 77*, 383–396. doi: 10.1037/ a0013877

Weisz, J. R., Suwanlert, S., Chaiyasit, W., Weiss, B., Walter, B. R., & Anderson, W. W. (1988). Thai and American perspectives on over- and undercontrolled child behavior problems: Exploring the threshold model among parents, teachers, and psychologists. *Journal of Consulting and Clinical Psychology, 56*, 601–609.

Wells, K. B., & Miranda, J. (2006). Promise of interventions and services research: Can it transform practice? *Clinical Psychology: Science and Practice, 13*, 99–104.

Welte, G. M., Barnes, G. M., Tidwell, M. C. O., & Hoffman, J. H. (2008). The prevalence of problem gambling among

U.S. adolescents and young adults: Results from a national survey. *Journal of Gambling Studies, 24,* 119–133.

Wenzel, A., Finstroma, N., Jordan, J., & Brendle, J. R. (2005). Memory and interpretation of visual representations of threat in socially anxious and nonanxious individuals. *Behaviour Research and Therapy, 43,* 1029–1044.

Wessell, R., & Edwards, C. (2010). Biological and psychological interventions: Trends in substance use disorders intervention research. *Addictive Behaviors, 35,* 1083–1088. doi:10.1016/j.addbeh.2010.07.009

Westen, D., & Gabbard, G. O. (2002). Developments in cognitive neuroscience: 1. Conflict, compromise, and connectionism. *Journal of the American Psychoanalytic Association, 50,* 53–98.

Wexler, B. E., Gottschalk, C. H., Fulbright, R. K., Prohovnik, I., Lacadie, C. M., Rounsaville, B. J., & Gore, J. C. (2001). Functional magnetic resonance imaging of cocaine craving. *American Journal of Psychiatry, 158,* 86–95.

Wheaton, M. G., Deacon, B. J., McGrath, P. B., Berman, N. C., & Abramowitz, J. S. (2012). Dimensions of anxiety sensitivity in the anxiety disorders: Evaluation of the ASI-3. *Journal of Anxiety Disorders, 26,* 401–408. http://dx.doi.org/10.1016/j.janxdis.2012.01.002

Wheaton, S (2001). Personal accounts: Memoirs of a compulsive firesetter. Psychiatric Service, 62, 1035–1036.

Whittal, M. L, Robichaud, M., Thordarson, D. S., & McLean, P. D. (2008). Group and individual treatment of obsessive-compulsive disorder using cognitive therapy and exposure plus response prevention: A 2-year follow-up of two randomized trials. *Journal of Consulting and Clinical Psychology, 76,* 1003–1014.

Whitten, L. (2009). Receptor complexes link dopamine to long-term neuronal effects. *NIDA Notes, 22* (4), 15–16.

Whooley, M. A., de Jonge, P., Vittinghoff, E., Otte, C., Moos, R., Carney, R. M., . . . Browner, W. S. (2008). Depressive symptoms, health behaviors, and risk of cardiovascular events in patients with coronary heart disease. *Journal of the American Medical Association, 300,* 2379–2388.

Whooley, M. A., Kiefe, C. I., Chesney, M. A., Markovitz, J. H., Matthews, K., & Hulley, S. B. (2002). Depressive symptoms, unemployment, and loss of income: The CARDIA Study. *Archives of Internal Medicine, 162,* 2614–2620.

Wicks, S., Hjern, A, & Dalman, C. (2010). Social risk or genetic liability for psychosis? A study of children born in Sweden and reared by adoptive parents. *American Journal of Psychiatry, 167,* 1240–1246. http://dx.doi.org/10.1176/appi.ajp.2010.09010114

Widaman, K. F. (2009). Phenylketonuria in children and mothers: Genes, environments, behavior. *Current Directions in Psychological Science, 18,* 48–52. doi: 10.1111/j.1467-8721.2009.01604.x

Widiger, T. A., & Simonsen, E. (2005). Alternative dimensional models of personality disorder: Finding a common ground. *Journal of Personality Disorders, 19,* 110–130.

Wierck, K., Van Caenegem, E., Elaut, E., Dedecker, D., Van de Peer, F., Toye, K., . . . Sjoen, G. (2011). Quality of life and sexual health after sex reassignment surgery in transsexual men. *Journal of Sexual Medicine, 8,* 3379–3388.

Wierman, M. E., Nappi, R. E., Avis, N., Davis, S. R., Labrie, F., Rosner, W., & Shifren, J. L. (2010). Endocrine aspects of women's sexual function. *Journal of Sexual Medicine, 7,* 561–585.

Wierman, M. E., Rossella, E., Nappi, E., Avis, N., Davis, S. R., Labrie, F., Rosner, W., . . . Shifren, J. L. (2010). Endocrine aspects of women's sexual function. *Journal of Sexual Medicine, 7,* 561–585. doi:10.1111/j.1743-6109.2009.01629.x

Wijeysundera H.C., Machado M, Farahati, F., Wang, X., Witteman, W., van der Velde, G. . . . . Capewell, S. (2010). Association of temporal trends in risk factors and treatment uptake with coronary heart disease mortality, 1994–2005. *Journal of the American Medical Association, 303,* 1841–1847.

Wilbur, C. B. (1986). Psychoanalysis and multiple personality disorder. In B. G. Braun (Ed.), *Treatment of multiple personality disorder* (pp. 6–28). Washington, DC: American Psychiatric Press.

Wilcox, H. C., Storr, C. L., & Breslau, N. (2009). Posttraumatic stress disorder and suicide attempts in a community sample of urban American young adults. *Archives of General Psychiatry, 66,* 305–311.

Wild Man brings back bad memories. (2009, June 4). *West Side Spirit,* p. 4.

Williams, D. (1992). *Nobody nowhere: The extraordinary autobiography of an autistic.* New York: Times Books.

Williams, N. M., Franke, B., Mick, E., Anney, R. J. L., Freitag, C. M., Gill, M., . . Faraone, S. V. (2012). Genome-wide analysis of copy number variants in attention deficit hyperactivity disorder: the role of rare variants and duplications at 15q13.3. *American Journal of Psychiatry, 169,* 195–204. doi: 10.1176/appi.ajp.2011.11060822

Williams, R. B., Marchuk, D. A., Gadde, K. M., Barefoot, J. C., Grichnik, K., Helms, M. J., et al.. . . Siegler, I. C. (2003). Serotonin-related gene polymorphisms and central nervous system serotonin function. *Neuropsychopharmacology, 28,* 533–541.

Wilson, D. (2011, April 13). As generics near, makers tweak erectile drugs. *The New York Times.* Retrieved from www.nytimes.com

Wilson, G. T., Grilo, C. M., & Vitousek, K. (2007). Psychological treatments for eating disorders. *American Psychologist, 62,* 199–216.

Wilson, G. T., Wilfley, D. E., Agras, W. S., & Bryson, S. W. (2010). Psychological treatments of binge eating disorder. *Archives of General Psychiatry, 67,* 94–101.

Wilson, K. A., & Hayward, C. (2006). Unique contributions of anxiety sensitivity to avoidance: A prospective study in adolescents. *Behaviour Research and Therapy, 44,* 601–609.

Winblad, B., Andreasen, N., Minthon, L., Floesser, A., Imbert, G., Dumortier, T., Maguire, R. P., . . Graf, A. (2012). Safety, tolerability, and antibody response of active Aß immunotherapy with CAD106 in patients with Alzheimer's disease: Randomised, double-blind, placebo-controlled, first-in-human study. *The Lancet Neurology, 11,* 597–604. doi: 10.1016/S1474-4422(12)70140-0

Winerip, M. (1998, January 4). Binge nights. *The New York Times,* 4A (Education Section), pp. 28–31, 42.

Winerman, L. (2004, May). Panel stresses youth suicide prevention. *Monitor on Psychology, 35* (5), 18.

Wingert, P. (2000, December 4). No more "afternoon nasties." *Newsweek,* p. 59.

Winstanley, C. A., Eagle, D. M., & Robbins, T. W. (2006). Behavioral models of impulsivity in relation to ADHD: Translation between clinical and preclinical studies. *Clinical Psychology Review, 26,* 379–395.

Wipfli, B., Landers, D., Nagoshi, C., & Ringenbach, S. (2010). An examination of serotonin and psychological variables in the relationship between exercise and mental health. *Scandinavian Journal of Medicine & Science in Sports, 21* (3), 474–481. doi:10.1111/j.1600-0838.2009.01049

Witkiewicz, K., & Marlatt, G. A. (2004). Relapse prevention for alcohol and drug problems: That was Zen, this is Tao. *American Psychologist, 59,* 224–235.

Witte, T. K., Timmons, K. A., Fink, E., Smith, A. R., & Joiner, T. E. (2009). Do major depressive disorder and dysthymic disorder confer differential risk for suicide? *Journal of Affective Disorders, 115,* 69–78. doi:10.1016/j.jad.2008.09.003

Wittstein, I. S., Thiemann, D. R., Lima, J. A. C., Baughman, K. L., Schulman, S. P., Gerstenblith, G., . . . Champion, H. C. (2006). Neurohumoral features of myocardial stunning due to sudden emotional stress. *New England Journal of Medicine, 352,* 539–548.

Witvliet, M., Brendgen, M., van Lier, P. A. C., Koot, H. M., & Vitaro, F. (2010). Early adolescent depressive symptoms: Prediction from clique isolation, loneliness, and perceived social acceptance. *Journal of Abnormal Child Psychology, 38,* 1045–1056. doi: 10.1007/s10802-010-9426-

Wolf, N. J., & Hopko, D. R. (2008). Psychosocial and pharmacological interventions for depressed adults in primary care: A critical review. *Clinical Psychology Review, 28,* 131–136.

Wolff, J. J., Gu, H., Gerig, G., Elison, J. T., Styner, M., Gouttard, S., . . . the IBIS. (2012). Network differences in white matter fiber tract development present from 6 to 24 months in infants with autism. *American Journal of Psychiatry, 169,* 589–600. 10.1176/appi.ajp.2011.11091447

Wolitzky, D. L. (2011). Psychoanalytic theories of psychotherapy. In J. C. Norcross, G. R. VandenBos, & D. K. Freedheim (Eds.), *History of psychotherapy: Continuity and change* (2nd ed.) (pp. 65–100). Washington, DC: American Psychological Association.

Wolitzky, D. L. (2011). Psychoanalytic theories of psychotherapy. In J. C. Norcross, G. R. VandenBos, & D. K. Freedheim (Eds.), *History of psychotherapy: Continuity and change* (2nd ed.,) (pp. 65–100). Washington, DC: American Psychological Association.

Wolpe, J. (1958). *Psychotherapy by reciprocal inhibition.* Palo Alto, CA: Stanford University Press

Wolpe, J., & Lazarus, A. A. (1966). *Behavior therapy techniques.* New York: Pergamon Press.

Women more at risk of mental illness than men (2012, January 20). *MSNBC.com.* Retrieved from http://www.msnbc.msn.com/id/46056751/ns/health-mental_health/#.TxiBj29Q6Ag.

Wong, C. L., Holroyd-Leduc, J., Simel, D. L., & Straus, S. E. (2010). Does this patient have delirium? *Journal of the American Medical Association, 304,* 779–786. doi:10.1001/jama.2010.118

Wong, C. L., Holroyd-Leduc, J., Simel, D. L., & Straus, S. E. (2010). Does this patient have delirium? Value of bedside instruments. *Journal of the American Medical Association, 304,* 779–786.

Wong, P. W. C., Fu, K.-W., Chan, K. Y. K., Chan, W. S. C., Liu, P. M. Y., Law, Y.-W., & Yip, P. S. F. (2012). Effectiveness of a universal school-based programme for preventing depression in Chinese adolescents: A quasi-experimental pilot study. *Journal of Affective Disorders, 142,* 106–114.

Woods, B., Spector, A. E., Prendergast, L., & Orrell, M. (2012). Cognitive stimulation to improve cognitive functioning in people with dementia. *The Cochrane Review,* published online. doi: 10.1002/14651858.CD005562

Woodward, N. D., Karbasforoushan, H., & Heckers, S. (2012). Thalamocortical dysconnectivity in schizophrenia. *American Journal of Psychiatry, 169,* 1092–1099.

Woody, G. E., Poole, S. A., Subramaniam, G., Dugosh, K., Bogenschutz, M., Abbott, P., . . . Fudala, P. (2008). Extended vs. short-term buprenorphine-naloxone for treatment of opioid-addicted youth: Randomized trial. *Journal of the American Medical Association, 300,* 2003–2011.

Wu, L.-T., Woody, G. E., Yang, C., Pan, J.-J., & Blazer, D. G. (2011). Racial/ethnic variations in substance-related disorders among adolescents in the United States. *Archives of General Psychiatry, 68,* 1176–1185. doi:10.1001/archgenpsychiatry.2011.120

Wu, R., Baob, J., Zhang, C., Deng, J., & Long, C. (2006). Comparison of sleep condition and sleep-related psychological activity after cognitive-behavior and pharmacological therapy for chronic insomnia. *Psychotherapy and Psychosomatics, 75,* 220–228.

Wykes, T., Huddy, V., Cellard, C., McGurk, S. R., & Czobor, P. (2011). A meta-analysis of cognitive remediation for schizophrenia: Methodology and effect sizes. *American Journal of Psychiatry, 168,* 472–485. doi: 10.1176/appi.ajp.2010.10060855

X

Xiao, L., Han, J., & Han, J. (2011). The adjustment of new recruits to military life in the Chinese Army: The longitudinal predictive power of MMPI-2. *Journal of Career Assessment, 19,* 392–404.

Xie, P., Kranzler, H. R., Poling, J., Stein, M. B., Anton, R. F., Brady, K., Weiss, R. D., Gelernter, J. (2009). Interactive effect of stressful life events and the serotonin transporter 5-httlpr genotype on posttraumatic stress disorder diagnosis in 2 independent populations. *Archives of General Psychiatry, 66,* 1201–1209.

Xiong P., Zeng, Y., Zhu, Z., Tan, D., Xu, F., Lu, J., Wan, J., & Ma, M. (2010). Reduced NGF serum levels and abnormal P300 event-related potential in first episode schizophrenia. *Schizophrenia Research, 119,* 34–39.

Y

Yücel, M., Solowij, N., Respondek, C., Whittle, S., Fornito, A., Pantelis, C., . . . Lubman, D. I. (2008). Regional brain abnormalities associated with long-term heavy cannabis use. *Archives of General Psychiatry, 65,* 694–701.

Yaccino, S. (2012, December 20). Arrests in a freshman's drinking death reflect a tougher approach. *The New York Times.* Retrieved from www.nytimes.com.

Yager, J. (2003, December 23). Is there something fishy about bipolar disorder? *Journal Watch Psychiatry.* Retrieved from http://psychiatry.jwatch.org/cgi/content/full/2003/1223/5?q=etoc

Yager, J. (2008, May 23). Attempted suicides in anorexia nervosa. *Journal Watch Psychiatry.* Retrieved from http://psychiatry.jwatch.org/cgi/content/full/2008/523/2

Yager, J. (2011). Eating disorders over 6 years: *DSM-IV* and *DSM-V* perspectives. *Journal Watch Psychiatry.* Retrieved from http://psychiatry.jwatch.org/cgi/content/full/2011/228/2?q=etoc_jwpsych

Yager, J. (2011, August 29). Genetics of psychosocial stress-induced alcohol consumption. *Journal Watch Psychiatry.* Retrieved from http://psychiatry.jwatch.org

Yager, J. (2011, January 10). Real-time study of substance use and psychotic symptoms. *Journal WatchPsychiatry.*

Retrieved from http://psychiatry.jwatch.org/cgi/content/full/2011/110/3 press.

Yang, M., Wong, S. C. P.W, & Coid, J. (2010). The efficacy of violence prediction: A meta-analytic comparison of nine risk assessment tools. *Psychological Bulletin, 136,* 740–746.

Yang, Q., Rasmussen, S. A., & Friedman, J. M. (2002). Mortality associated with Down's syndrome in the USA from 1983 to 1997: A population-based study. *The Lancet, 359,* 1019–1025.

Yang, Q., She, H., Gearing, M., Colla, E., Lee, M., Shacka, J. J., & Mao, Z. (2009). Regulation of neuronal survival factor MEF2D by chaperone-mediated autophagy. *Science, 323,* 124 – 127. doi: 10.1126/science.1166088

Yanovski, S. Z., & Yanovski, J. A. (2011). Obesity prevalence in the United States — up, down, or sideways? *New England Journal of Medicine, 364,* 987–989. http://healthpolicyandreform.nejm.org/?p=13941&query=home

Yates, P. M., Hucker, S. J., & Kingston,, D. A. (2008). Sexual sadism: Psychopathology and theory. In D. R. Laws & W. T. O'Donohue (Eds), *Sexual deviance: Theory, assessment, and treatment* (2nd ed., pp. 213–230). New York: Guilford Press.

Yatham, L. N. (2011). A clinical review of aripiprazole in bipolar depression and maintenance therapy of bipolar disorder. *Journal of Affective Disorders, 128,* S21–S28.

Yeargin-Allsopp, M., Rice, C., Karapurkan, T., Doernberg, N., Boyle, C., & Murphy, C. (2003). Prevalence of autism in a US metropolitan area. *Journal of the American Medical Association, 289,* 49–55.

Yeh, C. J. (2003). Age, acculturation, cultural adjustment, and mental health symptoms of Chinese, Korean, and Japanese immigrant youths. *Cultural Diversity and Ethnic Minority Psychology, 9,* 34–48.

Yeung, A., Howarth, S., Chan, R., Sonawalla, S., Nierenberg, A. A., & Fava, M. (2002). Use of the Chinese version of the Beck Depression Inventory for screening depression in primary care. *Journal of Nervous & Mental Disease, 190,* 94–99.

Young, E. A., McFatter, R., & Clopton, J. R. (2001). Family functioning, peer influence, and media influence as predictors of bulimic behavior. *Eating Behaviors, 2,* 323–337.

Youngstrom, E. A. (2009). Definitional issues in bipolar disorder across the life cycle. *Clinical Psychology: Science and Practice, 16,* 140–160. doi:10.1111/j.1468-2850.2009.01154.x

Young-Wolff, K. C., Enoch, M.-A., & Prescott, C. A. (2011). The influence of gene–environment interactions on alcohol consumption and alcohol use disorders: A comprehensive review. *Clinical Psychology Review, 31,* 800–816. doi:10.1016/j.cpr.2011.03.005

Yuen, E. K., Goetter, E. M., Herbert, J. D., & Forman, E. M. (2012). Challenges and opportunities in Internet-mediated telemental health. *Professional Psychology: Research and Practice, 43,* 1–8. doi: 10.1037/a0025524

Z

Zamanian, K., Thackrey, M., Starrett, R.A. & Brown, L.G. et al. (1992). Acculturation and depression in Mexican-American elderly. *Gerontologist, 11,* 109–121.

Zamanian, K., Thackreyb, M., Starretta, R. A., Browna, L. G., Lassmanc, D. K., & Blanchard, A. (1992). Acculturation and depression in Mexican-American elderly. *Gerontologist, 11,* 109–121.

Zanarini, M. C., Frankenburg, F. R., Reich, D. B., & Fitzmaurice, G. (2012). Attainment and stability of sustained symptomatic remission and recovery among patients with borderline personality disorder and Axis II comparison subjects: a 16-year prospective follow-up study. *American Journal of Psychiatry, 169,* 476–483.

Zanarini, M. C., Skodol, A. E., Bender, D., Dolan, R., Sanislow, C., Schaefer, E., . . . Gunderson, J. G. (2000). The Collaborative Longitudinal Personality Disorders Study: Reliability of Axis I and II diagnoses. *Journal of Personality Disorders, 14,* 291–299.

Zane, N., & Sue, S. (1991). Culturally responsive mental health services for Asian Americans: Treatment and training issues. In H. F. Myers et al. (Eds.), *Ethnic minority perspectives on clinical training and services in psychology* (pp. 49–58). Washington, DC: American Psychological Association.

Zapf, P. A., & Roesch, R. (2011). Future directions in the restoration of competency to stand trial. *Current Directions in Psychological Science, 20,* 43–47. doi:10.1177/0963721410396798

Zavos, H. M. S., Gregory, A. M., & Eley, T. C. (2012). Longitudinal genetic analysis of anxiety sensitivity. *Developmental Psychology, 48,* 204–212. doi:10.1037/a0024996

Zebenholzer, K., Rudel, E., Frantal, S., Brannath, W., Schmidt, K., & Wöber-Bingöl, C., (2011). Migraine and weather: A prospective diary-based analysis. *Cephalalgia, 31,* 391.

Zebenholzer, K., Rudel, E., Frantal, S., Brannath, W., Schmidt, K., Wöber-Bingöl, C., & Wöber, C.. (2011). Migraine and weather: A prospective diary-based analysis. *Cephalalgia, 31,* 391.

Zhang, T.-Y., & Meaney, M. J. (2010). Epigenetics and the environmental regulation of the genome and its function. *Annual Review of Psychology, 61,* 439–466. doi: 10.1146/annurev.psych.60.110707.163625Vol. 61: 439–466

Zhao, Y. L., Tan, S. P., Yang, F., Wang, L., Feng, W., Chan, R. C. K., & Zou, Y. Z. (2011). Dysfunction in different phases of working memory in schizophrenia: Evidence from ERP recordings. *Schizophrenia Research, 133,* 112–119.

Zhou, X., Dere, J., Zhu, X., Yao, S., Chentsova-Dutton, Y. E., & Ryder, A. J. (2011). Anxiety symptom presentations in Han Chinese and Euro-Canadian outpatients: Is distress always somatized in China? *Journal of Affective Disorders, 135,* 111–114.

Zickler, P. (2006) Smoking decreases key enzyme throughout body: Research findings. *NIDA Notes, 19.* Retrieved from www.drugabuse.gov

Ziermans, T. B., Schothorst, P. F., Sprong, M., Magnée, M. J. C. M., van Engeland, H., & Kemner, C. (2012). Reduced prepulse inhibition as an early vulnerability marker of the psychosis prodrome in adolescence. *Schizophrenia Research, 134,* 10–15.

Zimmermann, P., Brückl, T., Nocon, A., Pfister, H., Binder, E. B., . . . Ising, M. (2011). Interaction of FKBP5 gene variants and adverse life events in predicting depression onset: Results from a 10-year prospective community study. *American Journal of Psychiatry, 168,* 1107–1116. doi: 10.1176/appi.ajp.2011.10111577

Zivanovic, O., & Nedic, A. (2012). Kraepelin's concept of manic-depressive insanity: One hundred years. *Journal of Affective Disorders, 137,* 15–24.

Zlomuzica, A., Silva, M. D. S., Huston, J., & Dere, E. (2007). NMDA receptor modulation by D-cycloserine promotes episodic-like memory in mice. *Psychopharmacology.* Retrieved from http://lib.bioinfo.pl/pmid:17497136

Zou, J. B., Dear, B. F., Titov, N., Lorian, C. N., Johnston, L., Spence, J., . . . Sachdev, P. (2012). Brief Internet-delivered cognitive behavioral therapy for anxiety in older adults: A feasibility trial. *Journal of Anxiety Disorders, 26,* 650–655.

Zou, Y.-F., Wang, F., Feng, X.-L., Li, W.-F., Tian, Y.-H., Tao, J.-H., . . . Huang, F. (2012). Association of DRD2 gene polymorphisms with mood disorders: A meta-analysis. *Journal of Affective Disorders, 136,* 229–237.

Zuroff, D. C., & Blatt, S. (2006). Therapeutic relationship in the brief treatment of depression: Contributions to clinical improvement and enhanced adaptive capacities. *Journal of Consulting and Clinical Psychology, 74,* 130–140.

Zuvekas, S. H., & Vitiello, B. (2012). Stimulant medication use in children: A 12-year perspective. *American Journal of Psychiatry, 169,* 160–166.

Zvolensky, M. J., & Eifert, G. H. (2001). A review of psychological factors/processes affecting anxious responding during voluntary hyperventilation and inhalations of carbon dioxide-enriched air. *Clinical Psychology Review, 21,* 375–400.

Zvolensky, M. J., Kotov, R., Antipova, A. V., & Schmidt, N. B. (2005). Diathesis stress model for panic-related distress: A test in a Russian epidemiological sample. *Behaviour Research and Therapy, 43,* 521–532.

Zwilling, D., Huang, S.-Y., Sathyasaikumar, K. V., Notarangelo, F. M., Guidetti, P., Wu, H.-Q., Lee, J., . . . Muchowski, P. J. (2011). Kynurenine 3-monooxygenase inhibition in blood ameliorates neurodegeneration. *Cell, 145,* 863–874. doi: 10.1016/j.cell.2011.05.02

Photo Credits

Chapter 1 **page 1:** Millennium Images/SuperStock;**page 6:** Kenneth Benjamin Reed/ Shutterstock; **page 7:** Fotolia; **page 8:** Arne Hodalic/Corbis; **page 10:** Bierwert/American Museum of Natural History Library; **page 11:** (bottom) The Granger Collection, NYC; **page 11:** (top) The Granger Collection, NYC; **page 12:** The Granger Collection, NYC; **page 13:** Bettmann/Corbis; **page 14:** Guy Bell/Alamy; **page 15:** VStock/Alamy; **page 16:** Bettmann/Corbis; **page 17:** (left) The Granger Collection, NYC — All rights reserved; **page 17:** (right) The Granger Collection, NYC — All rights reserved; **page 18:** Ultra.F/ Alamy; **page 22:** Alix Minde/Getty Images; **page 25:** Image Source/Corbis; **page 29:** LadyInBlack/Fotolia.

Chapter 2 **page 35:** Yuri Arcurs Media/SuperStock; **page 40:** CNRI/Science Source; **page 43:** Gabriel M. Covian/Getty Images; **page 45:** Duman Laboratory/Nature Medicine; **page 48:** Aubord Dulac/Fotolia; **page 49:** (bottom) Getty Images; **page 49:** (top) Darren Brode/Fotolia; **page 50:** (bl) Bettmann/Corbis; **page 50:** (bm) Bettmann/Corbis; **page 50:** (br) PhotoEdit, Inc.; **page 50:** (top) Warner Brothers Pictures/Topham/The Image Works; **page 52:** The Granger Collection, NYC; **page 53:** Nina Leen/Time Life Pictures/Getty Images; **page 56:** Steven Puetzer/Getty Images; **page 57:** Alexander Yakovlev/Fotolia; **page 58:** (bottom) Ann Kaplan/Bettmann/Corbis; **page 58:** (top) Michael Rougier/Time & Life Pictures/Getty Images; **page 59:** (bottom) Albert Ellis Institute; **page 59:** (top) Fotolia; **page 60:** Aaron T. Beck, M.D.; **page 62:** Syracuse University Library; **page 68:** Zigy Kaluzny/Getty Images; **page 69:** Fotolia; **page 70:** Lisa F. Young/Fotolia; **page 71:** Drawing by Mike Ewers. Reprinted by permission.; **page 75:** (bottom) Michael Newman/ PhotoEdit, Inc; **page 75:** (top) Yuri Arcurs/Fotolia; **page 77:** Martinan/Fotolia; **page 80:** Nancy Sheehan/PhotoEdit, Inc.; **page 84:** © 2009 Dave Blazek. Distributed by Tribune Media Services, Inc.; **page 87:** Will McIntyre/Science Source.

Chapter 3 **page 91:** Ocean/Corbis; **page 97:** Marcel Jancovic/Shutterstock; **page 99:** Tom Wang/Fotolia; **page 104:** (bottom) The Image Works ; **page 104:** (top) Thomas A. Widiger; **page 105:** Iurii Sokolov/Fotolia; **page 107:** IT Stock Free/Jupiter Images/ Getty Images; **page 113:** Pearson Education/PH College; **page 114:** Reprinted by permission of the publishers from Henry A. Murray, THEMATIC APPERCEPTION TEST, Cambridge, Mass.: Harvard University Press, © 1943 by the President and Fellows of Harvard College, © 1971 by Henry A. Murray; **page 119:** Courtesy of the National Center for PTSD; **page 120:** Matthew Cole/Fotolia; **page 122:** Richard T. Nowitz/Corbis; **page 123:** (bottom) Science Source; **page 123:** (top) Scott Camazine/Photo Researchers, Inc.; **page 124:** (bottom left) Alexander Tsiaras/Science Source/Photo Researchers, Inc.; **page 124:** (top) Science Source; **page 125:** (bottom) Hank Morgan/Photo Researchers, Inc.; **page 125:** (middle) Tim Beddow/Photo Researchers, Inc.; **page 125:** (top) WDCN/ Univ. College London/Science Source.

Chapter 4 **page 129:** Science Photo Library/SuperStock; **page 133:** Biology Media/ Science Source/Photo Researchers, Inc.; **page 134:** Corbis/SuperStock; **page 135:** IN THE BLEACHERS ©2006 Steve Moore. Reprinted with permission of UNIVERSAL PRESS SYNDICATE. All rights reserved; **page 137:** (left) Katrina Brown/Fotolia; **page 137:** (right) Yuri Arcurs/Fotolia; **page 139:** Michael Newman/PhotoEdit, Inc.; **page 142:** Charles Negy, Ph.D.; **page 144:** Getty Images; **page 145:** Kadmy/Fotolia; **page 146:** Picture India/Corbis; **page 149:** Justin Lane/Epa/Landov; **page 150:** Dave Schwarz/St. Cloud Times/AP Images; **page 152:** Aaron Ontiveroz/Getty Images ; **page 154:** Pearson Education.

Chapter 5 **page 157:** Exactostock/SuperStock ; **page 161:** Petro Feketa/Fotolia; **page 169:** (bpttom right) Bill Aron/PhotoEdit, Inc.; ; **page 169:** (top left) Geri Engberg/Geri Engberg Photography; **page 169:** (top right) Denkou Images/Getty Images; ; **page 175:** National Institute of Mental Health, 2008; **page 176:** Peter Waters/Fotolia; **page 179:** Photo by Jim Whitmer; **page 181:** Bebeto Matthews/AP Images; **page 183:** Erin Patrice O'Brien/Photodisc/Getty Images; **page 189:** Pete Armstrong/Fotolia; **page 190:** Kasia Bialasiewicz/Fotolia; **page 191:** Auremar/Fotolia; **page 194:** Courtesy of Jamie Feusner, M.D; **page 195:** Michael Maloney/San Francisco Chronicle/Corbis.

Chapter 6 **page 198:** Holger Scheibe/Corbis; **page 203:** Diana Ong/SuperStock ; **page 206:** Photo courtesy of the Denver Police Department/The Olympian/MCT/Newscom; **page 207:** Nicole Bengiveno/The New York Times/Redux Pictures; **page 208:** Sergey Panychev/Fotolia; **page 211:** Jeff Siner/The Charlotte Observer; **page 214:** Jaimie Duplass/ Shutterstock; **page 217:** 20th Century-Fox Film Corp. All Rights Reserved/Everett Collection; **page 220:** Terry Vine/Getty Images; **page 223:** Image Source/Getty Images; **page 226:** Getty Images; **page 229:** Dalaprod/Fotolia; **page 233:** EastWest Imaging/ Fotolia; **page 234:** Littleny/Fotolia.

Chapter 7 **page 242:** Pixtal/SuperStock ; **page 244:** Sean Gallup/Getty Images; **page 246:** Voyagerix/Fotolia; **page 247:** The Corcoran Gallery of Art/Corbis; **page 250:** Dave Anthony/Taxi/Getty Images; **page 251:** Laurent/Laeticia/Photo Researchers, Inc.;

page 255: PacificCoastNews/Newscom; **page 256:** Loomis Dean/Time & Life Pictures/ Getty Images; **page 259:** Elwynn/Shutterstock; **page 261:** Yuri Arcurs/Fotolia; **page 262:** Corbis; **page 263:** Yuri Arcurs/Fotolia; **page 267:** Noel Hendrickson/Digital Vision/Getty Images; **page 270:** Lunamarina/Fotolia; **page 272:** Geoff Manasse/Getty Images; **page 277:** Will McIntyre/Photo Researchers, Inc.; **page 279:** Bonnie Weller/MCT /Landov ; **page 284:** Gemeente Museum, The Hague, Netherlands/SuperStock, Inc; **page 285:** Geri Engberg/The Image Works.

Chapter 8 **page 289:** Exactostock/SuperStock ; **page 293:** (left) Nyul/Fotolia; **page 293:** (right) Fotolia; **page 296:** Janine wiedel/Alamy; **page 299:** (bottom) Corbis; **page 299:** (top) Getty Images; **page 300:** Courtesy of The Sam Spady Foundation; **page 301:** Corbis; **page 304:** Don Farrall/Getty Images; **page 310:** Fotolia; **page 315:** Littleny/ Fotolia ; **page 319:** Shutterstock; **page 321:** Ted. S. Warren/AP Images; **page 322:** Yuri Arcurs/Fotolia; **page 326:** Kraevski/Fotolia.

Chapter 9 **page 333:** Tomas Rodriguez/Corbis; **page 338:** Hkannn/Shutterstock; **page 340:** Chamillew/Fotolia; **page 343:** REUTERS/L'Equipe Agence/ HO/Landov; **page 344:** The Image Works; **page 346:** Tom Raymond/Getty Images; **page 352:** Russell D. Curtis/Photo Researchers, Inc.; **page 355:** Pictor/ImageState; **page 356:** Fotolia; **page 360:** Ogust/The Image Works.

Chapter 10 **page 364:** Janice Alamanou/Alamy; **page 366:** Dr. Jayne Thomas, Deceased/Peg Greene; **page 367:** Barry King/Getty Images; **page 370:** (left) Getty Images; **page 370:** (right) George Holton/Photo Researchers, Inc.; **page 372:** Noel Hendrickson/ Getty Images; **page 377:** SuperStock; **page 380:** NBC/Getty Images; **page 385:** Randy Matusow; **page 388:** Getty Images; **page 391:** SuperStock; **page 394:** Shutterstock.

Chapter 11 **page 402:** Elena Kulikova/Getty Images; **page 404:** Bob Strong/AFP/ Getty Images; **page 408:** Ron Chapple/Taxi/Getty Images; **page 411:** (bottom) Robert Churchill/Getty Images; **page 411:** (top) Bettmann/Corbis; **page 413:** Peter Casolino/ ZUMAPRESS/Newscom; **page 415:** Grunnitus Studio/Science Source; **page 420:** (bottom) Nancy C. Andreasen, M.D./University of Iowa Hospitals & Clinics; **page 420:** (top) Courtesy of Paul Thompson, Laboratory of Neuro Imaging at UCLA.; **page 422:** David Lees/Corbis; **page 424:** Diego Cervo/Fotolia; **page 426:** Fotolia; **page 431:** Getty Images; **page 434:** Superstock.

Chapter 12 **page 438:** Mercè Bellera/Getty Images; **page 443:** Tony Savino/The Image Works; **page 444:** Mark Foley/AP Images; **page 446:** Bettmann/Corbis; **page 449:** Dr. P. Marazzi/Photo Researchers, Inc.; **page 451:** Catherine Ledner/Getty Images; **page 454:** Kzenon/Fotolia; **page 457:** Laima E. Druskis/Pearson Education/PH College; **page 458:** Marlene Ford/Flickr/Getty Images; **page 462:** Elena Efimova/Shutterstock; **page 463:** Hector Mata/AFP/Newscom; **page 465:** Diego Cervo/Fotolia; **page 467:** Science Photo Library/Custom Medical Stock Photo; **page 476:** Jerry L. Deffenbacher.

Chapter 13 **page 479:** Bastienne Schmidt/Gallery Stock/Galeries/Corbis; **page 482:** (bottom) Lee Lorenz/The New Yorker Collection/www.cartoonbank.com; **page 482:** (top) Tony Freeman/PhotoEdit, Inc.; **page 483:** M. Siluk/The Image Works; **page 487:** Robin Nelson/PhotoEdit, Inc.; **page 489:** Robin Nelson/PhotoEdit, Inc.; **page 491:** Michael Bergmann; **page 493:** Richard Hutchings/Photo Researchers, Inc.; **page 497:** Courtesy of American Institute of Physics; **page 498:** Dr. Judith Rumsey/National Institute of Mental Health; **page 499:** Bela Szandelszky/AP Images; **page 500:** Permission granted by DR. Marcel Just (Carnege Mellon University); **page 502:** Corbis; **page 504:** National Institute of Mental Health,Image Library. http://infocenter.nimh.nih.gov/il/public_il/image_details. cfm?id=291; **page 506:** SuperStock; **page 509:** Corbis; **page 511:** K Miragaya/Fotolia; **page 515:** Michael Newman/PhotoEdit, Inc.; **page 518:** Palco Labs, Inc.

Chapter 14 **page 522:** Exactostock/SuperStock; **page 525:** SuperStock; **page 531:** Mark J. Terrill/AP Images; **page 532:** Robert P. Friedland, MD, Case Western Reserve University; **page 533:** AP Images; **page 534:** Spike Walker/Getty Images; **page 535:** Shutterstock; **page 538:** George Gojkovich/Getty Images; **page 540:** JERRY LAMPEN/ Reuters/Corbis; **page 542:** Catherine Bauknight/ZUMA/Corbis; **page 543:** Robert Kneschke/Fotolia; **page 544:** Wissmann Design/Fotolia; **page 545:** Diego Cervo/Fotolia.

Chapter 15 **page 548:** Gary S Chapman/Getty Images; **page 550:** (bottom) Rj Sangosti/AFP/Getty Images/Newscom; **page 550:** (top) U.S. Marshals Service/ ZUMAPRESS/Newscom; **page 552:** Newscom; **page 555:** AP Images; **page 557:** (bottom) Charles Bennett/AP Images; **page 557:** (top) Republic Pictures/Getty Images; **page 561:** AP Images; **page 563:** Brendan Smialowski/Reuters/Corbis; **page 567:** Pool, Red Huber/ AP Images.

Text Credits

Chapter 1 **page 2:** Original Material; **page 2:** Excerpt from pp.27–8 from Moodswing by Ronald R. Fieve, M.D., Copyright © 1975 by Ronald Fieve. Reprinted by permission of Harper Collins Publishers.; **page 3:** Campbell, T. (2000). First person account: Falling on the pavement. Schizophrenia Bulletin, 26, 507–509; **page 4:** Source: Kessler, Chiu, et al., 2005a; Kessler, Kessler, Demler, et al., 2005b.; **page 4:** Satcher, 2000; USDHHS, 1999b; **page 8:** Kleinman, A. (1987). Anthropology and psychiatry: The role of culture in cross-cultural research on illness. British Journal of Psychiatry, 151, 447–454. Printed with permission.; **page 17:** as cited in Sulloway, 1983, p. 32.

Chapter 2   **page 61:** Source: Breslau et al., 2005, based on data from the National Comordibity Survey (NCS).; **page 63:** From Nevid. Psychology, 4E. © 2013 Wadsworth, a part of Cengage Learning Inc. Reproduced by permission. www.cengage.com/permissions; **page 66:** From Nevid. Psychology, 4E. © 2013 Wadsworth, a part of Cengage Learning Inc. Reproduced by permission. www.cengage.com/permissions; **page 69:** Reprinted by permission of Basic Books, a member of Perseus Books Group.; **page 82:** Sources: adapted from Cheung, 1991, López et al., 2012, Sanders Thompson, Bazile, & Akbar, 2004, Sue et al., 2012; Venner et al., 2012, and other sources.

Chapter 3   **page 92:** Source: Excerpted from "Panic Disorder: The Case of Jerry," found on the Videos in Abnormal Psychology CD-ROM that accompanies this textbook.; **page 98:** Source: Adapted from the DSM-5 (APA, 2013); Dzokoto & Adams (2005); and other sources.; **page 103:** Thomas Widiger; **page 108:** From Nevid. Psychology, 4E. © 2013 Wadsworth, a part of Cengage Learning Inc. Reproduced by permission. www.cengage.com/permissions; **page 109:** Sample items similar to those in the Wechsler Adult Intelligence Scale (WAIS). Copyright © 1955,1997 NCS Pearson, Inc. Reproduced with permission. All rights reserved.; **page 117:** —From the Author's Files; **page 119:** Source: US Department of Veterans Affairs.

Chapter 4   **page 130:** From, "Women at Ground Zero: Stories of Courage and Compassion," by Susan Hagen and Mary Carouba, Copyright © 2002, DK Publishing. Reprinted by permission of DK Publishing, a division of Penguin Group Inc. (USA). ; **page 132:** Source of data: Adapted from American Psychological Association (2010). Stress in America 2011: Executive Summary. ; **page 136:** Source: Reprinted from "Managing traumatic stress: Tips for recovering from disasters and other traumatic events," with permission of the American Psychological Association, ; **page 141:** Charles Negy; **page 143:** Kobasa, S. C., Maddi, S. R., & Kahn, S. (1982). Hardiness and health: A prospective study. Journal of Personality and Social Psychology, 42, 168–177.; **page 148:** Sources: APA, 2000, 2013; Conway et al., 2006; Grant et al., 2005a; Grant et al., 2006b, 2006c; Kessler et al., 1995, 2005a; Ozer & Weiss, 2004.; **page 150:** Sources: Afifi et al., 2010; Elwood et al., 2009; Goenjian et al., 2008; Koenen, Stellman, & Stellman, 2003; North et al., 2012; Ozer et al., 2003; Xie et al., 2009, among other sources.

Chapter 5   **page 178:** From RATHUS. Essentials of Psychology, 6E. © 2001 Wadsworth, a part of Cengage Learning, Inc. Reproduced bypermission. www.cengage.com/permissions; **page 187:** Ian Osborne, Tormenting Thoughts and Secret Rituals: The Hidden Epidemic of Obsessive-Compulsive Disorder, Random House, 1998. ; **page 192:** Pacemaker for brain may ease mental illness. (2008, November 12). Retrieved from http://www.msnbc.msn.com/id/27684083/ (602 words); **page 194:** Source: Obsessive-Compulsive Disorder: The Facts by Rachman & DeSilva (2009) 250 word excerpt from pp. 37–38. By permission of Oxford University Press. .

Chapter 6   **page 199:** Source: From "Quiet Storm," a pseudonym used by a woman who claims to have several personalities residing within her.; **page 207:** cited in Marx, R. F., & Didziulis, V. (2009, March 1). A life, interrupted. The New York Times, pp. CY1, CY7. ; **page 209:** Based on Spitzer, R. L., et al. (1994). DSM-IV case book (4th ed.). Washington, DC: American Psychiatric Association.; **page 210:** Elizabeth Loftus,Eyewitness Testimony (1996, p.356) Harvard University Press. ; **page 212:** Based on Spitzer, R. L., et al. (1994). DSM-IV case book (4th ed.). Washington, DC: American Psychiatric Association.; **page 216:** Adapted from Wilbur, C. B. (1986). Psychoanalysis and multiple personality disorder. In B. G. Braun (Ed.), Treatment of multiplepersonality disorder. Washington, DC: American Psychiatric Association.; **page 220:** Based on Spitzer, R. L., et al. (1994). DSM-IV case book (4th ed.). Washington, DC: American Psychiatric Association.; **page 223:** Source: Gregory, J. (2003). Sickened:The memoir of a Münchausen by proxy childhood. New York: Bantam.; **page 229:** Thiedke, C. C., Therapy and hypochondriacs often make poor mix, study Says. Nocturnal enuresis. American Family Physician,67,1509–1510.; **page 235:** Depression ups risk of complications following heart attack,study suggests. ScienceDaily. Retrieved from www.sciencedaily.com/releases/2008/07/080701194736.htm.

Chapter 7   **page 243:** William Styron, Darkness Visible: A Memoir of Madness, Random House. ; **page 246:** T. Thompson, "The Beast is Back". Printed with permission of Beth Vesel Literary Agency; **page 248:** Based on Spitzer, R. L., et al. (1994). DSM-IV case book (4th ed.). Washington, DC: American Psychiatric Association.; **page 250:** J. Joorman, et al., "Sticky Thoughts: Depression and Rumination are Associated with Difficulties Manipulating Emotional Material in Working Memory" Psychological Science 2011 Aug;22(8):979-83.; **page 252:** Source:. D. Blum & M. Kirchner (1997). Depression at work. Customs Today, Winter issue. Quotes used with permission of the National Mental Health Association. ; **page 253:** Based on Spitzer, R. L., et al. (1994). DSM-IV case book (4th ed.). Washington, DC: American Psychiatric Association.; **page 255:** From Jamison, K. R. (1995). An unquiet mind. New York: Knopf.; **page 256:** Behrman, Andy, Electroboy, (2002) New York: Random House. ; **page 258:** Based on Spitzer, R. L., et al.

(1994). DSM-IV case book (4th ed.). Washington, DC: American Psychiatric Association.; **page 273:** Beck, A. T., Rush, A. J., Shaw, B. F., & Emery, G. (1979). Cognitive therapy of depression. New York: Guilford Press.; **page 285:** From Nevid. Psychology, 4E. © 2013 Wadsworth, a part of Cengage Learning Inc. Reproduced by permission. www.cengage.com/permissions.

Chapter 8   **page 290:** From Weiss, R. D., & Mirin, S. M. (1987). Cocaine. Washington, DC:American Psychiatric Association.; **page 317:** From Nevid. Psychology, 4E. © 2013 Wadsworth, a part of Cengage Learning Inc. Reproduced by permission. www.cengage.com/permissions; **page 317:** Source: Childress et al., 2008.; **page 329:** Source: Childress et al., 2008.; **page 327:** Source: Pearson Education, Speaking Out: DVD for Abnormal Psychology Volume 2, 2nd Ed., ©2008. Reprinted and Electronically reproduced by permission of Pearson Education, Inc., Upper Saddle River, New Jersey.

Chapter 9   **page 334:** Copyright (1997) From Your Dieting Daughter: Is She Dying for Attention? by Carolyn Costin. Reproduced by permission of Taylor and Francis Group, LLC, a division of Informa plc. ; **page 341:** Source: Normandi & Rorak, 1998.; **page 342:** Source: Pearson Education, Speaking Out: DVD for Abnormal Psychology Volume 2, 2nd Ed., ©2008. Reprinted and Electronically reproduced by permission of Pearson Education, Inc., Upper Saddle River, New Jersey. ; **page 354:** Source: Pearson Education, Speaking Out: DVD for Abnormal Psychology Volume 2, 2nd Ed., ©2008. Reprinted and Electronically reproduced by permission of Pearson Education, Inc., Upper Saddle River, New Jersey. ; **page 358:** —From Hayes, B. (2001). Sleep demons:An insomniac's memoir. New York: Washington Square Press.

Chapter 10   **page 365:** Dr. Jayne Thomas; **page 368:** Dr. Jayne Thomas; **page 377:** Based on Spitzer, R. L., et al. (1994). DSM-IV case book (4th ed.). Washington, DC: American Psychiatric Association.; **page 388:** Based on Spitzer, R. L., et al. (1994). DSM-IV case book (4th ed.). Washington, DC: American Psychiatric Association.; **page 398:** Reprinted from Men Who Rape by A.N. Groth. Available from Basic Books, an imprint of The Perseus Books Group. Copyright © 1979.

Chapter 11   **page 403:** From The Quiet Room by Lori Schiller and Amanda Bennett. Copyright © 1994 by Lori Schiller and Amanda Bennett. By permission of Grand Central Publishing. All rights reserved.; **page 428:** From The Quiet Room by Lori Schiller and Amanda Bennett. Copyright © 1994 by Lori Schiller and Amanda Bennett. By permission of Grand Central Publishing. All rights reserved.; **page 434:** Adapted from Goldstein, 1986, p. 802; **page 433:** Based on Spitzer, R. L., et al. (1994). DSM-IV case book (4th ed.). Washington, DC: American Psychiatric Association.

Chapter 12   **page 442:** Based on Spitzer, R. L., et al. (1994). DSM-IV case book (4th ed.). Washington, DC: American Psychiatric Association.; **page 445:** Data from Kessler et al., 1994; **page 447:** Based on Spitzer, R. L., et al. (1994). DSM-IV case book (4th ed.). Washington, DC: American Psychiatric Association.; **page 453:** Source: Hotchkiss, S. (2002). Why is it always about you? The seven deadly sins of narcissism. Free Press. (Simon and Schuster); **page 455:** Based on Spitzer, R. L., et al. (1994). DSM-IV case book (4th ed.). Washington, DC: American Psychiatric Association.; **page 475:** — JERRY DEFFENBACHER.

Chapter 13   **page 480:** Williams, D. (1992). Nobody nowhere:The extraordinary autobiography of an autistic. New York: Times Books.; **page 488:** "There's a boy in here" published by Future Horizons--www.fhautism.com. Printed with permission.; **page 495:** Based on Spitzer, R. L., et al. (1994). DSM-IV case book (4th ed.). Washington, DC: American Psychiatric Association.; **page 504:** Based on Spitzer, R. L., et al. (1994). DSM-IV case book (4th ed.). Washington, DC: American Psychiatric Association.; **page 507:** Adapted from Kaplan, S. J. (1986). The private practice of behavior therapy: A guide for behavioral practitioners. New York: Plenum Press. With kind permission from Springer Science+Business Media B.V.

Chapter 14   **page 531:** Source: From McGowin, 1993. Living in the labyrinth: A personal journey through the maze of Alzheimer's. Dell Publishing.; **page 537:** Source: Adapted from Nevid, J. S., & Rathus, S. A. (2013). Adjustment and growth: The challenges of life (12th ed.), p. 484. Hoboken, NJ: John Wiley and Sons. Reprinted with permission.; **page 538:** Freemon, F. R. (1981). Organic mental disease. Jamaica, NY: Spectrum.

Chapter 15   **page 554:** Wild Man brings back bad memories. (2009, June 4). West Side Spirit, p. 4. New York Press. Printed with permission of New York Press.; **page 558:** Source: U.S. Supreme Court, O'Connor v. Donaldson; **page 559:** Source: U.S. Supreme Court, Youngberg v. Romeo; **page 562:** The John Hinckley trial (Hinkley's communications with Jodie Foster). Retrieved from http://www.law.umkc.edu/faculty/projects/ftrials/hinckley/hinckleytrial.html; **page 564:** The English M'Naghten case 1843; **page 564:** Source: U.S. Supreme Court, Durham v. United States of 1954; **page 566:** Source: U.S.Supreme Court, Jones v. United States.

author index

Cognitive triad of depression, 262

Cognitive-behavioral therapy (CBT), 60, 73
for binge-eating disorder, 349
for bipolar disorder, 280
for childhood anxiety disorders, 510–511
for childhood depression, 512
for disruptive behavior disorders, 508
for eating disorders, 345
for generalized anxiety disorder, 185
for obsessive-compulsive disorder, 191
for panic disorder, 166–167
for paraphilias, 393–395
for compulsive gambling, 328
for personality disorders, 470–471
for phobias, 181–182
for posttraumatic stress disorder, 153–154
for pyromania, 476
for schizophrenia, 431
for sleep disorders, 360
for somatoform disorders, 228–229

Cognitive-specificity hypothesis, 265–266
College students, drinking among, 298, 300–301
Command hallucinations, in schizophrenia, 413
Communication, autistic children and, 491
Communication deviance (CD), schizophrenia and, 423
Communication disorders, 484, 498–501
childhood-onset fluency disorder, 500–501
language disorder, 498–499
social (pragmatic), 501
speech sound disorder, 499–500
Community mental health centers (CMHCs), 14, 129–131
Comorbidity, 7
of avoidant personality disorder, 455
of intellectual disability, 495–496
of personality disorders, 459
Competency to stand trial, 567–568
Compulsions. See also Obsessive-compulsive disorder (OCD)
definition of, 186
obsessive-compulsive personality disorder and, 441, 456–457, 463
Compulsive fire setting, 294
Compulsive gambling, 326–328, 440
as nonchemical addiction, 328treatment of, 328
Compulsive stealing, 294, 472–474
Computed tomography (CT) scans, 122
Computerized axial tomography (CAT; CT), 122
Computerized interviews, 107

Concerta. See Methylphenidate (Concerta; Ritalin)
Conclusions, jumping to, depression and, 264
Concordance rates, 417
Conditional positive regard, 57
Conditioned response (CR), 53
Conditioned stimulus (CS), 54
Conditioning:
aversive, 71, 324, 393
classical, 53–54, 315, 353
operant, 55, 314
prepared, phobias and, 175
Conditions of worth, 57
Conduct disorder (CD), 476, 505–508
Confidentiality, 22
Congruence, in person-centered therapy, 71
Conscious, 46
Construct validity, 26, 104–105
Content scales110, 111
Content validity, 104
Contingency management (CM) programs, for substance abuse, 324
Continuous amnesia, 206
Control, as objective of science, 21
Control group, 24–25
attention-placebo, 25–26
Controlled drinking, 324
Conversion disorders, 217, 221–222
theoretical perspectives on, 225, 226
treatment of, 228
Coping, 142–143
development of, for panic disorder, 166
emotion-focused, 142
problem-focused, 142–143
writing about stress and trauma as, 134
Coprophilia, 391
Coronary heart disease (CHD), 233
Correlation coefficient, 23
Correlational method, 23
Cortical steroids (corticosteroids), 132–133
stress and, 132–133, 137
Countertransference, 68
Couple therapy, 76
Covert sensitization, for paraphilias, 393
Crack, 306
Craving(s), conditioning model of, 315
Craving-for-stimulation model, of antisocial personality disorder, 466
Creutzfeldt-Jakob disease, dementia due to, 543
Crime:
alcohol abuse and, 297
antisocial personality disorder and, 445–446, 448
criminal commitment and, 550, 565–566
duty to warn and, 560–561
guilty-but-mentally-ill verdict and, 563
insanity defense and. See Insanity defense
kleptomania and, 472–474
Criminal commitment, 550
determining length of, 565–566

Criterion validity, 104
Critical thinking, 31–32
Cross-fostering studies, 418
Cue exposure training, 315
Cultural barriers, to mental health service utilization, 83
Cultural mistrust, as barrier to mental health service utilization, 82
Cultural-familial retardation, 495
Culturally sensitive treatment approach, for alcoholism, 320–321
Culture. See also Ethnicity; Sociocultural entries; specific groups
abnormal behavior and, 8–9
beliefs about normal and abnormal behavior in childhood and adolescence and, 482
childhood depression and, 512
dependent personality disorder and, 456
dissociative identity disorder and, 204
DSM sensitivity to, 99
expressed emotion and, 423–424
postpartum depression and, 252
sexual dysfunctions and, 379–380
treatment and, 79–82
Culture-bound syndromes, 97–98
dissociative, 212–213
somatoform, 98, 224–225
Cybersex addiction, 394
D-Cycloserine, boosting of effects of psychotherapy by, 183
Cyclothymic disorder, 244, 258
Cymbalta (duloxetine), 86

Dangerousness. See also Aggressive behavior; Crime; Violence
as abnormal behavior, 7
phobias and, 176
predicting, 552–556
problems in defining, 552, 553
Date rape, 398
`Deep brain stimulation:
for depression, 192
for Parkinson's disease, 541
Defense mechanisms, 47
Deinstitutionalization, 13
psychiatric homeless population and, 14–15
unfilled promising service and, 15
Delayed ejaculation, 373
Deliriants, 309
Delirium, 526–528
causes of, 527–528
features of, 528
Delirium tremens (DTs), 292, 413, 527
Delusion(s), 6
love, 434
in schizophrenia, 408–409
Delusional disorders, 432–434, 435
Dementia, 528–529

of Alzheimer's type. See Alzheimer's disease (AD)
cognitive deficits in, 528, 529
in Creutzfeldt-Jakob disease, 543
HIV-related, 541–543
in Huntington's disease, 541
neurosyphilis causing, 528
in Parkinson's disease, 540–541
in Pick's disease, 537
presenile, 529
senile, 529
vascular. See Vascular neurocognitive disorder
Dementia praecox, 16. See also Schizophrenia
Demonological model of abnormal behavior, 9–10, 15
Dendrites, 38
Denial, 48
Deoxyribonucleic acid (DNA), 28
Dependence:
physical, 295
psychological, 295
Dependent personality disorder, 441, 455–456
Dependent variables, 24
Depersonalization disorder, 200, 209–212
Depressants, 41, 296–305
alcohol, 297–303. See also Alcohol/alcohol abuse
barbiturates, 303
opioids, 303–305
sexual dysfunction and, 379
Depression, 7–8. See also Bipolar disorders; Major depressive disorder (MDD)
acculturation and, 140
aging and, 544–545
anger and, 235
attributional theory of, 266–267
biological factors in, 268–269
cardiovascular disease and, 235
causes of, 258–269
in children and adolescents, 510–512
cognitive theories of, 262–266
common features of, 246
double, 253
humanistic theories of, 261
learning theories of, 261–262
neurotransmitters and, 39
obstructive sleep apnea and, 355
persistent depressive disorder and, 244, 252–253
phlegm and, 10
postpartum, 251–252
premenstrual dysphoric disorder and, 253–254
psychodynamic theories of, 260–261
seasonal affective disorder and, 249–251
stress and, 258–259
suicide and. See Suicide
treatment of, 271–277
Description, as objective of science, 20–21

Desipramine (Norpramin) for depression, 274
Desvenlafaxine (Pristiq), 86
Detoxification, 318, 322
Dexedrine (dextroamphetamine), 305
Dextroamphetamine (Dexedrine), 305
Dhat syndrome, 98, 225, 379
Diabetes mellitus, erectile dysfunction and, 378
Diagnostic and Statistical Manual of Mental Disorders (DSM), 94–102
advantages and disadvantages of, 4–5
axes of, 97
changes in, 99–101
concerns about, 100
controversy regarding, 103–104
culture-bound syndromes and, 97–98
determining level of care, 97
evaluation of, 98–99
features of, 96–97
homosexuality and, 18
substance use and abuse, 293–294
Dialectical behavior therapy (DBT), for borderline personality disorder, 470–471
Diathesis-stress model, 64
of depression, 278
depression and, 259
dissociative disorders and, 214–215, 218
of schizophrenia, 426–427
social anxiety disorder and, 171
Diazepam (Valium), 84, 86, 297
for panic disorder, 171
Dickinson, Emily, 256
Dimensional assessment, DSM, 100
Direct observation, 117
Disclosure, of threats of violence, unlikelihood of, 553
Diseases of adaptation, 137
Disinhibition, serotonin and, 284
Displacement, 47
Disqualifying the positive, depression and, 264
Disruptive mood dysregulation disorder, 101
Dissociation, in stress disorders, 148, 151
Dissociative amnesia, 200, 205–209
Dissociative disorders, 199–217
culture-bound, 212–213
definition of, 200–201
depersonalization disorder, 200, 209–212
dissociative amnesia, 200, 205–209
dissociative fugue, 208–209
dissociative identity disorder, 199, 200, 201–205
overview of, 201
theoretical perspectives on, 213–215
treatment of, 215–217
Dissociative Experiences Scale (DES), 213
Dissociative fugue, 208–209